COMPUTING &
INFORMATION TECHNOLOGY

FRENCH
DICTIONARY

French-English
English-French

COMPUTING &
INFORMATION TECHNOLOGY
FRENCH
DICTIONARY

French-English
English-French

PETER COLLIN PUBLISHING

Editorial Team

S.M.H. Collin

Françoise Laurendeau

Bernard Mouget

First edition published 1991
Revised edition first published in Great Britain 1996
by Peter Collin Publishing Ltd
1 Cambridge Road, Teddington, Middlesex, TW11 8DT

Reprinted 2000

British Library Cataloguing in Publication Data

A catalogue record for this book is available from the British Library

British edition: ISBN 0-948549-65-3
edition for France: ISBN 0-948549-84-X

Text typeset by Create Publishing Services, Bath
Printed in Finland by WS Bookwell

PREFACE

Languages change rapidly, and this new edition of the dictionary brings in many new words and expressions in English and French, while the original text has been widely revised. The aim of this dictionary is to give the user a basic vocabulary of terms relating to computers and information technology in French and English with translations into the other language.

The vocabulary covers the main areas of computer technology, including hardware, software, programming, networks, peripherals, together with many applications where computers are used; information technology in general, telecommunications, TV and radio, desk-top publishing, graphics and design, e-mail and the Internet; these are the situations in which the user may frequently require translations from one language into the other.

The dictionary covers not only international usage, but in some cases identifies words and expressions where American and British usages differ.

The dictionary gives many examples of usage, both to show how the words are used in context and how they can be translated; these examples are supplemented by short quotations in both languages from newspapers and magazines from all over the world; these show the worldwide applications of the two languages.

PREFACE

Cette nouvelle édition revue et corrigée a subi une mise à jour importante. Notre but est de vous offrir le vocabulaire essentiel de la langue de l'informatique qui s'est beaucoup enrichie au cours des dernières années, aussi bien en français qu'en anglais.

Outre les mots du langage courant employés dans le quotidien de l'informatique et de la micro-informatique, vous trouverez le vocabulaire des ordinateurs (matériels, logiciels, programmation, périphériques, réseaux, etc,), celui des applications multiples se rapportant au traitement des données (télécommunications, infographie, PAO, etc.), et des innovations plus récentes (CD ROM, messagerie électronique, Internet, etc).

Les exemples très nombreux sont des outils précieux qui permettent d'aider à résoudre les problèmes de traduction de cette langue spécialisée qui évolue sans cesse.

De multiples citations tirées de la presse spécialisée du monde anglophone et francophone vous permettront de mieux saisir le sens des mots dans leur contexte.

COMMENT UTILISER CE DICTIONNAIRE

Notre dictionnaire se veut clair et facile à utiliser.

Les entrées apparaissent en caractères gras.

Les mots dérivés figurent en sous-entrée et sont précédés d'un losange.

Les différentes catégories grammaticales sont introduites par une subdivision numérique en chiffres arabes: **1, 2**, etc.

Les lettres **(a)**, **(b)**, etc. introduisent une division sémantique souvent précédée d'une explication en italique entre parenthèses.

Les abréviations ont été réduites au minimum, en voici la liste:

adj	adjectif	adjective
adj num	adjectif numéral	numeral adjective
adv	adverbe	adverb
conj	conjonction	conjunction
f	féminin	feminine
GB	Grande-Bretagne	Great Britain
inf	infinitif	infinitive
inv	invariable	invariable
loc adv	locution adverbiale	adverb
loc prép	locution prépositive	preposition
m	masculin	masculine
n	nom	noun
nf	nom féminin	feminine noun
nfpl	nom féminin pluriel	plural feminine noun
nm	nom masculin	masculine noun
nm&f	nom masculin ou féminin	masculine or feminine noun
nmpl	nom masculin pluriel	plural masculine noun
npr	nom propre	proper noun
pl	pluriel	plural
prép	préposition	preposition
TM	nom déposé	registered trademark
vi	verbe intransitif	intransitive verb
vpr	verbe pronominal	reflexive verb
vtr	verbe transitif	transitive verb
US	Etats-Unis	United States

USING THE DICTIONARY

The dictionary aims to provide a clear layout which will help the user find the required translation as easily as possible. Each entry is formed of a headword in bold type, with clearly numbered divisions showing different parts of speech, or lettered divisions showing differences of meaning. Words which are derived from the main entry word are listed under that word, each time preceded by a lozenge.

As far as is possible, abbreviations are not used in the dictionary, apart from the following:

adj	adjectif	adjective
adj num	adjectif numéral	numeral adjective
adv	adverbe	adverb
conj	conjonction	conjunction
f	féminin	feminine
GB	Grande-Bretagne	Great Britain
inf	infinitif	infinitive
inv	invariable	invariable
loc adv	locution adverbiale	adverb
loc prép	locution prépositive	preposition
m	masculin	masculine
n	nom	noun
nf	nom féminin	feminine noun
nfpl	nom féminin pluriel	plural feminine noun
nm	nom masculin	masculine noun
nm&f	nom masculin ou féminin	masculine or feminine noun
nmpl	nom masculin pluriel	plural masculine noun
npr	nom propre	proper noun
pl	pluriel	plural
prép	préposition	preposition
TM	nom déposé	trademark
vi	verbe intransitif	intransitive verb
vpr	verbe pronominal	reflexive verb
vtr	verbe transitif	transitive verb
US	Etats-Unis	United States

FRANÇAIS-ANGLAIS
FRENCH-ENGLISH

Aa

A *(nombre hexadécimal équivalent du 10 décimal)* hexadecimal number equivalent to decimal 10 *ou* A

A = AMPERE

Å = ANGSTROM

A: *(dans certains systèmes d'exploitation)* **lecteur** *ou* **unité de disquettes A:** = disk drive A: (in some operating systems); **pour savoir quels fichiers sont enregistrés sur votre disquette, utilisez la commande DOS DIR A:** = to see what is stored on your floppy disk, use the DOS command DIR A:

@ *(d'adresse Internet)* @ (NOTE: se prononce 'at' en anglais)

abandonné, -ée *adj* abandoned; **affaire abandonnée** *ou* **sujet abandonné** = dead matter

◊ **abandonner** *vtr* *(un programme)* to abandon *ou* to exit *ou* to quit (a program); **abandonner prématurément** = to abort

abaque *nm* nomogram *ou* nomograph

aberration *nf* aberration *ou* distortion; **aberration chromatique** = chromatic aberration; **aberration de l'image** = image distortion; **aberration sphérique** = spherical aberration

abîmé, -ée *adj* damaged

◊ **abîmer** *vtr* to damage

ABIOS *(BIOS étendu)* Advanced Basic Input/Output System (ABIOS)

COMMENTAIRE: L'ABIOS est utilisé en plus des routines normales du BIOS. Les routines ABIOS sont utilisées pour contrôler le BUS MCA des ordinateurs IBM PS/2

abonné, -ée *n* subscriber; **les abonnés du téléphone** = telephone subscribers; **abonné du télex** = telex subscriber; **ligne de jonction d'abonné (au centre téléphonique)** = exchange line

abrégé, -ée *adj* abridged *ou* abbreviated; **adressage abrégé** = abbreviated addressing *ou* abb. add.; **adresse abrégée** = abbreviated address

◊ **abréviation** *nf* abbreviation; **RAM est l'abréviation de 'Random Access Memory'** = the acronym RAM means Random Access Memory; **dans le texte, on a remplacé le terme 'processeur' par l'abréviation 'proc'** = within the text, the abbreviation 'proc' is used instead of 'processor'

ABS *(fonction valeur absolue)* Absolute Function (ABS); **la commande ABS(-13) retourne**

la valeur 13 = command ABS(-13) will return the answer 13

abscisse *nf* X-coordinate; **axe d'abscisse** = X-axis *ou* horizontal axis

absolu,-e *adj* absolute; **adressage absolu** = absolute addressing; **adresse absolue** *ou* **adresse réelle** *ou* **adresse machine** = absolute address *ou* actual address *ou* machine address; **adresse absolue de la cellule** = absolute cell reference; **l'exécution d'un programme est un peu plus rapide si on utilise uniquement des adresses absolues dans le code** = program execution is slightly faster if you code only with absolute addresses; **assembleur absolu** = absolute assembler; **capacité théorique absolue** = absolute maximum rating; **chargeur absolu** = absolute loader; **codage (binaire) absolu** = absolute coding *ou* specific coding; **code (binaire) absolu** = absolute code *ou* specific code *ou* actual code; **coordonnées absolues** = absolute coordinates; **dispositif de pointage absolu** = absolute device; **erreur absolue** = absolute error; **expression absolue** = absolute expression; **fonction valeur absolue** *ou* **ABS** = absolute function (ABS); **instruction absolue** *ou* **code absolu** = absolute instruction *ou* code; **positionnement absolu** = absolute positioning; **priorité absolue** = absolute priority; **programme absolu** = absolute program; **valeur absolue** = absolute value; **la valeur absolue de −62,34 est 62,34** = the absolute value of −62.34 is 62.34; **il y a génération d'une valeur absolue des entrées** = an absolute value of the input is generated; *(sans signe négatif)* **en valeur absolue** = unsigned

absorber *vtr* to absorb

◊ **absorptance** *nf* absorptance

◊ **absorption** *nf* absorption; **absorption atmosphérique** = atmospheric absorption; **filtre d'absorption** = absorption filter; **indice d'absorption** = absorptance

ACC = ACCUMULATEUR

accédant *nm* *(utilisateur ayant un droit d'accès)* accessor

◊ **accéder (à)** *vi* to access *ou* to gain access to; **accéder à un fichier** = to access *ou* to gain access to a file; **elle a accédé au fichier de l'employé stocké sur l'ordinateur** = she accessed the employee's file stored on the computer; **vous ne pouvez accéder aux données que si le fichier est ouvert** = you cannot access the data unless the file is open; **il est impossible d'accéder aux renseignements confidentiels du fichier sans utiliser le mot de passe** = the user cannot gain access to the confidential information in the file without a password; **le gestionnaire du système peut accéder à toutes les** partitions à partir de sa partition privilégiée = the system manager can access anyone else's account from his privileged account; **le premier ordinateur individuel de la série ne peut accéder à plus de 640Ko de RAM** = the original PC cannot access more than 640Kbytes of RAM

accélérateur *nm* accelerator

◊ **accélérateur, -trice** *adj* **carte accélératrice** = accelerator board *ou* card

◊ **accélération** *nf* accélération; **carte d'accélération** = accelerator board *ou* card; **temps d'accélération** = acceleration time; *(raccourci clavier)* **touche d'accélération** = accelerator key; **au lieu de sélectionner le menu Fichier puis l'option Enregistrer, utilisez les touches d'accélération ALT-S pour sauvegarder votre fichier** = instead of selecting the File menu then the Save option, use the accelerator keys Alt and S to do the same thing and save the file

◊ **accéléré, -ée** *adj* **code accéléré** = optimized code *ou* optimum code

accent *nm* accent; **accent aigu** = acute accent; **accent circonflexe** = circumflex accent; **accent flottant** = floating accent; **accent grave** = grave accent; **accent mobile** *ou* **caractère accent** = piece accent

◊ **accentué, -ée** *adj* accented

acceptable *adj* acceptable; **le taux d'erreur était très bas et donc acceptable** = the error rate was very low, and is acceptable

◊ **acceptation** *nf* acceptance; **signal d'acceptation d'appel** = call accepted signal

◊ **accepté, -ée** *adj* **(a)** accepted; **signal d'appel accepté** = call accepted signal **(b)** agreed; **accepté d'avance** = pre-agreed

◊ **accepter** *vtr* **(a)** to accept; **il a accepté le devis de l'imprimeur** = he accepted the quoted price for printing; **il n'a pas accepté le poste de programmeur qu'on lui offrait** = he did not accept the programming job he was offered; **à ce prix-là, on peut accepter que la mallette ait une éraflure** = for the price, the scratched case is acceptable **(b)** to accept *ou* to read; **qui peut être accepté par l'imprimante** = printer-readable; **l'imprimante laser accepte même un imprimé de la taille d'une carte professionnelle** = the laser printer will accept a card as small as a business card; **ce lecteur multidisque accepte aussi bien les disquettes de format 3,5 pouces que 5,25 pouces** = the multi-disk reader will accept 3.5 inch disks as well as 5.25 inch formats; **l'ordinateur principal accepte jusqu'à six postes de travail** = the main computer supports six workstations **(c)** *(être d'accord)* to agree **(d)** *(approuver)* to approve

accès *nm* access; **accès aléatoire** = random access; **mémoire vidéo à accès aléatoire (VRAM)** = video random access memory (VRAM); **les lecteurs de disquettes permettent l'accès aléatoire** *ou* **direct des données alors qu'une bande magnétique en permet l'accès séquentiel** = disk drives are random access, magnetic tape is sequential access memory; **accès asynchrone** =

asynchronous access; **accès cyclique** = cyclic access; **accès sur demande (à la mémoire paginée)** = demand fetching; **accès direct** = direct access *ou* random access; **mémoire** *ou* **support à accès direct** = (i) direct access storage device (DASD); (ii) core memory *ou* primary memory; *(entre périphérique et mémoire principale d'un ordinateur)* **accès direct à la mémoire** = direct memory access (DMA); **accès direct à la mémoire par vol de cycle** = DMA cycle stealing; **contrôleur d'accès direct à la mémoire** *ou* **contrôleur DMA** = DMA controller; **transfert des données par accès direct à la mémoire entre la mémoire principale et le second processeur** = direct memory access transfer between the main memory and the second processor; **voie d'accès direct à la mémoire** = direct memory access channel; *(téléphone)* **accès direct au réseau** = direct outward dialling; **accès direct à un poste** = direct inward dialling; **accès au disque** = disk access; **(poste de travail) à accès illimité** = open access (workstation); **accès instantané** = instantaneous access; **mémoire à accès intermédiaire** = intermediate access memory (IAM); **accès multiple** = multiple access; **système à accès multiple** *ou* **système multi-accès** = multi-access system; *(circuit)* **accès multiple asservi à la demande** = demand assigned multiple access (DAMA); **accès multiple par division dans le temps** = time division multiple access; **accès non autorisé** *ou* **interdit** = access barred; **accès parallèle** = parallel access; **accès rapide** = rapid access; **mémoire à accès rapide** = rapid access memory *ou* fast access memory (FAM); **accès au réseau numérique intégré** = integrated digital access (IDA); **accès sélectif** = random access; **accès séquentiel** *ou* **accès série** = serial access *ou* sequential access; **mémoire à accès séquentiel** = sequential access storage *ou* serial access memory; **méthode d'accès séquentiel indexé (ISAM)** = indexed sequential access method (ISAM); **méthode d'accès séquentiel par clé** = keyed sequential access method (KSAM); *(communication)* **accès temporel multiplexé** = time division multiple access; **autorisation d'accès** = access authority; **avoir accès à** = to access; **avoir accès à quelque chose** = to have access to something; **avoir accès à un fichier (informatique)** = to have access *ou* to gain access to a file of data; **il a accès à de nombreux fichiers confidentiels** = he has access to numerous sensitive files; **il faut vous rappeler votre mot de passe** *ou* **code d'identification sinon vous ne pourrez pas avoir accès au système** = if you forget your user ID, you will not be able to log on; **catégorie d'accès** = access category; **chemin d'accès** = access path; **enregistrement des chemins d'accès** = access path journalling; **code d'accès (à un système)** = access code; **contrôle d'accès (au système)** = access control; **octet de contrôle d'accès** = access control byte; **contrôle des canaux d'accès** = access channel control; *(communication)* **mémoire à double accès** = dual port memory; **droits d'accès** = access rights; **fenêtre d'accès (d'un disque ou d'une disquette)** = access hole; **frais d'accès au système** = access charge; **gestion d'accès aux données** = data access management; **gestion d'accès aux disques** = disk access management; **interdire (à quelqu'un) l'accès à un système** = to bar access to a system *ou* to deny access to a system; **après avoir découvert qu'il** faisait du piratage, on lui a interdit l'accès au système = after he was discovered hacking, he was barred access to the system; **liberté d'accès à l'information** = freedom of information; *(communication)* **ligne d'accès** = access line; **mécanisme d'accès** = access mechanism; **méthode d'accès** = access method; **niveau d'accès** = access level; **nom d'accès (dans une base de données)** = access name; *(d'un enregistrement)* **numéro d'accès** = accession number; **période d'accès** = access period; **permission d'accès** = access permission; **point d'accès** = *(connexion)* port; *(de matériel ou logiciel)* access point; **privilège d'accès** = access privilege; **protection des accès mémoire** = fetch protect; **routines d'accès** = access method routines; **(formation) sans accès à l'ordinateur** = hands off (training); **temps d'accès** = *(aux données)* access time *ou* response time; *(de tête de lecture à une piste ou à une donnée)* seek time *ou* positioning time; **le nouveau disque a un temps d'accès de 35 ms** = the new hard disk drive has a seek time of 35ms; **le temps d'accès de cette RAM dynamique est d'environ 200ns - il existe une version plus rapide si votre fréquence d'horloge est plus élevée** = the access time of this dynamic RAM chip is around 200ns - we have faster versions if your system clock is running faster; **temps d'accès à la mémoire** = memory access time; **code à temps d'accès minimum** = optimum code; **temps d'accès moyen** = average access time; **code à temps d'accès optimisé** = minimum access code *ou* minimum delay code *ou* minimum latency coding *ou* optimum code; **type d'accès** = access category; *(dans un réseau Token-Ring)* **unité d'accès** = access unit

◊ **accessible** *adj* accessible; **les détails du fichier client de l'ordinateur principal sont facilement accessibles** = details of customers are easily accessible from the main computer files

accessoire *nm* accessory *ou* attachment; **accessoires** = accessories *ou* ancillary equipment; **plusieurs accessoires, dont un capot d'insonorisation, sont fournis avec l'imprimante** = the printer comes with several accessories, such as a soundproof hood; **il existe de nombreux accessoires pour cet ordinateur populaire** = this popular computer has a large range of accessories; **il existe un accessoire spécial pour l'alimentation du papier en feuille à feuille** = there is a special single sheet feed attachment; *(utilitaire Apple Macintosh)* **accessoire de bureau** = desk accessory (DA); **nous avons installé plusieurs accessoires de bureau qui nous aident à gérer les polices de caractères** = we have installed several DAs that help us manage our fonts

accidentel, -elle *adj* accidental; **si vous vous servez d'un disque protégé contre la destruction accidentelle, vous ne perdrez jamais vos données** = if the disk is crash-protected, you will never lose your data

accolades *nfpl (caractères { } utilisés dans certains programmes)* curly brackets *ou* braces

accommodation *nf (de l'oeil)* adaptation; **l'accommodation de l'oeil en réponse aux** variations d'intensité de lumière = the adaptation of the eye in response to different levels of brightness

accompagnement *nm* module **d'accompagnement** = coroutine

accord *nm* **(a)** *(compatibilité)* match; **non accord** = mismatch; **accord d'impédance** = impedance matching; **l'accord d'impédance entre un émetteur et un récepteur réduit la perte de puissance des signaux transmis** = impedance matching between a transmitter and a receiver minimizes power losses to transmitted signals **(b)** **être d'accord avec** = (i) to agree with; (ii) to approve of **(c)** *(contrat)* deal

accordé, -ée *adj* matched; **charge accordée** = matched load

accordéon *nm* **papier (plié) en accordéon** = accordion fold *ou* fanfold *ou* concertina fold paper

accorder *vtr* to match

◊ **s'accorder** *vpr* to match *ou* to agree

◊ **accordeur** *nm* **accordeur d'impédance** = cable matcher

accrochage *nm (erreur avec arrêt de programme)* lock up; **point d'accrochage (de test)** = hook

accroché, -ée *adj* hooked; *(combiné)* (receiver) on hook

◊ **accrocher** *vtr* **être accroché (dans une boucle)** = to hang (in a loop)

accu = ACCUMULATEUR

accumulateur *ou* **accu** *nm* **(a)** battery **(b)** *(registre d'une unité centrale de traitement)* accumulator *ou* accumulator register (ACC); **stockez les 2 octets de données dans les registres A et B et exécutez l'instruction 'add' - vous obtiendrez le résultat dans l'accumulateur** = store the two bytes of data in registers A and B and execute the add instruction - the answer will be in the accumulator; **accumulateur externe** = external register; **adresse d'accumulateur** = accumulator address

◊ **accumuler** *vtr* to accumulate

accusé *nm* accusé de réception = acknowledgement; *(d'un message)* **accusé de réception négatif** = negative acknowledge (NAK *ou* NACK); **accusé de réception positif** = affirmative acknowledge (ACK *ou* ACKNLG *ou* ACKNOWLEDGE); **caractère d'accusé de réception** = acknowledge character; **envoyer un accusé de réception** = to acknowledge; **message avec accusé de réception** = acknowledged mail

◊ **accuser** *vtr* **accuser réception** = to acknowledge; **accuser réception d'un message** = to acknowledge a message; **l'imprimante émet un signal pour accuser réception des données** = the printer generates an ACK signal when it has received data

achat *nm* purchase; **faire des achats** = (i) to buy *ou* to purchase; (ii) to shop *ou* to go shopping; **achats par téléphone** = teleshopping; **achats sur** *ou* **par ordinateur** = computer shopping *ou* electronic shopping

acheminement *nm* routing; **acheminement (en) delta** = delta routing; **acheminement de données** = data routing; **acheminement adaptatif** *ou* **dynamique** = adaptive routing; **acheminement de messages** = message routing; **acheminement fixe** *ou* **présélectionné** = fixed routing; **câble d'acheminement des signaux** = feeder cable; **procédure de contrôle d'acheminement** = routing overheads; **voie d'acheminement** = feeder; *(téléphone)* **système d'acheminement direct des appels** = direct dialling

◊ **acheminer** *vtr* to route *ou* to channel; to redirect; **il existe une nouvelle façon d'acheminer les données vers l'ordinateur central** = there is a new way of routing data to the central computer

acheter *vtr* to buy *ou* to purchase; **acheter un fichier d'adresses** = to buy a mailing list

achèvement *nm* completion

◊ **achever** *vtr* to complete

achromatique *adj* achromatic; *(gris)* **couleur achromatique** = achromatic colour

Ackerman *npr* **fonction d'Ackerman** = Ackerman's function

acoustique 1 *nf* acoustics 2 *adj* acoustic; **coupleur acoustique** = acoustic coupler; **j'utilise un coupleur acoustique avec mon (ordinateur) portatif** = I use an acoustic coupler with my lap-top computer; **enceinte acoustique** = set of loudspeakers; **ligne à retard acoustique** = acoustic delay line; **mémoire acoustique** = acoustic store *ou* acoustic memory; **niveau de pression acoustique** = sound pressure level (SPL)

acquisition *nf* **(a)** acquisition; **acquisition de données** = data acquisition *ou* data logging; **système à acquisition de connaissances et de règles** = self-learning (expert) system **(b)** *(dans une bibliothèque)* accession

Acrobat™ *(format de fichier graphique Adobe)* Acrobat

acronyme *nm* acronym; **l'acronyme FORTRAN signifie 'Formula Translator'** = the acronym FORTRAN means 'Formula Translator'

actif, -ive *adj (en cours)* active; **application active** = active application; **base de données active** = active database; **concentrateur** *ou* **hub actif** = active hub; **connexion** *ou* **liaison active** = active link; **dispositif (électronique) actif** = active device; **enregistrement actif** = active record; **fenêtre active** = active window; **fichier actif** = active file; *(reliée au port imprimante de l'ordinateur)* **imprimante active** = active printer; **ligne active** = active line;

matrice active = active matrix; **mode actif** = active state; *(relié à un autre noeud)* **noeud actif** = active node; **passerelle active** = active gateway; **programme actif** = active program; **réseau en étoile actif** = active star; **signal bas actif** = active low; **signal haut actif** = active high; **stockage actif** = active storage; **zone active** = active area *ou* hotspot; **l'image de la trompette est une zone active qui produit un son lorsqu'on la sélectionne avec le pointeur** = the image of the trumpet is a hotspot and will play a sound when you move the pointer over it

actinique *adj* actinic; **lumière actinique** = actinic light

action *nf* **(a)** action *(se rapporte à un menu)* **code action** = action code; *(serie d'actions)* **cycle d'action** = action cycle; *(liste de choix)* **liste d'actions** = action list; *(objet auquel se rapporte une action)* **objet d'action** = action-object **(b)** *(photographie)* **champ d'action** = action field

◊ **actionné, -ée** *adj* moved by *ou* driven by; *(logiciel* *ou* *procédure)* **actionné par évènement** = event-driven

◊ **actionner** *vtr* to move *ou* to drive; **actionner une touche** = to hit a key

activation *nf* **signal d'activation** = enabling signal; *(déclenche un programme)* **touche d'activation** = hot key

◊ **activé, -ée** *adj (logiciel* *ou* *procédure)* driven; *(commutateur)* enabled *ou* selected *ou* armed; **programme activé par commande** = command-driven program; **activé par événement** = event-driven; **activé par reconnaissance des données** = data-driven; **interruption activée** = armed interrupt

◊ **activer** *vtr* to enable *ou* to select *ou* to arm *ou* to wake up *ou* to activate; **activer un circuit intégré** = to chip select (CS)

activité *nf* active state *ou* activity; **niveau d'activité** = activity level; **suivi** *ou* **enregistrement** *ou* **traçage d'activité** = activity trail; **taux d'activité** = activity ratio; **taux** *ou* **ratio d'activité d'un fichier** = file activity ratio; **(mode de) chargement en fonction du taux d'activité** = activity loading; *(lampe)* **témoin d'activité** = activity light

actualisation *nf* **dispositif d'actualisation (d'un système)** = retrofit

actuel, -elle *adj* present *ou* current; **copiez les données du fichier précédent dans le fichier actuel** = copy data into the present workspace from the previous file

acuité *nf* acuity; **acuité visuelle** = visual acuity

acutance *nf* acutance

ADA *(langage)* Automatic Data Acquisition (ADA)

adaptable *adj* adaptable; **langage adaptable** = extensible language

adaptateur *nm* adapter *ou* adaptor; *(pour connexion)* adapter (plug); **l'adaptateur du câble permet de relier le scanner à une interface SCSI** = the cable adapter allows attachment of the scanner to the SCSI interface; **le câble de liaison entre le scanner et l'adaptateur est compris** = the cable to connect the scanner to the adapter is included in the package; **adaptateur de canal de transmission** = channel adapter; **adaptateur de canal de transmission de données** = data adapter unit; *(carte)* **adaptateur d'écran** = display adapter; **adaptateur graphique** = graphics adapter; **le nouvel adaptateur graphique améliore la résolution graphique de l'écran** = the new graphics adapter is capable of displaying higher resolution graphics; **adaptateur graphique couleur CGA** = colour graphics adapter (CGA); **adaptateur graphique couleur EGA** = enhanced graphics adapter (EGA); **adaptateur graphique couleur MCGA** = multicolor graphics adapter (MCGA); **adaptateur d'interface de communication** = communications interface adapter; **adaptateur de ligne** *ou* **de voie de communication** = data adapter unit; **adaptateur de l'ordinateur hôte** = host adapter; **adaptateur de réseau** = network adapter; **adaptateur de vitesse de transmission** = baud rate generator; *(changeur de genre d'une prise de courant)* **adaptateur mâle/femelle** *ou* **adaptateur femelle/mâle** = sex changer; *voir aussi* CARTE

◊ **adaptatif, -ive** *adj* adaptive; **routage adaptatif** = adaptive routing *ou* dynamic routing; **routage adaptatif protégé** = isolated adaptive routing

◊ **adaptation** *nf* adaptation; **l'adaptation de l'oeil pour répondre à différents niveaux de luminosité** *ou* **brillance** = the adaptation of the eye to respond to different levels of brightness

◊ **adapté, -ée** adapted *ou* conditioned *ou* modified; **(logiciel) adapté à l'ordinateur** = machine-intimate (software); **langage adapté aux problèmes** = problem-orientated language (POL)

◊ **adapter** *vtr* to adapt *ou* to condition *ou* to modify; **est-ce qu'il est possible d'adapter cet ordinateur pour les disquettes 5,25 pouces?** = can this computer be adapted to take 5.25 inch disks?; **le clavier a été adapté pour la vente en Europe** = the keyboard was modified for European users; **adaptez les données brutes à un format standard** = condition the raw data to a standard format

addition *nf (supplément)* addition; *(opération mathématique)* addition *ou* sum; **l'addition de chacune des colonnes du tableau donne un sous-total** = in the spreadsheet each column is added to make a subtotal; **addition destructive** = destructive addition; **addition sans retenue** = addition without carry; **registre d'addition** = add register; **le signe de l'addition (+)** = plus *ou* plus sign; **temps d'addition** = add time *ou* addition time; **premier terme d'une addition** = augend; **second terme d'une addition** = augmenter

◊ **additionnel, -elle** *adj (dispositif)* additional *ou* add-on *ou* add-in; **carte additionnelle** = add-in card; **sous-programme additionnel** = inserted subroutine; **un disque dur additionnel augmentera la capacité de mémoire de l'ordinateur** = the add-on hard disk will boost the computer's storage capabilities

◊ **additionner** *vtr* to add (up)

◊ **additionneur** *nm* adder; **additionneur binaire** *ou* **additionneur DCB** = BCD adder; **additionneur à deux entrées** = half adder *ou* two input adder; **additionneur complet** *ou* **à trois entrées** = full adder *ou* three input adder; **additionneur parallèle** = parallel adder; **additionneur à retenue automatique (très rapide)** = carry look ahead; **additionneur séquentiel** = serial adder

◊ **additionneur-soustracteur** *nm* adder-subtractor

additif, -ive *adj* **(a)** additive; **synthèse additive (de couleurs)** = additive colour mixing **(b)** add-on

adhésif *nm* adhesive *ou* glue

◊ **adhésif, -ive** *adj* adhesive *ou* sticky; **bande adhésive** = sticky tape; *(qui sert à tout dans un studio, l'outil favori du gaffeur)* **bande adhésive noire** = gaffer tape

adjacent, -e *adj* adjacent; **domaines adjacents** = adjacent domains; **noeuds adjacents** = adjacent nodes

administrateur *nm* administrator; *(gestionnaire de données)* **administrateur de programme** = data administrator

Adobe ™ *(société spécialisée en logiciels)* Adobe ™; **gestionnaire de police Adobe (ATM)** = Adobe Type Manager ™ (ATM)

adoucir *vtr (une couleur)* to deaden (a colour); *(une ligne)* to dither (a line)

ADPCM *(modulation dynamique de code de pulsion* *ou* *standard de conversion)* Adaptive Differential Pulse Code Modulation (ADPCM)

adressable *adj* addressable; **dans le nouveau système d'exploitation, la totalité des 5Mo de RAM installée est adressable** = with the new operating system, all of the 5MB of installed RAM is addressable; **adressable par le contenu** = content-addressable; **fichier** *ou* **location adressable par le contenu** = content-addressable file *ou* location; **mémoire adressable par le contenu** = content-addressable memory (CAM); **curseur adressable** = addressable cursor; **opération non adressable** = no-address operation; **point adressable** = addressable point

◊ **adressage** *nm* addressing; **adressage abrégé** *ou* **simplifié** = abbreviated addressing *ou* abb. add.; **adressage absolu** = absolute addressing; **adressage associatif** = associative addressing *ou* content-addressable addressing; **adressage binaire** = bit addressing; **infographie à adressage binaire** = bit-mapped graphics; **adressage direct** = direct addressing; **adressage élargi** = augmented addressing; **adressage des entrées/sorties** = I/O mapping; **adressage immédiat** = immediate addressing; **adressage implicite** = implied addressing; **l'adressage implicite pour l'accumulateur est inclus dans l'instruction LDA,16** = implied addressing for the accumulator is used in the instruction LDA,16;

adressage indexé = indexed addressing; **adressage indirect** = deferred addressing *ou* indirect addressing *ou* second-level addressing; **adressage inhérent** *ou* **particulier** = inherent addressing; **adressage de page** = page addressing; **terminal à adressage protégé** = addressable terminal; **adressage de registre** = register addressing; **adressage relatif** *ou* **adressage de base** = base addressing; **base d'adressage** = address base; **capacité** *ou* **disponibilité d'adressage** = addressability *ou* addressing capacity; **méthode d'adressage** = addressing method; **mode d'adressage** = addressing mode; **mode d'adressage à matrice active** = all points addressable (APA) mode; **niveau d'adressage** = addressing level; **définir une table d'adressage binaire** = to bit-map; **temps d'adressage** = address access time

adresse *nf* **(a)** *(en mémoire)* address; **chaque mot mémoire distinct a sa propre et unique adresse** = each separate memory word has its own unique address; **c'est l'adresse à laquelle les données commencent** = this is the address at which the data starts; **adresse absolue** *ou* **adresse réelle** *ou* **adresse machine** = absolute address *ou* actual address *ou* machine address *ou* real address; **adresse abrégée** = abbreviated address; **mon adresse complète de réseau comporte plus de 60 caractères; vous avez intérêt à utiliser mon adresse abrégée** = my full network address is over 60 characters long, so you will find it easier to use my abbreviated address; **adresse calculée** = generated address; **adresse courante** = current address; **registre d'adresse courante** = current address register (CAR); **adresse de base** = base address *ou* presumptive address; **voici l'adresse de début des données** = this is the address at which the data starts; **adresse de destination** = destination address; **adresse d'entrée** = entry point; **adresse d'exécution** = execution address; **adresse d'instruction** = instruction address; **registre d'adresse d'instruction** = instruction address register (IAR) *ou* instruction counter; **adresses d'octets** = byte addresses; **adresse de premier niveau** = first-level address; **adresse de piste** = track address; **adresse de référence** = reference address; **adresse de référence directe** = direct reference address; **adresse de réseau** = network address; **adresse directe** *ou* **à un niveau** = direct address *ou* one-level address; **adresse effective** = effective address; **adresse explicite** = explicit address; **adresse générée** = generated address; **adresse immédiate** = zero-level address *ou* immediate address; **adresse indexée** = indexed address; **adresse initiale** *ou* **de lancement** = initial address; **adresse machine** = machine address; **adresse origine (de la première instruction d'un programme)** = (program) origin *ou* initial address *ou* base address *ou* presumptive address; **adresse primitive** = base address *ou* presumptive address; **adresse réelle** = first-level address; **adresse relative** = relative address *ou* indirect address; **adresse symbolique** = tag *ou* floating address *ou* symbolic address; **instruction à adresse unique** = one address instruction; **code d'instruction à adresse unique** = single address code; **ordinateur à adresse unique** = one address computer; **adresse virtuelle** = virtual address; **bus d'adresses** = address bus *ou* address highway; **voies de liaison d'un bus d'adresses** = bus address lines;

calcul d'une adresse = address computation; **champ d'adresse** = address *ou* operand field; **changement d'adresse en mémoire** = relocation *ou* memory edit; **changer d'adresse** = to relocate (data); **l'adresse de cette donnée est changée au cours de l'éxécution** = the data is relocated during execution; **code adresse** = address code; **créer** *ou* **définir une adresse** = to address (data); **marque de début d'adresse** = address mark; **décodeur d'adresse** = address decoder; **espace adresse** = address space; **(code de) fin d'adresse** = end of address (EOA); **format d'adresse** = address format; **modification d'adresse** = address modification; **mot adresse** = address word; **plus le mot adresse est long, plus la mémoire adressable de l'ordinateur augmente** = a larger address word increases the amount of memory a computer can address; **piste d'adresses** = address track; **registre d'adresse** = address register *ou* base register; **registre des adresses en mémoire** = memory address register (MAR); **opération sans adresse** = no-address operation; **table de correspondance des adresses** = address mapping; **signal de validité d'adresse** = address strobe; **message à une seule adresse** = single address message; **une adresse plus une** = one-plus-one address; **instruction à deux adresses** = two-address-instruction; **instruction à deux adresses plus une** = two-plus-one-address instruction; **instruction à trois adresses** = three-address-instruction; **instruction à quatre adresses** = four-address instruction; **quatre adresses plus une** = four-plus-one address; **instruction à n adresse(s) plus une** = n-plus-one address instruction **(b)** *(domicile, etc.)* address; **adresse télégraphique** = cable address; **fichier d'adresses (destiné aux mailings)** = mailing list; **acheter un fichier d'adresses** = to buy a mailing list; **établir un fichier d'adresses** = to build up a mailing list; **son nom figure sur notre fichier d'adresses** = his name is on our mailing list; **notre fichier contient les adresses de deux mille sociétés en Europe** = we keep an address list of two thousand businesses in Europe; **répertoire d'adresses par rues** = street directory

◊ **adresser** *vtr* **(a)** *(informatique)* to address **(b)** *(courrier)* to address; **adresser une lettre** *ou* **un colis** = to address a letter *ou* a parcel

aérien, -ienne *adj* aerial; *(photo ou film)* **vue aérienne** = aerial image

aérographe *nm* airbrush; **nous avons utilisé l'aérographe pour créer un effet de nuage dans cette image** = we used the airbrush tool to create the cloud effects in this image

affaiblir *vtr (signal)* to attenuate; *(batterie)* to drain

◊ **s'affaiblir** *vpr* to fade *ou* to decay; **le signal s'est affaibli rapidement** = the signal decayed rapidly

◊ **affaiblissement** *nm* *(d'un signal)* attenuation *ou* loss *ou* fading *ou* decay *ou* leakage; **affaiblissement dû l'interférence** = interference fading; **affaiblissement d'insertion** = insertion loss; **enveloppe** *ou* **courbe d'affaiblissement** = envelope (in multimedia)

affectable *adj* **chiffre non affectable** = unallowable digit

affectation *nf (d'une tâche)* assignment; *(d'une somme)* allocation; **compatibilité d'affectation** = assignment compatible; **conversion d'affectation** = assignment conversion; **instruction d'affectation** = assignment statement; **affectation de capitaux à un projet** = allocation of capital to a project

◊ **affecter** *vtr* **(a)** *(une zone de mémoire ou une tâche)* to assign; **deux PC ont été affectés à la préparation des étiquettes** = two PCs have been assigned to outputting the labels **(b)** *(une somme à un projet)* to allocate

affichage *nm (sur écran)* display *ou* on-screen display *ou* readout; **le logiciel de PAO permet l'affichage des polices de caractères** = the dtp package offers on-screen font display; **affichage alphanumérique** = alphanumeric display; **affichage de caractères** *ou* **de texte** = character display; **affichage du contenu des registres** *ou* **affichage de la configuration des registres** = register map; **affichage couleur** = colour display; **affichage à cristaux liquides** *ou* **affichage LCD** = liquid crystal display (LCD); **affichage de données** = information output (on screen); **affichage destructif** = destructive readout (DRO); **affichage électroluminescent** = electroluminescent display; **affichage graphique** = graphic display; **définition d'affichage graphique** = graphic display resolution; **affichage noir sur blanc** = positive display; **affichage numérique** = digital readout; **cette horloge avait un affichage numérique** = the clock had a digital readout; **affichage d'une page** = page display; **affichage réduit** *ou* **d'une partie de page** = part page display; **affichage plasma** = gas discharge display *ou* gas plasma display *ou* plasma display; **affichage en positif** = positive presentation; **contrôleur** *ou* **pilote d'affichage** = display controller; **couleur d'affichage** = display colour; **dimension d'affichage** = display size; **dispositif** *ou* **écran d'affichage** = readout device; **espace d'affichage** = display space; **format d'affichage** = display format; **mode affichage** = display mode; **registre d'affichage** = display register; **tableau d'affichage** = notice board; *(sur un tableau télématique)* **tableau** *ou* **zone d'affichage** = Bulletin Board; **zone d'affichage de texte** = text screen

◊ **affiche** *nf* poster

◊ **afficher** *vtr (à l'écran)* to display *ou* to call up; *(faire apparaître à un moment précis)* to pop on; **l'heure était affichée** = the readout displayed the time; **les coordonnées du client étaient affichées sur l'écran** = the customer's details were displayed on the screen; **le système d'exploitation permet d'afficher d'autres programmes simultanément, chacun dans une fenêtre différente** = the operating system will allow other programs to be displayed on-screen at the same time in different windows; **un processeur d'images qui peut lire, afficher et manipuler les images vidéo** = an image processor that captures, displays and manipulates video

images; **on a affiché à l'écran les adresses de tous les clients** = all the customers addresses were called up; **on trouve habituellement quatre options affichées en haut de l'écran** = there are usually four options along the top of the screen; **pour afficher le menu déroulant cliquer sur l'icône en haut de l'écran** = the pull-down menu is viewed by clicking over the icon at the top of the screen

affirmatif, -ive *adj* affirmative *ou* positive; **réponse affirmative** = positive response

◊ **affirmation** *nf* assertion

AFIPS = AMERICAN FEDERATION OF INFORMATION PROCESSING SOCIETIES

AFNOR = ASSOCIATION FRANCAISE DE NORMALISATION

AFP *(protocole de gestion de fichiers Apple)* Apple Filing Protocol ™ (AFP)

AFX *(gestionnaire d'échange de fichiers Apple)* Apple File Exchange ™ (AFX)

agence *nf* agency; **agence de presse** = news agency

agenda *nm* **(a)** *(carnet)* diary; *(grande feuille)* planner; **agenda de bureau** = desk diary **(b)** **agenda électronique** = electronic agenda; **logiciel d'agenda** = scheduler

agent *nm* **(a)** *(programme ou logiciel d'un réseau)* agent **(b)** *(commandes ou actions exécutées automatiquement)* **agent intelligent** = agent

agglomérer *vtr (des données)* to gather write

agrandir *vtr* **(a)** to enlarge *ou* to expand; *(photo)* to enlarge *ou* to magnify; **cette photo a été agrandie 200 fois** = the photograph has been magnified 200 times **(b)** *(une fenêtre MS-Windows)* **agrandir au plein écran** = to maximise

COMMENTAIRE: vous agrandissez une fenêtre au plein écran en cliquant une fois sur la flèche de montée dans le coin en haut à droite

◊ **agrandissement** *nm* enlargement *ou* expansion; *(photo)* enlargement *ou* magnification; *(avec un zoom)* zooming; **on a utilisé un agrandissement de la photo pour voir les détails plus clairement** = an enlargement of the photograph was used to provide better detail

agréer *vtr* to approve *ou* to accept

agrégat *nm* aggregate

agrégé, -ée *adj* **données agrégées** = data aggregate

aide *nf (assistance)* help *ou* aid; **ils ont besoin d'aide pour la programmation** = they need some help with their programming; **aide au diagnostic** = diagnostic aid; **l'ordinateur est une aide importante pour le traitement d'une grande quantité de données** = the computer is a great aid to rapid processing of large amounts of information; **aides à la**

programmation dans un langage déterminé = language support environment; **système d'aide à la décision (SAID)** = decision support system (DSS); **aide en ligne** *ou* **aide contextuelle** = context sensitive help; **écran d'aide** = help screen; *(pour clavier)* **grille d'aide** = key *ou* keyboard overlay; **sans la grille d'aide, je ne saurais jamais quelle touche de fonction je dois utiliser** = without the key overlay, I would never remember which function key does what; **touche d'aide** *ou* **touche AIDE** = help key

COMMENTAIRE: la plupart des logiciels pour PC ont normalisé la touche F1 pour afficher le texte d'aide qui explique comment faire les choses

◊ **aider** *vtr (assister)* to help *ou* to aid; *(soutenir)* to back

aigu, -uë 1 *adj* acute; **accent aigu** = acute accent; **sons aigus** = high notes **2** *nmpl (sons aigus)* **haut-parleur d'aigus** = tweeter

aiguillage *nm (dans un programme)* switch

◊ **aiguille** *nf* needle; **imprimante à aiguilles** = dot-matrix printer

aimant *nm* magnet; **micro(phone) à aimant mobile** = moving coil microphone

◊ **aimanté, -ée** *adj* magnetic

aire *nf (surface)* area; **graphe à aires** = area graph

ajouté, -ée *adj* added; **réseau à valeur ajoutée** = value added network (VAN); **revendeur de systèmes à valeur ajoutée** = value added reseller (VAR)

◊ **ajouter** *vtr* **(a)** to add; *(introduire)* to insert; **avec les touches de fonction, il est facile d'ajouter au texte ou de le couper** = adding or deleting material from the text is easy using function keys; **les producteurs de logiciels ont ajouté un nouveau progiciel de gestion à leur gamme de produits** = the software house has added a new management package to its range of products **(b)** *(joindre un fichier à la suite d'un autre)* to append; **en utilisant la command DOS COPY A+B, vous ajoutez le fichier B à la fin du fichier A** = if you enter the DOS command COPY A+B, the file B will be appended to the end of file A

ajustement *nm* adjustment *ou* tuning

◊ **ajuster** *vtr (réguler* ou *mettre au point)* to adjust *ou* to tune *ou* to regulate; *(mettre en place)* to fit; **pour ajuster la luminosité de l'écran, tourner le bouton placé à l'arrière du moniteur** = the brightness can be regulated by turning a knob at the back of the monitor; **ajuster avec grande précision** = to fine tune; **ajuster la tête de lecture** = to align a read/write head

alarme *nf* alarm; **caractère (d')alarme** = bell character; **tout le personnel doit quitter le bâtiment dès que la sonnerie d'alarme retentit** = all staff must leave the building if the alarm sounds; **voyant d'alarme** = warning light

album *nm (utilitaire Apple Macintosh qui stocke les graphiques les plus utilisés)* **album de croquis** =

scrapbook; **nous conservons le logo dans l'album de croquis** = we store our logo in the scrapbook

albumen *nm* albumen; *(photo)* **plaque photosensible à l'albumen** = albumen plate

alcalin, -e *adj* **pile alcaline** = dry cell

alcool *nm* alcohol *ou* spirit; **duplicateur à alcool** = spirit duplicator

aléatoire *adj* random; **accès aléatoire** = random access; **les lecteurs de disquettes permettent l'accès aléatoire des données alors qu'une bande magnétique en permet l'accès séquentiel** = disk drives are random access, magnetic tape is sequential access memory; **mémoire à accès aléatoire** = random access memory (RAM) *ou* random access storage; **mémoire vidéo à accès aléatoire (VRAM)** = video random access memory (VRAM); **dispositif mémoire à accès aléatoire** = random access device; **nombre aléatoire** = random number; **générateur de nombres aléatoires** = random number generator; **génération de nombres aléatoires** = random number generation; **processus aléatoire** = random process; **test de lecture/écriture aléatoire des mémoires** = leapfrog test; **traitement aléatoire (des données)** = random processing; *voir aussi* PSEUDO

alerte *nf (indique une anomalie sur le réseau)* **alerte réseau** = network alert; *(message indiquant une erreur ou une anomalie)* **(message d')alerte** = alert; **boîte de message d'alerte** = alert box; **le message d'alerte m'a averti que j'étais sur le point d'effacer tous mes fichiers** = the alert box warned me that I was about to delete all my files; **condition d'alerte** = alert condition; **trame d'alerte** = beacon frame

◊ **alerter** *vtr* to alert; **alerter un système** = to wake up a system

◊ **alerteur** *nm (sur un réseau)* **alerteur d'évènement** *ou* **d'incident** = beacon

algèbre *nf* algebra; **algèbre booléenne** *ou* **algèbre de Boole** = Boolean algebra *ou* Boolean logic

◊ **algébrique** *adj* **langage algébrique** = algebraic language

ALGOL *voir* ALGORITHMIQUE

algorithme *nm* algorithm; *(des pages de mémoire)* **algorithme d'ancienneté** *ou* **de la page la moins récemment utilisée** = least recently used algorithm (LRU); **algorithme de compactage** = compacting algorithm; **algorithme cryptographique** *ou* **de cryptage** = cryptographic algorithm; **algorithme d'effacement de lignes cachées** = hidden line algorithm; **algorithme hash** = hashing function; **algorithme de pagination** = paging algorithm; *voir aussi* PREMIER

◊ **algorithmique** *adj* algorithmic; **langage algorithmique** = algorithmic language (ALGOL)

alias *nm* alias; **le système d'exploitation utilise l'alias COM1 pour désigner le port série à l'adresse**

3FCh = the operating system uses the alias COM1 to represent the serial port address 3FCh; **nom d'alias** = alias name

aligné, -ée *adj* aligned *ou* in alignment

◊ **alignement** *nm* **(a)** alignment; aligning; **alignement automatique des virgules** = automatic decimal adjustment **(b) alignement de la tête de lecture** = head alignment; **réglage d'alignement des têtes** *ou* **des angles d'azimut** = azimuth alignment; **c'est cette petite vis qui sert à régler l'alignement des têtes** *ou* **des angles d'azimut** = azimuth alignment is adjusted with this small screw; *(d'un scanner de texte)* **bord d'alignement** = aligning edge; **défaut d'alignement** = skew; *(assure la bonne position du papier dans l'imprimante)* **dispositif d'alignement** = aligner; **réaliser un mauvais alignement** = to skew; *(de la tête de lecture)* **perte d'alignement** = gap loss; **téton** *ou* **pige d'alignement** = alignment pin

◊ **aligner** *vtr (tête de lecture)* to align *ou* to line up; *(texte ou colonne)* to align *ou* to range *ou* to line up; **cette page est mal alignée** = this page is badly skewed; **les chiffres sont alignés l'un à la suite de l'autre plutôt que d'être présentés en colonnes** = the figures are presented in rows, not in columns; **en appuyant sur la touche de tabulation en début de ligne, pour se placer à la colonne 10, la liste avait été parfaitement alignée** = the list was neatly lined up by tabbing to column 10 at the start of each new line; *(justifier)* **aligner à gauche** = to range left

alimentation *nf* **(a)** *(papier)* feed *ou* paper feed; *(cartes perforées)* card feed; *(dans une imprimante)* **alimentation automatique du papier** = auto advance (of paper); **scanner avec alimentation automatique du papier** = paper-fed scanner; **alimentation par l'avant** = front feed; **alimentation du papier en continu** = continuous feed; **alimentation du papier feuille à feuille** = (single) sheet feed; **ce dispositif contrôle l'alimentation du papier feuille à feuille** = the device controls the copy flow; **système d'alimentation feuille à feuille** = cut sheet feeder; **système d'alimentation du papier** = feeder; *(bac)* sheet feed attachment; *(pour film)* **bobine d'alimentation** = feed reel **(b)** *(électricité)* power supply; **bloc d'alimentation** = power pack *ou* power supply unit (PSU); **alimentation auxiliaire** *ou* **de secours** = battery backup; **alimentation de secours de la mémoire** = memory backup capacitor; **brancher une ligne sur une source d'alimentation** = to pull up a line; **(dispositif de) contrôle de l'alimentation** = power monitor

◊ **alimenter** *vtr* **(a)** to feed **(b)** *(en courant électrique)* to power; **l'écran est alimenté par le transformateur du PC principal** = the monitor is powered from a supply in the main PC

> l'alimentation est assurée par une pile au lithium de 6V ou 4 piles au manganèse de 1,5V
> *Science et Vie*

alinéa *nm* indent *ou* indentation; **faire un alinéa** = to indent (a paragraph); **comptez deux espaces pour l'alinéa du premier paragraphe** = indent the first paragraph two spaces

aller *nm* outward direction *ou* journey; **canal (de transmission) aller** = forward channel; **temps de propagation aller (et) retour** = up and down propagation time

◊ **aller** *vi* to go; *(varier)* **aller (de ... à)** = to range (from ... to); **la gamme des produits de la société va du micro portable au gros ordinateur multiposte** = the company's products range from a cheap lapheld micro to a multistation mainframe; *(dans un texte)* **aller à la ligne** = to start a new line *ou* a new paragraph; **caractère indiquant d'aller à la ligne** = new line character

allocation *nf* allocation *ou* assignment; *(procédure de répartition de la mémoire nécessaire à une application)* **allocation de mémoire** = memory allocation; **allocation de temps a un projet** = allocation of time to a project; **allocation dynamique** = dynamic allocation; **allocation dynamique de canal** *ou* **de voie de communication** = adaptive channel allocation; **programme d'allocation** = allocation routine; *(secteur d'un disque dur où un fichier est stocké)* **unité d'allocation** = allocation unit

allonger *vtr* to extend

allophone *n&adj* allophone

alloué, -ée *adj* **fréquence allouée** = assigned frequency; **liste des emplacements non alloués** = uncommitted storage list

◊ **allouer** *vtr* to allocate *ou* to assign; **on peut allouer une étiquette aux touches de fonction** = tags can be allocated to function keys; **le système d'exploitation a alloué presque toute la mémoire principale au tableur** = the operating system allocated most of main memory to the spreadsheet program

allumer *vt (mettre sous tension)* **allumer (un ordinateur)** = to switch on *ou* to turn on (a computer)

ALPHA ™ *nm (processeur mis au point par Digital Equipment Corporation)* ALPHA ™ (chip)

alpha *nm (lettre de l'alphabet grec)* alpha; *(premier test effectué sur un ordinateur)* **alpha test** *ou* **test alpha** = alpha *ou* alpha test; **le nouveau logiciel en est au stade alpha** *ou* **existe en version alpha** = the new software is still in an alpha product stage; *(définit le propriétés d'un pixel)* **canal alpha** = alpha channel; **enrouleur alpha** = alpha wrap; **particule alpha** = alpha-particle; **rayons** *ou* **rayonnement alpha** = alpha radiation; **sensibilité aux rayons alpha** = alpha-particle sensitivity; *(technique d'intelligence artificielle)* **technique alpha bêta** = alpha beta technique

alphabet *nm* alphabet; *(police de caractères)* alphabetic character set

◊ **alphabétique** *adj* alphabetical; **chaîne de caractères alphabétiques** = alphabetic string; **ordre alphabétique** = alphabetical order; **en** *ou* **par ordre alphabétique** = in alphabetical order *ou* alphabetically; **classer (des données) en** *ou* **par**

ordre alphabétique = to alphasort *ou* to alphabetize; **les noms sont classés par ordre alphabétique** = the sequence of names is arranged alphabetically; **les fichiers sont classés en** *ou* **par ordre alphabétique sous le nom du client** = the files are arranged alphabetically under the customer's name; **veuillez saisir les données bibliographiques et les mettre en ordre alphabétique** = enter the bibliographical information and alphabetize it

◊ **alphabétiquement** *adv* alphabetically *ou* in alphabetical order

alphagéométrique *adj* alphageometric

alphamosaïque *adj* alphamosaic

alphanumérique *adj* alphanumeric; **affichage alphanumérique** = alphanumeric display; **caractères alphanumériques** = alphanumeric characters *ou* alphanumerics; **chaîne de caractères alphanumériques** = alphanumeric string; **clavier alphanumérique** = alphanumeric keyboard; **données alphanumériques** = alphanumeric data; **opérande alphanumérique** = alphanumeric operand; **touche alphanumérique** = alphanumeric key

alphaphotographique *adj* alpha-photographic

Alt *(touche d'un clavier d'ordinateur)* **touche Alt** = Alt key; **appuyez en même temps sur les touches Alt et P pour imprimer le document** = press Alt and P at the same time to print your document

COMMENTAIRE: la touche Alt est devenue le standard pour activer la barre de menu dans tous les logiciels destinés au PC; par exemple Alt F affiche normalement le menu Fichier d'un programme, Alt X ou Alt Q font sortir du programme

altération *nf (du signal)* distortion

◊ **altérer** *vtr (signal)* to distort; *(données ou fichier)* to mung up

alternance *nf* alternation; **redresseur (de) simple alternance** = half wave rectifier

◊ **alternat** *nm* **à l'alternat** = alternately; **mode de transmission bidirectionnelle à l'alternat** = either-way operation

◊ **alternateur** *nm* alternator

◊ **alternatif, -ive** *adj* **(a)** *(autre)* alternate **(b)** *(qui alterne)* alternating; **courant alternatif (CA)** = alternating current (AC)

◊ **alternative** *nf* alternative

◊ **alterné, -ée** *adj* alternate; **mode alterné** = alternate mode

◊ **alterner** *vtr* to alternate; **faire alterner** = to alternate

A-MAC *(basse fréquence multiplexée)* A-MAC

ambiant, -e *adj* ambient; **lumière ambiante** = available light *ou* ambient light; **niveau de bruit ambiant** = ambient noise level; **température ambiante** = ambient temperature

ambigu, -uë *adj* ambiguous; **nom de fichier ambigu** = ambiguous filename

◊ **ambiguïté** *nf* ambiguity; **erreur d'ambiguïté** = ambiguity error

ambisonique *adj* **enregistrement ambisonique** = ambisonics

âme *nf (d'un câble)* core

amélioration *nf* improvement; enhancement; **filtre d'amélioration du contraste** = contrast enhancement filter

◊ **amélioré, -ée** *adj* improved; upgraded *ou* enhanced *ou* optimized; **code amélioré** = optimum code *ou* optimized code

◊ **améliorer** *vtr* to improve; to upgrade *ou* to enhance *ou* to optimize; **le nouveau modèle peut être amélioré sans renvoi chez le fournisseur** = the new model has an on-site upgrade facility

Amiga ™ *(ordinateurs individuels mis au point par Commodore)* Amiga ™ (computer)

COMMENTAIRE: les ordinateurs Amiga sont basés sur la gamme de processeurs 68000 de Motorola et ne sont pas compatibles avec les IBM PC

amont *nm* **en amont** = above *ou* upstream; **chaînage en amont** = backward chaining

amorçage *nm (de système)* booting *ou* boot-up; *(automatique)* autoboot; **bloc** *ou* **enregistrement d'amorçage** = boot block *ou* record; **disque** *ou* **disquette d'amorçage** = boot disk *ou* startup disk; **après avoir mis l'ordinateur en route, insérez la disquette d'amorçage** = after you switch on the computer, insert the boot disk; **partition d'amorçage** = boot partition; **programme d'amorçage** = bootstrap; **chargeur de programme d'amorçage** = bootstrap loader

◊ **amorce** *nf* **(a)** *(d'une bande ou d'un film)* head *ou* leader **(b)** *(programme)* bootstrap **(c)** *(valeur de départ pour nombres aléatoires)* **amorce théorique** = seed

◊ **amorcer** *vtr* **(a)** *(système)* to boot up *ou* to bootstrap; *(automatiquement)* to autoboot **(b)** to warm up

amortir *vtr (un son ou bruit)* to deaden; **les capots d'insonorisation servent à amortir le bruit des imprimantes** = acoustic hoods are used to deaden the noise of printers

◊ **s'amortir** *vpr (signal)* to decay; **le signal s'est amorti rapidement** = the signal decayed rapidly

◊ **amortissement** *nm (d'un son)* decay; **avec un amortissement court, le son est très aigu** = with a short decay, it sounds very sharp; **délai d'amortissement d'un signal** = decay time

amovible *adj* exchangeable *ou* removable *ou* movable; **disque dur amovible** = exchangeable disk storage (EDS) *ou* removable hard disk *ou* disk cartridge; **disque (dur) non amovible** = fixed (hard) disk; **disque Winchester amovible** = removable Winchester; **ROM amovible** = ROM cartridge

ampère (A) *nm* ampere *ou* amp (A)

ampli *nm* = AMPLIFICATEUR amplifier; **ne placez pas le micro trop près du haut-parleur sinon le retour va saturer l'ampli** = make sure the microphone is not too close to the loudspeaker or positive feedback will occur and you will overload the amplifier

amplificateur *ou* **ampli** *nm* amplifier; **amplificateur audio** *ou* **amplificateur de basses fréquences** = audio amplifier; **amplificateur de courant (du bus)** = bus driver; **amplificateur à faible bruit** = low noise amplifier; **amplificateur d'image** = image enhancer; **amplificateur MASER** = microwave amplification by stimulated emission of radiation (MASER); **amplificateur operationnel** = operational amplifier *ou* op amp; **amplificateur de signal** = amplifier; regenerator *ou* repeater; **amplificateur de téléphone** = telephone repeater; **classe d'amplificateur** = amplifier class

◊ **amplification** *nf (du son ou du signal)* amplification; *(de l'image)* magnification; **augmentez l'amplification** = increase the amplification (of the input signal); **l'amplification est si grande qu'elle cause une distorsion du signal** = the amplification is so high that it distorts the signal; **boucle d'amplification** = positive feedback

◊ **amplifié, -ée** *adj (son ou signal)* amplified; *(image)* magnified; **téléphone amplifié** *ou* **à écoute amplifiée** = amplified telephone

◊ **amplifier** *vtr (son ou signal)* to amplify; *(image)* to magnify; **le signal reçu doit être amplifié avant d'être traité** = the received signal needs to be amplified before it can be processed

◊ **amplitude** *nf (d'un signal)* amplitude *ou* magnitude; *(du son)* **amplitude dynamique** = dynamic range; **amplitude maximum enregistrée** = maximum reading; **distorsion d'amplitude** = amplitude distortion; **modulation d'amplitude (MA)** = amplitude modulation (AM); **modulation d'impulsions en amplitude (MIA)** = pulse amplitude modulation (PAM); **quantification d'amplitude** = amplitude quantization

> l'amplitude des échos renvoyés renseigne sur la nature des tissus traversés et l'axe X, sur leur position
>
> *Techniques hospitalières*

analogique *adj* analog; **appareil analogique** = analog *ou* analogue; **boucle analogique** = analog loopback; **boucle analogique avec autotest** = analog loopback with selftest; **calculateur analogique** = analog computer; **carte d'entrée analogique** = analog input card; **carte de sortie analogique** = analog output card; **circuit analogique** = analog circuit *ou* gate; **données analogiques** = analog data; **écran analogique** = analog display; **enregistrement analogique** = analog recording; **ligne analogique** *ou* **commutée** = analog line; **moniteur analogique** = analog monitor; **multimètre analogique** = analog multimeter (AMM); **ordinateur analogique** = analog computer; **porte** *ou* **circuit analogique** = analog gate; **représentation analogique** = analog representation; **signal analogique** = analog signal;

signal analogique modulé = pseudo-digital signal; **transmission analogique** = analog transmission; **voie analogique** = analog channel

◊ **analogique-numérique** *ou* **analogique à digital** *adj* analog to digital (A to D *ou* A/D); **convertisseur analogique-numérique (CAN)** = analog to digital converter *ou* A to D converter (ADC); *(numériseur)* digitizer; **le signal vocal est d'abord passé par le convertisseur analogique-numérique avant d'être analysé** = the speech signal is first passed through an A to D converter before being analysed; **convertisseur analogique-numérique parallèle** = flash A/D; *voir aussi* NUMÉRIQUE-ANALOGIQUE

◊ **analogue** *nm&adj* analog *ou* analogue

analyse *nf* **(a)** analysis; **analyse cryptographique** = cryptanalysis; **analyse de données** = data analysis; *(d'un programme)* **analyse fonctionnelle** = functional specification; **analyse des médias** = media analysis *ou* media research; **analyse numérique** = numerical analysis; **analyse de réseaux** = network analysis; **analyse du signal dans le temps** = time domain analysis; **analyse de systèmes** = systems analysis **(b)** *(d'un langage informatique)* **analyse grammaticale** *ou* **syntaxique** = parsing; **faire l'analyse grammaticale** = to parse; **analyse lexicale** = lexical analysis **(c)** *(résumé)* abstract

◊ **analyser** *vtr* to analyse *ou* to analyze; **analyser un listing** = to analyse a computer printout

◊ **analyseur** *nm* analyzer; **analyseur de bruit** = decibel meter; **analyseur d'état logique** = logic state analyzer; **analyseur de fréquence** = frequency analyzer; **analyseur d'image** = image processor; **analyseur de spectre** = spectrum analyzer

◊ **analyste** *nm&f* analyst; **informaticien, -ienne analyste** *ou* **analyste (de systèmes)** = systems analyst

anamorphose *nf* anamorphic image

anastigmate *adj* anastigmatic

ancêtre *nm* ancestor; **fichier ancêtre** = ancestral file

ancrage *nm* ancrage (du pointage) = grid snap; **le plus simple pour tracer des lignes de manière précise est d'utiliser le dispositif d'ancrage du pointage** = if you want to draw accurate lines, you'll find it easier with grid snap turned on; **cellule d'ancrage** = anchor cell

angle *nm* angle; *(inclinaison)* **angle d'un caractère** = character skew; *(entre deux signaux)* **angle de phase** *ou* **de déphasage** = phase angle; *(d'une lentille)* **angle de réception** = acceptance angle

angström (Å) *nm* angstrom

animation *nf* animation; **animation sur ordinateur** = (computer) animation

◊ **animé, -ée** *adj* busy *ou* animated; **dessin animé** = cartoon; *(d'un film)* **fond animé** = busy background

◊ **animer** *vtr* to animate

anneau *nm* **(a)** *(dispositif)* ring; **anneau de protection d'écriture** = write-permit ring **(b)** *(réseau rapide)* **anneau collecteur** *ou* **backbone** = backbone ring; **réseau en anneau** = ring (data) network; **(réseau en) anneau de Cambridge** = Cambridge ring; **le système comprend cinq postes de travail reliés en anneau** = the system includes five workstations linked together in a ring network; **token ring utilise une topologie en anneau** = token ring uses a ring topology

annexe *nf* appendix; **voir annexes pour tout renseignement supplémentaire** = for further details see the appendices

◊ **annexer** *vtr* to append

annonciateur *nm* annunciator

◊ **annonciateur, -trice** *adj* **signal annonciateur** = annunciator

annotation *nf* annotation; **annotation typo(graphique)** = marking up

◊ **annoter** *vtr* to annotate; *(en spécifiant la typographie)* to mark up

annuaire *nm* directory; **annuaire des téléphones** *ou* **annuaire téléphonique** = telephone book *ou* phone book *ou* telephone directory; **cherche son adresse dans l'annuaire (téléphonique)** = look up his address in the directory *ou* in the phone book; **annuaire téléphonique par professions** = classified directory; **annuaire par rues** = street directory

annulaire *adj* ring; **compteur annulaire** = ring counter

annulation *nf* cancellation; *(effacement)* deletion *ou* removal; **l'annulation de cette instruction résoudrait le problème** = the removal of this instruction could solve the problem; **annulation de fichier** = file deletion; **caractère d'annulation** = cancel character (CAN); **le logiciel envoie automatiquement un caractère d'annulation à chaque erreur** = the software automatically sends a cancel character after any error

◊ **annuler** *vtr* to cancel; **annuler (une action)** = to undo; **vous venez de supprimer un paragraphe, vous pouvez annuler cette action avec l'option 'annuler frappe' (undo) du menu Edition** = you've just deleted the paragraph, but you can undo it from the option in the Edit menu

anode *nf* anode

anomale *adj* anomalistic; **période anomale** = anomalistic period

◊ **anomalie** *nf* fault *ou* error; **anomalie persistante** = hard error; **rapport d'anomalies** = exception report

anormal, -e *adj* abnormal; **arrêt anormal** = abnormal termination; **erreur anormale** = abnormal error; **fin anormale** *ou* **interruption anormale** = abnormal end *ou* abend *ou* abnormal termination; **code de fin anormale** *ou* **d'interruption** = abend code; **une commande d'interruption venant d'une imprimante défectueuse a provoqué une fin anormale de traitement** = an interrupt from a faulty printer caused an abend; **programme de récupération de fichier après une interruption anormale** = abend recovery program; **en cas de panne, la perte de données sera minimale grâce au nouveau programme de récupération des fichiers après interruption anormale** = if a fault occurs, data loss will be minimized due to the improved abend recovery program; **séquence de clôture anormale** = abort sequence

◊ **anormalement** *adv* abnormally; **le signal est anormalement faible** = the signal is abnormally weak

ANSI = AMERICAN NATIONAL STANDARDS INSTITUTE; *(version du langage de programmation C)* **C ANSI** = ANSI C; **clavier ANSI** = ANSI keyboard; **contrôle d'écran ANSI** = ANSI screen control; **logiciel de commande ANSI** = ANSI driver; **séquence d'échappement ANSI** = ANSI escape sequence

antémémoire *nf* cache *ou* cache memory *ou* RAM cache; **antémémoire d'instruction** = instruction cache

antenne *nf* antenna *ou* aerial; **antenne en boucle** = loop antenna; **antenne collective de télévision (câblée)** = community antenna television (CATV); **antenne contrarotative** = de-spun antenna; **antenne (uni)directionnelle** = directional antenna; **antenne (en) éventail** *ou* **semi-circulaire** = fan antenna; *(omnidirectionnelle)* **antenne isotrope** = isotropic radiator; **antenne linéaire** = linear array; **antenne parabolique** = dish aerial; **nous utilisons une antenne parabolique pour capter les signaux transmis par satellite** = we use a dish aerial to receive signals from the satellite; **antenne de relais régional** = master antenna television system (MATV); **antenne réseau** = array antenna; **(série de) modules d'émission-réception d'une antenne réseau** = antenna array; **câble d'antenne** = aerial cable; **câble antenne-circuit** = feeder cable; **gain d'antenne** = antenna gain

> pour qu'une antenne parabolique capte correctement les émissions renvoyées par les satellites géostationnaires, son axe doit être parallèle aux ondes acheminant ces émissions
> *Science et Vie*

antérieur, -e *adj* **(a)** prior *ou* previous; **instruction qui annule l'instruction antérieure** = instruction which cancels the instruction which precedes it **(b)** anterior *ou* front; **panneau antérieur** = fascia plate *ou* front panel

◊ **antérieurement** *adv* previously; **antérieurement à** = prior to

anthropomorphique *adj* **logiciel anthropomorphique** = anthropomorphic software

anti- *préfixe* anti-

◊ **anti-écho** *adj inv* **dispositif anti-écho** = echo suppressor

anticipation *nf* anticipation; **référence par anticipation** = forward reference

◊ **anticipé, -ée** *adj* anticipated; **appel d'instruction anticipé** = pre-fetch(ing); *(par processeur central)* **lecture anticipée** = look ahead; *(dans un réseau token ring)* **libération anticipée du jeton** = early token release; *(d'un calculateur rapide)* **retenue anticipée** = carry look ahead

anticopie *adj* **système** *ou* **dispositif anticopie** = copy protection *ou* copy protect device; **toutes les disquettes sont munies d'un dispositif anticopie** = all disks are copy protected; **il arrive qu'une protection anticopie défectueuse entraîne la détérioration du disque dur** = a hard disk may crash because of faulty copy protection

anticrénelage *nm* *(d'un graphique)* anti-aliasing

antiparasite *adj* **dispositif antiparasite** = interference suppressor

antirebond *nm&adj* de-bounce

antireflet *nm&adj* **filtre antireflet(s)** = glare filter

antislash (\) *nm* backslash

antistatique *adj* **tapis antistatique** = anti-static mat

antivirus *nm&adj* **(programme** *ou* **logiciel** *ou* **utilitaire) antivirus** = anti-virus program *ou* software; vaccine

APC = ASSISTANT PERSONNEL DE COMMUNICATION

aperçu *nm* viewing; *(prévisualisation)* **aperçu avant impression** = page preview; **fonction 'présentation-aperçu'** = previewer; **la fonction intégrée 'présentation-aperçu' permet de visualiser le document et de vérifier s'il s'est glissé des erreurs** = the built-in previewer allows the user to check for mistakes

APL *(langage de programmation)* A Programming Language (APL)

APPC *(programmation avancée des programmes de communications)* **protocole APPC** = advanced program to program communications (APPC)

apochromatique *adj* apochromatic; **objectif apochromatique** = apochromatic lens

apogée *nm* apogee

apostrophe (') *nf* apostrophe

apparaître *vi* to appear; **faire apparaître** = to reveal; *(sur l'écran)* to display; **la touche HELP fera apparaître sur l'écran une description des différentes options** = by keying HELP, the screen will display the options available to the user; **c'est la dernière image du film: faites apparaître les titres** = this is the last frame of the film so show the titles

appareil *nm* machine; *(électrique)* appliance; (de petite taille) device; **appareil en bon état de**

marche = functional unit; **appareil cinématographique** = cine camera; **tout appareil électrique doit être mis à la terre** = all electrical appliances should be properly earthed; **appareil d'entrée/sortie** = I/O device; **appareil photographique** *ou* **appareil photo** = camera; **appareil (photo) à plaques** = plate camera; **appareil de sortie** = output device; **appareils (de) téléinformatique** = data communications equipment (DCE); **appareil de traitement de texte** = word processor; **appareil de traitement de texte spécialisé** = dedicated word processor; **arrêt dû à une défaillance de l'appareil** = machine check; **(logiciel) qui ne fonctionne que sur un type d'appareil** = machine-dependent (software); **priorité d'un appareil** = device priority

apparence *nf* aspect *ou* appearance

apparié, -ée *adj* paired; **registres appariés** = paired registers

appel *nm* **(a)** *(d'un programme* *ou* *d'une instruction)* call; **appel d'instruction anticipé** = pre-fetch; **appel de page sur demande** = demand paging; **appel récursif** = recursive call; **instruction d'appel** = call instruction; **c'est ici qu'il faudrait introduire l'instruction d'appel** = the subroutine call instruction should be at this point; **reprise au point d'appel** = fall back recovery; **séquence d'appel** = calling sequence **(b)** *(entre stations)* call; **durée d'un appel** = call duration; **la durée de l'appel varie suivant la complexité de la transaction** = call duration depends on the complexity of the transaction; **les frais sont fonction de la durée de l'appel** = charges are related to call duration; **scanner de contrôle d'appel** = communications scanner; **signal d'appel accepté** *ou* **signal d'acceptation d'appel** = call accepted signal; **signal de contrôle d'appel** = call control signal; **unité** *ou* **système d'appel** = calling unit **(c)** *(de l'ordinateur principal aux terminaux* *ou* *périphériques)* **appel sélectif** = polling; **appel sélectif de groupe** = group poll; **temps d'appels sélectifs** = polling overhead; **caractères d'appel sélectif** = polling characters; **interruption d'appel sélectif** = polled interrupt; **intervalle d'appels sélectifs** = polling interval; **ordre d'appel (des terminaux)** = polling list **(d)** *(téléphonique)* (phone *ou* telephone) call; *(numérotation)* dialling; **(système d')appel automatique d'un correspondant** = auto-dial (system); *(relie l'ordinateur au téléphone)* **système** *ou* **unité d'appel automatique** = automatic calling unit (ACU); **appel en PCV** = reverse charge call *US* collect call; **(système d')acheminement direct des appels** = direct dialling; **enregistrer le nombre et la durée des appels** = to log calls; **faire un appel** = to make a (phone *ou* telephone) call; **personne qui fait un appel (téléphonique)** = caller; **faire un appel groupé** = to ring down; *(d'un système d'appel ACU)* **indicateur d'appel** = ring indicator (RI); **prendre un appel** = to answer the phone *ou* to take a (telephone) call; *(d'un serveur de télécopie)* **programmation d'appels** = call scheduling; *(aide en ligne)* **service d'appels** = dialup *ou* dial-up service; **tonalité (d'appel)** = dialling tone *ou* dial tone; **transfert d'appel (automatique)** = call forwarding; **dispositif de transfert** *ou* **de**

réacheminement *ou* de déroutage d'appel = call diverter; **nous avons demandé le transfert à la maison des appels que nous recevons au bureau** = we are having all calls forwarded from the office to home; *voir aussi* MODEM **(e)** *(signaleur d'appel)* **(système d')appel de personne** = (radio) paging; **appeler** *ou* **chercher à joindre quelqu'un par système d'appel** = to page someone

◊ **appeler** *vtr* **(a)** *(un programme ou une routine)* to call *ou* to invoke; **dès réception de l'entrée, on appelle la première fonction** = after an input is received, the first function is called up **(b)** *(un périphérique ou une station)* to call **(c)** *(afficher)* **appeler à l'écran** = to call up **(d)** *(au téléphone)* to telephone *ou* to phone *ou* to call (someone) *ou* to make a (telephone) call; **ne me téléphonez pas, c'est moi qui vous appellerai** = don't phone me, I'll phone you; **je vous appellerai au bureau demain** = I'll call you at your office tomorrow; **appeler en direct** = to dial direct; **vous pouvez appeler New York en direct depuis Londres** = you can dial New York direct from London; **appeler la standardiste** = to dial the operator; **appeler pour faire venir quelque chose** = to phone for something; **il a appelé un taxi** = he phoned for a taxi; **il a appelé à propos de la commande de papier listing** = he phoned about the order for computer stationery **(e)** **appeler quelqu'un par système d'appel (de personne)** *ou* **par signaleur d'appel** *ou* **par bip** = to page someone

appendice *nm* appendix; **vous trouverez la liste complète dans l'appendice** = a complete list is printed in the appendix

Apple *(société formée en 1975, qui a développé une série d'ordinateurs individuels dont: Apple II, Apple Lisa et, plus récemment, Apple Macintosh)* **(la société) Apple Computer Corporation** = Apple Computer Corporation; **bus Apple Desktop** = Apple Desktop Bus (ADB); **protocole de gestion de fichiers Apple (AFP)** = Apple filing protocol (AFP) ™; *(touche Pomme)* **touche Apple** = Apple Key

◊ **Appleshare** ™ *(logiciel qui permet aux utilisateurs de partager un fichier)* Appleshare ™

◊ **AppleTalk** ™ *(protocole de communication de réseau)* AppleTalk ™; **protocole de gestion de fichiers AppleTalk (AFP)** *ou* **protocole AFP** = AppleTalk Filing Protocol ™ (AFP)

application *nf* application; **applications informatiques** = computer applications; **architecture de système d'application** = Systems Application Architecture (SAA); **basculement** *ou* **changement d'application** = context-switching; **bibliothèque des routines d'applications** = run-time library; **ce logiciel a été conçu avec toutes les routines graphiques accessibles dans la bibliothèque des routines d'applications** = the software is designed with all the graphics routines in this run-time library file; **circuit intégré spécifique à une application (ASIC)** = application specific integrated circuit (ASIC); *(dans un réseau ISO/OSI)* **couche application** = application layer; **développeur d'application** = application developer; **fenêtre d'application** = application window; **fichier d'application** = application file;

générateur d'application = application generator; report program generator (RPG); **icône d'application** = application icon; **interface de programmation d'application (API)** = application programming interface (API); **si je développe mon programme conformément à l'API publié pour ce système, il marchera convenablement** = if I follow the published API for this system, my program will work properly; **langage d'application** = job-orientated language *ou* problem-orientated language (POL); **logiciel** *ou* **programme d'application** = applications software *ou* applications program; **l'éditeur multifenêtre est utilisé pour créer et éditer les programmes d'application** = the multi-window editor is used to create and edit applications programs; **progiciel d'application** = applications package; **programmeur d'application** = applications programmer; **terminal d'application** = job-orientated terminal

> COMMENTAIRE : contrairement à ce qu'il se passe dans un vrai système multitâche, le basculement d'application ne permet qu'à un seul programme de tourner

appliquer *vtr* to apply; **pour faire un circuit imprimé il faut d'abord recouvrir la carte d'une résine photosensible puis appliquer le masque du circuit, exposer, développer et graver pour finalement obtenir le tracé** = to make the PCB, coat the board with photoresist, place the opaque pattern above, expose, then develop and etch, leaving the conducting tracks

◊ **s'appliquer (à)** *vpr* to apply (to something)

APPN **réseau APPN** = Advanced Peer-to-Peer Networking (APPN); *voir aussi* RESEAU

apprécier *vtr* to appreciate *ou* to approve of (something)

apprendre *vtr* to learn *ou* to master (a subject *ou* a technique); **nous avons appris assez rapidement à utiliser le nouveau système de traitement de texte** = we mastered the new word-processor quite quickly

apprentissage *nm* training *ou* learning; **apprentissage assisté par ordinateur** = computer-aided training (CAT) *ou* computer-based training (CBT); **courbe d'apprentissage** = learning curve; **apprentissage difficile** = steep learning curve

approbation *nf* approval

approché, -ée *adj* approximate *ou* approximating

approuver *vtr&i* to approve something *ou* of something; **le conseil d'administration doit approuver le choix du logiciel** = the software has to be approved by the board

approximatif, -ive *adj* approximate *ou* rough; **calcul approximatif** = rough calculation; **j'ai fait un calcul approximatif sur le dos d'une enveloppe** = I made some rough calculations on the back of an envelope; **calcul approximatif du temps de saisie**

(au clavier) = approximation of keyboarding time; **nous avons calculé de façon approximative le temps nécessaire à la saisie du texte (par clavier)** = we have made an approximate calculation of the time needed for keyboarding; **résultat approximatif** = approximation; **ce résultat n'est qu'approximatif** = the final figure is only an approximation

◊ **approximation** *nf (résultat approximatif)* approximation; *(calcul approximatif)* rough calculation

◊ **approximativement** *adv* approximately

appuyer *vi* to press (on) *ou* to touch *ou* to push (something); **appuyer sur une touche** = to press *ou* to hit a key; **appuyez sur la touche ECHAPPEMENT pour arrêter le programme** = to end the program, press ESCAPE; **action d'appuyer sur une séquence de (deux) touches (en même temps)** = chord keying

> COMMENTAIRE: par exemple, vous pouvez accéder à une seconde fenêtre en appuyant en même temps sur les touches Control et F2; si vous choisissez d'appuyer sur la touche majuscule et sur la touche 'effacement', vous effacerez une ligne de texte

après *prép* **(a)** after; **édition après compilation** *ou* **après calculs** = post-editing **(b)** **d'après** = according to; **d'après les résultats de l'an dernier** = based on last year's figures

◊ **après-vente** *adj inv* **service après-vente (SAV)** = *(bureau)* customer service department; *(service offert)* maintenance service *ou* aftersales service *ou* backup service; **nous offrons à nos clients un service après-vente gratuit** = we offer a free backup service to customers

A propos de... *(renseignements sur l'auteur du programme, etc.)* About...

APT = AUTOMATICALLY PROGRAMME TOOLS; *voir* COMMANDE

arabe *adj* Arabic; **chiffres arabes** = Arabic numbers *ou* figures *ou* numerals; **les pages sont numérotées en chiffres arabes** = the page numbers are written in Arabic figures

arbitrage *nm* arbitration; **arbitrage de bus** = bus arbitration; **bus d'arbitrage** = contention bus

arborescence *nf (structure en arbre)* tree *ou* forest (structure); spanning tree; **une arborescence est formée de branches reliées les unes aux autres par des points de liaison ou noeuds** = a tree is made of branches that connect together at nodes; **arborescence optimale** = minimal tree; **arborescence en puits** = sink tree; **élément final d'une arborescence** = leaf; **tri en arborescence** = tree selection sort

◊ **arborescent, -e** *adj* **système arborescent** = tree and branch network system

arbre *nm (structure)* tree (structure); **arbre binaire** = binary tree; **arbre de décision** = decision tree

archétype *nm* archetype

Archimède *(ordinateur individuel de la société Acorn Computers)* Archimedes

architecture *nf* architecture; **architecture à bus multiples** = multiple bus architecture; **architecture d'un circuit intégré** = chip architecture; **architecture de micro-ordinateur** = microcomputer architecture; **architecture orientée vers l'objet** *ou* **adaptée à l'objet** = object architecture *ou* object-orientated architecture; **architecture en pelure d'oignon** = onion skin architecture; **cet ordinateur possède une architecture en pelure d'oignon comprenant un noyau central, un système d'exploitation, un langage de bas niveau et le programme utilisateur** = the onion skin architecture of this computer is made up of a kernel at the centre, an operating system, a low-level language and then the user's program; **architecture de réseau** = networking *ou* network architecture *ou* systems network architecture (SNA); **architecture d'un système** = computer architecture *ou* computer organization; **architecture en tranches** = bit-slice architecture *ou* design; *voir aussi* FLUX

archivage *nm* archiving; **attribut** *ou* **bit** *ou* **drapeau d'archivage** = archive attribute *ou* bit *ou* flag; **copie pour archivage** = archive copy *ou* file copy; **mémoire d'archivage** = archive storage; **la mémoire d'archivage a une capacité de 1200Mo pour sept stations de travail** = the archive storage has a total capacity of 1200Mb between seven workstations; **méthode d'archivage** = filing system; **qualité d'archivage** = archival quality

◊ **archivé, -ée** *adj* archived; **copie archivée** = archived copy

◊ **archiver** *vtr* to archive; **archiver des documents** = to file documents

◊ **archives** *fpl* archive(s); **copie d'archives** = archived copy; **fichier archives** = archive file

◊ **archiviste** *nm&f* archivist

ARCNET *ou* **ARCnet** réseau ARCNET *ou* ARCnet = Attached Resource Computer Network (ARCNET)

> COMMENTAIRE: ARCNET utilise un seul jeton qui passe d'une station à la suivante en portant des données. ARCNET transmet 2,5 Mbits par seconde et utilise une topologie en étoile.

arête *nf* **arête dorsale** = backbone

argument *nm* **(a)** argument; **argument décisif** = deciding factor; **l'excellence des graphiques a constitué l'argument décisif** = the deciding factor was the superb graphics **(b)** *(variable)* argument *ou* arg; **si vous entrez les mots 'MULTIPLY A, B',** **le processeur reconnaîtra l'opérateur MULTIPLY et l'utilisera avec les deux arguments A et B** = if you enter the words 'MULTIPLY A, B', the processor will recognise the operator, MULTIPLY, and use it with the two arguments, A and B; **séparateur d'arguments** = argument separator; **la commande 'MULTIPLY A, B'** **utilise une virgule comme séparateur d'arguments**

= the command 'MULTIPLY A, B' uses a comma as the argument separator

arithmétique 1 *nf* arithmetic; **arithmétique en double précision** = double precision arithmetic; **arithmétique externe** = external arithmetic; **arithmétique interne** = internal arithmetic; **arithmétique à virgule fixe** = fixed-point arithmetic; **arithmétique à virgule flottante** = floating point arithmetic **2** *adj* arithmetic; **capacité de calcul arithmétique** = arithmetic capability; **décalage arithmétique** = arithmetic shift; **élément arithmétique étendu** = extended arithmetic element; **fonctions arithmétiques** = arithmetic functions; **instruction arithmétique** = arithmetic instruction; **opérateur** *ou* **symbole (d'une opération) arithmétique** = arithmetic operator; **opération arithmétique** = arithmetic operation; **registre arithmétique** = arithmetic register; **unité arithmétique et logique (UAL)** = arithmetic logic unit (ALU) *ou* arithmetic unit; **vérification arithmétique** = arithmetic check

ARLL *(encodage)* Advanced Run-length Limited (ARLL)

armature *nf* **armature de déflexion** = deflection yokes

armé, -ée *adj* armed *ou* enabled; **dispositif armé** = armed *ou* active device

◊ **armer** *vtr* to arm *ou* to enable *ou* to activate

ARP *(protocole de liaison d'adresses TCP/IP)* Address Resolution Protocol (ARP)

ARQ *(système de correction d'erreurs pour modems)* Automatic Repeat Request (ARQ)

arrangement *nm* order *ou* pattern *ou* layout; **arrangement binaire** = bit pattern

arrêt *nm* **(a)** *(d'un appareil)* stop *ou* halt *ou* pause; *(fin d'une opération)* ending *ou* termination; *(défaillance)* failure *ou* check; *(position d'un commutateur)* 'power off' *ou* 'off'; **arrêt anormal** = abnormal termination; **arrêt automatique** = auto stop *ou* automatic power off; *(d'un programme)* **arrêt conditionnel** = conditional breakpoint; *(causé par un défaut du support magnétique)* **arrêt de courte durée** = check; **arrêt dû à une défaillance de l'appareil** = machine check; **arrêt désordonné** = disorderly close-down; **arrêt d'urgence manuel (avec perte du contenu des mémoires volatiles)** = cold standby; **arrêt dynamique** = dynamic stop; **arrêt de l'impression** = print pause; *(d'un programme)* **arrêt inattendu** = hangup; **arrêt pour manque de papier** = form stop; **arrêt programmé** = programmed halt; **arrêt de tabulation** = tab stop *ou* tabulation stop; *(panne)* **arrêt total** = dead halt *ou* drop dead halt; **le manuel n'explique pas la marche à suivre en cas d'arrêt total de la machine** = the manual does not say what to do if a dead halt occurs; **arrêt de transmission de données** = data break; *(appareil)* **à l'arrêt** = inactive (machine); *(pour téléphone)* **boîtier d'arrêt** = barrier box; **code d'arrêt** = stop code; *(d'un programme)* **condition d'arrêt** = halt condition; **instruction**

d'arrêt = halt instruction *ou* stop instruction *ou* breakpoint instruction; *(imprimerie)* **ligne d'arrêt** = holding line; **mécanisme d'arrêt** = shut-off mechanism; *(d'un programme)* **point d'arrêt** = breakpoint *ou* cutoff; **remise en marche** *ou* **reprise au point d'arrêt** = fall back recovery; **reprise sur l'instruction d'arrêt** *ou* **reprise au point d'arrêt** = warm start; **protocole de contrôle par signal d'arrêt** = stop and wait protocol; *(sur un clavier)* **touche Arrêt Défilement** = Scroll Lock key; **symbole d'arrêt (dynamique)** = breakpoint symbol; **temps d'arrêt** = stop time **(b) faire un arrêt sur image** = to freeze (frame); **le processeur d'images permet de faire un arrêt sur image** = with an image processor you can freeze a video frame

arrêter *vtr* to stop *ou* to halt *ou* to shut down; *(terminer)* to close *ou* to end; *(interrompre)* to interrupt; *(empêcher)* to inhibit; **arrêtez l'éxécution du programme, avant qu'il efface d'autres fichiers** = abort the program before it erases any more files; **arrêter (quelque chose) graduellement** = to phase out; **(instruction d') arrêter une tâche** = kill job

◊ **s'arrêter** *vpr* to stop

arrière 1 *nm* back; **pour ajuster la luminosité de l'écran, tourner le bouton placé à l'arrière du moniteur** = the brightness can be regulated by turning a knob at the back of the monitor **2** *adj* back; **panneau arrière** = back panel; **la prise est située sur le panneau arrière** = the socket is on the back panel; **on trouve une variété de connecteurs sur le panneau arrière de l'unité centrale** = there is a wide range of connectors at the back of the main unit **3** *adv* **marche arrière** = backward mode; **faire marche arrière** = to reverse; **en arrière** = backward *ou* backwards

◊ **arrière-plan** *nm* background; **ce nouveau processeur graphique permet de manipuler indépendamment les images d'arrière-plan et d'avant-plan ainsi que les plans-objets** = the new graphics processor chip can handle background, foreground and sprite movement independently; **communication en arrière-plan** = background communication; **image en arrière-plan** = background image; **impression en arrière-plan** = print spooling; **l'impression peut être exécutée en arrière-plan pendant que vous travaillez sur un autre document** = background printing can be carried out whilst you are editing another document; **recalcul en arrière-plan** = background recalculation; **tâche d'arrière-plan** = low-priority work; **traitement d'arrière-plan** = background processing

arrivée *nf* **(a)** arrival *ou* end; **(point d')arrivée** = far end *ou* receiving end; *(transmission)* **terminal d'arrivée** = receive only (RO) **(b) langue d'arrivée** = target language

arrondi *nm* *(au plus près)* rounding; *(par défaut)* truncation; **arrondi à un nombre fixe de décimales** = automatic decimal adjustment; **erreur d'arrondi** = approximation error *ou* round off error *ou* rounding error; *(par défaut)* truncation error

◊ **arrondir** *vtr (au plus près)* to round off; *(par défaut)* to truncate *ou* to round down; *(par excès)* to round up; **arrondir 23,456 à 23,46** = to round off 23.456 to 23.46; **3,5678 arrondi par défaut à 3,56** = 3.5678 truncated to 3.56; **on peut arrondir 2,651 à 2,65 par défaut** = we can round down 2.651 to 2.65; **on peut arrondir 2,647 à 2,65 par excès** = we can round up 2.647 to 2.65

◊ **arrondissement** *nm* rounding

arséniure *nm* arsenide; **arséniure de gallium** = gallium arsenide (GaAs)

article *nm* **(a)** *(d'un fichier)* article *ou* record; **votre article contient divers champs regroupés sous une même rubrique** = your record contains several fields that have been grouped together under the one heading; **article chaîné** = chained record; **fichier avec articles chaînés** = threaded file; **article logique** = logical record **(b)** *(de journal ou de revue)* article; **il a écrit, pour le journal local, un article concernant le groupe d'utilisateurs** = he wrote an article about the user group for the local newspaper **(c)** *(item de production)* article; **article en sus** *ou* **en option** = extra; **numérotation européenne des articles (NEA)** = European Article Number (EAN) **(d)** *(d'un contrat)* clause *ou* article; **voir l'article 8 du contrat** = see clause 8 of the contract

artificiel, -elle *adj* man-made; **intelligence artificielle (IA)** = artificial intelligence (AI) *ou* machine intelligence

l'intelligence artificielle n'est plus un domaine réservé: tous les utilisateurs peuvent y avoir accès

         L'Evénement

ASA *(sensibilité d'un film)* American Standard Association (ASA); **indice ASA** = ASA exposure index

ascendant, -e *adj* upward; **analyse ascendante** = bottom up analysis; **conception ascendante (d'un programme)** = bottom up method; *(d'un film)* **dispositif de défilement ascendant du générique** = crawl; *(dans un système expert)* **méthode ascendante** = hill climbing

ascenseur *nm (barre de défilement)* scroll bar

ASCII = AMERICAN STANDARD CODE FOR INFORMATION INTERCHANGE **caractère ASCII** = ASCII character; **chaîne de caractères ASCIIZ** = ASCIIZ string; **clavier ASCII** = ASCII keyboard; **code ASCII** = ASCII code; **le code ASCII est le code de caractères le plus fréquemment utilisé** = the ASCII code is the most frequently used character coding system; **fichier ASCII** = ASCII file; **utilisez un programme de traitement de texte ou un autre programme qui produira un fichier ASCII standard** = use a word processor or other program that generates a standard ASCII file; **texte ASCII** = ASCII text

aspect *nm* aspect

assemblage *nm* **(a)** *(conversion d'un programme en code machine)* assembly; **assemblage de caractères** = character assembly; **il y a un certain délai pendant lequel s'effectue l'assemblage du programme en code objet** = there is a short wait during which time the program is assembled into object code; **assemblage de documents** = document assembly *ou* document merge; **des erreurs de syntaxe repérées au cours de l'assemblage du programmme source** = syntax errors spotted whilst the source program is being assembled; **code d'assemblage** = assembly code; **code mnémonique d'assemblage** = assembler mnemonics *ou* mnemonic operation codes; **durée d'assemblage** = assembly time; **instruction d'assemblage** = pseudo-operation; **langage d'assemblage** = assembly language *ou* assembler language *ou* base language; **langage d'assemblage pour microprogramme** = microprogram assembly language; **liste** *ou* **listing** *ou* **impression d'un programme d'assemblage** = assembly listing; **période** *ou* **temps d'assemblage** = assembly time; **programme d'assemblage** = assembler (program) *ou* assembly (language) program *ou* assembly routine; **système d'assemblage** = assembly system **(b)** *(liaison de différents programmes ou fichiers)* linking *ou* merging; **(instruction d')assemblage de fichiers** = link files **(c)** *(montage d'un appareil)* assembly; **les pièces du lecteur de disquettes sont fabriquées au Japon, mais l'assemblage se fait en France** = the parts for the disk drive are made in Japan and assembled in France

assembler *vtr* **(a)** *(convertir un programme)* to assemble (a program) **(b)** *(relier différents programmes)* to link *ou* to join *ou* to merge **(c)** *(réunir les cahiers d'un livre)* to collate **(d)** *(monter un appareil)* to assemble

◊ **assembleur** *nm (programme)* assembler (program) *ou* assembly (language) program; language assembler; **assembleur absolu** = absolute assembler; **assembleur croisé** = cross-assembler; **assembleur de langage** = language assembler; **programme assembleur pour macrolangage** = macro assembler *ou* assembly program; **assembleur une passe** = one-pass assembler *ou* single-pass assembler; **ce nouvel assembleur une passe travaille très vite** = this new one-pass assembler is very quick in operation; **assembleur (en) deux passes** = two-pass assembler; **message d'erreur de l'assembleur** = assembler error message

◊ **assembleur/désassembleur** *nm* assembler/disassembler; **assembleur/désassembleur de paquets** = packet assembler/disassembler (PAD); **le terminal à distance est relié à un assembleur/désassembleur de paquets qui lui permet d'accéder à l'ordinateur hôte** = the remote terminal is connected to a PAD device through which it accesses the host computer **(b)** *(constructeur qui utilise des pièces provenant d'autres constructeurs)* OEM (Original Equipment Manufacturer)

◊ **assembleuse** *nf (machine pour assembler les cahiers d'un livres)* collator

assertion *nf* assertion

asservi, -e *adj* slave; *(puits ou collecteur de données)* **asservi à un bus** = bus slave; **asservi aux**

codes contrôle = control driven; **accès mutiple asservi à la demande** = demand assigned multiple access (DAMA); **multiplexage asservi à la demande** = demand multiplexing; **non asservi à l'horloge** = unclocked; **écran asservi** = slave tube; **processeur asservi** = slave processor; **terminal asservi** = slave terminal

> comme dans tout système asservi, des problèmes de stabilité interviennent lors de la conception, imposant telle ou telle architecture
> **Electronique Radio Plans**

assigné, -ée *adj* assigned; **fréquence assignée** = assigned frequency

◊ **assigner** *vtr* to assign

assistance *nf* backup *ou* support (service); **nous offrons à nos clients un service d'assistance gratuit** = we offer a free backup service to customers; **assistance technique** = *(par téléphone)* support hotline; *(sur le lieu de travail)* on-site maintenance **(b)** consultancy; **il offre une assistance technique** = he offers a consultancy service; **société d'assistance technique** = a consultancy firm

◊ **assistant, -e** *n (ultra-portatif)* **assistant personnel de communication (APC)** = personal digital assistant (PDA)

◊ **assisté, -ée** *adj* assisted; **assisté par ordinateur** = computer-aided *ou* computer-assisted; **apprentissage assisté par ordinateur** = computer-aided *ou* assisted training (CAT); computer-based training (CBT); **conception** *ou* **création assistée par ordinateur (CAO)** = computer-aided *ou* assisted design (CAD); **conception et fabrication assistées par ordinateur (CFAO)** = computer-aided *ou* assisted design/computer aided *ou* assisted manufacture (CAD/CAM); **dessin assisté par ordinateur (DAO)** = computer-aided drafting; **enseignement assisté par ordinateur (EAO)** = computer-aided *ou* assisted instruction (CAI); **fabrication assistée par ordinateur (FAO)** = computer-aided *ou* assisted manufacture (CAM); **formation assistée par ordinateur (FAO)** = computer-aided *ou* assisted learning (CAL); **ingénierie assistée par ordinateur (IAO)** = computer-aided *ou* assisted engineering (CAE); **présentation assistée par ordinateur (PréAO)** = computerized page layout; **publication assistée par ordinateur (PAO)** = desktop publishing (DTP) *ou* electronic publishing; **rencontres matrimoniales assistées par ordinateur** = computer dating; **test assisté par ordinateur (TAO)** = computer-aided *ou* assisted testing (CAT); **traduction assistée par ordinateur** = machine translation

◊ **assister** **1** *vtr (aider)* to help *ou* to aid **2** *vi (participer à)* to attend

associatif, -ive *adj* associative; **adressage associatif** = associative addressing *ou* content-addressable addressing; **mémoire associative** = associative memory *ou* storage; content-addressable memory (CAM) *ou* storage; **montage associatif** = associational editing; **processeur à mémoire associative** = associative processor;

recherche associative = chaining search; **registre de mémoire associative** = associative storage register

association *nf* **(a)** association; **Association française de normalisation (AFNOR)** = *(équivalent de)* British Standards Institute (BSI) **(b)** *(adresse)* **temps d'association** = binding time

◊ **associé, -ée 1** *n* associate **2** *adj* associate *ou* joined; associated; *(par deux)* paired; **document** *ou* **fichier associé** = associated document *ou* file; **registres associés** = paired registers

◊ **associer** *vtr* to associate; *(adresse)* to bind

assortir *vtr* to match

assourdir *vtr (un son)* to deaden

◊ **assourdissement** *nm (d'un son)* muting *ou* deadening

assurance *nf* assurance; **assurance de qualité** = quality assurance; **assurance qualité dans le domaine du génie logiciel** = software quality assurance (SQA)

◊ **assurer** *vtr (confirmer)* to ensure; **mettre en place le dispositif de protection d'écriture pour vous assurer de ne pas perdre vos données** = pushing the write-protect tab will ensure that the data on the disk cannot be erased

astable *adj* astable; **multivibrateur astable** = astable multivibrator

astérisque (*) *nm* asterisk; **pour voir tous les fichiers commençant par 'L', utiliser la commande DOS DIR L*.*** = to view all the files beginning with the letter 'L', use the DOS command DIR L*.*; **remplissage par des astérisques** = asterisk fill; **nous avons utilisé l'astérisque en remplissage pour obtenir la réponse '***122,33'** = we have used asterisk fill to produce the answer of '***122.33'

astigmatisme *nm* astigmatism

astucieux, -euse *adj* smart

asymétrique *adj* asymmetric; **compression vidéo asymétrique** = asymmetric video compression; **transmission asymétrique** = asymmetric transmission

> COMMENTAIRE: la transmission asymétrique divise le canal de communication en deux parties, la première supporte les transmissions à partir de 9600 bps, alors que la deuxième, plus lente, supporte les transmissions d'environs 300 bps et sert aussi aux données de contrôle et de correction d'erreurs. Le canal à grand débit sert à transmettre la plus grande partie des données.

asynchrone *adj* (i) asynchronous; (ii) unclocked; **accès asynchrone** = asynchronous access; **appel de procédure asynchrone** = asynchronous procedure call (APC); **communication asynchrone** = asynchronous communication; **émetteur/récepteur asynchrone universel** = universal asynchronous receiver/transmitter (UART); **contrôleur**

d'émetteur/récepteur asynchrone universel = UART controller; **interface de communications asynchrone** = asynchronous communications interface adapter (ACIA); **mode asynchrone** = asynchronous mode; **mode asynchrone équilibré** = asynchronous balanced mode (ABM); **mode asynchrone équilibré étendu** = asynchronous balanced mode extended (ABME); **ordinateur asynchrone** = asynchronous computer; **port (d'accès) asynchrone** = asynchronous port; **l'utilisation de ports asynchrones ne demande pas un matériel spécialisé** = when asynchronous ports are used no special hardware is required; **transmission asynchrone** = asynchronous transmission; **transfert asynchrone ATM** ou **commutation temporelle asynchrone** = asynchronous transfer mode (ATM); **transfert de données asynchrone** = asynchronous data transfer

AT *(norme)* bus AT = AT-bus; **clavier AT** = AT-keyboard; **code AT** = attention code; **jeu de commandes AT** = AT command set; **mode AT** = AT mode

> COMMENTAIRE: A l'origine AT désignait les ordinateurs personnels 'Advanced Technology' d'IBM. L'expression désigne maintenant tout compatible IBM qui utilise un processeur 16 bits

Atari ST ™ *(ordinateurs)* Atari ST ™ (computers)

ATD *(commande modem)* Attention, Dial (ATD)

atelier *nm (d'usine)* shop ou workshop; **atelier de composition** = composing room; **atelier flexible** = flexible manufacturing system (FMS)

atmosphère *nf* atmosphere

◊ **atmosphérique** *adj* atmospheric; **absorption atmosphérique** = atmospheric absorption; **bruit atmosphérique causé par le soleil** = helios noise; **conditions atmosphériques** = atmospheric conditions

atome *nm* atom

◊ **atomique** *adj* atomic; **horloge atomique** = atomic clock

> dans un atome, la plupart des électrons tournent autour du noyau et leur mouvement de rotation suffit encore à engendrer un champ magnétique
> *Science et Vie*

attachement *nm (fichier transmis en même temps qu'un message électronique)* attachment; **l'attachement joint au dernier message contient le rapport des ventes** = there is an attachment with my last mail message - it contains the sales report

attacher *vtr* to attach ou to fix; *(avec un trombone, etc.)* to clip; **les corrections sont attachées à la sortie d'imprimante** = the corrections are clipped to the computer printout

attaque *nf (d'une note)* attack; *(d'un signal)* **enveloppe d'attaque** = attack envelope

atteindre *vtr* to reach; **atteindre un niveau maximum** = to peak; **la tension a atteint le niveau maximum de 1200 volts** = the power peaked at 1,200 volts

attente *nf* **(a)** wait ou waiting state; **boucle d'attente** = wait loop; **délai d'attente** = wait time; **état d'attente** = sleep ou wait condition; **sans état d'attente** = zero wait state; **liste d'attente** = waiting list; **file d'attente des données d'entrée** = input work queue; **file d'attente de demandes de service** ou **de données à transmettre** = channel queue; **file d'attente à deux entrées** ou **à deux extrémités** = double-ended queue ou deque; **file d'attente de fichiers** = file queue; **file d'attente de périphériques** = device queue; **file d'attente des tâches** ou **des travaux à exécuter** = job queue ou job stream; **la file d'attente trop courte ne suffisait pas à la série de tâches à traiter** = the queue was too short for the backlog of tasks waiting to be processed; **file d'attente qui fonctionne sur le principe 'premier entré premier sorti'** = FIFO queue; **constitution de file d'attente** = scheduling; **gestionnaire de file d'attente** = queue manager ou queue management program; **ce nouveau logiciel de stockage des fichiers d'impression comporte un gestionnaire de file d'attente** = this is a new software spooler with a built-in queue management; **imprimer la file d'attente** = to despool; **se joindre à la file d'attente** = to form a queue ou to join a queue; **message d'attente de commande** = command prompt; **pile en file d'attente** = push-up list ou stack; **procédure de file d'attente** = queue discipline; **temps d'attente dans une file d'attente** = queuing time; **temps d'attente (entre deux opérations)** = idle time; **travail en attente** = backlog **(b)** *(communication)* **marque (d')attente** = mark hold; **mettre en attente** = to hold

attention *nf* attention

atténuation *nf (d'un signal)* attenuation ou loss ou fading ou decay

◊ **atténuer** *vtr (un signal)* to attenuate; *(un son ou un bruit ou une couleur)* to deaden; **les capots d'insonorisation servent à atténuer le bruit des imprimantes** = acoustic hoods are used to deaden the noise of printers; **si le câble est trop long, l'atténuation du signal va provoquer des erreurs** = if the cable is too long, the signal attenuation will start to cause data errors

◊ **s'atténuer** *vpr (signal)* to decay ou to fade

> le taux d'atténuation des signaux, compris entre 50 et 200 décibels par kilomètre, est encore trop élevé
> *Informatique et bureautique*

atterrissage *nm* **atterrissage de la tête de lecture** = head crash

attribuer *vtr* to allocate; *(une valeur)* to set; **le système d'exploitation a attribué presque toute la mémoire principale au tableur** = the operating system allocated most of main memory to the spreadsheet program

◊ **attribut** *nm* attribute; **attributs d'écran** = screen attributes; **cet attribut contrôle la couleur de l'écran** = this attribute controls the colour of the screen; **en appuyant sur (les touches) Ctrl et B en même temps, on donne l'attribut Gras à ce paragraphe** = pressing Ctrl and B keys at the same time will set the bold attribute for this paragraph of text; **table d'attributs** = image table

◊ **attribution** *nf* allocation *ou* assignment; **attribution de bandes de fréquences** = band allocation; **la nouvelle attribution de bandes de fréquences permettra d'avoir un plus grand nombre de voies de transmission** = the new band allocation means we will have more channels

audible *adj* audible; **fréquence audible** = audio frequency

audience *nf* audience

audimat *nm* (*télévision*) **bataille d'audimat** = ratings battle *ou* war

audio- *préfixe* audio-

◊ **audio** *adj* (*audible*) audio; **carte audio** = sound card; **ce logiciel vous permet de créer presque tous les sons, mais il vous faut une carte audio pour pouvoir les écouter** = this software lets you create almost any sound - but you can only hear them if you have a sound card fitted; **enregistreur de cassettes audio** = audio cassette recorder (ACR); **fichier audio** = audio file; **fréquence audio** = audio frequency; **limiteur** *ou* **réducteur de signal audio** = audio compressor; **système audio interactif** = audio active system

◊ **audiocassette** *nf* audio cassette

◊ **audioconférence** *nf* audio conferencing

◊ **audiofréquence** *nf* audio frequency; **gamme des audiofréquences** *ou* **limites de la bande des audiofréquences** = audio range

◊ **audionumérique** *adj* (enregistrement sur) **bande audionumérique** = digital audio tape *ou* DAT; **une bande audionumérique produit un son de très haute qualité** = DAT produces a very high quality sound; **lecteur de bande audionumérique** = DAT drive; **la sauvegarde du réseau est assurée par un lecteur de bande audionumérique** = we use a DAT drive as the backup device for our network; **cassette audionumérique** = digital cassette; **disque audionumérique** = digital audio disk (DAD)

◊ **audiovisuel, -elle** *adj* audiovisual (AV); **matériel audiovisuel** = audiovisual aids

audit *nm* audit (informatique) = audit; **faire un audit (informatique)** = to audit

augmentation *nf* increase *ou* boost; (*valeur*) increment; **pourcentage d'augmentation** = percentage increase; **quel est le pourcentage d'augmentation?** = what is the increase per cent?

◊ **augmenté, -ée** *adj* increased *ou* boosted; (en valeur) incremented *ou* increased; (en qualité ou en puissance) upgraded; **adressage augmenté** = augmented addressing; **code augmenté** = shift code

◊ **augmenter** *vtr* to increase *ou* to boost *ou* to augment; (en valeur) to increment *ou* to increase; (en qualité *ou* en puissance) to scale up *ou* to upgrade; (la dimension) to expand; **le disque dur supplémentaire va augmenter la capacité de mémoire de 25Mo** = the extra hard disk will boost our storage capacity by 25Mb; **il est possible d'augmenter la mémoire du processeur unique de 2Mo jusqu'à 4Mo** = the single processor with 2Mbytes of memory can be upgraded to 4Mbytes; **dont la dimension peut être augmentée** = expandable

AUI (*utilisé dans un système Ethernet câble lourd*) **connecteur AUI** = AUI connector

auteur *nm* **(a)** author; **droit d'auteur** = copyright; **Convention sur le droit d'auteur** = Copyright Act; **titulaire d'un droit d'auteur** = copyright owner; **violation du droit d'auteur** = infringement of copyright *ou* copyright infringement **(b)** **langage auteur** = authoring language; **système auteur** = authoring system

authentification *nf* authentication; **authentification de messages** = authentication of messages

◊ **authentifier** *vtr* to authenticate

◊ **authentique** *adj* authentic

auto- *préfixe* self-

◊ **auto-adaptable** *adj* adaptive; **système auto-adaptable** = adaptive *ou* dynamic system

◊ **auto-adaptatif, -ive** *adj* self-adapting; **système auto-adaptatif** = self-adapting system

◊ **autocommutateur** *nm* automatic exchange; **autocommutateur électronique** = electronic automatic exchange; **autocommutateur électronique privatif** = computerized branch exchange (CBX); **autocommutateur privatif (raccordé au réseau public)** = private branch exchange (PBX); **autocommutateur privatif (raccordé au réseau public) (PABX)** = private automatic branch exchange (PABX)

◊ **autocontrôle** *nm* **système avec autocontrôle** = self-checking system

◊ **autocopiant, -e** *adj* carbonless; **papier autocopiant** = carbonless paper *ou* NCR paper; **papier commercial avec double autocopiant** = two-part stationery; **nous utilisons des carnets de commandes autocopiants** = we use carbonless order pads

◊ **autocorrecteur, -trice** *adj* self-correcting; **code autocorrecteur** = self-correcting code

◊ **autodétecteur, -trice** *adj* self-checking; **code autodétecteur (d'erreur)** = self-checking code

◊ **autodiagnostic** *nm* self-diagnostic

◊ **autodidacte** *adj* (*système*) self-learning (system)

◊ **auto-enrichissant, -e** *adj* système auto-enrichissant = self-learning system

◊ **auto-entretenu, -e** *adj* **mémoire vive (RAM) auto-entretenue** = self-refreshing RAM

AUTOEXEC.BAT (*fichier de démarrage*) AUTOEXEC.BAT (batch file)

automate *nm* robot; **automate bancaire** = automated teller machine (ATM), *US* automatic telling machine

automatique 1 *nm (téléphone)* **l'automatique** = direct dialling system *ou* subscriber trunk dialling (STD) 2 *adj* automatic; **accord automatique des vitesses de transmission** = automatic speed matching; **adaptation automatique du mode** *ou* **de la fréquence (vidéo)** = automatic mode *ou* frequency switching; **alignement automatique des virgules** = automatic decimal adjustment; **alimentation automatique (du papier)** = auto advance; **(système d')appel automatique d'un correspondant** *ou* **numérotation automatique** = auto-dial (system); *(relie l'ordinateur au téléphone)* **système** *ou* **unité d'appel automatique** = automatic calling unit (ACU); **modem à appel automatique** = dial-in modem; **arrêt automatique** = auto stop; **(dispositif d')arrêt** *ou* **de mise hors tension automatique** = automatic power off; **central téléphonique automatique** = automatic telephone exchange; **changeur (de disques) automatique** = record changer; **chargeur automatique** = automatic loader; **composition automatique de lettres standard** = automatic letter writing; **compteur d'impulsions automatique (à domicile)** = automatic message accounting; **système avec contrôle automatique** = self-checking system; **correction automatique d'erreurs** = automatic error correction; **coupure automatique des mots** = automatic hyphenation; **demande de répétition automatique** = automatic repeat request (ARQ); **(système de) démarrage** *ou* **lancement automatique** = autoboot; **détection automatique d'erreurs** = automatic error detection; **(système de) distribution automatique des appels** *ou* **standard automatique** *ou* **distributeur d'appels automatique** = automatic call distribution (ACD); **distributeur automatique (de cigarettes, etc.)** = automatic vending machine; **distributeur automatique de billets** = *(de banque - DAB)* cash dispenser *ou* cash point; *(de parking, etc.)* ticket machine; **enregistrement automatique des erreurs** = error logging; **ce programme comprend un enregistrement automatique d'erreurs** = features of the program include error logging; **fonctionnement automatique (d'un système)** = unattended operation; **fonctionnement itératif automatique** = automatic sequencing; **contrôle de gain automatique** = automatic gain control (AGC) *ou* automatic level control (ALC); **guichet automatique de banque (GAB)** = automated teller machine, *US* automatic telling machine (ATM); **lancement automatique (d'un programme)** = auto start; *(modem* *ou* *téléphone)* **numérotation automatique** = auto-dial; **ouverture automatique de session** = auto-login *ou* auto-logon; **programmation automatique** = automatic programming; *(modem* *ou* *téléphone)* **(système de) rappel automatique d'un correspondant** = auto-redial; **recalcul automatique** = automatic recalculation; **reconnaissance automatique du débit d'une ligne** = auto-baud scanning; **reconnaissance automatique des numéros d'appels** = automatic number identification (ANI); **relance automatique** *ou* **redémarrage automatique** = auto restart; **horloge à relance automatique** = delta clock; **répétition automatique** = auto repeat *ou*

automatic repeat; **réponse automatique** = auto-answer; **retour à la ligne automatique** = automatic carriage return; **saisie automatique de données** = automatic data capture; **sauvegarde automatique** = auto save *ou* automatic backup; **suivi automatique** = auto trace; **système automatique = hands off system**; **système téléphonique automatique international** = international direct dialling (IDD); **traitement automatique de données** = automatic data processing (ADP); **transfert automatique** = automatic *ou* unconditional transfer; **vérification automatique** = auto verify; **equipement de vérification automatique (EVA)** = automatic test equipment (ATE)

◊ **automatiquement** *adv* automatically; **le compilateur a corrigé les fautes de syntaxe automatiquement** = the compiler automatically corrected the syntax errors; **le programme est lancé automatiquement lors de la mise sous tension de l'ordinateur** = the program is run automatically when the computer is switched on; **tâche qui peut être exécutée automatiquement** = unattended operation

automatisation *nf* automation

◊ **automatisé, -ée** *adj* automated; **bureau automatisé** = automated office

◊ **automatiser** *vtr* to automate

autonome *adj* (a) *(indépendant)* autonomous (b) *(indépendant de l'ordinateur principal)* offline; **impression par imprimante autonome** = off-line printing (c) *(poste non relié en réseau)* **poste autonome** = stand-alone *ou* standalone; on local; **les postes ont été reliés en réseau plutôt que d'être utilisés comme postes autonomes** = the workstations have been networked together rather than used as stand-alone systems; **système autonome** = stand-alone system; **terminal autonome** = stand-alone terminal

◊ **autonomie** *nf* independence; **autonomie des données** = data independence

autopositif, -ive *adj (procédé)* autopositive

autopsie *nf* post mortem; **vidage par autopsie** = post mortem dump

autorafraîchi, -e *adj* self-refreshing; **mémoire vive (RAM) autorafraîchie** = self-refreshing RAM

autoréponse *nf* auto-answer

autorisation *nf* authorization; *(à un fichier* *ou* *à une machine)* **autorisation d'accès** = clearance to access a file *ou* access permission; **cet utilisateur ne peut pas accéder au fichier du serveur parce qu'il n'a pas d'autorisation d'accès** = this user cannot access the file on the server because he does not have permission; **vous n'avez pas l'autorisation d'accéder à ce processeur** = you do not have the required clearance for this processor; **autorisation de copie d'un logiciel** = software licence; **autorisation de copier** *ou* **de dupliquer** = authorization to copy (ATC); **donner (à quelqu'un) l'autorisation (de faire quelque chose)** = to authorize (someone to do something)

◊ **autorisé, -ée** *adj* authorized; *(permis par la syntaxe du langage)* legal; **personne autorisée (à utiliser un système)** = authorized user; **la procédure d'authentification permet au système de reconnaître si un message est émis par un utilisateur autorisé** = authentication allows the system to recognize that a sender's message is genuine; **non autorisé** = unauthorized; **le mot de passe interdit aux personnes non autorisées d'avoir accès aux données** = the use of a password is to prevent unauthorized access to the data

◊ **autoriser** *vtr* to authorize; **autoriser quelque chose** *ou* **quelqu'un à faire quelque chose** = to authorize something *ou* someone to do something; **autoriser l'achat d'un nouveau système informatique** = to authorize the purchase of a new computer system

◊ **autorité** *nf* authority

autoroute *nf* **autoroute de l'information** = information superhighway

autotest *nm* automatic checking; **autotest à la mise sous tension** = power on self test (POST)

A/UX *(pour la gamme des ordinateurs Macintosh)* **version Unix A/UX** = A/UX

auxiliaire *adj* auxiliary *ou* secondary; *(appareil ou dispositif de secours)* standby *ou* backing (device) *ou* safety net; **alimentation auxiliaire** = battery backup; **clavier auxiliaire** = keypad; **équipement** *ou* **système auxiliaire** = standby equipment; **liaisons auxiliaires d'un réseau** = network redundancy; **mémoire auxiliaire** = secondary storage; backing memory *ou* storage *ou* store; auxiliary memory *ou* storage *ou* store; external memory; slave cache *ou* store; **cet appareil est équipé de lecteurs de disquettes et de bandes magnétiques qui servent de mémoire auxiliaire** = disk drives and magnetic tape are auxiliary storage on this machine; **je vais augmenter la capacité de mémoire auxiliaire en ajoutant un deuxième lecteur de disquettes** = by adding another disk drive, I will increase the backing store capabilities; **mémoire morte** *ou* **ROM auxiliaire** = sideways ROM; **mettre en mémoire auxiliaire** = to deposit; **pile auxiliaire** = battery backup; **processeur auxiliaire** = auxiliary processor *ou* support chip; **le processeur arithmétique auxiliaire peut être enfiché à cet endroit** = the maths support chip can be plugged in here; **registre auxiliaire de routage d'adresse** = B-line counter; **réseau auxiliaire** = back-end network; **station auxiliaire** = secondary station; **système auxiliaire** = satellite (system); **système à bus auxiliaire** = dual bus system

avalanche *nf* avalanche; **photodiode à avalanche** = avalanche photodiode (APD)

avance *nf* (a) *(du papier ou d'un film)* advance; **avance rapide du papier** = high-speed skip *ou* slew (b) *(progrès)* advance; **avance technologique** = sophistication

◊ **d'avance** *ou* **à l'avance** *loc adv* in advance *ou* pre- *ou* forward; **accepté d'avance** = pre-agreed;

définir d'avance = to predefine; **déterminer d'avance** = to predetermine *ou* to preset; **enregistrer d'avance** = to prerecord; *(plan)* **établir d'avance** = to predesign; **un grand choix de modèles de mise en page établis d'avance vous permet de formater automatiquement vos documents d'affaires ou vos documents techniques** = a wide selection of predesigned layouts help you automatically format typical business and technical documents; **fixer d'avance** = to preset; **formaté d'avance** = preformatted; **imprimé d'avance** = preprinted; **programmer d'avance** = to preprogram *ou* to preset; **on avait programmé d'avance les nouveaux paramètres de page de l'imprimante** = the printer was preset with new page parameters

◊ **avancé, -ée** *adj* advanced; *(de pointe)* sophisticated *ou* state-of-the-art; **un programme de PAO avancé** = a sophisticated desktop publishing program

avancer *vtr&i* to advance; **faire avancer** = to advance; **faites avancer le curseur de deux espaces (sur la ligne)** = advance the cursor two spaces along the line; *(incrémenter)* **faire avancer d'un pas** = to increment; **faire avancer image par image** *ou* **pas à pas** = to jog

avant 1 *nm* front; **alimentation par l'avant** = front feed **2** *adj inv* front; **bord avant** = leading edge; **palier avant** = front porch; **panneau avant** = front *ou* front panel *ou* fascia plate; **le panneau avant du lecteur de disquettes de ce modèle est plus petit que celui des autres modèles** = the fascia plate on the disk drive of this model is smaller than those on other models; **on insère les disquettes dans les fentes du panneau avant du terminal** = the disks are inserted in slots in the front of the terminal; **pointeur avant** = forward pointer **3** *prep & adv* before *ou* prior to; **il faut taper le mot de passe avant d'accéder au système** = the password has to be keyed in prior to accessing the system

avarie *nf* damage

avertir *vtr* to warn; **il a averti les opérateurs de saisie d'une surcharge possible du système** = he warned the keyboarders that the system might become overloaded

◊ **avertissement** *nm* warning; **donner un avertissement** = to issue a warning

◊ **avertisseur** *nm* (a) *(sonore)* buzzer (b) *(pour recherche de personne)* bleeper; **il doit être quelque part dans l'usine, nous essaierons de le joindre par son avertisseur** = he is in the factory somewhere - we'll try to find him on his bleeper

aveugle *adj* blind; **clavier aveugle** = blind keyboard; **transmission en aveugle** = blind dialling

avion *nm* aicraft *ou* plane; **enveloppe avion** = air mail envelope; **papier avion** = air mail paper

avis *nm* advice; **demander l'avis de quelqu'un** = to consult someone; **il a demandé l'avis du responsable de (la) maintenance sur le mauvais fonctionnement du disque** = he consulted the maintenance manager about the disk fault

avorter *vt* **(faire) avorter** = to abort *ou* to terminate; **connexion avortée** = aborted connection

axe *nm* **(a)** axis; **ce progiciel de CAO permet de positionner un axe où l'on veut** = the CAD package allows an axis to be placed anywhere; **axe d'abscisse** *ou* **axe des X** = X-axis *ou* horizontal axis; **axe de l'ordonnée** *ou* **axe des Y** = Y-axis *ou* vertical axis; **axe des Z** = Z-axis **(b)** *(qui fait tourner un disque)* spindle

AZERTY *(premières lettres du rang supérieur gauche de certains claviers utilisés surtout dans les pays francophones)* **clavier AZERTY** = AZERTY keyboard

azimut *nm* azimuth; **réglage d'alignement des angles d'azimut** = azimuth alignment; **c'est cette petite vis qui sert à régler l'alignement des angles d'azimut** = azimuth alignment is adjusted with this small screw

Bb

B *(nombre hexadécimal équivalent du 11 décimal)* hexadecimal number equivalent to decimal 11 *ou* B

b = BIT

B: lecteur *ou* **unité de disquettes B:** = (floppy) disk drive B: *ou* floppy drive B:; **copiez les fichiers du disque dur C: sur la disquette du lecteur B:** = copy the files from the hard drive C:, to the floppy drive B:

Babbage *npr* **machine de Babbage** = analytical engine

> COMMENTAIRE: Charles Babbage, mathématicien anglais (1792-1871), inventa la première machine différentielle ou machine de Babbage

babillard *nm* Bulletin Board

BABT *(Commission qui approuve et certifie les matériels de télécommunication avant leur mise en service dans le Royaume-Uni)* British Approval Board for Telecommunications (BABT); **(en Angleterre) si vous développez un nouveau modem, vous devrez obtenir l'approbation du BABT avant de le commercialiser** = if you design a new modem, you must have BABT approval before you can sell it

bac *nm (pour alimentation automatique du papier d'une imprimante)* **bac à feuilles** *ou* **à papier** = (paper) bin *ou* (paper) tray *ou* sheet feed attachment; **bac du dessous** *ou* **bac inférieur** = lower bin; **introduire le bac inférieur** = load lower bin; **bac du dessus** *ou* **bac supérieur** = upper bin

backbone *nm (collecteur à grand débit)* backbone

BACKUP *(commande sous MS-DOS)* BACKUP (command)

badge *nm* badge; **lecteur de badges** = badge reader; **le lecteur de badges garantit que seules les personnes autorisées ont accès à la salle des ordinateurs** = a badge reader makes sure that only authorized personnel can gain access to a computer room

bague *nf* **(a)** ring; **bague de protection d'écriture** = write-permit ring **(b)** *(pour lentille photographique)* **bague d'extension** *ou* **bague macro** = extension tube

baie *nf* **(a)** *(de cartes d'extension)* card cage *ou* card frame *ou* card chassis; **baie avec guide-cartes** = rack **(b)** *(de disquettes)* bay *ou* drive bay

baisse *nf (de signal)* fading; **baisse de courant** = brown-out

◊ **baisser** *vi (signal)* to fade

BAK *(sous MS-DOS: extension de fichier qui indique une sauvegarde)* BAK file extension

balade *nf (navigation sur Internet)* **balade sur Internet** = surfing the Internet *ou* surfing the net; netsurfing

◊ **se balader** *vpr (naviguer sur Internet)* to surf the Internet *ou* to surf the net; **utilisateur qui se balade sur Internet** = (net)surfer; *voir aussi* NAVIGATION, NAVIGUER, INTERNET

> dans le jargon des utilisateurs de l'Internet, le 'netsurfing' désigne la balade sur le réseau. A l'image du surfeur qui glisse sur le rouleau de la vague, à la recherche du plaisir
>
> *PC Magazine*

balai *nm* **manche à balai** = joystick; **connecteur** *ou* **port pour manche à balai** *ou* **de manche à balai** = joystick port; **ce modèle d'ordinateur personnel possède un connecteur pour manche à balai** = a joystick port is provided with the home computer

balance *nf (d'un ensemble stéréophonique)* balance

balayage *nm* scan; sweep; *(action)* scanning; **le balayage a fait apparaître les données périmées** = the scan revealed which records were out of date; **balayage de chaînes** = string scanning; **balayage dirigé** = directed scan; **balayage d'écran** = television scan; **balayage par faisceau mobile** = flying spot scan; **balayage hors champ** *ou* **en dehors des limites** = overscan; **(télévision à) balayage lent** = slow scan (television); **balayage de trame** = raster scanning; **graphisme par balayage de trame** = raster graphics; **processeur graphique à balayage de trame** = raster image processor (RIP); **balayage vertical** = field sweep; **impulsion de contrôle** *ou* **de synchronisation du balayage** = field sync pulse; **définition de balayage** = scanning resolution; **dispositif de lecture par balayage** = scanning device *ou* scanner; **erreur de balayage** = scanning error; **un pli ou une déchirure dans une page peut être la cause d'une erreur de balayage** *ou* **d'un balayage incorrect** = a wrinkled or torn page may be the cause of scanning errors; **faire un balayage** = to scan; **un télécopieur fait un balayage de l'image qu'il convertit en données numériques avant transmission** = a facsimile machine scans the picture and converts this to digital form before transmission; *(d'un satellite)* **faisceau de balayage** = scanning spot beam; **fréquence de balayage** = scanning rate; **les écrans à faible fréquence de balayage ont besoin de phosphore à longue persistance pour éviter l'instabilité de l'image** = slow scan rate monitors need long persistence phosphor to prevent the image flickering; **ligne de**

balayage = scanning line; **logiciel de saisie par balayage** = scanning software; **passe de balayage** = raster scan; **retour d'un balayage** = flyback; **signal (de début) de balayage** = line drive signal; **spot de balayage** = scanning spot; **vitesse de balayage** = scanning speed; **la vitesse de lecture par balayage est de 1,3 pouces par seconde** = throughput is 1.3 inches per second scanning speed; **zone de balayage** = scan area; **étendue de la zone de balayage** = scan length

◊ **balayer** *vtr* to scan; to sweep; **le lecteur optique utilise un rayon lumineux qui balaye les caractères, les symboles ou les lignes** = an optical reader uses a light beam to scan characters, patterns or lines; **le fax balaye l'image et la convertit en format numérique** *ou* **la numérise avant transmission** = the facsimile machine scans the picture and converts this to digital form before transmission

il faut un moniteur spécialisé ayant une fréquence de balayage compatible avec les performances et bien souvent un écran aux dimensions généreuses
L'Ordinateur Individuel

balisage *nm* flagging

◊ **balise** *nf* (indicator) flag

◊ **baliser** *vtr* to flag

balun *nm* *(équilibreur d'impédance)* balun

banal *adj* common; **canal banal** = common carrier; **signalisation par canal banal** = common channel signalling; **langage banal** = common language; **matériel banal** = common hardware; **mémoire banale** = working store *ou* scratch pad (memory)

◊ **banalisé, -ée** *adj* common *ou* general purpose; *(radio)* **bande banalisée** = Citizens Band (CB); **bus d'interface banalisé** = general purpose interface bus (GPIB); **ligne banalisée** = common carrier; **poste de travail banalisé** = general purpose computer *ou* open access workstation; **registre banalisé** = general register *ou* general purpose register (gpr)

◊ **banaliser** *vtr (une mémoire, un ordinateur)* to use as common storage *ou* to use as general purpose computer; **la mémoire centrale du serveur est en général banalisée en dehors de la partie réservée au système d'exploitation** = the file server memory is mainly common storage area, with a section reserved for the operating system

banc d'essai *nm* benchmark *ou* test bed; **les bancs d'essais consistent à évaluer la performance de plusieurs systèmes ou périphériques en utilisant le même test standard** = in benchmarking, the performances of several systems or devices are tested against a standard benchmark; **la revue a publié les résultats du banc d'essai du nouveau programme** = the magazine gave the new program's benchmark test results

bancatique *nf* electronic banking *ou* telebanking

bande *nf* **(a)** *(trait)* stripe; **bande de couleur** = colour stripe; **bande d'équilibrage (de tension)** =

balance stripe **(b)** **bande transporteuse** = conveyor (for paper); **imprimante à bande** = band printer **(c)** *(morceau long et étroit)* strip *ou* band; *(sur une bande magnétique)* **bande intermédiaire** = guard band **(d)** *(ruban)* tape; **bande (magnétique) audionumérique** *ou* **bande audio** = digital audio tape (DAT) *ou* DAT tape; **un enregistrement sur bande audionumérique produit un son de très haute qualité** = DAT produces a very high quality sound; **bande sur bobine ouverte** = open reel tape; **bande magnétique** = magnetic tape *ou* mag tape; **bande magnétique en cassette** = cassette tape; **bande idiote** *ou* **bande de texte non formaté** *ou* **sans paramètres d'impression** = idiot tape; **bande (de) mouvements** = change tape; **bande originale** = master tape *ou* magnetic master; **bande papier** = paper tape *ou* punched tape; **bande papier perforée** = punched (paper) tape *ou* perforated tape; **bande semi-perforée** *ou* **à confettis non détachés** = chadded *ou* chadless tape; **bande vidéo** = videotape *ou* video cassette tape; **largeur de bande vidéo** = video bandwidth; **bande vierge** = blank tape; **cartouche bande** *ou* **cartouche de bande magnétique** = (magnetic) tape cartridge; **cassette de bande magnétique** = (magnetic) tape cassette; **convertisseur bande magnétique/carte perforée** = tape to card converter; **début de bande** = tape header; **marque de début de bande** = beginning of tape (BOT) marker; **dérouleur de bande(s) magnétique(s)** = tape drive *ou* magnetic tape transport; **écarteur de bande** = lifter; **encodeur pour bande magnétique** = magnetic tape encoder; **en-tête de bande** = tape header; **entraînement de bande** = tape transport; **(code de) fin de la bande (magnétique)** = end of tape (EOT); **label de fin de bande** = tape trailer; **format de bande** = tape format; **lecteur de bandes (magnétiques)** = tape drive *ou* magnetic tape reader; **lecteur de bandes perforées** = paper tape reader; **tête de lecture** *ou* **d'écriture de bandes magnétiques** = tape head; **tête de lecture de bandes** = tape playback head **(e)** *(de fréquences)* (frequency) band; **bande de base** = baseband *ou* base band; **la bande de base des fréquences vocales varie de 20Hz à 15KHz** = voice base band ranges from 20Hz to 15KHz; **modem en bande de base** = base band modem; **n'utilisez jamais un modem en bande de base sur une ligne téléphonique normale** = do not use a base band modem with a normal phone line; **réseau local en bande de base** = baseband local area network; **les réseaux locaux en bande de base peuvent avoir des longueurs de câbles d'environ 300m au maximum** = baseband local area networks can support a maximum cable length of around 300m; **transmission en bande de base** = baseband signalling; **bande C** = C band; **bande étroite** = narrow band; **(système de) modulation de fréquence à bande étroite** = narrow band FM (NBFM); **bande de fréquences** = frequency band; **bande (de fréquences) intercalaire** *ou* **bande de protection** = guard band; **bande (de fréquences) vocale** *ou* **bande de basses fréquences** *ou* **bande téléphonique** = voice band; **filtre de bande de fréquences** = frequency equalizer; **(transmission en) large bande** = broadband *ou* wideband; **modulation de fréquence à large bande** = wideband frequency modulation (WBFM); **radio à large bande** = broadband radio; **largeur de bande (de** fréquences) = bandwidth; **largeur de bande effective** = effective bandwidth; **la largeur de bande d'un téléphone est de 3100Hz** = telephone bandwidth is 3100Hz; **bande latérale** = sideband; **double bande latérale** = double sideband; **bande latérale inférieure** = lower sideband; **bande latérale résiduelle** = vestigial sideband; **bande latérale supérieure** = upper sideband; **bande latérale unique** = single sideband; **double bande latérale sans porteuse** ou **à porteuse inhibée** = double sideband suppressed carrier (DSBSC); **bande (de fréquences) vocale** = voice band; **bande passante** = bandpass; bandwidth; **filtre passe-bande** ou **de bande passante** = bandpass filter; **le câble en fibre optique a une bande passante plus étendue que les anciens câbles de cuivre et peut transporter les données à des vitesses plus grandes** = this fibre-optic cable has a greater bandwidth than the old copper cable and so it can carry data at higher speeds; **signalisation en bande passante** = in-band signalling; **signalisation hors bande** = out-of-band signalling

> la bande de fréquence destinée à la radiodiffusion par satellite est la bande des 12 GHz
>
> *Electronique Radio Plans*

◊ **bandothèque** *nf* tape library

banque *nf (groupe)* bank; **banque de canaux** = channel bank; **banque de données** = *(sur ordinateur)* databank; *(centre* ou *service)* information retrieval centre; **banque de mémoire** = memory bank; **changement de banque de mémoire** = bank switching; **la carte d'extension possède une banque de mémoire de 128Ko constituée de 16 puces** = an add-on card has a 128Kb memory bank made up of 16 chips

> le petit disque (CD-ROM) permet aux professionnels d'accéder à des banques de données tout en restant dans l'environnement bureautique
>
> *Micro Systèmes*

barillet *nm* small barrel; **distorsion en barillet** = pin cushion distortion

barre *nf* **(a)** bar; *(d'un clavier)* **barre d'espacement** = space bar **(b)** *(trait)* **barre oblique inverse** (\) = backslash; **code (à) barres** = bar code; *(système)* universal product code (UPC); **lecteur (optique) de code (à) barres** = optical bar reader ou bar code reader ou optical wand; **graphique à barres** = bar chart ou bar graph; **imprimante (à) barres** = bar printer

barré, -ée *adj* crossed; **zéro barré d'un trait oblique** = slashed zero

barrette *nf* **barrette de mémoire vive de type SIMM** = single in-line memory module (SIMM); **pour augmenter la mémoire de votre ordinateur, installez deux barrettes SIMM supplémentaires** = you can expand the main memory of your PC by plugging in two more SIMMs; **barrette de type SIP** = single in-line package (SIP)

baryté, -ée *adj* **papier baryté** = baryta paper

bas *nm* bottom ou foot; *(imprimerie)* **bas de casse** = lower case; **bas de page** = bottom space; **note** ou **renvoi en bas de page** = footnote; **il a signé au bas de la lettre** = he signed his name at the foot of the letter; **vers le bas** = downward

◊ **bas, basse** *adj* **(a)** low; **basse définition** = low resolution ou low-res; **bas niveau** = low level; **formatage de bas niveau** = low-level formatting; **langage de bas niveau** = low-level language (LLL); **mémoire basse** = low-memory; **signal bas actif** = active low **(b)** **basse fréquence** = low frequency (LF); **canal de basses fréquences** = voice grade channel; **haut-parleur de basse fréquence** = woofer ou bass speaker ou bass driver; **réponse aux basses fréquences** = bass response; **signal de basse fréquence** = bass signal; **transmission de données (numérisées) sur basse fréquence** = data in voice (DIV); **basse fréquence multiplexée A-MAC** = A-MAC; **très basse fréquence** = very low frequency (VLF); **transmission de données (numérisées) sur très basse fréquence** = data under voice (DUV)

◊ **basse** *nf (note musicale)* **haut-parleur de basses** = bass driver ou bass speaker ou woofer

bascule *nf* bistable circuit ou multivibrator; **déclenchée par bascule de front d'impulsion** = edge-triggered; **commutateur à bascule** = DIP switch ou flip-flop (FF) ou toggle switch; **valider à l'aide d'un commutateur à bascule** = to toggle; **commutateur bascule à deux états** = RS-flip-flop ou reset-set flip-flop; **commutateur à bascule de type D** = D-(type) flip-flop; **commutateur à bascule de type JK** = JK-flip-flop

◊ **basculement** *nm (de programme)* swapping ou swap; **basculement d'application** = context-switching

◊ **basculer** *vtr* to roll; to swap; to toggle; *(des données)* to exchange; **basculer la communication d'un émetteur à l'autre** = to hand off

base *nf* **(a)** base ou basis; **base de la pile** = stack base; **base de temps** = time base; **base de temps réduite** = fast time-scale; **le coût de la saisie du texte (sur clavier) a été établi sur une base de 5500 frappes/heure** = we calculated keyboarding costs on the basis of 5,500 keystrokes per hour **(b)** **à base de** = based on; **système à base de connaissances** = knowledge-based system; **système intelligent à base de connaissances** = intelligent knowledge-based system (IKBS); **à base de procédure** = procedural **(c)** **de base** = basic; *(initial* ou *original)* base; **l'architecture de base est la même pour tous les modèles de la gamme** = the basic architecture is the same for all models in this range; **adressage de base** = base addressing; **adresse de base** = base address ou presumptive address; **bande de base** = base band; **modem en bande de base** = base band modem; **n'utilisez jamais un modem en bande de base sur une ligne téléphonique normale** = do not use a base band modem with a normal phone line; **réseau local en bande de base** = base band local area network; **cliché de base** = key plate; **code de base** = basic code ou skeletal code; **contrôleur de base** = basic controller; **débit de base (d'un RNIS)** = basic rate access (BRA); **format de base** = native format; **forme de base (dans un programme de graphisme)** =

primitive; **instructions de base** = basic instruction; **ligne de base** = base line; **mémoire de base** = base memory *ou* conventional memory *ou* base RAM; **méthode d'accès direct de base** = basic direct access method (BDAM); **méthode d'accès séquentiel de base** = basic sequential access method (BSAM); **police de caractères de base** = base font; **registre de base** = base register; **registre d'adresse de base** = base address register; **système d'exploitation de base** = basic operating system (BOS); **système satellite de base** = basic control system (satellite) (BCS) **(d)** *(de numération)* radix *ou* base; **complément à la base** = radix complement; **numération en base** = radix notation; **base binaire** *ou* **base 2** = base 2; **base décimale** *ou* **base 10** = base 10; **système à base dix** = decimal system; **base hexadécimale** *ou* **base 16** = base 16; **le nombre hexadécimal est en base 16** = the hexadecimal number has a radix of 16; **base octale** *ou* **base 8** = base 8 *ou* octal scale; **(numération) en base huit** = octal (notation); **nombre en base octale** = octal digit

◊ **base de données** *nf* database; **base de données hiérarchisée** = hierarchical database; **base de données en ligne** = on-line database; **base de données relationnelle** *ou* relational database; **base de données en réseau** = network database; **configuration** *ou* **implantation** *ou* **topologie d'une base de données** = database mapping; **consulter une base de données (avec** *ou* **sans autorisation)** = to browse; **langage de base de données** = database language; **machine dédiée au traitement de bases de données** = database machine; **moteur de base de données** = database engine; **responsable de base de données** = database administrator (DBA); **schéma de base de données** = database schema; **schéma de base de données standard** *ou* **canonique** = canonical schema; **service de base de données spécialisée (pour vidéotex)** = information provider (IP); **système de base de données** = database system; **système de base de données réparti** *ou* **en réseau** = distributed database system; **système de gestion de base de données (SGBD)** = database management system (DBMS) *ou* database manager; **système de gestion de base de données relationnelle (SGBDR)** = relational database management system

basé, -ée *adj* based on

◊ **baser** *vtr* to base; **nous avons basé nos calculs** *ou* **nos calculs sont basés sur la vitesse standard pour la saisie de texte (par clavier)** = we based our calculations on the basic keyboarding rate; **ce prix est basé sur diverses estimations des coûts de saisie** = the price is based on estimates of keyboarding costs

◊ **se baser (sur)** *vpr* to base oneself (on something)

BASIC = BEGINNER'S ALL-PURPOSE SYMBOLIC INSTRUCTION CODE **langage BASIC** = BASIC (language); **BASIC pour nombres entiers** = integer BASIC; **écrire un programme en BASIC** = to write a program in BASIC

BAT *(extension de fichier utilisée sous MS-DOS)* BAT file extension

battement *nm (défaut de synchronisation de tête de lecture)* flagging

batterie *nf* **(a)** *(pile)* battery **(b)** *(groupe d'objets)* **ce processus est contrôlé par une batterie de capteurs** = the process is monitored by a bank of sensors

> cet appareil peut fonctionner soit sur 220V, soit sur batterie 12V, avec une faible consommation
> *Opto électronique*

baud *nm* baud (rate); **le modem viewdata reçoit à 1200 bauds et transmet à 75** = the viewdata modem uses a 1200/75 split baud rate; **reconnaissance automatique de débit d'une ligne** = auto-baud scanning *ou* auto-baud sensing

> même si un bps n'est pas un baud (unité de mesure de la vitesse de modulation, et non du débit), on parle parfois de baud à la place de bps
> *Mon PC Multimédia*

Baudot *npr* code (télégraphique) **Baudot** = Baudot code

baver *vi (imprimerie)* to bleed

◊ **bavure** *nf* bleed *ou* slur

BBS *(zone d'affichage* ou *babillard)* Bulletin Board System (BBS)

BCH *(code de correction d'erreurs)* Bose-Chandhuri-Hocquenghem (BCH)

BCNF *(format normal de base de données)* Boyce-Codd Normal Form (BCNF)

BCPL *(langage de programmation de haut niveau)* Basic Combined Programming Language (BCPL)

BEL *(code ASCII 7)* **caractère BEL** = BEL (character)

bel *nm* bel; **le 'bel' est une unité de mesure de l'échelle logarithmique** = bel is a unit in the logarithmic scale

Bell *(modem qui fonctionne selon les normes AT&T)* **modem compatible Bell** = Bell-compatible modem

Bernoulli *npr* **boîte de Bernoulli** = Bernoulli box

bêta *nm (lettre de l'alphabet grec)* beta; *(deuxième série de tests)* **bêta test** *ou* **test bêta** = beta test; **cette application a passé le stade des tests alpha et entre juste en phase de bêta test** = the application has passed the alpha tests and is just entering the beta test phase; **site de bêta test** = beta site; **version bêta** = beta version; **logiciel (en version) bêta** = beta software; **nous allons essayer la version bêta sur autant de PC différents que nous pourrons pour tenter de trouver toutes les bogues** = we'll try out the beta version on as many different PCs as possible to try and find all the bugs

Bézier *npr* **courbe de Bézier** = Bézier curve

> COMMENTAIRE: Les courbes de Bézier font partie de la plupart des logiciels de dessin haut de gamme. Elles permettent de créer des courbes régulières passant par un grand nombre de points définis. La description de page de PostScript utilise les courbes de Bézier pour définir la forme des caractères imprimés.

biais *nm (inclinaison)* skew

◊ **biaisé, -ée** *adj* biased; **données biaisées** = biased data

biaural, -e *adj* binaural

bibliographie *nf* bibliography; **il a placé une bibliographie à la fin de chaque chapitre** = he printed a bibliography at the end of each chapter

◊ **bibliographique** *adj* bibliographic *ou* bibliographical; **liste bibliographique** = bibliography; **notice bibliographique** = bibliographical information

bibliothécaire *nm&f* librarian

◊ **bibliothèque** *nf* **(a)** *(collection de livres; bâtiment qui contient ces livres)* library; **consultez le catalogue de la bibliothèque pour obtenir les renseignements bibliographiques** = look up the bibliographical details in the library catalogue; **les éditeurs ont vérifié toutes les références à la bibliothèque locale** = the editors have checked all the references in the local library **(b)** *(collection de bandes, jeux, programmes. etc.)* **bibliothèque de bandes** = tape library; **il possède une grande bibliothèque de jeux informatiques** = he has a large library of computer games; **bibliothèque de logiciels** = software library; **bibliothèque de programmes** = program library **(c)** *(collection de routines ou fonctions spécialisées soit mathématiques, graphiques, etc.)* **bibliothèque graphique** *ou* **de graphiques** = graphics library; **bibliothèque de macros** = macro library; **bibliothèque de programmes d'entrée/sortie** = input/output library; **bibliothèque de symboles** = symbol library; *(fichiers qui contiennent le système d'exploitation)* **bibliothèque du système** = system library; **fonction bibliothèque** = library function; **forme de bibliothèque (dans un programme de graphisme)** = primitive; **image de bibliothèque** = clip-art; **nous avons utilisé des images de bibliothèque pour améliorer la présentation** = we have used some clip-art to enhance our presentation; **programme de bibliothèque** = library program *ou* library routine; **la fonction racine carrée se trouve déjà dans le programme de bibliothèque** = the square root function is already in the library program; **sous-programme de bibliothèque** = library subroutine

bidimensionnel, -elle *adj* two-dimensional; **fichier bidimensionnel** = flat file; **tableau bidimensionnel** = two-dimensional array

bidirectionnel, -elle *adj* bi-directional; **bus bidirectionnel** = bi-directional bus; **câble bidirectionnel** = two way cable; **circuit bidirectionnel** = two wire circuit; **imprimante bidirectionnelle** = bi-directional printer; **mode de transmission bidirectionnelle à l'alternat** = half duplex (transmission) *ou* either-way operation; **transfert de fichier bidirectionnel** = bi-directional file transfer

> en général, dans une liaison informatique bidirectionnelle, les échanges se font à la même vitesse dans les deux sens
> *Action PC*

bidouillage *nm (familier)* manipulation; **bidouillage du bit** = byte manipulation

◊ **bidouillé, -ée** *adj (familier)* manipulated *ou* altered; *(programme qui fonctionne tel que prévu parce qu'il n'a pas été manipulé)* **programme non bidouillé** = well-behaved program

bifilaire *adj* **circuit bifilaire** = two-wire circuit

bifurcation *nf (d'un système)* bifurcation; *(embranchement d'un programme)* switch

billet *nm (de banque)* banknote; **distributeur de billets** = ticket machine; **distributeur automatique de billets de banque** = cash dispenser *ou* cashpoint

◊ **billetterie** *nf* cash dispenser *ou* cashpoint

binaire 1 *adj* binary; **accélérateur binaire** = blitter; **le nouvel accélérateur binaire accélère l'affichage des images graphiques** = the new blitter chip speeds up the graphics display; **additionneur binaire** = BCD adder *ou* binary adder; **adressage binaire** = bit addressing; **infographie à adressage binaire** = bit-mapped graphics; **définir une table d'adressage binaire** = to bit-map; **arbre binaire** = binary tree *ou* btree; **arrangement binaire** = bit pattern; **base binaire** *ou* **base 2** = base 2; **calcul binaire** = binary arithmetic; **caractère codé binaire** = binary coded character; **cellule binaire** = binary cell; **chargeur binaire** = binary loader; **chiffre binaire** = binary digit *ou* bit; **groupe de 2 chiffres binaires** = dibit; **codage binaire** = binary encoding; **code binaire** = binary code *ou* pure code; **le code binaire du nombre décimal 8 est 1000** = the BCD representation of decimal 8 is 1000; **code binaire à 8 bits (EBCDIC)** = extended binary coded decimal interchange code (EBCDIC); **code binaire réfléchi** = cyclic code; **communication synchrone binaire** = binary synchronous communications (BSC); **compteur binaire** = binary counter; **conversion décimale-binaire** = decimal-to-binary conversion; *(dans une image graphique)* **couche** *ou* **plan binaire** = bit plane; **débit binaire** = bit rate *ou* debit; **décimal codé binaire (DCB)** = binary coded decimal (BCD); **demi-additionneur binaire** = binary half adder; **densité binaire** = bit density; **échelle binaire** = binary scale; **dans un mot à quatre bits, l'échelle binaire est 1,2,4,8** = in a four bit word, the binary scale is 1,2,4,8; **élément binaire** = binary digit *ou* bit; **encodage binaire** = binary encoding; **entrelaçage binaire** = bit interleaving; **exposant binaire** = binary exponent; **expression binaire d'un caractère** = character representation; **fichier binaire** = binary file; **les instructions du programme sont stockées dans un fichier binaire** = the program instructions are stored in the binary file; **votre lettre est un fichier texte et non un fichier binaire** = your letter is a text file, not a binary file; **fraction**

binaire = binary fraction; **la fraction binaire 0,011 est égale à un quart plus un huitième (ou trois huitièmes)** = the binary fraction 0.011 is equal to one quarter plus one eighth (i.e. three eighths); **image binaire** = bit image; **indicateur binaire** = flag bit; **indicateur binaire de dépassement de capacité** = overflow bit *ou* flag; **inversion binaire** = bit flipping; **logique binaire** = logic; **manipulation binaire** = bit manipulation; **mantisse binaire** = binary mantissa; **nombre binaire** = binary number *ou* bit; **numération binaire** = binary notation *ou* representation; **opération binaire** = binary operation; **opération effectuée au niveau binaire** = bit wise operation; **plan** *ou* **couche binaire (dans une image graphique)** = bit plane; **position binaire** = bit position; **recherche binaire** *ou* **par coupe binaire** = binary search *ou* binary chop *ou* binary look-up; **séparation binaire** = binary split; **séquence binaire** = binary sequence; **système binaire** = binary system; **valeur binaire** = truth value; **variable binaire** = binary variable; **vidage binaire** = binary dump; **virgule binaire** = binary point **2** *nm* **binaire de signe** = sign digit; **transmission de signaux en binaire** = binary signalling

◊ **binaire-décimale** *adj* binary-to-decimal; **conversion binaire-décimale** = binary-to-decimal conversion

> ces tensions sont ensuite codées en numération binaire: 011 pour 3 volts, 101 pour 5 volts, etc.
> *Science et Vie*

binaural, -e *adj* binaural

binding *nm* *(type de reliure)* **perfect binding** = perfect binding

binon *nm* *(élément binaire)* **binon 0** = logical low; **binon 1** = logical high

BIOS = BASIC INPUT/OUTPUT OPERATING SYSTEM **BIOS étendu** = Advanced Basic Input/Output System (ABIOS); *voir aussi* EXPLOITATION

bip *nm* **(a)** *(tonalité)* beep *ou* bleep; **bip d'appel** = decimonic ringing; **émettre** *ou* **faire un bip** = to beep *ou* to bleep; **lorsqu'on appuie sur la mauvaise touche, l'ordinateur émet un bip** = the computer beeps when the wrong key is hit; **lorsqu'il n'y a plus de papier, l'imprimante émet un bip** = the printer will make a beep *ou* a bleep when it runs out of paper **(b)** *(récepteur d'appel de personne)* pager; **appeler** *ou* **chercher à joindre quelqu'un par bip** = to page someone *ou* to call someone on his pager

> en effet, un avertisseur émet un bip si la résistance mesurée descend au-dessous d'une certaine valeur
> *Electronique pratique*

bipolaire *adj* bipolar; **codage bipolaire** = bipolar coding; **signal bipolaire** = bipolar signal; **transistor bipolaire** = bipolar transistor; **transistor à jonction bipolaire** = bipolar junction transistor (BJT)

biquinaire *adj* biquinary; **code biquinaire** = biquinary code

bistable *adj* bistable; **circuit** *ou* **multivibrateur bistable** = bistable circuit *ou* multivibrator

bit *nm* bit (b) *ou* binary digit *ou* binary bit; **(système) huit bits** = eight-bit (system); **code binaire à 8 bits (EBCDIC)** = extended binary coded decimal interchange code (EBCDIC); **registre à bits circulants** = circulating register; **bit de contrôle** = check bit *ou* service bit; **bit de dépassement de capacité** = overflow bit *ou* flag *ou* indicator; **bit indicateur** = flag bit; **bit lourd** = weighted bit; **bit marqué** = dirty bit; **bit (de) masque** = mask bit; **bit de parité** = parity bit; **bits par pixel** = bits per pixel (BPP); **bits par pouce** = bits per inch (bpi); **bit de protection** = guard bit; *(Apple Macintosh)* bozo bit; **(nombre de) bits par seconde (bps)** = bits per second (bps); **le débit est de 60 000 bits par seconde sur une liaison parallèle** = the transmission rate is 60,000 bits per second (bps) through a parallel connection; **bit de signe** = sign bit *ou* sign indicator; **bit significatif** = significant bit *ou* weighted bit; **bit le moins significatif** *ou* **le plus faible** = least significant bit (LSB); **bit le plus significatif** *ou* **le plus fort** = most significant bit (MSB); **bit supplémentaire** = overhead bit; **bit de synchronisation** = framing bit; **bloc de bits** = bit block; **déplacement de bit (en mémoire)** = bit blit *ou* bitblt; **effectuer un déplacement de bit (en mémoire)** = to blit *ou* to bitblt; **mot de quatre bits** = quadbit; **remplissage** *ou* **garnissage de bits** = bit stuffing; **train de bits** = bit stream; **traitement du bit** = bit handling; **transfert de bits par blocs** = bit block transfer; **transmission parallèle bit par bit** = bit parallel transmission

> sur une surface de 1 centimètre carré, ils savent faire tenir 100 (cent) millions de bits ou unités de base d'information, 1 ou 0 par exemple
> *Le Point*

bitmap *(mode point par point)* bitmap *ou* bitmap; *voir aussi* BINAIRE, POINT

blanc *nm* **(a)** *(couleur)* white (colour); **noir et blanc** = black and white; **photo en noir et blanc** = black and white photograph; **affichage noir sur blanc** = positive display; **impression blanc sur noir** = cameo; **imprimante à définition des blancs** = white writer; *(d'un affichage)* **niveau de blanc** = white level **(b)** *(typographie)* space *ou* blank; **blanc de pied** = bottom space *ou* foot margin; **blanc de tête** = top space *ou* top margin **(c)** *(d'un programme)* **essai à blanc** = desk check *ou* dry run; *voir aussi* MONOCHROME

◊ **blanc, blanche 1** *adj* **(a)** *(couleur)* white **(b)** *(sans signification)* blank; **bruit blanc** = white noise; **caractère blanc** = space character; **chambre blanche** = anechoic chamber; **signal blanc** = white flag

◊ **blanchir** *vtr* *(un disque)* to wipe clean; **si vous reformatez, vous blanchirez le disque** = by reformatting you will wipe the disk clean

blindage *nm* *(de protection)* screen *ou* shield; *(d'un câble)* shielding; **un blindage du bloc d'alimentation réduit les perturbations** = the PSU is screened against interference; **sans blindage, le signal transmis serait perturbé par les interférences**

= without RF shielding, the transmitted signal would be distorted by the interference; **blindage magnétique** = magnetic screen *ou* magnetic shield; **lorsqu'on enlevait le blindage métallique du bloc d'alimentation, l'ordinateur ne donnait plus rien de bon** = without the metal screen over the power supply unit, the computer just produced garbage; *(câble)* **avec blindage** = shielded; **sans blindage** = unshielded

◊ **blindé, -ée** *adj* shielded; **câble blindé** = shielded cable; **non blindé** = unshielded; **câble en paire(s) torsadée(s) blindé** = shielded twisted pair (STP) cable; **câble en paire(s) torsadée(s) non blindé (câble UTP)** = unshielded twisted-pair (UTP) cable

◊ **blinder** *vtr* to shield

blister *nm* blister pack

bloc *nm* **(a)** *(de texte)* block; **copie d'un bloc (de texte)** = block copy; *(instruction de déplacer un morceau de texte ou de déplacer en mémoire)* **déplacer le bloc** = move block; **manipulateur de bloc** = block device; **l'unité de disques est un manipulateur de blocs qui peut transférer 256 octets de données à la fois** = the disk drive is a block device that can transfer 256 bytes of data at a time; *(instruction)* **marquer le bloc** = mark block; **(code *ou* marque de) fin de bloc** = end of block (EOB); **en-tête de bloc** = block header; **protection de bloc** = block protection; *(instruction)* **supprimer le bloc** = block delete **(b)** *(groupe de caractères ou de données)* **bloc de caractères** = character block; **contrôle de bloc de caractères** = block character check (BCC); **bloc (de données) de contrôle** = control block; **bloc de contrôle de fichier** = file control block; **bloc de données** = data block; **bloc d'entrée** = input block; **bloc d'identification** = header *ou* header block; **changement de bloc de mémoire** = bank switching; **caractère de rejet d'un bloc (dont les données sont mauvaises)** = block ignore character; **(contrôle de) parité d'un bloc** = block parity; **code de contrôle de bloc** = block code; **traitement de contrôle de bloc à l'entrée** = block input processing; **compactage** *ou* **compression de bloc** = block compaction; **délimiteurs** *ou* **marques de bloc** = block markers; **entre blocs** = interblock; **espace entre blocs** = block gap *ou* interblock gap (IBG); **facteur de bloc** = blocking factor; **fichier d'enregistrement des blocs** = block list; **longueur** *ou* **taille d'un bloc** = block length; **manipulation de bloc(s)** = block operation; **marque de sélection d'un bloc** = block mark; **transfert d'un bloc** = block transfer; **recherche** *ou* **extraction de bloc** = block retrieval; **synchronisation de blocs** = block synchronization; **taux d'erreur par bloc** = block error rate; **effectuer un tri bloc par bloc** = to shell sort **(c) effacer en bloc** = to block delete; **lorsqu'il s'agit de supprimer un texte assez long, servez-vous de la commande qui permet d'effacer en bloc** = use the global delete command to remove large areas of unwanted text **(d)** *(groupe d'objets ou d'items)* bank; *(groupe de données transmises)* frame **(e)** *(source d'électricité)* **bloc d'alimentation** = power pack *ou* power supply unit (PSU)

blocage *nm (arrêt total de programme causé par une erreur)* lock up

bloc-notes *nm* notepad *ou* scratchpad; **champ bloc-notes** = comment field; **fenêtre bloc-notes** *ou* **bloc-notes d'écran** *ou* **bloc-notes en ligne** = screen notepad; **mémoire bloc-notes** = scratchpad memory *ou* working store

bloquer *vtr (arrêter)* to block; *(coincer)* to jam; **la sortie est restée bloquée au plus haut niveau jusqu'à la ré-initialisation du système** = the output latched high until we reset the computer

BMP *(extension d'un fichier graphique)* **ce logiciel de peinture permet l'importation de fichiers BMP** = this paint package lets you import BMP files

BNC *(adaptateur coaxial)* BNC connector; **adaptateur BNC en T** = BNC T-piece connector

BNF *(syntaxe d'un langage de programmation)* Backus-Naur-Form (BNF); **métalangage BNF étendu** *ou* **BNF étendu** = Extended BNF (EBNF)

bobine *nf* **(a)** *(de film)* reel *ou* spool; **il a laissé tomber la bobine et le ruban s'est déroulé** = he dropped the reel on the floor and the tape unwound itself; **bobine d'alimentation** = feed reel; **bobine réceptrice** *ou* **de réception** *ou* **d'enroulement** = take-up reel *ou* pickup reel *ou* pick-up reel; **(copie) de bobine à bobine** = reel to reel (copying); **bande sur bobine ouverte** = open reel tape; **tête de bobine** = head (of reel) **(b)** *(de fil conducteur)* coil; **microphone à bobine** = moving coil microphone; **bobine d'induction** = induction coil *ou* inductor; **un inducteur consiste en une bobine de fil (de cuivre)** = an inductor is made from a coil of (copper) wire

bof *ou* **BOF** = BEGINNING OF FILE; *voir* DEBUT

bogue *nf* bug; *voir aussi* DEBOGAGE, DEBOGUER

boîte *nf* **(a)** box; **boîte en carton** = cardboard box *ou* case; **les disquettes sont dans des boîtes de rangement rigides** = the disks are housed in hard protective cases **(b) boîte de connexion (sans soudure)** = breadboard; **boîte de jonction** *ou* **de raccordement** = junction box; **boîte noire** = black box **(c) boîte à outils** = *(de réparation)* toolbox; *(utilitaires pour programmes)* toolkit; *(zone de mémoire)* **boîte** *ou* **aux lettres (BAL)** = (electronic) mailbox *ou* mail box; **lorsque je me connecte au réseau, je vérifie toujours s'il y a des nouveaux messages dans ma boîte à lettres** *ou* **dans ma boîte aux lettres** = when I log onto the network, I always check my electronic mailbox for new messages; **boîtes d'aide et de formation en ligne** = cue cards

boîtier *nm* case; casing; **quand on a laissé tomber l'ordinateur, son boîtier s'est abîmé** = the computer casing was damaged when it fell on the floor; **le numéro de fabrication est gravé de façon permanente sur le panneau arrière du boîtier de l'ordinateur** = the production number is permanently engraved on the back of the computer casing; **boîtier d'arrêt** *ou* **d'isolation** = barrier box; *(de circuit intégré)* **boîtier plat** = flat pack; **boîtier protecteur** = enclosure

bolo-bolo *(police de caractères de trop petite taille)* en bolo-bolo = greeked

bombe *nf* bombe; **bombe logique** = logic bomb; **le programmeur système a installé une bombe logique lorsqu'il a été licencié** = the system programmer installed a logic bomb when they made him redundant

bond *nm (transmission)* hop

Boole *npr* **algèbre de Boole** = Boolean algebra *ou* Boolean logic; **table de Boole** = Boolean operation table

◊ **booléen, -éenne** *adj* Boolean; **algèbre booléenne** = Boolean algebra *ou* Boolean logic; **opérateur booléen** = Boolean operator; **opération booléenne** = Boolean operation; **opération booléenne à un opérande** = monadic Boolean operation; **opération booléenne dyadique** *ou* **opération booléenne à deux opérandes** = dyadic Boolean operation; **relation booléenne** = Boolean connective; **valeur booléenne** = Boolean value *ou* truth value; **variable booléenne** = Boolean variable *ou* data type

bord *nm* edge; *(d'un système de reconnaissance optique)* **bord d'alignement** *ou* **de référence** = aligning edge; *(d'une feuille de papier)* **bord déchiqueté** *ou* **non rogné** = deckle edge; *(d'une carte perforée)* **bord d'introduction** *ou* **bord avant** = leading edge

bordereau *nm (formulaire)* form

bordure *nf* border *ou* edge; **bordure d'écran** = screen border; *(par système de reconnaissance optique)* **détection de bordures** = edge detection

Borland *(société de logiciels spécialisée dans les langages et les bases de données)* Borland

borne *nf* **(a)** *(de raccordement)* terminal *ou* barrel; *(d'un transistor à effet de champ)* **borne d'entrée** = source; **borne positive** = positive terminal **(b)** *(limites)* bounds; **bornes d'un tableau** = array bounds

bouclage *nm* **fréquence de bouclage** = speed of loop

boucle *nf* loop; **boucle d'amplification** = positive feedback; **boucle d'attente** = wait loop; **boucle conditionnelle 'WHILE'** = while-loop; **boucle conditionnelle FOR...NEXT** = for-next loop; **boucle continue** *ou* **sans fin** = continuous loop *ou* infinite loop *ou* endless loop; **boucle emboîtée** = nested loop; **boucle de feedback** = feedback loop; **boucle fermée** = closed loop; **boucle de fond** = loop *ou* looping program; **boucle imbriquée** = nested loop; **boucle intérieure** = inner loop; **boucle d'itération** = loop *ou* looping program; **boucle de maintien** = holding loop; **boucle de modification** = modification loop; **boucle ouverte** = open loop; **boucle de programme** = loop *ou* looping program; **boucle de réaction** = feedback loop; **boucle de récurrence** = daisy-chain recursion; **boucle avec retour automatique à zéro** *ou* **aux paramètres de départ** = self-resetting *ou* self-restoring loop;

boucle de rétroaction *ou* **de correction** = loopback; **boucle de temporisation** *ou* **de synchronisation** = timing loop; **être accroché dans une boucle** = to hang (in a loop); **compteur de boucles** = loop counter; **contrôle de boucle** = loop check; **corps de la boucle** = loop body; **créer une boucle** = to loop; **fréquence de boucle** = speed of loop; **vérification de boucle** = loop check **(b) en boucle** = circular; **antenne en boucle** = loop antenna; **fichier en boucle** = circular file; **film en boucle** = loop film; **liste en boucle** = circular list; *(de calcul)* **report en boucle** = end-around carry

◊ **boucler** *vtr* to loop

bouffer *vtr (des données* *ou* *un fichier)* to mung up

bouger *vi* to move; **bouger avec un téléphone sans cordon** = to roam

boule *nf* ball; **boule d'impression** = golf-ball; **imprimante à boule** = golf-ball printer; **boule (de pointeur)** = trackball

bourdonnement *nm* hum

bourrage *nm* **(a)** *(de l'entraînement du papier)* jam (in the paper feed); **l'emploi de papier plus mince évite le bourrage** = lightweight copier paper will feed without jamming **(b)** *(remplissage)* padding *ou* stuffing

◊ **bourrer** *vtr* to pad *ou* stuff

bout *nm* end *ou* ending; **bouts de ligne** = line endings

bouton *nm* **(a)** *(de réglage, etc.)* knob *ou* dial; **pour obtenir la station de radio, tournez ce bouton-ci** = to tune into the radio station, turn this dial; **pour ajuster la luminosité de l'écran, tourner le bouton placé à l'arrière du moniteur** = the brightness can be regulated by turning a knob at the back of the monitor; **bouton (de) contraste** = contrast knob *ou* dial; **bouton de densité** = density dial; **si l'impression est trop pâle, réglez le bouton de densité (d'impression) sur le noir** = if the text fades, turn the density dial on the printer to full black; **bouton d'enregistrement** = record button; **tourner le bouton marche/arrêt** = to turn the on/off knob; **bouton du volume** = volume control **(b)** *(d'une souris ou d'une manette de jeu)* button; **utilisez la souris pour placer le curseur sur l'icône et démarrez l'application en appuyant sur le bouton (de la souris)** = use the mouse to move the cursor to the icon and start the application by pressing the mouse button **(c)** *(petite zone en forme de bouton sur laquelle on peut cliquer pour démarrer une action)* **bouton** *ou* **bouton radio** = button; **il y a deux boutons en bas de la fenêtre d'état, sélectionnez le bouton de gauche pour annuler l'opération et le bouton de droite pour continuer** = there are two buttons at the bottom of the status window, select the left button to cancel the operation or the right to continue; **bouton OK** = OK button

◊ **bouton-poussoir** *nm* pushbutton

Boyce-Codd *(structure des informations dans une base de données)* **format normal Boyce-Codd** *ou* **format BCNF** = Boyce-Codd normal form (BCNF)

bozo *nm (bit de protection Apple Macintosh)* bozo bit

bpi = BITS PAR POUCE

bps = BITS PAR SECONDE **débit corrigé en bps** = bps rate adjust

Bps *(octets par seconde)* bytes per second (Bps)

Braille *npr (écriture pour personnes aveugles)* Braille; **caractères Braille** = Braille marks; **elle lisait un livre en (caractères) Braille** = she was reading a Braille book; **il existe une édition en Braille de ce livre** = the book has been published in Braille

branche *nf* branch; **(programme) à plusieurs branches** = multithread (program); **branche d'un programme** = program branch; **une arborescence est formée de branches reliées les unes aux autres par des points de liaison ou noeuds** = a tree is made of branches that connect together at nodes

◊ **branchement** *nm* **(a)** *(dans un programme)* branch; jump; transfer; *(dans une routine)* leg; **branchement conditionnel** = conditional jump *ou* conditional transfer; **le branchement conditionnel choisira le programme 1 ou 2 suivant que la réponse est oui ou non** = the conditional branch will select routine one if the response is yes and routine two if no; **(instruction de) branchement conditionnel à l'indicateur zéro** = jump on zero; **branchement inconditionnel** = unconditional jump; **contrôle de branchement** = transfer control; **effectuer un branchement** = to jump; **effectuer un branchement conditionnel à zéro** = to jump on zero; **instruction de branchement** = branch instruction *ou* jump instruction *ou* transfer command; **opération de branchement** = jump operation; **point de branchement** = branchpoint; *(symbole graphique)* **symbole de branchement** = decision box; **table de branchement** = branch table **(b)** *(circuit secondaire)* branch; *(de télévision câblée)* drop line; **le poste défectueux est connecté sur ce branchement** = the faulty station is on this branch

brancher 1 *vi (faire un branchement)* to branch **2** *vtr* **(a)** *(un appareil)* to plug *ou* to plug in; **ne soyez pas surpris si l'ordinateur ne fonctionne pas, vous ne l'avez pas branché sur le secteur** = no wonder the computer does nothing, you haven't plugged it in at the mains **(b)** to connect; **brancher une ligne sur une table d'écoute** = to tap a line

bras *nm* arm; **bras de lecture/écriture** = access arm; actuator; **le bras de lecture est mis en position de parkage pendant le transport** = the access arm moves to the parking region during transport

bredouillage *nm (distorsion de la voix lors de la transmission)* slur

bricolé, -ée *adj* kludged *ou* kluged; **connexion bricolée** = dry joint; **programme** *ou* **système hâtivement bricolé** = kludge *ou* kluge

brillance *nf* brightness *ou* brilliance; **une trop forte brillance peut causer une fatigue oculaire** = the brightness of the monitor can hurt the eyes

brillant, -e *adj* **(a)** brilliant; **le fond est d'un rouge brillant** = the background colour is a brilliant red; **il utilise un blanc brillant pour les mises en valeur** = he uses brilliant white for the highlights **(b)** glossy; **papier (couché) brillant** = glossy paper; **les illustrations sont imprimées sur papier brillant** = the illustrations are printed on glossy art paper

broche *nf (de connecteur)* pin; **fiche** *ou* **connecteur à trois broches** = three-pin plug; **prise secteur à deux broches** *ou* **à trois broches** = two-pin *ou* three-pin mains socket; **il faut un fiche à trois broches pour connecter** *ou* **brancher le système sur le secteur** = use a three-pin plug to connect the printer to the mains; **disposition** *ou* **configuration des broches (d'un connecteur)** = pinout; **système à double rang de broches (parallèles)** = dual-in-line package (DIL *ou* DIP)

◊ **broché, -ée** *adj* **livre broché** = paperbound book *ou* paperback; **édition brochée** = paperbound edition *ou* paperback edition

brochure *nf* booklet *ou* brochure; **nous avons demandé une brochure sur les services de maintenance** = we sent off for a brochure about maintenance services

bromure *nm (imprimerie)* bromide *ou* bromide print; **24 heures plus tard nous avions reçu les bromures et pouvions faire les films** = in 24 hours we had bromides ready to film

brosse *nf (en infographie)* (paint) brush

brouillage *nm (parasites)* noise; *(d'un écran couleur)* bleed; **brouillage (de la réception)** = jamming *ou* blanketing; **brouillage de courte durée** = impulsive noise; **brouillage radio** = garbage; **zone de brouillage** = mush area; *voir aussi* EMBROUILLAGE

◊ **brouillard** *nm (de transmission)* mush

◊ **brouiller** *vtr (par interférence)* to jam; **cette tour brouille la transmission des émissions de télévision** = the TV signals are being jammed from that tower; **nous essayons de brouiller les signaux émis par cette station** = we are trying to jam the signals from that station; *voir aussi* EMBROUILLER

◊ **brouilleur** *nm voir* EMBROUILLEUR

brouillon *nm* draft *ou* rough copy; **faire un brouillon** = to draft *ou* to make a rough copy; **(sortie d'imprimante) qualité brouillon** = draft printing

bruit *nm* **(a)** noise *ou* sound; **(niveau de) bruit ambiant** *ou* **bruit de fond** = ambient noise level *ou* background noise; **le bruit de fond dans ce bureau est plus élevé que dans la bibliothèque** = the ambient noise level in the office is greater than in the library **(b)** *(parasites)* noise; static; **bruit atmosphérique causé par le soleil** = helios noise; **bruit blanc** = white noise; **bruits cosmiques** =

galactic noise; **bruit de courte durée** = impulsive noise; **bruit extra-terrestre** = extra-terrestrial noise; **bruit de fond** = background noise *ou* babble; **le modem est sensible au bruit de fond** = the modem is sensitive to background noise; **les autres appareils placés autour de cet équipement produiront un fort bruit de fond** = the other machines around this device will produce a lot of background noise; **bruit intermittent** = impulsive noise; **bruits de numérisation** = quantizing noise; *(sur un réseau: causé par une carte, un noeud défectueux)* **bruit parasite** = jabber; **bruit parasite causé par une machine** = man-made noise; **bruit thermique** = thermal noise; **analyseur de bruit** = decibel meter; **insensibilité au bruit** = noise immunity; **marge de bruit** = noise margin; **niveau de bruit d'un circuit** = circuit noise level; **réduction de bruit** = noise muting; **réduction du bruit d'interférence interstation** = interstation muting; **température de bruit** = noise temperature; **tolérance au bruit** = noise immunity; **limite de tolérance au bruit** = noise margin

brûlage *nm* **faire un brûlage d'écran** = to burn in; **brûlage laser** = ablation

◊ **brûler** *vtr (une PROM)* to blast *ou* to blow *ou* to burn

> COMMENTAIRE: un trou (qui représente un bit digital) est brûlé au laser dans la couche superficielle du support de stockage

brut, -e *adj* **(a)** raw; *(non traité)* **données brutes** = raw data; **ce petit ordinateur recueille les données brutes venant des capteurs, les convertit et les transmet au gros ordinateur** = this small computer collects raw data from the sensors, converts it and transmits it to the mainframe; **mode brut** = raw mode **(b)** gross; **poids brut** = gross weight

brutal, -e *adj (pour résoudre des problèmes informatiques)* **méthode brutale** = brute force method

bruyant, -e *adj* noisy; **les imprimantes laser sont beaucoup moins bruyantes que les imprimantes matricielles** = laser printers are much quieter than dot-matrix

BS *(caractère de marche arrière ou de rappel du curseur)* **caractère BS** = backspace *ou* BS

BTAM *(protocole d'accès de télécommunications britannique)* Basic Telecommunications Access Method (BTAM)

bug *nm (dans un programme)* bug; *voir aussi* DEBOGAGE, DEBOGUER

bulle *nf* **(a)** bubble; **emballage bulle** = blister pack **(b)** bubble; **mémoire à bulles (magnétiques)** = (magnetic) bubble memory; **cassette mémoire à bulles (magnétiques)** = bubble memory cassette; **la mémoire à bulles est une mémoire non-volatile** = bubble memory is a non-volatile storage; **effectuer un tri bulle** *ou* **un tri par permutation de bulles** = to bubble sort **(c)** **imprimante à bulle d'encre** = bubble jet printer ™

bulletin *nm (d'une société)* **bulletin d'informations** = (company) newsletter

◊ **Bulletin Board (BB)** *nm (zone d'affichage ou babillard)* Bulletin Board (BB)

bureau *nm* **(a)** *(meuble)* desk; **agenda de bureau** = desk diary; **lampe de bureau** = desk light; **ordinateur de bureau** = desk top unit *ou* desktop computer (system) **(b)** office; **il a ouvert son propre bureau d'ingénieur conseil en informatique** = he set up in business as an computer consultant; **bureau électronique** *ou* **automatisé** = automated office; **bureau d'études** = design department; **bureau informatisé** = electronic office; **bureau sans papier** *ou* **le bureau électronique** = paperless office; **copieur de bureau** = office copier; **ordinateur de bureau** = business computer *ou* office computer; **système informatique pour bureau** = computer office system **(c)** *(société de services)* bureau; facility; **bureau de photocopie** = photocopying bureau; **bureau de traitement de texte** = word-processing bureau; **nous avons ouvert un nouveau bureau de traitement de l'information** = we have opened our new data processing facility; **nous confions notre correspondance à un bureau de secrétariat local** = we farm out the office typing to a local bureau **(d)** *(fichier où sont stockés les renseignements sur tous les fichiers)* **fichier bureau** = *(Apple Macintosh)* Desktop file

> COMMENTAIRE: le bureau facilite l'utilisation d'un ordinateur par un débutant. Au lieu d'avoir à entrer des commandes au clavier, on pointe sur les icônes du bureau avec la souris.

◊ **bureautique** *nf* office automation (OA); **logiciel bureautique** = business system *ou* business package; **salon de la bureautique** = business efficiency exhibition; **système bureautique** = computer office system *ou* electronic office system; **système de bureautique intégrée** = integrated office

burst *nm (de signaux)* burst

bus *nm* bus *ou* highway; **bus A** *ou* **bus principal** = A-bus; **bus d'adresses** = address bus *ou* address highway; **voies de liaison d'un bus d'adresses** = bus address lines; **bus d'arbitrage** *ou* **de régulation** = contention bus; **système à bus auxiliaire** = dual bus system; **bus bidirectionnel** = bi-directional bus; **bus de chaîne** *ou* **bus série** = daisy chain bus; **bus de commande** = control bus; **bus de données** *ou* **bus de transfert de données** = data bus *ou* data highway; **système à bus double** *ou* **à bus auxiliaire** = dual bus system; **bus d'entrée** = data input bus (DIB); **bus d'extension** = expansion bus; **bus d'extension 16-bits** = 16-bit expansion bus; **bus (d')entrée/sortie** = I/O bus *ou* input/output (data) bus; **bus IEEE** *ou* **conforme aux normes IEEE** = IEEE bus; **bus d'interface universel** *ou* **banalisé** = general purpose interface bus (GPIB); **bus local** *ou* **local bus** = local bus; **bus de mémoire** = memory bus; **bus de micro-ordinateur** = microcomputer bus; **bus multiplexé** = multiplexed bus; **système multibus** *ou* **à bus multiples** = multi-bus system; **bus principal** *ou* **bus A** = A-bus; **bus de régulation** = contention bus; **bus série** *ou* **bus de chaîne** = daisy chain bus; **bus universel GPIB** = general purpose interface bus (GPIB); **arbitrage** *ou* **gestion de bus** = bus arbitration; **architecture à bus multiples** = multiple bus architecture; **(puits** *ou* **collecteur de données) asservi à un bus** = bus slave; **carte (de) bus**

= bus board; **carte d'extension de bus** = bus extender *ou* bus extension card (BEC); **esclave d'un bus** = bus slave; **gestion de (l'utilisation d'un) bus** = bus arbitration; **(émetteur de données) maître d'un bus** = bus master; **réseau de type bus** = bus network; **souris (de) bus** = bus mouse; **structure d'un bus** = bus structure; **système à bus fermé** = closed bus system; **topologie en bus** = bus topology; **Ethernet est un réseau qui utilise une topologie en bus** = Ethernet is a network that uses the bus topology

but *nm (visé ou atteint)* goal *ou* objective *ou* target

buzzer *nm* buzzer

Cc

C *(nombre hexadécimal équivalent du 12 décimal)* hexadecimal number equivalent to decimal 12 *ou* C

C *(fréquence)* **bande C** = C band

C *(langage)* C (language)

C++ *(langage de programmation orienté objets)* (high level programming language) C++

CA = COURANT ALTERNATIF

cabestan *nm (d'une bande)* **cabestan d'entraînement** = capstan

cabine *nf* booth; **cabine téléphonique** = call box *ou* telephone booth

câblage *nm* cabling *ou* wiring; **il a fallu refaire le câblage du système** = the wiring in the system had to be replaced; **en Angleterre, le câblage peut coûter jusqu'à 2 livres sterling pour 300mm** = cabling costs up to £2 a foot, in England; **câblage permanent** = hardwired connection; **boîte** *ou* **armoire de câblage** = wiring closet; **châssis** *ou* **cadre de câblage** = wiring frame; **schéma de câblage** = cabling diagram

◊ **câble** *nm* **(a)** *(de liaison)* cable *ou* flex *ou* lead; **câble d'acheminement des signaux** *ou* **câble antenne-circuit** = feeder cable; **câble blindé** = shielded cable; **câble non blindé** *ou* **sans blindage** = unshielded cable; **câble CATV** *ou* **câble de télévision (câblée)** = CATV cable; **câble coaxial** = co-axial cable; **câble d'entrée** = input lead; **câble étanche** = filled cable; **câble d'extension** = extension cable; **câble à fibres optiques** *ou* **câble optique** = fibre optic cable *ou* fibre optic connection; **les câbles à fibres optiques permettent de placer les noeuds jusqu'à un kilomètre l'un de l'autre** = fibre optic connections enable nodes up to one kilometre apart to be used; **câble de liaison** *ou* **de raccordement** *ou* **de raccord** = *(relie un poste de travail au câble principal du réseau)* drop cable; *(d'un tableau de distribution)* patchcord; *(câble qui permet à deux ordinateurs de communiquer par leur port série)* **câble de liaison directe** *ou* **de connexion série (sans modem)** = null modem (cable); modem eliminator; **câble ruban** *ou* **câble plat** = ribbon cable; **câble(s) souterrain(s)** = landline; **communication par câble** = line communications; **connecteur (de câble)** = cable connector; **section élémentaire de câble** = elementary cable section; **testeur de câble** = cable tester; *voir aussi* TORSADE **(b)** *(câblage)* cabling; **le câble peut coûter jusqu'à 12 francs les 30cm** = cabling costs up to 12 francs a foot; **les câbles de haute qualité vont permettre à l'utilisateur**

d'obtenir un taux de transfert de données très élevé = using high-quality cabling will allow the user to achieve very high data transfer rates; **les câbles (de) haute technologie doivent être manipulés avec soin** = high spec cabling needs to be very carefully handled **(c)** *(télégramme)* cable; **envoyer un câble** = to cable; **il a envoyé un câble au bureau pour redemander de l'argent** = he cabled his office to ask them to send more money **(d)** *(télévision)* **le câble** = cable television *ou* cable TV

◊ **câblé, -ée** *adj* **(a)** **réseau câblé** = cabling **(b)** **logique câblée** = hardwired logic; **logique câblée programmable** = programmable logic array (PLA); **ordinateur à logique câblée** = wired *ou* hardwired program computer *ou* fixed program computer; **programme en logique câblée** = hardwired program **(c)** **télévision câblée** = cable télévision *ou* cable TV; *(payante)* pay TV, *US* paycable; **télévision câblée interactive** = interactive cable television; **relais de télévision câblée** = cable TV relay station; **système de télévision câblée CATV** = community antenna television (CATV)

◊ **câbler** *vtr* **(a)** *(poser des câbles)* to wire *ou* to cable; **le studio est câblé pour la sonorisation** = the studio is wired for sound **(b)** *(envoyer un télégramme)* to wire *ou* to cable

◊ **câblogramme** *nm* cablegram *ou* telegram

cache *nm* **(a)** **cache** *ou* **mémoire cache** = cache *ou* cache memory; **contrôleur de cache** = cache controller; **donnée extraite (directement) du cache** = cache hit; **stocker en mémoire cache** *ou* **utiliser un cache** = to cache; **ce programme peut stocker une police de caractères, quelle qu'en soit la taille, dans la mémoire cache** = this program can cache any size font; **le temps d'accès est réduit lorsque les données les plus fréquemment utilisées sont stockées dans la mémoire cache** = file access time is much quicker if the most frequently used data is stored in cache memory; **ce processeur utilise un cache d'instructions et améliore ainsi les performances de 15 pour cent** = this CPU caches instructions so improves performance by 15 percent **(b)** *(masque pour film)* matt *ou* matte

◊ **caché, -ée** *adj* hidden; **fichiers cachés** = hidden files; **cela permet aux utilisateurs de sauvegarder ou de restaurer un par un les fichiers cachés** = it allows users to backup or restore hidden system files independently; **lignes cachées** = hidden lines; **effacement des lignes cachées** = hidden line removal; **algorithme d'effacement de lignes cachées** = hidden line algorithm; **vice** *ou* **défaut caché** = hidden defect in a program

◊ **cacher** *vtr* to hide *ou* to conceal

cacheté, -ée *adj* **enveloppe cachetée** = sealed envelope; **enveloppe non cachetée** = unsealed envelope

cadence *nf* speed; **prise de vue à cadence lente** = memomotion

cadrage *nm* *(d'une image)* framing; **cadrage d'une scène** = action frame; **dispositif de cadrage** = aligner; **marque de cadrage** = crop mark

cadran *nm* *(de téléphone)* dial; **impulsion de cadran** = dial pulse; **(composition de numéro d')appel au cadran (rotatif)** = pulse-dialling; **composer un numéro au cadran prend plus de temps qu'en utilisant le nouveau système à touches** = pulse-dialling takes longer to dial than the newer tone-dialling system

cadratin *nm* *(espace dont la longueur équivaut à un 'm')* em quad *ou* em space; *voir aussi* DEMI-CADRATIN

cadre *nm* **(a)** *(bordure)* border *ou* box; **les citations sont dans des cadres** = the quotations are printed in boxes **(b)** chassis *ou* frame; **cadre sous tension** = hot chassis **(c)** *(structure d'un programme)* framework; **on a d'abord établi le cadre du programme** = the program framework was designed first **(d)** *(administrateur)* **cadre de direction** *ou* **cadre supérieur** = director *ou* manager

◊ **cadre-réponse** *nm* *(d'une page vidéotex)* response frame

◊ **cadrer** *vtr* **cadrer une image** = to crop an image

cage *nf* cage; **cage de Faraday** = Faraday cage

cahier *nm* **(a)** *(section d'un livre)* signature; **ordre des cahiers** = collating sequence; **pliage en cahiers de 16, 32 ou 64 pages** = even working **(b)** **cahier des charges** = job specification(s); **le travail ne répond pas au cahier des charges** = the work is not up to specification *ou* does not meet the customer's specifications

caisse *nf* packing case; **mettre dans une caisse** = to pack in a case *ou* to case

calcul *nm* **(a)** calculation; **j'ai fait un calcul approximatif au dos d'une enveloppe** = I made some rough calculations on the back of an envelope; **d'après mes calculs, il nous reste du stock pour six mois** = according to my calculations, we have six months' stock left; **calcul approximatif** = rough calculation; **calcul des dimensions** = dimensioning; **le calcul des dimensions du tableau se fait à cette ligne-ci** = array dimensioning occurs at this line **(b)** *(fait par un ordinateur)* computation *ou* computing; **édition après calculs** = post-editing; **erreur de calcul** = computational error; **puissance de calcul** = computing power; **calcul ultra-rapide** = number crunching; **processeur mathématique pour calcul ultra-rapide** = number cruncher; **il faut un processeur puissant pour les applications graphiques qui exigent une possibilité de calcul ultra-rapide** = a very pposerful processor is needed for graphics applications which require extensive number crunching capabilities; *(processeur en tranches)* **unité**

centrale de calcul = central processing element (CPE); **vitesse de calcul (par ordinateur)** = computing speed **(c)** arithmetic; **calcul binaire** = binary arithmetic

◊ **calculable** *adj* *(par ordinateur)* computable

◊ **calculateur** *nm* computer; **calculateur analogique** = analog computer; **calculateur numérique** = electronic digital computer

◊ **calculatrice** *nf* calculator; **il a calculé la remise sur sa calculatrice** = he worked out the discount on his calculator; **calculatrice de poche** = pocket calculator; **j'ai besoin d'une pile pour ma calculatrice de poche** = my pocket calculator needs a new battery; **calculatrice avec fonctions scientifiques** = scientific calculator

◊ **calculé, -ée** *adj* calculated; *(sur ordinateur)* computed; **adresse calculée** = generated address *ou* synthetic address; **champ calculé** = calculated field

◊ **calculer** *vt* to calculate; *(ordinateur)* to compute; **il a calculé la remise sur sa calculatrice** = he calculated *ou* he worked out the discount on his calculator; **le directeur du centre de traitement a calculé le coût de saisie de texte sur clavier** = the DP manager calculated the rate for keyboarding; **vous devez calculer l'espace libre sur la disquette** = you need to calculate the remaining disk space; **les frais de connection ont été calculés sur une base horaire** = connect charges were computed on an hourly rate

◊ **calculette** *nf* pocket calculator

calendrier *nm* **(a)** calendar; **calendrier de bureau** = desk planner **(b)** **programme** *ou* **logiciel de calendrier** = calendar program; **logiciel de calendrier de groupe** = multi-user *ou* network calendar program

calibrage *nm* calibration; **calibrage d'un texte** = cast off *ou* casting off

◊ **calibrer** *vtr* **(a)** to gauge **(b)** **calibrer un texte** = to cast off (a text)

◊ **calibre** *nm* gauge

Callier *npr* **effet Callier** = callier effect

calligraphie *nf* calligraphy

calloc *(instruction en langage C)* calloc (in C programming)

Cambridge *npr* **(réseau en) anneau de Cambridge** = Cambridge ring

camembert *nm* *(diagramme)* pie chart; **l'attribution de mémoire est indiquée sur ce (diagramme en) camembert** = the memory allocation is shown on this pie chart

caméra *nf* cine camera *ou* film camera; **caméra de télévision** = television camera *ou* TV camera; **caméra de poursuite** = planetary camera; **caméra de traitement de l'image couleur** = process camera; **caméra de vision nocturne** = infrared camera; **ensemble caméra** = camera chain

Caméscope ™ *nm* camcorder

canal *nm* **(a)** *(voie de transmission)* channel; **canal (de transmission) aller** = forward channel; **canal banal** = common carrier; **signalisation par canal banal** = common channel signalling; **canal de basses fréquences** = voice grade channel; **canal dédié** = dedicated channel; **canal (d') entrée/sortie** = input/output channel *ou* I/O channel; **canal de retour** = backward channel; **canal sélecteur** *ou* **de sélection** = selector channel; **canal spécialisé** = dedicated channel; **canal de transmission** = transmission channel *ou* communications channel; **canal de transmission de données** = data channel; **adaptateur de canal de transmission de données** = data adapter unit; **canal de transmission de l'information** = information transfer channel; **canal (de type) P** = p-channel; **semi-conducteur MOS à canal (de type) P** = p-channel MOS; **banque de canaux** = channel bank; **commande de canal** = channel command; **débit d'un canal** *ou* **d'une voie** = channel capacity; **interface** *ou* **adaptateur de canal de transmission** = channel adapter; **isolation de canaux** = channel isolation; **liaison directe entre canaux** = channel-to-channel connection; **surcharge** *ou* **saturation d'un canal** = channel overload; **synchroniseur de canaux** = channel synchronizer **(b)** *(télévision)* channel; **Canal 5** = Channel 5 **(c)** *(sur carte perforée)* **canal d'entraînement (avec perforations centrales)** = centre sprocket feed

◊ **canalisation** *nf* channelling *ou* conduit; **les câbles de liaison de tous les terminaux sont acheminés par canalisation métallique jusqu'au centre informatique** = the cables from each terminal are channelled to the computer centre by metal conduit

candela *nf* candela; **candela par pied carré** = foot candle

canon *nm* **(a) canon à électrons** = electron gun **(b) microphone 'canon'** = shotgun microphone **(c)** *(qui tourne sans erreur du premier coup)* **programme canon** = blue-ribbon program

canonique *adj* canonical; **base de données canonique** = canonical schema

CAO = CONCEPTION ASSISTEE PAR ORDINATEUR computer-aided *ou* assisted design (CAD); **tous nos ingénieurs travaillent sur des postes de CAO** = all our engineers design on CAD workstations

> la CAO (conception assistée par ordinateur) est l'ensemble des procédés de création, de calcul, de description d'objets virtuels à l'aide d'un ordinateur
> *Science et Vie Micro*

capable *adj* capable

capacitance *nf* capacitance

capacité *nf* **(a)** *(espace)* capacity; **le modèle le plus récent possède un disque dur d'une capacité de 30Mo** = the latest model has a 30Mbyte hard disk; **la nouvelle unité de disquette(s) a une capacité de 100Ko** = the new disk drive has a 100Kb capacity; **capacité d'adressage** = *(espace adressable)*

addressing capacity; *(en infographie)* addressability; **capacité d'un circuit** = circuit capacity; **utiliser la capacité en excédent** = to use up spare *ou* excess capacity; **capacité maximale** = maximum capacity; **capacité de mémoire** = memory capacity *ou* storage capacity; **la capacité de mémoire est maintenant de 3Mo** = total storage capacity is now 3Mb; **(mémoire) tampon à capacité variable** = elastic buffer; *(capacité maximale d'un système)* **capacité théorique absolue** = absolute maximum rating; **capacité d'une voie de transmission** = channel capacity; **débordement de capacité (d'une ligne)** = overflow; **(nombre) qui dépasse la capacité (de mémoire) d'un ordinateur** = out of range (number); **dépassement de capacité** = overflow *ou* OV; **contrôle de dépassement de capacité** = overflow check; **bit** *ou* **indicateur** *ou* **drapeau** *ou* **marque de dépassement de capacité** = overflow bit *ou* flag *ou* indicator; **support de stockage de grande capacité** = bulk sotrage medium *ou* mass storage device **(b)** *(possibilité)* ability; capability; facility; **capacité de définition** = resolution capabilities; **capacité d'émulation** = emulation facility; **capacité de traitement (électronique) de données** = EDP capability; **la capacité de transmission** *ou* **de portage de cette liaison est excellente** = the information-carrying abilities of this link are very good **(c)** *(condensateur)* capacitor; **capacité variable** = variable capacitor

> la gamme propose un choix de disques durs d'une capacité de 20Mo à 660Mo
> *L'Ordinateur Individuel*

capacitif, -ive *adj* capacitative *ou* capacitive; **mémoire capacitive** = capacitor storage

capitale *nf* **(a)** *(imprimerie)* capital (letter) *ou* cap; **petites capitales** = small caps; *(d'une machine à écrire ou d'un clavier)* **touche (des) capitales** = shift key; **le voyant s'allume quand la touche (des) capitales est verrouillée** = the LED lights up when caps lock is pressed **(b)** *(écrit à la main)* **(lettres) capitales** = block capitals *ou* block letters; **écrire en capitales** = to write in block capitals *ou* to print; **écrivez votre nom et votre adresse en capitales** = write your name and address in block letters *ou* print your name and address

capot *nm* hood; **capot d'insonorisation** = acoustic hood

capteur *nm* sensor; *(médical)* biosensor; **ce processus est contrôlé par une batterie de capteurs** = the process is monitored by a bank of sensors; **le signal de sortie du capteur varie suivant la température** = the sensor's output varies with temperature; **capteur d'images** = image sensor; **capteur d'images vidéo** = frame grabber; *(pour ondes radio)* **capteur directionnel** = horn; **capteur de pression** = pressure pad

capture *nf (pour numériser une image)* **capture d'écran** = screen grab; *(photo)* screenshot

◊ **capturer** *vtr* to capture; to grab; **ce logiciel permet d'éditer les images capturées** = the software allows captured images to be edited; **en général, les scanners capturent les images avec une** résolution de 300 points par pouce (ppp) = scanners usually capture images at a resolution of 300 dots per inch (dpi)

caractère *nm* **(a)** character; **caractère (de déclenchement) d'alarme** = bell character; **caractères alpha-numériques** = alphanumeric characters; **caractère d'annulation** = cancel character (CAN); **le logiciel envoie automatiquement un caractère d'annulation à chaque erreur** = the software automatically sends a cancel character after any error; **caractère blanc** = space character; **insertion de caractères blancs** = character fill; **remplissage avec caractères blancs** character stuffing; **caractère clignotant** = flashing character; character blink; **caractères codés binaires** = binary coded characters; **caractère de contrôle** = check character *ou* control character; **caractère de contrôle d'impression** = print control character; **caractère de contrôle** *ou* **de commande de périphérique** = device control character; **caractère d'échappement** = escape character; *(sur écran vidéotex)* **caractères éclatés** = blast-through alphanumerics; **caractère d'écran** = display character; **caractère d'effacement** = delete character *ou* erase character; **caractère (d')espace** *ou* **(d')espacement** = blank character *ou* space character; **caractères (mis) en évidence** = highlights; **caractère de fonction** = function digit; **caractère graphique** = graphics character; **caractère d'identification** = identification character *ou* identifier; **caractère d'instruction** = instruction character; **caractère interdit** = forbidden character; **chaîne de caractères interdits** = forbidden combination; **caractère d'interrogation** = enquiry character (ENQ); **caractère invalide** = illegal character; **caractère nul** = idle character *ou* null character; **caractère (à valeur) numérique** = numeric character; **caractères parasites** = gibberish; **caractère de rejet d'un bloc (dont les données sont mauvaises)** = block ignore character; **caractère de remplissage** = fill character *ou* ignore character *ou* null character *ou* redundant character; **insertion de caractères de remplissage (en mémoire)** = character fill; **caractère de requête** = enquiry character (ENQ); **(nombre de) caractères par seconde (cps)** = characters per second (cps); **caractère de signal sonore** = bell character; **caractère de suppression** = delete character; **caractères en surbrillance** = highlights **(b)** **(système de) contrôle de périphérique utilisant des caractères** = device character control; **affichage de caractères** = character display; **assemblage de caractères** = character assembly; **bloc (de) caractères** = character block; **chaîne de caractères** = character string *ou* catena; **nombre de caractères dans une chaîne** = catena; **code de caractères** = character code; character coding system; **le code ASCII est le code de caractères le plus fréquemment utilisé** = the ASCII code is the most frequently used character coding system; **code de caractères interne** = internal character code; **contrôle de caractère** = character check; **contrôle de bloc de caractères** = block character check (BCC); **densité de caractère** = character density; **écrire en caractères d'imprimerie** = to print *ou* to write in capital letters; **ensemble de caractères** = character set; **ensemble de caractères nuls** = empty *ou* null set; **espacement**

(proportionnel) de caractères = intercharacter spacing; **expression binaire d'un caractère** = character representation; **générateur de caractères** = character generator; **on peut utiliser une ROM comme générateur de caractères pour obtenir les différentes polices** = the ROM used as a character generator can be changed to provide different fonts; **générateur de caractères fac-similés** = facsimile character generator; **groupage de caractères** = character assembly; **imprimante caractère (par caractère)** = character printer; **jeu de caractères** = character set; **jeu de caractères nuls** = empty *ou* null set; **lecteur optique de caractères** = optical character reader (OCR); **matrice de caractères** = character matrix; **mode caractère** = character mode; **ordinateur à mode caractère** = character orientated computer; **police de caractères** = font *ou* fount *ou* character set *ou* character repertoire; **police de caractères reconnaissable par lecture optique** = optical font *ou* OCR font; **police de caractères téléchargeable** = downloadable font; **police de caractères vectorielle** = dynamically redefinable character set; **processeur en mode caractère** = character machine; **reconnaissance optique de caractères** = optical character recognition (OCR); **système de reconnaissance de caractères CSM (par identification des caractéristiques combinées)** = combined symbol matching (CSM); **répertoire de caractères** = character repertoire; **support de polices de caractères** = image carrier; **touche de caractère** = character key; **vérification de caractère** = character check **(c)** *(lettre-bloc d'imprimerie)* **caractères d'imprimerie** = type *ou* font; **caractères fondus au moment de la composition** = hot metal type; **caractères utilisés pour le corps d'un texte** = body type; **caractère accent** = piece accent; **caractères Braille** = Braille marks; **caractère complet** = fully formed character; **la marguerite imprime des caractères complets** = a daisy wheel printer produces fully formed characters; **caractères Élite** = elite; **caractère gras** = bold face; **(donner une instruction d')imprimer en caractères gras** = to put in bold *ou* to embolden; **caractères de machine à écrire** = typewriter faces; **caractère spécial** = special character; **fonte de caractères spéciaux** = Dingbat ™; **(nombre de) caractères par pouce** = characters per inch (cpi); **le bouton vert vous permet de sélectionner 10 ou 12 caractères par pouce** = you can select 10 or 12 cpi with the green button; **(nombre de) caractères par seconde (cps)** = characters per second (cps); **imprimante à caractères pleins** = solid font printer; **mode caractère** = character mode; **style de caractère** = type style; **taille de caractère (mesurée en points)** = type size; **taille des caractères utilisés dans la composition** = composition size

caractéristique 1 *nf* characteristic *ou* feature *ou* aspect; **caractéristique essentielle** *ou* **principale** *ou* **la plus importante** = prime attribute *ou* main feature *ou* key feature *ou* highlight; **les principales caractéristiques de ce système sont les suivantes: 20Mo de mémoire formatée avec temps d'accès de 60ms** = the key features of this system are: 20Mb of formatted storage with an access time of 60ms; **caractéristique d'un circuit** = circuit grade; **caractéristique d'un fichier** = attribute;

dépassement de capacité de la caractéristique = characteristic overflow 2 *adj* characteristic; **courbe caractéristique** = characteristic curve; **c'est un défaut caractéristique de cette marque et de ce modèle d'ordinateur individuel en particulier** = this fault is characteristic of this make and model of personal computer

carbone *nm (papier)* carbon (paper); **vous avez oublié de mettre un carbone dans votre machine à écrire** = you forgot to put a carbon in the typewriter; **copie carbone** = carbon copy; **ruban carbone** = carbon ribbon

◊ **carboné, -ée** *adj* carbon-coated; **formulaire avec double carboné** = carbon set

cardinal, -e *adj* cardinal; **13, 19 et 27 sont des nombres cardinaux, −2,3 et 7,45 n'en sont pas** = 13, 19 and 27 are cardinal numbers, −2.3 and 7.45 are not

cardioïde *adj&nf* (réponse) **cardioïde** = cardioid response

caret *nm (symbole ^ de la touche Ctrl)* caret (sign)

carré *nm* square; **5 au carré égale 25** *ou* **le carré de 5 est 25** = 5 to the power 2 is equal to 25 *ou* 5 squared equals 25

◊ **carré, -ée** *adj* (a) square; *(poids du papier)* **grammes au mètre carré** = grams per square metre (gsm *ou* g/m²); **racine carrée** = square root (b) **onde carrée** = square wave

carte *nf* (a) *(de circuit)* card *ou* board; *(carte adaptateur)* adapter card; **carte accélératrice** *ou* **d'accélération** = accelerator card; **carte bus** = bus board; **carte CGA** = colour graphics adapter (CGA) *ou* CGA card; **carte de circuit imprimé** = printed circuit board (PCB) *ou* card; **carte à** *ou* **avec connecteur** = edge board *ou* card; **carte de contrôle** = control card; **carte contrôleur de disque(tte)** = disk-controller card; **carte courte** *ou* **carte demi-longueur** = half card; **carte de disque dur** = hard card; **carte EGA** = EGA card *ou* enhanced graphics adapter (EGA); **carte d'extension** = expansion card *ou* expansion board; add-on board *ou* add-in card; **carte fille** = daughter board; **carte graphique** = graphics board; **la carte graphique haute définition contrôle jusqu'à 300 pixels par pouce** = the HRG board can control up to 300 pixels per inch; **carte graphique couleur** *ou* **carte EGA** = enhanced graphics adapter (EGA) *ou* EGA card; **carte (d')interface** = interface card; **carte logique** = logic card *ou* logic board; **carte mémoire** = memory board; **carte mère** = motherboard; **carte mère d'un micro-ordinateur** = microcomputer backplane; **carte modem** = internal modem; **carte nue** *ou* **carte sans composants** = bare board; **carte processeur** = processor card; **vous pouvez soit vous servir d'un langage de description de pages soit ajouter une carte processeur** = you can use a page description language, or an add-in processor card; **carte son** = sound card; **micro-ordinateur à carte unique** = single board microcomputer; **ordinateur à carte unique** = single board computer (SBC *ou* sbc);

carte vidéo = video card; **circuit intégré de carte vidéo** = video interface chip; **connecteur de carte** = (card) edge connector; **connecteur** *ou* **emplacement pour carte d'extension** = (expansion) slot; **chassis avec guide cartes** = card cage *ou* card frame *ou* card chassis; **support de cartes** = card cage *ou* card frame *ou* card chassis; **support de carte d'extension** = card extender (b) **carte perforée** = punched card; *(pour microfilm)* **carte à encoches marginales** = edge notched card; **carte en-tête** = header card; **carte à fenêtre** = aperture card; **carte maîtresse** = master card; **carte à microfilm** *ou* **à microfiche** = aperture card; **(système d') alimentation** *ou* **entraînement de cartes perforées** = card feed; **champ de carte** = card field; **chargeur de cartes** = card loader *ou* hopper; **code de perforation de carte** = card code; **format de carte (perforée)** = card format; **jeu** *ou* **paquet de cartes perforées** = deck of punch cards; **image (mémoire) de carte** = card image; **lecteur de cartes perforées** = card reader *ou* punched card reader; **programme sur cartes perforées** = program cards (c) **carte magnétique** = (i) magnetic card; (ii) personal identification device (PID); (iii) smart card; **champ de carte (magnétique)** = card field; **lecteur de cartes magnétiques** = magnetic card reader; **carte accréditive** = charge card; **carte de crédit** = credit card; electronic money; **carte magnétique à mémoire** = smart card *ou* chip card; **à l'avenir, on pourrait inclure les empreintes digitales de l'utilisateur sur ses cartes à mémoire à fin d'identification** = future smart cards could contain an image of the user's fingerprint for identification; **carte à puce** = chip card *ou* smart card; **les cartes à puce aident à réduire le nombre de fraudes** = smart cards reduce fraud; **carte de retrait (bancaire)** = cash card; **téléphone à carte** = card phone (d) **carte graphitée** = mark sensing card; **carte d'identité** = identity card *ou* ID card (e) *(géographique)* map

cartésien, -ienne *adj* cartesian; **coordonnées cartésiennes** = cartesian coordinates; **structure cartésienne** = cartesian structure

carton *nm* (a) *(boîte)* cardboard box *ou* case; **le clavier est emballé dans du polystyrène expansé avant d'être mis dans son carton** = the keyboard is packed in expanded polystyrene before being put into the box (b) *(matériel plus épais que le papier)* card; *(très épais et solide ou pour boîtes)* cardboard; **nous avons fait imprimé les instructions sur carton blanc épais** = we have printed the instructions on thick white card

◊ **cartonnage** *nm (reliure cartonnée)* case

◊ **cartonné, -ée** *adj (reliure)* cased; **couverture cartonnée** = case binding; **relier avec couverture cartonnée** = to case (a book); **livre avec couverture cartonnée** *ou* **livre cartonné** = cased book *ou* hardbound book; **édition cartonnée** = hardback *ou* hardcover; **ce livre paraîtra en édition cartonnée et en livre de poche** = we are publishing the book as a hardback and as a paperback; **l'édition pour bibliothèques est cartonnée avec jaquette** = the library edition has a case and jacket; **nous avons imprimé 4000 exemplaires cartonnés et 10 000 brochés** = we printed 4,000 copies of the hardcover edition, and 10,000 of the paperback

◊ **cartonner** *vtr (un livre)* to case (a book); **machine à cartonner** = case-making machine

cartouche *nf* cartridge; **cartouche (de) bande** = tape cartridge; **cartouche (de) bande magnétique** = magnetic cartridge; **cartouche (de) disque (dur)** = disk cartridge; **cartouche de disquette** = flexible disk cartridge; **cartouche de données** = data cartridge; *(d'imprimante)* **cartouche d'encre** *ou* **de toner** = ink cartridge *ou* toner cartridge; **cartouche longue durée** = durable cartridge; **cartouche de police de caractères** = cartridge fonts; **cartouche ROM** = ROM cartridge; **cet ordinateur portatif n'est pas équipé de lecteur de disquettes mais possède un connecteur pour cartouches ROM** = the portable computer has no disk drives, but has a slot for ROM cartridges; **ruban d'imprimante en cartouche** = cartridge ribbon; **lecteur de cartouches** = cartridge drive

cascade *nf (en chaîne)* **bus en cascade** = daisy chain bus; **connexion (montée) en cascade** = cascade connection; **la connexion en cascade réduit le câblage** = daisy-chaining saves a lot of cable; **contrôle en cascade** = cascade control; *(dans un tableur à la suite d'un changement de valeur dans une cellule)* **effet de cascade** *ou* **mise à jour en cascade** = ripple-through effect; **(disposition de) fenêtres en cascade** = cascading windows; *(disposer en chaîne)* **relier en cascade** = to daisy-chain; *(de calcul)* **report en cascade** = cascade carry *ou* high speed carry

case *nf* **(a)** *(d'un formulaire)* **case vide** = blank (space); *(d'un formulaire graphité)* **case réservée à la réponse** *ou* **case à cocher** = response position **(b)** *(case où apparaît un x lorsqu'il y a sélection)* **case de sélection** *ou* **case de pointage** = check box; **pour faire un choix, déplacez le curseur sur une case de sélection et appuyez sur le bouton de la souris** = select the option by moving the cursor to the check box and pressing the mouse button

CASE *(commande CASE de branchement conditionnel)* CASE (command)

casque *nm (d'écoute)* headset *ou* headphones

casse *nf (imprimerie)* case; *(minuscule)* **bas de casse** = lower case; *(majuscule)* **haut de casse** = upper case

cassette *nf* cassette *ou* tape cassette *ou* cassette tape; **c'est en général avec les ordinateurs utilisés à la maison qu'on emploie les cassettes** = cassette tape is mainly used with home computers; **cassette audionumérique** = digital cassette; **cassette de bande magnétique** = magnetic cassette; **cassette compacte** = compact cassette; **cassette informatique** = data cassette; **cassette mémoire à bulles (magnétiques)** = bubble memory cassette; **il faut faire une cassette de sauvegarde pour vos données** = you must back up the information from the computer onto a cassette; **magnétophone à cassette** = cassette recorder

CAST *(commande CAST de conversion)* CAST (command); **pour convertir une variable de type nombre entier en une variable de type caractère,** utilisez la commande CAST = to convert the variable from an integer to a character type, use the CAST command

catalogue *nm* catalogue; *(bibliothèque)* **responsable de catalogue** = cataloguer

◊ **cataloguer** *vtr* to catalogue

catastrophe *nf* catastrophe; **erreur qui cause une catastrophe** = catastrophic error

cathode *nf* cathode

◊ **cathodique** *adj* **tube à rayons cathodiques** *ou* **tube cathodique** = cathode ray tube (CRT); **tube cathodique pour téléviseur** = television tube

CATV *voir* ANTENNE **câble CATV** = CATV cable

cavalier *nm* jumper; **(circuit** *ou* **dispositif) qui peut être sélectionné** *ou* **validé par cavalier** = jumper-selectable; **sur cette imprimante, la police de caractères peut être sélectionnée par cavalier** = the printer's typeface is jumper-selectable

caviardage *nm (familier)* **caviardage de la mémoire** = checkerboarding

CB = CITIZENS BAND; *(bande banalisé* *ou* *publique)* **radio CB** *ou* **radio à bande CB** = Citizens Band radio *ou* CB radio

CC = COURANT CONTINU

CCD *voir* DISPOSITIF **mémoire CCD** = CCD memory

CCITT = COMITE CONSULTATIF INTERNATIONAL TELEGRAPHIQUE ET TELEPHONIQUE

CD *(commande de changement de répertoire sous MS-DOS et UNIX)* Change Directory (CD); **entrez CD DOCS au clavier pour aller dans le sous-répertoire DOCS** = type in CD DOCS to move into the DOCS subdirectory

CD *(disque compact)* **disque CD** *ou* **CD** = compact disc *ou* CD; **platine de disques CD** = compact disc player *ou* CD player

◊ **CD-ROM** *(disque compact lecture seule)* Compact Disc-Read Only Memory *ou* compact disc ROM *ou* CD-ROM; **on peut stocker autant de données sur un (disque) CD-ROM que sur une douzaine de disques durs** = a CD-ROM can store as much data as a dozen hard disks; **platine** *ou* **lecteur de CD-ROM** = CD-ROM player

◊ **CD-ROM/XA** *(architecture étendue multimédia)* CD-ROM/XA *ou* CD-ROM Extended Architecture; *voir aussi* VITESSE

> le CD-ROM est un support technologiquement stable, fiable et de moins en moins cher
>
> *Micro Systèmes*

> contrairement à l'idée reçue, les coûts d'une diffusion de l'information sur support CD-ROM sont globalement inférieurs à ceux d'une impression papier
>
> *Micro Systèmes*

cédille *nf* cedilla

cellulaire *adj* cellular; **téléphone cellulaire** = cell phone *ou* cellular phone *ou* mobile radiophone *ou* private mobile radio (PMR)

◊ **cellule** *nf* **(a)** cell; *(d'un tableau)* element; **cellule binaire** = binary cell; **cellule courante** *ou* **active** = current *ou* active cell; **cellule de contrôle des couleurs** = colour cell; **cellule de mémoire** = memory cell; **cellule de travail** = active cell; **cellule magnétique** = magnetic cell; **adresse de cellule** = cell address; **définition de cellule** = cell definition; **format de cellule** = cell format; **le format de cette cellule est justification à droite et caractères gras** = the cell format is right-aligned and emboldened; **protection de cellule** = cell protection; **variable de location** *ou* **de référence d'une cellule** = cell reference variable **(b) cellule photoconductrice** = photoconductor; **cellule photoélectrique** = photoelectric cell *ou* photocell; **la cellule photoélectrique décèle la quantité de lumière qui traverse le liquide** = the photoelectric cell detects the amount of light passing through the liquid

cent *num* hundred; **pour cent** = per cent; **un pour cent** = one per cent *ou* one percentage point; **dix pour cent** = 10 per cent; **le taux d'erreur est tombé à douze pour cent** = the error rate has fallen to twelve per hundred

centi- *préf* centi-

centile *nm* percentile

centimètre *nm* centimetre

centrage *nm (d'un texte)* centering

central *nm (téléphonique)* telephone exchange; **central automatique** = automatic telephone exchange; **central automatique électronique** = electronic automatic exchange; **central répartiteur** = area exchange; **central téléphonique électromécanique** *ou* **central Strowger** = strowger exchange; **central téléphonique manuel privé (raccordé au secteur public)** = private manual branch exchange (PMBX); **central téléphonique privatif (non raccordé au réseau public)** = private automatic exchange (PAX); *voir aussi* AUTOCOMMUTATEUR

◊ **central, -e** *adj* central; **horloge centrale** = main clock; **mémoire centrale** = core memory *ou* core store; main memory *ou* central memory *ou* primary memory; **programme en mémoire centrale** = core program; **mémoire centrale rapide** = fast core; **dans ce système, la mémoire centrale rapide sert de bloc-notes pour tous les calculs** = the fast core is used as a scratchpad for all calculations in this system; **opérateur central** = centre operator; **ordinateur central** = mainframe (computer) *ou* central computer; *(d'une carte perforée)* **perforations centrales** = centre holes; **processeur central** = central processor *ou* central processing unit (CPU); **terminal central** = central terminal; *(processeur en tranches)* **unité centrale de calcul** = central processing element (CPE); **unité centrale (de traitement)** *ou* **processeur central** = central processing unit (CPU) *ou* central processor;

éléments de l'unité centrale = CPU elements; **(temps de) cycle de l'unité centrale** = CPU cycle; **temps d'utilisation de l'unité centrale** = CPU time

◊ **centrale** *nf* centre; **centrale d'information** = information retrieval centre

◊ **centralisé, -ée** *adj* centralized; **réseau informatique centralisé** = centralized computer network; **traitement centralisé de l'information** = centralized data processing

centre *nm* centre, *US* center; **centre de calcul** = computer centre; **centre de commutation des données** = data switching exchange; **centre de distribution** = distribution point; **centre de recherche documentaire** *ou* **centre serveur** = information retrieval centre; **centre de traitement de texte** = editorial processing centre; **nous avons ouvert un nouveau centre de traitement de l'information** = we have opened our new data processing facility

centrer *vtr* to centre, *US* to center; **sur quelle touche faut-il appuyer pour centrer l'en-tête?** = which key do you press to centre the heading?; **il est plutôt facile de centrer les en-têtes en utilisant cette touche de fonction** = centering of headings is easily done, using this function key

Centronics *(interface parallèle de Centronics Inc)* **interface Centronics** = Centronics interface

CEPT *(normes pour vidéotex)* Conference of European Post, Telephone and Telegraph standard *ou* CEPT standard

céramique *nf&adj* ceramic; **condensateur céramique** = ceramic capacitor

cercle *nm* circle; **décrire un cercle** = (i) to draw a circle; (ii) to circulate

certain, -e *adj* certain; **erreur certaine** = solid error

césure *nf* **(a)** *(procédure)* hyphenation *ou* (word) break; **césure et justification** = hyphenation and justification *ou* H & J; **(fonction de) césure et justification** = hyphenate and justify; **fonction césure intelligente** = intelligent spacer; **programme de césure et justification** = H & J program; **un programme de césure et justification établi aux Etats-Unis ne peut être utilisé pour un texte en anglais britannique** = an American hyphenation and justification program will not work with British English spellings; **remplacement de césures** = rehyphenation **(b)** *(trait d'union ou coupure d'un mot)* hyphen *ou* break; **césure d'écran** = soft *ou* discretionary hyphen; *(dont la longueur équivaut à un 'n')* **tiret de césure** = en dash *ou* en rule

CFAO = CONCEPTION ET FABRICATION ASSISTEES PAR ORDINATEUR

la CFAO (création et fabrication assistées par ordinateur) fait intervenir l'ordinateur d'un bout à l'autre du processus de production (conception d'un objet, simulation de son comportement et fabrication à l'aide de robots commandés par ordinateur)
Science et Vie Micro

CGA *(carte pour graphiques couleur)* Colour Graphics Adapter *ou* CGA card

CGM *(métafichier ou fichier graphique)* Computer Graphics Metafile (CGM)

chaînage *nm* chaining *ou* daisy-chaining; **chaînage arrière** *ou* **en amont** = backward chaining; **chaînage de données** = data chaining

◊ **chaîne** *nf* **(a)** *(série de caractères)* chain *ou* string *ou* catenation; *(d'appareils)* daisy chain; **(nombre de) caractères dans une chaîne** = catena; **chaîne de caractères** = character string *ou* catena; **chaîne de caractères alphabétiques** = alphabetic string; **chaîne de caractères alphanumériques** = alphanumeric string; **chaîne contenant des caractères d'espace** = blank string; **chaîne (de caractères) interdite** = forbidden combination; **chaîne de caractères numériques** = numeric string; **chaîne de commandes** = command chain; **chaîne d'éléments de données** = data element chain; **chaîne vide** = empty string *ou* null string *ou* blank string; **balayage de chaînes** = string scanning; **bus de chaîne** = daisy chain bus; **comparaison de chaînes** = string matching; **concaténation de chaînes** = string concatenation; **fonction (de) chaîne** = string function; **nom de chaîne** = string name; **taille d'une chaîne** = string length; **variable de chaîne** = string variable; **variable de type chaîne de caractères** = string type **(b) en chaîne** = chain(ed); **code en chaîne** = chain code; **la connexion en chaîne réduit le câblage** = daisy-chaining saves a lot of cable; **interruption en chaîne** = daisy chain interrupt; **liaison de données en chaîne** = data chaining; **liste en chaîne** = chain list; **recherche en chaîne** = chaining search; **relier en chaîne** = to daisy-chain; **données reliés en chaîne** = concatenated data set **(c)** *(série d'appareils)* **une chaîne haute fidélité** *ou* **une chaîne hi-fi** = a hi fi system *ou* a hi fi **(d) imprimante à chaîne** = chain printer

◊ **chaîné, -ée** *adj (en chaîne)* chained; **arborescence chaînée** = threaded tree; **article chaîné** = chained record; **code chaîné** = chain code; **données chaînées** = concatenated data set; **enregistrement chaîné** = chained record; **fichier chaîné** = chained file *ou* threaded file; **programme à fonctions chaînées** = thread; **langage chaîné** = threaded language; **liste chaînée** = chain(ed) list *ou* linked list; **sous-programme chaîné** = linked subroutine; **variable chaînée** = string type

◊ **chaîner** *vtr* to chain *ou* to daisy-chain; to catenate *ou* to concatenate

chaleur *nf* heat; *(radiateur à ailette(s))* **évacuateur de chaleur** = heat sink

chambre *nf* chamber *ou* room; *(sans écho)* **chambre blanche** = anechoic chamber; **chambre à** écho = echo chamber; *(pour photos)* **chambre noire** = darkroom

champ *nm* **(a)** *(section de fichier ou de carte)* field; **le dossier 'employés' possède un champ 'âge'** = the employee record has a field for age; **les commandes ont été triées sur le champ date** = the orders were sorted according to dates by assigning the date field as the sortkey; **champ (d')adresse** = address field; **champ bloc-notes** = comment field; **champ d'une carte magnétique** = magnetic card field; **champ de carte perforée** = punched card field; **champ clé** = key field; **champ de contrôle** = control field; **champ de données** = data field; **champ label** *ou* **champ d'identification** = label field; **champ magnétique** = magnetic field; **champ (d')opérande** = operand field; **champ d'opération** = operation field; **dispositif à champ programmable** = field programmable device; **champ protégé** = protected field; **champ de taille constante** *ou* **fixe** = fixed field; **champ de tri** = sortkey *ou* sort field; **dimension d'un champ** = field length; **élément** *ou* **item d'un champ** = member; **étiquette** *ou* **label d'un champ** = field label; **intensité de champ** = field strength; **marqueur de champ** = field marker; **programmation de champ** = field programming; **séparateur de champs** = field marker *ou* separator; **taille d'un champ** = field length **(b)** *(télévision)* **(action) hors champ** = off screen (action); **balayage hors champ** = overscan; **champ d'une scène** = action frame; *(photo)* **profondeur de champ** = depth of field **(c)** **champ magnétique** = magnetic field; **semi-conducteur à effet de champ MOSFET** = metal oxide semiconductor field effect transistor (MOSFET); **transistor à effet de champ (TEC)** = field effect transistor (FET)

certains champs comportent plusieurs options non visibles dans ce menu; pour les visualiser, vous utilisez la touche de fonction F1
L'Ordinateur Individuel

le champ magnétique apparaît donc comme créé par le mouvement de particules électrisées
Science et Vie

changement *nm* **(a)** *(dans un texte ou fichier)* alteration *ou* change *ou* modification; movement; **changement d'adresse en mémoire** = memory edit **(b)** *(d'un système à un autre)* change *ou* change-over *ou* crossover; **changement de banque** *ou* **de bloc de mémoire** = bank switching; **changement graduel** *ou* **progressif** = phased change-over; **(instruction de) changement de page** = form feed; **changement de police de caractères** = font change

◊ **changer** *vtr* **(a)** to alter *ou* to change *ou* to modify *ou* to vary; **sauvegarder le fichier mais changez-en le nom et appelez-le CLIENT** = save the file and rename it CLIENT; **qui peut être changé** = alterable **(b)** to change *ou* to switch over to *ou* to change over to; **changer d'appareil** = to change machines; **changer de place** = to move *ou* to change places **(c)** to replace; **un ruban qui a imprimé plusieurs milliers de caractères a besoin d'être changé** = a printer ribbon needs replacing after several thousand characters

◊ **changeur** *nm* changer; **changeur de disques (automatique)** = record changer; *(dispositif qui change une prise mâle en prise femelle et vice versa)* **changeur de genre** = gender changer *ou* sex changer; **il est possible de relier tous ces périphériques en utilisant seulement deux câbles et un changeur de genre** = you can interconnect all these peripherals with just two cables and a gender changer

chapelet *nm* **programme en chapelet** = thread

chapitre *nm* chapter; **tête de chapitre** = chapter heading; **les têtes de chapitre sont composées en caractères gras de 12 points** = chapter headings are in 12 point bold

char *(variable de type caractère)* char

charbon *nm* **microphone à charbon** = carbon microphone

charge *nf* **(a)** charge *ou* load; **charge électrique** = electric charge; **par charge électrostatique** = electrostatically; **(temps de) charge d'une pile** = battery charging; *(pour le toner d'une imprimante)* **charge statique** = corona; **fil de charge statique** = corona wire; **si vos sorties d'imprimante sont sales, il faut nettoyer le fil de charge statique** = if your printouts are smudged, you may have to clean the corona wire; **facteur de charge** = load factor **(b)** *(d'une ligne)* line load; **charge accordée** *ou* **équilibrée** = matched load; **facteur de charge** = load **(c)** **dispositif à couplage de charge** = charge-coupled device (CCD); **mémoire à couplage de charge** = CCD memory *ou* charge-coupled device memory **(d)** **charge de travail** = workload **(e)** **cahier des charges** = job specification; **le travail ne répond pas au cahier des charges** = the work is not up to specification *ou* does not meet the customer's specifications

◊ **chargement** *nm* *(d'un programme)* loading; **le chargement (d'un programme) peut être assez long à effectuer** = loading can be a long process; **chargement dispersé des données** = scatter load; **faire un chargement dispersé** *ou* **éclaté** = to scatter load; **chargement et exécution** = load and run *ou* load and go; **lanceur de programme de chargement** = initial program header; **programme de chargement de la mémoire vive** = RAM loader

◊ **charger** *vtr* **(a)** *(batterie)* to charge; **charger une ligne** = to load a line **(b)** *(programme)* to load; **charger des données** = to input (i/p *ou* I/P); **les données sont chargées à l'aide d'un modem** = the data is input via a modem **(c)** *(papier ou cartes)* to feed *ou* to load (into a printer, etc.); **le papier doit être chargé manuellement dans l'imprimante** = the paper should be manually fed into the printer **(d)** **charger un bit** = to set a bit

◊ **chargeur** *nm* **(a)** *(de programme)* loader *ou* bootstrap (loader); **chargeur absolu** = absolute loader; **chargeur automatique** = automatic loader; **chargeur binaire** = binary loader; **chargeur/éditeur de liens** = linking loader; **chargeur de programme**

de lancement = initial program loader (IPL); **(programme) chargeur de la mémoire vive** = RAM loader **(b)** **chargeur de cartes** = card loader; **chargeur de cartes perforées** = hopper

chariot *nm* **(a)** *(machine à écrire ou traitement de texte)* carriage; **commande de chariot** = carriage control; **les codes de commande de chariot peuvent être utilisés pour faire avancer le papier de deux interlignes** = carriage control codes can be used to move the paper forward two lines between each line of text; **retour de chariot** = carriage return; **touche de retour du chariot** = carriage return key **(b)** **chariot piloté par ordinateur** = buggy

chasse *nf* *(imprimerie)* set width

châssis *nm* chassis; **châssis avec guide cartes** = card cage *ou* card frame *ou* card chassis; **châssis sous tension** = hot chassis

chaud, -e *adj* **(a)** hot; warm; **test à chaud** = burn-in **(b)** *(nouveau lancement sans procédure de contrôle)* **amorçage à chaud** = warm boot; *(repérer et corriger une faute sans affecter l'opération)* **correction** *ou* **réparation à chaud** = hot fix **(c)** **point chaud** = hot spot *ou* hotspot; **zone chaude** = hot zone

chauffer *vi* to heat *ou* to overheat; **il se peut que le système chauffe si la pièce n'est pas climatisée** = the system may overheat if the room is not air-conditioned

CHCP *(commande de changement de page de code sous MS-DOS et OS/2)* CHCP

CHDIR *(commande de changement de répertoire sous MS-DOS et UNIX)* Change Directory (CHDIR)

chef *nm* head of department *ou* manager; **chef éclairagiste** = lighting director; **chef du service informatique** = data processing manager

chemin *nm* **(a)** path *ou* route; **le chemin choisi ne s'est pas révélé le plus direct du fait que de nombreux noeuds étaient occupés** = the route taken was not the most direct since a lot of nodes were busy **(b)** *(sous DOS)* **chemin d'accès** = path; **vous ne pouvez pas lancer le programme à partir du répertoire racine si vous n'avez pas ajouté le nom de son répertoire dans la commande de chemins d'accès** = you cannot run the program from the root directory until its directory is added to the path; **chemin complet** = full path; **nom du chemin** = pathname; **voici donc le nom du chemin pour trouver le fichier de la lettre:**

\FILES\SIMON\DOCS\LETTER.DOC = the pathname for the letter file is \FILES\SIMON\DOCS\LETTER.DOC; **chemin des données** = data path **(c)** *(maquette d'édition)* **chemin de fer** = editing plan *ou* flatplan

◊ **cheminement** *nm* route

chemise *nf (pour dossier)* cardboard file *ou* folder

chercher *vtr* **(a)** *(dans un programme ou un texte)* to search *ou* to seek; **(instruction) chercher** = get (instruction); **(instruction) chercher et remplacer** = search and replace; **chercher et remplacer globalement** *ou* **dans tout le texte** = global search and replace; **(instruction) aller chercher et lire** = fetch (instruction) **(b)** *(examiner attentivement)* **il a cherché Saint-Victor-de-Réno sur la carte** = he scanned the map for St Victor-de-Réno

cheval de Troie *nm (programme pirate)* Trojan Horse

chevauchement *nm* lap *ou* overlap

◊ **(se) chevaucher** *vi* to overlap

chiffrage *nm* encryption; **chiffrage de données** = data encryption; **clé de chiffrage** = cryptographic key *ou* cipher key

◊ **chiffre** *nm* **(a)** *(informatique)* digit *ou* figure *ou* number; **chiffre binaire** = binary digit *ou* bit; **groupe de 2 chiffres binaires** = dibit; **chiffre de contrôle** = check digit *ou* check number; **chiffre de remplissage** = gap digit; **chiffre (indicateur) de signe** = sign digit **(b)** number *ou* figure *ou* digit; **chiffre en exposant** = superior number; **chiffre le moins significatif** *ou* **de poids faible** = least significant digit (LSD) *ou* lower order digit; **chiffre le plus significatif** *ou* **de poids fort** = most significant character *ou* most significant digit (MSD); **la base de numération décimale utilise les chiffres 0123456789** = the decimal number system uses the digits 0123456789; **en chiffres ronds** = in round figures; **place d'un chiffre** = digit place *ou* position; **tableau de chiffres** = numeric array **(b)** *(caractère d'imprimerie)* numeral *ou* figure *ou* digit; **un numéro de téléphone de huit chiffres** = a phone number with eight digits *ou* an eight-digit phone number; **chiffres arabes** = Arabic numbers *ou* figures *ou* numerals; **chiffres et signes en code télégraphique** = figures case; **chiffres romains** = Roman numbers *ou* figures *ou* numerals

◊ **chiffré, -ée** *adj* code chiffré *ou* écriture chiffrée = cipher *ou* cipher system; **code chiffré à clé publique** = public key cipher; **nos concurrents ne peuvent lire nos fichiers qui sont en langage chiffré** = our competitors cannot understand our files - they have all been enciphered; **message chiffré** = coded message; **le message chiffré peut être transmis par téléphone sans que personne ne puisse le lire** = the encrypted text can be sent along ordinary telephone lines, and no one will be able to understand it; **texte non chiffré** = plaintext

◊ **chiffrement** *nm* encryption; **chiffrement de données** = data encryption

◊ **chiffrer** *vtr* to code *ou* to encipher *ou* to encrypt

chimique *adj* chemical; **produit chimique** = chemical; **réaction chimique** = chemical reaction

CHKDSK *(commande de contrôle de disque sous DOS)* CHKDSK (command)

choc *nm* jar *ou* jolt; **les disques durs sont très sensibles aux chocs** = hard disks are very sensitive to jarring

choix *nm* **(a)** choice; *(entre deux choses)* alternative; *(de plusieurs articles)* selection; **nous n'avons pas le choix** = we have no alternative; **au choix** = optional; **le système est équipé d'un lecteur de disquettes 3,5 ou 5,25 pouces au choix** = the system comes with optional 3.5 or 5.25 inch disk drives **(b) de choix** = high quality *ou* top quality; **meilleur choix** = best fit

Chooser ™ *(utilitaire d'Apple Macintosh)* Chooser ™

chroma *voir* CHROMINANCE

◊ **chromatique** *adj* chromatic; **aberration chromatique** = chromatic aberration; **contrôle chromatique** = chroma control; **détecteur chromatique** = chroma detector; **dispersion chromatique** = chromatic dispersion; **séparation** *ou* **sélection chromatique** = colour separation; **température chromatique** = colour temperature; **variation chromatique** = colour shift

◊ **chromaticité** *nf* chromaticity

chrominance *ou* **chroma** *nf* chrominance *ou* chroma; **signal de chrominance** = chrominance signal

chronique *nf (d'un journal)* column; **chronique économique** = business news; **chronique financière** = financial news *ou* column

chronologique *adj* chronological; **fichier chronologique** = journal file; **ordre chronologique** = chronological order

chronomètre *nm* timer

◊ **chronométrie** *nf* timing *ou* time measurement; **(à) double chronométrie** = dual clocking

chute *nf* fall; **chute de courant** = brown-out; **chute de tension** = power loss

cible *nf* target; **disque cible** = target disk; **niveau cible** = target level; **ordinateur cible** = target computer

cinéaste *nm* **équipe de cinéastes** = camera crew; **l'équipe de cinéastes a dû tourner toute la journée dans la neige** = the camera crew had to film all day in the snow

cinéma *nm* **(a)** *(art cinématographique)* cinema **(b)** *(bâtiment)* cinema

◊ **cinématographie** *nf* cinematography

◊ **cinématographique** *adj* (of) film *ou* (of the) cinema; **appareil cinématographique** = cine camera; **art cinématographique** = cinema; **équipe cinématographique** = camera crew

cinq *adj num* five

◊ **cinquième** *num* fifth; **ordinateur de cinquième génération** = fifth generation computer

circonflexe *adj* **accent circonflexe** = circumflex

circuit *nm* **(a)** circuit; **(ensemble de) circuits** = circuitry; **le programme de CAO peut tracer le circuit très rapidement** = the CAD program will plot the circuit diagram rapidly; **circuit à coïncidence** = coincidence circuit; **circuit à deux fils** = two wire circuit; **circuit à très haut niveau d'intégration** = jumbo chip; **circuit bifilaire** *ou* **bidirectionnel** = two wire circuit; **circuit bistable** = bistable circuit *ou* bistable multivibrator; **circuit combinatoire** = combinational circuit; **circuit composite** = composite circuit *ou* hybrid circuit; *(pour protection de logiciel)* **circuit crypté** = dongle; **circuit de décision** = decision circuit *ou* element; **circuit d'échange de données** = data circuit; **circuit de jonction** = trunk; **circuit de liaison directe (sans modem)** = null modem; **circuit de transmission de données** = data circuit; **circuit déparasité** = de-bounce circuit; **circuit duplex** = duplex circuit; **circuit équilibré** = balanced circuit; **il faut utiliser un circuit équilibré en fin de ligne pour éviter la réflexion des signaux** = you must use a balanced circuit at the end of the line to prevent signal reflections; **circuit d'équivalence** = equivalence gate; **circuit ET** = AND gate *ou* coincidence gate; **circuit hybride** = hybrid circuit; **(carte de) circuit imprimé (CI)** *ou* **plaque présensibilisée pour circuit imprimé** = printed circuit *ou* printed circuit board (PCB) *ou* circuit board *ou* card; **plaque (présensibilisée) double face pour circuit imprimé** = double-sided printed circuit board; **circuit intégré** = integrated circuit (IC) *ou* chip; **architecture d'un circuit intégré** = chip architecture; **ensemble des circuits intégrés** = chip set; **ligne de sélection** *ou* **de validation d'un circuit intégré** = chip select line; **circuit intégré de diagnostic** = diagnostic chip; **circuit intégré de carte vidéo** = video interface chip; **cet émulateur intégré au circuit sert à tester le contrôleur de la disquette, en simulant le fonctionnement d'un lecteur de disquettes** = this in-circuit emulator is used to test the floppy disk controller by emulating a disk drive; **circuit inverseur** = NOT gate; **circuit LC** = LC circuit; **circuit logique** = gate circuit *ou* logic array *ou* logic circuit *ou* logic gate; **circuit logique complexe** *ou* **en réseau** = gate array; **circuit logique non connecté** = uncommitted logic array (ULA); **circuit logique programmable** = programmable logic array (PLA); **circuit logique à trois états** = three state logic; **circuit loué ou de location** = leased circuit; **circuit mixte** = hybrid circuit; **circuit NI** = NOR circuit *ou* gate; **circuit NI exclusif** = exclusive NOR gate *ou* EXNOR gate; **circuit NON** = NOT gate *ou* negation gate; **circuit NON-ET** *ou* **circuit NAND** = NAND circuit *ou* gate; **circuit NON-OU** = NOR circuit *ou* gate; **circuit numérique** = digital circuit; **circuit optique intégré** = integrated optical circuit; **circuit OU** = OR gate; **circuit OU exclusif** = EXOR gate *ou* exclusive OR circuit *ou* gate; **circuit virtuel** = virtual circuit; **circuit vocal** = dry circuit **(b)**

analyseur de circuit = circuit analyzer; **câble antenne-circuit** = feeder cable; **capacité d'un circuit** = circuit capacity; **caractéristique d'un circuit** = circuit grade; **commutation de circuit** = circuit switching; **diagramme d'un circuit** = circuit diagram; **émulateur intégré au circuit** = in-circuit emulator; **niveau de bruit d'un circuit** = circuit noise level; **qualité d'un circuit** = circuit grade; **tracé d'un circuit** = circuit design **(c)** **télévision en circuit fermé** = closed circuit television (CCTV) **(d)** *(d'information ou communication)* channel; **créer de nouveaux circuits de communication** = to open up new channels of communication

◊ **circuiterie** *nf* circuitry; **la circuiterie demeure trop complexe** = the circuitry is still too complex

> le circuit imprimé pourra être gravé, d'après le dessin proposé, soit par un procédé photographique, soit en recopiant ce dessin à l'aide de pastilles et de rubans
> *Electronique pratique*

> en dernier lieu, on implantera les circuits intégrés
> *Electronique pratique*

circulaire *adj* circular; cyclic; **compteur (à décalage) circulaire** = ring counter; **décalage circulaire** = circular shift *ou* end about shift *ou* cyclic shift; **guide d'ondes circulaire** = circular waveguide; **liste circulaire** = ring; **orbite circulaire** = circular orbit; **permutation circulaire** = cyclic shift *ou* ring shift; **référence circulaire** = circular reference; *(d'un calculateur rapide)* **report circulaire** = end-around carry; **tampon circulaire** = circular buffer

circulant, -e *adj* circulating; **document circulant** = turnaround document; **mémoire circulante** = circulating storage; **registre à bits circulants** = circulating register

circulation *nf* circulation; **la société essaie d'améliorer la circulation de l'information dans les services** = the company is trying to improve the circulation of information between departments

circuler *vi* to flow; **faire circuler** = to circulate *ou* to distribute

citation *nf* quotation *ou* quote

◊ **citer** *vtr* to quote; **il a cité des chiffres mentionnés dans le journal** = he quoted figures from the newspaper report

clair, -e *adj* **(a)** *(non encrypté)* clear; **texte en clair** = plaintext; **les messages ont été transmis en clair par téléphone** = the messages were sent as plaintext by telephone **(b)** *(sans parasites)* **le signal est plus ou moins clair suivant les conditions atmosphériques** = the atmospheric conditions affect the clarity of the signal **(c)** *(pâle)* light

◊ **clairement** *adv* clearly; **la notice indique clairement comment relier les différents modules du système** = the booklet gives clear instructions how to connect the different parts of the system; **le manuel d'utilisation n'explique pas clairement la marche à suivre pour copier un fichier** = the program manual is not clear on copying files

clapet *nm* latch

clarté *nf* clarity; **les conditions atmosphériques influencent la clarté du signal** = the atmospheric conditions affect the clarity of the signal

classe *nf* **(a)** class *ou* grade; **(de) première classe** = first class *ou* top grade; **un expert-informaticien de première classe** = a top-grade computer expert **(b)** *(ensemble d'éléments d'une routine)* classe; *(valeurs des éléments d'une classe)* **intervalle de classe** = class interval

◊ **classement** *nm* **(a)** *(documents à classer)* filing *ou* indexing *ou* classification; *(de données)* **classement énumératif (de données)** = enumerated type; **méthode de classement** = filing system **(b)** *(des cahiers d'un livre)* **séquence de classement** = collating sequence

◊ **classer** *vtr* to classify *ou* to order *ou* to sort *ou* to file; **classer des documents** = to file documents; **on a classé les sorties d'imprimante avec diagnostics sous la rubrique 'Test'** = the diagnostic printouts have been classified under T for test results; **liste classée (en ordre alphabétique, etc.)** = ordered list; **classer en** *ou* **par ordre alphabétique** = to alphabetize *ou* to alphasort; **classer les adresses en ordre alphabétique** = to sort addresses into alphabetical order; **les noms sont classés par ordre alphabétique** = the sequence of names is arranged alphabetically; **classer par rang** *ou* **par ordre d'importance** = to rank; **documents à classer** = filing; **non classé, -ée** = unsorted; **il a fallu quatre fois plus de temps pour chercher dans les fichiers non classés** = it took four times as long to search the unsorted files

◊ **classeur** *nm* *(en carton)* file *ou* folder; *(meuble)* filing cabinet

◊ **classification** *nf* classification; **classification (suivant la méthode de) Dewey** = Dewey decimal classification; **classification hiérarchique** = hierarchical classification

clause *nf* *(d'un document)* article

clavier *nm* **(a)** *(de machine à écrire ou d'ordinateur)* keyboard; *(de petite dimension ou auxiliaire)* pad *ou* keypad; **le clavier comporte 84 touches** = there are 84 keys on the keyboard; **clavier ANSI** = ANSI keyboard; **clavier ASCII** = ASCII keyboard; **clavier auxiliaire** = keypad; **clavier aveugle** = blind keyboard; **clavier aveugle produisant une bande non justifiée** = noncounting keyboard; *(clavier utilisé surtout dans les pays francophones)* **clavier AZERTY** = AZERTY keyboard; **clavier à effleurement** = tactile keyboard *ou* touch-sensitive keyboard; **clavier électronique** = electronic keyboard; **clavier émetteur-récepteur** *ou* **de téléscripteur** = ASR keyboard; **clavier français accentué** = AZERTY keyboard; **clavier hexadécimal** = hex keypad *ou* hex pad; **clavier interactif** = interactive keyboard; **clavier numérique** = numeric keypad *ou* numeric pad; *(clavier international utilisé surtout dans les pays anglo-saxons)* **clavier QWERTY** = QWERTY keyboard; **clavier relié à un terminal** = terminal keyboard; **clavier tactile** = tactile keyboard *ou* touch-sensitive keyboard; **clavier à**

touches programmables = soft keyboard; **contrôle de clavier** = keyboard scan; **disposition des touches d'un clavier** = keyboard layout; **grille d'aide** *ou* **mémento (de fonction des touches) de clavier** = keyboard overlay; **implantation des touches d'un clavier** = keyboard layout *ou* key matrix; **mémoire tampon de clavier chronologique à n positions** = n-key rollover; **rebond d'une touche de clavier** = keyboard contact bounce; **saisie au** *ou* **sur** *ou* **par clavier** = keyboarding *ou* keying (in); manual entry *ou* manual input; **saisie directe sur disque(tte), par clavier** = keyboard to disk entry; **saisir (des données) au clavier** *ou* **par clavier** = to keyboard *ou* to key in; **saisie au clavier contrôlée par ordinateur** = processor-controlled keying **(b)** *(de téléphone)* keypad *ou* dial pad; **clavier tonal** = tone dialling pad; **numérotation sur clavier tonal** = tone dialling; **numérotation sur clavier** = pushbutton dialling; **téléphone à clavier** = pushbutton telephone; **terminal entrée-sortie** *ou* **émetteur-récepteur à clavier** = keyboard send/receive (KSR)

◊ **claviste** *nm&f* *(opérateur de saisie)* keyboarder; **le claviste a sauté plusieurs lignes du manuscrit** = several lines of manuscript have been missed by the keyboarder

> bien que la souris soit supportée, la totalité des fonctions peut être exécutée à partir du clavier
> *L'Ordinateur Individuel*

clé *ou* **clef** *nf* **(a)** key; *(de chiffrage ou de cryptage)* cipher key *ou* cryptographic key; **il a finalement trouvé la clé du code** = he finally broke the cipher system; **tapez la clé et vous pourrez décoder le dernier message** = type this key into the machine, that will decode the last message; **code chiffré** *ou* **cryptage à clé publique** = public key cipher (system); **clé à usage unique** = one-time pad **(b)** *(de programmation)* **clé de contrôle** = check key; **clé numérique de contrôle** = check bit *ou* check digit *ou* check number; **clé électronique** = dongle; **clé d'identification** = key; **clé d'index** = index key; **clé primaire** *ou* **principale** = primary key; **clé de protection** = protection key; **clé de recherche** = search key; **nous avons sélectionné les enregistrements en utilisant le mot DISK comme clé de recherche** = we selected all the records with the word DISK in their keys; **clé de tri** = sortkey; **champ clé** = key field; **gestion de clé** = key management; **méthode d'accès séquentiel par clé** = keyed sequential access method (KSAM); *voir aussi* MOT-CLE, TRI **(c)** *(de porte ou de système)* key; **système clé en main** = turnkey system

clef *nf* = CLE

clic *nm* click; **clic témoin (de fonctionnement) de touche** = key click; **un clic (sur le bouton de la souris) vous permet de vous déplacer dans les textes et graphiques** = you move through text and graphics with a click of the button

> par un simple clic sur un bouton, on se trouve dans la structure de la base, la procédure concernée s'affichant sur l'écran
> *L'Ordinateur Individuel*

cliché *nm* *(photographie)* negative; *(imprimerie)* plate; **cliché de base** = key plate

client, -e *n* **(a)** customer *ou* client; **maintenance du parc clients** = customer engineering; **service clients** = customer service department **(b)** client; **architecture client-serveur** = client-server architecture; **réseau client-serveur** = client-server network

clignotant *nm* flashing light

◊ **clignotant, -e** *adj* flashing *ou* blinking; **caractère clignotant** = flashing character *ou* character blink

◊ **clignotement** *nm* (*d'un caractère brillant*) blinking; (*télévision*) flicker; **sans clignotement** = flicker-free

◊ **clignoter** *vi* (*lumière ou voyant*) to blink *ou* to flash; (*télévision*) to flicker

clip *nm* (*extrait de film*) clip; **un clip de l'accident a été passé aux informations** = there was a clip of the disaster on the news

◊ **clip-art** *ou* **clipart** *ou* **clip art** *nm* (*image de bibliothèque*) clip-art

cliquer *vi* to click; **pour afficher le menu déroulant cliquer sur l'icône en haut de l'écran** = the pull-down menu is viewed by clicking over the icon at the top of the screen; **utilisez la souris pour agrandir un cadre: cliquez à l'intérieur des limites du cadre et glissez jusqu'à la position voulue** = use the mouse to enlarge a frame by clicking inside its border

avec la souris, il suffit de pointer et de cliquer
L'Ordinateur Individuel

clone *nm* clone; **ils ont copié notre nouveau modèle d'ordinateur pour commercialiser un clone qui se vend beaucoup moins cher** = they have copied our new personal computer and brought out a cheaper clone; **il existe des clones de tous nos modèles et tous sont plus performants** = higher performance clones are available for all the models in our range

clore *vtr* (*sur ordinateur*) **clore une session** = to log off *ou* log out

CLOSE (*commande de fin d'accès à un équipement ou à un fichier*) CLOSE (command)

clôture *nf* (*sur ordinateur*) **clôture de session** = logging off; **routines de clôture d'exécution (d'un programme)** = end of run routines

CLS (*commande MS-DOS de vidage d'écran*) CLS (command)

cluster *nm* (*équivaut à 4 secteurs d'un disque dur*) cluster; *voir aussi* SECTEUR

C-MAC (*norme de télévision*) **multiplexeur C-MAC** = C-MAC

CMIP (*protocole pour réseaux*) Common Management Information Protocol (CMIP)

CMIS (*système de gestion de réseau*) Common Management Information Specification (CMIS)

CMOS (*semi-conducteur*) Complementary Metal Oxide Semiconductor (CMOS)

CMOT (*gestionnaire de passerelle à base de CMIS et de CMIP*) CMIP/CMIS OVER TCP (CMOT)

CMYK (*système de définition de couleurs: cyan, magenta, jaune, noir*) Cyan-Magenta-Yellow-Black (CMYK)

coaxial, -e *adj* co-axial; **câble coaxial** = co-axial cable

COBOL (*langage de programmation de gestion*) Common Business Orientated Language (COBOL)

le COBOL étant le langage de programmation des applications de gestion le plus répandu au monde
L'Information professionnelle

codage *nm* coding *ou* encoding; **codage à adresse absolue** = specific coding; **codage binaire** = binary encoding; **codage bipolaire** = bipolar coding; **codage direct** = direct coding; **codage de Hamming** = Hamming code; **codage en ligne directe** = straight-line coding; **codage relatif** = relative coding; **codage spécifique** = specific coding; **modulation par impulsions et codage (MIC)** = pulse code modulation (PCM)

code *nm* **(a)** code; (*de chiffrage ou de cryptage*) cipher key *ou* cipher system; **code absolu** = absolute *ou* specific code; **code accéléré** = optimized code; **code d'accès (à un système)** = access code *ou* authorization code; **code amélioré** = optimized code; **code barres** = bar code; (*système*) universal product code (UPC); **lecteur de codes barres** = bar-code reader; **lecteur optique de codes barres** = optical bar reader *ou* bar code reader *ou* optical wand; **code de base** = basic code; **code binaire** = binary code; **le code binaire du nombre décimal 8 est 1000** = the BCD representation of decimal 8 is 1000; **code binaire absolu** = absolute *ou* specific code; **code binaire plus 3** = excess-3 code; **pour 6, le code binaire plus 3 est 1001** = the excess-3 code representation of 6 is 1001; **code binaire à 8 bits** = extended binary coded decimal interchange code (EBCDIC); **code binaire réfléchi** = cyclic code; **code biquinaire** = biquinary code; **code de caractères** = character code; character coding system; **code de caractères interne** = internal character code; **ASCII est le code de caractères le plus fréquemment utilisé** = the ASCII code is the most frequently used character coding system; **code en chaîne** *ou* **code chaîné** = chain code; **code chiffré** = cipher *ou* cipher system; **code chiffré à clé publique** = public key cipher; **il a finalement réussi à déchiffrer le code** *ou* **il a finalement trouvé la clé du code** = he finally broke the cipher system; **il faut toujours utiliser un code chiffré sûr quand vous transmettez des données par téléphone** = always use a secure cipher when sending data over a telephone line; **code de commande** = operating code *ou* op code *ou* order code; **processeur de codes de commande** = order code processor (OCP); **code compacté** = compact code; *(pour accès à un système)* **code confidentiel** = signature; **numéro de code confidentiel** = personal identification number (PIN) *ou* identity number; **code de contrôle de bloc** = block code; **code décimal réfléchi** = cyclic decimal code; **code direct** = direct code *ou* one-level code; **code drapeau** = flag code; **code EBCDIC** *ou* **code binaire à 8 bits** = extended binary coded decimal interchange code (EBCDIC); **code échappement** *ou* **code 'escape'** = escape code; **code élémentaire** = basic code; **code d'erreur** = error code; **code correcteur d'erreur** = error correcting code; **code détecteur d'erreur** *ou* **code de détection d'erreur** = error detecting code *ou* self-checking code; **code indicateur d'erreur** = error code; **code de vérification et correction d'erreur** = error checking and correcting code (ECCC); **code erroné** *ou* **erreur de code** = false code; **code ESC** = ESC code; **code à facettes** = faceted code; **code de fin anormale** *ou* **d'interruption anormale** = abend code; **code de fin de document** = end of document *ou* end of file (EOF); **code de fin de données** = end of data (EOD); **code de fonction** = function code *ou* function digit; **code (de) Gray** = Gray code *ou* cyclic code; **code de Hamming** = Hamming code; **code (de) Hollerith** = Hollerith code; **code de Huffman** = Huffman code; **code d'identification** = identity number *ou* ID code; **code d'identification de périphérique** = device code; **code d'instruction** = computer code *ou* instruction code; **code d'instruction imbriqué (dans un programme)** = embedded code; **code intermédiaire** = intermediate code; **code interprétatif** = interpretative code; **code en langage machine** *ou* **code machine** = computer code *ou* computer-readable code *ou* machine code *ou* actual code; **format de code machine** = machine code format; **instruction en code machine** = machine code instruction; *(d'un message)* **code de majuscules** = figures shift; *(pour bande papier)* **code de marquage** = tape code; **code à un niveau** = direct code *ou* one-level code; **code numérique d'une touche** = key number; **code objet** = object code; **code d'opération** = command code *ou* operation code *ou* operating code *ou* op code; **code optimal** = optimum code; **code optimisé** = optimized code; **code optimum** = optimum code; **code ouvert** = open code; **code de perforation de bande papier** = tape code *ou* punched code; **code de perforation de carte** = card code; **code personnel** = signature *ou* ID code; **numéro de code personnel** = personal identification number (PIN) *ou* identity number; **n'oublie pas d'entrer ton numéro de code personnel** = don't forget to log in your PIN number *ou* identity number; **après la mise en route du système, il faut tapez votre code personnel et votre mot de passe** = after you wake up the system, you have to input your ID code then your password; **code postal** = postcode, *US* ZIP code; **code pur** = pure code; **code à rapport (de bits) constant** *ou* **fixe** = constant ratio code; **code de redondance** = redundant code; **code réfléchi** = reflected code; **code source** = source code; **code spécifique** = specific code; **code de structure** = overhead; **code symbolique** = symbolic code; *(de l'image)* **code de synchronisation** = framing code; **code à temps d'accès minimum** = optimum code; **code à temps d'accès optimisé** = minimum access code *ou*

minimum delay code *ou* minimum latency coding **(b) bit de code** = code bit; **commandé par les codes CTRL** *ou* **asservi aux codes CTRL (générés par la touche contrôle)** = control-driven; **conversion de code** = code conversion; **élément d'un code** = code element; **erreur de code** = false code; **groupe code (de distribution par fibre optique)** = code group; **ligne de code (d'un programme)** = code line; **macro code** = macro code; **modifier les codes d'un programme** = to recode a program; **page de code** = code page; **pour entrer des caractères suédois avec un clavier britannique, il faut changer la page de code du système** = in order to enter Swedish characters from an English keyboard, you have to change the system code page; **segment (mémoire) de code** = code segment; **zone de code** = code area **(c) hash code** = hash code; **générer un hash code** = to hash; **index hash code** = hash index; **système de hash code** = hash-code system; **total de vérification pour hash code** = hash total; **valeur de vérification pour hash code** = hash value

◊ **codé, -ée** *adj* coded; **caractères codés binaires** = binary coded characters; **décimal codé binaire (DCB)** = binary coded decimal (BCD)

◊ **coder** *vtr* to code

◊ **codeur** *nm* coder; **codeur-décodeur** = coder/decoder (CODEC)

> ce code est une suite de trois nombres de 1 à 16, ce qui donne 4096 façons différentes de choisir son numéro secret
>
> *Electronique pratique*

coercibilité *nf* coercivity

coffret *nm* **coffret avec guide-cartes** = rack

cogniticien, -ienne *n* knowledge engineer

cohérence *nf* coherence; consistency; **contrôle de cohérence** = consistency check

◊ **cohérent, -e** *adj* coherent; **faisceau cohérent** = coherent bundle; **lumière cohérente** = coherent light; **le laser produit une lumière cohérente** = the laser produces coherent light

coin *nm* corner; **coin gauche supérieur de l'écran** = cursor home

coincement *nm (papier ou bande)* jam

◊ **coincer** *vtr (papier ou bande)* to jam; **le magnétophone ne fonctionne pas parce que la bande est coincée dans le moteur** = the recorder's not working because the tape is jammed in the motor

◊ **se coincer** *vpr* to jam *ou* to become jammed

coïncidence *nf* coincidence; **circuit à coïncidence** = coincidence circuit

collationner *vtr (les cahiers d'un livre)* to collate

◊ **collationnement** *nm (des cahiers d'un livre)* collating; **indices de collationnement** = collating marks

collecte *nf* collection; **collecte de données** = data collection; **plate-forme de collecte de données** = data collection platform

◊ **collecteur** *nm* collector; **collecteur de données** = (data) sink

collectif, -ive *adj* collective; **antenne collective de télévision (câblée)** = community antenna television (CATV)

collection *nf* collection

coller *vtr* (a) *(traitement de texte)* to paste; **après avoir coupé ce paragraphe à la fin du document, je peux le coller ici** = now that I have cut this paragraph from the end of the document, I can paste it in here; **(fonction) couper/coller** = cut and paste (b) *(film)* to splice

◊ **colleuse** *nf* **colleuse de film** *ou* **de bande** = splicing block

collision *nf* collision; **détection de collision** = collision detection; **méthode d'accès à test de porteuse et détection de collision** = carrier sense multiple access collision detection (CSMA-CD)

colonne *nf* column; **écrivez le total au bas de la colonne** = put the total at the bottom of the column; **additionner une colonne de chiffres** = to add up a column of figures; **écran (de) quatre-vingts colonnes** = eighty-column screen; **imprimante 80 colonnes** = 80-column printer; **le prix comprend une imprimante 80 colonnes** = an 80-column printer is included in the price; **colonne de perforations (d'une carte)** = perforations *ou* card row *ou* card column; **colonne double** = dual column; **en colonne(s)** = columnar *ou* in tabular form; **disposé en colonne(s)** = in tabular form; **disposer (des données) en colonne(s)** = to tab *ou* to tabulate; **diagramme** *ou* **graphique en colonnes** = columnar graph; *(dans une application de PAO)* **guide** *ou* **séparateur de colonnes** = column guide; **indicateur de colonne** = column indicator; **parité de colonnes** = column parity; **présentation graphique sous forme de colonne(s)** = columnar working

colophon *nm* *(symbole d'une société)* colophon; logo

colorier *vi* to colour; to paint

COM *(fichier binaire exécutable)* COM file; **pour démarrer le programme, entrez au clavier le fichier COM à l'invite MS-DOS** = to start the program, type the name of the COM file at the MS-DOS prompt

COM1 *(port)* COM1 (port)

coma *nm* *(aberration de lentille)* coma

COMAL *(langage de programmation structurée)* Common Algorithmic Language (COMAL)

combinaison *nf* combination

combinatoire *adj* combinational; **circuit combinatoire** = combinational circuit; **logique combinatoire** = combinational logic

combiné *nm* handset

◊ **combiner** *vtr&i* *(plusieurs fichiers)* to combine *ou* to merge *ou* to coalesce

COMMAND.COM *(fichier de commande sous MS-DOS)* COMMAND.COM (file); **MS-DOS ne marche pas parce que vous avez effacé le fichier COMMAND.COM par erreur** = MS-DOS will not work because you deleted the COMMAND.COM file by mistake

commande *nf* (a) *(d'un produit)* order; **donner une commande** = to order; **fabriquer sur commande** = to customize; **nous utilisons des logiciels écrits sur commande** = we use customized software; **fait sur commande** = custom-built; **articles vendus sur commande uniquement** = articles available to order only (b) *(instruction de programme)* command *ou* instruction; **en langage BASIC, la commande PRINT fera apparaître le texte sur l'écran** = the BASIC keyword PRINT will display text on the screen; **commande de canal** = channel command; **commande de chariot** = carriage control; **les codes de commande de chariot peuvent être utilisés pour faire avancer le papier de deux interlignes** = carriage control codes can be used to move the paper forward two lines between each line of text; **commande conditionnelle** = conditional statement; **commandes d'édition** = edit commands; **commandes et instructions d'édition** = editing terms; **commande d'exécution** = execute command; **RUN est la commande d'exécution du programme** = the command to execute the program is RUN; **commande imbriquée (dans le texte)** = embedded command; **commande d'interruption (de programme)** = interrupt command; **commande d'invalidation d'interruption** = disable interrupt; **(programme de) commandes numériques de machines-outils** = Automatically Programmed Tools (APT) *ou* Computer Numeric Control (CNC); **système de machines-outils à commandes numériques** = flexible machining system (FMS); **(caractère de) commande de périphérique** = device control character; **commande précédée d'un point** *ou* **commande point** = dot command; **commande de processus** = process control; **commande de stabilisation du signal (après échantillonnage)** = hold; **commande de tâches à distance** = remote job entry (RJE); **commandes de transmission** = line control (c) **chaîne de commandes** = command chain; **code de commande** = operating code *ou* op code *ou* order code; **processeur de codes de commande** = order code processor (OCP); **données de commande** = control data; *(d'un modem prêt à recevoir des commandes)* **état commande** = command state; **fenêtre de commande** = command window; **la fenêtre de commande est une simple ligne en bas de l'écran** = the command window is a single line at the bottom of the screen; **l'utilisateur peut définir la taille de la fenêtre de commande** = the user can define the size of the command window; **fichier de commandes** = batch file *ou* command file; **processeur de fichier de commandes** = command file processor; **instruction de commande** = control statement; **interface de commande** = command interface; **interpréteur de commandes** = command interpreter; **tapez la commande DIR pour obtenir**

la liste des fichiers = type in the command 'DIR' to get a list of files; **langage de commande** = command language *ou* control language; **langage de commande de tâche** = job control language (JCL); **ligne de commande** = command line; **argument de ligne de commande** = command line argument; **utilisez la commande DIR pour afficher la liste des fichiers du disque et ajoutez l'argument de ligne A: pour voir les fichiers du disque A:** = use the command 'DIR' to view the files on disk, add the command line argument 'A:' to view the files on drive A:; **système de ligne de commande** = command line operating system; **logiciel de commande de périphérique** = driver *ou* handler; *(invite)* **message d'attente de commande** = command prompt; **micro-ordinateur de commande** = microcontroller; **mot de commande** = keyword *ou* control word; *(d'un appareil)* **panneau de commande** = front panel *ou* control pannel; **procédure de commande** = operator procedure; **processeur de commande de console** = command console processor (CCP); **programme de commande** = master control program (MCP); **programme activé par commande** = command-driven program; **pupitre de commande d'un opérateur** = operator's console; **registre de commande** = command register *ou* control register; **registre de commande de contrôle** = control register; **séquence de commande (d'exécution)** = control sequence; **signal de commande** = control signal; *(d'un Apple Macintosh)* **touche de commande** = command key; control (key)

◊ **commandé, -ée** *adj* driven; **commandé par les codes CTRL (générés par la touche contrôle)** = control-driven

commencement *nm* beginning

◊ **commencer** *vtr* to begin; **commencer quelque chose graduellement** = to phase something in

commentaire *nm* **(a)** commentary *ou* narrative **(b)** *(écrit)* annotation *ou* comment *ou* commentary; **symbole de commentaire** = annotation symbol; **en BASIC il est possible d'inclure des commentaires à la suite de l'instruction REM** = BASIC allows comments to be written after a REM instruction; **mise en commentaire (d'une commande)** = comment out

commercial, -e *adj* commercial *ou* business; **correspondance commerciale** = business correspondence; **'et' commercial (&)** = ampersand

◊ **commercialisation** *nf* marketing; *(disque ou film ou logiciel)* release

◊ **commercialiser** *vtr* to market; **commercialiser (un nouveau produit)** = to release (a new product) on the market

commun, -e *adj* common *ou* general; **fichier commun** = shared file; **langage commun** = common language; **logiciel commun** = common software; **signalisation par voie commune** = common channel signalling; **variable commune** = global variable; **zone commune de mémoire** = common storage area

communauté *nf* community

communication *nf* **(a)** *(information)* communication; **créer de nouveaux circuits de communication** = to open up new channels of communication; **les communications avec le siège social sont plus rapides depuis que nous avons un télécopieur** = communicating with head office has been quicker since we installed a fax machine **(b)** *(télécommunication)* communications; **communication asynchrone** = asynchronous communications; **interface pour communication asynchrone** = asynchronous communications interface adapter (ACIA); **communication par câble** = line communications; **communication à faible débit** = low speed communications; **communications groupées** = batched communication; **système de communication hiérarchisé** = hierarchical communications system; **communication par infrarouge** = infrared communications; **moyens de communication interactifs** = interactive media; **communication entre ordinateurs** = computer conferencing; **communication par rayon laser** = laser beam communications; **communication synchrone binaire** = binary synchronous communications (BSC); **basculer la communication d'un émetteur à l'autre** = to hand off; **connecteur de communication** = communications port; **contrôleur de communication** = communications control unit (CCU); **interface de communication** = communications interface; **adaptateur d'interface de communication** = communications interface adapter; **système de traitement de texte doté d'une interface de communication** = communicating word processor (CWP); **ligne de communication** = communications link; **ligne de communication de données** = dataline; **contrôle de ligne de communication** = communications link control; **contrôle de mise en communication** = handshake I/O control; **logiciel de communication** = communications software; **progiciel de communication** = communications package; **protocole de communication** = communications protocol; **pour la plupart des services en lignes, le protocole de communication est un mot de huit bits, sans bit d'arrêt et bit de parité pair** = the communications protocol for most dial-up online services is eight-bit words, no stop bit and even parity; **protocole de mise en communication (de deux postes)** = full handshaking; **port de communication** = communications port; **réseau de communication** = communications network; **scanner de demande de communication** = communications scanner; **serveur de communication** = communications server **(c)** *(appel téléphonique)* call; **communication interurbaine** = long-distance call *ou* trunk call; **communication urbaine** = local call; **communication avec préavis** = person-to-person call

communiqué *nm* **communiqué de presse** = news release *ou* press release; **la société a diffusé *ou* a publié un communiqué au sujet de la nouvelle imprimante laser** = the company sent out a news release about the new laser printer

◊ **communiquer** *vi* to communicate; **il n'arrive pas à communiquer avec son personnel** = he finds it impossible to communicate with his staff; **l'affichage électronique du réseau permet aux systèmes reliés de communiquer entre eux** = the multi-user BBS has a computer conferencing facility; **communiquer avec le siège central est plus rapide depuis que nous avons installé un fax** = communicating with head office has been quicker since we installed the fax

commutateur *nm* **(a)** switch; **commutateur électronique** = electronic switching system; **commutateur à bascule** = flip-flop (FF) *ou* toggle switch; **valider à l'aide d'un commutateur à bascule** = to toggle; **commutateur à bascule de type D** *ou* **commutateur à deux sorties** = D-type flip-flop *ou* D-flip-flop; **commutateur à bascule de type JK** = JK-flip-flop; **commutateur à bascule à deux états** = RS-flip-flop *ou* reset-set flip-flop; **commutateur DIP** = DIP switch; **commutateur à effet (de champ) Hall** = Hall effect switch; **commutateurs (montés) en série** *ou* **groupement de commutateurs** *ou* **commutateurs chaînés** = switch train *ou* ganged switch; **avec des commutateurs montés en série, il est possible de choisir quel bus de données va activer l'imprimante** = a ganged switch is used to select which data bus a printer will respond to **(b)** *(caractère supplémentaire d'une ligne de commande)* **commutateur (de commande)** = switch; **ajoutez le commutateur '/W' à la commande DIR (sous DOS) pour afficher le répertoire sur toute la largeur de l'écran** = add the switch '/W' to the DOS command DIR and the directory listing will be displayed across the screen

◊ **commutation** *nf* switching; **commutation de circuit** = circuit switching; **commutation électromécanique** = electromechanical switching; **système de commutation électronique** = electronic switching system; **commutation de ligne** = line switching; **commutation de message** = message switching; **commutation de messages par paquets** = packet switching; **réseau de commutation de données par paquets** = packet switched data service *ou* packet switched network (PSN); **(système de) commutation numérique** = digital switching; **commutation de secours** = switched network backup; **commutation (en) tandem** = tandem switching; **commutation temporelle** = time division switching; **centre de commutation** = switching centre; **centre de commutation des données** = data switching exchange; **circuit de commutation** = switching circuit; **temps de commutation** = set-up time

◊ **commuté, -ée** *adj* switched; **circuiterie numérique commutée** = circuit-switched digital circuitry; **communication virtuelle commutée** = switched virtual call; **réseau commuté** = circuit switched network; **réseau commuté en étoile** = switched star; **connexion au réseau public commuté** = public dial port; *(via a modem)* **transmission de données sur le réseau commuté** = telephone (data carrier)

compact, -e *adj* compact; **cassette compacte** = compact cassette; **disque compact** = compact disc

ou CD; **disque compact lecture seule** *ou* **CD ROM** = compact disc ROM *ou* CD-ROM; **lecteur** *ou* **platine de CD-ROM** = CD-ROM player; **modèle compact** = compact model; *voir aussi* PLATINE

compactage *nm* packing *ou* compacting *ou* compaction; **compactage de bloc** = block compaction; **compactage de données** = data compacting; **algorithme de compactage** = compacting algorithm; **tous les fichiers ont pu être stockés sur une seule disquette grâce au nouveau programme de compactage** = all the files were stored on one disk with this new data compacting routine; **routine de compactage (de données)** = packing routine

◊ **compacté, -ée** *adj* code compacté = compact code

◊ **compacter** *vtr* to compact *ou* to concentrate *ou* to pack

Compaq ™ *(société qui fabrique des ordinateurs personnels)* COMPAQ ™

comparable *adj* comparable; **les deux séries de chiffres ne sont pas comparables** = the two sets of figures are not comparable; **les vitesses de traitement de texte de ces deux logiciels ne sont pas comparables** = there is no comparison between the speeds of the two word processors

comparaison *nf* comparison; **comparaison de chaînes** = string matching; **comparaison logique** = logical comparison

comparateur *nm* comparator

comparer *vtr* comparer (à *ou* avec) = to compare with; to contrast; **on a comparé les anciennes données aux informations les plus récentes** = the old data was contrasted with the latest information; **comparée à la version précédente, celle-ci est très facile à utiliser** = compared with the previous version this one is very user-friendly

compatibilité *nf* compatibility; **compatibilité de logiciel** = program compatibility; **compatibilité du matériel** = hardware compatibility; **compatibilité avec un système de niveau inférieur** = downwards compatibility, *US* downward compatibility; **fenêtre de compatibilité** = compatibility box; **OS/2 a une fenêtre de compatibilité qui permet de faire tourner les applications DOS** = OS/2 has a compatibility box to allow it to run DOS applications; **non compatibilité** = noncompatibility

compatible 1 *adj* compatible; *(avec une machine de niveau inférieur)* downwards compatible, *US* downward compatible; *(avec un système de niveau supérieur)* upwards compatible, *US* upward compatible; **l'unité centrale est compatible avec le micro** = the mainframe is downward compatible with the micro; **appareil** *ou* **machine à connecteur compatible** = plug-compatible machine; **fabricant de produits à connecteurs compatibles** = plug-compatible manufacturer (PCM); **le matériel est-il compatible IBM?** = is the hardware IBM-compatible?;

(système) compatible avec des logiciels écrits pour d'autres systèmes = software compatible (system); (logiciel *ou* appareil) compatible (avec un) PC = PC-compatible (software *ou* computer); compatible (avec) TTL = TTL compatible; non compatible = incompatible; disquette non compatible = alien disk; si la disquette n'est pas compatible, validez la fonction 'multidisque' qui permet au lecteur de lire une disquette non compatible = when you have an alien disk select the multi-disk reader option to allow you to turn the disk drive into an alien disk reader 2 *nm* a compatible; cet ordinateur est beaucoup moins cher que les autres compatibles = this computer is much cheaper than the other compatibles; un compatible IBM = an IBM compatible; achetez un IBM PC ou un compatible = buy an IBM PC or a compatible

compensateur *nm* compensateur de phase = phase equalizer *ou* delay equalizer

compilation *nf* compilation; faire la compilation = to compile; effectuer une nouvelle compilation = to recompile; il faut beaucoup de temps pour faire la compilation avec cette ancienne version du programme = compiling takes a long time with this old version of the software; (instruction de) compilation et exécution = compile and go; compilation et décompilation incrémentielles = incremental compilation and decompilation; compilation de programme = program compilation; un outil de diagnostic de compilation bien conçu facilite le débogage = thorough compiler diagnostics make debugging easy; durée de compilation = compilation time; erreur de compilation = compilation error; les erreurs de compilation provoquent l'interruption inopinée de la tâche = compilation errors result in the job being aborted; édition après compilation = post-editing; langage de compilation = compiler language; phase (de) compilation = compile phase; temps de compilation = compilation time

◊ **compilateur** *nm* compiler (program); ce compilateur génère un programme plus performant = this compiler produces a more efficient program; le nouveau compilateur possède un éditeur intégré = the new compiler has an in-built editor; compilateur croisé = cross-compiler; nous pouvons utiliser le compilateur croisé pour développer le logiciel avant l'arrivée du nouveau système = we can use the cross-compiler to develop the software before the new system arrives; (programme) compilateur d'un langage évolué = language compiler *ou* translator (program); outil de diagnostic du compilateur = compiler diagnostics; ordinateur compilateur = source machine

◊ **compiler** *vtr* to compile; déboguez votre programme avant de le compiler = debug your program, then compile it; les programmes en BASIC qui sont compilés sont plus rapides que les versions interprétées = compiled BASIC programs run much faster than the interpretor version; compiler en langage machine = to machine language compile

complément *nm* (a) *(dispositif additionnel)*

add-on *ou* add-in (b) complement; calculer un complément = to complement; on trouve les compléments en remplaçant les 1 par des 0 et les 0 par des 1 = the complement is found by changing the 1s to 0s and 0s to 1s; complément à 1 *ou* à un = one's complement; le complément à 1 de 10011 est 01100 = the one's complement of 10011 is 01100; complément à 2 *ou* à deux = two's complement; complément à 9 *ou* à neuf = nine's complement; complément à 10 *ou* à dix = ten's complement; complément à la base = radix complement; complément restreint = diminished radix complement; fonction complément = NOT function

◊ **complémenté, -ée** *adj (nombre binaire, etc.)* complemented

◊ **complémentaire** *adj* complementary; couleurs complémentaires = complementary colours; opération complémentaire = complementary operation; *(valeur ajoutée)* valeur complémentaire = offset

complet, -ète *adj* complete *ou* full; additionneur complet = full adder; caractère complet = fully formed character; la marguerite imprime des caractères complets = a daisy wheel printer produces fully formed characters; cycle complet d'exécution d'une opération = complete operation; index complet = dense index; liste complète = dense list; (ensemble des) nombres complets = complementation; opération complète = complete operation; soustracteur complet = full subtractor

◊ **complètement** *adv* fully

◊ **compléter** *vtr* (a) to fill in *ou* to complete; complétez le formulaire et introduisez-le dans le lecteur optique = fill in the blanks and insert the form into the OCR (b) *(ajouter des données à un fichier)* to append

complexe *adj* complex; cette formule mathématique complexe était difficile à résoudre = the complex mathematical formula was difficult to solve; circuit logique complexe = gate array; ordinateur à jeu d'instructions complexe = complex instruction set computer (CISC)

◊ **complexité** *nf* complexity; niveau de complexité = complexity measure

compliqué, -ée *adj* complicated; il s'agit d'un programme très compliqué = this program is very complicated; cet ordinateur est d'une conception plus compliquée que nécessaire = the computer design is more complicated than necessary

comporter *vtr* to include; ce circuit comporte un relais = there is a relay in the circuit; la disquette comporte un utilitaire qui permet la sauvegarde de fichiers sur disque dur = on the disk is a utility for backing up a hard disk

composant *nm (puce)* component *ou* chip; *(d'un tableau ou d'une matrice)* element *ou* item; ils ont ouvert une nouvelle usine de composants électroniques = they have opened a new components factory; erreur imputable à un composant défectueux = component error; carte avec (tous ses) composants = fully populated board; **carte sans composant** = unpopulated board; **densité des composants** = component density; **il y a une telle densité de composants sur la carte-mère qu'il sera impossible d'inclure un connecteur** = component density is so high on this motherboard, that no expansion connectors could be fitted; **la densité des composants augmente avec l'expertise du fabricant** = component density increases with production expertise; **nomenclature des composants** = component list

> les deux composants sont logés dans des boîtiers DIL en céramique ou plastique
> **Electronique**

composé, -ée *adj* compound; **élément logique composé** = compound logical element; **instruction composée** = compound statement; **le débogueur ne peut agir sur les instructions composées** = the debugger cannot handle compound statements

◊ **composer** *vtr* **(a)** *(typographie)* to set *ou* to typeset; **le texte est composé en Times romain corps 12** = the text is set in 12 point Times Roman; **composer un texte sur ordinateur** = to word-process; **on lit facilement les fichiers de texte composés sur ordinateur** = it is quite easy to read word-processed files; **composer à la suite** = to run on **(b)** *(téléphone)* **composer un numéro** = to dial (a number); **composer de nouveau** = to redial; **il a composé l'indicatif des Etats-Unis** = he dialled the code for the USA

composite *adj* composite; **circuit composite** = composite circuit *ou* hybrid circuit; **écran composite**; **affichage composite** = composite display; **signal vidéo composite** = composite video signal

compositeur *nm (personne ou machine)* compositor *ou* typesetter; **le texte est prêt à être envoyé au compositeur** = the text is ready to be sent to the typesetter; **compositeur électronique** = electronic compositor

◊ **composition** *nf* **(a)** *(typographie)* composition *ou* setting *ou* typesetting; **faire la composition d'un texte** = to typeset a text; **le manuscrit a été envoyé à l'atelier de composition** = the MS has been sent to the typesetter for setting; **les frais de composition ont augmenté depuis l'an dernier** = setting charges have increased since last year; **les frais de composition sont moins élevés si le texte est saisi sur disquette avant d'être envoyé au compositeur** = typesetting costs can be reduced by supplying the typesetter with prekeyed disks; **taille des caractères utilisés lors de la composition** = composition size; **atelier de composition** *ou* **la composition** = composing room; **composition informatisée** *ou* **assistée par ordinateur** = computer setting; **composition électronique** = electronic composition; **composition au plomb** *ou* **composition chaude** = hot metal composition *ou* hot type **(b)** *(d'un numéro de téléphone)* dialling

compresser *vtr* to concentrate *ou* to compress; **les données compressées ont pu être transmises à peu de frais** = the concentrated data was transmitted cheaply

◊ **compresseur** *nm* compressor

◊ **compression** *nf* compression; compaction; **compression de bloc** = block compaction; **compression de données** = data compression; data compacting; **les scanners utilisent la technique dite de compression de données qui peut réduire du tiers la mémoire nécessaire** = scanners use a technique called data compression which manages to reduce, even by a third, the storage required; **compression de texte** = text compression; **compression et expansion (de données)** = compressing and expanding *ou* companding; *(pour données vidéo)* **dispositif de compression-expansion** = compressor/expander *ou* compandor; **logiciel de compression de disque** = disk compression software; **routine de compression** = packing routine

comprimer *vtr* **(a)** *(des données)* to compress; to compact; **utilisez un programme d'archivage pour comprimer le fichier** = use the archiving program to compress the file **(b)** *(une photo)* to reduce *ou* to shrink

compris, -e *adj* included; **logiciel non compris dans l'offre d'achat** = unbundled software

comptabilité *nf* accounting *ou* accountancy; **logiciel comptabilité** = accounting package *ou* accounts package; **maintenant, nous entrons chaque transaction au clavier dans le nouveau logiciel de comptabilité au lieu de les inscrire dans le grand-livre** = we now type in each transaction into the new accounting package rather than write it into a ledger

comptage *nm* counting; **comptage d'images complètes** = full-frame time code

compte *nm* **(a)** account; **compte bancaire** = bank account; **consultation à domicile des comptes** = home banking **(b)** *(nom, mot de passe et droits d'un utilisateur)* account; **si vous êtes un nouvel utilisateur, vous devez demander à l'administrateur de vous créer un compte** = if you are a new user, you will have to ask the supervisor to create an account for you; **nom de compte** = account name; **le nom de compte de John Smith est JSMITH** = John Smith's account name is JSMITH **(c)** **tenir compte de** = to take account of; **ne pas tenir compte de** = to ignore; **cette commande donne ordre à l'ordinateur de ne pas tenir compte de la ponctuation** = this command instructs the computer to ignore all punctuation

compter *vi* **(a)** to count **(b)** **compter sur (quelque chose)** = to count on *ou* to rely on (something); **programme sur lequel on peut compter** = reliable program

◊ **compteur** *nm* counter *ou* meter *ou* comptometer; **le nombre de changements est enregistré sur le compteur** = the number of items changed are recorded by the counter; **la boucle se répétera jusqu'à ce que le compteur atteigne 100** = the loop will repeat itself until the counter reaches 100; **un compteur relié au photocopieur enregistre le nombre de photocopies** = a meter attached to the photocopier records the number of copies made;

compteur binaire = binary counter; **compteur de boucles** = loop counter; **compteur (à décalage) circulaire** *ou* **compteur annulaire** = ring counter; **compteur décadaire** = decade counter; **compteur de défilement** = tape timer; **compteur de déroulement** = tape counter; **compteur d'électricité** = electricity meter; *(téléphone)* **compteur d'impulsions automatique (à domicile)** = automatic message accounting; **compteur incrémenteur-décrémenteur** = up/down counter; **compteur d'instruction** *ou* **registre compteur** = instruction counter *ou* program counter (PC) *ou* instruction address register (IAR); *(de routines ou de tâches)* **compteur de répétitions** = repeat counter

CompuServe ™ *(service en ligne)* CompuServe ™

CON *(console avec écran et clavier, des compatibles IBM PC)* CON

concaténation *nf* catenation *ou* concatenation; **faire une concaténation** = to catenate *ou* to concatenate; **concaténation de données** = concatenated data set; **concaténation de (plusieurs) chaînes** = string concatenation; **(instruction de) concaténation de fichiers** = link files

◊ **concaténé, -ée** *adj* chained *ou* linked *ou* concatenated (data); **liste concaténée** = chained list *ou* linked list

◊ **concaténer** *vtr* to catenate *ou* to concatenate

concave *adj* concave; **lentille concave** = concave lens

concentrateur *nm* concentrator; **concentrateur de données** = data concentrator; **concentrateur de réseau** = concentrator; **concentrateur (de largeur de bande) vidéo** = video compressor; **concentrateur 10base-T** = concentrator in a 10Base-T Ethernet network

◊ **concentrateur-déconcentrateur** *nm* *(de données vidéo)* compressor/expander *ou* compandor

◊ **concentration** *nf* concentration; **concentration au point magnétique** *ou* **concentration magnétique** = magnetic focusing

◊ **concentrer** *vtr* to concentrate; **concentrer un rayon lumineux sur une lentille** = to concentrate a beam of light on a lens

concepteur, -trice *n* designer; **concepteur de logiciel** = software developer; **les concepteurs ont décidé de mettre en page sur format A4** = the designers have laid out the pages in A4 format; **les concepteurs travaillent à la mise en page de la nouvelle revue** = the design team is working on the layouts for the new magazine

◊ **conception** *nf* design; **un logiciel de CAO est indispensable à la réalisation d'une conception très précise** = CAD is essential for accurate project design; **conception ascendante d'un programme** = bottom up method; **conception assistée par ordinateur (CAO)** = computer-aided *ou* assisted design (CAD); **conception et fabrication assistées par ordinateur (CFAO)** = computer-assisted design/computer-assisted manufacture (CAD/CAM); **conception économique** = least cost design; **conception de produits** = product design; **langage de conception de programme** = program design language (PDL); **conception d'un système** = system design; **spécifications** *ou* **contraintes** *ou* **paramètres de conception** = design parameters

conceptuel, -elle *adj* **modèle conceptuel** = conceptual model

concevoir *vtr* to design; **formulaires et en-têtes de lettres peuvent être conçus sur ordinateur** = business forms and letterheads can now be designed on a PC

◊ **conçu, -e** *adj* designed; **conçu par ordinateur** = computer-generated; **programmation bien conçue** = elegant programming

concurrence *nf* competition; **les techniques du jet d'encre et du transfert thermique se font concurrence** = colour ink-jet technology and thermal transfer technology compete with each other

◊ **concurrent, -e** *adj* competing; **mise en place d'un programme concurrent** = counterprogramming

condensateur *nm* capacitor; **condensateur céramique** = ceramic capacitor; **condensateur électrolytique** = electrolytic capacitor; **condensateur non électrolytique** = non-electrolytic capacitor; **condensateur optique** = condenser lens; **condensateur variable** = variable capacitor; **condensateur pour mémoire RAM** = memory backup capacitor; **mémoire à condensateur** = capacitor storage; **microphone à condensateur** = capacitor microphone

◊ **condensation** *nf* *(de données ou lignes)* packing *ou* concentration

◊ **condensé, -ée** *adj* concentrated *ou* packed; **décimale condensée** = packed decimal; **format condensé** = packed format

◊ **condenser** *vtr* **(a)** *(des données ou lignes)* to concentrate *ou* to pack **(b)** *(image ou photo)* to shrink

condition *nf* **(a)** condition *ou* state; **condition d'arrêt** = halt condition; **condition d'entrée** = entry condition; **condition d'erreur** = error condition; **condition initiale** = initial condition; **registre des codes condition** = condition code register **(b)** **conditions atmosphériques** = atmospheric conditions

◊ **conditionnel, -elle** *adj* conditional; **arrêt conditionnel** = conditional breakpoint; **boucle conditionnelle 'WHILE'** = while-loop; **boucle conditionnelle FOR...NEXT** = for-next loop; **branchement conditionnel** = conditional jump *ou* branch *ou* transfer; case branch; **le branchement conditionnel choisira le programme 1 ou 2 suivant que la réponse est oui ou non** = the conditional branch will select routine one if the response is yes and routine two if no; **instruction de branchement** conditionnel à l'indicateur zéro = jump on zero; **effectuer un branchement conditionnel à zéro** = to jump on zero; **commande conditionnelle** = conditional statement; **décision conditionnelle** = decision *ou* discrimination instruction; **instruction conditionnelle** = conditional statement; **saut conditionnel** = conditional jump *ou* branch *ou* transfer; **transfert conditionnel** = conditional transfer

◊ **conditionnement** *nm* packing *ou* packaging

◊ **conditionner** *vtr* **(a)** *(des données)* to pack *ou* to package **(b)** *(un produit)* to package

conducteur *nm* **(a)** *(d'électricité)* conductor; **le cuivre est bon conducteur (d'électricité)** = copper is a good conductor of electricity *ou* copper conducts well **(b)** *(fil)* lead; *(fibre optique)* **conducteur de lumière** = light conduit

◊ **conductibilité** *nf* conduction

◊ **conductible** *adj* conductive

◊ **conduction** *nf* *(d'électricité)* conduction; **conduction (d'électricité) par broches de contact (en) or** = the conduction of electricity by gold contacts

◊ **conduire** *vtr* to conduct; **conduire l'électricité** = to conduct electricity

conduit *nm* duct

◊ **conduite** *nf* conduit *ou* channelling

cône *nm* *(d'un haut-parleur)* cone

conférence *nf* conference; **être en conférence** = to be in a meeting; **salle de conférence(s)** = conference room *ou* meeting room; **conférence de presse** = press conference; **téléphone de** *ou* **pour conférence** = conference telephone *ou* conference phone; *voir aussi* TELECONFERENCE

confetti *nm* chad; **bande à confettis non détachés** = chadded *ou* chadless tape

confiance *nf* confidence; **niveau de confiance** = confidence level

confidentialité *nf* privacy *ou* confidentiality; **confidentialité des données** = privacy of data; **confidentialité de l'information** = privacy of information; **cryptage de l'information pour en assurer la confidentialité** = privacy transformation

◊ **confidentiel, -elle** *adj* confidential *ou* private; **numéro de code confidentiel** = personal identification number *ou* PIN number

CONFIG.SYS *(fichier de configuration MS-DOS)* CONFIG.SYS (file); **si vous installez une nouvelle carte adaptateur sur votre PC, il faudra ajouter une nouvelle commande dans le fichier CONFIG.SYS** = if you add a new adapter card to your PC you will have to add a new command to the CONFIG.SYS file

configuration *nf* configuration *ou* mapping; *(graphique)* map; **configuration d'une base de données** = database mapping; *(disposition des broches)* **configuration d'un connecteur** = pinout; *(prêt à fonctionner)* **configuration disponible** = configured-in; **configuration d'entrée-sortie** = I/O mapping; **configuration invalidée** *ou* **indisponible** = configured-off *ou* configured out; **configuration logique** = logic map; **configuration du matériel** = hardware configuration; **configuration de mémoire** = memory map; **configuration prête à l'usage** = configured-in; **configuration des registres** = register map; **configuration de réseau** = network topology; networking; **configuration (d'un système)** = configuration state; **configuration validée** = configured-in; **délai de configuration** = setup time; **option de configuration** = set-up option

◊ **configurer** *vtr* to configure *ou* to set up; *(en mémoire)* to map out; **dès qu'il a été configuré par l'ingénieur système, le nouvel ordinateur a bien fonctionné** = the new computer worked well as soon as the engineer had set it up; **il suffit de configurer l'ordinateur individuel une seule fois, à l'achat** = you only have to configure the PC once - when you first buy it; **ce câble est configuré sans modem ce qui me permet de connecter les deux ordinateurs sans difficulté** = this cable is configured as a null modem, which will allow me to connect these two computers together easily; **ce terminal est configuré pour l'affichage de graphiques** = this terminal has been configured to display graphics; **configuré en mémoire** = memory-mapped; **un écran configuré en mémoire possède une adresse pour chaque pixel, permettant ainsi au processeur d'accéder directement à l'écran** = a memory-mapped screen has an address allocated to each pixel, allowing direct access to the screen by the CPU; **entrée-sortie configurée en mémoire** = memory-mapped I/O *ou* memory-mapped input/output; **configurer en réseau** = to network; *(prêt à fonctionner)* **(état) configuré** = configured-in

confirmation *nf* *(accusé de réception d'un message)* **confirmation positive** = affirmative acknowledgement

◊ **confirmer** *vt* to confirm; to OK; **cliquez sur le bouton OK pour confirmer que vous voulez effacer tous les fichiers** = click on the OK button to confirm that you want to delete all your files

conforme *adj* **être conforme à** = to conform to; **conforme aux normes** = up to standard

◊ **se conformer** *vpr* to conform to

conique *adj* conical; *(d'un haut-parleur)* **membrane conique** = cone

conjonction *nf* **conjonction logique** = AND operation *ou* coincidence operation *ou* conjunction *ou* meet

connaissance *nf* **(a)** knowledge; **connaissance globale** *ou* **exhaustive** = global knowledge; **ingénierie de la connaissance** = knowledge engineering; **système à base de connaissances** = knowledge-based system; **système intelligent à base de connaissances** = intelligent knowledge-based system (IKBS) *ou* expert system **(b)** **connaissances en informatique** = computer literacy; **personne qui a des connaissances en informatique** = computer-literate person; **personne qui ne possède aucune connaissance en informatique** = computer illiterate person

connecté, -ée *adj* connected; **le terminal est connecté à l'ordinateur principal** = the terminal is on-line to the mainframe; **circuit logique non connecté** = uncommitted logic array (ULA); **état connecté (d'un modem)** = connect state

◊ **connecter** *vtr (joindre)* to connect *ou* to link; *(brancher)* to connect *ou* to plug in; **les deux systèmes ont été connectés l'un à l'autre** = the two systems are coupled together; **vous n'avez qu'à déconnecter le lecteur et en connecter un nouveau à sa place** = simply unplug the old drive and plug-in a new one; **élevez le potentiel de la ligne de réception au niveau logique un, en la connectant sur une source de courant de 5 volts** = pull up the input line to a logic one by connecting it to 5 volts

◊ **se connecter** *vpr* to connect *ou* to link; *(à un noeud ou à un serveur de réseau)* = to attach; **j'ai entré la commande pour me connecter au serveur local** = I issued the command to attach to the local server

◊ **connecteur** *nm (électrique)* connector *ou* plug; *(d'un transistor à effet de champ)* gate; **le connecteur relié au câble s'adapte sur tout port série standard** = the connector at the end of the cable will fit any standard serial port; **connecteur à trois broches** = three-pin plug; *(appareil)* **à connecteur compatible** = plug-compatible (machine); **fabricant de produits à connecteurs compatibles** = plug-compatible manufacturer (PCM); **connecteur de carte** = (card) edge connector; **connecteur à une seule position d'enfichage** = polarized plug; **connecteur à enfichage dirigé** *ou* **à un seul bord d'enfichage** = polarized edge connector; *(emplacement)* **connecteur pour carte d'extension** = expansion slot; **connecteur (pour carte additionnelle) inutilisé** = empty slot; **il y a deux connecteurs libres sur ce micro, un seul suffit pour ajouter la carte d'extension** = there are two free slots in the micro, you only need one for the add-on board; **connecteur femelle** = female connector; connector receptacle *ou* socket; **connecteur mâle** = male connector; connector plug; **connecteur mâle à deux broches** = jumper; **configuration d'un connecteur** = pinout; **prise pour connecteur** = connector receptacle *ou* socket

◊ **connectique** *nf* connector technology *ou* connector engineering

◊ **connectif, -ive** *adj* connective

connexe *adj* **négation connexe** = joint denial

◊ **connectivité** *nf* connectivity

connexion *nf* connection *ou* contact; *(entre les postes d'un réseau)* nexus; *(par commutateur)* switching; *(pour transmission de données)* data connection; **le circuit ne fonctionne pas parce que la connexion est encrassée** = the circuit is not working because the contact is dirty; **connexion bricolée** = dry joint; **connexion (montée) en cascade** = cascade connection; **la connexion en** chaîne *ou* **en cascade réduit le câblage** = daisy-chaining saves a lot of cable; **connexion (en) delta** = delta connection; **(modem à) connexion directe** = direct connect (modem); **connexion enroulée** = wire wrap; **connexion fixe** = hardwired connection; **connexion (d'ordinateurs) en mode conversationnel** = computer conferencing; **connexion (en) parallèle** = parallel connection; **leur débit de transmission est de 60 000 bits par seconde sur connexion parallèle** = their transmission rate is 60,000 bps through parallel connection; **connexion au réseau public commuté** = public dial port; **connexion (en) triangle** = delta connection; *(pour prototype)* **boîte de connexion sans soudure** = breadboard; **carte à** *ou* **avec connexion** = edge board *ou* card; **coût de connexion** = connect charge; **point de connexion** = terminal; **temps de connexion** = connect time *ou* set-up time; *(d'une carte de circuits intégrés)* **zone de connexion** = terminal area

conscient, -e *adj* **erreur consciente** = conscious error

consécutif, -ive *adj* consecutive; **l'ordinateur a exploité trois fichiers consécutifs** = the computer ran three consecutive files; **de façon consécutive** = consecutively

◊ **consécutivement** *adv* consecutively

conseil *nm (firme ou bureau)* consultancy

conserver *vtr* to retain

console *nf* console; *(de compatible IBM PC)* CON; **console d'un opérateur** = operator's console; **la console comporte un périphérique d'entrée: par exemple un clavier, et un périphérique de sortie: soit une imprimante ou un écran** = the console consists of input device such as a keyboard, and an output device such as a printer or CRT; **processeur de commande de console** = command console processor (CCP)

> le groupe espère bien profiter de sa position stratégique pour transformer ses consoles de jeu en terminaux de communication
> *L'Express*

consommateur, -trice *n* **(logiciel) grand consommateur de mémoire** = memory-intensive (software)

◊ **consommation** *nf* **(a)** consumption **(b)** *(d'électricité, etc.)* consumption; **la consommation d'électricité de cette machine est beaucoup trop forte** = this machine uses too much electricity; **produits de consommation** = consumables; **il faut inclure les câbles pour imprimantes et le papier sous la rubrique 'produits de consommation'** = put all the printer leads and paper under the heading 'consumables'

◊ **consommer** *vtr (électricité, etc,)* to use *ou* to consume

constant, -e *adj* constant; **le moteur du lecteur de disquettes tourne à vitesse constante** = the disk drive motor spins at a constant velocity; **code à rapport (de bits) constant** = constant ratio code;

données constantes = fixed data; *(fonction logique)* **opération constante** = one element; *(dont la taille est limitée)* **champ de taille constante** = fixed field

◊ **constante** *nf* constant; **constante de translation** = relocation constant

constituer *vtr* to form *ou* to make up; **le système est constitué de cinq modules indépendants** = the system is formed of five separate modules; **nous avons constitué un dossier de coupures de presse sur le nouveau progiciel** = we have made up a file of press cuttings about the new software package

constructeur *nm* manufacturer; **constructeur de matériel informatique en pièces détachées** = original equipment manufacturer (OEM); **il a commencé (sa carrière) comme constructeur de PC pour le marché OEM** = he started in business as a manufacturer of PCs for the OEM market; **(logiciel) de constructeur** = machine-intimate (software); **format de fichier (de) constructeur** = proprietary file format; **vous ne pouvez pas lire ce fichier de tableur parce que mon logiciel le sauvegarde en format (de) constructeur** = you cannot read this spreadsheet file because my software saves it in a proprietary file format; **langage de constructeur** = native language; **syndicat européen des constructeurs d'ordinateurs** = European Computer Manufacturers Association (ECMA)

constructif, -ive *adj* constructive; **interférence constructive** = constructive interference

construction *nf* construction *ou* building; **la construction du prototype progresse rapidement** = construction of the prototype is advancing rapidly

◊ **construire** *vtr* to construct *ou* to build; to form

consultation *nf* consultation; **consultation d'une table de référence** = table lookup

◊ **consulter** *vtr* to consult *ou* to look up; **consulter une base de données sans autorisation** = to browse through a database; **le temps d'accès est le temps requis pour consulter une donnée en mémoire** = access time is the time taken to read from a location in memory

contact *nm* **(a)** contact; *(photo)* **épreuve** *ou* **planche de contact** = contact print; **(film) négatif contact** = contact negative **(b)** *(broche)* pin; **contacts (en) or** = gold contacts; **contact sec** *ou* **intermittent** = dry contact

◊ **contacter** *vtr* to contact (someone); **contacter par téléphone** = to phone; *(le bureau)* to call in

contenir *vtr* to contain *ou* to enclose; **chaque caisse contient deux ordinateurs et leurs périphériques** = each carton contains two computers and their peripherals; **nous avons égaré un dossier contenant des documents importants** = we have lost a file containing important documents

contention *nf* contention; **délai** *ou* **retard de contention** = contention delay

contenu *nm* **(a)** *(abstrait)* content; **le contenu d'une lettre** = the content of a letter; **adressable par le contenu** = content-addressable; **fichier** *ou* **location adressable par le contenu** = content-addressable file *ou* location; **mémoire adressable par son** *ou* **le contenu** = content-addressable memory (CAM) **(b)** *(physique)* contents; **le contenu de la bouteille s'est répandu sur le clavier de l'ordinateur** = the contents of the bottle poured out onto the computer keyboard; **les douaniers ont examiné le contenu de la caisse** = the customs officials inspected the contents of the box

contexte *nm* context; **l'exemple démontre l'emploi du mot dans son contexte** = the example shows how the word is used in context; **en fonction du contexte** *ou* **lié au contexte** = context-sensitive

◊ **contextuel, -elle** *adj (lié au contexte)* **aide contextuelle (en ligne)** = context-sensitive help

contigu, -ë *adj* contiguous *ou* adjacent; **fichier contigu** = contiguous file; **graphiques contigus** = contiguous graphics; **la plupart des écrans ne permettent pas l'affichage de graphiques contigus** = most display units do not provide contiguous graphics

continu, -e *adj* continuous *ou* endless; **boucle continue** = endless loop; **courant continu (CC)** = direct current (DC); **flux continu de données** = continuous data stream; **onde continue** = continuous wave; **signal continu** = continuous signal; **en continu** = continuous; **papier en continu** = continuous stationery *ou* listing paper; accordion fold *ou* fanfold paper; **(système d') alimentation du papier en continu** = continuous feed

continuation *nf* continuation

continuel, -elle *adj* continual; **les pannes continuelles du système ont ralenti le traitement** = the continual system breakdowns have slowed down the processing

◊ **continuellement** *adv* continually; continuously

continuité *nf* continuity

contraint, -e *adj* limited *ou* bound; **contraint par la vitesse de sortie** = output-bound *ou* output-limited

◊ **contrainte** *nf* restriction; **imposer une contrainte (à quelque chose)** = to restrict (something); **contraintes de conception** *ou* **de création** = design parameters; *(programme)* **avec contrainte de traitement** = process-bound (program); **avec contrainte de vitesse d'entrée** = input-bound *ou* input-limited (program); *(transmission)* **avec contrainte de vitesse de périphérique** = peripheral-limited (transmission)

contraire *nm* inverse; opposite; **le contraire de vrai est faux** = the inverse of true is false

contrarotatif, -ive *adj* **antenne contrarotative** = de-spun antenna

contrastant, -e *adj (effet, etc.)* contrasting

◊ **contraste** *nm* contrast; **bouton de contraste** = contrast dial; **ce bouton vous permet de régler la luminosité et le contraste** = this control allows you to adjust brightness and contrast; **filtre d'amélioration du contraste** = contrast enhancement filter; **rapport de contraste d'un imprimé** = print contrast ratio; **sans contraste** = flat

◊ **contrasté, -e** *adj* contrasting; **un dessin de couverture aux couleurs contrastées** = a cover design in contrasting colours; *(impression trop pâle)* **peu contrasté** = pale *ou* feint

les jeux d'ombres d'un objet en mouvement, mais restant à la même distance de la caméra, provoquent des variations de contraste que l'objectif cherche constamment à suivre
Audio Vidéo

contrat *nm* contract *ou* deal; **contrat global** = package deal; **il se sont mis d'accord sur un contrat global comprenant le développement d'un logiciel et la personnalisation du matériel** = they agreed a package deal, which involves the development of software and customizing hardware; **nous offrons un contrat global comprenant un système informatique complet pour le bureau, la formation du personnel et l'entretien du matériel** = we are offering a package deal which includes the whole office computer system, staff training and hardware maintenance; **contrat de maintenance** = maintenance contract *ou* service contract

contre- *préf* counter- *ou* cross-

◊ **contre-épreuve** *nf* cross-check

◊ **contrefaçon** *nf* **contrefaçon d'une oeuvre protégée par un copyright** *ou* **délit de contrefaçon** = infringement of copyright *ou* copyright infringement

◊ **contre-jour** *nm* *(d'un film)* cameo

◊ **contre-rotation** *nf* *(dans un réseau en anneau)* **anneau de contre-rotation** = counter-rotating ring

contrôlable *adj* controllable

contrôle *nm* *(vérification)* check *ou* checking *ou* control *ou* verification; supervision; *(bouton)* control; **contrôle d'accès (au système)** = access control; *(du courant)* **contrôle de l'alimentation** = power monitor; **contrôle de boucle** = loop check; **contrôle de caractère** = character check; **contrôle de bloc de caractères** = block character check (BCC); **contrôle en cascade** = cascade control; **contrôle chromatique** = chroma control; **contrôle de clavier** = keyboard scan; **contrôle croisé** = cross-check; **contrôle cyclique** = cyclic check; **contrôle de dépassement de capacité** = overflow check; **contrôle des données** = data control; **contrôle par écho** = echo check; **contrôle d'erreurs** = error control; **contrôle d'exécution des tâches** = job statement control; **contrôle du flux (de données)** = flow control; **contrôle de flux d'informations** = information flow control; **contrôle de frappe** = keystroke verification; **contrôle de gain** = gain control; **contrôle de gain automatique** = automatic gain control (AGC) *ou*

automatic level control (ALC); **contrôle des (sons) graves** = bass control; **contrôle horizontal** = horizontal check; **contrôle d'inférence** = inference control; **(opérations de) contrôle et exécution d'interruption** = interrupt servicing; **contrôle de liaison de données** = data link control; **contrôle de liaisons de données de haut niveau** = high-level data link control (HDLC); **contrôle de ligne de communication** *ou* **de transmission** = communications link control; **contrôle de mise en communication** = handshake I/O control; **contrôle numérique** = numerical control (NC) *ou* computer numerical control (CNC); *(d'un programme)* **contrôle sur papier** = desk check; **contrôle de parité** = parity check; **contrôle de parité impaire** = odd parity check; **contrôle de parité paire** = even parity check; **contrôle de parité paire-impaire** = odd-even parity check; **contrôle de processus** = process control; **contrôle de (la) qualité** = quality control; **responsable du contrôle de (la) qualité** = quality controller; **contrôle par le récepteur** = backwards supervision; **contrôle par redondance** = redundancy checking; **contrôle par redondance cyclique** = cyclic redundancy check (CRC); **contrôle par retour** = feedback control; **contrôle des touches** = keystroke verification; **contrôle d'utilisation de touches** = keyboard scan; **contrôle de travaux groupés en pile** = stacked job control; **contrôle et validation** = verification and validation (V & V); *(bouton)* **contrôle du volume (du son)** = volume control; **de contrôle** = supervisory; **bit de contrôle** = check bit *ou* service bit; **bloc (de données) de contrôle** = control block; **bloc de contrôle de fichier** = file control block; **caractère de contrôle** = check character *ou* control character; **caractère de contrôle de périphérique** = device control character; **caractère de contrôle d'impression** = print control character; **carte de contrôle** = control card; **cellule de contrôle des couleurs** = colour cell; **code de contrôle de bloc** = block code; **champ de contrôle** = control field; **chiffre de contrôle** = check digit; **clé de contrôle** = check number *ou* check key *ou* check bit; **clé numérique de contrôle** = check digit; **cycle de contrôle** = control cycle; *(en cas d'erreur ou de panne)* **dispositif de contrôle** = monitor; **données de contrôle** = test data *ou* control data; **fichier de contrôle de tâche** = job control file; *(groupe témoin)* **groupe de contrôle** = control group; **impulsion de contrôle du balayage vertical** = field sync pulse; **indicateur de contrôle** = check indicator; **indicateur de contrôle de parité** = parity flag; **instruction de contrôle** = control statement *ou* supervisory instruction *ou* control instruction; **la prochaine instruction de contrôle vous donnera les italiques** = the next control instruction will switch to italics; **interface de contrôle** = command interface; **jeton de contrôle (de réseau)** = control token; *(de périphériques)* **langage de contrôle** = command control language; **lignes de contrôle** = bus control lines; **menu de contrôle (MS-Windows)** = control menu; **micro-ordinateur de contrôle** = microcontroller; **micro-ordinateur de contrôle monopuce** *ou* **à puce unique** = single-chip microcontroller; **mode (de) contrôle** = control mode; **mot de contrôle** = control word; **ordinateur de contrôle** = control computer; **ordinateur de contrôle des transmissions** = communications computer; **panneau de contrôle** = control panel;

point de contrôle = access point; **poste de contrôle mixte** = combined station; **procédure de contrôle d'acheminement** = routing overheads; **programme de contrôle** = checking program *ou* monitor program; **programme de contrôle d'entrée-sortie** = input/output control program; **programme de contrôle de réseau** = network control program; **programme de contrôle de tâche** = job control program; *(pour contrôle d'erreurs ou d'utilisateurs)* **protocole de contrôle** = audit trail; **registre de données contrôle** = check register *ou* control register; **scanner de contrôle d'appel** = communications scanner; *(communication)* **séquence de contrôle** = supervisory sequence; **signal de contrôle** = control signal *ou* supervisory signal; **signal de contrôle d'appel** = call control signal; **système de contrôle** = control system; **système avec contrôle automatique** *ou* **avec autocontrôle** = self-checking system; **système de contrôle intégré** = built-in check; **tests de contrôle de liens** = link trials; **total de contrôle** = checksum *ou* check total *ou* control total; **les données sont sûrement erronées si le total de contrôle est faux** = the data must be corrupted if the checksum is different; *(sur le clavier d'un ordinateur)* **touche de contrôle** = control key *ou* Ctrl; **pour arrêter un programme, appuyez sur Ctrl-C, c'est-à-dire appuyez sur la touche de contrôle et la touche C en même temps** = to halt a program, press Ctrl-C - the control key and letter C - at the same time; **touches de contrôle du curseur** = cursor control keys *ou* cursor pad *ou* arrowed keys; **transmission sans contrôle de retour** = free wheeling; **unité de contrôle (de processus)** = control unit (CU); **vidage de contrôle (sur imprimante)** = check point dump; *(affichage des derniers caractères saisis)* **visualisation de contrôle d'entrée** = marching display

◊ **contrôlé, -ée** *adj* controlled; **qui peut être contrôlé** = controllable; **courant contrôlé** = regulated power supply; **interruption contrôlée** = transparent interrupt; **vocabulaire contrôlé** = controlled vocabulary

◊ **contrôler** *vtr* **(a)** *(vérifier)* to control *ou* to check *ou* to test *ou* to monitor *ou* to verify; to supervise; **ce processus est contrôlé par une batterie de capteurs** = the process is monitored by a bank of sensors; **il contrôle le progrès des programmeurs débutants** = he is monitoring the progress of the trainee programmers; **l'appareil contrôle chaque signal de sortie** = the machine monitors each signal as it is sent out; **l'ingénieur de maintenance a découvert des défauts en contrôlant le matériel** = the maintenance engineer found some defects whilst checking the hardware; **les différentes parties du système ont été contrôlées avant l'emballage** = the separate parts of the system were all checked for faults before being packaged **(b)** *(gérer)* to control *ou* to regulate; **l'ordinateur principal contrôle six postes de travail** = the main computer supports six workstations

◊ **contrôleur, -euse** *n* *(personne; programme)* supervisor; *(pilote)* controller; *(gestionnaire)* administrator; **contrôleur d'accès direct à la mémoire** *ou* **contrôleur DMA** = DMA controller; **contrôleur d'affichage** = display controller; **contrôleur de communication** = communications control unit (CCU); **contrôleur de disque** *ou* **de disquettes** = disk controller *ou* floppy disk controller (FDC); **carte contrôleur de disque** *ou* **de disquettes** = disk-controller card; **contrôleur d'écran** = display controller; **contrôleur d'émetteur-récepteur asynchrone universel** = UART controller; **contrôleur d'entrée-sortie** = input/output controller; **contrôleur d'imprimante** = printer controller; **contrôleur de périphérique(s)** = peripheral control unit (PCU); **contrôleur de réseau** = network controller; **contrôleur de terminal** = terminal controller; **contrôleur de transmission** *ou* **de communication** = communications control unit (CCU)

convenir (à) *vi* to apply (to); **cette formule ne convient qu'aux données reçues après le signal d'interruption** = this formula applies only to data received after the interrupt signal

convention *nf* convention; **Convention sur le droit d'auteur** = Copyright Act

conventionnel, -elle *adj* **mémoire conventionnelle** *ou* **RAM** = conventional memory *ou* RAM

conversation *nf* *(entre chambre de contrôle et studio)* talkback

◊ **conversationnel, -elle** *adj* interactive *ou* conversational; **mode conversationnel** = conversational mode *ou* interactive mode *ou* interactive processing; **connexion d'ordinateurs en mode conversationnel** = computer conferencing; **terminal conversationnel** = conversational *ou* interactive terminal

conversion *nf* conversion; **conversion binaire-décimale** = binary-to-decimal conversion; **conversion de code** = code conversion; **conversion décimale-binaire** = decimal-to-binary conversion; *(d'un format en un autre)* **conversion de données** = data translation; **conversion de fichier** = file conversion; *(d'une image couleur)* **conversion monochrome** = black crush; **conversion d'une onde en numérique** = waveform digitization; **conversion de signaux** = signal conditioning *ou* signal conversion; **délai de conversion** = sense recovery time; **programme de conversion** = conversion program; **tables de conversion** = translation tables *ou* conversion tables

convertibilité *nf* convertibility

◊ **convertible** *adj* convertible

◊ **convertir** *vtr* to convert *ou* to translate

◊ **convertisseur** *nm* converter *ou* convertor *ou* conversion equipment; **grâce au convertisseur les anciennes données sont acceptées par le nouveau système** = the convertor has allowed the old data to be used on the new system; **convertisseur analogique-numérique** = analog to digital converter *ou* A to D converter (ADC); *(numériseur)* digitizer; **le signal vocal est d'abord passé par le convertisseur analogique-numérique avant d'être analysé** = the speech signal was first passed through an A to D converter before being analysed; **convertisseur analogique-numérique parallèle** = flash A/D; **convertisseur de fréquence** = frequency changer *ou* set-top converter; **convertisseur de normes** = standards converter; **c'est grâce à un convertisseur de normes que nous pouvons regarder la télévision américaine** = the standards converter allows us to watch US television; **convertisseur numérique-analogique** = digital to analog converter *ou* D to A converter (DAC); **le convertisseur numérique-analogique du port de sortie contrôle la machine analogique** = the D/A converter on the output port controls the analog machine; **l'ordinateur émet un signal vocal via un convertisseur numérique-analogique** = speech is output from the computer via a D/A converter; *(de télévision)* **convertisseur de signal** = set-top converter; **convertisseur texte-signal vocal** = text-to-speech converter; **programme convertisseur** = conversion program

convexe *adj* convex; **lentille convexe** = convex lens

convivial,-e *adj* user-friendly; **appareil convivial** = user-friendly machine; **comparée à la version précédente, celle-ci est très conviviale** = compared with the previous version, this one is very user-friendly; **interface utilisateur conviviale** = friendly front-end

◊ **convivialité** *nf* user-friendliness *ou* being user-friendly; usability; **nous avons analysé les tests de convivialité et trouvé que l'interface (graphique) GUI est plus facile à maîtriser pour les débutants que les lignes de commandes** = we have studied usability tests and found that a GUI is easier for new users than a command line

> toutefois, ce que le logiciel gagne en convivialité pour le débutant, il le perd en rigueur
> **Science et Vie Micro**

convoyeur *nm* conveyor; *(d'alimentation du papier)* chain delivery mechanism

coopératif, -ive *adj* **processus coopératif** = cooperative processing

coordination *nf* coordination; *(entente pour réduire les bruits parasites)* **coordination inductive** = inductive coordination

coordonnée *nf* **(a)** *(math)* coordinate; **coordonnées** = X-Y coordinates; **coordonnées cartésiennes** = cartesian coordinates; **coordonnée horizontale** = X-coordinate; **coordonnées polaires** = polar coordinates; **diagramme en coordonnées polaires** = polar diagram; **coordonnées rectangulaires** = rectangular coordinates; **coordonnées relatives** = relative coordinates; **coordonnée verticale** = Y-coordinate **(b)** *(données)* data *ou* details; **les coordonnées des clients de la société sont entrées sur l'ordinateur principal** = the company stores data on customers in its main computer file *ou* customer details are stored on the company's main computer

◊ **coordonner** *vtr* to coordinate; **elle doit coordonner la saisie des diverses parties d'un fichier** qui se fait dans six centres différents = she has to coordinate the keyboarding of several parts of a file in six different locations

copie *nf* **(a)** *(action)* copying; duplication; *(illégal)* piracy; *(d'un logiciel)* **autorisation de copie** = software licence; authorization to copy (ATC); *(système ou dispositif ou codage)* **protection contre la copie** = copy protection *ou* copy protect; **tous les disques sont protégés contre la copie** = all disks are copy protected; **la nouvelle version du logiciel ne sera pas protégée contre la copie** = the new program will come without copy protection **(b)** *(double)* copy *ou* duplicate; *(d'un article de revue scientifique)* offprint; **copie pour archivage** = file copy; **copie d'un bloc (de texte)** = block copy; *(d'une lettre, etc.)* **copie carbone** = carbon copy; **passez-moi l'original et classez la copie dans le dossier** = give me the original, and file the carbon copy; **copie d'écran** = hard copy; **copie (de protection) d'original** = protection master; **copie de sauvegarde** = security backup; *(d'un texte)* **copie finale** = clean copy; *(pour imprimerie)* **copie finalisée** = camera-ready copy (crc); **copie illégale** = pirate copy; *(d'un bloc de données)* **copie image** = after-image; **copie piratée** = pirate copy; *(pour imprimerie)* **copie prête à reproduire** = camera-ready copy (crc); *(sur disquette)* **faire une copie** = to copy; **faire une copie d'une lettre** = to duplicate a letter; *(copier à l'identique)* **faire une copie-miroir** = to mirror; **maintenant que vous avez fait une copie-miroir du disque du serveur, vous avez moins de chance de perdre vos données** = there's less chance of losing your data now that you have mirrored the server's disk drive; *voir aussi* MIROIR

◊ **copier** *vtr* to copy *ou* to duplicate *ou* to replicate; **cette routine va copier vos résulats sans aucun problème** = the routine will replicate your results with very little effort; **il est impossible de copier quoi que ce soit sur une disquette non formatée** = it is impossible to copy to an unformatted disk; **il existe un utilitaire résident qui copie les fichiers les plus récents sur un support de sauvegarde toutes les 40 minutes** = there is a memory resident utility which copies the latest files onto backing store every 40 minutes; **copier à l'identique** = to mirror; **autorisation de copier (un logiciel)** = authorization to copy (ATC); software licence

◊ **copieur** *nm* copier *ou* copying machine *ou* photocopier; **copieur de bureau** *ou* **copieur professionnel** = office copier; **papier pour copieur** = copier paper *ou* paper for photocopier

co-processeur *ou* **coprocesseur** *nm* coprocessor; **coprocesseur graphique** = graphics coprocessor; **coprocesseur mathématique** = maths coprocessor chip *ou* maths coprocessor

COPY *(commande de copier)* COPY (command); **faites une copie de vos données avant de les modifier en utilisant la commande COPY** = make a copy of your data using the COPY command before you edit it

copyright *nm* copyright; **oeuvre protégée par un copyright** = copyright work *ou* copyrighted work *ou* work (still) in copyright; **photocopier une oeuvre protégée (par un copyright) est illégal** = it is illegal to take copies of a copyright work; **(document, etc.) qui n'est plus protégé par un copyright** = (document) which is out of copyright *ou* in the public domain; **déposer un copyright** = to copyright (a work); **mention de copyright (dans un livre)** = copyright notice; **titulaire d'un copyright** = copyright holder *ou* owner

coquille *nf* typographical error *ou* literal *ou* typo; **une erreur typographique à la composition donne ce qu'on appelle une 'coquille'** = a typographical error made while typesetting is called a 'typo'

CORAL *(langage)* Common Real-time Applications Language (CORAL)

corbeille *nf (icône sous Windows)* recycle bin *ou* wastepaper basket; *(Apple)* trashcan

cordon *nm (de liaison)* cord; *(d'un tableau de distribution)* patchcord; **cordon souple** = flex; **poste téléphonique** *ou* **téléphone sans cordon** = cordless telephone

co-résident, -e *adj* coresident

coroutine *nf* coroutine

corps *nm* body; **corps de boucle** = loop body; **corps d'un caractère** = body size *ou* set; *(en points)* typesize; **corps du texte** = body (of text); **caractères utilisés pour le corps d'un texte** = body type; **dimension (en points) du corps d'un texte** = body size

correct, -e *adj* accurate *ou* correct

◊ **correctement** *adv* accurately; **le lecteur optique n'arrivait pas à lire correctement toutes les lettres de la nouvelle police de caractères** *ou* **de la nouvelle fonte** = the OCR had difficulty in reading the new font accurately

correcteur, -trice 1 *n (d'épreuves)* proofreader **2** *adj* **code correcteur** = self-correcting code; **code correcteur d'erreurs** = error correcting code

correction *nf* **(a)** *(d'un texte imprimé)* correction; **corrections de l'imprimeur** = house corrections; **épreuve sans correction** = clean proof; **texte sans correction** = clean text; **signes de correction (d'épreuves d'imprimerie)** = proof correction marks **(b)** *(de données)* correction *ou* update; **correction d'erreurs** = error correction *ou* data cleaning; **correction automatique d'erreurs** = automatic error correction; **correction d'erreurs par retransmission** = backward error correction; **correction d'erreurs en cours de transmission** = forward error correction; **détection et correction d'erreurs** = error detection and correction (EDAC); **code de vérification et correction d'erreurs** = error checking and correcting code (ECCC); **correction provisoire** = patch; **fichier des corrections** = deletion record **(c)** *(de secteur de disque défectueux)* hot fix

◊ **correctif, -ive** *adj* corrective; **maintenance corrective** = corrective maintenance; repair

correspondance *nf* correspondence; **correspondance commerciale** *ou* **d'affaires** = business correspondence; **être en correspondance avec quelqu'un** = to correspond with someone *ou* to be in correspondence with someone

◊ **correspondant, -e** *n* **(a)** *(journaliste)* correspondent; **le correspondant (de la section) informatique** = the computer correspondent; **le correspondant économique du 'Figaro'** = the 'Figaro' business correspondent **(b)** *(d'une communication téléphonique)* called party

correspondre *vi* **(a)** *(coïncider)* to correspond; **correspondre à quelque chose** = to correspond with something **(b)** *(écrire)* **correspondre avec quelqu'un** = to correspond with someone

corriger *vtr* **(a)** to correct *ou* to rectify; *(mettre à jour)* to update; **erreur qui peut être corrigée** = recoverable error; **erreur impossible à corriger** = unrecoverable error; **fichier corrigé** = update (file); **le document original et le document corrigé se trouvent tous les deux sur disquette(s)** = we have the original and updated documents on disks **(b)** *(texte écrit)* to edit *ou* to correct; **corriger des épreuves** = to proofread; **ils ont dû corriger l'erreur à l'impression** = they had to rectify the error at the printout stage; **page corrigée qui en remplace une autre** = cancel page; **non corrigé** = unedited **(c)** *(un signal)* to equalize

corrompre *vtr* to corrupt; **les données de ce fichier n'ont pas été corrompues** = the data in this file has not been corrupted *ou* has integrity

◊ **corrompu, -e** *adj (fichier)* damaged; *(données* ou *fichier)* corrupt

◊ **corruption** *nf* corruption; **corruption de données** = data corruption; **la corruption des données stockées sur la disquette a rendu le fichier impossible à lire** = data corruption on the disk has made one file unreadable; **chaque fois qu'on met le système sous tension, il y a une corruption de données** = data corruption occurs each time the motor is switched on

cosmique *adj* **bruit cosmique** = galactic noise

côté *nm* side; **à côté de** = next to *ou* adjacent to; **l'adresse est rangée en mémoire à côté du champ nom du client** = the address is stored adjacent to the customer name field

couche *nf* **(a)** *(zone d'une structure)* layer; **couche application** = application layer; **couche (de) liaison de données** = data link layer; **couches multiples** = multilayer; *voir aussi* MULTICOUCHE **couche physique** = physical layer; **couche présentation** = presentation layer; **couche réseau** = network layer; **couche session** = session layer; **couche transport** = transport layer; **disposé en couches** = layered; **le noyau possède une structure en couches adaptée aux besoins de l'utilisateur** = the kernel has a layered structure according to user priority **(b)** *(enduit)* coating; **couche épitaxiale** = epitaxial layer; **couche de phosphore** *ou* **couche phosphorescente** = phosphor coating; **couche phosphorée à grande persistance** =

long persistence phosphor; **mémoire laser sur couche haute définition** = emulsion laser storage; **mémoire à couches minces magnétiques** = magnetic thin film storage **(c)** *(ionosphère)* **couche E** = E-region *ou* Heaviside-Kennelly layer

◊ **couché, -ée** *adj* **papier couché** = coated paper

couler *vi* to flow

couleur *nf* colour; **couleur d'affichage** = display colour; **couleurs complémentaires** = complementary colours; *(bleu, jaune, rouge)* **couleurs fondamentales** *ou* **primaires** = primary colours; **couleur de premier plan** = foreground colour; *(carte EGA)* **adaptateur graphique couleur EGA** = enhanced graphics adapter (EGA); *(carte CGA)* **adaptateur graphique couleur CGA** = colour graphics adapter (CGA); **affichage couleur** = colour display; **bits (de description) de couleur** = colour bits; **cellule de contrôle des couleurs** = colour cell; **décodeur de couleurs** = colour decoder; **diapositive couleur** = colour transparency; **écran couleur** = colour monitor; **encodeur de couleurs** = colour encoder; **équilibre des couleurs** = colour balance; **imprimante couleur** = colour printer; **moniteur couleur** = colour monitor; **le moniteur couleur est excellent pour les jeux électroniques** = the colour monitor is great for games; **photographie en couleur** *ou* **photo couleur** = colour photograph; **saturation de couleur** = colour saturation; **sélection** *ou* **séparation des couleurs** = colour separation; **négatifs de séparation des couleurs** = colour separations

coulomb *nm* coulomb

coup *nm* **(a)** blow *ou* knock; **éteindre l'ordinateur ou lui donner un mauvais coup quand la tête de lecture est en marche peut causer des ennuis** = you can cause trouble by turning off or jarring the PC while the disk read head is moving **(b) passer un coup de fil** = to make a phone call

coupe *nf* **(a)** cross-section; **une coupe de la fibre optique a révélé la source du problème** = the cross-section of the optical fibre showed the source of the problem **(b)** cut; *(d'un raccord)* **coupe (en) diagonale** *ou* **en biseau** = diagonal cut

◊ **coupe-circuit** *nm* circuit breaker

couper *vtr* **(a)** to cut (off); to clip; to scissor; *(très peu)* to trim; **on a coupé six mètres du rouleau de papier** = six metres of paper were cut off the reel; **il vous faudra couper légèrement le bord supérieur de la photo pour qu'elle ait les dimensions désirées** = you will need to trim the top part of the photograph to make it fit **(b) couper un mot** = to delete a word; **couper un texte** = to cut *ou* to shorten a text; **nous avons dû couper le fichier pour réussir à le sauvegarder sur une seule disquette** = we had to shorten the file to be able to save it on one floppy

◊ **couper/coller** *vtr&nm* *(traitement de texte)* cut and paste

couplage *nm* **(a)** linkage; **transformateur de couplage** = matching transformer **(b) dispositif à**

couplage de charge = charge-coupled device (CCD); **(dispositif) mémoire à couplage de charge** = charge-coupled device memory *ou* CCD memory

◊ **coupler** *vtr* to couple *ou* to lock onto; **les deux systèmes sont couplés l'un à l'autre** = the two systems are coupled together; **registre couplé** = adjunct register

◊ **coupleur** *nm* coupler; **coupleur acoustique** = acoustic coupler

le magnétophone peut être couplé à un micro-ordinateur

Science et Vie

coupure *nf* **(a)** *(dans un texte)* cut *ou* deletion; **les éditeurs ont demandé de faire des coupures au premier chapitre** = the editors have asked for cuts *ou* deletions in the first chapter; **fichier des coupures** = deletion record **(b)** *(découpure)* cutting; **coupure de journal** *ou* **de presse** = press cutting; **nous avons constitué un dossier de coupures de presse sur le nouveau progiciel** = we have kept a file of press cuttings about the new software package; **service de coupures de presse** = clipping service **(c)** *(césure d'un mot)* division *ou* hyphenation *ou* word break; **coupure impropre** *ou* **inappropriée** = bad break; **la coupure des mots trop longs se fait automatiquement en fin de ligne grâce au programme de césure** = in the hyphenation program, long words are automatically divided at the end of lines **(d)** *(de transmission)* **coupure au premier raccroché** = first party release; **coupure d'un signal** = breakup **(e)** *(d'électricité)* cut *ou* cutoff; **coupure de courant** = blackout *ou* black out; power cut *ou* power failure; **coupure d'alimentation de courant** = power dump; **il y a eu une coupure de courant** = the electricity supply was cut off; there was a power failure *ou* a power cut; **il y a eu une coupure de courant qui a été fatale à l'ordinateur** = the electricity was cut off, and the computer crashed; **fréquence de coupure** = cutoff frequency

courant *nm* *(électrique)* electric current; **courant alternatif (CA)** = alternating current (AC); **courant continu (CC)** = direct current (DC); **courant de décharge** = drain; **courant flottant** = floating voltage; **produire un courant induit** = to induce a current; **courant de maintien** = hold current; **courant noir** = dark current; *(d'une ligne)* **courant transitoire** = power transient; **limiteur** *ou* **éliminateur de courant transitoire** = transient suppressor; **courant de veille** = hold current; **amplificateur de courant de bus** = bus driver; **baisse** *ou* **chute de courant** = brown-out; **coupure de courant** = blackout *ou* black out; power failure *ou* power cut; **il y a eu une coupure de courant** = the electricity supply was cut off; there was a power cut *ou* a power failure; **coupure d'alimentation de courant** = power dump; **il y a eu une coupure de courant qui a été fatale à l'ordinateur** = the electricity was cut off, and the computer crashed; **inverseur de courant** = inverter (AC/DC); **panne de courant** = power failure *ou* power cut; **prise de courant** = electric outlet *ou* socket

◊ **courant, -e** *adj* **(a)** *(normal)* common *ou* standard; **c'est un défaut courant de ce modèle**

d'imprimante = this is a common fault with this printer model; **matériel courant** = common hardware; **maintenance courante** = housekeeping; **(bruit) parasite courant** = common mode noise **(b)** *(actuel)* current; **adresse courante** = current address; **registre d'adresse courante** = current address register (CAR); **(mise en) mémoire du format courant** = local format storage; **(lecteur de) disque courant** = current drive; **registre d'instruction courante** = current instruction register (CIR); **répertoire courant** = current directory **(c) titre courant** = running head; **titres et en-têtes courants** = rolling headers

courbe *nf* graph *ou* plot *ou* curve; **tracer une courbe (par points numérisés)** = to plot a graph *ou* a curve; **courbe d'apprentissage** = learning curve; **courbe caractéristique** = characteristic curve; **traceur de courbes** = X-Y plotter *ou* graph plotter; *voir aussi* TRACEUR

Courier *(police de caractères)* Courier

courir *vi* to run; *(un texte)* **laisser courir (sans interruption** *ou* **sans alinéa)** = to run on; **le texte peut courir sans alinéa** = the line can run on to the next without any space

courrier *nm* mail; **courrier 'arrivée'** = incoming mail; **courrier 'départ'** = outgoing mail; **courrier électronique** = electronic mail *ou* email *ou* e-mail; **fonction courrier électronique** = electronic mail capability; *(d'une imprimante)* **qualité courrier** = near-letter-quality *ou* NLQ (printing); **mettez l'imprimante en mode courrier pour imprimer ces lettres types** = switch the printer to NLQ for these form letters

course *nf* **course d'une touche** = key travel

court, -e *adj* short; **il est impossible de former convenablement un opérateur dans un délai aussi court** = there is insufficient time to train a keyboarder properly *ou* it is impossible to train the keyboarders properly in such a short space of time; **ondes courtes** = short wave (SW); **modem de courte portée** = short haul modem; *(trait d'union)* **tiret de césure** *ou* **tiret court (dont la longueur équivaut à un 'n')** = en dash *ou* en rule

◊ **court-circuit** *nm* short circuit; **créer un court-circuit** = to short-circuit; **qui a été mis en court-circuit** = short-circuited

◊ **court-circuiter** *vtr* to short-circuit

coussinet *nm* **distorsion en coussinet** = pin cushion distortion

couture *nf* seam; *(livre)* **relié sans couture** = perfect bound; **reliure sans couture** = perfect binding

couverture *nf* **(a)** *(d'un livre)* cover *ou* binding; **couverture cartonnée** = case binding; **livre avec couverture cartonnée** = hardbound book *ou* cased book; **relier avec couverture cartonnée** = to case a book; **c'est un livre avec couverture pelliculée** = the book has a laminated cover; **c'est un livre avec couverture plastique souple** = the book has a soft

plastic binding **(b)** *(suppression d'une émission)* blanketing **(c)** coverage; **couverture médiatique** = media coverage *ou* press coverage; **nous avons eu une bonne couverture médiatique pour le lancement du nouveau modèle** = we got good media coverage for the launch of the new model; *(zone de réception)* **zone terrestre de couverture** *ou* **couverture terrestre** = earth coverage

cp *(commande de copie de fichier UNIX)* cp (command)

CP/M *(système d'exploitation pour micros)* Control Program/Monitor *ou* Control Program for Microcomputers (CP/M); *voir aussi* EXPLOITATION

cps = CARACTERES PAR SECONDE

CPU = CENTRAL PROCESSING UNIT **protocole d'échange d'informations entre CPU et périphérique** = CPU handshaking; **cycle CPU** = CPU cycle; **éléments CPU** = CPU elements; **temps CPU** = CPU time; *voir aussi* UNITE

crash *nm* crash *ou* system crash; **crash du disque (dur)** = (hard) disk crash; **crash du disque dur causé par la tête de lecture** = head crash; **crash d'un programme** = program crash

crasse *nf* dirt; *(parasite sur bande)* drop in

crawl *nm* *(défilement de générique)* crawl

crayon *nm* pencil; *(sans clavier)* **ordinateur à crayon optique** = pen computer

créateur, -trice *n* **créateur de logiciel** = software developer

◊ **création** *nf* **(a)** creation *ou* origination *ou* generation; *(multimédia)* authoring; **la création de la maquette demandera plusieurs semaines** = the origination of the artwork will take several weeks; **allez à CREATION D'UN DOSSIER sur le menu** = move to the CREATE NEW FILE instruction on the menu; **création de données** = data origination; **création de fichier** = file creation; **création de liens** = linkage; **expert en création de logiciel** = software developer; **création d'un programme** = program generation **(b)** design; **studio de création** = design studio; **spécifications** *ou* **contraintes** *ou* **paramètres de création** = design parameters

crédit *nm* **(a)** *(d'argent)* credit; **carte de crédit** = credit card **(b)** *(de film ou revue)* **crédits** = credits

créer *vtr* to create *ou* to generate *ou* to originate; **créer une adresse** = to address; **créé à l'aide d'un ordinateur** = computer-generated; **document créé à partir de paragraphes standard** = boilerplate; **on a créé un nouveau fichier sur la disquette pour archiver le document** = a new file was created on disk to store the document; **créer une image à**

partir de données numériques = to generate an image from digitally recorded data; **ils ont fait l'analyse de l'image créée par l'ordinateur** = they analyzed the computer-generated image; **demandez l'aide d'un bon programmeur qui vous aidera à créer un nouveau programme de traitement de texte** = ask a specialist programmer to help you to devise a new word-processing program

crénage *nm (d'une photo)* kerning

créneau *nm* (a) *(emplacement pour carte)* slot; **créneau pour carte d'extension** = expansion slot; **créneau inutilisé** = empty slot; **cet ordinateur possède deux créneaux libres et votre carte d'extension n'en utilisera qu'un** = there are two free slots in the micro, you only need one for the add-on board; **enfichez la carte d'extension dans le créneau libre** = insert the board in the free expansion slot (b) *(transmission)* **créneau pour message** = message slot; **créneau de temps** = time slot

crénelage *nm* aliasing; *voir aussi* ANTICRÉNELAGE

crête *nf* peak; **veillez à ce que la tension de crête ne dépasse pas 60 watts sinon l'amplificateur surchauffera** = keep the peak power below 60 watts or the amplifier will overheat

creux *nm* trough; *(d'une onde)* **les pointes et les creux** = peaks and troughs

cristal *nm* crystal; **écran à cristaux liquides** *ou* **affichage à cristaux liquides** = Liquid Crystal Display (LCD); **imprimante à transfert LCD** = liquid crystal display shutter printer *ou* LCD shutter printer

le groupe électronique nippon est parvenu à réaliser un écran à cristaux liquides qui, contrairement aux écrans usuels, garantit sous tous les angles de vision une image nette et une haute définition

Electronique

critère *nm* criterion (NOTE: le pluriel est **criteria**)

critique *adj* (a) *(important)* critical; **critique (pour l'entreprise)** = mission-critical; **application critique pour l'entreprise** = mission-critical application; **erreur critique** = critical error; *(de l'image)* **fréquence critique de fusion** = critical fusion frequency; **ressource critique** = critical resource (b) *(dévaluation)* **résumé critique** = evaluative abstract

crochet(s) *nm(pl) (type de parenthèses* [] *)* square bracket(s); **mettre entre crochets** = to bracket together

croisé, -ée *adj* cross-; **assembleur croisé** = cross-assembler; **compilateur croisé** = cross-compiler; **nous pouvons utiliser un compilateur croisé pour développer le logiciel avant l'arrivée du nouveau système** = we can use a cross-compiler to develop the software before the new system arrives; **contrôle croisé** = cross-check; *(renvoi)* **référence croisée** = cross-reference

croissant, -e *adj* increasing; ascending; **en ordre croissant** = forward mode; **tri par ordre croissant** = forward sort

croix (†) *nf (signe typographique)* dagger; **croix double (‡)** = double dagger

cropping *nm (de photo)* cropping

crottes de souris *nfpl (pixels causés par la souris)* mouse trail

cryogénique *adj* cryogenic; **mémoire cryogénique** = cryogenic memory

cryptage *nm (système)* cipher; *(procédure)* encryption; **algorithme de cryptage** = cryptographic algorithm; **clé de cryptage** = cipher key *ou* cryptographic key; **cryptage à clé publique** = public key cipher system; **cryptage de données** = data encryption; **norme** *ou* **standard de cryptage de données** = data encryption standard (DES); **cryptage de l'information pour en assurer la confidentialité** = privacy transformation

◊ **crypter** *vtr* to code *ou* to encipher *ou* to encrypt; **circuit crypté (pour protection de logiciel)** = dongle; **message crypté** = ciphertext *ou* encrypted text; **le message crypté peut être transmis par téléphone sans que personne ne puisse le lire** = the encrypted text can be sent along ordinary telephone lines, and no one will be able to understand it

◊ **cryptographie** *nf* cryptography

◊ **cryptographique** *adj* cryptographic; **algorithme cryptographique** = cryptographic algorithm; **analyse cryptographique** = cryptanalysis

CSM = COMBINED SYMBOL MATCHING; *voir* SYSTEME

CSMA-CD = CARRIER SENSE MULTIPLE ACCESS-COLLISION DETECTION; *voir* COLLISION

CTR *ou* **CTRL** *ou* **Ctrl** *(touche 'contrôle')* Control (key); **mode CTRL** = control mode; **touche CTRL** = control key *ou* CONTROL *ou* Ctrl; **pour arrêter un programme, appuyez sur Ctrl-C, c'est-à-dire appuyez sur la touche de contrôle et la touche C en même temps** = to halt a program, press Ctrl-C - the control key and letter C - at the same time; **pour relancer votre PC, appuyez sur Ctrl-Alt-Del** = to reset your PC, press Ctrl-Alt-Del; **commandé par les codes CTRL** *ou* **asservi aux codes CTRL** = control-driven; *voir aussi* CONTROLE

CTS *(signal)* Clear To Send (CTS)

cuivre *nm* copper

cumul *nm* **de cumul** = cumulative; **registre de cumul** = accumulator register

◊ **cumulande** *nm (premier terme d'une addition)* augend

◊ **cumulateur** *nm (nombre ajouté au cumulande)* addend *ou* augmenter

◊ **cumulatif, -ive** *adj* cumulative; **index cumulatif** = cumulative index

curatif, -ive *adj* remedial; **maintenance curative** = remedial maintenance; repair; *voir aussi* CORRECTIF

curseur *nm* cursor; **curseur adressable** = addressable cursor; **curseur destructif** = destructive cursor; **l'écran devient presqu'illisible sans le curseur destructif** = reading the screen becomes difficult without a destructive cursor; **curseur non destructif** = non-destructive cursor; **curseur effaceur** = destructive cursor; **curseur (en) bâton** *ou* **en I** = I-beam (cursor shaped like 'I'); **curseur (en) pavé** = block cursor; **curseur secondaire** = ghost cursor; **touches de contrôle du curseur** = cursor control keys *ou* cursor pad *ou* arrowed keys

cyan-magenta-jaune-noir (CMYK) *(système de définition de couleurs)* Cyan-Magenta-Yellow-Black (CMYK)

cybernétique *nf* **la cybernétique** = cybernetics

cycle *nm* cycle; **cycle de contrôle** = control cycle; **cycle CPU** = CPU cycle; *(d'une instruction)* **cycle d'exécution** = execute cycle; **opération en cycle fixe** = fixed cycle operation; **cycle fonctionnel** = action cycle; **cycle d'horloge** = clock cycle *ou* CPU cycle; **cycle d'instruction** = instruction cycle; **temps de cycle d'instruction** = instruction cycle time; **cycle de lecture** = read cycle; **cycle de lecture d'une instruction** = fetch cycle; **cycle de lecture-exécution** = fetch-execute cycle *ou* execute cycle; **cycle de machine** = machine cycle; **cycle de mémoire** = memory cycle; **cycle d'opération** = operation cycle; **cycle principal** = major cycle; **cycle de production** = production run; **cycle de rotation des fichiers de sauvegarde** = grandfather cycle; **cycle de l'unité centrale** = CPU cycle; **cycle de vie d'un logiciel** = software life cycle; **(période de) disponiblité dans le cycle** = cycle availability; **(système) évalué en cycles possibles par unité de temps** = duty-rated (system); **index de cycle** = cycle index; **nombre de cycles** = cycle count; **temps de cycle** = cycle time; **(exploitation par) vol de cycle** = cycle stealing; **accès direct à la mémoire par vol de cycle** = DMA cycle stealing

◊ **cyclique** *adj* cyclic; **accès cyclique** = cyclic access; **contrôle cyclique** = cyclic check; **contrôle par redondance cyclique** = cyclic redundancy check (CRC)

cylindre *nm* cylinder *ou* drum; *(sur un disque)* cylinder; **cylindre d'impression** = impression cylinder; **cylindre porte-blanchet** = blanket cylinder; **imprimante à cylindre** = barrel printer

Dd

D *(nombre hexadécimal équivalent du 13 décimal)* hexadecimal number equivalent to decimal 13 *ou* D

D *(en D ou qui a la forme d'un D)* **commutateur à bascule de type D** = D-type flip-flop; **connecteur de type D** = D-type connector; **le port série du PC utilise un connecteur à neuf broches de type D** = the serial port on a PC uses a 9-pin D-type connector

D *(ionosphère)* **région D** = D-region; **la région D est la principale cause d'affaiblissement des ondes radioélectriques** = the D-region is the main cause of attenuation in transmitted radio signals

DAB = DISTRIBUTEUR AUTOMATIQUE DE BILLETS DE BANQUE

dactylo *nf* copy typist; **pool de dactylos** = typing pool

◊ **dactylographie** *nf* (copy) typing

◊ **dactylographié, -ée** *adj* typewritten; **texte** *ou* **manuscrit dactylographié** = typescript

daemon *nm (utilitaire UNIX)* daemon (disk and execution monitor)

DAO = DESSIN ASSISTE PAR ORDINATEUR

datagramme *nm* datagram

date *nf* date; **la date de création de ce fichier est le 10 juin** = the date of creation for the file was the 10th of June; **j'ai bien reçu votre message en date d'hier** = I have received your message of yesterday's date; **date limite** *ou* **date d'expiration de délai** = expiration date *ou* deadline; **nous avons dépassé notre date limite du 15 octobre** = we've missed our October 15th deadline; **date de péremption** = expiration date; *(d'un produit en magasin)* shelf life

◊ **dater** *vtr (un document)* to date

dB = DECIBEL

DB = DATA BUS CONNECTOR **connecteur DB** = DB connector; **les connecteurs DB les plus répandus sont DB-9, DB-25 et DB-50 qui portent respectivement 9, 25, 50 broches** = the most common DB connectors are DB-9, DB-25 and DB-50 with 9, 25 and 50 connections respectively

dBase™ *(logiciel de base de données)* dBASE™

COMMENTAIRE: dBase a fait l'objet de plusieurs versions: II, III et IV, le développement de ce progiciel est assuré par Borland International. Il y a eu plusieurs versions de dBase et les fichiers créés par dBase peuvent normalement être importés dans plusieurs autres programmes de base de données

DCB = DECIMAL CODE BINAIRE binary coded decimal; **additionneur DCB** = BCD adder

DD = DISQUETTE DOUBLE DENSITE

DDE *(procédure d'échange dynamique de données, de Microsoft Windows et OS/2)* Dynamic Data Exchange (DDE)

débit *nm* throughput *ou* transmission rate *ou* speed; baud rate; **communication à faible débit** = low speed communications; **débit binaire** = bit rate; **débit de données** = data transfer rate; **le débit d'électricité est régularisé par une résistance** = current flow is regulated by a resistor; **débit d'un canal** *ou* **d'une voie de transmission** = channel capacity; **débit d'une imprimante** = printer output; *(mesuré en 'ems')* ems per hour; **cette imprimante a un débit de 60 caractères/seconde** = the printer prints at 60 characters per second; **débit ligne** = *(d'une imprimante)* lines per minute (LPM); *(transmission de données)* line speed; **débit de transmission de données** = data signalling rate; **débit de transmission d'informations** = information rate; **débit maximal de transmission** = maximum transmission rate; **débit moyen de transmission** = medium (transmission) speed; **débit par défaut** *ou* **pré-déterminé** *ou* **implicite d'un modem** = default rate; **débit théorique (maximum)** *ou* **nominal (d'un appareil)** = rated throughput; **débit théorique de données dans un canal** = aggregate line speed; **carte vidéo à grand débit** = full motion video adapter; *(transmission)* **ligne de grand débit** = high usage trunk; *(d'un modem)* **reconnaissance automatique de débit d'une ligne** = auto-baud scanning *ou* auto-baud sensing; **un modem équipé d'une reconnaissance de débit s'ajuste automatiquement à la vitesse à laquelle il doit fonctionner** = a modem with auto-baud scanner can automatically sense at which baud rate it should operate; *(onduleur ou dispositif de secours)* **temps de débit** = holdup

débogage *nm* debugging; **débogage symbolique** = symbolic debugging; **logiciel de débogage** = debugger; **spécialiste en débogage** = troubleshooter; **système de débogage interactif** = interactive debugging system

◊ **débogué, -ée** *adj* debugged; **programme débogué** = debugged program

◊ **déboguer** *vtr* to debug; **il faut plus de temps pour déboguer un programme que pour en créer un** = debugging takes up more time than construction; **ils ont mis des semaines à déboguer le système** = they spent weeks debugging the system

◊ **débogueur** *nm* debugger

déborder *vtr&i* to overflow *ou* to go beyond; *(photo)* to bleed off; *(dans la marge de gauche)* **faire déborder une ligne** = to outdent

◊ **débordement** *nm (d'une mémoire tampon)* spillage; *(de capacité d'une ligne ou d'un ordinateur)* overflow; **débordement négatif** = underflow

débrancher *vtr* to disconnect *ou* to unplug; **ne déplacez pas le système sans l'avoir d'abord débranché** = do not move the system without unplugging it; **n'oubliez pas de débrancher (le câble de) l'imprimante avant de la changer de place** = do not forget to disconnect the cable before moving the printer

DEBUG ™ *(utilitaire MS-DOS)* DEBUG ™ (software utility in MS-DOS)

début *nm* beginning *ou* start; **début de bande** = tape header; *(pour le curseur)* **début de l'écran** = cursor home; *(données)* **début d'enregistrement** = home record; *(transmisssion)* **début d'en-tête** = start of header; **(caractère de) début de fichier** = beginning of file (bof *ou* BOF); **(données de) début de fichier** = head (of file); *(papier listing)* **début d'une page** = head of form (HOF); **(code de) début de texte** = start-of-text (SOT *ou* STX); **bit *ou* élément de début** = start bit *ou* start element; **marque de début de bande** = beginning of tape (bot) marker; **marque de début d'enregistrement** = beginning of information mark (bim); **marque de début de mot** *(d'une bande)* **point de début d'enregistrement** = (tape) loadpoint; *(sur un clavier)* **touche Début** = Home key

débuter *vtr* **débuter une session (à l'ordinateur)** = to log in *ou* log on

décadaire *adj* decade; **compteur décadaire** = decade counter

◊ **décade** *nf* decade

décalage *nm* **(a)** *(glissement d'un bit)* shift; **décalage arithmétique** = arithmetic shift; **décalage circulaire** = circular shift *ou* cyclic shift *ou* end about shift; **décalage à droite** = right shift; **faire *ou* effectuer un décalage à droite** = to right shift *ou* to shift right; **décalage à gauche** = left shift; **faire *ou* effectuer un décalage à gauche** = to left shift *ou* to shift left; **décalage logique** = logical shift *ou* non-arithmetic shift; **instruction de décalage** = shift instruction; **instruction de décalage dans le registre** = accumulator shift instruction; **registre à *ou* de décalage** = shift register *ou* circulating register **(b)** *(de données)* **(à) décalage de fréquence** = dual clocking **(c)** *(de temps)* **le décalage est perceptible sur les lignes téléphoniques internationales** = time lag is noticeable on international phone calls

◊ **décalé, -ée** *adj* shifted; **0110 décalé à gauche d'un pas, devient 1100** = 0110 left shifted once is 1100

◊ **décaler** *vtr* to shift

décelé, -ée *adj* detected *ou* found; **non décelé** = undetected

◊ **déceler** *vtr* to detect *ou* to find; **la cellule photo-électrique décèle la quantité de lumière qui traverse le liquide** = the photoelectric cell detects the amount of light passing through the liquid

décélération *nf* deceleration; **temps de décélération** = deceleration time *ou* stop time

décentralisé, -ée *adj* decentralized; **réseau décentralisé** = decentralized computer network; **système décentralisé** = distributed system; **traitement décentralisé des données** = decentralized data processing

décharge *nf (de pile)* discharge; **courant de décharge** = drain; **temps de décharge (d'un circuit d'impédance)** = load life

◊ **décharger** *vtr* to unload; *(pile)* to discharge *ou* to drain

déchiffrage *nm* decryption *ou* deciphering *ou* de-scrambling; **le déchiffrage se fait avec l'ordinateur pour aller plus vite** = decryption is done by computer to increase speed

◊ **déchiffrer** *vtr (un code)* to decipher *ou* to decrypt *ou* to break *ou* to de-scramble; **il a finalement réussi à déchiffrer le code** = he finally deciphered the code *ou* broke the cipher system

déchiqueté, -ée *adj* ragged; *(papier)* **bord déchiqueté** = deckle edge

déchirure *nf* tear *ou* tearing

déci- *préfixe* deci-

décibel *nm* decibel (dB)

◊ **décibelmètre** *nm* decibel meter

décile *nm* decile

décimal, -e *adj* decimal; **décimal codé binaire (DCB)** = binary coded decimal (BCD); **base décimale *ou* base 10** = base 10; **le chiffre décimal 8** = the decimal digit 8; **code décimal réfléchi** = cyclic decimal code; **numération décimale** = decimal notation *ou* denary notation; **système décimal** = decimal system; **tabulation décimale** = decimal tabbing; **touche de tabulation décimale** = decimal tab key; **virgule décimale** = decimal point

◊ **décimal-binaire** *adj* decimal-to-binary; **conversion décimale-binaire** = decimal-to-binary conversion

◊ **décimale** *nf* decimal; **la décimale 8** = the decimal digit 8; **décimale condensée** = packed decimal; **arrondi à un nombre fixe de décimales** = automatic decimal adjustment; **correct à la troisième décimale** = correct to three places of decimals

◊ **décimalisation** *nf* decimalization

◊ **décimaliser** *vtr* to decimalize

décimétrique *adj* decimetre; **ondes décimétriques** = ultra high frequency (UHF)

décimonique *adj* decimonic; **sonnerie décimonique** = decimonic ringing

décisif, -ive *adj* l'excellence des graphiques a constitué l'argument décisif = the deciding factor was the superb graphics

◊ **décision** *nf* decision; **décision logique** = logical decision; **arbre de décision** = decision tree; **circuit de décision** = decision circuit; **élément de décision** = decision element; **prendre une décision** = to come to a decision *ou* to reach a decision; **symbole de décision** = decision box; **système d'aide à la décision (SAID)** = decision support system (DSS); **table de décision** = decision table

déclaratif, -ive *adj* declarative *ou* narrative; **instruction déclarative** = narrative statement; **langage déclaratif** = declarative language

◊ **déclaration** *nf* declaration *ou* statement *ou* declarative statement *ou* narrative statement; **déclaration d'entrée** = input statement; **déclaration d'exécution** = execute statement; **déclaration de procédure** = procedure declaration; **déclaration d'une variable locale** = local declaration; **faire une déclaration** = to declare *ou* to state; **rubrique de déclaration des données** = data division

◊ **déclarer** *vtr* to declare *ou* to state; **au début du programme, X a été déclaré égal à 9** = he declared at the start of the program that X was equal to nine

déclenché, -ée *adj* triggered; **déclenché par bascule de front d'impulsion** = edge-triggered

◊ **déclencher** *vtr* to trigger *ou* to set off; **le détecteur de pression caché sous le tapis déclenche un système d'alarme si quelqu'un marche dessus** = the pressure pad under the carpet will set off the burglar alarm if anyone steps on it

décodage *nm* decoding

◊ **décoder** *vtr* to decode

◊ **décodeur** *nm* (*logiciel ou dispositif qui convertit les données*) decoder; (*de message*) descrambler; **décodeur d'adresse** = address decoder; **décodeur de couleurs** = colour decoder; **décodeur d'instruction** = operation decoder *ou* instruction decoder

décompilation *nf* decompilation; **compilation et décompilation incrémentielles** = incremental compilation and decompilation

décomposition *nf* decomposition; **décomposition de mouvements** = memomotion

décomprimer *vtr* to decompress *ou* to unpack; **ce sous-programme permet de décomprimer les fichiers archivés** = this routine unpacks the archived files

déconcentrateur *nm* **déconcentrateur pour transmission vidéo** = video expander

décondenser *vtr* (*des données*) to unpack

déconnecter *vtr* to disconnect *ou* to unplug; **vous n'avez qu'à déconnecter le lecteur et en connecter un nouveau à sa place** = simply unplug the old drive and plug-in a new one

décors *nmpl* (*film ou théâtre*) set

découpage *nm* cutting; (*photo ou image*) cropping; **les photos peuvent être éditées par découpage, dimensionnement, retouche, etc.** = photographs can be edited by cropping, sizing, touching up, etc.

◊ **découpe** *nf* cutting; (*du silicium*) **découpe en pastille** = slicing (from a bar of silicon crystal)

◊ **découper** *vtr* to cut; to clip; (*un fichier trop long*) to partition; (*la bordure d'une image*) to crop

décrémenter *vtr* to decrement; **le contenu du registre a été décrémenté à zéro** = the register contents were decremented until they reached zero

décrire *vtr* to describe; **décrire un cercle** = to go in a circle; **décrire une orbite** = to orbit; **ce satellite météorologique décrit une orbite autour de la terre toutes les quatre heures** = this weather satellite orbits the earth every four hours

décrochage *nm* (**a**) (*arrêt dans un programme ou dispositif*) holdup (**b**) (*distorsion d'image vidéo*) hooking (**c**) (*modem*) **transmission sans décrochage** = blind dialling

◊ **décroché, -ée** *adj* (*combiné du téléphone*) **(mode) décroché** = off-hook

décroissant, -e *adj* descending; **programmation structurée suivant un ordre décroissant** = top-down programming

décryptage *nm* decryption

◊ **décrypter** *vtr* to decrypt

dédié, -ée *adj* dedicated; **canal dédié** = dedicated channel; **ligne téléphonique dédiée** = dedicated line; **la logique dédiée réduit le nombre de puces** = dedicated logic cuts down the chip count; **ordinateur dédié** = dedicated computer; **système dédié** = special purpose system; **terminal dédié** = applications terminal *ou* dedicated computer

dédoublement *nm* division; dividing *ou* splitting; **dédoublement de faisceau** = beam diversity

déduction *nf* deduction *ou* inference

déduire *vtr* to deduct

de facto *ou* **de fait** *adv* **norme de facto** *ou* **de fait** = de facto standard

défaillance *nf* failure *ou* malfunction *ou* breakdown; (*totale*) crash; (*légère*) glitch; **les données ont été perdues par suite d'une défaillance du logiciel** = the data was lost due to a software malfunction; **défaillance induite** *ou* **ayant une cause externe** = induced failure; **défaillance du matériel** *ou* **de l'ordinateur** = equipment failure; **défaillance d'un programme** = program crash; **diagnostic (de cause) de défaillance** = problem diagnosis;

diagnostic de localisation de défaillance = fault diagnosis; **moyenne de temps de bon fonctionnement entre les défaillances (MTBF)** = mean time between failures (MTBF); **taux de défaillance** = failure rate

défaire *vtr* to undo

◊ **se défaire de** *vpr* to discard (something)

défaut *nm* **(a)** fault *ou* defect; *(de magnétisation)* drop out; **nous estimons qu'il y a un défaut dans la conception même du produit** = we think there is a basic fault in the product design; **défaut caché** = hidden defect; **défaut d'horloge** = hazard; **un défaut de l'ordinateur** = a computer defect *ou* a defect in the computer **(b)** default; *(état des paramètres définis par le constructeur)* **par défaut** = by default; **débit par défaut d'un modem** = default rate; **la largeur par défaut de cet écran est de 80** = screen width has a default value of 80; **lecteur par défaut** = default drive; **ce système d'exploitation permet à l'utilisateur de choisir le lecteur par défaut** = the operating system allows the user to select the default drive; **option par défaut** = default option; **réponse par défaut** = default response; **valeur par défaut** = default value **(c) 3,5678 arrondi par défaut à 3,56** = 3.5678 truncated to 3.56

le gestionnaire d'écran par défaut correspond aux écrans EGA (vous n'avez donc rien à faire si vous possédez un tel écran)

L'Ordinateur Individuel

défectueux, -euse *adj* defective *ou* faulty; **il arrive qu'une protection anticopie défectueuse entraîne la détérioration du disque dur** = a hard disk may crash because of faulty copy protection; **ils ont découvert que la défaillance était due à un câble défectueux** = they traced the fault to a faulty cable; **erreur imputable à un composant défectueux** = component error; **il doit sûrement y avoir un composant défectueux dans le système** = there must be a faulty piece of equipment in the system; *(d'un disque)* **secteur défectueux** = bad *ou* faulty *ou* defective sector; **l'appareil est tombé en panne parce que le système de refroidissement était défectueux** = the machine broke down because of a defective cooling system

défendre *vtr* **(a)** *(empêcher)* to forbid *ou* to bar **(b)** *(protéger)* to defend

◊ **défensif, -ive** *adj* defensive; **informatique** *ou* **programmation défensive** = defensive computing

défilement *nm* **(a)** *(du texte sur l'écran)* scrolling; scroll; **défilement vertical** = vertical scrolling; **barre de défilement** = scroll bar; **le marqueur est situé au milieu de la barre de défilement, je sais ainsi que je suis au milieu du document** = the marker is in the middle of the scroll bar so I know I am in the middle of the document; **flèches de défilement** = scroll arrows; **mode défilement** = scroll mode; **touche Arrêt Défilement** = Scroll Lock key **(b)** *(d'une bande magnétique)* running *ou* playing; **compteur de défilement** = tape timer; **vitesse de défilement** = playback speed

◊ **défiler** *vi* to pass; **faire défiler** = *(un texte)* to scroll; *(une bande)* to pass *ou* to play back; **faire défiler (un texte) ligne à ligne sur l'écran** = to roll scroll; **faire défiler (un texte) point par point** = to smooth scroll; **qu'on ne peut pas faire défiler (sur l'écran)** = non-scrollable

défini, -e *adj* defined; **défini d'avance** = predefined

◊ **définir** *vtr* **(a)** to define; *(une variable)* to define *ou* to assign; to set up; **toutes les variables ont été définies lors de l'initialisation** = all the variables were defined at initialization; **définir de nouveau** = to redefine; **nous avons défini les premiers paramètres de nouveau** = we redefined the initial parameters **(b)** **définir une adresse** = to address

◊ **définissable** *adj* selectable; *(par l'utilisateur)* user-selectable

définitif, -ive *adj* definitive; finished; **document définitif** = finished document; **texte définitif** = fair copy *ou* final copy

définition *nf* *(de l'image)* definition *ou* resolution; **définition de l'affichage graphique** = graphic display resolution; **définition de l'écran** = screen *ou* display resolution; **la plupart des écrans d'ordinateurs individuels ont une définition qui est à peine supérieure à 70 points par pouce** = the resolution of most personal computer screens is not much more than 70 dpi (dots per inch); **définition de lecture par balayage** = scanning resolution; **définition maximum** = limiting resolution; **basse** *ou* **faible définition** = low resolution *ou* low-res; **graphiques de basse définition** = low-resolution graphics *ou* low-res graphics; **capacité de définition** = resolution capabilities; **haute définition** = high definition *ou* high resolution *ou* hi-res; **avec un écran haute définition on obtient un affichage de 1824 par 768 pixels** = a high resolution screen can display 1824 by 768 pixels; **graphiques haute définition** = high-resolution graphics *ou* hi-res graphics; **cette carte graphique haute définition contrôle 300 pixels par pouce** = this HRG board can control 300 pixels per inch; **matrice d'impression à haute définition** = enhanced dot matrix; **ce nouveau moniteur haute définition permet un affichage de 1824 x 728 pixels** = this hi-res monitor can display 1824 x 728 pixels; **le nouveau scanner à main haute définition peut lire 400 points par pouce** = the new hi-res hand-held scanner can detect 400 dots per inch; **système vidéo haute définition** = high definition video system (HDVS)

ces super-consoles peuvent manier en un temps plus réduit davantage d'informations, et donc présenter des jeux avec une meilleure définition graphique

L'Express

définitivement *adv* permanently; **le numéro de fabrication est gravé définitivement sur le panneau**

arrière du boîtier de l'ordinateur = the production number is permanently engraved on the back of the computer casing

déflecteur *nm (pour téléviseur)* deflection yoke; *(de résonances parasites)* baffle

◊ **déflexion** *nf* deflection; **déflexion d'un rayon lumineux** = beam deflection; **dans un tube à rayons cathodiques, la déflexion du faisceau est effectuée par un champ magnétique** = a magnetic field is used for beam deflection in a CRT; **armature de déflexion** = deflection yoke

déformant, -e *adj* distorting; **lentille déformante** = distortion optics

◊ **déformation** *nf* distortion; **déformation de l'image** = image distortion

◊ **déformée** *nf* **calcul des déformées intermédiaires** = tweening

◊ **déformer** *vtr* to distort

DEFRAG ™ *(utilitaire de défragmentation sous MS-DOS)* DEFRAG ™ (defragmentation utility in MS-DOS)

défragmentation *nf* defragmentation; **utilitaire de défragmentation** = defragmentation utility

COMMENTAIRE: un fichier qu'on sauvegarde sur disque, n'est pas toujours stocké dans des secteurs adjacents ce qui augmente le temps de restitution. La défragmentation replace les fichiers dans des secteurs adjacents. De cette manière, la tête de lecture parcourt moins de chemin sur le disque, ce qui améliore les performances

dégradation *nf (des performances d'un appareil)* degradation; **dégradation de l'image** = image degradation; **dégradation limitée** *ou* **douce** *ou* **progressive** = graceful degradation

◊ **dégradé** *nm (de couleurs)* shading

dégrouper *vtr* to unpack; **dégrouper un bloc** *ou* **les éléments d'un bloc** = to deblock

DEL = DELETE; *(commande 'effacer' sous MS-DOS)* **commande DEL** = DEL (command); **pour effacer tous les fichiers avec l'extension BAK, entrez la commande DEL*.BAK** = to delete all files with the extension BAK, use the command DEL*.BAK; *(sur un clavier)* **touche d'effacement DEL** = DEL key; **pour effacer un mot à l'écran, appuyez sur la touche DEL plusieurs fois** = to remove a word from the screen, press the DEL key repeatedly

délai *nm* delay *ou* interval; *(date limite)* deadline; **l'imprimante a commencé à imprimer après un délai de trente secondes** = there was a delay of thirty seconds before the printer started printing; **le révélateur doit être utilisé dans un délai d'un an** = the developer has a shelf life of one year; **si vous ne répondez pas à la question dans la minute qui suit, le programme déclenche la question suivante parce que vous avez dépassé les délais** = if you do not

answer this question within one minute, the program times out and moves onto the next question; **délai d'amortissement d'un signal** = decay time; **délai d'attente** = wait time; **délai de contention** = contention delay; *(d'une mémoire vive)* **délai de conversion** = sense recovery time; **délai (de transmission) d'une enveloppe** = envelope delay; *(d'un ordinateur)* **délai d'installation** *ou* **de configuration** = set-up time; **délai d'inversion** *ou* **de retournement** = turnaround time (TAT); **délai moyen** = average delay; **délai de propagation** = propagation delay; *(d'une image)* **délai de retour de ligne** = line blanking interval; **délai de retour du signal en fin d'écran** = blanking interval; **date d'expiration de délai** = expiration date

déliasser *vtr (papier listing)* to decollate

◊ **déliasseuse** *nf* decollator

délimitation *nf* limit; *(de couleur *ou* d'image)* **ligne de délimitation** = holding line

◊ **délimiter** *vtr* to delimit; **délimité par virgule** = comma delimited

◊ **délimiteur** *nm (symbole)* **délimiteur de données** = data delimiter; **délimiteurs de bloc** = block markers

delta *nm (lettre de l'alphabet grec)* delta; **acheminement (en) delta** = delta routing; **horloge delta** = delta clock; **modulation (en) delta** = delta modulation

◊ **delta-delta** *nm (connexion)* delta-delta

démagnétiser *vtr* to demagnetize *ou* to bloop *ou* to degauss; **il faut démagnétiser les têtes de lecture/écriture une fois par semaine pour obtenir d'excellentes performances** = the R/W heads have to be degaussed each week to ensure optimum performance

◊ **démagnétiseur** *nm* demagnetizer; **démagnétiseur de tête** = head demagnetizer

demande *nf* request; *(impérative)* demand; *(de renseignement)* inquiry *ou* enquiry *ou* query; *(d'emploi, etc.)* application; **signal de demande d'invitation à émettre** = request to send signal (RTS); **demande d'interruption** = interrupt request; **demande de compte** *ou* **de partition sur le système** *ou* **d'accès à un système** = application for an account on the system; **(fonction) demande-réponse** = inquiry/response (function); **accès multiple asservi à la demande** = demand assigned multiple access (DAMA); **multiplexage asservi à la demande** = demand multiplexing; **faire une demande (de)** = to apply (for); **formulaire de demande** = application form; **remplir une demande de partition sur le système** = to fill in an application (form) for an account on the system; **sur demande** = on demand; **accès sur demande à la mémoire paginée** = demand fetching; **appel de page sur demande** = demand paging; **lecture-écriture sur demande** = demand reading/writing; **traitement (de données) sur demande** = demand processing *ou* immediate processing; **scanner de demande de communication** = communications scanner

◊ **demander** *vtr* **(a)** to request; *(impérativement)* to demand; **demander quelque chose par téléphone** = to phone for something; *(de transmission d'un réseau)* **demander la ligne** = to bid; **le terminal a dû demander trois fois la ligne avant d'obtenir un créneau sur le réseau** = the terminal had to bid three times before there was a gap in transmissions on the network **(b)** *(nécessiter)* to require; **les systèmes informatiques sont très fragiles et demandent à être manipulés avec soin** = delicate computer systems require careful handling

◊ **se demander** *vpr* to wonder; **nous nous demandons tous jusqu'à quel point la sortie d'imprimante est correcte** = we all question how accurate the computer printout is

◊ **demandeur** *nm (au téléphone)* caller

démarrage *nm* start; **(système de) démarrage automatique** = autoboot; **équipement de secours à démarrage semi-automatique** = warm standby; **démarrage à froid** = cold boot *ou* cold start; **erreur au démarrage** = cold fault

◊ **démarrer** **1** *vi* to start **2** *vtr* to start (something); **démarrer quelque chose graduellement** = to phase something in

demi, -e *adj* half *ou* semi-

◊ **demi-additionneur** *nm* half adder *ou* two input adder; **demi-additionneur binaire** = binary half adder

◊ **demi-cadratin** *nm (imprimerie)* quad *ou* en space

◊ **demi-carte** *nf (carte demi-longueur)* half card

◊ **demi-espace** *nm* half space

◊ **demi-hauteur** *nf* half height; **unité de disquettes (de) demi-hauteur** = half-height drive

◊ **demi-intensité** *nf* half intensity

◊ **demi-longueur** *nf (demi-carte)* **carte demi-longueur** = half card

◊ **demi-mot** *nm* half word

◊ **demi-octet** *nm* nibble *ou* nybble

◊ **demi-teinte** *nf* halftone *ou* half-tone; **en demi-teinte** = halftone; *(procédé)* **gravure en demi-teinte** = halftone process; **ce livre est contient vingt planches en demi-teinte** = the book is illustrated with twenty halftones

démo *nf (démonstration)* demo

démocratique *adj* democratic; **réseau démocratique** = democratic network

démodé, -ée *adj* out of date

démodulateur *nm* demodulator; *voir aussi* MODULATEUR

◊ **démodulation** *nf* demodulation; *voir aussi* MODULATION

démon *nm (utilitaire UNIX)* daemon (disk and execution monitor)

démonstration *ou* **démo** *nf* demonstration *ou* demo; **faire une démonstration** = to demonstrate; **il a fait une démonstration du programme de gestion de fichiers** = he demonstrated the file management program; **disquette de démonstration** = demo disk; **logiciel de démonstration** *ou* **de démo** = demonstration software; **l'entreprise a distribué gratuitement un logiciel de démonstration qui permet de tout faire sauf sauvegarder les données** = the company gave away demonstration software that lets you do everything except save your data; **modèle de démonstration** = demonstration model; **version de démonstration** = demo disk

> grâce à la disquette de démonstration jointe à ce numéro, vous découvrirez par vous-même le nouveau système d'exploitation de Microsoft
> *l'Ordinateur Individuel*

démontage *nm* taking down; *(entre deux tâches)* takedown

◊ **démonter** *vtr* to take down; **démonter un disque en utilisant la fonction 'unmount'** = to unmount

démontrer *vtr* to demonstrate

démultiplexer *vtr* to demultiplex

◊ **démultiplexeur** *nm* demultiplexor

dénaire *adj* denary; **numération dénaire** = denary notation

dense *adj* dense *ou* compact

◊ **densité** *nf* density; **densité binaire** = bit density; **densité de caractère** = character density *ou* pitch; **densité des composants** = component density; **il y a une telle densité de composants sur la carte-mère** = component density is so high on this motherboard; **la densité des composants augmente avec l'expertise du fabricant** = component density increases with production expertise; **densité d'enregistrement** = recording density *ou* packing density; **densité de mémoire** = storage density; *(sur une ligne)* **densité du trafic** = traffic density; **bouton** *ou* **réglage de densité d'impression** = density dial; **si l'impression est trop pâle, réglez le bouton de densité (d'impression) sur le noir** = if the text fades, turn the density dial on the printer to full black; **disquette double densité (DD)** = double-density disk (DD); **disquette haute densité (HD)** = high density disk (HD); **mémoire** *ou* **support magnétique haute densité** = high density storage; **un disque dur est un support de haute densité par rapport à une bande perforée** = a hard disk is a high density storage medium compared to paper tape; *(vidéo disque)* **très haute densité** = very high density (VHD); **quadruple densité** = quad density; **disquette quadruple densité (QD)** = quad density disk (QD); **disquette à simple densité (SD)** = single density disk (SD)

◊ **densitomètre** *nm* densitometer

dépannage *nm* repair *ou* corrective maintenance

déparasitage *nm* *(blindage d'un câble)* RF shielding; **sans déparasitage, le signal transmis serait perturbé par les interférences** = without RF shielding, the transmitted signal would be distorted by the interference

départ *nm* start; **au départ** = at the beginning; **erreur au départ** = initial error; **langue de départ** = source language; **boucle avec retour automatique aux paramètres de départ** = self-resetting *ou* self-restoring loop; **point de départ** = starting point; *(du curseur)* **position de départ** = Home; **prix départ usine** = factory price *ou* price ex factory

dépassé, -ée *adj* out of date; **leur système informatique est totalement dépassé** = their computer system is years out of date; **ils utilisent toujours du matériel dépassé** = they are still using out-of-date equipment; *(d'un produit qui ne supporte pas certaines fonctions)* **version dépassée** = back-level

◊ **dépassement** *nm* *(de capacité)* overflow *ou* OV; **bit** *ou* **indicateur** *ou* **drapeau** *ou* **marque de dépassement de capacité** = overflow bit *ou* flag *ou* indicator; **contrôle de dépassement de capacité** = overflow check; **dépassement négatif** = underflow

dépendant, -e *adj* dependent; **procédé dépendant des résultats d'un autre procédé** = a process which is dependent on the result of another process; **dépendant du matériel** = hardware dependent; **le logiciel de communication est dépendant du matériel et ne fonctionne qu'avec un modem compatible Hayes** = the communications software is hardware dependent and will only work with Hayes-compatible modems; **dépendant du processeur** = processor-limited

déphasage *nm* phase displacement; **angle de déphasage** = phase angle

◊ **déphasé, -ée** *adj* out of phase

déplacement *nm* displacement *ou* shift *ou* relocation; *(d'une adresse relative)* float; **déplacement dynamique** = dynamic relocation (program); **caractère de déplacement** = shift character; **code de déplacement** = shift code; *(d'une adresse relative)* **facteur de déplacement** = float factor; **afficher (une image) par déplacement horizontal** = to pan; **modulation par déplacement de fréquence** = frequency shift keying (FSK); *(en ajoutant une adresse origine à une adresse relative)* **ré-adressage par déplacement** = float relocate

◊ **déplacer** *vtr* to move *ou* to displace *ou* to relocate; **(instruction de) déplacer un bloc** = move block; **déplacer de mémoire auxiliaire en mémoire centrale** = to roll in; **déplacer une souris (sur son tapis)** = to drag a mouse

◊ **se déplacer** *vpr* **se dépacer avec un téléphone sans cordon** = to roam

déposer *vtr* to deposit; **il faut déposer un exemplaire de toute nouvelle publication à la Bibliothèque Nationale** = a copy of each new book has to be deposited in the Bibliothèque Nationale; **déposer un copyright** = to copyright (a book)

◊ **dépôt** *nm* **(a)** deposit **(b)** *(d'un enduit)* deposition

dépouiller *vtr* *(enlever les codes de contrôle d'un message)* to strip (a message)

dérangement *nm* failure *ou* fault; **être en dérangement** = to malfunction; **ce modem est en dérangement** = the modem has broken down; **(marge de) tolérance aux dérangements** = fault tolerance

déréglage *nm* maladjustment; *(d'un appareil photo)* defocussing; *(d'un télécopieur)* **déréglage de la qualité d'impression** = hangover

◊ **dérégler** *vtr* to adjust badly; *(d'un appareil photo, etc.)* **dérégler la mise au point** = to defocus

dérivation *nf* **(a)** *(communication)* bridge *ou* bridging product; **mise en place d'une dérivation** = bridging **(b)** *(système de secours)* bypass; **il y a dérivation automatique lorsqu'une des machines tombe en panne** = there is an automatic bypass around any faulty equipment **(c)** *(d'une télévision câblée)* drop line

dérive *nf* *(changement dans un circuit)* drift

dérivé, -ée *adj* derived; **indexage dérivé** = derived indexing; **son dérivé** = derived sound; **voie dérivée en temps** = time derived channel

◊ **dériver (de)** *vi* *(venir de)* to derive (from)

dernier, -ière *adj* final; **apporter les dernières corrections à un document** = to make the final changes to a document; **saisir les derniers fichiers de données** = to keyboard the final data files; **dernier entré premier sorti** = last in first out (LIFO); *voir aussi* LIFO

déroulant, -e *adj* **liste déroulante** = drop-down list box; **menu déroulant** = pull-down menu *ou* drop-down menu; **on affiche le menu déroulant en cliquant sur la barre de menu au sommet de l'écran** = the pull-down menu is viewed by clicking on the menu bar at the top of the screen

déroulement *nm* **compteur de déroulement** = tape counter

◊ **dérouleur** *nm* **dérouleur de bande(s) magnétique(s)** = tape drive

déroutage *nm* **dispositif de déroutage** = diverter; **dispositif de déroutage d'appel** = call diverter

◊ **déroutement** *nm* *(communication)* **voie de déroutement** = alternate route

DES *(norme de cryptage de données)* Data Encryption Standard (DES) = S-box; *voir aussi* NORME

désaccord *nm* mismatch; **désaccord d'impédance** = impedance mismatch

désactivé, -ée *adj* disactivated *ou* disarmed; **état désactivé** = disarmed state

◊ **désactiver** *vtr* to disactivate *ou* to disarm

désaffecter *vtr* to deallocate

désaligné, -ée *adj* nonaligned *ou* out of alignment; **la bande est désalignée parce qu'un guide-bande est cassé** = the tape is out of alignment because one of the tape guides has broken; **tête de lecture désalignée** = nonaligned read head

désallouer *vtr (une ressource)* to deallocate *ou* to blast; **lorsque vous appuyez sur la touche de ré-initialisation, toutes les ressources sont désallouées** = when a reset button is pressed all resources are deallocated

désassemblage *nm* disassembling; **désassemblage de macro** = macro expansion

◊ **désassembler** *vtr* to disassemble

◊ **désassembleur** *nm* disassembler

descripteur *nm* descriptor; **descripteur de fichier** = file descriptor *ou* file label; **système de recherche** *ou* **de stockage par descripteurs** = aspect system

◊ **descriptif, -ive** *adj* **donnée descriptive** = physical parameter; **liste descriptive** = description list

◊ **description** *nf* **(a)** description; **le prospectus contient une description des services offerts par la société** = the leaflet describes the services the company can offer; **on trouve une description plus détaillée des spécifications à la fin du manuel** = the specifications are described in greater detail at the back of the manual **(b)** *(utilitaire)* **description de projet** = outliner; **langage de description de données** = data description language (DDL); **plusieurs des avantages d'un langage de description de données vient du fait qu'il s'agit d'un langage de deuxième génération** = many of DDL's advantages come from the fact that it is a second generation language; **langage de description de pages** = page description language (PDL)

désembrouillage *nm* de-scrambling

◊ **désembrouiller** *vtr* to de-scramble *ou* to decode

◊ **désembrouilleur** *nm* de-scrambler

déséquipement *nm* *(entre deux tâches)* takedown

design *nm* *(conception)* design; **le design a été complètement exécuté sur ordinateur** = the design project was entirely worked out on computer; **design d'un système** = system design; **design économique** = least cost design; **studio de design** = design studio

◊ **designer** *nm&f* designer

désordonné, -ée *adj* disorderly; **arrêt désordonné** *ou* **panne désordonnée** = disorderly close-down

despotique *adj* **réseau (avec synchronisation) despotique** = despotic network

DESQview ™ *(logiciel multitâche sous MS-DOS)* (multitasking function) DESQview ™

dessin *nm* **(a)** *(illustration ou image)* drawing *ou* picture; **vous pouvez voir le nouveau modèle sur ce dessin** = this picture shows the new design; **dessin assisté par ordinateur (DAO)** = computer-aided *ou* computer-assisted design; **dessin au trait** = line drawing; **on trouve dans ce livre des dessins au trait et des similigravures** = the book is illustrated with line drawings and halftones; **logiciel de dessin** = graphics software; drawing program; paint program; **j'ai fait une esquisse de notre nouveau logo en utilisant ce logiciel de dessin** = I drew a rough of our new logo with this paint program; **utilitaire de stockage de dessin** = scrapbook **(b)** *(représentation d'une forme)* pattern; **avec dessins** = patterned

> COMMENTAIRE: les logiciels de dessin ou de conception graphique travaillent normalement sur des images vectorielles

◊ **dessinateur, -trice** *adj* designer

◊ **dessiner** *vtr* to draw *ou* to design; **dessiner de nouveau** = to redraw *ou* to redesign

dessouder *vtr* to desolder

◊ **dessoudeur** *nm* desoldering tool

dessous *nm* bottom; *(pour papier d'imprimante)* **bac du dessous** = lower bin

dessus *nm* top; **dessus de pile** = top of stack; *(pour papier d'imprimante)* **bac du dessus** = upper bin

destinataire *nm&f* addressee

◊ **destination** *nf* destination

destructif, -ive *adj* destructive; **addition destructive** = destructive addition; **interférence destructive** = destructive interference; **lecture destructive** = destructive read *ou* readout; **non destructif** = non-destructive; **curseur non destructif** = non-destructive cursor; **l'écran devient rapidement illisible lorsqu'on utilise le curseur non destructif** = the screen quickly becomes unreadable when using a non-destructive cursor; **essai non destructif** = non-destructive test; **lecture non destructive** = non-destructive readout (NDR); **je vais effectuer une série de tests non destructifs sur votre machine; si tout se passe bien, vous pourrez vous en servir de nouveau** = I will carry out a number of non-destructive tests on your computer: if it passes, you can start using it again

◊ **destruction** *nf* destruction; **destruction accidentelle** = crash; **protégé contre toute destruction accidentelle** = crash-protected; **si vous vous servez d'un disque protégé contre la destruction accidentelle, vous ne perdrez jamais vos données** = if the disk is crash-protected, you will never lose your data; **destruction de fichier** = file deletion

détaché, -ée *adj* detached; **pièce détachée** = spare part

détail *nm* detail; **en détail** = in detail; **expliquer en détail** = to explain in detail

◊ **détaillé, -ée** *adj* detailed; **le catalogue présente une liste détaillée de tous les composants** = the catalogue lists all the components in detail

◊ **détailler** *vtr* to detail

détecté, -ée *adj* detected; **erreur détectée** = detected error; **erreur non détectée** = undetected error

◊ **détecter** *vtr* to detect *ou* to sense; **l'appareil peut détecter les signaux faibles émis par le transducteur** = the equipment can detect faint signals from the transducer; **l'erreur de programmation n'a été détectée qu'après un certain temps** = the programming error was undetected for some time; **le programme a pu détecter l'état du connecteur** = the condition of the switch was sensed by the program

◊ **détecteur** *nm* detector; sensor; **détecteur chromatique** = chroma detector; **détecteur d'infrarouge** = infrared detector; **détecteur de métal** = metal detector; **détecteur d'onde porteuse** = data carrier detect (DCD) (signal); **détecteur photoélectrique** *ou* **photosensible** = photosensor; **le détecteur de pression caché sous le tapis déclenche un système d'alarme si quelqu'un marche dessus** = the pressure pad under the carpet will set off the burglar alarm if anyone steps on it; **code détecteur d'erreurs** = error detecting code *ou* self-checking code; **commutateur détecteur** = sense switch

◊ **détection** *nf* detection *ou* sense; **détection automatique d'erreurs** = automatic error detection; **détection de collision** = collision detection; **détection d'enveloppe** = envelope detection; **détection d'erreurs** = error trapping *ou* error detection; **détection et correction d'erreurs** = error detection and correction (EDAC); **détection de limites** *ou* **de bordures** = edge detection; **codes de détection d'erreurs** = error detecting codes; **signal de détection de porteuse (du modem)** = data carrier detect (DCD); **l'appel est bloqué si le logiciel ne reçoit pas de signal de détection de porteuse** = the call is stopped if the software does not receive a DCD signal from the modem; *(pour stylo optique)* **symbole de détection** *ou* **zone de détection** = aiming symbol *ou* field

détérioration *nf* **(a)** corruption; **détérioration de données** = data corruption **(b)** *(disque)* crash; **protégé contre toute détérioration accidentelle** = crash-protected **(c)** *(d'un signal)* decay

◊ **détérioré, -ée** *adj (fichier)* damaged; *(données)* corrupted; *(disque)* crashed

◊ **détériorer** *vtr (fichier)* to damage; *(données)* to corrupt; **un problème de tension pendant l'accès au disque peut détériorer les données** = power loss during disk access can corrupt the data; **est-il possible de récupérer les fichiers détériorés?** = is it possible to repair the damaged files?

◊ **se détériorer** *vpr (disque)* to crash; *(données)* to become corrupt; *(signal)* to decay

détermination *nf* **détermination de priorité des tâches** = job scheduling

◊ **déterminé, -ée** *adj* determined; **enregistrement de longueur déterminée** = fixed-

length record; **mot de longueur déterminée** = fixed-length word; **déterminé d'avance** = predetermined

◊ **déterministe** *adj* deterministic

détritus *nm* garbage

détruire *vtr* **(a)** *(disque)* to crash **(b)** *(donnée ou fichier)* to erase *ou* to delete *ou* to wipe *ou* to kill *ou* to scrub *ou* to scratch; **(instruction de) détruire un fichier** = kill file; **détruire des données par superposition d'écriture** = to overwrite; **détruisez tous les fichiers avec l'extension .BAK** = scrub all files with the .BAK extension; **si vous reformatez, vous détruirez toutes les données du disque** = by reformatting you will wipe the disk clean

◊ **détruit, -e** *adj* **(a)** *(disque)* crashed **(b)** *(donnée ou fichier)* erased *ou* deleted *ou* wiped *ou* killed *ou* scrubbed *ou* scratched

deux *adj num & nm* two; **complément à deux** = two's complement; **instruction à deux adresses** = two-address instruction; **instruction à deux adresses plus une** = two-plus-one-address instruction; **file d'attente à deux entrées** *ou* **à deux extrémités** = double-ended queue *ou* deque; **en deux exemplaires** = in duplicate; **établir une facture en deux exemplaires** = to print an invoice in duplicate

◊ **deuxième** *adj num & nm* second; **ordinateurs de deuxième génération** = second generation computers

développement *nm* development; **développement d'un programme** = program development; **environnement de développement de programmes** = program development system; **logiciel de développement** = development software; **recherche et développement** = research and development; **temps de développement d'un nouveau produit** = development time

◊ **développer** *vtr* to develop; **développer un nouveau produit** = to develop a new product

◊ **développeur, -euse** *n* **développeur de logiciel** = software developer

déverminage *nm* debugging; **système de déverminage interactif** = interactive debugging system

◊ **déverminé, -ée** *adj* debugged; **programme déverminé** = debugged program

◊ **déverminer** *vtr* to debug

déverrouiller *vtr (donner accès à un fichier)* to unlock

déviation *nf* **(a)** alternate route **(b)** *(de rayon)* deflection

◊ **dévier** *vtr (rayon)* to deflect

dévideur *nm* streamer

devis *nm* quote *ou* estimate; **faire un devis** = to give a quote *ou* to give an estimate

Dewey *npr* **classification (suivant la méthode de) Dewey** = Dewey decimal classification

Dhrystone *(test comparatif de performance)* benchmark Dhrystone = Dhrystone benchmark

diacritique *adj* **un signe diacritique** = a diacritic

diagnostic *nm* **(a)** diagnosis *ou* diagnostic; **diagnostic (de cause) de défaillance** = problem diagnosis; **diagnostic d'erreurs** = error diagnosis; **diagnostic de localisation de panne** *ou* **de défaillance** = fault diagnosis; **diagnostic de la mémoire** = memory diagnostic; **diagnostic de système** = system check; **aide au diagnostic** = diagnostic aid; **circuit intégré** *ou* **puce de diagnostic** = diagnostic chip; **logiciel de diagnostic** = diagnostic program; **message de diagnostic** = diagnostic message; **message de diagnostic d'erreur** = diagnostic error message; **programme de diagnostic** = maintenance routine; **programme diagnostic de dysfonctionnement** = malfunction routine; **puce de diagnostic** = diagnostic chip; **ils font des recherches sur les puces de diagnostic destinées au contrôle des ordinateurs équipés de processeurs** = they are carrying out research on diagnostic chips to test computers that contain processors; **routine de diagnostic** = diagnostic routine; **test de diagnostic** = diagnostic test **(b) outils de diagnostic** = diagnostics *ou* system diagnostics; **outils de diagnostic du compilateur** = compiler diagnostics; **des outils de diagnostic de compilation bien conçus facilitent le débogage** = thorough compiler diagnostics make debugging easy; **outils de diagnostic d'erreurs** = error diagnostics

◊ **diagnostique** *adj* diagnostic

◊ **diagnostiquer** *vtr* to diagnose

diagonal, -e *adj* diagonal

◊ **diagonale** *nf* **coupe en diagonale** = diagonal cut

diagramme *nm* diagram *ou* chart *ou* flowchart *ou* schema *ou* graph; **diagramme en camembert** *ou* **en secteurs** = pie chart; **diagramme d'un circuit** = circuit diagram; **diagramme en colonnes** *ou* **en tuyaux d'orgue** = columnar graph *ou* bar graph; **les ventes du mois dernier avaient meilleure mine grâce à l'utilisation de diagrammes** = the sales for last month looked even better thanks to the use of presentation graphics; **diagramme de flux de données** = data flow diagram (DFD); **diagramme d'opérations** = flowchart; **diagramme fonctionnel** = functional diagram; **diagramme logique** = logical chart *ou* logical flowchart; **diagramme en secteurs** = pie chart; **diagramme de Venn** = Venn diagram; **sous forme d'un diagramme** = diagramatically *ou* in schematic form; **le tableau présente la courbe des ventes sous forme de diagramme** = the chart shows the sales pattern diagramatically

dialecte *nm* dialect

dialogue *nm* dialogue; *(entre chambre de contrôle et studio)* talkback; **boîte** *ou* **fenêtre de dialogue** = dialogue box; **dialogue vidéotex** = interactive videotext

◊ **dialogué, -ée** *adj* conversational *ou* interactive; **mode dialogué** = conversational *ou* interactive mode

◊ **dialoguer** *vi (ordinateurs)* to communicate (with) *ou* to talk (to)

diamant *nm* diamond; **diamant de lecture** = stylus

diamètre *nm* diameter

DIANE *(service d'information en ligne)* Direct Information Access Network for Europe (DIANE)

diaph *ou* **diaphragme** *nm (d'appareil photo)* **ouverture de diaphragme** *ou* **diaph** = f-number

diaphonie *nf* crosstalk *ou* babble; **diaphonie induite** = crossfire; **il y avait une telle diaphonie que le signal était illisible** = the crosstalk was so bad, the signal was unreadable

> sa gamme d'appareils s'est grandement élargie avec, en particulier, un suppresseur de diaphonie
>
> *Audio Tech*

diaphragme *nm* diaphragm; **le diaphragme d'un microphone capte les ondes sonores** = the diaphragm in the microphone picks up sound waves; *(d'appareil-photo)* **ouverture de diaphragme** *ou* **diaph** = f-number

diapo *nf* = DIAPOSITIVE slide *ou* transparency; **magnétophone avec interface synchro pour projecteur de diapos** = slide/sync recorder; **diapo-son** = audio slide

diapositive *ou* **diapo** *nf* slide *ou* transparency; **diapositive couleur** = colour transparency *ou* colour slide; **projecteur pour diapositives** = slide projector *ou* diascope

diazocopie *nf* diazo (process)

dibit *nm (deux bits binaires)* dibit

dichotomie *nf* dichotomy; **recherche par dichotomie** = binary search *ou* binary chop *ou* dichotomizing search

◊ **dichotomique** *adj* **recherche dichotomique** = binary search *ou* binary chop *ou* dichotomizing search

dichroïque *adj* dichroic

Dictaphone ™ *nm* dictating machine

dictée *nf* dictation; **prendre en dictée** = to take dictation *ou* to take down

◊ **dicter** *vtr* to dictate; **dicter une lettre à quelqu'un** = to dictate a letter to someone; **machine à dicter** = dictating machine

dictionnaire *nm* dictionary; **dictionnaire-répertoire de données** = data dictionary/directory (DD/D); **dictionnaire par thèmes** = thesaurus

didacticiel *nm* courseware; **formation à l'aide de didacticiel** = programmed learning

Didot *npr (imprimerie)* **11 points Didot** = pica (NOTE: un point Didot = 0,324mm; 11 points Didot = environ 12 points anglais)

diélectrique *adj* dielectric

DIF *(format de tableur)* Data Interchange Format (DIF); **fichier DIF** = DIF file

différé *nm* **(a) en différé** = off-line; **impression en différé** = off-line printing *ou* print spooling; **mémoire auxiliaire pour impression en différé** = spooler *ou* spooling device; **traitement en différé** = off-line processing *(Radio, TV)* pre-recorded (programme); **(système avec facilité de) transmission en différé** = store and forward (system)

◊ **différé, -ée** *adj* deferred; **mode différé** = deferred mode; **visualisation en temps différé** = time shift viewing

différence *nf* **(a)** difference; **il existe une grande différence entre les deux produits** = the two products differ considerably **(b) différence de potentiel** = potential difference

◊ **différent, -e** *adj* different; **être différent (de)** = to differ (from); **notre gamme de produits est d'une conception entièrement différente de celle des modèles japonais** = our product range is quite different in design from the Japanese models

◊ **différentiel, -elle** *adj* differential; **modulation différentielle par impulsions et codage (MIC)** = differential pulse code modulation (PCM)

◊ **différer** *vi* to differ

diffusé, -ée *adj* **onde diffusée** = scatter

◊ **diffuser** *vtr* **(a)** to send out; **la société a diffusé un communiqué au sujet de la nouvelle imprimante laser** = the company sent out a news release about the new laser printer **(b)** *(radio, etc.)* to broadcast; **il a diffusé les dernières informations à la radio** *ou* **via le réseau étendu** = he broadcast the latest news over the radio *ou* over the WAN

◊ **se diffuser** *vpr (gaz ou fumée)* to diffuse

◊ **diffusion** *nf* **(a)** diffusion; **entreprise de diffusion d'informations grand public** = common carrier **(b) diffusion radiophonique** = broadcast; **diffusion sur (tout) un réseau** = networking; **réseau de diffusion** = broadcast network; **satellite de diffusion directe** = direct broadcast satellite (DBS); **technique de diffusion par satellite** = broadcast satellite technique **(c)** *(de gaz ou fumée)* **il y a eu diffusion du produit chimique dans le substrat** = the chemical was diffused into the substrate **(d) dopage par diffusion** = (doping by) diffusion; **jonction pn à diffusion** = diffused pn-junction; **zone interface pn à diffusion** = diffused pn-junction

Digipulse ™ *nm* **téléphone Digipulse** = Digipulse telephone

digital, -e *adj* digital; **écran digital** = digital display; *voir aussi* NUMÉRIQUE

dimension *nf* dimension *ou* size *ou* measurements; **noter les dimensions d'un paquet** = to write down the measurements of a package; **dispositif** *ou* **composant de très petite dimension** = microdevice; **dimension d'affichage** = display size; **dimension d'un champ** = field length; *(imprimerie)* **dimension (en points) du corps d'un texte** = body size; **dimension de l'écran** = screen size; **dimension d'un enregistrement** = record length; **dimension d'un fichier** = file length; **dimension d'un registre** = register length; **à deux dimensions** = two-dimensional; **tableau à deux dimensions** = two-dimensional array; **à trois dimensions** = three-dimensional *ou* **3D**; **calcul des dimensions** = dimensioning; **le calcul des dimensions du tableau se fait à cette ligne-ci** = array dimensioning occurs at this line; *(d'une image ou d'une photo)* **modification des dimensions** = sizing

◊ **dimensionnement** *nm (d'image ou photo)* sizing; **les photos peuvent être éditées par découpage, dimensionnement, retouche, etc.** = photographs can be edited by cropping, sizing, touching up, etc.

◊ **dimensionner** *vtr (image ou photo)* to size

diminuteur *nm (d'une soustraction)* subtrahend

DIN *(normes allemandes pour l'industrie)* Deutsche Industrienorm

Dingbat ™ *(police de caractères spéciaux)* Dingbat ™

diode *nf* diode; **diode électroluminescente** = light-emitting diode (LED); *(imprimante LED)* **imprimante à diodes** = LED printer

petit clavier auxiliaire où chaque touche est accompagnée d'une diode
Audio Tech

des diodes électroluminescentes permettent de contrôler si l'installation s'est effectuée correctement
Electronique

dioptrie *nf* dioptre, *US* diopter

◊ **dioptrique** *adj* dioptre, *US* diopter; **lentille dioptrique** = dioptre lens

DIP *(procédé de traitement d'image)* Document Image processing (DIP)

DIP = DUAL-IN-LINE PACKAGE **commutateur DIP** = DIP switch; *voir aussi* BROCHE

dipôle *nm* dipole

DIR = DIRECTORY; *(commande MS-DOS de recherche de fichier)* DIR (command)

direct *nm* **en direct** = direct; **appeler** *ou* **téléphoner en direct** = to dial direct; **vous pouvez appeler New York en direct depuis Londres** = you can dial New York direct from London; **émission en direct** = live broadcast, *US* program shown in real time

◊ **direct, -e** *adj* direct; **accès direct** = direct access; random access; **accès direct à la mémoire (DMA)** = direct memory access (DMA); **transfert des données par accès direct (à la mémoire) entre la mémoire principale et le second processeur** = direct memory access transfer between the main memory and the second processor; **accès direct à la mémoire par vol de cycle** = DMA cycle stealing; **contrôleur d'accès direct à la mémoire** = DMA controller; **voie d'accès direct à la mémoire** = direct memory access channel; **accès direct au réseau** = direct outward dialling; **accès direct au système** = direct inward dialling; **fichiers à accès direct** = random access files; **mémoire** *ou* **support à accès direct** = random access storage *ou* direct access storage device (DASD); **les lecteurs de disquettes permettent l'accès direct des données alors qu'une bande magnétique en permet l'accès séquentiel** = disk drives are random access, magnetic tape is sequential access memory; *(téléphone)* **système d'acheminement direct des appels** = direct dialling; **adressage direct** = direct addressing; **adresse directe** = one-level address *ou* direct (access) address *ou* zero-level address *ou* immediate address; **adresse de référence directe** = direct reference address; **instruction à adresse directe** = one address instruction *ou* single address instruction; **code d'instruction à adresse directe** = single address code; **codage direct** = direct coding; **code direct** = direct code *ou* one-level code *ou* specific code *ou* single address code; **commande numérique directe** = direct digital control (DDC); *(d'un modem)* **connexion directe** = direct connect; **satellite de diffusion directe** = direct broadcast satellite (DBS); **impression directe** = direct impression; **programme** *ou* **sous-programme d'insertion directe** = direct-insert routine *ou* subroutine; **instruction directe** = direct instruction; **lecture-écriture directe** = demand reading/writing; *(transmission en ligne droite)* **ligne directe** = line of sight; **mode direct** = direct mode *ou* raw mode; **publicité directe** = direct mailing; **saisie directe de données (par clavier)** *ou* **entrée directe de données** = direct data entry (DDE); **sous-programme direct** = one-level subroutine; **traitement direct (des données)** = random processing; **transfert direct** = direct change-over *ou* direct transfer; **transmission directe de signaux** = DC signalling

◊ **directement** *adv* directly *ou* direct

directeur, -trice 1 *n* director; **le directeur de l'institut de recherche informatique gouvernemental** = the director of the government computer research institute; **elle a été nommée directrice de l'organisation** = she was appointed director of the organization; **directeur (du service) informatique** = computer manager; *(film ou télévision)* **directeur de production** = executive producer; **directeur de programme** = administrator; **directeur technique** = technical director **2** *adj* **schéma directeur** = outline flowchart; **terminal directeur** = executive terminal

◊ **direction** *nf (sens)* direction; **direction du flux** = flow direction

◊ **directionnel, -elle** *adj* directional; **antenne**

directionnelle = directional antenna; **capteur directionnel** = horn; *(antenne ou microphone)* **empreinte directionnelle** = directional pattern; **(dispositif de) guidage directionnel** = feed horn

directive *nf (instruction)* directive statement

dirigé, -ée *adj* directed; *(balayage cavalier)* **balayage dirigé** = directed scan

◊ **diriger** *vtr* **(a)** *(pointer)* to direct; **la camera est dirigée sur le premier plan** = the camera is focused on the foreground **(b)** *(gérer)* to manage

discordance *nf* mismatch

discret, -ète *adj* discrete; **le mot de données est formé de bits discrets** = the data word is made up of discrete bits; **avis de réception de copie discrète** = blind copy receipt

discrétionnaire *adj* discretionary

disjoint, -e *adj* disjointed

disjoncteur *nm (de courant)* circuit breaker; **disjoncteur à air** = air circuit breaker; **système disjoncteur progressif** = fail soft system

disjonction *nf* disjunction *ou* exjunction; *(fonction logique)* **fonction de disjonction** = non-equivalence function *ou* NEQ function

disparaître *vi* to disappear; **faire disparaître** = to remove; **faire disparaître de l'écran** = to clear (the screen) *ou* to zap; **tapez CLS pour faire disparaître ce qu'il y a sur l'écran** = type CLS to clear the screen; **faire disparaître progressivement** = to fade out

dispersé, -ée *adj* scattered; **chargement dispersé de données** = scatter load

◊ **dispersion** *nf* dispersion; **dispersion chromatique** = chromatic dispersion; **dispersion modale** = mode dispersion; **routage par dispersion** = flooding

disponibilité *nf* **(a)** availability; **(période de) disponibilité dans le cycle** = cycle availability; *(d'un appareil)* **temps de disponibilité** = available time; **temps de non disponibilité** = outage **(b)** capacity; **disponibilité d'adressage** = addressing capacity

◊ **disponible** *adj* **(a)** available; *(en mémoire)* **liste des emplacements disponibles** = uncommitted storage list; *(en programmation orientée objet)* **objet disponible** = instance; **puissance maximale** *ou* **réelle disponible** = available power; **liste des ressources disponibles** = available list; **temps disponible** = available time **(b)** *(d'un dispositif)* **configuration disponible** = configured-in

◊ **disposé, -ée** *adj* set *ou* laid out; **disposé en tableau** *ou* **en table** *ou* **en colonnes** = (set) in tabular form *ou* in columns

◊ **disposer** *vtr* to set *ou* to lay out; **disposer en réseau** = to network; **disposer en tableau** *ou* **en table, en colonnes** = to set in tabular form, in columns

dispositif *nm* device; **dispositif d'affichage** = readout device; **dispositif anticopie** = copy protect device; **toutes les disquettes sont munies d'un dispositif anticopie** = all disks are copy protected; **dispositif anti-écho** = echo suppressor; **dispositif antirebond** = de-bounce (device); **dispositif à champ programmable** = field programmable device; **dispositif de compression-expansion** *ou* **dispositif concentrateur-déconcentrateur (de données vidéo)** = compressor/expander *ou* compandor; **dispositif à couplage de charge** = charge coupled device (CCD); **dispositif d'effacement** = eraser; **dispositif d'entrée-sortie** = input-output device *ou* I/O device; **dispositif externe** = external device; **dispositif de fin de ligne** = line terminator; **dispositif (électronique) d'identification** = personal identification device (PID); **dispositif intégré** = integrated device; *(scanner)* **dispositif de lecture par balayage** = scanning device; **dispositif de protection (contre la copie)** = copy protect device; **dispositif de protection d'écriture (de fichier)** = file protect tab; *(téléphone)* **dispositif de réacheminement** *ou* **de déroutage d'appel** = call diverter; **dispositif de sortie** = output device; **dispositif de transfert** *ou* **de déroutage** = diverter; **dispositif de transfert d'appel** = call diverter; **dispositif transistorisé** *ou* **à semi-conducteurs** = solid-state device; **dispositif (à bascule) de type D** = D-type flip-flop

disposition *nf (arrangement)* layout; **disposition des touches d'un clavier** = keyboard layout; **le logiciel de PAO permet à l'utilisateur de juger de la bonne disposition d'une page** = the DTP package allows the user to see if the overall page balance is correct

disque *nm* **(a)** *(disque magnétique)* disk; *(disque compact)* disc; *(disque simple ou plateau de disque dur)* platter; *(disque audionumérique lu par faisceau laser)* **disque compact** *ou* **disque CD** = compact disc *ou* CD; **disque dur** = hard disk; *(unité)* (hard) disk drive; **disque dur amovible** = removable hard disk; disk cartridge; **disque dur fixe** *ou* **non amovible** = fixed disk; **carte de disque dur** = hard card; **modèle d'ordinateur avec disque dur** = hard disk model; **système d'exploitation utilisant un disque dur** = disk-based operating system; **un disque dur est un support de haute densité par rapport à une bande perforée** = a hard disk is a high density storage medium compared to paper tape; **disque magnétique** = magnetic disk; **disque mémoire** = storage disk; **disque optique** = laser disk *ou* optical disk; **disque original** = master disk *ou* magnetic master; **disque RAM** = RAM disk *ou* silicon disk *ou* virtual disk; **les résultats comptables ont été transférés sur le disque de sauvegarde** = the account results were copied to the backup disk; *(disquette)* **disque souple** = flexible disk *ou* floppy disk *ou* floppy *ou* FD; **disque de travail** *ou* **de manoeuvre** *ou* **d'enregistrement** = work disk; **disque vidéo** = videodisk; **disque vierge** = blank disk; **disque virtuel** = virtual disk *ou* RAM disk *ou* silicon disk; **disque (dur) Winchester** = Winchester disk; **disque Winchester amovible** = removable Winchester; **accès au disque** = disk access; **gestion des accès aux disques** = disk access management; **contrôleur de disque** = disk controller; **carte contrôleur de disque** = disk-controller card; **cartouche disque** = disk cartridge; **crash** *ou* **panne totale d'un disque** = disk crash; **fichier sur disque** = disk file; **formatage de disque** = disk formatting; **formater un disque** = to format a disk; **lecteur de disques compacts** *ou* **de disques CD** = compact disc player; **mémoire à disque** = disk memory; **perforation de disque** = hard-sectoring; **perforations de marquage (du bord) d'un disque** = disk index holes; **piste d'un disque** = disk track; **disque de quatre-vingts pistes** = eighty-track disk; **plateau de disque dur** = platter; **répertoire des fichiers d'un disque** = disk catalogue; **le nom d'un fichier qui est effacé disparaît aussi du répertoire du disque** = the entry in the disk catalogue is removed when the file is deleted; **saisie directe sur disque, par clavier** = keyboard to disk entry *ou* key-to-disk; **secteur de disque** = disk sector; **système d'exploitation de disque** = disk operating system (DOS); **table (de classement) des fichiers du disque** = disk map; **tête de lecture de disque** = disk playback head; **tri sur disque** = external sort; **unité de disque** = disk unit; **qui utilise un disque** = disk-based; **système qui utilise un disque** = disk-based system; **qui n'utilise pas de disque** *ou* **sans disque** = diskless; **système qui n'utilise pas de disque** = diskless system; **ils veulent créer un poste de travail qui n'utilise pas de disque** = they want to create a diskless workstation **(b)** *(non magnétique)* record; **changeur de disques automatique** = record changer; **nouveaux disques** = new releases

COMMENTAIRE : les disques sont faits de métal ou de verre recouvert d'un composé magnétisable; chaque disque possède une tête de lecture/écriture qui se déplace sur la surface pour accéder aux données enregistrées

le disque dur fait désormais partie du quotidien: il est devenu un élément indispensable, voire vital, du poste de travail
L'Ordinateur Individuel

disquette *nf* disk *ou* diskette *ou* floppy disk *ou* floppy *ou* flexible disk *ou* FD; **microdisquette** = microfloppy; **minidisquette** = minidisk; **disquette compatible** = compatible disk; **disquette non compatible** = alien disk; **disquette double densité (DD)** = double density disk (DD); **disquette haute densité (HD)** = high density disk (HD); **disquette quadruple densité (QD)** = quad density disk (QD); **disquette simple densité** = single density disk (SD); **disquette (à) double face** = double-sided disk; **disquette de 3,5 pouces** = 3.5 inch disk; **disquette de 5,25 pouces** = 5.25 inch disk; **disquette de huit pouces** = eight-inch disk; **disquette (de) mémoire** = storage disk; **disquette de nettoyage** = head cleaning disk; **il faut passer la disquette de nettoyage une fois par semaine** = use a head cleaning disk every week; **vous aurez des erreurs d'écriture si vous ne vous servez pas régulièrement de votre disquette de nettoyage** = write errors occur if you do not use a head cleaning kit regularly; **disquette de polices de caractères** *ou* **de fontes** = font disk; **disquette réversible** = flippy; **disquette de sauvegarde** = backup (disk); **disquette (de programme) système** = system disk; **contrôleur de disquettes** = disk controller *ou* floppy disk controller (FDC); **carte contrôleur de disquettes** = disk-controller card; **cartouche de disquette** = flexible disk cartridge; **crash** *ou* **panne totale d'une**

disquette = disk crash; **fichier sur disquette** = disk file; **formatage de disquette** = disk formatting; **formater une disquette** = to format a disk; **il faut formater toutes les nouvelles disquettes avant de les utiliser** = you have to format new disks before you can use them; **lecteur de disquette(s)** = (floppy) disk drive; disk unit; **lecteur de disquette(s) double face** = double-sided disk drive; **lecteur de disquettes de huit pouces** ou **de 5,25 pouces** ou **3,5 pouces** = eight-inch disk drive ou 5.25 inch disk drive ou 3.5 inch disk drive; **lecteur de disquettes externe** = external disk drive; **mémoire à disquette** = disk memory ou storage; **piste d'une disquette** = disk track; **disquette (de) quarante pistes** = forty-track disk; **secteur de disquette** = disk sector; **système utilisant des disquettes** = disk-based system; **système d'exploitation utilisant des disquettes** = disk-based operating system; **système qui n'utilise pas de disquette** = diskless system; **tête de lecture** ou **de lecture-écriture de disquettes** = disk head; **unité de disquette(s)** = disk drive

dissipateur nm **dissipateur thermique** = heat sink

distance nf distance; **distance entre signaux** = signal distance; **distance focale** = focal length; **distance de Hamming** = Hamming distance; **à distance** = distant ou remote; **accès à distance** = remote access; **appel de procédure à distance** ou **appel RPC** = remote procedure call (RPC); **console** ou **poste de commande** ou **périphérique à distance** = remote console ou device; **contrôle à distance** ou **pilotage à distance** = remote control; **logiciel de prise de contrôle à distance** ou **de pilotage à distance** = remote control software; **ce logiciel de prise de contrôle à distance travaille sous Windows et me permet d'utiliser de chez moi le PC de mon bureau relié par modem** = this remote control software will work with Windows and lets me operate my office PC from home over a modem link; **lancement de tâches à distance** = remote job entry (RJE); **les utilisateurs peuvent imprimer leurs rapports sur des imprimantes à distance** = users can print reports on remote printers; **les imprimantes à distance sont reliées par câbles** = the distant printers are connected with cables; **modem à distance de transmission limitée** = limited distance modem; **réseau à distance** ou **réseau étendu** = wide area network (WAN); **réseau à grande distance** = long haul network; **terminal à distance** = remote terminal

◊ **distant, -e** adj distant ou far; **plusieurs postes de travail à distance sont connectées au réseau, chacune disposant d'une fenêtre sur le disque dur** = several remote stations are connected to the network and each has its own window onto the hard disk

distorsion nf distortion ou aberration ou breakup; **distorsion d'amplitude** = amplitude distortion; **distorsion en barillet** ou **en oreiller** ou **en coussinet** = barrel distortion ou pin cushion distortion; **distorsion géométrique** = geometric distortion; **distorsion d'harmoniques** = harmonic distortion; **distorsion de l'image** = image distortion; **distorsion due au retard du signal** = delay distortion

distribuer vtr to distribute ou to circulate

◊ **distributeur** nm (appareil) dispenser; **distributeur automatique (de cigarettes, etc.)** = automatic vending machine; (de parking, etc.) **distributeur de billets** = ticket machine; **distributeur automatique de billets de banque (DAB)** = cash dispenser; cashpoint

◊ **distribution** nf (a) distribution; (télévision ou téléphone) **centre de distribution** = distribution point; (informatique) **réseau de distribution** = distribution network (b) (de connecteurs) **tableau de distribution** = plugboard ou patchboard; (téléphonique) **tableau de distribution principal** = main distributing frame (c) (film ou théâtre) casting; **responsable de la distribution** = casting director

divergence nf divergence

diversité nf diversity

divisé, -ée adj (a) divided ou split ou partitioned; **écran divisé** = split screen; **fichier divisé en plusieurs parties** = partitioned file (b) (math) **vingt-et-un divisé par trois égale sept** = twenty-one divided by three gives seven

◊ **diviser** vtr (a) to divide ou to partition ou to split (b) (math) **diviser un nombre par quatre** = to divide a number by four

◊ **diviseur** nm (a) divider ou dividor ou splitter; **diviseur optique** = beam splitter; **diviseur de fréquence** = frequency divider (b) (math) divisor

◊ **division** nf (a) division ou partition (b) (math) division

divulguer vtr to leak

dix adj num & nm ten; **complément à dix** = ten's complement

10Base2 (norme IEEE pour Ethernet avec câble coaxial fin) 10Base2

10Base5 (norme IEEE pour Ethernet avec câble coaxial lourd) 10Base5

10BaseT (norme IEEE pour Ethernet avec câble en paires torsadées sans blindage) 10BaseT

DLL (bibliothèque dynamique des liens sous Windows et OS/2) Dynamic Link Library (DLL) (utility program); **le traitement de texte appelle le vérificateur d'orthographe stocké dans la (bibliothèque) DLL** = the word-processor calls a spell-check program that is stored as a DLL; **fichier DLL** = DLL file

DMA = DIRECT MEMORY ACCESS **contrôleur DMA (d'accès direct à la mémoire)** = DMA controller; **accès direct à la mémoire par vol de cycle** = DMA cycle stealing

DNS (base de données des adresses et des domaines dans Internet) Domain Name System (DNS)

document *nm* document *ou* copy; **document définitif** = finished document; **document imprimé** = printed document; **document monté** *ou* **créé (à partir de paragraphes standard)** = boilerplate; **montage d'un document (à partir de paragraphes standard)** = boilerplating; **document original** *ou* **d'origine** = source document; *(format de document IBM)* **architecture de description de document** = document content architecture (DCA); **classer** *ou* **archiver des documents** = to file documents; **(code de) fin de document** = end of document *ou* end of file (EOF); **fusion** *ou* **assemblage de documents** = document assembly *ou* document merge; **lecteur de documents** = document reader; **projecteur de documents opaques** = episcope *ou* epidiascope; **récupération** *ou* **régénération de document** = document recovery; **système de recherche de documents** = document retrieval system; **traitement de document** = document processing

◊ **documentaire** *adj* **recherche documentaire** = data retrieval *ou* information retrieval (IR); **recherche documentaire en ligne** = on-line information retrieval; **centre de recherche documentaire** = information retrieval centre; **système de recherche documentaire** = document retrieval system

◊ **documentation** *nf* documentation; **documentation relative à l'utilisation d'un programme** = program documentation; **programme avec documentation en ligne** = self-documenting program

◊ **documenter** *vtr* to document

dollar *nm* dollar; **signe du dollar ($)** = dollar sign

domaine *nm* **(a)** domain; *(dans Internet)* **base de données des adresses et des domaines** = domain name system (DNS) **(b)** **domaine de fréquence** = frequency domain **(c)** **domaine public** = public domain (PD); *(non protégé par un copyright)* **oeuvre qui est dans le domaine public** = work which is out of copyright *ou* in the public domain; **programme du domaine public** = program which is in the public domain

domestique *adj* domestic; **ordinateur domestique** = home computer; **satellite domestique** = domestic satellite

domicile *nm* home; **consultation des comptes à domicile** = home banking

dommage *nm* damage; **les dommages causés par la panne d'électricité s'élèvent à environ 100 millions de francs** = the breakdown of the electricity supply caused damage estimated at 100 million francs; **subir des dommages** = to suffer damage

domotique *nf* integrated home system

donnée(s) *nf(pl)* **(a)** *(valeur ou chaîne non réductible)* **donnée absolue** = atom **(b)** data *ou* information; **données agrégées** = data aggregate; **données alphanumériques** = alphanumeric data; **données biaisées** = biased data; **données brutes** = raw data; **données chaînées** = concatenated data set; **données de commande** *ou* **de contrôle** = control

data; **données constantes** *ou* **permanentes** = fixed data; **données d'entrée** = input (data); **données graphiques** = graphic data; **données incrémentielles** = incremental data; **données numériques** *ou* **numérisées** = digital data; **données orientées** = biased data; **données permanentes** *ou* **de base** = master data *ou* fixed data; **(nombre de) données reçues** = incoming traffic; **données reliées en chaîne** = concatenated data set; **données relatives** = relative data; **données saisies** = (computer) input; **données de sortie** = computer output; **données structurées** = data aggregate; **données supravocales** = data above voice (DAV); **données de type général** = abstract data type; **la pile est une structure de données de type général, elle peut stocker des données de tous types comme des nombres entiers ou des adresses** = the stack is a structure of abstract data types, it can store any type of data from an integer to an address; **accéder aux données** = to access data; **l'utilisateur doit utiliser un mot de passe pour accéder aux données** = a user needs a password to access data; **accès aux données** = data access; **gestion d'accès aux données** = data access management; **acheminement de données** = data routing; **acquisition de données** = data acquisition; **affichage de données** = information output; information display; **analyse de données** = data analysis; **autonomie des données** = data independence; **banque de données** = databank; **basculer des données** = to exchange data; **base de données** = database; *voir aussi* BASE; **bloc de données** = data block; **bus de données** = data bus *ou* data highway; **cartouche de données** = data cartridge; **chaînage de données** = data chaining; **champ de données** = data field; **chemin des données** = data path; **chiffrage** *ou* **chiffrement de données** = data encryption; **collecte de données** = data collection; **plate-forme de collecte de données** = data collection platform; **collecteur de données** = data sink; **ligne de communication de données** = dataline; **centre de commutation des données** = data switching exchange; **compactage de données** = data compacting; **compression de données** = data compression; **les scanners utilisent la technique dite de compression de données qui peut réduire du tiers la mémoire nécessaire** = scanners use a technique called data compression which manages to reduce, even by a third, the storage required; **contrôle de données** = data control; **conversion de données** = data translation; **corruption de données** = data corruption; **la corruption de données sur la disquette a rendu le fichier impossible à lire** = data corruption on the disk has made one file unreadable; **chaque fois qu'on met le système sous tension, il y a corruption de données** = data corruption occurs each time the motor is switched on; **création de données** = data origination; **cryptage de données** = data encryption; **norme** *ou* **standard de cryptage de données** = data encryption standard (DES); *(d'un programme en COBOL)* **rubrique de déclaration des données** = data division; **(symbole) délimiteur de données** = data delimiter; **langage de description de données** = data description language (DDL); **plusieurs des avantages d'un langage de description de données viennent du fait qu'il s'agit d'un langage de deuxième génération** = many of DDL's advantages come from the fact that it is a second generation language; **détérioration de données** = data corruption; **les coupleurs acoustiques sont plus susceptibles aux détériorations de données que les modems branchés directement sur la ligne** = acoustic couplers suffer from data corruption more than the direct connect form of modem; **dictionnaire-répertoire de données** = data dictionary/directory (DD/D); **échanger** *ou* **permuter des données** = to exchange data; **circuit d'échange de données** = data circuit; **élément de données** = data element *ou* data item; **chaîne d'éléments de données** = data element chain; **émetteur de données** = data source; **enregistrement de données** = data record; **enregistrement (automatique et chronologique) de données** = data logging; **entrée de données** = data input *ou* data entry; **bus d'entrée de données** = data input bus (DIB); **routine d'entrée** *ou* **d'introduction de données** = input routine; **erreur de données** = data error; **à données erronées, résultats erronés** *ou* **des données douteuses produisent des résultats douteux** = garbage in garbage out (GIGO); **extraction de données** = data retrieval *ou* information retrieval (IR); **fiabilité des données** = data reliability; **fichier de données** = data file; **fichier de données externe** = external data file; **il faut analyser le fichier de données** = the data file has to be analysed; **file d'attente des données d'entrée** = input work queue; **(code de) fin de données** = end of data (EOD); **flot de données** = data stream; **flux de données** *ou* **flow; diagramme de flux de données** = data flow diagram (DFD); **format de données** = data format; **génération de données** = data origination; **gestion de données** = data management; **gestionnaire de données** = data administrator; **hiérarchie des données** = data hierarchy; **système avec intégration de données** = firmware; **intégrité des données** = data integrity; **un problème de tension pendant l'accès au disque peut faire perdre l'intégrité des données** = power loss during disk access can corrupt the data; **introduction de données** = data input *ou* data entry; **lecture optique de données numériques** = digital optical reading (DOR); **liaison de données** = data link; **liaison de données en chaîne** = data chaining; **contrôle de liaison de données** = data link control; **couche de liaison de données** = data link layer; **langage de manipulation de données** = data manipulation language (DML); **mémoire de données** = data memory *ou* storage; **mise en mémoire de données** = data storage; **migration de données** *ou* **transfert de données (sur dispositif hors ligne)** = data migration; **nettoyage des données** = data cleaning; **niveau de données** = data level; **ordinogramme de données** = data flowchart; **l'ordinogramme des données nous a permis d'améliorer nos résultats à l'aide d'une meilleure structure** = the data flowchart allowed us to improve throughput, by using a better structure; **partage de données; données partagées** = data sharing; **permuter des données** = to exchange data; **pointeur (de position) de données** = data pointer; **(onde) porteuse de données** = data carrier; **préparation des données** = data preparation; **protection des données** = data protection; **qualité des données** = data reliability; **activé par reconnaissance des données** = data-driven; **récupérer des données (et les transférer dans un registre)** = to collect transfer; **réduction de données** = data reduction; **registre de données** = data register; **réseau de transmission de données** = data network; **routage de données** = data routing; **saisie de données** = data input *ou* data capture; **saisie directe de données (au clavier)** *ou* **entrée directe de données** = direct data entry (DDE); **les données ont été saisies** = the data has been entered; **les données sont saisies sur l'un des nombreux postes de travail** = data is input at one of several workstations; **sécurité des données** = data security *ou* data protection; **source de donnés** = data source; **stockage de données** = data storage *ou* information storage; **stockage de données sur disque** *ou* **disquette** = disk storage; **stockage et restitution de données** = information storage and retrieval (ISR); **structure des données** = data structure *ou* information structure; **structure dynamique de données** = dynamic data structure; **structure hiérarchique de données** = data hierarchy; **support de données** = data *ou* information medium; **support de données d'un fichier** = file storage; **(mémoire) tampon de données** = data buffer; **traduction de données** = data translation; **traitement de données** = data processing (DP *ou* dp) *ou* information processing; **traitement décentralisé des données** = decentralized data processing; **traitement électronique de données** = electronic data processing (EDP); **capacité** *ou* **facilité de traitement électronique de données** = EDP capability *ou* electronic data processing capability; **vitesse de traitement de données** = data rate; **trajet des données** = data path; **transaction de données** = data transaction; **transfert de données** = data transfer *ou* data migration; **transfert des données par accès direct (à la mémoire) entre la mémoire principale et le second processeur** = direct memory access transfer between the main memory and the second processor; **bus de transfert de données** = data highway; **vitesse de transfert de données** *ou* **débit de données** = data transfer rate; **transmission de données** = data communication(s); **transmission de données vocales** = data in voice (DIV); **transmission de données subvocales** = data under voice (DUV); **arrêt de transmission de données** = data break; *(causé par un défaut du support magnétique)* data check; **canal de transmission de données** = data channel; **adaptateur de canal de transmission de données** = data adapter unit; **connexion pour transmission de données** = data connection; *(causée par un défaut du support magnétique)* **brève interruption de transmission de données** = data check; **lignes de transmission de données** = bus data lines; **réseau de transmission de données** = data communications network; **service de transmission de données** = data services; **signaux de transmission de données** = data signals; **(mémoire) tampon de transmission de données** = data communications buffer; **vitesse de transmission de données** = data rate *ou* data signalling rate; **voie de transmission de données** = data path; **type de données** = data type; **validation de données** = data validation; **validation** *ou* **vérification de données** = data vetting; **signal de validation de données transmises** = data strobe; *(en mémoire)* **zone de données** = data area *ou* data field

donner *vtr* to give; **donner un avertissement** = to issue a warning; **donner une commande** *ou* **une**

instruction = to give an instruction *ou* a command *ou* an order

dopage *nm* doping; **dopage par diffusion** = (doping by) diffusion

◊ **dopant** *nm* dopant; **enduit d'un dopant** = doped

◊ **dopé, -ée** *adj* doped

◊ **doper** *vtr* to dope

DOS = DISK OPERATING SYSTEM **système (d'exploitation) DOS** = DOS; **lancez le système DOS après la mise en route de l'ordinateur** = boot up the DOS after you switch on the PC; *(développé par Microsoft)* **système d'exploitation MS-DOS ™** = MS-DOS ™; *(développé par Digital Research)* **système d'exploitation DR-DOS ™** = DR-DOS ™

dos *nm* back; *(d'un livre)* spine; **on trouve une variété de connecteurs au dos de l'unité centrale** = there is a wide range of connectors at the back of the main unit; **de façon générale, le nom de l'auteur et le titre apparaissent au dos du livre et sur la page de titre** = the author's name and the title usually are shown on the spine as well as on the title page; **il y aura une photographie en couleur de l'auteur au dos de la jaquette** = we will be using a colour photograph of the author on the back of the jacket

dossier *nm* **(a)** file *ou* (complete) documentation on a subject; **classez ces lettres dans le dossier 'clients'** = put these letters in the customer file; **insérer un document au dossier** = to place a document on file **(b) dossier (Macintosh, eMAIL)** = folder (Apple Macintosh group of files); **dossier préférentiel (Macintosh)** = blessed folder

doublage *nm* *(d'un film)* dubbing

double 1 *nm* duplicate *ou* copy; *(avec carbone)* carbon copy *ou* carbon; *(action)* replication *ou* copying; **faites un original et deux doubles** = make a top copy and two carbons; **formulaire avec double carboné** = carbon set; **papier avec double autocopiant** = two-part stationery **2** *adj* double *ou* dual; *(double épaisseur)* two-part; **mémoire à double accès** = dual port memory; **double bande latérale** = double sideband; **(modulation d'amplitude à) double bande latérale sans porteuse *ou* à porteuse inhibée** = double sideband suppressed carrier (DSBSC); **(à) double chronométrie** = dual clocking; **double contrôle** = cross-check; **disquette double densité (DD)** = double density disk (DD); **travail qui fait double emploi** = duplication of work; *(papier, etc.)* **en double épaisseur** = two-part; **papier listing en double épaisseur** = two part computer stationery; **en double exemplaire** = in duplicate; **reçu en double exemplaire** = receipt in duplicate; *(photo)* **double exposition** = double exposure; **disquette (à) double face** = double-sided disk; **lecteur de disquettes (à) double face** = double-sided disk drive; **papier photosensible double face** = duplex; **plaque (présensibilisée) double face pour circuit imprimé** = double-sided printed circuit board; **utilisation de double mémoire tampon** = double buffering;

double précision = double-length precision *ou* double precision; **calcul en double précision** = double precision arithmetic; **double processeur** = dual processor; **station à double connexion (sur réseau FDDI)** = dual attachment station (DAS); **système à double rang de broches (parallèles)** = dual-in-line package (DIL *ou* DIP); **système à bus double** = dual bus system; **colonne double** = dual column; *(symbole typographique)* **croix double (‡)** = double dagger; *(typographie)* **guillemets doubles** = double quotes; *(code informatique)* **mot double** = double word; **processeur double** = dual processor; **système double** = dual system; *(transmission)* **voie double** = dual channel

◊ **double-clic** *nm* double-click; **déplacer le pointeur sur l'icône puis démarrez le programme avec un double-clic** = move the pointer to the icon then start the program with a double-click

◊ **double-cliquer** *vi* *(appuyer deux fois sur le bouton de la souris)* to double-click

◊ **doubler** *vtr* *(un film)* to dub

◊ **doublet** *nm* *(mot de deux bits)* dyad *ou* doublet; *(antenne radio)* dipole; *(erreur d'imprimerie)* dittogram

doubleur *nm* **doubleur d'horloge** = clock doubler; **le nouveau processeur d'Intel a un doubleur d'horloge en option qui permet de doubler ses performances** = the new CPU from Intel has an optional clock doubler that will double performance

doublon *nm* *(erreur typographique)* double line, double word, etc.

douchette *nf* bar-code reader

douille *nf* socket

doute *nm* doubt; **mettre en doute** = to doubt *ou* to question (something)

◊ **doux, douce** *adj* **(a)** soft; **dégradation douce** = graceful degradation; **panne douce** = soft-fail **(b) impression en taille douce** = copperplate printing

DPA **architecture DPA** = Demand Protocol Architecture (DPA)

drapeau *nm* flag *ou* indicator flag; **drapeau de dépassement de capacité** = overflow bit *ou* flag *ou* indicator; **code drapeau** = flag code; **mise en place d'un drapeau** = flagging; **condition *ou* fonction de mise en place d'un drapeau** = flag event; **registre des drapeaux** = flag register; **séquence de drapeaux** = flag sequence

DR-DOS *(développé par Digital Research)* **système d'exploitation DR-DOS** = DR-DOS

driver *nm* (bus) driver

droit *nm* **(a)** *(ce qui est exigible ou conforme à un règlement)* right; **droit d'auteur** = copyright; **Convention sur le droit d'auteur** = Copyright Act; **titulaire d'un droit d'auteur** = copyright owner; **violation du droit d'auteur** = infringement of copyright *ou* copyright infringement; **oeuvre dont les droits de reproduction sont réservés** = work still in copyright **(b)** *(somme d'argent)* charge; **l'utilisateur paie un droit pour visualiser les pages de la messagerie** = the user has to pay a charge for viewing pages on a bulletin board

◊ **droit, -e** *adj* right

◊ **droite** *nf* right; **décalage** *ou* **glissement à droite** = right shift; **effectuer un décalage à droite** = to right shift *ou* to shift right; **au fer à droite** = flush right; **justification à droite** = right justification; **justifié à droite** = flush right *ou* right justified; **justifier à droite** = to right justify; **(instruction de) justifier à droite** = right justify

DSP *(circuit intégré)* **circuit DSP** = Digital Signal Processing (DSP)

DTMF = DUAL TONE, MULTIFREQUENCY; *voir* SIGNALISATION

duodécimal, -e *adj* duodecimal; **système duodécimal** = duodecimal number system

duplex *nm&adj* duplex *ou* diplex; **circuit duplex** = duplex circuit; **opération** *ou* **transmission en duplex** = duplex operation; **système duplex** = duplex computer; **full duplex** = full duplex (FDX *ou* fdx); **half-duplex** = half duplex; **modem half-duplex** = half-duplex modem

duplicateur *nm* duplicator *ou* duplicating machine; **duplicateur à alcool** = spirit duplicator; **duplicateur grande vitesse** = high-speed duplicator; **papier pour duplicateur** = duplicating paper *ou* duplicator paper

◊ **duplication** *nf* duplication *ou* replication; *(action)* duplicating

◊ **dupliquer** *vtr* to duplicate *ou* to replicate

dur, -e *adj* hard *ou* rigid; **disque dur** = hard disk; *(unité)* hard disk drive; **disque dur amovible** = removable hard disk; disk cartridge; *(de type Winchester)* removable Winchester; **carte de disque dur** = hard card

durable *adj* durable

◊ **durée** *nf* duration; **durée d'appel** = call duration; **la durée de l'appel varie suivant la complexité de la transaction** = call duration depends on the complexity of the transaction; **le prix est fonction de la durée de l'appel** = charges are related to call duration; **durée d'assemblage (d'un programme)** = assembly time; **durée de compilation (d'un programme)** = compilation time; **durée d'exécution (d'un programme)** = run-time *ou* run-duration *ou* execute time; **durée moyenne de bon fonctionnement entre les défaillances** = mean time between failures (MTBF); **durée d'une panne** = fault time; **durée de**

vie = lifetime; **ce nouvel ordinateur a une durée de vie de quatre ans** = this new computer has a four-year lifetime; **durée de vie d'un système** = system life cycle; **durée de vie de la tête (de lecture)** = headlife; **de courte durée** = impulsive *ou* transient; **interférence de courte durée** = impulsive *ou* transient noise; **cartouche longue durée** = durable cartridge; **modulation d'impulsions en durée (MID)** = pulse duration modulation (PDM) *ou* pulse width modulation (PWM)

DV-I *(systèmes vidéo et audio)* **système DV-I** = Digital Video Interactive (DV-I)

DVORAK **clavier DVORAK** = DVORAK keyboard

dyade *nf (mot de deux bits)* doublet *ou* dyad

dyadique *adj* dyadic; **opération dyadique** = dyadic operation; **opération booléenne dyadique** = dyadic Boolean operation

dynamique *adj* dynamic; adaptive; **acheminement dynamique** = adaptive routing; **allocation dynamique** = dynamic allocation; **allocation dynamique de la mémoire** = dynamic storage allocation; **arrêt dynamique** = dynamic stop; *(sous Windows and OS/2)* **bibliothèque dynamique des liens (DLL)** = dynamic link library (DLL); **déplacement dynamique** = dynamic relocation (program); *(sous Windows et OS/2)* **échange dynamique des données (DDE)** = dynamic data exchange (DDE); **gamme** *ou* **amplitude dynamique** = dynamic range; **mémoire dynamique** = dynamic memory *ou* dynamic storage; **mémoire dynamique permanente** = permanent dynamic memory; **mémoire tampon dynamique** = dynamic buffer; **mémoire vive dynamique** = dynamic RAM *ou* dynamic random access memory (DRAM); **micro(phone) dynamique** = dynamic microphone; **multiplexage dynamique** = dynamic multiplexing; **(mémoire) RAM dynamique** = dynamic RAM *ou* dynamic random access memory (DRAM); **routage dynamique** = dynamic routing *ou* adaptive routing; **structure de données dynamique** = dynamic data structure; **système dynamique** = adaptive system; **tampon dynamique** = dynamic *ou* elastic buffer; **translation dynamique** = dynamic relocation; **vidage dynamique** = dynamic dump

dysfonction *nf* malfunction; malfunctioning

◊ **dysfonctionnement** *nm* malfunction; malfunctioning; **(programme) diagnostic de dysfonctionnement** = malfunction routine

la première branche du réseau dut être recâblée à la suite de dysfonctionnement
L'Information professionnelle

Ee

E *(nombre décimal équivalent du 14 décimal)* hexadecimal number equivalent to decimal 14 *ou* E

E *(ionosphère)* **couche E** = E-region *ou* Heaviside-Kennelly layer

EAO = ENSEIGNEMENT ASSISTE PAR ORDINATEUR **langage de programmation EAO** = authoring language; **système adapté aux langages EAO** = authoring system

EAPROM *(mémoire)* Electrically Alterable Programmable Read-Only Memory (EAPROM); *voir aussi* MEMOIRE

EAROM *(mémoire)* Electrically Alterable Read-Only Memory (EAROM); *voir aussi* MEMOIRE

ébauche *nf* rough copy *ou* draft

◊ **ébaucher** *vtr* to draft

EBCDIC *(code binaire)* Extended Binary Coded Decimal Interchange Code (EBCDIC); *voir aussi* CODE BINAIRE

écart *nm (statistiques)* deviation

◊ **écarteur** *nm (éloigne la bande de la tête pendant le rembobinage)* lifter

échange *nm* exchange; interchange; transfer; **échange d'informations** *ou* **de données** = data transfer; **protocole d'échange d'informations** *ou* **de données entre unité centrale et périphérique** = CPU handshaking; **circuit d'échange (bi-directionnel) de données** = data circuit; **tri par échange** = exchange selection

◊ **échangeable** *adj* exchangeable

◊ **échanger** *vtr* to exchange; to transfer; *(permuter)* to interchange

échantillon *nm* sample; **selon échantillon** = as per sample

◊ **échantillonnage** *nm* sampling; *(de réception de signal ou de qualité)* acceptance sampling; **fréquence d'échantillonnage** = sampling rate; **pas d'échantillonnage** = sampling interval

◊ **échantillonner** *vtr* to sample; *(par impulsion)* to strobe

◊ **échantillonneur** *nm* sampler

◊ **échantillonneur-bloqueur** *nm&adj* **(circuit) échantillonneur-bloqueur** = sample and hold circuit

le signal radio analogique qui entre dans ce magnétophone est transformé en numérique avec une fréquence d'échantillonnage de 44,1 ou 48kHz
Audio Tech

échappement *nm* **(a)** escape (ESC); **caractère d'échappement** = escape character; **code d'échappement** = escape code; *(d'un clavier)* **touche d'échappement** = escape key (ESC); **appuyez sur la touche ECHAPPEMENT pour arrêter le programme** = to end the program, press ESCAPE **(b)** *(mouvement du papier dans une machine à écrire)* escapement

échauffement *nm* (over)heating; **panne par échauffement** = burn out

échéance *nf* **planning à courte échéance** = short-term planning; **planning à longue échéance** = long-term planning

échec *nm* failure; **le premier essai du prototype de lecteur de disquettes a été un échec** = the prototype disk drive failed its first test

échelle *nf* scale; **échelle binaire** = binary scale; **dans un mot à quatre bits, l'échelle binaire est 1,2,4,8** = in a four bit word, the binary scale is 1,2,4,8; **échelle de gris**, *US* gray scale; **le 'bel' est mesuré sur une échelle logarithmique** = bel is a unit in the logarithmic scale; **grande échelle** = large scale; *(de composants)* **intégration à grande échelle** = large-scale integration (LSI); **intégration à très grande échelle** = very large scale integration (VLSI); **intégration à super grande échelle** = super large scale integration (SLSI); **intégration à moyenne échelle** = medium scale integration (MSI); **petite** *ou* **faible échelle** = small scale; **intégration à petite échelle** = small scale integration (SSI); *(adaptable au nombre d'utilisateurs)* **logiciel à échelle variable** = scalable software; **police de caractères à échelle variable** = scalable font; **augmenter l'échelle** = to scale up; **réduire l'échelle** = to scale down; **mise à la bonne échelle (d'un système informatique)** = rightsizing

écho *nm* echo; **chambre à écho** = echo chamber; **contrôle par écho** = echo check; **(dispositif) éliminateur d'écho** = echo suppressor; **faire écho** = to echo; **sans écho** = anechoic

échouer *vi* to fail

ECL **logique ECL** = Emitter-Coupled Logic (ECL)

éclairage *nm* lighting *ou* illumination

◊ **éclairagiste** *nm&f* *(film ou télévision)* lighting engineer; **chef éclairagiste** = lighting director

◊ **éclairement** *nm* illuminance

◊ **éclairer** *vtr* to light *ou* to illuminate; **l'écran est éclairé par une lampe de très faible puissance** = the screen is illuminated by a low-power light

éclaté, -ée *adj* scattered; *(sur écran vidéotex en mode graphique)* **caractères éclatés** = blast-through alphanumerics; **faire un chargement éclaté** = to scatter load; **onde éclatée progressante** = forward scatter

◊ **éclater** *vtr&i* **éclater (les éléments d')un bloc** = to deblock

◊ **éclateur** *nm* *(de papier listing)* burster

ECMA = EUROPEAN COMPUTER MANUFACTURERS ASSOCIATION **symboles ECMA** = ECMA symbols; *voir aussi* SYNDICAT

économie *nf* saving *ou* economy; **la société met en place des mesures d'économie d'énergie** = the company is introducing energy-saving measures

◊ **économique** *adj* economical; **conception** *ou* **design économique** = least cost design; **le budget n'étant que de 4000 francs, il nous faut un design économique pour ce nouveau circuit** = the budget is only 4000 francs, we need the least cost design for the new circuit

◊ **économiser** *vtr* to save; **qui économise l'énergie** = energy-saving; **vous économiserez de l'énergie en limitant la température de la pièce à 18 degrés** = if you reduce the room temperature to eighteen degrees, you will save energy

écoulé, -ée *adj* *(temps)* passed; **signal de contrôle du temps écoulé** = time address code

écoute *nf* **(a)** listening; *(télévision)* **heures de grande écoute** *ou* **d'écoute maximale** = prime time; **nous commençons à diffuser des spots publicitaires aux heures de grande écoute** = we are putting out a series of prime-time commercials; **indice d'écoute** = audience rating; **potentiel d'écoute** = coverage; **taux d'écoute** = ratings **(b)** **table d'écoute** = wiretap; **brancher une ligne sur une table d'écoute** = to tap (a telephone)

écran *nm* **(a)** *(d'ordinateur ou pour projections)* screen; **écran (d'affichage** *ou* **d'ordinateur)** = screen *ou* monitor *ou* visual display unit (VDU); cathode ray tube (CRT); **écran asservi** *ou* **second écran** = slave tube; **écran couleur** = colour monitor; **écran électroluminescent** = electroluminescent display screen; **écran électrostatique** = electrostatic screen; **écran EGA** = enhanced graphics adapter screen *ou* EGA screen; **écran (à affichage) graphique** = graphics VDU; **terminal avec écran (à affichage) graphique** = graphics art terminal; **écran magnétique** = magnetic screen; **écran à mémoire** = storage tube; **écran monochrome** *ou* **écran noir et blanc** = monochrome monitor; **écran multistandard** = multi-scan *ou* multi-sync monitor; **écran partagé** *ou* **divisé** = split screen; **écran plasma** = gas discharge display *ou* gas plasma display; **écran plat à matrice active** = thin film transistor (TFT) screen; **écran pleine page** = full-size *ou* full-screen display; **écran (de) quatre-vingts colonnes** = eighty-column screen; **écran rétroéclairé** = backlit display; **écran tactile** = touch screen; **écran texte** = text screen; **écran vidéo** = video monitor; **écran vidéo avec clavier** = video terminal; **écran de visualisation** = display screen *ou* readout device *ou* visual display terminal (VDT) *ou* visual display unit (VDU); **à l'écran** = *(données)* on-screen; *(film)* on general release; **adaptateur d'écran** = display adapter; **afficher** *ou* **appeler** *ou* **rappeler** *ou* **faire apparaître des données à l'écran** = to call up data; **rappelez le fichier précédent à l'écran** = call up the previous file; **la touche HELP fera apparaître sur l'écran une description des différentes options** = by keying HELP, the screen will display the options available to the user; **on a affiché à l'écran les adresses de tous les clients** = all the customers addresses were called up; **les coordonnées du client étaient affichées sur l'écran** = the customer's details were displayed on the screen; **attribut d'écran** = screen attribute; display attribute; **bordure d'écran** = screen border; **faire un brûlage d'écran** = to burn in; **capture d'écran** = screen grab; **caractère d'écran** = display character; **générateur de caractères d'écran** = display character generator; **césure d'écran** = soft *ou* discretionary hyphen; **coin gauche supérieur (de l'écran)** *ou* **début de l'écran** = cursor home; **contrôleur** *ou* **pilote d'écran** = display controller; *(texte imprimé)* **copie d'écran** = hard copy; **défilement du texte sur l'écran** = display scrolling; **définition de l'écran** = display resolution *ou* screen resolution; **économiseur d'écran** = screen saver; **éditeur d'écran** = screen editor; **format d'écran** = display format *ou* screen format; **grille d'écran** = form; **kit de nettoyage pour écran** = screen cleaning kit; **ligne d'écran** = display line; **mémoire (d')écran** = screen memory; **mémoire tampon d'écran** = screen buffer; **plein écran** = screenful; **police (d')écran** = screen font; **la police d'écran est affichée à 72 ppp sur le moniteur plutôt qu'à 300 ppp sur l'imprimante laser** = the screen font is displayed at 72dpi on a monitor, rather than printed at 300dpi on this laser printer; **processeur d'écran** = display processor; **texte (d')écran** = soft copy; **vidage d'écran (sur imprimante)** = screen dump **(b)** *(de protection)* **écran** *ou* shield; *(d'un haut-parleur)* baffle; **écran électromagnétique** = electromagnetic shield; **faire écran** = to block; **la montagne fait écran à ces habitations qui ne reçoivent aucune émission radio** = the mountain casts a shadow over those houses, so they cannot receive any radio broadcasts; **protéger à l'aide d'un écran** = to screen *ou* to shield

---

il s'agit d'une machine sans clavier, de la classe et de la puissance d'une station de travail et équipée d'un écran qui est au moins de la taille d'une page

Science et Vie Micro

---

les écrans tactiles permettent de sélectionner la fonction désirée, sans apprentissage préalable, par simple pointage d'un menu sur un écran

Electronique (Suisse)

écrasement *nm (de l'image)* crushing

écrêtage *nm* clipping; **écrêtage de phase** = phase clipping

◊ **écrêter** *vtr* to clip; **le signal a été écrêté pour éviter une amplitude excessive** = the voltage signal was clipped to prevent excess signal level

écrire *vtr* to write; *(échanger des lettres)* to correspond; **écrire à la machine** = to type; **machine à écrire** = typewriter; **machine à écrire électrique** = electric typewriter; **machine à écrire électronique** = electronic typewriter; **écrire en majuscules** *ou* **en capitales** *ou* **en caractères d'imprimerie** = to write in capitals *ou* to print; **écrivez votre nom en majuscules en début de page** = write your name in capitals *ou* print your name at the top of the sheet of paper; **écrire de nouveau** = to rewrite; **écrire un programme** = to write a program *ou* to program; **(mot) qui s'écrit avec un trait d'union** = hyphenated (word); **le mot 'arrière-plan' s'écrit habituellement avec un trait d'union** = the word 'arrière-plan' is usually hyphenated *ou* is usually written with a hyphen *ou* is usually spelled with a hyphen

◊ **écrit** *nm* written document *ou* printed document; publication; **les écrits officiels sont en vente dans des librairies spécialisées** = government publications can be bought at special shops; **par écrit** = in writing

◊ **écrit, -e** *adj* written; **écrit à la machine** = typewritten; **écrit à la main** = handwritten; **règlements écrits** = printed regulations

◊ **écriture** *nf* **(a)** *(à la main)* writing *ou* handwriting; **il trouve mon écriture difficile à lire** = he has difficulty in reading my writing; **les opérateurs de saisie trouvent que l'écriture de l'auteur est difficile à lire** = the keyboarders are having difficulty in reading the author's handwriting; **reconnaissance d'écriture** = handwriting recognition; **ce nouvel APC (assistant personnel de communication) est doté d'un excellent système de reconnaissance de l'écriture** = the new PDA has excellent handwriting recognition **(b)** *(d'une disquette)* anneau *ou* bague de protection d'écriture = write-permit ring; **dispositif de protection d'écriture de fichier** = file protect tab; **erreur d'écriture** = write error; **mémoire cache à écriture différée** = write *ou* write-back *ou* write-behind cache; **le cache à écriture différée améliore les performances mais peut être difficile à utiliser** = write-back cacheing improves performance, but can be dangerous; **temps d'écriture** = write time; **tête d'écriture** = *(d'un disque)* record head *ou* write head; *(d'une bande)* tape head; *(d'une disquette)* **volet de protection d'écriture** = write-protect tab **(c)** **écriture chiffrée** = cipher

EDI *(système électronique d'échange de données)* Electronic Data Interchange (EDI)

édité, -ée *adj* edited; **non édité** = unedited

◊ **éditer** *vtr* to edit; **éditer sous forme de liste** = to list; **éditer un texte sur ordinateur** = to edit a text on screen

◊ **éditeur** *nm (programme)* editor program; **éditeur d'écran** = screen editor; **éditeur de liens** = linkage editor; **éditeur de ligne** = line editor; **éditeur de programme** = program editor; **éditeur de texte** = text editor; **cet éditeur de texte ne peut lire que les fichiers de moins de 64Ko** = the text editor will only read files smaller than 64Kbytes long

◊ **éditeur, -trice** *n (qui s'occupe de la publication d'oeuvres littéraires)* publisher; **nom de l'éditeur** = publisher's imprint

◊ **édition** *nf* **(a)** *(de programme ou de texte sur ordinateur)* editing; **édition après compilation** *ou* **après calculs** = post-editing; **(programme d')édition de lettres types** = mail-merge; **commandes et instructions d'édition** = edit commands; **fenêtre d'édition** = edit window; **programme d'édition de texte** = text editor; **exécution d'un programme d'édition (pour contrôle)** = editing run; **touche (de fonction) d'édition** = edit key; **il y a plusieurs touches d'édition - celle-ci permet de reformater le texte** = there are several special edit keys - this one will re-format the text **(b)** *(fabrication de livres)* publishing; **édition électronique** = electronic publishing *ou* desktop publishing (dtp); **maison d'édition** = publishing firm *ou* publisher **(c)** *(livre, journal, revue)* edition; *(livre)* **édition cartonnée** *ou* **reliée** = hardback *ou* hardcover (edition); **l'édition pour bibliothèques est cartonnée avec jaquette** = the library edition has a case and jacket; **avez-vous lu la dernière édition du journal du soir?** = did you see the last edition of the evening paper?; **le texte de la seconde édition a été modifié** = the second edition has had some changes to the text **(d)** *(d'un film)* editing; **maquette d'édition** = editing plan

◊ **éditorial** *nm (article)* editorial *ou* leading article

EDLIN *(utilitaire MS-DOS)* (MS-DOS system utility) EDLIN

éducatif, -ive *adj* educational; **programme de télévision de caractère éducatif** = educational TV (ETV)

EEMS *(gestion avancée de la mémoire étendue)* **mémoire EEMS** = Enhanced Expanded Memory System (EEMS)

EEPROM *(mémoire)* Electrically Erasable Programmable Read-Only Memory (EEPROM); *voir aussi* MEMOIRE

EEROM *(mémoire)* Electrically Erasable Read-Only Memory (EEROM); *voir aussi* MEMOIRE

effaçable *adj* erasable; *(données)* soft; **mémoire effaçable** = erasable memory; **mémoire morte programmable (PROM) effaçable par ultraviolet** = ultraviolet erasable PROM; **mémoire ROM effaçable électriquement** = electrically erasable read-only memory (EEROM); **mémoire ROM programmable et effaçable** = erasable programmable read-only memory (EPROM); **mémoire ROM programmable et effaçable électriquement** = electrically programmable read-only memory (EEPROM); **support (magnétique) effaçable** = erasable storage *ou* erasable memory

◊ **effacement** *nm* deletion; **effacement des lignes cachées** = hidden line removal; *(d'un disque ou d'une bande)* **effacement en masse** = bulk erase; **caractère d'effacement** = delete character *ou* erase character; **dispositif d'effacement** = eraser; **outil d'effacement** = eraser tool; **tête d'effacement** = erase head

◊ **effacer** *vtr* to erase *ou* to delete; to remove *ou* to clear *ou* to wipe; to kill; **effacer en bloc** = to block delete; **lorsqu'il s'agit de supprimer un texte assez long, servez-vous de la commande de suppression de bloc** = use the global delete command to remove large areas of unwanted text; **effacer les données d'un disque** = to wipe a disk clean; **effacer des données par superposition d'écriture** = to overwrite; **tapez CLS pour effacer ce qu'il y a sur l'écran** = type CLS to clear the screen; **effacer un fichier** = to delete *ou* to kill *ou* to junk *ou* to zero a file; *(faire disparaître à un moment déterminé)* **effacer une image** = to pop off an image; **(instruction d')effacer une PROM** = wash PROM; **qui peut être effacé** = erasable; **qui ne peut être effacé** = nonerasable; **mémoire qui ne peut être effacée** = nonerasable storage; **une bande papier perforée est une mémoire qui ne peut pas être effacée** = paper tape is a nonerasable storage

◊ **effaceur** *nm* **effaceur magnétique** = degausser *ou* demagnetizer; **il s'est servi d'un effaceur magnétique pour démagnétiser les têtes de lecture** = he used the demagnetizer to degauss the tape heads

effectif, -ive *adj* effective; **adresse effective** = effective address; **instruction effective** = effective instruction; **largeur de bande effective** = effective bandwidth; **puissance d'ouverture effective** = effective aperture; **rendement effectif** = effective throughput; **vitesse de recherche effective** = effective search speed

effectuer *vtr* to carry out; **il faut quand même un certain temps pour effectuer la mise en route de l'ordinateur** = the process of setting up the computer takes quite a long time; **la société ne s'est pas souciée d'effectuer la maintenance de routine de son matériel** = the company failed to carry out routine maintenance of its equipment; **je vais effectuer une série de tests non destructifs sur votre machine; si tout se passe bien, vous pourrez vous en servir de nouveau** = I will carry out a number of non-destructive tests on your computer: if it passes, you can start using it again; **effectuer un branchement** = to jump; **effectuer un traitement** = to process; **effectuer un tri bulle** *ou* **un tri par permutation de paires** *ou* **de bulles** = to bubble sort

effet *nm* effect; **effet (de champ) Hall** = Hall effect; **commutateur à effet (de champ) Hall** = Hall effect switch; **semi-conducteur à effet de champ MOSFET** = metal oxide semiconductor field effect transistor (MOSFET); **transistor à effet de champ (TEC)** = field effect transistor (FET); *(d'une ligne courbe ou diagonale, causé par les pixels)* **effet d'escalier** = aliasing; **effet optronique** = electro-optic effect; **effets sonores** = sound effects; **tous les effets sonores dans le film sont produits électroniquement** = all the sound effects for the film were produced electronically; **effet sonore postsynchronisé** = dubbed sound; **instruction sans effet** = do-nothing (instruction)

efficace *adj* efficient; **intensité efficace d'une ligne** = RMS line current; **rendre plus efficace** = to upgrade; *(d'amplitude ou d'intensité, etc.)* **valeur efficace** = root mean square (RMS); **la valeur efficace d'une sinusoïde parfaite équivaut à 0,7071 de son amplitude** = the root mean square of the pure sinusoidal signal is 0.7071 of its amplitude

◊ **efficacement** *adv* efficiently

◊ **efficacité** *nf* efficiency

efficience *nf* efficiency

◊ **efficient, -e** *adj* efficient

effleurement *nm (clavier tactile)* **clavier à effleurement** = tactile keyboard *ou* touch-sensitive keyboard; **pavé à effleurement** = touch pad

EGA = ENHANCED GRAPHICS ADAPTER **carte EGA** = EGA card; **écran EGA** = EGA screen; *voir aussi* GRAPHIQUE

égal, -e *adj* equal; **être égal à** = to equal

◊ **égal-à-égal** *adj* **réseau égal-à-égal** = peer-to-peer network

◊ **également** *adv* equally

◊ **égaler** *vtr* to equate *ou* to equal; **5 à la puissance deux** *ou* **5 au carré égale 25** = 5 to the power 2 is equal to 25 *ou* equals 25

égalisateur *nm* equalizer; **égalisateur de phases** = delay equalizer

◊ **égalisation** *nf* equalization

◊ **égaliser** to equalize *ou* to balance; *(à l'aide d'un filtre)* to equalize

◊ **égaliseur** *nm* equalizer; **égaliseur de fréquence** = frequency equalizer; **égaliseur de phase** = phase equalizer

◊ **égalité** *nf* equality

égaré, -ée *adj* stray

égratignure *nf* scratch

EIA *(norme d'interface)* Electronics Industry Association (EIA); **interface EIA** = EIA interface

EISA *(standard de bus)* Electronics Industry Standards Association (EISA)

| COMMENTAIRE: le standard de bus d'extension EISA est rétro-compatible avec les anciens standards ISA; il dispose aussi de 32 bits pour déplacer les données et d'une gestion du bus.

éjecter *vtr (un fichier)* to junk (a file)

élargi, -e *adj* augmented *ou* expanded; **adressage élargi** = augmented addressing

◊ **élargir** *vtr* to expand

électret *nm* electret; **microphone à électret** = electret microphone son nom s'explique par le fait que ce microphone miniature ne comporte pas moins de 3 capsules à électret

Audio Tech

électricien *nm* electrician; **chef-électricien** = gaffer

électricité *nf* electricity; **électricité statique** = static; **à l'électricité** = electrically; **conduire l'électricité** = to conduct electricity; **les frais d'électricité constituent un élément important des coûts de production** = electricity prices are an important factor in the production costs; **moteur qui marche** *ou* **qui fonctionne à l'électricité** = electric motor *ou* electrically-powered motor; **panne d'électricité** = power cut *ou* power failure; blackout

◊ **électrique** *adj* electric *ou* electrical; **charge électrique** = electric charge; **courant électrique** = electric current; **machine à écrire électrique** = electric typewriter; **moteur électrique** = electric motor *ou* electrically-powered motor; **les ingénieurs essaient de réparer une panne du système électrique** = the engineers are trying to repair an electrical fault; **polarité électrique** = electrical polarity

◊ **électriquement** *adv* electrically; **mémoire ROM effaçable électriquement** = electrically erasable read-only memory (EEROM); **mémoire ROM modifiable électriquement** = electrically alterable read-only memory (EAROM); **mémoire ROM programmable et effaçable électriquement** = electrically erasable programmable read-only memory (EEPROM); **mémoire ROM programmable, modifiable électriquement** = electrically alterable, programmable read-only memory (EAPROM)

électro-aimant *nm* electromagnet; **qui fonctionne grâce à un électro-aimant** = electromagnetically powered

électrode *nf* electrode; *(pour mesurer les impulsions biologiques)* biosensor; **l'activité nerveuse peut se mesurer en plaçant une électrode sur le bras** = the nerve activity can be measured by attaching a biosensor to your arm

électroluminescence *nf* electro-luminescence

◊ **électroluminescent, -e** *adj* electro-luminescent *ou* electroluminescing; **affichage** *ou* **écran électroluminescent** = electroluminescent display; **l'écran est recouvert d'une couche électroluminescente** = the screen coating is electroluminescent; **diode électroluminescente** = light emitting diode (LED)

électrolytique *adj* electrolytic; **condensateur électrolytique** = electrolytic capacitor; **condensateur non électrolytique** = non-electrolytic capacitor

électromagnétique *adj* electromagnetic; **écran** *ou* **blindage électromagnétique** = electromagnetic shield; **le blindage protège l'unité**

centrale des pertes *ou* fuites électromagnétiques du bloc d'alimentation = the metal screen protects the CPU against stray electromagnetic effects from the PSU; **interférence électromagnétique** = electromagnetic interference (EMI); **rayonnement électromagnétique** = electromagnetic radiation; **spectre de fréquences électromagnétiques** = electromagnetic spectrum

électromécanique *adj* electromechanical; **central téléphonique électromécanique** = strowger exchange; **commutation électromécanique** = electromechanical switching

électromoteur, -trice *adj* electromotive; **force électromotrice** = electromotive force (EMF)

électron *nm* electron; **canon à électrons** = electron gun; **faisceau d'électrons** = electron beam

électronicien, -ienne *n* electronic specialist; **ingénieur électronicien** = electronic(s) engineer

électronique 1 *nf* **l'électronique** = electronics; **un expert en électronique** = an electronics specialist **2** *adj* electronic; **autocommutateur électronique** *ou* **central automatique électronique** = electronic automatic exchange; **autocommutateur électronique privé** *ou* **PBX électronique** = computerized branch exchange (CBX); **boîte aux lettres électronique** = electronic mail box; **bureau électronique** = automated office *ou* paperless office; **clavier électronique** = electronic keyboard; **clé électronique** = dongle; **commutateur électronique** *ou* **système de commutation électronique** = electronic switching system; **compositeur électronique** = electronic compositor; **composition électronique** = electronic composition; **courrier électronique** = electronic mail *ou* email *ou* e-mail; **dispositif électronique d'identification** = personal identification device (PID); **édition électronique** = electronic publishing *ou* desktop publishing; **faisceau électronique** = electron beam; **le faisceau électronique dessine l'image à l'intérieur de l'écran cathodique** = the electron beam draws the image on the inside of a CRT screen; **enregistrement par faisceau électronique (sur microfilm)** = electron beam recording (EBR); **impulsion électronique** = electronic pulse; **jeu électronique** = computer game; **l'industrie électronique** = the electronics industry; **journalisme** *ou* **reportage électronique** = electronic news gathering (ENG); **machine à écrire électronique** = electronic typewriter; **messagerie électronique** = electronic mail *ou* email *ou* e-mail; *(dans une société)* computer-based message system (CBMS); **monnaie électronique** = electronic money; *(de vidéofilm)* **montage électronique** = electronic editing; **point de vente électronique** = electronic point-of-sale (EPOS); **pollution (par rayonnement) électronique** = electronic smog; **signature électronique** = electronic signature; **stylo électronique** = electronic wand *ou* stylus; **par système électronique** = electronically; **le texte est transmis au compositeur externe par système électronique** = the text is electronically transmitted to an outside typesetter; **système électronique d'échange de données** *ou* **EDI** = electronic data interchange

(EDI); **tableau d'affichage électronique** = bulletin board system (BBS); **tableau noir électronique** = electronic blackboard; **traitement électronique de données** = electronic data processing (EDP); **facilité de traitement électronique de données** = electronic data processing capability; **transfert électronique de fonds** = electronic funds transfer (system) (EFT); **terminal de transfert électronique de fonds** = electronic funds transfer point of sale (EFTPOS); **transmission électronique** = electronic traffic; **verrou (de sécurité) électronique** = electronic lock; *(d'une caméra)* **viseur électronique** = electronic viewfinder

◊ **électroniquement** *adv* electronically; **tous les effets sonores dans le film sont produits électroniquement** = all the sound effects for the film are produced electronically

électrophotographie *nf* electrophotography

électrosensible *adj* electrosensitive; **papier électrosensible** = electrosensitive paper

électrostatique *adj* electrostatic; **par charge électrostatique** = electrostatically; **écran électrostatique** = electrostatic screen; **haut-parleur électrostatique** = electrostatic speaker; **imprimante électrostatique** = electrostatic printer; **mémoire électrostatique** = electrostatic storage

élégant, -e *adj* elegant; **programmation élégante** = elegant programming

élément *nm* element *ou* item *ou* unit; building block; *(d'un champ)* member; **élément final d'une arborescence** = leaf; **élément arithmétique étendu** = extended arithmetic element; **élément binaire** = binary digit *ou* bit; **élément d'un code** = code element; **élément de décision** = decision element; **élément de données** = data element *ou* data item; **élément d'image** = picture element *ou* pixel; **élément logique** = logic element; **élément logique composé** *ou* **élément logique multiple** = compound logical element; *(code)* **élément de structure** = overhead; **élément d'un signal** = signal element; **élément dans un tableau** = array element; **éléments de l'unité centrale** *ou* **éléments CPU** = CPU elements; **chaîne d'éléments de données** = data element chain

élémentaire *adj* elementary *ou* primary; **code élémentaire** = basic code; **forme** *ou* **ligne élémentaire** = graphics primitive; **guide élémentaire** *ou* **manuel d'utilisation élémentaire** = primer; **section élémentaire de câble** = elementary cable section; **tampon élémentaire** = unit buffer

élévation *nf (math)* **élévation (d'un nombre) à la puissance x** = exponentiation

◊ **élever** *vtr* (a) **élever (un nombre) à la puissance x** = to exponentiate (b) **élever le potentiel d'une ligne** = to pull up a line; **élever le potentiel de la ligne de réception au niveau logique un, en la connectant sur une source de courant de 5 volts** = to pull up the input line to a logic one by connecting it to 5 volts

◊ **s'élever à** *vpr* to amount to

éliminateur *nm* suppressor; **éliminateur de courant transitoire** = transient suppressor; **éliminateur d'écho** = echo suppressor

◊ **élimination** *nf* suppression *ou* elimination; **élimination des zéros (non significatifs)** = zero compression *ou* zero suppression; **facteur d'élimination** = elimination factor

◊ **éliminer** *vtr* to eliminate; *(par filtrage)* to filter; **l'ordinateur devrait servir à éliminer toute possibilité d'erreur dans le système d'adresses** = using a computer should eliminate all possibility of error in the address system; **un correcteur orthographique n'élimine pas toutes les fautes d'orthographe** = a spelling checker does not eliminate all spelling mistakes

Elite *(caractères typographiques)* **caractères Elite** = elite font *ou* elite characters

ellipse *nf* ellipse

◊ **elliptique** *adj* elliptical; **orbite elliptique** = elliptical orbit

éloigné, -ée *adj* distant *ou* remote; **accès éloigné** = remote access; **console éloignée** *ou* **poste de commande** *ou* **périphérique éloigné** = remote console *ou* device; *(centre de communication)* **poste éloigné** = remote station; **terminal éloigné** = remote terminal

ELSE *(sinon)* **instruction ELSE** = else rule

emballage *adj nm* packing *ou* packaging; **emballage bulle** = blister pack; **emballage hermétique** = airtight packaging

◊ **emballement** *nm (activité excessive d'un disque; erreur de configuration de la mémoire virtuelle)* thrashing

◊ **emballer** *vtr* to pack; *(dans une caisse)* to case

emboîté, -ée *adj* nested; **boucles emboîtées** = nested loop

◊ **emboîter** *vtr* to nest

embranchement *nm* branch

embrouillage *nm (codage)* scrambling

◊ **embrouiller** *vtr (coder)* to scramble

◊ **embrouilleur** *nm* scrambler

émetteur *nm* emitter *ou* sender *ou* send-only device; **remise à l'état initial commandée par l'émetteur** = forward clearing; **émetteur à bande** = tape transmitter; **émetteur de données** = data source; *(antenne)* **émetteur isotrope** = isotropic radiator; **le signal de cet émetteur radio est très faible** = the signal from this radio station is very weak

◊ **émetteur, -trice** *adj* **le signal de cette station émettrice est très faible** = the signal from this radio station is very weak

◊ **émetteur-récepteur 1** *nm* transceiver *ou* receiver-transmitter; **émetteur-récepteur radio** = radio transceiver; **émetteur-récepteur asynchrone universel** = universal asynchronous receiver-transmitter (UART); **contrôleur d'émetteur-récepteur asynchrone universel** = UART controller; **émetteur-récepteur synchrone universel** = universal synchronous receiver-transmitter (USRT); **émetteur-récepteur synchrone asynchrone universel** = universal synchronous asynchronous receiver-transmitter (USART) **2** *adj* **appareil émetteur-récepteur** = automatic send/receive (ASR); **clavier émetteur-récepteur** = ASR keyboard; **poste émetteur-récepteur** = two way radio; **terminal émetteur-récepteur à clavier** = keyboard send/receive (KSR)

◊ **émettre** *vtr* to emit; **un multiplexeur 4/1 reçoit sur 4 canaux et émet sur un seul** = a 4 to 1 multiplexor combines four inputs into a single output; **émettre un bip** = to bleep; **émettre des impulsions** = to pulse; **émettre un signal** = to signal; **nous avons émis le signal d'entrée mais toujours sans succès** = we pulsed the input but it still would not work; **émettre un signal d'échantillonnage** *ou* **de validation** = to strobe; **signal d'interruption émis par un périphérique** = external interrupt; **émettre une vibration sonore** = to buzz; *(entre ordinateurs)* **invitation à émettre** = polling; **inviter à émettre** = to poll; *(transmission)* **(signal de) demande d'invitation** *ou* **sollicitation à émettre** = request to send signal (RTS)

émission *nf* emission; **l'émission du faisceau électronique** = the emission of the electron beam; *(transmission de données)* **émission en duplex** = duplex operation; **émission radiophonique** = broadcast; **le récepteur a capté l'émission radiophonique** = the receiver picked up the radio broadcast; *(radio, TV)* **fin des émissions** = close-down; *(télévision)* **grille d'émission** = format

empagement *nm* type area

empattement *nm* serif; **caractère avec empattements** = serif character; **avec empattements elzéviriens** = bracketed (serif); **(caractère) sans empattement** = sans serif

empêcher *vtr* to prevent *ou* to block; **nous avons changé les mots de passe pour empêcher le piratage de la base de données** = we have changed the passwords to prevent hackers getting into the database

emplacement *nm* location *ou* site; **emplacement de carte** *ou* **pour carte d'extension** = (expansion) slot; **emplacement pour lecteur de disquette(s)** = bay *ou* bay drive; **emplacement de mémoire** = memory location; **emplacement protégé** = protected location; **emplacement de rangement (en mémoire)** = bucket; *(d'un formulaire)* **emplacement réservé à la réponse** = response position; **(algorithme du) premier emplacement libre** = first fit

emploi *nm* **(a)** use; **mode d'emploi** = directions for use **(b)** **travail qui fait double emploi** = duplication of work

◊ **employer** *vtr* to use something *ou* to make use of something

empreinte *nf* print *ou* pattern; *(d'un faisceau, etc.)* footprint; *(d'antenne ou de microphone)* **empreinte directionnelle** = directional pattern;

empreinte d'interférence = interference pattern; **empreinte vocale** = voice print

emprunter *vtr* to borrow; **elle a emprunté un livre sur la fabrication des ordinateurs** = she borrowed a book on computer construction

EMS **mémoire étendue EMS** = expanded memory system (EMS); *voir aussi* LIM EMS

émulateur *nm* emulator; **émulateur intégré** = integrated emulator; **émulateur intégré au circuit** = in-circuit emulator

◊ **émulation** *nf* emulation; **émulation d'imprimante** = printer emulation; **cette émulation permet à mon imprimante NEC d'émuler une Epsom** = this printer emulation allows my NEC printer to emulate an Epsom; **capacité d'émulation** = emulation facility

◊ **émuler** *vtr* to emulate; **une imprimante laser qui peut émuler une série d'autres imprimantes de bureau** = laser printer which emulates a wide range of office printers

émulsion *nf* emulsion

ENAO = ENTRAINEMENT ASSISTE PAR ORDINATEUR

encapsulation *nf* encapsulation

◊ **encapsulé, -ée** *adj* encapsulated; **fichier PostScript encapsulé** *ou* **EPSF** = encapsulated PostScript file (EPSF); **PostScript encapsulé** *ou* **EPS** = encapsulated PostScript (EPS)

encodage *nm* **encodage ARLL** = advanced run-length limited (ARLL)

encadré, -ée *adj* framed *ou* boxed in; **les citations sont encadrées** = the quotations are printed in boxes

◊ **encadrement** *nm* frame *ou* box *ou* border

◊ **encadrer** *vtr* to frame *ou* to box in

encarté, -ée *adj* *(inclus sur une carte de circuit imprimé)* on-board

enceinte *nf* **enceinte acoustique** = set of loudspeakers

enchaîné, -ée *adj* chained; *(signal)* **fondu enchaîné** = cross fade; **programme à fonctions enchaînées** = thread

◊ **enchaînement** *nm* chaining *ou* linking *ou* catenation; **ordre d'enchaînement des opérations** = operator precedence; **page (vidéotex) à enchaînement programmé** = time coded page

◊ **enchaîner** *vtr* to chain *ou* to link; to concatenate *ou* to catenate; **plus de 1000 articles ou chapitres peuvent être enchaînés à l'impression** = more than 1,000 articles or chapters can be chained together when printing; **le film enchaîne sur un ralenti** = the film switches to slow motion

◊ **s'enchaîner** *vpr* to be chained *ou* to be linked

encoche *nf* notch; **carte à encoches marginales** = edge notched card

encodage *nm* encoding; **encodage binaire** = binary encoding; **encodage magnétique** *ou* **sur support magnétique** = magnetic encoding; **format d'encodage** = encoding format

◊ **encoder** *vtr* to encode

◊ **encodeur** *nm* **encodeur pour bandes magnétiques** = magnetic tape encoder; **encodeur couleurs** = colour encoder; **encodeur de touches** = keyboard encoder

encombrement *nm* **(a)** dimension(s) *ou* measurements; *(surface utilisée par un ordinateur sur un bureau)* footprint **(b)** *(d'un réseau de transmission)* congestion

encre *nf* ink; *(poudre d'encre pour photocopieur, imprimante laser, etc.)* toner; **encre magnétique** = magnetic ink; *(d'une imprimante laser ou de toner)* **cartouche d'encre** = toner cartridge; **lorsque l'encre est épuisée, on remplace la cartouche et le tambour ensemble** = the toner cartridge and the imaging drum can be replaced as one unit when the toner runs out; **pour remettre de l'encre ou changer la cartouche, voir la marche à suivre dans le manuel d'utilisation** = change toner and toner cartridge according to the manual; **excès d'encre** = overinking; **mettre un excès d'encre** *ou* **mettre trop d'encre** = to overink; **deux cahiers ont été gâchés par excès d'encre** = two signatures were spoilt by overinking; **imprégner** *ou* **couvrir d'encre** = to ink; **imprimante à jet d'encre** = ink-jet printer; **les techniques du jet d'encre couleur et du transfert thermique sont concurrentielles** = colour ink-jet technology and thermal transfer technology compete with each other; **imprimante à transfert d'encre** = write black printer

| COMMENTAIRE: une imprimante à transfert d'encre donne des arêtes et des graphiques nets mais les grandes surfaces noires sont teintées de manière irrégulière

◊ **encrer** *vtr* to ink; **encrer de façon excessive** = to overink

end *(sur clavier)* **touche End** = end key

endommagé, -ée *adj* damaged

◊ **endommager** *vtr* to damage *ou* to cause damage; **le disque dur a été endommagé quand on l'a laissé tomber** = the hard disk was damaged when it was dropped; **il semble que la tête de lecture défectueuse ait endommagé le disque** = the faulty read/write head appears to have damaged the disk

endroit *nm* **(a)** *(emplacement)* point *ou* position **(b)** *(d'une feuille)* recto

enduction *nf* *(procédé)* deposition

◊ **enduire** *vtr* to coat (a surface) *ou* to deposit (a substance on a surface)

◊ **enduit** *nm* coating; *(sur semi-conducteur; enduction)* **pose** *ou* **dépôt d'un enduit** = deposition (process)

◊ **enduit, -e** *adj* coated; **papier enduit d'une fine couche de kaolin** = paper which has a coating of clay; **enduit d'un dopant** = doped

énergie *nf* energy; **nous essayons d'économiser de l'énergie en éteignant les lumières lorsque les pièces sont vides** = we try to save energy by switching off the lights when the rooms are empty; **vous économiserez de l'énergie en limitant la température de la pièce à 18 degrés** = if you reduce the room temperature to eighteen degrees, you will save energy; **qui économise l'énergie** = energy-saving; **notre société met en place des mesures d'économie d'énergie** = our company is introducing energy-saving measures

enfermer *vtr* to enclose

enfichable *adj* *(qui se branche)* plug-in; *(qui ne demande pas d'adaptateur)* plug-compatible; *(qui ne demande pas de soudure)* solderless; **extension enfichable** = plug-in unit; **cette nouvelle carte directement enfichable travaille beaucoup plus vite que ses concurrentes, vous l'installez en l'enfichant simplement dans le connecteur d'extension** = this new plug-compatible board works much faster than any of its rivals, you can install it by simply plugging it into the expansion port; **ROM enfichable** = ROM cartridge

◊ **enfichage** *nm* plugging; **bloc d'enfichage (de câble de réseau local)** = punch-down block; **compatible à l'enfichage** = pin-compatible; **il est facile d'augmenter la puissance de ce processeur, la nouvelle puce est compatible à l'enfichage avec l'ancienne** = it's easy to upgrade the processor because the new one is pin-compatible; **connecteur** *ou* **fiche à une seule position d'enfichage** = polarized plug; **connecteur (de carte) à enfichage dirigé** *ou* **à un seul bord d'enfichage** = polarized edge connector

◊ **enficher** *vtr* to plug in

enfoncer *vtr* to press *ou* to push in

engorgement *nm* *(transmission)* overrun

enlever *vtr* to remove; *(un disque du lecteur)* to unmount

enregistré, -ée *adj* recorded; **amplitude maximum enregistrée** = maximum reading; *(pour film)* **commentaire enregistré** = voice-over; **des données enregistrées numériquement servent à générer des images** = digitally recorded data are used to generate images; **programme enregistré** = stored program

◊ **enregistrement** *nm* **(a)** *(support)* record *ou* recording; *(procédure)* recording; *(entrée dans un journal ou livre de bord)* log; *(procédure)* logging; **votre enregistrement contient divers champs regroupés sous une même rubrique** = your record contains several fields that have been grouped together under one heading; **cet enregistrement contient toutes leurs coordonnées** = this record contains all their personal details; **enregistrement ambisonique** *ou* **d'ambiance** = ambisonics; **enregistrement chaîné** = chained record; **enregistrement de données** = data record; *(automatique et chronologique)* data logging; **enregistrement (automatique) des erreurs** = error logging; **ce programme permet l'enregistrement (automatique) des erreurs** = features of the program include error logging; **enregistrement d'erreur dans un système** = fault trace; **enregistrement par faisceau électronique (sur microfilm)** = electron beam recording (EBR); **(nombre d')enregistrements dans un fichier** = record count; **enregistrement de labels** ou **d'étiquettes** ou **d'identificateurs** = label record; **enregistrement logique** = logical record; **enregistrement de longueur fixe** ou **déterminée** = fixed-length record; **enregistrement à longueur variable** = variable length record; **enregistrement de mouvements** ou **de modifications** ou **de détails** = change record ou amendment record; **enregistrement numérique** ou **digital** = digital recording ou sound capture; **enregistrement physique** = physical record; **enregistrement par rayon laser** = laser beam recording; **enregistrement sur support magnétique** = magnetic recording; **enregistrement de tête** = leader record; **enregistrement de transactions** = transaction record; *(dans un fichier)* **début d'enregistrement** = home record; **point de début d'enregistrement** = loadpoint; **densité d'enregistrement** = recording density ou packing density; **dernier enregistrement** ou **enregistrement de fin de fichier** = trailer record; **disque d'enregistrement** = work disk; **espace entre deux enregistrements** = record gap; **fichier d'enregistrement des blocs** = block list; **(code de) fin d'enregistrement** = end of record (EOR); **format** ou **présentation d'un enregistrement** = record format ou layout; **programme de gestion d'enregistrements** = records management; **gestionnaire d'enregistrements** = records manager; **(instructions d') enregistrement** = log on script; **intervalle blanc entre deux enregistrements** = record gap; **longueur** ou **dimension** ou **taille d'un enregistrement** = record length; **structure des enregistrements** = record structure; **temps d'enregistrement** = write time; **tête d'enregistrement** = record head ou write head; **touche** ou **bouton d'enregistrement** = record button; **verrouillage des enregistrements** = record locking **(b)** *(surtout musique)* **un nouvel enregistrement des quatuors de Beethoven** = a new recording of Beethoven's quartets; **nouveaux enregistrements** = new releases **(c)** *(téléphone)* **enregistrement d'appels** = call logging

◊ **enregistrer** *vtr* **(a)** *(données)* to record ou to read-in ou to read in ou to write ou to post; *(en mémoire auxiliaire)* to deposit; *(dans un journal ou livre de bord)* to log ou to write; *(le nombre et la durée)* to meter; **ce dispositif enregistre les signaux sur bande magnétique** = this device records signals onto magnetic tape; *(dicter)* **il enregistrait ses instructions sur son Dictaphone de poche** = he was dictating orders into his pocket dictating machine; *(musique ou effet sonore)* **enregistrer d'avance** = to prerecord **(b)** *(téléphone)* **enregistrer les appels** = to log calls **(c)** *(sauvegarder sous un titre déterminé)* **enregistrer sous ...** = to save as ...

◊ **enregistreur** *nm* **(a)** recorder; *(d'une imprimante)* **enregistreur graphique** = pen recorder ou plotter; **enregistreur à tambour** = drum plotter **(b)** *(téléphone)* logger; **enregistreur d'appels** = call logger; **le nombre et la durée des**

appels effectués dans chacun des bureaux sont enregistrés sur l'enregistreur (d'appels) = the calls from each office are metered by the call logger

enroulé, -ée *adj* wound; **connexion enroulée** = wire wrap

◊ **enroulement** *nm* *(d'un fil ou d'un film)* winding; **bobine d'enroulement** = pickup reel ou pick-up reel ou take-up reel; *(télévision)* **déflecteur à enroulement** = deflection yoke

◊ **enrouler** *vtr* to wind

◊ **s'enrouler** *vpr* to wind ou to rewind; **le film s'enroule automatiquement sur la bobine** = the tape rewinds onto the spool automatically

◊ **enrouleur-presseur** *nm* **enrouleur-presseur de bande magnétique** = omega wrap

enseignement *nm* teaching ou instruction; training; **enseignement assisté par ordinateur (EAO)** = computer-aided ou -assisted instruction (CAI) ou teaching (CAT); computer-based training (CBT); **enseignement interactif géré par ordinateur** = computer-managed instruction (CMI)

ensemble *nm* set; **ensemble de caractères** = character set; **ensemble de caractères nuls** = empty set ou null set; **ensemble référentiel** = universal set; **ensemble des tâches** ou **travaux en cours d'exécution** = job mix; *(math)* **théorie des ensembles** = set theory

ensemblier *nm* *(qui construit des ordinateurs à partir de pièces détachées)* original equipment manufacturer (OEM)

ensoleillement *nm* period of sunshine; **durée de non ensoleillement** = sun outage

entendre *vtr* to hear; *(son)* **qu'on peut entendre** = audible

enter *(touche Entrée, sur un clavier)* **touche ENTER** = Enter key

en-tête *nm* heading; **formulaires et en-têtes de lettres peuvent être conçus sur un PC** = business forms and letterheads can be designed on a PC; **en-tête de bande** = tape header; **en-tête de bloc** = block header; **en-tête courant** = form flash; **en-tête de fichier** = (file) header; **en-tête de lettre** = letterhead; **en-tête de message** = message heading; **en-tête pré-établi** = form overlay ou form flash; **carte en-tête** = header card; **(code de) début d'en-tête** = start of header; **papier à en-tête** = headed paper ou preprinted stationery

entier, -ière *adj* full ou complete; **nombre entier** = integer; **BASIC pour nombres entiers** = integer BASIC; **nombre entier en double précision** = double-precision integer

entité *nf* entity

entraînement *nm* *(pour bande ou cartes ou film ou papier)* feed ou advance ou transport; **(dispositif d')entraînement de la bande papier** = paper tape feed; (**système d')entraînement de cartes perforées** = card feed; **entraînement feuille à feuille** = single sheet feed; **entraînement d'un film** = film advance; **entraînement par friction** *ou* **par rouleaux** = friction feed; (**dispositif d')entraînement du papier** = paper feed *ou* feeder; **ce bouton sert à l'entraînement du papier** = the paper is advanced by turning this knob; **entraînement par picots** = tractor feed *ou* pinfeed *ou* sprocket feed; *(de cartes)* **canal d'entraînement (avec perforations centrales)** = centre sprocket feed; **perforations d'entraînement** = feed holes *ou* sprocket holes

◊ **entraîner** *vtr* (a) *(bande ou cartes ou film ou papier)* to move *ou* to advance *ou* to feed (b) to drive; **un moteur entraîne le disque** = the disk is driven by a motor (c) to produce *ou* to cause; **les fluctuations de courant peuvent entraîner la perte de données** = data loss can occur because of power supply variations

> un moteur commande l'entraînement du film
> *Science et Vie*

entrance *nf* *(facteur d'entrée d'un circuit)* fan-in

entré, -ée *adj* entered *ou* input; **dernier entré premier sorti** = last in first out (LIFO); **cet ordinateur gère la pile suivant la méthode du 'dernier entré premier sorti'** = this computer stack uses a last in first out data retrieval method; (**méthode du) premier entré premier sorti (FIFO)** = first in first out (FIFO); **mémoire qui fonctionne** *ou* **qui est basée sur le principe 'premier entré premier sorti'** = FIFO memory *ou* first in first out memory; **les deux ordinateurs fonctionnent à des vitesses différentes mais peuvent transmettre des données en utilisant une mémoire tampon fonctionnant sur le système 'premier entré premier sorti'** = the two computers operate at different rates, but can transmit data using a FIFO memory

entrée *nf* (a) input (i/p *ou* I/P) *ou* entry; *(action)* entering; **entrée de données** = data input *ou* data entry; **entrée directe de données** = direct data entry (DDE); **entrée à partir de** *ou* **par lecture de microfilm** = computer input from microfilm (CIM); **entrée sur un système avec un mot de passe piraté** *ou* **sur un terminal mal verrouillé** = piggyback entry; **entrée en temps réel** = real-time input; **additionneur à deux entrées** = half adder *ou* two input adder; **additionneur à trois entrées** = full adder *ou* three input adder; **bloc d'entrée** = input block; **traitement de contrôle de bloc à l'entrée** = block input processing; **bus d'entrée** = data input bus (DIB); **câble d'entrée** *ou* **liaison d'un périphérique d'entrée** = input lead; **condition d'entrée** = entry condition; **visualisation de contrôle d'entrée** = marching display; **déclaration d'entrée** = input statement; **données d'entrée** = input data; *(d'un circuit)* **facteur pyramidal d'entrée** = fan-in; **file d'attente des données d'entrée** = input work queue; **file d'attente à deux entrées** = double-ended queue *ou* deque; **heure d'entrée** = entry time; **instruction d'entrée** = entry instruction; **instruction d'entrée dans la pile** = push instruction *ou* operation; **lecteur optique de microfilms pour entrée de données sur ordinateur** = film optical scanning device for input into

computers (FOSDIC); (**programme) limité par la vitesse d'entrée** *ou* **avec contrainte de vitesse d'entrée** = input-bound *ou* input-limited; **mémoire d'entrée** = input storage; **mode (d')entrée** = input mode; **périphérique d'entrée** = input device *ou* unit; **point** *ou* **adresse d'entrée** = *(de logiciel)* entry point *ou* access point; *(dans un système)* access point *ou* trapdoor; **port (d')entrée** = input port; **registre d'entrée** = input register *ou* receiver register; **registre tampon des entrées** = input buffer register; **routine d'entrée** = input routine; **section d'entrée** = input section; **signal d'entrée** = input signal; **soustracteur à trois entrées** = full subtractor; **terminal d'entrée (de données) vidéotex** = ip terminal; **zone d'entrée** = input area (b) **touche Entrée** = enter key *ou* return (key) *ou* carriage return (CR); **tapez votre nom et numéro de code, puis appuyez sur la touche 'entrée'** = you type in your name and code number then press return (c) *(dans un index ou dictionnaire)* entry *ou* headword; *(dans un journal ou livre de bord)* log; **entrée principale** = main entry; **entrée secondaire** = added entry

◊ **entrée/sortie** *nf* input/output *ou* I/O; **entrée/sortie configurée en mémoire** = memory-mapped input/output; *(en FORTRAN)* **entrée/sortie graphique** = graphical input/output (GINO); **entrée/sortie utilisant une mémoire tampon** = buffered input/output; **entrée/sortie parallèle** = parallel input/output (PIO); **circuit intégré d'entrée/sortie parallèle** = parallel input/output chip; **entrée parallèle/sortie parallèle** = parallel input/parallel output (PIPO); **entrée parallèle/sortie série** = parallel input/serial output (PISO); **entrée/sortie série** = serial input/output (SIO); **entrée série/sortie parallèle** = serial input/parallel output (SIPO); **entrée série/sortie série** = serial input/serial output (SISO); **adressage des entrées/sorties** = input/output mapping; **adresse des ports d'entrée/sortie** = I/O address; **appareil** *ou* **dispositif d'entrée/sortie** = I/O device; **bus (d')entrée/sortie** = input/output bus *ou* input/output data bus; **canal d'entrée/sortie** = input/output channel; **configuration d'entrées/sortie** = input/output mapping; **contrôleur d'entrée/sortie** = input/output controller; **fichier (d')entrée/sortie** = input/output file; **instruction d'entrée/sortie** = input/output instruction; **interface d'entrée/sortie** = input/output interface; **(signal d')interruption d'entrée/sortie** = input/output interrupt; (**programme) limité par la vitesse d'entrée/sortie** = input/output bound (program); **mot d'état d'entrée/sortie** = input/output status word; **périphérique d'entrée/sortie** = input/output device *ou* unit; **point** *ou* **port (d')entrée/sortie** = input/output port; **le manche à balai peut être connecté sur le port entrée/sortie** = the joystick can be connected to the input/output port; **processeur d'entrée/sortie** = input/output processor (IOP); **bibliothèque de programmes d'entrée/sortie** = input/output library; **programme de contrôle d'entrée/sortie** = input/output control program; **référençage d'entrée/sortie** = input/output referencing; **registre d'entrée/sortie** = input/output register; **requête d'entrée/sortie** = input/output request (IORQ); **superviseur d'entrée/sortie** = input/output executive; **tampon (d')entrée/sortie** = input/output buffer; **terminal à** clavier d'entrée/sortie = keyboard send/receive (KSR); **voie (d')entrée/sortie** = input/output channel (NOTE: on peut utiliser la forme abrégée **I/O** dans tous les exemples ci-dessus: **I/O channel; I/O buffer; serial I/O)**

entrefer *nm* air gap *ou* head gap

entrelacé, -ée *adj* (a) *(balayage d'image)* interlaced; **non entrelacé** = non-interlaced (b) *(programme, mémoire: imbriqué)* interleaved

◊ **entrelacement** *nm* interleaving; *(des secteurs d'un disque)* sector interleave; *(d'un disque)* **facteur d'entrelacement** = interleave factor

COMMENTAIRE: sur un disque dur avec un facteur d'entrelacement de 3, le premier secteur est lu, puis trois secteurs sont sautés et le secteur suivant est lu. Ceci permet à des disques ayant des temps d'accès longs de stocker plus de données sur le disque.

◊ **entrelacer** *vtr* to interleave; *(balayage d'image)* to interlace

entrepôt *nm* warehouse *ou* storage facilities

entreprendre *vtr* to undertake; **il a entrepris de reprogrammer tout le système** = he has undertaken to reprogram the whole system

◊ **entreprise** *nf (société)* business *ou* firm *ou* company; **il possède une petite entreprise de réparation d'ordinateurs** = he owns a small computer repair business; **dans l'entreprise** = in-house; **tout le travail informatique se fait dans l'entreprise** = all the data processing is done in-house; **répertoire d'entreprises** = commercial directory *ou* trade directory; **réseau d'entreprise** = enterprise network

entrer 1 *vtr (des données)* to enter *ou* to input; *(par lecture)* to read in; *(au clavier)* to keyboard *ou* to type; **entrer un nom sur une liste** = to enter a name on a list **2** *vi* (a) to access *ou* to enter *ou* to dial into; **avec un code d'accès valide, il est possible d'entrer dans le système du client et d'extraire les fichiers utiles pour établir le rapport** = with the right access code it is possible to dial into a customer's computer to extract the files needed for the report (b) **entrer en vigueur** = to come into force; **les nouveaux règlements entreront en vigueur le 1er janvier** = the new regulations will come into force on January 1st

entretenir *vtr* (a) *(appareil)* to maintain (b) *(image ou mémoire)* to refresh

◊ **entretenu, -e** *adj* (a) *(appareil)* serviced *ou* maintained; **bien entretenu** = well maintained *ou* well looked after (b) *(continu)* continuous; **onde entretenue** = continuous wave

◊ **entretien** *nm (d'appareil)* maintenance *ou* upkeep; *(opération d'entretien)* service; **entretien régulier** = preventive maintenance; **ingénieur d'entretien (sur le site)** = field engineer

énumératif, -ive *adj* enumerative

◊ **énumérer** *vtr* to detail *ou* to list

enveloppe *nf* (a) *(d'un paquet de données; de messagerie électronique; de multimédia)* envelope; **effectuer un tri 'enveloppe'** = to shell sort (b) *(amplitude)* **enveloppe d'attaque (d'un signal)** = attack envelope; **enveloppe tonale** = pitch envelope; **délai (de transmission) d'une enveloppe** = envelope delay; **détection d'enveloppe** = envelope detection (c) *(pour envoyer une lettre)* envelope; **enveloppe avion** = air mail envelope; **enveloppe à fenêtre** = window envelope; **enveloppe fermée** *ou* **cachetée** = sealed envelope; **enveloppe longue (pour papier ministre)** = foolscap envelope; **enveloppe ouverte** *ou* **non cachetée** = unsealed envelope; **bac d'alimentation pour enveloppes** = envelope feeder; **imprimante d'enveloppes** = envelope printer

environ *adv* approximately; **le temps de traitement est d'environ 10% inférieur à celui du trimestre précédent** = processing time is approximately 10% lower than during the previous quarter

environnement *nm* (a) *(espace ou zone de réseau)* environment; **environnement universitaire** = campus environment; **taille de l'environnement** = environment space; **variable d'environnement** = environment variable (b) *(matériel)* platform; **environnement de développement de programmes** = program development system *ou* environment; **ce logiciel ne fonctionne que dans un environnement IBM** = this software will only work on the IBM PC platform; *(logiciel ou réseau)* **indépendant de l'environnement (de travail)** = platform independent; **environnement graphique WIMP** = WIMP (window, icon, mouse, pointers)

COMMENTAIRE: les environnements graphiques utilisent les fenêtres, icônes et souris pour contrôler le système d'exploitation; dans de nombreuses interfaces graphiques comme Windows de Microsoft, System 7 d'Apple ou DR GEM, on peut contrôler toutes les fonctions du système d'exploitation avec la souris; des icônes figurent le programmes et les fichiers; au lieu d'entrer au clavier le nom du fichier, on le sélectionne en déplaçant un pointeur à l'aide d'une souris.

envoi *nm* (a) dispatch *ou* despatch; *(par la poste)* mailing; *(prospectus envoyé par la poste)* mail shot *ou* mailing piece; **l'envoi (par la poste) de prospectus publicitaires** = the mailing of publicity material (b) *(messagerie électronique)* **envoi différé** = store and forward

◊ **envoyer** *vtr* to dispatch *ou* to despatch *ou* to send; **envoyer par la poste** = to mail *ou* to post; **envoyer par télécopie** *ou* **envoyer par fax** = to fax *ou* to send by fax; **envoyer un télex** = to telex

EOF *(code de fin de fichier)* End of file; *voir aussi* FIN

EOM *(code de fin de message)* End of Message; *voir aussi* FIN

EOT *(code de fin de transmission)* End of Transmission; *voir aussi* FIN

épais, épaisse *adj* thick; **couche épaisse** = thick film

◊ **épaisseur** *nf* **papier listing en double épaisseur** = two-part computer stationery; **papier listing en plusieurs épaisseurs** = multi-part computer stationery

éphémère *adj* transient

épidiascope *nm* episcope *ou* epidiascope

épine *nf (connexion)* **épine dorsale** = backbone

épitaxial, -e *adj* epitaxial; **couche épitaxiale** = epitaxial layer

◊ **épitaxie** *nf* epitaxy

épreuve *nf* **(a)** *(imprimerie)* proof; **épreuve finale** = master proof; **épreuve de machine** = machine proof; **épreuve de mise en page** *ou* **dernière épreuve** = page proof; **épreuves en placard** *ou* **en première** = galley proofs *ou* slip pages *ou* slip proofs; **épreuve sans correction** = clean proof; **épreuve de reproduction** = repro proof; **épreuves en vrac** = scatter proofs; **correcteur, -trice d'épreuves** = proofreader; **correction** *ou* **relecture d'épreuves** = proofreading; **corriger des épreuves** = to proofread; **imprimante (destinée au tirage) d'épreuves** = proofer; **des périphériques tels qu'imprimantes laser destinées au tirage d'épreuves et photocomposeuses** = output devices such as laser proofers and typesetters; **la relecture des épreuves est-elle terminée?** = has all the text been proofread yet?; **signes de correction d'épreuve** = proof correction marks; **tirage d'épreuves** = proofing; **tirer les épreuves (d'un texte)** = to proof **(b)** *(photo)* print; **épreuve de contact** = contact print; **épreuve positive** = photoprint

EPROM *(mémoire)* Erasable Programmable Read-Only Memory (EPROM); *voir aussi* MÉMOIRE

épuiser *vtr (une pile)* to drain

épure *nf* blueprint

équateur *nm* equator

équation *nf* equation; **équation machine** = machine equation

équatorial, -e *adj* equatorial; **orbite équatoriale** = equatorial orbit

équilibrage *nm* balance; balancing; **équilibrage des colonnes** = column balance; **équilibrage des lignes de transmission** = balanced routing; **bande d'équilibrage (de tension)** = balance stripe

◊ **équilibré, -ée** *adj* balanced; **charge équilibrée** = matched load; **circuit équilibré** = balanced circuit; **il faut utiliser un circuit équilibré en fin de ligne pour éviter la réflexion des signaux** = you must use a balanced circuit at the end of the line to prevent signal reflections; **erreur équilibrée** = balanced error; **ligne équilibrée** = balanced line

◊ **équilibre** *nm* balance; **le logiciel de PAO permet à l'utilisateur de juger du bon équilibre d'une page** = the DTP package allows the user to see if the overall page balance is correct; **équilibre des couleurs** = colour balance

◊ **équilibrer** *vtr* to balance; to match

◊ **équilibreur** *nm* **équilibreur d'impédance** *ou* **de ligne** = balun *ou* line adapter; **nous avons utilisé un équilibreur d'impédance pour connecter le câble coaxial au circuit à paire torsadée** = we have used a balun to connect the coaxial cable to the twisted-pair circuit

équipe *nf* team *ou* crew; **équipe cinématographique** *ou* **de cinéastes** = camera crew; **l'équipe de cinéastes a dû tourner toute la journée dans la neige** = the camera crew had to film all day in the snow

équipé, -ée *adj* fitted with; **équipé d'une pile auxiliaire** *ou* **de secours** = battery-backed; **carte équipée** = fully populated board; **la carte RAM peut être équipée, en option, d'une pile de secours** = the RAM disk card has the option to be battery-backed; **(carte) non équipée** = unpopulated (board)

◊ **équipement** *nm* **(a)** equipment; **fournisseur** *ou* **revendeur d'équipements informatiques** = computer equipment supplier; **équipement de traitement de papier listing (en sortie d'imprimante)** = form handling equipment; **équipement de vérification automatique (EVA)** = automatic test equipment (ATE) **(b)** installation(s) *ou* facilities

◊ **équiper** *vtr* to equip

équivalence *nf* **(a)** *(fonction logique)* equivalence; **fonction** *ou* **opération d'équivalence** = equivalence function *ou* operation; **fonction non équivalence** = non-equivalence function (NEQ) *ou* symmetric difference; **porte** *ou* **circuit d'équivalence** = equivalence gate **(b)** **table d'équivalence** = look-up table (LUT) *ou* conversion table *ou* translation table *ou* substitution table; **les tables d'équivalence sont préprogrammées et permettent de gagner du temps de traitement en évitant de recalculer les mêmes valeurs** = lookup tables are preprogrammed then used in processing so saving calculations for each result required; **on peut établir des tables d'équivalence qui serviront à convertir les données clients aux codes utilisés par notre système** = conversion tables may be created and used in conjunction with the customer's data to convert it to our system codes

◊ **équivalent, -e** *adj* equivalent; **être équivalent (à)** = to be equivalent to *ou* to amount to

◊ **équivaloir (à)** *vi* to be equivalent to *ou* to amount to; **le nombre de caractères saisis (par clavier) jusqu'ici équivaut à une journée de temps d'impression** = the total number of characters keyboarded so far is equivalent to one day's printing time

équivoque *adj* ambiguous

éraflure *nf (sur un disque)* scratch

ergonome *nm&f* ergonomist
◊ **ergonomie** *nf* ergonomics
◊ **ergonomiste** *nm&f* ergonomist

erratum *nm* erratum

erreur *nf* error *ou* fault *ou* inaccuracy; *(d'horloge)* hazard; *(inexplicable)* gremlin; **on trouve des tas d'erreurs dans la bibliographie** = the bibliography is full of inaccuracies; **il me faut tout recommencer; je viens d'effacer le seul fichier qui ne contenait aucune erreur** = I'll have to start again - I just erased the only clean file; **nous estimons qu'il y a une erreur fondamentale dans la conception du produit** = we think there is a basic fault in the product design; **par erreur** = by error; **application qui tolère toutes les erreurs possibles** = hazard-free implementation; **erreur d'ambiguïté** = ambiguity error; **erreur anormale** = abnormal error; **erreur d'arrondi** = approximation error; **erreur de balayage** = scanning error; **un pli ou une déchirure dans une page peut être la cause d'une erreur de balayage** = a wrinkled or torn page may be the cause of scanning errors; **erreur de calcul** = computational error; **erreur certaine** = solid error; **erreur de code** = false code; **erreur de compilation** = compilation error; **les erreurs de compilation provoquent l'interruption inopinée de la tâche** = compilation errors result in the job being aborted; **erreur consciente** = conscious error; **erreur qui peut être corrigée** *ou* **redressée** = recoverable error; **erreur au démarrage** = cold fault; **erreur au départ** = initial error; **erreur détectée** = detected error; **erreur de données** = data error; **erreur équilibrée** = balanced error; **erreur à l'exécution** = run-time error *ou* execution error; **erreur fatale** = fatal error *ou* catastrophic error; **erreur générée (par des arrondis)** = generated error; **erreur héritée** = inherited error; **erreur imputable à un composant défectueux** = component error; **erreur inexplicable** = gremlin; **erreur intermittente** = intermittent error; **erreur irrécupérable** *ou* **impossible à corriger** = unrecoverable error; **erreur de logiciel** = soft error; **erreur logique** = logical error; **erreur momentanée** = transient error; **erreur monstre** = howler; **erreur non détectée** = undetected error; **erreur notifiée** = detected error; **erreur de numérisation** = quantization error; **erreur due à l'ordinateur** = computer error; **erreur passagère** = transient error; **erreur permanente** = permanent error; **erreur persistante** = hard error; **la tête de lecture fait une erreur de piste** = the read head is not tracking the recorded track correctly; **les techniciens essayent de corriger une erreur de programmation** = the technical staff are trying to correct a programming fault; **erreur qui se propage** = propagating error; **erreur propagée** = propagated error; **erreur de quantification** = quantization error; **erreur de rejet** = rejection error; **erreur relative** = relative error; **erreur sporadique** = sporadic fault; **erreur de substitution** = substitution error; **faire une erreur de synchronisation (en transmettant trop vite)** = to overrun; **il a fait une erreur de total** = he made an error in calculating the total; **erreur de trame** = frame error; **erreur transmise** = inherited error; **erreur de transmission** = transmission error; **erreur à valeur moyenne nulle** = balanced error; **code d'erreur** *ou* **code indicateur d'erreur** = error code; **condition d'erreur** = error condition; **contrôle d'erreurs** = error control; **correction d'erreurs** = error correction *ou* data cleaning; **correction automatique d'erreurs** = automatic error correction; **code de correction d'erreurs** *ou* **code correcteur d'erreurs** = error correcting code; **code de vérification et correction d'erreurs (ECCC)** = error checking and correcting code (ECCC); **correction d'erreurs en cours de transmission** = forward error correction; **correction d'erreurs par retransmission** = backward error correction; **détection d'erreurs** = error detection; **détection et correction d'erreurs** = error detection and correction (EDAC); **détection** *ou* **recherche** *ou* **prévention d'erreurs** = automatic error detection *ou* error trapping; **code de détection d'erreurs** *ou* **code détecteur d'erreurs** = error detecting code *ou* self-checking code; **diagnostic d'erreurs** = error diagnosis; **outils de diagnostic d'erreurs** = error diagnostics; **enregistrement automatique des erreurs** = error logging; **ce programme permet l'enregistrement des erreurs** = features of the program include error logging; **fausse erreur** = false error; **(signal d') interruption sur erreur** = error interrupt; **marge d'erreur** = margin of error; **message d'erreur** = error message; **message de diagnostic d'erreurs** = diagnostic (error) message; **propagation d'erreurs** = error propagation; **rafale d'erreurs** *ou* **série d'erreurs consécutives** = error burst; **reprise après erreur (sans repartir à zéro)** = error recovery; **routine (de traitement) d'erreur** = error routine; **sans erreur** = accurate; **texte sans erreur** = clean copy *ou* clean text; **taux d'erreur** = error rate; **le taux d'erreur est inférieur à 1%** = the error rate is less than 1%; **taux d'erreur par bloc** = block error rate; **taux d'erreur de transmission (sur fibre optique)** = bit error rate (BER); **(procédure de) traitement des erreurs** *ou* **gestion des erreurs** = error handling *ou* management

erroné, -ée *adj* incorrect *ou* false; *(corrompu)* corrupt; **code erroné** = false code; **résultat erroné (d'une recherche)** = false drop *ou* retrieval

E/S = ENTREE/SORTIE

ESC *(échappement)* Escape; **code ESC** = escape code *ou* ESC code; *(touche d'Echappement)* **touche ESC** = escape key *ou* ESC key

escalade *nf (dans un système expert)* hill climbing

escalier *nm (d'une ligne courbe* ou *diagonale; causé par les pixels)* **effet d'escalier** = aliasing; jagged edges *ou* jaggies

escargot *nm (@ d'adresse Internet)* @ (NOTE: se prononce: '**at**' en anglais)

esclave *nm* slave; **(puits** *ou* **collecteur de données) esclave d'un bus** = bus slave

ESDI *(interface)* Enhanced Small Device Interface (ESDI)

espace *nm* **(a)** *(blanc)* space *ou* spacing *ou* blank; **il y a quelques lignes où les espaces sont très inégaux** = the spacing on some lines is very uneven; **caractère d'espace** = blank character *ou* space character; **chaîne contenant des caractères d'espace** = blank string; **gestionnaire d'espaces** = spacer; *(imprimerie)* **insertion d'espaces** = quadding **(b)** *(étendue)* space *ou* area; **espace adresse** = address space; **espace d'affichage** = display space; **espace de manoeuvre** *ou* **de travail** = workspace *ou* work area; **espace mémoire de l'image** = image storage space **(c)** *(distance)* gap; **espace entre deux enregistrements** = record gap; **espace interbloc** = interblock gap (IBG); *(séparant deux fichiers)* **espace neutre** = file gap **(d)** **l'espace** = space *ou* free space media; **perte dans l'espace** = free space loss **(e)** *(forme de signal)* **marque espace** = mark space

◊ **espacement** *nm* *(d'imprimante)* space *ou* spacing; *(de film)* film advance; **espacement (proportionnel) de caractères** = intercharacter spacing; **espacement entre les mots** = interword spacing; **espacement proportionnel** = proportional spacing; **espacement uniforme** = monospacing; *(d'un clavier)* **barre d'espacement** = space bar; **caractère d'espacement** = space character

◊ **espacé, -ée** *adj* spaced; **caractères graphiques espacés** = separated graphics; **les caractères régulièrement espacés s'alignaient sur la page** = the line of characters was evenly spaced out across the page

◊ **espacer** *vtr* to space out

esperluette (&) *nf* ampersand

espion *nm* spy; **micro espion** = bug; **surveiller par micro espion** *ou* **installer des micros espions** = to bug

esprit *nm* *(symbole mobile d'infographie)* sprite

esquisse *nf* outline *ou* sketch *ou* design; **faire une esquisse** = to sketch *ou* to outline

◊ **esquisser** *vtr* to sketch *ou* to outline; to draft; **il a esquissé un projet de programme sur une feuille de papier** = he drafted out the details of the program on a piece of paper

essai *nm* test *ou* trial; *(d'un programme)* test run; **un essai fera tout de suite apparaître les erreurs** = a test run will soon show up any errors; **essai à blanc** = desk check *ou* dry run; **essai comparatif** = benchmark; **essai opérationnel** = operation trial; **à l'essai** = on approval; **banc d'essai** = benchmark(ing); test bed; **les bancs d'essais consistent à évaluer la performance de plusieurs systèmes ou périphériques en utilisant le même test standard** = in benchmarking, the performances of several systems or devices are tested against a standard benchmark; **faire un essai** = to test *ou* to pilot; **ils font l'essai du nouveau système** = they are piloting the new system; **ingénieur d'essai** = trials engineer

essentiel, -elle *adj* main *ou* essential *ou* prime; **caractéristique essentielle** = prime attribute

esthétique *nf* **esthétique industrielle** = industrial design

estimation *nf* approximation *ou* estimate

◊ **estimé, -ée** *adj* estimated *ou* calculated *ou* rated; **rendement estimé** = rated throughput

◊ **estimer** *vtr* to estimate *ou* to calculate; **j'estime que nous avons du stock pour six mois encore** = I calculate that we have six months' stock left

estomper *vtr* to blur; to soften

ET (a) AND; **circuit ET** *ou* **porte ET** = AND gate *ou* coincidence gate *ou* circuit; **opération ET** = coincidence operation **(b)** **et commercial (&)** = ampersand

établi, -e *adj* established; **travailler suivant des normes établies** = to work to standard specifications; **établi d'avance** = predetermined *ou* predesigned

◊ **établir** *vtr* to establish; **demande de communication qui ne peut être établie** = lost call; **établir un fichier d'adresses** = to build up a mailing list; **établir d'avance** = to preset *ou* to predetermine *ou* to predesign

étalonnage *nm* **(a)** standardization *ou* calibration **(b)** **étalonnage des performances** = benchmarking; **problème d'étalonnage** = benchmark problem

étanche *adj* watertight; *(par remplissage)* **câble étanche** = filled cable

étape *nf* stage *ou* step; **étape de programmation** = program step; **étape d'un travail** = job step; **effectué par étapes** = staged; **le processus compte cinq étapes** = there are five stages in the process

état *nm* **(a)** *(d'un ordinateur ou périphérique)* state *ou* status; **état d'attente** *ou* **de latence** = wait condition *ou* state; **état désactivé** = disarmed state; **remise à l'état initial commandée par l'émetteur** = forward clearing; **état logique** = logic state; **état logique bas** = logical low; **état logique haut** = logical high; **analyseur d'état logique** = logic state analyzer; *(appareil)* **en (bon) état de marche** = in working order; **état prêt** = ready state; **état stable** = stable state; **état stationnaire** = steady state; *(d'un périphérique)* **appel de contrôle d'état** = status poll; **bit d'état** *ou* **bit indicateur d'état** *ou* **marqueur d'état** = status bit *ou* device flag; **circuit logique à trois états** = three state logic; **indicateur d'état** = status word; **cette routine vérifie l'indicateur d'état et ne transmet pas le signal si le bit occupé est présent** = this routine checks the device status word and will not transmit data if the busy bit is set; **ligne d'état** = information line *ou* status line; **mot d'état** *ou* **mot indicateur d'état** = status word *ou* device status word (DSW); **mot d'état d'entrée/sortie** = input/output status word; **mot d'état d'un processeur** = processor status word (PSW); **registre d'état** = status register; **registre des mots d'état** = program status word register (PSW register) **(b)** report; **générateur d'état** = report generator

éteindre *vtr* **(a)** *(un appareil)* to shut down *ou* to switch off *ou* to turn off; **il faut éteindre l'appareil avant de déconnecter le moniteur** = turn off the power before unplugging the monitor; **éteindre l'ordinateur ou lui donner un coup quand la tête de lecture est en marche peut causer des ennuis** = you can cause trouble by turning off or jarring the PC while the disk read head is moving **(b)** *(s'affaiblir)* to decay *ou* to fade; **le signal s'est éteint rapidement** = the signal decayed rapidly

étendre *vtr* to extend

◊ **s'étendre** *vpr* **(a)** s'étendre (de ... à) = to range (from ... to); **la gamme des radiofréquences s'étend de seulement quelques hertz à des centaines de gigahertz** = the radio frequency range extends from a few hertz to hundreds of gigahertz **(b)** *(se répandre)* to propagate

étendu, -e *adj* *(augmenté ou amélioré)* extended; expanded; enhanced; **clavier étendu** = enhanced keyboard; **élément arithmétique étendu** = extended arithmetic element; **métalangage BNF étendu** *ou* **BNF étendu** = extended Backus-Naur Form *ou* extended BNF (EBNF); **mémoire étendue EMS** = expanded memory system (EMS); **gestion avancée de la mémoire étendue (EEMS)** = enhanced expanded memory system (EEMS); **gestionnaire de mémoire étendue** = expanded memory manager (EMM); **gestionnaire de mémoire étendue XMS** = extended memory specification (XMS); **mode étendu** = enhanced mode; **réseau étendu** = wide area network (WAN); **réseau très étendu** = long haul network

◊ **étendue** *nf (grandeur)* extent; *(choix)* range

Ethernet *(norme IEEE 802.3 de réseau)* Ethernet; **Ethernet câble fin** = thin-Ethernet *ou* cheapernet; **Ethernet câble lourd** = thick-Ethernet; **câblage léger (et bon marché) Ethernet** = cheapernet cable

COMMENTAIRE: Ethernet se présente sous diverses formes: 10 Base5 (le plus courant) basé sur une topologie en bus et utilisant des liaisons en câble coaxial; 10 BaseT qui utilise des câbles sans blindage en doubles paires torsadées. Ethernet a un débit de 10 Mbps

EtherTalk *(version Apple)* Apple Macintosh variation of Ethernet *ou* EtherTalk

étincelle *nf* spark; **imprimante thermique à étincelle** = spark printer

étiquetage *nm* labelling

◊ **étiqueter** *vtr* to label

◊ **étiquette** *nf* **(a)** *(informatique)* label *ou* tag *ou* quasi-instruction; **étiquette en-tête de bande** = tape label; **étiquette d'un champ** = field label; **étiquette de fichier** = file label; **chaque fichier est identifié rapidement par son étiquette de trois lettres** = each file has a three letter tag for rapid identification; **on peut allouer une étiquette aux touches de fonction** = tags can be allocated to function keys; **enregistrement d'étiquettes** = label record; **production d'étiquettes (pour un programme)** = labelling (of a program); **produire une étiquette (pour un programme)** = to label (a program) **(b)** *(d'un produit)* label *ou* tag; **étiquette externe** *ou* **extérieure** *ou* **apposée à l'extérieur** =

external label; **étiquette Kimball** = Kimball tag; *(d'une cassette, etc.)* **étiquette interne** = inlay card; **étiquette perforée** = punched tag; **étiquettes en continu** = continuous labels; **imprimante d'étiquettes** = label printer; **impression d'étiquettes** = labelling *ou* label printing; **ce traitement de texte dispose d'un utilitaire spécial qui permet d'imprimer des étiquettes facilement et rapidement** = the word-processor has a special utility allowing simple and rapid labelling

étoile *nf* **(a)** star; **réseau en étoile** = star network; star topology (of a network); **réseau commuté en étoile** = switched star **(b)** *(caractère d'imprimerie)* asterisk; **pour voir tous les fichiers commençant par 'L', utiliser la commande DOS DIR L*.*** = to view all the files beginning with the letter 'L', use the DOS command DIR L*.*

étouffer *vtr* *(un son ou bruit)* to deaden

étranger, -ère *n&adj* alien *ou* foreign

étroit, -e *adj* narrow; **bande étroite** = narrow band; **modulation de fréquence à bande étroite** = narrow band FM (NBFM); *(d'un affichage)* **fenêtre étroite** = thin window

étude *nf* **(a)** study **(b)** design; **il a fait l'étude de la nouvelle usine de composants** = he designed a new chip factory; **bureau d'études** = design department

ETX = END OF TEXT; *voir* FIN

Euronet *(réseau téléphonique)* Euronet

européen, -enne *adj* European; **numérotation européenne des articles (NEA)** = European Article Number (EAN)

EVA = EQUIPEMENT DE VERIFICATION AUTOMATIQUE

évacuateur *nm* **évacuateur de chaleur** = heat sink

évaluation *nf* evaluation *ou* measurement; **évaluation comparative des performances** = benchmarking; **problème d'évaluation** = benchmark problem; **technique d'évaluation et de révision de programme** = program evaluation and review technique (PERT); **test d'évaluation de performances** = benchmark; **la revue a publié les résultats du test d'évaluation des performances du nouveau programme** = the magazine gave the new program's benchmark test results

◊ **évaluer** *vtr* to evaluate *ou* to rate; **les bancs d'essais consistent à évaluer la performance de plusieurs systèmes ou périphériques en utilisant le même test standard** = in benchmarking, the performances of several systems or devices are tested against a standard benchmark

s'évanouir *vpr* *(signal)* to fade

◊ **évanouissement** *nm* *(du signal)* fading; **évanouissement (du signal) dû au brouillage** = interference fading

évènement *nm* event; **activé, -ée** *ou* **actionné, -ée par évènement** = event-driven

éventail *nm* fan; **antenne (en) éventail** = fan antenna; **papier en éventail** = accordion fold *ou* fanfold paper

évidence *nf* evidence; **mettre en évidence** = to highlight; **mots** *ou* **caractères (mis) en évidence** = highlights; **mots** *ou* **caractères mis en évidence (par affichage plus lumineux ou couleur contrastée)** = display highlights

évolué, -ée *adj* sophisticated *ou* advanced; **langage de programmation évolué** = high-level programming language (HLL); **un programme de PAO évolué** = a sophisticated desktop publishing program; **langage peu évolué** = low-level language (LLL)

◊ **évoluer** *vi* to move *ou* to develop; **qui n'évolue pas** = static

exact, -e *adj* correct *ou* precise *ou* accurate

◊ **exactitude** *nf* accuracy *ou* precision

examen *nm* checking *ou* scanning

◊ **examiner** *vtr* **(a)** *(attentivement)* to examine *ou* to scan **(b)** *(vérifier)* to check

excellent, -e *adj* excellent *ou* fine; **ce programme est excellent pour le tri des fichiers** = the program is highly efficient at sorting files

excepté 1 *prep* except **2** *adj* excepted

◊ **exception** *nf* **(a)** exception; **liste** *ou* **répertoire d'exceptions** = exception dictionary; **rapport d'exceptions** = exception report; **traitement des exceptions** = exception handling **(b)** **à l'exception de** = excluding

excès *nm* excess; *(de données dans une mémoire tampon)* spillage

◊ **excessif, -ive** *adj* excessive; **ce programme a utilisé une quantité excessive de mémoire pour exécuter la tâche en question** = the program used an excessive amount of memory to accomplish the job

excitation *nf* *(électrique)* impulse

exclamation *nf* exclamation; **point d'exclamation (!)** = exclamation mark

exclure *vtr* to exclude

exclusif, -ive *adj* exclusive; **(fonction) NI exclusif** = exclusive NOR (EXNOR); **porte** *ou* **circuit NI exclusif** = exclusive NOR gate *ou* EXNOR gate; **(fonction) OU exclusif** = exclusive OR (EXOR) *ou* non-equivalence function *ou* NEQ function; **porte** *ou* **circuit OU exclusif** = exclusive OR gate *ou* EXOR gate

◊ **exclusion** *nf* exclusion

EXE *(exécutable)* **fichier (à extension) EXE** = EXE file; **pour démarrer un programme sous DOS, tapez le nom de son fichier EXE** = in DOS, to start a program type in its EXE file name

exécutable *adj* executable; **fichier exécutable** = executable file

◊ **exécuter** *vtr* to execute *ou* to implement; *(un programme)* to run *ou* to execute (a program); **une fois cette tâche exécutée, ce sera le tour de la suivante dans la file d'attente** = when this job is complete, the next in the queue is processed; **on peut exécuter le programme sur un ordinateur indépendant ou un système multiposte** = the program runs on a standalone machine or a multi-user system; *(programme)* **prêt à être exécuté** = executable (form); **tâche qui peut être exécutée automatiquement** = unattended operation

◊ **exécutif, -ive** *adj* executive

◊ **exécution** *nf* execution *ou* run; **(instruction de) compilation et exécution** = compile and go; **exécution d'un programme** = computer run *ou* machine run *ou* production run *ou* program execution *ou* program run; **exécution (d'un programme) en temps réel** = real time execution; **exécution de commandes (à la mise sous tension)** = boot up *ou* booting; **exécution d'un programme d'édition (pour contrôle)** = editing run; **adresse d'exécution** = execution address; **(opérations de) contrôle et exécution d'interruption** = interrupt servicing; **contrôle d'exécution des tâches** = job statement control; **cycle d'exécution** = execute cycle *ou* execution cycle; **cycle de lecture/exécution** *ou* **cycle d'exécution (d'une instruction)** = fetch-execute cycle *ou* execute cycle; **déclaration** *ou* **message d'exécution** = execute statement; **durée** *ou* **temps d'exécution (d'un programme)** = execute time *ou* run-time *ou* run-duration; **erreur à l'exécution** = run-time error *ou* execution error; **mode d'exécution** = execute mode; **ordinateur d'exécution** = target computer *ou* object computer; **phase d'exécution** = execute phase *ou* run phase *ou* target phase; **routines de clôture (d'exécution)** = end of run routines; **signal d'exécution** = execute signal; **temps d'exécution** = *(d'une instruction)* instruction execution time *ou* instruction time; *(d'une opération)* operation time; *(d'un programme)* execution time *ou* run-time *ou* run-duration, *US* turnaround time (TAT); *(d'une tâche)* operating time *ou* elapsed time

exemplaire *nm* **(a)** *(d'un journal ou revue)* copy; **je l'ai lu dans l'exemplaire de 'Science et Vie' que nous avons au bureau** = I read it in the office copy of 'Science et Vie' **(b)** **en double exemplaire** *ou* **en deux exemplaires** = in duplicate; **établir une facture en deux exemplaires** = to print an invoice in duplicate; **reçu en double exemplaire** = receipt in duplicate; **en quatre exemplaires** = in quadruplicate; **les relevés sont imprimés en quatre exemplaires** = the statements are printed in quadruplicate

exemple *nm* example

exhaustif, -ive *adj* exhaustive *ou* global; **connaissance exhaustive** = global knowledge; **recherche exhaustive** = exhaustive search

exigence(s) *nf(pl)* requirement(s)

◊ **exiger** *vtr* to demand *ou* to require

EXIT *(commande MS-DOS)* (MS-DOS system command) EXIT

expansion *nf* expansion; **boîtier d'expansion** = expansion box; *voir aussi* EXTENSION

expérience *nf* experience *ou* background; **il a une bonne expérience de l'industrie informatique** = his background is in the computer industry

expert *nm* expert *ou* specialist *ou* consultant; **un expert en électronique** = an electronics specialist; **ils ont fait venir un expert en informatique pour les conseiller sur la conception du système** = they called in a computer consultant to advise them on the system design

◊ **expert, -e** *adj* (a) **être expert (en** *ou* **dans)** = to specialize (in); **c'est un expert en DAO** = he specializes in the design of CAD systems **(b) système expert** = expert system *ou* knowledge-based system *ou* intelligent knowledge-based system (IKBS); **formation assistée par système expert** = intelligent tutoring system

> les systèmes experts sont les premiers produits de l'intelligence artificielle
> *L'Ordinateur Individuel*

expiration *nf* expiration; **date d'expiration (d'un délai)** = expiration date

◊ **expirer** *vi* to expire

explication *nf* explanation; comment

explicite *adj* explicit; **adresse explicite** = explicit address

expliquer *vtr* to explain; *(le fonctionnement de quelque chose)* to demonstrate

exploitable *adj* **exploitable par l'ordinateur** = machine-readable; **le disque garde en mémoire des données sous une forme exploitable par l'ordinateur** = the disk stores data in machine-readable form; **(commandes** *ou* **données) directement exploitables** = machine-readable (instructions *ou* data)

◊ **exploitation** *nf* operation *ou* running *ou* working; **exploitation en parallèle** *ou* **en double** = parallel running; **logiciel d'exploitation** = systems software; **système d'exploitation** = operating system *ou* op sys (OS); **système d'exploitation de disque** *ou* **système d'exploitation DOS** = disk operating system (DOS); **système d'exploitation CP** = control program/monitor *ou* control program for microcomputers (CP/M); **le système d'exploitation des entrées/sorties** = basic input/output operating system (BIOS)

exploration *nf* *(par balayage)* scanning; **faisceau d'exploration** = scanning spot beam

exporter *vt* to export; **pour utiliser ces données avec dBase, il faut les exporter sous la forme d'un fichier de format dBase** = to use this data with dBASE, you will have to export it as a DBF file

exposant *nm* exponent *ou* characteristic; *(dans un système à virgule flottante)* biased exponent; **la valeur de l'exposant du nombre à virgule flottante 1,345 x 10³ est 3** = the floating point number 1.345

x 10^3 has a characteristic of 3; **exposant binaire** = binary exponent; **chiffre en exposant** = superior number *ou* superscript

exposé *nm* statement; **exposé d'un problème** = problem definition

exposer *vtr* *(photo)* to expose

◊ **exposition** *nf* *(photo)* exposure; **double exposition** = double exposure

expression *nf* **(a)** expression *ou* representation; **expression binaire d'un caractère** = character representation; **expression logique** = logical expression **(b) liberté d'expression** = freedom of speech

◊ **exprimer** *vtr* to express

extensible *adj* extensible *ou* expandable; **le processeur unique possède une mémoire de 2Mo extensible jusqu'à 4Mo** = the single processor with 2Mbytes of memory can be upgraded to 4Mbytes; **langage extensible** = extensible language; **programme extensible** = open-ended program; **système extensible** = expandable system

◊ **extension** *nf* **(a)** extension *ou* expansion; **les trois modèles offrent des possibilités d'extension sur site** = all three models have an on-site upgrade facility; **extension du nom du fichier** = filename extension; **l'extension SYS ajoutée au nom du fichier indique qu'il s'agit d'un fichier système** = the filename extension SYS indicates that this is a system file; **pour conserver une telle quantité de données, il vous faudra une extension de votre disque** = if you want to hold so much data, you will have to expand the disk capacity; **extension de mémoire** = memory extension; *(pour lentille photographique)* **bague d'extension** *ou* **macro** = extension tube; **câble d'extension** = extension cable; **kit d'extension de micro-ordinateur** = microcomputer development kit **(b) carte d'extension** = expansion card *ou* expansion board *ou* add-in card *ou* add-on board; **carte d'extension enfichable** = plug-in unit; **cette nouvelle carte d'extension permet l'affichage graphique en couleur** = the new add-on board allows colour graphics to be displayed; **pourriez-vous expliquer comment fonctionne le système de carte d'extension?** = can you explain the add-in card method?; **le traitement s'effectue beaucoup plus rapidement avec les cartes d'extension** = processing is much faster with add-in cards; **carte d'extension de mémoire étendue** = expanded memory board; **carte d'extension multifonction** = multifunction card; **créneau** *ou* **connecteur pour carte d'extension** = expansion slot; **support de carte d'extension** = card extender; **unité d'extension d'une ligne** = line extender

extérieur *nm* **(a) (prise de vue) en extérieur** = on location (filming); **les extérieurs (d'un film)** = location shots; **les extérieurs pour ce programme ont été tournés en Espagne** = the programme was shot on location in Spain **(b) qui vient de l'extérieur** = incoming

◊ **extérieur, -e** *adj* external; **étiquette extérieure** = external label; **horloge extérieure** = external clock

externe *adj* external; **défaillance ayant une cause externe** = induced failure; **dispositif externe** = external device; **fichier de données externe** = external data file; **horloge externe** = external clock; **lecteur de disquette(s) externe** = external disk drive; **mémoire externe** = external memory *ou* external storage *ou* external store; **modem externe** = external modem; **registre externe** = external register; **signal d'appel externe** = external interrupt; **tri sur support externe** = external sort

extinction *nf (d'un son, d'un signal)* extinction *ou* decay; **temps d'extinction d'un signal** = decay time

extra-terrestre *adj* extra-terrrestrial; **bruit extra-terrestre** = extra-terrestrial noise

extracode *nm (routine)* extracode

extracteur *nm (masque)* extractor

◊ **extraction** *nf* extraction; *(de données ou de fichiers)* extraction *ou* retrieval; **extraction de bloc** = block retrieval; **extraction de données** = data retrieval *ou* information retrieval (IR); **instruction d'extraction** = extract instruction

extraire *vtr* to extract; *(données ou fichiers)* to retrieve *ou* to extract; to read; *(une donnée d'une pile)* to pull; **extraire des données rangées en mémoire** = to obtain data from a storage device; **il est impossible d'extraire les fichiers depuis la panne** = the files are irretrievable since the computer crashed; **nous pouvons extraire les dossiers qui doivent aller à la composition** = we can extract the files required for typesetting; **on utilise cette commande pour extraire la liste de tous les noms qui commencent par S** = this command will retrieve all names beginning with S

◊ **extrait** *nm* **(a)** *(d'un article)* abstract; **extrait critique** = evaluative abstract **(b)** **extrait de film** = clip

◊ **extrait, -e** *adj* retrieved; **qui peut être extrait** = retrievable; **qui ne peut être extrait** = irretrievable

extrapolation *nf (déduction)* extrapolation

extrémité *nf* end; **file d'attente à deux extrémités** = double-ended queue *ou* deque

Ff

F *(nombre hexadécimal équivalent du 15 décimal)* hexadecimal number equivalent to decimal 15 *ou* F

F = FARAD

f = FEMTO

F *(ionosphère)* **région F** = F-region

fabricant *nm* manufacturer; **le fabricant garantit le système (pendant) un an** = the manufacturer guarantees the system for 12 months; **en cas de mauvais fonctionnement, renvoyer le système au fabricant** = if the system develops a fault it should be returned to the manufacturer

◊ **fabrication** *nf* construction *ou* production; **chacune des pièces de l'ordinateur possède un numéro de fabrication** = each piece of hardware has a production number; **le numéro de fabrication est gravé définitivement sur le panneau arrière du boîtier de l'ordinateur** = the production number is permanently engraved on the back of the computer casing; **les techniques de fabrication ont évolué au cours des dernières années** = construction techniques have changed over the past few years; **fabrication assistée par ordinateur (FAO)** = computer-aided *ou* assisted manufacture (CAM); *voir aussi* CFAO

fabriquer *vtr* to construct *ou* to manufacture; to produce; **cette société fabrique des disquettes et des bandes magnétiques** = the company manufactures diskettes and magnetic tape; **fabriquer sur commande** = to customize

façade *nf* **(panneau de) façade** = front panel *ou* bezel

◊ **face** *nf* *(d'un appareil)* front; *(d'un disque)* side; **disquette simple face** = single-sided disk (SSD); **disquette double face** = double-sided disk; **lecteur de disquettes double face** = double-sided disk drive; **papier photosensible double face** = duplex (paper); **plaque présensibilisée double face pour circuit imprimé** = double-sided printed circuit board

facette *nf* facet; **code à facettes** = faceted code

facile *adj* easy; **rendre quelque chose plus facile** = to make something easy *ou* to simplify something; **facile à utiliser** *ou* **d'utilisation facile** = user-friendly *ou* easy-to-use; **c'est un appareil extrêmement facile à utiliser** = it's a very user-friendly machine; **les données devraient être réparties en fichiers plus faciles à utiliser** = data should be split into more manageable files

◊ **facilité** *nf* capacity *ou* capability; **facilité de traitement électronique de données** = electronic data processing capability

façon *nf* **imprimerie à façon** = print shop; **imprimeur à façon** = jobbing printer

fac-similé *nm* fax *ou* facsimile (copy); **générateur de caractères fac-similés** = facsimile character generator; **transmission de fac-similé** = fax transmission; *(anciennement)* phototelegraphy; *voir aussi* FAX, TELECOPIE

facteur *nm* **(a)** factor; *(nombre d'enregistrements dans un bloc)* **facteur de bloc** = blocking factor; *(électricité)* **facteur de charge** = load (factor); *(le plus important)* **facteur décisif** = deciding factor; *(d'une adresse relative)* **facteur de déplacement** = float factor; *(d'une recherche)* **facteur d'élimination** = elimination factor; *(de lumière)* **facteur de filtre** = filter factor; *(d'une recherche)* **facteur d'omission** *ou* **de silence** = omission factor; *(de circuit)* **facteur pyramidal d'entrée** = fan-in; **facteur pyramidal de sortie** = fan-out **(b)** *(math)* factor; **mettre en facteur** = to factorize; **la mise en facteur de 15 nous donne les facteurs suivants: 1, 15 ou 3, 5** = when factorized, 15 gives the factors 1, 15 or 3, 5

factice *adj* false; **instruction factice** = no-operation instruction *ou* no-op instruction *ou* non-operable instruction *ou* null instruction; **variable factice** = dummy variable

factorielle *nf* factorial; **la factorielle de 4 (qui s'écrit 4!) est 1x2x3x4 ou 24** = 4 factorial (written 4!) is 1x2x3x4 or 24

◊ **factoriser** *vtr* to factorize

faible *adj* weak *ou* low; **communication à faible débit** = low speed communications; **graphique de faible définition** = low-resolution graphics *ou* low-res graphics; **bit de poids faible** = least significant bit (LSB); **chiffre de poids faible** = least significant digit (LSD) *ou* low-order digit; *(état logique)* **tension faible** = logical low

◊ **faiblir** *vi* *(signal)* to fade *ou* to decay

faire *vtr* **(a)** *(agir)* to do (something); **ne pas faire quelque chose** = to fail to do something; **homme à tout faire** = general assistant; *(dans un studio de cinématographie)* gaffer, US gofer **(b)** *(produire)* to make (something); **il a fait six photos de la nouvelle machine** = he took six photographs of the new machine

faisceau *nm* **(a)** *(rayon)* beam; **faisceau de balayage** = scanning spot beam; **faisceau électronique** *ou* **d'électrons** = electron beam; **enregistrement par faisceau électronique (sur**

microfilm) = electron beam recording (EBR); **faisceau étroit** = spot beam; **faisceau d'exploration** = scanning spot beam; **faisceau d'image** = picture beam; **faisceau lumineux** = light beam; **balayage par faisceau mobile** = flying spot scan; **dédoublement de faisceau** = beam diversity; **largeur d'un faisceau** = beam width **(b)** *(groupement de fibres optiques)* bundle; **faisceau cohérent** = coherent bundle **(c)** *(de connexions)* **faisceau de jonction** = trunk

```
un faisceau lumineux de longueur d'onde
inférieure à 950nm ne sera détecté que par la
photodiode supérieure et sera entièrement
absorbé par celle-ci
                              Opto électronique
```

famille *nf* family *ou* group

fana *nm&f (familier)* **fana d'informatique** = terminal junky (TJ)

faner *vi (couleur ou photo)* to fade

fantôme *nm* ghost *ou* phantom; *(télévision)* **image fantôme** = ghost (image)

FAO **(a)** **fabrication assistée par ordinateur (FAO)** = computer-aided *ou* assisted manufacture (CAM) **(b)** **formation assistée par ordinateur (FAO)** = computer-aided *ou* assisted learning (CAL); **langage de programmation FAO** = authoring language; **système adapté aux langages FAO** = authoring system

farad (F) *nm* farad (F)

Faraday *npr* **cage de Faraday** = Faraday cage

FAT *(table d'allocation des fichiers)* **table FAT** = File Allocation Table (FAT)

fatal, -e *adj* fatal *ou* terminal; **erreur fatale** = fatal error *ou* catastrophic error; **panne fatale** = catastrophic failure

fatigue *nf* tiredness; **fatigue oculaire** = eye-strain

faute *nf* **(a)** *(erreur)* error; **faute de frappe** = typing error; **elle doit avoir fait une faute de frappe** = she must have made a typing error; **faute de syntaxe** = grammatical error *ou* syntax error **(b)** *(défaut)* defect *ou* fault

faux, fausse *adj* false; **fausse erreur** = false error; *(en caractères trop petits pour être affichés)* **en faux texte** = greeked

◊ **faux-titre** *nm (d'un livre)* half title

fax *nm* **(a)** *(message par télécopie)* fax *ou* facsimile transmission; **nous n'avons reçu que deux fax ce matin** = we received only two faxes this morning **(b)** *(machine ou télécopieur)* fax (machine); **notre fax est tout à côté du standard téléphonique** = the fax machine is next to the telephone switchboard; **envoyer quelque chose par fax** = to fax something; **adaptateur fax** = fax adapter; **carte fax** = fax card *ou* board; **serveur de fax** = fax server

◊ **faxer** *vtr* to fax; **j'ai faxé les documents à notre bureau de New York** = I've faxed the documents to our New York office; *voir aussi* TELECOPIE

FDDI *(pour réseaux à fibres optiques)* Fibre Distributed Data Interface (FDDI) (for high-speed networks); **standard FDDI II** = FDDI II

FDISK *(utilitaire de formatage de disque sous MS-DOS)* (MS-DOS system utility) FDISK

FDM *(multiplexage en fréquence)* Frequency Division Multiplexing (FDM)

fdx = FULL DUPLEX; *voir* DUPLEX

fédérateur *adj* **réseau fédérateur** = fibre distributed data interface (FDDI) (for high-speed networks)

feedback *nm* feedback; **feedback acoustique** = acoustical feedback; **feedback négatif** = negative feedback; **feedback positif** = positive feedback; **boucle de feedback** = feedback loop

femelle *adj* female; **connecteur femelle** = female connector; **prise femelle** = female socket; *voir aussi* MALE, CHANGEUR

femto- (f) *préfixe* femto- (f)

◊ **femtoseconde** *nf* femtosecond

fenêtrage *nm (d'écran)* windowing

fenêtre *nf* **(a)** window; **le système d'exploitation permet d'afficher d'autres programmes simultanément, chacun dans une fenêtre différente** = the operating system will allow other programs to be displayed on-screen at the same time in different windows; **plusieurs postes de travail à distance sont connectés au réseau, chacun disposant d'une fenêtre sur le disque dur** = several remote stations are connected to the network and each has its own window onto the hard disk; **fenêtre active** = active window; **fenêtre bloc-notes** = screen notepad; **fenêtre de commande** = command window; **la fenêtre de commande est une seule ligne en bas de l'écran** = the command window is a single line at the bottom of the screen; **l'utilisateur peut définir la taille de la fenêtre de commande** = the user can define the size of the command window; **fenêtre de contrôle d'interface** = breakout box; **l'interface série ne semble pas fonctionner - ouvrez la fenêtre de contrôle pour voir quels signaux fonctionnent** = the serial interface doesn't seem to be working - use the breakout box to see which signals are present; **fenêtre de dialogue** = dialogue box; **fenêtre d'édition** = edit window; **fenêtre étroite** *ou* **fenêtre d'une ligne** = strip window *ou* thin window; **fenêtre de texte** = text window; **fenêtre de transmission** = transmission window **(b)** **enveloppe à fenêtre** = window envelope

◊ **fenêtrer** *vi (écran)* to window

fente *nf* slot *ou* aperture; **insérer dans une fente** = to slot in(to); **la disquette s'insère dans l'une des deux fentes du lecteur de disquettes** = the disk slots into one of the floppy drive apertures; **insérer la disquette dans la fente gauche du panneau avant de l'ordinateur** = insert the disk into the left-hand slot on the front of the computer

fer *nm* **(a)** iron; **oxyde de fer** = ferric oxide **(b)** *(imprimerie)* **au fer à droite** = flush right; **au fer à gauche** = flush left

fermé, -ée *adj* closed; **boucle fermée** = closed loop; **enveloppe fermée** = sealed envelope; **groupe fermé d'utilisateurs** = closed user group (CUG); **sous-programme fermé** = closed *ou* linked subroutine; **télévision en circuit fermé** = closed circuit television (CCTV)

◊ **fermer** *vtr* to close *ou* to shut down; *(un appareil sous tension)* to power down *ou* power off; **fermer hermétiquement** = to seal; **fermer un fichier** = to close a file; **fermer une session** = to log off *ou* log out

◊ **fermeture** *nf* (opération de) fermeture de fichier = close file

ferrique *adj* oxyde ferrique = ferric oxide

◊ **ferrite** *nf* ferrite; **noyau de ferrite** = ferrite core

◊ **ferromagnétique** *adj* ferromagnetic; **matériau ferromagnétique** = ferromagnetic material

feuille *nf* sheet (of paper); *(imprimerie)* leaf; **placé entre deux feuilles** = interleaved; **on avait placé des feuilles blanches entre les pages nouvellement imprimées pour éviter les coulures d'encre** = blank paper was interleaved with the newly printed text to prevent the ink running; **alimentation feuille à feuille** = (single) sheet feed; **bac d'alimentation feuille à feuille** *ou* **bac à feuilles** = sheet feed attachment; **système d'alimentation feuille à feuille** = cut sheet feeder; **entraînement feuille à feuille** = single sheet feed; **feuille de programmation** = coding sheet *ou* coding form; **feuille de style** = style sheet *ou* image master; **la feuille de style comporte 125 symboles programmables (par l'utilisateur)** = the style sheet contains 125 user-definable symbols

◊ **feuillet** *nm* **(a)** *(d'ancien manuscrit)* folio **(b)** **feuillet publicitaire** = leaflet

fiabilité *nf* reliability; **cette appareil est reconnu pour sa fiabilité** = this machine has an excellent reliability record; **ce produit a réussi tous les tests de fiabilité** = the product has passed its reliability tests; **fiabilité des données** = data reliability; **fiabilité d'un logiciel** = software reliability

◊ **fiable** *adj* reliable

fibre *nf* fibre, *US* fiber; **fibre optique** = optical fibre; **technologie de la fibre optique** *ou* **de la transmission par fibre optique** = fibre optics; **fibre optique monomode** = monomode fibre; **fibre optique multimode** = multimode fibre; **câble à fibres optiques** = fibre optic cable *ou* fibre optic connection; **les câbles à fibres optiques permettent de placer les noeuds jusqu'à un kilomètre l'un de l'autre** = fibre optic connections enable nodes up to one kilometre apart to be used; **faisceau de fibres optiques** = bundle (of optical fibres); **liaison à fibres optiques** = fibre optic cable *ou* fibre optic connection

fiche *nf* **(a)** *(carte)* filing card *ou* index card; **faire une fiche** = to place something on file; **mettre sur fiches** = to card-index; **mise sur fiches** = card-indexing **(b)** *(d'un appareil électrique)* plug; *(pour téléphone)* jack; **la fiche est fournie avec l'imprimante** = the printer is supplied with a plug

◊ **fichier** *nm* **(a)** *(sur cartes)* card index; **personne ne comprend sa méthode de classement du fichier** = no one can understand her card-indexing system **(b)** **fichier d'adresses** (destiné aux mailings) = mailing list; **son nom figure sur notre fichier d'adresses** = his name is on our mailing list; **établir un fichier d'adresses** = to build up a mailing list; **acheter un fichier d'adresses** = to buy a mailing list **(c)** *(informatique)* file *ou* data file; **fichier à accès séquentiel** = serial file; **fichier bidimensionnel** = flat file; **fichier binaire exécutable** *ou* **fichier COM** = COM file; **fichier en boucle** = circular file; **fichiers cachés** = hidden files; **cela permet aux utilisateurs de sauvegarder ou de restaurer un par un les fichiers cachés** = it allows users to backup or restore hidden system files independently; **fichier chaîné** = chained file; **fichier avec articles chaînés** = threaded file; **fichier chronologique** = journal file; **fichier COM** *ou* **fichier binaire exécutable** = COM file; **fichier de commande(s)** = batch file *ou* command file; **ce fichier de commande(s) est utilisé pour économiser du temps et des efforts lorsqu'on effectue des tâches de routine** = this batch file is used to save time and effort when carrying out a routine task; **processeur de fichier de commandes** = command file processor; **fichier contigu** = contiguous file; **fichier de contrôle de tâche** = job control file; **fichier corrigé** = corrected file *ou* update (file); **fichier des coupures** *ou* **des corrections** = deletion record; **fichier sur disque** *ou* **sur disquette** = disk file; **fichier divisé en plusieurs parties** = partitioned file; **fichier de données** = data file; **il faut analyser le fichier de données** = the data file has to be analysed; **fichier de données externe** = external data file; **fichier d'enregistrement des blocs** = block list; **fichier (d')entrée/sortie** = I/O file; **fichiers dans une file d'attente** = file queue; **fichier fils** = son file; **fichier grand-père** = grandfather file; **fichier indexé** = indexed file; **fichier informatique** = computer file; **avoir accès à un fichier informatique** = to have access to a file of data; **fichier intermédiaire** = intermediate file; **fichier inversé** = inverted file; **fichier-journal** = journal file; **fichier maître** = master file; **fichier de manoeuvre** = scratch file *ou* work file; **(ensemble des) fichiers en mémoire** = file store; **fichier mis à jour** = update (file); **fichier de mise à jour** = change file *ou* transaction file *ou* addition record; **fichier de modifications** = change *ou* movement file; **fichier (de) mouvements** = detail file *ou* movement file *ou* change file *ou* transaction file *ou* update file; **fichier d'ordinateur** = computer file; **fichier ouvert** = open file; **laisser le fichier ouvert** = leave file open; **(système à) fichiers partagés** = distributed file (system); **fichier père** = father file; **le fichier père est un fichier de sauvegarde de première génération** = the father file is a first generation backup; **fichier**

permanent = permanent file *ou* master file; **fichier plat** = flat file; **fichier de pointeurs** = pointer file; **fichier principal** = master file; **fichier programme** = program file; **fichier de programme maître** = master program file; **fichier de référence** = authority file *ou* authority list *ou* reference file; **fichier des registres** = register file; **(système à) fichiers répartis** = distributed file (system); **fichier de sauvegarde** *ou* backup *ou* backup file; **cycle de rotation des fichiers de sauvegarde** = grandfather cycle; **fichier série extensible** = extending serial file; **fichier de sortie** = output file; **fichier source** = source file; **fichier subdivisé** = partitioned file; **fichier de tâches (à exécuter)** = job file; **fichier texte** = text file; **fichier de transactions** = transaction file; **fichier de travail** = scratch file *ou* work file; **avoir accès à** *ou* **accéder à un fichier** = to gain access to a file; **annulation de fichier** = file deletion; **archivage de fichiers** = file sort; **attributs de fichiers** = file attributes; **bloc de contrôle de fichier** = file control block; **conversion de fichier** = file conversion; **création de fichier** = file creation; **(données de) début de fichier** = head (of file); **défragmentation de fichier** = file defragmentation; **descripteur de fichier** = file descriptor *ou* file label; **destruction de fichier** = file deletion; **dimension d'un fichier** = file length; **dispositif de protection d'écriture de fichier** = file protect tab; **enregistrement en fin de fichier** = trailer record; **en-tête de fichier** = file header; **l'en-tête du fichier de la base de données indique le nombre total d'enregistrements et la liste des champs indexés** = the file header in the database file shows the total number of records and lists the index fields; **étiquette de fichier** = file label; **extension (du nom) d'un fichier** = *voir plus bas* NOM DE FICHIER **fermer un fichier** = to close a file; **(instruction de) fermeture de fichier** = close file; **file d'attente de fichiers** = file queue; **format de fichier image** = tag image file format (TIFF); **fragmentation de fichier** = file fragmentation; **fusion de fichiers** = file merger *ou* file collating; **(instruction de) fusion de fichier** = join *ou* merge files; **(méthode de) gestion, accès et transfert de fichiers (méthode FTAM)** = file transfer access and management (FTAM); **(système de) gestion de fichier** = file management (system); **programme de gestion de fichier** = records management; **gestionnaire de fichier** = file manager; **groupe de fichiers (connexes)** = file set; **identification de fichier** = file identification; **index des fichiers** = file index; **intégrité d'un fichier** = integrity of a file; **interclassement de fichiers** = file collating; **interrogation de fichier** = file interrogation; **label de fichier** = file label; **label de fin de fichier** = trailer; **longueur d'un fichier** = file length; **maintenance de fichier** = file maintenance; **mise en mémoire d'un fichier** = file storage; **mise à jour d'un fichier** = file update *ou* file maintenance; **nettoyage de fichier** = file cleanup; **nom d'un fichier** = file name *ou* filename; **extension du nom d'un fichier** = filename extension; **l'extension SYS ajoutée au nom du fichier indique qu'il s'agit d'un fichier système** = the filename extension SYS indicates that this is a system file; **sous MS-DOS, le nom de fichier peut comporter jusqu'à huit caractères et une extension (de nom) de trois caractères** = in MS-DOS, a filename can be up to eight characters long together with a three character filename extension; **les fichiers avec une extension EXE contiennent un code exécutable** = files with the extension EXE are file types that contain program code; **longueur du nom d'un fichier** = length of filename; **spécification du nom du fichier** = filename extension; **numéro de fichier** = file handle; **les nouvelles données sont écrites dans un fichier identifié par le numéro 1** = the new data is written to the file identified by file handle 1; **partage de fichier** = file sharing; **protection** *ou* **verrouillage de fichier** = file security; file locking; **(logiciel** *ou* **dispositif de) protection de fichier** = file protection (software *ou* device); **ratio d'activité d'un fichier** = file activity ratio; **logiciel de récupération de fichiers (après incident)** = file-recovery utility; **il est impossible de retrouver un fichier perdu sans l'aide d'un logiciel de récupération de fichiers** = a lost file cannot be found without a file-recovery utility; **répertoire de fichiers** = file directory; **routine de manipulation de fichier** = file handling routine; **sécurisation de fichiers** = file security; **(logiciel** *ou* **dispositif de) sécurisation de fichier** = file protection; **serveur de fichier** = file server; **stockage de fichier** = file storage; **structure d'un fichier** = file layout *ou* file structure; **système à fichiers** = distributed file system; *(table FAT)* **table d'allocation des fichiers** = file allocation table (FAT); **taille d'un fichier** = file extent *ou* file size; **taux d'activité d'un fichier** = file activity ratio; **traitement de fichier** = file processing; **transfert de fichier** = file transfer; **protocole de transfert de fichiers** *ou* **protocole FTP** = file transfer protocol (FTP); **utilitaire de transfert de fichiers** = file transfer utility; **tri de fichiers** = file sort; **type de fichier** = file type; **validation de fichier** = file validation; **verrouillage de fichier** = file locking; **version améliorée** *ou* **nouvelle version d'un fichier** = file update; **vidage de fichier** = file purge *ou* file cleanup

> pour créer un nouveau fichier, exécutez la commande 'Nouveau document'
> *L'Ordinateur Individuel*

> en apparence, rien n'est plus simple que de copier un fichier sur disquette, puis d'utiliser cette disquette sur un second ordinateur
> *Action PC*

fidélité *nf* fidelity; **haute fidélité** = high fidelity *ou* hifi *ou* hi fi *ou* hi-fi; **chaîne haute fidélité** *ou* **système haute fidélité** = high fidelity system *ou* hi fi system *ou* hifi *ou* hi-fi

se fier *vpr (appareil)* **auquel on peut se fier** = reliable (machine)

FIFO *(méthode du premier entré premier sorti)* First in First out (FIFO); **mémoire FIFO** = FIFO memory *ou* first in first out memory; **pile en mode FIFO** = push-up list *ou* stack; *voir aussi* PREMIER

figer *vtr* to freeze; **figer une image** = to freeze a frame; **le processeur d'images permet de figer une image** = with an image processor you can freeze a video frame

fignoler *vtr (apporter de légères modifications au logiciel ou au matériel pour améliorer les performances)* to tweak

figure 106 **fin**

figure *nf* figure; **voir figure 10: tableau des codes ASCII** = see figure 10 for a chart of ASCII codes

◊ **figurer** *vi* to appear (on) *ou* to be on; **son nom figure sur notre fichier d'adresses** = his name is on our mailing list

fil *nm* (a) *(métallique ou électrique)* wire; *(de liaison)* lead *ou* flex *ou* cord *ou* cable; **circuit à deux fils** = two wire circuit; **fils téléphoniques** = telephone wires; **fil de terre** *ou* **de mise à la masse** = earth wire; **sans fil** = wireless; **micro** *ou* **microphone sans fil** = radio microphone (b) **passer un coup de fil** = to make a phone call

file *nf* queue; **méthode d'accès séquentiel en file** = queued sequential access method (QSAM); **méthode d'accès séquentiel indexé en file** = queued indexed sequential access method (QISAM); **prendre la file** = to queue; **file d'attente** = queue *ou* waiting list; *(de demandes de transmission ou de données à transmettre)* channel queue; *(des données d'entrée)* input work queue; *(de fichiers)* file queue; *(de périphériques)* device queue; *(de tâches ou de travaux à exécuter)* job queue *ou* job stream *ou* task queue; **imprimer la file d'attente** = to despool; **se joindre à la file d'attente** = to form a queue *ou* to join a queue; **placer (des données** *ou* **des tâches) dans la file d'attente** = to place in the queue; **file d'attente à deux entrées** *ou* **à deux extrémités** = double-ended queue *ou* deque; **file d'attente qui fonctionne sur le principe 'premier entré premier sorti'** = FIFO queue; **fichiers dans une file d'attente** = file queue; **méthode de gestion de la file d'attente** = queued access method; **programme de gestion** *ou* **gestionnaire de file d'attente** = queue management program *ou* queue manager; **ce nouveau logiciel de spouling comporte un gestionnaire de file d'attente** = this is a new software spooler with built-in queue management; **pile en file d'attente** = push-up list *ou* stack; **procédure de file d'attente** = queue discipline; **les périphériques tels que les imprimantes laser sont reliés en ligne et les fichiers sont gérés par un système de file d'attente automatique** = output devices such as laser printers are connected on-line with an automatic file queue; **temps d'attente dans la file** = queuing time

filet *nm* *(imprimerie)* bar *ou* line *ou* rule; **filet ultra-fin** = hairline rule

filière *nf* *(d'un programme)* path

fille *nf* **carte fille** = daughter board

film *nm* (a) *(matériau)* film; **film lith** = lith film; **film de transfert** = carbon tissue (b) photographic film; **film en boucle** = loop film; **photo avec film sensible aux infrarouges** = infrared photography; **traitement de film instantané** *ou* **intégré dans l'appareil** = in camera process; **entraînement d'un film** = film advance (c) *(cinématographique)* film *ou* motion picture; **film fixe** = film strip; **extrait de film** = clip; **l'équipement de prise de vue et de projection de films** = film chain; **image orientée en film** = cine-orientated image; **montage d'un film** = film assembly; **repiquage vidéo d'un film** = film pickup; **tourner un film** = to film *ou* to shoot

◊ **filmer** *vtr* to film *ou* to shoot; *(imprimerie)* **filmer un texte** = to film copy; *(télévision)* **programme filmé** = canned programme

fils *nm* **fichier fils** = son file

filtrage *nm* filtering; **éliminer par filtrage** = to filter

◊ **filtre** *nm* (a) *(de lumière ou couleur)* filter; **filtre d'absorption** = absorption filter; **filtre d'amélioration du contraste** = contrast enhancement filter; *(pour écran d'ordinateur)* **filtre antireflet(s)** = glare filter; **filtre d'optimisation de caractères et de protection de la vue** = character enhancement filter; **filtre polaroïde** = polaroid filter; **facteur de filtre** = filter factor (b) *(de fréquence, etc.)* **filtre de bande de fréquences** = frequency equalizer; **filtre passe-bande** = bandpass filter; **filtre passe-bas** = low pass filter; **filtre passe-haut** = high pass filter; **filtre de sélection du signal maximal** *ou* **minimal** = auctioneering device (c) **filtre de microphone** = pop filter; **chaque fois que vous prononcez un 'p' vous saturez l'enregistrement, placez donc ce filtre pour que cela cesse** = every time you say a 'p' you overload the tape recorder, so put this pop filter in to stop it

◊ **filtré, -ée** *adj* (a) filtered (b) **signal filtré** = bandlimited signal

◊ **filtrer** *vtr* to filter; **le signal d'entrée a été filtré pour obtenir une forme optimale** = the received signal was equalized to an optimum shape

fin *nf* (a) end *ou* completion *ou* ending *ou* finish; *(radio ou télévision)* **fin des émissions** = close-down; **mettre fin à quelque chose graduellement** = to phase something out; **prendre fin** = to end *ou* to finish; **à la fin** = *(au bout)* at the end; *(finalement)* in the end *ou* finaly; **à la fin de la transmission des données** = at the end of the data transmission (b) **(code de) fin d'adresse** = end of address (EOA); *(de traitement informatique)* **fin anormale** = abend *ou* abnormal end; **(code de) fin de la bande (magnétique)** = end of tape (EOT); **label de fin de bande** = tape trailer; **(marque** *ou* **code de) fin de bloc** = end of block (EOB); **(code de) fin de document** = end of document *ou* end of file (EOF); **(code de) fin de données** = end of data (EOD); **(code de) fin d'enregistrement** = end of record (EOR); **enregistrement de fin de fichier** = trailer record; **(caractère) fin de fichier** = end of file (EOF); **label de fin de fichier** = trailer; **marque** *ou* **marqueur de fin de fichier** = rogue value *ou* terminator; **fin de ligne** = line ending; **(caractère de) fin de ligne** = end of line (EOL); **dispositif de fin de ligne** = line terminator; **fin de liste** = tail; **marqueur de fin de liste** = terminator; **marqueur de fin de liste chaînée** = nil pointer; **(code de) fin de message** = end of message (EOM) *ou* tail; **(code) fin de module** = chapter stop; **(caractère** *ou* **instruction de) fin de page** = page break (instruction); *(sur machine à écrire)* **signal de fin de page** = end of page indicator; **(code de) fin de paragraphe** = hard return; **signal de fin de report** = carry complete signal; **(code de) fin de support de données** = end of medium (EM); **(code de) fin de tâche** = end of job (EOJ); **(code de) fin de texte** = end of text (EOT *ou* ETX); **(code** *ou* **signal de) fin de la transmission** =

end of transmission (EOT); **sans fin** = endless; **boucle sans fin** = continuous loop *ou* infinite loop *ou* endless loop; *(sur un clavier)* **touche Fin** = End key

fin, -e *adj* fine; **on trouve quelques lignes très fines dans cette gravure** = the engraving has some very fine lines

final , -e *adj* final *ou* finished; **copie finale** = clean copy; **épreuve finale** = master proof

◊ **finaliser** *vtr* to finalize; *(prête pour la reproduction)* **copie finalisée** = camera-ready copy (crc)

Finder ™ (Apple Macintosh graphical user interface) Finder ™

fini *nm* finish; **ce produit a un très beau fini** = the product has an attractive finish

◊ **fini, -e** *adj* **(a)** finished; **produit fini** = end product **(b)** finite; **nombres à précision finie** = finite-precision numbers

◊ **finir 1** *vtr&i* to end *ou* to finish *ou* to complete **2** *vtr* to finish

◊ **finition** *nf* finish; **ce produit présente une très belle finition** = the product has an attractive finish

firmware *nm* *(logiciel microprogrammé intégré à l'ordinateur)* firmware

fisheye *nm* *(lentille)* fisheye lens

fixage *nm* = FIXATION

fixation *nf* *(stade de développement d'un film)* fixing

fixe *adj* **(a)** fixed; **connexion fixe** = hardwired connection; **disque (dur) fixe** = fixed disk; **unité comprenant des disques fixes et des disques amovibles** = fixed and exchangeable disk storage (FEDS) **(b)** **film fixe** = film strip; **image fixe** = still frame **(c)** **cycle fixe** = fixed cycle; **opération en cycle fixe** = fixed cycle operation; **longueur fixe** = fixed length; **enregistrement de longueur fixe** = fixed-length record; **mot de longueur fixe** = fixed-length word; **ordinateur à longueur de mots fixe** = fixed word length computer; **mémoire fixe** = control memory *ou* ROM *ou* read only memory; **code à rapport de bits fixe** = constant ratio code; **taille fixe** = fixed length; **champ de taille fixe** = constant length field *ou* fixed field; **tête de lecture fixe** = fixed head disk (drive); **virgule fixe** = fixed point; **arithmétique à virgule fixe** = fixed-point arithmetic; **notation à virgule fixe** = fixed-point notation; **la mise en mémoire de nombres à virgule fixe utilise deux octets pour le nombre entier et un octet pour la partie décimale** = storage of fixed point numbers has two bytes allocated for the whole number and one byte for the fraction part

fixer *vtr* to fix *ou* to set; **l'ordinateur est fixé au poste de travail** = the computer is fixed to the workstation; **fixer d'avance** = to preset; **fixer une marge** = to set a margin; **nous avons fixé la marge de droite à 80 caractères** = we set the right-hand margin at 80 characters

flare *nm* *(effet Callier)* Callier effect

flash *nm* **carte 'flash'** = flash card; **mémoire flash** = flash memory

flashage *nm* *(imprimerie)* **flashage d'un texte** = filming of copy

◊ **flasheur** *nm* *(imprimerie)* output bureau

flatbed *nm* *(à plat)* **de type 'flatbed'** = flatbed; **lecteur de transmission de type 'flatbed'** = flatbed transmitter; **les scanners sont de type 'flatbed', ou possèdent un système d'entraînement du papier par rouleau** = scanners are either flatbed models or platen type, paper-fed models

fléché, -ée *adj* arrowed *ou* with an arrow; *(de direction du curseur)* **touches fléchées** = arrow keys *ou* arrowed pad *ou* cursor pad

flexibilité *nf* flexibility

◊ **flexible** *adj* flexible; **atelier flexible** = flexible manufacturing system (FMS); **routage flexible** = distributed adaptive routing

flot *nm* flow *ou* stream; **flot de données** = data stream

flottant, -e *adj* floating; **accent flottant** = floating accent; **courant flottant** = floating voltage; **tête flottante** = floating head *ou* flying head; **calcul en virgule flottante** = floating point arithmetic; **dans un calcul en virgule flottante, le nombre 56,47 serait écrit 0,5647 puissance 2** = the fixed number 56.47 in floating-point arithmetic would be 0.5647 and a power of 2; **nombre à virgule flottante** = floating point number; **numération à virgule flottante** = floating point notation; **opération en virgule flottante** = floating point operation (FLOP); **(nombre d')opérations en virgule flottante par seconde** = floating point operations *ou* FLOPs per second; **(nombre de) millions d'opérations en virgule flottante par seconde** = mega floating point operations per second *ou* megaflops *ou* MFLOPS; **processeur à virgule flottante** = floating point unit (FPU) *ou* floating point processor; **le processeur à virgule flottante accélère le traitement de ce logiciel graphique** = the floating point processor speeds up the processing of the graphics software; **ce modèle est livré avec un processeur à virgule flottante installé** = this model includes a built-in floating point processor

flottement *nm* swim

flou, -e 1 *adj* **(a)** fuzzy; **rendre flou** = to blur; **un papier de qualité supérieure donnera des caractères moins flous** = top quality paper will eliminate fuzzy characters; **l'image est floue** = the picture is out of focus *ou* is not in focus; **en tournant le bouton de mise au point l'image devient floue** = the image becomes blurred when you turn the focus knob **(b)** **logique floue** = fuzzy logic *ou* fuzzy theory **2** *nm* blur

fluctuation *nf* fluctuation; **fluctuation de l'intensité du signal** = fluctuating signal strength;

les **fluctuations de courant peuvent entraîner la perte de données** = data loss can occur because of power supply variations

◊ **fluctuer** *vi* to fluctuate; **le courant fluctue entre 1Amp et 1,3Amp** = the electric current fluctuates between 1Amp and 1.3Amp; **courant qui fluctue** = fluctuating current

flux *nm* flow *ou* stream; **flux de données** = data flow; **flux (de données) de sortie** = output stream; **flux continu** *ou* **ininterrompu de données** = continuous data stream; **flux magnétique** = magnetic flux; **flux multiple d'instructions, flux multiple de données** = multiple instruction stream, multiple data stream (MIMD); **flux multiple d'instructions, flux unique de données** = multiple instruction stream, single data stream (MISD); **flux unique d'instructions, flux multiple de données** = single instruction stream multiple data stream (SIMD); **flux unique d'instructions, flux unique de données** = single instruction stream single data stream (SISD); **flux des tâches** = job stream; **contrôle du flux** = flow control; **contrôle de flux d'informations** = information flow control; **diagramme de flux de données** = data flow diagram (DFD); **direction du flux** = flow direction; **(logiciel de gestion de) flux de travaux** = workflow

focal, -e *adj* focal; **distance focale** = focal length; **plan focal** = image plane

◊ **focale** *nf (distance)* **objectif de focale moyenne** = medium lens; **objectif à focale variable** = zoom lens

folding *nm (méthode de génération d'adresses)* folding

folio *nm* folio

◊ **folioter** *vtr* to folio *ou* to number the pages of a book

fonction *nf* (a) function *ou* capability; **le temps d'ordinateur requis pour le traitement d'une page de texte varie en fonction de la complexité du document** = page processing time depends on the complexity of a given page; **le résultat de sortie est fonction de l'état (physique) des liaisons** = the output is dependent on the physical state of the link; **multiplexage temporel en fonction des appels** = statistical time division multiplexing (STDM) (b) *(informatique)* **fonction bibliothèque** = library function; **cette machine de traitement de texte possédait une fonction correction orthographique mais n'était pas équipée d'éditeur intégré** = the word-processor had a spelling-checker function but no built-in text-editing function; **fonction avancée de communication** = advanced communications function (ACF); **fonction courrier électronique** = electronic mail capabilities; **fonction d'agrégation** *ou* **de globalisation** = aggregate function; **fonctions graphiques GKS** = graphics kernel system (GKS); **fonction hash** = hashing function; **fonction incorporée** = built-in function; **fonction linéaire** = linear function; **l'expression Y (10 + 5X²) n'est pas une fonction linéaire** = the expression $Y (10 + 5X^2)$ is not a linear function; **l'expression Y 10 + 5X - 3W est une fonction linéaire** = the expression Y 10

+ 5X - 3W is a linear function; **appel de fonction** = function call; **bibliothèque de fonctions** = function library; **code** *ou* **caractère de fonction** = function digit; function code; **indicateur de fonction** = role indicator; **liste des fonctions** = capability list; **mémento de fonction des touches** = key overlay; **système de programmation à surcharge de fonctions** = function overloading; **table de fonctions** = function table; **touche de fonction** = (programmable) function key; *(qui ne produit pas de caractère)* dead key; **en appuyant sur la touche de fonction F5 on se met en mode entrée** = hitting F5 will put you into insert mode; **on peut allouer des étiquettes aux touches de fonction** = tags can be allocated to function keys **(c)** *(fonction logique)* function; **fonction de disjonction** = non-equivalence function *ou* NEQ function; **fonction d'équivalence** = equivalence function; **fonction logique spécialisée** = dedicated logic (function); **fonction NON** *ou* **fonction complément** = NOT function; **fonction NON-ET** *ou* **NAND** = NOT-AND *ou* NAND function *ou* dispersion; **fonction NON-OU** *ou* **NI** = NOR function *ou* neither-nor function; **fonction d'union** = join (function)

◊ **fonctionnel, -elle** *adj* functional; **analyse** *ou* **spécification fonctionnelle** = functional specification; **cycle fonctionnel** = action cycle; **diagramme** *ou* **schéma fonctionnel** = functional diagram

◊ **fonctionnement** *nm (d'un appareil)* working *ou* operation *ou* running; **fonctionnement automatique (d'un système)** = unattended operation; **durée moyenne de bon fonctionnement** = mean time to failure (MTF); **durée moyenne de bon fonctionnement** *ou* **moyenne de temps de bon fonctionnement entre les défaillances** = mean time between failures (MTBF); **temps de bon fonctionnement** = up time *ou* uptime; **mauvais fonctionnement** = malfunctioning

◊ **fonctionner** *vi* to function *ou* to run *ou* to work; **l'imprimante fonctionne depuis deux heures** = the printer has been in use for the last two hours; **l'ordinateur fonctionne jusqu'à dix heures par jour** = the computer has been running ten hours a day; **le service de maintenance espère que le système sera de nouveau en état de fonctionner dans les 24 heures** = the maintenance people hope that the system will be ready for use *ou* up and running in 24 hours; **faire fonctionner** = to drive *ou* to operate; **ce modem ne fonctionne pas** = the modem has broken down; **fonctionner bien** *ou* **mal** = to perform well *ou* badly; **il n'est pas vraiment sûr que le nouveau système multiposte fonctionne bien** = he is doubtful about the efficiency of the new networking system; **ils ont sûrement trouvé la source du problème puisque l'ordinateur fonctionne à merveille** = they must have found the fault - the computer is finally up and running; **quelques-unes des touches du clavier ne fonctionnent déjà plus très bien** = some of the keys on the keyboard have started to malfunction; **depuis que nous l'avons, l'ordinateur n'a jamais très bien fonctionné** = the computer system has never worked properly since it was installed; **mal fonctionner** = to malfunction; **(appareil) qui fonctionne à l'électricité** = (machine) powered by electricity *ou* driven by electricity; **un** moteur qui fonctionne à l'électricité = an electrically-powered motor; **(appareil) qui fonctionne grâce à un électro-aimant** = device which works electromagnetically; **logiciel qui fonctionne sur la plupart des ordinateurs** = machine-independent software; **logiciel qui ne fonctionne que sur un type d'ordinateur** = machine-dependent software; **installation de secours prête à fonctionner** = hot standby

fond *nm* (a) background; **un texte en noir sur fond blanc est moins fatigant pour la vue** = black text on a white background is less stressful for the eyes; **bruit de fond** = background noise; **le modem est sensible au bruit de fond** = the modem is sensitive to background noise; **les autres appareils placés autour de cet équipement produiront un fort bruit de fond** = the other machines around this device will produce a lot of background noise; **couleur de fond** = background colour; **traitement de fond** = background processing **(b)** *(d'un film)* **fond animé** = busy background **(c)** *(circuits)* **fond de panier** = (microcomputer) backplane; **processeur de fond** = back-end processor **(d)** *(arts graphiques)* **photo à fond perdu** = photograph which is bled off

fondamental, -e *adj* basic; *(bleu, jaune, rouge)* **couleurs fondamentales** = primary colours; **fréquence fondamentale** = fundamental frequency

◊ **fondamentalement** *adv* basically

fonderie *nf* foundry; **fonderie de silicium** = silicon foundry

fondeuse *nf (de caractères d'imprimerie)* caster machine

fondre *vi (fusionner des fichiers)* to merge *ou* to join *ou* to coalesce (files)

fonds *nm* funds; **transfert électronique de fonds** = electronic funds transfer (system) (EFT); **terminal de transfert électronique de fonds** = electronic funds transfer point of sale (EFTPOS)

fondu *nm (signal audio)* cross fade; **faire un fondu** = to fade out; *(dans une application multimédia)* **fondu enchaîné** = AB roll

◊ **fondu, -e** *adj (métal)* melted; **caractères fondus** *ou* **ligne-bloc fondue au moment de la composition** = hot metal characters *ou* hot type

fonte *nf* font *ou* fount *ou* character set; typeface *ou* typestyle; **fonte logicielle** *ou* **téléchargeable** = soft font; **fonte spéciale** = special sort; **disquette de fontes** = font disk

force *nf* force; **force électromotrice** = electromotive force (EMF)

forfait *nm* flat rate *ou* package deal

◊ **forfaitaire** *adj* **tarif forfaitaire** = set tariff *ou* fixed rate; **il existe un tarif forfaitaire d'utilisation plus un taux/minute de temps d'ordinateur** = there is a set tariff for logging on, then a rate for every minute of computer time used

format *nm* (a) *(dimensions)* format; **format de** carte (perforée) = card format; **format d'écran** = display format *ou* screen format; **écran monochrome standard de format A4, avec une définition de 300 points par pouce** = a standard 300 d.p.i. black and white A4 monitor; **format d'impression** = print format; *(de papier)* **l'imprimante peut accommoder tous les formats jusqu'au quarto** = the printer can deal with all formats up to quarto; **nos formats de pages varient de 220 x 110mm à 360 x 220mm** = our page sizes vary from 220 x 110mm to 360 x 220mm; **papier format A1, A2, A3, A4, A5** = A1, A2, A3, A4, A5 paper; **vous devez photocopier le tableau sur une feuille de format A3** = you must photocopy the spreadsheet on A3 paper; **(papier) format ministre** = foolscap; **la lettre était écrite sur six feuilles format ministre** = the letter was on six sheets of foolscap; **format de la page** = page size; *(de photos)* **format professionnel** = ideal format; **format standard** = normal format *ou* standard format **(b)** *(informatique)* **format d'adresse** = address format; **format d'affichage** = display format; **format de base** = native format; **format de code machine** = machine code format; **format condensé** = packed format; **(mise en) mémoire d'un format courant** = local format storage; **format de données** = data format; **format (standard) d'échange** = (basic) exchange format; *(masque de saisie)* **format d'écran (de saisie)** = form; **il a été facile de former les opérateurs à l'utilisation de ce nouveau logiciel, parce que les formats d'écran ressemblent aux rapports d'impression existants** = it's been easy to train the operators to use the new software since its display looks like the existing printed forms; **format d'encodage** = encoding format; **format d'un enregistrement** = record format *ou* layout; **format initial** = native format; **format d'instruction** = instruction format; *(de données dans l'unité centrale)* **format interne** = internal format; **format de langage symbolique** = symbolic-coding format; **format de message** = message format; **format normal** = normal format; *(de données)* **format variable** = variable format *ou* V format; **vidage au format** = formatted dump **(c)** *(de programme de télévision)* **format magazine** = magazine format

◊ **formatage** *nm (d'un texte)* make up *ou* makeup; *(de nombres ou données)* normalization; *(d'un disque ou d'une disquette)* (disk) formatting; *(d'un disque)* **formatage de bas niveau** = low-level format; **formatage de secteurs (d'un disque)** = (disk) sector formatting; **formatage de secteurs permanents** = hard-sectoring; **(disque) avec formatage physique** = hard-sectored (disk); **logiciel** *ou* **matériel de formatage** = formatter; **logiciel de formatage d'impression** = print formatter; **logiciel** *ou* **programme de formatage de texte** = text formatter; **on utilise le formatage de texte comme programme de base de PAO** = people use the text formatter as a basic desk-top publishing program; **commande de formatage (de paragraphe, etc.)** = template command; **une commande de formatage permet à l'utilisateur de préciser l'alinéa de chaque paragraphe** = a template paragraph command enables the user to specify the number of spaces each paragraph should be indented; **unité de formatage vertical** = vertical format unit (VFU)

◊ **formaté, -ée** *adj (disque ou disquette)* formatted; **formaté d'avance** = preformatted; **(disque) formaté par logiciel** = soft-sectored (disk); **non formaté, -ée** = unformatted; **le lecteur de cartouche a une capacité de stockage non formaté de 12,7Mo** = the cartridge drive provides 12.7Mbyte of unformatted storage; **bande de texte non formaté** = idiot tape; **capacité non formatée** = unformatted capacity; **disque non formaté** = unformatted disk; **il est impossible de copier quoi que ce soit sur une disquette non formatée** = it is impossible to copy to an unformatted disk *ou* to a disk which has not been formatted

◊ **formater** *vtr (un texte)* to make up; *(un nombre, une donnée)* to normalize; *(un disque ou une disquette)* to format; **vous devez formater toutes les nouvelles disquettes avant de les utiliser** = you have to format new disks before one can use them

◊ **formateur** *nm* formatter; **formateur de données de sortie** = output formatter

le formatage consiste donc à poser des marques sur la couche magnétique de la disquette
Science et Vie Micro

lorsqu'un disque est formaté, des codes magnétiques sont inscrits sur sa surface, la divisant en secteurs (les parts de gâteau) et en pistes (les arcs de cercles concentriques)
Science et Vie Micro

formation *nf* teaching *ou* instruction *ou* learning; **formation pratique** = hands-on instruction; **la société informatique offre une formation pratique de deux jours** = the computer firm gives a two day hands-on training course; **formation à l'aide de didacticiels** = programmed learning; **formation assistée par ordinateur (FAO)** = computer-aided *ou* -assisted learning (CAL); computer-managed learning (CML) *ou* computer-based learning (CBL); **formation assistée par système expert** = intelligent tutoring system

forme *nf* form *ou* pattern; **sous forme de diagramme** = diagrammatically *ou* in diagrammatic form; **sous forme numérique** = digitally; **mettre en forme** = to format; **(texte) mis en forme à l'impression** = post-formatted (text); **on utilise des feuilles de style pour mettre en forme les documents** = style sheets are used to format documents; **forme d'impression** = (printing) form; **forme d'onde** = waveform; **reconnaissance de formes** = pattern recognition

formel, -elle *adj* **logique formelle** = formal logic

former *vtr* to form

formulaire *nm* form; **formulaires et en-têtes de lettres peuvent être conçus sur un PC** = business forms and letterheads can now be designed on a PC; **formulaire de demande** = application form; **formulaire de programmation** = (program) coding sheet *ou* coding form; **formulaire préimprimé** = preprinted form; preprinted stationery

◊ **formule** *nf* formula *ou* expression; **portabilité d'une formule** = formula portability; **réduire une**

formule à sa plus simple expression = to express a formula in its simplest form; *(langage FORTRAN)* **traducteur de formule** = formula translator (FORTRAN)

◊ **formuler** *vtr* to express

fort, -e *adj* important *ou* significant; **de poids fort** = high order; **bit de poids fort** = most significant bit (MSB); **chiffre de poids fort** = most significant character *ou* most significant digit (MSD); **forte réduction** = high reduction

FORTH *(langage)* FORTH

FORTRAN *(langage de programmation)* Formula Translation (FORTRAN); *voir aussi* FORMULE

FOSDIC = FILM OPTICAL SCANNING DEVICE FOR INPUT INTO COMPUTERS; *voir* LECTEUR

fou, folle *n* **fou d'informatique** = terminal junky (TJ)

fourchette *nf* range *ou* span; **fourchette normale** = normal range

Fourier *npr* série de Fourier = Fourier series

fournir *vtr* to supply; **ils ont signé un contrat pour fournir des informations en ligne** = they have signed a contract to supply on-line information

fournisseur *nm* supplier; dealer; **un fournisseur de composants pour ordinateurs** = a supplier of computer parts; **un fournisseur d'équipements informatiques** = a computer equipment supplier; **un fournisseur de lecteurs de disquettes** = a supplier of disk drives *ou* a disk drive supplier; **l'ordinateur vient de chez un fournisseur connu** = the computer was supplied by a recognized dealer; **service fournisseur d'information** = information provider (IP)

foyer *nm (de lentille)* focus; **profondeur de foyer** = depth of focus

fractal *nm* fractal

fraction *nf* fraction; **fraction binaire** = binary fraction; **la fraction binaire 0,011 est égale à un quart plus un huitième (ou trois huitièmes)** = the binary fraction 0.011 is equal to one quarter plus one eighth (i.e. three eighths); *(d'une imprimante)* **caractère de fraction** = piece fraction

◊ **fractionnaire** *adj* fractional; **partie fractionnaire** = fractional part; **puissance fractionnaire** = root *ou* fractional power; **la racine est la puissance fractionnaire d'un nombre** = the root is the fractional power of a number

◊ **fractionnement** *nm* division; fragmentation

fragmentation *nf* fragmentation

frais *nmpl* costs; **frais fixes** = fixed costs *ou* above-the-line costs

français, -e *adj* French; **clavier français accentué** = AZERTY keyboard

frappe *nf* keystroke *ou* stroke; **contrôle de la frappe** = keystroke verification; **faute de frappe** = typing error; **faire une faute de frappe** = to make a typing error; **nombre de frappes** = keystroke count; **nombre de frappes par heure** *ou* **frappes/heure** = keystrokes per hour; **elle peut saisir un texte au rythme de 3500 frappes/heure** = she keyboards at a rate of 3500 keystrokes per hour; **vitesse de frappe** = keystroke rate; **il a une vitesse de frappe assez rapide** = he can type quite fast

fraude *nf* fraud; *(passible du tribunal correctionnel)* **fraude informatique** = computer crime *ou* computer fraud

◊ **frauduleux, -euse** *adj* fraudulent; **depuis quelque temps déjà, la société fait des copies frauduleuses de logiciels protégés par un copyright** = the company has been illegally copying copyright software for some time

fréquence *nf* frequency; *(vitesse)* rate; **fréquence allouée** *ou* **assignée** = assigned frequency; **fréquence audio** *ou* **fréquence audible** = audio frequency; **fréquence de balayage** = scanning rate; **fréquence de balayage de ligne** = line frequency; **fréquence de boucle** *ou* **de bouclage** = speed of loop; **fréquence de coupure** = cutoff frequency; **fréquence d'horloge** = clock frequency; *(télévision)* **fréquence de l'image** = frame frequency; **la télévision britannique utilise une fréquence de 25 images par seconde** *ou* **25 images/seconde** = in the UK the frame frequency is 25 fps; *(balayage)* **fréquence de trame** = field frequency; **fréquence fondamentale** = fundamental frequency; **fréquence (critique) de fusion** = (critical) fusion frequency; **la principale fréquence d'horloge est de 10MHz** = the main clock frequency is 10MHz; **fréquence inaudible** *ou* **infrasonore** = subaudio frequency; **fréquence infrasonique** = infrasonic frequency; **fréquence intermédiaire** = intermediate frequency (if *ou* IF); **fréquence maximale utilisable** = maximum usable frequency; **fréquence radio** *ou* **radiofréquence** = radio frequency (RF); **bande de fréquences** = frequency band; **bande (de fréquences) intercalaire** = guard band; **bande des fréquences vocales** *ou* **bande de basses fréquences** = voice band; **la bande de base des fréquences vocales varie de 20Hz à 15KHz** = voice base band ranges from 20Hz to 15KHz; **basse fréquence** = low frequency (LF); **basse fréquence multiplexée (A-MAC)** = A-MAC; **très basse fréquence** = very low frequency (VLF); **canal de basses fréquences** = voice grade channel; **canal de fréquences subvocales** = subvoice grade channel; **haut-parleur de basses fréquences** = woofer; **réponse aux basses fréquences** = bass response; **signal de basse fréquence** = bass signal; **convertisseur de fréquence** = frequency changer; **décalage de fréquence** = dual clocking; **(système de) modulation par décalage de fréquence** = frequency shift keying (FSK); **diviseur de fréquence** = frequency divider; **domaine de fréquence** = frequency domain; **égaliseur de fréquence** *ou* **filtre de bande de fréquences** = frequency equalizer; **gamme de fréquences** = frequency range; **haute fréquence** = high frequency (HF); **très haute fréquence** = very high frequency (VHF); **ultra-haute fréquence** = ultra

high frequency (UHF); **modulation de fréquence (MF)** = frequency modulation (FM); **modulation de fréquence à large bande** = wideband frequency modulation (WBFM); **réducteur de fréquence** = frequency divider; **multiplexage par répartition en fréquence** = frequency division multiplexing (FDM); **réponse en fréquence** = frequency response; **sonnerie à résonnance de fréquence** = decimonic ringing; **variation de fréquence** = frequency variation

> pour avoir une chance d'obtenir un filtre fonctionnant à une fréquence d'horloge assez élevée (quelques dizaines de hertz), il est nécessaire d'écrire le programme en langage machine
>
> **Electronique Applications**

fréquent, -e *adj* frequent

friction *nf* friction; *(d'un connecteur)* **insertion sans friction** = zero insertion force (ZIF); *(du papier, etc.)* **entraînement par friction** = friction feed

frisure *nf (sur un courant)* ripple

froid, -e *adj* **(a)** cold; **les appareils fonctionnent mal par temps froid** = the machines work badly in cold weather **(b)** **démarrage à froid** = cold start

front *nm* front; **déclenché par bascule de front d'impulsion** = edge-triggered

◊ **frontal, -e** *adj* front-end; **chargement frontal des polices de caractères** = automatic font downloading; **mode d'exécution frontal/masqué** = foreground/background modes; **ordinateur frontal** = front-end computer; **processeur frontal** = front-end processor (FEP); **système frontal** = front-end system; **traitement frontal** = foreground processing *ou* foregrounding; **mémoire de traitement frontal** = foreground processing memory

frontière *nf (entre deux pays)* border *ou* frontier; **flux de données passant les frontières** = transborder data flow

FTAM *(méthode de gestion, accès et transfert de fichiers)* **méthode FTAM** = File Transfer Access and Management (FTAM)

FTP *(protocole de transfert de fichier)* **protocole FTP** = File Transfer Protocol (FTP)

fuir *vi (robinet, etc.)* to leak

◊ **fuite** *nf (d'un robinet ou d'un secret)* leak *ou* leakage; **c'est grâce à une fuite que la presse a eu vent de notre nouveau modèle** = a leak informed the press of our new designs

fumée *nf* smoke; **test de la fumée** = smoke test; *(produits fictifs)* **rideau de fumée** = vapourware

fusée *nf* rocket; **fusée porteuse** *ou* **de lancement** = launch vehicle

fusible 1 *nm* fuse; **mémoire ROM** *ou* **mémoire morte à fusibles** = fusible read only memory (FROM) **2** *adj* **élément fusible** = fusible link

fusion *nf* fusion *ou* merge *ou* merger *ou* merging; **fusion de documents** = document assembly *ou* document merge; **fusion de fichiers** = file collating *ou* file merger; **(instruction de) fusion de fichiers** = join *ou* merge files; **(application de) tri et fusion** = merge sort; *(de l'image)* **fréquence critique de fusion** = critical fusion frequency

◊ **fusionnement** *nm* *(données)* collating; **séquence de fusionnement** = collating sequence; **programme de fusionnement de données** = collator

◊ **fusionner** *vtr&i* *(fichiers)* to combine *ou* to merge *ou* to join (files); *(données)* to collate (data)

futur *nm* the future; **le bureau du futur** = the office of the future

Gg

G = GIGA

g = GRAMME

GAB = GUICHET AUTOMATIQUE DE BANQUE

gabarit *nm* **gabarit (de traçage)** = template

gaffeur *nm* gaffer, *US* gofer

gain *nm* gain; **augmentez le gain du signal d'entrée** = increase the amplification of the input signal; **contrôle de gain** = gain control; **contrôle de gain automatique** = automatic gain control (AGC) *ou* automatic level control (ALC)

gaine *nf* cladding; **la fibre optique sera moins performante si sa gaine est endommagée** = if the cladding is chipped, the fibre-optic cable will not function well

galet *nm* **galet presseur** = head wheel

gallium *nm* **arséniure de gallium** = gallium arsenide

gamma *nm* **(rayon)** gamma

gamme *nf* range *ou* family; **gamme des audiofréquences** = audio range; **gamme de fréquences** = frequency range; **la transmisison par téléphone accepte des signaux dans la gamme de fréquences 300 à 3400 Hz** = the telephone channel can accept signals in the frequency range 300 - 3400Hz; **gamme dynamique** = dynamic range; **gamme normale** = normal range; **une gamme de produits** = a wide range of products; **on trouve dans le catalogue toute une gamme de papiers listing** = the catalogue lists a wide range of computer stationery; **gamme de valeurs** = number range; **bas de gamme** = cheap *ou* down market; **haut de gamme** = up market *ou* high quality *ou* top quality *ou* top of the range

garantie *nf* guarantee; **le système est toujours sous garantie et la réparation sera faite gratuitement** = the system is still under guarantee and will be repaired free of charge

◊ **garantir** *vtr* **le fabricant garantit le système un an** = the manufacturer guarantees the system for 12 months

garde *nf* *(de signal de télévision)* **intervalle de garde** = breezeway

garder *vtr* **(a)** to keep; **garder (un fichier) à jour** = to keep something up to date **(b)** *(en mémoire)* to hold

garnir *vtr* *(fixer des composants)* **garnir une carte** = to populate a board; **carte complètement garnie (de composants)** = fully-populated PCB; *(une section de la mémoire)* **garnir de zéros** = to zero fill

◊ **garnissage** *nm* *(pour transmission)* **garnissage de bits** = bit stuffing

gauche 1 *nf* left; **décalage** *ou* **glissement à gauche** = left shift; **effectuer un décalage à gauche** = to left shift; *(imprimerie)* **(au) fer à gauche** = flush left; **justification à gauche** = left justification; **justifié à gauche** = flush left *ou* left justified; **justifier à gauche** = to left justify; **(instruction de) justifier à gauche** = left justify; **page de gauche** = left-hand page **2** *adj* left

gaz *nm* gas; **gaz inerte** = inert gas

géant, -e *adj* giant *ou* jumbo; **modèle géant** = huge model; **ordinateur géant** = supercomputer; **puce géante** = jumbo chip

général, -e *adj* general; **index général** = main index; **registre général** = general register *ou* general purpose register (gpr); *(d'un programme)* **variable générale** = global variable

générateur *nm* **(a)** *(d'électricité)* generator **(b)** *(appareil)* **générateur d'impulsions** = pulse generator; *(circuit intégré)* **générateur de son** = sound chip *ou* music chip **(c)** *(programme)* **générateur d'application** = report program generator (RPG); **générateur de caractères** = character generator; **on peut utiliser une ROM comme générateur de caractères pour obtenir les différentes polices** = the ROM used as a character generator can be changed to provide different fonts; **générateur de caractères fac-similés** = facsimile character generator; **générateur de liens** = linkage software; **les graphiques et le texte sont réunis sans l'aide d'un générateur de liens** = graphics and text are joined without linkage software; **générateur de nombres aléatoires** = random number generator; **générateur de programme** = program generator; **générateur de renvois** = cross-reference generator

◊ **génération** *nf* **(a)** *(période dans le temps)* generation; **génération d'ordinateurs** = computer generation; **génération d'un système** *ou* **à laquelle appartient un système** = system generation *ou* sysgen; **première génération** = first generation; **le fichier père est un fichier de sauvegarde de première génération** = the father file is a first generation backup; **copie** *ou* **image de première génération** = first generation image; **ordinateur de première génération** = first generation computer; **deuxième génération** = second generation; **ordinateurs de deuxième génération** = second generation computers; **troisième génération** = third generation; **ordinateurs de troisième génération** =

third generation computers; **langages de quatrième génération** = fourth generation languages; **ordinateurs de quatrième génération** = fourth generation computers; **ordinateurs de cinquième génération** = fifth generation computers **(b)** *(création* ou *production)* origination; **génération de données** = data origination

◊ **génératrice** *nf* génératrice (d'électricité) = generator; **en cas de panne de courant, le centre informatique possède sa propre génératrice (d'électricité)** = the computer centre has its own independent generator, in case of mains power failure

◊ **généré, -ée** *adj* generated; **généré par ordinateur** = computer-generated; **adresse générée** = generated address; **le code est généré automatiquement** = code generation is automatic; **erreur générée (par des arrondis)** = generated error

◊ **générer** *vtr* to generate; **une tablette graphique permet de générer deux coordonnées à chaque position du stylo** = the graphics tablet generates a pair of co-ordinates each time the pen is moved

générique 1 *nm (de film)* credits; **défilement ascendant du générique** = crawl **2** *adj (qui n'est pas spécifique d'un constructeur)* generic

génie *nm* engineering; **génie logiciel** = software engineering

genre *nm* gender; **changeur de genre** = gender changer; **il est possible de relier tous ces périphériques en utilisant seulement deux câbles et un changeur de genre** = you can interconnect all these peripherals with just two cables and a gender changer

géométrie *nf* geometry

◊ **géométrique** *adj* **distorsion géométrique** = geometric distortion

géostationnaire *adj (de satellite)* **orbite géostationnaire** = geostationary orbit; **satellite géostationnaire** = geostationary satellite

la durée de vie de ces deux tubes est inférieure à celle de l'ensemble du système TDF1-TDF2, évaluée à environ huit ans à partir de sa mise en orbite géostationnaire
Le Figaro

l'ensemble des satellites géostationnaires étant situé dans le plan de l'équateur terrestre, le mât principal fixe de l'antenne aura donc une orientation telle qu'il soit perpendiculaire au plan de l'équateur
Science et Vie

géré, -ée *adj* **géré par ordinateur** = computer-managed; **enseignement interactif géré par ordinateur** = computer-managed instruction (CMI)

◊ **gérer** *vtr* to manage

germanium (Ge) *nm* germanium

gestion *nf* direction ou management; **gestion**

d'accès aux données = data access management; **gestion des accès au(x) disque(s)** = disk access management; **gestion de (l'utilisation d'un) bus** = bus arbitration; **gestion de clé** = key management; **gestion de données** = data management; **gestion des erreurs** = error handling ou error management; **gestion de fichier** = file management; **gestion de mémoire** = memory management; **gestion de réseau** = network management; **gestion de tâches** = job scheduling ou task management; **gestion de texte** = text management; **ordinateur de gestion** = business computer; **programme de gestion d'enregistrements** ou **de fichiers** = records manager; **programme de gestion de file d'attente** = queue management program ou queue manager; **routine de gestion de périphérique** = peripheral software driver; **système de gestion de base de données** = database management system (DBMS) ou database manager; **logiciel de gestion** = information management system; **système de gestion informatisée** = management information system (MIS); **terminal de gestion** = executive terminal

◊ **gestionnaire** *nm* manager; administrator; **gestionnaire de base de données** = database management program; **un gestionnaire de base de données ultra-rapide permet la manipulation d'une très grande quantité de données** = a high-speed database management program allows the manipulation of very large amounts of data; **le code du gestionnaire du disque se trouve dans la bibliothèque** = the disk drive handler code is supplied in the library; **gestionnaire de données** = data administrator; **gestionnaire d'enregistrements** = records manager; **gestionnaire d'erreurs** = error handler; **gestionnaire d'espaces** = spacer; **gestionnaire d'espaces intelligent** = intelligent spacer; **gestionnaire de fichiers** = file manager; **gestionnaire de file d'attente** = queue management program ou queue manager; **ce nouveau logiciel de spouling comporte un gestionnaire de file d'attente** = this is a new software spooler with a built-in queue management; **gestionnaire d'imprimante** = printer driver; **gestionnaire d'interruptions** = interrupt handler (IH); **gestionnaire de périphérique** = driver ou device driver ou handler ou device handler; **gestionnaire de priorités** = priority scheduler; **gestionnaire de segments de recouvrement** = overlay manager; **gestionnaire de tâches** = scheduler; **gestionnaire de télécommunication** = communications executive; **gestionnaire de texte** = text manager

GHz = GIGAHERTZ

GIF = GRAPHICS FILE FORMAT **fichier (graphique) GIF** = GIF file

giga- (G) *(un milliard)* giga- (G)

◊ **gigaflop** *nm* gigaflop

◊ **gigahertz (GHz)** *nm* gigahertz (GHz)

◊ **giga-octet (Go)** *nm* gigabyte

il supporte des capacités mémoire pouvant aller jusqu'à 4 giga-octets
L'Ordinateur Individuel

GKS *(fonctions graphiques)* Graphics Kernel System (GKS)

glacé, -ée *adj (papier)* glossy; **on utilise du papier glacé pour l'impression de similigravures** = glossy paper is used for printing half-tones

glissement *nm* shift; **glissement à gauche** = left shift

◊ **glisser** *vtr* to slide; *(une souris)* to drag; **pour agrandir un cadre, vous cliquez à l'intérieur de ses limites et vous glissez jusqu'à la position voulue** = you can enlarge a frame by clicking inside its border and dragging to the position wanted

◊ **se glisser** *vpr* (a) to slide; **la disquette se glisse dans la pochette et s'en retire tout aussi facilement** = the disk cover slides on and off easily (b) to creep in; **il s'est glissé des erreurs au cours de la saisie du texte** = errors crept *ou* were introduced into the text at keyboarding

◊ **glisser/lâcher** *vtr (transporter une icône sur une autre)* to drag and drop

global, -e *adj* global; *(d'un sujet ou d'un problème)* **connaissance globale** = global knowledge; **contrat global** = package deal; **nous offrons un contrat global comprenant un système informatique complet pour le bureau, la formation du personnel et l'entretien du matériel** = we are offering a package deal which includes the whole office computer system, staff training and hardware maintenance; *(traitement de texte)* **recherche globale** = full-text search; *(réseau, disque dur, serveur)* **sauvegarde globale** = global backup; **variable globale** = global variable

◊ **globalement** *adv* globally; **chercher et remplacer globalement** = global search and replace

◊ **globalisation** *nf* **fonction de globalisation** = aggregate function; **opérateur de globalisation** = aggregate operator

gobo *nm (pour film)* matt *ou* matte

gomme *nf (dans un programme graphique)* eraser tool

gondolage *nm* buckling

gonfler *vtr* (a) *(avec de l'air)* to blow (b) *(augmenter l'importance)* to boost; **le disque dur supplémentaire va gonfler la capacité de mémoire de 25Mo** = the extra hard disk will boost our storage capacity by 25Mb

GOSIP *(standard de compatibilité)* Government Open Systems Interconnect Profile (GOSIP)

GOSUB *(exécute une routine et retourne à l'instruction suivante)* **(commande) GOSUB** = GOSUB (command)

GOTO *(instruction de saut)* GOTO (instruction); **GOTO 105 indique un saut à la ligne 105** = GOTO 105 instructs a jump to line 105

gourmand, -e *adjective (logiciel)* **gourmand en mémoire** = memory-intensive (software)

GPI = GESTIONNAIRE PERSONNEL D'INFORMATION Personal Information manager (PIM)

GPIA *(interface universelle)* General Purpose Interface Adapter (GPIA)

GPIB *(bus universel)* General Purpose Interface Bus (GPIB)

gradué, -ée *adj* graduated

graduel, -elle *adj* gradual *ou* phased *ou* staged; **changement graduel** *ou* **passage graduel (à un nouveau système)** = staged change-over (to a new system)

◊ **graduellement** *adv* **arrêter** *ou* **mettre fin à quelque chose graduellement** = to phase out something *ou* to phase something out; **commencer** *ou* **démarrer** *ou* **introduire quelque chose graduellement** = to phase in something *ou* to phase something in

grain *nm (du papier)* grain

grammage *nm (du papier)* grammage *ou* paper weight

> en dehors des classiques papiers blancs aux divers grammages, les imprimantes laser acceptent de nombreux autres types de support
> *L'Ordinateur Individuel*

> ne pas employer de papiers trop légers, d'un grammage inférieur à 80 grammes
> *L'Ordinateur Individuel*

grammaire *nf* grammar; *(vérificateur grammatical)* **utilitaire de vérification de grammaire** = grammar checker

◊ **grammatical, -e** *adj* **vérificateur grammatical** = grammar checker

gramme (g) *nm* gram (g); *(poids du papier)* **gramme au mètre carré (g/m²)** = grams per square metre (gsm); **le livre est imprimé sur du papier 80 grammes** = the book is printed on 80gsm paper; **nous avons du papier de 70 - 90 grammes** = our paper weights are 70 - 90 gsm; **ce livre est imprimé sur papier couché de 70g** = the book is printed on 70 gram *ou* 70 gsm coated paper

grand, -e *adj (taille)* tall *ou* big *ou* large; *(quantité)* large; **ligne de grand débit** = high usage trunk; **grand modèle (de mémoire des processeurs Intel)** = large model (of Intel processor memory); **grande vitesse** = high-speed; **duplicateur grande vitesse** = high-speed duplicator

◊ **grand-angle** *ou* **grand-angulaire** *nm&adj* **(objectif) grand-angle** *ou* **grand-angulaire** = wide angle lens

◊ **grandeur** *nf* size; *(d'un signal, etc.)* magnitude; **grandeur de page** = page size

◊ **grand-père** *nm* **fichier grand-père** = grandfather file

granularité *nf (degré de segmentation de la mémoire)* granularity

graphe *nm* graph *ou* plot; *(exprimé en coordonnées)* coordinate graph; **graphe logarithmique** = logarithmic graph; **graphe à pavés** = block diagram; **graphe de relation** = derivation graph; **mode graphe** = plotting mode; **tracer un graphe (par points numérisés)** = to plot a graph

◊ **grapheur** *nm* graph plotter

◊ **graphique 1** *nm* **(a)** chart *ou* diagram *ou* graph *ou* schema; **graphique à barres** *ou* **en colonnes** *ou* **en tuyaux d'orgue** = bar chart *ou* columnar graph; **à l'aide d'un graphique** = graphically; **graphique de points** = scatter graph **(b)** *(représentations graphiques)* graphics; presentation graphics; **graphiques contigus** = contiguous graphics; **la plupart des écrans ne permettent pas l'affichage de graphiques contigus; chaque caractère (graphique) est bordé de chaque côté par un espace qui améliore sa lisibilité** = most display units do not provide contiguous graphics: their characters have a small space on each side to improve legibility; **graphiques de basse définition** = low-resolution graphics *ou* low-res graphics; **graphiques haute définition** = high resolution graphics *ou* hi-res graphics; **graphiques interactifs** = interactive graphics; **le jeu (électronique) 'les envahisseurs de l'espace' présente d'excellents graphiques interactifs; le joueur contrôle la position de son vaisseau spatial avec la manette (de jeu)** = the space invaders machine has great interactive graphics, the player controls the position of his spaceship on the screen with the joystick **2** *adj* graphic *ou* graphical; **adaptateur** *ou* **carte graphique** = graphics adapter; **cette nouvelle carte graphique permet un affichage de haute définition** = the new graphics adapter is capable of displaying higher resolution graphics; **adaptateur** *ou* **carte graphique couleur EGA** = enhanced graphics adapter (EGA); **adaptateur** *ou* **carte graphique couleur MCGA** = multicolor graphics adapter (MCGA); **affichage graphique** = graphic display; **définition de l'affichage graphique** = graphic display resolution; **caractère graphique** = graphics character; **la carte graphique haute définition contrôle jusqu'à 300 pixels par pouce** = the HRG board can control up to 300 pixels per inch; **coprocesseur graphique** = graphics coprocessor; **cette carte graphique, équipée d'un coprocesseur graphique, est beaucoup plus rapide** = this graphics adapter has a graphics coprocessor fitted and is much faster; **données graphiques** = graphic data; **écran (à affichage) graphique** = graphics VDU; **enregistreur graphique** = chart recorder; **entrée-sortie graphique** = graphical input/output (GINO); **fichier graphique** = graphics file; **il existe de nombreux formats de fichiers graphiques comme TIFF, IMG et EPS** = there are many standards for graphics files including TIFF, IMG and EPS; **format de fichier graphique** = graphics file format; **fonctions graphiques GKS** = graphics kernel system (GKS); **imprimante graphique** = graphics printer; **intégrateur graphique (à fenêtre, icône, souris, pointeur)** = window, icon, mouse, pointer (WIMP); **interface graphique (d'utilisateur) (GUI)** = graphical user interface (GUI); **langage graphique** = graphic language; **avec ce langage graphique, on peut tracer des lignes, cercles et graphes avec une seule commande** = this graphic language can plot lines, circles and graphs with a single command; **logiciel graphique** = graphics software; **mode graphique** = graphics mode; **palette graphique** = graphics software; **processeur graphique** = graphics processor; **représentation graphique** = graphic display *ou* graphics; **les représentations graphiques telles que histogrammes, camemberts, etc.** = graphics output such as bar charts, pie charts, etc.; *(infographie)* **représentations graphiques sur ordinateur** = computer-generated graphics; **stylo optique graphique** = graphics light pen; **symbole graphique** = graphic symbol; **bibliothèque de symboles graphiques** = graphics library; **tablette graphique** = graphics pad *ou* graphics tablet *ou* digitizing pad; **terminal graphique** *ou* **terminal avec écran à affichage graphique** = graphics terminal *ou* graphics art terminal; **traceur** *ou* **enregistreur graphique** = pen recorder

◊ **graphiquement** *adv* graphically; **les chiffres de vente sont reproduits graphiquement sous forme de camembert** = the sales figures are graphically represented as a pie chart

◊ **graphisme** *nm* line art; **graphisme par balayage de trame** = raster graphics

> les langages graphiques permettent la présentation de résultats sous forme de graphiques plus ou moins riches
> *L'Information professionnelle*

graphité, -ée *adj* **carte graphitée** = mark sensing card

◊ **graphiter** *vtr (une marque)* to mark sense

grappe *nf (de périphériques, etc.)* cluster; **unité de contrôle de périphériques disposés en grappe** = cluster controller; **liaison en grappe de plusieurs périphériques** = clustering

gras, grasse *adj (caractère)* bold; **(en) caractère gras** = bold face; **(instruction d') imprimer en caractères gras** = bold *ou* embolden

gratuit, -e *adj* **logiciel gratuit** = freeware

grave *adj&nm (son)* bass; **contrôle des (sons) graves** = bass control; **haut-parleur de graves** = bass driver *ou* bass speaker *ou* woofer

gravé, -ée *adj* **caractère gravé** = etched type

◊ **graver** *vtr* to etch; **pour faire un circuit imprimé il faut d'abord recouvrir la carte d'une résine photosensible puis appliquer le masque du circuit, exposer, développer et graver pour finalement obtenir le tracé** = to make the PCB, coat the board with photoresist, place the opaque pattern above, expose, then develop and etch, leaving the conducting tracks

◊ **gravure** *nf* **(a)** *(oeuvre)* print; **il fait collection de gravures du 18e siècle** = he collects 18th century prints **(b)** *(procédé)* engraving; **gravure en demi-teinte** = halftone process *ou* half-toning

Gray *n* **code (de) Gray** = Gray code *ou* cyclic code

grille *nf* **(a)** grid; **grille d'aide (de fonction des touches) de clavier** = key overlay *ou* keyboard overlay; **sans la grille d'aide, je ne saurais jamais quelle touche de fonction je dois utiliser** = without the key overlay, I would never remember which function key does what **(b)** *(masque de saisie)* **grille d'écran** = form; *(de programme de télévision)* **grille d'émission** = format; **grille pour ordinogramme** = flowchart template *ou* flowchart stencil **(c)** *(de dessin)* mesh

gris *nm* grey, *US* gray; **échelle de gris** = grey scale, *US* gray scale; **niveaux de gris** = (i) shades of grey, *US* shades of gray; (ii) grey scale, *US* gray scale

◊ **gris, -e** *adj* grey, *US* gray

> l'image est recueillie en échelle de gris sur l'enregistreur à fibres optiques utilisant un papier sensible aux ultraviolets et à développement immédiat
>
> *Techniques hospitalières*

gros, grosse *adj* large *ou* big; **gros ordinateur** = mainframe computer; *(photographie)* **gros plan** = close-up

◊ **grossir** *vtr* to enlarge *ou* to magnify; **cette lentille grossit 10 fois** = the lens gives a magnification of 10 times

◊ **grossissement** *nm* enlargement *ou* magnification

groupage *nm* assembly; **groupage de caractères** = character assembly

◊ **groupe** *nm* **(a)** group; *(de caractères ou de mots)* group *ou* batch *ou* set; *(collection de données ou d'objets semblables)* bank; **un groupe de mini-ordinateurs traite toutes les données brutes** = a bank of minicomputers process all the raw data; **groupe de contrôle** = control group; **groupe de fichiers (connexes)** = file set; **groupe témoin** = control group; *(de périphériques)* **appel sélectif de groupe** = group poll; **marqueur (de début** *ou* **de fin) de groupe** = group mark *ou* marker; *(pour vérification d'erreurs)* **total par groupe** = batch total **(b)** *(voies de communication)* **groupe primaire** = primary group; **groupe tertiaire** = mastergroup **(c)** **groupe d'utilisateurs** = user group; **groupe fermé d'utilisateurs** = closed user group (CUG); **le groupe ACCOUNTS contient tous les utilisateurs des services comptables** = the group ACCOUNTS contains all the users who work in the accounts department; **groupe d'intérêt particulier** = special interest group (SIG); **notre club informatique local a constitué un groupe de travail qui s'intéresse aux communications et aux réseaux** = our local computer club has a SIG for comms and networking **(d)** **groupe de travail** *ou* **de projet (relié par réseau** *ou* **messagerie)** = workgroup; **qui permet** *ou* **qui facilite le travail de groupe** = workgroup enabled; **ce traitement de texte est orienté sur les groupes de travail et comporte un passerelle de messagerie électronique dans le menu courant** = this word-processor is

workgroup enabled which adds an email gateway from the standard menus; **logiciel de groupe (de travail)** = workgroup software *ou* groupware **(e)** **groupe d'icônes** = icon group; **icône de groupe** = group icon; **toutes les icônes de ce groupe concernent la peinture** = all the icons in this group are to do with painting

◊ **groupé, -e** *adj* batched; *(offre de vente)* bundled; **communications groupées** = batched communication; **signal groupé** = M signal; *(commutateurs)* **groupés en série** = ganged

◊ **groupement** *nm* group; **groupement de commutateurs (en série)** = ganged switch; **groupement de voies** = channel group

◊ **grouper** *vtr* **(a)** to group *ou* to bracket together; **grouper des données** = to gather write **(b)** *(dispositifs)* to group

GUI *(interface graphique d'utilisateur)* Graphical User Interface (GUI)

> COMMENTAIRE: une interface graphique d'utilisateur (GUI) utilise normalement une combinaison de fenêtres, icônes et souris pour contrôler le système d'exploitation. De nombreux GUIs comme Microsoft Windows, Apple Macintosh System 7 and DR-GEM, permettent de contrôler toutes les fonctions du système d'exploitation en utilisant seulement la souris. Les icônes représentent des programmes et des fichiers que l'on sélectionne en déplaçant un pointeur avec la souris au lieu d'entrer le nom du fichier au clavier

guichet *nm* **guichet automatique de banque (GAB)** = automated teller machine, *US* automatic telling machine (ATM); cashpoint

guidage *nm* *(de signaux)* **dispositif de guidage directionnel** = feed horn

◊ **guide** *nm* **(a)** *(livre ou manuel)* guide; **guide élémentaire** = primer **(b)** *(dispositif)* **guide d'ondes** = waveguide; **guide d'ondes circulaire** = circular waveguide; **guide d'ondes rectangulaire** = rectangular waveguide; **guide optique** = light guide **(c)** *(d'un code barres)* **lignes guides** = guide bars; **les lignes guides standard se présentent sous la forme de deux lignes fines un peu plus longues que les lignes codes** = the standard guide bars are two thin lines that are a little longer than the coding lines **(d)** *(de vidéotex)* **page guide** = lead in page

◊ **guide-bande** *nm* tape guide; **la bande est désalignée parce qu'un guide-bande est cassé** = the tape is out of alignment because one of the tape guides has broken

guillemets *nmpl* quotation marks *ou* quotes *ou* inverted commas; **guillemets doubles (" ")** = double quotes; **il faut mettre le nom de la société entre guillemets (doubles)** = the name of the company should be put in double quotes; **guillemets simples (' ')** = single quotes

Hh

habillage *nm (d'une gravure* ou *d'une image)* **faire l'habillage** = to run around

◊ **habiller** *vtr (fixer des composants)* **habiller une carte** = to populate a printed circuit board

hachures *nfpl (d'un dessin)* shading

Hall *npr* **effet (de champ) Hall** = Hall effect; **commutateur à effet (de champ) Hall** = Hall effect switch

halo *nm (photographie)* halo; **effet de halo** = halation

halogénure *nf* **halogénure (d'argent)** = halide

Hamming *npr* **code** ou **codage de Hamming** = Hamming code; **distance de Hamming** = signal distance ou Hamming distance

hampe *nf (d'une lettre)* ascender

handshaking *nm* handshaking; *voir aussi* ECHANGE

harmonique *nf* harmonic; **distorsion d'harmoniques** = harmonic distortion; **sonnerie d'appel à harmoniques** = harmonic telephone ringer

hartley *nm (mesure d'information)* hartley

hasard *nm* chance; **au hazard** = at random; **nombre choisi au hasard** = random number

hash *nm* hash; **table des adresses hash codées** = hash table; **algorithme** ou **fonction hash** = hashing function; **hash code** = hash code; **générer un hash code** = to hash; **index hash code** = hash index; **système de hash code** = hash-code system; **total de vérification pour hash code** = hash total; **valeur d'un code hash** = hash value

haut *nm* **(a)** top; *(caractère d'imprimerie)* **haut de casse** = upper case **(b) haut de gamme** = high quality ou top quality ou up market; high-end (device)

◊ **haut, -e** *adj* **(a)** high; **haute définition** = high resolution ou hi-res; *(vidéo)* high definition; **graphiques haute définition** = high-resolution graphics ou hi-res graphics; **carte graphique haute définition** = HRG board; **matrice d'impression à haute définition** = enhanced dot matrix; **ce moniteur haute définition permet un affichage de 1824 x 768 pixels** = this high-resolution monitor can display 1824 x 768 pixels; **système vidéo haute définition** = high definition video system (HDVS); **haute densité** = high density; **disquette haute**

densité (HD) = high density disk (HD); **très haute densité** = very high density (VHD); **haute fréquence** = high frequency (HF); **haut-parleur de hautes fréquences** = tweeter; **très haute fréquence (THF)** = very high frequency (VHF); **ultra-haute fréquence** = ultra high frequency (UHF); **on demande aux programmeurs une connaissance des langages de haut niveau, dont PASCAL** = programmers should have a knowledge of high-level languages, particularly PASCAL; **(de) haute performance** = high performance; **matériel (de) haute performance** = high performance equipment; **(de) haute précision** ou **haute technologie** = high specification ou high spec; **les câbles (de) haute technologie doivent être manipulés avec soin** = high spec cabling needs to be handled very carefully **(b) mémoire haute** = high memory; **bloc de mémoire haute** = upper memory block (UMB) **(c) signal haut actif** = active high; **état logique haut** ou **1** = logical high **(d) filtre passe haut** = high pass filter

◊ **haute-fidélité** *nf* high fidelity ou hifi ou hi-fi ou hi fi; **chaîne haute-fidélité** = high fidelity system ou hi-fi

> le système comprend, dans une mallette, un boîtier, un casque haute-fidélité, un cordon de raccordement pour chaîne hi-fi, magnétophone ou téléviseur
>
> **L'Evénement**

hauteur *nf* height; **hauteur d'un son** = pitch

haut-parleur *nm* loudspeaker; **ne placez surtout pas le micro trop près du haut-parleur sinon le retour va saturer l'ampli** = make sure the microphone is not too close to the loudspeaker or positive feedback will occur and you will overload the amplifier; **haut-parleur d'aigus** ou **de hautes fréquences** = tweeter; **haut-parleur de graves** ou **de basses fréquences** = bass driver ou bass speaker ou woofer; **haut-parleur électrostatique** = electrostatic speaker

Hayes Corporation ™ *(société spécialisée en modems et qui a développé des normes pour modems)* **jeu de commandes Hayes AT** = Hayes AT command set; **pour appeler le numéro 1234, utilisez la commande Hayes ATD1234** = to dial the number 1234, use the Hayes AT command ATD1234; **compatible Hayes** = Hayes compatible

HD = HAUTE DENSITE **disquette HD** = high density disk

HDLC *(protocole d'interfaçage)* High-Level Data Link Control (HDLC); **poste** ou **équipement interfacé HDLC** = high-level data link control station

hebdomadaire 1 *adj* weekly; **une revue hebdomadaire** = a weekly magazine 2 *nm (revue, journal, etc.)* a weekly

hectométrique *adj* hectometric; *(moyennes fréquences)* **ondes hectométriques** = medium frequency

hélicoïdal, -e *adj* **balayage hélicoïdal** *ou* **lecture hélicoïdale** = helical scan

HELP *(touche de clavier d'aide à l'utilisateur ou touche AIDE)* **tapez la touche HELP pour connaître la marche à suivre** = hit the HELP key if you want information about what to do next

Hercules™ *(carte ou adaptateur graphique)* Hercules graphics adapter (HGA)

héritage *nm (des caractéristiques d'un objet ou d'une classe)* inheritance

◊ **hériter** *vtr&i (des caractéristiques d'un autre objet)* to inherit

hermétique *adj* airtight; **emballage hermétique** = airtight packaging

◊ **hermétiquement** *adv* **fermer hermétiquement** = to seal

hertz *nm* Hertz

◊ **hertzien, -ienne** *adj* hertzian; **liaison hertzienne** = microwave communications link; **relais hertzien** = microwave relay; **transmission hertzienne** = microwave transmission

hétérodyne *adj* heterodyne

hétérogène *adj* heteregeneous; **multiplexage hétérogène** = heterogeneous multiplexing; **réseau informatique hétérogène** = heterogeneous network

heure *nf* **(a)** hour; **à** *ou* **de l'heure** = per hour; **(nombre de) frappes/heure** = keystrokes per hour **(b)** time; **heure d'entrée** = entry time; *(télévision)* **heures de grande écoute** *ou* **d'écoute maximale** = prime time

heuristique *adj* heuristic; **un programme heuristique exploite ses actions et décisions antérieures** = a heuristic program learns from its previous actions and decisions

Hewlett Packard™ *(société spécialisée en informatique et en ordinateurs, imprimantes, etc.)* *voir aussi* HP, HPGL

hexadécimal, -e *adj* **base hexadécimale** = base 16; **clavier hexadécimal** = hexadecimal *ou* hex (key)pad; **numération hexadécimale** = hexadecimal *ou* hex notation; **vidage hexadécimal** = hex dump; *voir aussi* A, B, C, D, E, F

hiérarchie *nf* hierarchy; **hiérarchie des données** = data hierarchy; **hiérarchie des mémoires** = memory hierarchy

◊ **hiérarchique** *adj* hierarchical; **classification hiérarchique** = hierarchical classification; **répertoire hiérarchique** = hierarchical directory; **structure hiérarchique de données** = data hierarchy

◊ **hiérarchisé, -ée** *adj* hierarchical; **base de données hiérarchisées** = hierarchical database; **réseau (d'ordinateurs) hiérarchisé** = hierarchical computer network; **système de communication hiérarchisé** = hierarchical communications system; **système de fichiers hiérarchisés** = hierarchical file system (HFS)

hi-fi *n&adj* high fidelity *ou* hifi *ou* hi-fi; **système hi-fi** = high fidelity system *ou* hi-fi; **une chaîne hi-fi** = a hi fi system *ou* a hi-fi; *voir aussi* HAUTE-FIDELITE

High Sierra *(norme de stockage sur CD-ROM)* High Sierra specification

histogramme *nm* bar chart *ou* bar graph *ou* histogram *ou* columnar graph; **présentation (graphique) sous forme d'histogramme** = columnar working

HMA *(mémoire supérieure)* **mémoire HMA** = High Memory Area (HMA); *voir aussi* MEMOIRE, UMB

Hollerith *npr* **code (de) Hollerith** = Hollerith code

hologramme *nm* hologram *ou* holographic image; **stockage** *ou* **mémoire d'hologramme** = holographic storage

◊ **holographie** *nf* holography

◊ **holographique** *adj* **stockage** *ou* **mémoire holographique** = holographic storage

homme *nm* **(a)** man; **homme à tout faire** = general assistant; *(dans un studio de cinématographie)* gaffer, *US* gofer **(b)** **interface homme-machine** = man machine interface (MMI) *ou* human-computer *ou* human-machine interface (HMI)

homogène *adj* homogeneous; **multiplexage homogène** = homogeneous multiplexing; **réseau informatique homogène** = homogeneous computer network

homologation *nf* (official) approval; **certificat d'homologation** = certificate of approval; **test d'homologation** = acceptance test *ou* testing

◊ **homologuer** *vtr* to approve officially; **le nouveau moniteur graphique a été homologué par le conseil de sécurité avant d'être commercialisé** = the new graphics monitor was approved by the safety council before being sold

horaire 1 *nm* schedule; **établir un horaire de programmes (de télévision** *ou* **radio)** = to schedule programmes; **établissement d'un horaire de programmes (de télévision** *ou* **radio)** = programme scheduling; **personne qui établit un horaire de programmes (de télévision** *ou* **radio)** = scheduler 2 *adj* hourly; per hour; **tranche horaire** = time slice

horizontal, -e *adj* horizontal; **abscisse** *ou* **coordonnée horizontale** = X-coordinate; *(pour* *détection d'erreurs de transmission)* **contrôle horizontal** = horizontal check; **défilement horizontal** = horizontal scrolling; **barre de défilement horizontal** = horizontal scrollbar; **impulsion de synchronisation horizontale** = horizontal synchronization pulse; **inhibition** *ou* **suppression horizontale (du signal)** = horizontal blanking

◊ **horizontale** *nf* **(a)** horizontal line **(b)** *(coordonnées)* X direction

◊ **horizontalement** *adv* horizontally

horloge *nf* **(a)** *(qui marque l'heure)* clock; *(qui affiche l'heure sur l'écran)* time display; **l'heure est affichée à l'horloge placée dans un coin de l'écran** = the time is shown by the clock in the corner of the screen; **le micro possède une horloge incorporée** = the micro has a built-in clock; **horloge atomique** = atomic clock; **horloge numérique** = digital clock **(b)** *(de synchronisation)* clock; **cycle d'horloge** = clock cycle *ou* CPU cycle; **fréquence d'horloge** = clock frequency; **fréquence d'horloge du processeur** = microprocessor timing; **la principale fréquence d'horloge est de 10MHz** = the main clock frequency is 10MHz; **impulsion d'horloge** = clock pulse; **signaux synchrones aux impulsions d'horloge** = clocked signals; **piste d'horloge** = clock track; **vitesse d'horloge** = clock rate; **horloge centrale** = main clock; **horloge delta** *ou* **à relance automatique** = delta clock; **horloge en temps réel** = real-time clock; **horloge externe** *ou* **extérieure** = external clock; **horloge maîtresse** *ou* **horloge principale** = main clock *ou* master clock *ou* timing master; **horloge programmable** = programmable clock; **horloge relative** = relative-time clock

hors *prép* out of; **hors service** = out of service *ou* dead

hôte *nm* host; **ordinateur hôte** = central computer *ou* host computer; **on peut manipuler l'image avant son téléchargement sur l'ordinateur hôte** = the image can be manipulated before uploading to the host computer; **adaptateur de l'ordinateur hôte** = host adapter; **le cordon qui relie le scanner et (l'adaptateur de) l'ordinateur hôte est fourni** = the cable to connect the scanner to the host adapter is included in the package

housse *nf* *(de protection d'un appareil)* dustcover

HP = HEWLETT PACKARD **bus d'interface HP** = Hewlett Packard Interface Bus (HPIB); **imprimante graphique HP Laserjet** = Hewlett Packard LaserJet *ou* HP LaserJet; **langage de contrôle d'imprimante HP** = Hewlett Packard

Printer Control Language (HP-PCL); **langage graphique HP** = Hewlett Packard Graphics Language (HPGL)

HPFS *(gestionnaire de fichiers)* High Performance Filing System (HPFS)

HPGL *(langage de programmation graphique HP)* **langage HPGL** = Hewlett Packard Graphics Language (HPGL)

HP-PCL *(langage de contrôle d'imprimante HP)* **langage HP-PCL** = Hewlett Packard Printer Control Language (HP-PCL)

hub *nm* hub

Huffman *npr* **code de Huffman** = Huffman code

huit 1 *nm* **base huit** = octal scale *ou* octal notation **2** *adj num* eight; **(système) huit bits** = eight-bit (system); **disquette de huit pouces** = eight-inch disk; **lecteur de disquettes de huit pouces** = eight-inch drive

hybride *adj* hybrid; **circuit hybride** = hybrid circuit; **interface hybride** = hybrid interface; **ordinateur hybride** = hybrid computer; **système hybride** = hybrid system

hyper *préfixe* ultra-

HyperCard ™ *(système de base de données pour HyperTalk)* HyperCard ™

hyperfréquence *nf* ultra high frequency (UHF) *ou* microwave; **relais d'hyperfréquences** = microwave relay; **transmission par hyperfréquences** = microwave transmission; **liaison de transmission par hyperfréquences** = microwave communications link

hypermedia *nm* hypermedia

HyperTalk ™ *(langage de programmation pour HyperCard)* HyperTalk ™

hypertext(e) *nm* hypertext; **dans cette page hypertext(e), cliquez sur le mot 'ordinateur' et on vous expliquera ce qu'est un ordinateur** = in this hypertext page, click once on the word 'computer' and it will tell you what a computer is

hyposulfite *nm* *(pour fixage en photographie)* **hyposulfite de sodium** = sodium thiosulfate; *(familier)* hypo; *voir aussi* THIOSULFATE

Hz = HERTZ

Ii

I curseur en **I** = I-beam *ou* cursor shaped like 'I'

IA = INTELLIGENCE ARTIFICIELLE

IAO = INGENIERIE ASSISTEE PAR ORDINATEUR

IBM la société IBM = IBM (International Business Machines); *(familier)* Big Blue; (ordinateur) IBM AT = IBM AT (computer); clavier (IBM) AT = IBM AT keyboard; compatible IBM = IBM compatible; (ordinateur) IBM PC = IBM PC; clavier IBM PC = IBM PC keyboard; (ordinateur) IBM PS/2 = IBM PS/2 *ou* IBM Personal System/2; (ordinateur) IBM-XT = IBM XT

icône *nf* icon *ou* ikon; **l'icône du programme graphique a la forme d'une petite palette** = the icon for the graphics program is a small picture of a palette; **cliquer deux fois sur l'icône du traitement de texte** = click twice over the wordprocessor icon; **pour afficher le menu déroulant cliquer sur l'icône en haut de l'écran** = the pull-down menu is viewed by clicking over the icon at the top of the screen

◊ **iconographie** *nf (ensemble des illustrations d'un livre ou d'une revue)* visuals *ou* illustrations; *(familier)* pix

IDE = INTEGRATED DRIVE ELECTRONICS *ou* INTELLIGENT DEVICE ELECTRONICS **contrôleur de disque IDE** = Integrated Device Electronics (IDE); **le disque dur IDE est devenu l'équipement standard de la plupart des PC** = IDE drives are the standard fitted to most PCs

idéal,-e *adj* ideal

identificateur *nm* identifier (word) *ou* label; **enregistrement d'identificateurs** = label record

◊ **identification** *nf* identification; *(de message)* authentication; **identification de fichier** = file identification; **bloc d'identification** = header (block); **caractère d'identification** = identification character *ou* identifier; **champ d'identification** = label field; **code d'identification de périphérique** = device code; **(code d') identification d'un terminal** = terminal identity; *(indique sur quelle touche on a appuyé)* **code d'identification de touche** = scan code; *(d'une personne)* **numéro de code d'identification** = personal identification number (PIN); **dispositif électronique d'identification** = personal identification device (PID); **label d'identification (sur le support magnétique)** = interior label; **label d'identification de bande** = header label; **mot d'identification** = identifier word; **division avec paramètres d'identification (d'un programme en COBOL)** = identification division; *(qui définit le format d'une bande magnétique)* **séquence d'identification** = identity burst

◊ **identifier** *vtr* to identify; **l'utilisateur doit s'identifier par un mot de passe qui lui permet d'avoir accès au système** = the user has to identify himself to the system by using a password before access is allowed

identique *adj* identical; **les deux systèmes utilisent des logiciels identiques** = the two systems use identical software; **copier** *ou* **reproduire à l'identique** = to mirror

identité *nf* **(a)** identity; **carte d'identité** = identity card *ou* ID card **(b)** *(fonction logique)* **opération d'identité** = identity operation; **porte d'identité** = identity gate *ou* element

idiot, -e *adj (non formaté)* **bande idiote** = idiot tape

IEC *(connecteur)* IEC connector; **tous les PC utilisent un connecteur mâle IEC et un câble d'alimentation avec un connecteur femelle IEC** = all PCs use a male IEC connector and a mains lead with a female IEC connector

IEEE *USA* = INSTITUTE OF ELECTRICAL AND ELECTRONIC ENGINEERS (IEEE) **bus (conforme aux normes du) IEEE** = IEEE bus; *(pour interface parallèle standard)* **norme IEEE-488** = IEEE-488

IF *(si)* **instruction IF** = IF statement

◊ **IF-THEN-ELSE** *(branchement conditionnel)* **instruction IF-THEN-ELSE** = IF-THEN-ELSE

ignorer *vtr* to ignore

IIL *ou* **I2L** = INTEGRATED INJECTION LOGIC; *(logique intégrée à injection)* **logique IIL** *ou* **logique I2L** = integrated injection logic (IIL)

illégal, -e *adj* **(a)** *(document)* illegal; **copie illégale** = *(d'un programme)* bootleg (copy); *(d'un livre ou d'un programme)* pirated copy **(b)** *(action)* **copie illégale** *ou* **reproduction illégale (d'une oeuvre)** = infringement of copyright *ou* copyright infringement

◊ **illégalement** *adv* illegally

illimité, -ée *adj* **(poste de travail) à accès illimité** = open access (station)

illisible *adj* illegible; **si le manuscrit est illisible, il faut le renvoyer à l'auteur et lui demander de le faire taper à la machine** = if the manuscript is illegible, send it back to the author to have it typed; **texte illisible** = bad copy

illumination *nf* illumination; *(d'une antenne)* **illumination de l'ouverture** = aperture illumination

◊ **illuminer** *vtr* to illuminate

illustration *nf (de livre ou revue)* illustration *ou* picture; *(l'ensemble des illustrations)* **illustrations** = illustrations *ou* visuals; *(familier)* pix; **ce livre comporte des illustrations en couleur** = the book is illustrated in colour; **on trouve dans le livre 25 pages d'illustrations en couleur** = the book has twenty-five pages of full-colour illustrations; **le manuel contient des graphiques et des illustrations de configurations de réseaux** = the manual is illustrated with charts and pictures of the networking connections

◊ **illustrer** *vtr* to illustrate

image *nf* picture; *(vidéo ou télévision)* **image complète** = frame; **image de bibliothèque** = clip-art; **nous avons utilisé des images de bibliothèque pour améliorer la présentation** = we have used some clip-art to enhance our presentation; **image d'écran** = video frame *ou* image; **image fantôme** = ghost image; **image latente** = latent image; **image mémoire de carte** = card image; **image orientée en film** = cine-oriented image; **image originale** *ou* **de première génération** = first generation image; **(nombre d')images par seconde** *ou* **images/seconde** = frames per second (fps); **image de synthèse** = computer-generated image; **image vidéo** *ou* **image d'écran** = video image *ou* video frame; **capteur d'images vidéo** = frame grabber; **le processeur d'images permet le stockage d'une image vidéo dans une mémoire intégrée de 8 bits** = the image processor allows you to store a video frame in a built-in 8-bit frame store; **amplificateur** *ou* **intensificateur d'image** = image enhancer; **analyseur d'image** = image processor; **(faire un) arrêt sur image** = (to) freeze (frame); **le processeur d'image permet de faire un arrêt sur image** = with an image processor you can freeze a video frame; **capteur d'image** = image sensor; **compression d'image** = image compression; **comptage d'images (complètes)** = full-frame time code; **déformation** *ou* **distorsion** *ou* **aberration de l'image** = image distortion; **dégradation de l'image** = image degradation; **distorsion de l'image** = image distortion; **élément d'image** = picture element *ou* pixel; **faisceau d'image** = picture beam; **figer une image** = to freeze a frame; **fréquence d'image** = frame frequency; **la télévision britannique utilise une fréquence de 25 images par seconde** *ou* **25 images/seconde** = in the UK the frame frequency is 25 frames per second *ou* 25 fps; **mémoire image** = *(télévision)* frame store; *(vidéo)* video memory *ou* video RAM (VRAM); **espace mémoire de l'image** = image storage space; **la mémoire image peut servir à l'affichage des images météorologiques transmises par satellite** = the frame store can be used to display weather satellite pictures; **mémoire d'images optiques** = scanner memory; *(onde)* **porteuse d'image** = image carrier; **processeur d'image** = image processor; **le processeur d'image peut figer une image de télévision isolée** = the image processor will freeze a single TV frame; **rémanence de l'image** = image retention *ou* hangover; **saut d'image** = frame flyback; **scanner d'images** = image scanner; **stabilité de l'image** =

image stability; **traînée d'image** = hangover; **traitement de l'image** = image processing *ou* picture processing; **traitement informatique de l'image** = computer image processing; **machine** *ou* **système de traitement de l'image** = image processor; **transmission d'images** = picture transmission; **zone d'image** = image area; **zone d'image reçue** = safe area; **zone de stockage de l'image** = image storage space

◊ **imagerie** *nf* **imagerie médicale** = imaging; **imagerie par résonance magnétique (IRM)** = magnetic resonance imaging

> des affections non décelables par examens classiques sont maintenant détectées précocement grâce à l'imagerie médicale, augmentant ainsi considérablement les chances de guérison
>
> *01 Informatique*

imbrication *nf* interleaving; *(de boucles ou instructions)* nesting; *(code, etc.)* embedding; **niveau d'imbrication (de boucles)** = nesting level

◊ **imbriqué, -ée** *adj* interleaved; *(boucle ou instruction)* nested; *(code, etc.)* embedded; **appel de macro imbriqué** = nested macro call; **boucle imbriquée** = nested loop; **code imbriqué (dans un programme)** = embedded code; **commande imbriquée (dans le texte)** = embedded command; **ordinateur** *ou* **système imbriqué (dans un autre)** = embedded computer *ou* system; **mémoire imbriquée** = interleaved memory; **structure imbriquée** = nested structure

◊ **imbriquer** *vtr (une boucle ou une instruction)* to nest; **macro-instruction imbriquée** = nested macrocall

immédiat, -e *adj* immediate; **adressage immédiat** = immediate addressing; **adresse immédiate** = zero-level address *ou* immediate address; **instruction immédiate** = immediate instruction; **mode immédiat** = immediate mode; **opérande immédiat** = immediate operand; *(de données, de musique enregistrées)* **relecture immédiate** = instant replay; **traitement (de données) immédiat** = demand processing *ou* immediate processing; *(d'un film)* **visionnage immédiat** = instant replay

◊ **immédiatement** *adv* immediately *ou* directly

immobilisation *nf* immobilisation; **temps d'immobilisation** = stop time

◊ **immobiliser** *vtr* to stop

Imp *(sur un clavier)* **touche Imp Ecran** *ou* **impression d'écran** = PrtSc *ou* Print Screen

impact *nm* impact; **imprimante à impact** = impact printer; **imprimante sans impact** = non-impact printer

> la compétition entre les imprimantes à 'impact' (marguerite et aiguilles) et les 'non impact' (jet d'encre, laser, thermique) est de plus en plus vive
>
> *L'Ordinateur Individuel*

impair, -e *adj* odd; **(contrôle de) parité impaire** = odd parity (check)

◊ **imparité** *nf* (contrôle d')imparité = odd parity (check)

impasse *nf* deadlock

impeccable *adj* perfect

◊ **impeccablement** *adv* perfectly

impédance *nf* impedance *ou* load; **impédance de charge** = load impedance; **impédance de ligne** = line impedance; **accord d'impédance** = impedance matching; **l'accord d'impédance entre un émetteur et un récepteur réduit la perte de puissance des signaux transmis** = impedance matching between a transmitter and a receiver minimizes power losses to transmitted signals; **charge d'impédance** = load; **temps de décharge d'un circuit d'impédance** = load life; **désaccord d'impédance** = impedance mismatch

implantation *nf* **implantation d'une base de données** = database mapping; **implantation des touches d'un clavier** = keyboard layout *ou* key matrix

◊ **implanter** *vtr* (a) *(ranger dans la mémoire)* to plant (b) to implant; **le dopant est implanté dans le substrat** = the dopant is implanted into the substrate

implémentation *nf* implementation

◊ **implémenter** *vtr* to implement

implication *nf* implication

implicite *adj* implied *ou* (by) default; **adressage implicite** = implied addressing; **l'adressage implicite pour l'accumulateur est inclus dans l'instruction LDA,16** = implied addressing for the accumulator is used in the instruction LDA,16; **débit implicite (d'un modem)** = default rate (of a modem); **la largeur implicite de cet écran est de 80** = screen width has a default value of 80; **lecteur implicite** = default drive; **option implicite** = default option

important, -e *adj* important *ou* significant; **très important** = most important *ou* prime; **caractéristique la plus importante** = key feature

importation *nf* importation

◊ **importé, -e** *adj* **signal importé** = imported signal

◊ **importer** *vtr* to import; **il est possible d'importer des images d'un logiciel CAO dans un programme de PAO** = you can import images from the CAD package into the DTP program

impression *nf* impression *ou* printing *ou* print; **si l'impression est trop pâle, réglez le bouton de densité (d'impression) sur le noir** = when fading occurs, turn the density dial on the printer to full black; **impression en arrière-plan** = background printing; **l'impression peut être exécutée en arrière-plan pendant que vous travaillez sur un autre document** = background printing can be carried out whilst you are editing another document; **impression en différé** = print spooling *ou* off-line printing; **impression directe** = direct impression; **impression d'étiquettes** = labelling *ou* label printing; **impression hors ligne** *ou* **par imprimante autonome** = off-line printing; *(blanc sur noir)* **impression inversée** = cameo; **impression à passages multiples** = multipass overlap; **impression d'un programme d'assemblage** = assembly listing; **impression (en) offset** = offset printing; **impression par spouling** = print spooling; **impression en taille douce** = copperplate printing; **impression thermique** = electrosensitive printing; **arrêt de l'impression** = print pause; **bande sans paramètres d'impression** = idiot tape; **boule d'impression** = golf-ball; **caractères de contrôle d'impression** = print *ou* printer control characters; **cylindre** *ou* **tambour d'impression** = impression cylinder; *(télévision ou télécopie)* **déréglage de la qualité d'impression** = hangover; **file d'attente à l'impression** = print queue; **format d'impression** = print format; **logiciel de formatage d'impression** = print formatter; *(plaque ou bloc)* **marteau d'impression** = print hammer; **matrice d'impression à haute définition** = enhanced dot matrix; **modificateurs** *ou* **paramètres d'impression** = print modifiers; **qualité d'impression** = print quality; **une imprimante graphique avec une résolution de 600 dpi fournit une bonne qualité d'impression** = a desktop printer with a resolution of 600dpi provides good print quality; *(copieur ou imprimante)* **réglage de densité d'impression** = density dial; **serveur d'impression** = print server; **style d'impression** = print style; **tâche d'impression** = print job; **tête d'impression** = printhead; **la tête d'impression peut imprimer plus de 400 millions de caractères** = the printhead has a print life of over 400 million characters

◊ **imprimable** *adj* printer-readable; **une image vidéo imprimable peut être envoyée sur une imprimante laser classique par le port vidéo** = a printer-readable video image can be sent to a basic laser printer through a video port

◊ **imprimante** *nf* *(d'ordinateur)* (computer) printer; **imprimante à aiguilles** = stylus printer *ou* dot-matrix printer; **imprimante à bande** = band printer; **imprimante à barres** = bar printer; **imprimante bidirectionnelle** = bi-directional printer; **imprimante à boule** = ball printer; golf-ball printer; **imprimante à bulle d'encre** = bubble jet printer ™; **imprimante caractère (par caractère)** = character printer; **imprimante à caractères pleins** = solid font printer; **imprimante à chaîne** = chain printer; **imprimante 80 colonnes** = 80-column printer; **le prix comprend une imprimante 80 colonnes** = an 80-column printer is included in the price; **imprimante à cylindre** *ou* **à tambour** = barrel printer; **imprimante à définition des blancs** = white writer; **imprimante à définition des noirs** = black writer; **imprimante électrostatique** = electrostatic printer; **imprimante graphique** = printer-plotter; **imprimante à impact** = impact printer; **imprimante sans impact** = non-impact printer; **imprimante à jet d'encre** = ink-jet printer; **imprimante (à) laser** = laser printer; **imprimante ligne à ligne** = line printer; **imprimante à marguerite** = daisy-wheel printer; **l'imprimante à marguerite donne un bien meilleur résultat que l'imprimante matricielle mais elle est plus lente** = a daisy-wheel printer produces much better quality text than a dot-matrix, but is slower; **l'imprimante à marguerite imprime un caractère à la fois** = a daisy-wheel printer is a character printer *ou* prints one character at a time; **imprimante matricielle** = dot-matrix printer *ou* stylus printer *ou* wire printer; **imprimante (en mode) page** = page printer; **imprimante parallèle** = parallel printer; **imprimante à tambour** = barrel printer; **imprimante thermique** = thermal *ou* electrothermal printer; **imprimante thermique (à étincelle)** = spark printer; **imprimante à transfert thermique** = thermal transfer printer; **imprimante à tulipe** = thimble printer; **contrôleur** *ou* **pilote d'imprimante** = printer's controller; **débit d'une imprimante (mesuré en 'ems')** = printer output *ou* ems per hour; **durée de vie d'une imprimante** = print life; **gestionnaire d'imprimante** = printer driver; **interface d'imprimante** = hard copy interface; **pilote d'imprimante** = printer driver; **port (d')imprimante** = printer port; **ruban d'imprimante** = printer ribbon; **sortie d'imprimante** = computer printout *ou* computer listing; hard copy; **tampon d'imprimante** = printer buffer; **vidage sur imprimante** = dump; **vidage d'écran sur imprimante** = screen dump; **vidage de mouvements (sur imprimante)** = change dump; **vider sur l'imprimante (le contenu d'une mémoire)** = to deposit

◊ **imprimé** *nm* **(a)** *(document)* printed matter; **imprimé publicitaire** = publicity matter; **rapport de contraste d'un imprimé** = print contrast ratio **(b)** *(sortie d'imprimante ou texte d'écran)* hard copy

imprimantes à aiguilles, à jet d'encre, à laser, thermiques: les technologies d'impression progressent et les choix de matériels se diversifient

L'Ordinateur Individuel

◊ **imprimé, -e** *adj* **(a)** *(document)* printed; **document imprimé** = printed document; **texte imprimé** = hard copy; **imprimé d'avance** = preprinted **(b)** **circuit imprimé (CI)** = printed circuit *ou* printed circuit board (PCB); **carte de circuit imprimé** *ou* **plaque (présensibilisée) pour circuit imprimé** = printed circuit card *ou* printed circuit board *ou* PCB; **plaque (présensibilisée) double face pour circuit imprimé** = double-sided printed circuit board

◊ **imprimer** *vtr* to print; **le livre est imprimé sur du papier 80 grammes** = the book is printed on 80gsm paper; **nous faisons imprimer quelques-unes de nos revues au Japon** = we are using Japanese printers for some of our magazines; **nous n'imprimons pas les prochaines factures avant vendredi** = the next invoice run will be on Friday; **il était ravi de voir son livre imprimé** = he was very pleased to see his book in print; **ce livre a été imprimé à Hong Kong** = the book was printed in Hong Kong; **imprimer (des données)** = to print out (data); **(instruction d')imprimer en caractères gras** = bold *ou* embolden; **imprimer la file d'attente** = to despool; **trait d'union qui ne s'imprime pas** = discretionary hyphen *ou* soft hyphen

◊ **imprimerie** *nf* *(l'art)* printing; *(atelier)* printing house *ou* printing press *ou* printer's; **le texte a été envoyé à l'imprimerie la semaine dernière** = the text was sent to the printer's last

week; **imprimerie à façon** = print shop; **imprimerie et reliure** = bookwork; **écrire en caractères d'imprimerie** = to print

◊ **imprimeur** *nm* printer; **on doit envoyer le livre chez l'imprimeur la semaine prochaine** = the book will be sent to the printer next week; **corrections de l'imprimeur** = house corrections; **imprimeur à façon** = jobbing printer; **nom de l'imprimeur** = imprint

impulsion *nf* impulse *ou* pulse; **impulsion de cadran** = dial pulse; **impulsion électronique** = electronic pulse; **impulsion d'horloge** = clock pulse; **signaux synchrones aux impulsions d'horloge** = clocked signals; **impulsion d'inhibition du signal** = blanking pulse; **impulsion de synchronisation horizontale** = horizontal synchronization pulse; **impulsion de synchronisation du balayage vertical** = field sync pulse; **impulsion électrique** = strobe; **(composition de numéro d')appel par impulsion** = pulse-dialling; **émettre des impulsions** = to pulse; **(d'échantillonnage ou de validation)** to strobe; **déclenché par bascule de front d'impulsion** = edge-triggered; **générateur d'impulsions** = pulse generator; **micro à impulsion** = dynamic microphone; **modulation d'impulsions** = pulse modulation; **modulation d'impulsions en amplitude (MIA)** = pulse amplitude modulation (PAM); **modulation d'impulsions en durée (MID)** = pulse duration modulation (PDM); **modulation d'impulsions en largeur** *ou* **en durée (MIL** *ou* **MID)** = pulse width modulation (PWM); **modulation d'impulsions en position (MIP)** = pulse position modulation (PPM); **modulation par impulsions et codage (MIC)** = pulse code modulation (PCM); **train d'impulsions** = pulse stream

d'un point de vue pratique, ce codage qui ne fait appel qu'aux chiffres 1 et 0 est traduit en impulsions électriques (les 1) séparées par l'absence de signal (les 0)

Science et Vie

imputable *adj* attributable; **erreur imputable à un composant défectueux** = component error

inacceptable *adj* unacceptable *ou* not acceptable; **texte inacceptable** = bad copy

inaccessible *adj* out of range

inactif, -ive *adj* inactive; **fenêtre inactive** = inactive window; **instruction inactive** = no-op instruction

inapproprié, -ée *adj* improper; **coupure inappropriée** = bad break

inattendu, -e *adj* unexpected; *(d'un programme)* **arrêt inattendu** = hangup

inaudible *adj* inaudible; **fréquences inaudibles** = subaudio frequencies

incandescence *nf* incandescence

◊ **incandescent, -e** *adj* incandescent; **le passage du courant qui chauffe le filament dans une** ampoule contenant un gaz, produit une lumière **incandescente** = current passing through gas and heating a filament in a light bulb causes it to produce incandescent light

incident *nm (d'un ordinateur* ou *d'un programme)* failure ou fault; **enregistrement (automatique) des états d'incidents** = failure logging; **(signal d')interruption sur incident** = error interrupt; *(sans repartir à zéro)* **reprise sur incident** = failure recovery ou error recovery

inclinaison *nf (d'un caractère)* skew

◊ **incliné, -ée** *adj* inclined ou tilted; **orbite inclinée** = inclined orbit

inclure *vtr* (a) *(contenir)* to enclose; **les frais financiers n'ont pas été inclus dans le document** = the interest charges have been excluded from the document (b) *(comprendre)* to involve

◊ **inclus, -use** *adj* enclosed; **logiciel inclus à l'achat d'un ordinateur** = bundled software; **logiciel non inclus (dans l'offre d'achat)** = unbundled software

◊ **inclusif, -ive** *adj* inclusive; *(fonction logique)* **OU inclusif** = inclusive OR; **opération OU inclusif** = either-or operation

◊ **inclusion** *nf* inclusion

incompatibilité *nf* noncompatibility

◊ **incompatible** *adj* incompatible; **en essayant de relier les deux systèmes, ils les ont trouvés incompatibles** = they tried to link the two systems, but found they were incompatible

incomplet, -ète *adj* incomplete; **code incomplet** = skeletal code; **(mémoire) RAM incomplète** = partial RAM

inconditionnel, -elle *adj* unconditional; **branchement** ou **saut inconditionnel** = unconditional branch ou jump

incontrôlable *adj* uncontrollable; *(d'un dispositif* ou *d'un ordinateur)* **opération incontrôlable** = runaway

incorporé, -ée *adj* built-in; **fonction incorporée** = built-in function

incorrect, -e *adj* false ou inaccurate ou incorrect; **les données saisies étant incorrectes, les résultats à la sortie étaient par le fait même erronés** = the input data was incorrect, so the output was also incorrect

◊ **incorrectement** *adv* incorrectly; **les données ont été incorrectement saisies** = the data was incorrectly keyboarded

incrément *nm* increment; **incrément de ligne** = line increment; **augmentez l'incrément à trois** = increase the increment to three

◊ **incrémentation** *nf* increment; **traceur à incrémentation** = incremental plotter

◊ **incrémenter** *vtr* to increment; **le compteur est**

incrémenté à chaque instruction exécutée = the counter is incremented each time an instruction is executed

◊ **incrémenteur-décrémenteur** *nm* **compteur incrémenteur-décrémenteur** = up/down counter

◊ **incrémentiel, -elle** *adj* incremental; **compilation et décompilation incrémentielles** = incremental compilation and decompilation; **donnée(s) incrémentielle(s)** = incremental data; **ordinateur incrémentiel** = incremental computer; **sauvegarde incrémentielle** = incremental backup; **traceur incrémentiel** = incremental plotter

indépendamment *adv* independently; separately; **lors d'un spooling, l'imprimante fonctionne indépendamment du clavier** = in spooling, the printer is acting independently of the keyboard

◊ **indépendant, -e** *adj* independent ou separate; **indépendant du constructeur** = vendor independent; **émission de signaux par canaux indépendants** = separate channel signalling; **langage informatique indépendant** = computer independent language; **on peut exécuter le programme sur un ordinateur indépendant ou un système multiposte** = the program runs on a standalone machine or a multi-user system; **ordinateur indépendant** = standalone (machine); **programme indépendant** = device-independent program

indéterminé, -ée *adj* indeterminate; **système indéterminé** = indeterminate system

index *nm (d'un livre* ou *d'un programme)* index; *(système de recherche)* reference retrieval system; **l'index de ce livre est très mal fait** = the book has been badly indexed; **index complet** = dense index; **index cumulatif** = cumulative index; **index de cycle** = cycle index; **index des fichiers** = file index; **index général** ou **principal** = main index; **index hash code** = hash index; **préparation de l'index d'un livre** = indexing; **préparation d'un index à l'aide d'un ordinateur** = computer indexing; **le livre a été envoyé à l'extérieur pour la préparation de l'index** = the book was sent out for indexing; **personne qui prépare un index** ou **auteur d'un index** = indexer; **clé d'index** = index key; **mot d'index** = index value word; **page index** = index page; *(informatique)* **registre d'index** = index register (IR)

◊ **indexage** *nm* indexing; **indexage libre** = free indexing; **indexage dérivé** = derived indexing

◊ **indexation** *nf* indexing; **indexation sur ordinateur** = computer indexing; **langage d'indexation** = indexing language; **résumé et indexation** = abstracting & indexing (A&I)

◊ **indexé, -ée** *adj* indexed; **adressage indexé** = indexed addressing; **adresse indexée** = indexed address; **fichier indexé** = indexed file; **instruction indexée** = indexed instruction; **mémoire séquentielle indexée** = indexed sequential storage; **méthode d'accès séquentiel indexé (ISAM)** = indexed sequential access method (ISAM); **méthode d'accès séquentiel indexé en file** = queued indexed sequential access method (QISAM); **registre (d'adresse) indexé** = B register

◊ **indexer** *vtr* to index

indicateur *nm* **(a)** *(symbole ou code)* indicator *ou* (indicator) flag *ou* marker; **indicateur binaire** = flag bit; **indicateur binaire de dépassement de capacité** = overflow bit *ou* flag; **indicateur de contrôle** = check indicator *ou* rogue indicator; **indicateur de contrôle de parité** = parity flag; **(bit) indicateur d'état** *ou* **d'utilisation** = device flag; **cette routine vérifie l'indicateur d'état et ne transmet pas le signal si le bit occupé est présent** = this routine checks the device status word and will not transmit data if the busy bit is set; **indicateur de mot** = word marker; **indicateur de retenue** = carry flag; **indicateur de signe** = sign bit *ou* sign indicator; **indicateur (binaire) zéro** = zero flag; **si le résultat est zéro, l'indicateur zéro est activé** = if the result is zero, the zero flag is set; **bit indicateur** = flag bit; **mise en place d'un indicateur** = flag event; **mot indicateur d'état** = device status word (DSW); **séquence d'indicateurs** = flag sequence; **tableau des indicateurs** = indicator chart **(b)** *(dispositif)* **(commutateur) indicateur d'état** = sense switch; **indicateur de fin de papier** = form stop

indicatif *nm* **(a)** *(téléphonique)* (dialling) code; **quel est l'indicatif de Bruxelles?** = what is the code for Brussels?; **indicatif international** = international dialling code; **indicatif du pays** = country code; *(Canada)* **indicatif régional** = area code; **indicatif de zone** = area code; **l'indicatif (de zone) de Londres est 0171** = the area code for central London is 0171; **indicatif du pays suivi de l'indicatif de zone suivi du numéro de votre correspondant** = country code followed by area code followed by customer's number **(b) indicatif littéral** = index letter; **indicatif numérique** = index number

indice *nm* **(a)** subscript *ou* inferior figure; **variable caractérisée par un indice** = subscripted variable **(b)** *(des cahiers d'un livre)* **indices de collationnement** = collating marks; *(sur film)* **indice de position** = index **(c)** *(télévision)* **indice d'écoute** = audience rating **(d)** *(de la lumière)* **indice de réfraction** = refractive index

◊ **indicé, -ée** *adj* **variable indicée** = subscripted variable

indiquer *vtr* to mark *ou* specify *ou* to indicate

indirect, -e *adj* indirect; **adressage indirect** = deferred *ou* indirect *ou* second-level addressing; **rayonnement indirect** = indirect ray

indisponible *adj* *(non-activé)* **configuration indisponible** = configured off *ou* configured out

individuel, -elle *adj* **(a)** individual; **ordinateur individuel** = personal computer *ou* PC **(b) poste individuel** = stand-alone *ou* standalone; **les postes ont été reliés en réseau plutôt que d'être utilisés comme postes individuels** = the workstations have been networked together rather than used as stand-alone systems

inductance *nf* inductance

◊ **inducteur** *nm* inductor

◊ **inductif, -ive** *adj* **coordination inductive** = inductive coordination

◊ **induction** *nf* *(électricité)* induction; **bobine d'induction** = induction coil *ou* inductor; **produire une induction** = to induce (a current)

◊ **induire** *vtr* *(un courant)* to induce (a current)

◊ **induit, -e** *adj* **(a)** *(électricité)* **produire un courant induit** = to induce a current **(b)** *(produite par une cause externe)* **défaillance induite** = induced failure **(c)** *(produite par d'autres machines)* **diaphonie** *ou* **interférence induite** = crossfire *ou* induced interference

industrie *nf* industry; **l'industrie électronique** = the electronics industry

◊ **industriel, -elle** *adj* industrial; **esthétique industrielle** = industrial design; **ordinateur industriel** = process control computer

ineffaçable *adj* **mémoire ineffaçable** = nonerasable memory

ineffectif, -ive *adj* ineffective; **instruction ineffective** = do-nothing (instruction)

inégalité *nf* **opérateur d'inégalité** = inequality operator; **le langage C utilise le symbole '!='** **comme opérateur d'inégalité** = the C programming language uses the symbol '!=' as its inequality operator

inerte *adj* inert; **gaz inerte** = inert gas

inexact, -e *adj* inaccurate *ou* incorrect

◊ **inexactitude** *nf* inaccuracy

inexplicable *adj* inexplicable *ou* strange; **erreur inexplicable** = gremlin; **perte de transmission inexplicable** = line gremlin

infecté, -ée *adj* *(dans lequel il y a un virus)* **ordinateur infecté** = infected computer

inférence *nf* inference; **(nombre d')inférences logiques par seconde** = logical inference per second (LIPS); **contrôle d'inférence** = inference control; **moteur d'inférence** = inference engine *ou* machine

inférieur, -e *adj* lower; *(pour papier d'une imprimante)* **bac inférieur** = lower bin; **introduire le bac inférieur** = load lower bin

infini *nm* infinity

◊ **infini, -e** *adj* infinite

infixé, -ée *adj* **notation infixée** = infix notation

influer *vi* to affect; **les sautes** *ou* **les variations de tension vont influer sur le fonctionnement de l'ordinateur** = changes in voltage will affect the way the computer functions

infographie *nf* computer graphics *ou* computer-generated graphics *ou* raster graphics; **infographie interactive** = interactive graphics; **infographie par**

points *ou* **à adressage binaire** = bit-mapped graphics

◊ **infographiste** *nm&f (dessinateur travaillant sur ordinateur)* designer

> il a animé pendant près d'un an une équipe d'une soixantaine d'infographistes, animateurs ou spécialistes d'effets spéciaux, pour réaliser 26 minutes d'un bonheur de synthèse qui ressemble comme deux gouttes d'eau au vrai
>
> *Mon PC Multimédia*

in-folio *nm&adj* folio

infomaniaque *nm&f* terminal junky (TJ); **mon fils est devenu un véritable infomaniaque** = my son has turned into a real terminal junky

informaticien, -ienne *n&adj* ingénieur **informaticien** = computer engineer

information *nf* **(a)** *(ensemble de données)* information; **information sans intérêt** *ou* **de rebut** = garbage; **canal** *ou* **voie de transmission de l'information** = information transfer channel; **contrôle de flux d'information** = information flow control; **liberté d'accès à l'information** = freedom of information; **ligne d'information** = information line; **ordinateur utilisé pour le traitement de l'information** = information processor; **quantité d'information** = information content; **réseaux d'information** = information networks; **sécurité de l'information** = data security; **source d'information** *ou* **service (fournisseur) d'information** = information provider (IP); **stockage de l'information** = information storage; **support d'information** = information *ou* data medium; **système de gestion de l'information** = information management system; **techniques de l'information** = information technology (IT); **théorie de l'information** = information theory; **traitement de l'information** = data processing (DP *ou* dp) *ou* information processing; **traitement centralisé de l'information** = centralized data processing; **traitement électronique de l'information** = electronic data processing (EDP); **unité d'information** = computer word; **vitesse de sortie de l'information** = information rate; **voie de transmission d'information** = information bearer channel **(b)** *(nouvelles)* **informations** = news; **bulletin d'informations de la société** = company newsletter

informatique 1 *nf* **(science de) l'informatique** = computer science *ou* computing; electronic data processing (EDP); information technology (IT); **informatique défensive** = defensive computing; *(loi)* **loi Informatique et Libertés** = Data Protection Act; **informatique répartie** = distributed (data) processing (DDP); **connaissances en informatique** = computer literacy; **(personne) qui a des connaissances en informatique** = computer-literate (person); **le directeur général n'a aucune notion de l'informatique** = the managing director is simply not computer-literate *ou* is computer-illiterate **2** *adj* computer; **applications informatiques** = computer applications; **cassette informatique** = data cassette; **(personne) qui ne possède aucune connaissance informatique** *ou* **qui ne comprend pas le jargon informatique** = computer-illiterate; **fournisseur** *ou* **revendeur d'équipements informatiques** = computer equipment supplier; **fichier informatique** = computer file; *(passible du tribunal correctionnel)* **fraude informatique** = computer crime *ou* computer fraud; **langage informatique** = computer language; **langage informatique indépendant** = computer independent language; **logique informatique** = computer logic; **matériel informatique** = hardware; *(ensemble du matériel et de l'équipement)* installation; **personnel informatique** = liveware; **pirate (de système) informatique** = hacker; **poste informatique de télétransmission** = data station; **réseau informatique** = computer network *ou* information network; **réseau informatique centralisé** = centralized computer network; **réseau informatique homogène** = homogeneous computer network; **l'éditeur de la rubrique informatique du journal** = the paper's computer editor; *(dans une entreprise)* **service informatique** = management information service (MIS); computer department; **directeur, -trice** *ou* **responsable** *ou* **chef du service informatique** = computer manager *ou* data processing manager (DPM); **système informatique** = information system *ou* computer system; **système informatique pour bureau** = computer office system; **cette entreprise est un fournisseur réputé de systèmes informatiques intégrés qui permettent à la fois la pagination de très longs documents et le traitement personnalisé de chaque page** = this firm is a very well-known supplier of computer-integrated systems which allow batch pagination of very long documents with alteration of individual pages; **terminal** *ou* **poste informatique** = data terminal; **traitement informatique de l'image** = computer image processing; **société de services et d'ingénierie informatique (SSII)** = computer bureau

◊ **informatisation** *nf* computerization; **l'informatisation du secteur financier progresse très rapidement** = computerization of the financial sector is proceeding very fast

◊ **informatisé, -ée** *adj* computer-managed; **bureau informatisé** = electronic office; **entraînement informatisé** = computer-based training (CBT); **formation informatisée** = computer-based learning (CBL) *ou* computer-managed learning (CML); **leur facturation est informatisée** = they operate a computerized invoicing system; **système de gestion informatisé** = management information system (MIS); **notre gestion des stocks est totalement informatisée** = our stock control has been completely computerized; **système de réapprovisionnement informatisé** = computerized stock system

◊ **informatiser** *vtr* to computerize

infra- *préfixe* infra-

◊ **infrarouge 1** *nm* infrared; **communication par infrarouge** = infrared communications; **détecteur d'infrarouge** = infrared detector; **instruments de vision aux infrarouges** = infrared sights; **photo avec film sensible aux infrarouges** = infrared photography; **vidéocamera à infrarouge** = infrared video camera **2** *adj* **rayons infrarouges** *ou* **rayonnement infrarouge** = infrared light (IR light)

◊ **infrasonique** *adj* infrasonic; **fréquence infrasonique** = infrasonic frequency

◊ **infrasonore** *adj* **fréquences infrasonores** = subaudio frequencies

◊ **infrastructure** *nf* infrastructure

ingénierie *nf* engineering; **ingénierie assistée par ordinateur (IAO)** = computer-aided *ou* assisted engineering (CAE); **ingénierie de la connaissance** = knowledge engineering; **société de services et d'ingénierie informatique (SSII)** = computer bureau

◊ **ingénieur** *nm* engineer; **ingénieur électronicien** = electronic(s) engineer; **ingénieur d'entretien** *ou* **d'après-vente** *ou* **de maintenance (sur le site)** = field engineer; **ingénieur d'essai** = trials engineer; **ingénieur informaticien** = computer engineer; **ingénieur logiciel** *ou* **ingénieur programmeur** = software engineer; **ingénieur système** = systems engineer

◊ **ingénieur-conseil** *nm* consulting engineer *ou* engineering consultant

inhérent, -e *adj* inherent; **adressage inhérent** = inherent addressing

inhibé, -ée *adj* inhibited *ou* suppressed; **modulation d'amplitude à porteuse inhibée** = suppressed carrier modulation; *(de modulation d'amplitude)* **bande latérale unique à porteuse inhibée** = single sideband suppressed carrier (SSBSC); **double bande latérale à porteuse inhibée** = double sideband suppressed carrier (DSBSC)

◊ **inhiber** *vtr* to inhibit *ou* to suppress

◊ **inhibition** *nf* inhibition *ou* suppression; **inhibition du signal** = blanking; **impulsion d'inhibition du signal** = blanking pulse; **inhibition horizontale (du signal)** = horizontal blanking

ininterrompu, -e *adj* continuous; **flux ininterrompu de données** = continuous data stream

initiale *nf (lettre)* initial; **signer de ses initiales** = to initial (a document)

◊ **initial, -e** *adj* **(a)** initial; **adresse initiale** = initial address; **condition initiale** = initial condition; **format initial** = native format; **instruction initiale** = initial instruction; **instruction dans sa forme initiale** = unmodified instruction; *(du curseur)* **position initiale** = home; **valeur initiale** = initial value **(b) lettre initiale** = initial

◊ **initialisation** *nf (d'un système)* initialization; **l'initialisation peut souvent s'effectuer à l'insu de l'utilisateur** = initialization is often carried out without the user knowing

◊ **initialiser** *vtr (un système)* to set up *ou* to initialize; **l'ingénieur a initialisé le nouvel ordinateur qui a tout de suite bien fonctionné** = the new computer worked well as soon as the engineer had set it up

injecter *vtr (instruction de PAO)* **injecter du texte (dans un cadre)** = flow text

◊ **injection** *nf* injection; *(par fibre optique)* **laser d'injection** = injection laser; **logique intégrée à injection** = integrated injection logic (IIL)

in-quarto *nm&adj* **(format) in-quarto** = quarto

Ins *(sur un clavier)* **touche Ins** = Ins key (insert key)

inscrire *vtr* to enter *ou* to record; **inscrire un nom sur une liste** = to enter a name on a list; **inscrivez les résultats dans cette colonne** = record the results in this column

in-seize *ou* **in-16** *nm&adj (format)* sixteenmo *ou* 16mo

insensibilité *nf* **insensibilité au bruit** = noise immunity; **insensibilité aux interférences** = interference immunity

insérer *vtr* to introduce *ou* to load; **insérer au dossier** = to place something on file; **insérer dans une fente** *ou* **une ouverture** = to slot (in *ou* into); **la disquette s'insère dans l'une des deux fentes du lecteur de disquettes** = the disk slots into one of the floppy drive apertures

◊ **insertion** *nf* **(a)** *(dans un texte)* **insertion d'un bloc** *ou* **d'un paragraphe** = block transfer; **mode insertion** = insert mode; *(dans un programme: moment où on introduit un test de débogage, etc.)* **point d'insertion (de test)** = hook; **programme** *ou* **sous-programme d'insertion directe** = direct-insert routine *ou* subroutine **(b)** *(connecteur)* **insertion sans friction** *ou* **à force d'insertion zéro** = zero insertion force (ZIF); *(de signal)* **perte** *ou* **affaiblissement d'insertion** = insertion loss

insonorisation *nf* soundproofing; **capot** *ou* **hotte d'insonorisation** = acoustic hood; **grâce au capot d'insonorisation, il est possible d'avoir une conversation lorsque l'imprimante fonctionne** = an acoustic hood allows us to talk while the printer is working

◊ **insonorisé, -ée** *adj* soundproof; **le téléphone est dans une cabine insonorisée** = the telephone is installed in a soundproof booth

instabilité *nf* instabilité; *(de l'image)* flickering

installable *adj* **gestionnaire de périphérique installable** = installable device driver

◊ **installation** *nf* installation; **installation de secours prête à fonctionner** = hot standby; **installation simplifiée** = abbreviated installation; **délai d'installation** = setup time; **programme d'installation** = install program

◊ **installer** *vtr* to install *ou* to set up; **on nous installera une nouvelle machine** *ou* **un nouveau photocopieur Xerox demain** = we are having a new xerox machine installed tomorrow; **qu'on peut installer** = installable

instance *nf (objet disponible en programmation orientée objet)* instance

instantané *nm* snapshot

◊ **instantané, -ée** *adj* instantaneous *ou* instant; **accès instantané** = instantaneous access; **l'accès instantané au disque RAM a été bien accueilli** = the instantaneous access of the RAM disk was welcome; **traitement instantané d'un film** = in camera process; *(de mémoire ou de registre)* **vidage instantané** = snapshot dump

instruction *nf* instruction *ou* command *ou* order *ou* (program) statement; *(mot)* instruction word; **l'instruction PRINT est un opérande employé en langage BASIC pour l'affichage des données suivantes** = the instruction PRINT is used in this BASIC dialect as an operand to display the following data; **instruction absolue** = absolute instruction; **instruction à adresse unique** *ou* **à adresse directe** = one-address instruction; **instruction à deux adresses** = two-address instruction; **instruction à deux adresses plus une** = two-plus-one-address instruction; **instruction à n adresse(s) plus une** = n-plus-one address instruction; **instruction à trois adresses** = three-address instruction; **instruction à quatre adresses** = four-address instruction; **instruction à quatre adresses plus une** = four-plus-one address instruction; **instruction d'affectation** = assignment statement; **instruction d'appel** = call instruction; **c'est ici qu'il faudrait introduire l'instruction d'appel** = the subroutine call instruction should be at this point; **instruction arithmétique** = arithmetic instruction; **instruction d'arrêt (dans un programme)** = breakpoint instruction *ou* halt instruction; **instruction d'assemblage** = pseudo-operation; **instruction de base** = basic instruction *ou* reference instruction; **instruction de branchement** *ou* **de saut** = branch instruction *ou* jump instruction; **les fabricants du CPU ont décidé que l'instruction JMP servirait à faire un branchement** = the manufacturers of this CPU have decided that JMP will be the instruction word to call the jump function; **instruction en code** *ou* **en langage machine** = machine code instruction; **instruction composée** = compound statement; **le débogueur ne peut agir sur les instructions composées** = the debugger cannot handle compound statements; **instruction conditionnelle** = conditional statement; **instruction d'opération conditionnelle** = discrimination instruction *ou* decision instruction; **instruction de contrôle** = control statement *ou* control instruction; *(de surveillance)* supervisory instruction; **la prochaine instruction de contrôle vous donnera les italiques** = the next control instruction will switch to italics; **instruction déclarative** = narrative statement; **instruction directe** = direct instruction; **instruction directive** = directive statement; **commandes et instructions d'édition** = editing terms; **instruction effective** = effective instruction; **instruction d'entrée** = entry instruction; **instruction d'entrée dans la pile** = push instruction *ou* operation; **instruction (d')entrée/sortie** = I/O instruction *ou* input/output instruction; **instruction d'extraction** = extract instruction; **instruction factice** = no-operation instruction *ou* no-op instruction *ou* null instruction; **instruction dans sa forme initiale** = unmodified instruction; **instruction 'GET'** *ou*

instruction 'chercher' = get instruction; **instruction 'GOTO'** *ou* **instruction de saut** = GOTO instruction; **instruction IF (si)** = IF statement; **instructions IF-THEN-ELSE (de branchement conditionnel)** = IF-THEN-ELSE; **instruction immédiate** = immediate instruction; **instruction inactive** *ou* **de remplissage** = no-op instruction; **instruction indexée** = indexed instruction; **instruction ineffective** *ou* **sans effet** = do-nothing (instruction); **instruction invalide** = illegal instruction; **instructions de lancement** *ou* **instructions initiales** = initial instructions; **instruction en langage machine** = machine instruction; **instruction de lecture d'une instruction** = fetch instruction; **instruction multi-adresse** = multi-address *ou* multi-address instruction; **instruction nulle** = blank *ou* dummy *ou* null instruction; **instruction d'origine** *ou* **primitive** = presumptive instruction; **instructions privilégiées** = privileged instructions; **instruction de remplissage** = blank instruction *ou* dummy instruction *ou* pseudo-instruction *ou* null instruction; **instruction de superviseur** = executive instruction; **instruction de vidage et reprise** = dump and restart instruction; **instruction vide** = no-operation instruction *ou* no-op instruction; **adresse d'instruction** = instruction address; **antémémoire d'instruction** = instruction cache; **avancer le registre d'une instruction** = to increment the register; **caractère d'instruction** = instruction character; **code d'instruction** = computer code *ou* instruction code *ou* machine code; **compteur d'instruction** = instruction counter *ou* program counter (PC) *ou* instruction address register (IAR); **cycle d'instruction** = instruction cycle; **cycle de lecture d'une instruction** = fetch cycle; **décodeur d'instruction** = instruction decoder *ou* operation decoder; *(à quelqu'un ou à un ordinateur)* **donner une instruction** = to order *ou* to instruct; **format d'instruction** = instruction format; **jeu d'instructions** = instruction repertoire *ou* set; **langage d'instruction** = command language; **phase de lecture d'une instruction** = fetch phase; **signal de lecture d'instruction** = fetch signal; **ligne d'instruction (d'un programme)** = command line; **mémoire d'instruction** = instruction storage; **mise en mémoire** *ou* **stockage d'instruction** = instruction storage; **mode d'exécution d'instructions en pipeline** *ou* **enchaînement d'instructions avec recouvrement** = instruction pipelining; **modification d'une instruction** = instruction modification; **mot instruction** = instruction word; **pointeur d'instruction** = instruction pointer; **processeur d'instruction** = instruction processor; **processeur à jeu d'instructions réduit** = reduced instruction set computer (RISC); **registre d'adresse d'instruction** = instruction address register (IAR); **registre d'instruction** = command register *ou* instruction register (IR); **registre d'instruction courante** = current instruction register (CIR); **registre d'instruction à exécuter** *ou* **de la prochaine instruction** = next instruction register; **registre d'instruction à suivre** = sequence control register (SCR); **répertoire d'instructions** = instruction repertoire; **temps de cycle d'instruction** = instruction cycle time; **temps d'exécution d'une instruction** *ou* **temps d'instruction** = instruction (execution) time; **zone d'instruction (dans une mémoire)** = instruction area

instrument *nm* tool; **instruments (de précision)** = instrumentation; **instruments de vision aux infrarouges** = infrared sights

◊ **instrumentation** *nf* instrumentation; **nous avons amélioré l'instrumentation se rapportant à ce modèle pour que vous puissiez mieux suivre l'état de la machine** = we've improved the instrumentation on this model to keep you better informed of the machine's position

insuffisant, -e *adj* insufficient

intégral, -e *adj* integral; **structure à maillage intégral** = plex structure

intégrateur *nm* intégrateur graphique (à fenêtre, icône, souris, pointeur) = window, icon, mouse, pointer (WIMP)

◊ **intégration** *nf* **(a)** integration; **ce système assure l'intégration automatique du texte et des illustrations dans le document** = the system automatically merges text and illustrations into the document; **intégration parfaite** *ou* **sans couture** *ou* **sans hiatus** = seamless integration; **cela nous a demandé beaucoup de préparation, mais nous avons réussi une intégration sans couture de la nouvelle application** = it took a lot of careful planning, but we succeeded in a seamless integration of the new application **(b)** *(de composants)* **intégration à grande échelle** = large-scale integration (LSI); **intégration à très grande échelle** = very large scale integration (VLSI); **intégration à super grande échelle** = super large scale integration (SLSI); **intégration à moyenne échelle** = medium scale integration (MSI); **intégration à faible** *ou* **petite échelle** = small scale integration (SSI); **intégration sur tranche de silicium** = wafer scale integration **(c)** **réseau numérique à intégration de services (RNIS)** = integrated services digital network (ISDN); **système avec intégration de données** = system firmware

l'intégration de textes, tables et graphiques au sein d'un document est dynamique
Informatique & Bureautique

intégré, -ée *adj* integrated *ou* integral *ou* built-in *ou* inbuilt *ou* on-board; **(logiciel) intégré à une puce** = on-chip (software); **base de données intégrée** = integrated database; **(système de) bureautique intégrée** = integrated office; **la carte adaptateur intégrée rend l'appareil compatible IBM** = the built-in adapter card makes it fully IBM compatible; **circuit intégré** = integrated circuit (IC); **circuit intégré de diagnostic** = diagnostic chip; **circuit intégré d'entrée/sortie en parallèle** = parallel input/output chip; **circuit intégré linéaire** = linear integrated circuit; **architecture d'un circuit intégré** = chip architecture; **ensemble des circuits intégrés** = chip set; **circuit optique intégré** = integrated optical circuit; **ligne de sélection** *ou* **de validation d'un circuit intégré** = chip select line; **système de contrôle intégré** = built-in check; **logiciel possède un système de correction d'erreurs intégré** = this software has inbuilt error correction; **dispositif intégré** = integrated device; **l'ordinateur est équipé d'un disque dur intégré** = the

computer has a built-in hard disk; **émulateur intégré au circuit** = in-circuit emulator; **cet émulateur intégré au circuit sert à tester le contrôleur de la disquette, en simulant le fonctionnement d'un lecteur de disquettes** = this in-circuit emulator is used to test the floppy disk controller by emulating a disk drive; **puisque les lecteurs de disquettes et le modem sont intégrés l'encombrement est réduit** = the integral disk drives and modem reduce desk space; **l'ordinateur concurrent ne possède pas de lecteur de disquettes intégré comme ce modèle-ci** = our competitor's computer doesn't have an integrated disk drive like this model; **logiciel intégré** = integrated software; **le processeur utilise un logiciel de lancement intégré à la puce, pour permettre le chargement rapide des programmes** = the processor uses on-chip bootstrap software to allow programs to be loaded rapidly; **logique intégrée à injection** *ou* **logique IIL** *ou* **logique I2L** = integrated injection logic (IIL); **modem intégré** = integrated modem; **moniteur intégré** = firmware monitor; **tous les modems possèdent des ports de communication intégrés** = there are communications ports built into all modems; **productique intégrée** = computer-integrated manufacturing (CIM); **programme intégré** = integrated program *ou* integrated software; **réseau numérique intégré (RNI)** = integrated digital network; **accès au réseau numérique intégré** = integrated digital access (IDA); **systèmes d'exploitation intégrés** = computer-integrated systems; **cette entreprise est un fournisseur réputé de systèmes informatiques intégrés qui permettent à la fois la pagination de très longs documents et le traitement personnalisé de chaque page** = this firm is a very well-known supplier of computer-integrated systems which allow batch pagination of very long documents with alteration of individual pages; **(système de) traitement de données intégré** = integrated data processing (IDP); **traitement de film intégré dans l'appareil** = in camera process

◊ **intégrer** *vtr* **(a)** to build (a disk drive, etc.) into **(b)** *(des fichiers, etc.)* to merge

le circuit intégré se présente sous forme d'un boîtier comportant 16 broches 'dual in line' (2 rangées de 8). La broche no 16 est affectée au 'plus' alimentation tandis que la broche no 8 est à relier au 'moins'
Electronique pratique

intégrité *nf* integrity; **intégrité des données** = data integrity; **faire perdre l'intégrité des données** = to corrupt data; **un problème de tension pendant l'accès au disque peut faire perdre l'intégrité des données** = power loss during disk access can corrupt the data; **intégrité d'un fichier** = integrity of a file

Intel™ *(société qui a mis au point et commercialisé le premier microprocesseur, et un grand nombre d'autres depuis)* Intel ™; **(microprocesseurs) Intel 8086, 8088, 80286, 80386, 80486** = (Intel microprocessors) Intel 8086, 8088,

80286, 80386, 80486; **Intel Pentium** ™ = Intel Pentium ™

intelligence *nf* intelligence; **intelligence artificielle (IA)** = artificial intelligence (AI) *ou* machine intelligence; **intelligence répartie** = distributed intelligence

◊ **intelligent, -e** *adj* intelligent *ou* smart; **boîtier de câblage intelligent** *ou* **concentrateur** *ou* **hub intelligent** = intelligent *ou* smart wiring hub; **avec ce logiciel de gestion, je peux fermer à distance le port de Tom sur le concentrateur intelligent** = using this management software, I can shut down Tom's port on the remote smart wiring hub; **fonction césure intelligente** = intelligent spacer; **gestionnaire d'espaces intelligent** = intelligent spacer; **machine intelligente** = intelligent device; **terminal intelligent** = intelligent terminal *ou* smart terminal; **le nouveau terminal intelligent comporte un éditeur de texte** = the new intelligent terminal has a built-in text editor; **terminal non intelligent** = dumb terminal

intensificateur *nm* intensificateur d'image = image enhancer

◊ **intensité** *nf* intensity; **intensité de champ** = field strength; **intensité de trafic** = traffic intensity; **fluctuation de l'intensité du signal** = fluctuating signal strength; **perdre de l'intensité** = to fade

interactif, -ive *adj* interactive; **clavier interactif** = interactive keyboard; **disque audionumérique interactif** *ou* **disque compact interactif** *ou* **CD interactif** = CD-I *ou* compact disc interactive; **enseignement interactif géré par ordinateur** = computer-managed instruction (CMI); **graphiques interactifs** *ou* **infographie interactive** = interactive graphics; **le jeu (électronique)** 'les **envahisseurs de l'espace' présente d'excellents graphiques interactifs; le joueur contrôle la position de son vaisseau spatial avec la manette (de jeu)** = the space invaders machine has great interactive graphics, the player controls the position of his spaceship with the joystick; **mode interactif** = conversational mode *ou* interactive mode *ou* interactive processing; **moyens de communication interactifs** = interactive media; **routine interactive** = interactive routine; **système interactif** = interactive system; **système audio interactif** = active audio system; **système de déverminage interactif** *ou* **de débogage interactif** = interactive debugging system; **(système) multimédia interactif** = interactive multimedia; **ce logiciel multimédia interactif permet à l'utilisateur de faire de la musique avec un programme de synthétiseur** = this interactive multimedia title allows a user to make music with a synthesizer program; **télévision câblée interactive** = interactive cable television; **terminal interactif** = interactive terminal; **vidéo** *ou* **vidéographie interactive** = interactive video

◊ **interaction** *nf* interaction

◊ **interagir** *vi* to interact

interbloc *adj* interblock; **espace interbloc** = interblock gap (IBG) *ou* block gap

intercalaire *adj* (*entre deux bandes de communication*) **bande (de fréquences) intercalaire** = guard band; (*d'un programme*) **symbole intercalaire** = separator

interchangeable *adj* interchangeable

interclassement *nm* (*cartes perforées*) collating; **interclassement de fichier(s)** = file collating

◊ **interclasser** *vtr* (*des cartes perforées ou des fichiers*) to collate

◊ **interclasseuse** *nf* (*de cartes perforées*) collator

interconnecté, -ée *adj* interconnected; **réseau intégralement interconnecté** = plex structure

◊ **interconnecter** *vtr* to interconnect

◊ **interconnexion** *nf* interconnection; **interconnexion de systèmes ouverts (ISO)** *ou* **normes ISO (pour systèmes ouverts)** = Open System Interconnection (OSI)

intercouche *adj* **transfert intercouche** = radial transfer

interdiction *nf* interdiction; **liste d'interdictions** = stop list; **signal d'interdiction de transmission** = inhibiting input

◊ **interdire** *vtr* (*quelque chose ou de faire quelque chose*) to forbid (something); (*l'accès à un circuit ou à un système*) to deny *ou* to bar access (to a circuit *ou* to a system); **le mot de passe interdit aux personnes non autorisées d'avoir accès aux données** = the use of a password is to prevent unauthorized access to the data; **interdire l'accès à un fichier** *ou* **à un dossier** = to bar entry to a file; **interdire une interruption** = to interrupt disable

◊ **interdit, -e** *adj* unauthorized; **caractère interdit** = forbidden character; **chaîne (de caractères) interdite** = forbidden combination; **code** *ou* **chiffre interdit** = unallowable digit; (*dans une indexation*) **liste des mots interdits** = stop list

interfaçage *nm* interfacing; **protocole d'interfaçage HDLC** = high-level data link control (HDLC)

◊ **interface** *nf* interface; **interface de canal de transmission** = channel adapter; **interface de commande** *ou* **de contrôle** = command interface; **interface de communication asynchrone** = asynchronous communications interface adapter (ACIA); **adaptateur d'interface de communication** = communications interface adapter; **interface d'entrée/sortie** = input/output interface; **interface de transition** = bridge *ou* bridging product; **interface EIA** = electronic industry association interface *ou* EIA interface; **interface ESDI** = enhanced small device interface (ESDI); **interface graphique** = graphics interface; **interface homme/machine** = man/machine interface (MMI); **interface hybride** = hybrid interface; **interface d'imprimante** = hard copy interface; **interface magnétophone** = ACR interface; **interface parallèle** = parallel interface; **interface parallèle (de type) Centronics** = Centronics interface; **interface de périphérique** = peripheral interface adapter (PIA); **interface SCSI pour petit ordinateur** = small computer system interface (SCSI); **interface série** = serial interface; **interface standard** = standard interface; **interface système/utilisateur** = user interface; **interface (pour) téléimprimeur** = teleprinter interface; **interface pour** *ou* **de terminal** = terminal interface; **le contrôleur de réseau possède 16 interfaces pour terminaux** = the network controller has 16 terminal interfaces; **interface universelle** = standard interface; **interface universelle GPIA** = general purpose interface adapter (GPIA); **interface utilisateur** = front-end; **ce programme est très facile à utiliser du fait de la simplicité de son interface utilisateur** = the program is very easy to use thanks to the uncomplicated front-end; **interface utilisateur-machine** = human-computer *ou* human-machine interface (HMI); **carte (d')interface** = interface card; **processeur d'interface** = interface processor; **relier avec une interface** = to interface with; **routines d'interface** = interface routines

◊ **interfacé, -ée** *adj* interfaced; **équipement interfacé HDLC** = high-level data link control station

◊ **interfacer** *vtr* to interface (with) *ou* to link

> ce produit est une interface qui, placée entre le lecteur de disquettes et son contrôleur, interdit physiquement l'écriture sur la disquette mais en autorise la lecture
> *Le Monde informatique*

interférence *nf* interference; **interférence constructive** = constructive interference; **interférence de courte durée** = impulsive noise; **interférence de fichiers** = cross-linked files; **interférence destructive** = destructive interference; **interférence électromagnétique** = electromagnetic interference (EMI); **interférence induite** = induced interference; *(par un autre canal de transmission)* crosstalk *ou* crossfire; **interférence interligne** = transverse mode noise; **interférence lumineuse** = flare; **réduction du bruit d'interférence interstation** = interstation muting; **interférence entre porteuses** = intercarrier noise; **on note des interférences de porteuses sur une télévision lorsque la porteuse son et la porteuse image se rencontrent** = television intercarrier noise is noticed when the picture and the sound signal carriers clash; **interférences radio** = garbage; **empreinte d'interférence** = interference pattern; **insensibilité** *ou* **tolérance aux interférences** = interference immunity

◊ **interférer** *vi* to interfere with something

interfoliage *nm* interleaving

◊ **interfolié, -ée** *adj* interleaved

intérieur, -e *adj* internal *ou* inner; **boucle intérieure** = inner loop; *(d'un livre)* **marge intérieure** = gutter

interlignage *nm* *(imprimerie)* leading; *(imprimante d'ordinateur)* line feed (LF)

◊ **interligne 1** *nf (lame de métal)* lead **2** *nm* **(a)** *(espace entre les lignes d'imprimerie)* leading *ou* line spacing *ou* interlinear spacing; **est-il possible**

d'ajouter un interligne supplémentaire entre les paragraphes? = can we insert an extra line of spacing between the paragraphs?; **texte sans interligne** = solid text **(b)** *(entre deux lignes de communication)* **interférence interligne** = transverse mode noise

interlude *nm* interlude

intermédiaire *adj* intermediate; **bande intermédiaire** = guard band; **code intermédiaire** = intermediate code; **fichier intermédiaire** = intermediate file; **fréquence intermédiaire** = intermediate frequency (if *ou* IF); **mémoire intermédiaire** = intermediate storage *ou* secondary storage; **mémoire à accès intermédiaire** = intermediate access memory (IAM); **support intermédiaire** = intermediate materials; **ces diapositives et photos sont les supports intermédiaires qui doivent être recopiés sur le vidéodisque** = those slides and photographs are the intermediate materials to be mastered onto the video disk; **utilisateur intermédiaire** = mid-user **(b)** **par l'intermédiaire de** = via; **les données ont été transmises à l'ordinateur par l'intermédiaire du téléphone** = the computer received data via the telephone line; **le téléchargement des données dans l'unité centrale peut se faire par l'intermédiaire d'un modem** = you can download the data to the CPU via a modem

intermittent, -e *adj* intermittent; **bruit intermittent** = impulsive noise; **contact intermittent** = dry contact; **erreur intermittente** = intermittent error

intermodulation *nf* cross modulation

international, -e *adj* **(a)** international; **indicatif (téléphonique) international** = international dialling code; **système téléphonique automatique international** = international direct dialling (IDD) **(b)** *(utilisé surtout dans les pays anglo-saxons)* **clavier international** = QWERTY keyboard

interne *adj* **(a)** internal; **arithmétique interne** = internal arithmetic; **commande interne** = internal command; **la commande interne DIR est fréquemment employée lorsqu'on travaille avec MS-DOS** = in MS-DOS, the internal command DIR is used frequently; **code de caractères interne** = internal character code; **disque dur interne** = internal hard disk; **étiquette interne** = inlay card; **format interne** = internal format; **langage interne** = internal language; **mémoire interne** = internal memory *ou* store; **tri en mémoire interne** = internal sort; **mémoire interne à accès immédiat** = immediate access store (IAS) **(b)** in-house; **téléphone interne** = house phone *ou* house telephone *ou* internal telephone

internet *nm* internet; **adresse internet** = internet protocol address (IP Address); **protocole internet (assurant l'interconnexion de réseau)** = internet protocol (IP) (TCP/IP standard)

◊ **Internet** *(réseau public étendu)* Internet (international wide area network)

Interphone ™ *nm* intercom

interpolation *nf* interpolation; **interpolation de signaux sur bande vocale** = time assigned speech interpolation (TASI)

interprétatif, -ive *adj* interpretative; **code interprétatif** = interpretative code; **programme interprétatif** = interpretative program

◊ **interprétation** *nf* interpretation; **programme d'interprétation** = translator (program)

◊ **interprété, -ée** *adj* interpreted; **langage interprété** = interpreted language

◊ **interpréter** *vtr* to interpret

◊ **interpréteur** *nm* (language) interpreter

interrogation *nf* enquiry (ENQ) *ou* inquiry *ou* query *ou* interrogation; *(de plusieurs postes de travail)* polling; **interrogation de fichier** = file interrogation; **(fonction) interrogation-réponse** = inquiry/response (function); **caractère d'interrogation** = inquiry character (ENQ); **langage d'interrogation** = query language; **ordre d'interrogation (des terminaux)** = polling list; **point d'interrogation (?)** = question mark; **poste d'interrogation** = inquiry station; **utilitaire d'interrogation** = query facility

interroger *vtr* to query; *(une série de postes de travail)* to poll; **interroger quelqu'un** = to question someone

interrompre *vtr* to halt *ou* to interrupt; **taper CTRL S pour interrompre le programme** = hitting CTRL S will halt the program; **on a interrompu le programme en appuyant sur la touche rouge** = the program was aborted by pressing the red button

interrupteur *nm (de courant)* circuit breaker *ou* switch; **interrupteur de reprise** = hardware reset; **interrupteur temporaire** = momentary switch

◊ **interruption** *nf* **(a)** break *ou* interrupt; **interruption anormale** = abnormal end *ou* abend *ou* abnormal termination; **programme de récupération de fichier après une interruption anormale** = abend recovery program; **en cas de panne, la perte de données sera minimale grâce au nouveau programme de récupération des fichiers après interruption anormale** = if a fault occurs, data loss will be minimized due to the improved abend recovery program; **interruption d'appel** = polled interrupt; **interruption d'entrée/sortie** = input/output interrupt; **interruption sur (une) erreur** *ou* **sur (un) incident** = error interrupt; **interruption d'intervention** = attention interruption; **interruption qui peut être masquée** *ou* **invalidée** = maskable interrupt; **interruption obligatoire** *ou* **qui ne peut être invalidée** *ou* **qui ne peut être masquée** = non-maskable interrupt (NMI); **interruption (de contrôle) de parité** = parity interrupt; **interruption prioritaire** = priority interrupt; **interruption provenant d'une machine** = hardware interrupt; *(instruction)* **interruption du processeur** *ou* **du traitement** = processor interrupt; **interruption en série** *ou* **en chaîne** = daisy chain interrupt; **interruption transparente** *ou* **contrôlée** = transparent interrupt; **interruption vectorisée** = vectored interrupt; **commande d'interruption (de programme)** = interrupt command; **contrôle et**

exécution d'interruption = interrupt servicing; **brève interruption de transmission de données (causée par un défaut du support magnétique)** = data check; **commande d'invalidation d'interruption** = disable interrupt; **demande d'interruption** = interrupt request; **gestionnaire d'interruptions** = interrupt handler (IH); **invalider** *ou* **interdire une interruption** = to interrupt disable; **ligne d'interruption** = interrupt line; *(logiciel gestionnaire d'interruptions)* **manipulateur d'interruption** = trap handler; **masque d'interruption** = interrupt mask; **niveau d'interruption** = interrupt level; **constitution de pile d'interruptions** = interrupt stacking; **point d'interruption** = breakpoint; **priorité d'interruption** = interrupt priority; **table de priorité des interruptions** = priority interrupt table; **signal d'interruption** = interrupt signal; **touche (d') interruption** = Break key; **j'ai résolu le problème en pressant les touches CTRL et Interruption** = I stopped the problem by pressing Ctrl-Break; **valider une interruption** = to interrupt enable **(b)** *(d'un appareil)* **interruption de service** = outage; **sans interruption** = continuously; **l'imprimante se mettait à chauffer après cinq heures de marche sans interruption** = the printer overheated after working continuously for five hours

intersection *nf* *(logique)* intersection *ou* conjunction; *(fonction logique)* **fonction d'intersection** = coincidence function

interstation *adj* between stations; **réduction du bruit d'interférence interstation** = interstation muting

interurbain, -e *adj* **appel interurbain** = long-distance call *GB* trunk call; **central téléphonique pour réseau interurbain** = *GB* trunk exchange; **communication interurbaine** = long-distance call *GB* trunk call

intervalle *nm* gap *ou* interval; **il y a eu un intervalle entre le moment où on a appuyé sur la touche et la mise en marche de l'imprimante** = there was an interval between pressing the key and the starting of the printout; **intervalle d'appels** = polling interval; **intervalle blanc entre deux enregistrements** = record gap; *(de signal de télévision)* **intervalle de garde** = breezeway; **intervalle de marquage** = marking interval; **l'horloge émet un signal à intervalles réguliers** = the clock signal is periodic

intervenir *vi* to take action

◊ **intervention** *nf* intervention; attention; **ce programme exige l'intervention constante du processeur** = this routine requires the attention of the processor every minute; **interruption d'intervention** = attention interruption; **message d'intervention** = action message; **touche d'intervention** = attention key

interversion *nf* transposition; **une série d'interversions a donné de faux résultats** = a series of transposition errors caused faulty results

intrinsèque *adj* **(a)** intrinsic; **le matériau de base**

utilisé dans la fabrication des circuits intégrés est un semi-conducteur intrinsèque auquel on ajoute un dopant = the base material for ICs is an intrinsic semiconductor which is then doped **(b)** default; **réponse intrinsèque** = default response; **option intrinsèque** = default option; **valeur intrinsèque** = default value

introduction *nf* **(a)** entry; **introduction de données** = data entry *ou* input; **routine d'introduction de données** = input routine **(b)** *(d'une carte)* **bord d'introduction** = leading edge

◊ **introduire** *vtr* **(a)** *(dans un ordinateur)* to enter *ou* to input; *(par lecture)* to read in; **introduire des données** = to input *ou* to enter data; **les données ont été introduites par l'intermédiaire d'un modem** = the data was input via a modem; **les données sont introduites dans l'ordinateur** = data is fed into the computer; **introduire des données dans la pile (de mémoire)** = to put data onto a stack **(b)** *(dispositif, etc.)* to insert *ou* to introduce *ou* to load; **introduire ensuite le bac inférieur** = then load lower bin; **introduire d'abord la disquette système dans le lecteur gauche** = first insert the system disk in the left slot **(c)** *(un système, etc.)* to introduce; **introduire quelque chose graduellement** = to phase something in

◊ **s'introduire** *vpr* to get into; **s'introduire sans autorisation dans un système** = to hack into a system

intrus *nm* intruder

◊ **intrusion** *nf* intrusion

inutilisé, -ée *adj* (i) unused; (ii) empty; **connecteur** *ou* **créneau inutilisé** = empty slot

invalidation *nf* **commande d'invalidation d'interruption** = disable interrupt; **signal d'invalidation de transmission** = inhibiting input

◊ **invalide** *adj* invalid *ou* illegal; **caractère invalide** = illegal character; **de façon invalide** = illegally; **instruction invalide** = illegal instruction; **d'après le message, l'instruction était invalide** = the message was that the instruction was invalid; **opération invalide** = illegal operation

◊ **invalidé, -ée** *adj* **(a)** *(dispositif)* disarmed *ou* disabled; **configuration invalidée** = configured off *ou* configured out **(b) interruption invalidée** = masked interrupt

◊ **invalider** *vtr* **(a)** *(un dispositif)* to disable *ou* to disarm **(b)** to mask *ou* to inhibit; **invalider (une option ou un évènement) lorsque le temps imparti est écoulé** = to time out; **(instruction d')invalider une interruption** = interrupt disable; **interruption qui peut être invalidée** = maskable interrupt; **interruption qui ne peut être invalidée** = non-maskable interrupt (NMI); **(instruction d')invalider la justification** = justify inhibit

inverse *adj* reverse; **vidéo inverse** = inverse video *ou* reverse video

◊ **inversé, -ée** *adj* reverse; **fichier inversé** = inverted file; **impression inversée** *ou* **caractère inversé** = cameo; **index inversé** = reverse index; **liste inversée** = pushdown list; **notation polonaise**

inversée = reverse Polish notation (RPN) *ou* postfix notation *ou* suffix notation; **la notation conventionnelle s'écrit: (x-y) + z, la notation polonaise inversée s'écrit: xy - z +** = normal notation: (x-y) + z, but using postfix notation: xy - z +; **pile inversée (utilisée suivant la méthode LIFO)** = push-down list *ou* stack; **polarité inversée** = reverse polarity; **vidéo inversée** = inverse *ou* reverse video

◊ **inverser** *vtr* to reverse *ou* to invert; *(une valeur)* to negate

◊ **inverseur** *nm* inverter; **inverseur de courant** = inverter (AC/DC); **circuit inverseur** = NOT gate

◊ **inversion** *nf* inversion *ou* transposition; *(d'une valeur)* negation; **il y a inversion du chiffre binaire dans le complément à un** = the inversion of a binary digit takes place in one's complement; *(d'une image)* **inversion latérale** = lateral reversal; **inversion vidéo** = inverse video *ou* reverse video; *(de la direction du flux de données)* **délai d'inversion** = turnaround time (TAT); *(pour terminaison de transmission)* **interruption d'inversion** = reverse interrupt

investiguer *vtr* **investiguer un système (sans autorisation)** = to hack

invitation *nf* **(a)** **(message d')invitation à taper une instruction** = prompt *ou* cue **(b)** **(signal d')invitation à transmettre** = go ahead *ou* invitation to send (ITS)

invite *nf* **invite (de commande)** = command prompt; **MS-DOS affiche normalement l'invite (de commande) C:\> pour indiquer qu'il est prêt à traiter les commandes entrées par l'utilisateur** = MS-DOS normally displays the command prompt C:\> to indicate that it is ready to process instructions typed in by a user

IP = INTERNET PROTOCOL **paquet IP** = IP Datagram

ion *nm* ion

◊ **ionosphère** *nf* ionosphere

IRM = IMAGERIE PAR RESONNANCE MAGNETIQUE

irradier *vtr* to radiate

irrécupérable *adj* **erreur irrécupérable** = unrecoverable error

irrégulier, -ière *adj* irregular; *(d'un satellite)* **période irrégulière** = anomalistic period

irréparable *adj* **l'ordinateur souffre d'une panne irréparable** = the computer has a terminal fault

irréversible *adj* irreversible; **processus irréversible** = irreversible process; **vidage irréversible** = disaster dump

ISA *(architecture de bus d'extension de 16 bits)* Industry Standard Architecture (ISA)

ISBN = INTERNATIONAL STANDARD BOOK NUMBER

ISO = INTERCONNEXION DE SYSTEMES OUVERTS; *voir aussi* INTERCONNEXION

ISO = INTERNATIONAL STANDARDS ORGANIZATION; *voir aussi* ORGANISME

ISO/OSI = INTERNATIONAL STANDARDS ORGANIZATION/OPEN SYSTEM INTERCONNECTION **modèle ISO/OSI** = ISO/OSI model; **système ISO/OSI** = ISO/OSI system

isolant *nm* insulator *ou* insulation material; **le plastique est un bon isolant** = plastic is a good insulator

◊ **isolant, -e** *adj* **matériau isolant** = insulator *ou* insulation material

◊ **isolateur** *nm* **(a)** insulator **(b)** isolator

◊ **isolation** *nf* **(a)** insulation **(b)** isolation; **isolation de canaux** = channel isolation; **boîtier d'isolation** = barrier box

◊ **isolement** *nm* **(a)** insulation **(b)** isolation; **transformateur d'isolement** = isolation transformer

◊ **isoler** *vtr* **(a)** to insulate **(b)** to isolate

isotrope *adj* isotropic; **émetteur** *ou* **antenne isotrope** = isotropic radiator

ISSN = INTERNATIONAL STANDARD SERIAL NUMBER

italique 1 *nm* italic; **tapez CTRL I pour imprimer les italiques** = hit CTRL I to print the text in italics; **les notes de bas de page sont toutes en italique** = all the footnotes are printed in italics; **le titre est en italique souligné** = the headline is printed in italic and underlined; **ils ont changé de police de caractères et imprimé l'en-tête en italique** = they switched to italic type for the heading **2** *adj* italic; **lettres italiques** = italics

item *nm* item; **dimension d'un item** = item size

itératif, -ive *adj* **fonctionnement itératif automatique** = automatic sequencing; **processus itératif** = iterative process; **programme itératif** = loop program *ou* looping program; **routine itérative** = iterate *ou* iterative routine

◊ **itération** *nf* **boucle d'itération** = iteration *ou* loop program *ou* looping program

Jj

jack *nm (fiche)* jack

jambage *nm (d'un caractère)* descender *ou* down stroke

jaquette *nf* jacket; **on trouve le nom de l'auteur sur la jaquette du livre** = the book jacket has the author's name on it

jauge *nf* gauge

◊ **jauger** *vtr* to gauge

jet *nm* jet; **imprimante à jet d'encre** = ink-jet printer; **les techniques du jet d'encre couleur et du transfert thermique sont concurrentielles** = colour ink-jet technology and thermal transfer technology compete with each other

jeton *nm* token; **jeton de contrôle (de réseau)** = control token; **réseau à jeton (circulant)** = token ring network; **réseau en bus à jeton** = token bus network; **passage du jeton** = token passing; **prélever le jeton** = to capture the token

jeu *nm* **(a)** set; **jeu de caractères** = character set; **jeu de caractères nuls** = empty *ou* null set; **jeu de cartes perforées** = (card) deck; *(qui contient un programme)* **jeu (de cartes) objet** = object deck; **jeu d'instructions** = instruction repertoire *ou* instruction set; **jeu d'instructions réduit** = reduced instruction set; **contrôle avec un jeu d'essai** = dry run **(b)** game; **jeu d'arcade** = arcade game; **jeu électronique** *ou* **jeu (sur) ordinateur** = computer game; **jeu (électronique) d'aventure** = adventure game; **jeu vidéo** = video game; **cartouche de jeu** = game cartridge; **console de jeu** = game console; **manette de jeu** = game paddle; joystick; **port de jeu** *ou* **port pour manette de jeu** = game port; joystick port **(c)** **jeu vertical d'une touche** = key travel

> une station de travail portable achitecturée autour d'un processeur à jeu d'instructions réduit Mips
> *Le Monde informatique*

> deux ans auparavant, le marché des jeux vidéo à domicile était encore l'un des plus florissants de l'industrie du jouet
> *L'Express*

JK *(type de commutateur à bascule)* JK-flip-flop

joindre *vtr* **(a)** *(réunir)* to join *ou* to couple *ou* to combine *ou* to link **(b)** *(attacher)* to attach *ou* to append **(c)** *(contacter)* to contact; **chercher à joindre quelqu'un par système d'appel (de personne)** *ou* **par signaleur d'appel** *ou* **par bip** = to call someone on a bleeper *ou* to page someone

joker *nm* wild card; **on peut utiliser un joker pour chercher tous les fichiers commençant par DIC** = a wild card can be used to find all files names beginning with DIC; **caractère joker** = wild card character *ou* question mark; **un caractère joker peut être utilisé pour trouver tous les noms de fichiers commençant par DIC** = a wild card can be used to find all file names beginning with DIC; **pour trouver toute les lettres, utilisez la commande avec joker DIR LETTER?.DOC qui produira la liste LETTER1.DOC, LETTER2.DOC, LETTER3.DOC** = to find all the letters, use the command DIR LETTER?.DOC which will list LETTER1.DOC, LETTER2.DOC and LETTER3.DOC

> COMMENTAIRE: dans les systèmes d'exploitation pour PC, comme DOS ou UNIX, le caractère joker ? remplace à cet emplacement n'importe quel caractère; d'autre part, le caractère * remplace un nombre indéfini de caractères

jonction *nf* junction; *(dans un réseau)* spur; **jonction pn** = pn-junction; **jonction pn à diffusion** = diffused pn-junction; **jonction pn à seuil** = step pn-junction; **boîte de jonction** = junction box; **circuit** *ou* **faisceau de jonction** = trunk; **ligne de jonction d'abonné (au centre téléphonique)** = exchange line; **ligne de jonction privée** = tie line *ou* tie trunk; **transistor à jonction bipolaire** = bipolar junction transistor (BJT); **transistor à jonction pnp** *ou* **npn** = bipolar (junction) transistor (BJT) *ou* pnp transistor

jouer *vtr (un enregistrement)* to play (back); **après avoir enregistré la musique, appuyez sur ce bouton-ci pour faire jouer la bande et vous assurer de la bonne qualité du son (enregistré)** = after you have recorded the music, press this button to play back the tape and hear what it sounds like; **faire jouer une bande nouvellement enregistrée** = to replay a new recording

jour *nm* **(a)** day; **à jour** = up to date; **garder** *ou* **maintenir (un fichier) à jour** = to keep (a file) up to date; **nous passons beaucoup de temps à maintenir nos fichiers à jour** = we spend a lot of time keeping our files up to date; **mettre à jour** = *(un fichier)* to update *ou* to bring up to date; *(mémoire)* to refresh; **mise à jour** = *(file)* update *ou* upkeep *ou* maintenance; **la mise à jour des fichiers doit se faire tous les six mois** = the upkeep of the files means reviewing them every six months; **enregistrement** *ou* **fichier de mise à jour** = addition record *ou* change file *ou* movement file *ou* update; **terminal de mise à jour rapide** = bulk update terminal **(b)** *(faire apparaître)* **mettre à jour** = to reveal **(c)** **mot du jour** = buzzword

journal *nm* **(a)** diary *ou* journal; **les enregistrements modifiés ont été ajoutés au fichier maître et inscrits au journal des modifications** = the modified records were added to the master file and noted in the journal; **journal de bord** = log; **journal de bord d'un système** = system log; **enregistrer dans un journal (de bord)** = to log; **entrée dans un journal de bord** = log; **tenir un journal** = to log **(b)** newspaper; **coupure de journal** = press cutting; **papier journal** = mechanical paper *ou* newsprint; **les journaux** = the press; **aucun journal n'a mentionné le nouveau produit** = there was no mention of the new product in the press; **les grands journaux** *ou* **les journaux à gros tirage** = the national press; **les journaux régionaux** = regional newspaper *ou* the local press

◊ **journalisme** *nm* journalism; **journalisme électronique** = electronic news gathering (ENG)

◊ **journaliste** *nm&f* journalist; (newspaper) correspondent

joystick *nm (manette de jeu)* joystick

juger *vi* to calculate *ou* to evaluate *ou* to measure; **pour juger de la performance du système** = to measure the system's performance *ou* as a measure of the system's performance

jumelé, -ée *adj* **ordinateurs jumelés** = duplex computer

justification *nf (imprimerie)* justification; **justification à droite** = right justification; **justification à gauche** = left justification; **césure et justification** = hyphenation and justification *ou* H & J; *(fonction)* hyphenate and justify; **un programme de césure et justification établi aux Etats-Unis ne peut être utilisé pour un texte en anglais britannique** = an American hyphenation and justification program will not work with British English spellings; **(instruction d')invalider la justification** = justify inhibit

◊ **justifié, -ée** *adj (texte)* justified; **justifié à droite** = right justified; **justifié à gauche** = left justified; **texte non justifié** = ragged text; **non justifié à droite** = ragged right; **non justifié à gauche** = ragged left

◊ **justifier** *vtr* **(a)** *(un texte)* to justify *ou* to align (a text); **justifier à droite** = to right justify *ou* to flush right; *(instruction)* right justify *ou* flush right; **justifier à gauche** = to left justify *ou* to flush left; *(instruction)* left justify *ou* flush left **(b)** *(registre)* to justify

juxtaposition *nf* juxtaposition

Kk

k = KILO

K = KILO-

Karnaugh *npr* **table de Karnaugh** = Karnaugh map; **le prototype a fait l'objet d'un contrôle de fiabilité statistique sur la base des tables de Karnaugh** = the prototype was checked for hazards with a Karnaugh map

KB = KILOBYTE

Kb (a) = KILOBYTE **(b)** KILOBIT

Kbit = KILOBIT

Kbyte = KILOBYTE

Kermit *(protocole de communication)* Kermit (file transfer protocol)

kerning *nm (crénage d'image ou de photo)* kerning

kg = KILOGRAMME

kHz = KILOHERTZ

kilo 1 *nm (abréviation)* = KILOGRAMME **2** *(abréviation)* = 1000 (k) **3** *(quantité d'information)* = 1024 (K)

◊ **kilobaud** *nm* kilobaud

◊ **kilobit (Kbit)** *nm* kilobit (Kbit *ou* Kb)

◊ **kilobyte (KB** *ou* **Kb)** *voir* KILO-OCTET

◊ **kilogramme (kg)** *nm* kilogram; **mètre kilogramme seconde (ampère)** *ou* **mks(A)** = metre kilogram second (Ampere) *ou* MKS(A)

◊ **kilohertz (kHz)** *nm* kilohertz (kHz)

◊ **kilométrique** *adj* **ondes kilométriques** = infra-low frequency (ILF)

◊ **kilomot** *nm* kiloword (KW)

◊ **kilo-octet (Ko)** *nm* kilobyte *ou* Kbyte *ou* KB *ou* Kb

◊ **kilo-ohm** *nm* kilo-ohm

◊ **kilowatt (kW)** *nm* kilowatt (kW)

Kimball *npr* **étiquette Kimball** ™ = Kimball tag

kiosque *nm* **kiosque (à livres)** = bookstall

KIPS = KILO INSTRUCTIONS PER SECOND; *voir* MILLIER

kit *nm* kit *ou* pack; **kit d'extension de micro-ordinateur** = microcomputer development kit; **kit de nettoyage pour écran** = screen cleaning kit

Ko = KILO-OCTET kilobyte *ou* Kbyte (KB *ou* Kb); **le lecteur de disquettes a une capacité de 100Ko** = the disk drive has a 100Kb capacity; **le premier ordinateur individuel de la série ne peut accéder à plus de 640Ko de RAM** = the original PC cannot access more than 640Kbytes of RAM

kva = KILOVOLT-AMPERE OUTPUT **mesure du travail en kva** = kiloVolt-Ampere output rating (KVA)

kW = KILOWATT

LI

label *nm* **(a)** *(étiquette)* label; *(sur support magnétique)* **label d'identification interne** = interior *ou* internal label; **label de qualité** = quality label **(b)** *(d'un programme)* label *ou* quasi-instruction; **les programmes en langage BASIC contiennent plusieurs labels dont la numérotation des lignes** = BASIC uses many program labels such as line numbers; **label d'un champ** = field label; **champ label** = label field; **enregistrement de labels** = label record

laboratoire *nm* laboratory; **le travail de recherche et développement sur la nouvelle puce se fait dans les laboratoires de l'université** = the new chip is being developed in the university laboratories; **technicien de laboratoire** = laboratory technician

lacet *nm* *(mouvement de satellite)* yaw

lampe *nf* **(a)** **lampe de bureau** = desk light **(b)** **lampe témoin** = warning light; *(voyant lumineux)* light emitting diode **(c)** *(dans un ordinateur)* valve

lancement *nm* **(a)** *(d'un programme)* start; **lancement automatique** = auto-start; **lancement de tâches à distance** = remote job entry (RJE); **adresse de lancement** = initial address; **chargeur de programme de lancement** = initial program loader (IPL); **instructions de lancement** = initial instructions **(b)** *(d'un système)* boot-up *ou* booting; *(automatique)* auto-boot; **bloc** *ou* **enregistrement de lancement** = boot block *ou* record; **disque** *ou* **disquette de lancement** = startup disk *ou* boot disk; **après avoir mis l'ordinateur en route, insérez la disquette de lancement** = after you switch on the computer, insert the boot disk; **mémoire de lancement** = bootstrap memory; **partition de lancement** = boot partition; **programme de lancement** = bootstrap **(c)** launch; **fusée de lancement** = launch vehicle **(d)** *(un nouveau produit)* launch; **le lancement du nouvel ordinateur individuel se fera avec six mois de retard** = the launch of the new PC has been put back six months; **le lancement du réseau aura lieu en septembre** = the launch date for the network will be September

◊ **lancer** *vtr* **(a)** *(un programme)* to launch *ou* to start; **on lance le traitement de texte avec un double clic sur cette icône** = you launch the word-processor by double-clicking on this icon **(b)** *(un système)* to boot (up) **(c)** *(une fusée)* to launch **(d)** *(un nouveau produit)* to launch *ou* to release; **on a lancé le nouvel ordinateur personnel au Salon de l'Informatique** = the new PC was launched at the Personal Computer Show

◊ **lanceur** *nm* **lanceur de programme de chargement** = initial program header

langage *nm* **(a)** language; **langage algébrique** *ou*

documentaire = algebraic language; **langage algorithmique** *ou* **ALGOL** = algorithmic language *ou* ALGOL; **langage (de programmation) APL** = A programming language (APL); **langage (de haut niveau) BASIC** = Beginner's All-Purpose Symbolic Instruction Code (BASIC); **langage (de haut niveau) BCPL** = BCPL (language); **(langage) C** = C (language); **langage (de programmation) COBOL** = common business-orientated language (COBOL); **langage (de programmation structurée) COMAL** = common algorithmic language (COMAL); **langage (d'application temps réel) CORAL** = common real-time applications language (CORAL); **système adapté aux langages EAO** *ou* **FAO** = authoring system; **langage FORTH** = FORTH (language); **langage FORTRAN** = formula translator (FORTRAN); **langage LISP** = list processing (LISP); **langage LOGO** = LOGO; **on demande aux programmeurs une connaissance des langages de haut niveau, plus spécialement PASCAL** = programmers should have a knowledge of high-level languages, particularly PASCAL; **langage (de traitement et de manipulation de chaînes) SNOBOL** = string-orientated symbolic language (SNOBOL) **(b)** **langage adaptable** *ou* **extensible** = extensible language; **langage d'application** = job-orientated language *ou* problem orientated language (POL); **langage d'application temps réel** = common real-time applications language (CORAL); **langage d'assemblage** = assembly language *ou* assembler language *ou* base language; **langage d'assemblage pour microprogramme** = microprogram assembly language; **langage de base de données** = database language; **langage de commande** *ou* **d'instruction** = command language *ou* control language; **langage de commande de tâche** = job control language (JCL); **langage commun** *ou* **banal** *ou* **partagé** = common language; **langage de compilation** = compiler language; **langage de conception de programme** = program design language (PDL); **langage de contrôle** *ou* **de pilotage (de périphériques)** = command control language; **langage de description de données** = data description language (DDL); **plusieurs des avantages du langage de description de données vient du fait qu'il s'agit d'un langage de deuxième génération** = many of DDL's advantages come from the fact that it is a second generation language; **langage de description de page** = page description language (PDL); **langage évolué** = high-level language (HLL); **langage peu évolué** = low-level language (LLL); **langage graphique** = graphic language; **avec ce langage graphique, on peut tracer des lignes, cercles et graphes avec une seule commande** = this graphic language can plot lines, circles and graphs with a single command; *voir aussi* HP, HPGL **langage informatique** = computer language; **langage d'indexation** = indexing language; **langage d'instruction** =

command language *ou* control language; **langage interne** *ou* **langage machine** = internal language; **langage interprété** = interpreted language; **langage d'interrogation** = query language (QL); **langage machine** = machine code *ou* machine language; *(commandes ou données)* **en langage machine** = machine-readable; **codes en langage machine** = machine-readable codes; **compiler en langage machine** = machine language compile; **instruction en langage machine** = machine (code) instruction; **programmation en langage machine** = machine language programming; **langage de manipulation de données** = data manipulation language (DML); **langage multidimensionnel** *ou* **multiniveau** = multidimensional language; **langage naturel** = natural language; **le système expert peut être programmé en langage naturel** = the expert system can be programmed in a natural language; **langage de bas niveau** *ou* **peu évolué** = low-level language (LLL); **langage de haut niveau** *ou* **évolué** = high-level language (HLL); **langage objet** = object language *ou* target language; **pour ce qui est de ce programme en PASCAL, le langage machine constitue le langage objet** = the target language for this PASCAL program is machine code; **langage d'origine** *ou* **langage source** = source language; **langage partagé** = common language; **langage en pelure d'oignon** = onion skin language; **langage de pilotage (de périphériques)** = command control language; **langage de procédure** *ou* **langage adapté à la procédure** = procedure-orientated language *ou* procedural language; **langage de programmation** = programming language; **langage de programmation EAO** = authoring language; **langage de programmation évoluée** *ou* **de haut niveau** = high-level (programming) language (HLL); **langages de quatrième génération** = fourth generation languages; **langage de requête** *ou* **d'interrogation** = query language (QL); structured query language (SQL); **langage de résolution de problème** *ou* **langage adapté au problème** = problem-orientated language (POL); **langage source** = source language; *(langage de requête)* **langage SQL** = structured query language (SQL); **langage standard** *ou* **universel** = machine-independent language *ou* computer independent language; **langage symbolique** = symbolic language; **format de langage symbolique** = symbolic-coding format; **langage de synthèse** = synthetic language; **processeur de langage** = language processor

langue *nf* language; **il parle plusieurs langues européennes** = he speaks several European languages; *(en traduction)* **langue d'arrivée** = target language; **langue de départ** = source language; **langue étrangère** = foreign language

LAN Manager ™ *(système d'exploitation de réseau, de Microsoft)* LAN Manager ™ (MicroSoft network operating system)

LAN Server ™ *(système d'exploitation IBM)* LAN Server ™ (IBM network operating system)

LAP *(protocole de liens de réseau)* Link Access Protocol (LAP); *(protocole de liens entre ordinateur et modem)* **routine d'installation LAP-B** = LAP-B; *(protocole pour modems avec*

correction d'erreurs) **protocole LAP-M** = Link Access Protocol for Modems (LAP-M) (a variation of LAP-B protocol)

laptop *nm (ordinateur portable)* laptop (computer) *ou* lapheld (computer)

large *adj* broad *ou* wide; **large bande** = broadband *ou* wideband; **modulation de fréquence à large bande** = wideband frequency modulation (WBFM); **radio à large bande** = broadband radio

◊ **largeur** *nf* **(a)** width; **la largeur par défaut de cet écran est de 80** = screen width has a default value of 80; **largeur de page (en caractères)** = page width **(b)** **largeur de bande (de fréquences)** = bandwidth; **largeur de bande agréée** *ou* **autorisée** = aggregate bandwidth; **largeur de bande effective** = effective bandwidth; **largeur de bande vidéo** = video bandwidth; **concentrateur** *ou* **réducteur de largeur de bande vidéo** = video compressor; **la largeur de bande d'un téléphone est de 3100Hz** = telephone bandwidth is 3100Hz; **largeur d'un faisceau** *ou* **d'un lobe** = beam width; **modulation d'impulsions en largeur (MIL)** = pulse width modulation (PWM)

laser *nm* Light Amplification by Stimulated Emission of Radiation (Laser); **laser à composant solide** = solid-state laser; **laser d'injection (dans une fibre optique)** = injection laser; **laser de portance** = injection laser; **laser transistorisé** = semiconductor laser; **communication par rayon laser** = laser beam communications; **disque laser** = compact disc (CD) *ou* laser disc; **enregistrement par rayon laser** = laser beam recording; **imprimante (à) laser** = laser printer; **mémoire laser sur couche haute définition** = emulsion laser storage; **trou laser** *ou* **brûlage laser** = ablation

COMMENTAIRE: un trou (qui représente un bit digital) est brûlé au laser dans la couche superficielle du support de stockage.

grâce à un laser à semi-conducteur émettant une lumière bleue (au lieu de l'infrarouge proche), le diamètre du faisceau est réduit de moitié (0,4 micron), ce qui double la densité d'information du disque
Science et Vie Micro

LaserJet ™ *(imprimante laser de Hewlett Packard)* Hewlett Packard LaserJet *ou* HP LaserJet

LaserWriter ™ *(imprimante laser Apple)* (Apple) LaserWriter ™

latence *nf* wait time; **état de latence** = wait condition *ou* state; **période** *ou* **temps de latence** = latency

◊ **latent, -e** *adj* latent; **image latente** = latent image

latéral, -e *adj* lateral *ou* side; **bande latérale** = sideband; **bande latérale inférieure** = lower sideband; **bande latérale résiduelle** = vestigial sideband; **bande latérale supérieure** = upper sideband; **bande latérale unique** = single sideband; **bande latérale unique sans porteuse** *ou* **à porteuse**

inhibée = single sideband suppressed carrier (SSBSC); **double bande latérale** = double sideband; **double bande latérale sans porteuse** *ou* **à porteuse inhibée** = double sideband suppressed carrier (DSBSC); **inversion latérale** = lateral reversal; **lobe latéral** = side lobe

LB *(local bus)* local bus

LC *(circuit)* LC circuit

LCD *(affichage à cristaux liquides)* Liquid Crystal Display (LCD); **imprimante à transfert LCD** = crystal shutter printer

lecteur, -trice *n* **(a)** *(personne)* reader; *(d'épreuves)* copy reader *ou* proofreader **(b)** *(machine)* **lecteur de badges** = badge reader; **le lecteur de badges garantit que seules les personnes autorisées ont accès à la salle des ordinateurs** = a badge reader makes sure that only authorized personnel can gain access to a computer room; **lecteur de bandes (magnétiques)** = tape drive *ou* tape reader *ou* magnetic tape reader; **lecteur de bandes perforées** = (paper) tape reader; **lecteur de cartes (magnétiques)** = card reader *ou* magnetic card reader; **lecteur de cartes perforées** = punched card reader; **lecteur de cartouche** = cartridge drive; **lecteur (optique) de code barres** = bar-code reader; **lecteur par défaut** *ou* **implicite** = default drive; **ce système d'exploitation permet à l'utilisateur de choisir le lecteur par défaut** = the operating system allows the user to select the default drive; *(platine laser)* **lecteur de disque compact** *ou* **de disque CD** = compact disc player *ou* CD player; **lecteur de (disque) CD-ROM** = CD-ROM player; **lecteur de disquette(s)** = (floppy) disk drive *ou* unit; **lecteur de disquettes (à) double face** = double-sided disk drive; **lecteurs de disquettes de 5,25 pouces et de 3,5 pouces** = 5.25 and 3.5 disk drives; **lecteur de disquettes de huit pouces** = eight-inch drive; **lecteur de disquettes externe** = external disk drive; **lecteur de documents** = document reader; **lecteur de marques magnétiques** = mark sense device *ou* reader; **lecteur multidisque** *ou* **lecteur de disquettes non compatibles** = alien disk reader *ou* multi-disk reader; **si la disquette n'est pas compatible, validez la fonction 'multidisque' qui permet au lecteur de lire une disquette non compatible** = when you have an alien disk select the multi-disk reader option to allow you to turn the disk drive into an alien disk reader; **lecteur optique** = optical scanner; **un lecteur optique utilise un rayon lumineux qui balaye les caractères, les symboles ou les lignes** = an optical reader uses a light beam to scan characters, patterns or lines; **lecteur optique de caractères** = optical character reader (OCR); **police de caractères reconnaissable par lecteur optique** = optical font *ou* OCR font; **lecteur optique de code barres** = optical bar reader *ou* bar code reader *ou* optical wand; **lecteur optique de marques** = optical mark reader (OMR); **lecteur optique de microfilms pour entrée de données sur ordinateur** = film optical scanning device for input into computers (FOSDIC); **lecteur de pistes magnétiques** = magnetic strip reader; **lecteur vidéo** = video player

en introduisant la carte dans le lecteur, les trois chiffres sont lus par un dispositif optique approprié

Electronique pratique

lecture *nf* **(a)** reading *ou* readout; **lecture anticipée** = look ahead; **lecture par balayage** *ou* **par scanner** = scanning; **la lecture par scanner se fait avec une définition de 300 ppp** = the machine scans at up to 300 dpi resolution; *(scanner)* **dispositif de lecture par balayage** = scanning device; **définition de lecture par balayage** = scanning resolution; **la vitesse de lecture par balayage est de 1,3 pouces par seconde** = throughput is 1.3 inches per second scanning speed; **lecture destructive** = destructive read *ou* destructive readout; **lecture hélicoïdale** = helical scan; **lecture optique** = optical reading; **police de caractères reconnaissable par lecture optique** = optical font *ou* OCR font; **lecture optique de données numériques** = digital optical reading (DOR); **lecture régénératrice (de données)** = regenerative reading; **le temps d'accès peut être le temps requis pour la lecture de données (mises) en mémoire** = access time can be the time taken to read from a record; **attribut lecture seule** = read only attribute; **cycle de lecture** = read cycle; **cycle de lecture d'une instruction** = fetch cycle; **cycle de lecture-exécution (d'une instruction)** = fetch-execute cycle *ou* execute cycle; **erreur de lecture** = read error; **instruction de lecture d'une instruction** = fetch instruction; **phase de lecture d'une instruction** = fetch phase; **signal de lecture d'instruction** = fetch signal; **tête de lecture** = playback head *ou* read head *ou* sound head; *(pour bande magnétique)* tape head *ou* tape playback head; *(de disque ou de disquette)* disk head *ou* read head *ou* disk playback head; **tête de lecture fixe** = fixed head; **vitesse de lecture** = read rate **(b)** *(reconnaissance ou identification automatique)* sense

◊ **lecture-écriture** *nf* **(i)** read/write; **(ii)** reading/writing; **lecture-écriture directe** *ou* **sur demande** = demand reading/writing; **bras de lecture-écriture** = access arm *ou* read/write arm; **cycle de lecture-écriture** = read/write cycle *ou* R/W cycle; **mémoire lecture-écriture** = read/write memory; **tête de lecture-écriture** = combined head *ou* read/write head *ou* R/W head; **voie de lecture-écriture** = read/write channel

LED *voir* DIODE

légal, -e *adj* legal

légende *nf* *(texte explicatif d'une illustration)* caption; **les légendes sont imprimées en italique** = the captions are printed in italics

léger, -ère *adj* lightweight; **un ordinateur léger qui tient facilement dans une valise** = a lightweight computer which can easily fit into a suitcase

lent, -e *adj* slow; **périphérique lent** = slow peripheral; **prise de vue à cadence lente** = memomotion

lentille *nf* lens; **lentille concave** = concave lens; **lentille convexe** = convex lens; **lentille déformante**

= distortion optics; **lentille dioptrique** = dioptre lens, *US* diopter lens

lettre *nf* **(a)** *(message)* letter; **lettre type** *ou* **lettre standard** = form letter *ou* standard letter *ou* repetitive letter *ou* template (letter); **composition automatique de lettres standard** = automatic letter writing; **boîte à** *ou* **aux lettres** = letter box *ou* mailbox; **boîte aux lettres électronique** = electronic mailbox; **en-tête de lettre** = letterhead; **faire une copie d'une lettre** = to copy *ou* to duplicate a letter **(b)** *(caractère)* letter; **lettres italiques** = italics; **lettre majuscule** = capital letter; **lettre minuscule** = lower case; **lettre numérale** = numeric character **(c)** *(caractère ou code d'identification)* **lettre d'identification du lecteur** *ou* **de l'unité de disque** = drive letter *ou* designator; logical drive

◊ **lettré, -ée** *adj* literate

◊ **lettrine** *nf* drop cap

lexical, -e *adj* **analyse lexicale** = lexical analysis *ou* parsing

lexicographique *adj* lexicographical; **ordre lexicographique** = lexicographical order

LH = LOAD HIGH

liaison *nf* line *ou* link; *(action)* linking; *(entre plusieurs machines ou dispositifs)* interconnection; **liaison de données** = data link; **liaison (de données) en chaîne** = data chaining; **contrôle de liaison de données** = data link control; **contrôle de liaison de données de haut niveau** = high-level data link control (HDLC); **couche (de) liaison de données** = data link layer; **liaison directe entre canaux** = channel-to-channel connection; **pour une transmission plus rapide, vous pouvez utiliser la liaison directe avec le gros ordinateur** = to transmit faster, you can use the direct link with the mainframe; **liaison à fibres optiques** = fibre optic cable *ou* connection; **liaison optique pour transmission de données** = optical data link; **(câble de) liaison d'un périphérique d'entrée** = input lead; **liaison par satellite** = satellite link; **liaison (de transmission) hertzienne** *ou* **liaison de transmission par hyperfréquence** = microwave communications link; **liaison terre/satellite** = uplink; **cordon de liaison** = cord; **cordon de liaison d'un tableau de distribution** = patchcord; **fil de liaison** = cord; **une arborescence est formée de branches reliées les unes aux autres par des points de liaison ou noeuds** = a tree is made of branches that connect together at nodes

libérer *vtr (de l'espace dans la mémoire)* to free *ou* to deallocate *ou* to blast; *(un bloc de mémoire ou un fichier)* to release; *(une ligne lorsque la transmission est terminée)* to clear

liberté *nf* freedom; **loi Informatique et Libertés** = Data Protection Act; **liberté d'accès à l'information** = freedom of information; **liberté d'expression** = freedom of speech; **liberté de la presse** = freedom of the press

libraire *nm&f* bookseller

◊ **librairie** *nf* bookshop, *US* bookstore

libre *adj* clear *ou* free; **base de données à structure (de champs) libre** = free form database; **indexage libre** = free indexing; **ligne libre** = free line; **logiciel en libre service** = freeware

◊ **librement** *adv* freely

licence *nf* licence; **ici, ce logiciel est fabriqué sous licence** = the software is manufactured in this country under licence

lien *nm (entre programmes)* link; **création de liens** = linkage; **chargeur-éditeur de liens** = linking loader; **éditeur de liens** = linkage editor; **(programme) générateur de liens** = linkage software; **les graphiques et le texte sont réunis sans l'aide d'un générateur de liens** = graphics and text are joined without linkage software; **mise en place de liens (à l'aide d'un éditeur de liens)** = linkage editing; **tests de contrôle de liens** = link trials

lier *vtr (des données)* to catenate *ou* to concatenate (data)

lieu *nm* **(a)** place; **publicité lieu de vente (PLV)** = point-of-sale material **(b)** **avoir lieu** = to occur

LIFO = LAST IN FIRST OUT **liste en mode LIFO** = pushdown list; **pile en mode LIFO** = push-down list *ou* stack; **cet ordinateur gère la pile suivant la méthode LIFO** = this computer stack uses a last in first out data retrieval method; *voir aussi* DERNIER

ligature *nf* ligature

ligne *nf* **(a)** *(d'un texte)* line; **on compte 52 lignes de texte par page** = each page has 52 lines of text; **l'opérateur de saisie a sauté plusieurs lignes du manuscrit** = several lines of manuscript have been missed by the keyboarder; **ligne de base** = base line; **ligne de code (d'un programme)** = code line; **ligne de commande** *ou* **d'instruction d'un programme** = command line *ou* program line; **ligne d'écran** = display line; *(sur l'écran)* **ligne d'état** *ou* **d'information** = status ligne; information line; **ligne multi-instruction** = multi-statement line; *(vitesse d'une imprimante)* **lignes par minute** = lines per minute (lpm); **caractère** *ou* **symbole de fin de ligne** = line ending; **caractère indiquant d'aller à la ligne** = new line character; *(d'une imprimante)* **débit ligne** = lines per minute (lpm); **écran d'une ligne** *ou* **affichage d'une seule ligne** = single line display; **éditeur de ligne** = line editor; **enroulement d'une ligne** = line folding; **enroulement** *ou* **retour à la ligne (automatique)** = horizontal wraparound; **fenêtre d'une ligne** = thin window; **fins de lignes** = line endings; **imprimante ligne à ligne** = line printer; **l'imprimante à marguerite donne un meilleur résultat que l'imprimante ligne à ligne** = the print from the daisy-wheel printer is clearer than that from the line printer; **longueur d'une ligne** *ou* **nombre de caractères par ligne** = line length *ou* line width; **numéro d'une ligne (de programme)** = (program) line number; **retour de chariot-retour à la ligne** = carriage return/line feed (CR/LF); **retour à la ligne automatique** *ou* **saut de ligne automatique (en limite d'écran)** =

wraparound *ou* horizontal wraparound *ou* word wrap **(b)** *(trait)* line; **l'imprimante ne réussit pas très bien à imprimer les lignes trop fines** = the printer has difficulty in reproducing very fine lines; **(papier à) lignes très pâles** = feint; *(d'affichage 3D)* **lignes cachées** = hidden lines; **effacement de ligne cachée** = hidden line removal; **algorithme d'effacement de ligne cachée** = hidden line algorithm; *(de code barres)* **lignes guides** *ou* **lignes de référence** = guide bars; **les lignes guides standard se présentent sous la forme de deux lignes fines un peu plus longues que les lignes codes** = the standard guide bars are two thin lines that are a little longer than the coding lines; *(de dessin ou de couleur)* **ligne de délimitation** *ou* **d'arrêt** = holding line; **ligne de jonction des symboles d'un ordinogramme** = flowline **(c)** *(rang d'une série d'items)* row; *(ligne d'un tableau ou d'une matrice)* row; **ligne pointillée** = dotted line; **ligne de perforations** *ou* **ligne perforée** = perforated line *ou* perforations; **une ligne pointillée sépare les entrées les unes des autres** = each entry is separated by a row of dots **(d)** *(d'image de télévision)* line; **ligne de balayage** = scan line; **délai de retour de ligne** = line blanking interval; **fréquence (de balayage) de ligne** = line frequency; **retour de ligne** = line flyback **(e)** *(de communication)* line; **ligne d'accès** = access line; **ligne banalisée** = common carrier; **ligne de communication** *ou* **de transmission** = communications link; **ligne optique** *ou* **directe** = line of sight; **ligne d'interruption** = interrupt line; **ligne (de communication) rapide** = fast line; **ligne à** *ou* **de retard** = delay line; **mémoire à ligne de retard** = delay line store; **ligne de sélection** *ou* **de validation d'un circuit intégré** = chip select line; **ligne téléphonique** = telephone line; **lignes de transmission de données** = bus data lines; **la ligne de validation de données est reliée à la ligne de sélection de la bascule** = the data strobe line is connected to the latch chip select line; **ligne équilibrée** = balanced line; **analyseur de ligne** = line analyzer; **brancher une ligne sur une source d'alimentation** = to pull up a line; **charge d'une ligne** = line load; **charger une ligne** = to load a line; **contrôle de ligne de communication** *ou* **de transmission** = communications link control; **courant transitoire d'une ligne** = line transient; **élever le potentiel d'une ligne** = to pull up a line; **élever le potentiel de la ligne de réception au niveau logique un, en la connectant sur une source de courant 5 volts** = to pull up the input line to a logic one by connecting it to 5 volts; **équilibreur de ligne** *ou* **d'impédance** = line adapter; **impédance de ligne** = line impedance; *(lorsque la transmission est terminée)* **libérer la ligne** = to clear the line; **maintenance de ligne** = line conditioning; **signal ligne occupée** = line busy tone; **temps d'occupation de la ligne** = holding time; **trafic** *ou* **charge d'une ligne** = line load; **unité d'extension d'une ligne** = line extender **(f)** **en ligne** = on-line; **le terminal est en ligne avec l'ordinateur principal** = the terminal is on-line to the mainframe; **aide en ligne** = on-line help; **base de données en ligne** = on-line database; **recherche documentaire en ligne** = on-line information retrieval; **stockage de données en ligne** = on-line storage; **système en ligne** = on-line system; **traitement en ligne** = on-line processing; **traitement transactionnel en ligne** = on-line transaction processing; **hors ligne** = off-line; **avant de remplacer le papier de l'imprimante, assurez-vous que l'imprimante est hors ligne** = before changing the paper in the printer, switch it off-line; **impression hors ligne** = off-line printing; **stockage hors ligne** = off-line storage; **traitement hors ligne** = off-line processing **(g)** *(téléphonique)* **ligne de grand débit** = high usage trunk; **ligne de jonction d'abonné (au centre téléphonique)** = exchange line; **ligne libre** = free line; **ligne louée** *ou* **de location** = leased line; **ligne privée** *ou* **réservée** *ou* **privative** = private line; **ligne téléphonique spécialisée** *ou* **dédiée** = dedicated line *ou* scheduled circuit; **être en ligne (avec quelqu'un)** = to be on the phone; **elle est en ligne avec Hong Kong** = she's on the phone to Hong Kong **(h)** **codage en ligne directe** = straight-line coding

◊ **ligne-bloc** *nf* slug; *(fondue au moment de la composition)* hot metal type

LIM EMS *(mémoire étendue)* Lotus, Intel, Microsoft Expanded Memory System (LIM EMS)

limitateur *nm* limiter

◊ **limite** *nf* **(a)** *(d'étendue)* edge *ou* boundary *ou* limit; **limite de page** = page boundary; **limites de tableau** = array bounds; **balayage en dehors des limites** = overscan; **détection de limites** = edge detection; **marquage de limites (d'un fichier)** = boundary punctuation; **protection des limites (de mémoire)** = boundary protection; **registre (d'adresses) de limites** = boundary register **(b)** *(de niveau)* restriction; **limites de la bande des audiofréquences** = audio range; **limite de tolérance au bruit** = noise margin **(c)** **date limite** = deadline *ou* expiration date; **nous avons dépassé notre date limite du 15 octobre** = we've missed our October 15th deadline

◊ **limité, -ée** *adj* limited; **(ordinateur) limité par les entrées** *ou* **limité par le débit d'entrée des données** = input bound (computer); **limité par le processeur** = processor limited; **limité par les sorties** *ou* **limité par le débit de sortie des données** = output bound; **(programme) limité par l'entrée/sortie** = I/O bound (program); **limité par (la vitesse d') un périphérique** = peripheral limited; **dégradation limitée** = graceful degradation; **modem à distance de transmission limitée** = limited distance modem; **test sélectif limité** = crippled leapfrog test; *(imprimerie)* **tirage limité** = short run; **l'imprimante laser est très utile pour les tirages limités** = a laser printer is good for short-run printing

◊ **limiter** *vtr* to limit *ou* to restrict; **limiter l'accès** *ou* **l'utilisation (de quelque chose)** = to restrict access to (something)

◊ **limiteur** *nm* **limiteur de courant transitoire** = transient suppressor; **limiteur de signal audio** = audio compressor; **limiteur de tension** = surge protector

linéaire *adj* linear; **antenne linéaire** = linear array (antenna); **base de données linéaire (non relationnelle)** = flat file database; **circuit intégré linéaire** = in-line *ou* linear circuit; **circuit intégré linéaire** = linear integrated circuit; **fonction linéaire** = linear function; **l'expression Y 10 + 5X - 3W est une**

fonction linéaire = the expression Y 10 + 5X - 3W is a linear function; **l'expression Y (10 + 5X²) n'est pas une fonction linéaire** = the expression Y (10 + 5X²) is not a linear function; **programmation linéaire** = linear programming; **programme linéaire** = in-line program *ou* linear program; **traitement linéaire** = in-line processing

liquide *adj* liquid; **affichage à cristaux liquides** = liquid crystal display (LCD)

> tout se fait par l'intermédiaire d'un petit écran à cristaux liquides par simple branchement sur le réseau secteur
>
> **L'Evénement**

lire *vtr* **(a)** *(personne)* to read; **les opérateurs de saisie trouvent ce manuscrit difficile à lire** = the keyboarders find the manuscript lacks legibility; **les conditions de vente sont imprimées en caractères si petits qu'il est très difficile de les lire** = conditions of sale are printed in such small characters that they are difficult to read **(b)** *(par tête de lecture, etc.)* to read; *(par détection)* to sense; **qui peut être lu** = readable; **qui peut être lu par l'imprimante** = printer-readable; **le texte électronique est converti en image vidéo qui peut être lue par l'imprimante** = the electronic page is converted to a printer-readable video image; **l'ordinateur a lu automatiquement trente valeurs données par le convertisseur analogique-numérique** = the computer automatically reads in thirty values from the A/D converter; **est-ce qu'un lecteur optique peut lire les caractères d'imprimerie?** = can an OCR read typeset characters?; **il lui faut 9,9 secondes pour lire un document de 8,5 x 11 pouces** = its scanning speed is 9.9 seconds for an 8.5 inch by 11 inch document; **un processeur d'images qui peut lire, afficher et manipuler les images vidéo** = an image processor that captures, displays and manipulates video images; **ce scanner peut lire des images avec une définition de 300 points par pouce** = this scanner captures images at a resolution of 300 dots per inch (dpi); **aller chercher et lire (une instruction)** = fetch (instruction); **cette instruction va lire le premier enregistrement du fichier** = this instruction reads the first record of a file; **ce dispositif lit les perforations de la bande papier** = this device senses the holes punched in a paper tape

◊ **lisibilité** *nf* legibility; **la lisibilité du manuscrit laisse à désirer** = the manuscript lacks legibility

◊ **lisible** *adj* legible; **le manuscrit est écrit au crayon et est à peine lisible** = the manuscript is written in pencil and is hardly legible

LISP *(langage de haut niveau)* List Processing (LISP)

lissage *nm (d'une courbe)* anti-aliasing

listage *nm* listing; **listage de mémoire** = memory dump; **listage (du texte) source** *ou* **original** = source listing

◊ **liste** *nf* **(a)** list; **liste d'adresses** = address list; **liste (d'un programme) d'assemblage** = assembly listing; **liste en boucle** = circular list; **liste en chaîne** *ou* **liste d'articles chaînés** = chain list *ou* chained list

ou linked list; **liste complète** = dense list; **liste concaténée** = chain list *ou* chained list *ou* linked list; **liste déroulante** *ou* **boîte de liste** = drop-down list box; **liste descriptive** = description list; **liste d'exceptions** = exception dictionary; **liste des fonctions** = capability list; **liste d'interdictions** = stop list; **liste inversée** *ou* **en mode LIFO** = pushdown list; **liste des modifications** = journal; **liste des possibilités** = capability list; **liste d'un programme source** = source listing; **liste de références** = authority file *ou* reference list; **liste séquentielle** = linear list; **liste vide** = empty *ou* null list; **éditer sous forme de liste** = to list; **entrer** *ou* **inscrire un nom sur une liste** = to enter a name on a list; **marqueur de fin de liste** = nil pointer; **traitement de liste** = list processing **(b)** *(des films ou pièces à l'affiche)* listings

◊ **lister** *vtr* to list; **lister (les lignes d'instruction d')** **un programme** = to list a program; **édition listée d'un programme sur imprimante** = program listing

◊ **listing** *nm* **listing d'imprimante** = (computer) listing *ou* printout; **le directeur des ventes a demandé un listing des commissions d'agents** = the sales director asked for a printout of the agents' commissions; **listing (du texte) d'origine** = source listing; **listing d'un programme** = program listing; **listing d'un programme d'assemblage** = assembly listing; **listing de programme source** = source listing; **papier listing** = listing paper *ou* continuous stationery; *(sortie d'imprimante)* **qualité listing** = draft printing

lith *adj* **film lith** = lith film

litho = LITHOGRAPHIE

◊ **lithographie** *ou* **litho** *nf* lithography *ou* litho; **lithographie offset** = offset lithography

◊ **lithographique** *adj* lithographic

littéral, -e *adj* **symbole littéral** = literal; **indicatif littéral** = index letter; **opérande littéral** = literal operand

livre *nm* book; **ils peuvent imprimer des livres qui ont jusqu'à 96 pages** = they can print books of up to 96 pages; **livre broché** *ou* **livre de poche** = paperback; **livre cartonné** = cased book; **ce livre existe en édition brochée et en édition cartonnée** = the book is available in paperback and hard cover; **création de livres (par des maisons spécialisées)** = packaging

◊ **livret** *nm* booklet

LLC *(norme IEEE)* Logical Link Control (LLC) (IEEE 802.2 standard)

LLL *(langage de bas niveau)* Low-Level Language (LLL)

LOAD HIGH *(commande MS-DOS de transfert en mémoire supérieure)* Load High (LH)

lobe *nm* lobe; **lobe latéral** = side lobe

local, -e 1 *nm* room; **locaux** = facilities **2** *adj* **(a)** *(rattaché à l'ordinateur)* local; **bus local** *ou* **local bus** *ou* **LB** = local bus; **les cartes d'extension les plus**

rapides se placent dans ce connecteur **local bus** = the fastest expansion cards fit into this local bus connector; **imprimante locale** = local printer; **lecteur de disque local** *ou* **unité de disque locale** = local drive; **mémoire locale** = local memory; **pont local** = local bridge; **nous utilisons un pont local pour connecter les deux réseaux locaux du bureau** = we use a local bridge to link the two LANs in the office; **réseau local (d'entreprise)** = local area network (LAN); **modem pour réseau local** = limited distance modem; **serveur de réseau local** = local area network server *ou* LAN server **(b)** *(variable ou argument)* local; **variable locale** = local variable; **déclaration d'une variable locale** = local declaration **(c)** *(à accès limité)* **à accès local** = local; **mode local** = local mode

localisation *nf* **(a)** location; **localisation (automatique) de panne** = fault detection; **diagnostic de localisation de panne** *ou* **de défaillance** = fault diagnosis; **programme de localisation de panne** = fault location program **(b)** **fichier localisation** = country file

◊ **localiser** *vtr* to locate *ou* to track; **avez-vous réussi à localiser l'erreur de programmation?** = have you managed to locate the programming fault?; **localiser (et réparer) une panne** = to troubleshoot

LocalTalk ™ *(système de câblage de réseau AppleTalk)* LocalTalk ™ (cabling system in AppleTalk network)

location *nf* hiring *ou* leasing; **circuit de location** = leased circuit; **ligne de location** = leased line

lockout *nm* lockout

logarithme *nm* logarithm; **le logarithme décimal de 1000 est 3 (= 10 x 10 x 10)** = decimal logarithm of 1,000 is 3 (= 10 x 10 x 10)

◊ **logarithmique** *adj* logarithmic; **le 'bel' est mesuré sur une échelle logarithmique** = bel is a unit in the logarithmic scale; **graphe logarithmique** = logarithmic graph

loger *vtr* to house

logiciel *nm* software; *(pour lequel une contribution volontaire est demandée)* shareware; **logiciel commun** *ou* **partagé** = common software; **logiciel comptabilité-gestion** *ou* **logiciel bureautique** = business system *ou* business package; **logiciel convivial** *ou* **d'utilisation facile** = user-friendly software; **logiciel d'application** = applications software; **logiciel d'archivage** = filing system; **logiciel de commande de périphérique** = handler *ou* driver; **logiciel de débogage** = debugger; **logiciel de développement** = development software; **logiciel de diagnostic** = diagnostic program; **logiciel d'exploitation** = systems software; **logiciel de formatage** = formatter; **logiciel de formatage d'impression** = print formatter; **logiciel de formatage de texte** = text formatter; **logiciel de récupération de fichiers (après incident)** = file-recovery utility; **il est impossible de retrouver un fichier perdu sans l'aide d'un logiciel de récupération de fichiers** = a lost file cannot be found without a file-recovery utility; **logiciel de réseau** = network software; **logiciel de série** = canned software; **logiciel graphique** = graphics software; *(à l'achat d'un ordinateur)* **logiciel inclus** *ou* **fourni** = bundled software; **logiciel non inclus** *ou* **non fourni** = unbundled software; **logiciel intégré** = integrated software; **logiciel paramétrique** = parameter-driven software; **nous utilisons des logiciels personnalisés** *ou* **écrits sur commande** = we use customized software; **logiciel piraté** = pirate software; **logiciel résident** = resident software *ou* memory-resident software; **logiciel non standard** *ou* **qui ne fonctionne que sur un type d'appareil** = machine-dependent software; **logiciel système** = systems software; **logiciel de traitement de texte** = word-processing program *ou* word-processing software; **logiciel téléchargé** = telesoftware (TSW); **bibliothèque de logiciels** = software library; **(système) compatible logiciels** *ou* **compatible avec des logiciels écrits pour d'autres systèmes** = software compatible (system); **compatibilité de logiciel** = program compatibility; **créateur** *ou* **concepteur de logiciel** *ou* **expert en création de logiciels** = software writer; **cycle de vie d'un logiciel** = software life cycle; **définition et standards de qualité d'un logiciel** = software specification; **développement d'un logiciel** = software development; **développeur de logiciel** = software developer; **erreur de logiciel** = soft error; **fiabilité d'un logiciel** = software reliability; **disque formaté** *ou* **sectorisé par logiciel** = soft-sectored disk; **génie logiciel** = software engineering; **assurance qualité dans le domaine du génie logiciel** = software quality assurance (SQA); **ingénieur logiciel** = software engineer; **interruption programmée** *ou* **générée par logiciel** = software interrupt; **maintenance de logiciel** = software maintenance; **piratage de logiciel** = software piracy; **spécifications d'un logiciel** = software specification; **société spécialisée en logiciels** = software house

logique 1 *nf* logic; **la personne nommée devra connaître le matériel micro-informatique et la logique qui s'y rapporte** = the person appointed should have a knowledge of micro-based hardware and dedicated logic; **logique binaire** = logic; **logique câblée** = hardwired logic; **ordinateur à logique câblée** = fixed program computer; **programme en logique câblée** = hardwired program; **logique câblée programmable** = programmable logic array (PLA); **logique combinatoire** = combinational logic; **la logique dédiée réduit le nombre de puces** = the dedicated logic cuts down the chip count; **logique ECL** = emitter-coupled logic (ECL); **logique floue** = fuzzy logic *ou* fuzzy theory; **logique formelle** = formal logic; **logique intégrée à injection** = integrated injection logic (IIL); **logique machine** = machine equation; **logique négative** = negative-true logic; **logique à n niveau(x)** = n-level logic; **logique numérique** = digital logic; **logique des ordinateurs** *ou* **logique informatique** = computer logic; **logique positive** = positive logic; **logique de reconnaissance** = recognition logic; **logique séquentielle** = sequential logic; **logique transistor résistance (LTR)** = transistor-resistor logic (TRL); **logique transistor transistor (LTT)** = transistor-transistor logic (TTL) **2** *adj* logical *ou* logic; **anneau** *ou* **chemin**

logique = logical ring; **bombe logique** = logic bomb; **un programmeur système a installé une bombe logique lorsqu'il a été licencié** = a system programmer installed a logic bomb when they made him redundant; **carte logique** = logic card *ou* logic board; **circuit logique** = gate circuit *ou* logic circuit; **circuit logique complexe** *ou* **en réseau** = gate array; **circuit logique non connecté** = uncommitted logic array (ULA); **circuit logique programmable** = programmable logic array (PLA); **circuit logique à trois états** = three state logic; **comparaison logique** = logical comparison; **configuration logique** = logic map; **décalage logique** = logical shift *ou* non-arithmetic shift; **décision logique** = logical decision; **diagramme logique** = logic flowchart *ou* logical chart; **élément logique** = logic element; **élément logique composé** *ou* **élément logique multiple** = compound logical element; **enregistrement** *ou* **article logique** = logical record; **équivalence logique** = equivalence function *ou* operation; **erreur logique** = logical error; **état logique** = logic state; **analyseur d'état logique** = logic state analyzer; **état logique bas** *ou* **0** = logical low; **état logique haut** *ou* **1** = logical high; **expression logique** = logical expression; **fonction logique spécialisée** = dedicated logic; **(nombre d') inférences logiques par seconde (LIPS)** = logical inference per second (LIPS); **marque logique** = logical mark; **niveau logique** = logic level; **opérateur logique** = relational operator *ou* logical operator; **opération logique** = logic operation; **ordinogramme logique** = logical flowchart; **porte** *ou* **circuit logique** = logic gate; **le raisonnement logique peut être simulé par une machine intelligente** *ou* **un système expert** = logical reasoning can be simulated by an artificial intelligence machine; **(imprimante à) recherche logique** = logic-seeking (printer); **réseau** *ou* **circuit logique** = logic array; **symbole logique** = logic symbol; **unité logique** = logical drive; **en fait, l'unité logique F: est une partie du disque du serveur utilisée pour stocker les données** = the logical drive F: actually stores data on part of the server's disk drive; **voie logique** = logical channel

◊ **logithèque** *nf* software library

LOGO *(langage de programmation de haut niveau)* LOGO (language)

logo *nm* = LOGOTYPE

◊ **logotype** *nm* logotype *ou* logo

loi *nf* law; **loi d'Ohm** = Ohm's Law; *voir aussi* LIBERTE

lointain, -e *adj* far

long, longue *adj* **(a)** long; **enveloppe longue (pour papier ministre)** = foolscap envelope; **mot long** = double word **(b) cartouche longue durée** = durable cartridge

longitudinal, -e *adj* longitudinal

longueur *nf* length; *(d'un document)* extent; **longueur d'un bloc** = block length; **longueur d'un enregistrement** = record length; **longueur d'un fichier** = file length; **longueur du nom d'un fichier** = length of filename; **enregistrement de longueur fixe**

ou **déterminée** = fixed-length record; **mot de longueur fixe** *ou* **déterminée** = fixed-length word; **longueur d'une ligne** = line length *ou* line width; **longueur d'un mot** = (data) word length; **ordinateur à mots de longueur fixe** = fixed word length computer; **ordinateur à mots de longueur variable** = variable word length computer; **longueur d'onde** = wavelength; **longueur de page** = page length; **enregistrement à longueur variable** = variable length record

lot *nm* **(a)** *(d'un produit)* batch; **les lecteurs de disquettes du dernier lot sont défectueux** = the last batch of disk drives are faulty; **numéro de lot** = batch number **(b)** *(de données)* **total par lot** = batch total; **traitement par lots** = batch processing; **mode de traitement par lots** = (processing data in) batch mode; **traitement par lots en mode séquentiel** = sequential batch processing; **partition** *ou* **zone de traitement par lots** = batch region; **processeur de traitement par lots** = batch processor; **système de traitement par lots** = batch system

Lotus™ *(société spécialisée en logiciels)* Lotus™

loué, -ée *adj* leased; **circuit loué** = leased circuit; **ligne louée** = leased line

◊ **louer** *vtr* to lease; **la société loue tous ses ordinateurs** = the company leases all its computers; **la société a pour politique de louer son matériel** = the company has a policy of only using leased equipment

lourd, -e *adj* **bit lourd** = weighted bit

LPT1 *(sur un PC)* **port parallèle (imprimante) LPT1** = first parallel printer port (LPT1)

LTR = LOGIQUE TRANSISTOR RESISTANCE

LTT = LOGIQUE TRANSISTOR TRANSISTOR

ludiciel *nm* games software

lumen *nm* lumen

lumière *nf* light; **il faut éviter de placer l'écran sous une lumière trop forte** = the VDU should not be placed under a bright light; **lumière actinique** = actinic light; **lumière ambiante** = available light; **lumière cohérente** *ou* **monochrome** = coherent light; **lumière ultraviolette** = ultra-violet light *ou* UV light; **lumière visible** = visible light; **conducteur de lumière** = light conduit

luminance *nf* luminance; **signal de luminance** = luminance signal

lumineux, -euse *adj* **rayon lumineux** = (light) beam; **déflexion d'un rayon lumineux** = beam deflection; **tache lumineuse** *ou* **interférence lumineuse** = *(photographie)* flare; *(sur écran)* bloom

luminosité *nf* brightness; **un bouton vous permet de régler la luminosité et les contrastes** = a control knob allows you to adjust brightness and contrast; **niveaux de luminosité** = brightness range

lux *nm* *(unité d'éclairement)* lux (lx)

Mm

M = MEGA

m = METRE, MILLI-

mA = MILLIAMPERE

MA = MODULATION D'AMPLITUDE

MAC *(transmission: code d'identification de message)* Message Authentification Code (MAC); *(télévision)* Multiplex Analog Components (MAC); **format MAC** = MAC

Mac *(ordinateur Mac ou Macintosh ™)* Apple *ou* Apple Macintosh ™ computer

MacBinary ™ *(système de transfert de fichier)* MacBinary ™ (file storage and transfer system)

machine *nf* **(a)** *(appareil)* machine; *(l'ensemble des machines)* machinery; **bruit parasite causé par une machine** = man-made noise *ou* induced interference; **machine à cartonner** = case-making machine; **machine à dicter** = dictating machine; **machine à écrire** = typewriter; **caractères de machine à écrire** = typewriter faces; **machine à écrire électrique** = electric typewriter; **machine à écrire électronique** = electronic typewriter; **il fait moins d'erreurs depuis qu'il utilise une machine à écrire électronique** = he makes fewer mistakes now he is using an electronic typewriter; **écrit à la machine** = typewritten; **machine de Turing** = Turing machine; *(d'imprimante ou presse)* **épreuve de machine** = machine proof **(b)** *(ordinateur)* machine; **machine de traitement de texte** = word-processor; **machine dédiée au traitement de bases de données** = database machine; **machine intelligente** = intelligent device; **machine nue** = clean machine; **machine source** = source machine; **machine virtuelle** = virtual machine; **cycle de machine** = machine cycle; **équation ou logique machine** = machine equation; **erreur (causée par la) machine** = machine error; **langage machine** *ou* **code machine** = computer code *ou* machine code *ou* machine language *ou* internal language; **format de code machine** = machine code format; *(instruction ou donnée)* **en langage machine** = machine-readable; **codes en langage machine** = computer-readable codes *ou* machine-readable codes; **compiler en langage machine** = machine language compile; **instruction en code** *ou* **en langage machine** = machine code instruction *ou* machine instruction; **programmation en langage machine** = machine language programming; **programme en langage machine** = absolute program; **interface utilisateur-machine** *ou* **interface homme-machine** = human-computer *ou* human-machine interface (HMI); **mot machine** = machine word; **(logiciel) propre à la machine** = intimate *ou* machine-intimate (software); **(signal d') interruption provenant d'une machine** = hardware interrupt

◊ **machine-outil** *nf* machine-tool; **(programme de) commandes numériques de machines-outils** = Automatically Programmed Tools (APT); Computer Numeric Control (CNC); **système de machines-outils à commandes numériques** = flexible machining system (FMS)

◊ **machiniste** *nm&f* *(opérateur)* machinist; *(théâtre ou film)* grip

Macintosh ™ *(ordinateurs)* **les ordinateurs Macintosh ne sont pas compatibles avec les IBM PC à moins que vous n'utilisiez un logiciel d'émulation** = Macintosh computers are not compatible with an IBM PC unless you use special emulation software

macro- *préfixe* macro-

macro *nf* = MACROCOMMANDE, MACRO-INSTRUCTION macro; **bibliothèque de macros** = macro library; **désassemblage de macro** = macro expansion

◊ **macro-assembleur** *nm* macro assembler *ou* assembly program

◊ **macrocode** *nm* macro code

◊ **macrocommande** *nf* *(routine ou bloc de commandes)* macro command *ou* macro instruction; *voir aussi* MACRO

◊ **macrodéfinition** *nf* macro definition

◊ **macro-élément** *nm* macroelement

◊ **macro-expansion** *nf* macro expansion

◊ **macro-instruction** *nf* macro instruction *ou* macro command *ou* macro call *ou* macro; **macro-instruction imbriquée** = nested macro call

◊ **macrolangage** *nm* macro language; **programme assembleur pour macrolangage** = macro assembler *ou* macro assembly program

◊ **macro-ordinogramme** *nm* macro flowchart

◊ **macroprogrammation** *nf* macro programming

macule *nf* *(d'image)* slur

magasin *nm* *(pour pellicule)* magazine

magazine *nm* *(vidéotex)* magazine; **format magazine** = magazine format

magnétique *adj* magnetic; **bande magnétique** = magnetic tape *ou* mag tape; *(en cassette)* cassette tape; **cartouche** *ou* **cassette de bande magnétique** = magnetic tape cartridge *ou* cassette; **dérouleur de bandes magnétiques** = magnetic tape drive; magnetic tape transport; **encodeur pour bandes**

magnétiques = magnetic tape encoder; **lecteur de bandes magnétiques** = magnetic tape reader; **mémoire à bulles magnétiques** = magnetic bubble memory; **carte magnétique** = magnetic card *ou* smart card *ou* personal identification device (PID); **champ d'une carte magnétique** = card field; **lecteur de cartes magnétiques** = magnetic card reader; **cellule magnétique** = magnetic cell; **champ magnétique** = magnetic field; **disque magnétique** = magnetic disk; **écran magnétique** = magnetic screen; **effaceur magnétique** = degausser *ou* demagnetizer; **il s'est servi d'un effaceur magnétique pour démagnétiser les têtes de lecture** = he used a demagnetizer to degauss the tape heads; **encodage magnétique** *ou* **sur support magnétique** = magnetic encoding; **encre magnétique** = magnetic ink; **flux magnétique** = magnetic flux; **lecteur de marques magnétiques** = mark sense device *ou* reader; **mémoire magnétique** = magnetic memory *ou* store; **mémoire à couches minces magnétiques** = magnetic thin film storage; **mise au point magnétique** = magnetic focusing; **orage magnétique** = magnetic storm; *(d'une carte)* **piste magnétique** = magnetic strip; **lecteur de pistes magnétiques** = magnetic strip reader; **polarité magnétique** = magnetic polarity; **reconnaissance de caractères magnétiques** = magnetic ink character recognition (MICR); **imagerie par résonnance magnétique (IRM)** = magnetic resonance imaging; **support magnétique** = magnetic material *ou* medium; **les supports magnétiques** = magnetic media; **support magnétique original** = magnetic master; **support magnétique vierge** = empty medium; **données sur support magnétique** = soft data; **enregistrement sur support magnétique** = magnetic recording; **tambour magnétique** = magnetic drum; *(pour enregistrement)* **tête magnétique** = magnetic head; **tore magnétique** = magnetic core; **transfert d'un support magnétique à un autre** *ou* **transfert magnétique** = magnetic transfer

◊ **magnétisation** *nf* magnetization; **perte** *ou* **défaut de magnétisation** = drop out

◊ **magnétiser** *vtr* to magnetize

le champ ainsi créé magnétise les particules métalliques prisonnières de la surface du disque, forçant l'alignement de leurs pôles
Science et Vie Micro

magnétocassette *nm* tape unit; **platine magnétocassette** = tape deck

magnéto-optique *adj* **disque magnéto-optique** *ou* **disque optique** = magneto-optical disc; **enregistrement magnéto-optique** = magneto-optical recording

COMMENTAIRE: le disque magnéto-optique *ou* optique est couvert d'une couche mince de film magnétique qui est chauffée par un laser. Les particules sont alors polarisées par un faible champ magnétique. Les supports magnéto-optiques ont de très grandes capacités de stockage.

magnétophone *nm* (magnetic) tape recorder *ou* audio cassette recorder (ACR) *ou* tape unit *ou* reel to reel recorder; **magnétophone à cassette** =

cassette recorder; **magnétophone à quatre pistes** = four-track recorder; **magnétophone stéréophonique** = stereophonic recorder; **interface magnétophone** = ACR interface; **platine magnétophone** = tape deck

magnétoscope *nm* video recorder *ou* video cassette recorder (VCR) *ou* videotape recorder

maigre *adj* *(imprimerie)* **caractères maigres** = light face; *voir aussi* GRAS

mailing *nm* (direct) mailing

maillage *nm* *(de réseau ou de données)* **structure à maillage intégral** = plex structure

◊ **maille** *nf* mesh

◊ **maillé, -ée** *adj* **réseau maillé** = mesh network; **réseau totalement maillé** = fully connected network; **système maillé** = multilink system

main *nf* hand; **(qui fonctionne) à la main** = (which works) manually; **écrit à la main** = handwritten; *(d'un ordinateur)* **mise en main** = hands-on training; **une mise en main du nouvel ordinateur a été organisée pour les délégués commerciaux** = the sales representatives have received hands-on experience of the new computer; **(petit appareil) qu'on tient à la main** = hand-held (device)

mainframe *nm* mainframe computer

maintenabilité *nf* maintainability

maintenance *nf* *(d'un appareil)* maintenance *ou* service; upkeep; **contrat de maintenance** = maintenance contract *ou* service contract; *(réparation)* **maintenance corrective** *ou* **curative** = corrective maintenance *ou* remedial maintenance; repair; **maintenance courante** = housekeeping; **maintenance de fichier** = file maintenance; **maintenance de logiciel** = software maintenance; **maintenance du parc clients** = customer engineering; *(vérification)* **maintenance préventive** = preventive maintenance; **nous offrons un contrat de maintenance préventive qui s'applique à ce système** = we offer a preventive maintenance contract for the system; **maintenance d'un programme** = program maintenance *ou* maintenance routine *ou* housekeeping routine; **maintenance sur site** = on-site maintenance; **ingénieur de maintenance (sur site)** = field engineer; **programme de maintenance** = service program; **service de maintenance** = maintenance (service)

maintenir *vtr* **(a)** to retain *ou* to sustain **(b)** **maintenir (un fichier) à jour** = to keep (a file) up to date; **nous passons beaucoup de temps à maintenir nos fichiers à jour** = we spend a lot of time keeping our files up to date

◊ **maintien** *nm* **boucle de maintien** = holding loop; **courant de maintien** = hold current; **délai** *ou* **retard de maintien** = contention delay

maison *nf* *(société)* house; **maison d'édition** = publisher *ou* publishing house; **une des plus grandes maisons de logiciel aux Etats-Unis** = one of the biggest software houses in the US; **de la maison** = in-house; **tous nos équipements sont suivis par l'équipe de maintenance de la maison** = the in-house maintenance staff deal with all our equipment; **style (de la) maison** = house style

maître, maîtresse *n* master; *(émetteur de données)* **maître d'un bus** = bus master; **adaptateur maître** = bus master adapter; **l'adaptateur maître du réseau a un débit de transfert de données beaucoup plus élevé que l'ancien** = the bus master network adapter provides much faster data throughput than the old adapter; **carte maîtresse** = master card; **fichier maître** = master file; **fichier de programme maître** = master program file; **horloge maîtresse** = main clock *ou* master clock *ou* timing master; **ordinateur maître** = master computer; **l'ordinateur maître contrôle tout** = the master computer controls everything else; **terminal maître** = master terminal

◊ **maître-esclave** *nm* système informatique **maître-esclave** = master/slave computer system

◊ **maître-maître** *nm* système **maître-maître** = master/master computer system

◊ **maîtriser** *vtr* to control *ou* to manage; **qui peut être maîtrisé** = manageable

majuscule *nf&adj* (lettre) majuscule = capital *ou* cap *ou* capital letter *ou* block capital; *(imprimerie)* upper case; **écrire en majuscules** = to write in capital letters *ou* to print; **BASIC s'écrit toujours avec des majuscules** = the word BASIC is always written in caps; **son nom était écrit en majuscules** = his name was written in capital letters; **écrivez votre nom et votre adresse en majuscules en haut du formulaire** = please print your name and address *ou* write your name and address in block letters at the top of the form; **M majuscule** = capital M *ou* upper case M; **il a remplacé le M majuscule de 'coMputer' par une minuscule** = he corrected the word 'coMputer', replacing the upper case M with a lower case letter; **mettre en mode majuscule ou minuscule** *ou* **uniformiser (en majuscules ou minuscules)** = to normalize; *(d'un texte)* **mise en majuscule** = capitalization; **passer en majuscule** = to use the shift key; **(procédure) qui distingue les majuscules des minuscules** = case sensitive; **recherche (de texte) qui distingue les majuscules des minuscules** = case sensitive search; **le mot de passe tient compte des majuscules** = the password is case sensitive; **touche des majuscules** = shift key; **touche de verrouillage des majuscules** = caps lock

mal *adv* wrongly; incorrectly; **mal fonctionner** = to malfunction *ou* to function badly *ou* not to work properly

mâle *adj* male; **connecteur mâle** = male connector; **connecteur mâle à deux broches** = jumper; *voir aussi* FEMELLE, CHANGER

manager *nm* manager

manche *nm* **manche à balai** = joystick; **port pour manche à balai** = joystick port; **l'ordinateur personnel possède un port pour le manche à balai** = the computer comes with a joystick port

Manchester *npr (communications)* encodage **Manchester** = Manchester coding

manchettes *nfpl* banner headlines

Mandlebrot *npr* équation de **Mandlebrot** = Mandlebrot set

manette *nf* **manette (de jeu)** = games paddle *ou* joystick; **port (pour) manette de jeu** *ou* **port jeu** = joystick port

manipulation *nf (de données ou d'images)* manipulation; **manipulation binaire** = bit manipulation; **manipulation de bloc** = block operation; **routine de manipulation de fichier** = file handling routine; **manipulation d'octets** = byte manipulation; **manipulation de texte** = text manipulation; **un gestionnaire de base de données ultra-rapide permet la manipulation d'une très grande quantité de données** = a high-speed database management program allows the manipulation of very large amounts of data; **langage de manipulation de données** = data manipulation language (DML)

◊ **manipuler** *vtr* to manipulate; **les câbles de technologie avancée doivent être manipulés avec grand soin** = high spec cabling needs to be very carefully handled; **on peut manipuler l'image avant son téléchargement sur l'ordinateur hôte** = the image can be manipulated before uploading to the host computer; **un processeur d'images qui peut lire, afficher et manipuler les images vidéo** = an image processor that captures, displays and manipulates video images

manoeuvre *nf* **disque de manoeuvre** = work disk; **espace de manoeuvre** = workspace; **fichier de manoeuvre** = scratch file *ou* work file

manomètre *nm* gauge

manquement *nm* failure

mantisse *nf* mantissa *ou* argument *ou* fractional part; **mantisse binaire** = binary mantissa; **la mantisse du nombre 45,897 est 0,897** = the mantissa of the number 45.897 is 0.897

manuel *nm* manual; **manuel d'installation** = installation manual *ou* technical manual; **manuel d'utilisation** = user guide *ou* instruction manual; **un manuel d'utilisation est inclus avec le système** = a user guide *ou* an instruction manual is included with the system; **manuel d'utilisation élémentaire** = primer

◊ **manuel, -elle** *adj* manual

◊ **manuellement** *adv* manually; **l'alimentation du papier se fait manuellement** = the paper has to be fed into the printer manually

manufacturer *vtr* to manufacture

manuscrit *nm* manuscript *ou* MS; **ce manuscrit a été écrit directement sur ordinateur** = this manuscript was all written on computer; **l'auteur**

a envoyé un manuscrit de deux cents pages entièrement écrit à la main = the author sent in two hundred pages of handwritten manuscript; **manuscrit dactylographié** = typescript

◊ **manuscrit, -e** *adj* handwritten

manutention *nf* (materials) handling

MAQ = MODULATION D'AMPLITUDE EN QUADRATURE

maquette *nf (illustrations)* artwork; *(d'un livre ou d'une revue) (prototype de test)* mock-up; *(modèle réduit)* model; **la maquette a été envoyée au flashage** = the artwork has been sent for filming; **il nous a fait voir la maquette du nouveau centre informatique** = he showed us a model of the new computer centre building; *(chemin de fer)* **maquette d'édition** = editing plan

marche *nf* (a) **marche/arrêt** = on/off; **tourner le bouton marche/arrêt** = turn the on/off knob; 'marche' = 'power on'; **indicateur (lumineux) de marche** = run indicator; **mettre en marche** = to power up *ou* to switch on *ou* to turn on *ou* to bring up; to activate; to operate; **en appuyant sur la touche CR, on met l'imprimante en marche** = pressing CR activates the printer; **appareil en (bon) état de marche** = functional unit *ou* machine which is up and running; **remise en marche automatique** = auto restart; **remise en marche au point de reprise** *ou* **au point d'arrêt** = failure recovery *ou* fall back recovery; **marche arrière** = backward mode; **faire marche arrière** = to backtrack (b) **marche à suivre** = procedure; **voici la marche à suivre pour retrouver des fichiers perdus** = you should use this procedure to retrieve lost files

◊ **marcher** *vi* to function *ou* to perform; **ce système informatique n'a jamais bien marché depuis son installation** = the computer system has never worked properly since it was installed; **faire marcher** = to operate *ou* to drive; **êtes-vous capable de faire marcher le standard téléphonique?** = do you know how to operate the telephone switchboard?; *(appareil)* **qui marche (à l'électricité, etc.)** = powered (by electricity, etc.); **un moteur qui marche à l'électricité** = an electrically-powered motor

marge *nf* (a) *(espace blanc autour d'un texte)* margin; **en tapant le contrat à la machine, n'oubliez pas de laisser des marges très larges** = when typing the contract don't forget to leave wide margins; **les marges de droite et de gauche sont les blancs de chaque côté d'une page** = the left margin and right margin are the two sections of blank paper on either side of the page; **marge de reliure** *ou* **d'agrafage** = binding offset; *(d'un livre)* **marge intérieure** = gutter; **marge supérieure** = top space; **fixer** *ou* **paramétrer une marge** = to set a margin; **paramétrage de marges** = margination *ou* setting of margins (b) *(limite)* margin; **marge de tolérance au bruit** = noise margin; **marge d'erreur** = margin of error; **marge de sécurité** = safety margin

◊ **marginal** *adj* **carte à encoches marginales** = edge notched card; *(d'un texte)* **notes marginales** = cut-in notes; *(d'une carte perforée ou papier listing)* **perforations marginales** = feed holes *ou* sprocket holes

marguerite *nf* daisy-wheel *ou* printwheel; **imprimante à marguerite** = daisy-wheel printer; **l'imprimante à marguerite donne un bien meilleur résultat que l'imprimante matricielle mais elle est plus lente** = a daisy-wheel printer produces much better quality text than a dot-matrix, but is slower

marquage *nm* marking; *(avec drapeau ou balise)* flagging; **marquage (mnémotechnique) des touches (de clavier)** = key strip; *(d'un fichier)* **marquage de limites** = boundary punctuation; *(de bande papier)* **code de marquage** = tape code; *(entre des signaux)* **intervalle de marquage** = marking interval; *(du bord d'un disque)* **perforation de marquage** = (disk) index hole

◊ **marque** *nf* (a) mark *ou* marker; *(logique)* mark; *(drapeau ou balise)* flag *ou* indicator; *(qui permet de retrouver facilement une partie de programme)* bookmark; **marque (de début) d'adresse** = address mark; *(signal)* **marque attente** = mark hold; **marques de bloc** *ou* **de sélection d'un bloc** = block markers *ou* block marks; **marque de début d'enregistrement** = beginning of information mark (bim); **marque de début de mot** = word marker; **marque de dépassement de capacité** = overflow bit *ou* flag *ou* indicator; **marque de fin de fichier** = terminator; *(sur microfilm)* **marque de positionnement** = editing symbol; **lecteur de marques magnétiques** = mark sense device *ou* mark reader; **lecteur optique de marques** = optical mark reader (OMR); **reconnaissance optique de marques** = optical mark recognition (OMR) (b) *(d'un produit)* **nom de marque** = brand name; **marque de l'éditeur** *ou* **de l'imprimeur** = colophon

◊ **marqué, -ée** *adj* **bit marqué** = dirty bit; **image marquée d'un reflet** = flared image

◊ **marquer** *vtr* to mark; *(d'un drapeau ou d'une balise)* to flag; **(instruction de) marquer un bloc** = mark block

◊ **marqueur** *nm* (a) marker; *(drapeau ou balise)* flag *ou* indicator flag; **marqueur de champ** = field marker; *(imprimerie: sous forme de point)* **marqueur d'énumération** = bullet; **marqueur d'état** *ou* **d'utilisation** = device flag; **marqueur de fin de fichier** = terminator; **marqueur (de début** *ou* **de fin) de groupe** = group mark *ou* marker; **marqueur de fin de liste** = nil pointer; **séquence de marqueurs** = flag sequence (b) *(stylo feutre)* marker pen

marteau *nm* **marteau d'impression** = print hammer

MASER *(amplificateur)* Microwave Amplification by Stimulated Emission of Radiation (MASER)

masquage *nm* masking

◊ **masque** *nm* (a) mask; **on se sert d'un masque ou d'un stencil pour reproduire le tracé du circuit du transistor sur le silicium** = a mask or stencil is used to transfer the transistor design onto silicon **(b)** **bit masque** = mask bit; **masque d'interruption** = interrupt mask; **registre de masque** = mask register **(c)** *(de saisie)* form *ou* template; **mode masque** = form mode **(d)** *(télévision)* **masque filtre** = shadowmask; **masque de séparation** = aperture mask

◊ **masqué, -ée** *adj* masked; **mémoire morte masquée** = masked ROM; **mode d'exécution frontal-masqué** = foreground/background modes

◊ **masquer** *vtr* to mask *ou* to conceal; **le signal a été masqué par le bruit** = we have lost the signal in the noise; **les lignes qu'on ne veut pas montrer sont masquées par cet algorithme** = the hidden lines are concealed from view with this algorithm; **qui peut être masqué** = maskable; **interruption qui peut être masquée** = maskable interrupt; **interruption qui ne peut être masquée** = non-maskable interrupt (NMI)

mass-media *nm* **les mass-medias** = the mass media

masse *nf* **(a)** bulk; *(d'un disque ou d'une bande)* **effacement en masse** = bulk erase; **mémoire de masse** = bulk storage *ou* mass storage; **en masse** = in bulk **(b)** *(d'un appareil électrique)* **mettre à la masse** = to earth; **fil de mise à la masse** = earth wire; **tresse de mise à la masse** = fanning strip

massicot *nm* guillotine

mat, matte *adj (qui n'est pas brillant)* matt *ou* matte

matériau *nm* material; **l'or est le matériau idéal pour la fabrication des connecteurs électriques** = gold is the ideal material for electrical connections; **matériau ferromagnétique** = ferromagnetic material; **matériau isolant** = insulator *ou* insulation material; **matériau semi-conducteur (de type) n** = n-type material *ou* N-type material *ou* n-type semi-conductor; **matériaux synthétiques** = synthetic materials; **contrôle d'approvisionnement en matériaux** = materials control

matériel *nm* **(a)** *(informatique)* hardware; **matériels annexes** = ancillary equipment; **matériel courant** *ou* **banal** *ou* **partagé** = common hardware; **matériel de formatage** = formatter; **compatibilité du matériel** = hardware compatibility; **configuration du matériel** = hardware configuration; **défaillance du matériel** = equipment failure; **dépendant, -e du matériel** = hardware dependent; **le logiciel de communication est dépendant du matériel et ne fonctionne qu'avec un modem compatible Hayes** = the communications software is hardware dependent and will only work with Hayes-compatible modems; **fiabilité** *ou* **bonne qualité du matériel** = hardware reliability; **plate-forme de matériel** = hardware platform; **sécurité du matériel** = hardware security **(b)** equipment; **matériel audiovisuel** = audiovisual aids; **matériel de bureau** = office equipment *ou* business equipment; **matériel (de) haute performance** = high performance equipment; **matériel publicitaire** =

publicity matter *ou* display material; **matériel de secours** = auxiliary equipment; **matériel (de) téléinformatique** = data communications equipment (DCE); **manutention du matériel** = materials handling

◊ **math** *nf* = MATHEMATIQUE maths, *US* math

◊ **mathématique 1** *nf* **les mathématiques** = mathematics **2** *adj* mathematical; **coprocesseur mathématique** = maths chip *ou* maths coprocessor; **modèle mathématique** = mathematical model; **ordre de mise en oeuvre des opérateurs mathématiques** = operator precedence; **sous-programme mathématique** = mathematical subroutine

◊ **maths** *nf* = MATH

matrice *nf* **(a)** *(tableau de nombres ou données)* matrix; **matrice réduite** = sparse array; **rotation de matrice** = matrix rotation **(b)** *(connexions)* **matrice de relation** = matrix; **matrice des touches sur un clavier** = key matrix **(c)** *(graphique)* **matrice active** = active matrix; **matrice de caractères** = character matrix; **matrice d'impression à haute définition** = enhanced dot matrix; **matrice de points** = dot matrix

◊ **matriciel, -elle** *adj* **imprimante matricielle** = matrix printer *ou* dot-matrix printer *ou* wire printer; **processeur d'image matricielle** = raster image processor; **une page électronique peut être convertie en image vidéo imprimable à l'aide d'un processeur d'image matricielle** = an electronic page can be converted to a printer-readable video image by an on-board raster image processor

◊ **matricielle** *nf (imprimante)* matrix printer *ou* dot-matrix printer *ou* wire printer

les matricielles à aiguilles sont aussi capables de travailler en couleur. De très beaux résultats mais une limitation: les teintes ne peuvent pas se mélanger

L'Ordinateur Individuel

mauvais, -e *adj* **(a)** wrong *ou* inaccurate; **il a tapé le mauvais mot de passe** = he entered an inaccurate password *ou* the wrong password; **l'erreur provenait d'une mauvaise saisie des données** = the error was caused because the data had not been accurately keyed **(b)** anomalous; *(due à des perturbations atmosphériques)* **mauvaise transmission d'images** = anomalous propagation (ANAPROP)

maximal, -e *adj* maximum; **capacité maximale** = maximum capacity; **débit maximal de transmission** = maximum transmission rate; **fréquence maximale utilisable** = maximum usable frequency; **vitesse maximale de transmission** = maximum transmission rate

◊ **maximaliser** *vtr* to maximize

◊ **maximizer** *vtr* to maximize

◊ **maximum 1** *nm* maximum; **porter à son maximum** = to maximize **2** *adj* maximum; **amplitude maximum enregistrée** = maximum reading; **définition maximum** = limiting resolution; **période de demande maximum** = time of peak demand; **niveau maximum de production** = peak output; **atteindre un niveau maximum** = to peak; **la tension a atteint le niveau maximum de 1200 volts** = the power peaked at 1,200 volts; **nombre maximum d'utilisateurs** = maximum users; **le marqueur du thermomètre indique la température maximum d'aujourd'hui** = the marker on the thermometer shows the peak temperature *ou* the maximum temperature for today; **c'est la vitesse maximum que peut atteindre cette imprimante** = that is the highest speed that this printer is capable of

MB *ou* **Mb** *ou* **Mbyte** = MEGABYTE

Mb *ou* **Mbit** = MEGABIT

Mbps = MEGABITS PAR SECONDE

mC = MILLICOULOMB

MCA *(architecture d'un bus d'extension)* Micro Channel Architecture (MCA); **jeu de composants MCA** = Micro Channel Architecture chipset *ou* MCA chipset; **bus Micro-Channel** *ou* **bus MCA** = Micro Channel Bus

MD *ou* **MKDIR** *(commande de création de répertoire sous MS-DOS and OS/2)* Make Directory *ou* MD *ou* MKDIR

MDA *(standard d'adaptateur monochrome)* Monochrome Display Adapter (MDA)

mécanique *adj* mechanical; **souris mécanique** = mechanical mouse

◊ **mécanisme** *nm* mechanism; **l'imprimante possède un mécanisme très simple** = the printer mechanism is very simple; **il semble que le mécanisme du lecteur ne fonctionne pas très bien** = the drive mechanism appears to be faulty

média *nm* media; **les médias** *ou* **les mass-medias** = the media *ou* the mass media; **le produit a beaucoup fait parler de lui dans les medias** = the product attracted a lot of interest in the media *ou* a lot of media interest; **analyse des médias** = media analysis *ou* media research; **coût média** = above-the-line costs

◊ **médiatique** *adj* **couverture médiatique** = media coverage *ou* press coverage; **le produit a eu un gros intérêt médiatique** = the product attracted a lot of interest in the media *ou* a lot of media interest; **nous avons eu une bonne couverture médiatique pour le lancement du nouveau modèle** = we got good media coverage for the launch of the new model

médical, -e *adj* **imagerie médicale** = imaging

méga = MEGA-OCTET meg; **cet ordinateur a un disque de quatre-vingts mégas** = this computer has a ninety-meg hard disk

méga- *préfixe* mega-

◊ **mégabit (Mb)** *nm* megabit *ou* Mbit (Mb); **(nombre de) mégabits par seconde (Mbps)** = megabits per second (Mbps)

◊ **mégaflops (Mflops)** *nm (million d'instructions en virgule flottante par seconde)* megaflops *ou* Mflops

◊ **mégahertz (MHz)** *nm* megahertz (MHz)

◊ **méga-octet** *ou* **Moctet (Mo)** *nm* megabyte *ou* Mbyte (MB *ou* Mb); **carte mémoire de plusieurs méga-octets** = multimegabyte memory card

Megastream ™ *(connexion)* Megastream ™

mélange *nm (sonore)* mix

◊ **mélanger** *vtr (des signaux audio)* to mix *ou* to mix down; **fichiers mélangés** = cross-linked files

◊ **mélangeur** *nm (de signaux audio)* mixer

membrane *nf (d'un haut-parleur)* **membrane conique** = cone; **clavier à membrane** = membrane keyboard

> COMMENTAIRE: les touches d'un clavier à membrane ont moins de course que celles d'un clavier mécanique mais comme ces derniers ne comportent pas de pièces mobiles ils sont plus robustes et plus fiables

mémento *nm* **mémento de clavier** = keyboard overlay; **mémento de fonction des touches** = key overlay

mémo *nm* **champ mémo** = memo field

mémoire *nf* memory *ou* store *ou* storage; **mémoire à accès aléatoire** *ou* **sélectif** *ou* **direct** = random access storage *ou* memory; **mémoire à accès direct** = direct access storage device (DASD); **mémoire à accès intermédiaire** = intermediate access memory (IAM); **mémoire à accès rapide** = rapid access memory *ou* fast access memory (FAM); **mémoire à accès séquentiel** = serial access memory (SAM) *ou* sequential access storage; **mémoire à double accès** = dual port memory; **mémoire acoustique** = acoustic store *ou* acoustic memory; **mémoire adressable par son contenu** *ou* **mémoire associative** = content-addressable memory (CAM) *ou* associative memory; **mémoire d'archivage** = archive storage; **mémoire associative** = associative memory *ou* content-addressable storage *ou* parallel search storage; search memory *ou* searching storage; **processeur à mémoire associative** = associative processor; **registre de mémoire associative** = associative storage register; **mémoire auxiliaire** = auxiliary storage *ou* memory *ou* store; backing memory; **cet appareil est équipé de lecteurs de disquettes et de bandes magnétiques qui servent de mémoire auxiliaire** = disk drives and magnetic tapes are auxiliary storage on this machine; **mémoire banale** *ou* **mémoire 'bloc-notes'** = scratchpad memory *ou* working store; **mémoire de base** *ou* **mémoire conventionnelle** = base memory *ou* conventional memory *ou* base RAM; **mémoire à bulles (magnétiques)** = (magnetic) bubble memory; **cassette mémoire à bulles (magnétiques)** = bubble memory cassette; **mémoire cache** = cache memory; **le temps d'accès est réduit lorsque les données les plus fréquemment utilisées sont placées dans la mémoire cache** = file access time is much quicker if the most frequently used data is stored in cache memory; **stocker dans la mémoire cache** = to cache; **mémoire capacitive** *ou* **à condensateur** = capacitor storage; **mémoire CCD** *ou* **à couplage de charge** = charge coupled device memory *ou* CCD memory; **mémoire centrale** = core memory *ou* store *ou* central memory; **dans ce système, la mémoire centrale rapide sert de bloc-notes pour tous les calculs** = the fast core is used as a scratchpad for all calculations in this system; **programme en mémoire centrale** = core program; **mémoire centrale à accès direct** = core memory *ou* primary memory; **mémoire centrale rapide** = fast core; **mémoire circulante** *ou* **mémoire dynamique** = circulating storage; **mémoire de contrôles** = control memory; **mémoire à couches minces (magnétiques)** = (magnetic) thin film storage *ou* memory; **mémoire cryogénique** = cryogenic memory; **mémoire à disque** = disk memory; **mémoire de données** = data memory *ou* data storage; **mémoire dynamique** = dynamic memory *ou* dynamic storage; **mémoire dynamique permanente** = permanent dynamic memory; **mémoire EAPROM** = electrically alterable programmable read-only memory (EAPROM); **mémoire EAROM** = electrically alterable read-only memory (EAROM); **mémoire écran** = screen memory; **mémoire EEPROM** = electrically erasable programmable read-only memory (EEPROM); **mémoire EEROM** = electrically erasable read-only memory (EEROM); **mémoire effaçable** = erasable memory; **mémoire électrostatique** = electrostatic storage; **mémoire d'entrée** = input storage; **mémoire EPROM** = erasable programmable read-only memory (EPROM); **mémoire étendue** = extended memory; **mémoire externe (auxiliaire)** = external memory *ou* external storage *ou* external store; **(mise en) mémoire de fichiers** = file storage; **(mise en) mémoire du format courant** = local format storage; **mémoire FIFO** *ou* **mémoire qui fonctionne sur le principe du premier entré premier sorti** = FIFO memory *ou* first in first out memory; **mémoire fixe** = control memory *ou* ROM; **mémoire haute** = high memory; **bloc de mémoire haute** = upper memory block (UMB); **mémoire holographique** *ou* **d'hologramme** = holographic storage; **mémoire image** = frame store; **la mémoire image peut servir à l'affichage des images météorologiques transmises par satellites** = the frame store can be used to display weather satellite pictures; **le processeur d'images permet le stockage d'une image vidéo dans une mémoire intégrée de 8 bits** = the image processor allows you to store a video frame in a built-in 8-bit frame store; **espace mémoire de l'image** = image storage space; **mémoire d'images optiques** = scanner memory; **mémoire ineffaçable** = nonerasable storage; **mémoire d'instruction** = instruction storage; **mémoire intermédiaire** = intermediate storage; **mémoire interne** = internal memory *ou* store; **mémoire interne à accès immédiat** = immediate access store (IAS); **tri en mémoire interne** = internal sort; *(d'un système)* **mémoire de lancement** = bootstrap memory; **mémoire (à) laser sur couche haute définition** = laser emulsion storage; **mémoire à ligne de retard** = delay line store; **mémoire à liste permutée** = nesting store; **mémoire locale** = local memory; **mémoire magnétique** = magnetic memory *ou* magnetic

store; **mémoire magnétique haute densité** = high density storage; **mémoire de masse** = mass storage *ou* bulk storage; **mémoire morte** = read only memory (ROM); **(support de) mémoire morte** *ou* **fixe** *ou* **à lecture seule** = read only memory; **mémoire morte auxiliaire** = sideways ROM; **mémoire morte à fusibles** = fusible read only memory (FROM); **mémoire morte masquée** = masked ROM; **mémoire morte programmable** = programmable memory (PROM) *ou* programmable read only memory (PROM); **mémoire morte programmable effaçable par ultraviolet** = ultraviolet erasable PROM; **programmeur de mémoire morte** = burner; **mémoire MOS** *ou* **à semi-conducteurs** = MOS memory; **mémoire à un niveau** = one-level store; **mémoire non-volatile** = non-volatile memory; **mémoire optique** = optical storage *ou* optical memory; **mémoire optonumérique** = photodigital memory; **mémoire paginée** = paged memory; **accès sur demande à la mémoire paginée** = demand fetching; **mémoire (de) périphérique** = peripheral memory; **mémoire permanente** = permanent memory *ou* nonerasable storage; **mémoire principale** = primary memory *ou* primary store *ou* primary storage *ou* central memory (CM) *ou* main memory *ou* main storage; **le système de 16 bits contient une mémoire principale d'une capacité allant jusqu'à 3Mo** = the 16-bit system includes up to 3Mb of main memory; **mémoire (de) programme** = program storage; **mémoire PROM** = programmable memory (PROM) *ou* programmable read only memory (PROM); **PROM effaçable par ultraviolet** = ultraviolet erasable PROM; **mémoire protégée** = protected storage; *(mémoire vive)* **mémoire RAM** = random access memory; **condensateur pour mémoire RAM** = memory backup capacitor; **la bande perforée est une des mémoires de rangement les plus lentes d'accès** = paper tape is one of the slowest access backing stores; **mémoire réelle** = real memory; *(mémoire morte)* **mémoire ROM** = read only memory; **mémoire ROM effaçable électriquement** = electrically erasable read-only memory (EEROM); **mémoire ROM fantôme** = phantom ROM; **mémoire ROM à fusibles** = fusible read only memory (FROM); **mémoire ROM modifiable électriquement** = electrically alterable read-only memory (EAROM); **mémoire ROM programmable et effaçable** = erasable programmable read-only memory (EPROM); **mémoire ROM programmable et effaçable électriquement** = electrically erasable programmable read-only memory (EEPROM); **mémoire ROM programmable, modifiable électriquement** = electrically alterable, programmable read-only memory (EAPROM); **mémoire secondaire** *ou* **intermédiaire** = secondary storage; **mémoire séquentielle** = serial memory *ou* sequential memory *ou* storage; **la bande magnétique constitue une mémoire séquentielle d'une grande capacité** = magnetic tape is a high capacity serial memory; **mémoire séquentielle indexée** = indexed sequential storage; **mémoire statique** = static memory *ou* static storage; **mémoire tampon** = buffer (memory); **mémoire tampon d'entrée/sortie** = I/O buffer; **registre de mémoire tampon** = memory buffer register (MBR); **taille de la mémoire tampon** = buffer length *ou* buffer size; **mémoire tampon de transmission de données** = data communications buffer; **mémoire tampon dynamique** = dynamic buffer; **qui possède une mémoire tampon** = buffered; **utilisation de mémoire tampon** = buffering; **entrée/sortie utilisant une mémoire tampon** = buffered input/output; **utilisation de double mémoire tampon** = double buffering; **utiliser une mémoire tampon** = to buffer; **les deux ordinateurs fonctionnent à des vitesses différentes mais peuvent transmettre des données en utilisant une mémoire tampon fonctionnant sur le système 'premier entré premier sorti'** = the two computers operate at different rates, but can transmit data using a FIFO memory; **mémoire temporaire** = temporary storage *ou* erasable storage *ou* erasable memory; *(bloc-notes)* working store *ou* scratchpad; **mémoire vidéo** = video memory; **mémoire vidéo à accès aléatoire** = video random access memory (VRAM); **mémoire virtuelle** = virtual memory *ou* virtual storage (VS); **mémoire vive** *ou* **mémoire RAM** = random access memory (RAM); **mémoire vive dynamique** = dynamic RAM *ou* dynamic random access memory (DRAM); **(programme) chargeur** *ou* **programme de chargement de la mémoire vive** = RAM loader; **mémoire volatile** = volatile memory *ou* volatile store *ou* storage *ou* volatile dynamic storage; **accès direct à la mémoire** = direct memory access (DMA); **accès direct à la mémoire par vol de cycle** = DMA cycle stealing; **contrôleur d'accès direct à la mémoire** *ou* **contrôleur DMA** = DMA controller; **temps d'accès à la mémoire** = memory access time; **changement d'adresse en mémoire** = memory edit; **registre d'adresse en mémoire** = memory address register (MAR) *ou* store address register (SAR); **alimentation de secours de la mémoire** = memory backup capacitor; **allocation de mémoire** = storage allocation; **allocation dynamique de la mémoire** = dynamic storage allocation; **banque de mémoire** = memory bank; **la carte d'extension possède une banque de mémoire de 128Ko constituée de 16 puces** = an add-on card has a 128Kb memory bank made up of 16 chips; **bus de mémoire** = memory bus; **capacité de mémoire** = memory capacity *ou* storage capacity; **la capacité de mémoire est de 3Mo** = total storage capacity is 3Mb; **capacité de mémoire de disque** *ou* **de disquette** = disk storage capacity; *(circuit intégré)* **carte mémoire** = memory board; *(carte magnétique)* **carte (magnétique) à mémoire** = chip card *ou* smart card; **cellule de mémoire** = memory cell *ou* store cell; **clavier à mémoire** = key rollover; **configuration de la mémoire** = memory map; **configuré en mémoire** = memory-mapped; **entrée/sortie configurée en mémoire** = memory-mapped I/O *ou* memory-mapped input/output; **un écran configuré en mémoire possède une adresse pour chaque pixel, permettant ainsi au processeur d'accéder directement à l'écran** = a memory-mapped screen has an address allocated to each pixel, allowing direct access to the screen by the CPU; **cycle de mémoire** = memory cycle; **densité de mémoire** = storage density; **diagnostic de la mémoire** = memory diagnostic; **dispositif mémoire** = storage device; **disquette** *ou* **disque de mémoire** = storage disk; **écran à mémoire** = storage tube; **emplacement de mémoire** = store location; **fichiers en mémoire** = file store; **gestion de mémoire** =

memory management; **unité de gestion de la mémoire** = memory management unit (MMU); **(logiciel) grand consommateur de mémoire** *ou* **gourmand en mémoire** = memory-intensive (software); **hiérarchie des mémoires** = memory hierarchy; **implanter** *ou* **ranger** *ou* **stocker dans la** *ou* **en mémoire** = to plant *ou* to store; **listage de mémoire** = memory dump; **mettre en mémoire** = to memorize *ou* to store *ou* to deposit (data); **programme mis en mémoire** = stored program; **mise en mémoire** = storage; **mise en mémoire de données** = data storage; **mise en mémoire de fichier** = file storage; **mise en mémoire du format courant** = local format storage; **mise en mémoire d'instruction** = instruction storage; **modèle de (gestion des accès à la) mémoire** = memory model; **nettoyage de mémoire** = garbage collection; **page mémoire** = memory page; **protection des accès mémoire** = fetch protect; **(dispositif de) protection de la mémoire** = memory protect; **puce mémoire** = memory chip; **(signal de) régénération** *ou* **rafraîchissement de la mémoire RAM** = RAM refresh; **registre d'adresse en mémoire** = store address register (SAR) *ou* memory adress register (MAR); **registre des données en mémoire** = store data register (SDR); **(logiciel) qui requiert beaucoup de mémoire** = memory-intensive (software); **segmentation** *ou* **modularité de la mémoire** = granularity; **système à transfert de mémoire** = memory switching system; **taille (de la) mémoire** = storage capacity; **tube à mémoire** = storage tube; **vidage de mémoire (sur imprimante)** = memory dump; **voie d'accès direct à la mémoire** = direct memory access channel; **zone mémoire** = storage area; **zone mémoire de stockage de variables** = string area; **zone commune de la mémoire** = common storage area; **zone de mémoire supérieure** = high memory area (HMA); **zone de travail en mémoire** = memory workspace

d'autres constructeurs ont adopté des cartes de mémoire vive permanente comme mémoire de masse sur des portables légers
L'Ordinateur Individuel

mémorisé, -ée *adj* memorized *ou* stored; **programme mémorisé** = stored program

◊ **mémoriser** *vtr* to memorize *ou* to store; **il faudra jusqu'à 3Mo pour mémoriser une page de données graphiques haute-définition** = storing a page of high resolution graphics can require 3MB

mentionner *vtr* to quote *ou* to refer to; **en cas de réclamation, mentionnez toujours le numéro de lot qui apparaît sur le boîtier de l'ordinateur** = when making a complaint please quote the batch number printed on the computer case; **le manuel mentionne un port série, mais je n'en vois aucun** = the manual refers to the serial port, but I cannot find it

menu *nm* menu; **menu déroulant** = pull-down menu; **le menu déroulant est affiché en cliquant sur la barre de menu au sommet de l'écran** = the pull-down menu is viewed by clicking on the menu bar at the top of the screen; **menu principal** = main menu; **barre de menu** = action bar *ou* menu-bar; **logiciel avec menu** *ou* **à base de menu** = menu-driven software; **déroulement du menu** = action bar pull-down; **élément de menu** = menu item; **fenêtre de menu** = pop-up menu *ou* pop-down menu; **sélection par menu** = menu selection

mercure *nm* mercury; **ligne à** *ou* **de retard au mercure** = mercury delay line

mère *nf* mother; **carte mère** = motherboard; **carte mère d'un micro-ordinateur** = microcomputer backplane

message *nm* **(a)** message; *(affiché à l'écran)* **message de diagnostic** = diagnostic message; **message de diagnostic d'erreur** = diagnostic (error) message; **message d'entrée** = input statement; **message d'erreur** = error message; **vous obtiendrez des messages d'erreur si vous essayez de copier des fichiers implantés sur des secteurs défectueux d'une disquette** = you will receive error messages when you copy files that are stored on bad sectors on a disk; **message d'exécution** = execute statement **(b) message d'invitation à taper une commande** = (command) prompt; **le message READY signifie que le système est prêt à recevoir des instructions** = the prompt READY indicates that the system is available to receive instructions **(c)** *(informations transmises)* **message chiffré** *ou* **crypté** = ciphertext; *(sur un réseau)* **message diffusé** = broadcast message; **cinq minutes avant de fermer le réseau local, nous diffusons un message à tous les utilisateurs** = five minutes before we shut down the LAN, we send a broadcast message to all users; **message multimédia** = multimedia mail; **message reçu** = incoming message; **(nombre de) messages reçus** = incoming traffic; **acheminement des messages** = message routing; **authentification de messages** = authentication of messages; **code d'identification de message** = message authentication code (MAC); **commutation de message** = message switching; **créneau pour message** = message slot; *(séquence qui contient le routage et la destination)* **en-tête de message** = message header; **(code de) fin de message (EOM)** = end of message (EOM); **format de message** = message format; **numérotation des messages** = message numbering; **serveur de message** = interface message processor; **texte d'un message** = message text

messagerie *nf* **messagerie électronique** = computer mail *ou* electronic mail *ou* email *ou* E-mail; *(dans une société)* computer-based message system (CBMS); **utilisable avec une messagerie électronique** = mail-enabled; **ce traitement de texte peut être utlisé avec la messagerie électronique: vous pouvez envoyer des messages aux autres utilisateurs sans sortir du programme** = this word-processor is mail-enabled - you can send messages to other users from within it

mesure *nf* **(a)** *(dimension)* measure *ou* measurement; **mesure de surface** = square measure **(b) (fait) sur mesure** = custom-built; **logiciel sur mesure** = customized software *ou* machine-intimate software *ou* intimate software **(c)** *(action)* measure; **mesures de sécurité** = safety measures; **prendre des mesures** = to take action; **prendre des mesures pour éviter quelque chose** = to take measures to prevent something happening;

on a pris les mesures nécessaires pour remédier au défaut *ou* **pour rectifier** *ou* **réparer ce qui n'allait pas** = action has been taken to repair the fault

◊ **mesurer** *vtr* to measure *ou* to gauge; **la performance est mesurée à l'aide d'un programme test** = performance measurement *ou* measurement of performance is carried out by running a benchmark program

◊ **mesureur** *nm* gauge *ou* meter

métabit *nm* metabit

métacompilation *nf* metacompilation

métafichier *nm* metafile; **le système d'exploitation utilise un métafichier qui contient les données qui définissent l'emplacement de chaque fichier sur le disque** = the operating system uses a metafile to hold data that defines where each file is stored on disk

métal *nm* metal; **détecteur de métal** = metal detector

métalangage *nm* metalanguage; **métalangage BNF** = Backus-Naur-Form (BNF); **métalangage BNF étendu** = extended BNF (EBNF)

méthode *nf* procedure *ou* technique; **méthode ascendante** = hill climbing method; **méthode brutale** = brute force method; **méthode de classement** *ou* **d'archivage** = filing system

mètre (m) *nm* metre, *US* meter; *(poids du papier, par feuille)* **gramme au mètre carré** = grams per square metre (gsm *ou* g/m^2); **mètre kilogramme seconde (ampère) (mks(A))** = metre kilogram second (Ampere) (MKS(A)) **(b) mètre (à ruban)** = tape measure

◊ **métrique** *adj* metric; **ondes métriques** = very high frequency (VHF)

mettre *vtr* to put; *(une ligne)* **mettre en attente** = to hold; to put on hold; **mettre sur fiche** = to place something on file; **mettre en forme** = to format; **texte mis en forme à l'impression** = post-formatted text; *(un fichier, etc.)* **mettre à jour** = to update a file *ou* to bring a file up to date; **mettre en marche** = *(faire fonctionner)* to operate; *(mettre sous tension)* to switch on; **mettre à la masse** *ou* **à la terre** = to earth; **tous les appareils doivent être mis à la masse** = all appliances must be earthed; **mettre en mémoire** = to store; **programme mis en mémoire** = stored program; **mettre au point** = *(un produit)* to develop *ou* to perfect; *(une lentille)* to focus; *(un appareil)* to tune; **il a mis au point le procédé de fabrication d'un acier de haute qualité** = he perfected the process for making high grade steel; **mettre au point (avec grande précision)** = to fine tune; **mettre en place** = to install *ou* to set up *ou* to position; **il n'a fallu que quelques heures pour mettre l'équipement en place** = the installation of the equipment took only a few hours; **mettre en page** = to do the page layout *ou* the page makeup; to lay out the pages; **les concepteurs ont décidé de mettre en page sur format A4** = the designers have laid out the pages in A4 format; **mettre (des données) dans la pile** = to put data onto a stack;

mettre sous tension = to power up *ou* to switch on; **mettre à la terre** *ou* **à la masse** = to earth; **tous les fils non rattachés doivent être mis à la terre** *ou* **à la masse** = all loose wires should be earthed; *voir aussi* MISE

MF = MODULATION DE FREQUENCE

MFLOPS *(million d'instructions en virgule flottante par seconde)* Mega Floating Point Instructions per Second (megaflops *ou* MFLOPS)

MFM *(norme de codage)* Modified Frequency Modulation (MFM)

MFS *(logiciel d'archivage)* Macintosh Filing System (MFS)

MIA = MODULATION D'IMPULSION EN AMPLITUDE

MIC = MODULATION PAR IMPULSIONS ET CODAGE

micro[1] *nm* = MICRO-ORDINATEUR micro *ou* microcomputer; **l'unité centrale de traitement peut piloter un micro** = the mainframe is downward compatible with the micro

l'Institut a depuis longtemps mis en place des micros pour répondre à ses besoins de gestion mais aussi dans un but pédagogique
L'Information professionnelle

micro[2] *nm* = MICROPHONE mike *ou* microphone; **micro à aimant mobile** = moving coil microphone; **micro dynamique** *ou* **à impulsion** = dynamic microphone; **micro radio** = radio microphone; **micro sans fil** = wireless microphone; **filtre de micro** = pop filter

micro- *préfixe (petit)* micro-

microbe *nm* bacterium

microcassette *nf* microcassette

Micro-Channel Architecture (MCA) *(architecture de bus IBM pour la série des PS/2)* **bus Micro-Channel (bus MCA)** = Micro Channel Bus (MCA)

microcircuit *nm* microcircuit

◊ **microcode** *nm* microcode

Microcom *(protocole de communication de réseau)* Microcom Networking Protocol ™ (MNP)

micro-cravate *nm* lapel microphone

microcycle *nm* microcycle

◊ **microdisquette** *nf* microfloppy

◊ **micro-électronique** *nf* **la micro-électronique** = microelectronics

micro-espion *nm* bug; **placer un micro-espion** *ou* **surveiller par micro espion** = to bug; **il y avait des**

micros-espions dans la salle de conférence = the conference room was bugged

microfiche *nf* microfiche *ou* microform; *(avec réduction de plus de 90X)* ultrafiche

◊ **microfilm** *nm* microfilm; **toutes nos archives sont sur microfilms** = we hold all our records on microfilm; **lecteur optique de microfilms pour entrée de données sur ordinateur** = film optical scanning device for input into computers (FOSDIC); **entrée à partir de** *ou* **par lecture de microfilm** = computer input from microfilm (CIM); **stockage sur microfilm** = computer output on microfilm (COM)

◊ **microfilmer** *vtr* to microfilm; **nous avons envoyé les archives de 1989 pour les faire microfilmer** *ou* **pour les faire mettre sur microfilm(s)** = the 1989 records have been sent away for microfilming

◊ **micrographie** *nf* micrographics

◊ **micro-image** *nf* microimage

◊ **micro-informatique** *nf* microcomputing; **il travaille à la rédaction d'une revue de micro-informatique** = he edits a computer magazine

◊ **micro-instruction** *nf* microcode *ou* microinstruction

◊ **micromètre** *nm* micrometre

micron *nm* micrometre

micro-onde *nf* microwave

micro-ordinateur *ou* **micro**[1] *nm* microcomputer *ou* micro; **micro-ordinateur à carte unique** = single board microcomputer; **micro-ordinateur de contrôle** *ou* **de commande** = microcontroller; **micro-ordinateur de contrôle à puce unique** *ou* **monopuce** = single chip microcontroller; **micro-ordinateur portatif** = microwriter; **bus d'un micro-ordinateur** = microcomputer bus; **kit d'extension de micro-ordinateur** = microcomputer development kit; **l'industrie des micro-ordinateurs** = the microcomputing industry

microphone *ou* **micro**[2] *nm* microphone; *(familier)* mike; **microphone à bobine** *ou* **à aimant mobile** = moving coil microphone; **microphone à charbon** = carbon microphone; **microphone à condensateur** = capacitor microphone; **microphone dynamique** = dynamic microphone; **microphone à électret** = electret microphone; **microphone omnidirectionnel** = omnidirectional microphone; **microphone à quartz** = crystal microphone; **microphone sans fil (pour transmission)** = wireless microphone

microphotographie *nf* microphotography

microprocesseur *nm* microprocessor *ou* microprocessor unit (MPU) *ou* microdevice; **microprocesseur en tranches** = bit-slice microprocessor; **le microprocesseur en tranches utilise quatre processeurs à 4 bits pour réaliser un microprocesseur à 16 bits** = the bit-slice microprocessor uses four 4-bit processors to make a 16-bit word processor; **architecture d'un microprocesseur** = microprocessor architecture; **capacité** *ou* **facilité d'adressage mémoire d'un microprocesseur** = microprocessor addressing capabilities; **puce microprocesseur** = microprocessor chip

microprogrammation   *nf*   microprogramming

◊ **microprogramme** *nm* microprogram; **compteur de microprogramme** = microprogram counter; **ensemble des instructions** *ou* **jeu d'instructions d'un microprogramme** = microprogram instruction set; **langage d'assemblage pour microprogramme** = microprogram assembly language; **mémoire qui contient un microprogramme** = microprogram store; **registre de microprogramme** = microprogram counter; **séquence de micro-instructions** *ou* **d'instructions d'un microprogramme** = microsequence

◊ **microprogrammé, -ée** *adj* **logiciel microprogrammé** = firmware

microseconde *nf* microsecond (ms)

Microsoft ™ *(la plus grande société de logiciels pour PC et Macintosh)* Microsoft ™; **interface graphique Microsoft Windows** = Microsoft Windows

MID = MODULATION D'IMPULSIONS EN DUREE

MIDI *(interface numérisée pour instruments de musique)* **interface MIDI** = Musical Instrument Digital Interface (MIDI)

COMMENTAIRE: l'interface MIDI transmet les signaux d'un contrôleur ou d'un ordinateur pour faire jouer des notes à divers instruments de musique

migration *nf* migration; **migration de données** = data migration

MIL = MODULATION D'IMPULSIONS EN LARGEUR

milli- (m) *préfixe* milli- (m)

◊ **milliampère (mA)** *nm* milliampere (mA)

◊ **millicoulomb (mC)** *nm* millicoulomb (mC)

millier *nm* thousand; *(mesure de puissance d'un ordinateur)* **milliers d'instructions par seconde** = kilo instructions per second (KIPS)

millimétré, -ée *adj* **papier millimétré** = graph paper

◊ **millimétrique** *adj* **onde millimétrique** = extremely high frequency (EHF)

million *nm* million; **million de millions** = billion; **million d'instructions par seconde (MIPS)** = million instructions per second (MIPS); **million d'instructions en virgule flottante par seconde (MFLOPS)** = million floating point instructions per second (megaflops *ou* MFLOPS)

l'un des chiffres les plus significatifs est le coût du 'million d'instructions par seconde', unité de mesure de puissance des processeurs informatiques

L'Information professionnelle

milliseconde (ms) *nf* millisecond (ms)

MIMD *(d'un processeur parallèle)* **architecture MIMD** = Multiple Instruction Stream - Multiple Data Stream (MIMD); *voir aussi* FLUX

mince *adj* fine *ou* thin; **couche mince** = thin film; **mémoire à couches minces** = thin film memory; **mémoire à couches minces magnétiques** = magnetic thin film storage

mini 1 *nm* = MINI-ORDINATEUR **2** *préfixe* mini-

miniaturisation *nf* miniaturization

minidisquette *nf* minidisk

mini/maxi *adj inv* **méthode mini/maxi** = minmax (method)

minimiser *vtr* to minimize

minimum 1 *nm* minimum **2** *adj* minimum; **code à temps d'accès minimum** = optimum code

mini-ordinateur *ou* **mini** *nm* minicomputer *ou* mini

ministre *nm* (papier) **format ministre** = foolscap; **la lettre était écrite sur six feuilles format ministre** = the letter was on six sheets of foolscap

Minitel ™ *nm* système de télécommunication français équivalent au système britannique Viewdata ™

minuscule *nf&adj* (lettre) **minuscule** = lower case *ou* minuscule; **mettre en mode majuscule ou minuscule** *ou* **uniformiser en majuscules ou minuscules** = to normalize

minute *nf* minute; **(nombre de) lignes par minute (lpm)** = lines per minute (lpm); **(nombre de) pages par minute (ppm)** = pages per minute (ppm)

◊ **minuter** *vtr* to time

MIP = MODULATION D'IMPULSIONS EN POSITION

MIPS = MILLION D'INSTRUCTIONS PAR SECONDE

mire *nf* *(télévision)* **mire de contrôle** = test pattern

miroir *nm* mirror; *(action)* **copie miroir** *ou* **duplication de données sur un disque miroir** = disk mirroring; **disque miroir** = mirror disk; **effet miroir** = lateral reversal

◊ **mirroring** *nm* *(duplication de données sur un disque miroir)* disk mirroring

MISD *(architecture d'un type d'ordinateur parallèle)* Multiple Instruction Stream - Single Data Stream (MISD)

mise *nf (nouvelle version d'un logiciel)* mise à jour = update *ou* (new) release; **mise à jour corrective** = maintenance release; **la mise à jour corrective de ce programme de base de données, version 2.01, corrige le problème des marges** = the maintenance release of the database program, version 2.01, corrects the problem with the margins; *(action)* **mise à jour de fichier** = file maintenance *ou* updating; upkeep of a file; **la mise à jour des fichiers doit se faire tous les six mois** = the upkeep of the files means reviewing them every six months; **fichier de mise à jour** = change file *ou* transaction file; **publier une mise à jour** = to release a new version; **mise à la masse** = earthing; **fil de mise à la masse** = earth (wire); *(d'une photo)* **mise à la taille** = sizing; **mise au point** = *(d'un appareil)* tuning; *(d'un produit)* development; *(d'une lentille)* focusing; **mise au point magnétique** = magnetic focusing; **dérégler la mise au point** = to defocus; **logiciel de mise au point** = debugger; **temps de mise au point d'un nouveau produit** = development time; **mise en main** = hands-on training; **une mise en main du nouvel ordinateur a été organisée pour les délégués commerciaux** = the sales representatives have received hands-on experience of the new computer; **mise en mémoire de données** = information storage *ou* data storage; **mise en mémoire de fichier** = file storage; **ordre de mise en oeuvre des opérateurs (mathématiques)** = operator precedence; **mise en orbite** = launch (into orbit); **mise en page** = page layout *ou* page makeup; **les concepteurs travaillent à la mise en page de la nouvelle revue** = the design team is working on the layouts for the new magazine; **les corrections faites après la mise en page coûtent très cher** = corrections after the page makeup are very expensive; **mise en piggyback** = piggybacking; **mise en place** = installation; **temps de mise en place** = positioning time; **mise en place de liens (à l'aide d'un éditeur de liens)** = linkage editing; **mise en place d'un programme concurrent** = counterprogramming; **mise en réseau (d'ordinateurs)** = networking; **mise en route** = cold boot *ou* cold start; **(dispositif de) mise hors tension automatique** = automatic power off; **mise sous tension** = power on; **réinitialisation automatique à la mise sous tension** = power-on reset; **mise sur fiches** = card-indexing; *voir aussi* METTRE

mixage *nm* **(a)** *(signaux audio)* mix *ou* mixing; **faire un mixage** = to mix; **studio de mixage** = mixing studio **(b)** *(polices de caractères)* mixing

◊ **mixer** *vtr (signaux audio)* to mix down

◊ **mixeur** *nm (circuit électronique)* mixer

mixte *adj* circuit mixte = hybrid circuit; **poste de contrôle mixte** = combined station

mks(A) = METRE KILOGRAMME SECONDE (AMPERE)

mnémonique *adj* mnemonic; **code mnémonique d'assemblage** = assembler mnemonics *ou* mnemonic operation codes

Mo = MEGA-OCTET megabyte *ou* Mbyte (MB); **le modèle le plus récent possède un disque dur d'une capacité de 30Mo** = the latest model has a 30Mbyte hard disk

mobile *adj* mobile *ou* movable; **accent mobile** = piece accent; **balayage par faisceau mobile** = flying spot scan; **microphone à aimant mobile** = moving coil microphone; **radiotéléphone mobile** = mobile radiophone; **station terrestre mobile** = mobile earth terminal; **téléphone mobile** = mobile phone *ou* telephone; **unité mobile** = mobile unit

Moctet = MEGA-OCTET

modal, -e *adj* modal; **dispersion modale** = mode dispersion

mode *nm* mode; **mode actif** = active state; **mode d'adressage** = addressing mode; **mode affichage** = display mode; **pour saisir un texte, appuyer d'abord sur cette touche de fonction qui met le terminal en mode alphanumérique** = when you want to type in text, press this function key which will put the terminal into its alphanumeric mode; *(en virgule flottante)* **mode asynchrone** = asynchronous mode; **mode bruyant** = noisy mode; **(ordinateur) à mode caractère** = character orientated (computer); **mode (de) contrôle** *ou* **mode CTRL** = control mode; **mode conversationnel** = conversational mode *ou* interactive mode; **mode défilement** = scroll mode; **mode dialogué** = conversational mode; **mode différé** *ou* **en (mode) différé** = deferred mode; **mode direct** *ou* **en (mode) direct** = direct mode; **mode (d') entrée** = input mode; **mode (d') exécution** = execute mode; **mode d'exécution frontal/masqué** = foreground/ background modes; **mode graphe** = plotting mode; **mode graphique** = graphics mode; **mode immédiat** = immediate mode; **mode insertion** = insert mode; **mode interactif** = interactive mode; **mode local** = local mode; **mode masque (de saisie)** = form mode; **mode multi-utilisateur** = free running mode; **mode octet** = byte mode; **mode point** = bit-map mode; **mode remplacement** = replace mode; **mode séquentiel** = sequential mode; **mode sortie** = output mode; **mode standard** = standard mode; **mode de traitement de données par paquets** *ou* **par lots** = batch mode; **mode de transfert par paquets** = burst mode **(b)** *(d'un produit)* **mode d'emploi** = directions for use

modèle *nm* **(a)** *(d'un produit)* model; **voici notre dernier modèle** = this is the latest model; **nouveau modèle B remplace le modèle A** = the new model B has taken the place of model A; **modèle de démonstration** = demonstration model; *(police de caractères)* **modèle de fonte** = outline font; **modèle d'un système** = system design; **création de modèles (sur ordinateur)** = modelling **(b)** *(maquette)* **modèle réduit** = (scale) model **(c)** **modèle pour ordinogramme** = flowchart stencil *ou* flowchart template **(d)** **modèle mathématique** = mathematical model

◊ **modéliser** *vtr* to model

modem *nm (modulateur-démodulateur)* modulator-demodulator *ou* modem, *US* dataset; **notre modem ne fonctionne pas** *ou* **est en dérangement** *ou* **en panne** = the modem has broken down; **certains modems peuvent fonctionner en mode semi-duplex si nécessaire** = some modems can operate in half-duplex mode if required; **modem à appel automatique** = dial-in modem; **modem à deux vitesses (réception et émission)** = split baud rate modem; **modem d'appel** ou **modem demandeur** = originate modem; **modem de courte portée** = short haul modem; **modem de rappel** = call back modem; **modem en bande de base** = base band modem; **n'utilisez jamais un modem en bande de base sur une ligne téléphonique normale** = do not use a base band modem with a normal phone line; **modem half-duplex** = half-duplex modem; **modem intégré** = integrated modem; **modem pour réseau local** ou **modem à distance de transmission limitée** = limited distance modem; **le modem viewdata reçoit à 1200 et transmet à 75** = the viewdata modem uses a 1200/75 split baud rate; **carte modem** = internal modem; **débit par défaut d'un modem** = default rate; **sans modem** = null modem; **ce câble est configuré pour fonctionner sans modem et me permet de connecter ces deux ordinateurs facilement** = this cable is configured as a null modem, which will allow me to connect these two computers together easily

le modem permet la transmission de données informatiques par l'intermédiaire d'une ligne téléphonique classique
Science et Vie Micro

modifiable *adj* alterable; **mémoire ROM modifiable électriquement** = electrically alterable read-only memory (EAROM); **mémoire ROM programmable, modifiable électriquement** = electrically alterable, programmable read-only memory (EAPROM); **ordinateur à jeu d'instructions modifiable** = writable instruction set computer (WISC)

modificateur *nm* modifier; **modificateurs d'impression** = print modifiers

◊ **modification** *nf* alteration ou change ou modification ou adjustment; **les modifications apportées au système permettent de l'utiliser sur un réseau local d'entreprise** = the modifications to the system allow it to be run as part of a LAN; **la nouvelle version du logiciel comporte de nombreuses modifications et améliorations** = the new version of the software has many alterations and improvements; **modification d'adresse** = address modification; **modification d'une instruction** = instruction modification; **modification provisoire** = patch; **boucle de modification** = modification loop; **enregistrement de modifications** = change record ou amendment record; **fichier de modifications** = change ou movement file; **les enregistrements modifiés ont été ajoutés au fichier maître et inscrits au journal des modifications** = the modified records were added to the master file and noted in the journal; **liste des modifications** = journal; **page mémoire sans modification** = clean page; **texte sans modification** = clean copy

◊ **modifié, -ée** *adj* modified; **nous utilisons une version modifiée du programme d'édition de lettres types** = we are running a modified version of

the mail-merge system; **modulation de fréquence modifiée** = modified frequency modulation

◊ **modifier** *vtr* to adjust ou to alter ou to change ou to modify ou to vary; **les spécifications du programme viennent d'être modifiées** = the program specifications have just been altered; **il faudra modifier le logiciel pour pouvoir l'utiliser sur un ordinateur individuel** = the software will have to be modified to run on a small PC; **modifier les codes d'un programme** = to recode a program; **qui peut être modifié** = alterable ou selectable; *(débit, vitesse, etc.)* **qui peut être modifié suivant les besoins de l'utilisateur** = user-selectable

Modula-2 *(langage de haut niveau)* Modula-2 (language)

modulaire *adj* modular; **programmation modulaire** = modular programming ou modularization

la quatrième version offre désormais un environnement intégré et permet la programmation modulaire
Informatique & Bureautique

modularité *nf* modularity; **la modularité du logiciel ou du matériel permet de modifier le système** = the modularity of the software or hardware allows the system to be changed; **modularité de la mémoire** = granularity

modulateur *nm* modulator; **modulateur de fréquence radio** = radio frequency modulator ou RF modulator

◊ **modulateur-démodulateur** *nm* modulator-demodulator ou modem, *US* dataset; *voir aussi* MODEM

modulation *nf* modulation; **modulation d'amplitude (MA)** = amplitude modulation (AM); **modulation d'amplitude en quadrature** = quadrature amplitude modulation (QAM); **modulation de fréquence (MF)** = frequency modulation (FM); **modulation de fréquence à large bande** = wideband frequency modulation (WBFM); **modulation de fréquence modifiée** = modified frequency modulation; **modulation (en) delta** = delta modulation; **modulation d'impulsions** = pulse modulation; **modulation d'impulsions en amplitude (MIA)** = pulse amplitude modulation (PAM); **modulation d'impulsions en durée (MID)** = pulse duration modulation (PDM); **modulation d'impulsions en largeur** ou **en durée (MIL** ou **MID)** = pulse width modulation (PWM); **modulation d'impulsions en position (MIP)** = pulse position modulation (PPM); **modulation de phase** = phase modulation; **(système de) modulation par décalage de fréquence** = frequency shift keying (FSK); **modulation par impulsions et codage (MIC)** = pulse code modulation (PCM); **modulation différentielle par impulsions et codage** = differential pulse code modulation; **modulation différentielle dynamique par impulsions et codage (ADPCM** ou **standard de conversion ADPCM)** = adaptive differential pulse code modulation (ADPCM); **signal de modulation** = modulating signal

module *nm* *(d'un programme)* bead; *(d'un programme ou d'un système)* module; *(d'un programme ou d'un vidéodisque)* chapter; *(d'un système)* building block; *(d'un programme)* **module d'accompagnement** = coroutine; **un module d'interface analogique multifonction comprend un convertisseur analogique-numérique et un convertisseur numérique-analogique** = a multifunction analog interface module includes analog to digital and digital to analog converters; **(code) fin de module** = chapter stop

> ce logiciel est intégré, ce qui signifie qu'il possède différents modules (au nombre de quatre) ayant chacun une vocation propre: traitement de texte, tableur et graphiques, gestion de fichiers et rapports, communication
> *L'Ordinateur Individuel*

modulé, -ée *adj* **signal modulé** = modulated signal; **(signal) analogique modulé** = pseudo-digital; **non modulé** = unmodulated

◊ **moduler** *vtr* to modulate

modulo *nm* (a) **modulo-n** = modulo-N; **contrôle par modulo-n** = modulo-N check (b) **modulus** *ou* mod; **7 modulo-3 égale 1** = 7 mod 3 is 1; **signe et modulo** = sign and modulus

moins *nm* **le signe moins (-)** = minus *ou* minus sign

mois *nm* month; **pendant quelques mois** = for a period of months

moitié *nf* half; **la moitié des données ont été perdues au cours de la transmission** = half the data was lost in transmission

molette *nf* serrated wheel; **molette de pressage** = head wheel; **molette de serrage** = pinchwheel

momentané, -ée *adj* temporary; **erreur momentanée** = transient error

monadique *adj* monadic; **opérateur monadique** = monadic (Boolean) operator; **l'opérateur monadique NOT peut être utilisé ici** = the monadic operator NOT can be used here; **opération monadique** = monadic Boolean operation *ou* unary operation

monaural, -e *adj* monoaural

moniteur *nm* (a) *(écran de visualisation)* monitor (unit); **moniteur couleur** = colour monitor; **le moniteur couleur est excellent pour les jeux électroniques** = the colour monitor is great for games; **moniteur intégré** = firmware monitor; **moniteur multistandard** = multi-scan *ou* multi-sync monitor; **moniteur (de) télévision** = television monitor; **moniteur vidéo** = video monitor (b) *(programme)* **programme moniteur** = monitor program (c) *(de contrôle d'image de télévision)* monitor (d) *(haut-parleur)* **moniteur (retour de son)** = monitor

◊ **moniteur/téléviseur** *nm* television receiver/monitor

monnaie *nf* money; **monnaie électronique** = electronic money

mono- *préfixe* mono-

◊ **monocarte** *nm&adj* **ordinateur monocarte** = single board computer (sbc)

◊ **monochrome** *adj* *(moniteur ou écran)* black and white *ou* monochrome; **conversion monochrome (d'une image couleur)** = black crush; **écran monochrome** = monochrome monitor *ou* black and white screen; **lumière monochrome** = coherent light

◊ **monoflux** *nm&adj* **architecture multiflux d'instruction-monoflux de données** = multiple instruction stream - single data stream (MISD)

◊ **monofréquence** *nf&adj* **signalisation monofréquence** = single frequency signalling *ou* sf signalling

◊ **monolithique** *adj* *(circuit intégré)* monolithic

◊ **monomode** *nm&adj* single mode *ou* monomode; **fibre optique monomode** = monomode fibre

◊ **monopasse** *adj* **opération monopasse** = single pass operation

◊ **monophonique** *adj* monophonic

◊ **monoprogrammation** *nf* **système de monoprogrammation** = monoprogramming system

◊ **monopuce** *adj* **ordinateur monopuce** = single chip computer

◊ **monostable** *adj* *(circuit)* monostable

◊ **mono-utilisateur** *nm&adj* **système mono-utilisateur** = single-user system

◊ **monotâche** *adj* single-tasking

montage *nm* (a) *(d'une machine ou d'un appareil)* assembly; **il n'y a pas de notice de montage pour aider à la mise en place de l'ordinateur** = there are no assembly instructions to show you how to put the computer together; **carte de montage (de circuits)** = breadboard; **usine de montage** = assembly plant (b) *(d'une feuille isolée ou d'une illustration)* **montage sur onglet** = guarding (c) *(des parties d'un texte)* editing; *(à partir de paragraphes standard)* **montage d'un document** = boilerplating (d) *(d'un film)* film editing; **montage associatif** = associational editing; **montage électronique** = electronic editing; **salle de montage** = cutting room (e) *(imprimerie)* film assembly

Monte Carlo *npr* *(statistiques)* **méthode de Monte Carlo** = Monte Carlo method

monté, -ée *adj* **(a)** mounted; **cartes montées sur supports** *ou* **en rack** = rack mounted cards **(b)** **monté en série** = ganged; **commutateurs montés en série** = ganged switch; **avec des commutateurs montés en série, il est possible de choisir le bus de données qui va activer l'imprimante** = a ganged switch is used to select which data bus a printer will respond to **(c)** **document monté à partir de paragraphes standard** = boilerplate

◊ **montée** *nf* **temps de montée** = rise time *ou* acceleration time; **le temps de montée du circuit est très rapide** = the circuit has a fast rise time; **il faut inclure le temps de montée dans le temps d'accès** = allow for acceleration time in the access time

◊ **monter** *vtr* **(a)** *(fixer des composants, un disque dur)* to mount (chips; a disk); **les puces sont montées dans des prises de la carte de circuit imprimé** = the chips are mounted in sockets on the PCB; **monter en surface** = to piggyback **(b)** *(mettre en marche)* **faire monter (un système)** = to bring-up **(c)** *(augmenter)* to increase; to climb; **le nouveau modèle a fait monter les chiffres de vente** = the new model gave a boost to the sales figures

◊ **se monter à** *vpr* to amount to

montrer *vtr* to indicate *ou* to point out

morse *nm* morse *ou* **alphabet morse** = Morse code; **télégraphe** *ou* **manipulateur morse** = Morse key

mort, -e *adj* **(a)** **mémoire morte** = read only memory (ROM); **mémoire morte masquée** = masked ROM; **mémoire morte programmable** *ou* **PROM** = programmable ROM (PROM); **mémoire morte programmable effaçable par ultraviolet** = ultraviolet erasable PROM; **programmeur de mémoires mortes** = burner **(b)** **temps mort** = *(dû au mauvais fonctionnement)* dead time *ou* down time; *(lorsque la machine n'est pas utilisée)* idle time *ou* lost time

MOS *(semi-conducteur)* Metal Oxide Semiconductor (MOS); **mémoire MOS** *ou* **à semi-conducteurs** = MOS memory; **semi-conducteur MOS à canal (de type) P** = p-channel MOS

mosaïque *nf* mosaic; *(dans GUI)* **(disposition en) mosaïque** = tile; **disposer en mosaïque** = to tile

MOSFET **semi-conducteur à effet de champ MOSFET** = Metal Oxide Semiconductor Field Effect Transistor (MOSFET)

mot *nm* **(a)** *(d'un texte)* word; **mot du jour** *ou* **mot à la mode** = buzzword; **(nombre de) mots par minute** = words per minute (wpm *ou* WPM); **mot de passe** = access code *ou* authorization code *ou* identification (ID) code *ou* password; **entrée sur un système avec un mot de passe piraté** = piggyback entry; **il faut vous rappeler votre mot de passe sinon vous ne pourrez pas avoir accès au système** = if you forget your user ID, you will not be able to logon; **l'utilisateur doit d'abord taper le mot de passe pour avoir accès à la base de données** = the user has to key in the password before he can access the database; **mot principal** = keyword; **mots (mis) en évidence** *ou* **en surbrillance** = highlights; **nombre de** mots contenus dans un fichier *ou* un texte = word count **(b)** *(informatique)* word *ou* computer word *ou* data word; **mot adresse** = address word; **mot de commande** = keyword; **mot de contrôle** = control word; **mot double** *ou* **mot long** = double word; **mot d'état** *ou* **mot indicateur d'état** = processor status word (PSW) *ou* device status word (DSW); **mot d'état d'entrée/sortie** = input/output status word; **registre des mots d'état** = program status word register (PSW register); **mot d'identification** = identifier word; **mot d'index** = index value word; **mot instruction** = instruction word; **mot de longueur fixe** *ou* **déterminée** = fixed-length word; **(ordinateur) à longueur de mots fixe** = fixed word length; **mot machine** = machine word; **mot réservé** = reserved word; **processeur à mots variables** = byte machine *ou* character machine; **espacement entre les mots** = interword spacing; **indicateur de mot** = word marker; **longueur d'un mot** = data word length *ou* word length; **marque de début de mot** = word marker; **série de mots (l'un à la suite de l'autre)** = word serial; **temps de transfert d'un mot** = word time

◊ **mot-clé** *nm* key *ou* keyword *ou* descriptor; **le mot 'ordinateur' est un mot-clé en informatique** = 'computer' is a keyword in IT; **recherche par mots-clés** = disjunctive search

◊ **mot-paramètre** *nm* parameter word

> en contrepartie, l'égarement de ce mot de passe interdit tout accès à la structure, ce qui signifie à plus ou moins long terme la 'mort' de la base
> *L'Ordinateur Individuel*

> développé en LISP et récrit en COBOL, ce programme fonctionne par repérage des mots-clés
> *L'Ordinateur Individuel*

moteur *nm* motor; **un moteur électrique** *ou* **un moteur qui marche** *ou* **qui fonctionne à l'électricité** = an electrically-powered motor; **moteur d'inférence** = inference engine *ou* machine

motif *nm* pattern; **avec motifs** = patterned

Motorola ™ *(société de composants électroniques)* Motorola ™; **(puces) Motorola 68000, 68020, 68030** = Motorola 68000, 68020, 68030 (processors used in Apple Macintosh computers)

mouture *nf* **première mouture** = draft; **le programme en est à sa troisième mouture** = the program is in its second rewrite; **c'est la dernière mouture du nouveau logiciel** = this is the latest build of the new software

mouvement *nm* **(a)** *(déplacement)* movement; *(de transmissions)* traffic; **ce dispositif contrôle le mouvement des feuilles** = the device controls the copy flow **(b)** *(modifications)* movement *ou* transaction; **bande (de) mouvements** = change tape; **décomposition de mouvement** = memomotion; **enregistrement de mouvements** = amendment record *ou* change record *ou* transaction record; **fichier (de) mouvements** = change file *ou* detail file *ou* movement file *ou* update file; **traitement de mouvements** = transaction processing (TP); **vidage de mouvements (sur imprimante)** = change dump

Mover *(gestionnaire de polices et d'accessoires de bureau Apple Macintosh)* Font/DA Mover (Apple Macintosh system utility)

moyen *nm* **(a)** mean **(b)** medium; **moyens de transmission** = transmission media; **moyens de communication interactifs** = interactive media

moyen, -enne *adj* average *ou* mean *ou* medium; **temps d'accès moyen** = average access time; **délai moyen** = average delay; **durée moyenne de bon fonctionnement** = mean time to failure (MTF); **intégration à moyenne échelle** = medium scale integration (MSI); *(de gestion de mémoire, pour processeurs Intel 8086)* **modèle moyen** = medium model; **objectif de focale moyenne** = medium lens; **un système informatique de taille moyenne** = a medium-sized computer system; **après 9h30, le temps d'attente moyen est beaucoup plus long lorsque chacun tente de se loger sur le système pour travailler** = the average delay increases at nine-thirty when everyone tries to log-in; **vitesse moyenne** = medium speed

moyenne *nf* average *ou* mean; **moyenne de temps de bon fonctionnement entre les défaillances (MTBF)** = mean time between failures (MTBF); **moyenne de temps requis pour réparation** = mean time to repair; **moyenne pondérée** = weighted average; **atteindre une moyenne (de)** *ou* **faire en moyenne** = to average (out); **en moyenne** = on an average; **nous vendons en moyenne cinq ordinateurs par jour** = we sell on an average, five computers a day; **cela fait en moyenne 120 points par pouce** *ou* **une moyenne de 120 points par pouce** = it averages out at 120 dpi

moyeu *nm* hub

MPC = MULTIMEDIA PC; *voir* MULTIMEDIA

MRT = MULTIPLEXAGE PAR REPARTITION DANS LE TEMPS

ms = MILLISECONDE

MS-DOS ™ *(système d'exploitation MS-DOS)* Microsoft Disk Operating System (Microsoft DOS ™ *ou* MS-DOS ™); *voir aussi* DOS

MS-Windows = MICROSOFT WINDOWS; *voir aussi* Windows

MSX *(pour ordinateurs individuels)* **norme** *ou* **standard MSX** = MSX

MTBF = MEAN TIME BETWEEN FAILURES; *voir* MOYENNE

muet, -ette *adj* dumb; *(en faux texte ou en bolo-bolo)* **en texte muet** = greeked

multi- *préfixe* multi-

◊ **multi-accès** *adj* **système multi-accès** = multi-access system

◊ **multi-adresse** *adj* **code multi-adresse** = multiple address code; **instruction multi-adresse** = multi-address instruction

◊ **multibus** *adj* **système multibus** = multi-bus system

◊ **multicarte** *adj* **ordinateur multicarte** = multi-board computer

◊ **multicible** *adj* **transmission multicible** = multicasting

◊ **multiclé** *adj* **méthode d'accès séquentiel indexé multiclé** = keyed sequential access method (KSAM)

◊ **multicolore** *adj* multicolour

◊ **multicouche** *adj* multilayer

◊ **multidimensionnel, -elle** *adj* multidimensionnel; **langage multidimensionnel** = multidimensional language; **tableau multidimensionnel** = multidimensional array

◊ **multidisque** *adj* multi-disk; **lecteur multidisque** = multi-disk reader; **option multidisque** = multi-disk option

◊ **multifenêtrage** *nm* multi-windowing

◊ **multifenêtre** *adj* **logiciel (de traitement de texte) multifenêtre** = multi-window editor

MultiFinder ™ *(version Apple-Macintosh)* MultiFinder ™

multiflux *nm&adj* **architecture multiflux d'instruction-monoflux de données** = multiple instruction stream - single data stream (MISD); **architecture multiflux d'instruction-multiflux de données** = multiple instruction stream - multiple data stream (MIMD)

◊ **multifonction** *adj* multifunction; **multifonctionnel; carte d'extension multifonction** = multifunction card; **un module d'interface analogique multifonction comprend un convertisseur analogique-numérique et un convertisseur numérique-analogique** = a multifunction analog interface module includes analog to digital and digital to analog converters; **poste de travail multifonction** = multifunction workstation; **programme multifonction** = general purpose program; **scanner multifonction** = multifunctional scanner

◊ **multifrappe** *adj* **ruban multifrappe** = multi-strike printer ribbon

◊ **multifréquence** *nf&adj* multifrequency; **(appel à) tonalité multifréquence DTMF** = dual tone multifrequency (DTMF)

◊ **multi-instruction** *adj* **ligne multi-instruction** = multi-statement line

◊ **multiligne** *adj* *(système de transmission)* multi-line; **système multiligne** = multilink system

◊ **multimédia** *nm&adj* multimedia; **architecture étendue multimédia (CD-ROM/XA)** = CD-ROM Extended Architecture *ou* CD-ROM/XA; **message multimédia** = multimedia mail; **PC multimédia** = multimedia PC (MPC)

◊ **multimètre** *nm* multimeter; **multimètre analogique** = analog multimeter (AMM); **multimètre numérique** = digital multimeter (DMM)

◊ **multimode** *adj* multimode; **fibre optique multimode** = multimode fibre

les noeuds sont réunis 2 à 2 par deux fibres optiques multimodes. La distance maximale entre noeuds est de 2000m
Opto électronique

multiniveau *adj* multilevel; **langage multiniveau** = multidimensional language

◊ **multinorme** *nm&adj* multistandard; **unité multinorme** = a multistandard unit

◊ **multipage** *adj* système multipage = multiple base page

◊ **multipaquet** *adj* signal **multipaquet** = multiburst signal

◊ **multiphase** *adj* programme **multiphase** = multiphase program

multiple *adj* multiple; **(à) accès multiple** = multiple access; **système à accès multiple** = multi-access system; **accès multiple asservi à la demande** = demand assigned multiple access (DAMA); **accès multiple par division dans le temps** = time division multiple access; **architecture à bus multiples** = multiple bus architecture; **système à bus multiples** = multi-bus system; **(en) multiple précision** = multiprecision *ou* multiple precision; **(à) couches multiples** = multilayer; **élément logique multiple** = compound logical element; **programme à usage multiple** = general purpose program

multiplet *nm* n-bit byte

multiplex *nm&adj* multiplex; **système multiplex** = carrier system

◊ **multiplexage** *nm* multiplexing *ou* dataplex; **multiplexage asservi à la demande** = demand multiplexing; **multiplexage dynamique** = dynamic multiplexing; **multiplexage hétérogène** = heterogeneous multiplexing; **multiplexage homogène** = homogeneous multiplexing; **multiplexage optique** = optical multiplexing; **multiplexage en fréquence (FDM)** = frequency division multiplexing (FDM); **le multiplexage en fréquence permet de transférer 100 appels téléphoniques sur un seul câble** = using FDM we can transmit 100 telephone calls along one main cable; **multiplexage temporel** *ou* **multiplexage (par répartition) dans le temps (MRT)** = time division multiplexing (TDM); **multiplexage temporel statistique** *ou* **en fonction des appels** = statistical time division multiplexing (STDM)

◊ **multiplexé, -ée** *adj* multiplexed; **accès temporel multiplexé** = time division multiple access; **bus multiplexé** = multiplexed bus

◊ **multiplexeur** *nm* multiplexor (MUX); **un multiplexeur 4/1 reçoit sur 4 canaux et émet sur un seul** = a 4 to 1 multiplexor combines four inputs into a single output; **multiplexeur C-MAC** = C-MAC

il est à remarquer que le multiplexage de 12 canaux vidéo sur une seule fibre est une première avec la qualité de transmission obtenue
Opto électronique

multiplicande *nm* multiplicand

◊ **multiplicateur** *nm* multiplier

◊ **multiplication** *nf* multiplication; **le résultat de la multiplication de 5 par 3 est 15** = the result of the multiplication of 5 and 3 equals 15; **signe de la multiplication (x)** = multiplication sign

◊ **multiplié, -ée** *adj* multiplied; **multiplié par dix** = by a factor of ten; multiplied by ten

◊ **multiplier** *vtr* to multiply; **les erreurs n'ont cessé de se multiplier lorsque j'ai appuyé sur la mauvaise touche** = there was an avalanche of errors after I pressed the wrong key

multipoint *adj* multipoint; **circuit multipoint** = multidrop circuit

◊ **multiposte** *nm&adj* système **multiposte** = multi-terminal system *ou* multi-user system; **on peut exécuter le programme sur un ordinateur indépendant ou un système multiposte** = the program runs on a standalone machine or a multi-user system

l'utilisation des bases de données en multiposte s'est par ailleurs considérablement améliorée grâce au regroupement des fichiers sur le disque: un fichier contenant les données et un second contenant la structure du programme
L'Ordinateur Individuel

multiprocesseur *nm&adj* multiprocessor; **entrelacement (de traitement) par multiprocesseur** = multiprocessor interleaving; **système multiprocesseur** = multiprocessing system

◊ **multiprogrammation** *nf* multi-programming *ou* concurrent programming *ou* multiprocessor interleaving

◊ **multiprogramme** *nm&adj* **système d'exploitation multiprogramme** = concurrent operating system

◊ **multistandard** *nm&adj* *inv* **moniteur multistandard** *ou* **multisync** = multi-scan *ou* multi-sync monitor; **unité multistandard** = a multistandard unit

◊ **multitâche** *adj* multitasking *ou* multi-tasking; **multitâche en temps réel** = real-time multitasking; **environnement multitâche** = multitasking environment; **c'est un système multi-utilisateur et multitâche** = the system is multi-user and multi-tasking; **traitement multitâche en temps réel** = real-time multitasking

les participants auront cinq jours pour apprendre à utiliser un ordinateur dans un environnement multitâche et multi-utilisateur
Informatique & Bureautique

multitraitement *nm* multiprocessing; concurrent processing; **trois transordinateurs procurent une capacité de multitraitement suffisante pour tout le département** = three transputers provide concurrent processing capabilities for the entire department

multi-utilisateur *nm&adj* **mode multi-utilisateur** = free running mode; **système multi-utilisateur** = multi-user system *ou* shared resources system; **c'est un système multi-utilisateur et multitâche** = the system is multi-user and multi-tasking

◊ **multivibrateur** *nm* multivibrator; **multivibrateur astable** = astable multivibrator;

multivibrateur bistable = bistable circuit *ou* multivibrator

◊ **multivoie** *adj (protocole d'accès au réseau)* multichannel

musique *nf* music; **instrument de musique** = musical instrument; **interface numérisée pour instruments de musique (interface MIDI)** = musical instrument digital interface (MIDI)

myriamétrique *adj* **onde myriamétrique** = very low frequency (VLF) *ou* extremely low frequency (ELF)

Nn

n = NANO-

N *(code de détection d'erreur)* **code N dont M** = M out of N code

N matériau semi-conducteur de type N = n-type material *ou* N-type material *ou* n-type semiconductor; **semi-conducteur MOS à canal (de type) N** = n-channel metal oxide semiconductor

n instruction à n adresse(s) plus une = n-plus-one address instruction; **logique à n niveau(x)** = n-level logic; **mémoire tampon (de clavier) chronologique à n positions** = n-key rollover

NACK *ou* **NAK** = NEGATIVE ACKNOWLEDGE *ou* NEGATIVE ACKNOWLEDGEMENT; *voir* NEGATIF

NAND = NOT-AND **circuit NAND** = NAND gate; **fonction NAND** = NAND function *ou* NOT-AND; **porte NAND** = NAND gate; *voir aussi* NON-ET

nano- (n) *préfixe* nano- (n)

◊ **nanomètre** *nm* nanometre (nm)

◊ **nanoseconde (ns)** *nf* nanosecond (ns); **circuit (électronique** *ou* **logique) à délai de réponse de l'ordre de la nanoseconde** = nanocircuit *ou* nanosecond circuit

le temps de base d'un cycle est passé de 18,5 nanosecondes à 17,2 et la mémoire d'arrière plan passe de 256Mo à 1Go
L'Information professionnelle

natif, -ive *adj* native; **compilateur natif** = native compiler; **format natif** = native format; **format de fichier natif** = native file format; **langage natif** *ou* **de constructeur** = native language

national, -e *adj* national; **la presse nationale** = the national press

naturel, -elle *adj* natural; **décimal codé binaire naturel** = natural binary coded decimal (NBCD); **langage naturel** = natural language; **le système expert peut être programmé en langage naturel** = the expert system can be programmed in a natural language

navigation *nf* **navigation sur Internet** = surfing the Internet *ou* surfing the net; netsurfing

◊ **naviguer** *vi* **naviguer sur Internet** = to surf the Internet *ou* to surf the net

Quarterdeck, réputé pour ses utilitaires propose ici une trousse d'outils pour naviguer sur Internet
l'Ordinateur Individuel

NCR = NO CARBON REQUIRED **papier NCR** = NCR paper

NDIS *(norme d'interface gestionnaire de réseaux)* **norme NDIS** = Network Driver Interface Specification (NDIS)

NEA = NUMEROTATION EUROPEENNE DES ARTICLES

nécessaire *adj* necessary; **la quantité de mémoire nécessaire varie suivant le logiciel utilisé** = memory requirements depend on the application software in use

négatif *nm (film)* negative; **négatif contact** = contact negative; **négatifs (de séparation des) couleurs** = colour separations

négatif, -ive *adj* negative; **accusé de réception négatif (NACK)** = negative acknowledge (NAK *ou* NACK); **affecter (un nombre) d'un signe négatif** = to negate (a number); **dépassement** *ou* **débordement négatif** = underflow; **nombre négatif** = negative number; **rétroaction négative** = negative feedback; **la valeur négative de 23,4 est −23,4** = if you negate 23.4 the result is −23.4

◊ **négation** *nf (fonction logique)* negation *ou* denial; **négation connexe** = joint denial

◊ **négativement** *adv* **qualifier négativement** = to negate

neige *nf (distorsion de l'image de télévision)* **(effet de) neige (sur l'écran)** = snow

net, nette *adj* **(a)** *(déductions faites)* **poids net** = net weight **(b)** *(clair)* **un papier de qualité supérieure donnera des caractères plus nets** = top quality paper will eliminate fuzzy characters

NetBIOS *(système de base pour gérer les entrées et sorties de réseau)* Network Basic Input Output System (NetBIOS); **ce logiciel utilise les appels NetBios pour gérer le partage des fichiers** = this software uses NetBIOS calls to manage file sharing

netteté *nf* **en tournant le bouton de mise au point l'image perd de sa netteté** = the image becomes blurred when you turn the focus knob

nettoyage *nm* **(a)** cleaning; **disquette de nettoyage (des têtes)** = head cleaning disk; **il faut passer la disquette de nettoyage une fois par semaine** = use a head cleaning disk every week; **vous aurez des erreurs d'écriture si vous ne vous servez pas régulièrement de votre disquette de nettoyage** = write errors will occur if you do not use a head cleaning kit regularly; **kit de nettoyage**

pour écran = screen cleaning kit **(b)** *(faire disparaître les erreurs)* cleaning *ou* cleanup; **nettoyage de données** = data cleaning; **nettoyage de fichier** = file cleanup; **nettoyage de mémoire** = garbage collection

◊ **nettoyer** *vtr* **(a)** to clean **(b)** *(faire disparaître le texte)* **nettoyer l'écran** = to zap; **nettoyer un dispositif programmable** = to zero a device

neuf *nm&adj num* nine; **complément à neuf** = nine's complement

neural, -e *adj* **réseau neural** = neural network

neuro-réseau *nm* neural network

neutre *adj* neutral; *(séparant deux fichiers)* **espace neutre** = file gap; **transmission neutre** = neutral transmission

NI *(logique)* NOR; **fonction NI** = neither-nor function *ou* NOR function; **opération NI** = joint denial; **porte** *ou* **circuit NI** = NOR gate; **NI exclusif** = exclusive NOR (EXNOR); **porte** *ou* **circuit NI exclusif** = exclusive NOR gate *ou* EXNOR gate

niveau *nm* **(a)** *(hauteur)* level; **vérifier le niveau** = to gauge the level (of something); **au même niveau** *ou* **de niveau** = flush; **la couverture est rognée de niveau avec les pages** = the cover is trimmed flush with the pages **(b)** **niveau de production** = production level; **niveau maximum de production** = peak output; **atteindre un niveau maximum** = to peak; **la tension a atteint le niveau maximum de 1200 volts** = the power peaked at 1,200 volts; **niveau de qualité d'un service téléphonique** = grade of service **(c)** **niveau d'adressage** = addressing level; **niveau de bruit d'un circuit** = circuit noise level; **niveau cible** = target level; **niveau de complexité** = complexity measure; **niveau de confiance** = confidence level; **niveau de données** = data level; **niveau d'imbrication (de boucles)** = nesting level; **niveau d'interruption** = interrupt level; **niveau logique** = logic level; **niveaux de luminosité** = brightness range; **niveau de pression acoustique** = sound pressure level (SPL); **niveau de référence** = reference level; **niveau d'un signal** = signal level; **perte de niveau (d'un signal)** = drop out; **niveau de transmission (d'une ligne)** = line level; **adresse à un niveau** = one-level address; **adresse de premier niveau** = first-level address; **code à un niveau** = direct code *ou* one-level code *ou* specific code; **mémoire à un niveau** = one-level store; **à plusieurs niveaux** *ou* **multiniveau** = multilevel; **langage de bas niveau** = low-level language (LLL); **langage de haut niveau** = high-level language (HLL); **langage de programmation de haut niveau** = high-level (programming) language (HLL) *ou* high-order language; **on demande aux programmeurs une connaissance des langages de haut niveau, plus spécialement PASCAL** = programmers should have a knowledge of high-level languages, particularly PASCAL; **sous-programme à deux niveaux** = two-level subroutine **(d)** *(saturation)* **niveau de blanc** = white level; **niveaux de gris** = (i) grey scale, *US* gray scale; (ii) shades of grey, *US* shades of gray; **niveau de noir** = black level

NMOS *(semi-conducteur)* N-channel Metal Oxide Semiconductor (NMOS); *voir aussi* N

nocturne *adj* nocturnal; **caméra de vision nocturne** = infrared sights

noeud *nm* node; **une arborescence est formée de branches reliées les unes aux autres par des points de liaison ou noeuds** = a tree is made of branches that connect together at nodes; **ce réseau est relié par fibres optiques avec des noeuds pouvant être positionnés jusqu'à un kilomètre les uns des autres** = this network has fibre optic connection with nodes up to one kilometre apart; *(d'un réseau FDDI)* **noeud d'accès au réseau** = concentrator

noir *nm* black; **noir et blanc** = black and white *ou* monochrome; **écran (en) noir et blanc** = black and white monitor *ou* monochrome monitor; **photo en noir et blanc** = black and white photograph; **affichage noir sur blanc** = positive display; **imprimante à définition des noirs** = black writer; **niveau de noir** = black level

◊ **noir, -e** *adj* black; **boîte noire** = black box; **chambre noire** = darkroom; **courant noir** = dark current; **tableau noir** = blackboard; **tableau noir électronique** = electronic blackboard

nom *nm* **(a)** name; **nom de chaîne** = string name; **nom d'un fichier** = file name *ou* filename; **l'extension SYS ajoutée au nom du fichier indique qu'il s'agit d'un fichier système** = the filename extension SYS indicates that this is a system file; **changer le nom (d'un fichier)** = to rename (a file); **extension du nom d'un fichier** = filename extension; **longueur du nom d'un fichier** = length of filename; **nom d'un programme** = program name; **nom de variable** = variable name **(b)** title; **nom sur une disquette** = title of disk **(c)** *(de l'éditeur ou de l'imprimeur)* imprint

nombre *nm* **(a)** *(math)* number; **nombre aléatoire** *ou* **choisi au hasard** = random number; **nombre en base octale** = octal digit; **nombre binaire** = binary number *ou* bit; **(ensemble des) nombres complets** = complementation; **nombre entier** = integer; **nombre entier en double précision** = double-precision integer; *(nombre représenté par plusieurs octets de données)* **nombre entier long** = long integer *ou* integer represented by several bytes of data; **BASIC pour nombres entiers** = integer BASIC; **nombre négatif** = negative number; **nombres à précision finie** = finite-precision numbers; **nombre premier** = prime; **sept est un nombre premier** = the number seven is a prime; **nombre rationnel** = rational number; **nombre réel** = real number **(b)** quantity *ou* number; **nombre de cycles** = cycle count; **nombre de frappes** = keystroke count; **nombre de mots (contenus dans un fichier** *ou* **un texte)** = word count; **nombre maximum d'utilisateurs** = maximum number of users; **nombre total de pages (d'un document)** = extent (of a document); **un petit nombre de disquettes piratées de ce programme se sont infiltrées à l'importation** = a small quantity of illegal copies of the program have been imported; **la société fait une remise sur les achats en nombre** = the company offers a discount for quantity purchases

nomenclature *nf* nomenclature *ou* list; **nomenclature des composants** = component list

nominal, -e *adj* **débit nominal** = rated throughput

nomographe *nm* nomogram *ou* nomograph

NON *(logique)* NOT; **fonction NON** = NOT function *ou* negation; **porte** *ou* **circuit NON** = NOT gate; *voir aussi* NON-ET, NON-OU

non- *préfixe* non- *ou* un-

◊ **non-aligné, -ée** *adj* nonaligned

◊ **non-connecté, -ée** *adj* (i) unconnected; (ii) off-line

◊ **non-dédié, -ée** *adj* **serveur non-dédié** = non-dedicated server

◊ **non-équivalence** *nf* symmetric difference

NON-ET *(logique)* NAND; **fonction NON-ET** *ou* **opération** NON-ET = NAND function *ou* NOT-AND *ou* alternative denial *ou* dispersion; **porte** *ou* **circuit NON-ET** = NAND gate

non-linéaire *adj* nonlinear

NON-OU *(logique)* **fonction NON-OU** = neither-nor function *ou* NOR function; **opération** NON-OU = joint denial; **porte** *ou* **circuit** NON-OU = NOR gate; *voir aussi* NI

non-remise *nf* **non-remise à zéro** = non return to zero (NRZ)

◊ **non-retour** *nm* **non-retour à zéro** = non return to zero (NRZ)

◊ **non-système** *nm&adj* **disquette non-système** = non-system disk

◊ **non-volatile** *adj* non-volatile; **mémoire non-volatile** = non-volatile memory *ou* non-volatile store *ou* storage; **la mémoire à bulles est une mémoire non-volatile** = bubble memory is a non-volatile storage; **une bande magnétique constitue une mémoire non-volatile** = magnetic tape provides non-volatile memory

normal, -e *adj* **(a)** normal *ou* standard; **format normal** = normal format; **forme normale** = normal form; **fourchette** *ou* **gamme** *ou* **plage normale** = normal range; **la procédure normale préconise une sauvegarde de tout le travail en fin de journée** = the normal procedure is for backup copies to be made at the end of each day's work **(b) en notation normale on écrit: (x-y) + z, en notation suffixée on écrit: xy- z+** = normal notation: (x-y) + z, but using postfix notation: xy - z + **(c) il n'est pas normal que deux lecteurs de disquettes tombent en panne l'un après l'autre** = it's abnormal for two consecutive disk drives to break down

◊ **normalisation** *nf* **(a)** *(de données)* normalization; **routine de normalisation** = normalization routine **(b)** standardization; **Comité National de Normalisation de la Télévision** = National Television Standards Committee (NTSC); **organisme international de normalisation ISO** = International Standards Organization (ISO)

> bénificiant d'un numéro et d'un protocole de normalisation de l'ISO (International Standards Organization), il est déjà utilisé par les organisations internationales, certaines administrations et quelques grandes entreprises
> *Informatique & Bureautique (Suisse)*

normalisé, -ée *adj* **(a)** *(d'un nombre à virgule flottante)* **forme normalisée** = normalized form **(b)** standardized; **le contrôle normalisé des voies de transmission** = the standardized control of transmission links; **les protocoles (de transmissions) normalisés** = protocol standards

◊ **normaliser** *vtr* to normalize *ou* to standardize; **toutes les nouvelles données sont normalisées à dix positions décimales** = all the new data has been normalized to 10 decimal places

norme *nf* standard; **travailler suivant des normes établies** = to work to standard specifications; **(qui est) conforme aux normes** = up to standard; **norme CEPT** = CEPT standard; **norme de cryptage de données** = data encryption standard (DES); **interface aux normes EIA** = EIA interface *ou* electronic industry association interface (EIA); **normes pour modems** = modem standards; **norme NDIS** *ou* **norme d'interface gestionnaire de réseaux** = network driver interface specification (NDIS); **normes NTSC** = NTSC standards; **normes de production** = standards of quality; production standards; **normes de programmation** = programming standards; **normes de qualité** = quality standards; production standards; **ce lot de disquettes ne répond pas aux normes** = this batch of disks is not up to standard; **nous pouvons utiliser votre présentation multimédia pour la publicité à condition qu'elle soit conforme aux normes télévision** = we can use your multimedia presentation as the advert on TV if it's of broadcast quality; **normes vidéo** = video standards; **convertisseur de normes** = standards converter

NOS *(système d'exploitation de réseau)* Network Operating System (NOS)

notation *nf* notation; **notation infixée** = infix notation; **notation polonaise inversée** *ou* **notation suffixée** = reverse Polish notation (RPN) *ou* postfix notation *ou* suffix notation; **alors que la notation conventionnelle s'écrit: (x-y) + z, la notation polonaise inversée s'écrit: xy - z+** = normal notation: (x-y) + z, but using RPN: xy - z+; **notation préfixée** *ou* **notation polonaise préfixée** = prefix notation; **notation normale: (x-y) + z, notation polonaise préfixée: - xy + z** = normal notation: (x-y) + z, but using prefix notation: - xy + z; *(notation polonaise inversée)* **notation suffixée** = postfix notation *ou* suffix notation; **notation à virgule fixe** = fixed-point notation; *voir aussi* NUMERATION, BASE

note *nf* comment *ou* note; **note en bas de page** = footnote; **notes marginales** = cut-in notes

notice *nf* **(a)** **notice bibliographique** = bibliographical information **(b)** **notice d'utilisation** = *(d'un produit)* directions for use; *(d'un appareil)* operational information *ou* documentation; **l'excellente notice d'utilisation facilitait l'emploi du progiciel** = using the package was easy with the excellent user documentation

notifié, -ée *adj* **erreur notifiée** = detected error

nouveau, nouvelle *adj* new; **ils ont installé un nouveau système informatique** *ou* **un nouvel ordinateur** = they have installed a new computer system; *(commande de lancement)* **nouvelle tâche** = new; **nouvelle technologie** *ou* **techniques nouvelles** = new technology; **nouvelle version d'un fichier** = file update

◊ **nouvelle** *nf* piece of news; **nouvelles** = news

Novell ™ *(importante société de logiciels)* Novell ™

noyau *nm (du système d'exploitation)* kernel; **noyau de ferrite** = ferrite core

npn *ou* **NPN** **transistor (de type) npn** = npn transistor; **transistor à jonction npn** = bipolar (junction) transistor (BJT)

le constructeur prétend avoir réalisé un circuit ECL avec des transistors bipolaires de type PNP dont le temps de communication est de 35 picosecondes, soit six fois mieux que le record précédent (qui remonte à 1986) et aussi bien que si on utilisait des transistors de type NPN
01 Informatique

ns = NANOSECONDE

NTSC *(normes américaines de télévision et vidéo)* **normes NTSC** = NTSC standards; *voir aussi* NORMALISATION

nu, nue *adj (sans composants)* **carte nue** = unpopulated card; **vous pouvez acheter une carte RAM nue et installer vos propres plaquettes** = you can buy an unpopulated RAM card and fit your own RAM chips; **machine nue** *ou* **processeur nu** = clean machine

nuance *nf* shade *ou* nuance *ou* tone; **le progiciel graphique offre plusieurs nuances de bleu** = the graphics package can give several tones of blue

◊ **nuancier** *nm* **nuancier Pantone** = Pantone Matching System (PMS)

NuBus ™ *(extension de bus à 96 connecteurs utilisé par les Macintosh de Apple)* NuBus ™

nuire (à) *vi* to interfere with something

nul, nulle *adj* null; **caractère nul** = null character *ou* idle character; **chaîne de caractères terminée par un caractère nul** = null terminated string; **jeu** *ou* **ensemble de caractères nuls** = empty *ou* null set; **instruction nulle** = blank *ou* dummy *ou* null instruction *ou* non-operable instruction *ou* no-op instruction; *(circuit ou câble de liaison directe)* **null modem** = null modem

numéral, -ale *adj* numeric; **lettre numérale** = numeric character

◊ **numération** *nf* number representation; notation; **numération à base** = radix notation; **numération binaire** *ou* **en base binaire** = binary notation; **numération décimale** = decimal notation; **numération hexadécimale** = hex *ou* hexadecimal notation; **numération octale** = octal notation

numérique *adj* **(a)** *(se rapportant à un nombre)* numeric *ou* numerical; **analyse numérique** = numerical analysis; **caractère (à valeur) numérique** = numeric character; **clavier numérique** = numeric keypad *ou* numeric pad *ou* numerical pad; **code numérique d'une touche** = key number; **commande** *ou* **contrôle numérique** = numerical control (NC) *ou* computer numerical control (CNC); **indicatif numérique** = index number; **opérande numérique** = numeric operand; **opérations numériques (en masse) ultra-rapides** = number crunching; **pavé numérique** = numeric keypad *ou* numeric pad *ou* numerical keypad; **utilisez le pavé numérique pour saisir les chiffres** = you can use the numeric keypad to enter the figures; **perforation numérique** = numeric punch; **tableau numérique** = numeric array **(b)** *(représenté par un nombre)* digital; **affichage numérique** = digital readout; **calculateur** *ou* **ordinateur numérique** = (electronic) digital computer; **caméra numérique** = digital camera; **circuit numérique** = digital circuit; **circuiterie numérique commutée** = circuit-switched digital circuitry; **commande numérique directe** = direct digital control (DDC); **(système de) commutation numérique** = digital switching; **données numériques** = digital data; **lecture optique de données numériques** = digital optical reading (DOR); **écran numérique; affichage numérique** = digital display; **enregistrement numérique** = digital recording; **horloge numérique** = digital clock; *(qui affiche l'heure sur l'écran)* time display; **logique numérique** = digital logic; **multimètre numérique** = digital multimeter (DMM); **ordinateur numérique** = digital computer; **représentation numérique** = digital representation; **réseau numérique à intégration de services (RNIS)** = integrated services digital network (ISDN); **réseau numérique intégré (RNI)** = integrated digital network; **accès au réseau numérique intégré** = integrated digital access (IDA); **signal numérique** = digital signal; **signature numérique** = digital signature; **sortie numérique** = digital output; **sous forme numérique** = digitally; **l'appareil produit une image à partir de données enregistrées sous forme numérique** = the machine takes digitally recorded data and generates an image; **système numérique** = digital system; **système de transmission numérique** = digital transmission system; **traceur**

numérique = digital plotter; **transmission de signaux numériques** = digital signalling

numérique-analogique *adj* **convertisseur numérique-analogique** = digital to analog converter *ou* D to A converter *ou* DAC *ou* d/a converter; **l'ordinateur émet un signal vocal via un convertisseur numérique-analogique** = speech is output from the computer via a D/A converter; **le convertisseur numérique-analogique du port de sortie contrôle l'ordinateur analogique** = the D/A converter on the output port controls the analog machine

◊ **numériquement** *adv* digitally

◊ **numérisation** *nf* digitization; **numérisation d'une onde** = waveform digitization; **circuit de numérisation des signaux** = digital signal processing (DSP)

◊ **numérisé, -ée** *adj* digitized *ou* digital; **données numérisées** = digital data; **photographie numérisée** = digitized photograph; *(système DV-I)* **vidéo numérisée interactive** = digital video interactive (DV-I); **voix numérisée** = digital speech

◊ **numériser** *vtr* to digitize; **il nous est possible de numériser votre signature pour qu'elle puisse être imprimée par n'importe quelle imprimante laser** = we can digitize your signature to allow it to be printed with any laser printer; **tablette à numériser** = data tablet *ou* digitizing pad *ou* graphics pad *ou* tablet; *(pour saisie de l'écriture manuelle)* writing pad

◊ **numériseur** *nm* digitizer

numéro *nm* (a) number; **numéro de code confidentiel** = personal identification number (PIN); **numéro de code personnel** *ou* **de code d'identification** = identity number; **n'oublie pas d'entrer ton numéro de code personnel** = don't forget to log in your identity number; **chaque pièce**

d'équipement possède un numéro de fabrication = each piece of hardware has a production number; **le numéro de fabrication est gravé de façon permanente sur le panneau arrière du boîtier de l'ordinateur** = the production number is permanently engraved on the back of the computer casing; **numéro d'identification de fichier (actif)** = handle; **numéro d'instruction** = statement number; **numéro de ligne d'un programme** = program line number; **numéro de lot** = batch number; **numéro de référence** *ou* **d'entrée** = accession number; **numéro de stock** = stock code; **numéro de suite d'une tâche dans la file d'attente** = job number; **numéro de téléphone** = phone number *ou* telephone number; **composer un numéro (de téléphone)** = to dial a number; **le numéro de téléphone figure sur le papier à en-tête de la société** = the phone number is on the company notepaper; **pouvez-vous me donner votre numéro de téléphone?** = can you give me your telephone number? (b) *(d'un journal ou d'une revue)* copy; **numéro déjà paru** *ou* **vieux numéro** = back number; **j'ai toujours le numéro du 'Figaro' d'hier** = I kept yesterday's copy of 'Le Figaro'

> il inscrira également le numéro du central vidéotex de son arrondissement, son numéro personnel d'identification et son mot de passe
> *Informatique & Bureautique (Suisse)*

numérotation *nf* (a) numbering; **numérotation européenne des articles (NEA)** = European Article Number (EAN); **numérotation des messages** = message numbering; **refaire la numérotation** = to renumber (b) *(d'appel)* dialling; **système de numérotation automatique** = auto-dial; **numérotation sur clavier** = pushbutton dialling; **numérotation sur clavier tonal** = tone dialling

◊ **numéroter** *vtr* to number; **les pages de ce manuel sont numérotées de 1 à 395** = the pages of the manual are numbered 1 to 395

Oo

o = OCTET

obéir *vi* obéir à = to conform to *ou* to obey to

objectif *nm* **(a)** objective *ou* target **(b)** *(lentille)* lens; **objectif à focale variable** = zoom lens; **objectif grand-angle** = wide angle lens; **objectif standard** *ou* **de focale moyenne** = medium lens; **ouverture d'objectif** = lens stop; **vitesse d'ouverture d'un objectif** = lens speed

> des chercheurs de l'Université d'Edimbourg viennent de faire tenir une caméra vidéo sur une surface de 8 millimètres carrés, avec des objectifs de la taille d'une tête d'épingle
> *Le Point*

objet *nm* object; **code objet** = object code; **phase (en) code objet** = run phase *ou* target phase; **fichier objet** = object file; **jeu (de cartes) objet** = object deck; **langage objet** = object language *ou* target language; **pour ce qui est de ce programme en PASCAL, le langage machine constitue le langage objet** = the target language for this PASCAL program is machine code; **programme objet** = object program *ou* target program; **architecture orientée vers l'objet** *ou* **adaptée à l'objet** = object architecture *ou* object-orientated architecture; *(sous Windows de Microsoft)* **(procédé de) liaison et incorporation d'objets** *ou* **procédé OLE** = object linking and embedding (OLE)

obligatoire *adj* **(a)** compulsory *ou* forced; **saut de page obligatoire** = forced page break; **trait d'union obligatoire** = hard hyphen *ou* required hyphen **(b)** **interruption obligatoire** = nonmaskable interrupt (NMI)

oblique *adj* oblique; *(d'un caractère)* character skew; **trait oblique** = slash *ou* oblique stroke; **zéro barré d'un trait oblique** = slashed zero

◊ **obliquité** *nf* skew

obtenir *vtr* to obtain; **le filtrage permet d'obtenir un signal très clair** = a clear signal is obtained after filtering; **ce que vous voyez est ce que vous obtenez** = What-You-See-Is-What-You-Get (WYSIWYG); **ce que vous voyez est tout ce que vous obtenez** = What-You-See-Is-All-You-Get (WYSIAYG)

obturateur *nm* shutter

OCCAM *(langage de programmation)* OCCAM

occasion *nf* **d'occasion** = used; **(équipement) d'occasion** = second-user *ou* second-hand (equipment)

occupation *nf* **temps d'occupation de la ligne** = holding time

◊ **occupé, -ée** *adj (signal ou tonalité)* busy; **tonalité 'occupé'** = line busy tone *ou* engaged tone; **la ligne est occupée** = the line is busy; **quand le signal 'occupé' s'éteint, l'imprimante peut de nouveau accepter des données** = when the busy line goes low, the printer will accept more data

octal, -e *adj* octal; **base octale** *ou* **base 8** = base 8; **nombre en base octale** = octal digit; **numération octale** = octal notation

octave *nf* octave

octet (o) *nm* byte (B); *(de caractère)* character byte; **octet de placement** = postbyte; **octets par pouce** = bytes-per-inch; **octets par seconde (Bps)** = bytes per second (Bps); **adresses d'octets** = byte addresses; **giga-octet (Go)** = gigabyte *ou* Gbyte; **groupe d'octets** = gulp; **manipulation d'octets** = byte manipulation; **mode octet** = byte mode; **protocole (de communication) à niveau octet** = byte-orientated protocol; **transmission d'octets en série** = byte serial transmission *ou* mode

> tout repose sur un bus 64 bits bénéficiant d'un débit de 150 millions d'octets par seconde
> *L'Information professionnelle*

oculaire **1** *nm (d'un appareil photo)* eyepiece **2** *adj* of the eye; **fatigue oculaire** = eye-strain

ODI *(interface)* Open Datalink Interface (ODI)

OEM = ORIGINAL EQUIPMENT MANUFACTURER **un OEM fournit l'unité de disques, un autre le moniteur** = one OEM supplies the disk drive, another the monitor; *voir aussi* CONSTRUCTEUR, ENSEMBLIER

oeuvre *nf* **(a)** work; **oeuvre protégée par un copyright** *ou* **dont les droits de reproduction sont réservés** *ou* **oeuvre sous copyright** = work still in copyright **(b)** **ordre de mise en oeuvre des opérateurs (mathématiques)** = operator precedence

off *adv* **voix off** = voice over

off-line *adj* **(a)** *(non connecté)* off-line; **avant de remplacer le papier de l'imprimante, assurez-vous que l'imprimante est off-line** = before changing the paper in the printer, switch it off-line; **traitement off-line** = off-line processing **(b)** *(système)* autonome; *voir aussi* LIGNE

offre *nf (offre promotionnelle)* **l'offre comprend** *ou* **regroupe un PC avec un tableur et une base de données** = the bundle includes a PC with spreadsheet and database applications

offset *nm* offset; **impression (en) offset** = offset printing; **lithographie offset** = offset lithography

Ohm *npr* **loi d'Ohm** = Ohm's Law

◊ **ohm** *nm* ohm; **la valeur de cette résistance est de 100 ohms** = this resistance has a value of 100 ohms

oignon *nm* onion; **architecture en pelure d'oignon** = onion skin architecture; **l'architecture en pelure d'oignon de cet ordinateur consiste en un noyau central, une couche système d'exploitation, une couche langage de bas niveau et enfin une couche programmes utilisateur** = the onion skin architecture of this computer is made up of a kernel at the centre, an operating system, a low-level language and then the user's programs; **langage en pelure d'oignon** = onion skin language

OK *adv (prêt - message d'invitation à taper une instruction)* OK; *(utilisé sous GUI pour confirmer une action)* OK button

OLE *(liaison et incorporation d'objets)* **procédé OLE** = Object Linking and Embedding (OLE)

ombrage *nm (d'un dessin)* shading

◊ **ombre** *nf* **(a)** *(d'un dessin)* shading; *(créée par un corps opaque)* shadow; **durée d'ombre** = sun outage

◊ **ombré, -ée** *adj* **tube ombré** = dark trace tube

omettre *vtr* to skip

omission *nf (de correction d'épreuves)* **signe d'omission** = caret mark *ou* caret sign; *(d'une recherche)* **facteur d'omission** = omission factor

omnidirectionnel, -elle *adj* omnidirectional; **antenne omnidirectionnelle** = omnidirectional aerial; **microphone omnidirectionnel** = omnidirectional microphone

onde *nf* wave *ou* waveform; **onde carrée** = square wave; **onde continue** *ou* **entretenue** = continuous wave; **onde courte** = short wave (SW); **récepteur** *ou* **radio à ondes courtes** = short-wave receiver; **ondes décimétriques** = ultra high frequency (UHF); **onde en dents de scie** = sawtooth waveform; **onde diffusée** = scatter; **onde éclatée progressante** = forward scatter; **onde hectométrique** = medium frequency; **onde kilométrique** = low frequency (LF); **onde métrique** = very high frequency (VHF); **onde millimétrique** = extremely high frequency (EHF); **onde myriamétrique** = very low frequency (VLF) *ou* extremely low frequency (ELF); **onde porteuse** = carrier wave; **onde porteuse de données** = data carrier; **détecteur d'onde porteuse** = data carrier detect (DCD); **télégraphie par onde porteuse** = carrier telegraphy; **onde (radio) réfléchie** = backscatter; **onde sinusoïdale** = sine wave; **onde sonore** = sound wave; **conversion d'une onde en numérique** = waveform digitization; **forme d'onde** = waveform; **guide d'onde** = waveguide; **guide d'ondes circulaire** = circular waveguide; **longueur d'onde** = wavelength; **numérisation d'une onde** = waveform digitization

onduleur *nm* uninterruptable power supply (UPS); **temps de débit d'un onduleur** = holdup

onglet *nm* **(a)** *(de fenêtre sous Windows)* tab *ou* tag **(b)** *(d'une feuille isolée ou d'une illustration)* guard; **montage sur onglet** = guarding

on-line *adj* on-line; **traitement on-line** = on-line processing; *voir aussi* LIGNE

opacité *nf* opacity

◊ **opaque** *adj* opaque; **l'écran étant opaque, il est impossible de voir au travers** = the screen is opaque - you cannot see through it; **projecteur de documents opaques** = episcope *ou* epidiascope

opérande *nm* operand *ou* argument; *(d'une opération ET ou d'une conjonction)* conjunct; **par effet de l'instruction ADD 74, l'opérateur ADD va ajouter l'opérande 74 à l'accumulateur** = in the instruction ADD 74, the operator ADD will add the operand 74 to the accumulator; **opérande alphanumérique** = alphanumeric operand; **opérande immédiat** = immediate operand; **opérande littéral** = literal operand; **opérande numérique** = numeric operand; **champ d'opérande** = address *ou* operand field; **instruction à un opérande** = single operand instruction; **opérateur à un opérande** = monadic (Boolean) operator; **opération à un opérande** = unary operation; **opération booléenne à un opérande** = monadic Boolean operation; **opération booléenne à deux opérandes** = dyadic Boolean operation

opérateur, -trice *n* **(a)** *(personne)* operator; **l'opérateur était assis devant l'écran de son ordinateur** *ou* **à son pupitre** = the operator was sitting at his console; **console** *ou* **pupitre de commande** *ou* **poste de travail d'un opérateur** = operator's console; **opérateur d'ordinateur** = computer operator; **opérateur de saisie** = keyboard operator *ou* keyboarder; **opérateur de télex** = telex operator **(b)** *(d'une multiplication)* operator; **x est l'opérateur de la multiplication** = x is the multiplication operator; **opérateur arithmétique** = arithmetic operator; **opérateur booléen** = Boolean operator; **opérateur central** = centre operator; *(sous Unix)* **opérateur de dérivation** *ou* **de transfert (de données)** = pipe; **opérateur logique** = logical operator; **opérateur monadique** *ou* **à un opérande** = monadic (Boolean) operator; **opérateur relationnel** *ou* **logique** = relational operator *ou* logical operator; **(ordre de) priorité des opérateurs** = operator precedence; **surcharge d'un opérateur** = operator overloading

◊ **opération** *nf* **(a)** *(math)* operation; **opération arithmétique** = arithmetic operation; **opération binaire** = binary operation; **opération booléenne** = Boolean operation; **opération booléenne à deux opérandes** = dyadic Boolean operation; **opération booléenne à un opérande** = monadic Boolean operation; **opération (booléenne) dyadique** = dyadic (Boolean) operation; **opération en virgule flottante** = floating point operation (FLOP); **(nombre d') opérations en virgule flottante par seconde** = FLOPs per second **(b)** *(activité)* operation; **opération de branchement** = jump operation; **opération complémentaire** = complementary operation; **opération complète** = complete operation; **opération en cycle fixe** *ou* **opération synchronisée** = fixed cycle operation; **opération en duplex** = duplex operation; **opération d'identité** = identity operation; **opération invalide** = illegal operation; **opération logique** = logic operation; **opération monadique** = monadic operation; **opération non adressable** = no-address operation; **opération surveillée** = attended operation; **champ d'opération** = operation field; **code d'opération** = command code *ou* operating code *ou* op code *ou* order code; **cycle d'opération** = operation cycle; **cycle complet d'exécution d'une opération** = complete operation; **ordre d'enchaînement des opérations** = operator precedence; **ordre de priorité des opérations** = operation priority; **registre d'opération** = operation register; **registre de code d'opération** = op register; **temps d'exécution d'une opération** = operation time **(c)** *(logique)* **opération d'équivalence** = equivalence function *ou* operation; **opération ET** = AND operation *ou* conjunction; **opération NON-ET** = NAND operation; **opération NON-OU** *ou* **NI** = NOR operation *ou* joint denial; **opération OU** = OR operation *ou* disjunction; **opération OU inclusif** = inclusive OR operation *ou* either-or operation; **opérations numériques ultra-rapides** = number crunching

◊ **operationnel, -elle** *adj* operational; **amplificateur operationnel** = operational amplifier (op amp); **essai** *ou* **test opérationnel** = operation trial

opposé *nm* inverse *ou* opposite; **l'opposé de 1 est 0** = the inverse of 1 is 0; **l'opposé de 23,4 est −23,4** = if you negate 23.4 the result is −23.4

opposition *nf* **faire opposition (à)** = to block; **le directeur du système a fait opposition à sa demande de temps supplémentaire sur l'unité centrale** = the system manager blocked his request for more CPU time

optimal, -e *adj* optimum; **arborescence optimale** = minimal tree; **code optimal** = optimum code

◊ **optimisation** *nf* enhancement *ou* optimization; **compilateur d'optimisation** = optimizing compiler

◊ **optimisé, -ée** *adj* optimized; **code optimisé** = optimized code; **code à temps d'accès optimisé** = minimum access code *ou* minimum delay code *ou* minimum latency coding; **routage optimisé** = minimum weight routing

◊ **optimiser** *vtr* to enhance *ou* to optimize *ou* to upgrade; **ils peuvent optimiser l'imprimante** = they can upgrade the printer; **le nouveau modèle peut être optimisé sans renvoi chez le fournisseur** = the new model has an on-site upgrade facility

◊ **optimiseur** *nm* enhancer; **(programme) optimiseur** = optimizer

optimum *nm&adj* optimum; **code optimum** = optimum code

option *nf* **(a)** option; **les options disponibles sont décrites dans le menu principal** = the options available are described in the main menu; **on trouve habituellement quatre options affichées en haut de l'écran** = there are usually four options along the top of the screen; *(d'un système)* **option**

de configuration = setup option; **option par défaut** *ou* **implicite** *ou* **intrinsèque** *ou* **pré-caractérisée** = default option; **option multidisque** = multi-disk option; *(carte)* **avec toutes les options** = fully-populated (card) **(b)** **article en option** = extra; **la souris et le câble sont en option** = the mouse and cabling are sold as extras

◊ **optionnel, -elle** *adj* optional

optique *adj* optical *ou* optic; **câble** *ou* **liaison à fibres optiques** *ou* **câble optique** = fibre optic cable *ou* connection; **les câbles à fibres optiques permettent de placer les noeuds jusqu'à un kilomètre l'un de l'autre** = fibre optic connections enable nodes up to one kilometre apart to be used; **circuit optique intégré** = integrated optical circuit; **condensateur optique** = condenser lens; **disque optique** = laser disk *ou* optical disk; **diviseur optique** = beam splitter; **fibre optique** = optical fibre; **technologie de la fibre optique** *ou* **de la transmission par fibre optique** = fibre optics; **fibre optique monomode** = monomode fibre; **fibre optique multimode** = multimode fibre; **guide optique** = light guide; **mémoire d'images optiques** = scanner memory; **lecteur optique** = optical scanner; **un lecteur optique utilise un rayon lumineux qui balaye les caractères, les symboles ou les lignes** = an optical reader uses a light beam to scan characters, patterns or lines; **lecteur optique de caractères** = optical character reader (OCR); **lecteur optique de code barres** = bar reader *ou* optical bar code reader *ou* optical wand; **lecteur optique de marques** = optical mark reader (OMR); **lecture optique** = optical reading; **police de caractères reconnaissable par lecture optique** = optical font *ou* OCR font; **lecture optique de données numériques** = digital optical reading (DOR); **liaison optique pour transmission de données** = optical data link; **ligne optique** = line of sight; **mémoire optique** = optical memory *ou* optical storage; **multiplexage optique** = optical multiplexing; **reconnaissance optique de caractères** = optical character recognition (OCR); **reconnaissance optique de marques** *ou* **de signes** *ou* **de symboles** = optical mark recognition (OMR); **souris optique** = optical mouse; **stylo optique** = electronic pen *ou* stylus *ou* wand; light pen *ou* optical wand *ou* bar-code reader; **stylo optique graphique** = graphics light pen; **stockage de données sur support optique** = optical storage

optoélectrique *adj* optoelectrical

optoélectronique **1** *nf* *(science)* optoelectronics **2** *adj* optoelectronic; **système de communication optoélectronique** = optical communications system; **transmission par système optoélectronique** = optical transmission

optomécanique *adj* **souris optomécanique** = optomechanical mouse

optonumérique *adj* **mémoire optonumérique** = photodigital memory

optronique **1** *nf* *(science)* optoelectronics **2** *adj* optoelectronic; **effet optronique** = electro-optic effect

on n'utilise plus uniquement radar et électronique, mais l'optronique - ce sont des systèmes de détection optique

Opto électronique

or *nm* gold; **contacts (en) or** = gold contacts

OR **porte** *ou* **circuit OR** = OR gate; *voir aussi* OU

orage *nm* storm; **orage magnétique** = magnetic storm

orbite *nf* orbit; **le satellite se déplace sur une orbite à 100km de la surface de la terre** = the satellite's orbit is 100km from the earth's surface; **orbite circulaire** = circular orbit; **orbite elliptique** = elliptical orbit; **orbite équatoriale** = equatorial orbit; **orbite géostationnaire** = geostationary orbit; **orbite inclinée** = inclined orbit; **orbite polaire** = polar orbit; **décrire une orbite** = to orbit; **ce satellite météorologique décrit une orbite autour de la terre toutes les quatre heures** = this weather satellite orbits the earth every four hours; **mettre en orbite** = to launch into orbit; **mise en orbite** = launching into orbit; **parcourir une orbite** = to orbit

◊ **orbiter** *vtr* to orbit

ordinateur *nm* computer *ou* computer system *ou* machine; *(utilisé pour le traitement de l'information)* information processor; **ordinateur à adresse unique** = one address computer; **ordinateur asynchrone** = asynchronous computer; **ordinateur de bureau** *ou* **à usage professionnel** = business computer *ou* desk top unit *ou* office computer; **ordinateur central** = *(gros ordinateur)* mainframe (computer); *(ordinateur hôte)* central computer; **ordinateur de contrôle** = control computer; **ordinateur de contrôle de processus** *ou* **ordinateur industriel** = process control computer; **ordinateur de contrôle des transmissions** = communications computer; **ordinateur dédié** = dedicated computer; **ordinateur d'exécution de programme objet** = object computer; **ordinateur familial** *ou* **pour toute la famille** = home computer; **ordinateur géant** *ou* **de grande puissance** = supercomputer; **ordinateur de gestion** *ou* **de bureau** = business computer; **ordinateur hôte** = host computer; **adaptateur de l'ordinateur hôte** = host adapter; **ordinateur hybride** = hybrid computer; **ordinateur imbriqué (dans un autre)** = embedded computer *ou* system; **ordinateur incrémentiel** *ou* **à valeurs variables** = incremental computer; **ordinateur individuel** = personal computer (PC); single-user system; **ordinateurs jumelés** = duplex computer; **ordinateur à logique câblée** = fixed program computer; **ordinateur maître** *ou* **principal** = master computer; **ordinateur monocarte** *ou* **à carte unique** = single board computer (sbc); **ordinateur monopuce** *ou* **à puce unique** = single chip computer; **ordinateur à mots de longueur variable** = variable word length computer; **ordinateur multicarte** = multi-board computer; **ordinateur numérique** = digital computer; **ordinateur parallèle** = parallel computer; **ordinateur personnel** = personal computer *ou* PC; **ordinateur de poche** *ou* **qui tient dans la main** *ou* **ultra-portatif** = hand-held programmable *ou* hand-held computer; **ordinateur polyvalent** *ou* **non spécialisé** = general purpose computer; **ordinateur principal** = *(gros ordinateur)* mainframe (computer); *(ordinateur hôte)* host computer; **accès à l'ordinateur principal (par l'intermédiaire d'un micro)** = mainframe access; **ordinateur série** = sequential computer; **ordinateur de table** *ou* **de bureau** = desktop computer (system); **(formation) sans accès à l'ordinateur** = hands-off (training); **achats sur** *ou* **par ordinateur** = electronic shopping; **(logiciel) adapté à l'ordinateur** = machine-intimate (software); **animation (d'images) sur ordinateur** = computer animation; **archivage sur ordinateur** = electronic filing; **assisté par ordinateur** = computer-aided *ou* computer-assisted; *voir aussi* ASSISTE **commandes numériques par ordinateur (pour machine-outil)** = computer numeric control (CNC); **communication entre ordinateurs** = computer conferencing; **conçu** *ou* **généré par ordinateur** = computer-generated; **créé** *ou* **produit à l'aide d'un ordinateur** = computer-generated; **ils ont fait l'analyse de l'image créée par l'ordinateur** = they analyzed the computer-generated image; **défaillance de l'ordinateur** = equipment failure; **défaut de l'ordinateur** = computer defect *ou* defect in the computer; **erreur due à l'ordinateur** = computer error; **exploitable par l'ordinateur** = machine-readable; **fichier d'ordinateur** = computer file; **génération d'ordinateurs** = computer generation; **ordinateurs de première génération** = first generation computers; **ordinateurs de deuxième génération** = second generation computers; **ordinateurs de troisième, de quatrième, de cinquième génération** = third, fourth, fifth generation computers; **géré par ordinateur** = computer-managed; **enseignement interactif géré par ordinateur** = computer-managed instruction (CMI); **système de réapprovisionnement géré par ordinateur** = teleordering; **gros ordinateur** *ou* **ordinateur central** = mainframe (computer) *ou* large-scale computer; **indexation sur ordinateur** *ou* **préparation d'un index à l'aide d'un ordinateur** = computer indexing; **lecteur optique de microfilms pour entrée de données sur ordinateur** = film optical scanning device for input into computers (FOSDIC); **logiciel qui fonctionne sur la plupart des ordinateurs** = machine-independent software; **logiciel qui ne fonctionne que sur un type d'ordinateur** = machine-dependent software; **logique des ordinateurs** = computer logic; **modèle d'ordinateur avec disque dur** = hard disk model; **opérateur d'ordinateur** = computer operator; **chariot piloté par ordinateur** = buggy; **puissance d'un ordinateur** = computer power; **représentations graphiques sur ordinateur** = computer-generated graphics *ou* computer graphics; **réseau d'ordinateurs** = computer network; **réseau d'ordinateurs hiérarchisé** = hierarchical computer network; **saisie au clavier contrôlée par ordinateur** = processor-controlled keying; **temps d'ordinateur** = computer time; **tous ces rapports de vente coûtent cher en temps d'ordinateur** = running all those sales reports costs a lot in computer time; **terminal d'ordinateur** = computer terminal; **terminal (i) de traitement de données (ii) de transmission de données** = data terminal equipment (DTE); **traitement de l'information sans l'aide d'un ordinateur** = manual data processing; **usine de construction d'ordinateurs** = computer factory

ordinogramme *nm* flow diagram *ou* flowchart; **l'ordinogramme est à la base d'un programme bien conçu** = a flowchart is the first step to a well designed program; **ordinogramme à pavés** = block diagram; **ordinogramme de données** = data flowchart; **l'ordinogramme des données nous a permis d'améliorer nos résultats à l'aide d'une meilleure structure** = the data flowchart allowed us to improve throughput, by using a better structure; **ordinogramme logique** = logical flowchart; **ordinogramme d'un système** = system flowchart; **grille** *ou* **modèle pour ordinogramme** = flowchart template; **ligne de jonction des symboles d'un ordinogramme** = flowline; **symboles d'un ordinogramme** = flowchart symbols

ordonnancement *nm* scheduling

◊ **ordonnanceur** *nm* scheduler

ordonnée *nf* Y-coordinate; **axe des ordonnées** = Y-axis *ou* vertical axis

ordonner *vtr* to order; **les instructions sont ordonnées suivant le numéro de ligne** = the program instructions are arranged in sequence according to line numbers

ordre *nm* order *ou* sequence; **en** *ou* **par ordre alphabétique** = in alphabetical order; **les noms sont classés par ordre alphabétique** = the sequence of names is arranged alphabetically; **liste triée** *ou* **classée en ordre alphabétique, etc.** = ordered list; **ordre d'appel (des teminaux)** = polling list; *(d'un livre)* **ordre des cahiers** = collating sequence; **ordre chronologique** = chronological order; **(tri, etc.) en ordre croissant** = forward mode; **ordre d'enchaînement des opérations** = operator precedence; **ordre d'interrogation (des terminaux)** = polling list; **ordre lexicographique** = lexicographical order; **ordre de priorité** = priority sequence; **ordre de priorité des opérations** = operation priority

oreiller *nm* pillow; **distorsion en oreiller** = pin cushion distortion

organe *nm* unit; **organe d'entrée/sortie** = input/output unit; **organe de traitement** = processing unit

organigramme *nm* organization chart; **organigramme de programmation** = program flowchart

organisation *nf* organization

◊ **organisationnel, -elle** *adj* organizational

◊ **organiser** *vtr* to organize *ou* to structure *ou* to map out; **vous organisez d'abord le document pour répondre à vos besoins, puis vous remplissez les blancs** = you first structure a document to meet your requirements and then fill in the blanks

organisme *nm* **Organisme international de normalisation ISO** = International Standards Organization (ISO)

orientable *adj (écran)* tilt and swivel (screen)

◊ **orientation** *nf* orientation; *(d'une page: paysage ou portrait)* orientation

◊ **orienté, -ée** *adj* **(a)** orientated; *(sur un microfilm)* **image orientée en film** = cine-orientated image **(b)** **orienté objet** = object-oriented; **graphique orienté objet** = object-oriented graphics; **ce programme graphique orienté objet vous permet de déplacer les formes très facilement** = this object-oriented graphics program lets you move shapes around very easily; **langage orienté objet** = object-oriented language; **programmation orientée objet (POO) (c)** *(biaisé)* biased; **données orientées** = biased data

original *nm* original; *(d'une lettre ou d'un document écrit à la machine)* top copy; **l'original n'est pas assez contrasté pour être photocopié** = the original is too faint to photocopy well; *(d'une disquette)* **original sauvegardé** *ou* **copie d'original** = protection master

◊ **original, -e** *adj (bande ou disque ou film)* original; **bande originale** = master tape *ou* original tape; **disque original** = master disk *ou* original disk; **document original** = source document; **image originale** *ou* **de première génération** = first generation image *ou* master copy; *(de cartes perforées)* **jeu original** = source deck *ou* pack; *(bande ou disque)* **support magnétique original** = magnetic master; **le texte original est chez l'éditeur pour correction** = the unedited text is with the publisher for editing

origine *nf* origin *ou* source; **adresse origine** = origin *ou* presumptive address; *(de la première instruction d'un programme)* = program origin; **document d'origine** = source document; **instruction d'origine** = presumptive instruction; **listing (du texte) d'origine** = source listing; **programme d'origine** = source program; *(signal ou donnée)* **retour à l'origine** = homing

◊ **originel, -elle** *adj* **compilateur originel** = native compiler

orthochromatique *adj* orthochromatic; **film orthochromatique** = orthochromatic film *ou* ortho film

orthogonal, -e *adj* orthogonal

orthographe *nf* spelling; **vérificateur d'orthographe** = spelling checker *ou* spellchecker; **on va optimiser le programme en ajoutant un traitement de texte et un vérificateur d'orthographe** = the program will be upgraded with a word-processor and a spelling checker; **vérifier l'orthographe** = to spellcheck; **vérifiez d'abord l'orthographe, vous pourrez ensuite imprimer votre texte** = after spellchecking the text, you can proceed to the printing stage

◊ **orthographique** *adj* **faire une vérification orthographique** = to spellcheck *ou* to do a spellcheck; **programme de vérification orthographique** = spelling checker *ou* spellchecker

OS/2 ™ *(système d'exploitation multitâche)*
OS/2 ™

oscillateur *nm* oscillator; **oscillateur à quartz** =
crystal oscillator

◊ **oscillation** *nf* oscillation; **oscillations
résiduelles (sur un courant)** = ripple

◊ **oscilloscope** *nm* oscilloscope

les deux oscilloscopes portables disposent de
quatre voies, d'une bande passante de 100MHz
et ont des possibilités de mesures intégrées
Electronique pratique

OU *(logique)* OR; **fonction OU** = OR function;
opération OU = join *ou* union *ou* disjunction; **porte**
ou **circuit OU** = OR gate; **OU exclusif** = exclusive
OR (EXOR); **fonction OU exclusif** = non-
equivalence function *ou* NEQ function *ou*
anticoincidence function; **porte** *ou* **circuit OU
exclusif** = exclusive OR gate *ou* EXOR gate *ou*
anticoincidence circuit; **OU inclusif** = inclusive
OR; **opération OU inclusif** = either-or operation

outil *nm* tool; **l'ordinateur est un outil très utile à
l'esthétique industrielle** = industrial design is aided
by computers; **outils de diagnostic** = system
diagnostics *ou* diagnostics; **outils de diagnostic du
compilateur** = compiler diagnostics; **un outil de
diagnostic de compilation bien conçu facilite le
débogage** = thorough compiler diagnostics make
debugging easy; **outils de diagnostic d'erreurs** =
error diagnostics; **outil de programmation** =
software tool; *(routines)* **boîte à outils** = toolbox
ou toolkit; **boîte à outils Macintosh** = Toolbox ™;
voir aussi MACHINE-OUTIL

ouvert, -e *adj* **(a)** open; *(qui permet l'addition de
cartes supplémentaires)* **architecture ouverte** =
open architecture; **bande sur bobine ouverte** =
open reel tape; **boucle ouverte** = open loop; **code
ouvert** = open code; **fichier ouvert** = open file; **vous
ne pouvez accéder aux données que si le fichier est
ouvert** = you cannot access the data unless the file
is open; **poste de travail ouvert** = open access
terminal; **programme ouvert** = open-ended
program; **routine ouverte** = open routine; **sous-
programme ouvert** = open subroutine; **système
ouvert** = open system; **interconnexion de systèmes
ouverts (ISO)** *ou* **normes ISO (pour systèmes
ouverts)** = Open System Interconnection (OSI)
(b) enveloppe ouverte = open *ou* unsealed envelope

ouverture *nf* **(a)** *(fente)* mouth *ou* slot; **insérer
dans une ouverture** = to slot (in *ou* into) **(b)**
ouverture d'objectif = lens stop *ou* aperture;
ouverture utile = effective aperture; **vitesse
d'ouverture d'un objectif** = lens speed **(c)**
(d'antenne) **illumination de l'ouverture** = aperture
illumination **(d)** *(d'une session d'ordinateur)*
ouverture de session = logging in *ou* logging on;
ouverture automatique de session = auto-login *ou*
auto-logon *ou* automatic log on

ouvrir *vtr* **(a)** to open; **ouvrez d'abord la porte du
lecteur de disquettes** = first, open the disk drive
door; **soulevez le couvercle de l'ordinateur pour
l'ouvrir** = open the top of the computer by lifting
(b) ouvrir un fichier = to open a file; **vous ne pouvez
pas accéder aux données avant d'avoir ouvert le
fichier** = you cannot access the data unless the file
has been opened **(c) ouvrir une session** = to log in
ou to log on

overlay *nm* overlay; **segment d'overlay** = overlay
segments; *voir aussi* RECOUVREMENT

OVL = OVERLAY **fichier OVL** = overlay

oxyde *nm* oxide; **oxyde de fer** *ou* **oxyde ferrique** =
ferric oxide *ou* ferrite

Pp

p = PETA

p = PICO

P *(section d'un semiconducteur)* **canal (de type) P** = p-channel; **semi-conducteur de type P** = p-type semiconductor; **semi-conducteur MOS à canal (de type) P** = p-channel MOS

PABX = PRIVATE AUTOMATIC BRANCH EXCHANGE; *voir* AUTOCOMMUTATEUR

package *nm (progiciel)* software package *ou* packaged software

◊ **packager** *ou* **packageur** *nm (de livres, etc.)* (book, etc.) packager

page *nf* **(a)** page; *(de papier listing)* form; **en ajoutant l'appendice, nous ferons 256 pages au total** = by adding the appendix, we will increase the page extent to 256; **page corrigée (qui en remplace une autre)** = cancel page; *(d'un livre)* **page de droite** *ou* **belle page** = recto *ou* right-hand page; **page de gauche** *ou* verso *ou* left-hand page; **page de titre** = title page; **belle page** = recto *ou* right-hand page; *(de papier listing)* **début d'une page** = head of form (HOF); **définition de page** = page setup; **disposition de page** = area composition; **épreuve en page** = page proof; *(traitement de texte)* **fin de page** = page break; **format de la page** = page size; **imprimante (par) page** = page printer; **cette imprimante matricielle n'est pas une imprimante page, elle n'imprime qu'une ligne à la fois** = this dot-matrix printer is not a page printer, it only prints one line at a time; *(contrôle une imprimante)* **langage de description de page** = page description language (PDL); **largeur de page (en caractères)** = page width; **lecteur de page (avec reconnaissance de caractères)** = page reader; **longueur de page** *ou* **nombre de lignes par page** = page length; *(d'une imprimante page)* **mémoire image de page** = page image buffer; **mettre en page** = to do the page layout *ou* the page makeup; to lay out the pages; **les designers ont décidé de mettre en page sur format A4** = the designers have laid out the pages in A4 format; **mise en page** = layout *ou* makeup; **les concepteurs travaillent à la mise en page de la nouvelle revue** = the design team is working on the layouts for the new magazine; **nous faisons toute notre mise en page avec un logiciel de PAO** = we do all our page layouts using desktop publishing software; **les corrections faites après la mise en page coûtent très cher** = corrections after page makeup are very expensive; **nombre total de pages (d'un document)** = extent (of a document); *(vitesse d'une imprimante)* **(nombre de) pages par minute (ppm)** = pages per minute (ppm); **cette imprimante laser peut imprimer huit pages par minute** = this laser printer can output eight pages per minute;

(portrait ou paysage) **orientation de la page** = page orientation; **pied de page** = footer *ou* footing; **présentation de page** = desktop presentation; page layout *ou* page makeup; **nous faisons toute notre présentation de page avec un logiciel de PAO** = we do all our page layouts using desktop publishing software; *(pour imprimante)* **(instruction de) saut de page** *ou* **changement de page** = form feed; **scanner page (avec reconnaissance de caractères)** = page reader; **taille de la page** = page size; **tête d'une page (de papier listing)** = head of form (HOF) **(b)** *(d'écran)* page; **affichage d'une page** = page display; **caractère d'instruction de fin de page** = page break character *ou* indicator; **écran pleine page** = full-size display; **touche page précédente** = page up key; **touche page suivante** = page down key; **signal de fin de page** = end of page indicator **(c)** *(de système vidéotex)* **page guide** = lead in page; **page index** = index page; **(nombre de) pages** = magazine **(d)** *(en mémoire)* **page mémoire** = memory page; **page mémoire sans modification** = clean page; **page de routage** = routing page; **adressage de page** = page addressing; **appel de page sur demande** = demand paging; **limite de page** = page boundary; **mémoire (RAM en mode) page** = page-mode RAM; **protection de page** = page protection; *(de mémoire paginée)* **table de pages** = page table; *(adresse physique en mémoire paginée)* **trame de page** = page frame

◊ **pagination** *nf* **(a)** *(d'un document)* pagination *ou* paging; **refaire la pagination** = to repaginate; **la pagination a été refaite avec une nouvelle largeur de ligne** = the text was repaginated with a new line width **(b)** *(de mémoire paginée)* **pagination transparente** = transparent paging; **algorithme de pagination** = paging algorithm; **méthode de pagination (de la mémoire)** = paged-memory scheme; **registre de pagination à accès direct** = direct page register

◊ **paginé, -ée** *adj* **adresse paginée** = paged address; **mémoire paginée** = paged memory *ou* page-mode RAM; **l'adaptateur vidéo utilise la mémoire paginée pour accélérer l'affichage** = the video adapter uses page-mode RAM to speed up the display; **unité de gestion de la mémoire paginée** = paged-memory management unit

◊ **paginer** *vtr (un livre)* to folio *ou* to paginate; **paginer de nouveau** = to repaginate

pair *nm* peer

pair, -e *adj* even; **les trois premiers nombres pairs sont 2, 4 et 6** = the first three even numbers are 2, 4, 6; **(contrôle de) parité paire** = even parity (check)

◊ **pair-impair, paire-impaire** *adj* **contrôle de parité paire-impaire** = odd-even check

◊ **paire** *nf* pair; **effectuer un tri par permutation de paires** = to bubble sort

PAL *(norme de télévision couleur)* Phase Altermating Line (PAL)

pâle *adj* pale; **si l'impression est trop pâle, réglez le bouton de densité (d'impression) sur le noir** = when fading occurs turn the density dial on the printer to full black

palette *nf (de couleurs)* palette; **palette graphique** = graphics software

palier *nm* (a) step *ou* stage; **effectué par paliers** = staged (b) *(élément du signal télévisé)* **palier avant** = front porch

pâlir *vi (couleur)* to fade

panier *nm* panier **(à bits)** = bit bucket; **(circuits de) fond de panier** = (microcomputer) backplane

panne *nf* (a) breakdown *ou* failure *ou* fault; *(complète)* crash; **nous ne pouvons pas joindre notre bureau à New York à cause d'une panne des lignes de télex** = we cannot communicate with our New York office because of the breakdown of the telex lines; **panne désordonnée** = disorderly close-down; **panne douce** = soft-fail; **panne de courant** *ou* **de secteur** = power cut *ou* power failure; blackout; **il y a eu une panne de courant** *ou* **de secteur** = the electricity supply has failed *ou* the electricity supply was cut off; **panne par échauffement** = burn out; **panne d'électricité** = electrical failure; **les ingénieurs essaient de réparer une panne d'électricité** = the engineers are trying to repair an electrical failure; **panne fatale** = catastrophic failure *ou* crash; **panne sérieuse (d'équipement)** = hard failure; **la panne était due à la défaillance d'un composant** = the hard failure was due to a burnt-out chip; **panne totale d'un disque** = disk crash; **panne de système** = system crash; **durée d'une panne** = fault time; **enregistrement** *ou* **traçage de panne** = fault trace; **localisation (automatique) de panne** = fault detection; **diagnostic de localisation de panne** = fault diagnosis; **programme de localisation de panne** = fault location program; **tolérance de pannes** = fault tolerance (b) **être en panne** *ou* **tomber en panne** = to break down *ou* to fail; **ce modem est en panne** = the modem has broken down; **l'imprimante est en panne, il faut remplacer une pièce** = the printer won't work - we need to get a spare part; **on peut dire que l'ordinateur est en panne si rien ne se produit à la mise sous tension** = a computer has failed if you turn on the power supply and nothing happens; **que faut-il faire quand l'imprimante ligne tombe en panne?** = what do you do when your line printer breaks down?; **l'ordinateur est tombé en panne deux fois cet après-midi** = the computer system went down twice during the afternoon; **la tête de lecture du disque est tombée en panne et il se peut que les données aient été perdues** = the disk head has crashed and the data may have been lost

panneau *nm* (a) *(d'un appareil)* panel; **panneau avant** = front *ou* front panel *ou* fascia plate *ou* bezel; **le panneau avant du lecteur de disquettes de ce modèle est plus petit que celui des autres modèles** = the fascia plate on the disk drive of this model is smaller than those on other models; **panneau**

arrière = back panel; **la prise est située sur le panneau arrière** = the socket is on the back panel; **le numéro de fabrication est gravé de façon permanente sur le panneau arrière du boîtier de l'ordinateur** = the production number is permanently engraved on the back of the computer casing; **panneau de commande** *ou* **panneau de contrôle** = control panel; **panneau de commandes d'un système** = system control panel; **panneau de raccordement** = plugboard *ou* patchboard (b) *(pour affiches)* **on a placé des panneaux d'avertissement autour du laser de puissance** = warning notices were put up around the high powered laser

panoplie *nf* **toute la panoplie** = bells and whistles; **ce traitement de texte est doté de toute la panoplie y compris l'aperçu avant impression** = this word-processor has all the bells and whistles you would expect - including page preview

Pantone *(nuancier ou système de référence de couleurs)* Pantone Matching System ™ (PMS)

PAO = PUBLICATION ASSISTEE PAR ORDINATEUR

papier *nm* paper; *(à lettre, etc.)* stationery; **un papier de mauvaise qualité est beaucoup trop transparent** = bad quality paper gives too much show-through; **le papier doit être chargé manuellement dans l'imprimante** = the paper should be manually fed into the printer; **nous avons du papier de 70 - 90 grammes** = our paper weight is 70 - 90 gsm; **le livre est imprimé sur du papier 80 grammes** = the book is printed on 80gsm paper; **papier en accordéon** = fanfold *ou* accordion fold paper; **papier autocopiant** = carbonless paper; **papier baryté** = baryta paper; **papier en continu** = continuous stationery; **papier couché** = coated paper; **papier enduit d'une fine couche de kaolin** = paper which has a coating of clay; **papier à dessin (de type 'cartridge')** = cartridge paper; **papier pour copieur** = copier paper *ou* paper for (photo)copier; **papier électrosensible** = electrosensitive paper; **papier à en-tête** = headed paper *ou* letterhead; **papier à lettre** = writing paper; **papier à lettre commercial** = bond paper; **on utilise du papier glacé pour l'impression de similigravures** = glossy paper is used for printing half-tones; **papier journal** = newspaper; newsprint *ou* mechanical paper; **papier listing** = continuous stationery *ou* listing paper; **équipement de traitement de papier listing (en sortie d'imprimante)** = form handling equipment; **indicateur de fin de papier (listing)** = form stop; **page de papier listing** = form; **papier millimétré** = graph paper; **papier (plié) en paravent** = accordion fold *ou* fanfold paper; *(fond d'écran du bureau Windows)* **papier peint** = wallpaper; **papier photosensible double face** = duplex paper; **papier préimprimé** = preprinted stationery; **papier quadrillé** = graph paper; **papier thermique** = heat sensitive paper *ou* thermal paper; **(dispositif d') alimentation** *ou* **entraînement du papier** = paper feed; **arrêt pour manque de papier** = form stop; *(pour l'alimentation en feuille à feuille)* **bac à papier** = paper bin *ou* paper tray; **bande papier** = (paper) tape *ou* punched tape; **(dispositif d')**

entraînement de la bande papier = paper tape feed; poinçon de perforation pour bandes papier = paper tape punch; le bureau sans papier = the paperless office; contrôle d'un programme sur papier = desk check of a program; feuille de papier = sheet (of paper); rouleau de papier de *ou* pour télécopieur = fax roll; saut du papier = paper throw

◊ **papier-calque** *nm* detail paper

papillotement *nm (d'une image)* flicker *ou* blinking; sans papillotement = flicker-free

paquet *nm* **(a)** pack; paquet de cartes perforées = card deck **(b)** *(groupes de données)* batch; traitement par paquets = batch processing; mode de traitement par paquets = batch mode; processeur de traitement par paquets = batch processor; système de traitement par paquets = batch system **(c)** *(données de tailles uniformes)* packet; commutation (de messages) par paquets = packet switching; réseau de commutation de données par paquets = packet switched data service *ou* packet switched network (PSN); système de transmission par paquets (PSS) = packet switching system (PSS) **(d)** *(rafales ou signaux intermittents)* burst; mode de transmission *ou* de transfert par paquets = burst mode **(e)** paquet promotionnel = bundle; le paquet comporte un PC avec un tableur et une base de données pour seulement 999£ = the bundle now includes a PC with spreadsheet and database applications for just £999

par *prép* **(a)** per; par année = per year; par heure = per hour; par jour = per day; par semaine = per week **(b)** par *ou* par l'intermédiaire de *ou* en passant par = by *ou* via; les signaux nous ont été transmis par satellite = the signals have reached us via satellite

parabolique *adj* antenne parabolique = dish aerial; nous utilisons une antenne parabolique pour capter les signaux transmis par satellite = we use a dish aerial to receive signals from the satellite

paragraphe *nm* paragraph; paragraphe standard = template paragraph; bloc paragraphe (de mémoire) = paragraph; *(traitement de texte)* marqueur de paragraphe (d'un texte) = paragraph marker; transfert *ou* insertion d'un paragraphe = block transfer

paraître *vi* to be published; ce livre paraîtra en édition cartonnée et en livre de poche = the book will be published as a hardback and as a paperback; *(d'une revue ou d'un journal)* numéro déjà paru = back number

parallèle *adj* parallel; accès parallèle = parallel access; additionneur parallèle = parallel adder; connexion (en) parallèle = parallel connection; leur débit de transmission est de 60 000 bits par seconde en connexion parallèle = their average transmission rate is 60,000 bps through parallel connection; convertisseur analogique-numérique parallèle = flash A/D; entrée/sortie parallèle = parallel input/output (PIO); circuit intégré d'entrée/sortie en parallèle = parallel input/output chip; entrée parallèle/sortie parallèle = parallel

input/parallel output (PIPO); entrée parallèle/sortie série = parallel input/serial output (PISO); entrée série/sortie parallèle = serial input/parallel output (SIPO); exploitation (en) parallèle = parallel running; système de gestion des priorités en parallèle = parallel priority system; imprimante parallèle = parallel printer; interface parallèle = parallel interface; opération (en) parallèle = parallel operation; ordinateur parallèle = parallel computer; port parallèle = parallel port; traitement (en) parallèle = parallel processing; transfert (en) parallèle = parallel transfer; transmission (en) parallèle = parallel transmission; transmission de données en parallèle = parallel data transmission

paramétrable *adj* programmable *ou* dynamic; code paramétrable = skeletal code; sous-programme paramétrable = dynamic subroutine

◊ **paramétrage** *nm* parameterization; paramétrage de marges = margination; code de paramétrage de l'imprimante = non-printing codes

◊ **paramètre** *nm* parameter; la taille du tableau est fixée par ce paramètre = the size of the array is set with this parameter; le paramètre X définit le nombre de caractères contenus dans une ligne d'écran = the X parameter defines the number of characters displayed across a screen; paramètres de conception *ou* de création = design parameters; paramètres d'impression = print modifiers; bande sans paramètres d'impression = idiot tape; paramètre physique = physical parameter; paramètres programmables à l'installation = set-up options; *(dans un programme)* passage de paramètre = parameter passing; test des paramètres = parameter testing

◊ **paramétré, -ée** *adj* programmed *ou* set; sous-programme paramétré = parametric (subroutine)

◊ **paramétrer** *vtr* to set *ou* to program; paramétrer une marge = to set a margin

◊ **paramétrique** *adj* code paramétrique de l'imprimante = non-printing code; la largeur des lignes peut être définie par le code paramétrique .LW suivi d'un chiffre = the line width can be set using one of the non-printing codes, .LW, then a number; logiciel paramétrique = parameter-driven software; sous-programme paramétrique = parametric (subroutine); test paramétrique = parameter testing

parasite 1 *nm* **(a)** *(qui nuit à l'enregistrement sur disque)* drop in **(b)** *(bruits)* parasites = noise *ou* static; *(causés par une autre voie de transmission)* crosstalk **2** *adj* bruits parasites = noise *ou* static; *(causés par une autre voie de transmission)* crosstalk; bruit parasite courant = common mode noise; caractères parasites = garbage

paravent *nm* papier en paravent = accordion fold *ou* fanfold *ou* concertina fold paper

parc *nm* total number (of computers *ou* of clients, etc.); maintenance du parc clients = customer engineering

parcage *nm* parcage de la tête de lecture = head park; **zone de parcage (de la tête de lecture)** = landing zone

parcourir *vtr* parcourir une orbite = to orbit

parent *nm (système Macintosh)* fichier parent = parent folder; **programme parent** = parent program; **répertoire parent** = parent directory

parenthèse(s) *nf(pl)* (round) brackets; **mettre entre parenthèses** = to put between *ou* in brackets

parité *nf* parity; **parité de bloc** = block parity; **parité de colonne** = column parity; **bit de parité** = parity bit; **sans (bit de) parité** = no parity; **contrôle de parité** = parity check; **(contrôle de) parité d'un bloc** = block parity (check); **(contrôle de) parité impaire** = odd parity (check); **(contrôle de) parité paire** = even parity (check); **(contrôle de) parité paire-impaire** = odd-even (check); **(contrôle de) parité verticale** = vertical parity (check); **indicateur de contrôle de parité** = parity flag; **interruption (de contrôle) de parité** = parity interrupt; **piste de parité** = parity track

théoriquement, le bit de parité placé en fin des 7 ou 8 bits utiles du caractère, sert à contrôler la qualité de la transmission
Action PC

parole *nf* speech; voice; **processeur de la parole** = speech processor; **reconnaissance de la parole** = speech recognition *ou* voice recognition; **synthèse de la parole** = speech synthesis; **synthétiseur de la parole** = speech synthesizer

parquer *vt (la tête de lecture du disque)* to park; **en position parquée, la tête du disque ne peut plus endommager les données en touchant la surface du disque** = when parked, the disk head will not damage any data if it touches the disk surface

partage *nm* division *ou* sharing; **(en) partage de port** = port sharing; **partage de ressources** = resource sharing; **partage des tâches** = load sharing; **partage de temps** = time-sharing

◊ **partagé, -ée** *adj* **(a)** *(utilisé par plusieurs persones)* shared; common; **accès partagé** = shared access; **bus partagé** = shared bus; **fichier partagé** = shared file; **système à fichiers partagés** = distributed file system; **imprimante non partagée** = local printer; **langage partagé** = common language; **ligne partagée** = party line *ou* shared line; **logiciel partagé** = common software; **processeur à logique partagée** = shared logic text processor; **matériel partagé** = common hardware; **mémoire partagée** = shared memory; **(en) port partagé** = port sharing; **répertoire partagé** = shared directory; **répertoire de réseau partagé** = shared network directory; **services partagés** = fractional services; **l'opérateur (commercial) vous vendra des services partagés qui permettent de transmettre des données à 64Kbps** = the commercial carrier will sell you fractional services that provide 64Kbps data transmission; **système logique partagé** = shared logic system; **système à ressources partagées** = shared resources system;

système en temps partagé = time-sharing system; **système multitâche en temps partagé** = preemptive multitasking **(b)** *(divisé)* split; **écran partagé** = split screen; **nous utilisons le mode d'écran partagé pour comparer le texte en cours de travail à un texte de référence conservé en mémoire** = we use split screen mode to show the text being worked on and another text from memory for comparison

◊ **partager** *vtr* to divide *ou* to share *ou* to split; **plusieurs sociétés indépendantes se partagent le système** = the system is shared by several independent companies

partial, -e *adj* biased

particule *nf* particle; **particule alpha** = alpha-particle; **sensibilité aux particules alpha** = alpha-particle sensitivity

particulier, -ière *adj* **adressage particulier** = inherent addressing

partie *nf* part; section; region; **partie fractionnaire** = fractional part; **affichage d'une partie de page** = part page display

◊ **partiel, -ielle** *adj* **(mémoire) RAM partielle** = partial RAM; **report partiel** = partial carry

◊ **partiellement** *adv* partially; **données partiellement (pré)traitées** = semi-processed data

partition *nf* **(a)** *(d'un disque dur)* partition; **effectuer une partition** = to partition; **j'ai défini deux partitions sur ce disque dur désignées par C: et D:** = I defined two partitions on this hard disk - called drive C: and D: **(b)** partition *ou* area; **partition privée** = private address space; **partition privilégiée (avec niveau d'accès prioritaire)** = privileged account; **le gestionnaire d'un système jouit d'une partition privilégiée qui lui permet d'accéder à tous les fichiers de ce système** = the systems manager has a privileged status so he can access any file on the system; **partition de traitement par lots** = batch region

paru *voir* PARAITRE

parution *nf* publication; **la date de parution du livre est fixée au 15 novembre** = the publication date of the book is November 15th

parvenir *vi* parvenir à = to achieve; **les concepteurs de matériel informatique tentent de parvenir à une compatibilité totale entre tous les composants du système** = the hardware designers are trying to achieve compatibility between all the components of the system

pas *nm* **(a)** *(d'un programme)* step; **pas de programmation** = program step; **avancer d'un pas** *ou* **faire un pas (en avant)** = to step (forward); **faire avancer d'un pas** = to increment; **exécution** *ou* **opération pas à pas** = single step opération; **reculer d'un pas** *ou* **faire un pas en arrière** = to step backward **(b)** *(d'un moteur)* step; **moteur à pas** = stepper motor *ou* stepping motor **(c)** *(taille de caractères)* pitch **(d)** *(d'un film)* film advance

PASCAL *(langage de programmation de haut niveau)* PASCAL

passage *nm* (a) pass; **ruban à un seul passage** = single strike ribbon; **passage de tri** = sorting pass (b) *(d'un système à un autre)* crossover

passager, -ère *adj* transient; **erreur passagère** = transient error

◊ **passe** *nf* (a) pass; **passe de balayage** = raster scan; **balayage une passe sans segmentation d'image** *ou* **balayage d'image complète en une passe** = single scan non segmented; **assembleur une passe** = one-pass assembler *ou* single-pass assembler; **ce nouvel assembleur une passe travaille très vite** = this new one-pass assembler is very quick in operation; **assembleur deux passes** = two-pass assembler; **impression en plusieurs passes légèrement décalées** = multipass overlap; **opération (en) une passe** = single pass operation (b) **mot de passe** = password; *(code personnel)* identification code *ou* ID code; **il faut vous rappeler votre mot de passe sinon vous ne pourrez pas avoir accès au système** = if you forget your user ID, you will not be able to logon; **l'utilisateur doit d'abord taper le mot de passe pour avoir accès à la base de données** = the user has to key in the password before he can access the database; **protection par mot de passe** = password protection; **protégé par mot de passe** = password-protected

◊ **passe-bande** *adj inv* **filtre passe-bande** = bandpass filter

◊ **passe-bas** *adj inv* **filtre passe-bas** = low pass filter

◊ **passe-haut** *adj inv* **filtre passe-haut** = high pass filter

◊ **passer 1** *vtr* **passer un coup de fil** = to make a phone call; **demande de communication qui ne passe pas** = lost call **2** *vi* **passer à** = to proceed; **passer d'un système à un autre** = to change over; **il a été difficile de passer à un système d'index informatisé** = the crossover to computerized file indexing was difficult

passerelle *nf (d'accès entre réseaux différents)* gateway; **nous utilisons une passerelle pour relier le réseau local au réseau étendu** = we use a gateway to link the LAN to WAN; **passerelle fax** *ou* **de télécopie** = fax gateway; **pour envoyer des messages par fax au lieu de les envoyer par le réseau, vous devez installer une passerelle fax** = to send messages by fax instead of across the network, you'll have to install a fax gateway

COMMENTAIRE: Un pont relie deux réseaux similaires, une passerelle relie deux réseaux différents. Pour relier deux réseaux Ethernet, utilisez un pont

et, surtout, il dispose de passerelles qui lui permettent d'être utilisé dans un environnement industriel
L'Événement

passionné, -ée *adj & n* **passionné d'informatique** = hacker

pastille *nf* **pastille de silicium** = silicon chip; *(du silicium)* **découpe en pastille** = slicing

patch *nm (correction provisoire d'un logiciel)* patch

pause *nf* pause *ou* short stop; **pause accidentelle** = holdup; **touche Pause** = pause key

pavé *nm* (a) pad *ou* keypad; **pavé à effleurement** *ou* **pavé tactile** = touch pad; **pavé de commandes du curseur** = cursor pad; **pavé numérique** = numeric keypad; **utilisez le pavé numérique pour saisir les chiffres** = you can use the numeric keypad to enter the figures; **touche de blocage du pavé numérique** = Num Lock key (b) **graphe** *ou* **ordinogramme à pavés** = block diagram

payer *vtr* to pay; **l'utilisateur paie un droit pour visualiser le tableau d'affichage** = the user has to pay a charge for viewing pages on a bulletin board

pays *nm* country; **fichier pays** = country file; **indicatif (téléphonique) du pays** = country code

paysage *nm (orientation d'une page)* landscape

PBX = PRIVATE BRANCH EXCHANGE **PBX électronique** = computerized branch exchange (CBX); *voir aussi* AUTOCOMMUTATEUR

PC *(ordinateur personnel)* Personal Computer (PC); **compatible PC** = PC-compatible

◊ **PC/AT** *(ordinateur compatible IBM PC, avec processeur Intel 80286)* PC/AT; **clavier PC/AT** = PC/AT keyboard

◊ **PC/XT** *(ordinateur compatible IBM PC, avec processeur Intel 8086)* PC/XT; **clavier PC/XT** = PC/XT keyboard

PC-DOS ™ *(version IBM de MS-DOS)* PC-DOS ™

PCI *(modèle de bus local)* Peripheral Component Interconnect (PCI)

PCL ™ *(langage ou jeu de commandes de contrôle d'imprimante)* Printer Control Language ™ (PCL)

PCMCIA *(norme de carte d'extension)* Personal Computer Memory Card International Association (PCMCIA); **carte PCMCIA** = PCMCIA card; **la mémoire additionnelle est stockée sur une carte PCMCIA et je l'utilise sur mon (ordinateur) portable** = the extra memory is stored on this PCMCIA card and I use it on my laptop; **connecteur PCMCIA** = PCMCIA connector; **emplacement (avec connecteur) pour carte PCMCIA** = PCMCIA slot

PCV *(communication téléphonique payable par le destinataire)* **appel en PCV** = reverse charge call, *US* collect call

PDA = PERSONAL DIGITAL ASSISTANT; *voir* ASSISTANT

PEEK *(lecture directe de la mémoire)* **instruction PEEK** = PEEK instruction; **vous devez utliser l'instruction PEEK 1452 pour regarder le contenu de la mémoire à l'emplacement 1452** = you need the instruction PEEK 1452 here to examine the contents of memory location 1452

peindre *vi* to paint

◊ **peinture** *nf* paint

pellicule *nf* (i) film; (ii) film base; **pellicule photographique** = (photographic) film; **il a mis une nouvelle pellicule dans son appareil photo** = he put a new roll of film into the camera

◊ **pelliculé, -ée** *adj* laminated; **c'est un livre avec couverture pelliculée** = the book is bound in laminated paper

◊ **pelliculer** *vtr* to laminate

pelure *nf* skin; **architecture en pelure d'oignon** = onion skin architecture; **cet ordinateur possède une architecture en pelure d'oignon comprenant un noyau central, un système d'exploitation, un langage de bas niveau et le programme utilisateur** = the onion skin architecture of this computer is made up of a kernel at the centre, an operating system, a low-level language and then the user's program; **langage en pelure d'oignon** = onion skin language

pendant *prép* for *ou* during; **pendant quelque temps** *ou* **pendant un certain temps** = for a period of time; **pendant quelques mois** = for a period of months; **pendant six ans** = for a six-year period

pense-bête *nm* *(indiquant la fonction des touches)* key strip

Pentium ™ *(processeur 32 bits développé par Intel)* Pentium ™

pépin *nm* glitch

perceptible *adj* **perceptible à l'oreille** = audible

perche *nf* *(d'un microphone)* boom

perdre *vtr* **(a)** to lose; **tous les fichiers courants ont été perdus lors de la panne d'ordinateur et nous n'avions pas de copie de sauvegarde** = all the current files were lost when the system crashed and we had no backup copies **(b)** *(condensateur)* **perdre sa charge** = to leak; **dans ce circuit, le condensateur perd 10% de sa charge par seconde** = in this circuit, the capacitor charge leaks out at 10% per second

◊ **se perdre** *vpr* to be lost; **se perdre dans une boucle** = to hang

◊ **perdu, -e** *adj* lost; *(égaré)* stray; **grappe de données perdue** *ou* **cluster perdu** = lost cluster

père *nm* father; **fichier père** = father file

péremption *nf* expiration; **date de péremption** = expiration date; *(d'un produit en magasin)* sell-by date

perfect binding *nm* *(type de reliure)* perfect binding; **(livre) avec perfect binding** = perfect bound (book)

perforateur *nm* *(pour cartes)* card punch (CP)

◊ **perforateur-compteur** *nm* *(de bandes papier)* counting perforator

◊ **perforation** *nf* **(a)** *(de bande papier)* hole *ou* perforation; **perforations centrales** = centre holes; **perforations d'entraînement** *ou* **perforations marginales** = feed holes *ou* sprocket holes; **code de perforation** = tape code; **poinçon de perforation** = paper tape punch *ou* perforator **(b)** *(de carte perforée)* **perforation numérique** = numeric punch; **perforation (de la ligne) 11** *ou* **perforation X** = x punch; **perforation (de la ligne) 12** *ou* **perforation Y** = y punch; **code de perforation de carte** = card code *ou* punched code; **colonne de perforation (d'une carte)** = card row *ou* card column; **poinçon de perforation (pour cartes)** = card punch (CP) **(c)** *(de disque)* **perforations** = hard-sectoring; **perforations de marquage (du bord) d'un disque** = disk index holes; **perforation de positionnement** = sectoring hole

◊ **perforatrice** *nf* perforator *ou* reperforator; **perforatrice (à clavier)** = key punch

◊ **perforé, -ée** *adj* **bande (papier) perforée** = punched (paper) tape *ou* perforated tape; *(pour télex hors ligne)* torn tape; **lecteur de bandes perforées** = paper tape reader; **carte perforée** = punched card; **(système d') alimentation** *ou* **entraînement de cartes perforées** = card feed; **chargeur de cartes perforées** = hopper; **lecteur de cartes perforées** = punched card reader; **étiquette perforée** = punched tag; **ligne perforée** = perforations; *(sur carte)* card row *ou* card column; **ruban perforé** = perforated tape

◊ **perforer** *vtr* to punch

performance *nf* performance; *(d'un appareil)* **bonne performance** = efficiency; **dégradation** *ou* **réduction des performances** = degradation; **étalonnage des performances** *ou* **évaluation comparative des performances** = benchmarking; **les bancs d'essais consistent à évaluer la performance de plusieurs systèmes ou périphériques en utilisant le même test standard** = in benchmarking, the performances of several systems or devices are tested against a standard benchmark; **pour juger de la performance du système** = as a measure of the system's performance; **(de) haute performance** = high performance; **matériel (de) haute performance** = high performance equipment

◊ **performant, -e** *adj* efficient; **ce progiciel de traitement de texte a produit, de façon très performante, une série de lettres personnalisées** = the word-processing package has produced a series of addressed letters very efficiently

périgée *nm* perigee

périmé, -ée *adj* old *ou* out of date; *(d'un produit qui ne supporte pas certaines fonctions)* **version périmée** = back-level

période *nf* period *ou* time; **période d'assemblage** = assembly time; **période de latence** = latency; **période de référence** = reference time; **période de travail** = session

◊ **périodique 1** *nm* *(revue)* magazine *ou* periodical **2** *adj* periodic *ou* periodical

◊ **périodiquement** *adv* periodically

périphérique *nm* (external) device *ou* peripheral (unit) *ou* peripheral equipment; **les périphériques, tels que les lecteurs de disquettes et les imprimantes, qui permettent le transfert de données sont asservis à un système (central) mais fonctionnent grâce à des circuits indépendants** = peripherals such as disk drives or printers allow data transfer and are controlled by a system, but contain independent circuits for their operation; **périphérique d'entrée** = input device *ou* input unit; **(câble de) liaison d'un périphérique d'entrée** = input lead; **périphérique d'entrée/sortie** = input/output device *ou* unit; I/O device *ou* unit; **périphérique lent** = slow peripheral; **périphérique rapide** = fast peripheral; **périphérique de sortie** = output device *ou* unit; **adresse de contrôleur de périphérique** = device address; **caractère de contrôle de périphérique** = device control character; **(système de) commande** *ou* **contrôle de périphérique utilisant des caractères** = device character control; **nom de commande de périphérique** = device name; **unité de commande** *ou* **unité de contrôle de périphérique** *ou* **contrôleur de périphérique** = peripheral control unit (PCU) *ou* peripheral controller; **échange d'information entre CPU et périphérique** = CPU handshaking *ou* peripheral transfer; **file d'attente de périphériques** = device queue; **gestion de périphérique** = device control; **routine de gestion de périphérique** = peripheral software driver; **gestionnaire de périphérique** = device driver *ou* device handler *ou* peripheral driver; **code d'identification de périphérique** = device code; **interface** *ou* **connecteur de périphérique** = peripheral interface adapter (PIA); **limité par (la vitesse d') un périphérique** *ou* **avec contrainte de vitesse de périphérique** = peripheral-limited; **mémoire (de) périphérique** = peripheral memory; **langage de pilotage de périphérique** = peripheral command control language; **pilote de périphérique** = device driver *ou* peripheral controller; **port pour périphérique(s)** = user port; **priorité d'un périphérique** = device priority; **processeur périphérique** = peripheral processing unit (PPU); **signal d'appel émis par un périphérique** = external interrupt

permanence *nf* **(service de) permanence téléphonique** = answering service; **en permanence** = permanently

◊ **permanent, -e** *adj* (a) permanent; **câblage permanent** = hardwired connection; **données permanentes** = fixed data; **erreur permanente** = permanent error; **fichier permanent** = permanent file *ou* master file; **fichier d'échange permanent** = permanent swap file; **mémoire permanente** = permanent memory *ou* nonerasable storage; **mémoire dynamique permanente** = permanent dynamic memory (b) **de façon permanente** = permanently

perméabilité *nf* permeability

permettre *vtr* to allow *ou* to authorize; to enable; **permettre quelque chose** = to authorize something; **ce logiciel permet d'exécuter des fonctions beaucoup plus complexes** = the software is capable of far more complex functions; **un gestionnaire de base de données ultra-rapide permet la manipulation d'une très grande quantité**

de données = a high-speed database management program allows the manipulation of very large amounts of data; **un programme de spouling permet d'éditer un texte tout en imprimant** = a spooling program enables editing work to be carried out while printing is going on

◊ **permis** *nm* licence

◊ **permis, -e** *adj* authorized *ou* legal

◊ **permission** *nf* authorization

permutable *adj* **registre permutable** = circulating register

◊ **permutation** *nf* permutation *ou* interchange *ou* change-over; *(de programmes)* swapping *ou* swap; *(de bits ou de mots de données)* shift *ou* rotation; **ce code chiffré est très sûr puisqu'il comporte une clé avec un très grand nombre de permutations possibles** = this cipher system is very secure since there are so many possible permutations for the key; **permutation de bits** = bit rotation *ou* rotate operation; **permutation circulaire** = cyclic shift *ou* cycle shift; **tri par permutation (de paires** *ou* **de bulles)** = bubble sort; **effectuer un tri par permutation de paires** *ou* **de bulles** = to bubble sort

◊ **permuté, -ée** *adj* **mémoire à liste permutée** = nesting store

◊ **permuter** *vtr* to interchange; *(programmes)* to swap; *(bits ou mots de données)* to shift *ou* to rotate; **permuter des données** = to exchange data

persistance *nf* persistence *ou* afterglow; **persistance de l'image** = image retention *ou* lag; **phosphore à longue persistance** *ou* **couche phosphorée à grande persistance** = long persistence phosphor; **les écrans à faible fréquence de balayage ont besoin de phosphore à longue persistance pour éviter l'instabilité de l'image** = slow scan rate monitors need long persistence phosphor to prevent the image flickering

◊ **persistant, -e** *adj* **anomalie** *ou* **erreur persistante** = hard error

personnalisé, -ée *adj* custom-built *ou* customized; **nous utilisons des logiciels personnalisés** = we use customized software; **papier à lettre personnalisé** = preprinted stationery; **ROM personnalisée** = custom ROM (PROM)

◊ **personnaliser** *vtr* to customize *ou* to personalize

personne *nf* person *ou* individual; **chaque personne possède son propre mot de passe pour accéder au système** = each individual has his own password to access the system

◊ **personnel** *nm* personnel; **personnel informatique** = liveware

◊ **personnel, -elle** *adj* personal *ou* individual; *(ordinateur qui tient dans la main)* **assistant personnel de communication (APC)** = personal digital assistant (PDA); **code personnel** = ID code; **après la mise en route du système, il faut tapez votre code personnel et votre mot de passe** = after you wake up the system, you have to input your ID code then your password; **gestionnaire personnel d'information (GPI)** = personal information manager (PIM); **numéro de code personnel** = identity number *ou* personal identification number *ou* PIN number; **ordinateur personnel** = personal computer (PC); home computer

perte *nf* loss; *(fuite)* leakage *ou* leak; **perte d'alignement** = gap loss; **perte de charge** = leak *ou* leakage; **perte dans l'espace** = free space loss; **perte d'insertion** = insertion loss; **perte de magnétisation** = drop out; *(d'un signal)* **perte de niveau** = drop out; *(radio ou télévision)* **perte d'un signal** = attenuation; **perte de terre** = ground absorption; **perte de transmission** = link loss; **perte de transmission inexplicable** = line gremlin

pertinence *nf* relevance

◊ **pertinent, -e** *adj* relevant; **relation pertinente** = relevance

perturbation *nf* disturbance; interference; **courte perturbation sur la ligne** = hit on the line; **perturbation électromagnétique** = electromagnetic disturbance *ou* electromagnetic interference (EMI)

péta *nm* peta (P)

◊ **péta-octet** *nm* petabyte (PB)

petit, -e *adj* small; **petites capitales** = small caps; **petit modèle (de mémoire Intel de 64Ko)** = tiny model; **interface pour petits ordinateurs** = small computer system interface (SCSI)

PF = PICOFARAD

PgDn *(touche page suivante)* page down key *ou* PgDn key

PgUp *(touche page précédente)* page up key *ou* pgUp key

phase *nf* **(a)** *(étape)* phase *ou* stage; **nous n'en sommes qu'à la phase de rodage du système d'exploitation** = we are in the first stage of running in the new computer system; **phase de compilation** = compile phase; **phase d'exécution** = execute phase *ou* execution phase; **phase exécution en code objet** = target phase *ou* run phase; **phase de lecture d'une instruction** = fetch phase **(b)** *(d'un signal)* phase; **angle de phase** = phase angle; **écrêtage de phase** = phase clipping; **égaliseur** *ou* **compensateur de phase** = delay equalizer *ou* phase equalizer; **modulation de phase** = phase modulation; **en phase** = in phase; *voir aussi* DEPHASE

phone *nm (unité de puissance sonore)* phon

◊ **phonème** *nm* phoneme; **les mots 'tout' et 'roue' contiennent le phonème 'ou'** = the phoneme 'ou' is present in the words 'tout' and 'roue'

◊ **phonétique 1** *nf (science)* phonetics **2** *adj* phonetic; **il y a une transcription phonétique de la prononciation** = the pronunciation is indicated in phonetic script

phosphore *nm* phosphor; **phosphore à longue persistance** = long persistence phosphor; **phosphore vert** = green phosphor; **couche de phosphore** = phosphor coating; **points de phosphore** = phosphor dots

◊ **phosphoré, -ée** *adj* **couche phosphorée à longue persistance** = long persistence phosphor coating

◊ **phosphorescence** *nf* phosphorescence; **points de phosphorescence** = phosphor dots; **rendement de phosphorescence** = phosphor efficiency

◊ **phosphorescent, -e** *adj* **couche phosphorescente** = phosphor coating

photo *nf* = PHOTOGRAPHIE **(a)** *(image)* photo *ou* photograph *ou* picture; *(l'ensemble des photos d'une revue, etc.)* pix; **c'est une photo de l'auteur** = it's a photograph of the author; **il a fait six photos du nouvel ordinateur** = he took six photographs of the new machine; **vous pouvez voir le nouveau modèle sur cette photo** = this picture shows the new design; **photo couleur** = colour photograph; **photo en noir et blanc** = black and white photograph **(b)** *(art)* photography; **photo avec film sensible aux infrarouges** = infrared photography; **appareil photo** = camera

photo- *préf* photo-

photocellule *nf* photocell

photocomposé, -ée *adj* **texte photocomposé** = phototypeset text

◊ **photocomposeuse** *nf* phototypesetter

◊ **photocomposition** *nf* filmsetting *ou* photocomposition *ou* phototypesetting; **la PAO devrait produire un texte dont la qualité est à peu près égale à celle de la photocomposition** = in desktop publishing, the finished work should look almost as if it had been typeset

photoconductivité *nf* photoconductivity

◊ **photoconducteur, -trice** *adj* **cellule photoconductrice** = photoconductor

photocopie *nf* **(a)** photocopy; *(faite avec une machine de marque Xerox)* Xerox (copy); **faites six photocopies du contrat** = make six photocopies of the contract; **envoyer une photocopie du contrat à l'autre partie** = to send the other party a xerox of the contract; **nous avons envoyé des photocopies à chacun des agents** = we have sent photocopies to each of the agents **(b)** *(action)* photocopying; **bureau de photocopie** = photocopying bureau; **les frais de photocopie augmentent d'année en année** = photocopying costs are rising each year

◊ **photocopier** *vtr* to photocopy; *(avec une machine de marque Xerox ™)* to xerox; **elle a photocopié le contrat et tout le dossier** = she photocopied the contract and the entire file; **photocopier un document** = to xerox a document; **photocopier une lettre** = to make a xerox copy *ou* a photocopy of a letter

◊ **photocopieur** *nm* photocopier *ou* copier *ou* copying machine; *(de marque Xerox ™)* Xerox ™ (machine); **on nous installera un nouveau photocopieur Xerox demain** = we are having a new Xerox machine installed tomorrow

photodiode *nf* photodiode; **photodiode à avalanche** = avalanche photodiode (APD); **photodiode (de type) PIN** = pin photodiode

ce détecteur est composé de deux photodiodes au silicium superposées, chacune ayant une réponse spectrale différente
Opto électronique

photoélectricité *nf* photoelectricity

◊ **photoélectrique** *adj* photoelectric; **cellule photoélectrique** = photocell *ou* photoelectric cell; **la cellule photoélectrique décèle la quantité de lumière qui traverse le liquide** = the photoelectric cell detects the amount of light passing through the liquid; **détecteur photoélectrique** = photosensor

photoémission *nf* photoemission

photographie *nf* (a) *(image)* photograph; **photographie en couleur** = colour photograph; **il y aura une photographie en couleur de l'auteur au dos de la jaquette** = we will be using a colour photograph of the author on the back of the jacket; **photographie numérisée** = digitized photograph (b) *(art, method)* photography; **le film du texte peut être reproduit par photographie** = the text film can be reproduced photographically; **photographie de la même scène avec plusieurs ouvertures** = bracketing

◊ **photographier** *vtr* to photograph; **le copieur photographie le texte imprimé pour le reproduire** = the copier makes a photographic reproduction of the printed page

◊ **photographique** *adj* photographic; **appareil photographique** *ou* **appareil photo** = camera; **pellicule photographique** = (photographic) film; **plaque photographique** = (photographic) plate

◊ **photographiquement** *adv* photographically

◊ **photogravure** *nf* photogravure

photo-litho *nf* photolithography

◊ **photolithographie** *nf* photolithography

photomécanique *adj* photomechanical; **transfert photomécanique** = photomechanical transfer (PMT)

photométrie *nf* photometry

photon *nm* photon

photosensible *adj* light-sensitive; **détecteur photosensible** = photosensor; **dispositif photosensible** = light-sensitive device; **les films photosensibles réagissent à la lumière** = light-sensitive films change when exposed to light; **papier photosensible** = light-sensitive paper; **la photo est imprimée sur papier photosensible** = the photograph is printed on light-sensitive paper; **papier photosensible double face** = duplex (paper); **plaque photosensible** = (photographic) plate; **résine photosensible** = photoresist; **(méthode de la) résine photosensible en positif** = positive photoresist

photostat *nm* photostat; **faire un photostat (d'un document)** = to photostat (a document)

phototransistor *nm* phototransistor

photovoltaïque *adj* photovoltaic; **calculatrice à batteries photovoltaïques** = solar-powered calculator

ces photodiodes sont de type photovoltaïque et ne nécessitent pas de polarisation
Opto électronique

physique *adj* physical; **adresse physique** = physical address; **couche physique** = physical layer; **enregistrement physique** = physical record; **(disque) avec formatage physique** = hard-sectored (disk); **mémoire physique** = physical memory; **paramètre physique** = physical parameter; **base de données physique** = physical database; **topologie physique** = physical topology; **unité physique** = physical record

pic *nm* peak

pica *nm (12 points anglais, environ 11 points Didot)* pica

PICK ™ *(système d'exploitation multi-utilisateur et multitâche)* PICK ™ (operating system)

pick-up *nm* pickup

pico- (p) *préf (un million de millions de fois plus petit)* pico-

◊ **picofarad (pF)** *nm* picofarad (pF)

◊ **picoseconde (ps)** *nf* picosecond (ps)

picot *nm* **entraînement (du papier) par picots** = tractor feed *ou* sprocket feed *ou* pinfeed; **roue à picots** = sprocket wheel

pièce *nf* part *ou* component; **pièce détachée** = spare part; **l'imprimante est en panne, il faut remplacer une pièce** = the printer won't work - we need to get a spare part

pied *nm* foot; *(d'une page)* **blanc de pied** = bottom space *ou* foot margin; **pied de page** = foot (of page)

piézoélectrique *adj* piezoelectric

ce système piézoélectrique fonctionne même à travers les obstacles perturbants du type vitre ou eau
Hi-fi Vidéo

PIF *(fichier d'information d'un programme, sous MS-Windows)* **fichier PIF** = Program Information File (PIF)

piggyback *nm* piggyback; **mettre en piggyback** = to piggyback; **mise en piggyback** = piggybacking

pile *nf* **(a)** *(binaire)* heap; *(de données en mémoire)* stack; *(pour stockage de données en mode LIFO)* cellar; **pile en file d'attente (en mode FIFO)** = push-up list *ou* stack; **pile d'instructions d'un programme** = program stack; **constitution de pile d'interruptions** = interrupt stacking; **pile inversée (en mode LIFO)** = push-down list *ou* stack; **pile de mémoire virtuelle** = virtual memory stack; **processeur de pile de tâches** = stack job processor; **adresse de pile** = stack address; **base de la pile** = stack base; **dessus de la pile** = top of stack; **introduire** *ou* **mettre (des données) dans la pile** = to put data onto a stack; **pointeur de pile** = stack pointer (SP) **(b)** battery; **pile auxiliaire ou de secours** = battery backup; **équipé d'une pile auxiliaire** *ou* **de secours** = battery-backed; **dans ce portable, le lecteur de disquettes est remplacé par une mémoire CMOS avec pile auxiliaire** = battery-backed CMOS memory replaces a disk drive in this portable; **la carte RAM peut être équipée, en option, d'une pile de secours** = the RAM disk card has the option to be battery-backed; **pile rechargeable** = re-chargeable battery; **pile sèche** *ou* **alcaline** = dry cell; **pile solaire** = solar cell; **niveau de tension** *ou* **différence de potentiel d'une pile** = battery voltage level

piller *vtr (sans permission)* **piller une base de données** = to browse; to break into a database *ou* to scavenge a database

PILOT *(langage utilisé principalement pour les didacticiels)* PILOT

pilotage *nm* control; **langage de pilotage (de périphériques)** = (peripheral) command control language

◊ **pilote** *nm* **(a)** controller *ou* pilot; **pilote d'écran** *ou* **d'affichage** = display controller; **pilote d'imprimante** = printer's controller *ou* printer driver; **pilote de périphérique(s)** = device driver *ou* peripheral driver; **(programme) pilote de souris** = mouse driver; **pilote de traceur (de courbes)** = plotter driver **(b)** **la société a mis sur pied un projet-pilote pour évaluer le procédé de fabrication proposé** = the company set up a pilot project to see if the proposed manufacturing system was efficient; **système-pilote** = pilot system; **l'usine-pilote a été construite pour tester le nouveau procédé de fabrication** = the pilot factory has been built to test the new production process

◊ **piloté, -ée** *adj* **chariot piloté par ordinateur** = buggy

◊ **piloter** *vtr* to control *ou* to drive

les pilotes de périphériques ou 'device drivers' sont des programmes ajoutés au système d'exploitation (DOS) pour piloter des accessoires et des périphériques
L'Ordinateur Individuel

PIM *(gestionnaire personnel d'information)* Personal Information Manager (PIM)

PIN = P-TYPE, INTRINSIC AND N-TYPE **photodiode PIN** = pin photodiode

pinceau *nm (brosse)* brush; **le logiciel de dessin vous permet de changer la largeur du pinceau (en pixels) et la couleur qu'il étale** = the paint package lets you vary the width of the brush (in pixels) and the colour it produces; **type de pinceau** = brush style; **pour couvrir une grande surface, j'utilise un pinceau large et à bout carré** = to fill in a big area, I select a wide, square brush style

pipe-line *ou* **pipeline** *nm* ordinateur avec architecture en pipeline = pipeline computer; **exécuter** *ou* **traiter (des instructions) en pipeline** = to pipeline; **mode d'exécution** *ou* **de traitement en pipeline** = pipelining; **mode d'exécution d'instructions en pipeline** = instruction pipelining; **organisation en pipeline** = pipelining; **organiser en pipeline** = to pipeline

piqué *nm (de lentille)* acutance

piratage *nm* piracy; **faire du piratage informatique** = to hack; **nous avons changé les mots de passe pour empêcher le piratage de la base de données** = we have changed the passwords to prevent hackers getting into the database; **piratage de logiciel** = software piracy

◊ **pirate** *nm (de logiciels)* pirate; *(pirate de système informatique)* hacker; **la société tente d'amener les pirates de logiciel devant les tribunaux** = the company is trying to take the software pirates to court; **copie pirate** = pirate copy *ou* pirated copy

Quatre ans de prison et deux millions de francs d'amende: c'est la peine maximale encourue par le pirate informatique
l'Ordinateur Individuel

◊ **piraté, -ée** *adj* pirated; **une bande piratée** = a pirated tape; *(d'enregistrement)* **copie piratée** = bootleg; **exemplaire piraté d'un programme d'ordinateur** = pirate copy of a computer program; **logiciel piraté** = pirate software *ou* pirate copy (of a computer program); **entrée sur un système avec un mot de passe piraté** = piggyback entry

◊ **pirater** *vtr* to pirate; **pirater un système** = to hack; **logiciel qui a été piraté** = pirate software; **il a utilisé une disquette piratée bon marché et a découvert que le programme contenait des bogues** = he used a cheap pirated disk and found the program had bugs in it; **les différents schémas du nouveau système ont été piratés en Extrême-Orient** = the designs for the new system were pirated in the Far East

piste *nf* **(a)** *(de disque ou de bande)* track; **piste d'adresses** = address track; **piste de données binaires** = bit track; **piste d'horloge** = clock track; **piste de parité** = parity track; **(nombre de) pistes par pouce** = tracks per inch (TPI); **piste de référence** = library track; **piste sonore** = sound track; **adresse de piste** = track address; **la tête de**

lecture fait une erreur de piste = the read head is not tracking the recorded track correctly; **disque de quatre-vingts pistes** = eighty-track disk; **disquette (de) quarante pistes** = forty-track disk; **magnétophone à quatre pistes** = four-track recorder **(b)** *(de carte magnétique)* **piste magnétique** = magnetic strip; **lecteur de pistes magnétiques** = magnetic strip reader

pitch *nm (espacement)* pitch

pixel *nm* picture element *ou* pixel; **adaptateur d'écran de résolution supérieure à 1024 x 1024 pixels** = megapixel display

le pixel correspond à la plus petite unité d'information d'une image numérique
Science et Vie Micro

un pixel est le plus petit élément d'une image. En noir et blanc, c'est un simple point sur l'écran, défini par un bit. En couleur, chaque point correspond à trois faisceaux: un rouge, un vert, un bleu (R,G,B en anglais).
Mon PC Multimédia

PL/1 = PROGRAMMING LANGUAGE/1 ; *voir* PROGRAMMATION

placard *nm* broadsheet; **épreuves en placard** = galley proof *ou* slip pages *ou* slip proofs

place *nf* place; **place d'un chiffre** = digit place *ou* position; **changer (quelque chose) de place** = to move (something); **mettre en place** = to install *ou* to position; **mise en place** = installation; **mise en place de liens** = linkage editing; **temps de mise en place** = positioning time; *(permuter)* **mettre une chose à la place d'une autre** = to interchange; **sur place** = on-site *ou* in-house; *(ordinateur)* on local

◊ **placement** *nm* **octet de placement** = postbyte

◊ **placer** *vtr* to position; **il faut éviter de placer l'écran devant une fenêtre** = the VDU should not be positioned in front of a window; **on avait placé des feuilles blanches entre les pages nouvellement imprimées pour éviter les coulures d'encre** = blank paper was interleaved with the newly printed text to prevent the ink running

plage *nf* **(a)** *(écart)* gap; *(d'erreurs)* error range; **plage normale** = normal (error) range **(b)** *(d'un disque)* track

cela assure une très grande précision dans le positionnement du laser, la recherche d'une plage déterminée est du même coup facilitée et se fait dans des temps extrêmement courts
Hi-fi Vidéo

plan *nm* **(a)** *(photo)* **plan focal** = image plane; **gros plan** = close-up **(b)** *(avant)* **premier plan** = foreground; **couleur de premier plan** = foreground colour **(c)** *(prioritaire)* **tâche de premier plan** = foreground job; *voir aussi* ARRIÈRE-PLAN **(d)** *(design)* blueprint *ou* plan; **il a fait les plans de la nouvelle usine de composants** = he designed the new chip factory; *(d'un étage)* **plan d'ensemble** = floor plan; **armoire** *ou* **meuble à plans** = planchest;

jeu de plans = plans **(e)** *(des rues d'une ville)* street plan *ou* town plan **(f)** *(planning)* plan; *(suivant un horaire)* schedule; **plan d'urgence** = contingency plan; **logiciel de plan de travail** = scheduler

plan, -e *adj* flat; **surface plane** = flat *ou* plane surface

PLAN *(langage de bas niveau)* PLAN (language)

planar *adj (de production de circuits intégrés)* **procédé planar** = planar **(b)** **graphe planar** = planar

planche *nf (illustration)* plate

planète *nf* planet

planification *nf* planning; scheduling; **planification de la séquence d'exécution des tâches** = job scheduling

◊ **planifier** *vtr&i* to plan *ou* to map out

◊ **planning** *nm* **(a)** *(planification)* planning; **planning à longue échéance** *ou* **à courte échéance** = long-term planning *ou* short-term planning **(b)** *(calendrier)* **planning mural** = wall planner

plantage *nm (d'un système)* crash

◊ **(se) planter** *vpr* to bomb *ou* to crash; **le programme s'est planté, nous avons perdu toutes les données** = the program bombed, and we lost all the data

plaque *nf* **(a)** board *ou* card; **plaque (présensibilisée) pour circuit imprimé** = printed circuit board (PCB); **plaque double face pour circuit imprimé** = double-sided printed circuit board **(b)** plate; **plaque photographique** *ou* **photosensible** = photographic plate; **appareil photo à plaques** = plate camera

plaquette *nf (pour circuit imprimé)* board

plasma *nm* plasma; **affichage** *ou* **écran (au) plasma** = (gas) plasma display *ou* gas discharge display

plat, -e *adj* **(a)** flat; **boîtier plat** = flat pack; **câble plat** = tape cable *ou* ribbon cable; **fichier plat** = flat file

◊ **à plat** *adv (scanner, etc.)* flatbed; **le papier n'est pas entraîné par rouleaux dans un scanner à plat** = in flatbed scanners the paper is not fed in through rollers; **lecteur de transmission à plat** = flatbed transmitter

plateau *nm (chacun des disques du disque dur)* platter; **pile de plateaux qui constituent le disque dur** = disk pack

un disque dur comporte un ou plusieurs disques rigides empilés les uns sur les autres: les plateaux
l'Ordinateur Individuel

plate-forme *nf* platform; **plate-forme de collecte de données** = data collection platform;

(d'un logiciel ou d'un réseau) **indépendance de la plate-forme** = platform independence

platine *nf* **(a)** *(tourne-disque)* turntable *ou* deck; **platine laser** = CD player *ou* compact disc player; **platine magnétophone** *ou* **platine magnétocassette** = tape deck **(b) presse à platine** = platen press *ou* flatbed press

> le marché de la hi-fi est ici composé des produits suivants: platines CD, platines tourne-disques, platine K7, tuners, amplis, chaînes composées
> *Audio Vidéo*

plein, -e *adj* full; **cette disquette est pleine, il faudra donc saisir les données sur une autre disquette** = the disk is full, so the material will have to be stored on another disk; **la disquette a été très vite pleine** = the disk was quickly filled up; **carte vidéo pleine animation** = full motion video adapter; **écran pleine page** = full-size display; **plein écran** = full-screen

pleurage *nm (d'une bande)* wow

pli *nm* fold; *(papier)* **(à) quatre plis** = sixteenmo *ou* 16mo

◊ **pliage** *nm (papier)* fold *ou* folding; **pliage en cahiers de 16, 32 ou 64 pages** = even working

◊ **plier** *vtr* to fold

◊ **plieuse** *nf (pour papier)* folding machine

◊ **pliure** *nf* folding

plomb *nm* **(a)** lead; **composition au plomb** = hot metal setting **(b)** fuse; **faire sauter un plomb** = to blow a fuse; **on a fait sauter les plombs en branchant le climatiseur** = when the air-conditioning was switched on, it fused the whole system

plongeant, -e *adj* **vue plongeante** = aerial image

plume *nf* pen; *(de traceur)* plotter pen; **traceur à plumes** = pen plotter

plus 1 *conj* **code (binaire) plus 3** = excess-3 code; **pour 6, le code (binaire) plus 3 est 1001** = the excess-3 code representation of 6 is 1001; **une adresse plus une** = one-plus-one address; **instruction à n adresse(s) plus une** = n-plus-one address instruction **2** *nm (le signe de l'addition)* **le signe plus (+)** = plus *ou* plus sign

PLV = PUBLICITE LIEU DE VENTE; *voir* LIEU

pn jonction pn *ou* **zone interface pn** = pn-junction; **jonction pn à diffusion** *ou* **zone interface pn à diffusion** = diffused pn-junction; **jonction pn à seuil** *ou* **zone interface pn à seuil** = step pn-junction

◊ **pnp transistor (de type) pnp** = pnp transistor; **transistor bipolaire** *ou* **à jonction pnp** = bipolar (junction) transistor (BJT)

poche *nf* **(a)** pocket; **calculatrice de poche** = pocket calculator; **ordinateur de poche** = hand-held computer; palmtop; **cet ordinateur de poche a un clavier minuscule et un écran à cristaux liquides de 20 lignes** = this palmtop has a tiny keyboard and twenty-line LCD screen **(b) livre de poche** = paperback; **ce livre paraîtra en édition cartonnée et en livre de poche** = we are publishing the book as a hardback and as a paperback

◊ **pochette** *nf (d'un disque)* jacket *ou* sleeve

pochoir *nm* **pochoir de traçage** = stencil; **ce pochoir contient toutes les formes pour composants électroniques** = the stencil has all the electronic components on it

poids *nm* **(a)** weight; **poids brut** = gross weight; **poids net** = net weight; *(d'une rame de papier)* **poids unitaire** = basic weight **(b) bit de poids faible** = least significant bit (LSB); **chiffre de poids faible** = least significant digit (LSD) *ou* low-order digit; **bit de poids fort** = weighted bit *ou* most significant bit (MSB); **chiffre de poids fort** = high order digit *ou* most significant digit (MSD) *ou* most significant character

poignée *nf* **poignées (de manipulation)** = handle; **dans ce programme de PAO, on sélectionne d'abord la boîte qu'on veut agrandir pour faire apparaître les poignées, puis on tire une des poignées pour modifier la forme de la boîte** = to stretch the box in the DTP program, select it once to display the handles then drag one handle to change its shape

poinçon *nm (de perforation)* punch; *(de cartes)* card punch (CP); *(de bandes papier)* perforator *ou* (paper) tape punch

point *nm* **(a)** dot; **(nombre de) points par pouce** = dots per inch *ou* d.p.i. *ou* dpi; **certaines imprimantes laser sont dotées d'une définition de 400 points par pouce** = some laser printers offer high resolution printing at 400 dpi; **un moniteur monochrome format A4 avec une définition de 300 points par pouce** = a 300 d.p.i. black and white A4 monitor; **un scanner d'image avec définition de 300 points par pouce** = a 300 dpi image scanner; **point de contrôle** = available point; **point d'image** = scanning spot; *(d'un écran)* **points de phosphore** *ou* **de phosphorescence** = phosphor dots *ou* spots; **matrice de points** = dot matrix; **commande (précédée d'un) point** = dot command; **graphique de points** = scatter graph **(b)** *(typographie)* full stop, *US* period; **point d'exclamation (!)** = exclamation mark; **point d'interrogation (?)** = question mark; **point-virgule (;)** = semi-colon; **deux points (:)** = colon **(c)** *(placé devant chaque élément d'une liste)* bullet; **point indicateur de couleur** = colour bullet **(d)** *(mesure de taille de caractères)* point; **est-ce qu'en augmentant la taille des caractères à 10 points on augmente ainsi le nombre de pages?** = if we increase the point size to 10, will the page extent increase?; *(0.324 mm)* **point Didot** *ou* **point typographique** = point; *(environ 11 points Didot)* **12 points anglais** = pica; **le texte du livre est (composé) en Times 9 points** = the text of the book is set in 9 point Times **(e)** *(endroit)* **point d'accès** = *(port d'entrée ou sortie)* port; *(pour contrôle d'une carte ou d'un logiciel)* access point; **point d'arrêt** = cutoff; *(d'exécution d'un programme)* breakpoint; **point d'arrêt variable** = regional breakpoint; *(après incident)* remise en marche au point d'arrêt *ou* au point de reprise *ou* reprise au point d'appel = fall back recovery *ou* failure recovery; (point d') arrivée = far end *ou* receiving end; *(de film ou écran)* point chaud = hot spot; point de branchement = branchpoint; point de connexion = terminal; point de contrôle = check point; point de début d'enregistrement = loadpoint; point de départ = starting point; point d'entrée = entry point; point d'entrée dans un système = trapdoor; (liaison) point à point = point to point (connection); point de raccordement = terminal; point de réception = receiving point; point de ré-entrée *ou* de rentrée = re-entry point; point de reprise = re-entry point *ou* check point; point de sortie = exit point; point de vidage = dump point (f) point de vente = point-of-sale (POS); point de vente électronique = electronic point-of-sale (EPOS); terminal de point de vente = point-of-sale terminal *ou* POS terminal (g) *(sujet)* matter (h) *(valeur)* percentage point (i) au point = *(image)* in focus; *(appareil)* tuned *ou* adjusted; *(program)* debugged; l'image n'est pas au point = the picture is out of focus *ou* is not in focus; mettre au point = *(une image)* to focus; *(un appareil)* to tune *ou* to adjust; *(un programme ou un détail d'installation)* to tweak; *(un produit)* to develop; to perfect; la position de la lentille a été ajustée de façon à bien mettre au point le rayon lumineux = they adjusted the lens position so that the beam focused correctly; mettre au point (avec grande précision) = to fine tune; il a mis au point le procédé de fabrication d'un acier de haute qualité = he perfected the process for making high grade steel; mise au point = *(d'une image)* focusing; *(d'un appareil)* tuning *ou* adjustment; *(d'un programme)* tweaking; *(d'un produit)* development; mise au point magnétique = magnetic focusing; dérégler la mise au point = to defocus; une mise au point très précise améliore la vitesse de dix pour cent = fine-tuning improved the speed by ten per cent; logiciel de mise au point = debugger; temps de mise au point d'un nouveau produit = development time

---

sur des réseaux privés point à point, le codeur-décodeur d'images fonctionne dans une plage de débit comprise entre 9600bps et 384Kbps

Informatique & Bureautique (Suisse)

---

pointage *nm* dispositif de pointage = pointing device

pointe *nf* (a) *(de tension)* spike; voltage transient (b) *(d'une onde)* les pointes et les creux = peaks and troughs (c) heure(s) de pointe = peak period; techniques de pointe = high technology

pointeur *nm* pointer; *(poignée)* handle; fichier de pointeurs = pointer file; pointeur (de position) de données = data pointer; pointeur de pile = stack pointer (SP); la PAO sur ordinateur personnel est facilitée par l'emploi d'un pointeur et d'une souris = desktop publishing on a PC is greatly helped by the use of a pointer and mouse; incrémenter le pointeur jusqu'à l'adresse (d'instruction) suivante = increment the contents of the pointer to the address of the next instruction

pointillé *nm* (a) dotted line (b) *(perforé)* perforated line *ou* perforations

◊ **pointillé, -ée** *adj* ligne pointillée = dotted line

point-virgule (;) *nm* semi-colon

POKE *(de modification en mémoire)* instruction POKE = POKE instruction; l'instruction POKE 1423,74 écrira 74 à l'emplacement 1423 = POKE 1423,74 will write the data 74 into location 1423

polaire *adj* (a) polar; coordonnées polaires = polar coordinates; diagramme en coordonnées polaires = polar diagram (b) orbite polaire = polar orbit

◊ **polarisation** *nf* polarization *ou* bias; *(antenne ou signal)* à *ou* avec polarisation verticale = vertically polarized; signal avec polarisation verticale = vertically polarized signal

◊ **polarisé, -ée** *adj* biased *ou* polarized

◊ **polarité** *nf* polarity; polarité électrique = electrical polarity; polarité inversée = reverse polarity; polarité magnétique = magnetic polarity; test de polarité = polarity test

polaroïde *adj* filtre polaroïde = polaroid filter

police *nf* police de caractères = font *ou* fount *ou* typeface *ou* typestyle *ou* character set; police de caractères de base *ou* par défaut = base font; police de caractères du corps de texte = body type; police de caractères reconnaissable par lecture optique = optical font *ou* OCR font; police de caractères téléchargeable = downloadable fonts; police de caractères utilisable par un terminal = terminal character set; police de caractères vectorielle = dynamically redefinable character set; police résidente = resident font; carte de polices de caractères = font card; cartouche de police de caractères = cartridge fonts; changement de police de caractères = font change; disquette de polices de caractères = font disk; gestionnaire de polices et d'accessoires de bureau (Mover Apple Macintosh) = Font/DA Mover (Apple Macintosh system utility); support de polices de caractères = image carrier; utilisation de plusieurs polices de caractères = font mixing

policé, -ée *adj (programme)* well-behaved

pollution *nf* pollution (par rayonnement) électronique = electronic smog

polonais, -e *adj (notation suffixée)* notation polonaise inversée = reverse Polish notation (RPN) *ou* postfix notation *ou* suffix notation; alors que la notation conventionnelle s'écrit: (x-y) + z, la notation polonaise inversée s'écrit: xy - z+ = normal notation: (x-y) + z, but using RPN: xy - z+; notation polonaise (préfixée) = prefix notation; la notation normale: (x-y) + z, la notation polonaise (préfixée): - xy + z = normal notation: (x-y) + z, but using prefix notation: - xy + z

polymérisé, -ée *adj* enregistrement sur couche polymérisée = dye-polymer recording

polynomial, -e *adj* polynomial; code polynomial = polynomial code

polyvalent, -e *adj* ordinateur polyvalent = general purpose computer; **registre polyvalent** = general register *ou* general purpose register (gpr)

pomme *nf* apple; *(sur un Apple Macintosh)* **touche Pomme** = Apple Key

pompage *nm (erreur dans un circuit numérique)* race

ponctuation *nf* punctuation; **signe de ponctuation** = punctuation mark

pondération *nf* weighting

◊ **pondéré, -ée** *adj* weighted; **moyenne pondérée** = weighted average

◊ **pondérer** *vtr* to weight

pont *nm* **(a)** *(connecteur)* jumper **(b)** *(logiciel ou équipement de transition)* bridge *ou* brigeware *ou* bridging product; **établir un pont** = to bridge; **pont de routage** = brouter; **le pont de routage permet un routage dynamique entre les deux réseaux locaux** = the brouter provides dynamic routing and can bridge two local area networks

> COMMENTAIRE: Un pont relie deux réseaux similaires, une passerelle relie deux réseaux différents. Pour relier deux réseaux Ethernet, utilisez un pont

POO = PROGRAMMATION ORIENTEE OBJET

pool *nm (groupe de dactylos)* **pool de dactylos** = typing pool

POP 2 *(langage de haut niveau pour traitement de listes)* POP 2 (language)

port *nm* port; **port asynchrone** = asynchronous port; **l'utilisation de ports asynchrones ne demande pas un matériel spécialisé** = when asynchronous ports are used no special hardware is required; **port de communication** = communications port; **port (d') entrée** = input port; **port (d') entrée/sortie** = I/O port *ou* input/output port; **le manche à balai peut être connecté sur le port entrée/sortie** = the joystick can be connected to the input/output port; **port (pour** *ou* **d')imprimante** = printer port; **port jeu** *ou* **port (pour** *ou* **de) manche à balai** *ou* **manette de jeu** = joystick port; **port (de) sortie** = output port; **connectez l'imprimante au port de sortie (d')imprimante** = connect the printer to the printer output port; **port parallèle** = parallel port; **(en) port partagé** *ou* **partage de port** = port sharing; **port pour périphériques** = user port; **port privatif** *ou* **réservé** = private dial port; **port série** = serial port; **port vidéo** = video port; **sélecteur de port** = port selector

portabilité *nf* portability; **portabilité d'une formule** = formula portability

◊ **portable 1** *adj* **(a)** portable *ou* transportable; **équipement de prise de vue portable sur le dos** = back pack; **ordinateur portable** = portable (computer); laptop (computer); *voir aussi* PORTATIF **(b) programmes portables** = portable software *ou* portable programs *ou* canned programs **2** *nm&f (un ordinateur portable)* **un portable** = a portable

portage *nm* **la capacité de portage de cette liaison est excellente** = the information-carrying abilities of this link are very good

portance *nf* **laser de portance** = injection laser

portatif, -ive 1 *adj* portable; **petit (ordinateur) portatif (autonome)** = laptop computer *ou* lapheld computer; *(ultra-portatif)* **petit ordinateur portatif (qu'on tient à la main)** = hand-held computer **2** *n (ordinateur)* **un portatif** = a portable; *(machine à écrire)* **une portative** = a portable (typewriter); **elle a écrit la lettre sur sa petite portative** = she wrote the letter on her portable typewriter

porte *nf* gate; **porte d'équivalence** = equivalence gate; **porte ET** = AND gate *ou* coincidence gate; **porte d'identité** = identity gate *ou* element; **porte logique** = logic gate; **porte NI** = NOR gate; **porte NI exclusif** = exclusive NOR gate *ou* EXNOR gate; **porte NON** = NOT gate; **porte NON-ET** *ou* NAND = NAND gate; **porte NON-OU** *ou* **NI** = NOR gate; **porte OU** = OR gate; **porte OU exclusif** = except gate *ou* exclusive OR gate *ou* EXOR gate *ou* non-equivalence gate

portée *nf* range; **modem de courte portée** = short haul modem *ou* short range modem; **hors de portée** = out of range

porteur, -euse *adj* **(a)** **onde porteuse** = carrier wave; **détecteur d'onde porteuse** = data carrier detect (DCD); **télégraphie par onde porteuse** = carrier telegraphy; **transmission par onde porteuse** = carrier signalling; **elle n'utilise pas de modem: il n'existe aucun signal porteur sur la ligne** = she's not using a modem - there's no carrier signal on the line **(b) fusée porteuse** = launch vehicle

◊ **porteuse** *nf (onde)* carrier (wave); **porteuse de données** = data carrier; **interférence entre porteuses** = intercarrier noise; **on note des interférences de porteuses sur une télévision lorsque la porteuse son et la porteuse image se rencontrent** = television intercarrier noise is noticed when the picture and the sound signal carriers clash; **modulation d'amplitude sans porteuse** *ou* **à porteuse inhibée** = suppressed carrier modulation; **bande latérale unique sans porteuse** *ou* **à porteuse inhibée** = single sideband suppressed carrier (SSBSC); **bandes latérales** *ou* **double bande latérale sans porteuse** *ou* **à porteuse inhibée** = double sideband suppressed carrier (DSBSC); **l'appel est bloqué si le logiciel ne reçoit pas de signal de détection de porteuse** = the call is stopped if the software does not receive a DCD signal from the modem; **porteuse d'image** *ou* **de signal vidéo** = image carrier; **porteuse principale** = main beam; **signal CD** *ou* **de détection de porteuse** = carrier detect (CD)

pose *nf (d'un enduit)* deposition

positif *nm (photo ou film)* positive; **affichage en positif** = positive presentation; **(méthode de la) résine photosensible en positif** = positive photoresist (technique)

◊ **positif, -ive** *adj* positive; **accusé de réception positif (d'un message)** = affirmative acknowledgement; **borne positive** = positive terminal; **épreuve positive** = photoprint; **feedback positif** *ou* **rétroaction positive** = positive feedback; **film positif** = positive film *ou* direct image film; **logique positive** = positive logic; **réponse positive** = positive response

position *nf* place *ou* position; **position binaire** = bit position; *(du curseur, etc.)* **position initiale** *ou* **de départ** = home; **mise en position de transport de la tête** = head park; **modulation d'impulsions en position (MIP)** = pulse position modulation (PPM)

◊ **positionnel, -elle** *adj* positional

◊ **positionnement** *nm* positioning; **positionnement de la tête de lecture** = head positioning; *(sur microfilm)* **marque** *ou* **repère** *ou* **symbole de positionnement** = editing symbol; *(marque de secteur de disque)* **perforation de positionnement** = sectoring hole

◊ **positionner** *vtr* to position *ou* to align; **positionnez la photo dans le coin droit du haut de la page** = position this photograph at the top right-hand corner of the page; *(deux images)* **positionner sur repères** = to register

POSIX *(norme UNIX)* Portable Operating System Interface (POSIX)

possibilité *nf* possibility; capability; **liste des possibilités** = capability list

◊ **possible** *adj* possible; **rendre possible** = to enable

post- *préfixe* post-

postal *adj* postal; **code postal** = post code, *US* ZIP code

◊ **poste 1** *nf (courrier)* mail; **bureau de poste** = post office; **envoi par la poste** = mailing; **envoyer par la poste** *ou* **mettre à la poste** = to mail *ou* to post; **prospectus envoyé par la poste** = mailing piece; **poste électronique** = E-mail *ou* email **2** *nm* **(a)** *(ordinateur)* station *ou* terminal; **poste de contrôle mixte** = combined station; **poste éloigné** = remote station; **poste informatique de télétransmission** = data terminal *ou* data station; **poste d'interrogation** = inquiry station; **poste de travail** = workstation *ou* (operating) console *ou* terminal; **poste de travail multifonction** = multifunction workstation; **poste de travail d'un opérateur** = operator's console; **le système comprend cinq postes de travail reliés en anneau** = the system includes five workstations linked together in a ring network **(b) (de) poste (de) radio** *ou* **(de) T.S.F.** = radio (set); **poste (de) télévision** = television (TV) *ou* television receiver *ou* television set; **foyers qui possèdent au moins un poste de télévision ou de radio** = broadcast homes

◊ **poster 1** *nm (affiche)* poster **2** *vtr* **poster une lettre** = to post *ou* to mail a letter

post-processeur *nm* postprocessor

PostScript ™ *(langage de description de page de Adobe)* PostScript ™; **si vous utilisez beaucoup la PAO, vous tirerez profit d'une imprimante** PostScript = if you do a lot of DTP work, you will benefit from a PostScript printer; **affichage PostScript** = Display PostScript ™

postsynchronisation *nf* dubbing

◊ **postsynchronisé, -ée** *adj* dubbed; **effet sonore postsynchronisé** = dubbed sound

potentiel *nm* **(a)** *(possibilité)* potential; **potentiel d'écoute** = coverage **(b)** *(tension)* potential *ou* voltage level; **différence de potentiel** = potential difference; **différence de potentiel d'une pile** = battery voltage level; **élever le potentiel d'une ligne** = to pull up a line; **élever le potentiel de la ligne de réception au niveau logique un, en la connectant sur une source de courant de 5 volts** = to pull up the input line to a logic one by connecting it to 5 volts

◊ **potentiomètre** *nm* potentiometer

poubelle *nf (icône Apple)* trashcan; *voir aussi* CORBEILLE **poubelle à bits** = bit bucket; **mettre à la poubelle** = to junk

pouce *nm* **(a)** *(mesure de longueur)* inch; **disquette de 3,5 pouces, de 5,25 pouces** = three and a half inch disk, five and a quarter inch disk; **disquette de huit pouces** = eight inch disk; **lecteur de disquettes de 3,5 pouces, de 5,25 pouces, de 8 pouces** = three and a half inch, five and a quarter inch, eight inch (disk) drive **(b) (nombre de) pouces par seconde** *ou* **pouces/seconde** = inches per second (ips); **la vitesse de balayage de cette machine est de 1,3 pouce par seconde (ppp)** = for this machine throughput is 1.3 inches per second (ips) scanning speed; **(nombre de) bits par pouce** = bits per inch (bpi); **(nombre de) caractères par pouce** = characters per inch (cpi); **le bouton vert vous permet de sélectionner 10 ou 12 caractères par pouce** = you can select 10 or 12 cpi with the green button; **(nombre de) pistes par pouce** = tracks per inch (tpi); **(nombre de) points par pouce** = dots per inch (d.p.i. *ou* dpi); **un moniteur monochrome format A4 avec une définition de 300 points par pouce** = a 300 d.p.i. black and white A4 monitor; **un scanner d'image avec définition de 300 points par pouce** = a 300 dpi image scanner; **certaines imprimantes laser sont dotées d'une définition de 400 points par pouce** = some laser printers offer high resolution printing at 400 dpi

pourcentage *nm* percentage; **pourcentage d'augmentation** = percentage increase; **quel est le pourcentage d'augmentation?** = what is the increase per cent?

poursuite *nf* **caméra de poursuite** = planetary camera

poussé, -ée *adj* **recherche très poussée** = exhaustive search

PowerBook ™ *(laptop de Macintosh)* PowerBook ™

pratique *adj (mise en main)* **formation pratique** = hands-on training; **la société informatique offre une formation pratique de deux jours** = the computer firm gives a two day hands-on training course

PPP = PROTOCOLE POINT A POINT

pré- *préfixe* pre-
◊ **préallocation** *nf* pre-allocation

préampli *nm* = PREAMPLIFICATEUR
◊ **préamplificateur** *nm* pre-amplifier
◊ **préamplifier** *vtr* *(fréquence)* to pre-emphasise

PréAO = PRESENTATION ASSISTEE PAR ORDINATEUR

préavis *nm* **appel** *ou* **communication (téléphonique) avec préavis** = person-to-person call

précaution *nf* precaution; **mesure de précaution** = safety measure *ou* safety net

précédemment *adv* previously

◊ **précédent, -e** *adj* prior *ou* previous; **comparée à la version précédente, celle-ci est très facile à utiliser** = compared with the previous version this one is very user-friendly; **copiez les données du fichier précédent dans le fichier actuel** = copy data into the present workspace from the previous file

◊ **précéder** *vtr* to precede

précis, -e *adj* precise *ou* accurate; **l'horloge atomique indiquera l'heure précise du début du processus** = the atomic clock will give the precise time of starting the process

◊ **préciser** *vtr* to specify

◊ **précision** *nf* accuracy *ou* precision; **avec précision** = accurately; **le code barres doit être imprimé avec une précision de l'ordre du millième de micron** = the printed bar code has to be accurate to within a thousandth of a micron; **régler un appareil avec grande précision** = to fine tune a machine; **caractère (de contrôle) de précision** = accuracy control character; **précision d'un nombre** = precision of a number; **nombres à précision finie** = finite-precision numbers; **double précision** = double-length precision *ou* double precision; **calcul en double précision** = double precision arithmetic; **(de) haute précision** = high specification *ou* high spec; **(en) multiple précision** = multiple precision *ou* multiprecision; **(en) simple précision** = single-length precision *ou* single precision

précompilé, -ée *adj* precompiled; **code précompilé** = precompiled code

préconditionner *vtr* to precondition

préconiser *vtr* to recommend; to specify; **la procédure normale préconise une sauvegarde de tout le travail en fin de journée** = the normal procedure is for backup copies to be made at the end of each day's work

prédéfini, -e *adj* predefined

prédéterminé, -ée *adj* predetermined; **débit prédéterminé d'un modem** = default rate; **valeur prédéterminée** = default value

prédicat *nm* predicate

prééditer *vtr* to pre-edit

préemptif, -ive *adj* preemptive; **(système) multitâche préemptif** = preemptive multitasking

préenregistré, -ée *adj* prerecorded; **(module de) texte pré-enregistré** = prerecord; **le répondeur téléphonique fait entendre un message pré-enregistré** = the answerphone plays a prerecorded message

◊ **préenregistrer** *vtr* to prerecord

préétabli, -e *adj* predesigned; **en-tête préétabli** = form flash; *(gardé en mémoire)* **texte** *ou* **graphique préétabli** = form overlay; **un grand choix de modèles de mise en page préétablis vous permet de formater automatiquement vos documents techniques** = a wide selection of predesigned layouts helps you automatically format typical business and technical documents

préférentiel, -elle *adj* **dossier préférentiel (Macintosh)** = blessed folder

préfixe *nm* prefix

◊ **préfixé, -ée** *adj* **notation préfixée** *ou* **notation polonaise (préfixée)** = prefix notation; *voir aussi* NOTATION

préformaté, -ée *adj* preformatted; **disquette préformatée** = preformatted disk; **ces données ont été copiées sur des disquettes préformatées** = the data is copied onto previously formatted disks

préimprimé, -ée *adj* preprinted; **formulaire préimprimé** = preprinted form

prélever *vtr* *(dans un réseau Token-Ring)* **prélever (le jeton)** = to capture (the token)

prématuré, -ée *adj* premature; unexpected; **interruption prématurée** = abnormal end *ou* abend *ou* abnormal termination

◊ **prématurément** *adv* prematurely; **abandonner** *ou* **interrompre (un programme) prématurément** = to abort (a program)

premier, -ière 1 *n* **(a)** first; **épreuve en première** = galley proof; *(téléphone)* **coupure au premier raccroché** = first party release; **(méthode du) premier entré premier sorti (FIFO)** = first in first out (FIFO); **file d'attente qui fonctionne sur le principe 'premier entré premier sorti'** = FIFO queue; **mémoire basée sur le principe 'premier entré premier sorti'** = FIFO memory *ou* first in first out memory; **les deux ordinateurs fonctionnent à des vitesses différentes mais peuvent transmettre des données en utilisant une mémoire tampon fonctionnant sur le système 'premier entré premier sorti'** = the two computers operate at different rates, but can transmit data using a FIFO memory **2** *adj* **(a) première génération** = first generation; **le fichier père est un fichier de sauvegarde de première génération** = the father file is a first generation backup; **image de première génération** = first generation image; **ordinateur de première génération** = first generation computer; **adresse de premier niveau** = first-level address; **algorithme du premier emplacement capable** = first fit (algorithm) **(b)** *(avant ou prioritaire)* **premier plan** = foreground; **couleur de premier plan** = foreground colour; **tâche de premier plan** = foreground task **(c) nombre premier** = prime; **sept (7) est un nombre premier** = the number seven is a prime

prémixage *nm* premix

préparation *nf* preparation; **la préparation de ces étiquettes se fera beaucoup plus rapidement avec l'ordinateur** = if you use the computer for processing the labels, it will be much quicker; **préparation de données** = data preparation; **temps de préparation** = make-ready time; **temps de préparation entre deux tâches** = takedown time

préprocesseur *nm* preprocessor

préproduction *nf* preproduction

préprogrammé, -ée *adj* preprogrammed

◊ **préprogrammer** *vtr* to preprogram; **les tables d'équivalence sont préprogrammées et permettent de gagner du temps de traitement en évitant de recalculer les mêmes valeurs** = lookup tables are preprogrammed and then used in processing to save redoing the calculations for each result required

◊ **préréglé, -ée** *adj* preset; **qui n'est pas préréglé** = selectable

◊ **pré-sélectionné, -ée** *adj* preselected; **acheminement pré-sélectionné** = fixed routing

présent, -e *adj* present; **être présent à** = to attend (a meeting, etc.)

présentation *nf* presentation; **présentation assistée par ordinateur (PréAO)** = desktop presentation; computerized page layout; *(format)* **présentation d'un enregistrement** = record format *ou* layout; *(d'un réseau)* **couche présentation** = presentation layer; *(prévisualisation)* **fonction 'présentation-aperçu'** = previewer; **la fonction intégrée 'présentation - aperçu' permet de visualiser le document et de vérifier s'il s'est glissé des erreurs** = the built-in previewer allows the user to check for mistakes

Presentation Manager ™ *(interface de présentation graphique OS/2)* Presentation Manager ™

présenter *vtr* to present; **les disquettes sont présentées sous emballage plastique** = the diskettes are packed in plastic wrappers

◊ **présentoir** *nm* (display) rack

presse *nf* **(a) la presse** = the press; **nous avons été très déçus par ce que la presse a écrit sur le nouvel ordinateur individuel** = we were very disappointed by the press coverage of the new PC; **nous avons l'intention de faire beaucoup de publicité dans la presse pour le produit** = we plan to give the product a lot of press publicity; **la presse nationale** = the national press; **la publicité pour la nouvelle voiture a été faite dans la presse nationale** = the new car has been advertised in the national press; **agence de presse** = news agency; **communiqué de presse** = news release *ou* press release; **la société a publié un communiqué de presse au sujet du lancement du nouveau scanner** = the company sent out a press release about the launch of the new scanner; **conférence de presse** = press conference; **coupure de presse** = press cutting; **nous avons constitué un dossier de coupures de presse sur le nouveau progiciel** = we have kept a file of press cuttings about the new software package; **service de coupures de presse** = clipping service; **liberté de la presse** = freedom of the press **(b)** *(d'imprimerie)* printing press; **le livre est sous presse** = the book is printing; **le livre est sous presse, nous recevrons donc les exemplaires reliés vers la fin du mois** = the book is printing at the moment, so we will have bound copies at the end of the month

◊ **presse-papiers** *nm* clipboard; **copiez le texte dans le presse-papiers, puis collez-le dans le nouveau document** = copy the text to the clipboard, then paste it back into a new document

◊ **presseur** *nm (d'une imprimante matricielle)* clapper; *(d'un appareil photo)* platen; **presseur de bande** = capstan; **galet presseur** = head wheel

◊ **pression** *nf* pression; **pression acoustique** = sound pressure; **niveau de pression acoustique** = sound pressure level (SPL); **pression nécessaire pour actionner une touche** = key force; **capteur** *ou* **détecteur de pression** = pressure pad; **le détecteur de pression caché sous le tapis déclenche une alarme si quelqu'un marche dessus** = the pressure pad under the carpet will set off the burglar alarm if anyone steps on it; **vérifier la pression** = to gauge (pressure)

prêt *nm* loan; **prêt interbibliothèque** = inter-library loan (ILL)

prêt, -e *adj* ready; **le texte est prêt pour l'impression** = the text is ready for the printing stage *ou* for the printer; **le voyant vert allumé signifie que le système est prêt à accepter le programme suivant** = the green light indicates the system is ready for another program; **(signal de) prêt à transmettre** = clear to send (CTS) *ou* data terminal ready (DTR); *(signal de modem)* **prêt à transmettre/recevoir** = dataset ready (DSR); **configuration prête à l'usage** = configured-in; **état prêt** = ready state

prétraitement *nm* **programme de prétraitement** = preprocessor

◊ **prétraiter** *vtr* **prétraiter des données** = to preprocess data; **données partiellement prétraitées** = semi-processed data

préventif, -ive *adj* preventive *ou* preventative; **maintenance préventive** = preventive maintenance; **nous offrons un contrat de maintenance préventive qui s'applique à ce système** = we offer a preventive maintenance contract for the system

◊ **prévention** *nf* prevention; **prévention d'erreur** = error trapping

prévisualisation *nf* page preview; **fonction de prévisualisation** = previewer

◊ **prévisualiser** *vtr* to preview

primaire *adj* primary; **clé primaire** = primary key; *(voies de communication)* **groupe primaire** = primary group; **station primaire** = primary station

primitif, -ive *adj* **adresse primitive** = presumptive address; *(dans un programme de graphisme)* **forme primitive** = primitive; **instruction primitive** = presumptive instruction; **routine primitive** = primitive

primitive *nf (unité de base de programme, de graphique)* primitive

principal, -e *adj* principal *ou* main *ou* primary; central; **boucle principale (d'un programme)** = main loop (of a program); **canal principal** = primary channel; **caractéristique principale** = key feature *ou* highlight; **les principales caractéristiques de ce système sont les suivantes: 20Mo de mémoire formatée avec temps d'accès de 60ms** = the key features of this system are: 20MB of formatted storage with an access time of 60ms; *(de recherche)* **clé principale** = primary key; **corps principal (d'un programme)** = main body (of a program); **cycle principal** = major cycle; **entrée principale** = main entry; **fichier principal** = master file; **horloge principale** = master clock *ou* timing master; **index principal** = main index; **mémoire principale** = primary memory *ou* core *ou* storage; main memory *ou* store *ou* storage; central memory (CM); **ce système de 16 bits contient une mémoire principale d'une capacité allant jusqu'à 3Mo** = this 16-bit system includes up to 3MB of main memory; **menu principal** = main menu; **mot principal** = keyword; **ordinateur principal** = master computer *ou* host computer; *(gros ordinateur)* mainframe; **accès à l'ordinateur principal** = mainframe access; **porteuse principale** = main beam; **processeur principal** = back-end processor; **routine principale** = main routine; **tableau de distribution principal** = main distributing frame; **terminal principal** = key terminal *ou* central terminal *ou* master terminal; **le gestionnaire de système utilise le terminal principal pour relancer** = the system manager uses the master terminal to restart the system

◊ **principalement** *adv* primarily *ou* mainly

Print Screen *(touche 'impression d'écran')* touche Print Screen = PrtSc (print screen)

prioritaire *adj* priority *ou* foregroung (task, etc.); *(d'arrière plan)* **non prioritaire** = low-priority *ou* background (task, etc.); **communication non prioritaire** = background communication; **interruption prioritaire** = priority interrupt; **opération non prioritaire** = background operation; **programme prioritaire** = high priority program *ou* foreground program; **programme non prioritaire** = background program; **tâche prioritaire** = foreground task; **tâche non prioritaire** = background *ou* low-priority task *ou* work; **traitement non prioritaire** = background processing; *(film)* **(procédé de) transparence non prioritaire** *ou* **d'arrière-plan** = background projection

◊ **priorité** *nf* precedence *ou* priority; **la console de commande a priorité sur l'imprimante et les autres terminaux** = the master console has a higher device priority than the printers and other terminals; **le lecteur de disquettes est plus important que l'imprimante, il a donc la priorité sur cette dernière** = the disk drive is more important than the printer, so it has a higher priority; **le système d'exploitation a priorité sur les applications en ce qui concerne l'espace alloué sur la disquette** = the operating system has priority over applications when disk space is allocated; **priorité d'interruption** = interrupt priority; **table des priorités d'interruption** = priority interrupt table; **priorité d'un périphérique** *ou* **d'un appareil** = device priority; **priorité d'une tâche** *ou* **d'un travail** = job priority; **détermination de priorité des tâches** = job scheduling; **(système de) gestion des priorités en (fonctionnement) parallèle** = parallel priority (system); **gestionnaire de priorités** = priority scheduler; **ordre de priorité** = order of priority; **ordre de priorité des opérations** = operation priority *ou* operator precedence *ou* priority sequence; **détermination de l'ordre de priorité** = scheduling

prise *nf* **(a)** *(de courant)* socket *ou* outlet; **prise de terre** = earth, *US* ground; **prise secteur à deux broches** = two-pin mains socket; **prise secteur à trois broches** = three-pin mains socket; **il faut une prise à trois broches pour connecter** *ou* **brancher le système sur le secteur** = a three-pin socket is needed to connect the printer to the mains **(b)** taking; **prise de vue** = shooting *ou* filming; **prise de vue à cadence lente** = memomotion; **prise de vue en extérieur** = filming *ou* shooting on location **(c)** **prise d'échantillon** = sampling; **la prise d'échantillon toutes les trois secondes a révélé une augmentation** = the sample at three seconds showed an increase

privatif, -ive *adj* private; **autocommutateur privatif (raccordé au réseau public)** = private branch exchange (PBX); **central téléphonique privatif (non raccordé au réseau public)** = private automatic exchange (PAX); **ligne privative** = private line; **port privatif** = private dial port; **système téléphonique privatif** = private telephone system

privé, -ée *adj* **(a)** private; **autocommutateur privé (raccordé au réseau public) (PABX)** = private automatic branch exchange (PABX); **central téléphonique manuel privé (raccordé au secteur public)** = private manual branch exchange (PMBX); **ligne privée** = private line **(b)** *(d'un seul* *utilisateur)* **partition privée** = private address space

privilège *nm* privilege

◊ **privilégié, -ée** *adj* priviledged; **instructions privilégiées** = privileged instructions; *(avec niveau d'accès prioritaire)* **partition privilégiée** = privileged account; **le gestionnaire d'un système jouit d'une partition privilégiée qui lui permet d'accéder à tous les fichiers de ce système** = the systems manager has a privileged status so he can access any file on the system; **le gestionnaire du système peut accéder à toutes les partitions à partir de sa partition privilégiée** = the systems manager can access anyone else's account from his privileged account

PRN = PRINTER; *(abréviation DOS pour désigner l'imprimante)* PRN

problème *nm* **(a)** problem *ou* question; **le problème essentiel est celui du coût** = the main question is that of cost **(b)** problem; *(pépin)* glitch; **problème d'étalonnage** = benchmark problem; **exposé d'un problème** = problem definition; **résoudre un problème** = to solve a problem; **langage de résolution de problèmes** *ou* **langage adapté aux problèmes** = problem-orientated language (POL)

procédé *nm* process

◊ **procédure** *nf* procedure; **cette procédure qui sert à classer les fichiers par ordre alphabétique peut être sélectionnée depuis le programme principal par la commande SORT** = this procedure sorts all the files into alphabetic order, you can call it from the main program by the instruction SORT; **la procédure est expliquée dans le manuel d'utilisation** = the procedure is given in the manual; **la procédure normale préconise une sauvegarde de tout le travail en fin de journée** = the normal procedure is for backup copies to be made at the end of each day's work; **procédure de commande** = operator procedure; **procédure de contrôle d'acheminement** = routing overheads; **procédure de contrôle de liaison de données** *ou* **procédure SDLC** = synchronous data link control (SDLC); **procédure de deuxième génération** *ou* **procédure fille** = child process *ou* program; **procédure de file d'attente** = queue discipline; **procédure de sauvegarde** = backup procedure; **procédures de secours** = fall back routines; **procédure de traitement des erreurs** = error handling *ou* management; **procédure récursive** = recursive call; **à base de procédure** = procedural; **déclaration de procédure** = procedure declaration; **diagramme de procédure** = process chart; **langage de procédure** *ou* **langage adapté à la procédure** = procedure-orientated language *ou* procedural language; **schéma de procédure** = process chart

processeur *nm* processor; **processeur à architecture RISC** = reduced instruction set computer (RISC); **processeur auxiliaire** = auxiliary processor *ou* coprocessor; **processeur auxiliaire relié au processeur central** = attached processor; **processeur central** = central processing unit (CPU) *ou* central processor; **processeur de**

codes commande = order code processor; **processeur de console** = command console processor (CCP); **processeur double** = dual processor; **processeur d'écran** = display processor; **processeur d'entrée/sortie** = input/output processor (IOP); **processeur de fichier de commandes** = command file processor; **processeur de fond** *ou* **processeur principal** = back-end processor; **processeur frontal** = front-end processor (FEP); **processeur graphique** = graphics processor; **processeur d'image** = image processor; **processeur d'image matricielle** = raster image processor; **processeur d'instruction** = instruction processor; **processeur d'interface** = interface processor; **processeur de langage** = language processor; **processeur mathématique pour calcul ultra-rapide** = number cruncher; **processeur à mémoire associative** = associative processor; **processeur en mode caractère** = character machine; **processeur à mots variables** = byte machine; **processeur nu** = clean machine; **processeur de la parole** *ou* **du signal vocal** = speech processor; **processeur périphérique** = peripheral processing unit (PPU); **processeur de programme source** = source machine; **processeur de réseau** = network processor; **processeur de réseau de communication** = communications network processor; **processeur de traitement par lots** *ou* **par paquets** = batch processor; **processeur en tranches** = bit-slice processor; **le processeur en tranches utilise quatre processeurs à 4 bits pour réaliser un processeur à 16 bits** = the bit slice design uses four 4-bit word processors to construct a 16-bit processor; **processeur vectoriel** = array processor; **le processeur vectoriel permet de faire pivoter le tableau qui contient l'image écran à l'aide d'une seule commande** = an array processor allows the array that contains the screen image to be rotated with one simple command; **processeur à virgule flottante** = floating point processor; **un processeur à virgule flottante est installé sur ce modèle** = this model includes a built-in floating point processor; **le processeur à virgule flottante accélère la vitesse de traitement de ce logiciel graphique** = a floating point processor speeds up the processing of the graphics software; **dépendant du processeur** *ou* **limité par le processeur** = processor-limited; **double processeur** = dual processor; **post-processeur** = postprocessor; **temps d'utilisation du processeur** = CPU time

processus *nm* process; **ce processus est contrôlé par une batterie de capteurs** = the process is monitored by a bank of sensors; **le processus compte cinq étapes** = there are five stages in the process; **processus aléatoire** = random process; **processus irréversible** = irreversible process; **processus itératif** = iterative process; **commande** *ou* **contrôle** *ou* **conduite de processus** = process control; **ordinateur de contrôle de processus** = process control computer; **système de contrôle** *ou* **de conduite de processus** = process control system

productif, -ive *adj* productive; **temps productif** = up time *ou* uptime *ou* productive time

◊ **production** *nf* **(a)** creation *ou* generation *ou* origination **(b)** *(d'un produit)* production; **l'avant-production** = preproduction; **cycle de production** = production run; **niveau maximum de** production *ou* **production record** = peak output **(c)** *(d'un film)* **directeur de production** = executive producer

◊ **productique** *nf* **productique intégrée** = computer-integrated manufacturing (CIM)

◊ **produire** *vtr* to produce *ou* to create *ou* to generate *ou* to originate; **on utilise l'ordinateur pour produire des images graphiques** = the computer is used in the generation of graphic images; **produire un label** *ou* **une étiquette (pour un programme)** = to label (a program); **cette clé produit trois réponses** = there are three hits for this search key

◊ **se produire** *vpr* to occur

◊ **produit** *nm* product; **produit fini** = end product; **produits fictifs** = vapourware; *(pont)* **produit de transition** = bridge *ou* bridging product; *(progiciel)* **produit logiciel** = software package *ou* packaged software; **conception de produits** = product design

◊ **produit, -e** *adj* created *ou* generated *ou* originated; **le code est produit automatiquement** = code generation is automatic; **produit à l'aide d'un ordinateur** = computer-generated

profession *nf* profession; **annuaire par professions** = classified directory

◊ **professionnel, -elle** *adj* **copieur professionnel** = office copier; **ordinateur** *ou* **terminal à usage professionnel** = office computer *ou* executive terminal

profil *nm* outline

profondeur *nf* depth; **profondeur de champ** = depth of field; **profondeur de foyer** = depth of focus

PROFS ™ *(messagerie électronique mise au point par IBM)* PROFS ™ (electronic mail system)

progiciel *nm* applications software *ou* software system *ou* applications package; **l'ordinateur se vend avec un progiciel de comptabilité et traitement de texte** = the computer is sold with accounting and word-processing packages; **progiciel adapté aux besoins de l'utilisateur** *ou* **progiciel personnalisé** = customized software *ou* middleware; **progiciel en coffret** *ou* **progiciel plus manuel d'utilisation** = packaged software *ou* software package

programmable *adj* programmable *ou* selectable; **programmable par l'utilisateur** = user-selectable *ou* user-definable; **attributs programmables par l'utilisateur** = user-selectable attributes; **calculatrice programmable** = programmable calculator; **circuit logique programmable** = programmable logic array (PLA); **contrôleur d'interruptions programmable** = programmable interrupt controller; **dispositif à champ programmable** = field programmable device; **horloge programmable** = programmable clock; **logique câblée programmable** = programmable logic device (PLD); **mémoire morte programmable** = programmable memory *ou* programmable read only memory (PROM);

mémoire morte programmable (PROM) effaçable par ultraviolet = ultraviolet erasable PROM; **mémoire ROM programmable et effaçable** = erasable programmable read-only memory (EPROM); **mémoire ROM programmable et effaçable électriquement** = electrically erasable programmable read-only memory (EEPROM); **touche (de fonction) programmable** = programmable key *ou* soft key; **la feuille de style comporte 125 symboles programmables (selon les besoins de l'utilisateur)** = the style sheet contains 125 user-definable symbols

◊ **programmateur** *nm* = PROGRAMMEUR

◊ **programmathèque** *nf* program library

◊ **programmation** *nf* programming; **programmation automatique** = automatic programming; **programmation de champ** = field programming; **programmation défensive** = defensive computing; **programmation élégante** *ou* **bien conçue** = elegant programming; **programmation en langage machine** = machine language programming; **programmation linéaire** = linear programming; **programmation modulaire** = modular programming *ou* modularization; **programmation visuelle** = visual programming; **aides à la programmation (dans un langage déterminé)** = language support environment; **feuille** *ou* **formulaire de programmation** = program coding sheet *ou* form; **langage de programmation** = programming language; **langage de programmation évolué** *ou* **de haut niveau** = high-level (programming) language (HLL); **langage de programmation PL/1** = programming langage/1 *ou* PL/1; **normes** *ou* **standards de programmation** = programming standards; **ordinogramme de programmation** = program flowchart; **outil de programmation** = software tool; **pas** *ou* **étape de programmation** = program step

programme *nm* **(a)** *(d'ordinateur)* (computer) program; **j'ai omis une instruction importante ce qui a produit le crash du programme et détruit tous les fichiers contenus sur le disque** = I forgot to insert an important instruction which caused a program to crash, erasing all the files on the disk; **programme activé par commande** = command-driven program; **programme agenda** = diary management; **programme d'application** = applications program; **programme d'amorçage** = bootstrap loader; **programme d'assemblage** = assembly (language) program; **programme de bibliothèque** = library program *ou* library routine; *(qui tourne sans erreur du premier coup)* **programme canon** = blue-ribbon program; **programme sur cartes perforées** = program cards; **programme en chapelet** = thread; **programme de commande** = master control program (MCP); **programme compilateur** = compiler (program); **programme de contrôle** *ou* monitor program; **programme de contrôle d'entrée/sortie** = input/output control program; **programme de contrôle de tâche** = job control program; **programme convertisseur** *ou* **programme de conversion** = conversion program; **programme débogué** *ou* **déverminé** = debugged program; **programme de diagnostic** = maintenance routine; **programme du domaine public** *ou* **qui n'est plus protégé par un copyright** = program which is in the public domain; **programme éditeur** = editor program; **programme d'édition de texte** = text editor; **exécution d'un programme d'édition** = editing run; **programme extensible** *ou* **ouvert** = open-ended program; **programme de fusionnement de données** = collator; **programme d'insertion directe** = direct-insert routine *ou* subroutine; **programme intégré** = integrated program *ou* integrated software; **programme interpréteur** = interpreter; **programme interprétatif** = interpretative program; **programme itératif** = loop program *ou* looping program; **programme de lancement (d'un système)** = bootstrap; **programme linéaire** = linear program; **programme de localisation de panne** = fault location program; **programme en logique câblée** = hardwired program; **programme de maintenance** = housekeeping routine *ou* maintenance program; **programme en mémoire centrale** = core program; **programme (élémentaire) de mise en route** = bootstrap (loader); **programme multiphase** = multiphase program; **programme objet** = object program; **programme portable** *ou* **transportable** *ou* **programme d'une grande portabilité** = portable program; **programme prêt à être exécuté** = executable form; **programme prioritaire** = high priority program *ou* foreground program; **programme non prioritaire** = background program; **programme résident** = internally stored program; **programme de retraitement** = postprocessor; **programme source** *ou* **d'origine** = source program; **programme superviseur** = executive program *ou* supervisor program; **programme système** = systems program; **programme de test** = exerciser; **programme de traduction** *ou* **d'interprétation** *ou* **programme traducteur** = translator (program); **programme (d') utilisateur** = user program; **programme à usage multiple** *ou* **multi-fonction** = general purpose program; **programme utilitaire** = utility (program); **programme (utilitaire) de service** = application service element; **appeler un programme** = to call a program; **bibliothèque de programmes** = program library; **bibliothèque de programmes d'entrée/sortie** = input/output library; **boucle de programme** = loop program *ou* looping program; **branche d'un programme** = program branch; **chargeur de programme de lancement** = initial program loader (IPL); **commande** *ou* **instruction d'un programme** = program instruction; **compilation de programme** = program compilation; **contrôle d'un programme sur papier** = desk check; **crash** *ou* **défaillance d'un programme** = program crash; **création d'un programme** = program generation; **développement d'un programme** = program development; **documentation relative à l'utilisation d'un programme** = program documentation; **écrire un programme** = to program *ou* to write a program; **l'utilisateur ne peut pas écrire de programme avec ce système** = the user cannot write a computer program with this system; **éditeur de programme** = program editor; **édition listée d'un programme** *ou* **listage d'un programme** = program listing; **élément de programme** = program item; **environnement de développement de programmes** = program development system; **essai d'un programme** = program testing; **exécution d'un programme** =

computer run *ou* program execution *ou* program run; **fichier programme** = program file; **générateur de programme** = program generator; **icône de programme** = program icon; **pour lancer le programme, faites un double clic sur l'icône du programme** = to run the program, double-click on the program icon; **lanceur de programme de chargement** = initial program header; **instruction dans un programme** = program instruction; **langage de conception de programme** = program design language (PDL); **ligne (d'instruction) d'un programme** = program line; **numéro de référence d'une ligne d'un programme** = program line number; **maintenance d'un programme** = program maintenance; **mémoire (de) programme** = program storage; **mise en place d'un programme concurrent** = counterprogramming; **nom d'un programme** = program name; **pile d'instructions d'un programme** = program stack; **segment de programme** = overlay *ou* program segment; **spécifications d'un programme** = program specifications; **structure d'un programme** = program structure; **technique d'évaluation et de révision de programme** = program evaluation and review technique (PERT); **test de programme** = program testing; **translation** *ou* **déplacement** *ou* **transfert (en mémoire) d'un programme (relogeable)** = program relocation; **vérification (du bon fonctionnement) d'un programme** = program verification; **(b)** *(de radio* *ou* *de télévision)* programme, *US* program; **les programmes destinés aux enfants sont présentés tôt dans la soirée** = children's programmes are scheduled for early evening viewing; **ils tournaient un programme sur les animaux sauvages** = they were filming a wild life programme; **programme de télévision à caractère éducatif** = educational TV (ETV) programme; **programme filmé** *ou* **en différé** = pre-recorded programme

◊ **programmé, -ée** *adj* programmed *ou* set; **arrêt programmé** = programmed halt; **saut de page programmé** = forced page break; **signalisation à contrôle programmé (en mémoire)** = stored program signalling; **programmé d'avance** = preprogrammed *ou* preset

◊ **programmer** *vtr* to code *ou* to program *ou* to set; *(une PROM)* to blow *ou* to burn *ou* to blast; **nous avons programmé la marge de droite à 80 caractères** = we set the right-hand margin at 80 characters; **qui peut être programmé suivant les besoins de l'utilisateur** = user-selectable; **programmer les points d'arrêt** = to set breakpoints; **programmer d'avance** = to preprogram *ou* to preset; **on avait programmé d'avance les nouveaux paramètres de page de l'imprimante** = the printer was preset with new page parameters; **programmer de nouveau** = to reprogram *ou* to reset

◊ **programmeur, -euse** *n* **(a)** (computer) programmer; **le programmeur n'a pas encore terminé le nouveau logiciel** = the programmer is still working on the new software; **programmeur d'application** = applications programmer; **programmeur (de) système** = systems programmer; **ingénieur programmeur** = software engineer **(b) programmeur de ROM** *ou* **de mémoire morte** = burner

progressif, -ive *adj* progressive; **changement progressif** = phased change-over; **dégradation progressive** = graceful degradation; **système disjoncteur progressif** = fail soft system

projecteur *nm* projector; **projecteur de diapositives** = slide projector *ou* diascope; **magnétophone avec interface synchro pour projecteur de diapos** = slide/sync recorder; **projecteur de documents opaques** = episcope *ou* epidiascope; **projecteur de cinéma** *ou* **de films** = film projector; **projecteur synchronisé** = interlock projector; **projecteur (de) télévision** = television projector

◊ **projection** *nf* projection; **la projection du film est commencée** = the film is now being screened; **salle de projection** = projection room

projet *nm* plan *ou* project

◊ **projeter** *vtr* **(a)** *(un film)* to screen; **nous avons projeté le film image par image** = we played *ou* stepped forward the film one frame at a time **(b)** to plan; **il projette maintenant d'informatiser le service des ventes** = his latest project is computerizing the sales team *ou* now he's planning to computerize the sales team

◊ **projeteur** *nm* designer

PROLOG *(langage pour systèmes experts)* Programming in Logic (PROLOG)

PROM = PROGRAMMABLE READ ONLY MEMORY **brûler** *ou* **programmer une PROM** = to blow a PROM; **effacer une PROM** = to wash PROM; **mémoire PROM** = programmable memory (PROM); **PROM effaçable par ultraviolet** = ultraviolet erasable PROM; **programmeur de PROM** = PROM burner *ou* programmer; *voir aussi* MEMOIRE

promouvoir *vtr* *(par publicité)* to plug *ou* to promote

prompt *nm* *(invite)* prompt

propagation *nf* **(a)** propagation; **propagation d'erreurs** = error propagation **(b)** délai *ou* temps de propagation = gate delay *ou* propagation time; **le délai de propagation dans une voie de communication crée une distorsion du signal** = propagation delay in the transmission path causes signal distortion; **temps de propagation aller (et) retour** = up and down propagation time

◊ **propagé, -ée** *adj* **erreur propagée** = propagated error

◊ **propager** *vtr* to propagate

◊ **se propager** *vpr* to propagate; **erreur qui se propage** = propagating error

proportion *nf* proportion

◊ **proportionnel, -elle** *adj* **espacement proportionnel** = proportional spacing

◊ **proportionnellement** *adv* proportionally *ou* in proportion

propriétaire *nm&f* **format de fichier propriétaire** = proprietary file format; *voir aussi* CONSTRUCTEUR

◊ **propriété** *nf* **propriété littéraire** = copyright

prospectus *nm* booklet; **prospectus publicitaire** = brochure, *US* broadside; **envoi de prospectus publicitaires** = mailing shot; **prospectus envoyé par la poste** = mailing piece; **prospectus publicitaires sans intérêt** = junk mail

protecteur, -trice *adj* protective

◊ **protection** *nf* **(a)** *(de logiciel ou de mémoire)* protection; **protection des accès mémoire** = fetch protect; **(dispositif de) protection anticopie** *ou* **contre la copie** = copy protect *ou* copy protection (device); **une protection anticopie défectueuse peut provoquer une défaillance du disque dur** = a hard disk may crash because of faulty copy protection; **protection des données** = data protection; **(logiciel** *ou* **dispositif de) protection de fichier** = file protection *ou* file security; **protection des limites (de mémoire)** = boundary protection; **(dispositif de) protection de la mémoire** = memory protect (device); **(dispositif de) protection par mot de passe** = interlock; **protection de page** = page protection; **de protection** = protective; **anneau** *ou* **bague de protection d'écriture** = write-permit ring; **bande de protection** = guard band; **bit de protection** = guard bit; **blocage de protection** = advisory lock; **clé de protection** = protection key; **volet de protection d'écriture** = write-protect tab; **dispositif de protection d'écriture (de fichier)** = file protect tab; **verrouillage de protection** = advisory lock **(b)** *(d'un fil)* **mise à nu de protection** = demarcation strip; *(électrique)* **transformateur de protection** = isolation transformer

◊ **protégé, -ée** *adj* **(a)** protected; **non protégé** = unprotected; **protégé contre toute détérioration** *ou* **destruction (accidentelle)** = crash-protected; **si vous vous servez d'un disque protégé contre la destruction accidentelle, vous ne perdrez jamais vos données** = if the disk is crash-protected, you will never lose your data; **champ protégé** = protected field; **champ non protégé** = unprotected field; **emplacement protégé** = protected location; **mémoire protégée** = protected storage; **mode protégé** = privileged mode; **mode non protégé** = real mode; **routage adaptatif protégé** = isolated adaptive routing; **zone protégée** = isolated location **(b)** *(par un copyright)* copyright *ou* copyrighted; **oeuvre protégée par un copyright** = copyright work *ou* work still in copyright; **programme qui n'est plus protégé par un copyright** = program which is out of copyright *ou* which is in the public domain

◊ **protéger** *vtr* **(a)** to protect; **une boîte rigide protège les disques** = the disks are housed in hard protective cases; **tous les disques sont protégés contre la copie** = all disks are copy protected; **le programme n'est pas protégé contre la copie** = the program is not copy protected; **le nouveau programme ne sera pas protégé contre la copie** = the new program will come without copy protection; **protéger (une disquette) contre l'écriture indésirée** = to write protect (a disk); **le mot de passe est censé protéger la base de données contre le piratage** = the password is supposed to exclude hackers from the database; **il est protégé par un relais à 5A** = it is relay-rated at 5 Amps **(b)** *(à l'aide d'un écran)* to screen *ou* to shield

protocole *nm* protocol; **protocole de communication** = line control *ou* link control procedure (LCP); *(entre deux postes)* full handshaking; *(entre CPU et périphérique)* CPU handshaking; **protocole (de communication) caractère par caractère** *ou* **à niveau octet** = byte-orientated protocol; *(entre deux postes)* **protocole d'interfaçage HDLC** = high-level data link control (HDLC); **protocole point à point (PPP)** = point to point protocol; **protocole de résolution d'adresse** *ou* **protocole ARP** = address resolution protocol (ARP); *(de message)* **protocole de routage** = routing overheads; **protocole standard de contrôle de liaisons** = basic mode link control; *(d'un système)* **protocole de traçage** *ou* **de contrôle** *ou* **de vérification** = audit trail; **protocole de validation de transfert (de données)** = handshake *ou* handshaking; **normes de protocoles (de communication)** = protocol standards

prototypage *nm* prototyping

◊ **prototype** *nm* prototype; **fabrication de prototype(s)** = prototyping

provenant *adj* coming from *ou* generated by; **interruption provenant d'une machine** = hardware interrupt

◊ **provenir (de)** *vi* to come *ou* to derive (from)

provisoire *adj* temporary; **correction** *ou* **modification provisoire** = patch

PrtSc = PRINT SCREEN; *(touche d'impression d'écran)* PrtSc (print screen)

ps = PICOSECONDE

PS/2 ™ *(modèle de PC IBM avec bus d'extension MCA)* PS/2 ™ (IBM PC computers)

pseudo- *préfixe* pseudo-

◊ **pseudo-aléatoire** *adj* pseudo-random; **générateur de nombres pseudo-aléatoires** = pseudo-random number generator

◊ **pseudocode** *nm* pseudo-code *ou* P-code

◊ **pseudo-instruction** *nf* pseudo-instruction *ou* quasi-instruction *ou* P-code

PSS *(système de transmission par paquets)* Packet Switching System (PSS)

pub *nf (familier)* commercial; **ils ont fait un véritable matraquage publicitaire avec leurs six pubs sur les séjours en Espagne** = they ran six commercials plugging holidays in Spain

public *nm* **entreprise de diffusion d'informations grand public** = common carrier; **revue grand public** = mass market magazine

◊ **public, publique** *adj* public; **code chiffré** *ou* **cryptage à clé publique** = public key cipher (system); **domaine public** = public domain (PD);

progiciel du domaine public = program in the public domain *ou* program which is out of copyright; **réseau public de transmission de données** = public data network; **réseau téléphonique public commuté** = public switched telephone network (PSTN); **point d'accès au réseau public commuté** = public dial port; **satellite de transmission publique** = domestic satellite

publication *nf* **(a)** *(action)* publication *ou* publishing; **la publication du rapport sur la confidentialité de l'information** = the publication of the report on data protection; **publication assistée par ordinateur (PAO)** = desktop publishing (DTP) *ou* electronic publishing **(b)** *(écrit)* publication

publicitaire *adj* **(a)** imprimé *ou* matériel **publicitaire** = publicity matter *ou* display material; **prospectus publicitaire** = leaflet *ou* mailing piece; **envoi de prospectus publicitaires** = mailing shot; **support publicitaire** = advertising medium

◊ **publicité** *nf* **(a)** publicity; **la publicité pour la nouvelle voiture a été faite dans la presse nationale** = the new car has been advertised in the national press; **publicité directe** = direct mailing; **publicité lieu de vente (PLV)** = point-of-sale material **(b)** *(à la télévision)* **la publicité** = commercials

publier *vtr* to publish; **la maison d'édition publie principalement des livres de référence** = the company specializes in publishing reference books; **la maison publie des revues destinées aux hommes/femmes d'affaires** = the company specializes in publications for the business reader; **la société a publié un communiqué de presse au sujet du lancement du nouveau scanner** = the company sent out a press release about the launch of the new scanner

publipostage *nm* direct mailing; *(traitement de texte: fusion lettre type/adresse)* **fonction publipostage** = mail-merge

puce *nf* **(a)** chip *ou* microchip; **nombre de puces (sur une carte, etc.)** = chip count; **le nombre de puces est malheureusement encore trop élevé** = it's no good, the chip count is still too high; **puce de diagnostic** = diagnostic chip; **ils font des recherches sur les puces de diagnostic destinées au contrôle des ordinateurs équipés de processeurs** = they are carrying out research on diagnostic chips to test computers that contain processors; **puce géante** = jumbo chip; **puce mémoire** = memory chip; **puce microprocesseur** = microprocessor chip; **puce musicale** = music chip *ou* sound chip; **puce RAM** = RAM chip; **puce de silicium** = silicon chip; **puce de synthèse vocale** = speech chip; **carte à puce** = chip card *ou* smart card; **les cartes à puce aident à réduire le nombre de fraudes** = smart cards reduce fraud; **micro-ordinateur de contrôle à puce unique** = single chip microcontroller; **ordinateur à puce unique** = single chip computer **(b)** *(imprimerie)* bullet

bourrer les armes de puces électroniques ne suffit pas; il faut aussi des programmes pour les faire fonctionner

L'Express

puissance *nf* **(a)** power; **puissance de calcul** = computing power; **puissance maximale** *ou* **réelle disponible** = available power; **puissance d'un ordinateur** = computer power; *((i) antenne; (ii) photographie)* **puissance d'ouverture effective** = effective aperture; **ordinateur de grande puissance** = supercomputer; **unité de puissance vocale** = voice unit **(b)** *(math)* **5 à la puissance deux égale 25** = 5 to the power 2 is equal to 25; **élévation (d'un nombre) à la puissance x** = exponentiation; **puissance fractionnaire** = root

puits *nm* (data) sink; **arborescence en puits** = sink tree

pupitre *nm* console; **pupitre de commande d'un opérateur** = operator's console

◊ **pupitreur, -euse** *n* keyboarder; *voir aussi* OPÉRATEUR

pur, -e *adj* pure; **code pur** = pure code; **son pur** = pure tone

purée *nf (familier)* mush; **zone de purée** = mush area

purger *vtr (la mémoire)* to purge; **chaque mois, je purge le disque de tous les messages périmés** = each month, I purge the disk of all the old email messages

pylône *nm (de radio ou de télévision)* radio mast *ou* TV mast

pyramidal, -e *adj* **facteur pyramidal d'entrée** = fan-in; **facteur pyramidal de sortie** = fan-out

Qq

QD = QUADRUPLE DENSITE; *voir* QUADRUPLE

QBE *(langage utilisé pour recherche d'information)* Query By Example (QBE); **dans la plupart des base de données QBE, les requêtes ont sensiblement la même forme que les enregistrements dans la base de données; faire une requête est aussi facile que remplir un formulaire** = in most QBE databases, the query form looks like the record format in the database - retrieving data is as easy as filling in a form

quadr- *préf* quadr-

quadrat *nm (papier)* quad

quadrature *nf (vidéo)* quadrature; **encodage en quadrature** = quadrature encoding; **modulation d'amplitude en quadrature (MAQ)** = Quadrature Amplitude Modulation (QAM)

quadrillé, -ée *adj* **papier quadrillé** = graph paper

quadriphonique *adj* quadrophonic

quadruple 1 *nm* quadruple **2** *adj* quadruple *ou* quad; **quadruple densité** = quad density; **disquette quadruple densité (QD)** = quad density disk (QD); *(lecteur de CD-ROM)* **quadruple vitesse** = quadruple speed *ou* 4x speed

◊ **quadruplex** *nm (signaux)* quadruplex

qualité *nf* **(a)** grade *ou* quality; **nous vérifions chaque lot pour nous assurer de la qualité** = we check each batch to make sure it is perfect; **qualité d'un circuit** = circuit grade; **qualité des données** = data reliability; **qualité du matériel** = hardware reliability; **qualité de transmission** *ou* **qualité broadcast** = broadcast quality; **de qualité supérieure** = high quality *ou* top quality; **assurance de (la) qualité** = quality assurance; **bonne qualité** = good quality; **il existe un marché pour les ordinateurs d'occasion de bonne qualité** = there is a market for good quality secondhand computers; **contrôle de (la) qualité** = quality control; **responsable du contrôle de (la) qualité** = quality controller; **label de qualité** = quality label **(b)** *(sortie d'imprimante)* **qualité brouillon** *ou* **qualité listing** = draft printing; **qualité courrier** = near-letter-quality (NLQ); **qualité d'impression d'une imprimante** = printer quality

---

doté d'une tête à 18 aiguilles, cette imprimante matricielle atteint la vitesse de 600cps (caractères par seconde) en qualité brouillon, et 150cps en qualité courrier

Action PC

---

quantifiable *adj* quantifiable

◊ **quantificateur** *nm* **(a)** *(d'une quantité)* quantifier **(b)** *(d'une grandeur physique)* quantizer

◊ **quantification** *nf* **(a)** *(attribution d'une quantité)* quantification **(b)** *(d'une grandeur physique)* quantization; **erreur de quantification** = quantization error; **quantification d'amplitude** = amplitude quantization; **quantification de niveau quatre** = quaternary level quantization; **bruits de quantification** = quantizing noise

◊ **quantifier** *vtr* **(a)** *(attribuer une quantité)* to quantify; **il est impossible de quantifier l'effet du nouveau système informatique sur notre production** = it is impossible to quantify the effect of the new computer system on our production **(b)** *(une grandeur physique)* to quantize

quantité *nf* amount *ou* quantity; **grande quantité** = large quantity; **il a acheté une grande quantité de pièces détachées** = he bought a large quantity of spare parts; **quelle est la quantité maximale de données qu'on puisse traiter en une heure?** = what is the largest amount of data which can be processed in one hour?; **en grande quantité** = in bulk

quantum *nm* quantum

quarante *adj num* forty; **disquette (de) quarante pistes** = forty-track disk

quartile *nm* quartile

quartz *nm* quartz; **horloge à quartz** = quartz (crystal) clock; **microphone à quartz** = crystal microphone; **oscillateur à quartz** = crystal oscillator

quasi- *préf* quasi-

quaternaire *adj* quaternary; *(voies de communication)* **groupe quaternaire** = super mastergroup

quatre 1 *nm* **quantification de niveau quatre** = quaternary level quantization **2** *adj num* four; **instruction à quatre adresses** = four-address instruction; **instruction à quatre adresses plus une** = four-plus-one address instruction; **en quatre exemplaires** = in quadruplicate; **les relevés sont imprimés en quatre exemplaires** = the statements are printed in quadruplicate; **magnétophone à quatre pistes** = four-track recorder

◊ **quatrième** *nm&adj* fourth; **langages de quatrième génération** = fourth generation languages; **ordinateurs de quatrième génération** = fourth generation computers

◊ **quatre-vingts** *adj num* eighty; **disque de quatre-vingts pistes** = eighty-track disk; **écran de quatre-vingts colonnes** = eighty-column screen

question *nf* question *ou* query; **poser une question** = to ask a question; to query (something); **poser une question à quelqu'un** = to ask someone a question; **répondre à une question** = to answer a question; **elle a refusé de répondre aux questions concernant les claviers défectueux** = she refused to answer questions about faulty keyboards

◊ **questionnaire** *nm* questionnaire; **remplir** *ou* **compléter un questionnaire** = to answer *ou* to fill in a questionnaire; **envoyer un questionnaire concernant le système pour faire un sondage d'opinion auprès des utilisateurs** = to send out a questionnaire to test the opinions of users of the system

QuickDraw ™ *(routine graphique de Apple Macintosh)* QuickDraw ™

QuickTime ™ *(routine graphique de Apple Macintosh)* QuickTime ™

quintet *nm* quintet

quitter *vtr* to quit; *(abandonner sans sauvegarder)* to abandon; **n'oubliez pas de sauvegarder votre texte avant de quitter le système** = do not forget to save your text before you quit the system; **pour mettre des en-têtes, il faut quitter ce programme et entrer dans un autre** = you have to exit to another editing system to add headlines; **si vous quittez votre feuille de calcul sans sauvegarder, vous ne pourrez pas la récupérer** = once you have abandoned your spreadsheet, you cannot retrieve it again

quotidien *nm* *(journal qui paraît tous les jours)* daily (newspaper); **les grands quotidiens** = the main dailies *ou* the national press

quotient *nm* quotient

QWERTY *(utilisé surtout dans les pays anglo-saxons)* **clavier QWERTY** = QWERTY keyboard; **l'ordinateur possède un clavier QWERTY conventionnel** = the computer has a normal QWERTY keyboard

Rr

R et D = RECHERCHE ET DEVELOPPEMENT

raccord *nm* (*de bande ou de film*) **faire un raccord** = to splice; **ruban de raccord** = splicing tape

◊ **raccordement** *nm* interconnection; **boîte de raccordement** = junction box; **câble de raccordement** = *(d'un tableau de distribution)* patch cord; *(de télévision)* drop line; *(de téléphone)* **panneau de raccordement** = patch panel *ou* patch board; **point de raccordement** = terminal

◊ **raccorder** *vtr* to join; *(film)* to splice; **utilisez de la colle ou du ruban gommé pour raccorder les extrémités du film** = you can use glue or splicing tape to splice the ends of the film

raccourci *nm* *(touche(s) d'accélération)* **raccourci clavier** = accelerator key

◊ **raccourcir** *vtr* to shorten; **nous avons dû raccourcir le fichier pour réussir à le sauvegarder sur une seule disquette** = we had to shorten the file to be able to save it on one floppy

raccroché, -ée *adj (téléphone)* **(en mode) raccroché** = on hook; **coupure au premier raccroché** = first party release

◊ **raccrocher** *vtr&i* to hang up; **à la fin de la conversation téléphonique, elle a raccroché** = after she had finished talking (on the phone) she hung up

racine *nf* **(a)** root; **répertoire racine** = root directory; **sous DOS, le répertoire racine du disque C: est désigné par C:** = in DOS, the root directory on drive C: is called C:\ **(b) racine carrée** = square root; **la racine carrée de 25 est 5** = the square root of 25 is 5

rack *nm* rack; **(cartes) montées en rack** = rack mounted (boards)

radar *nm* *(appareil ou système de détection)* Radio Detecting And Ranging *ou* radar

radial, -e *adj* radial; *(données ou programmes)* **transfert radial** = radial transfer

radiateur *nm* radiator; **radiateur à ailette(s)** = heat sink

radiation *nf* radiation

radier *vtr* to remove *ou* to delete; **le fichier a été radié du répertoire de la disquette** = the file entry was removed from the floppy disk directory

radio *nf* **(a)** *(GUI: cercle indiquant une option)* **bouton radio** = radio button **(b)** *(radiodiffusion)* radio; **j'ai entendu la nouvelle à la radio** = I heard the news on the radio; **il a diffusé les dernières informations à la radio** = he broadcast the latest news over the radio; **radio à large bande** = broadband radio; **radio CB** *ou* **radio à bande CB** = citizens band radio (CB); **émetteur/récepteur radio** = radio transceiver; **fréquence radio** = radio frequency (RF); **micro radio** = radio microphone; **poste (de) radio** = radio; **récepteur radio** = radio receiver; **spectre de fréquences radio** = radio spectrum; **station de radio** = broadcasting station *ou* radio station; **transmission de données par radio** = radio transmission of data **(c)** = RADIOGRAPHIE

◊ **radioamateur** *nm* radio ham

◊ **radiocassette** *nf* radiorecorder

◊ **radiocommunication** *nf (transmission et réception par radio)* radiocommunications

◊ **radiodiffusion** *nf* (radio) broadcast *ou* broadcasting; **radiodiffusion par satellite** = satellite broadcasting; **réseau de radiodiffusion** = broadcast(ing) network

◊ **radioélectrique** *adj* **ondes radioélectriques** = radio waves

◊ **radiofréquence** *nf* radio frequency (RF); **la gamme des radiofréquences s'étend de seulement quelques hertz à des centaines de gigahertz** = the radio frequency range extends from a few hertz to hundreds of gigahertz

radiographie *nf* X-ray

◊ **radiographier** *vtr* to X-ray

radiophonique *adj* **diffusion radiophonique** = broadcast; **le récepteur a capté l'émission radiophonique** = the receiver picked up the broacast; **réseau radiophonique** = radio network

radiorecherche *nf* **(système de) radiorecherche de personne** = radio paging

radioscopie *nf* X-ray imaging

radiotélégraphie *nf* radio telegraphy *ou* carrier telegraphy

radiotéléphone *ou* **radio-téléphone** *nm* radio telephone *ou* radio phone; **radiotéléphone (de type) cellulaire** = cellular radio; **radiotéléphone mobile** = mobile radiophone

◊ **radiotéléphonique** *adj* **réseau radiotéléphonique** = cellular service

radiotransmission *nf* radio transmission (of data)

rafale *nf* burst; **rafale d'erreurs** = error burst; **rafale de signaux couleur** = colour burst

rafraîchir *vtr* to refresh; *(une connexion)* to retrain; **(instruction de) rafraîchir l'écran** = screen refresh; **mémoire qui demande à être rafraîchie** = regenerative memory; **une RAM dynamique a besoin d'être rafraîchie toutes les 250ns** = dynamic RAM is regenerative memory - it needs to be refreshed every 250ns; **l'écran peut être comparé à une mémoire qui demande à être rafraîchie; il doit être balayé régulièrement pour éviter de présenter des images instables** = the CRT display can be thought of as regenerative memory, it requires regular refresh picture scans to prevent flicker

◊ **rafraîchissement** *nm* **rafraîchissement de l'image (de l'écran)** = screen refresh; **rafraîchissement de la mémoire** = memory refresh; *(de l'écran ou de la mémoire)* **cycle** *ou* **temps de rafraîchissement** = refresh cycle; **fréquence de rafraîchissement** = refresh rate; **fréquence de rafraîchissement de l'image** = image refresh rate; **fréquence de rafraîchissement de la mémoire RAM** *ou* **de la mémoire vive** = RAM refresh rate; **signal de rafraîchissement de la mémoire** = memory refresh signal; **signal de rafraîchissement de la mémoire RAM** = RAM refresh signal

RAID *(système de stockage rapide sur disques multiples)* Redundant Array of Inexpensive Disks (RAID)

raie *nf* stripe; **raie de couleur** = colour stripe

ralenti *nm* slow motion; **repassez ce film au ralenti** = play the film again in slow motion; **le film enchaîne sur un ralenti** = the film switches to slow motion

◊ **ralenti, -e** *adj (ordinateur)* **ralenti par le débit d'entrée des données** = input bound

◊ **ralentir** *vtr&i* to slow down

RAM *nf* = RANDOM ACCESS MEMORY **RAM autorafraîchie** *ou* **auto-entretenue** *ou* **autorégénérable** = self-refreshing RAM; **RAM dynamique** = dynamic RAM *ou* dynamic random access memory (DRAM); **RAM partielle** = partial RAM; **(mémoire) RAM statique** = static RAM; **RAM vidéo** = video memory *ou* video RAM (VRAM); **carte RAM** = RAM card; **cartouche RAM** = RAM cartridge; **vous pouvez augmenter la mémoire de l'imprimante en enfichant une cartouche RAM supplémentaire** = you can increase the printer's memory by plugging in another RAM cartridge; **disque RAM** = silicon disk *ou* RAM disk; **mémoire RAM** = random access memory (RAM); **puce RAM** = RAM chip; *voir aussi* MEMOIRE

rang *nm* row; **système à double rang de broches (parallèles)** = dual-in-line package (DIL *ou* DIP)

rangement *nm* storing; filing; *(en mémoire)* **emplacement de rangement** = bucket

◊ **ranger** *vtr (en mémoire)* to plant *ou* to store *ou* to write; **le temps d'accès est le temps requis pour lire ou pour ranger une donnée en mémoire** = access time is the time taken to read from or write to a location in memory

rapide *adj* fast *ou* quick *ou* rapid; **c'est un disque dur très rapide avec un temps d'accès de 28ms** = this hard disk is fast, it has an access time of 28ms; **accès rapide** = rapid access; **mémoire à accès rapide** = fast access memory (FAM); *(avec mémoire tampon)* **clavier rapide** = key rollover *ou* N-key rollover; **exécution rapide d'un programme** = fast program execution; **ligne de transmission rapide** = fast line; **mémoire centrale rapide** = fast core; **dans ce système, la mémoire centrale rapide sert de bloc-notes pour tous les calculs** = the fast core is used as a scratchpad for all calculations in this system; **périphérique rapide** = fast peripheral; **report rapide** = high speed carry *ou* ripple-through carry; **saut rapide** = high-speed skip; **terminal de mise à jour rapide** = bulk update terminal; **tri rapide** = quicksort

◊ **rapidement** *adv* quickly

◊ **rapidité** *nf* speed

rappel *nm* **(a)** *(de données en mémoire)* recall **(b)** *(téléphone)* redial; **système de rappel automatique** = ring back system; **modem** *ou* **téléphone avec système de rappel automatique** = auto-redial modem *ou* telephone; **modem de rappel** = call back modem **(c)** *(machine à écrire ou traitement de texte)* backspace; **caractère de rappel (du curseur)** = backspace character

◊ **rappeler** *vtr* **(a)** *(ce qui est en mémoire)* to recall; *(de mémoire centrale en mémoire auxiliaire)* to roll out; **rappelez le fichier précédent à l'écran** = call up the previous file **(b)** *(au téléphone)* to phone back; **M. Dubois a téléphoné en votre absence et a demandé que vous le rappeliez** = Mr Dubois called while you were out and asked if you would phone him back; **le président est en conférence, pourriez-vous rappeler dans une demi-heure environ?** = the chairman is in a meeting, can you phone back in about half an hour? **(c)** to quote; **veuillez rappeler ce numéro de référence dans votre réponse** = in your reply please quote this number

rapport *nm* **(a)** ratio; **le rapport 10 sur 5 est égal à 2:1** = the ratio of 10 to 5 is 2:1; **code à rapport (de bits) constant** *ou* **fixe** = constant ratio code; **rapport de contraste d'un imprimé** = print contrast ratio; **rapport de discrimination** *ou* **rapport un à zéro** = one to zero ratio; **rapport longueur/largeur (d'un pixel)** = aspect ratio; **rapport signal/bruit (d'une transmission)** = signal to noise ratio *ou* S/N ratio **(b)** relationship; **(données) qui n'ont aucun rapport (entre elles)** = disjointed (data) **(c)** report; **rapport d'exceptions** *ou* **d'anomalies** = exception report

le laboratoire de la FNAC a réalisé des mesures et obtenu un rapport signal/bruit de 76 à 83dB, selon les appareils
Science et Vie

rapprocher *vtr (lignes ou caractères)* to close up

rassemblement *nm* collection

◊ **rassembler** *vtr* to collect *ou* to gather; to accumulate; **nous avons rassemblé progressivement un impressionnant fichier d'adresses** = we have gradually accumulated a large databank of names and addresses

raster *nm* raster image processor (RIP)

ratelier *nm* **un ratelier pour bandes magnétiques** = a rack for holding mag tapes

rater *vtr* to fail

ratio *nm* ratio; **ratio d'activité d'un fichier** = file activity ratio

rationnel, -elle *adj* rational; **nombre rationnel** = rational number; **24/7 est un nombre rationnel** = 24 over 7 is a rational number; **on peut écrire 0,333 sous la forme du nombre rationnel 1/3** = 0.333 can be written as the rational number 1/3

rayer *vtr* to delete

rayon *nm* beam *ou* ray; **les rayons lumineux se propagent dans la fibre optique** = rays of light pass down the optical fibre; **le laser émet un mince rayon lumineux** = a laser produces a thin beam of light; **l'imprimante utilise un rayon laser pour obtenir une haute résolution graphique** = a beam of laser light is used in this printer to produce high-resolution graphics; **rayons X** = X-rays; **déviation d'un rayon lumineux** = beam deflection; **tube à rayons cathodiques** = cathode ray tube (CRT)

◊ **rayonnant, -e** *adj* radiant; **élément rayonnant** = radiating element; *(d'une antenne)* radiator; **énergie rayonnante** = radiant energy

◊ **rayonnement** *nm* radiation *ou* ray *ou* light; **rayonnement électromagnétique** = electromagnetic radiation; **rayonnement indirect** = indirect ray; **rayonnement infrarouge** = infrared light (IR light); **rayonnement ultraviolet** = ultraviolet light (UV light); **de rayonnement** = radiant; **énergie de rayonnement** = radiant energy

◊ **rayonner** *vi* to radiate

rayure *nf (sur image)* streaking; *(sur un disque)* scratch; **cette rayure rend impossible la lecture du disque** = this scratch makes the disk unreadable

RD *(pour supprimer un répertoire sous DOS)* **commande d'effacement de répertoire** = Remove Directory *ou* RD

réacheminement *nm* redirection *ou* re-routing; *(téléphone)* **dispositif de réacheminement d'appel** = call diverter

◊ **réacheminer** *vtr* to redirect *ou* to re-route; **le dispositif de transfert d'appel sert à réacheminer les appels** = the call diverter will re-route calls

réactance *nf* reactance

◊ **réactif, -ive** *adj* **mode réactif** = reactive mode

◊ **réaction** *nf* **(a)** reaction *ou* response; **réaction chimique** = chemical reaction; **la réaction des films photosensibles varie suivant l'intensité de la lumière** = light-sensitive films register light intensity; **entrer en réaction avec une autre substance** = to react with something **(b)** *(information)* feedback; **nous commençons à connaître les réactions des clients face au nouveau système** = we are getting customer feedback on the new system; **boucle de réaction** = feedback loop

réadressable *adj (relogeable)* relocatable; **programme réadressable** = relocatable program

◊ **réadressage** *nm* relocation

réagir *vi* to react; **réagir à quelque chose** = to react to something

réalisateur, -trice *n (d'un film)* director

◊ **réalisation** *nf* **(a)** *(d'un projet)* realization; implementation **(b)** *(d'un film)* direction

◊ **réaliser** *vtr* **(a)** *(un projet)* to realize; to implement **(b)** *(un film)* to direct **(c)** *(dessiner)* **c'est elle qui a réalisé le nouvel ordinateur** = she is the designer of the new computer

réassemblage *nm (hashing)* folding

rebond *nm* bounce; **rebond de contact** = contact bounce; **rebond d'une touche de clavier** = keyboard contact bounce

rebours *nm* **à rebours** = backward *ou* backwards; **aller à rebours** = to backtrack

rebut *nm* junk; **informations de rebut** = garbage *ou* gibberish; **mettre au rebut** = to discard

recadrage *nm (d'une image sur l'écran)* elastic banding *ou* rubber banding; **le recadrage d'une image est plus facile à réaliser avec la souris** = elastic banding is much easier to control with a mouse

récemment *adv* recently; *(algorithme d'ancienneté de la mémoire paginée)* **algorithme de la page la moins récemment utilisée** = least recently used algorithm

◊ **récent, -e** *adj* recent *ou* new *ou* up to date; **un système informatique de modèle récent** = an up-to-date computer system

récepteur *nm* receiver; *(pour système d'appel de personne)* **récepteur de poche** = pager *ou* radio pager *ou* radio paging device; **vous pourriez contacter votre vendeur s'il était équipé d'un récepteur de poche** = you could contact your salesman if he had a radio pager; **récepteur portatif** = hand receiver; **récepteur radio** = radio receiver; **votre signal a été capté très clairement par le récepteur radio** = the radio receiver picked up your signal very strongly; **contrôle par le récepteur** = backwards supervision

◊ **récepteur, -trice** *adj* **bobine réceptrice** = pickup reel; **terminal récepteur (de données)** = data sink

◊ **réception** *nf* **(a)** *(d'un signal)* reception; **cette antenne ne donne pas un bonne réception** = signal reception is bad with that aerial; **accusé de réception** = acknowledgement; *(d'un message)* acknowledge; **caractère d'accusé de réception** = acknowledge character; **accusé de réception négatif** = negative acknowledge (NAK *ou* NACK); **accusé de réception positif** = affirmative acknowledge (ACK *ou* ACKNLG); **accuser réception** *ou* **envoyer un accusé de réception** = to acknowledge; **point de réception** = far end *ou* receiving end; **terminal de réception** = receive only terminal **(b)** *(de lentille ou de fibre optique)* **angle de réception** = acceptance angle; **un rayon lumineux d'incidence supérieure à l'angle de réception de la lentille ne sera pas transmis** = a light beam at an angle greater than the acceptance angle of the lens will not be transmitted **(c) bobine de réception** = take-up reel; **placez la bobine pleine sur cet axe-ci et la bobine de réception sur celui-là** = put the full reel on this spindle, and feed the tape into the take-up reel on the other spindle

◊ **réceptrice** *voir* RECEPTEUR

recevoir *vtr (signal)* to receive; **un multiplexeur 4/1 reçoit sur 4 canaux et émet sur un seul** = a 4 to 1 multiplexor combines four inputs into a single output; **le signal reçu devrait être amplifié** = the received ou RXed signal needs to be amplified; **(signal de) prêt à transmettre/recevoir** = data set ready (DSR)

rechargeable *adj* rechargeable; **batterie** *ou* **pile rechargeable** = rechargeable battery; **on utilise une pile rechargeable comme alimentation auxiliaire pour la mémoire RAM quand le système est éteint** = a rechargeable battery is used for RAM back-up when the system is switched off

◊ **rechargement** *nm* **(a)** *(d'une pile)* recharging **(b)** *(d'un programme, après incident)* reloading *ou* rollback

◊ **recharger** *vtr* **(a)** *(une batterie d'accumulateurs)* to replenish; *(une pile)* to recharge **(b)** *(un programme)* to reload; **nous avons rechargé le programme après la panne** = we reloaded the program after the crash

recherche *nf* **(a)** search; *(avec extraction de données)* retrieval; **recherche arrière** *ou* **en amont** = backwards search; **recherche associative** = chaining search; **recherche (par coupe) binaire** = binary search *ou* binary chop *ou* binary look-up; **recherche de bloc** = block retrieval; **recherche en chaîne** = chaining search; **(système de) recherche par descripteurs** = aspect system; **(méthode de) recherche par dichotomie** *ou* **recherche dichotomique** = dichotomizing search *ou* binary chop; **recherche documentaire** = information retrieval (IR); data retrieval *ou* text retrieval; **recherche documentaire en ligne** = on-line information retrieval; **centre de recherche documentaire** = information retrieval centre; **système de recherche documentaire** = information retrieval system; **recherche effective** = effective search; **vitesse de recherche effective** = effective search speed; **recherche exhaustive** *ou* **très poussée** = exhaustive search; **recherche par mots-clés** = disjunctive search; **clé de recherche** = (search) key; **nous avons sélectionné les enregistrements en utilisant le mot DISK comme clé de recherche** = we selected all the records with the word DISK in their keys; **recherche rétrospective** = retrospective search; **recherche séquentielle** = sequential search *ou* linear search; **recherche (et extraction) de texte** = text retrieval; **recherche de zone** = area search; **faire une recherche** = to search; **zone de recherche** = seek area **(b) (imprimante à) recherche logique** = logic-seeking (printer); **récepteur à recherche de signal** = scanning radio receiver **(c)** *(de produits,*

etc.) research; **recherche et développement (R et D)** = research and development (R & D); **service de Recherche et Développement** *ou* **service R et D** = R & D department; **la société a dépensé des millions de dollars pour la recherche et le développement** = the company has spent millions of dollars on R & D

◊ **rechercher** *vt (une donnée)* to search

réciproque *adj (fonction logique)* **exclusion réciproque** = inequivalence *ou* symmetric difference

réclame *nf* publicity

recommencer *vtr* to start again; **recommencer l'exécution** = to rerun (a program)

reconfiguration *nf* reconfiguration

◊ **reconfigurer** *vtr* to reconfigure; **avec ce programme, il est possible de reconfigurer le système selon nos besoins** = this program allows us to reconfigure the system to our own requirements; **j'ai reconfiguré la structure des champs du fichier** = I reconfigured the field structure in the file

reconnaissable *adj* recognizable; **police de caractères reconnaissable par lecture optique** = optical font *ou* OCR font

reconnaissance *nf* **(a)** recognition; sensing *ou* sense; **reconnaissance automatique de débit d'une ligne** = auto-baud sensing; auto-baud scanning; **reconnaissance de caractères magnétiques** = magnetic ink character recognition (MICR); **système de reconnaissance de caractères CSM (par identification des caractéristiques combinées)** = combined symbol matching (CSM); **reconnaissance de formes** = pattern recognition; **reconnaissance (optique) de caractères** = character recognition *ou* optical character recognition (OCR); **reconnaissance optique de marques** *ou* **de signes** *ou* **de symboles** = optical mark recognition (OMR); **reconnaissance de la parole** *ou* **reconnaissance vocale** = speech recognition *ou* voice recognition; **activé par reconnaissance des données** = data-driven; **logique de reconnaissance** = recognition logic **(b) label de reconnaissance de bande** = header label

◊ **reconnaître** *vtr* to recognize *ou* to distinguish; to sense; **le lecteur optique reconnaît difficilement certains caractères** = an OCR has difficulty in distinguishing certain characters; **le scanner reconnaît la plupart des polices de caractères** = the scanner will recognize most character fonts; **ne pas reconnaître** = to ignore

reconnecter *vtr* to reconnect

reconstituer *vtr (un message crypté)* to descramble; *(des données)* to reconstitute

◊ **reconstitution** *nf* **(a)** *(d'un message)* descrambling **(b)** *(de données)* reconstitution; **reconstitution de procédure** = backward recovery

recopier *vtr* to copy

record *nm* record; **production record** = peak output

recouvrement *nm* overlap; *(de segments de programme)* overlay; **segment de recouvrement** = overlay segment; **gestionnaire de segment de recouvrement** = overlay manager; **zone de segment de recouvrement** = overlay region; **utilisation d'une technique de recouvrement** = overlaying; **réseau à zone de recouvrement** = overlay network

recouvrir *vtr* **(a)** to cover; *(d'une mince couche)* to coat with a thin layer *ou* to deposit a thin layer (of something) **(b)** *(chevaucher)* to overlap

◊ **se recouvrir** *vpr (se chevaucher)* to overlap

recréer *vtr* to regenerate

rectangulaire *adj* rectangular; **coordonnées rectangulaires** = rectangular coordinates; **guide d'ondes rectangulaire** = rectangular waveguide

recto *nm (d'une feuille)* recto; *(d'une page d'un livre)* right-hand page; **imprimante recto/verso** = duplex printer

reçu *nm* receipt; **reçu en double exemplaire** = receipt in duplicate

◊ **reçu, -e** *adj* **message reçu** = incoming message; **(nombre de) messages reçus** *ou* **données reçues** = incoming traffic

récupérable *adj* recoverable; **les données sont récupérables mais il faudra beaucoup de temps pour y arriver** = it is possible to recover the data but it can take a long time; **erreur récupérable** = recoverable error

◊ **récupération** *nf* recovery; **récupération de document** = document recovery; **récupération de fichier** = file recovery; *(à rebours)* backward recovery; **procédure de récupération** = recovery procedure; **programme** *ou* **logiciel de récupération de fichier(s)** = file-recovery program *ou* file-recovery utility; **les fichiers perdus peuvent être récupérés en suivant une procédure de récupération** = the recovery of lost files can be carried out using a recovery procedure

◊ **récupérer** *vtr (un texte non sauvegardé)* to recover *ou* to restore *ou* to retrieve; *(un fichier ou un texte supprimé)* to undelete; **ne vous faites pas de soucis, cette fonction vous permet de récupérer les parties coupées de votre lettre** = don't worry, this function will undelete your cuts to the letter; **il est impossible de récupérer un fichier perdu sans l'aide d'un programme de récupération de fichier** = a lost file cannot be found without a file-recovery utility; **(instruction de) récupérer des données et les transférer dans un registre** = collect transfer

récurrence *nf* **boucle de récurrence** = daisy-chain recursion

◊ **récurrent, -e** *adj* **balayage récurrent** = raster scanning

récursif, -ive *adj* recursive; **appel récursif** *ou* **procédure récursive** = recursive call; **routine récursive** = recursive routine *ou* recursion

rédaction *nf* editing; *(le bureau)* **la rédaction** = (i) editorial office; (ii) editorial board; **il travaille à la rédaction d'une revue de micro-informatique** = he edits a computer magazine

redéfinir *vtr* to redefine; **redéfinir la fonction d'une touche** = to redefine a key; **j'ai redéfini cette touche pour obtenir un 5** = I have redefined this key to display the figure five when pressed; **touche qui peut être redéfinie** = redefinable key

redémarrage *nm* restart; **redémarrage automatique** = auto restart

◊ **redémarrer** *vtr* to restart

redessiner *vtr* to redraw

rédiger *vtr* to write *ou* to put in writing; **rédiger un accord** = to put the agreement in writing

redirection *nf (caractère > sous DOS)* **opérateur** *ou* **caractère de redirection** = redirect operator *ou* redirection operator

◊ **rediriger** *vtr* to redirect

redistribution *nf* **routage par redistribution** = flooding

redondance *nf* redundancy; **bit de redondance** = redundant bit; **caractère de redondance** = redundant character; **contrôle par redondance** = redundancy checking; **contrôle par redondance cyclique** = cyclic redundancy check (CRC); **contrôle par redondance longitudinale** = longitudinal redundancy check; **contrôle par redondance verticale** = vertical redundancy check

◊ **redondant, -e** *adj* redundant; **équipement redondant** = redundant equipment; **liaisons redondantes d'un réseau** = network redundancy

redonner *vtr* to give back *ou* to send back; **l'instruction RETOUR à la fin d'une routine permet de redonner la main au programme principal** = the RETURN instruction at the end of the routine sends control back to the main program

redressé, -ée *adj* rectified; **erreur qui peut être redressée** = recoverable error

◊ **redresser** *vtr* to rectify

◊ **redresseur** *nm&adj* **redresseur (de) simple alternance** = half wave rectifier; **circuit redresseur** = rectifier

réducteur *nm (de bruit)* muting device; **réducteur de fréquence** = frequency divider; **réducteur de signal audio** = audio compressor; **réducteur (de largeur de bande) vidéo** = video compressor

◊ **réduction** *nf* **(a)** reduction; **réduction de bruit** = muting; **réduction du bruit d'interférence interstation** = interstation muting; **réduction de données** = data reduction; **réduction des performances** = (efficiency) degradation; **forte réduction** = high reduction **(b)** **réduction d'échelle** = downsizing; **la réduction d'échelle est très** efficace sur le plan des coûts et donne plus de puissance de traitement à l'utilisateur = downsizing is more cost effective and gives more processing power to the end-user

◊ **réduire** *vtr* to reduce *ou* to cut (down) *ou* to minimize; **il nous faut réduire la reproduction en simili de 25% pour pouvoir l'insérer dans l'espace fixé** = we need a 25% reduction to fit the halftone in the space; **nous avons réduit les frais en diminuant le nombre des composants** = we minimized costs by cutting down the number of components; **les éditeurs ont demandé de réduire le premier chapitre** = the editors have asked for cuts in the first chapter; **on a demandé à l'auteur de réduire son manuscrit à 250 pages** = the author was asked to cut his manuscript to 250 pages; **on a réduit le dessin pour le faire entrer dans l'emplacement prévu** = the drawing was shrunk to fit the space; **réduire l'échelle** = to scale down; *(d'une configuration informatique)* = to downsize; *(en imprimerie)* **réduire l'espace entre deux caractères** = to kern; **nous avons réduit l'espace entre le T et le o pour les rapprocher** = we have kerned 'T' and 'o' so they are closer together; *(sous MS-Windows)* **réduire une fenêtre en icône** = to minimise a window

> COMMENTAIRE: l'application peut continuer à tourner en tâche de fond, vous réduisez la fenêtre en cliquant une fois sur la flèche descendante dans le coin supérieur droit

◊ **réduit, -e** *adj* reduced; shortened; **affichage réduit** = part page display; **base de temps réduite** = fast time-scale; *(carte courte ou demi-longueur)* **carte (de taille) réduite** = short card; half card; **processeur à jeu d'instructions réduit** = reduced instruction set computer (RISC); **matrice réduite** *ou* **tableau réduit** = sparse array; *(d'un livre)* **tirage réduit** = short run; **livre à tirage réduit** = short-run book

réécrire *vtr* to rewrite

réel, -elle *adj* real; **adresse réelle** = actual address *ou* absolute address *ou* first-level address; **débit réel de transfert de données** = actual data transfer rate; **mémoire réelle** = real memory; **mode réel** = real mode; **nombre réel** = real number; **temps réel** = real time; **animation en temps réel** = real-time animation; **entrée en temps réel** = real-time input; **exécution (d'un programme) en temps réel** = real time execution; **horloge en temps réel** = real-time clock; **multitâche en temps réel** = real-time multitasking; **système en temps réel** = real-time system; **dans un système en temps réel, le déplacement de l'image vers la gauche est parfaitement synchronisé au mouvement du manche à balai vers la gauche; s'il se produit un délai entre l'action et le résultat, il ne s'agit pas d'un véritable système en temps réel** = in a real-time system, as you move the joystick left, the image on the screen moves left; if there is a pause for processing it is not a true real-time system; **système d'exploitation en temps réel** = real-time operating system; **traitement en temps réel** = real-time processing

ré-entrant *adj* re-entrant; **programme ré-entrant** = re-entrant program *ou* code *ou* routine; **sous-**programme ré-entrant** = closed *ou* linked subroutine

◊ **ré-entrée** *nf* re-entry; **point de ré-entrée** = re-entry point

refaire *vtr* to redo; **refaire à partir du début** = to redo from start; **est-ce que l'ordinateur peut refaire le graphique du produit de façon à en présenter une vue plongeante?** = can the computer redraw the graphics showing the product from the top view?

référençage *nm* referencing; **référençage d'entrée/sortie** = input/output referencing

◊ **référence** *nf* **(a)** reference; **référence par anticipation** = forward reference; *(dans un livre, un document, etc.)* **référence croisée** = cross reference; **adresse de référence** = reference address; **adresse de référence directe** = direct reference address; **faire référence (à)** = to refer (to); **fichier** *ou* **liste de référence** = authority file *ou* reference file *ou* list; **liste de référence** = reference list; **niveau de référence** = reference level; **période de référence** = reference time; **piste de référence** = library track; **système de référence** = reference retrieval system; **table** *ou* **tableau de référence** = reference table *ou* look-up table (LUT) *ou* translation table *ou* conversion table; **variable de référence d'une cellule** = cell reference variable **(b)** *(lignes guides)* **bord de référence** = aligning edge; **lignes de référence** = guide bars

◊ **référencé, -ée** *adj* **extrait référencé** = quote

◊ **référencer** *vtr* to reference

référentiel, -elle *adj* **ensemble référentiel** = universal set; **l'ensemble référentiel des nombres premiers inférieurs à dix et plus grands que deux est 3,5,7** = the universal set of prime numbers less than ten and greater than two is 3,5,7

référer *vtr* *(à une autre section d'un document)* to cross-reference

◊ **se référer (à)** *vpr* to refer (to)

refermer *vtr* to close up

réfléchi, -ie *adj* **code réfléchi** = reflected code; **code binaire réfléchi** = cyclic code; **code décimal réfléchi** = cyclic decimal code; **onde (radio) réfléchie** = backscatter; **signal réfléchi** = signal reflection

◊ **réfléchir** *vtr* to reflect; **dans un appareil reflex, l'image est réfléchie par un miroir interne** = in a reflex camera, the image is reflected by an inbuilt mirror

◊ **réfléchissant, -e** *adj* reflective; **disque laser à surface réfléchissante** = reflective disk

◊ **réflectance** *nf* reflectance; **réflectance de fond** *ou* **d'arrière-plan** = background reflectance

◊ **réflectométrie** *nf* reflectometry; **test de câble par réflectométrie** = time domain reflectometry (TDR)

reflet *nm* *(sur l'écran)* glare; *(sur un film)* flare; **filtre anti-reflet(s)** *ou* **antireflet(s)** = glare filter; **marqué d'un reflet** = flared

◊ **refléter** *vtr (une image)* to mirror

reflex *nm* appareil (photo) **reflex** = reflex (camera); **dans un appareil reflex, l'image est réfléchie par un miroir interne** = in a reflex camera, the image is reflected by an inbuilt mirror

réflexion *nf* **(a)** glare *ou* reflection; **disque laser à réflexion** = reflective disk; **la réflexion sur l'écran me fatigue la vue** = the glare from the screen makes my eyes hurt **(b) coefficient de réflexion d'un signal** = signal reflection

reformatage *nm* reformatting; **toutes les données contenues sur un disque sont détruites par le reformatage** = reformatting destroys all the data on a disk

◊ **reformater** *vtr* to reformat; **si vous reformatez, vous détruirez toutes les données du disque** *ou* **vous blanchirez le disque** = by reformatting you will wipe the disk clean; **évitez de reformater votre disque dur à moins qu'il n'y ait aucune autre solution** = do not reformat your hard disk unless you can't do anything else

réfracter *vtr* to refract

◊ **réfraction** *nf* refraction; **indice de réfraction** = refractive index

refus *nm* refusal; **erreur de refus** = rejection error

régénérateur *nm* regenerator

◊ **régénérateur, -trice** *adj* **lecture régénératrice (de données)** = regenerative reading

◊ **régénération** *nf* regeneration; recovery; **régénération de document** = document recovery; **régénération de signal** = signal regeneration

◊ **régénérer** *vtr* to regenerate

régime *nm* **travailler à plein régime** = to work at full capacity

région *nf* region; *(ionosphère)* **région D** = D-region; **la région D est la principale cause d'affaiblissement des ondes radioélectriques** = the D-region is the main cause of attenuation in transmitted radio signals; **région F** = F-region

◊ **régional, -e** *adj* **antenne de relais régional** = master antenna television system (MATV); *(Québec)* **indicatif (téléphonique) régional** = area code; **les journaux régionaux** = the regional papers *ou* the local press

registre *nm* register; **registre banalisé** *ou* **général** *ou* **polyvalent** = general register *ou* general purpose register (gpr); **registre compteur** = instruction *ou* program counter (PC) *ou* instruction address register (IAR); **registre couplé** = adjunct register; **registre d'addition** = add register; **registre d'adresse** = address register; **registre d'adresse courante** = current address register (CAR); **registre d'adresse indexé** = B register; **registre d'adresse d'instruction** = instruction address register (IAR) *ou* instruction counter; **registre (d'adresse) de limites** = boundary register; **registre d'adresse en mémoire** = memory address register

(MAR); **pour obtenir un registre d'adresse de 16 bits avec un processeur de 8 bits, on lui associe un deuxième registre (de 8 bits)** = the 8-bit CPU uses a paired register to provide a 16-bit address register; **registre d'affichage** = display register; **registre auxiliaire de routage d'adresse** = B-line counter; **registre des balises** = flag register; **registre de base** = base register; **registre à bits circulants** = circulating register; **registre de commande** = command register; **registre de contrôle** = *(commande)* control register; *(vérification)* check register; **registre à décalage** = circulating register *ou* shift register; **registre de données** = data register; **registre des données en mémoire** = memory data register (MDR); **vider le registre de données** = to clear the data register; **registre d'entrée** = input register *ou* receiver register; **registre d'entrée/sortie** = input/output register; **registre d'index** = index register (IR); **registre d'instruction** = instruction register (IR) *ou* program register; **registre d'instruction courante** = current instruction register (CIR); **registre d'instruction à exécuter** *ou* **registre de la prochaine instruction** = next instruction register; **registre de masque** = mask register; **registre de mémoire associative** = associative storage register; **registre de mémoire tampon** = memory buffer register (MBR); **registre des mots d'état** = program status word register (PSW register); **registre d'opération** *ou* **de code d'opération** = operation register *ou* op register; **registre de pagination à accès direct** = direct page register; **registre (de) sortie** = output register; **registre des témoins** = flag register; **registre de texte** = text register; **registre externe** = external register; **registre programme** = program counter (PC); **registre secondaire** = B box; **registre tampon** = buffer register; **registre tampon des entrées** = input buffer register; **registre tampon de sortie** = output buffer register; **registre temporaire** = temporary register; **adressage de registre** = register addressing; **fichier de registre** = register file; **instruction de décalage dans le registre** = accumulator shift instruction; **mettre en registre** = to deposit in the register; **taille d'un registre** = register length

réglable *adj* **(a)** *(son, densité, contraste)* adjustable **(b)** *(vitesse, etc.)* selectable *ou* programmable; **réglable (par l'utilisateur)** = user-selectable; **les vitesses (de réception et de transmission) de ce modem sont réglables par l'utilisateur** = this modem has user-selectable baud rates

◊ **réglage** *nm* **(a)** *(action)* adjustment *ou* setting; **réglage des contrastes** = contrast setting; **réglage de la luminosité** = brightness setting; **la luminosité a besoin d'un réglage** = the brightness needs adjustment **(b)** *(touche ou bouton)* dial *ou* control; **réglage de densité d'impression** = density dial; **réglage du volume** = volume control

règle *nf* **(a)** *(dispositif de mesure)* **règle graduée** = ruler; **règle de tabulation** = tab rack *ou* ruler line; **la règle de tabulation indique les marges de gauche et de droite** = a tab rack shows you the left and right margins **(b)** *(lignes directrices)* rule; **il est de règle d'attendre le signal CTS avant de commencer à transmettre** = the rule states that you wait for the clear signal before transmitting; **règles propres à**

un **langage** = language rules; *(en donnant des instructions, des commandes, etc.)* **agir contre les règles** = to act illegally; *(en informatique)* **qui va contre les règles de la syntaxe** = illegal (instruction); **système à base de règles** = rule-based system

◊ **règlement** *nm* rule *ou* regulation; **règlements écrits** = printed regulations

réglé, -ée *adj (appareil)* set *ou* tuned; *(son, densité, contraste)* adjusted; *(paramètres de vitesse, etc.)* selected *ou* programmed

◊ **régler** *vtr (un appareil)* to set *ou* to tune; *(courant)* to regulate; *(son, densité, contraste)* to adjust; *(paramètres)* to program *ou* to select; **vous n'avez qu'à tourner un bouton pour régler la luminosité et le contraste** = you can adjust the brightness and contrast by turning a knob; **régler (un appareil) avec grande précision** = to fine tune (a machine); **la camera est réglée pour le premier plan** = the camera is focused on the foreground; **qui peut être réglé suivant les besoins de l'utilisateur** = user-selectable

réglure *nf (imprimerie: ligne mince)* rule

regroupé, -ée *adj* grouped; *(en série)* ganged

◊ **regroupement** *nm* group; **regroupement de commutateurs (en série)** = ganged switch

◊ **regrouper** *vtr* to group *ou* to batch *ou* to bracket together; to gather

régulateur *nm* regulator; **régulateur de tension** = voltage regulator

◊ **régulation** *nf* **bus de régulation** = contention bus

◊ **régulé, -ée** *adj* regulated; **courant régulé** = regulated power supply

◊ **réguler** *vtr* to regulate

régulier, -ière *adj* regular; **l'horloge émet un signal à intervalles réguliers** = the clock signal is periodic

réimpression *nf* reprint; **faire une réimpression** = to reprint

◊ **réimprimer** *vtr* to reprint; **nous réimprimons 10 000 exemplaires** = we have ordered a 10,000 copy reprint

ré-initialisation *ou* **réinitialisation** *nf* reset; **ré-initialisation automatique à la mise sous tension** = power-on reset; **ré-initialisation (du système) par commande** = soft reset; **ré-initialisation (du système) en utilisant le contacteur** = hard reset; **bouton de ré-initialisation** = reset button *ou* key; **signal de ré-initialisation** = return to zero signal

◊ **ré-initialiser** *vtr* to reset

ré-injecter *vtr* to redirect; **vous pouvez trier les résultats d'une commande DIR en les ré-injectant dans la commande SORT** = you can sort the results from a DIR command by redirecting to the SORT command

rejet *nm* rejection; **caractère de rejet d'un bloc (dont les données sont mauvaises)** = block ignore character; *(du scanner qui ne peut lire un caractère)* **erreur de rejet** = rejection error

◊ **rejeter** *vtr* to reject *ou* to ignore; **l'ordinateur rejette toute donnée venant de sources non compatibles** = the computer rejects all incoming data from incompatible sources

rejouer *vtr* to replay *ou* to play back; **rejouer une bande** = to replay a tape *ou* to re-run a tape

relâcher *vtr (un bloc de mémoire ou un fichier)* to release

relais *nm* relay; **ce circuit comporte un relais** = there is a relay in the circuit; **il est protégé par un relais de 5A** = it is relay-rated at 5 Amps; **relais hertzien** = microwave relay; **relais de télévision câblée** = cable TV relay station; **disque relais** = milk disk; *(de télévision)* **station relais** = local distribution service (LDS)

relance *nf* restart; **relance automatique** = auto restart; **horloge à relance automatique** = delta clock

◊ **relancer** *vtr* to restart *ou* to reboot *ou* to reload; **essayez d'abord de relancer (votre système)** = first try to restart your system; **nous avons relancé le système et les fichiers ont réapparu sur l'écran** = we rebooted and the files reappeared on the screen

> le système est tel que l'utilisateur peut lui-même identifier la panne, autorisant ainsi la relance automatique ou la reconfiguration à distance de l'élément déficient
> *Le Monde informatique*

relatif, -ive *adj* relative; **adressage relatif** = base addressing; **adresse relative** = relative address *ou* indirect address; floating address; **codage relatif** = relative coding; **coordonnées relatives** = relative coordinates; **données relatives** = relative data; **erreur relative** = relative error; **horloge relative** = relative-time clock; **pointeur relatif** *ou* **dispositif de pointage relatif** = relative pointing device; **valeur (adresse) relative** = offset value *ou* offset word

relation *nf* relationship; **(données) qui n'ont aucune relation** = disjointed (data); **relation booléenne** = Boolean connective; **graphe de relation** = derivation graph

◊ **relationnel, -elle** *adj* **base de données relationnelle** = relational database *ou* plex database; **si vous recherchez un patronyme dans une base de données relationnelle, il est aussi possible d'extraire le salaire du livre de comptes qui lui est relié** = if you search the relational database for the surname, you can pull out his salary from the related accounts database; **système de gestion de base de donnés relationnelle (SGBDR)** = relational database management system (RDBMS); **opérateur relationnel** = relational operator *ou* logical operator; **requête relationnelle** = relational query

> il faut prévoir le nombre et les types de rubriques et la séparation de celles-ci en fichiers pour bénéficier des structures relationnelles construites visuellement à l'aide de la souris
>
> *L'Ordinateur Individuel*

relecture *nf* **(a)** *(d'épreuves d'imprimerie)* proofreading; **la relecture des épreuves est-elle terminée?** = has all the text been proofread yet? **(b)** *(disque ou bande)* read back *ou* replay; **relecture immédiate** *ou* **instantanée** = instant replay; **contrôle par relecture** = read back check

relève *nf* **prendre la relève** = to take over (from); **en cas de panne d'électricité, nous avons un onduleur qui peut prendre la relève** = if there is a power failure, we have a safety net in the form of a UPS

relever *vtr* to enhance

relié, -ée *adj* **(a)** linked *ou* joined; **procédé relié aux résultats d'un autre procédé** = a process which is dependent on the result of another process **(b)** connected *ou* linked *ou* joined; *(en ligne)* on-line; **les deux ordinateurs sont reliés** = the two computers are linked; **processeur auxiliaire relié au processeur central** = attached processor; **une série de postes reliés les uns aux autres** = a series of interconnected terminals **(c)** *(livre)* bound; **relié sans couture** = perfect bound; **édition reliée** = hardcover edition *ou* hardback

relief *nm* relief; **impression en relief** = relief printing

relier *vtr* **(a)** *(joindre)* to join *ou* to link **(b)** *(connecter)* to connect (to) *ou* to link *ou* to attach; *(utilisant une interface)* to interface (with); **relier les un(e)s aux autres** = to interconnect; **relier en chaîne** *ou* **en cascade** *ou* **en série** = to daisy-chain; **relier en réseau** = to network; **les postes ont été reliés en réseau plutôt que d'être utilisés comme postes autonomes** *ou* **comme postes individuels** = the workstations have been networked together rather than used as stand-alone systems **(c)** *(livre)* **relier avec couverture cartonnée** = to case (a book)

◊ **relieur, -euse** *n (personne)* binder

◊ **reliure** *nf* **(a)** binding; **reliure sans couture** = perfect binding **(b)** **(l'art de) la reliure** = binding; **atelier de reliure** = bindery; **les feuilles ont été envoyées à la reliure** = the sheets have been sent to the bindery for binding

relogeable *adj* relocatable; **programme relogeable** = relocatable program; **programme automatiquement relogeable** = self-relocating program

◊ **relogement** *nm (de programme)* relocation

◊ **reloger** *vtr* to relocate

REM *(déclaration de remarque dans un programme BASIC)* **instruction REM** = remark *ou* REM

rémanence *nf* lag; **rémanence cathodique** = cathode ray tube storage; **rémanence de l'image** = image retention *ou* hangover

remarque *nf* **déclaration de remarque dans un programme BASIC** = remark (REM)

rembobiner *vtr (un film, etc.)* to rewind

remerciement *nm (dans un livre)* **remerciements** = acknowledgements

remettre *vtr* to put back; **il a remis la bande** = he replayed the tape; **remettre en bon état** = to restore; **remettre en marche** = to restart; **essayez d'abord de remettre votre système en marche** = first try to restart your system; **remettre à zéro** = to reset *ou* to zero; **remettre à zéro un dispositif programmable** = to zero a device

◊ **remise** *nf* **remise en état** = *(machine)* repair; *(fichier)* recovery; **programme de remise en état automatique** = automatic recovery program; **remise à l'état initial commandée par l'émetteur** = forward clearing; **remise en marche** = restart; *(après une panne)* **remise en marche** *ou* **remise en route au point de reprise** *ou* **au point d'arrêt** = failure recovery *ou* fall back recovery

remove directory *voir* REPERTOIRE

remplacement *nm* **mode remplacement** = replace mode

◊ **remplacer** *vtr* to replace *ou* to supersede; **le nouveau programme, qui remplace le précédent, est beaucoup plus rapide** = the new program supersedes the earlier one, and is much faster; **remplacer des données par superposition d'écriture** = to overwrite (data); **les nouvelles données ont remplacé les données anciennes (par superposition d'écriture)** = the latest data input has overwritten the old information; *(instruction)* **chercher et remplacer** = search and replace; *voir aussi* CHERCHER

remplir *vtr* to fill (up) *ou* to pad

◊ **remplissage** *nm* filling *ou* padding; **remplissage de bits** = bit stuffing; **remplissage avec caractères blancs** = character fill *ou* character stuffing *ou* padding; **remplissage de zone** = region fill; **caractère de remplissage** = fill character *ou* pad character; *(utilisés comme caractères de remplissage)* null character *ou* redundant character *ou* ignore character *ou* gap character; **insertion (en mémoire) de caractères de remplissage** = character fill; **chiffre de remplissage** = gap digit; **instruction de remplissage** = dummy instruction *ou* waste instruction; *(utilisées comme instructions de remplissage)* blank instruction *ou* null instruction *ou* no-operation *ou* no-op instruction *ou* pseudo-instruction

rendement *nm* **(a)** efficiency; capacity; **rendement de phosphorescence** = phosphor efficiency; **travailler à plein rendement** = to work at full capacity **(b)** *(d'un appareil)* throughput; **rendement effectif** = effective throughput; **rendement estimé** = rated throughput

rentrée *nf* re-entry; **point de rentrée** = re-entry point

renvoi *nm* *(note dans un document)* cross-reference; *(signe de la note)* reference mark; **renvoi en bas de page** = footnote; **faire un renvoi** = to cross-reference *ou* to cross-refer; **les unités SI font l'objet d'un renvoi à l'appendice** = the SI units are cross-referenced to the appendix; **générateur de renvois** = cross-reference generator

réorganiser *vtr* to reorganize; **il faut attendre que la base de données du correcteur orthographique soit réorganisée** = wait while the spelling checker database is being reorganized

repagination *nf* repagination; **le logiciel de PAO permet de faire une simple repagination** = the dtp package allows simple repagination

◊ **repaginer** *vtr* to repaginate *ou* to renumber the pages; **le système de PAO permet de repaginer** = the dtp package allows simple repagination; **le texte a été repaginé après modification de la longueur des lignes** = the text was repaginated with a new line width

réparable *adj* *(machine)* repairable; **erreur réparable** = recoverable error

◊ **réparation** *nf* repair *ou* corrective maintenance; **moyenne de temps requis pour réparation** = mean time to repair

◊ **réparer** *vtr* to repair *ou* to fix; **l'ordinateur ne peut être réparé** = the computer has a terminal fault; **pouvez-vous réparer le photocopieur?** = can you fix the photocopier?; **les techniciens essayent de réparer le standard téléphonique** = the technicians are trying to repair the switchboard; **réparer une panne** = to repair a fault

réparti, -e *adj* distributed; **informatique répartie** = distributed data processing (DDP); **répartie** = distributed intelligence; **système réparti** = distributed system; **système de base de données réparti** = distributed database system; **système à fichiers répartis** = distributed file system

◊ **répartir** *vtr* to allocate *ou* to distribute

repartir *vi* to resume

répartiteur *nm* *(d'une ligne)* splitter

◊ **répartition** *nf* **(a)** allocation; **répartition des tâches** = job scheduling **(b)** multiplexage par répartition en fréquence = frequency division multiplexing (FDM); **multiplexage par répartition dans le temps (MRT)** = time division multiplexing (TDM)

repasser *vtr* *(un film ou une bande)* to play again *ou* to replay; **il a repassé la bande** = he replayed the tape; **repassez ce film au ralenti** = play the film again in slow motion

repérage *nm* register; *(imprimerie)* **en repérage** = in register; **les deux couleurs ne sont pas en repérage** = the two colours are out of register

◊ **repère** *nm* mark *ou* indicator; *(d'alignement)* register marks; *(on a tape or film)* blip; **repère de positionnement (sur microfilm)** = editing symbol; **repères de tabulation** = tabulation markers

◊ **repérer** *vtr* to find *ou* to locate; **ils ont repéré le composant défectueux** = they established which component was faulty; **le débogueur a repéré la faute très rapidement** = the debugger found the error very quickly; **les ingénieurs de maintenance ont repéré la source de la panne du système** = the maintenance engineers have identified the cause of the system failure

reperforatrice *nf* reperforator

répertoire *nm* **(a)** list *ou* directory; **répertoire d'adresses** = address list *ou* directory; **répertoire d'adresses par rues** = street directory; **répertoire d'entreprises** = commercial directory *ou* trade directory **(b)** *(liste des fonctions possibles d'un appareil ou d'un logiciel)* repertoire; **le répertoire entier est inclus dans le manuel** = the manual describes the full repertoire; **répertoire de caractères** *ou* **répertoire typographique** = character repertoire; **répertoire d'exceptions** = exception dictionary; **répertoire d'instructions** = instruction repertoire **(c)** *(films ou pièces à l'affiche)* listings **(d)** *(informatique)* disk directory *ou* disk catalogue; **on trouve les titres des fichiers, la date et l'heure de leur création dans le répertoire** = the disk directory shows the file names, date and time of creation; **le nom d'un fichier qui est effacé disparaît aussi du répertoire du disque** = the entry in the disk catalogue is removed when the file is deleted; **répertoire de fichiers** = file directory; **répertoire des fichiers d'un disque** *ou* **d'une disquette** = disk catalogue *ou* directory; **répertoire hiérarchique** = hierarchical directory; **répertoire racine** *ou* **de départ** = root directory; *(sous MS-DOS, OS/2 et UNIX)* **commande de changement de répertoire** = change directory (CD); *(sous MS-DOS, OS/2)* **commande de création de répertoire** = make directory (MD); *(sous MS-DOS, OS/2)* **commande d'effacement de répertoire** = remove directory (RD); **routage par répertoire** = directory routing

COMMENTAIRE: un répertoire peut être imaginé comme un dossier rangé dans le tiroir d'un classeur qui peut contenir des fichiers ou d'autres dossiers

◊ **répertorier** *vtr* to catalogue; **tous les terminaux sont répertoriés avec (indication de) leur emplacement, leur code** *ou* **signe d'appel et leur table d'attributs** = all the terminals were catalogued, with their location, call sign and attribute table

répéter *vtr* to repeat; **groupe (de données) qui se répètent de façon périodique** = repeating group

◊ **répéteur** *nm* *(relais amplificateur)* repeater; **ce répéteur bon marché ne régénère pas les signaux** = this cheap repeater does not regenerate signals

◊ **répétiteur** *nm* *(dispositif qui répète les signaux)* repeater

◊ **répétition** *nf* **(a)** repeat; **répétition automatique** = automatic repeat *ou* auto repeat; **compteur de répétitions** = repeat counter; **groupe** (de données) à répétition = repeating group; **touche répétition** = repeat key **(b)** *(d'une séquence de film, au ralenti)* replay

repiquage *nm (transmission d'un film à la télévision)* **repiquage vidéo d'un film** = film pickup

replâtrage *nm (corrections temporaires d'un programme)* bug patches

replier *vtr* to fold

répondeur *nm* **répondeur téléphonique** = (telephone) answering machine *ou* answerphone; **répondeur avec message vocal de synthèse** = voice answer back; **répondeur vocal** = audio response unit

◊ **répondre** *vi* **(a)** *(à quelqu'un ou à une lettre ou au téléphone)* to answer (someone *ou* a letter *ou* the telephone); **répondre à un appel** *ou* **répondre au téléphone** = to answer the phone *ou* to take a (phone) call; **le premier modem transmet l'appel tandis que le second y répond** = the first modem originates the call and the second answers it **(b)** *(satisfaire)* **ce lot de disquettes ne répond pas aux normes de qualité** = this batch of disks is not up to standard; **le logiciel ne fonctionnera pas s'il ne répond pas aux normes du système d'exploitation** = the software will not run if it does not conform to the operating system standards; **le travail ne répond pas aux spécifications du client** *ou* **au cahier des charges** = the work is not up to specification *ou* does not meet the customer's specifications

◊ **réponse** *nf* **(a)** *(téléphone ou modem)* answer; **réponse automatique** = auto-answer; **mode réponse** = answer mode; *(modem qui émet un signal de réponse)* **modem de réponse** = answer modem; **signal de réponse** = answertone **(b)** response *ou* answer; *(signal)* **réponse affirmative** *ou* **positive** = positive response; **réponse aux basses fréquences** = bass response; **réponse en fréquence** = frequency response; **réponse intrinsèque** *ou* **par défaut** = default response; **délai de réponse** = gate delay; **temps de réponse** = answer time *ou* access time *ou* response time; **le temps de réponse de ce simulateur de vol est excellent** = the response time of this flight simulator is very good **(c)** **emplacement** *ou* **case réservé(e) à la réponse** = response position; **(fonction) interrogation/réponse** *ou* **demande/réponse** = inquiry/response (function)

report *nm (math)* carry; **report en cascade** = cascade carry *ou* high speed carry; **report circulaire** *ou* **en boucle** = end-around carry; **report partiel** = partial carry; **report rapide** *ou* **simultané** = ripple-through carry; **bit de report** = carry bit *ou* flag; **signal de fin de report** = carry complete signal; **signe de report** = carry bit *ou* flag; **temps de report** = carry time

reportage *nm* press coverage *ou* media coverage; **reportage électronique** = electronic news gathering (ENG)

reporter *vtr* to transfer

repos *nm* **au repos** = *(machine)* idle *ou* inactive; *(circuit ou dispositif)* quiescent

reprendre *vtr* to repeat *ou* to resume; **le travail reprend normalement après la panne de l'imprimante** = work is flowing normally again after the breakdown of the printer; **nous avons repris le fichier, entrée par entrée** = we stepped forward through the file one record at a time; **reprendre l'exécution d'un programme** = to rerun a program

représentatif, -ive *adj* representative

◊ **représentation** *nf* representation; **vous pouvez voir le nouveau modèle sur cette représentation** = this picture shows the new design; **représentation graphique** = graphics *ou* graphic display; **les représentations graphiques telles que histogrammes, camemberts, etc** = graphics output such as bar charts, pie charts, etc.; **représentations graphiques sur ordinateur** = computer graphics *ou* computer-generated graphics; **représentation numérique** = digital representation

◊ **représenter** *vtr* to represent; **l'architecture** *ou* **la structure de l'ordinateur était représentée graphiquement** = the computer structure was expressed graphically

reprise *nf* **(a)** restart; *(sans repartir à zéro)* **reprise sur incident** *ou* **remise en marche au point de reprise** = fall back recovery *ou* error recovery *ou* failure recovery; **reprise sur l'instruction d'arrêt** *ou* **reprise au point d'arrêt** = warm start; **reprise après interruption de l'alimentation** = cold start; **point de reprise** = check point *ou* rerun point; **(instruction de) vidage et reprise** = dump and restart **(b)** *(contre achat)* part exchange

repro = REPROGRAPHIE

reproduction *nf (d'un document)* duplication *ou* reproduction; **reproduction illégale d'une oeuvre protégée** = infringement of copyright *ou* copyright infringement; **oeuvre dont les droits de reproduction sont réservés** = work (still) in copyright

◊ **reproduire** *vtr (un document)* to reproduce *ou* to duplicate *ou* to copy

reprogrammer *vtr* to reprogram

reprographie *nf* reprography

requête *nf* query *ou* request; enquiry *ou* inquiry; **requête d'entrée/sortie** = input/output request (IORQ); **requête relationnelle** = relational query; **la requête relationnelle 'trouver tous les individus mâles de moins de 35 ans' ne peut pas être traitée par ce système** = the relational query 'find all men under 35 years old' will not work on this system; **caractère de requête** = inquiry character (ENQ); **langage de requête** = query language (QL); **langage de requête par l'exemple** *ou* **langage QBE** = Query by example *ou* QBE language; **dans la plupart des bases de données QBE, les requêtes ont sensiblement la même forme que les enregistrements dans la base de données; faire une requête est aussi facile que remplir un formulaire** = in most QBE databases, the query form looks like the record format in the database - retrieving data is as easy as filling in a form; **traitement de requête** = query processing; **utilitaire de requête** = query facility

requis, -e *adj* wanted; **non requis** = unwanted

réseau *nm* **(a)** *(d'ordinateurs)* network; **cette société informatique est une société britannique spécialisée en réseaux** = this computer firm is a UK networking specialist; **réseau en anneau** = ring (data) network; **réseau de type bus** = bus network; **réseau centralisé** = centralized (computer) network; **réseau décentralisé** = decentralized (computer) network; **réseau démocratique** = democratic network; **réseau d'entreprise** = enterprise network; **réseau (avec synchronisation) despotique** = despotic network; **réseau à distance** *ou* **réseau étendu** = wide area network (WAN); **réseau à grande distance** = long haul network; **réseau de distribution** = distribution network; **réseau égal à égal avancé** *ou* **réseau poste à poste avancé** *ou* **réseau sans serveur dédié (SSD)** *or* **réseau APPN** = advanced peer-to-peer networking (APPN); **réseau étendu** = wide area network (WAN); **réseau très étendu** = long haul network; **il a diffusé les dernières informations via le réseau étendu** = he broadcast the latest news over the WAN; **réseau hétérogène** = heterogeneous network; **réseau hiérarchisé** = hierarchical computer network; **réseau homogène** = homogeneous network; **réseau informatique** *ou* **d'information** = information network; **expert** *ou* **spécialiste en réseaux informatiques** = networking specialist; **réseau intégralement interconnecté** = plex structure; **réseau local (d'entreprise)** = local area network (LAN); **réseau local en bande de base** = base band local area network; **réseau local utilisant les ports séries ou un adaptateur externe** = zero slot LAN; **modem pour réseau local d'entreprise** = limited distance modem; **segment de réseau local** = LAN segment; **serveur de réseau local d'entreprise** = local area network server *ou* LAN server; **réseau maillé** = mesh network; **réseau totalement maillé** = fully connected network; **ils exploitent un réseau de micros** = they run a system of networked micros; **réseau neural** = neural network; **réseau d'ordinateurs** *ou* **réseau informatique** = computer network; **réseau urbain** = metropolitan area network (MAN); **adaptateur de réseau** = network adapter; **administrateur de réseau** = network administrator; **architecture** *ou* **configuration de réseau** = network architecture *ou* systems network architecture (SNA); **base de données en réseau** = network database; **système de base de données en réseau** = distributed database system; **carte (interface) de réseau** = network interface card (NIC); network adapter card; **configuration en réseau** = networking; **configurer en réseau** = to network; **contrôleur de réseau** = network controller; **couche réseau** = network layer; **diagramme (de configuration** *ou* **de topologie) de réseau** = network diagram; **disque réseau** = network drive; **disposer en réseau** = to network; **gestion de réseau** = network management; **gestionnaire de périphérique de réseau** = network device driver; **imprimante de réseau** = network printer; **liaisons redondantes** *ou* **auxiliaires d'un réseau** = network redundancy; **logiciel de** *ou* **pour réseau** = networking software *ou* network

software *ou* common software; **matériel** *ou* **équipements de réseau (informatique)** = network hardware *ou* networking hardware; **mise en réseau (d'ordinateurs)** = networking; **norme d'interface gestionnaire de réseau** = network driver interface specification (NDIS); **processeur de réseau** = network processor; **processeur de réseau de communication** = communications network processor; **programme de contrôle de réseau** = network control program; **protocole (de communication) de réseau** = network protocol; **relier en réseau** to network; **les postes de travail ont été reliés en réseau plutôt que d'être utilisés indépendamment** = the workstations have been networked together rather than used as standalone systems; **répertoire de réseau** = network directory; **serveur de réseau** = network server; **structure en réseau** = network structure; **synchronisation de réseau** = network timing; **système d'exploitation de réseau (NOS)** = network operating system (NOS); **tête de réseau** = head end; **topologie de réseau** = network topology **(b)** *(téléphonique* *ou* *télécommunication* *ou* *radio* *ou* *télévision)* network; **réseau de communication** *ou* **de télécommunications** = communications network; **réseau commuté** = circuit switched network; **réseau numérique à intégration de services (RNIS)** = integrated services digital network (ISDN); **réseau numérique intégré (RNI)** = integrated digital network (IDN); **accès au réseau numérique intégré** = integrated digital access (IDA); **réseau public (de transmission de données)** = public data network; **réseau radiophonique** *ou* **de radiodiffusion** = broadcast network *ou* radio network; **réseau radiotéléphonique** = cellular service; **réseau téléinformatique** *ou* **de transmission de données** = data communications network *ou* data network; **réseau téléphonique** = telephone network; **accès direct au réseau (téléphonique)** = direct outward dialling; **réseau téléphonique (public) commuté** = public switched telephone network (PSTN); **réseau de télévision** = television network; **programme transmis sur (tout) un réseau de télévision** = networked TV programme; **transmission** *ou* **diffusion sur (tout) un réseau** = networking; **réseau à valeur ajoutée** = value added network (VAN); **réseau à zone de recouvrement** = overlay network **(c)** array; **réseau logique** = logic array; **circuit logique en réseau** = gate array; **antenne en réseau** = array antenna **(d)** *(câbles)* **réseau câblé** = cabling

réserve *nf* **(a) avec réserve** = (i) conditional; (ii) conditionally; **sans réserve** = (i) unconditional; (ii) unconditionally **(b) (appareil** *ou* **dispositif) de réserve** = standby (device)

◊ **réservé, -ée** *adj* reserved; **caractère réservé** = reserved character; **sous DOS, le caractère \ est réservé pour représenter un chemin du répertoire** = in DOS, the reserved character \ is used to represent a directory path; **espace mémoire réservé (à l'usage d'un utilisateur)** = private address space; **ligne réservée** = private line; **mot réservé** = reserved word; **port réservé** = private dial port; **il n'y a qu'un seul poste réservé aux graphiques sur ce réseau** = there's only one dedicated graphics workstation in this network; **secteur réservé** = reserved sector

résident, -e *adj* resident *ou* memory-resident; **logiciel résident** = resident software *ou* memory-resident software; **police (de caractères)** *ou* **fonte résidente** = internal *ou* resident font; **programme résident** = memory-resident program *ou* internally stored program; **le système peut se planter si vous introduisez un trop grand nombre de programmes résidents** = the system can bomb if you set up too many memory-resident programs at the same time; **programme résident TSR** = terminate and stay resident (TSR) program *ou* terminate and stay resident (TSR) software *ou* RAM resident program; **tapez Ctrl et F5, vous activez ainsi le module résident (TSR) et il affiche l'agenda du jour** = when you hit Ctrl-F5, you will activate the RAM resident program and it will display your day's diary; **zone (de mémoire) des programmes non résidents** = transient area

ces produits sont constitués de programmes de communication résidents, qui possèdent toutes les caractéristiques des réseaux, mais sont limités à deux PC

Action PC

résiduel, -elle *adj* residual; **bande latérale résiduelle** = vestigial sideband; **oscillations résiduelles (sur un courant)** = ripple; **taux d'erreur résiduel** = residual error rate

résine *nf* resin; **résine photosensible** = photoresist; **(méthode de la) résine photosensible en positif** = positive photoresist; **pour faire un circuit imprimé il faut d'abord recouvrir la carte d'une résine photosensible** = to make the PCB, first coat the board with photoresist

résistance *nf* (a) resistance (b) *(device)* resistor; **résistance variable** = variable resistor; **logique (à) transistors (et) résistances (LTR)** = resistor transistor logic (RTL)

◊ **résister (à)** *vi* to resist

résolution *nf* (a) solving *ou* resolving; **langage de résolution de problème** = problem-orientated language (POL); **pouvoir de résolution** = resolving power (b) *(définition)* resolution; **résolution d'un nombre (binaire)** = digital resolution; *(d'un écran)* **haute résolution** = high resolution *ou* hi-res; *voir aussi* DEFINITION

la plupart ont une résolution de 300 x 300 points avec un débit de l'ordre de 6 pages/minute, la résolution des meilleurs modèles atteignant les 400 points par pouce

L'Ordinateur Individuel

résonance *ou* **résonnance** *nf* resonance; **sonnerie à résonance de fréquence** = decimonic ringing; **imagerie par résonance magnétique (IRM)** = magnetic resonance imaging

résoudre *vtr* to solve; **résoudre un problème** = to solve a problem

respecter *vtr* to respect; **respecter un délai** = to meet a deadline

responsable *adj* *(de département)* (department) director *ou* manager *ou* head *ou* chief; **responsable de base de données** = database administrator (DBA); **responsable du contrôle de (la) qualité** = quality controller; **responsable du service informatique** = data processing manager (DPM); *(d'un film)* **responsable de la distribution** = casting director

resserrer *vtr* to close up; **en resserrant les lignes, nous gagnerons une page** = if we close up the lines, we should save a page

ressortir *vi* (a) *(une ligne de paragraphe)* **faire ressortir** = to outdent (b) *(mettre en évidence ou mettre en surbrillance)* **faire ressortir** = to highlight; **les titres sont en caractères gras pour les faire ressortir** = the headings are highlighted in bold

ressource *nf* resource; **ressource critique** = critical resource; **allocation de ressources** = resource allocation; *(de fichier Apple Macintosh)* **fourche de ressources** = resource fork; **partage de ressources** = resource sharing

resquilleur, -euse *n* intruder

restauration *nf* recovery; **procédure de restauration** = recovery procedure; **programme de restauration automatique** = automatic recovery program

◊ **restaurer** *vtr* to restore; *(des données)* to reconstitute (data); *(un fichier dans sa forme originale)* to backout

reste *nm* remainder *ou* residue; **contrôle sur reste** = residue check

◊ **rester** *vi* to remain; **7 divisé par 3 égale 2 reste 1** = 7 divided by 3 is equal to 2 remainder 1

restituer *vtr* *(donnée ou fichier)* to retrieve *ou* to call up; **(fichier) qui ne peut être restitué** = irretrievable (file); **il est impossible restituer les fichiers depuis la panne** = the files are irretrievable since the computer crashed

◊ **restitution** *nf* (a) *(de donnés stockées en mémoire)* retrieval; **restitution de données** = information retrieval (IR); **stockage et restitution de données** = information storage and retrieval (ISR) (b) *(d'un fichier perdu)* **procédure de restitution** = recovery procedure

restreint, -e *adj* restricted; **ce document de diffusion restreinte ne doit pas être rendu public** = the document is restricted, and cannot be placed on open access; **complément restreint** = diminished radix complement; **test sélectif restreint** = crippled leapfrog test

◊ **restriction** *nf* restriction

résultat *nm* result; **procédé dépendant des résultats** *ou* **relié aux résultats d'un autre procédé** = a process which is dependent on the result of another process; **le résultat de sortie est fonction de l'état (physique) des liaisons** = the output is dependent on the physical state of the link; **à**

données erronées, résultats erronés *ou* des données douteuses produisent des résultats douteux = garbage in garbage out (GIGO); **code résultat** = result code

résumé *nm* abstract *ou* summary of a (document); **il est plus rapide de chercher dans les résumés que dans le texte complet** = it's quicker to search through the abstracts than the full text; **dans notre bibliothèque, les résumés sont réunis en volumes distincts ce qui assure la facilité et la rapidité des recherches sur un sujet particulier** = in our library, abstracts are gathered together in separate volumes allowing an easy and rapid search for a particular subject; **résumé critique** = evaluative abstract; **résumé et indexation** = abstracting & indexing (A&I)

◊ **résumer** *vtr (un article)* to summarize (an article); to make a summary *ou* to make an abstract (of an article)

rétablir *vtr* **rétablir une liaison** = to reconnect; **les techniciens du téléphone essayent de rétablir la liaison téléphonique** = the telephone engineers are trying to reconnect the telephone

retaper *vtr* **(a)** *(taper de nouveau sur le clavier)* to type again *ou* to retype; **j'ai retapé cette commande, mais ça ne marche pas** = I typed in the command again, but it still didn't work **(b)** *(refaire ou reconstruire)* **programme** *ou* **système qui a été retapé** = kludge

retard *nm* **(a)** delay *ou* lag; **retard de contention** *ou* **de maintien** = contention delay; **retard d'effacement (d'une image)** = lag; **distorsion due au retard du signal** = delay distortion; **ligne à** *ou* **de retard** = delay line; **ligne à** *ou* **de retard au mercure** = mercury delay line; **mémoire à ligne de retard** = delay line store; **vecteur de retard** = delay vector **(b)** delay; **en retard** = late; **travail en retard** = backlog; **les programmeurs ne réussissent pas à venir à bout de toute la programmation en retard** = the programmers can't deal with the backlog of programming work

◊ **retarder** *vtr* to delay

retenir *vtr (math)* to carry; **lorsqu'on additionne 5 et 7, on abaisse 2 et on retient 1 sur la colonne des dizaines, ce qui fait 12** = when 5 and 7 are added, there is an answer of 2 and a carry which is put in the next column, giving 12

rétention *nf* retention

retenue *nf (math)* carry; **retenue anticipée** = carry look ahead; **addition sans retenue** = addition without carry; **additionneur à retenue automatique (très rapide)** = carry look ahead; **indicateur** *ou* **témoin de retenue** = carry flag

retouche *nf* touching (up) *ou* retouching; **il y a quelques retouches à faire au dessin** = the artwork for the line drawings needs retouching in places

◊ **retoucher** *vtr* to retouch *ou* to touch up

retour *nm* **(a)** *(instruction)* return; **(code** *ou* **touche de) retour (du) chariot** *ou* **retour à la ligne** =

carriage return (CR); **les opérateurs de saisie trouvent que la touche de retour est mal placée** = the carriage return key is badly placed for touch-typists; **retour (du) chariot/retour à la ligne** = carriage return/line feed (CR/LF); **retour à la ligne (en limite d'écran)** = (horizontal) wraparound *ou* word wrap; **retour à la ligne automatique** = automatic carriage return *ou* word wrap *ou* wraparound **(b)** *(du curseur)* **retour arrière** = backspace; **caractère de retour arrière** = backspace character; **pointeur retour** = back pointer; **touche de retour arrière** = backspace key; **pour corriger une erreur de saisie de texte, utilisez la touche de retour arrière** = if you make a mistake entering data, use the backspace key to correct it; **retour à la source** *ou* **à l'origine** = homing **(c)** *(d'un balayage)* flyback; **retour de ligne** = line flyback; **délai de retour de ligne** = line blanking interval; **retour de trame** = field flyback **(d)** *(transmission)* **canal** *ou* **voie de retour** = reverse channel *ou* backward channel; **contrôle par retour** = feedback control; **dispositif de retour/d'appel** = answer/originate (device); **modem de retour** = answer modem; **transmission sans contrôle de retour** = free wheeling; **voie de retour du réseau local** = backward LAN channel **(e)** *(rétroaction)* feedback; **ne placez pas le micro trop près du haut-parleur sinon le retour va saturer l'ampli** = make sure the microphone is not too close to the loudspeaker or positive feedback will occur and you will overload the amplifier; **retour acoustique** = acoustical feedback **(f)** **commande de retour au texte original** = revert command

◊ **retournement** *nm* turnaround; **délai de retournement** = turnaround time (TAT) *ou* sense recovery time

retrait *nm* withdrawal; **carte de retrait bancaire** = cash card

retraitement *nm* postprocessing; **programme de retraitement** = postprocessor

retransmettre *vtr* to relay *ou* to retransmit; **tous les messages sont retransmis par l'intermédiaire de ce petit micro** = all messages are relayed through this small micro

◊ **retransmission** *nf* retransmission; **correction d'erreurs par retransmission** = backward error correction; **(système avec facilité de) stockage et retransmission** = store and forward (system)

rétro- *préf* retro-

◊ **rétroaction** *nf* feedback; **rétroaction négative** = negative feedback; **rétroaction positive** = positive feedback; **boucle de rétroaction** = feedback loop

◊ **rétroéclairage** *nm (d'un écran à cristaux liquides)* backlight

◊ **rétroéclairé, -ée** *adj* **écran (à cristaux liquides) rétroéclairé** = backlit display

◊ **rétro-ingénierie** *nf* reverse engineering

◊ **rétroprojecteur** *nm* overhead projector

◊ **rétroprojection** *nf* front projection

◊ **rétrospectif, -ive** *adj* retrospective; **recherche rétrospective** = retrospective search; **test rétrospectif en parallèle** = retrospective parallel running

retrouver *vtr* to find *ou* to recover

réunion *nf* conference; *(opération logique)* **opération de réunion** *ou* **d'union** = disjunction *ou* either-or operation

réussir *vtr&i* to achieve (something) *ou* to master (something) *ou* to manage to do (something); **ne pas réussir quelque chose** = to fail (to do something); **l'imprimante ne réussit pas très bien à imprimer les lignes trop fines** = the printer has difficulty in reproducing very fine lines

réutilisable *ou* **ré-utilisable** *adj* re-usable; **ruban non ré-utilisable** = single-strike ribbon; **support (magnétique) réutilisable** = erasable storage *ou* erasable memory

révélateur *nm* *(photographique)* developer

◊ **révéler** *vtr* to reveal

revendeur, -euse *n* dealer; reseller; **n'achetez votre matériel informatique que chez un revendeur agréé** = always buy hardware from a recognized dealer; **revendeur à valeur ajoutée** *ou* **revendeur à intégration de service** = value-added reseller (VAR); **revendeur d'équipements informatiques** = computer equipment supplier; **revendeur de systèmes à valeur ajoutée** = value added reseller (VAR)

réversible *adj* **disquette réversible** = flippy

revêtir *vtr* *(d'une substance)* to coat

réviser *vtr* to review *ou* to revise; *(un texte avant l'impression)* to edit *ou* to sub-edit *ou* to sub; *(une machine ou une voiture)* to service; **nous avons fait réviser les lecteurs de disquettes hier et tout fonctionne très bien** = the disk drives were serviced yesterday and are working well

◊ **révision** *nf* *(d'un article ou d'un manuscrit)* editing *ou* sub-editing *ou* subbing; *(d'une machine)* service

revoir *vtr* to revise; **la version revue et corrigée ne contient aucune erreur** = the revised version has no mistakes

révolution *nf* revolution; **la révolution technologique** = the technological revolution

revue *nf* magazine; **la maison publie des revues detinées aux hommes/femmes d'affaires** = the company specializes in publications for the business reader; **il travaille à la rédaction d'une revue de micro-informatique** = he edits a computer magazine; **une revue hebdomadaire** = a weekly magazine; **les revues de luxe** = *(familier)* the glossies; **revue spécialisée** *ou* **revue savante** = learned journal

rhéostat *nm* rheostat

rideau *nm* *(produit non existant)* **rideau de fumée** = vapourware

rigide *adj* rigid; **disque rigide** = rigid disk; **les disques sont dans des boîtes rigides par mesure de protection** = the disks are housed in hard protective cases

RISC = REDUCED INSTRUCTION SET COMPUTER; *voir* INSTRUCTION

RJ11 *(connecteur)* RJ11 connector

RJ45 *(connecteur de réseau)* RJ45 connector

RLL *(système de codage pour disques durs)* Run-Length Limited Encoding (RLL)

rm *(commande de suppression d'un sous-répertoire UNIX)* rm (command)

RNI = RESEAU NUMERIQUE INTEGRE

◊ **RNIS** = RESEAU NUMERIQUE A INTEGRATION DE SERVICES

robot *nm* robot

◊ **robotique** *nf* **la robotique** = robotics

robuste *adj* *(face aux situations imprévues)* robust; **ce disque dur n'est pas très robuste** = this hard disk is not very robust

◊ **robustesse** *nf* robustness

le principal avantage de Netscape est sa robustesse. Il n'est pas rare de voir Mosaic 'planter' ou donner des résultats aberrants. Ici, les plantages sont presque inexistants

PC Magazine

roder *vtr* to run in

rogné, -ée *adj* *(pages)* trimmed; **non rogné** = ragged; **bord non rogné** = deckle edge; **livre dont les pages ne sont pas rognées** = uncut book

◊ **rogner** *vtr* *(pages)* to trim; **après l'impression, on rogne pour obtenir des pages de 198 x 129mm** = the printed pages are trimmed to 198 x 129mm

ROM *nf* *(mémoire à lecture seule)* Read Only Memory; **ROM auxiliaire** = sideways ROM; **ROM enfichable** *ou* **ROM amovible** *ou* **cartouche ROM** = ROM cartridge; **cet ordinateur portatif n'est pas équipé d'un lecteur de disquettes mais possède un connecteur pour cartouches ROM** = the portable computer has no disk drives, but has a slot for ROM cartridges; **le constructeur a fourni le programme de commande du moniteur sur deux circuits ROM** = the manufacturer provided the monitor program in two ROM chips; **mémoire ROM** = read only memory (ROM); **ROM effaçable électriquement** = electrically erasable read-only memory (EEROM); **ROM modifiable électriquement** = electrically alterable read-only memory (EAROM); **ROM programmable et effaçable** = erasable programmable read-only memory (EPROM); **ROM programmable et effaçable électriquement** = electrically erasable programmable read-only memory (EEPROM); **ROM programmable, modifiable électriquement** = electrically alterable, programmable read-only memory (EAPROM); **ROM personnalisée** = custom ROM (PROM); **programmes sur ROM** = romware; **programmeur de ROM** = burner; *voir aussi* MEMOIRE

◊ **ROM BIOS** *(BIOS sur ROM)* ROM BIOS

romain, -e *adj* **(a)** roman; **chiffres romains** = Roman numerals **(b)** *(typographie)* **le texte est (composé) en Times Romain** = the text is set in Times Roman

rond, -e *adj* round; **en chiffres ronds** = in round figures

rotatif, -ive *adj* rotary; **caméra rotative** = rotary camera; **presse rotative** = rotary press

◊ **rotation** *nf* rotation; **rotation de matrice** = matrix rotation; *(transmis manuellement)* **mouvement de rotation** = spindling

roue *nf* wheel; **roue à picots** = sprocket wheel

rouge *nm&adj* red; *(couleurs utilisées pour la télévision)* **rouge, vert, bleu** = red, green, blue (RGB); *(met une partie d'un texte en évidence)* **surligné rouge** = redliner

rouleau *nm* **(a)** *(de papier, etc.)* roll; **rouleau de papier pour télécopieur** = roll of fax paper **(b)** *(de machine à écrire ou d'imprimante)* platen; **entraînement par rouleaux** = friction feed

routage *nm* routing; **routage adaptatif** *ou* **flexible** = distributed adaptive routing; **routage adaptatif protégé** = isolated adaptive routing; **routage par dispersion** *ou* **par redistribution** = flooding; **routage des données** = data routing; **routage dynamique** = adaptive routing; **routage optimisé** = minimum weight routing; **routage par répertoire** = directory routing; **routage transparent** = transparent routing; *(de réseau)* **dispositif** *ou* **gestionnaire de routage** = router; **page de routage** = routing page; **pont de routage** = brouter; **le pont de routage permet un routage dynamique entre deux réseaux locaux** = the brouter provides dynamic routing and can bridge two local area networks; **protocole de routage (d'un message)** = routing overheads; **la vitesse de transmission d'informations est beaucoup moins grande une fois qu'on tient compte du protocole de routage** = the information transfer rate is very much less once all routing overheads have been accommodated; **registre auxiliaire de routage d'adresse** = B-line counter; **table de routage** = routing table

◊ **route** *nf* route *ou* path; **mettre en route** = to start; **mise en route** = start; **chargeur** *ou* **programme (élémentaire) de mise en route** = bootstrap (loader); **n'arrêtez pas la vérification de l'orthographe en cours de route** = do not interrupt the spelling checker while it is running

◊ **routeur** *nm* router

routine *nf* routine; **la routine permet d'imprimer le contenu de l'écran** = the routine copies the screen display onto a printer; **l'instruction**

RETOUR à la fin d'une routine permet de redonner la main au programme principal = the RETURN instruction at the end of the routine sends control back to the main program; **routines de clôture (d'exécution)** = end of run routines; **routine de compression** = packing routine; **routine de diagnostic** = diagnostic routine; **routine d'entrée** *ou* **d'introduction de données** = input routine; **routine de gestion de périphérique** = peripheral software driver; **routine interactive** = interactive routine; **routines d'interface** = interface routines; **routine itérative** = iterate *ou* iterative routine; **routine de manipulation de fichier** = file handling routine; **routine de normalisation** = normalization routine; **routine ouverte** = open routine; **routine principale** = main routine; *(en cas de panne)* **routines de secours** = fall back routines; **routine de traitement d'erreur** = error routine; **routines de traitement de la virgule flottante** = floating-point routines; **appeler une routine** = to call a routine

RPC *(appel de procédure à distance)* **appel RPC** = Remote Procedure Call (RPC)

RS-232C *(pour interface série)* **norme RS-232C** = RS-232C (standard)

RS-422 *(norme)* RS-422 (standard)

RS-423 *(norme)* RS-423 (standard)

RSA = RIVEST, SHAMIR AND ADLEMAN **code de cryptage RSA** = RSA cipher system

RTL *(configuration de circuit)* **logique RTL** = Resistor Transistor Logic (RTL)

ruban *nm* **(a)** **mètre à ruban** = tape measure **(b)** *(pour machine à écrire ou imprimante)* ribbon; **ruban (en) tissu** = fibre ribbon; **ruban carbone** = carbon ribbon; **ruban en cartouche** = cartridge ribbon; **ruban d'imprimante** = printer ribbon; **ruban multifrappe** = multi-strike printer ribbon; **ruban à un seul passage** *ou* **non réutilisable** = single strike ribbon; **cartouche de ruban** = ribbon cartridge **(c)** *(pour film)* **ruban de raccord** = splicing tape **(d)** *(bande papier)* **ruban perforé** = perforated tape

rubrique *nf* heading *ou* rubric; **rubrique de déclaration des données** = data division

ruiner *vtr (des données ou un fichier)* to mung up

run-time *n&adj (utilisable seulement avec l'interpréteur d'une application maître)* **version run-time** = run-time version

rupteur *nm (de papier listing)* burster

◊ **rupture** *nf* **(a)** break; *(traitement de texte)* **espace sans rupture** = non-breaking space **(b)** *(électricité)* **rupture de courant** = power failure; **système de sécurité en cas de rupture de courant** = fail safe system

rustine *nf* bug patches

RVB = ROUGE, VERT, BLEU red, green, blue(RGB); **moniteur couleur RVB** = RGB display *ou* monitor

rythme *nm (d'horloge)* clock pulse

Ss

S-100 *(bus)* S-100 bus

SAA *(norme d'une application non spécialement adaptée au matériel, mise au point par IBM)* **norme SAA** = Systems Application Architecture (SAA)

SAFE *(technique d'identification)* Signature Analysis using Functional Analysis (SAFE)

saisie *nf (de données)* (data) input (i/p *ou* I/P) *ou* data entry; data capture; **la saisie commence dès réception du signal d'interruption** = data capture starts when an interrupt is received; **saisie automatique de données** = automatic data capture; **saisie par balayage** = scanning; **logiciel de saisie par balayage** = scanning software; **saisie au** *ou* **sur** *ou* **par clavier** = keyboarding *ou* keying; manual entry *ou* manual input; **le coût de saisie (par clavier) est calculé sur une base de frappes/heure** = the cost of keyboarding is calculated in keystrokes per hour; **saisie au clavier contrôlée par ordinateur** = processor-controlled keying; **saisie directe de données au clavier** = direct data entry (DDE); **saisie directe sur disque(tte), par clavier** = keyboard to disk entry *ou* key-to-disk; **saisie vocale** = voice data entry *ou* input; **masque de saisie** = form *ou* template

◊ **saisi, -e** *adj* input *ou* captured; **données saisies** = input (data)

◊ **saisir** *vtr* **(a)** *(mécaniquement)* to grab *ou* to grip; **dans l'entraînement par friction le papier est saisi par les rouleaux** = in friction feed, the paper is gripped by the rollers **(b)** *(données)* to input *ou* to enter; to capture; **les données ont été saisies** = the data has been entered; **saisir (des données) au clavier** *ou* **par clavier** *ou* **sur clavier** = to keyboard *ou* to key in (data); **il était plus économique de faire saisir le manuscrit par une société de services informatiques** = it was cheaper to have the manuscript keyboarded by another company; **ils ont saisi les toutes dernières données (sur clavier)** = they keyed in the latest data; **utilisez le pavé numérique pour saisir les chiffres** = you can use the numeric keypad to enter the figures

salle *nf* room; **salle de conférence(s)** = conference room; *(de films)* **salle de montage** = cutting room; **salle de projection** = projection room

salon *nm* exhibition; **salon de la bureautique** = business efficiency exhibition

saphir *nm* sapphire

satellite *nm* **(a)** satellite; **satellite de diffusion directe** = direct broadcast satellite (DBS); **satellite domestique** *ou* **national** = domestic satellite; **satellite géostationnaire** = geostationary satellite;

satellite météorologique = weather satellite; **satellite de télécommunications** = communications satellite; **liaison par satellite** = satellite link; **radiodiffusion par satellite** = satellite broadcasting; **technique de diffusion par satellite** = broadcast satellite technique; **(re)transmission par satellite** = satellite transmission **(b)** *(système dépendant)* **ordinateur satellite** = satellite computer; **système satellite** = satellite (system); **terminal satellite** = satellite terminal

> un PC 'satellite' communique avec un PC 'serveur', soit par le port série à une vitesse maximale de 115 200bps, soit par le port parallèle à 50 000bps
>
> *Action PC*

satisfaction *nf* satisfaction; **qui donne satisfaction** = satisfactory *ou* reliable; **les premières versions du logiciel ne donnaient pas complète satisfaction** = the early versions of the software were not completely reliable

saturation *nf* saturation; **saturation d'un canal** *ou* **d'une voie** = channel overload; **saturation de couleur** = colour saturation; **bruit de saturation (magnétique)** = saturation noise; **tests de saturation** = saturation testing

◊ **saturer** *vtr* to saturate *ou* to overload; **ne placez pas le micro trop près du haut-parleur sinon le retour va saturer l'ampli** = make sure the microphone is not too close to the loudspeaker or positive feedback will occur and you will overload the amplifier; **chaque fois que vous prononcez un 'p' vous saturez l'enregistrement, placez donc ce filtre pour que cela cesse** = every time you say a 'p' you overload the tape recorder, so put this pop filter in to stop it

saut *nm* **(a)** *(movement)* jump *ou* skip; **saut du papier** = paper throw; *(de l'imprimante)* **saut rapide** = high-speed skip **(b)** **saut d'image** = frame flyback; **saut de ligne** = line feed (LF); **saut de ligne automatique (en limite d'écran)** = horizontal wraparound; **(instruction de) saut de page** = form feed; **saut de page obligatoire** *ou* **programmé** = forced page break; *(traitement de texte)* **capacité de saut** = skip capability **(c)** *(branchement)* jump *ou* transfer; **saut conditionnel** = conditional jump *ou* branch *ou* transfer; **instruction de saut** = jump instruction *ou* branch instruction *ou* skip instruction; **GOTO est une instruction de saut** = GOTO is a jump instruction **(d)** *(dans la mémoire)* **test saut de puces** = leapfrog test; **test saut de puce limité à un seul emplacement** = crippled leapfrog test

◊ **saute** *nf (de courant)* fluctuation; **les sautes de courant peuvent nuire au bon fonctionnement de l'ordinateur** = voltage fluctuations can affect the functioning of the computer system

◊ **sauter** *vi* **(a)** *(oublier)* to jump *ou* to skip; **l'opérateur de saisie a sauté plusieurs lignes du manuscrit** = several lines of manuscript have been missed by the keyboarder; **l'imprimante a sauté les trois lignes suivantes** = the printer skipped the next three lines of text; **le système de pagination a sauté deux numéros de pages** = the paging system has jumped two folio numbers **(b)** *(exploser)* to blow; *(système)* to bomb; **faire sauter un plomb** *ou* **un fusible** = to blow a fuse; **on a fait sauter les plombs en branchant le climatiseur** = when the air-conditioning was switched on, it fused the whole system; **vous pouvez faire sauter le système si vous installez en même temps des accessoires de bureau ou plusieurs programmes résidents** = the system can bomb if you set up several desk accessories or memory-resident programs at the same time

◊ **sautillement** *nm (de l'image d'écran)* jitter *ou* flicker

sauvegarde *nf* backup; **nous mettons toujours la plus récente (copie de) sauvegarde dans le coffre fort** = the most recent backup copy is kept in the safe; **sauvegarde sur bande** = tape backup; **sauvegarde programmée** = timed backup; **chemin de sauvegarde** = backup path; **contrôleur de sauvegarde par domaine** = backup domain controller; **copie de sauvegarde** = security backup *ou* backup copy; **cycle de rotation des fichiers de sauvegarde** = grandfather cycle; **disquette de sauvegarde** = backup disk; **faire une sauvegarde** = to do a backup *ou* to back up *ou* to save (a text *ou* a file); **ce système de traitement de texte fait une sauvegarde toutes les 15 minutes pour prévenir une défaillance** = this WP system saves the text every 15 minutes in case of a fault; **faire une sauvegarde sur deux disques** = to mirror (text *ou* file); **fichier de sauvegarde** = backup file; **plan de sauvegarde** = backup plan; **l'onduleur est tombé en panne, il faut donc mettre en oeuvre notre plan de sauvegarde** = the normal UPS has gone wrong, so we will have to use our backup plan to try and restore power; **procédure de sauvegarde** = backup procedure; **la procédure normale préconise une sauvegarde de tout le travail en fin de journée** = the normal procedure is for backup copies to be made at the end of each day's work; **serveur de sauvegarde** = backup server; **unité de sauvegarde rapide sur bande magnétique** = tape streamer *ou* streaming tape drive *ou* stringy floppy; **utilitaire de sauvegarde** = backup utility; **version** *ou* **copie de sauvegarde** = backup version; **vidage de sauvegarde** = rescue dump; **zone de sauvegarde** = save area

◊ **sauvegardé, -ée** *adj* saved; **original sauvegardé** = protection master

◊ **sauvegarder** *vtr* to save *ou* to back up (text *ou* file); **sauvegardez toujours vos données sur disquettes pour le cas où le fichier principal serait endommagé** = always keep backup copies in case of accidental damage to the master file; **ce programme permet aux utilisateurs de sauvegarder les fichiers du disque dur grâce à une seule commande** = the program enables users to back up hard disk files with a single command; **la comptabilité de l'entreprise a été sauvegardée sur disque pour la protéger contre les risques d'incendie** = the company accounts were backed up on disk

as a protection against fire damage; **n'oubliez pas de sauvegarder le fichier avant d'éteindre votre appareil** = don't forget to save the file before switching off; **sauvegarder de nouveau** = to resave; **cela permet de sauvegarder le texte de nouveau automatiquement** = it automatically resaves the text

> lorsque vous ne désirez plus travailler sur un fichier donné, sauvegardez-le grâce à la commande 'Enregistrer', du même fichier
> *L'Ordinateur Individuel*

savant, -e *adj* learned; **revue savante** = learned journal

scalaire *adj* scalar; **données scalaires** = scalar data; **grandeur scalaire** = scalar; **une grandeur scalaire n'a qu'une dimension, un vecteur en possède au moins deux** = a scalar has a single magnitude value, a vector has two or more positional values; **processeur scalaire** = scalar processor; **architecture de processeur scalaire** *ou* **architecture SPARC ™** = scalar processor architecture (SPARC) ™; **valeur scalaire** = scalar value; **variable scalaire** = scalar variable

scan *nm* scan

◊ **scannage** *nm* scan *ou* scanning; **faire un scannage** = to scan; **cet appareil peut faire un scannage avec définition allant jusqu'à 300 points par pouce** = the machine scans at up to 300 dpi resolution

◊ **scanner** *nm* (optical) scanner *ou* scanning device; **l'examen au scanner a très vite repéré le composant qui surchauffait** = the heat scan of the computer quickly showed which component was overheating; **scanner à main** = hand-held scanner; **scanner à plat** = flat-bed scanner; **les scanners sont de type 'flatbed' (scanners à plat), ou possèdent un système d'entraînement du papier par rouleau** = scanners are either flatbed models, or platen type paper-fed models; **scanner de contrôle d'appel** *ou* **de demande de communication** = communications scanner; **scanner d'images** = image scanner; **scanner vidéo** = video scanner; **les nouveaux scanners vidéo sont conçus pour saisir des objets en trois dimensions** = new video scanners are designed to scan three-dimensional objects; **scanner multifonction** = a multifunctional scanner

◊ **scanneur** *nm* (optical) scanner *ou* scanning device; **le scanneur peut lire les codes barres sur les étiquettes des produits grâce à un rayon laser et une photodiode** = a scanner reads the bar-code on the product label using a laser beam and photodiode; *voir aussi* SCANNER

◊ **scanning** *nm* scan *ou* scanning; **faire un scanning** = to scan; **le scanning a fait apparaître les données périmées** = the scan revealed which records were out of date

sceller *vtr* to seal; **le disque dur est contenu dans un boîtier scellé** = the hard disk is in a sealed case

scénario *nm (d'un film)* script

◊ **scénariste** *nm&f (auteur d'un scénario)* scriptwriter

schéma *nm* schema *ou* diagram; *(du point de vue de l'utilisateur)* external schema; **schéma de base de données** = database schema; **schéma directeur** = outline flowchart; **schéma fonctionnel** = functional diagram; **schéma de procédure** = process chart; **schéma synoptique** *ou* **fonctionnel** = block diagram; **la première étape de la conception d'un ordinateur consiste à établir le schéma synoptique de ses principaux composants** = the first step to designing a new computer is to draw out a block diagram of its main components; **sous forme de schéma** = *(schématique)* schematic; *(schématiquement)* in diagrammatic form *ou* diagrammatically

◊ **schématique** *adj* schematic; **plan schématique** = schema *ou* schematic plan

schmilblic *nm* *(familier)* gremlin; **schmilblic sur la ligne** = line gremlin

scie *nf* saw; **onde en dents de scie** = sawtooth waveform

scientifique *adj* scientific; **calculatrice avec fonctions scientifiques** = scientific calculator

scintillement *nm* *(d'enregistrement)* flutter; *(de l'image)* (screen) flicker; **le pleurage et le scintillement sont des défauts courants des magnétophones bon marché** = wow and flutter are common faults on cheap tape recorders

script *nm* *(instruction d'une fonction)* script; **script de début de session** *ou* **de mise en route** = logon script; **je débute automatiquement la session en utilisant ce script avec mon logiciel de communication** = I log in automatically using this script with my communications software; **langage de script** = scripting language; **ce logiciel de communication possède un langage de script qui me permet de composer les numéros d'appels et de débuter la session automatiquement** = this communications software has a scripting language that lets me dial and log in automatically

Scroll lock *(sur un clavier)* **touche Scroll lock** = Scroll Lock key

scrutation *nf* *(par appel)* polling

SCSI = SMALL COMPUTER SYSTEM INTERFACE (NOTE: se prononce '**scousi**') **interface SCSI** = Small Computer System Interface (SCSI); **interface Fast-SCSI** = Fast-SCSI; **interface SCSI-2** = SCSI-2; **interface Wide-SCSI** *ou* **SCSI large** = Wide-SCSI

COMMENTAIRE: SCSI est l'interface standard pour connecter des unités de disques à hautes performances aux ordinateurs, les unités moins puissantes sont connectées avec l'interface IDE qui est plus lente mais moins coûteuse. SCSI a remplacé l'ancienne interface ESDI et permet de relier en chaîne jusqu'à huit unités à un seul contrôleur

ainsi le protocole SCSI (Small Computer System Interface) a-t-il été systématiquement choisi en haut de gamme pour ses performances en terme de débit (5Mo/s) et pour ses capacités de connexion de périphériques (256 par contrôleur contre 2 floppies et 2 disques durs par contrôleur ESDI)
L'Ordinateur Individuel

SDLC *(protocole de transmission de données en mode synchrone)* **protocole SDLC** = Synchronous Data Link Control (SDLC)

sec, sèche *adj* dry; **connexion sèche** = dry joint; **contact sec** = dry contact; **pile sèche** = dry cell

SECAM *(standard de télévision couleur)* = SEQUENTIEL COULEUR A MEMOIRE

second, -e *adj (deuxième)* second; **la seconde partie du programme contient des erreurs** = the second half of the program contains some errors; **utilisation d'une seconde source de composants** = second-sourcing

◊ **secondaire** *adj* secondary *ou* sub-; **adresse secondaire** = subaddress; **canal** *ou* **voie secondaire** = secondary channel; **couleur secondaire** = secondary colour; **curseur secondaire** = ghost cursor; **entrée secondaire** = added entry; *(de voies de transmission à fréquence vocale)* **groupe secondaire** = supergroup; **mémoire secondaire** = secondary storage; **registre secondaire** = B box; **station secondaire** = tributary station; *(qui reçoit des données)* secondary station

seconde *nf (unité de temps)* second; **(nombre de) bits par seconde (bps)** = bits per second (bps); **(nombre de) caractères par seconde (cps)** = characters per second (cps); **(nombre d') images par seconde** *ou* **images/seconde** = frames per second (fps); **(nombre d') inférences logiques par seconde** = logical inference per second (LIPS); **(nombre de) mégabits par seconde** = megabits per second (Mbps); **(nombre de) pouces par seconde (pps)** *ou* **pouces/seconde** = inches per second (ips); **million(s) d'opérations en virgule flottante par seconde** = megaflops (MFLOPS)

secours *nm* help; **alimentation** *ou* **pile de secours** = battery backup *ou* auxiliary battery; **la salle des ordinateurs est équipée d'un bloc d'alimentation de secours en cas de panne de secteur** = the computer room has an auxiliary power supply in case there is a mains failure; **alimentation de secours de la mémoire** = memory backup capacitor; **dispositif de secours** = auxiliary *ou* standby (device); **temps de débit d'un dispositif de secours** = holdup; **équipement** *ou* **matériel** *ou* **système de secours** = standby equipment *ou* auxiliary equipment; **installation de secours prête à fonctionner** = hot standby; **procédure de secours** = fall back procedure; **routines de secours** = fall back routines; *(arrêt d'urgence manuel)* **système de secours lancé manuellement** = cold standby; **système de secours prêt à fonctionner** = hot standby; **système de secours à démarrage semi-automatique** = warm standby

secousse *nf* les disques durs sont très sensibles aux secousses = hard disks are very sensitive to jarring

secteur *nm* **(a)** *(d'électricité)* **le secteur** = mains (electricity); **fiche secteur à deux broches** = two-pin mains plug; **fiche secteur à trois broches** = three-pin mains plug; **panne de secteur** = power failure *ou* power cut; blackout *ou* black out; **il y a eu une panne de secteur** = the electricity supply was cut off **(b)** *(de disque)* disk sector; *(de disquette)* floppy disk sector; **secteur défectueux** *ou* **mauvais secteur** = faulty sector *ou* bad sector; **secteur réservé** = reserved sector; **diviser (un disque) en secteurs** = to sector (a disk); **formatage de secteurs (d'un disque)** = (disk) sector formatting; **formatage de secteurs permanents** = hard-sectoring; **table d'adresses des secteurs marqués inutilisables** = sector map **(c)** **diagramme à secteurs** = pie chart **(d)** *(d'une ville)* zone

> sur les disques modernes, chaque secteur renferme 512 octets. Quatre secteurs forment un 'cluster'. Il y a entre 17 et 34 secteurs par piste
>
> *PC Expert*

section *nf* section *ou* part; **section élémentaire de câble** = elementary cable section; **section d'entrée** = input section

sectoriser *vtr* to sector; **(disque) sectorisé par logiciel** = soft-sectored (disk)

sécurisation *nf* **(logiciel** *ou* **dispositif de) sécurisation de fichier** = file security *ou* file protection (software *ou* device); **sécurisation d'un système** = system security

◊ **sécurisé, -ée** *adj* secured *ou* protected; **système sécurisé** = secure system

◊ **sécuriser** *vtr* to secure *ou* to make secure *ou* to protect

◊ **sécurité** *nf* security *ou* protection; **la conception du système assure la sécurité des données en mémoire** = the system has been designed to assure the security of the stored data; **sécurité des données** *ou* **de l'information** = data security *ou* data protection; **sécurité du matériel** = hardware security; **sécurité par niveau d'opération** = share level security; **contrôle de sécurité** = security check; **formatage de sécurité** = safe format; **marge de sécurité** = safety margin; *(en cas de défaillance ou de rupture de courant)* **système de sécurité** = fail safe system

segment *nm* **(a)** *(exécutable)* (program) section *ou* segment; **segment de format superposable** = form overlay; **segment de recouvrement** = overlay segment; **gestionnaire de segment de recouvrement** = overlay manager; **zone de segment de recouvrement** = overlay region **(b)** *((i) câble; (ii) section d'un réseau)* **segment de réseau local** = LAN segment

◊ **segmentation** *nf* fragmentation; **(degré de) segmentation de la mémoire** = granularity

◊ **segmenter** *vtr* to segment; **espace d'adresse segmenté** = segmented address space

seize *adj num & nm* sixteen; **(système à) seize bits** = sixteen-bit *ou* 16-bit; *(format de pages)* **in seize** *ou* **in-16** = sixteenmo *ou* 16mo

sélecteur *nm* selector control *ou* knob; **tournez le sélecteur** = turn the selector control; **c'est là que se trouve le sélecteur d'amplitude** = the selector knob for the amplification is located there; **sélecteur de port** = port selector

◊ **sélecteur, -trice** *adj* selector; **canal sélecteur** = selector channel

◊ **sélectif, -ive** *adj* selective; **accès sélectif** = random access; **fichiers à accès sélectif** = random access files; **mémoire à accès sélectif** = random access storage; **appel sélectif** = polling *ou* selective calling; **appel sélectif de groupe** = group poll; **temps d'appels sélectifs** = polling overhead; **faire une lecture sélective** = to scatter read; *(recherche de zone)* **recherche sélective** = area search; *(de mémoire)* **test sélectif** = leapfrog test; **test sélectif limité** *ou* **restreint** = crippled leapfrog test; **tri sélectif** = selective sort; **vidage sélectif** = selective dump

◊ **sélection** *nf* sélection; **la sélection d'informations dans une grande base de données peut prendre un certain temps** = selection of information from a large database may take some time; **sélection automatique de vitesse de transmission** *ou* **de débit d'une ligne** = auto-baud scanning *ou* auto-baud sensing; **sélection des couleurs** = colour separation; **sélection par menu** = menu selection; **canal de sélection** = selector channel; **filtre de sélection du signal maximal** *ou* **minimal** = auctioneering device; **ligne de sélection d'un circuit intégré** = chip select line; **la ligne de validation de données est reliée à la ligne de sélection de la bascule** = the data strobe line is connected to the latch chip select line; **marque de sélection d'un bloc** = block mark; **signal de sélection** = enabling signal

◊ **sélectionner** *vtr* to select *ou* to screen; *(activer)* to enable; *(par filtre)* to filter; **qui peut être sélectionné** = selectable; **(circuit** *ou* **dispositif) qui peut être sélectionné par cavalier** = jumper-selectable (circuit *ou* device); **(paramètre) qui peut être sélectionné suivant les besoins de l'utilisateur** = user-selectable (value)

◊ **sélectivité** *nf* selectivity

selon *prép* as per; **selon échantillon** = as per sample; **selon les spécifications** = as per specification

sémantique *nf&adj* **la sémantique** = semantics; **erreur de sémantique** = semantic error

sémaphore *nm* *(fonction* *ou* *technique)* semaphore

semblable *adj* identical

semi- *préfixe* semi-

◊ **semi-automatique** *adj* semi-automatic; **équipement de secours à démarrage semi-automatique** = warm standby

◊ **semicirculaire** *adj* semi-circular; **antenne semi-circulaire** = fan antenna

◊ **semi-compilé, -ée** *adj (programme)* semicompiled

◊ **semi-conducteur** *nm (composant)* semiconductor (device); **semi-conducteur CMOS** = complementary metal oxide semiconductor (CMOS); **semi-conducteur MOS** = metal oxide semiconductor (MOS); **semi-conducteur MOS à canal (de type) P** = p-channel MOS; **semi-conducteur à effet de champ MOSFET** = metal oxide semiconductor field effect transistor (MOSFET); **semi-conducteur de type P** = p-type semiconductor; **semi-conducteur au silicium** = silicon gate; **semi-conducteur simple** = pure semiconductor; **dispositif à (base de) semi-conducteurs** = solid-state device; **mémoire à semi-conducteurs** = semiconductor memory

◊ **semi-conducteur, -trice** *adj* semiconductor; **matériau semi-conducteur de type N** = n-type material *ou* N-type material *ou* n-type semiconductor

semi-perforé, -ée *adj* **bande semi-perforée** = chadded *ou* chadless tape

sensibilité *nf* sensitivity; **la sensibilité du scanner aux petits objets** = the scanner's sensitivity to small objects

◊ **sensible** *adj* sensitive; **cet ordinateur est sensible aux moindres variations du courant** = the computer is sensitive even to very slight changes in current; **les disques durs sont très sensibles aux secousses** *ou* **aux chocs** = hard disks are very sensitive to jarring; **sensible à la lumière** = light-sensitive; *(à tolérance de panne)* **(système) peu sensible aux dérangements** = fault-tolerant (system)

séparateur *nm* **(a)** *(symbole ou code)* delimiter; **séparateur de champs** = field marker *ou* separator **(b)** *(de papier listing)* burster

◊ **séparation** *nf* separation; **séparation chromatique** *ou* **séparation des couleurs** = colour separation; **masque de séparation** = aperture mask; **négatifs de séparation des couleurs** = colour separations

◊ **séparé, -ée** *adj* separated; **caractères graphiques séparés** = separated graphics

◊ **séparément** *adv* separately *ou* independently; **ces articles sont indexés séparément** = each item is indexed independently

◊ **séparer** *vtr* to separate; *(par filtre)* to filter

sept *adj num & nm* seven

◊ **septet** *nm (mot de sept bits)* septet

séquence *nf* sequence *ou* set; *(de mots ou caractères)* string; **séquence d'appel** = calling sequence; **séquence binaire** = binary sequence; **séquence de commande (d'exécution)** = control sequence; **planification de la séquence d'exécution des tâches** = job scheduling; **séquence de fusionnement** *ou* **de classement** = collating sequence; **séquence de marqueurs** *ou* **d'indicateurs** = flag sequence; **séquence d'ouverture de session** *ou* **d'identification** = logon sequence; *(en bits)* **séquence d'identification** = identity burst; **contrôle de séquence** = sequence check; **registre de contrôle de séquence** = sequence control register (SCR) *ou* sequence counter *ou* sequence register

◊ **séquenceur** *nm* sequencer

séquentiel, -ielle *adj* sequential *ou* serial *ou* linear; **accès séquentiel** = sequential access *ou* serial access; **fichier à accès séquentiel** = sequential file *ou* serial file; **mémoire à accès séquentiel** = sequential access storage *ou* serial access memory (SAM); **méthode d'accès séquentiel par clé** = keyed sequential access method (KSAM); **méthode d'accès séquentiel en file (d'attente)** = queued sequential access method (QSAM); **méthode d'accès séquentiel indexé (ISAM)** = indexed sequential access method (ISAM); **méthode d'accès séquentiel indexé en file (d'attente)** = queued indexed sequential access method (QISAM); **additionneur séquentiel** = serial adder; **si l'entrée dans le circuit séquentiel logique est 1101, la sortie sera toujours zéro (0)** = if the input sequence to the sequential logic circuit is 1101 the output will always be zero (0); **liste séquentielle** = linear list; **logique séquentielle** = sequential logic; **mémoire séquentielle** = sequential access memory *ou* storage; serial memory *ou* storage; **la bande magnétique constitue une mémoire séquentielle d'une grande capacité** = magnetic tape is a high capacity serial memory; **mémoire séquentielle indexée** = indexed sequential storage; **mode séquentiel** = sequential mode; **traitement par lots en mode séquentiel** = sequential batch processing; **opération séquentielle** = sequential operation *ou* serial operation; **suivant un ordre séquentiel** = sequentially; **recherche séquentielle** = linear search *ou* sequential search; **stockage séquentiel** = serial storage; **traitement séquentiel** = serial processing *ou* sequential processing

série *nf* **(a)** series *ou* suite *ou* set; chain; *(de produits)* family; **série de commutateurs** = switch train; **série d'erreurs consécutives** = error burst; *(math)* **série de Fourier** = Fourier series; **série de mots** = word serial; **série de programmes (l'un à la suite de l'autre)** = suite of programs; **le système de traitement de texte utilise une série de trois programmes reliés: un éditeur de texte, un correcteur d'orthographe et un contrôleur d'impression** = the word-processing system uses a suite of three programs: editor, spelling checker and printing controller **(b) en série** = serial; *(disposé ou monté)* serially; *(exécuté)* sequentially; **accès série** = serial access; **additionneur (en) série** = serial adder; **bus série** = daisy chain bus; **circuit (disposé en) série** = series circuit; **communication** *ou* **transmission (en mode) série** = serial data transmission *ou* communications; **commutateurs en série** = switch train; **leur vitesse de transmission est de 64 000 bits par seconde avec connexion parallèle ou 19 200 avec connexion série** = their transmission rate is 64,000 bits per second through a parallel connection or 19,200 serially; **convertisseur série/parallèle** = serial to parallel converter; **entrée/sortie en série** = serial input/output (SIO); **entrée série/sortie parallèle** = serial input/parallel output (SIPO); **entrée parallèle/sortie série** = parallel input/serial output (PISO); **entrée**

série/sortie série = serial input/serial output (SISO); **fichier série extensible** = extending serial file; **imprimante série** = serial printer; **interface série** = serial interface; *de façon générale, les* **connexions parallèles sont moins difficiles à mettre en place et à utiliser que les interfaces série, mais leur longueur est limitée à environ 6 mètres** = parallel connections are usually less trouble to set up and use than serial interfaces, but are usually limited to 20 feet in length; **interruption en série** = daisy chain interrupt; **ordinateur série** *ou* serial computer; **port série** = serial port; **relier en série** = to daisy-chain; **souris série** = serial mouse; **traitement en série** = serial processing; **transmission (en) série** = serial transmission; **transmission de données en série** = serial data transmission; **transmission d'octets en série** = byte serial transmission *ou* mode

sérieux, -ieuse *adj* serious; *(d'équipement)* **panne sérieuse** = hard failure

serrage *nm* **molette de serrage** = pinchwheel

◊ **serré, -ée** *adj* compact

◊ **serrer** *vtr* to close *ou* to tighten; *(imprimerie)* **serrer l'espace entre deux caractères** = to kern

serveur *nm* **(a)** *(ordinateur)* server; **serveur de contrôle des accès** = log on server; **serveur de fichier** = file server; **serveur de fond** *ou* **serveur auxiliaire** = back-end server; **serveur d'impression** = print server; **serveur de message** = interface message processor; **serveur de réseau local** = local area network server *ou* LAN server; **serveur de secours** = backup server; *(unité de disque dur du serveur d'un réseau)* **disque serveur** = network drive; **réseau sans serveur dédié** = peer-to-peer network; **nous avons connecté les quatre PCs de notre petit bureau avec un réseau sans serveur** = we have linked the four PCs in our small office using a peer-to-peer network **(b)** *(centre de recherche documentaire)* **centre serveur** = information retrieval centre

service *nm* **(a)** service *ou* facility; **service de coupures de presse** = press-cutting service *ou* clipping service; **la société offre, entre autres, des services d'imprimerie et de saisie de données** = the company offers a number of bureau services, such as printing and data capture; **service (fournisseur) d'informations** *ou* **service de base de données spécialisée (pour vidéotex)** = information provider (IP); **services informatiques** = computer services; **nous offrons à nos clients un service de traitement de leurs propres disquettes** = we offer facilities for processing a customer's own disks; **service de maintenance** = maintenance (service); **service de téléinformatique** *ou* **de transmission de données** = data service; **fonctions de service** = services; **réseau numérique à intégration de services (RNIS)** = integrated services digital network (ISDN); **société de services** = (service) bureau; **nous faisons faire la manipulation de données par une société de services informatiques** = our data manipulation is handled by a bureau; **société de services et d'ingénierie informatique (SSII)** = computer bureau; **société de services en PAO** = word-processing bureau **(b)** *(section)* department;

service après-vente *ou* **service clients** = customer service department; **service informatique** = computer department; **responsable** *ou* **chef du service informatique** = data processing manager **(c)** *(appareil)* **en service** = in use *ou* busy; **hors service** = out of use

se servir de *vpr* to use; **je regrette, mais il y a déjà quelqu'un qui se sert de l'imprimante** = sorry, the printer is already in use *ou* is already being used

servomécanisme *nm* servomechanism *ou* servo

session *nf* session; *(5ème couche d'un modèle ISO/OSI)* **couche session** = session layer; **clore une session** = to log off *ou* log out; **clôture de session** = logging off *ou* logging out; **ouverture de session** = logging in *ou* logging on; **clé d'ouverture d'une session** = session key; **ouverture automatique d'une session** = automatic log on *ou* automatic log in; **auto-login** *ou* auto-logon; **ouvrir** *ou* **débuter une session** = to log in *ou* to log on; *(en s'identifiant)* to sign on; **sortie de session** = timeout; **terminer une session** = to log off *ou* to log out; *(en s'identifiant)* to sign off

seuil *nm* threshold; **circuit à seuil** = threshold gate; **jonction pn à seuil** = step pn-junction; **valeur de seuil** = threshold value; **zone interface pn à seuil** = step pn-junction

sextet *nm* *(mot de six bits)* sextet

SGBDR = SYSTEME DE GESTION DE BASE DE DONNEES RELATIONNELLES

SGML *(langage ou norme de balisage)* Standard Generalized Markup Language (SGML)

Shadow RAM *(mémoire haute)* Shadow RAM

Shannon *npr* **loi de Shannon** = Shannon's Law

◊ **shannon** *nm* *(unité d'information)* shannon

shell *(programme de définition de l'environnement ou interpréteur de commandes)* **(programme) shell** = shell; **COMMAND.COM de MS-DOS est un programme shell indispensable qui interprète les commandes entrées au clavier en réponse à l'invite de DOS** = MS-DOS's COMMAND.COM is a basic shell that interprets commands typed in at the prompt; **Finder de Macintosh est un programme shell intelligent qui utilise une interface graphique (GUI)** = the Macintosh Finder is a sophisticated shell with a GUI front-end

SI = SYSTEME INTERNATIONAL D'UNITES **unités SI** = SI units

sibilance *nf* sibilance

SID = SYSTEME D'INFORMATION POUR LA DIRECTION Executive Information System (EIS); **le logiciel de SID est très facile à utiliser** = the EIS software is very easy to use; **avec ce logiciel de SID on peut connaître l'efficacité de**

chaque section de l'entreprise = with this EIS software, we can see how every part of the company performs

sifflement *nm* hiss *ou* sibilance

sigle *nm* initials; **que signifie le sigle IBM?** = what do the initials IBM stand for?

signal *nm* signal; **le signal s'est affaibli** *ou* **s'est éteint rapidement** = the signal decayed rapidly; **signal d'appel** = call signal *ou* calling signal; **signal d'appel accepté** *ou* **d'acceptation d'appel** = call accepted signal; **signal de basse fréquence** = bass signal; **signal bipolaire** = bipolar signal; *(sur disque vidéo)* **signal blanc** = white flag; **signal de chrominance** = chrominance signal; **signal continu** = continuous signal; **signal de contrôle** *ou* **de commande** = control signal; **signal de contrôle d'appel** = call control signal; **signal de détection de porteuse** = data carrier detect signal *ou* DCD signal; **l'appel est bloqué si le logiciel ne reçoit pas de signal de détection de porteuse du modem** = the call is stopped if the software does not receive a DCD signal from the modem; **les signaux élémentaires de ce système de radiotransmission sont 10ms à 40kHz pour le bit zéro (0) et 10 ms à 60 kHz pour le bit chargé (1)** = the signal elements for the radio transmission system are 10ms of 40KHz and 10ms of 60KHz for binary 0 and 1 respectively; **signal d'entrée** = input signal; **signal d'exécution** = execute signal; **signal de fin de page** = end of page indicator; **signal de fin de report** = carry complete signal; *(d'un système stéréophonique)* **signal groupé** = M signal; **signal importé** = imported signal; **signal (d') interruption** = interrupt signal; **signal d'invalidation** *ou* **d'interdiction de transmission** = inhibiting input; **signal de lecture d'instruction** = fetch signal; **signal de luminance** = luminance signal; **signal numérique** = digital signal; **transmission de signaux numériques** = digital signalling; **signaux parasites** = garbage; **signal polarisé** = polar signal; **signal de sélection** = enabling signal; **signal sonore** = alarm *ou* bleep; **un signal sonore prévient qu'il ne reste plus de papier dans l'imprimante** = an alarm rings when the printer has run out of paper; **caractère (de déclenchement) de signal sonore** = bell character; **signaux synchrones aux impulsions d'horloge** = clocked signals; *(télévision)* **signal de synchronisation** = hold (signal); **signaux de transmission de données** = data signals; **signal unipolaire** = unipolar signal; **signal de validation** = enabling signal; **signal vidéo** = video signal; **porteuse de signal vidéo** = image carrier; **signal vidéo composite** = composite video signal; **amplificateur de signal** = line driver; *(TV)* launch amplifier; **conversion de signaux** = signal conversion; **convertisseur de signaux** = signal converter; **coupure** *ou* **perte** *ou* **distorsion d'un signal** = signal breakup; **distance entre signaux** = signal distance *ou* Hamming distance; **élément (d'un) signal** = signal element; **l'élément signal de ce système est une courte impulsion de tension qui représente un 1 binaire** = the signal element in this system is a short voltage pulse, indicating a binary one; **émettre un signal** = to signal; *(de validation ou d'échantillonnage)* to strobe; **le signal émis par l'ordinateur contenait la réponse** = the signal

received from the computer contained the answer; **envoie un signal au réseau pour prévenir que nous sommes occupés** = signal to the network that we are busy; **générateur de signaux** = signal generator; **inhibition du signal** = signal blanking; **limiteur** *ou* **réducteur de signal audio** = audio compressor; **impulsion d'inhibition du signal** = blanking pulse; **mise en forme** *ou* **conversion de signaux** = signal conditioning; **niveau d'un signal** = signal level; **rapport signal/bruit** = signal to noise ratio *ou* S/N *ou* s/n ratio; **suppression du signal** = signal blanking; **traitement du signal** = signal processing; **ce système est à la disposition des étudiants qui se spécialisent dans la recherche sur les techniques de traitement du signal** = the system is used by students doing research on signal processing techniques; **transmettre un signal** = to signal; **transmission de signaux** = signalling; **transmission de signaux sur la bande vocale** = in band signalling; **transmission directe de signaux** = DC signalling

◊ **signaler** *vtr&i* to signal; *ou* to send a signal; **signale au réseau que nous sommes occupés** = signal to the network that we are busy

◊ **signaleur** *nm (pour système d'appel de personne)* **signaleur d'appel** = pager *ou* radio pager *ou* radio paging device; **appeler** *ou* **chercher à joindre quelqu'un par signaleur d'appel** = to page someone *ou* to bleep someone

◊ **signalisation** *nf* signalling; **signalisation par canal banal** *ou* **par voie commune** = common channel signalling; **signalisation hors bande (vocale)** = out of band signalling; **signalisation multifréquence DTMF** = dual tone, multifrequency (DTMF); **signalisation tonale** = tone signalling

signature *nf* signature; **reconnais-tu la signature sur le chèque?** = do you recognize the signature on the cheque?; **signature électronique** = electronic signature; **signature numérique** = digital signature

signe *nm* sign; mark; **signe de l'addition (+)** = plus (sign); **signes de correction (d'épreuves d'imprimerie)** = proof correction marks; **signe diacritique** = diacritic; **signe de la division (÷)** = division sign; **signe du dollar ($)** = dollar sign; **signe et modulo** = sign and modulus; **signe de la multiplication (x)** = multiplication sign; **signe de polarité** = polarity sign; **signe de ponctuation** = punctuation mark; **signe de la soustraction (-)** = minus (sign); **binaire de signe** *ou* **bit de signe** *ou* **chiffre (indicateur) de signe** = sign digit *ou* sign bit *ou* sign indicator; **champ (de) signe** = signed field; **chiffre (de) signe** = sign and magnitude *ou* signed magnitude; **position du signe** = sign position; **reconnaissance optique de signes** = optical mark recognition (OMR); **sans signe** = unsigned

signet *nm (permet de retrouver une section de programme)* bookmark

significatif, -ive *adj* significant; **bit le moins significatif** = least significant bit (LSB); **chiffre le moins significatif** = least significant digit (LSD) *ou* low-order digit; **6 est le chiffre le moins significatif du nombre 234156** = the number 234156 has a low-order digit of 6; **bit significatif** *ou* **le plus**

significatif = most significant bit (MSB); **le bit le plus significatif dans un mot de huit bits représente 128 en numération décimale** = the most significant bit in an eight bit binary word represents 128 in decimal notation; **le chiffre le plus significatif** = most significant character *ou* most significant digit (MSD); **codes significatifs** = significant digit codes *ou* faceted codes

◊ **signification** *nf* significance

◊ **signifier** *vtr* to signify *ou* to represent *ou* to mean; **l'envoi d'un code CR signifie que la ligne saisie est terminée** = a carriage return code signifies the end of an input line; **le message DISK FULL signifie que le disque n'a plus l'espace voulu pour enregistrer de nouvelles données** = the message DISK FULL means that there is no more room on the disk for further data; **sauvegarder signifie faire la copie du fichier de travail actuel sur une deuxième disquette** = backing up involves copying current working files onto a separate storage disk

silence *nm* silence; **facteur de silence** = omission factor

◊ **silencieux, -ieuse** *adj* quiet; **les imprimantes laser sont beaucoup plus silencieuses que les imprimantes matricielles** = laser printers are much quieter than dot-matrix

silicium *nm* silicon; **silicium sur saphir** = silicon on sapphire (SOS); **fonderie de silicium** = silicon foundry; **pastille** *ou* **puce de silicium** = silicon chip; **tranche de silicium** = silicon wafer; **intégration sur tranche de silicium** = wafer scale integration; **transistor silicium** = silicon transistor

SIMD **architecture SIMD** = Single Instruction stream, Multiple Data stream (SIMD)

simili = SIMILIGRAVURE

◊ **similigravure** *nf (planche)* halftone; *(procédé)* halftone process *ou* halftoning; **on utilise du papier glacé pour l'impression de similigravures** = glossy paper is used for printing halftones

SIMM *(mémoire)* **barrette** *ou* **module de mémoire SIMM** = Single In-line Memory Module (SIMM); **pour augmenter la mémoire de votre ordinateur, installez deux barrettes SIMM supplémentaires** = you can expand the main memory of your PC by plugging in two more SIMMs

simple *adj* simple *ou* single; *(math)* **simple précision** = single precision; **disquette à simple densité** = single density disk (SD); **disquette simple face** = single-sided disk (SSD); **espace d'adressage simple** = flat address space; **guillemets simples** = single quotes; **semi-conducteur simple** = pure semiconductor

◊ **simplex** *nm* simplex *ou* single operation

◊ **simplifié, -ée** *adj* **(a)** simplified **(b)** abbreviated; **adressage simplifié** = abbreviated addressing *ou* abb. add.; **installation simplifiée** = abbreviated installation

◊ **simplifier** *vtr* **(a)** to simplify; **les touches de fonction simplifient l'exploitation d'un programme** = function keys simplify program operation **(b)** to abbreviate

simulateur *nm* simulator; **simulateur (de) Turing** = Turing machine; **simulateur de vol** = flight simulator

◊ **simulation** *nf* simulation; **simulation en temps réel** = real-time simulation; **les techniques de simulation sont devenues très sophistiquées** = simulation techniques have reached a high degree of sophistication; **logiciel de simulation** = simulation software

◊ **simuler** *vtr* to simulate; **ce logiciel simule les manoeuvres aériennes** *ou* **est un simulateur de vol** = this software simulates the action of an aeroplane

> d'un côté, l'électronique rend la bataille de plus en plus abstraite - comme dans les simulateurs, le conducteur de char voit sa cible non plus à l'oeil nu, mais sur l'écran
>
> *L'Express*

simultané, -ée *adj* **(a)** simultaneous *ou* concurrent; **de façon simultanée** = simultaneously; **traitement simultané** = simultaneous processing; **transmission simultanée** = simultaneous transmission **(b)** **report simultané** = ripple-through carry

◊ **simultanéité** *nf* simultaneity

◊ **simultanément** *adv* simultaneously *ou* concurrently; **chacune des applications exécutées simultanément possède sa propre fenêtre** = each concurrent process has its own window

singulièrement *adv (étrangement)* abnormally; **le taux d'erreur de cette disquette est singulièrement élevé** = the error rate with this disk is abnormally high

sinon *voir* ELSE

sinus *nm* sin *ou* sine

◊ **sinusoïdal, -e** *adj* sinusoidal; **onde sinusoïdale** = sine wave *ou* sinusoidal waveform

◊ **sinusoïde 1** *nf* sine wave *ou* sinusoidal waveform; **la porteuse est une onde sinusoïde** = the carrier has a sinusoidal waveform **2** *adj* sinusoidal

SIP *(composant)* Single In-line Package (SIP)

siphonage *nm* siphoning

SIT = SYSTEME INTERBANCAIRE DE TELECOMPENSATION Bankers Automated Clearance System (BACS)

site *nm* site; **les trois modèles offrent des possibilités d'extension sur site** = all three models have an on-site upgrade facility; **site de bêta test** = beta site; **appel (à émettre) à tous les terminaux d'un site** = site poll; *(permettant l'utilisation d'un logiciel par plusieurs utilisateurs)* **licence de site** = site licence; **nous avons négocié longtemps pour obtenir une licence de site pour les 1200 employés**

du siège = we have negotiated a good deal for the site licence for our 1200 employees in our HQ; **maintenance sur site** = on-site maintenance

situer *vtr* to locate

six *adj num & nm* six

Smalltalk ™ *(langage de programmation orienté objet mis au point par Xerox)* Smalltalk ™

SMB *(système de partage de fichiers)* Server Message Block (SMB)

SMT *(gestion de station)* Station Management (SMT)

SMT *(procédé d'assemblage de cartes de circuits intégrés)* Surface-Mount Technology (SMT); **la technologie d'assemblage SMT est plus rapide et utilise mieux l'espace que la soudure** = surface-mount technology is faster and more space-efficient than soldering

SMTP *(protocole de messagerie électronique)* Simple Mail Transfer Protocol (SMTP)

SNA *(architecture de réseau)* Systems Network Architecture (SNA)

SNMP *(protocole de gestion de réseau)* Simple Network Management Protocol (SNMP)

SNOBOL *(langage de programmation de haut niveau)* String Orientated Symbolic Language (SNOBOL)

société *nf* company *ou* firm; **société d'assistance technique** = consultancy firm; **société de services** = bureau; **société de services et d'ingénierie informatique (SSII)** = computer bureau; **société de traitement de texte** = word-processing bureau

sodium *nm (utilisé en photographie)* **hyposulfite** *ou* **thiosulfate de sodium** = sodium thiosulfate; *(familier)* hypo

sol *nm* ground; **station au sol** = ground station

solaire *adj* solar; **énergie solaire** = solar power; **pile solaire** = solar cell; **calculatrice à pile(s) solaire(s)** = solar-powered calculator

solénoïde *nm* solenoid

solide *adj* **(a)** *(résistant)* solid *ou* robust **(b) laser à composant solide** = solid-state laser

◊ **solidité** *nf* robustness

solution *nf* **(a)** *(liquid)* solution **(b)** *(réponse à un problème)* solution

sommaire *nm* summary; *(page vidéotex)* lead-in page

somme *nf* sum

son *nm* sound; **son dérivé** = derived sound; **son pur** = pure tone; **capture** *ou* **prise de son** = sound

capture; **circuit intégré générateur de son** = sound chip *ou* music chip; **décalage en avance de la bande son** = sound advance; **synthétiseur de son** = music synthesizer *ou* sound synthesizer; *voir aussi* AUDIO

sonar *nm* = SOUND NAVIGATION AND RANGING (SONAR)

sonde *nf* biosensor

sonique *adj* sonic

sonner *vi* to ring; *(vibreur)* to buzz

◊ **sonnerie** *nf* **(a)** *(dispositif)* bell; *(vibreur)* buzzer; **sonnerie d'appel à harmonique** = harmonic telephone ringer **(b)** *(action)* ringing; **sonnerie décimonique** *ou* **sonnerie à résonnance de fréquence** = decimonic ringing

◊ **sonore** *adj* sound; **effets sonores** = sound effects; **tous les effets sonores du film sont produits électroniquement** = all the sound effects for the film are produced electronically; **effets sonores postsynchronisés** = dubbed sound; **onde sonore** = sound wave; **piste sonore** = sound track; **signal sonore** = bleep *ou* buzz *ou* alarm; **un signal sonore prévient qu'il ne reste plus de papier dans l'imprimante** = an alarm rings when the printer has run out of paper; **vibration sonore** = buzz; **émettre une vibration sonore** = to buzz

◊ **sonorisation** *nf* sound; *(système)* public address system (PA); **le studio est câblé pour la sonorisation** = the studio is wired for sound

sophistication *nf* sophistication

◊ **sophistiqué, -ée** *adj* sophisticated; **le nouveau progiciel est tout à fait sophistiqué** = the sophistication of the new package is remarkable; **les techniques de simulation sont devenues très sophistiquées** = simulation techniques have reached a high degree of sophistication

sortance *nf (d'un circuit)* fan-out

sorti, -e *adj* **dernier entré premier sorti** = last in first out (LIFO); **cet ordinateur gère la pile suivant la méthode du dernier entré premier sorti** = this computer stack uses a last in first out data retrieval method; **premier entré premier sorti** = first in first out (FIFO); **mémoire qui fonctionne sur le principe du premier entré premier sorti** = FIFO memory

◊ **sortie** *nf* **(a)** *(point de connexion ou de circuit)* outlet **(b) sortie de session** = timeout **(c)** *(de données)* output (o/p *ou* O/P); **sortie d'imprimante** = computer printout *ou* computer listing *ou* hard copy *ou* information output; **sortie (sur) microfilm** = computer output on microfilm (COM); **sortie numérique** = digital output; **sortie d'ordinateur** = computer output; **sortie vocale** = voice output; **appareil** *ou* **périphérique** *ou* **dispositif de sortie** = output device; **commutateur à deux sorties** = D-type flip-flop; **données de sortie** = computer output *ou* output data; **facteur pyramidal de sortie** = fan-out; **fichier de sortie** = output file; **flux (de données) de sortie** = output stream; **formateur de données de sortie** = output formatter; **mode sortie**

= output mode; *(d'une routine)* **point de sortie** = exit point; **port (de) sortie** = output port; **port de sortie audio** = audio port; **port de sortie vidéo** = video port; **registre (de) sortie** = output register; **registre tampon de sortie** = output buffer register; **vitesse de sortie de l'information** = information rate; **zone sortie (de la mémoire)** = output area *ou* block; *voir aussi* ENTREE/SORTIE

◊ **sortir** *vi* **(a)** to leave *ou* to quit; **sortir du program (en cours) et revenir au DOS** = to shell out; **je suis sorti du traitement de texte pour vérifier quels étaient les fichiers disponibles sur la disquette, puis je suis retourné dans le programme** = I shelled out from the word-processor to check which files were on the floppy, then went back to the program **(b)** to originate from; **les données sortent du nouvel ordinateur** = the data originated from the new computer

---

il possède également une sortie vidéo et une sortie audio pour se connecter à un téléviseur
Hi-fi Vidéo

---

souche *nf* **(programme) souche** = stub

souder *vtr* to solder

◊ **soudure** *nf* solder; **sans soudure** = solderless; *voir aussi* DESSOUDER

soulignage *nm* underlining *ou* underscoring

◊ **soulignement** *nm* underlining *ou* underscoring

◊ **souligner** *vtr* to underline *ou* to underscore; **on souligne deux fois l'en-tête d'un chapitre et une seule fois celui d'un paragraphe** = the chapter headings are given a double underline and the paragraphs a single underline

souple *adj* flexible; **disque souple** = flexible disk *ou* floppy disk *ou* floppy *ou* FD *ou* fd

◊ **souplesse** *nf* flexibility

source *nf* **(a)** source; **source de données** = data source; *(société)* **source d'informations** = information provider (IP); **code source** = source code; **éditeur de (programme) source** = source editor; **fichier source** = source file; **filtrage des adresses sources** = source address filtering; **langage source** = source language; **listage source** *ou* **listage des sources (d'un programme)** = source listing; **listing de (programme) source** = source listing; **ordinateur de source** = source machine; **processeur de programme source** = source machine; **programme source** = source program; *(du curseur)* **retour à la source** = homing; **routage source** = source routing **(b)** *(électricité)* **source d'alimentation** = power supply; **brancher une ligne sur une source d'alimentation** = to pull up a line **(c)** **utilisation d'une seconde source de composants** = second-sourcing

sourd, -e *adj (personne)* deaf; *(chambre)* anechoic (chamber)

souris *nf* mouse; **souris (de) bus** = bus mouse; **souris mécanique** = mechanical mouse; **souris optique** = optical mouse; **souris série** = serial mouse; **(logiciel) contrôlé** *ou* **piloté par une souris** = mouse-driven (software); **(programme) pilote de souris** = mouse driver; **pointeur de souris** = mouse pointer

sous- *préfixe* sub-

◊ **sous-classe** *nf* subclass

◊ **sous-ensemble** *nm* subset; *(d'un programme)* bead

◊ **sous-exposé, -ée** *adj (film)* underexposed

◊ **sous-programme** *nm* subroutine *ou* subprogram; **appel d'un sous-programme** = subroutine call; **sous-programme additionnel** = inserted subroutine; **sous-programme de bibliothèque** = library subroutine; **sous-programme chaîné** = linked subroutine; **sous-programme à deux niveaux** = two-level subroutine; **sous-programme direct** = one-level subroutine; **sous-programme fermé** *ou* **ré-entrant** = closed subroutine *ou* linked subroutine; **sous-programme d'insertion directe** = direct-insert subroutine; **sous-programme mathématique** = mathematical subroutine; **sous-programme ouvert** = open subroutine; **sous-programme paramétrable** = dynamic subroutine; **sous-programme statique** = static subroutine

◊ **sous-répertoire** *nm* sub-directory

---

les fichiers MS-DOS d'un utilisateur sont stockés dans un sous-répertoire
L'Information professionnelle

---

sous-segment *nm* subsegment

◊ **sous-système** *nm* subsystem

◊ **sous-total** *nm* subtotal

soustracteur *nm* subtractor; **soustracteur complet** *ou* **à trois entrées** = full subtractor

◊ **soustraction** *nf* subtraction; **signe de la soustraction (-)** = minus (sign)

◊ **soustraire** *vtr* to subtract *ou* to deduct; **nombre à soustraire d'un autre** = subtrahend; **nombre duquel on soustrait** = minuend

soutenir *vtr (étayer)* to back (up); **il a apporté un dossier de documents pour soutenir sa plainte** *ou* **sa réclamation** = he brought along a file of documents to back up his claim; **les documents imprimés sont venus soutenir ses arguments en faveur d'un nouveau système** = the printout backed up his argument for a new system

SPARC ™ *(architecture de processeur scalaire)* **architecture SPARC** ™ = Scalar Processor Architecture (SPARC) ™

spatial, -e *adj* space; **station spatiale** = space station; **véhicule** *ou* **engin spatial** = space craft

spécial, -e *adj* special; **caractère spécial** = special character; **effets spéciaux** = special effects; **fonte spéciale** = special sort; *(police de caractères qui contient des petits dessins: symboles, puces, étoiles, etc.)* **police de caractères spéciaux** = Dingbat ™; **pour insérer une marque de copyright,**

utilisez les **caractères spéciaux** = to insert a copyright symbol, use the Dingbat font; **système spécial** = special purpose system

◊ **spécialisé, -ée** *adj* (a) dedicated; **appareil de traitement de texte spécialisé** = dedicated word processor; **canal spécialisé** = dedicated channel; **fonction logique spécialisée** = dedicated logic; **ligne téléphonique spécialisée** = dedicated line; **logiciel d'application spécialisée** = single function software; **logiciel non spécialisé** = device-independent software; **ordinateur spécialisé** = applications terminal; **ordinateur non spécialisé** = general purpose computer; **terminal spécialisé** = applications terminal *ou* job-orientated terminal; **voie spécialisée** = dedicated channel (b) **revue spécialisée** = learned journal; **service de base de données spécialisées (pour vidéotex)** = information provider (IP)

◊ **se spécialiser (en)** *vpr* to specialize (in)

◊ **spécialiste** 1 *nm&f* expert *ou* specialist; consultant; **c'est un spécialiste en informatique** = he is a computer expert; **c'est une spécialiste des langages de programmation** = she is an expert in programming languages; **c'est un spécialiste des systèmes CAO** = he specializes in the design of CAD systems 2 *adj* specialist

spécification *nf* (a) specification; *(copie d'un dessin)* blueprint; **le travail ne répond pas aux spécifications du client** = the work does not meet the customer's specifications; **spécifications de conception** *ou* **de création** = design parameters; **spécification fonctionnelle** = functional specification; **spécifications du système** = system specifications; **selon les spécifications** = as per specification (b) *(d'un programme)* **spécifications de présentation des données** = layout specifications; **spécifications d'un programme** *ou* **relatives à un programme** = program specifications (c) **spécification (du nom) du fichier** = filename extension

◊ **spécificité** *nf* specificity

◊ **spécifier** *vtr* to specify

◊ **spécifique** *adj* **adresse spécifique** = specific address; **codage spécifique** = specific coding; **code spécifique** = direct *ou* one-level *ou* specific code

spectre *nm* spectrum; **spectre de fréquences électromagnétiques** = electromagnetic spectrum; **spectre de fréquences radio** = radio spectrum; **analyseur de spectre** = spectrum analyzer

sphérique *adj* spherical; **aberration sphérique** = spherical aberration

spooling = SPOULE

sporadique *adj* sporadic; **erreur sporadique** = sporadic fault

spot *nm* **spot de balayage** = scanning spot

spoule *nm* spooling; **faire un spoule** = to spool; **impression par spoule** = print spooling; **mémoire auxiliaire pour spoule** = spooler *ou* spooling device; **unité de bande magnétique pour spoule** = spooler *ou* spooling device

sprite *nm* sprite

SQL *(langage de requête)* **langage SQL** = Structured Query Language (SQL)

SSD = SANS SERVEUR DEDIE **réseau SSD** = Advanced Peer-to-Peer Networking (APPN)

SSII = SOCIETE DE SERVICES ET D'INGENIERIE INFORMATIQUE; *voir* SERVICE

ST *(connecteur)* ST connector

ST506 *(norme d'interface de disque dur)* ST506 standard; **la norme ST506 a été remplacée par IDE et SCSI** = the ST506 standard has now been replaced by IDE and SCSI

stabilisation *nf* *(après échantillonnage)* **commande de stabilisation du signal** = hold

◊ **stabilité** *nf* stability; **stabilité de l'image** = image stability

◊ **stable** *adj* stable; **la bande magnétique est stable entre 0° et 40°** = magnetic tape is stable within a temperature range of 0° to 40°C; **état stable** = stable state

stade *nm* stage; **le texte (en) est au stade de l'impression** = the text is ready for printing

standard 1 *nm* (a) *(norme)* **standard de conversion ADPCM** = Adaptive Differential Pulse Code Modulation (ADPCM); **standard de cryptage de données** = Data Encryption Standard (DES); **standards de production** = production standards; **standards de programmation** = programming standards; **standards vidéo** = video standards (b) **standard téléphonique** = (telephone) switchboard 2 *adj inv* standard *ou* universal; basic; *(document ou formulaire ou paragraphe ou texte)* standard (document *ou* form *ou* paragraph *ou* text); **fonction standard** = standard function; **format standard** = normal format; **interface standard** = standard interface; **langage standard** = machine-independent language; **lettre standard** = form letter *ou* repetitive letter *ou* standard letter; **logiciel non standard** = machine-dependent software; **objectif standard** = medium lens; **protocole standard de contrôle de liaisons** = basic mode link control; **schéma (de base de données) standard** = canonical schema; **sous-programme standard** = standard subroutine

◊ **standardisé, -ée** *adj* **le contrôle standardisé des voies de transmission** = the standardized control of transmission links

◊ **standardiser** *vtr* to standardize

standardiste *nm&f* (telephone) operator *ou* switchboard operator *ou* telephonist; **appeler la standardiste** = to dial the operator

station *nf* (a) *(ordinateur)* station; **station auxiliaire** = secondary station; **station primaire** = primary station; **station secondaire** = tributary station; **station de travail** = workstation *ou* operating console; **la mémoire d'archivage a une capacité de 1200 Mo pour sept stations de travail**

(CAO) = the archive storage has a total capacity of 1200 MB between seven workstations **(b)** *(de radio ou télévision)* station; **le signal de cette station émettrice est très faible** = the signal from this radio station is very weak; **nous essayons de brouiller les signaux émis par cette station** = we are trying to jam the signals from that station; **station de radio** = broadcasting station *ou* radio station; *(de télévision)* **station relais** = local distribution service (LDS); *(antennes)* **station au sol** = ground station; **station terrestre** = earth station; **station terrestre mobile** = mobile earth terminal

stationnaire *adj* stationary; **état stationnaire** = steady state

statique *adj* static; **électricité statique** = static electricity; **mémoire statique** = static memory *ou* static storage; **mémoire vive** *ou* **mémoire RAM statique** = static RAM; **sous-programme statique** = static subroutine; **translation statique** = static relocation; **vidage statique** = static dump

statisticien, -ienne *n* statistician

◊ **statistique** 1 *nf (science)* statistics 2 *adj* statistical; **multiplexage temporel statistique** = statistical time division multiplexing (STDM)

statut *nm* status

stencil *nm* stencil; **on se sert d'un masque ou d'un stencil pour reproduire le tracé du circuit du transistor sur le silicium** = a mask or stencil is used to transfer the transistor design onto silicon

stéradian *nm* steradian

stéréo *adj inv* = STEREOPHONIQUE

stéréophonique *ou* **stéréo** *adj* stereophonic *ou* stereo; **disque stéréophonique** *ou* **disque stéréo** = stereo record; **magnétophone stéréophonique** = stereophonic recorder; **microphone stéréophonique** = stereophonic microphone

stérile *adj* **chambre stérile** = clean room

stochastique *adj* stochastic; **modèle stochastique** = stochastic model

stock *nm* stock; **numéro de stock** = stock code *ou* stock number

◊ **stockage** *nm* storage; **stockage de données** *ou* **de l'information** = data storage *ou* information storage; **stockage de données sur disque** *ou* **disquette** = disk storage; **stockage de données sur support optique** = optical storage; **stockage de fichier** = file storage; **stockage holographique** *ou* **d'hologramme** = holographic storage; **stockage d'instruction** = instruction storage; **stockage et restitution de données** = information storage and retrieval (ISR); **(système avec facilité de) stockage et retransmission** = store and forward (system); **stockage temporaire** = temporary storage; *(presse-papiers)* clipboard; **système de stockage par descripteurs** = aspect system; **zone de stockage de l'image** = image storage space; **zone de stockage des variables** = string area

◊ **stocker** *vtr (en mémoire)* to store; **stocker (des données) avant traitement** = to prestore; **stocker dans la mémoire cache** = to cache; **ce programme peut stocker une police de caractères, quelle qu'en soit la taille, dans la mémoire cache** = this program can cache any size font

> sa capacité énorme permet de stocker sur l'une de ses faces une très grande quantité de données
> *Micro Systèmes*

stopper *vtr* to inhibit *ou* to interrupt *ou* to stop

streamer *nm* floppy tape *ou* tape streamer *ou* streaming tape drive *ou* stringy floppy; **notre nouveau modèle est équipé d'un streamer de 96 Mo** = our new product has a 96MB streaming tape drive; *voir aussi* DEVIDEUR

stroboscope *nm* stroboscope *ou* strobe

Strowger *npr (pour téléphone)* **central Strowger** = strowger exchange

structure *nf* structure *ou* framework; **structure d'un bus** = bus structure; **structure cartésienne** = cartesian structure; **structure de données** = data structure *ou* information structure; **structure dynamique de données** = dynamic data structure; **structure hiérarchique de données** = data hierarchy; **structure d'un fichier** = file layout *ou* file structure; *(d'un réseau)* **structure à maillage intégral** = plex structure; **structure d'un programme** = program structure; **on a d'abord établi la structure du programme** = the program framework was designed first; **structure en réseau** = network structure; **code** *ou* **élément de structure** = overhead; **les numéros de lignes sont des éléments de structure en BASIC** = the line numbers in a BASIC program are an overhead

◊ **structuré, -ée** *adj* structured; **câblage structuré** = structured cabling; **données structurées** = data aggregate; **modèle structuré** = structured design; **programmation structurée** = structured programming

◊ **structurer** *vtr* to structure

studio *nm (de création ou d'enregistrement ou de prise de vues)* studio; **studio de création** *ou* **de design** = design studio; **studio de mixage** = mixing studio

STX = START OF TEXT; *voir* DEBUT

style *nm* style; **style d'impression** = print style; **style (de la) maison** = house style; **feuille de style** = image master *ou* style sheet; **la feuille de style comporte 125 symboles programmables (selon les besoins de l'utilisateur)** = the style sheet contains 125 user-definable symbols

stylet *nm (de tablette graphique)* stylus

> le stylet Ultrapen Eraser permet de gommer ce que l'on désire dans un logiciel de dessin, de traitement de texte ou de mise en page. La gomme est sensible à la pression et à l'inclinaison, et peut être programmée pour devenir un deuxième outil de dessin
> *l'Ordinateur Individuel*

stylo *nm* pen; **stylo électronique** = electronic pen *ou* stylus *ou* wand; **stylo optique** = light pen; *(pour code barres)* optical bar reader *ou* bar code reader *ou* optical wand; **stylo optique graphique** = graphics light pen

subdivisé, -ée *adj* subdivided *ou* partitioned; **fichier subdivisé** = partitioned file

◊ **subdiviser** *vtr* to subdivide *ou* to partition

sublimation *nf* **imprimante à sublimation thermique** = dye-sublimation printer; thermal wax transfer printer; **la nouvelle imprimante à sublimation thermique peut fournir une image couleur avec une définition de 300 dpi** = the new dye-sublimation printer can produce colour images at a resolution of 300dpi

substance *nf* substance

substituer *vtr* to substitute

◊ **substitution** *nf* substitution; **caractère de substitution** = substitute character; **erreur de substitution** = substitution error; **table de substitution** = substitution table

substrat *nm* substrate

subvocal, -e *adj* **canal de fréquences subvocales** = subvoice grade channel

successif, -ive *adj* successive; **chacune des opérations successives ajoute de nouveaux caractères à la chaîne** = each successive operation adds further characters to the string

suffixe *nm* suffix; postfix; **suffixe d'un fichier** = filename extension

◊ **suffixé, -ée** *adj (notation polonaise inversée)* **notation suffixée** = postfix notation *ou* reverse Polish notation; **alors que la notation conventionnelle s'écrit: (x-y) + z, la notation suffixée s'écrit: xy- z+** = normal notation: (x-y) + z, but using postfix notation: xy - z +

suite *nf* **(a)** suite *ou* sequence; **suite de programmes** = suite of programs; **suite de tâches** = job stream; **l'un(e) à la suite de l'autre** = consecutively; **les différentes sections du programme s'exécutent l'une à la suite de l'autre** = the sections of the program run consecutively **(b)** *(d'une page)* continuation page

suivi *nm* follow up; **utilitaire de suivi de version** = version control

suivre *vtr* **(a)** to follow; **marche à suivre** = procedure **(b)** *(un appel ou une lettre)* **faire suivre** = to forward; **faire suivre les appels veut dire les réacheminer automatiquement** = call forwarding is automatic redirection of calls **(c)** *(surveiller)* to monitor; **il suit le progrès des programmeurs débutants** = he is monitoring the progress of the trainee programmers

super- *préfixe* super-; **intégration à super grande échelle** = super large scale integration (SLSI)

◊ **super VGA (SVGA)** *(standard d'écran couleur)* Super VGA (SVGA)

superflu, -e *adj* redundant; **les bits de parité des données reçues sont superflus et peuvent être supprimés** = the parity bits on the received data are redundant and can be removed

superhétérodyne *adj* superheterodyne; **radio superhétérodyne** = superheterodyne radio

supérieur, -e *adj* **(a)** upper *ou* top; *(de papier d'imprimante)* **bac supérieur** = upper bin; **coin gauche supérieur de l'écran** = top left corner of a screen *ou* cursor home; **marge supérieure** = top margin *ou* top space; **partie supérieure** = top part **(b)** **de qualité supérieure** = high quality *ou* top quality

superposable *adj* **section de programme superposable** = overlay; **segment superposable** = overlay segments

◊ **superposer** *vtr* **(a)** to put on top (of something else); *(chevaucher)* to overlap; *(pour créer un nouveau caractère)* **superposer des caractères** = to overstrike; *(en détruisant les données en mémoire)* **superposer des données** = to overwrite data **(b)** *(deux circuits)* to piggyback; **superposez ces deux puces pour augmenter la capacité de la mémoire** = piggyback those two memory chips to boost the memory capacity

◊ **superposition** *nf* **(a)** putting on top (of something else); *(chevauchement)* overlap *ou* overlapping; **remplacer** *ou* **effacer** *ou* **détruire des données par superposition d'écriture** = to overwrite data; **les nouvelles données ont remplacé les anciennes par superposition d'écriture** = the latest data input has overwritten the old information **(b)** **superposition d'un accusé de réception au message suivant** = piggybacking

superstation *nf US* superstation

superviser *vtr* to supervise

◊ **superviseur** *nm&adj* supervisor *ou* administrator *ou* executive; **(programme) superviseur** = supervisor (program) *ou* executive program *ou* supervisory program; *(pour multiprogrammation)* scheduler; **superviseur d'entrée/sortie** = input/output executive; **instruction de superviseur** = executive instruction; **terminal superviseur** = executive terminal

◊ **supervision** *nf* supervision; **de supervision** = supervisory; **signal de supervision** = supervisory signal

supplémentaire *adj* additional *ou* extra; *(dispositif)* add-on *ou* add-in (device); **peut-on ajouter trois postes de travail supplémentaires au réseau?** = can we add three additional workstations to the network?; **bit supplémentaire** = overhead bit

support *nm* **(a)** *(physique)* support *ou* carrier; **support de cartes** = card cage *ou* card frame *ou* card chassis; **support de carte d'extension** = card extender; **cartes montées sur supports** = rack mounted cards **(b)** medium *ou* media; support *ou* carrier; **support à accès direct** = direct access storage device (DASD); **support de données** *ou* d'information = data medium; **(code de) fin de support de données** = end of medium (EM); **tri sur support externe** = external sort; **support de données d'un fichier** = file storage; *(en photocomposition)* **support de polices de caractères** = image carrier; **support intermédiaire** = intermediate materials; **ces diapositives et photos sont les supports intermédiaires qui doivent être recopiés sur le vidéodisque** = those slides and photographs are the intermediate materials to be mastered onto the video disk; **support magnétique** = magnetic material *ou* magnetic medium; **enregistrement sur support magnétique** = magnetic recording; **vidage de transfert sur support magnétique** = dump; **support magnétique effaçable** *ou* **réutilisable** = erasable storage *ou* erasable memory; **support magnétique haute densité** = high density storage (medium); **un disque dur est un support de haute densité par rapport à une bande perforée** = a hard disk is a high density storage medium compared to paper tape; **support magnétique original** = magnetic master; **support magnétique vierge** = empty medium; **support de stockage** = storage medium; **il existe différents types de supports de stockage dont les bandes papier, les disques et bandes magnétiques, les cartes et microfiches** = data storage mediums such as paper tape, magnetic disk, magnetic tape, card and microfiche are available; **les ordinateurs utilisent toutes sortes de supports pour stocker les données comme les disques, les cartes perforées ou le CD-ROM** = computers can store data on a variety of media, such as disk, punched card or CD-ROM; **support de stockage de grande capacité** = bulk storage medium *ou* mass storage device; **un disque dur constitue un véritable support de stockage de grande capacité** = a hard disk is definitely a mass storage device; **la bande magnétique constitue un support de stockage de grande capacité très sûr** = magnetic tape is a reliable bulk storage medium; **support publicitaire** = advertising medium; **support de transmission** = transmission medium; **support vierge** = empty medium; **code support** = skeletal code; **conversion de support(s)** = media conversion; **pour transférer le contenu d'une bande magnétique sur disquette, vous avez besoin d'un équipement de conversion de support(s)** = to transfer from magnetic tape to floppy disk, you need a media conversion device; **erreur causée par le support** = media error

◊ **supporter** *vtr* to back *ou* to support

Suppr *(sur claviers français: suppression)* **touche d'effacement** *ou* **touche Suppr** = DEL key; **pour effacer un mot à l'écran, appuyez sur la touche Suppr plusieurs fois** = to remove a word from the screen, press the DEL key repeatedly

suppresseur *nm* suppressor

◊ **suppression** *nf* suppression *ou* deletion *ou* removal; **suppression du signal** = blanking; **(bouton de) suppression de signal d'appel parasite** = anti-tinkle suppression; **suppression horizontale (du signal)** = horizontal blanking; **suppression verticale (du signal)** = field blanking (interval); **caractère de suppression** = delete character; **suivi** *ou* **traçage des suppressions** = deletion tracking

◊ **supprimer** *vtr* to suppress *ou* to delete *ou* to remove; *(d'un disque ou d'une mémoire)* to delete *ou* to scrub *ou* to scratch; **le traitement de texte permet de supprimer un fichier complet en appuyant sur cette touche** = the word-processor allows us to delete a whole file by pressing this key; **lorsqu'il s'agit de supprimer un texte assez long, servez-vous de la commande qui permet d'effacer en bloc** = use the global delete command to remove large areas of unwanted text; **ce filtre sert à supprimer les bruits parasites** = the filter is used to suppress the noise due to static interference

supravocal, -e *adj* above voice; *(transmission)* **données supravocales** = data above voice (DAV)

sûr, -e *adj* safe *ou* secure; **ce code chiffré est très sûr puisqu'il comporte une clé avec un très grand nombre de permutations possibles** = this cipher system is very secure since there are so many possible permutations for the key

sur- *préfixe* super-

◊ **surbrillance** *nf* **mettre en surbrillance** = to highlight; **mot** *ou* **caractères en surbrillance** = (display) highlights

◊ **surcharge** *nf* **(a)** overload; overloading; **surcharge d'une voie** *ou* **d'un canal** = channel overload; **surcharge d'un opérateur** = operator overloading **(b)** *(pour créer un nouveau caractère)* **faire une surcharge** = to overstrike

◊ **surcharger** *vtr* *(canal ou voie ou système)* to overload; **l'ordinateur est vraiment surchargé par tout ce travail** = the computer is overloaded with that amount of processing

◊ **surchauffer** *vi* to overheat

◊ **suréquipement** *nm* redundant equipment

surface *nf* **(a)** *(dessus)* surface; *(d'un disque)* **défaut de surface** = scratch **(b)** *(mesure)* area; **mesure de surface** = square measure

surimposer *vtr* to superimpose

◊ **surimpression** *nf* multipass overlap; *(pour créer un nouveau caractère)* **faire une surimpression** = to overstrike

surintensité *nf (de courant)* surge

surligneur *nm* marker pen

surmodulation *nf* overmodulation

surperforation *nf* overpunching

surtension *nf* surge *ou* over-voltage; **(dispositif de) protection contre la surtension** = over-voltage protection (device)

surveillance *nf* supervision *ou* control; **de surveillance** = supervisory; **instruction de surveillance** = supervisory instruction; *(micro espion)* **dispositif de surveillance** = bug

◊ **surveillant, -e** *n* supervisor

◊ **surveillé, -ée** *adj* supervised *ou* monitored *ou* controlled *ou* attended; **opération surveillée** = attended operation

◊ **surveiller** *vtr* to supervise *ou* to monitor *ou* to control; **la confection des cartes de circuits imprimés est très étroitement surveillée** = the manufacture of circuit boards is very carefully supervised; **surveiller par micro-espion** = to bug

survenir *vi* to occur

survoltage *nm* surge *ou* over-voltage; **(dispositif de) protection contre le survoltage** = over-voltage protection (device)

symbole *nm* **(a)** symbol; **ce langage utilise le symbole ? pour la commande d'impression** = this language uses the symbol ? to represent the print command; **symbole d'arrêt (dynamique)** = breakpoint symbol; **symbole de décision** = decision box; **symboles ECMA** = ECMA symbols; **symbole graphique** = graphic symbol; **symbole logique** = logic symbol; **symboles d'un ordinogramme** = flowchart symbols; **symbole de positionnement (sur microfilm)** = editing symbol; **bibliothèque de symboles** = symbol library; **ligne de jonction des symboles d'un ordinogramme** = flowline; **reconnaissance optique de symboles** = optical mark recognition (OMR); **table de symboles** = symbol table **(b) symbole (d'une opération) arithmétique** = arithmetic operator

◊ **symbolique** *adj* symbolic; **adresse symbolique** = (floating) symbolic address; **code** *ou* **instruction symbolique** = symbolic code *ou* instruction; **(programme de) débogage symbolique** = symbolic debugging; **langage symbolique** = symbolic language; **format de langage symbolique** = symbolic-coding format; **logique symbolique** = symbolic logic; **nom symbolique** = symbolic name; **programmation symbolique** = symbolic programming

symétrie *nf* symmetry; balance

synchro = SYNCHRONISATION sync; **bit de synchro** = sync bit; **caractère de synchro** = sync character; **impulsions de synchro** = sync pulses; **magnétophone avec interface synchro pour projecteur de diapos** = slide/sync recorder

◊ **synchrone** *adj* synchronous *ou* in sync; **communication synchrone binaire** = binary synchronous communications (BSC); **mode synchrone** = synchronous mode; **ordinateur synchrone** = synchronous computer; **repérage synchrone** = synchronous detection; **réseau synchrone** = synchronous network; **réseau de données synchrone** = synchronous data network; **système synchrone** = synchronous system; **transmission synchrone** = synchronous transmission; *voir aussi* SYNCHRONISE

◊ **synchronisation** *ou* **synchro** *nf* synchronization; *(de bandes audio et vidéo)* interlock; *(de bande vidéo)* pix lock; **synchronisation de réseau** = network timing; **bit de synchronisation de trame** = framing bit; **boucle de synchronisation** = timing loop; **caractère de synchronisation** = synchronous idle character; **code de synchronisation de trame** = framing code;

impulsions de synchronisation = synchronization pulses; **impulsion de synchronisation du balayage vertical** = field sync pulse; **impulsion de synchronisation horizontale** = horizontal synchronization pulse; **unité de synchronisation** = synchronizer

◊ **synchronisé, -ée** *adj* synchronized *ou* in phase *ou* in sync; **ces deux dispositifs ne sont pas parfaitement synchronisés** = the two devices are out of sync; *(d'horloge)* **opération synchronisée** = fixed cycle operation; *(imagelson)* **projecteur synchronisé** = interlock projector

◊ **synchroniser** *vtr* to synchronize *ou* to clock; *(signal avec horloge interne)* to lock onto; *(film avec piste sonore)* to lay in

◊ **synchroniseur** *nm* synchronizer; **synchroniseur de canaux** *ou* **de voies** = channel synchronizer

◊ **synchronisme** *nm* **en synchronisme** = in sync

dès lors, le rôle du programme de gestion de données consiste aussi à synchroniser la lecture des différents blocs texte/image et son

Micro Systèmes

Syndicat européen des constructeurs d'ordinateurs
European Computer Manufacturers Association (ECMA)

synonyme 1 *nm* synonym; **'erreur' et 'faute' sont des synonymes** = the words 'error' and 'mistake' are synonymous **2** *adj* synonymous

syntactique *adj* syntactical; **analyse syntactique** = syntax analysis *ou* syntactical analysis *ou* parsing

◊ **syntaxe** *nf* **(a)** syntax *ou* grammar; **faute de syntaxe** = grammatical error *ou* syntactic error *ou* syntax error; **utilitaire de contrôle de syntaxe** = grammar checker **(b)** *(en informatique)* language rules; **qui va contre les règles de la syntaxe** = illegal

◊ **syntaxique** *adj* **analyse syntaxique** = syntax analysis *ou* syntactical analysis *ou* parsing

synthèse *nf* synthesis; **synthèse additive (de couleurs)** = additive colour mixing; **synthèse vocale** *ou* **de la parole** = voice synthesis *ou* speech synthesis; **langage de synthèse** = synthetic language; **puce de synthèse vocale** = speech chip; **voix de synthèse** = digital speech

◊ **synthétique** *adj* synthetic; **matériaux synthétiques** = synthetic materials

◊ **synthétiser** *vtr* to synthesize

◊ **synthétiseur** *nm* **synthétiseur de son** = music synthesizer *ou* sound synthesizer; **synthétiseur vocal** *ou* **de la parole** = voice synthesizer *ou* speech synthesizer

System 7 ™ *ou* **Système 7** ™ *(version de système d'exploitation pour Apple Macintosh)* System 7 ™

systématique *adj* systematic *ou* unconditional; **transfert systématique** = unconditional transfer

système *nm* **(a)** *(informatique)* system; **les ingénieurs n'ont pas terminé l'essai du nouveau système** = the engineers are still testing the new system *ou* the new installation; **système d'aide à la décision (SAID)** = decision support system (DSS); **système à base de connaissances** *ou* **système expert** = (intelligent) knowledge-based system (IKBS) *ou* expert system; **système de base de données** = database system; **système de gestion de base de données** = database management system (DBMS) *ou* database manager; **système de base de données réparti** *ou* **en réseau** = distributed database system; **système binaire** = binary system; **système bureautique** *ou* **système informatique pour bureau** = computer office system; **système à bus auxiliaire** *ou* **à bus double** = dual bus system; **système-conseil** = advisory system; **système de débogage interactif** *ou* **de déverminage interactif** = interactive debugging system; **système disjoncteur progressif** = fail soft system; **système double** = dual system; **système duplex** = duplex computer; **système évalué en cycles possibles par unité de temps** = duty-rated system; **système expert** = expert system; **système d'exploitation** = operating system (OS); **système d'exploitation de base** = basic operating system (BOS); **système d'exploitation CP** = control program/monitor *ou* control program for microcomputers (CP/M); **système d'exploitation de disque** *ou* **système d'exploitation DOS** *ou* **système DOS** = disk operating system (DOS); **système d'exploitation MS-DOS** ™ = MS disk operating system *ou* Microsoft DOS ™ (MS-DOS); **système extensible** = expandable system; **système à fichiers répartis** *ou* **partagés** = distributed file system; **système frontal** = front-end system; **système de gestion de l'information** = information management system; **système de hash code** = hash-code system; **système hybride** = hybrid system; **système imbriqué (dans un autre)** = embedded system; **système indéterminé** = indeterminate system; **système d'information pour la direction (SID)** = executive information system (EIS); **système informatique** = computer system *ou* information system; **système informatique intégré** = computer-integrated system; **cette entreprise est un fournisseur réputé de systèmes informatiques intégrés qui permettent à la fois la pagination de très longs documents et le traitement personnalisé de chaque page** = this firm is a very well-known supplier of computer-integrated systems which allow both batch pagination of very long documents with alteration of individual pages; **système interactif** = interactive system; **système ISO/OSI** = International Standards Organization Open System Interconnection (ISO/OSI); **système multiposte** = multi-terminal system; **système numérique** = digital system; **système ouvert** = open system; **système pilote** = pilot system; **système de recherche documentaire** = document retrieval system; **système de reconnaissance de caractères CSM (par identification des caractéristiques combinées)** = combined symbol matching (CSM); **système sécurisé** = secure system; **système de sécurité** = fail safe system; **système en temps réel** = real-time system; **système de traitement de l'image** = image processor; **système de traitement par lots** *ou* **par paquets** = batch system; **système de traitement de texte** = word processing system *ou* word processor **(b)** **analyse de systèmes** = systems analysis; **architecture d'un système** = computer architecture; **bibliothèque du système** = system library; **conception** *ou* **design d'un système** = system design; **console système** = system console; **diagnostic de système** = system check; **disquette (de programme) système** = system disk; **dossier système** = system folder; **durée de vie d'un système** = system life cycle; **formation assistée par système expert** = intelligent tutoring system; **génération d'un système** *ou* **à laquelle appartient un système** = system generation *ou* sysgen; **ingénieur système** = systems engineer; **interface système/utilisateur** = user interface; man/machine interface; **intégration de systèmes** = systems integration; **invite du système** = system prompt; **journal d'un système** = system log; **logiciel (de) système** = system software *ou* system firmware; **ordinogramme d'un système** = system flowchart; **panne de système** = system crash; **panneau de commandes d'un système** = system control panel; **programme système** = systems software *ou* program; **programmeur système** = systems programmer; **sécurisation d'un système** = system security; **spécifications du système** = system specifications; **unité système** = system unit **(c)** *(autres systèmes)* **système d'alimentation** *ou* **d'entraînement (du papier)** = (paper) feeder; **système d'appel** = calling unit; **système d'appel automatique (d'un correspondant)** *ou* **système de numérotation automatique** = auto-dial system; **système auto-adaptable** *ou* **dynamique** = adaptive system; **système de communication** = communications system; **système de communication hiérarchisé** = hierarchical communications system; **système de commutation électronique** = electronic switching system; **systèmes de contrôle** = control systems; *(analogique)* **système à courants porteurs** = carrier system; **système haute-fidélité** *ou* **hi-fi** = high fidelity system (hi fi); **système multiplex** = carrier system; **système téléphonique automatique international** = international direct dialling (IDD); **système de transmission numérique** = digital transmission system; **système vidéo haute définition** = high definition video system (HDVS) **(d)** *(math)* **système décimal** *ou* **à base dix** = decimal system; **système duodécimal** = duodecimal number system

Tt

T connecteur *ou* **coupleur en T** = T connector; **jonction en T** = T junction; **réseau en T** = T network

T1 *(commission ANSI)* T1 committee (which sets digital communications standards); **liaison T1** = T1 link

tab *nm (caractère ASCII 09hex)* tab character; *(touche de tabulation)* **touche Tab** = tab key

table *nf* **(a)** *(meuble)* table; **ordinateur de table** = desktop computer (system) **(b)** **table d'écoute** = wiretap; **brancher une ligne sur une table d'écoute** = to tap (a phone line) **(c)** *(format)* table; **disposé en table** = in tabular form; **disposer en table** = to tab *ou* to tabulate **(d)** *(liste)* **définir une table d'adressage binaire** = to bit-map; **table des adresses hash codées** = hash table; **table d'attributs** = image table; **table de Boole** = Boolean operation table; **table de branchements** = branch table; **table de contrôle des paramètres d'écran couleur** = video lookup table; **tables de conversion** = translation tables *ou* conversion tables; **table de décision** = decision table; **table (de classement des fichiers) du disque** = disk map; **table d'équivalence** = look-up table (LUT) *ou* translation table *ou* conversion table; **voici la fonction de cette touche, pour la traduire en ASCII consultez la table d'équivalence** = this is the value of the key pressed, use a lookup table to find its ASCII value; **les tables d'équivalence sont préprogrammées et permettent de gagner du temps de traitement en évitant de recalculer les mêmes valeurs** = lookup tables are preprogrammed then used in processing to save calculating each result required; **on peut établir des tables d'équivalence qui serviront à convertir les données clients aux codes utilisés par notre système** = conversion tables may be created and used in conjunction with the customer's data to convert it to our systems codes; *(sous DOS)* **table des fichiers système** = system file table; **table de fonctions** = function table; **table de Karnaugh** = Karnaugh map; **table des matières** = table of contents; **table de noms** *ou* **de symboles** = name table; *(de la mémoire paginée)* **table des pages** *ou* **table Page** = page table; **table des priorités d'interruption** = priority interrupt table; **table de référence** = reference table *ou* look-up table (LUT); translation table *ou* conversion table; **table de référence de programme** = reference program table; **consultation d'une table de référence** = table lookup; **table de routage** = routing table; **table de substitution** = substitution table; **table de symboles** = symbol table; **table de vérité** = truth table **(e)** **table traçante** = (flatbed) plotter

tableau *nm* **(a)** table; *(sortie d'imprimante d'un tableur)* spreadsheet; **tableau de référence** = reference table; **disposé en tableau** = in tabular form; **disposer en tableau** = to tab *ou* to tabulate **(b)** *(structures pour données)* array; **tableau alphanumérique** = alphanumeric array; **tableau de chaînes de caractères** = string array; **tableau de chiffres** = numeric array; **tableau à deux dimensions** *ou* **bidimensionnel** = two-dimensional array; **tableau à trois dimensions** = three-dimensional array; **tableau à dimensions variables** = flexible array; **tableau multidimensionnel** = multidimensional array; **tableau numérique** = numeric array; **tableau réduit** = sparse array; **bornes d'un tableau** = array bounds; **dimension d'un tableau** = array dimension; **élément d'un tableau** = array element; **limites de tableau** = array bounds; **valeur dans un tableau** = array element **(c)** *(panneau)* **tableau d'affichage** = notice board; *(e-mail)* **tableau d'affichage électronique** = bulletin board system (BBS); *(téléphone)* **tableau de distribution** = plugboard *ou* patchboard; **tableau de distribution principal** = main distributing frame; **tableau des indicateurs** = indicator chart; **tableau noir** = blackboard; **tableau noir électronique** = electronic blackboard

tablette *nf* pad; **tablette graphique** = graphics pad *ou* tablet; **tablette à numériser** = digitizing pad; *(pour saisie de l'écriture manuelle)* writing pad *ou* data tablet; **un dessin précis s'obtient beaucoup plus facilement avec une tablette à numériser qu'avec une souris** = it is much easier to draw accurately with a tablet than with a mouse

tableur *nm (programme)* spreadsheet

tabulaire *adj* in tabular form; **disposition tabulaire** = layout in tabular form

◊ **tabulateur** *nm* tabulator

◊ **tabulation** *nf* tabulation *ou* tabbing; **la tabulation peut être incorporée au programme** = tabbing can be done from inside the program; **tabulation décimale** *ou* **sur la virgule** = decimal tabbing; **touche de tabulation décimale** = decimal tab key; **tabulation verticale** = vertical tab; **arrêt de tabulation** = tabulation stop *ou* tab stop; **faire une tabulation arrière** = to backtab; **mémoire de tabulation** = tab memory; **règle de tabulation** = tab rack *ou* ruler line; **la règle de tabulation indique les marges de gauche et de droite** = a tab rack shows you the left and right margins; **repères de tabulation** = tabulation markers; **touche de tabulation** = tab key; **en appuyant sur la touche de tabulation en début de ligne, pour se placer à la colonne 10, la liste avait été parfaitement alignée** = the list was neatly lined up by tabbing to column 10 at the start of each new line

◊ **tabulatrice** *nf (pour cartes perforées)* tabulator *ou* tabulating machine; **traitement de données par tabulatrice** = data tabulating

◊ **tabuler** *vtr* to tabulate *ou* to tab

tache *nf* tache lumineuse = *(sur film)* flare; *(sur l'écran)* bloom

◊ **taché, -ée** *adj (film)* taché d'un reflet lumineux = flared

tâche *nf* job *ou* load *ou* task; *(l'ensemble des tâches d'un ordinateur)* activities *ou* work load; **la tâche suivante consistera à trier tous les enregistrements** = the next job to be processed is to sort all the records; *(non prioritaire)* **tâche de fond** = background operation *ou* backgroung task; **recalcul en tâche de fond** = background recalculation; **tâche de premier plan** *ou* **prioritaire** = foreground task; **tâche non prioritaire** *ou* **d'arrière-plan** = low-priority work *ou* background task; **(instruction d') arrêter** *ou* **(de) virer une tâche** = kill job; **contrôle d'exécution des tâches** = job statement control; **fichier de contrôle de tâche** = job control file; **programme de contrôle de tâche** = job control program; **ensemble des tâches en cours d'exécution** = job mix; **fichier de tâches (à exécuter)** = job file; **(code de) fin de tâche** = end of job (EOJ); **flux des tâches** = job stream; **gestion de tâches** = job scheduling *ou* task management; **lancement** *ou* **commande de tâches à distance** = remote job entry (RJE); **langage de commande de tâche** = job control language (JCL); **numéro (de suite) d'une tâche dans la file d'attente** = job number; **partage des tâches** = load sharing; *(passage d'une tâche à une autre)* **permutation** *ou* **basculement de tâche** = task swapping *ou* switching; **priorité d'une tâche** = job priority; **traitement de tâche** = job processing; **planification de la séquence d'exécution des tâches** *ou* **répartition des tâches** = job scheduling; **temps d'exécution d'une tâche** = operating time *ou* elapsed time

TACS *(norme pour système de radio-téléphone cellulaire)* **norme TACS** = TACS (standard)

tactile *adj* tactile; **clavier tactile** = tactile keyboard *ou* touch pad *ou* touch-sensitive keyboard; **écran tactile** = touch screen; **information tactile** = tactile feedback; **pavé tactile** = touch pad

taille *nf* **(a)** size *ou* length; **taille d'un bloc** = block length; **taille d'un caractère (en points)** = typesize; **taille des caractères utilisés dans la composition** = composition size; **taille d'une chaîne** = string length; **taille d'un champ** = field length; **taille d'un enregistrement** = record length; **taille d'un fichier** = file extent; **la taille d'impression a été augmentée pour la rendre plus lisible** = the size of the print has been increased to make it easier to read; **taille (de la) mémoire** = storage capacity; **taille de la mémoire tampon** = buffer length *ou* buffer size; **taille de la page** = page size; **taille d'un registre** = register length; **un système informatique de taille moyenne** = a medium-sized computer system; **champ de taille constante** *ou* **fixe** = fixed field; *(d'une illustration ou photo)* **mise à la taille** = sizing **(b)** *(gravure)* **impression en taille douce** = copperplate printing

talon *nm* **talon de caractère** = beard

tambour *nm* drum *ou* cylinder; **tambour d'impression** = impression cylinder; **tambour**

magnétique = magnetic drum; **imprimante à tambour** = barrel printer; **traceur** *ou* **enregistreur à tambour** = drum plotter

tampon *nm (circuit ou mémoire)* buffer; **tampon à capacité variable** = elastic buffer; **tampon circulaire** = circular buffer; **tampon de clavier** = key rollover; **tampon de données** = data buffer; **tampon de transmission de données** = communications buffer *ou* data communications buffer; **tampon dynamique** *ou* **variable** = dynamic buffer *ou* elastic buffer; **tampon (d') entrée/sortie** = input/output buffer *ou* I/O buffer; **tampon d'imprimante** = printer buffer; **mémoire avec tampon** = buffered memory; **mémoire tampon** = buffer (memory); **entrée/sortie utilisant une mémoire tampon** = buffered input/output; **registre de mémoire tampon** = memory buffer register (MBR); **taille de la mémoire tampon** = buffer length *ou* buffer size; **utilisation de mémoire tampon** = buffering; *(entre périphérique lent et processeur rapide)* **utilisation de mémoire tampon auxiliaire** = spooling; **utilisation de double mémoire tampon** = double buffering; **utiliser une mémoire tampon** = to buffer; **vider la mémoire tampon** = to flush buffers; **registre tampon** = buffer register; **registre tampon des entrées** = input buffer register; **registre tampon des sorties** = output buffer register

tandem *nm* tandem; **commutation (en) tandem** = tandem switching; **fonctionnement en tandem** = working in tandem; **processeurs en tandem** = tandem processors

tangage *nm (mouvement autour d'un axe)* pitch

TAO = TEST ASSISTE PAR ORDINATEUR

taper *vtr* **(a)** *(écrire à la machine)* to type; **tous ses rapports sont tapés sur sa petite (machine) portative** = all his reports are typed on his portable typewriter; **tapez la clé et vous pourrez décoder le dernier message** = type this key into the machine, that will decode the last message **(b)** *(entrer une donnée, une instruction au clavier)* to enter; to key in *ou* to keyboard; *(appuyer sur une touche)* to hit *ou* to press (a key); **taper une commande** = to key in a command; **taper un code** = to enter a code; **il a tapé CONTROL Z pour vider l'écran** = he pressed CONTROL Z and zapped all the text

◊ **tapuscrit** *nm* typescript

taquer *vtr (cartes perforées)* to joggle

taux *nm* **(a)** *(rapport)* ratio; **taux d'activité** = activity ratio; **taux d'activité d'un fichier** = file activity ratio **(b)** rate; **taux de défaillance** = failure rate; **taux d'écoute** = ratings; **guerre de taux d'écoute** = ratings battle *ou* war; **taux d'erreur** = error rate; **taux d'erreur par bloc** = block error rate; **le taux d'erreur est inférieur à 1%** = the error rate is less than 1%; **taux par minute** *ou* **taux/minute** = rate per minute; **il existe un tarif forfaitaire d'utilisation plus un taux/minute de temps d'ordinateur** = there is a set tariff for logging on, then a rate for every minute of computer time used

TCP *(protocole de contrôle de transmission)* **protocole TCP** = Transmission Control Protocol (TCP)

TCP/IP *(protocole de communication de réseau)* Transmission Control Protocol/Interface Program (TCP/IP)

TEC = TRANSISTOR A EFFET DE CHAMP

technicien, -ienne *n* technician; **le nouveau système a été mis en place par les techniciens** = the computer technicians installed the new system; **technicien de laboratoire** = laboratory technician; **technicien/réparateur** = troubleshooter

technique 1 *nf* **(a)** technique *ou* method; **le société a mis au point une nouvelle technique de traitement des disquettes clients** = the company has developed a new technique for processing customers' disks **(b) techniques** = technology; **techniques de l'information** = information technology (IT); **techniques de pointe** *ou* **techniques nouvelles** = new technology; **l'introduction de techniques nouvelles** = the introduction of new technology **2** *adj* technical *ou* technological; **assistance technique** = technical support; **il offre une assistance technique** = he offers a consultancy service; **société d'assistance technique** = consultancy firm; **manuel technique** = installation manual *ou* technical manual; **ce document contient tous les renseignements d'ordre technique concernant le nouvel ordinateur** = the document gives all the technical details on the new computer

technologie *nf* technology; **technologie de la fibre optique** *ou* **de la transmission par fibre optique** = fibre optics; **technologie avancée** *ou* **haute technologie** = high technology *ou* high tech; **high specification** *ou* high spec; **les câbles (de) haute technologie doivent être manipulés avec soin** = high spec cabling needs to be very carefully handled; **nouvelle technologie** = new technology

◊ **technologique** *adj* technological; **la révolution technologique** = the technological revolution

télé- *préfixe* tele-

◊ **télébanque** *nf* home banking

◊ **Télécarte ™** *nf* phonecard

◊ **téléchargeable** *adj* downloadable; **police de caractères téléchargeable** = downloadable font

◊ **téléchargement** *nm (de données, etc., d'un gros à un petit ordinateur; de données, d'un ordinateur à distance à un autre ordinateur, par modem; de police de caractères - sur disque - vers l'imprimante)* downloading; *(de données d'un petit vers un gros ordinateur)* uploading; **le téléchargement des données dans l'unité centrale peut se faire par l'intermédiaire d'un modem** = you can download the data to the CPU via a modem; **on peut manipuler l'image avant son téléchargement sur l'ordinateur hôte** = the image can be manipulated before uploading to the host computer

◊ **télécharger** *vtr (de données, etc., d'un gros à un petit ordinateur; de données, d'un ordinateur à distance à un autre ordinateur, par modem; de police de caractères - sur disque - vers l'imprimante)* to download; *(de données d'un petit vers un gros ordinateur)* to upload; **on a téléchargé le logiciel hier** = the telesoftware was downloaded yesterday; **il n'en coûte rien de télécharger, depuis le tableau d'affichage, un logiciel qui n'est pas protégé par un copyright** = there is no charge for downloading public domain software from the BBS; **logiciel téléchargé** = telesoftware (TSW)

pour pallier ces limites, certaines machines autorisent le téléchargement de fontes dans leur mémoire interne
L'Ordinateur Individuel

◊ **télécinéma** *nm* telecine

TELECOM *(pour modem)* **prise TELECOM** = data jack

télécommande *nf* remote control *ou* telecontrol; **ce magnétoscope est équipé d'une télécommande** = the video recorder has a remote control facility

télécommunication(s) *nf(pl)* telecommunications *ou* communications; **gestionnaire de télécommunication** = communications executive; **réseau de télécommunications** = communications network; **satellite de télécommunications** = communications satellite

télécompensation *nf* **Système Interbancaire de Télécompensation (SIT)** = Bankers Automated Clearance System (BACS)

télécomposition *nf* teletypesetting

téléconférence *nf (téléphone)* teleconference *ou* teleconferencing *ou* conference call; *(modems, ordinateurs)* conferencing *ou* teleconferencing; **téléconférence par sélection** *ou* **par composition** = dial conference; **téléconférence sur réseau informatique** = computer conferencing

télécopie *nf* facsimile transmission *ou* fax *ou* FAX; **envoyer par télécopie** = to fax; **nous enverrons les plans par télécopie** = we will send a fax of the design plan; **j'ai envoyé les documents par télécopie à notre bureau de New York** = I've faxed the documents to our New York office; **serveur de télécopie** = fax server

◊ **télécopieur** *nm* fax (machine *ou* system); **rouleau de papier pour télécopieur** = roll of fax paper

télégramme *nm* telegram *also GB* telemessage; **envoyer un télégramme** = to cable *ou* to telegraph; to send a telegram *ou* a telemessage; **il a envoyé un télégramme au bureau pour redemander de l'argent** = he sent a cable to his office asking for more money; **ils ont envoyé un télégramme confirmant leur accord** = they telegraphed their agreement

◊ **télégraphe** *nm* telegraph

◊ **télégraphie** *nf* telegraphy; **télégraphie par onde porteuse** = carrier telegraphy

◊ **télégraphier** *vtr* to cable *ou* to telegraph *ou* to send a telegram; **on a télégraphié les photos à New York** = the photographs were telegraphed to New York; **message télégraphié** = telegram *GB* telemessage

◊ **télégraphique** *adj* telegraphic; **adresse télégraphique** = cable address *ou* telegraphic address; **chiffres et signes en code télégraphique** = figures case; **le bureau lui a envoyé un mandat télégraphique de 1000 francs pour couvrir ses frais** = the office cabled him 1,000 francs to cover his expenses

téléimprimeur *nm* teleprinter *ou* teletypewriter; **vous pouvez connecter un téléimprimeur sur ce port série modifié** = you can drive a teleprinter from this modified serial port; **interface (pour) téléimprimeur** = teleprinter interface; **opérateur, -trice de téléimprimeur** = teleprinter operator; **rouleau de papier de** *ou* **pour téléimprimeur** = teleprinter roll

téléinformatique *nf* data communications; **appareils** *ou* **matériel téléinformatique** = data communications equipment (DCE); **réseau téléinformatique** = data communications network *ou* data network; **service (de) téléinformatique** = teleinformatic services *ou* data services

télémaintenance *nf* remote maintenance

télématique *nf* telematics *ou* data communications

télémétrie *nf* telemetry

téléphone *nm* (a) telephone *ou* phone; **téléphone à carte** = card phone; **téléphone cellulaire** = cellular telephone *ou* cell phone; **téléphone à clavier** = pushbutton telephone; **téléphone de conférence** = conference telephone; **téléphone à impulsion numérique (de marque) Digipulse™** = Digipulse telephone; **téléphone interne** = house phone *ou* internal phone; **téléphone mobile** = mobile radiophone *ou* mobile (tele)phone; **téléphone sans cordon** = cordless telephone; **les abonnés du téléphone** = telephone subscribers; **amplificateur de téléphone** = telephone repeater; **annuaire du téléphone** = telephone directory *ou* telephone book; **numéro de téléphone** = telephone number *ou* phone number; **pouvez-vous me donner votre numéro de téléphone?** = can you give me your (tele)phone number?; **le numéro de téléphone figure sur le papier à en-tête de la société** = the phone number is on the company notepaper; **il a une liste de numéros de téléphone dans un petit carnet noir** = he keeps a list of phone numbers in a little black book; **parler au téléphone** = to be on the phone; **elle a passé la matinée (à parler) au téléphone** = she has been on the phone all morning; **il a parlé au directeur** *ou* **il a eu le directeur au téléphone** = he spoke to the manager on the phone; **répondre au téléphone** = to answer the phone *ou* to take a (phone) call **(b) par téléphone** = by telephone *ou* by phone; **achats par téléphone** = teleshopping; **contacter quelqu'un par téléphone** = to call someone *ou* to contact someone by phone; **contacter son bureau par téléphone** = to call in; **demander quelque chose par téléphone** = to phone

for something; **faire une commmande par téléphone** = to place an order by telephone; **il a passé la commande directement à l'entrepôt par téléphone** = he phoned the order through to the warehouse; **ventes par téléphone** = telesales

◊ **téléphoner** *vtr* to make a phone call *ou* to make a telephone call *ou* to ring (up); *(être en ligne)* **elle est en train de téléphoner à Hong Kong** = she is on the telephone to Hong Kong; **M. Dubois a téléphoné en votre absence et a demandé que vous le rappeliez** = Mr Dubois called while you were out and asked if you would phone him back; **sa secrétaire a téléphoné pour prévenir de son retard** = his secretary phoned to say he would be late; **téléphoner (à quelqu'un)** = to telephone (someone) *ou* to make a call (to someone) *ou* to call (someone) *ou* to phone (someone); **ne me téléphonez pas, c'est moi qui vous appellerai** = don't phone me, I'll phone you; **téléphoner au sujet de quelque chose** = to phone about something; **il a téléphoné au sujet de la commande de papier listing** = he telephoned about the order for computer stationery; **téléphoner en direct** = to dial direct

◊ **téléphonie** *nf* telephony

◊ **téléphonique** *adj* telephone *ou* phone; **nous avons une nouvelle installation téléphonique depuis la semaine dernière** = we had a new phone system installed last week; **annuaire téléphonique** = phone book *ou* telephone book *ou* telephone directory; **bande téléphonique** = voice band; **cabine téléphonique** = call box *ou* telephone booth; **central téléphonique** = telephone exchange; **indicatif téléphonique** = dialling code; *voir aussi* INDICATIF **ligne téléphonique spécialisée** *ou* **dédiée** = dedicated line; **répondeur téléphonique** = (telephone) answering machine *ou* answerphone; **réseau téléphonique (public) commuté** = public switched telephone network (PSTN); **standard téléphonique** = (telephone) switchboard; **système téléphonique automatique international** = international direct dialling (IDD)

◊ **téléphoniste** *nm&f* telephonist

téléscripteur *nm* teleprinter *ou* teletype (TTY); **clavier de téléscripteur** = ASR keyboard

téléspectateur, -trice *n* viewer

Télétex™ *nm* Teletext

mal connu et, de ce fait, peu aimé, le mode télétex combine cependant des avantages. Il fonctionne à 2400 bits/seconde, une vitesse tout à fait correcte pour transmettre de l'information codée. Les 309 symboles permettent la transmission de documents bien préparés avec un minimum de graphisme

Temps Micro

télétraitement *nm* teleprocessing (TP)

télétransmission *nf* **poste informatique de télétransmission** = data station

télétravail *nm* telecommuting

télétype *nm* teleprinter

◊ **télétypiste** *nm&f* teleprinter operator

téléviseur *nm* television (receiver) *ou* television set *ou* TV set *ou* TV

◊ **télévision** *nf* **la télévision** = television *ou* TV; **télévision câblée** = cable télévision *ou* cable TV; **télévision câblée interactive** = interactive cable television; **télévision câblée payante** = pay TV, *US* paycable; *(familier)* feevee; **antenne collective de télévision câblée** *ou* **système de télévision câblée CATV** = community antenna television (CATV); **relais de télévision câblée** = cable TV relay station; **télévision en circuit fermé** = closed circuit television (CCTV); **câble de télévision** = CATV cable; **caméra de télévision** = television camera *ou* TV camera; **Comité National de Normalisation de la Télévision (NTSC)** = National Television Standards Committee (NTSC); **moniteur (de) télévision** = television monitor; **poste (de) télévision** = television set *ou* television *ou* TV set *ou* TV; **projecteur (de) télévision** = television projector; **programme de télévision** = television programme *ou* TV programme; **programme de télévision (à caractère) éducatif** = educational TV (ETV) programme; **réseau de télévision** = television network

télex *nm* **(a)** *(machine ou système)* telex; **nous n'avons pas le télex** = we don't have a telex; **il nous est impossible de joindre nos bureaux au Nigéria parce que le télex est en panne** = we cannot communicate with our Nigerian office because of the breakdown of the telex lines; **abonné du télex** = telex subscriber; **envoyer des renseignements par télex** = to send information by telex; **ligne (de) télex** = telex line; **opérateur de télex** = telex operator **(b)** *(message)* **un télex** = a telex; **envoyer un télex** = to telex; **il a envoyé un télex à son bureau** = he sent a telex to his office; **pouvez-vous envoyer un télex au bureau canadien avant son ouverture?** = can you telex the Canadian office before they open ?; **nous avons reçu son télex ce matin** = we received his telex this morning

◊ **télexer** *vtr* to telex; **télexer des renseignements** = to send information by telex; **la commande nous a été télexée** = the order came by telex

◊ **télexiste** *nm&f* telex operator

le télex est lent (50 bits/seconde) et ses capacités de représentation de l'information sont limitées (48 symboles seulement). Son atout principal est sa valeur juridique
Temps Micro

témoin *nm* **(a)** *(symbole)* flag *ou* indicator flag; **témoin de retenue** = carry flag; *(d'un appareil)* **témoin d'utilisation** = device flag; **clic témoin (de fonctionnement) de touche** = key click; **mise en place d'un témoin** = flag event; **registre des témoins** = flag register **(b)** *(voyant lumineux)* **témoin** *ou* **lampe témoin** = indicator light *ou* light emitting diode; **témoin d'activité** *ou* **lampe témoin** = activity light **(c)** **groupe témoin** = control group

température *nf* **(a)** temperature; **le marqueur du thermomètre indique la température maximum d'aujourd'hui** = the marker on the thermometer shows the peak temperature for today **(b)**

température de bruit = noise temperature; **température chromatique** = colour temperature

temporaire *adj* temporary; **fichier (d'échange) temporaire** = temporary swap file; **interrupteur temporaire** = momentary switch; **mémoire temporaire** = temporary storage; erasable storage *ou* erasable memory; working store; scratchpad; **registre temporaire** = temporary register; **stockage temporaire** = temporary storage

◊ **temporairement** *adv* temporarily

temporel, -elle *adj* **accès temporel multiplexé** = time division multiple access; **commutation temporelle** = time division switching; **multiplexage temporel** = time division multiplexing (TDM)

temporisation *nf* **boucle de temporisation** = timing loop

temps *nm* **(a)** time; **de temps en temps** = periodic *ou* periodical *ou* periodically; **pendant quelque temps** *ou* **pendant un certain temps** = for a period of time **(b)** **temps d'accélération** = acceleration time; **temps d'accès moyen** = average access time; **temps d'addition** = add time *ou* addition time; **temps d'adressage** = address access time; **temps d'arrêt** *ou* **d'immobilisation** = stop time; **temps d'assemblage** = assembly time; **temps d'association (d'une adresse)** = binding time; **temps d'attente** = queuing time; **temps de compilation** = compilation time; **temps de connexion** = connect time; **temps de cycle** = cycle time; **temps de cycle d'instruction** = instruction cycle time; *(d'un onduleur ou d'un dispositif de secours)* **temps de débit** = holdup; **temps de développement** *ou* **de mise au point d'un nouveau produit** = development time; **temps disponible** *ou* **de disponibilité** = available time; **temps d'exécution** = execution time *ou* execute time; **temps d'exécution d'une instruction** *ou* **temps d'instruction** = instruction execution time *ou* instruction time; **temps d'exécution d'un programme** *ou* **temps de traitement** = run-time *ou* run-duration; **temps d'exécution d'une tâche** *ou* **temps passé à une tâche** = operating time *ou* elapsed time; **temps d'extinction d'un signal** = decay time; **temps de latence** = latency; **temps de mise en place** = positioning time; **temps de montée** *ou* **temps d'accélération** = rise time; **temps mort** = dead time *ou* down time *ou* idle time; **temps d'occupation de la ligne** = holding time; **temps d'ordinateur** = computer time; **tous ces rapports de vente coûtent cher en temps d'ordinateur** = running all those sales reports costs a lot in computer time; **temps de préparation** = make-ready time; **temps productif** *ou* **de bon fonctionnement** = up time *ou* uptime; **temps de réponse** = response time; **temps de report** = carry time; **temps d'utilisation de l'unité centrale** *ou* **du processeur** *ou* **temps CPU** = CPU time; **temps de traitement** = run-time *ou* run-duration **(c)** **temps réel** = real time; **un système de navigation doit pouvoir faire le point en temps réel et prendre les mesures nécessaires pour éviter de heurter un écueil** = a navigation system needs to be able to process the position of a ship in real time and take suitable action before she hits a rock; **entrée en temps réel** = real-time input; **exécution (d'un programme) en temps réel** = real-time execution; **horloge en temps réel** = real-time clock; **(traitement) multitâche en temps réel** = real-time multitasking; **simulation en temps réel** = real-time simulation; **système en temps réel** = real-time system; **traitement en temps réel** = real-time processing **(d) accès multiple par division dans le temps** = time division multiple access; **analyse du signal dans le temps** = time domain analysis; **base de temps; base de temps réduite** = fast time-scale; **créneau de temps** = time slot; **moyenne de temps de bon fonctionnement (entre les défaillances) (MTBF)** = mean time between failures (MTBF); **multiplexage par répartition dans le temps (MRT)** = time division multiplexing (TDM); **partage de temps** ou **(système) en temps partagé** = time-sharing; **signal de contrôle du temps écoulé** = time address code; **tranche de temps** = time slice; **visualisation en temps différé** = time shift viewing; **voie dérivée en temps** = time derived channel

tension *nf* voltage; **veillez à ce que la tension de crête ne dépasse pas 60 watts sinon l'amplificateur surchauffera** = keep the peak power below 60 watts or the amplifier will overheat; **chute** ou **baisse de tension** = voltage dip ou dip in voltage ou power loss; **'hors tension'** = 'power off' ou 'off'; *(éteindre)* **mettre hors tension** = to power off ou to power down ou to turn off; **lorsque vous avez quitté le programme, vous pouvez mettre le serveur hors tension** = once you have shut down the software, you can power off the server; **mise hors tension automatique** = automatic power off; **niveau de tension d'une pile** = battery voltage level; **pointe de tension** = voltage transient; **régulateur de tension** = voltage regulator; **'sous tension'** = 'power on' ou 'on'; **cadre sous tension** = hot frame; **chassis sous tension** = hot chassis; *(un appareil)* **mettre sous tension** = to power up ou to switch on ou to turn on; **ré-initialisation automatique à la mise sous tension** = power-on reset

cette fonction permet de mesurer la chute de tension d'une fonction de semi-conducteur traversée par une intensité d'environ un milliampère
Electronique pratique

téra- *préfixe (10¹²)* tera- (T)

◊ **térahertz** *nm* terahertz

◊ **téraoctet** *nm* terabyte

terminaison *nf* termination

terminal *nm* station ou terminal; **terminal à adressage protégé** = addressable terminal; **tous les messages sont transmis à tous les terminaux puisqu'aucun d'eux ne possède un adressage protégé** = all the messages go to all the terminals since none are addressable terminals; **terminal d'application** ou **terminal spécialisé** = job orientated terminal; **terminal asservi** = slave terminal; **terminal de CAO** = graphics terminal; **terminal central** = central terminal; **terminal conversationnel** = interactive terminal ou conversational terminal; **terminal dédié** ou **spécialisé** = dedicated computer ou applications

terminal; **terminal directeur** = executive terminal; **terminal à distance** ou **éloigné** = remote terminal; **terminal d'entrée (de données)** = input ou i/p terminal; **terminal entrée/sortie** = input/output terminal ou keyboard send/receive (KSR); **terminal graphique** ou **avec écran (à affichage) graphique** = graphics terminal; **terminal informatique** = data terminal; **terminal intelligent** = intelligent terminal; **le nouveau terminal intelligent comporte un éditeur de texte** = the new intelligent terminal has a built-in text editor; **terminal non intelligent** = dumb terminal; **terminal interactif** = interactive terminal; **terminal maître** = master terminal; **terminal de mise à jour rapide** = bulk update terminal; **terminal d'ordinateur** = data terminal equipment (DTE); **terminal de point de vente** = point-of-sale terminal ou POS terminal; **terminal principal** = key terminal ou central terminal ou master terminal; **le gestionnaire de système utilise le terminal principal pour relancer le système** = the system manager uses the master terminal to restart the system; **terminal public** = public access terminal; **terminal récepteur (de données)** = data sink; **terminal de réception** = receive only terminal; **l'imprimante est un terminal de sortie d'ordinateur** = a printer is a data terminal for computer output; **terminal de transfert électronique de fonds** = electronic funds transfer point of sale (EFTPOS); **terminal vidéo** = video terminal; **terminal virtuel** = virtual terminal; **barrette de connexion du terminal** = terminal strip; **contrôleur de terminal** = terminal controller; **émulation de terminal** = terminal emulation; **(code d') identification d'un terminal** = terminal identity; **interface de** ou **pour terminal** = terminal interface; **le contrôleur de réseau possède 16 interfaces pour terminaux** = the network controller has 16 terminal interfaces; **police de caractères utilisable par un terminal** = terminal character set; **session** ou **temps de connexion d'un terminal** = terminal session; **système à plusieurs terminaux** = multi-terminal system

terminateur *nm (résistance)* **terminateur de réseau** = terminator; LAN resistor; **terminateur SCSI** = terminator; SCSI resistor

terminé, -ée *adj* complete ou finished ou closed

◊ **terminer** *vtr* to complete ou to close ou to finish ou to terminate; **la vérification orthographique est terminée** = the spelling check is complete; **une fois la saisie du texte terminée, servez-vous du correcteur orthographique pour corriger les fautes** = when you have completed the keyboarding, pass the text through the spelling checker; **elle a terminé la saisie avant le déjeuner** = she finished all the keyboarding before lunch; **la programmation ne sera pas terminée avant la semaine prochaine** = the programming will not be ready until next week; **terminer une session** = to log off ou log out

◊ **se terminer** *vpr* to finish ou to end

ternaire *adj* ternary

terre *nf* earth; **fil de terre** = earth (wire); **mettre à la terre** = to earth, *US* to ground; **tous les appareils doivent être mis à la terre** = all appliances must be earthed; **tous les fils non rattachés doivent être mis à la terre** = all loose wires should be tied to earth; **perte de terre** = ground absorption; **prise de terre** = earth, *US* ground

◊ **terrestre** *adj* **liaison** *ou* **ligne terrestre** = landline; **station terrestre** = earth station; **station terrestre mobile** = mobile earth terminal; *(de transmission par satellite)* **zone terrestre de couverture** = earth coverage

tertiaire *adj (voies de transmission)* **groupe tertiaire** = mastergroup

test *nm* test *ou* trial *ou* check; **faire un test** = to test; **l'ingénieur possède un équipement spécialisé pour effectuer les tests sur ce modèle** = the engineer has special test equipment for this model; **test à chaud** = burn-in; **test assisté par ordinateur (TAO)** = computer-aided *ou* assisted testing (CAT); **tests de contrôle de liens** = link trials; **test de diagnostic** = diagnostic test; **test d'évaluation des performances** = test run; **benchmark(ing)**; **test de la fumée** = smoke test; **test opérationnel** = operation trial; **test de polarité** = polarity test; **tests de saturation** = saturation testing; **test sélectif** = leapfrog test; **test sélectif limité** *ou* **restreint** = crippled leapfrog test; **test de Turing** = Turing test; **équipement pour tests** = test equipment; **programme de test** = exerciser

◊ **tester** *vtr* to test *ou* to check; **tester en continu sur une longue période** = to soak; **l'appareil a été testé sous tous les angles avant la livraison** = the device was soak-tested prior to delivery; **tester un système** = to test a system

◊ **testeur** *nm (de logiciel et de machine)* test equipment; *(de dispositif)* exerciser

tête *nf* **(a)** *(partie supérieure)* head; *(commencement)* **tête de chapitre** = chapter heading; **les têtes de chapitres sont en caractères gras de 12 points** = chapter headings are in 12 point bold; *(de papier listing)* **tête d'une page** = head of form (HOF); *(marge supérieure)* **blanc de tête** = top margin *ou* top space **(b)** *(de film ou de bande)* **tête de bobine** = head (of reel); *(titre, etc.)* **enregistrement de tête** = leader record; *(de données en mémoire)* **zéro de tête** = leading zero **(c)** *(de connection)* **tête de réseau** = head end **(d)** **être à la tête de** *ou* **être en tête de** = to head (something); **c'est lui qui est maintenant à la tête du groupe de diffusion de logiciels** = he took over the direction of a software distribution group; **mon fichier était en tête de la file d'attente** = the queue was headed by my file **(e)** *(dispositif de lecture)* head; **tête d'écriture** *ou* **d'enregistrement** = write head *ou* record head; **tête d'effacement** = erase head; **tête flottante** = floating head *ou* flying head; **tête d'impression** = printhead; **la tête d'impression peut imprimer plus de 400 millions de caractères** = the printhead has a print life of over 400 million characters; **tête de lecture** = playback head *ou* read head *ou* sound head; *(de bandes magnétiques)* tape head *ou* tape playback head; *(de disque ou disquettes)* disk head *ou* disk playback head; **tête de lecture/écriture** = combined head *ou* read/write head; *(lecteur à)* **tête de lecture fixe** = fixed head (disk drive); **crash causé par la tête de lecture** = head crash; **tête magnétique** = magnetic head; **l'alignement des têtes va peut être demandé un**

réglage différent lorsqu'il s'agit de bandes enregistrées sur d'autres machines = azimuth alignment might not be correct for tape recorded on a different machine; **réglage d'alignement des têtes** = azimuth alignment; **démagnétiseur de tête** = head demagnetizer; **durée de vie de la tête** = headlife; **mise en position de transport de la tête** = head park

tétra- *préfixe* quadr-

◊ **tétraphonique** *adj* quadrophonic

texte *nm* text *ou* copy; **les éditeurs ont généreusement annoté le texte avant le renvoi des épreuves pour correction** = the editors made many textual changes before the proofs were sent back for correction; **texte en clair** *ou* **non chiffré** = plaintext; **texte dactylographié** = typescript; **texte définitif** = fair copy *ou* final copy; **texte imprimé** = hard copy; **texte non justifié (à droite)** = ragged text; **texte au kilomètre avec changement de page automatique** = automatic text flow across pages; **texte d'un message** = message text; **texte publicitaire** = publicity copy; **le texte publicitaire doit nous arriver mardi, dernier délai** = Tuesday is the last date for copy for the advertisement; **texte sans erreur** *ou* **sans modification** = clean copy; **affichage de texte** = character display; **zone d'affichage de texte** *ou* **écran texte** = text screen; *(pour une fonte donnée)* **calibrage d'un texte** = cast off *ou* casting off; **faire le calibrage d'un texte** = to cast off; **compression de texte** = text compression; **convertisseur texte/signal vocal** = text-to-speech converter; **(code de) début de texte** = start of text (SOT *ou* STX); **écran texte** = text screen; **éditer** *ou* **traiter un texte sur ordinateur** = to word-process; **éditeur de texte** *ou* **programme d'édition de texte** = text editor; **cet éditeur de texte ne peut lire que les fichiers de moins de 64Ko** = the text editor will only read files smaller than 64Kbytes long; **fenêtre de texte** = text window; **fichier texte** = text file; **(code de) fin de texte** = end of text (EOT *ou* ETX); **logiciel** *ou* **programme de formatage de texte** = text formatter; **on utilise le formatage de texte comme programme de base de PAO** = people use the text formatter as a basic desk-top publishing program; **gestion de texte** = text management; **gestionnaire de texte** = text manager; **manipulation de texte** = text manipulation; **recherche (et extraction) de texte** = text retrieval; **registre de texte** = text register; **traitement de texte** = word-processing (WP) *ou* text processing *ou* document processing; **appareil de traitement de texte spécialisé** = dedicated word processor; **bureau de traitement de texte** = word-processing bureau; **centre de traitement de texte** = editorial processing centre; **fonction (de) traitement de texte** = text-editing function; **une fonction traitement de texte est intégrée au programme** = the program includes a built-in text-editing function; **logiciel** *ou* **programme de traitement de texte** = word-processing program; **chargez le programme de traitement de texte avant de commencer à saisir le texte** = load the word-processing program before you start keyboarding; **machine de traitement de texte** = word-processor; **système de traitement de texte** = word processing system

◊ **textuel, -elle** *adj* textual

théorie *nf* theory; **théorie des ensembles** = set theory; **théorie de l'information** = information theory

◊ **théorique** *adj* theoretical; **débit théorique** = rated throughput; **formation théorique** = hands off training

thermique *adj* thermal; **bruit thermique** = thermal noise; **dissipateur thermique** = heat sink; **impression thermique** = electrosensitive printing; **imprimante thermique** = thermal *ou* electrothermal printer; **imprimante thermique à étincelle** = spark printer; **imprimante à jet d'encre thermique** = thermal inkjet printer; **papier thermique** = heat sensitive paper *ou* thermal paper; **transfert thermique** = thermal transfer; **imprimante à sublimation thermique** = thermal transfer *ou* thermal wax *ou* thermal wax transfer printer; **les techniques du jet d'encre et du transfert thermique se font concurrence** = colour ink-jet technology and thermal transfer technology compete with each other; **la technologie de transfert par sublimation thermique produit encore les meilleures représentations de couleurs sur papier pour les sorties sur PC** = thermal wax transfer technology still provides the best colour representation on paper for PC output; **papier à transfert thermique** = electrosensitive paper

thermistor *nm* thermistor

thermosensible *adj* thermo-sensitive

thésaurus *nm* thesaurus

thiosulfate *nm* *(pour fixage en photographie)* **thiosulfate de sodium** = sodium thiosulfate; *(familier)* hypo

thyristor *nm* thyristor

tierce *nf* *(imprimerie: troisième épreuve)* page proof

tiers *nm* **(a)** *(fraction)* **un tiers** = one third **(b)** third party

TIFF *(format de fichier graphique)* Tag Image File Format (TIFF)

tilde *nm* *(accent)* tilde

tirage *nm* **(a)** *(imprimerie)* impression *ou* print *ou* printrun; **tirage d'épreuves** = proofing; **tirage réduit** *ou* **limité** = short-run; **un imprimeur qui se spécialise dans les petits tirages** = a printer specializing in short-run printing; **tirage à la suite** = run-on; **faire un tirage à la suite** = to run on; **nous avons décidé de faire un tirage à la suite de 3000 exemplaires** = we decided to run on 3,000 copies to the first printing; **prix du tirage à la suite** = run-on price **(b)** circulation; **quel est le tirage de cette revue d'informatique?** *ou* **à combien d'exemplaires tire cette revue d'informatique?** = what is the circulation of this computer magazine?; **les journaux à gros tirage** = the national press

◊ **tiré** *nm* tiré à part = offprint

◊ **tirer** *vtr* **(a)** to drag; *(sous GUI)* **tirer une poignée** = to drag a handle **(b)** *(imprimerie)* **tirer**

les épreuves (d'un texte) = to proof *ou* to print; **un journal spécialisé qui tire à plus de 10 000 exemplaires** = a specialized magazine with a circulation of over 10,000; **tirer à la suite** = to run on

tiret *nm* dash; *(dont la longueur équivaut à un 'm')* em dash *ou* em rule; *(dont la longueur équivaut à un 'n')* **tiret court** *ou* **tiret de césure** = en dash *ou* en rule

tissu *nm* *(pour machine à écrire)* **ruban (en) tissu** = fibre ribbon

titre *nm* **(a)** title; **c'est la dernière image du film, faites apparaître les titres** = this is the last frame of the film so pop on the titles; **titre d'une disquette** = title of disk **(b)** *(d'un livre)* title; **faux-titre** = half title; **page de titre** = title page **(c)** *(d'une page ou d'un chapitre)* heading; **titre courant** = running heading *ou* headline; *(d'un journal)* **gros titres à la une** = banner headlines **(d)** *(livres d'une bibliothèque)* **nouveaux titres** = accessions

titulaire *nm* owner; **titulaire d'un droit d'auteur** *ou* **d'un copyright** = copyright owner

Token Ring *(réseau)* Token Ring network; **les réseaux Token Ring sont très démocratiques et conservent leurs performances en cas d'accroissement de la charge** = Token Ring networks are very democratic and retain performance against increasing load

tolérance *nf* tolerance *ou* robustness; **tolérance au bruit** = noise immunity; **limite de tolérance au bruit** = noise margin; **tolérance aux interférences** = interference immunity; **tolérance de panne** = fault tolerance; **(système) à tolérance de panne** = fault-tolerant (system); **ils ont commercialisé, avec beaucoup de succès, une gamme de minis à tolérance de panne** = they market a highly successful range of fault-tolerant minis

tombée *nf* off-cut

◊ **tomber** *vi* **l'ordinateur est tombé en panne deux fois cet après-midi** = the computer system went down twice during the afternoon

tomo- *préfixe* tomo-

◊ **tomodensitométrie** *nf* Computerized Axial Tomography (CAT)

◊ **tomographie** *nf* tomography

◊ **tomographique** *adj* **image tomographique** = tomogram

ton *nm* **(a)** *(son)* tone **(b)** *(couleur)* tone *ou* shade

◊ **tonal, -e** *adj* *(de son)* **numérotation sur clavier tonal** = tone dialling; **enveloppe tonale** = pitch envelope; **signalisation tonale** = tone signalling

◊ **tonalité** *nf* tone; **tonalité d'appel** = dial tone *ou* dialling tone; **tonalité 'occupé'** = line busy tone *ou* engaged tone

◊ **toner** *nm* *(pour photocopieur, imprimante laser, etc.)* toner; **si vous vous êtes mis du toner sur les mains, il faut absolument les laver à l'eau froide**

= if you get toner on your hands, you can only wash it off with cold water; **cartouche de toner** = toner cartridge

Toolbox ™ *(boîte à outils Macintosh)* Toolbox ™

topage *nm (de signal vidéo)* pix lock

topologie *nf* topology; **topologie en anneau** = ring topology; **Token Ring utilise une typologie en anneau** = Token Ring uses a ring topology; **topologie en bus** = bus topology; **Ethernet est un réseau qui utilise une topologie en bus** = Ethernet is a network that uses the bus topology; **topologie en étoile** = star topology; **si le câble d'une station est défaillant dans une topologie en étoile, les autres stations continuent à travailler, ce qui n'est pas le cas dans une topologie en bus** = if one workstation cable snaps in a star topology, the rest continue, unlike a bus topology; **topologie d'une base de données** = database mapping; **topologie de réseau** = network topology

TOPS ™ *(logiciel de communication entre IBM PCs et ordinateurs Macintosh)* TOPS ™

tore *nf* **tore magnétique** = magnetic core

torsadé, -ée *adj* twisted; **câble en paire(s) torsadée(s)** = twisted-pair cable; **câble en paire(s) torsadée(s) blindé** *ou* **avec blindage** = shielded twisted pair (STP) cable; **câble en paire torsadée non blindé** *ou* **sans blindage** = unshielded twisted pair (UTP) cable

tortue *nf* turtle; **graphisme généré avec une tortue** = turtle graphics; **la présentation graphique a été préparée à l'aide d'une tortue** = the charts were prepared using turtle graphics

total *nm* total; **le total des caractères saisis est de dix millions** = the total keyboarded characters amount to ten million; **en ajoutant l'appendice, nous ferons 256 pages au total** = by adding the appendix, we will increase the page extent to 256; **total de contrôle** = control total *ou* checksum *ou* check total; **les données sont sûrement corrompues si le total de contrôle est faux** = the data must be corrupted if the checksum is different; **total par groupe** *ou* **par lot** = batch total; **total de vérification** = checksum *ou* check total *ou* control total; **total de vérification pour hash code** = hash total

◊ **total, -e** *adj* total; global; **arrêt total** = dead halt *ou* drop dead halt; **le manuel n'explique pas la marche à suivre en cas d'arrêt total de la machine** = the manual does not say what to do if a dead halt occurs; **nombre total de pages (d'un document)** = extent (of a document)

◊ **totalement** *adv* totally *ou* fully; **réseau totalement maillé** = fully connected network

◊ **totalisation** *nf* adding up *ou* addition (to make a total); **contrôle par totalisation** = summation check

touche *nf (d'un clavier)* key; *(d'un téléphone)* pushbutton; **le clavier comporte 84 touches** = there are 84 keys on the keyboard; **touche alphanumérique** = alphanumeric key; **touche des capitales** = shift key; *(de verrouillage)* caps lock; **le témoin s'allume quand la touche (des) capitales est verrouillée** = the LED lights up when caps lock is pressed; **touche de caractère** = character key; **touches qui ne produisent pas de caractères** = dead keys; **touche (du) chariot** = carriage return (CR); **touche (de) contraste** = contrast key *ou* button; **touche de contrôle** = control (key) *ou* CTRL; **touches de contrôle du curseur** *ou* **touches fléchées** = cursor control keys *ou* arrow keys; cursor pad; **touche d'échappement** *ou* **touche ESC** = escape key *ou* ESC; **appuyez sur la touche ECHAPPEMENT pour arrêter le programme** = to end the program, press ESCAPE; **touche d'édition** = edit key; **il y a plusieurs touches d'édition - celle-ci permet de reformater le texte** = there are several special edit keys - this one will re-format the text; **touche d'enregistrement** = record button; **touches fléchées** = cursor control keys *ou* arrow keys; cursor pad; **touche de fonction** = function key; **en appuyant sur la touche de fonction F5 on se met en mode entrée** = hitting F5 will put you into insert mode; **on peut allouer des étiquettes aux touches de fonction** = tags can be allocated to function keys; **touche de fonction programmable** = programmable function key; **touche d'intervention** = attention key; **touche des majuscules** = shift key; *(de verrouillage)* caps lock; **touches programmables** = soft keys; programmable keys; **touche répétition** = repeat key; **touche de retour arrière (du curseur)** = backspace key; **pour corriger une erreur de saisie de texte, utilisez la touche de retour arrière** = if you make a mistake entering data, use the backspace key to correct it; **touche de retour du chariot** = carriage return key *ou* carriage return (CR); **les opérateurs de saisie trouvent que la touche de retour est mal placée** = the carriage return key is badly placed for touch-typists; **touche de tabulation décimale** = decimal tab key; **touche de validation d'entrée** = enter key; **touche de verrouillage des majuscules** = caps lock; **touche 'page précédente'** = 'PgUp' key *ou* 'page up' key; **touche 'page suivante'** = 'PgDn' key *ou* 'page down' key; **touche secondaire** = alternate key; **action sur deux touches en même temps** = chord keying; **actionner une touche** = to key; **pression nécessaire pour actionner une touche** = key force; **(logiciel) activé par une seule touche** = single key response; **clic témoin (de fonctionnement) de touche** = key click; **code numérique d'une touche** = key number; **contrôle des touches** = keystroke verification; **contrôle (par balayage)** *ou* **reconnaissance d'utilisation de touches** = keyboard scan; **course d'une touche** = key travel; **encodeur des touches** = keyboard encoder; **implantation** *ou* **disposition des touches d'un clavier** = keyboard layout; **jeu vertical d'une touche** = key travel; **matrice des touches sur un clavier** = key matrix; **mémento de fonction des touches** = key overlay; **rebond d'une touche de clavier** = keyboard contact bounce

◊ **toucher** *vtr* to touch

tour *nm* **(a)** turn; *(utilisation d'un appareil)* **à tour de rôle** = round robin; **tour à tour** = alternately **(b)** *(d'enroulement)* loop

tournage *nm* filming *ou* shooting; **tournage d'une scène** = action shot; **le tournage commencera la semaine prochaine s'il fait beau** = filming will start next week if the weather is fine

◊ **tourner** *vi* **(a)** to spin *ou* to roll; *(autour d'un axe)* to rotate; **le lecteur faisait tourner la disquette** = the disk was spun by the drive; **le moteur du lecteur de disquettes tourne à vitesse constante** = the disk drive motor spins at a constant velocity **(b)** *(un film)* to film *ou* to shoot a film; **ils tournaient un programme sur les animaux sauvages** = they were filming a wild life programme; **les extérieurs pour ce programme ont été tournés en Espagne** = the programme was shot on location in Spain

traçage *nm* **(a)** outlining *ou* drawing; **gabarit de traçage** = template; **pochoir de traçage** = stencil **(b)** *(d'un programme ou d'un procédé)* **traçage de panne** = fault trace; **point de contrôle (du registre) dans un programme de traçage** = trace trap; **programme de traçage** = trace program; **protocole de traçage** = audit trail

◊ **traçant, -e** *adj* **table traçante** = flatbed plotter; pen plotter

◊ **tracé** *nm* line *ou* design; *(courbe)* plot; **tracé d'un circuit** = circuit design

◊ **tracer** *vtr* **tracer une courbe** *ou* **un graphe (par points numérisés)** = to plot a curve

◊ **traceur** *nm* printer plotter *ou* plotter; **traceur de courbes** *ou* **de graphiques** = X-Y plotter *ou* graph plotter; **pilote de traceur de courbes** = plotter driver; **traceur incrémentiel** *ou* **à incrémentation** = incremental plotter; **traceur numérique** = digital plotter; **traceur à plat** = flatbed plotter; **traceur à plumes** = pen plotter; **plume de traceur** = plotter pen; **traceur à tambour** = drum plotter

traducteur *nm* **(a)** *(personne)* translator **(b)** *(programme)* **traducteur de langage** = language translator *ou* translator program

◊ **traduction** *nf* **(a)** *(en langue étrangère)* translation; **traduction assistée par ordinateur** = machine translation **(b)** *(informatique)* **traduction de données** = data translation; **traduction d'un langage (informatique)** = language translation; **programme de traduction** = translator (program)

◊ **traduire** *vtr* **(a)** *(en langue étrangère)* to translate **(b)** *(langage informatique)* to translate; *(à l'exécution)* to interpret

trafic *nm* *(sur une ligne)* traffic; **notre réseau Ethernet commence à ralentir lorsque le trafic atteint 60 pour cent de la bande passante** = our Ethernet network begins to slow down if the traffic reaches 60 per cent of the bandwidth; **trafic d'entrée** *ou* **d'arrivée** = incoming traffic; **trafic d'une ligne** = line load; **analyse du trafic** = traffic analysis; **densité du trafic** = traffic density

train *nm* train *ou* stream; **train de bits** = bit stream; **train d'impulsions** = pulse stream

traînage *nm* *(distorsion d'image)* streaking

◊ **traînée** *nf* **traînée d'image** = hangover *ou* extra

◊ **traîner** *vtr* to drag; **traînez l'icône du document sur l'icône du traitement de texte, puis lâchez la touche, le système démarrera le programme et chargera le document** = drag and drop the document icon onto the word-processor icon and the system will start the program and load the document

◊ **traîner/lâcher** *vtr* to drag and drop

trait *nm* **(a)** bar *ou* line; *(sous un mot ou une ligne de texte)* underline *ou* underscore; **trait oblique** = slash *ou* oblique stroke; **dessin au trait** = line drawing **(b)** **trait d'union** = hyphen *ou* dash; **mot qui s'écrit avec un trait d'union** = hyphenated word; **le mot 'porte-clés' s'écrit toujours avec un trait d'union** = the word 'porte-clés' is always hyphenated; **trait d'union obligatoire** = hard hyphen

traité, -ée *adj* processed; **données non traitées** = raw data

◊ **traitement** *nm* process *ou* processing; **effectuer un traitement** = to process (data, etc.); **traitement d'arrière-plan** *ou* **traitement de fond** = background processing; **traitement de bases de données** = database processing; **machine dédiée au traitement de bases de données** = database machine; **traitement de contrôle de bloc à l'entrée** = block input processing; **traitement (en) différé** *ou* **hors ligne** *ou* **off-line** = off-line processing; **traitement de données** = data processing (DP *ou* dp) *ou* information processing; **le traitement des données sera assez long** = processing all the information will take a long time; **traitement de données sur demande** *ou* **immédiat** = demand processing; **traitement aléatoire** *ou* **direct des données** = random processing; **traitement automatique de données** = automatic data processing (ADP); **traitement centralisé des données** *ou* **de l'information** = centralized data processing; **traitement décentralisé des données** = decentralized data processing; **traitement électronique de données** = electronic data processing (EDP); **capacité de traitement électronique de données** = electronic data processing capability *ou* EDP capability; **système de traitement de données intégré** = integrated data processing (IDP); **vitesse de traitement de données** = data rate; **(procédure de) traitement des erreurs** = error handling *ou* management; **traitement de fichier** = file processing; **traitement instantané d'un film** = in camera process; **traitement frontal** = foreground processing *ou* foregrounding; **traitement de l'image** = image processing *ou* picture processing; **traitement informatique de l'image** = computer image processing; **caméra de traitement de l'image** = process camera; **système de traitement de l'image** = image processor; **traitement immédiat** *ou* **sur demande** = immediate processing *ou* demand processing; **traitement de l'information** = data processing (DP *ou* dp) *ou* information processing; **traitement en ligne** *ou* **on-line** = on-line processing; **traitement hors ligne** *ou* **off-line** = off-line processing; **traitement linéaire** = in-line processing; **traitement de liste** = list processing; **traitement par lots** *ou* **par paquets** = batch processing; **mode de traitement par paquets** = (processing data in) batch mode; **partition** *ou* zone de traitement par lots = batch region; processeur de traitement par lots *ou* par paquets = batch processor; système de traitement par lots *ou* par paquets = batch system; traitement multitâche en temps réel = real-time multi-tasking; traitement non prioritaire = background processing; traitement de requête = query processing; traitement en série = serial processing; traitement de tâche = job processing; traitement en temps réel = real-time processing; traitement de texte = *(logiciel)* word-processor *ou* text-processor; *(action)* word-processing (WP) *ou* text-processing; le temps d'ordinateur requis pour le traitement d'une page de texte varie en fonction de la complexité du document = page processing time depends on the complexity of a given page; machine de traitement de texte = word-processor *ou* text-processor; machine de traitement de texte spécialisé = dedicated word-processor; bureau de traitement de texte = word-processing bureau; centre de traitement de texte = editorial processing centre; fonction (de) traitement de texte = text-editing function; une fonction traitement de texte est intégrée au programme = the program includes a built-in text-editing function; logiciel de traitement de texte = word-processing program *ou* word-processing software *ou* word-processor; machine de traitement de texte = word-processor; programme de traitement de texte = word-processing program; chargez le programme de traitement de texte avant de commencer à taper au clavier = load the word-processing program before you start keyboarding; (programme) limité par le traitement *ou* avec contrainte de traitement = process-bound (program); système de traitement de texte = word-processing system

◊ traiter *vtr (des données, etc.)* to process (data, etc.); nous avons traité les nouvelles données = we processed the new data; traiter un texte sur ordinateur = to word-process a text; disque à traiter = milk disk

trajectoire *nf* trajectory; trajectoire elliptique = elliptical orbit

trajet *nm (de données)* data path

trame *nf* (a) *(télévision)* trame d'image = field; balayage (vertical) de trame = raster scanning; impulsion de contrôle du balayage de la trame = field sync pulse; fréquence de trame = field frequency; retour de trame = field flyback; intervalle de trame *ou* suppression verticale de la trame = field blanking (interval) (b) *(de transmission)* message slot; *(de réseau sous protocole FDDI)* trame d'initialisation = claim frame; *(protocole de communication)* échange de trames = frame relay (c) *(de données sur bande)* frame; erreur de trame = frame error; synchronisation de trame = framing

tranche *nf* (a) slice; tranche (de silicium) = silicon wafer; intégration sur tranche de silicium = wafer scale integration (b) architecture de (processeur) en tranches = bit-slice architecture; microprocesseur en tranches = bit-slice microprocessor; processeur en tranches = bit-slice processor; le processeur en tranches utilise quatre processeurs à 4 bits pour réaliser un processeur à 16

bits = the bit slice design uses four 4-bit word processors to construct a 16-bit processor (c) tranche de temps *ou* tranche horaire = time slice

transaction *nf* transaction; transaction de données = data transaction; enregistrement de transactions = transaction record; fichier de transactions = transaction file

◊ transactionnel, -elle *adj* système transactionnel = transaction-driven system (TDS); traitement transactionnel en ligne = on-line transaction processing

transcodeur *nm* transcoder; utilisez le transcodeur pour la conversion de PAL en SECAM = use the transcoder to convert PAL to SECAM

transcription *nf* transcription

◊ transcrire *vtr* to transcribe

transducteur *nm* transducer; un transducteur de pression transforme un signal physique de pression en signal électrique = a pressure transducer converts physical pressure signals into electrical signals

transférer *vtr* to transfer *ou* to output; *(d'un gros processeur à un plus petit)* to download; *(d'un petit ordinateur à un plus gros)* to upload; *(entre périphérique lent et processeur rapide)* to spool; *(vider sur disque)* to dump; *(sur imprimante)* to deposit; toutes les opérations de traitement ont été transférées sur l'ordinateur principal = all processing activities have been transferred to the mainframe; avec cette machine, on peut transférer des documents d'une machine à l'autre sans qu'il soit nécessaire de reformater = the machine allows document interchange between it and other machines without reformatting; l'utilisateur peut transférer les données d'un micro sur un gros ordinateur, pour mettre les applications à jour = the user can upload PC data to update mainframe applications; les résultats comptables ont été transférés sur le disque de sauvegarde = the account results were dumped to the backup disk; récupérer des données et les transférer dans un registre = to collect transfer

◊ transfert *nm* (a) *(de données)* transfer; *(échange)* interchange *ou* change-over; transfert d'un bloc *ou* d'un paragraphe = block transfer; transfert conditionnel = conditional transfer; transfert de contrôle à l'unité centrale = control transfer to the CPU; transfert direct = direct change-over *ou* direct transfer; *(des données en mémoire)* transfert sur disque *ou* sur support magnétique = dump; *(sur dispositif hors ligne)* transfert de données = data migration; transfert des données par accès direct (à la mémoire) entre la mémoire principale et le second processeur = direct memory access transfer between the main memory and the second processor; bus de transfert des données = data highway; transfert de fichier = file transfer; transfert de fichier bidirectionnel = bi-directional file transfer; transfert électronique de fonds = electronic funds transfer (system) (EFT); terminal de transfert électronique de fonds = electronic funds transfer point of sale (EFTPOS); transfert intercouche =

radial transfer; *(de signaux)* **mode de transfert par paquets** = burst mode; **transferts de page incontrôlés (entre la mémoire et le disque)** = thrashing; *(dans la mémoire)* **transfert d'un programme** = program relocation; **transfert radial** = radial transfer; *(de mots binaires)* **transfert en série** = word serial; **transfert d'un support magnétique à un autre** *ou* **transfert magnétique** = magnetic transfer; **transfert systématique** *ou* **automatique** = unconditional transfer; **dispositif de transfert** = diverter; **instruction de transfert** = transfer command; **temps de transfert** = transfer time; **protocole de validation de transfert (de données)** = handshake *ou* handshaking; **système à transfert de mémoire** = memory switching system; **vitesse de transfert** = transfer rate; **taux** *ou* **vitesse de transfert de données** = data transfer rate; **avec une bonne ligne téléphonique, cette paire de modems peut atteindre un taux de transfert de 14,4 Kbps** = with a good telephone line, this pair of modems can achieve a transfer rate of 14.4Kbps (b) *(téléphonique)* **transfert d'appel (automatique)** = call forwarding; **nous avons demandé le transfert à la maison des appels que nous recevons au bureau** = we are having all calls forwarded from the office to home; **dispositif de transfert d'appel** = call diverter (c) *(photogravure)* **film de transfert** = carbon tissue; **transfert (par sublimation) thermique** = thermal transfer; thermal wax transfer; **les techniques du jet d'encre et du transfert thermique se font concurrence** = colour ink-jet technology and thermal transfer technology compete with each other; **papier à transfert thermique** = thermal paper *ou* electrosensitive paper; *voir aussi* SUBLIMATION, THERMIQUE (d) **transfert photomécanique** = photomechanical transfer (PMT)

transformateur *nm* transformer; **transformateur de couplage** = matching transformer; **transformateur d'isolement** *ou* **de protection** = isolation transformer

transformation *nf* transformation; **transformation sérielle** = tweening; **en utilisant le procédé de transformation sérielle nous pouvons montrer une grenouille qui se transforme en princesse en cinq étapes** = using tweening, we can show how a frog turns into a princess in five steps; **régles de transformation** = transformational rules

◊ **transformer** *vtr* to transform

transfrontière *adj* **flux de données transfrontière** = transborder data flow

transgression *nf* infringement

transistor *nm* transistor; **transistor bipolaire** = bipolar transistor; **transistor à effet de champ (TEC)** = field effect transistor (FET); **transistor à jonction bipolaire** = bipolar junction transistor (BJT); **transistor à jonction pnp** *ou* **npn** = bipolar junction transistor (BJT); **transistor (de type) npn** = npn transistor; **transistor (de type) pnp** = pnp transistor; **transistor silicium** = silicon transistor; **transistor unipolaire** = unipolar transistor; **logique transistor résistance (LTR)** = transistor-resistor logic (TRL); **logique transistor transistor (LTT)** = transistor-transistor logic (TTL)

◊ **transistorisé, -ée** *adj* dispositif transistorisé = solid-state device; **laser transistorisé** = semiconductor laser; **mémoire transistorisée** = solid-state memory device

transit *nm* **de transit** = transient; **courant de transit** = line transient *ou* voltage transient

transitif *adj* **disque optique transitif** = transmissive disk

transition *nf* transition; **équipement** *ou* **interface** *ou* **logiciel de transition** = bridge *ou* bridging product *ou* bridgeware; **établir une transition** = to bridge; **point de transition** = transition point

transitoire *adj* *(d'un courant électrique)* **courant transitoire** = power transient; **limiteur** *ou* **éliminateur de courant transitoire** = transient suppressor

translatable *adj* *(relogeable)* relocatable; **programme translatable** = relocatable program; **ce système d'exploitation peut charger et exécuter un programme translatable sans distinction de la zone d'origine** = the operating system can load and run a relocatable program from any area of memory

◊ **translater** *vtr* to relocate

◊ **translation** *nf* *(d'adresse)* relocation; **translation dynamique** = dynamic relocation; **translation statique** = static relocation; **constante de translation** = relocation constant

transmetteur *nm* transmitter (TX)

◊ **transmetteur/répondeur** *nm* transponder

transmettre *vtr* (a) to transmit *ou* to carry *ou* to channel; **transmettre de nouveau** = to retransmit; **transmettre un signal** = to send a signal *ou* to signal; **toutes les données ont été transmises par fibres optiques** = the fibre optic link carried all the data; **les données ont été transmises à l'ordinateur par l'intermédiaire de la ligne téléphonique** = the computer received data via the telephone line; **les signaux nous ont été transmis par satellite** = the signals have reached us via satellite; **(signal d') invitation à transmettre** = go ahead (signal); **(signal de) prêt à transmettre** = clear to send (CTS) (signal); *(modem)* **prêt à transmettre/recevoir** = dataset ready (DSR) *ou* data terminal ready (DTR) (b) *(à un périphérique)* to output; **les documents qui sont prêts peuvent être transmis à l'imprimante laser** = finished documents can be output to the laser printer

◊ **transmis, -e** *adj* **erreur transmise** = inherited error

◊ **transmission** *nf* (a) *(des caractéristiques d'un objet ou d'une classe)* inheritance (b) transmission *ou* communications; **transmission asynchrone** = asynchronous transmission; *(téléphonique)* **transmission en aveugle** *ou* **sans décrochage** = blind dialling; **transmission en bande de base** *ou* **en modulation de tension** = baseband signalling; **transmission bidirectionnelle à l'alternat** = either-way operation; **transmission sans contrôle de retour** = free wheeling;

transmission de données = data transmission *ou* data communications; **transmission de données en parallèle** = parallel data transmission; **transmission de données subvocales** = data under voice (DUV) (transmission); **transmission de données vocales** = data in voice (DIV) (transmission); **arrêt de transmission de données** = data break; **canal de transmission de données** = data channel; **circuit de transmission de données** = data circuit; *(causée par un défaut du support magnétique)* **brève interruption de transmission de données** = data check; **lignes de transmission de données** = bus data lines; *(burst)* **mode de transmission de données par paquets** = burst mode; **protocole de contrôle de transmission** = transmission control protocol (TCP); **réseau de transmission de données** = data communications network; **service de transmission de données** = data services; **signaux de transmission de données** = data signals; **(mémoire) tampon de transmission de données** = (data) communications buffer; **vitesse de transmission de données** = data rate *ou* data signalling rate; **voie de transmission de données** = data path; **transmission électronique** = electronic traffic; **transmission de fac-similé** = fax transmission; **(technologie de la) transmission par fibre optique** = fibre optics; **transmission hertzienne** *ou* **par hyperfréquence** = microwave transmission; **transmission d'images** = picture transmission; **transmission de l'information** = data communications; **canal** *ou* **voie de transmission de l'information** = information transfer channel *ou* information bearer channel; **transmission multicible** = multicasting; **transmission neutre** = neutral transmission; **(système de) transmission numérique** = digital transmission (system); **transmission par onde porteuse** = carrier signalling; **transmission (en) parallèle** = parallel transmission; **transmission par satellite** = satellite transmission; **transmission (en) série** = serial transmission; **transmission d'octets en série** = byte serial transmission *ou* mode; **transmission de signaux sur la bande vocale** = in-band signalling; **transmission de signaux en binaire** = binary signalling; **transmission de signaux numériques** = digital signalling; **transmission directe de signaux** = DC signalling; **transmission simultanée** = simultaneous transmission; **transmission synchrone** = synchronous transmission; **transmission de télécopie** = fax transmission; **transmission unidirectionnelle** = simplex *ou* unidirectional transmission; **transmission vidéo** = video transmission; **déconcentrateur pour transmission vidéo** = video expander; **(code** *ou* **signal de) fin de la transmission** = end of transmission (EOT) (signal); **canal de transmission** = communications channel; **la capacité de transmission de cette liaison est excellente** = the information-carrying abilities of this link are very good; **centrale** *ou* **base de transmission** = base station; **contrôle de ligne de transmission** = communications link control; **ordinateur de contrôle des transmissions** = communications computer; **contrôleur de transmission** = communications control unit (CCU); **débit maximal de transmission** = maximum transmission rate; **erreur de transmission** = transmission error; **correction d'erreur en cours de transmission** = forward error correction; **fenêtre de transmission** = transmission window; **ligne de transmission** = communications link; **moyens** *ou* **supports de transmission** = transmission media; **perte de transmission** = link loss; **protocole de transmission** = link control procedure (LCP); **système avec facilité de transmission en différé** = store and forward system; **vitesse de transmission** = transmission rate; baud rate; **vitesse maximale de transmission** = maximum transmission rate; **adaptateur de vitesse de transmission** = baud rate generator; **la vitesse moyenne de transmission est de 64 000 bits par seconde en connexion parallèle et 19 200 bits par seconde en connexion série** = the average transmission is 64,000 bits per second (bps) through a parallel connection or 19,200 bps through a serial connection; **la vitesse de transmission du signal binaire était de 300 bits par seconde** = the baud rate of the binary signal was 300 bits per second; **voie** *ou* **canal de transmission** = transmission channel *ou* feeder

transmittance *nf* transmittance

transordinateur *nm* transputer

transparence *nf* **(a)** show-through; *(informatique)* transparency **(b)** *(de film)* **(procédé de) transparence** = back projection; **(procédé de) transparence non prioritaire** *ou* **d'arrière-plan** = background projection

◊ **transparent** *nm (pour rétroprojecteur)* transparency *ou* acetate; **les graphiques avaient été dessinés sur des transparents pour être montrés au rétroprojecteur** = the graphs were plotted on acetate, for use on an overhead projector

◊ **transparent, -e** *adj* **(a)** transparent; **le papier de mauvaise qualité est beaucoup trop transparent** = bad quality paper gives too much show-through **(b)** *(informatique)* **interruption transparente** = transparent interrupt; **pagination transparente** = transparent paging; **routage transparent** = transparent routing

transphaseur *nm* transphasor

transpondeur *nm* transponder

transport *nm* transport; **couche transport** = transport layer

◊ **transportable** *adj* transportable; portable; **programme transportable d'une machine à une autre** = portable program

◊ **transporter** *vtr* to carry *ou* to transport *ou* to convey

◊ **transporteur, -euse** *adj* **bande transporteuse** = conveyor belt

transposition *nf* transposition

Transputer ™ *nm* transputer

transversal, -e *adj* transverse; **balayage transversal** *ou* **lecture transversale** = transverse scan

trappe *nf* trap

travail *nm* **(a)** work; **bande (magnétique) de travail** = scratch tape; **charge de travail** = workload *ou* work load; **disque de travail** = work disk; **espace de travail** = workspace *ou* work area; **feuille de travail** = worksheet; **fichier de travail** = scratch file *ou* work file; **poste de travail** = workstation; operating console *ou* terminal; **poste de travail multifonction** = multifunction workstation; **poste de travail d'un opérateur** = operator's console; **le système comprend cinq postes de travail reliés en anneau** = the system includes five workstations linked together in a ring network; **station de travail** = workstation; **la mémoire d'archivage a une capacité de 1200 Mo pour sept stations de travail** = the archive storage has a total capacity of 1200 MB between seven workstations; **zone de travail** = *(en mémoire)* work area *ou* memory workspace **(b)** *(tâche)* job *ou* task; **contrôle de travaux groupés (en pile)** = stacked job control; **ensemble des travaux en cours d'exécution** = job mix; **fichier de travaux à exécuter** = job file; **file d'attente des travaux à exécuter** = task queue; **ordonnancement des travaux** = job scheduling

◊ **travailler** *vi* to work; **travailler à plein régime** *ou* **à plein rendement** = to work at full capacity

treillis *nm (pour transmission de données de plus de 9600 bits par seconde)* **codage treillis** = trellis coding

tréma *nm* dieresis; *(utilisé en allemand)* umlaut

tremblement *nm (de la lumière)* flicker; *(de l'image)* jitter

◊ **trembler** *vi (lumière)* to flicker

◊ **trembloter** *vi (image)* to jitter; **j'ai mal à la tête à force de regarder cet écran qui tremblote** = looking at this screen jitter is giving me a headache

trente-deux *adj num* thirty-two; **système (informatique) de 32 bits** = thirty-two bit system

tresse *nf (câble)* **tresse de mise à la masse** = fanning strip

tri *nm* sort; *(action)* sorting; **tri par arborescence** = tree selection sort; **tri bulle** = bubble sort; **effectuer un tri bulle** *ou* **un tri par permutation de bulles** = to bubble sort; **tri sur disque** = external sort; **tri par échange** = exchange selection; **tri enveloppe** = shell sort; **effectuer un tri enveloppe** *ou* **un tri bloc par bloc** = to shell sort; **tri de fichiers** = file sort; **(application de) tri et fusion** = merge sort; **tri en mémoire interne** = internal sort; **tri par permutation de paires** = bubble sort; **tri rapide** = quicksort; **tri sélectif** = selective sort; **tri sur support externe** = external sort; **champ de tri** = sort field; **clé de tri** = sortkey; **les commandes ont été triées par dates en donnant le champ date comme clé de tri** = the orders were sorted according to dates by assigning the date field as sortkey; **passage de tri** = sorting pass

entrez le nom du champ sur lequel doit porter le tri; définissez ensuite l'ordre du tri, croissant (A à Z) ou décroissant (Z à A). Validez la définition

L'Ordinateur Individuel

triade *nf* triad

triangle *nm* triangle; **(en delta) connection (en) triangle** = delta (connexion)

tributaire *adj* dependent; **(programme) non tributaire** = device-independent (software)

tridimensionnel, -elle *adj (à 3 dimensions)* three-dimensional *ou* 3D

trier *vtr* to order *ou* to sort; **trier sur une clé** = to order *ou* to sort using a sortkey; **non trié** = unsorted; **les commandes ont été triées sur le champ date** = the orders were sorted according to dates *ou* by assigning the date field as the sortkey; **liste triée en ordre (alphabétique, etc.)** = ordered list; **(instruction *ou* fonction de) trier/fusionner** = sort/merge (instruction *ou* function)

Troie *npr* **cheval de Troie** = Trojan Horse

trois *adj num & nm* three; **instruction à trois adresses** = three-address instruction; **à trois dimensions** = three-dimensional *ou* 3D; **circuit logique à trois états** = three state logic

◊ **troisième** *adj* third; **ordinateur de troisième génération** = third generation computer

troncature *nf* rounding *ou* truncation; **erreur de troncature** = truncation error *ou* rounding error

◊ **tronquer** *vtr* to truncate; **3,5678 tronqué à 3,56** = 3.5678 truncated to 3.56

trop *adv&n* too much; too many; **en trop** = redundant

troposphère *nf* troposphere

trou *nm* hole; *(sur un disque)* **trou laser** = ablation

trousse *nf (d'outils *ou* de nettoyage, etc.)* pack *ou* kit

trouvaille *nf* hit

◊ **trouver** *vtr* to find *ou* to detect *ou* to diagnose *ou* to locate; **il a fallu beaucoup de temps pour trouver la puce défectueuse** = it took a lot of time to find the faulty chip; **il est difficile de trouver la source du problème** = the detection of the cause of the fault is proving difficult; **on a trouvé au bout de quelques secondes à peine** = there was a hit after just a few seconds; **on trouve le nouveau progiciel dans presque tous les magasins** = you can find the new software package in any shop *ou* the availability of the latest software package is very good

◊ **se trouver** *vpr* to be located; **l'ordinateur se trouve dans l'édifice principal** = the computer is located in the main office building

TrueType™ *(fonte de caractères de base)* TrueType™ (outline font technology)

T.S.F. = TELEGRAPHIE SANS FIL **poste de T.S.F.** *ou* **une T.S.F.** = radio *ou* wireless

TSR *(programme résident)* Terminate and Stay Resident (TSR) program *ou* Terminate and Stay Resident software (TSR) *ou* RAM resident program

TTL = TRANSISTOR-TRANSISTOR LOGIC **compatible TTL** = TTL compatible; **logique TTL** = TTL logic *ou* transistor-transistor logic; **moniteur TTL** = TTL monitor; *voir aussi* TRANSISTOR

tube *nm* tube; **tube à rayons cathodiques** *ou* **tube cathodique** = cathode ray tube (CRT); *(pour télévision)* television tube; **tube ombré** = dark trace tube; **tube à vide** = vacuum tube *ou* valve

tulipe *nf* **imprimante à tulipe** = thimble printer

Turing *npr* **machine de Turing** *ou* **simulateur (de) Turing** = Turing machine; **test de Turing** = Turing test

tutoriel *nm* tutorial

tuyau *nm* conduit *ou* pipe

type *nm* **(a)** *nm* type; **type de données** = data type; *voir aussi* DONNÉE **(b)** **lettre type** = form letter *ou* standard letter

typographe *ou* **typo** *nm* typographer *ou* typesetter

◊ **typographie** *nf* typography; *(composition)* typesetting; **ce travail ne demande aucune expérience en typographie** = no typographical skills are required for this job

◊ **typographique** *adj* typographic *ou* typographical; **annotation typographique** = marking up; **une erreur typographique à la composition donne ce qu'on appelle une 'coquille'** = a typographical error made while typesetting is called a 'typo'; **point typographique (0.324 mm)** = point; **répertoire typographique** = character repertoire

Uu

UAL = UNITE ARITHMETIQUE ET LOGIQUE

UHF *(ultra-hautes fréquences)* Ultra High Frequency (UHF)

ultra *préfixe* ultra-

◊ **ultra-fin, -e** *adj (imprimerie)* **filet ultra-fin** = hairline rule

◊ **ultra-haut, -e** *adj (ondes décimétriques)* **ultra-haute fréquence** = ultra high frequency (UHF)

◊ **ultraportatif** *nm* hand-held (computer)

◊ **ultraportatif, -ive** *adj (petit ordinateur qui tient dans la main)* **appareil ultraportatif** = hand-held (computer)

◊ **ultra-rapide** *adj* high-speed; **un gestionnaire de base de données ultra-rapide permet la manipulation d'une très grande quantité de données** = a high-speed database management program allows the manipulation of very large amounts of data

◊ **ultrasensible** *ou* **ultra-sensible** *adj (film)* high-speed (film)

◊ **ultrason** *ou* **ultra-son** *nm* ultrasound

◊ **ultrasonique** *adj* ultrasonic

◊ **ultrasonore** *adj* ultrasonic

> les premières applications médicales des ultrasons à des fins thérapeutiques datant de 1941, il faut attendre 1945 pour que les applications à des fins diagnostiques apparaissent pour la première fois
>
> *Techniques hospitalières*

ultraviolet *ou* **ultra-violet** *nm* ultraviolet (light *ou* radiation); **mémoire morte programmable (PROM) effaçable par ultraviolet** = ultraviolet erasable PROM

◊ **ultraviolet, -ette** *ou* **ultra-violet, -ette** *adj* ultraviolet *ou* UV; **rayonnement ultraviolet** = ultraviolet radiation *ou* ultraviolet light *ou* UV light

UMB *(mémoire haute)* Upper Memory Block (UMB)

un *nm* one; **complément à 1** = one's complement; **le complément à 1 de 10011 est 01100** = the one's complement of 10011 is 01100

◊ **un, -e** *adj num* **une adresse plus une** = one-plus-one address; *(langage de programmation)* **un pour un** = one for one

undo *vtr (fonction qui annule une action)* (to) undo

uni- *préf* uni-

◊ **unidirectionnel, -elle** *adj* unidirectional; **antenne unidirectionnelle** = directional antenna; **microphone unidirectionnel** = unidirectional microphone; **transmission unidirectionnelle** = simplex *ou* single operation transmission

uniforme *adj* uniform; *(imprimerie)* **espacement uniforme** = monospacing

◊ **uniformiser** *verb* to make uniform; *(traitement de texte)* **uniformiser (en majuscules *ou* en minuscules)** = to normalize

union *nf* union; **fonction logique d'union** = join (function); **opération d'union** = disjunction *ou* either-or operation *ou* OR operation

◊ **trait d'union** *nm* hyphen; **trait d'union d'écran** = soft hyphen; **trait d'union obligatoire** = hard hyphen

unipolaire *adj* unipolar; **commutateur unipolaire** = single pole switch; **signal unipolaire** = unipolar signal; **transistor unipolaire** = unipolar transistor

unique *adj* (a) single *ou* unique; **adresse unique** = single *ou* unique address; **chaque octet de mémoire a une adresse unique** = each separate memory byte has its own unique address; **instruction à adresse unique** = one address instruction *ou* single address instruction; **code d'instruction à adresse unique** = single address code; **ordinateur à adresse unique** = one address computer; **bande latérale unique** = single sideband; **micro-ordinateur à carte unique** = single board microcomputer; **ordinateur à carte unique** = single board computer (SBC); **station à connexion unique *ou* à liaison unique** = single attachment station (SAS); **enregistrement unique** = unit record; **micro-ordinateur de contrôle à puce unique** = single chip microcontroller; **ordinateur à puce unique** = single chip computer; **code à usage unique** = one-time pad **(b)** **tarif unique** = flat rate

unitaire *adj (d'une rame de papier)* **poids unitaire** = basic weight

unité *nf* **(a)** *(appareil *ou* système)* unit; **unité centrale (de traitement)** = central processing unit (CPU) *ou* central processor; **bridé *ou* limité par l'unité centrale** = CPU bound; **éléments de l'unité centrale** = CPU elements; **(temps de) cycle de l'unité centrale** = CPU cycle; **temps d'utilisation de l'unité centrale** = CPU time; *(processeur en tranches)* **unité centrale de calcul** = central processing element (CPE); **unité de commande *ou* unité de contrôle de périphérique** = peripheral control unit (PCU); **unité de contrôle (de processus)** = control unit (CU); **unité de disque** = *(disque dur)* disk unit *ou* hard disk drive; *(lecteur* *de disquettes)* disk unit *ou* floppy disk drive; *(pour disquettes)* **unité de disque demi-hauteur** = half-height drive; **unité de disquette** = disk unit *ou* floppy disk drive; **unité d'extension d'une ligne** = line extender; *(d'appareils pour télévision)* **unité mobile** = mobile unit; **unité multinorme** *ou* **unité multistandard** = a multistandard unit; **unité de visualisation** *ou* **de visu** = visual display unit **(b)** *(le plus petit élément)* unit *ou* item; **unité d'appel** = calling unit; **unité arithmétique et logique** = arithmetic and logic unit (ALU); **unité d'information** = computer word; **dimension d'une unité d'information** = item size; **une unité d'information peut être soit un mot, une série de chiffres ou une entrée dans un fichier** = a data item can be a word or a series of figures or a record in a file; **unité physique** = physical record; **unité de puissance vocale** = voice unit; **système évalué en cycles possibles par unité de temps** = duty-rated system

universel, -elle *adj* universal; **bus universel GPIB** *ou* **bus d'interface universel** = general purpose interface bus (GPIB); **canal universel de transmission par blocs** = universal block channel (UBC); **dispositif universel** = universal device (UART, USRT, USART); **émetteur/récepteur asynchrone universel** = universal asynchronous receiver/transmitter (UART); **contrôleur d'émetteur/récepteur asynchrone universel** = UART controller; **émetteur/récepteur synchrone asynchrone universel** = universal synchronous asynchronous receiver/transmitter (USART); **émetteur/récepteur synchrone universel** = universal synchronous receiver/transmitter (USRT); **interface universelle** = standard interface; **interface universelle GPIA** = general purpose interface adapter (GPIA); **langage universel** = machine-independent language; **programmation e.1 langage universel** = universal programming

UNIX™ *(système d'exploitation mis au point par AT&T Bell Laboratories)* UNIX (operating system)

◊ **UNIX (BSD)** *(version de système UNIX qui vient de l'Université de Californie, Berkeley)* Berkeley UNIX (BSD)

unmount *vtr (instruction qui indique que le disque n'est pas utilisable)* **instruction 'unmount'** = (to) unmount

urbain , -e *adj* **communication (téléphonique) urbaine** = local call

urgence *nf* emergency; **plan d'urgence** = contingency plan

usage *nm* use; **faire usage de quelque chose** = to make use of something; **terminal à usage professionnel** = executive terminal

usinage *nm* machining

◊ **usine** *nf* factory; **ils ont ouvert une nouvelle usine de composants électroniques** = they have opened a new components factory; **usine de construction d'ordinateurs** = computer factory

utile *adj* **(a)** helpful *ou* useful; **document utile se rapportant à un logiciel** = software documentation; **il trouve la machine de traitement de texte très utile pour le travail de bureau** = he finds his word-processor a great help in the office **(b)** *(efficace)* **ouverture utile** = effective aperture

utilisable *adj* usable; **maximum de fréquence utilisable** = maximum usable frequency; **cet ordinateur individuel possède 512K de mémoire utilisable** = the PC has 512K of usable memory

utilisateur, -trice *n* **(a)** user *ou* end user; **la société cherche à créer un ordinateur adapté aux besoins de l'utilisateur** = the company is creating a computer with a specific end user in mind; **utilisateur avancé** *ou* **ayant besoin d'une configuration puissante** = power user; **utilisateur intermédiaire** = mid-user; **code personnel** *ou* **mot de passe d'un utilisateur** = user ID; **compte (d') utilisateur** = user account; **j'ai un nouveau compte d'utilisateur sur ce réseau, mais j'ai oublié mon mot de passe** = I have a new user account on this LAN but I cannot remember my password; **groupe d'utilisateurs** = user group; **j'ai trouvé la solution au problème en me renseignant auprès des autres utilisateurs rencontrés à la réunion des membres du groupe** = I found how to solve the problem by asking people at the user group meeting; **groupe fermé d'utilisateurs** = closed user group (CUG); **langage (d') utilisateur** = user language *ou* user-operated language; **interface utilisateur/machine** = man/machine interface (MMI); **nom d'utilisateur** = user name; **nombre maximum d'utilisateurs** = maximum users; **notice d'utilisation destinée à l'utilisateur** = user documentation; **programmable** *ou* **modifiable** *ou* **réglable par l'utilisateur** = user-selectable *ou* user-definable; **qui peut être programmé** *ou* **modifié** *ou* **réglé** *ou* **sélectionné** *ou* **validé suivant les besoins de l'utilisateur** = user-selectable *ou* user-definable; **l'utilisateur peut sélectionner une résolution d'écran de 640 x 300, 240 ou 200 pixels** = the video resolution of 640 by 300, 240 or 200 pixels is user-selectable; **caractères programmés par l'utilisateur** = user-defined characters; **programme (d') utilisateur** *ou* **programme écrit par l'utilisateur** = user's program *ou* user program; **zone pour programme utilisateur** *ou* **zone utilisateur** = user area; **schéma de l'utilisateur** = external schema

◊ **utilisation** *nf* use; *(convivial)* **d'utilisation facile** = user-friendly *ou* simple to use; **logiciel d'utilisation facile** = user-friendly software; **utilisation de mémoire tampon** = buffering; **utilisation de double mémoire tampon** = double buffering; **(mode de) chargement en fonction de la fréquence d'utilisation** = activity loading; **contrôle d'utilisation de touches** = keyboard scan; **facilité d'utilisation** = usability; **licence d'utilisation** = run-time licence; **(bit) indicateur** *ou* **marqueur** *ou* **témoin d'utilisation** = device flag; **manuel d'utilisation** = user guide *ou* instruction manual *ou* user manual *ou* operations manual; **manuel d'utilisation élémentaire** = primer; **notice d'utilisation** = operational information; **notice d'utilisation destinée à l'utilisateur** = user documentation; **notice d'utilisation d'un logiciel** = software documentation; **l'excellente notice d'utilisation facilitait l'emploi du progiciel** = using the package was easy with the excellent user documentation; **temps d'utilisation de l'unité centrale** *ou* **du processeur** = CPU time

> l'utilisateur moyen risque de ne pas exploiter toute la capacité de son ordinateur
>
> *Temps Micro*

utilisé, -ée *adj* used *ou* in use

◊ **utiliser** *vtr* to use; **utiliser quelque chose** = to make use of something; **utiliser une mémoire tampon** = to buffer; **utilisez le pavé numérique pour saisir les chiffres** = you can use the numeric keypad to enter the figures; **les commerciaux utilisent l'ordinateur trop souvent** = the computer is used too often by the sales staff; **le nouveau progiciel peut être utilisé sur notre PC** = the new package runs on our PC; *(convivial)* **facile à utiliser** = user-friendly *ou* easy-to-use; **c'est un appareil extrêmement facile à utiliser** = it's such a

user-friendly machine; **les données devraient être réparties en fichiers plus courts et plus faciles à utiliser** = data should be split into manageable files

utilitaire *nm&adj* **(programme) utilitaire** = utility (program) *ou* service program; *(in Microsoft Windows, etc.)* applet; **il est impossible de récupérer un fichier perdu sans l'aide d'un utilitaire de récupération de fichier** = a lost file cannot be found without a file-recovery utility; **il y a un utilitaire qui permet de copier tous les fichiers du disque dur** = on the disk is a utility for backing up a hard disk; **il existe des utilitaires pour vous aider à formater les disques et configurer le clavier** = there are applets to help format your disk and configure your keyboard; **utilitaire de plan** = outliner; **utilitaire de requête** *ou* **d'interrogation** = query facility; **utilitaire de suivi de version** *ou* **de modifications** = version control

Vv

V = VOLTAGE

V *(normes ou protocoles de transmission pour modems)* **avis de série V** = V series; *(transmission en duplex à 300 bits par seconde en émission et réception)* **norme V21** = V.21; *(transmission en semi-duplex à 1200 bits par seconde en émission et réception)* **norme V22** = V.22; *(transmission en duplex à 1200 bits par seconde en émission et réception)* **norme V22 bis** = V.22 BIS; *(transmission en semi-duplex à 75 bits par seconde en émission et 1200 bits par seconde en réception)* **norme V23** = V.23; *(circuits d'échange entre système central et terminal)* **norme V24** = V.24; *(équipement d'appel et de réponse automatique sur le réseau public commuté)* **norme V25 bis** = V.25 BIS; *(transmission à 2400 bits par seconde sur des lignes louées)* **norme V26** = V.26; *(transmission en semi-duplex à 2400 bits par seconde en émission et 1200 bits par seconde en réception sur le réseau public commuté)* **norme V26 bis** = V.26 BIS; *(transmission en duplex à 2400 bits par seconde en émission et 1200 bits par seconde en réception sur le réseau public commuté)* **norme V26 ter** = V.26 TER; *(modem à 4800 bits par seconde sur lignes louées)* **norme V27** = V.27; *(transmission à 4800 bits par seconde en émission et 2400 bits par seconde en réception sur lignes louées)* **norme V27 bis** = V.27 BIS; *(transmission à 4800 bits par seconde en émission et 2400 bits par seconde en réception sur le réseau public commuté)* **norme V27 ter** = V.27 TER; *(modem à 9600 bits par seconde sur le réseau public commuté ou sur lignes louées)* **norme V29** = V.29; *(protocole de contrôle et de correction d'erreurs)* **norme V42** = V.42; *(compression de données avec contrôle d'erreurs V42)* **norme V42 bis** = V.42 BIS

V & V *(test pour s'assurer de la bonne marche d'un système)* **vérification et validation** = Verification and Validation (V & V)

V20, V30 *(processeurs NEC compatibles avec Intel 8088 et 8086)* V20, V30 (processor chips)

vacillement *nm* flicker; **(image ou affichage) sans vacillement** = flicker-free (screen ou display)

◊ **vaciller** *vi* to flicker; **l'image sur l'écran vacille à la mise sous tension de l'imprimante** = the image flickers when the printer is switched on

vacuum *nm* vacuum

valeur *nf* **(a)** value; **la variable a pris la valeur de la donnée saisie** = the variable was equated to the input data; **valeur absolue** = absolute value; **la valeur absolue de −62,34 est 62,34** = the absolute value of −62.34 is 62.34; **valeur binaire** *ou* **booléenne** = truth value *ou* Boolean value; **valeur complémentaire (d'un nombre)** = offset value; **valeur par défaut** *ou* **intrinsèque** *ou* **pré-programmée** = default value; *(de valeurs aléatoires ou pseudo-aléatoires)* **valeur de départ** = seed; *(d'amplitude ou d'intensité, etc.)* **valeur efficace** = root mean square (RMS); **la valeur efficace d'une sinusoïde parfaite équivaut à 0,7071 de son amplitude** = the root mean square of the pure sinusoidal signal is 0.7071 of its amplitude; *(en début de programme)* **valeur initiale** = initial value; *(d'une adresse)* **valeur relative** = offset value *ou* offset word; **valeur de vérification pour hash code** = hash value; **charger** *ou* **affecter la valeur 1 à un bit** = to set a bit value of 1; **erreur à valeur moyenne nulle** = balanced error; **gamme de valeurs** = number range; **ordinateur à valeurs variables** = incremental computer **(b) valeur dans un tableau** = array element **(c) valeur ajoutée** = value added; **réseau à valeur ajoutée** = value added network (VAN); **revendeur de systèmes à valeur ajoutée** = value added reseller (VAR)

validation *nf* validation; **validation de données** = data validation *ou* data vetting; **validation de fichier** = file validation; *(ligne de caractères)* **(commande de) validation de ligne** = line input; **protocole de validation de transfert de données** = handshake *ou* handshaking; **vérification et validation** = verification and validation (V & V); **ligne de validation d'un circuit intégré** = chip select line; **signal de validation** = enabling signal; **signal de validation d'adresse** = address strobe; **signal de validation de données (transmises)** = data strobe; **touche de validation d'entrée** = enter key

◊ **valide** *adj* valid; **non valide** = invalid; **il a tenté d'utiliser un mot de passe qui n'était pas valide** = he tried to use an invalid password; **adresse valide** = valid memory address

◊ **validé, -ée** *adj (activé)* armed *ou* selected *ou* enabled *ou* activated; **(avec) configuration validée** = configured-in; **interruption validée** = armed interrupt

◊ **valider** *vtr* **(a)** *(données, etc.)* to validate **(b)** *(activer)* to select *ou* to arm *ou* to enable *ou* to activate; **valider un circuit intégré** = to chip select (CS); **(circuit** *ou* **dispositif) qui peut être validé par cavalier** = jumper-selectable (device); **qui peut être validé suivant les besoins de l'utilisateur** = user-selectable (device); **valider une interruption** = to interrupt enable **(c)** *(par une impulsion)* to strobe

◊ **validité** *nf* **(a)** validity; **(test de) vérification de validité des données** = validity check **(b) signal de validité d'adresse** = address strobe

valise *nf (icône de police de caractères)* suitcase

valve *nf* valve

variable 1 *nf* variable; **nom de variable** = variable name; **variable binaire** = binary variable; **variable booléenne** = Boolean variable; **variable de chaîne** = string variable; **variable chaînée** *ou* **de type chaîne de caractères** = string type variable; **variable factice** = dummy variable; **variable globale** *ou* **commune** *ou* **générale** = global variable; **variable indicée** *ou* **caractérisée par un indice** = subscripted variable; **variable locale** = local variable; **variable de location** *ou* **de référence d'une cellule** = cell reference variable; **variable de type non précisé** = variable data type 2 *adj* variable *ou* fluctuating; **condensateur variable** = variable capacitor; **tableau à dimensions variables** = flexible array; **donnée(s) variable(s)** = variable data; **objectif à focale variable** = zoom lens; **format variable** = variable format *ou* V format; **intensité variable du signal** = signal strength; **enregistrement à longueur variable** = variable length record; **ordinateur à mots de longueur variable** = variable word length computer; **processeur à mots variables** = byte machine; *(d'un programme)* **point d'arrêt variable** = regional breakpoint; **résistance variable** = variable resistor; **tampon (de capacité) variable** = dynamic *ou* elastic buffer; **ordinateur à valeurs variables** = incremental computer

> pendant longtemps le traitement du signal s'est essentiellement intéressé aux signaux dépendant d'une seule variable (le temps)
> *Traitement du signal*

variante *nf* alternative

variateur *nm* *(d'un potentiomètre)* wiper

◊ **variation** *nf* variation *ou* fluctuation; *(non voulue)* **variation chromatique** = colour shift; *(d'un magnétophone)* **variation de vitesse** = flutter; **variation de fréquence** = frequency variation; **le pleurage et les variations de vitesse sont des défauts courants des magnétophones bon marché** = wow and flutter are common faults on cheap tape recorders

◊ **varier** *vi* (a) to vary *ou* to fluctuate; **la clarté du signal peut varier avec la tension du courant d'alimentation** = the clarity of the signal can vary with the power supply; **qui varie** = fluctuating (b) **varier (de ... à)** = to range (from ... to)

vecteur *nm* vector; **vecteur de retard** = delay vector

◊ **vectoriel, -ielle** *adj* vector; **image** *ou* **infographie vectorielle** = vector graphics *ou* vector image *ou* vector scan; **fonte vectorielle** *ou* **police de caractères vectorielle** = scalable font; dynamically redefinable character set; **processeur vectoriel** = vector processor *ou* array processor; **le processeur vectoriel permet de faire pivoter le tableau qui contient l'image écran, à l'aide d'une seule commande** = the array processor allows the array that contains the screen image to be rotated with one simple command

◊ **vectorisé, -ée** *adj* vectored; **interruption vectorisée** = vectored interrupt

vedette *nf* star; **programme vedette** = star program

véhiculer *vtr* *(données* *ou* *signaux)* to channel *ou* to carry

veille *nf* **courant de veille** = hold current

Veitch *npr* **diagramme de Veitch** = Veitch diagram

vendeur *nm* vendor

◊ **vendre** *vtr* to sell; *(livres)* **vendre à bas prix** = to remainder; **articles vendus sur commande uniquement** = articles available to order only

venir de *vi* (a) to originate from; **les données viennent du nouvel ordinateur** = the data originated from the new computer (b) **qui vient de l'extérieur** = incoming (message *ou* data)

Venn *npr* **diagramme de Venn** = Venn diagram

vente *nf* sale; **vente(s) par téléphone** = telesales; **publicité lieu de vente (PLV)** = point-of-sale material; **point de vente** = point-of-sale (POS); **point de vente électronique** = electronic point-of-sale (EPOS); **terminal de point de vente** = point-of-sale terminal *ou* POS terminal

ventilateur *nm* fan; **si le ventilateur tombe en panne, le système va bientôt surchauffer** = if the fan fails, the system will rapidly overheat

ventiler *vtr* to fan

vérificateur, -trice *n&adj* **vérificateur grammatical** = grammar checker; **vérificateur d'orthographe** = spellchecker *ou* spelling checker

◊ **vérificatrice** *nf* verifier

◊ **vérification** *nf* (a) control *ou* check *ou* verification *ou* test; **vérification automatique** = auto verify; **équipement de vérification automatique (EVA)** = automatic test equipment (ATE); **vérification de boucle** = loop check; **vérification de caractère** = character check; **vérification de données** = data vetting; **code de vérification et correction d'erreurs** = error checking and correcting code (ECCC); **faire une vérification orthographique** = to spellcheck; **programme de vérification orthographique** = spellchecker *ou* spelling checker; **vérification d'un programme** = program verification; **vérification et validation** = verification and validation (V & V); **protocole de vérification (d'utilisation)** = audit trail; **total de vérification** = checksum *ou* check total (b) *(de maintenance)* service *ou* preventive maintenance; **la vérification des lecteurs de disquette a été faite hier et tout fonctionne très bien** = the disk drives were serviced yesterday and are working well (c) *(relecture)* **vérification (d'un article** *ou* **d'un manuscrit)** = subbing *ou* sub-editing

◊ **vérifier** (a) *vtr* to verify *ou* to check *ou* to control *ou* to monitor; *(pression* *ou* *niveau)* to gauge; **le programme permet de vérifier l'orthographe** = the program allows the user to review all wrongly spelled words; **les éditeurs ont vérifié toutes les références à la bibliothèque locale** = the editors have checked all the references in the local library; **nous vérifions chaque lot pour nous** assurer de la qualité = we check each batch to make sure it is perfect; **il faudrait vérifier la manette de commande qui reste parfois coincée** = I think the joystick needs adjustment as it sometimes gets stuck **(b)** *(un texte)* to sub-edit *ou* to sub (a text)

vérin *nm* actuator

véritable *adj* genuine

vérité *nf* truth; **table de vérité** = Boolean operation table *ou* truth table

véroler *vtr (familier)* to corrupt; **un problème de tension pendant l'accès au disque peut véroler les données** = power loss during disk access can corrupt the data

verrou *nm* **(a)** lock; **verrou électronique** = electronic lock **(b)** *(du niveau de sortie)* latch

◊ **verrouillage** *nm,* **(a)** locking; **verrouillage d'un fichier** = locking a file; **verrouillage des enregistrements** = record locking **(b)** *(du niveau de sortie)* **dispositif de verrouillage** = latch **(c)** *(par logiciel)* interlock

◊ **verrouillé, -ée** *adj* locked; **entrée sur un système** *ou* **sur un terminal mal verrouillé** = piggyback entry; **système verrouillé** = secure system

◊ **verrouiller** *vtr* **(a)** to lock; **verrouiller (l'accès d')** **un fichier** = to lock a file **(b)** *(par logiciel)* to interlock **(c)** *(un niveau de sortie)* to latch **(d)** *(le voltage d'un signal)* to clamp

verser *vtr* verser du texte (dans un cadre PAO) = (to) flow text

version *nf (d'un programme)* version *ou* implementation *ou* release; **version avancée** *ou* **évoluée** = advanced version; *(utilisable seulement avec l'interpréteur d'une application maître)* **version exécutable** *ou* **version run-time** = run-time version; **dernière** *ou* **nouvelle version** = rewrite *ou* update (of a program); **publier une nouvelle version** = to release a new version; **le programme en est à sa troisième version** = the program is in its second rewrite; **cette version du BASIC offerte par le fabricant est légèrement différente de celle que j'utilise** = this manufacturer's dialect of BASIC is a little different to the one I'm used to; **comparée à la version précédente, celle-ci est très conviviale** = compared with the previous version this one is very user-friendly; **la dernière version du logiciel comprend une routine graphique améliorée** = the latest version of the software includes an improved graphics routine; **la dernière version du logiciel est beaucoup plus rapide** = the latest implementation of the software runs much faster; **numéro de version** = version number *ou* release number; **la dernière version du logiciel porte le numéro 5** = the latest software is release 5

verso *nm* verso; *voir aussi* RECTO

vert , -e *adj* green; **phosphore vert** = green phosphor

vertical, -e *adj* vertical; **application verticale** = vertical application; **votre nouveau progiciel pour gérer une boutique de fleuriste est une bonne application verticale** = your new software to manage a florist's is a good vertical application; **balayage vertical** = field sweep; **impulsion de contrôle** *ou* **de synchronisation du balayage vertical** = field sync pulse; **coordonnée verticale** = Y-coordinate; **défilement vertical** = vertical scrolling; **délai de retour vertical** = vertical blanking interval; **jeu vertical d'une touche** = key travel; **(antenne, etc.) à polarisation verticale** = vertically polarized (antenna); **signal avec polarisation verticale** = vertically polarized signal; **signal vidéo vertical** = vertical sync signal; **suppression verticale de la trame** = field blanking (interval); **tabulation verticale** = vertical tab; **unité de formatage vertical** = vertical format unit (VFU)

◊ **verticale** *nf* vertical line; *(coordonnée)* Y-direction

◊ **verticalement** *adv* vertically; **signal polarisé verticalement** = vertically polarized signal

VESA *(norme)* Video Electronics Standards Association; **bus local VESA** = VESA local bus *ou* VL-bus; **pour avoir un PC de hautes performances, choisissez un modèle avec bus local VESA** = for a high-performance PC, choose one with a VESA bus

VGA *(norme d'adaptateur d'écran vidéo à matrice graphique IBM)* Video Graphics Array (VGA)

◊ **Super VGA** *ou* **SVGA** *(norme améliorée)* Super VGA (SVGA)

via *prép* via

vibration *nf* **(a)** judder **(b)** **vibration sonore** = buzz; **émettre une vibration sonore** = to buzz

◊ **vibreur** *nm* vibreur sonore = buzzer

vice *nm* defect; *(dans un programme)* **vice caché** = hidden defect (in a program)

vidage *nm (sur imprimante* *ou* *sur support magnétique)* dump; **vidage par autopsie** = post mortem (dump); **vidage binaire** = binary dump; **vidage de contrôle (sur imprimante)** = check point dump; **vidage dynamique** = dynamic dump; **vidage d'écran (sur imprimante)** = screen dump; **vidage de fichier** = file cleanup *ou* file purge; **vidage au format** = formatted dump; **vidage hexadécimal** = hex dump; **vidage sur imprimante** = dump; **vidage irréversible** = disaster dump; **vidage de mémoire (sur imprimante)** = storage dump *ou* memory dump; **vidage (sur imprimante) après mouvements** = change dump; **point de vidage** = dump point; **(instruction de) vidage et reprise** = dump and restart; **vidage de sauvegarde** = rescue dump; **vidage sélectif** = selective dump; **vidage statique** = static dump

◊ **vide 1** *nm* vacuum; **on a fait le vide dans le tube cathodique scellé** = there is a vacuum in the sealed CRT; **tube à vide** = vacuum tube **2** *adj* **(a)** empty; **case vide** = *(d'un formulaire)* blank; *(pour carte d'extension)* empty slot **(b)** **cellule vide** = blank cell; **chaîne vide** = empty *ou* null *ou* blank string;

instruction vide = no-operation instruction *ou* no-op instruction; **liste vide** = empty *ou* null list

vidéo *nf & adj inv* video; **vidéo interactive** = interactive video; **vidéo inverse** *ou* **inversion vidéo** = inverse video *ou* reverse video; **adaptateur vidéo** = video adapter; **bande vidéo** = video cassette tape *ou* videotape; **films d'épouvante** *ou* **d'horreur sur bandes vidéo** = video nasties; **largeur de bande vidéo** = video bandwidth; **concentrateur** *ou* **réducteur (de largeur de bande) vidéo** = video compressor; **carte vidéo** = video card; **circuit intégré de carte vidéo** = video interface chip; **contrôleur vidéo** = video controller; **disque vidéo** = videodisk; **écran** *ou* **moniteur vidéo** = video monitor *ou* video display; **norme (d'adaptateur) d'écran vidéo à matrice graphique (VGA)** = video graphics array (VGA); **image vidéo** = video image *ou* video frame; **une image vidéo imprimable peut être envoyée sur une imprimante laser classique par le port vidéo** = a printer-readable video image can be sent to a basic laserprinter through a video port; **capteur d'image vidéo** = frame grabber; **scanner d'image vidéo** = video scanner; **jeu vidéo** = video game; **lecteur vidéo** = video player; **mémoire vidéo** = video memory; **mémoire vidéo à accès aléatoire** = video random access memory (VRAM); **mémoire (tampon) vidéo** = video buffer; **moniteur** *ou* **écran vidéo** = video monitor *ou* video display; **normes vidéo** = video standards; **numériseur vidéo** = video digitiser; **port vidéo** = video port; **déconcentrateur pour transmission vidéo** = video expander; **RAM vidéo** = video RAM (VRAM); **repiquage vidéo d'un film** = film pickup; **signal vidéo** = video signal; **porteuse de signal vidéo** = image carrier; **signal vidéo composite** = composite video signal; **standards vidéo** = video standards; **système vidéo haute définition** = high definition video system (HDVS); **terminal vidéo** = video terminal

◊ **vidéocaméra** *nf* video camera; **vidéocamera à infrarouge** = infrared video camera; **certains instructeurs utilisent une vidéocaméra à infrarouge pour suivre leurs élèves** = some instructors monitor their trainees with an infrared video camera

◊ **vidéocassette** *nf* video cassette

◊ **vidéoconférence** *nf* video conferencing

◊ **vidéodisque** *nm* videodisk

> il assure l'acquisition, le traitement et le stockage sur vidéodisque
>
> *01 Informatique*

◊ **vidéographie** *nf (vidéotex)* **vidéographie interactive** = interactive videography *ou* videotext

◊ **vidéophone** *nm* videophone *ou* video phone

◊ **vidéoscanner** *nm* video scanner; **les nouveaux vidéoscanners ont été conçus pour le balayage d'objets à trois dimensions** = new video scanners are designed to scan three-dimensional objects

◊ **vidéotex** *nm* videotext; **dialogue vidéotex** = interactive videotext

◊ **vidéothèque** *nf* video library

vider *vtr* **(a)** to clear; **vider le registre de données** = to clear the data register; **vider l'écran** = to clear *ou* to zap (the screen); **il a tapé CONTROL Z pour vider l'écran** = he pressed CONTROL Z and zapped all the text; **tous les tableaux sont vidés chaque fois que le programme est lancé** = all arrays are cleared each time the program is run; **vider une zone de mémoire** = to clear an area of memory **(b)** *(transférer le contenu de la mémoire vers l'imprimante)* to deposit **(c)** to flush *ou* to purge; **vider la mémoire tampon** = to flush buffers

vie *nf* life; **durée de vie d'un produit en magasin** = shelf life of a product; **durée de vie d'une imprimante** = print life; **durée de vie de la tête de lecture** = headlife

vierge *adj (disquette ou bande)* virgin *ou* clean *ou* blank (disk *ou* tape); **support magnétique vierge** = empty medium

vieux, vieille *adj (journal ou revue)* **vieux numéro** = back number

vif, vive *adj* **(a)** fast *ou* rapid **(b)** **mémoire vive** = random access memory *ou* RAM; **mémoire vive dynamique** = dynamic RAM *ou* dynamic random access memory (DRAM)

vigueur *nf* **entrer en vigueur** = to come into force; **les nouveaux règlements entreront en vigueur le 10 janvier** = the new regulations will come into force on January 10th; **page de codes en vigueur** = active code page

violation *nf* infringement; **violation du droit d'auteur** = infringement of copyright *ou* copyright infringement

virement *nm* **virement électronique de fonds** = electronic funds transfer (EFT)

◊ **virer** *vtr (familier)* **virer un fichier** = to junk a file; **(instruction de) virer une tâche** = kill job

virgule (,) *nf* **(a)** *(signe de ponctuation)* comma; **point-virgule (;)** = semi-colon; **fichier délimité par virgule** = comma-delimited file; **à partir de toutes bases de données on peut soit importer des données d'un fichier délimité par virgule, soit en exporter** = all databases can import and export to a comma-delimited file format **(b)** **virgule (décimale)** = decimal point; **alignement automatique des virgules** = automatic decimal adjustment; **tabulation sur la virgule** = decimal tabbing; **virgule binaire** = binary point **(c)** **calcul en virgule fixe** = fixed-point arithmetic; **numération à virgule fixe** = fixed-point notation; **la mise en mémoire de nombres à virgule fixe utilise deux octets pour le nombre entier et un octet pour la partie décimale** = storage of fixed point numbers has two bytes allocated for the whole number and one byte for the fraction part; **calcul en virgule flottante** = floating point arithmetic; **dans un calcul en virgule flottante, le nombre 56,47 serait écrit 0,5647 puissance 2** = the fixed number 56.47 in floating-point arithmetic would be 0.5647 and a power of 2; **nombre à virgule flottante** = floating point number; **numération à virgule flottante** = floating point notation; **opération en virgule flottante** = floating point operation (FLOP); **(nombre d')**

opérations en virgule flottante par seconde = FLOPs per second; **million(s) d'opérations en virgule flottante par seconde** = mega floating point operations per second *ou* megaflops *ou* MFLOPS; **processeur à virgule flottante** = floating point processor; **ce modèle est équipé d'un processeur à virgule flottante** = this model includes a built-in floating point processor; **le processeur à virgule flottante accélère la vitesse de traitement de ce logiciel graphique** = the floating point processor speeds up the processing of the graphics software; **routines de traitement de la virgule flottante** = floating-point routines

virtuel, -elle *adj* virtual; **adresse virtuelle** = virtual address; **appareil virtuel** = virtual terminal; **circuit virtuel** = virtual circuit; **communication virtuelle commutée** = switched virtual call; **disque virtuel** = virtual disk *ou* RAM disk; silicon disk; **machine virtuelle** = virtual machine; **mémoire virtuelle** = virtual memory *ou* virtual storage (VS); **réalité virtuelle** = virtual reality; **ce nouveau logiciel de réalité virtuelle peut créer une pièce en trois dimensions dans laquelle vous pouvez vous déplacer** = this new virtual reality software can create a three-dimensional room that you can navigate around; **terminal virtuel** = virtual terminal

virus *nm* *(dans un programme)* virus *ou* bacterium; **si vous avez un virus dans votre PC, vos données sont en danger** = if your PC is infected with a virus, your data is at risk; **virus informatique** = computer virus; **détecteur de virus** = virus detector

COMMENTAIRE: les virus se répandent en téléchargeant sans contrôle des fichiers venant de BBS ou de réseaux non contrôlés, ou encore en lisant une disquette non contrôlée dans votre PC - il faut toujours utiliser un détecteur de virus

viseur *nm* *(d'une caméra)* eyepiece *ou* viewfinder; **viseur électronique** = electronic viewfinder

visible *adj* visible; **lumière visible** = visible light

vision *nf* sight; **instruments de vision aux infrarouges** *ou* **caméra de vision nocturne** = infrared sights

visionnage *nm* *(d'un film)* viewing *ou* replay; *(d'une séquence de TV ou vidéo)* action replay; **visionnage immédiat** *ou* **instantané** = instant replay; **ce magnétoscope possède une fonction 'visionnage'** = this video recorder has a replay feature; **visionnage (d'une séquence de film) au ralenti** = slow-action replay; **le visionnage du ralenti ne laisse aucun doute sur le vainqueur** = the action replay clearly showed the winner; **visionnage en temps différé** = time shift viewing

◊ **visionner** *vtr* *(film)* to view *ou* to replay; **elle a enregistré le programme de télévision sur une bande vidéo et l'a visionné le lendemain soir** = she recorded the TV programme on a videotape and replayed it the next evening

◊ **visionneuse** *nf* viewer; *(qu'on tient à la main)* hand viewer

visiophone *nm* video phone *ou* videophone

visu *nf* = VISUEL

visualisation *nf* display; **visualisation de contrôle d'entrée** = marching display; **attributs de visualisation** = screen attributes; **console de visualisation** = visual display unit *ou* VDU; **mode visualisation** = display mode; **unité de visualisation** *ou* **écran de visualisation** = visual display unit (VDU) *ou* visual display terminal (VDT) *ou* display screen

◊ **visualiser** *vtr* **(a)** to display *ou* to view; **l'utilisateur paie un droit pour visualiser le tableau d'affichage** = the user has to pay a charge for viewing pages on a bulletin board **(b)** *(imaginer)* to picture *ou* to visualize; **essayer de visualiser l'implantation avant de commencer à dessiner** = try to picture the layout before starting to draw it in

◊ **visuel** *nm* visual display unit *ou* VDU

◊ **visuel, -elle** *adj* visual; **programmation visuelle** = visual programming

vital, -e *adj* vital **(pour l'entreprise)** = mission-critical

vitesse *nf* **(a)** speed; **vitesse de balayage** = scanning speed; **vitesse de calcul (par ordinateur)** = computing speed; *(d'une bande magnétique)* **vitesse de défilement** = playback speed; **vitesse moyenne** = medium speed; **vitesse d'ouverture d'un objectif** = lens speed; **vitesse de recherche effective** = effective search speed; **vitesse en sténographie** = dictation speed; **grande vitesse** = high-speed; **duplicateur grande vitesse** = high-speed duplicator; **lecteurs de CD-ROM double vitesse, quadruple vitesse, sextuple vitesse** = double speed, quadruple speed, sextuple speed CD-ROM players *ou* 2x speed, 4x speed, 6x speed CD-ROM players **(b)** rate; **modem à deux vitesses** = split baud rate modem; **vitesse d'entrée** = input rate; **(programme) limité par la vitesse d'entrée** *ou* **avec contrainte de vitesse d'entrée** = input-bound *ou* input-limited (program); **(programme) limité par la vitesse d'entrée/sortie** = I/O bound (program); **vitesse d'exécution** = execution rate; **la vitesse d'exécution des commandes de ce processeur est plus grande qu'avec l'ancienne version** = the processor's instruction execution rate is better than the older version; **vitesse de frappe** = keystroke rate; **vitesse d'horloge** = clock rate; **vitesse de lecture** = read rate; **avec contrainte de vitesse de périphérique** = peripheral-limited; **vitesse de sortie de l'information** = information rate; **vitesse de traitement de données** = data rate; **vitesse de transfert** = transfer rate; **vitesse de transfert (de données)** = data transfer rate; **vitesse de transmission** = transmission rate; *(d'un modem)* bits per second; baud rate; **vitesse maximale de transmission** = maximum transmission rate; **la vitesse de transmission du signal binaire était de 300 bits par seconde** = the baud rate of the binary signal was 300 bits per second; **la vitesse moyenne de transmission est de 64 000 bits par seconde en connexion parallèle et 19 200 bits par seconde en connexion série** = the average transmission is 64,000 bits per second (bps) through a parallel connection or 19,200 bps through a serial connection; **adaptateur de vitesse de transmission** = baud rate generator; **reconnaissance automatique de vitesse de transmission** = auto-baud scanning *ou* auto-baud sensing; **vitesse de transmission de données** = data signalling rate **(c)** velocity; **le moteur du lecteur de disquettes tourne à vitesse constante** = the disk drive motor spins at a constant velocity

VLB *(bus)* VL-bus *ou* VL local bus; **pour avoir un PC de hautes performances, choisissez un modèle avec bus VLB** = for a high-performance PC, choose one with a VL-bus

vocabulaire *nm* vocabulary; **vocabulaire contrôlé** = controlled vocabulary

vocal, -e *adj* (of) speech; (of) voice; **bande (de fréquence) vocale** = voice band; **interpolation de signaux sur bande vocale** = time assigned speech interpolation (TASI); **transmission de signaux sur la bande vocale** = in-band signalling; **circuit vocal** = dry circuit; **empreinte vocale** = voice print; **messagerie vocale** *ou* **boîte à lettre vocale** = voice mail; **j'ai vérifié ma boîte à lettre vocale pour voir si quelqu'un m'avait laissé un message** = I checked my voice mail to see if anyone had left me a message; **reconnaissance vocale** = voice recognition *ou* speech recognition; **répondeur vocal** *ou* **répondeur avec message vocal de synthèse** = voice answer back *ou* audio response unit; **saisie vocale** = voice data entry *ou* input; **signal vocal** = speech signal; **processeur du signal vocal** = speech processor; **sortie vocale** = voice output; **synthèse vocale** = voice synthesis *ou* speech synthesis; **puce de synthèse vocale** = speech chip; **synthétiseur vocal** = voice synthesizer; **transmission vocale étendue** = speech plus; **unité de puissance vocale** = voice unit

voie *nf* **(a)** *(de communication)* channel *ou* line *ou* path; **voie d'accès direct à la mémoire** = direct memory access channel; **voie d'acheminement** *ou* **de transmission de signaux** = transmission channel *ou* feeder; **signalisation par voie commune** = common channel signalling; **voie double** = dual channel; **voie (d') entrée/sortie** = I/O channel; **voie de lecture/écriture** = read/write channel; **voies de liaison d'un bus d'adresses** = bus address lines; **voie logique** = logical channel; **voie de retour** = backward channel; **voie spécialisée** = dedicated channel; **voie de transmission** = transmission channel; **capacité** *ou* **débit d'une voie de transmission** = channel capacity; **voie de transmission de données** = data path; **voie de transmission de l'information** = information transfer channel; **groupement de voies** = channel group; **saturation** *ou* **surcharge d'une voie** = channel overload; **synchroniseur de voies** = channel synchronizer **(b)** means; **la publicité pour le produit s'est faite par voie de presse spécialisée** = the product was advertised through the medium of the trade press

voile *nm (photographie)* fog

voir *vtr* to see; **ce que vous voyez est ce que vous obtenez** = What-You-See-Is-What-You-Get (WYSIWYG); **ce que vous voyez est tout ce que vous obtenez** = What-You-See-Is-All-You-Get (WYSIAYG)

voix *nf* voice; *(parole)* speech; **voix hors champ** *ou* **voix off** = voice-over; **voix numérisée** *ou* **de synthèse** = digital speech

vol *nm* **(exploitation par) vol de cycle** = cycle stealing; **accès direct à la mémoire par vol de cycle** = DMA cycle stealing; *voir aussi* ACCES

volatile *adj* volatile; **mémoire volatile** = volatile memory *ou* volatile (dynamic) storage

◊ **volatilité** *nf* volatility

volée *nf (vérification de données)* **à la volée** = on the fly

voler 1 *vtr (dérober)* to steal **2** *vi (se mouvoir dans l'air)* to fly

volet *nm (d'une disquette)* **volet de protection d'écriture** = write-protect tab

volt *nm* volt

◊ **voltage** *nm* voltage; **verrouiller le voltage (d'un signal)** = to clamp a voltage

volume *nm* **(a)** *(du son)* volume *ou* loudness *ou* level; **baissez le volume (du son) qui est vraiment trop fort** = turn the sound level down, it's far too loud; **bouton** *ou* **contrôle** *ou* **réglage du volume** = volume control **(b)** *(disque, etc.)* **nom** *ou* **étiquette** *ou* **label de volume** = volume label *ou* name **(c)** *(espace occupé par les données sur un dispositif de stockage)* volume

voyant *nm* **voyant (lumineux)** = (i) indicator light; (ii) light emitting diode; **voyant d'alarme** = warning light; **lorsque le voyant placé sur le panneau avant s'allume, il faut éteindre le système** = when the warning light on the front panel comes on, switch off the system

vrac (en) *loc adv* in bulk; **épreuves en vrac** = scatter proofs

vrai, -e *adj* genuine *ou* real; *(logique)* true

VRAM = VIDEO RANDOM ACCESS MEMORY; *voir* VIDEO

VT *(émulation de terminal de Digital Equipment Corporation)* VT-terminal emulation; **standard VT-52** = VT-52 (standard)

vue *nf* view; **vue plongeante** *ou* **aérienne** = aerial image; **prise de vue** = shot; **prise de vue d'une scène** = action shot; **prise de vue à cadence lente** = memomotion; **prise de vue en extérieur** = shot on location *ou* location shot

Ww

watt (W) *nm* Watt (W)

WHILE *(alors que)* **boucle conditionnelle 'WHILE'** = while-loop

WIMP *(environnement graphique avec fenêtre, icône, souris, pointeur)* Window, Icon, Mouse, Pointer (WIMP)

COMMENTAIRE: les environnements graphiques utilisent les fenêtres, icônes et souris pour contrôler le système d'exploitation; dans de nombreuses interfaces graphiques comme Windows de Microsoft, System 7 d'Apple ou DR GEM, on peut contrôler toutes les fonctions du système d'exploitation avec la souris; des icônes figurent le programmes et les fichiers; au lieu d'entrer au clavier le nom du fichier, on le sélectionne en déplaçant un pointeur à l'aide d'une souris.

Winchester *npr (disque dur)* **disque (de type) Winchester** = Winchester disk; **disque Winchester amovible** = removable Winchester; **lecteur de disque Winchester** = Winchester drive; **minidisque (de type) Winchester** = miniwinny

Windows ™ *(interface graphique de Microsoft)* Windows ™ (graphical user interface developed by Microsoft); **Windows for Workgroups** ™ = Windows for Workgroups ™; **système d'exploitation Windows NT** ™ = Windows NT ™

WISC = WRITABLE INSTRUCTION SET COMPUTER; *voir aussi* MODIFIABLE

Word ™ *(progiciel de traitement de texte de Microsoft)* Word ™

WordPerfect ™ *(progiciel de traitement de texte mis au point par WordPerfect Corp.)* WordPerfect ™

WordStar ™ *(progiciel de traitement de texte de MicroPro International)* WordStar ™ (word-processing application)

WORM = WRITE ONCE, READ MANY TIMES MEMORY; *(permet une seule écriture et des lectures multiples)* **disque optique WORM** = WORM

WYSIAYG = WHAT YOU SEE IS ALL YOU GET; *voir* VOIR

WYSIWYG = WHAT YOU SEE IS WHAT YOU GET; *voir* VOIR

Xx

X = EXTENSION

X (a) *(coordonnée)* **axe des X** = X-axis; **distance sur l'axe des X** = X distance **(b)** *(de carte perforée)* **perforation X** = x punch **(c)** *(communication)* **protocoles de télétransmission de la série X** = X-series **(d) rayon X** = X-ray

X 25 *(connexion entre un terminal et un réseau de transfert par paquets)* **standard CCITT X 25** = X.25

X 400 *(transfert de messages électroniques)* **standard CCITT X 400** = X.400

X 500 *(gestion de nom et de transfert de message)* **standard CCITT X 500** = X.500

xérographie *nf* xerography

◊ **xérographique** *adj* **imprimante xérographique** = xerographic printer

◊ **Xerox** ™ *(société bien connue, entre autres, pour ses photocopieurs)* **photocopieur Xerox** = Xerox machine; **photocopie faite avec une machine Xerox** = xerox; **photocopier une lettre avec une machine Xerox** = to make a xerox copy of a letter; **il faut commander de nouveau du papier Xerox pour le photocopieur** = we must order some more xerox paper for the copier; **on nous installera une nouvelle machine** *ou* **un nouveau photocopieur Xerox demain** = we are having a new Xerox machine installed tomorrow

XGA *(norme d'adaptateur graphique)* Extended Graphics Array (XGA)

XMODEM *(protocole de transmission de fichiers)* XMODEM; **protocole XMODEM 1K** = XMODEM 1K; *(comprend un dispositif de contrôle d'erreurs)* **protocole XMODEM CRC** = XMODEM CRC

XMS *(spécification de mémoire étendue)* Extended Memory Specification *ou* XMS

XNS *(protocole de réseau local de Xerox)* Xerox Networking System (XNS)

XON/XOFF *(protocole de transmission asynchrone)* XON/XOFF

X/OPEN *(groupe de vendeurs de systèmes ouverts)* X/OPEN

XT *(version originale du IBM PC basée sur le processeur Intel 8088)* XT; **clavier XT** = XT keyboard

X-Window System *ou* **X-Windows** *(système de commandes API)* X-Window System *ou* X-Windows

Yy

Y (a) *(coordonnée)* **axe des Y** = Y-axis; **distance sur l'axe des Y** = Y-distance **(b)** *(de carte perforée)* **perforation Y** = y punch

YMCK *(définition de couleurs basée sur: jaune, magenta, cyan, noir)* Yellow, Magenta, Cyan, Black (YMCK)

YMODEM *(protocole de transmission de fichiers)* YMODEM

YMODEM apporte relativement peu d'améliorations techniques à XMODEM-1K; c'est principalement en autorisant le transfert de plusieurs fichiers en une seule session qu'il innove, de même qu'en transmettant leur nom et leurs principaux attributs (dans des blocs numérotés 0)

PC Expert

Zz

Z *(coordonnée)* **axe des Z** = Z-axis

Z80 *(processeur)* Z80 (processor)

zébrure *nf* streaking

zéro *nm* zero; **le compteur revient automatiquement à zéro dès qu'il atteint 999** = when it reaches 999 this counter resets to zero; **pour appeler Paris, depuis Londres, faites d'abord: zéro zéro, trente-trois, un, puis le numéro du correspondant** = to call Paris from London, first dial zero zero, thirty-three, one, followed by the subscriber's phone number; **(instruction de) branchement conditionnel à l'indicateur zéro** = jump on zero; **l'instruction de branchement conditionnel à zéro teste l'indicateur zéro** = the jump on zero instruction tests the zero flag; **effectuer un branchement (conditionnel) à zéro** = to jump on zero (instruction); **élimination des zéros (non significatifs)** = zero compression *ou* zero suppression; **garnir de zéros** = to zero fill; **(connecteur) à force d'insertion zéro** = zero insertion force (ZIF); **indicateur (binaire) zéro** = zero flag; **remettre à zéro** = *(un dispositif)* to reset *ou* to zero; *(un fichier)* to erase *ou* to rub out; **remettre à zéro un dispositif (programmable)** = to zero a device; **signal de remise** *ou* **de retour à zéro** = return to zero signal; **boucle avec retour automatique à zéro** = self-resetting *ou* self-restoring loop; **non-retour** *ou* **non-remise à zéro** = non return to zero (NRZ); **zéro de tête** = leading zero

ZMODEM *(protocole de transmission de fichiers)* ZMODEM

zonage *nm* fielding

◊ **zone** *nf* **(a)** *(de mémoire)* area *ou* region *ou* zone; **zone active** = active area *ou* hotspot; **zone de code** = code area; **zone commune de la mémoire** = common storage area; **zone de données** = data area *ou* data field; **zone d'entrée de données** = input area; **zone d'image** = image area; **zone d'image reçue** = safe area; *(dans une mémoire)* **zone d'instruction** = instruction area; **zone de recherche** = seek area; **zone de segment de recouvrement** = overlay region; **zone sortie (de la mémoire)** = output area *ou* output block; **zone de stockage de l'image** = image storage space; **zone de traitement par lots** = batch region; **zone de travail (en mémoire)** = memory workspace *ou* work area; **recherche de zone** *(d'écran)* = area search; **zone d'affichage** = bulletin board system (BBS); **zone d'image** = image area; **remplissage de zone** = area fill **(c)** *(transmission)* **zone de brouillage** *ou* **de purée** = mush area; **zone terrestre de couverture** = earth coverage; *(téléphone)* **indicatif (téléphonique) de zone** = area code **(d)** **zone de connexions** = terminal area; *(de matériel)* **zone protégée** = (hardware) isolated location; **réseau à zone de recouvrement** = overlay network **(e)** *(entre deux marges)* **zone de texte** = hot zone *ou* soft zone

zoom *nm* **(a)** *(action)* zooming; **faire un zoom** = to zoom **(b)** *(lentille)* zoom lens

ENGLISH-FRENCH
ANGLAIS-FRANÇAIS

Aa

A *(hexadecimal number equivalent to decimal 10)* nombre hexadécimal équivalent du 10 décimal *or* A

A = AMPERE

Å = ANGSTROM

A: *(in some operating systems denotes the first disk drive)* (lecteur de disquette) A:; **to see what is stored on your floppy disk, use the DOS command DIR A:** = pour savoir quels fichiers sont enregistrés sur votre disquette, utilisez la commande DOS DIR A:

A-bus *noun* bus *m* principal *or* bus A

A programming language (APL) *noun* langage *m* (de programmation) APL

A1, A2, A3, A4, A5 *noun* papier format A1, A2, A3, A4, A5; **you must photocopy the spreadsheet on A3 paper** = vous devez photocopier le tableau sur une feuille de format A3; **a standard 300 d.p.i. black and white A4 monitor** = écran monochrome standard de format A4, avec une définition de 300 points par pouce

A to D *or* **A/D** = ANALOG TO DIGITAL (conversion) analogique-numérique; **A to D converter** = convertisseur *m* analogique-numérique; **the speech signal was first passed through an A to D converter before being analysed** = le signal vocal est d'abord passé par le convertisseur analogique-numérique avant d'être analysé

abandon *verb* quitter *or* abandonner (sans sauvegarder); **once you have abandoned your spreadsheet, you cannot retrieve it again** = si vous quittez votre feuille de calcul sans sauvegarder, vous ne pourrez pas la récupérer

abbreviated address *noun (a user name that has fewer characters than the full name)* adresse *f* abrégée; **my full network address is over 60 characters long, so you will find it easier to use my abbreviated address** = mon adresse complète de réseau comporte plus de 60 caractères; vous avez intérêt à utiliser mon adresse abrégée

◊ **abbreviated installation** *noun (installation without restoring the previous backup settings)* installation *f* simplifiée

abbreviation *noun* abréviation *f*; **within the text, the abbreviation 'proc' is used instead of processor** = dans le texte, on a remplacé le terme processeur par l'abréviation 'proc'; **abbreviated addressing** *or* **abb. add.** = adressage *m* abrégé *or* simplifié

ABD = APPLE DESKTOP BUS ™

abend *noun* = ABNORMAL END fin *f or* interruption *f* anormale *or* prématurée; **an interrupt from a faulty printer caused an abend** = une commande *or* un signal d'interruption venant d'une imprimante défectueuse a provoqué une fin anormale de traitement; *(special number that identifies type of error)* **abend code** = code *m* de fin anormale *or* d'interruption; **abend recovery program** = programme *m* de récupération de fichiers après une interruption; **if a fault occurs, data loss will be minimized due to the improved abend recovery program** = en cas de panne, la perte de données sera minimale grâce au nouveau programme de récupération des fichiers après une interruption

aberration *noun* **(a)** *(of light beam or image, etc.)* aberration *f* **(b)** *(of TV picture - caused by corrupt signal or incorrect adjustment)* distorsion *f*

ABIOS = ADVANCED BASIC INPUT/OUTPUT SYSTEM

| COMMENT: the ABIOS is used in addition to the normal BIOS routines; ABIOS routines are used to control the MCA bus in an IBM PS/2 computer

ablation *noun (method of writing data to an optical storage device)* trou *m* laser *or* brûlage *m* laser

| COMMENT: a laser burns a hole or pit (that represents digital bits of data) into the thin metal surface of the storage device

ABM = ASYNCHRONOUS BALANCED MODE

ABME = ASYNCHRONOUS BALANCED MODE EXTENDED

abnormal *adjective* anormal, -e; **it's abnormal for two consecutive disk drives to break down** = il n'est pas normal que deux lecteurs de disquettes tombent en panne l'un après l'autre; **abnormal error** = erreur anormale; **abnormal end** *or* **abend** *or* **abnormal termination** = fin *or* interruption anormale; fin *or* interruption prématurée

◊ **abnormally** *adverb* anormalement *or* singulièrement; **the signal is abnormally weak** = le signal est anormalement faible; **the error rate with this disk is abnormally high** = le taux d'erreur de cette disquette est singulièrement élevé

abort *verb* (faire) avorter; abandonner prématurément *or* interrompre *or* arrêter l'éxécution (d'un programme); **the program was aborted by pressing the red button** = on a interrompu le programme en appuyant sur la touche rouge; **abort the program before it erases**

any more files = arrêtez l'éxécution du programme, avant qu'il efface d'autres fichiers; *(connexion to a network that has not been shut down correctly)* **aborted connection** = connexion *f* avortée; *(unique sequence of bits that indicates that the transmission will be abnormally terminated)* **abort sequence** = séquence *f* de fin *or* de clôture anormale; séquence d'interruption prématurée

About... *(menu selection that tells you who developed the program and gives copyright information)* A propos de...

above-the-line costs *plural noun (in making TV films)* coût *m* média; frais *m* fixes

AB roll *noun (two video or music segments that are synchronised)* fondu *m* enchaîné

ABS = ABSOLUTE FUNCTION

absolute address *or* **actual address** *or* **machine address** *noun* adresse *f* absolue *or* adresse réelle *or* adresse machine; **program execution is slightly faster if you code only with absolute addresses** = l'exécution d'un programme est un peu plus rapide si on utilise uniquement des adresses absolues dans le code; **absolute addressing** = adressage absolu; **absolute assembler** = assembleur absolu; *(reference that always refers to the same cell)* **absolute cell reference** = adresse absolue de la cellule; **absolute code** = code (binaire) absolu; *(describe the distance of a point from the intersection of axes)* **absolute coordinates** = coordonnées *fpl* absolues; *compare* RELATIVE COORDINATES; *(input device such as a tablet or mouse)* **absolute device** = dispositif *m* de pointage absolu; *(value or magnitude of an error, ignoring its sign)* **absolute error** = erreur *f* absolue; **absolute expression** = expression *f* absolue; *(programming instruction that returns the magnitude of a number without the number's sign)* **absolute function (ABS)** = ABS *or* fonction valeur absolue; **command ABS(-13) will return the answer 13** = la commande ABS(-13) retourne la valeur 13; *(instruction describing completely the operation to be performed; graphics command that uses absolute coordinates)* **absolute instruction** *or* **code** = instruction absolue *or* code absolu; **absolute loader** = chargeur absolu; **absolute maximum rating** = capacité théorique absolue; *(position of an object in relation to an origin)* **absolute positioning** = positionnement *m* absolu; *(in the OS/2 operating system: priority of a process that cannot be changed)* **absolute priority** = priorité *f* absolue; **absolute program** = programme absolu *or* en langage machine; **absolute value** = valeur absolue (d'un nombre); **the absolute value of −62.34 is 62.34** = la valeur absolue de −62,34 est 62,34; **an absolute value of the input is generated** = il y a génération d'une valeur absolue des entrées

absorb *verb* absorber

◊ **absorptance** *noun* absorptance *f or* indice *m* d'absorption

◊ **absorption** *noun* absorption *f*; *(for colour)* **absorption filter** = filtre *m* d'absorption

abstract 1 *noun (summary of a document)* résumé *m* ; extrait *m*; **it's quicker to search through the abstracts than the full text** = il est plus rapide de chercher dans les résumés que dans le texte complet; **in our library, abstracts are gathered together in separate volumes allowing an easy and rapid search for a particular subject** = dans notre bibliothèque, les résumés sont réunis en volumes distincts ce qui assure la facilité et la rapidité des recherches sur un sujet particulier **2** *verb* **(a)** extraire (de) *or* retirer (de) *or* soustraire (de) **(b)** résumer (un article)

◊ **abstract data type** *noun (general data type that can store any kind of information)* données *fpl* de type général; **the stack is a structure of abstract data types, it can store any type of data from an integer to an address** = la pile est une structure de données de type général, elle peut stocker des données de tous types comme des nombres entiers ou des adresses

◊ **abstracting & indexing (A&I)** *noun* résumé et indexation

AC = ALTERNATING CURRENT

ACC = ACCUMULATOR

acceleration time *noun* **(a)** *(to spin a disk at correct speed)* temps *m* de montée *or* d'accélération; **allow for acceleration time in the access time** = il faut inclure le temps de montée dans le temps d'accès **(b)** *(total time between access instruction and data transfer)* temps de réponse

◊ **accelerator** *noun* accélérateur *m*; **accelerator board** *or* **card** = carte *f* accélératrice *or* carte d'accélération

◊ **accelerator key** *noun (usually a combination of keys that carry out a function)* touche *f* d'accélération *or* raccourci *m* clavier; séquence *f* de touches; **instead of selecting the File menu then the Save option, use the accelerator keys Alt and S to do the same thing and save the file** = au lieu de sélectionner le menu Fichier puis l'option Enregistrer, utilisez les touches d'accélération ALT-S *or* le raccourci clavier ALT-S pour sauvegarder votre fichier

accent *noun (mark above a character)* accent *m*; **acute accent** = accent aigu; **circumflex accent** = accent circonflexe; **grave accent** = accent grave

◊ **accented** *adjective* accentué, -ée

accept *verb* **(a)** *(to agree)* accepter (de); **he accepted the quoted price for printing** = il a accepté le devis de l'imprimeur; **he did not accept the programming job he was offered** = il n'a pas accepté *or* il a refusé le poste de programmeur qu'on lui offrait **(b)** *(to take as compatible)* accepter; **the laser printer will accept a card as small as a business card** = l'imprimante (à) laser accepte même un imprimé de la taille d'une carte professionnelle; **the multi-disk reader will accept 3.5 inch disks as well as 5.25 inch formats** = ce lecteur multidisque accepte aussi bien les disquettes de 3,5 pouces que celles de 5,25 pouces **(c)** *(to establish a session or connection)* accepter;

call **accepted signal** = signal *m* d'acceptation d'appel

◊ **acceptable** *adjective* acceptable; **the error rate was very low, and is acceptable** = le taux d'erreur était très bas et donc acceptable; **for the price, the scratched case is acceptable** = à ce prix-là, on peut accepter que la mallette ait une éraflure

◊ **acceptance** *noun* acceptation *f or* réception *f*; *(of lens or optic fibre)* **acceptance angle** = angle *m* de réception; **a light beam at an angle greater than the acceptance angle of the lens will not be transmitted** = un rayon lumineux d'incidence supérieure à l'angle de réception ne sera pas transmis; *(for quality)* **acceptance sampling** = échantillonnage *m* (de qualité); **acceptance test** *or* **testing** = test *m* d'homologation

access 1 *noun* accès *m*; **to have access to something** = avoir accès à quelque chose; **to have access to a file of data** = avoir accès à un fichier informatique; **he has access to numerous sensitive files** = il a accès à de nombreux fichiers confidentiels; **to bar access to a system** = interdire (à quelqu'un) l'accès à un système; **after he was discovered hacking, he was barred access to the system** = après avoir découvert qu'il faisait du piratage, on lui a interdit l'accès au système; **access arm** = bras *m* de lecture/écriture; **the access arm moves to the parking region during transport** = le bras de lecture est mis en position de parkage pendant le transport; *(permission to carry out a particular operation)* **access authority** = autorisation *f* d'accès; *(preventing a user accessing data)* **access barred** = accès non autorisé *or* interdit; *(one of several possible predefined access levels)* **access category** = type *m or* catégorie *f* d'accès; *(in Token-Ring network: protocols that manage data transfer)* **access channel control** = contrôle *m* des canaux d'accès; **access charge** = frais *mpl* d'accès au système; **access code** = mot *m* de passe *or* code *m* d'accès (à un système); *(opening in a floppy disk's casing)* **access hole** = fenêtre *f* d'accès (d'un disque ou d'une disquette); *(one of various predefined access categories)* **access level** = niveau *m* d'accès; **access line** = ligne *f* d'accès; *(device that moves an access arm over the surface of a disk)* **access mechanism** = mécanisme *m* d'accès; **access method** = méthode *f* d'accès; *(move data between main storage and an output device)* **access method routines** = routines *fpl* d'accès; *(name that identifies an object in a database)* **access name** = nom *m* d'accès (dans une base de données); *(location of a stored file within a directory structure of a disk)* **access path** = chemin *m* d'accès; *(recording changes to an access path)* **access path journalling** = enregistrement des chemins d'accès; *(time during which a user can access data)* **access period** = période *f* d'accès; *(for a particular user)* **access permission** = permission *f* d'accès; *(on circuit board or in software)* **access point** = point *m* d'accès *or* de contrôle; *(status allowing a user to see or read or alter files)* **access privilege** = privilège *m* d'accès; *(permission to access a particular file)* **access rights** = droits *mpl* d'accès; *(in Token-Ring network)* **access unit** = unité *f* d'accès; **direct access storage device (DASD)** = mémoire *f or* support *m* à accès direct;

(direct link between a peripheral and a computer's main memory) **direct memory access (DMA)** = accès direct à la mémoire; **disk access** = accès au disque; **disk access management** = gestion *f* d'accès aux disques; **instantaneous access** = accès instantané; **the instantaneous access of the RAM disk was welcome** = l'accès instantané au disque RAM a été bien accueilli; **parallel access** = accès parallèle; **public access terminal** = terminal *m* public; **random access** = accès aléatoire *or* sélectif *or* direct; **sequential access** = accès séquentiel; **serial access** = accès séquentiel **2** *verb* *(a file or a system)* accéder à *or* avoir accès à; **she accessed the employee's file stored on the computer** = elle a accédé au fichier (informatique) de l'employé stocké sur l'ordinateur

◊ **access control** *noun* contrôle *m* d'accès (au système); *(in Token-Ring network: byte following start marker)* **access control byte** = octet *m* de contrôle d'accès

◊ **access time** *noun* **(a)** *(time needed between request and data being shown)* temps *m* d'accès; **the access time of this dynamic RAM chip is around 200ns - we have faster versions if your system clock is running faster** = le temps d'accès de cette RAM dynamique est d'environ 200ns - il existe une version plus rapide si votre fréquence d'horloge est plus élevée **(b)** *(time needed to find a file, etc.)* temps *m* d'accès (à un fichier, etc.)

accessible *adjective* accessible; **details of customers are easily accessible from the main computer files** = les détails du fichier client de l'ordinateur principal sont facilement accessibles

accessions *plural noun* *(in libraries, etc.)* nouveaux titres *mpl or* acquisitions *fpl*; **accession number** = numéro *m* de référence *or* d'entrée; *(number that shows in which order each record was entered)* numéro *m* d'accès

accessor *noun* *(person who accesses data)* accédant *m or* utilisateur ayant un droit d'accès

accessory *noun* accessoire *m*; **the printer comes with several accessories, such as a soundproof hood** = plusieurs accessoires, dont un capot d'insonorisation, sont fournis avec l'imprimante; **this popular home computer has a large range of accessories** = il existe de nombreux accessoires pour cet ordinateur individuel très populaire

accidental *adjective* accidentel, -elle; **always keep backup copies in case of accidental damage to the master file** = sauvegardez toujours vos données (sur disquettes) pour le cas où le fichier principal serait endommagé

accordion fold *or* **fanfold** *noun* papier *m* (plié) en éventail *or* en paravent *or* en accordéon; papier en continu

account 1 *noun* *(record of a user's name, password and rights)* compte *m*; **if you are a new user, you will have to ask the supervisor to create an account for you** = si vous êtes un nouvel utilisateur, vous devez demander à l'administrateur de vous créer un compte; *(unique* *name of a user)* **account name** = nom *m* de compte; **John Smith's account name is JSMITH** = le nom de compte de John Smith est JSMITH **2** *verb (logging how much time and resources each user uses)* comptabiliser

accounting *or* **accounts package** *noun (software for business accounting functions)* logiciel *m* de comptabilité; **we now type in each transaction into the new accounting package rather than write it into a ledger** = maintenant, nous entrons chaque transaction au clavier dans le nouveau logiciel de comptabilité au lieu de les inscrire dans le grand-livre

accumulate *verb* accumuler *or* rassembler; **we have gradually accumulated a large databank of names and addresses** = nous avons rassemblé progressivement un impressionnant fichier d'adresses

◊ **accumulator** *or* **ACC** *or* **accumulator register** *noun* accumulateur *m or* ACC; **store the two bytes of data in registers A and B and execute the add instruction - the answer will be in the accumulator** = stockez les 2 octets de données dans les registres A et B et exécutez l'instruction 'add' - vous obtiendrez le résultat dans l'accumulateur; *(address accessed by instruction held in the accumulator)* **accumulator address** = adresse *f* d'accumulateur; **accumulator shift instruction** = commande *f* de décalage dans le registre

accuracy précision *f*; **accuracy control character** = caractère (de contrôle) de précision

◊ **accurate** *adjective* juste *or* précis, -e *or* sans erreur; **the printed bar code has to be accurate to within a thousandth of a micron** = le code (à) barres doit être imprimé avec une précision de l'ordre du millième de micron

◊ **accurately** *adverb* correctement *or* avec précision; **the OCR had difficulty in reading the new font accurately** = le lecteur optique n'arrivait pas à lire correctement toutes les lettres de la nouvelle police de caractères *or* de la nouvelle fonte; **the error was caused because the data had not been accurately keyed** = l'erreur provenait d'une mauvaise saisie des données

ACD = AUTOMATIC CALL DISTRIBUTION

ACDI = ASYNCHRONOUS COMMUNICATIONS DEVICE INTERFACE

acetate *noun* transparent *m* (d'acétate); **the graphs were plotted on acetate, for use on an overhead projector** = les graphiques avaient été dessinés sur des transparents pour être montrés au rétroprojecteur

ACF = ADVANCED COMMUNICATIONS FUNCTION

achieve *verb* réussir *or* parvenir à; **hardware designers are trying to achieve compatibility between all the components of the system** = les concepteurs de matériel informatique tentent de parvenir à une compatibilité totale entre tous les composants du système

achromatic *adjective* achromatique; *(grey)* **achromatic colour** = couleur *f* achromatique

ACIA = ASYNCHRONOUS COMMUNICATIONS INTERFACE ADAPTER

ACK *or* **ACKNLG** = ACKNOWLEDGE (caractère d') accusé *m* de réception (positif); **the printer generates an ACK signal when it has received data** = l'imprimante émet un signal pour accuser réception des données

Ackerman's function *noun* fonction *f* d'Ackerman

acknowledge 1 *noun* (signal *or* caractère d') accusé *m* de réception **2** *verb* accuser réception (d'un message) *or* envoyer un accusé de réception; **acknowledge character** = caractère *m* d'accusé de réception

◊ **acknowledged mail** *noun (signals to the sender when an electronic mail message has been read)* message *m* avec accusé de réception

◊ **acknowledgements** *noun (in books)* remerciements *mpl (in magazines)* crédits *mpl*

ACM = ASSOCIATION OF COMPUTING MACHINERY

acoustic *adjective* acoustique; **acoustic hood** = hotte *f or* capot *m* d'insonorisation; **an acoustic hood allows us to talk and print in the same room** = grâce au capot d'insonorisation, il est possible d'avoir une conversation dans la pièce où l'imprimante fonctionne; *(original data storage method)* **acoustic delay line** = ligne *f* à retard acoustique; **acoustic store** *or* **acoustic memory** = mémoire *f* acoustique

◊ **acoustical feedback** *noun* retour *m* acoustique

◊ **acoustics** *noun* l'acoustique *f*

acoustic coupler *noun* coupleur *m* acoustique; **I use an acoustic coupler with my laptop computer** = j'utilise un coupleur acoustique avec mon (ordinateur) portable

acquisition *noun* acquisition *f*; **data acquisition** = acquisition *f* de données

ACR = AUDIO CASSETTE RECORDER enregistreur *m* de cassettes audio; magnétophone *m*; **ACR interface** = interface *f* ACR

Acrobat™ *noun (file format developed by Adobe Systems)* (format de fichier graphique Adobe) Acrobat

acronym *noun* acronyme *m*; **the acronym FORTRAN means Formula Translator** = l'acronyme FORTRAN signifie 'Formula Translator'; **the acronym RAM means Random Access Memory** = RAM est l'abréviation de 'Random Access Memory'

actintic light *noun* lumière *f* actinique

action *noun* **(a)** action *f*; **action has been taken to repair the fault** = on a pris les mesures nécessaires pour remédier au défaut *or* pour rectifier *or* réparer ce qui n'allait pas; **to take action** = agir *or* prendre des mesures *or* intervenir **(b)** *(in SAA CUA frontend: user event, such as pressing a key)* action *f (top line of the screen that displays the menu names)* **action bar** = barre *f* de menu; **action bar pull-down** = déroulement *m* du menu; *(associated with a particular menu option)* **action code** = code *m* action; *(set of actions)* **action cycle** = cycle *m* fonctionnel; **action list** = liste *f* d'actions; **action message** = message *m* d'intervention; *(object to which an action should be applied)* **action-object** = objet *m* d'action **(c)** *(photography)* **action field** = champ *m* (d'action); **action frame** = champ *m or* cadrage *m* d'une scène; **action shot** = (i) prise *f* de vue *or* tournage *m* d'une scène; (ii) image *f* d'une scène

activate *verb* activer *or* mettre en marche; **pressing CR activates the printer** = en appuyant sur la touche CR, on met l'imprimante en marche

active *adjective* actif, -ive; *(application being used)* **active application** = application active; *(area that contains data; area that will start or select a function)* **active area** = zone active; *(spreadsheet cell currently selected)* **active cell** = cellule de travail; **active code page** = code page en vigueur; *(database file currently being accessed)* **active database** = base de données active; **active device** = dispositif (électronique) actif *or* armé; **active file** = fichier actif; **active gateway** = passerelle active; **active high** = signal haut actif; *(hub that directs packets of data)* **active hub** = concentrateur *or* hub actif; *(line being used to transfer data)* **active line** = ligne active; *(link currently being used to transfer information)* **active link** = connexion *or* liaison active; **active low** = signal bas actif; *(of screen)* **active matrix** = (écran à) matrice active; **active matrix liquid crystal display** = écran *m* à cristaux liquides à matrice active; *(node connected to another node)* **active node** = noeud actif; *(printer currently connected to the computer's printer port)* **active printer** = imprimante active; *(program currently in control of the processor)* **active program** = programme actif; *(record being updated or accessed)* **active record** = enregistrement actif; **active star** = réseau en étoile actif; **active state** = mode actif; **active storage** = stockage actif; *(area of display screen or window in use)* **active window** = fenêtre active; *see also* WINDOW

◊ **activity** *noun* **(a)** activité *f*; *(in a multitasking system)* **activity level** = niveau *m* d'activité; *(small light on the front of a computer that indicates when the disk drive is reading or writing data)* **activity light** = témoin *m* d'activité *or* lampe *f* témoin; *(organizing of activities)* **activity loading** = (mode de) chargement *m* en fonction du taux d'activité *or* de la fréquence d'utilisation; **activity ratio** = taux *m* d'activité; *(record of activities)* **activity trail** = suivi *m or* enregistrement *m or* traçage *m* d'activité **(b)** **activities** = tâches *fpl* (d'un ordinateur)

actual address *or* **absolute address** *noun* adresse *f* réelle *or* adresse absolue; **actual code** = code *m* absolu *or* code machine; *(average number*

of data bits transferred in a period) **actual data transfer rate** = débit *m* réel de transfert de données; **actual instruction** = instruction absolue

actuator *noun* (i) bras *m* de lecture; (ii) vérin *m*

ACU = AUTOMATIC CALLING UNIT

acuity *noun* *(sight)* acuité *f* visuelle; *(hearing)* acuité auditive

acutance *noun* acutance *f or* piqué *m*

acute *adjective* **(a)** *(pointed)* aigu, -uë **(b)** **acute accent** = accent aigu

A/D *or* **A to D** = ANALOG TO DIGITAL

ADA *noun* langage ADA

adapt *verb* adapter; **can this computer be adapted to 5.25 inch disks?** = est-ce qu'il est possible d'adapter cet ordinateur pour les disquettes 5,25 pouces?

◊ **adaptation** *noun* adaptation *f*; **the adaptation of the eye to respond to different levels of brightness** = l'adaptation de l'oeil pour répondre à différents niveaux de luminosité *or* de brillance

◊ **adapter** *or* **adaptor** *noun* **(a)** *(connector)* adaptateur *m*; **the cable adapter allows attachment of the scanner to the SCSI interface** = l'adaptateur du câble permet de relier le scanner à une interface SCSI; **adapter plug** = adaptateur; **data adapter unit** = adaptateur de ligne *or* de voie de communication **(b)** *(add-on interface board)* **adapter card** = carte *f or* adaptateur; *(device in a computer that provides software commands that display graphics)* **graphics adapter** = carte graphique; **the new graphics adapter is capable of displaying higher resolution graphics** = la nouvelle carte graphique améliore la résolution graphique de l'écran; **the cable to connect the scanner to the adapter is included in the package** = le câble de liaison entre le scanner et l'adaptateur est compris; *see also* CGA, EGA, VGA; *(add-in board that connects a computer to a network)* **network adapter** = carte réseau *or* adaptateur de réseau

◊ **adaptive channel allocation** *noun* allocation *f* dynamique de canal; *(standard that defines a method of converting an analog signal into a compressed digital signal)* **adaptive differential pulse code modulation (ADPCM)** = modulation *f* différentielle dynamique par impulsions et codage *or* norme *f* de conversion ADPCM; *(used to adjust the size of data packets)* **adaptive packet assembly** = assemblage *m* adaptatif de paquets *or* groupage *m* adaptatif de données (en correction d'erreur MNP); **adaptive routing** = acheminement *m or* routage *m* dynamique; **adaptive system** = système *m* auto-adaptable *or* dynamique

adaptor *see* ADAPTER

ADC = ANALOG TO DIGITAL CONVERTER

add *verb* **(a)** *(figures)* additionner; **in the spreadsheet each column should be added to make a subtotal** = l'addition de chacune des colonnes du tableau donne un sous-total; **add time** = temps *m*

d'addition; **add register** = registre *m* d'addition
(b) *(parts or text)* ajouter; **the software house has added a new management package to its range of products** = les producteurs de logiciels ont ajouté un nouveau progiciel de gestion à leur gamme de produits; **adding or deleting material from the text is easy using function keys** = avec les touches de fonction, il est facile d'ajouter ou de supprimer du texte

◊ **added entry** *noun* entrée *f* secondaire

◊ **addend** *noun* cumulateur *m or* second terme d'une addition

◊ **adder** *noun* additionneur *m*; **adder-subtractor** = additionneur-soustracteur *m*; **full adder or three input adder** = additionneur complet *or* à trois entrées; **half adder or two input adder** = demi-additionneur *or* additionneur à deux entrées; **parallel adder** = additionneur parallèle; **serial adder** = additionneur séquentiel

add-in *noun & adjective* (dispositif, etc.) supplémentaire *or* additionnel, -elle; **add-in card** = carte additionnelle *or* carte d'extension; **the first method is to use a page description language, the second is to use an add-in processor card** = vous pouvez soit vous servir d'un langage de description de pages soit ajouter une carte processeur; **can you explain the add-in card method?** = pourriez-vous expliquer comment fonctionne le système de carte d'extension?; **processing is much faster with add-in cards** = le traitement s'effectue beaucoup plus rapidement avec les cartes d'extension

addition *noun* addition *f*; **addition record** = enregistrement *m or* fichier *m* de mise à jour; **addition time** = temps *m* d'addition; **addition without carry** = (i) addition sans retenue; (ii); *(same as EXOR function)* exclusion *f* réciproque *or* OU exclusif; **destructive addition** = addition destructive

◊ **additional** *adjective* additionnel, -elle *or* supplémentaire; **can we add three additional workstations to the network?** = peut-on ajouter trois postes *or* stations de travail supplémentaires au réseau?

◊ **additive colour mixing** *noun* synthèse *f* additive (de couleurs)

add-on *noun & adjective* complément *m* ; (dispositif) supplémentaire *or* additionnel, -elle *or* additif, -ive; **the add-on hard disk will boost the computer's storage capabilities** = un disque dur supplémentaire augmentera la capacité de stockage de l'ordinateur; **add-on board** = carte d'extension; **the new add-on board allows colour graphics to be displayed** = cette nouvelle carte d'extension permet l'affichage graphique en couleur (NOTE: opposite is **built-in**)

address 1 *noun* **(a)** *(street, town, etc.)* adresse *f*; **address list** = répertoire *m or* liste *f* d'adresses; **we keep an address list of two thousand businesses in Europe** = notre fichier contient les adresses de deux mille sociétés en Europe **(b)** *(in central processing unit)* adresse; **each separate memory word has its own unique address** = chaque mot

mémoire distinct a sa propre et unique adresse; **this is the address at which the data starts** = c'est l'adresse à laquelle les données commencent; **absolute address or actual address or direct address** = adresse absolue *or* adresse réelle *or* adresse machine; **address access time** = temps *m* d'adressage; **address base** = base *f* d'adressage; *(list of node addresses; list of the network addresses)* **address book** = livre *m* d'adresses; **address bus** = bus *m* d'adresses; *(special code that identifies an address)* **address code** = code *m* adresse; **address computation** = calcul *m* d'une adresse; **address decoder** = décodeur *m* d'adresse; **address field** = champ *m* (d') adresse; **address format** = format *m* d'adresse; **address mapping** = table *f* de correspondance des adresses; **address mark** = marque *f* (de début) d'adresse; **address modification** = modification *f* d'adresse; **address register** = registre *m* d'adresse; *(used to link one IP address to a low-level physical address)* **address resolution protocol (ARP)** = protocole *m* de résolution d'adresse *or* protocole ARP; *see also* TCP/IP **address space** = espace *m* adresse; **address strobe** = signal *m* de validité d'adresse; **address track** = piste *f* d'adresses; *(address produced by calculating an expression)* **address translation** = adresse calculée; **address word** = mot *m* adresse; **base address** = adresse de base; *(address of the node to which data is being sent)* **destination address** = adresse de destination; **initial address** = adresse d'origine; **machine address** = adresse machine; **network address** = adresse de réseau; **relative address** = adresse relative **2** *verb* **(a)** *(letter)* adresser; **to address a letter or a parcel** = adresser une lettre *or* un colis **(b)** *(in CPU)* créer *or* définir une adresse; **a larger address word increases the amount of memory a computer can address** = plus le mot adresse est long, plus la mémoire adressable de l'ordinateur augmente

QUOTE The world's largest open data network, the Internet, links more than 10,000 local networks and 3 million workstations in 50 countries. It has grown so fast that its address space is 'bust' and is being redesigned to allow further expansion.

Computing

addressability *noun (of pixels)* capacité *f* d'adressage

◊ **addressable** *adjective* adressable; **with the new operating system, all of the 5MB of RAM is addressable** = dans le nouveau système d'exploitation, la totalité des 5Mo de RAM installée est adressable; **addressable cursor** = curseur adressable; *(point or pixel that can be directly addressed)* **addressable point** = point *m* adressable; **addressable terminal** = terminal à adressage protégé

◊ **addressee** *noun (person)* destinataire *m&f*

◊ **addressing** *noun (accessing a location in memory)* adressage *m*; **absolute addressing** = adressage absolu; **abbreviated addressing** = adressage abrégé *or* simplifié; **bit addressing** = adressage binaire; **deferred addressing** = adressage différé *or* indirect; **direct addressing** = adressage direct; **immediate addressing** = adressage immédiat; **indexed addressing** =

adrassage indexé; **indirect addressing** = adressage indirect; **addressing capacity** = disponibilité *f or* capacité *f* d'adressage *or* de mémoire; **addressing level** = niveau *m* d'adressage; **addressing method** = méthode *f* d'adressage; **addressing mode** = mode *m* d'adressage

adjacent *adjective* adjacent, -e *or* contigu, -uë; **the address is stored adjacent to the customer name field** = l'adresse est rangée en mémoire à côté du champ nom du client; *(two domains linked by two adjacent nodes)* **adjacent domains** = domaines adjacents; *(two nodes connected by a path)* **adjacent nodes** = noeuds adjacents

adjunct register *noun (where the top 16 bits are used for control information and the bottom 16 bits are available for use by a program)* registre *m* couplé

adjust *verb* ajuster *or* régler *or* modifier; **you can adjust the brightness and contrast by turning a knob** = vous n'avez qu'à tourner un bouton pour régler la luminosité et le contraste

◊ **adjustment** *noun* ajustement *m or* réglage *m or* mise *f* au point *or* modification *f*; **the brightness needs adjustment** = la luminosité a besoin d'un réglage; **I think the joystick needs adjustment as it sometimes gets stuck** = il faudrait vérifier la manette de commande qui reste parfois coincée

administrator *noun* **(a)** *(person who is responsible for looking after a network)* administrateur *m* **(b)** *(software or person)* contrôleur *m or* superviseur *m or* directeur *m* de programme; *(of a database management system)* **data administrator** = gestionnaire *m* de données; *(personne)* **database administrator (DBA)** = administrateur de base de données

Adobe™ *(software company that developed products including Acrobat, ATM, and PostScript)* (la société) Adobe™

◊ **Adobe Type Manager™** *or* **ATM™** *(standard for describing scalable fonts)* gestionnaire *m* de police Adobe *or* ATM; *see also* OUTLINE FONTS

ADP = AUTOMATIC DATA PROCESSING

ADPCM = ADAPTIVE DIFFERENTIAL PULSE CODE MODULATION

advance *verb* (faire) avancer; *(paper or film)* entraîner; **the paper is advanced by turning this knob** = ce bouton sert à l'entraînement du papier; **advance the cursor two spaces along the line** = faites avancer le curseur de deux espaces (sur la ligne)

◊ **advanced** *adjective* avancé, -ée *or* évolué, -ée; *(routines stored on a ROM chip in the IBM PS/2 range of PCs)* **advanced basic input/output system (ABIOS)** = ABIOS *or* BIOS étendu; **advanced communications function (ACF)** = fonction *f* avancée de communication; *(version of UNIX produced by IBM to run its range of PCs)* **Advanced Interactive Executive (AIX)** = (version UNIX) AIX; **advanced peer-to-peer networking (APPN)** = réseau égal à égal avancé *or* réseau poste à poste avancé *or* réseau sans serveur dédié (SSD) *or* réseau APPN; *(protocols that allow peer-to-peer communication between workstations)* **advanced program to program communications (APPC)** = programmation *f* avancée des programmes de communications (APPC) *or* protocole *m* APPC; *(method of storing data onto a hard disk)* **advanced run-length limited (ARLL)** = encodage *m* ARLL; **advanced version** = version avancée *or* évoluée

adventure game *noun* jeu *m* (électronique) d'aventure

advisory lock *noun (lock placed on a region of a file)* blocage *m or* verrouillage *m* de protection

◊ **advisory system** *noun (expert system that provides advice to a user)* système-conseil *m*

aerial 1 *noun* antenne *f*; **aerial cable** = câble *m* d'antenne **2** *adjective (in the air)* aérien, -ienne; **aerial image** = vue *f* plongeante *or* aérienne

affect *verb* affecter *or* influer sur *or* avoir une incidence sur; **changes in voltage will affect the way the computer functions** = les sautes *or* les variations de tension vont influer sur *or* affecter le fonctionnement de l'ordinateur

affirmative *adjective* affirmatif, -ive; positif, -ive; **affirmative acknowledgement** = accusé *m* de réception positif *or* confirmation positive (d'un message)

AFIPS = AMERICAN FEDERATION OF INFORMATION PROCESSING SOCIETIES

AFNOR = ASSOCIATION FRANCAISE DE NORMALISATION

AFP = APPLETALK FILING PROTOCOL™

afterglow *see* PERSISTENCE

after-image *noun (copy of a block of data that has been modified)* copie *f* image

aftersales service *noun* service *m* après-vente (SAV)

AGC = AUTOMATIC GAIN CONTROL

agenda *noun (list of tasks or appointments or activities that have to be carried out)* agenda *m*; *(for appointments)* **electronic agenda** = agenda électronique

agent *noun* **(a)** agent *m* *(program or software that runs on a workstation in a network)* (programme) agent intelligent **(b)** *(series of commands or actions carried out automatically)* agent

aggregate *noun* agrégat *m*; *(total bandwidth of a channel)* **aggregate bandwidth** = largeur *f* de bande agréée *or* autorisée; **aggregate function** = fonction *f* d'agrégation *or* de globalisation; **aggregate line speed** = débit *m* théorique (de données dans un canal); *(command that starts an aggregate function)* **aggregate operator** = opérateur *m* de globalisation; **data aggregate** = données *fpl* structurées

AI = ARTIFICIAL INTELLIGENCE

A & I = ABSTRACTING AND INDEXING

aid 1 *noun* aide *f or* assistance *f*; **the computer is a great aid to rapid processing of large amounts of information** = l'ordinateur est une aide importante pour le traitement d'une grande quantité de données; **diagnostic aid** = aide au diagnostic **2** *verb* aider *or* assister; **industrial design is aided by computers** = l'ordinateur est un outil très utile à l'esthétique industrielle; *see also* COMPUTER-AIDED

aiming symbol *or* **field** *noun (defines the area in which a light-pen can be detected)* symbole *m* de détection *or* zone *f* de détection

airbrush *noun (painting tool that creates a diffuse pattern of dots)* aérographe *m*; **we used the airbrush tool to create the cloud effects in this image** = nous avons utilisé l'aérographe pour créer un effet de nuage dans cette image

◊ **air circuit breaker** *noun* disjoncteur *m* à air

◊ **air gap** *noun* entrefer *m*

AIX™ = ADVANCED INTERACTIVE EXECUTIVE

alarm *noun* alarme *f or* signal *m* sonore; **all staff must leave the building if the alarm sounds** = tout le personnel doit quitter le bâtiment dès que la sonnerie d'alarme retentit; **an alarm rings when the printer has run out of paper** = un signal sonore prévient qu'il ne reste plus de papier dans l'imprimante

albumen plate *noun (photography)* plaque *f* photosensible à l'albumen

ALC = AUTOMATIC LEVEL CONTROL

alert *noun (warning message)* (message d') alerte *f*; *(warning panel displayed on screen)* **alert box** = (boîte de) message *m* d'alerte; **the alert box warned me that I was about to delete all my files** = le message d'alerte m'a averti que j'étais sur le point d'effacer tous mes fichiers; *(that triggers an alarm)* **alert condition** = condition *f* d'alerte; *(warning that network hardware is not working properly)* **network alert** = alerte réseau

algebra *noun* algèbre *f*; **Boolean algebra** = algèbre de Boole *or* algèbre booléenne

◊ **algebraic language** *noun (context-free language)* langage *m* documentaire *or* algébrique

ALGOL = ALGORITHMIC LANGUAGE langage *m* algorithmique *or* ALGOL

algorithm *noun* algorithme *m*

◊ **algorithmic** *adjective* algorithmique; **algorithmic language** *or* **ALGOL** = langage algorithmique *or* ALGOL; *see also* FIRST

> QUOTE image processing algorithms are stepby step procedures for performing image processing operations
> *Byte*

> QUOTE the steps are: acquiring a digitized image, developing an algorithm to process it, processing the image, modifying the algorithm until you are satisfied with the result
> *Byte*

> QUOTE the complex algorithms needed for geometrical calculations make heavy demands on the processor
> *PC Business World*

alias *noun (name given to a file, port, device, etc.)* alias *m*; **the operating system uses the alias COM1 to represent the serial port address 3FCh** = le système d'exploitation utilise l'alias COM1 pour désigner le port série à l'adresse 3FCh; *(another name that is used instead of the user name)* **alias name** = nom d'alias *m*

◊ **aliasing** *noun (jagged edges along diagonal or curved lines on a computer screen)* crénelage *m or* effet *m* d'escalier; *(method of reducing the jagged edges or adding sound signals to create a smoother sound)* **anti-aliasing** = anticrénelage *m or* lissage *m* (de courbes)

alien *adjective* étranger, -ère; **alien disk** = disquette non compatible; **alien disk reader** = lecteur de disquettes non compatibles *or* lecteur multidisque; **when you have an alien disk select the multi-disk option to allow you to turn the disk drive into an alien disk reader** = si la disquette n'est pas compatible, validez la fonction 'multidisque' qui permet au lecteur de lire une disquette non compatible

align *verb* **(a)** *(make sure that characters are spaced and levelled correctly)* aligner; **align text** = justifier le texte; *see also* JUSTIFY **(b)** *(read/write head)* positionner *or* aligner

◊ **aligner** *noun (on typewriter, etc.)* dispositif *m* d'alignement *or* de cadrage *or* de positionnement

◊ **aligning edge** *noun (of optical character recognition system)* bord *m* d'alignement *or* de référence

◊ **alignment** *noun* alignement *m*; **in alignment** = aligné, -ée; **out of alignment** = désaligné, -ée; **alignment pin** = téton *m or* pige *f* d'alignement

allocate *verb* allouer *or* répartir *or* attribuer *or* affecter; **the operating system allocated most of main memory to the spreadsheet program** = le système d'exploitation a alloué *or* attribué presque toute la mémoire principale au tableur

◊ **allocation** *noun* **(a)** allocation *f or* attribution *f*; **band allocation** = attribution de bandes de fréquences *or* de longueurs d'ondes; **the new band allocation means we will have more channels** = la nouvelle attribution de bandes de fréquences permettra d'avoir un plus grand nombre de voies de transmission **(b)** *(dividing memory or disk space, etc.* in various ways)* allocation *f*; **allocation routine** = programme d'allocation; *(sector on a hard disk used to store a file)* **allocation unit** = unité *f* d'allocation; **dynamic allocation** = allocation dynamique; *(process of providing an application with the memory it requires)* **memory allocation** = allocation de mémoire

QUOTE IBM has issued a fix to correct bugs in the latest version of its OS/2 PC operating system which could cause screen crashes. The fix is meant to correct seven problems with OS/2 2.0, which began shipping just three months ago. They include problems with swapper files and DOS memory allocation.

Computing

allophone *noun* allophone *m&f*

all points addressable (APA) mode *noun (graphics mode in which each pixel can be individually addressed)* mode *m* d'adressage à matrice active

ALPHA™ *noun (processor chip developed by Digital Equipment Corporation)* ALPHA™

alpha *or* **alpha test** *noun (first test of a computer product)* alpha test *m*; **the new software is still in an alpha product stage** = le nouveau logiciel en est au stade alpha; *see also* BETA TEST

◊ **alpha beta technique** *noun (technique used in artificial intelligence)* technique *f* alpha bêta

◊ **alpha channel** *noun (top eight bits that define the properties of a pixel)* canal *m* alpha

◊ **alpha-particle** *noun* particule *f* alpha; **alpha-particle sensitivity** = sensibilité *f* aux rayons alpha

◊ **alpha radiation** *noun* rayonnement *m or* rayons *mpl* alpha

◊ **alpha wrap** *noun* enrouleur *m* alpha

alphabet *noun* alphabet *m*

◊ **alphabetic character (set)** *noun* lettres *fpl* de l'alphabet; **alphabetic string** = chaîne de caractères alphabétiques

◊ **alphabetical order** *noun* ordre *m* alphabétique

◊ **alphabetically** *adverb* alphabétiquement; en *or* par ordre alphabétique; **the files are arranged alphabetically under the customer's name** = les fichiers sont classés en *or* par ordre alphabétique sous le nom du client

◊ **alphabetize** *verb* classer par ordre alphabétique; **enter the bibliographical information and alphabetize it** = veuillez saisir les données bibliographiques et les mettre en ordre alphabétique

alphageometric *adjective* alphagéométrique

alphameric *US* = ALPHANUMERIC

alphamosaic *adjective* alphamosaïque

alphanumeric *adjective* alphanumérique; **alphanumeric characters** *or* **alphanumerics** =

caractères *mpl* alphanumériques; **alphanumeric data** = données *fpl* alphanumériques; **alphanumeric display** = affichage *m* alphanumérique; **alphanumeric keyboard** = clavier *m* alphanumérique; **alphanumeric operand** = opérande *m* alphanumérique; **alphanumeric string** = chaîne *f* de caractères alphanumériques

QUOTE geometrical data takes up more storage space than alphanumeric data
PC Business World

alphaphotographic *adjective* alphaphotographique

◊ **alphasort** *verb* classer (des données) en *or* par ordre alphabétique

Alt key *noun* touche *f* Alt; **press Alt and P at the same time to print your document** = appuyez en même temps sur les touches Alt et P pour imprimer le document

COMMENT: the Alt key has become the standard method of activating a menu bar in any software running on a PC; for example, Alt-F normally displays the File menu of a program, Alt-X normally exits the program

alter *verb* changer *or* modifier; **the program specifications have just been altered** = les spécifications du programme viennent d'être modifiées

◊ **alterable** *adjective* modifiable *or* qui peut être changé *or* qui peut être modifié; *see also* EAPROM, EAROM

◊ **alteration** *noun* changement *m or* modification *f*; **the new version of the software has many alterations and improvements** = la nouvelle version du logiciel comporte de nombreuses modifications et améliorations

alternate 1 *verb* (faire) alterner **2** *adjective* **(a)** alterné, -ée; **alternate mode** = (en) mode alterné; **alternate route** = voie *f* de déroutement *or* déviation *f* **(b)** autre *or* alternatif, -ive; *(set of special characters)* **alternate character set** = jeu *m or* police *f* de caractères disponible; **we can print Greek characters by selecting the alternate character set** = nous pouvons imprimer des caractères grecs en utilisant un second jeu de caractères; *(key that is not the primary key)* **alternate key** = touche *f* secondaire

◊ **alternately** *adverb* tour à tour *or* alternativement *or* à l'alternat

◊ **alternating current (AC)** *noun* courant *m* alternatif (CA)

◊ **alternation** *noun* alternance *f*

◊ **alternator** *noun* alternateur *m*

alternative 1 *noun* alternative *f or* variante *f* ; choix *m*; **what is the alternative to re-keying all the data?** = que peut-on faire sinon saisir de nouveau toutes les données?; **we have no alternative** = nous n'avons pas le choix *or* il n'y a rien d'autre à faire *or* il n'y a pas d'alternative **2** *adjective* autre; *(logical function)* **alternative denial** = fonction *f* NON-ET

ALU = ARITHMETIC LOGIC UNIT

AM = AMPLITUDE MODULATION

A-MAC *(low bandwidth variation of MAC)* basse fréquence multiplexée *or* A-MAC

ambient *adjective* ambiant, -e; **ambient noise level** = niveau *m* de bruit de fond *or* de bruit ambiant; **the ambient noise level in the office is greater than in the library** = le bruit de fond dans ce bureau est plus élevé que dans la bibliothèque; **ambient temperature** = température ambiante

ambiguous *adjective* ambigu, -uë *or* équivoque; **ambiguous filename** = nom de fichier ambigu

◊ **ambiguity** *noun* ambiguïté *f*; **ambiguity error** = erreur *f* d'ambiguïté; **error ambiguity** = incertitude causée par une erreur

ambisonics *noun* enregistrement *m* ambisonique *or* d'ambiance

AMM = ANALOG MULTIMETER

amendment record *noun* enregistrement *m* des détails *or* des mouvements *or* des modifications

American National Standards Institute (ANSI) *(American equivalent of)* Association française de normalisation (AFNOR)

American Standard Code for Information Interchange (ASCII) (code) ASCII

Amiga™ *(range of personal computers developed by Commodore)* (ordinateurs) Amiga™

COMMENT: Amiga computers are based on the Motorola 68000 range of CPUs and are not IBM PC compatible

amount 1 *noun* quantité *f*; **what is the largest amount of data which can be processed in one hour?** = quelle est la quantité maximale de données qu'on puisse traiter en une heure? **2** *verb* **to amount to** = se monter à *or* s'élever à *or* équivaloir à; **the total keyboarded characters amount to ten million** = le total des caractères saisis (par clavier) est de dix millions

amp *or* **ampere (A)** *noun* ampère (A) *m* (NOTE: used with figures: **a 13-amp fuse)**

ampersand (&) *noun* 'et' commercial *or* esperluette *f*

amplifier *noun* amplificateur *m*; **audio amplifier** = amplificateur audio *or* de basse fréquence; **low noise amplifier** = amplificateur à faible bruit; **amplifier class** = classe *f* d'amplificateur

◊ **amplification** *noun* amplification *f*; **increase the amplification of the input signal** = augmentez l'amplification *or* le gain du signal d'entrée; **the amplification is so high, the signal is distorting** = l'amplification est si grande qu'elle cause une distorsion du signal

◊ **amplify** *verb* amplifier; **the received signal needs to be amplified before it can be processed** = le signal reçu doit être amplifié avant d'être traité; **amplified telephone** = téléphone *m* amplifié *or* à écoute amplifiée

amplitude *noun* amplitude *f*; **amplitude distortion** = distorsion *f* d'amplitude; **amplitude modulation (AM)** = modulation *f* d'amplitude (MA); **amplitude quantization** = quantification *f* d'amplitude

analog *or* **analogue** *noun* **(a)** analogue *m or* appareil *m* analogique; **analog channel** = voie *f* analogique; **analog computer** = calculateur analogique; *(data represented as a continuously variable signal)* **analog data** = données *fpl* analogiques; *(monitor that can display an infinite range of colours or shades of grey)* **analog display** = écran *m* analogique; **analog gate** = porte *f or* circuit *m* analogique; *(communications line that carries analog signals)* **analog line** = ligne *f* analogique *or* commutée; *(test mode used to test the serial port of the local computer or terminal)* **analog loopback** = boucle *f* analogique; *(test mode on a modem)* **analog loopback with selftest** = boucle *f* analogique avec autotest; **analog monitor** = moniteur *m* analogique; **analog multimeter (AMM)** = multimètre *m* analogique; **analog output card** = carte de sortie analogique; **analog recording** = enregistrement *m* analogique; **analog representation** = représentation *f* analogique; **analog signal** = signal *m* analogique; **analog transmission** = transmission *f* analogique **(b) analog to digital (A to D** *or* **A/D)** = (conversion) analogique-numérique *or* analogique à digital; **analog to digital converter (ADC** *or* **A to D converter)** = convertisseur *m* analogique-numérique; **digital to analog converter (DAC** *or* **D to A converter)** = convertisseur numérique-analogique *or* digital à analogique

analyse *or* **analyze** *verb* analyser; **to analyse a computer printout** = analyser une sortie d'imprimante *or* un listing; **to analyse the market potential for a new computer** = faire l'analyse du potentiel du marché pour un nouvel ordinateur

◊ **analysis** *noun* analyse *f*; **data analysis** = analyse de données; **systems analysis** = analyse de systèmes (NOTE: plural is **analyses**)

◊ **analyst** *noun* analyste *m&f*; **systems analyst** = informaticien, -ienne analyste *or* analyste (de) systèmes

◊ **analytical engine** *noun* machine *f* de Babbage

COMMENT: mechanical calculating machine developed by Charles Babbage in 1833 that is generally considered the first general-purpose digital computer

◊ **analyzer** *noun* analyseur *m*; **frequency analyzer** = analyseur de fréquence

anamorphic image *noun* anamorphose *f*

ANAPROP = ANOMALOUS PROPAGATION

anastigmatic *adjective (lens)* anastigmate

ancestral file *noun* fichier *m* ancêtre

anchor cell *noun (cell that defines the start of a range of cells)* cellule *f* d'ancrage

ancillary equipment *noun* accessoires *mpl or* matériels *mpl* annexes

AND *or* **coincidence function** *noun* ET *or* fonction d'intersection; AND *or* **coincidence gate** *or* **circuit** *or* **element** = ET *or* circuit ET *or* porte ET; **AND** *or* **coincidence operation** = ET *or* opération ET *or* intersection logique *or* conjonction logique

anechoic *adjective* (chambre) blanche *or* sourde *or* sans écho

angle *noun (measure of the change in direction)* angle *m*

angstrom (Å) *noun* angström *m*

ANI = AUTOMATIC NUMBER IDENTIFICATION

animate *verb* animer

◊ **animation** *or* **computer animation** *noun (creating the illusion of movement)* animation *f or* animation sur ordinateur

annotation *noun* annotation *f or* commentaire *m*; **annotation symbol** = symbole *m* de commentaire

annunciator *noun* & *adjective (signal)* annonciateur *m*

anode *noun* anode *f*

anomalistic period *noun* période *f* anomale *or* irrégulière

◊ **anomalous** *adj* **anomalous propagation** (ANAPROP) = mauvaise transmission d'images (due à des perturbations atmosphériques)

ANSI *US* = AMERICAN NATIONAL STANDARDS INSTITUTE; *(standard version of the C programming language)* ANSI C = C ANSI; *(resident software program that interprets ANSI screen control codes)* ANSI driver = logiciel *m* de commande ANSI; **ANSI escape sequence** = séquence *f* d'échappement ANSI; **ANSI screen control** = contrôle *m* d'écran ANSI

answer 1 *noun* réponse *f* **2** *verb* **(a)** répondre (à quelqu'un *or* à une lettre *or* au téléphone) **(b)** répondre à un appel; **the first modem originates the call and the second answers it** = le premier modem transmet l'appel tandis que le second y répond; **answer back** = signal *m* de réponse; *(mode of a modem that emits an answertone)* **answer mode** = mode *m* réponse; *(modem that is waiting to receive a call and establish a connection)* **answer modem** = modem *m* de retour *or* de réponse; **answer time** = temps *m* de réponse

◊ **answering machine** *noun* répondeur *m* téléphonique

◊ **answering service** *noun* (service de) permanence *f* téléphonique

◊ **answer/originate (device)** *noun (device, such as a modem, that can receive or send data)* dispositif *m* de retour/d'appel

◊ **answerphone** *noun* répondeur *m* téléphonique

◊ **answertone** *noun (tone an answering modem emits before the carrier is exchanged)* signal *m* de réponse (d'un modem)

antenna *noun* antenne *f*; **antenna array** = (série de) modules *mpl* d'émission-réception d'une antenne réseau; **antenna gain** = gain *m* d'antenne; **array antenna** = antenne réseau

anthropomorphic software *noun (software that appears to react to what a user says)* logiciel *m* anthropomorphique

anti- *prefix* anti-; **anti-aliasing** = anticrénelage *m or* lissage *m* (de courbes); **anticoincidence circuit** *or* **function** = porte *f or* circuit *m* OU exclusif *or* fonction *f* OU exclusif; **anti-static mat** = tapis *m* antistatique; *(in a modem)* **anti-tinkle suppression** (bouton de) suppression *f* de signal d'appel parasite; **anti-virus program** = programme *m or* utilitaire *m* antivirus

APA = ALL POINTS ADDRESSABLE

APD = AVALANCHE PHOTODIODE

aperture *noun* ouverture *f* (d'un objectif); **aperture card** = carte *f* à fenêtre *or* à microfilm *or* à microfiche; *(of antenna)* **aperture illumination** = illumination *f* de l'ouverture; *(in colour TV or monitors)* **aperture mask** = masque *m* de séparation

API = APPLICATION PROGRAMMING INTERFACE

APL = A PROGRAMMING LANGUAGE langage *m* (de programmation) APL

apochromatic lens *noun* objectif *m* apochromatique

apogee *noun (in a satellite's orbit)* apogée *m*

apostrophe (') *noun (typography)* apostrophe *f*

APPC = ADVANCED PROGRAM TO PROGRAM COMMUNICATION

append *verb* annexer *or* joindre *or* ajouter; *(add a file or data to the end of an existing file)* **if you enter the DOS command COPY A+B, the file B will be appended to the end of file A** = en utilisant la command DOS COPY A+B, vous ajoutez le fichier B à la fin du fichier A

◊ **appendix** *noun (in a book)* appendice *m*; *(of a document)* annexe *f*; **for further details see the appendices** = voir annexes pour tout renseignement supplémentaire; **a complete list is printed in the appendix** = vous trouverez la liste complète dans l'appendice (NOTE: plural is **appendices**)

Apple Computer Corporation *(company, formed in 1975, which has developed a range of personal computers including the Apple II, Apple Lisa and, more recently, the Apple Macintosh)* (la société) Apple Computer Corporation

◊ **Apple Desktop Bus (ADB)** *noun (serial bus built into Apple Macintosh computers)* bus *m* Apple Desktop

◊ **Apple file exchange** ™ *noun (program on an Apple Macintosh computer allowing it to read disks from a PC)* (gestionnaire d'échange de fichiers) AFX

◊ **Apple filing protocol (AFP)** ™ *noun (method of storing files on a network server so that they can be accessed from an Apple Macintosh computer)* protocole *m* de gestion de fichier Apple *or* protocole AFP

◊ **Apple Key** *noun (key on the keyboard of an Apple Macintosh that provides a short cut to a menu selection)* touche pomme *or* touche Apple

◊ **Apple** *or* **Apple Macintosh** ™ **computer** *noun (range of personal computers developed by Apple Inc.)* ordinateur Mac *or* Macintosh ™

◊ **Appleshare** ™ *noun (software that allows Apple Macintosh computers to share files)* (logiciel) Appleshare ™

◊ **AppleTalk** ™ *noun (communications protocol developed by Apple Computer that carries data over network hardware between two or more Apple Macintosh computers)* (protocole) AppleTalk ™; *(protocol used to communicate between workstations and servers in a network of Apple Macintosh computers)* **AppleTalk Filing Protocol** ™ **(AFP)** = protocole de gestion de fichier AppleTalk *or* protocole AFP

> QUOTE Apple Computer has fleshed out details of a migration path to the PowerPC RISC architecture for its 7 million Apple Macintosh users. Developments in the pipeline include PowerPC versions of the AppleTalk Remote Access networking protocol.
>
> *Computing*

applet *noun (utility application program)* utilitaire *m*; **there are applets to help format your disk and configure your keyboard** = il existe des utilitaires pour vous aider à formater les disques et configurer le clavier

appliance *noun* appareil *m* (électrique); **all electrical appliances should be properly earthed** = tout appareil électrique doit être mis à la terre

◊ **appliance computer** *noun* ordinateur *m*

application *noun* **(a)** *(asking for something)* demande *f*; **application for an account on the system** = demande d'accès à un système *or* de partition sur le système; demande de compte; **application form** = formulaire *m* de demande; **to fill in an application (form) for an account on the system** = remplir une demande de compte sur le réseau **(b)** *(task which a computer performs or problem that a computer solves)* application *f*; *(programmer who designs an application)*

application developer = développeur d'application; *(binary file that contains the machine code instructions of a program)* **application file** = fichier *m* d'application; *(special software that allows a programmer to define the main functions and look of an application)* **application generator** = générateur *m* d'application; *(small graphical symbol that represents an application program)* **application icon** = icône *f* d'application; *(in ISO/OSI network)* **application layer** = couche application; **application orientated language** = langage *m* d'application; **application package** = progiciel *m* d'application; *(standard program functions that allow any programmer to interface a program with another application)* **application programming interface (API)** = interface *f* de programmation d'application *or* API; **if I follow the published API for this system, my program will work properly** = si je développe mon programme conformément à l'API publié pour ce système, il marchera convenablement; *(part of a program of an OSI environment that interacts with the layers beneath it)* **application service element** = programme (utilitaire) de service; **application software** *or* **application program** = logiciel *m* *or* programme *m* d'application; **the multi-window editor is used to create and edit applications programs** = l'éditeur multifenêtre est utilisé pour créer et éditer les programmes d'application; **application specific integrated circuit (ASIC)** = circuit *m* intégré spécialisé *or* sur mesure *or* circuit spécifique à une application (ASIC); **applications terminal** = ordinateur *m* dédié *or* spécialisé; **application window** = fenêtre *f* d'application; *see also* GUI

> QUOTE they have announced a fourth generation application development tool which allows users of PCs and PC networks to exchange data with mainframe databases
>
> *Minicomputer News*

> QUOTE How do users interact with a computer system? Via a terminal or PC. So what application layer OSI protocol do we need first? The Virtual Terminal. And what do we get? File Transfer Access and Maintenance.
>
> *Computing*

apply *verb* **(a)** *(to ask for something)* faire une demande (de) **(b)** *(to affect or to touch)* s'appliquer (à) *or* convenir (à); **this formula applies only to data received after the interrupt signal** = cette formule ne convient qu'aux données reçues après le signal d'interruption

APPN = ADVANCED PEER-TO-PEER NETWORKING

approve *verb* **(a) to approve of** = approuver *or* être d'accord avec *or* apprécier; **the new graphics monitor was approved by the safety council before being sold** = le nouveau moniteur graphique a été homologué par le conseil de sécurité avant d'être commercialisé; **I approve of the new editor - it's much easier to use** = le nouvel éditeur de texte est tout à fait ce qu'il faut, et beaucoup plus facile à utiliser **(b)** *(to agree to something)* accepter *or* agréer; **the software has to be approved by the**

board = le conseil d'administration doit ratifier le choix du logiciel; **an approved modem should carry a label with a green circle and the words 'Approved by ....'** = un modem agréé (par BABT) doit être muni de l'étiquette au cercle vert portant la mention 'Approved by...'

◊ **approval** *noun* **(a)** approbation *f or* homologation *f*; **a BABT approval is needed for modems** = les modems doivent être agréés par BABT (et porter la mention 'Approved by ...'); **certificate of approval** = certificat *m* d'homologation **(b) on approval** = à condition *or* à l'essai

approximate *adjective* approximatif, -ive; **we have made an approximate calculation of the time needed for keyboarding** = nous avons calculé de façon approximative le temps nécessaire à la saisie du texte (au clavier)

◊ **approximately** *adverb* environ *or* approximativement; **processing time is approximately 10% lower than during the previous quarter** = le temps de traitement est d'environ 10% inférieur à celui du trimestre précédent

◊ **approximating** *adjective* approché, -ée; **using approximating A to D** = en utilisant une valeur approchée de A à la place de D

◊ **approximation** *noun* approximation *f or* résultat *m* approximatif *or* estimation *f*; **approximation of keyboarding time** = calcul approximatif du temps de saisie (au *or* sur *or* par clavier); **the final figure is only an approximation** = ce résultat n'est qu'approximatif; **approximation error** = erreur *f* d'arrondi

APT = AUTOMATICALLY PROGRAMMED TOOLS

Arabic *adjective* **Arabic numbers** *or* **figures** = chiffres *mpl* arabes; **the page numbers are written in Arabic figures** = les pages sont numérotées en chiffres arabes

arbitration *noun* (*ensuring fair usage by several users*) **bus arbitration** = arbitrage *m or* gestion *f* de l'utilisation d'un bus

arcade game *noun* jeu *m* électronique dans une salle de jeux publique *or* jeu d'arcade

archetype *noun* archétype *m*

Archimedes™ *noun* (*personal computer developed by Acorn Computers*) (ordinateur) Archimède

architecture *noun* architecture *f*; **network architecture** = architecture d'un réseau; **onion skin architecture** = architecture en pelure d'oignon; **the onion skin architecture of this computer is made up of a kernel at the centre, an operating system, a low-level language and then the user's programs** = l'architecture en pelure d'oignon de cet ordinateur consiste en un noyau central, une couche système d'exploitation, une couche langage de bas niveau et enfin une couche programmes (d') utilisateur

archive 1 *noun* archives *fpl*; (*special attribute attached to a file that indicates if the file has been archived*) **archive attribute** *or* **bit** *or* **flag** = attribut *m or* bit *m or* drapeau *m* d'archivage; *see also* ATTRIBUTE **archive file** = fichier archives **2** *verb* archiver; **archived copy** = copie archivée *or* copie d'archives

◊ **archival quality** *noun* qualité *f* d'archivage

ARCNET *or* **ARCnet** = ATTACHED RESOURCE COMPUTER NETWORK

COMMENT: network hardware and cable standard developed by Datapoint Corporation; it is a token bus network that transmits data at between 2.5 and 4Mbps. ARCNET uses a single token that moves from one workstation to the next carrying data; ARCNET transmits data at 2.5Mbits per second and uses a star-wired cable topology

area *noun* **(a)** (mesure de) surface *f or* aire *f*; **area composition** = composition *f or* mise *f* en page *or* disposition *f* de page; (*in graphics: instruction to fill an area of the screen*) **area fill** = remplissage *m* de zone; (*line graph in which the area below the line is filled with a pattern*) **area graph** = graphe *m* à aires; **type area** = empagement *m* **(b)** (*section of memory*) zone *f*; **area search** = recherche *f* de zone *or* recherche sélective; (*of monitor*) **image area** = zone d'affichage; (*section of main memory*) **input area** = zone d'entrée (de données) **(c)** (*part of a country*) région *f*; (*of town*) quartier *m or* secteur *m* (d'une ville); (*telephone*) **area code** = indicatif *m* (téléphonique) de zone; *Canada* indicatif régional; **the area code for central London is 0171** = l'indicatif (de zone) de Londres est 0171; **area exchange** = central *m* répartiteur

arg *see* ARGUMENT

argument *or* **arg** *noun* argument *m*; **if you enter the words 'MULTIPLY A, B', the processor will recognise the operator, MULTIPLY, and use it with the two arguments, A and B** = si vous entrez les mots 'MULTIPLY A, B', le processeur reconnaîtra l'opérateur MULTIPLY et l'utilisera avec les deux arguments A et B; *see also* OPERAND; (*punctuation mark or symbol that separates several arguments*) **argument separator** = séparateur *m* d'arguments; **the command 'MULTIPLY A, B' uses a comma as the argument separator** = la commande 'MULTIPLY A, B' utilise une virgule comme séparateur d'arguments

arithmetic *noun* arithmétique *f or* calcul *m*; **arithmetic capability** = capacité *f* de calcul arithmétique; **arithmetic check** = vérification *f* arithmétique; **arithmetic functions** = fonctions *fpl* arithmétiques; **arithmetic instruction** = instruction *f* arithmétique; **arithmetic logic unit (ALU)** *or* **arithmetic unit** = unité *f* arithmétique et logique (UAL); **arithmetic operation** = opération *f* arithmétique; **arithmetic operator** = opérateur *m* arithmétique; **arithmetic register** = registre *m* arithmétique; **arithmetic shift** = décalage *m* arithmétique; **external arithmetic** = arithmétique externe; **internal arithmetic** = arithmétique interne

arm 1 *noun (mechanical device in a disk drive)* bras *m*; **access arm** = bras de lecture/écriture **2** *verb (to prepare)* préparer *or* armer; *(to activate)* valider *or* activer; **armed interrupt** = interruption validée *or* activée

ARP = ADDRESS RESOLUTION PROTOCOL

ARQ = AUTOMATIC REPEAT REQUEST

array *noun (of figures or data)* tableau *m*; *(antennae or circuits)* (en) réseau *m*; **alphanumeric array** = tableau *m* alphanumérique; **array bounds** = bornes *fpl* d'un tableau; **array dimension** = dimension *f* d'un tableau; **array element** = valeur *f or* élément *m* dans un tableau; **array processor** = processeur vectoriel; **the array processor allows the array that contains the screen image to be rotated with one simple command** = le processeur vectoriel permet de faire pivoter le tableau qui contient l'image écran à l'aide d'une seule commande; **logic array** = réseau *or* circuit logique; **string array** = tableau de chaînes de caractères; **three-dimensional array** = tableau à trois dimensions; **two-dimensional array** = tableau à deux dimensions; *see also* ANTENNA

arrow keys *noun (set of four keys that move the cursor around the screen)* touches *fpl* fléchées

arsenide *see* GALLIUM

article *noun* **(a)** *(of newspaper or magazine)* article *m*; **he wrote an article about the user group for the local newspaper** = il a écrit, pour le journal local, un article concernant le groupe d'utilisateurs **(b)** *(of file)* article **(c)** *(of contract)* clause *f or* article *m*; **see article 8 of the contract** = voir l'article 8 du contrat

artificial intelligence (AI) *noun* intelligence *f* artificielle (IA)

artwork *noun (graphical work or images which are to be printed)* maquette *f*; **the artwork has been sent for filming** = la maquette a été envoyée au flashage

ASA = AMERICAN STANDARDS ASSOCIATION **ASA exposure index** = indice ASA (de sensibilité d'un film) (NOTE: see DIN)

ascend *verb (increase)* monter; augmenter; *(arrange data with the smallest value first)* **ascending order** = ordre *m* croissant

◊ **ascender** *noun (of a character)* hampe *m* (d'une lettre)

ASCII = AMERICAN STANDARD CODE FOR INFORMATION INTERCHANGE **ASCII character** = caractère *m* ASCII; **ASCII file** = fichier *m* ASCII; **use a word processor or other program that generates a standard ASCII file** = utilisez un programme de traitement de texte ou un autre programme qui produira un fichier ASCII standard; **ASCII keyboard** = clavier *m* ASCII; **ASCII text** = texte *m* ASCII; *(sequence of ASCII characters followed by the ASCII code zero indicating the end of the sequence)* **ASCIIZ string** = chaîne *f* de caractères ASCIIZ (NOTE: when speaking say **'ass-key'**)

ASIC = APPLICATION SPECIFIC INTEGRATED CIRCUIT

aspect *noun* (i) aspect *m or* apparence *f* ; (ii) descripteurs *mpl or* caractéristiques *fpl*; *(in an information retrieval system)* **aspect card** = carte *f* d'indentification; *(of pixel shapes)* **aspect ratio** = rapport *m* longueur/largeur (d'un pixel); **aspect system** = système *m* de recherche *or* de stockage par descripteurs

ASR = AUTOMATIC SEND/RECEIVE (appareil) émetteur-récepteur

assemble *verb* **(a)** *(to put together)* assembler *or* monter; **the parts for the disk drive are made in Japan and assembled in France** = les pièces du lecteur de disquettes sont fabriquées au Japon, mais l'assemblage se fait en France **(b)** *(to translate assembly code into machine code)* assembler; **there is a short wait during which time the program is assembled into object code** = il y a un certain délai pendant lequel s'effectue l'assemblage en code objet du programme; **syntax errors spotted whilst the source program is being assembled** = des erreurs de syntaxe repérées au cours de l'assemblage du programmme source **(c)** assembler un programme (routines, macros, paramètres)

◊ **assembler (program)** *noun (assembly program)* assembleur *m or* programme *m* d'assemblage; **assembler language** = langage *m* d'assemblage; **absolute assembler** = assembleur absolu; **assembler error message** = message *m* d'erreur de l'assembleur; **cross-assembler** = assembleur croisé; **single-pass assembler** = assembleur une passe; **two-pass assembler** = assembleur deux passes

◊ **assembly** *noun* **(a)** *(putting together)* assemblage *m or* montage *m*; **there are no assembly instructions to show you how to put the computer together** = il n'y a pas de notice de montage pour aider à la mise en place de l'ordinateur; **assembly plant** = usine *f* de montage **(b)** *(converting a program into machine code)* assemblage; **assembly code** = code d'assemblage; *(assembler language)* **assembly language** = langage *m* d'assemblage; **assembly listing** = *(display)* liste *f* (d'un programme) d'assemblage; *(in print)* listing *m or* impression *f* d'un programme d'assemblage; **assembly (language) program** = assembleur *m or* programme *m* d'assemblage; **assembly routine** = routine *f* d'assemblage; **assembly system** = système *m* d'assemblage; **assembly time** = (i) durée *f* d'assemblage; (ii) temps *m* *or* période *f* d'assemblage

assertion *noun (program statement of a fact or rule)* assertion *f*; *(fact that is true or defined as being true)* affirmation *f or* assertion *f*

assign *verb* **(a)** assigner à *or* affecter à *or* allouer; **two PCs have been assigned to outputting the labels** = deux PC ont été affectés à la préparation des étiquettes **(b)** *(a variable)* définir (une variable); *(part of memory)* affecter (une zone de mémoire à une tâche); **assigned frequency** = fréquence *f* assignée *or* allouée

◊ **assignment** *noun* affectation *f or* attribution *f or* allocation *f*; *(in Pascal: check to see if a value is allowed according to its type)* **assignment compatible** = compatibilité *f* d'affectation; *(in C and Fortran: operation to change the type of a value)* **assignment conversion** = conversion d'affectation; **assignment statement** = instruction *f or* déclaration *f* d'affectation

assisted *see* COMPUTER-AIDED

associate **1** *adjective (linked)* associé, -ée **2** *noun (person)* associé, -ée *or* collègue *m&f*

◊ **associated document** *or* **file** *noun (document or file linked to its originating application)* document *m or* fichier *m* associé

◊ **associative addressing** *or* **content-addressable addressing** *noun* adressage *m* associatif; **associative processor** = processeur avec mémoire associative; **associative memory** *or* **storage** *or* **content-addressable storage** = mémoire *f* associative; **associative storage register** = registre *m* de mémoire associative

astable multivibrator *noun* multivibrateur *m* astable

asterisk (*) *noun* astérisque *m or* étoile *f*; **to view all the files beginning with the letter 'L', use the DOS command DIR L*.*** = pour voir tous les fichiers commençant par 'L', utiliser la commande DOS DIR L*.*; *(filling unused decimal places with the asterisk symbol)* **asterisk fill** = remplissage *m* par des astérisques; **we have used asterisk fill to produce the answer of '***122.33'** = nous avons utilisé l'astérisque en remplissage pour obtenir la réponse '***122,33'

asymmetric transmission *noun (data transmission used in high-speed modems)* transmission *f* asymétrique

COMMENT: asymmetric transmission splits a communications channel into two, one that can support fast data transmission at 9,600bps or higher and a slower channel that can support transmission of around 300bps. The slower channel is used to carry control and error-correcting data, the high-speed channel used to transfer the bulk of the data

◊ **asymmetric video compression** *noun (using a powerful computer to compress video)* compression *f* vidéo asymétrique

async *(informal)* = ASYNCHRONOUS

asynchronous *adjective* asynchrone; **asynchronous access** = accès *m* asynchrone; **asynchronous balanced mode (ABM)** = mode *m* asynchrone équilibré; **asynchronous balanced mode extended (ABME)** = mode asynchrone équilibré étendu; **asynchronous communications** = communication *f* asynchrone; **asynchronous communications device interface (ACDI)** = interface *f* de communication asynchrone; **asynchronous communications interface adapter (ACIA)** = interface *f* pour communication asynchrone; **asynchronous computer** = ordinateur *m* asynchrone; *(transfer of data that takes place without any regular timing signal)* **asynchronous data transfer** = transfert *m* de données asynchrone; **asynchronous mode** = mode *m* asynchrone; **asynchronous port** = port *m* (d'accès) asynchrone; **when asynchronous ports are used no special hardware is required** = l'utilisation de ports asynchrones ne demande pas un matériel spécialisé; **asynchronous procedure call (APC)** = appel *m* de procédure asynchrone; *(method of transferring data very rapidly; CCITT and ANSI standard defining cell relay transmission)* **asynchronous transfer mode (ATM)** = transfert *m* asynchrone ATM *or* commutation *f* temporelle asynchrone; *see also* CELL RELAY TRANSMISSION **asynchronous transmission** = transmission *f* asynchrone

QUOTE each channel handles two forms of communication: asynchronous communication is mainly for transferring data between computers and peripheral devices, while character communication is for data transfer between computers
Electronics & Power

AT *noun (standard of PC that uses a 16-bit 80286 processor)* (norme) AT; *(expansion bus standard developed by IBM)* **AT-bus** = bus AT; *(standard keyboard layout for IBM AT personal computers)* **AT-keyboard** = clavier AT

COMMENT: AT originally meant IBM's Advanced Technology personal computer, but is now used to describe any IBM PC compatible that uses a 16-bit processor

AT command set *(standard set of commands to control a modem)* jeu *m* de commandes AT; *(mode of a modem that is ready to accept commands using the AT command set)* **AT mode** = mode *m* AT

Atari ST™ *(range of personal computers developed by Atari Corp)* (ordinateurs) Atari ST™

ATC = AUTHORIZATION TO COPY

ATD = ATTENTION, DIAL; *(standard command for compatible modems used to dial a telephone number)* (commande modem) ATD

ATE = AUTOMATIC TEST EQUIPMENT

ATM *see* ADOBE TYPE MANAGER

ATM = ASYNCHRONOUS TRANSFER MODE

ATM = AUTOMATED TELLER MACHINE

atmosphere *noun* atmosphère *f*

◊ **atmospheric** *adjective* atmosphérique; **atmospheric absorption** = absorption *f* atmosphérique; **atmospheric conditions** = conditions *fpl* atmosphériques

atom *noun* **(a)** *(smallest particle of an element)* atome *m* **(b)** *(value or string that cannot be reduced to a simpler form)* donnée absolue *or* atome

◊ **atomic** *adjective* *(referring to atoms; operation that returns data to its original state if it is stopped during processing)* atomique; **atomic clock** = horloge *f* atomique

attach *verb* **(a)** attacher *or* joindre *or* relier; **attached processor** = processeur *m* auxiliaire (indépendant) relié au processeur central **(b)** *(to connect a node or login to a server on a network)* se connecter (à un noeud *or* à un serveur de réseau); **I issued the command to attach to the local server** = j'ai entré la commande pour me connecter au serveur local

◊ **attached resource computer network (ARCNET)** réseau ARCNET *or* ARCnet

◊ **attachment** *noun* **(a)** accessoire *m*; **there is a special single sheet feed attachment** = il existe un accessoire spécial pour l'alimentation du papier en feuille à feuille **(b)** *(named file with an electronic mail message)* attachement *m*; **there is an attachment with my last mail message - it contains the sales report** = l'attachement joint au dernier message contient le rapport des ventes

attack *noun* *(start of a sound)* attaque *f* (d'un signal, etc.); **attack envelope** = enveloppe *f* d'attaque

attend *verb* assister à *or* être présent à; **attended operation** = opération *f* surveillée

◊ **attention** *noun* (i) attention *f*; (ii) intervention *f*; **this routine requires the attention of the processor every minute** = ce programme exige l'intervention constante du processeur; **attention interruption** = interruption *f* d'intervention; **attention key** = touche *f* d'intervention

◊ **attention code** *noun* *(the characters AT used within the Hayes AT command set to tell a modem that a command follows)* code *m* AT

attenuate *verb* atténuer *or* affaiblir

◊ **attenuation** *noun* *(reduction of a signal)* atténuation *f* *or* affaiblissement *m* *or* perte *f* (de signal); **if the cable is too long, the signal attenuation will start to cause data errors** = si le câble est trop long, l'atténuation du signal va provoquer des erreurs (NOTE: opposite of **gain**)

attribute *noun* **(a)** attribut *m* *or* caractéristique *f*; **this attribute controls the colour of the screen** = cet attribut contrôle la couleur de l'écran; **screen attributes** = attributs d'écran; **pressing Ctrl and B keys at the same time will set the bold attribute for this paragraph of text** = en appuyant sur (les touches) Ctrl et B en même temps, on donne

l'attribut Gras à ce paragraphe **(b)** *(set of control data attached to a file)* attribut; *(indicates if the file has been archived)* **archive attribute** = attribut archive; *(only allows the contents of the file to be viewed)* **read-only attribute** = attribut lecture seule; *(attached to a file used by the operating system)* **system attribute** = attribut système

auctioneering device *noun* filtre *m* de sélection du signal maximal *or* minimal

audible *adjective* audible *or* perceptible à l'oreille *or* qu'on peut entendre; **the printer makes an audible signal when it runs out of paper** = l'imprimante est munie d'un dispositif d'alarme sonore pour avertir qu'il ne reste plus de papier

audience *noun* *(of TV or radio programmes)* audience *f*; **audience rating** = indice *m* d'écoute

audio *adjective & noun* **active audio system** = (système) audio interactif; **audio cassette** = audiocassette *f* *or* cassette *f* audio; **audio cassette recorder (ACR)** = enregistreur *m* de cassettes audio; magnétophone *m*; **audio compressor** = limiteur *m* *or* réducteur *m* de signal audio; **audio conferencing** = audioconférence *f*; *(digital sound sample stored on disk)* **audio file** = fichier *m* audio; **audio frequency** = fréquence *f* audio *or* audiofréquence *f*; **audio port** = port *m* audio; *(frequency range between 50-20 000Hz)* **audio range** = limites *fpl* de la bande des audiofréquences *or* gamme *f* des audiofréquences; **audio response unit** = répondeur *m* vocal; **audio slide** = diapo-son *f*

◊ **audiovisual (AV)** *adjective* audiovisuel, -elle; **audiovisual aids** = matériel audiovisuel

audit 1 *noun* *(noting tasks carried out by a computer)* audit *m* (informatique); **audit trail** = protocole *m* de traçage *or* de contrôle *or* de vérification **2** *verb* *(examine the state of a system and check that it is still working properly)* faire un audit

augend *noun* *(in an addition: the number to which another number is added)* cumulande *m* *or* premier terme d'une addition

augment *verb* augmenter; **augmented addressing** = adressage *m* augmenté

◊ **augmenter** *noun* *(value added to another)* cumulateur *m* *or* second terme d'une addition

AUI connector *noun* *(connector used to connect Ethernet cable to a network adapter)* connecteur *m* AUI

aural *adjective* sonore *or* acoustique

authentic *adjective* authentique

◊ **authenticate** *verb* authentifier

◊ **authentication** *noun* authentification *f*; **authentication of messages** = authentification de messages

author *noun* *(person who wrote a program)* auteur *m*

◊ **authoring** *noun (creating a multimedia application)* création *f* (multimédia); *(programming language used to write CAL and training programs)* **authoring language** = langage *m* auteur; *(tools normally used to develop multimedia applications)* **authoring system** = système auteur

QUOTE The authoring system is a software product that integrates text and fractally compressed images, using any word-processor line editor, to create an electronic book with hypertext links between different pages.

Computing

authority *noun* autorité *f*; **authority file** *or* **list** = fichier *m* *or* liste *f* de référence

authorize *verb* **(a)** *(to give permission)* autoriser (qch) *or* permettre (qch); **to authorize the purchase of a new computer system** = autoriser l'achat d'un nouveau système informatique **(b)** *(to give someone the authority to do something)* autoriser (quelqu'un à faire quelque chose) *or* donner (à quelqu'un) l'autorisation (de faire quelque chose)

◊ **authorization** *noun* **(a)** *(permission or power to do something)* autorisation *f* *or* permission *f*; **authorization to copy (ATC)** = autorisation *f* de copier *or* de dupliquer **(b)** *(permission to access a system)* autorisation; **authorization code** = mot *m* de passe *or* code *m* d'accès

◊ **authorized** *adjective* autorisé, -ée *or* permis, -e; **authorized user** = personne *f* autorisée (à utiliser un système)

auto *adjective & prefix* automatique *or* auto-; *(of paper in printer)* **auto advance** = alimentation *f* *or* entraînement *m* automatique du papier; *(of modem)* **auto-answer** = auto-réponse *f* *or* réponse *f* automatique; **auto-baud scanning** = reconnaissance *f* automatique du débit d'une ligne; **autoboot** = amorçage *m* *or* lancement *m* automatique (d'un système); *(telephone or modem)* **auto-dial** = (avec) système d'appel automatique (d'un correspondant) *or* numérotation *f* automatique; **auto-login** *or* **auto-logon** = ouverture *f* automatique de session; **auto-redial** = (modem *or* téléphone avec) système de rappel automatique d'un correspondant; **auto repeat** = répétition *f* automatique; *(feature that can reload its operating system if there is a fault)* **auto restart** = relance *f* automatique; **auto save** = sauvegarde *f* automatique; **auto start** = lancement *m* *or* mise *f* en route automatique *or* démarrage *m* automatique; **auto stop** = arrêt *m* automatique; *(feature that transforms a bit-mapped image into a vector image)* **auto trace** = suivi *m* automatique; **auto verify** = vérification *f* automatique

QUOTE expansion accessories include auto-dial and auto-answer

Electronic & Wireless World

AUTOEXEC.BAT *(batch file which contains commands that are executed when the computer is first switched on)* (fichier de démarrage) autoexec.bat; *see also* CONFIG.SYS, BATCH FILE

automate *verb* automatiser; **automated office** = bureau *m* électronique; *(system)* bureautique *f*; *US* **automated teller machine (ATM)** = guichet *m* automatique de banque (GAB) *or* automate *m* bancaire

◊ **automation** *noun* automatisation *f*

automatic *noun* automatique; **automatic backup** = sauvegarde *f* automatique; *(telephone system that can handle lots of incoming calls)* **automatic call distribution (ACD)** = (système de) distribution automatique des appels *or* standard *m* automatique *or* distributeur *m* d'appels automatique; **automatic calling unit (ACU)** = système *m* *or* unité *f* d'appel automatique; *(of cursor)* **automatic carriage return** = retour *m* à la ligne automatique; **automatic checking** = auto-test *m*; **automatic data capture** = saisie *f* automatique de données; **automatic data processing (ADP)** = traitement *m* automatique de données; **automatic decimal adjustment** = *(lining up the decimal points in a column)* alignement *m* automatique des virgules; *(rounding to a certain number of decimals)* arrondi *m* à un nombre fixe de décimales; **automatic error correction** = correction *f* automatique d'erreurs; **automatic error detection** = détection *f* automatique d'erreurs; *(process in which special font information is sent to a printer)* **automatic font downloading** = chargement frontal des polices de caractères; **automatic gain control (AGC)** *or* **automatic level control (ALC)** = contrôle *m* de gain automatique; *(feature of a software program used to correctly split and hyphenate words)* **automatic hyphenation** = coupure *f* automatique des mots; *(word-processing)* **automatic letter writing** = composition *f* automatique de lettres types; *(short program)* **automatic loader** = chargeur *m* automatique; *(for telephone)* **automatic message accounting** = compteur *m* d'impulsions automatique (à domicile); *(of monitor)* **automatic mode** *or* **frequency switching** = adaptation *f* automatique du mode *or* de la fréquence (vidéo); *(telephone system which displays the telephone number of the caller)* **automatic number identification (ANI)** = reconnaissance *f* automatique des numéros d'appels; **automatic programming** = programmation *f* automatique; *(spreadsheet mode in which the answers to new formula are calculated every time any value or cell changes)* **automatic recalculation** = recalcul *m* automatique; *(of character)* **automatic repeat** = répétition *f* automatique; *(error correction system used in some modems)* **automatic repeat request (ARQ)** = demande de répétition automatique; correction *f* (d'erreurs) ARQ; **automatic sequencing** = fonctionnement *m* itératif automatique; *(ability of a modem to adjust its data rate to the speed of the remote modem)* **automatic speed matching** = accord *m* automatique des vitesses de transmission; **automatic telephone exchange** = central *m* (téléphonique) automatique *or* autocommutateur *m* (téléphonique); **automatic telling machine** *or* *US* **automated teller machine (ATM)** = guichet *m* automatique de banque

(GAB) *or* automate *m* bancaire; **automatic test equipment (ATE)** = équipement *m* de vérification automatique (EVA); **automatic vending machine** = distributeur *m* automatique (de cigarettes, etc.)

◊ **automatically** *adverb* automatiquement; **the compiler automatically corrected the syntax errors** = le compilateur a corrigé les fautes de syntaxe automatiquement; **a SBC automatically limits the movement of the machine** = un ordinateur à carte unique est, par le fait même, limité dans ses opérations; **the program is run automatically when the computer is switched on** = le programme est lancé automatiquement lors de la mise sous tension de l'ordinateur; **Automatically Programmed Tools (APT)** = (programme de) commandes numériques de machines-outils *or* programme APT

automation *noun* automatisation *f*; **office automation** = bureautique *f*

autopositive *noun* procédé *m* autopositif

A/UX *(version of the Unix operating system for the Apple Macintosh range)* (version Unix) A/UX (pour la gamme des ordinateurs Macintosh); *see also* UNIX

AUX = AUXILIARY; *see also* COM1 *or* SERIAL PORT

auxiliary *adjective* auxiliaire *or* de secours; **the computer room has an auxiliary power supply in case there is a mains failure** = la salle des ordinateurs est équipée d'un bloc d'alimentation de secours en cas de panne de secteur; *(in case of breakdown)* **auxiliary equipment** = matériel *m* de secours; **auxiliary processor** = processeur *m* auxiliaire; **auxiliary storage** *or* **memory** *or* **store** = mémoire *f* auxiliaire; **disk drives and magnetic tapes are auxiliary storage on this machine** = cet appareil est équipé de lecteurs de disquettes et de bandes magnétiques qui servent de mémoire auxiliaire

AV = AUDIOVISUAL

available *adjective* disponible; **available to order only** = articles *mpl* vendus sur commande uniquement; **available light** = lumière ambiante; **available list** = liste *f* des ressources disponibles; **available point** = point *m or* élément *m* d'image;

available power = puissance *f* maximale *or* réelle disponible; *(time during which a system may be used)* **available time** = temps *m* disponible *or* de disponibilité

◊ **availability** *noun* disponibilité *f*; **the availability of the latest software package is very good** = on trouve le nouveau progiciel dans presque tous les magasins

avalanche *noun (one action starting a number of other actions)* avalanche *f*; **there was an avalanche of errors after I pressed the wrong key** = les erreurs n'ont cessé de se multiplier lorsque j'ai appuyé sur la mauvaise touche; **avalanche photodiode (APD)** = photodiode *f* à avalanche

average 1 *noun* moyenne *f*; **on an average** = en moyenne; **we sell on an average five computers a day** = nous vendons en moyenne cinq ordinateurs par jour **2** *adjective* moyen, -enne; **average access time** = temps *m* d'accès moyen; **average delay** = délai *m* moyen; **the average delay increases at nine-thirty when everyone tries to log-in** = après 9h30, le temps d'attente moyen est beaucoup plus long lorsque chacun tente de se loger ou d'entrer dans le système **3** *verb (to produce as an average figure)* atteindre une moyenne (de)

◊ **average out** *verb* atteindre une moyenne (de) *or* faire en moyenne; **it averages out at 120 dpi** = cela fait en moyenne 120 points par pouce *or* une moyenne de 120 ppp

axis *noun (around which something turns)* axe *m*; *(on a graph)* axe (de coordonnées); **the CAD package allows an axis to be placed anywhere** = ce progiciel de CAO permet de positionner un axe où l'on veut; **horizontal axis** = axe des abscisses; **vertical axis** = axe des ordonnées (NOTE: plural is **axes**)

azerty keyboard *noun* clavier *m* AZERTY; *compare with* QWERTY

azimuth *noun* azimut *m*; **azimuth alignment** = réglage *m* d'alignement des têtes *or* des angles d'azimut; **azimuth alignment is adjusted with this small screw** = c'est cette petite vis qui sert à régler l'alignement des têtes *or* des angles d'azimut; **azimuth alignment might not be correct for tape recorded on a different machine** = l'alignement des têtes va peut-être demander un réglage différent pour les bandes enregistrées sur d'autres machines

Bb

B *(hexadecimal number equivalent to decimal 11)* nombre hexadécimal équivalent du 11 décimal *or* B

b *abbreviation (one bit)* b *or* bit *m*; **bps (bits per second)** = bit(s) par seconde (NOTE: compare **B**)

B *abbreviation (one byte)* o *or* octet *m or* B; *(1024 bytes)* **KB (kilobyte)** = Ko *or* kilo-octet *m or* KB

B: *(second disk drive)* (lecteur de disquette) B:; **copy the files from the hard drive C:, to the floppy drive B:** = copiez les fichiers à partir du lecteur de disque dur C: sur la disquette du lecteur B:

Babbage, Charles mathématicien anglais qui inventa la première machine différentielle ou machine de Babbage

| COMMENT: Charles Babbage (1792-1871) was the English inventor of the first automatic calculator and inventor of the forerunner of today's digital computers

babble *noun* diaphonie *f or* bruit *m* de fond

BABT = BRITISH APPROVAL BOARD FOR TELECOMMUNICATIONS; *(organisation that tests and certifies telecommunications equipment)* BABT (Commission qui approuve et certifie les matériels de télécommunication avant leur mise en service dans le Royaume-Uni); **if you design a new modem, you must have BABT approval before you can sell it** = si vous développez un nouveau modem, vous devrez obtenir l'approbation du BABT avant de le commercialiser

back 1 *noun* arrière *m or* dos *m*; **there is a wide range of connectors at the back of the main unit** = on trouve une variété de connecteurs au dos *or* sur le panneau arrière de l'unité centrale; *(panel at the rear of a computer)* **back panel** = panneau *m* arrière; *(in a tree structure)* **back pointer** = pointeur *m* en retour **2** *verb* aider; **battery-backed** = équipé, -ée d'une pile auxiliaire *or* d'une pile de secours; **the RAM disk card has the option to be battery-backed** = la carte RAM peut être équipée, en option, d'une pile de secours; **battery-backed CMOS memory replaces a disk drive in this portable** = dans ce portable, le lecteur de disquettes est remplacé par une mémoire CMOS avec pile auxiliaire

| QUOTE The V3500 has on-board Ethernet and SCSI interfaces, up to 32Mb local DRAM, two programmable timers, a battery-backed real-time clock with 32Kb RAM and four serial ports.
| *Computing*

backbone *noun (high-speed, high-capacity connection path)* (réseau) collecteur *m or* arête *f* dorsale *or* épine *f* dorsale *or* backbone *m*; **we have linked the networks in each office using a high-speed backbone** = nous avons relié les réseaux de chaque établissement par un collecteur à grand débit; *(high-speed ring network)* **backbone ring** = anneau *m* collecteur *or* backbone

backdoor *see* TRAP DOOR

back-end network *noun (connection between a mainframe computer and a high-speed mass storage device)* réseau *m* auxiliaire

◊ **back-end processor** *noun (special purpose auxiliary processor)* processeur *m* de fond *or* processeur principal

◊ **back-end server** *noun (computer that carries out tasks requested by client workstations)* serveur *m* de fond *or* serveur auxiliaire *m*

background *noun* **(a)** *(past work or experience)* expérience *f*; **his background is in the computer industry** = il a une bonne expérience de l'industrie informatique **(b)** *(part of a picture)* arrière-plan *m or* fond *m*; **the new graphics processor chip can handle background, foreground and sprite movement independently** = le nouveau processeur graphique permet de manipuler indépendamment les images d'arrière-plan et d'avant-plan ainsi que les plans-objets; *(of a computer screen)* **background colour** = (couleur de) fond *m*; **black text on a white background is less stressful for the eyes** = un texte en noir sur fond blanc est moins fatigant pour la vue; *(image displayed as a backdrop)* **background image** = image *f* en arrière plan; *(light reflected from paper that is being scanned)* **background reflectance** = réflectance *f* de fond *or* d'arrière-plan **(c)** *(which is present along with the required signal)* **background noise** = bruit *m* de fond; **the other machines around this device will produce a lot of background noise** = les autres appareils placés autour de cet équipement produiront un fort bruit de fond; **the modem is sensitive to background noise** = le modem est sensible au bruit de fond **(d)** *(activity carried out as a low-priority task)* non prioritaire *or* d'arrière-plan *or* en arrière plan; **background communication** = communication *f* en arrière-plan *or* non prioritaire; **background job** = tâche *f* non prioritaire *or* tâche de fond; **background operation** = opération *f* non prioritaire; **background printing** = impression *f* en arrière-plan; **background printing can be carried out whilst you are editing another document** = l'impression peut être exécutée en arrière-plan pendant que vous travaillez sur un autre document; **background program** = programme *m* non prioritaire; *(facility in a spreadsheet program that allows a user to enter new numbers while the program recalculates the solutions in the background)* **background**

recalculation = recalcul *m* en arrière-plan *or* en tâche de fond; **background task** = tâche non prioritaire *or* tâche de fond

◊ **background processing** *noun* **(a)** *(low priority job)* traitement *m* non prioritaire **(b)** *(not using the on-line capabilities)* traitement d'arrière-plan *or* de fond (NOTE: opposite is **foreground**)

backing *noun & adjective* auxiliaire *(m&f)* **backing store** *or* **storage** *or* **memory** = mémoire *f* de masse *or* mémoire auxiliaire; **by adding another disk drive, I will increase the backing store capabilities** = je vais augmenter la capacité de mémoire auxiliaire en ajoutant un deuxième lecteur de disquettes; **paper tape is one of the slowest access backing stores** = la bande perforée est une des mémoires de rangement les plus lentes d'accès

back-level *noun (earlier release of a product)* version *f* dépassée *or* périmée (d'un produit qui ne supporte pas certaines fonctions)

backlight *noun (light behind a LCD)* rétroéclairage *m* (d'un écran à cristaux liquides)

◊ **backlit** *adj (screen or display)* rétroéclairé, -ée

◊ **backlit display** *noun (LCD unit that has a backlight fitted)* écran *m* (à cristaux liquides) rétroéclairé

backlog *noun* travail *m* en retard *or* en attente *or* en souffrance; **the programmers can't deal with the backlog of programming work** = les programmeurs ne réussissent pas à venir à bout de toute la programmation en retard; **the queue was too short for the backlog of tasks waiting to be processed** = la file d'attente trop courte ne suffisait pas à la série de tâches à traiter

backout *verb (restore a file to its original condition)* restaurer (un fichier dans sa forme originale)

backplane *noun* (circuits de) fond *m* de panier

back projection *noun (cinema)* (procédé de) transparence *f*

backscatter *noun (radio wave)* onde *f* (radio) réfléchie

backslash *noun (ASCII character 92: the sign* \) barre *f* oblique inverse *or* antislash *m*

back number *noun (of newspaper or magazine)* numéro *m* déjà paru *or* vieux numéro

back pack *noun (lightweight TV equipment)* équipement *m* de prise de vue portable sur le dos

backspace *noun (of cursor)* retour *m* arrière *or* rappel *m*; **backspace character** = caractère *m* de retour arrière *or* de rappel (du curseur); **backspace key** = touche *f* de retour arrière (du curseur); **if you make a mistake entering data, use the backspace key to correct it** = pour corriger une erreur de saisie de texte, utilisez la touche de retour arrière

backtab *verb (move the cursor back to the previous field)* faire une tabulation arrière

backtrack *verb* aller à rebours *or* faire marche arrière

back up *verb* **(a)** *(to make a copy of a file or data or disk)* sauvegarder *or* faire une copie de sauvegarde; **the company accounts were backed up on disk as a protection against fire damage** = la comptabilité de la société avait été sauvegardée sur une disquette pour la protéger contre les risques d'incendie; **the program enables users to back up hard disk files with a single command** = ce programme permet de sauvegarder un fichier sur disque dur grâce à une seule commande **(b)** *(to help)* soutenir *or* supporter *or* étayer; **he brought along a file of documents to back up his claim** = il a apporté un dossier de documents pour soutenir sa réclamation; **the printout backed up his argument for a new system** = les documents imprimés sont venus soutenir ses arguments en faveur d'un nouveau système

◊ **backup** *adjective & noun* **(a)** *(which helps)* de secours *or* auxiliaire; **we offer a free backup service to customers** = nous offrons à nos clients un service d'assistance gratuit *or* un service après-vente gratuit; **battery backup** = pile *f or* alimentation *f* auxiliaire *or* de secours **(b)** backup *or* **backup copy** = (copie de) sauvegarde *f*; *(server that keeps a copy of database)* **backup domain controller** = contrôleur *m* de sauvegarde par domaine; **backup file** = fichier *m* de sauvegarde; **the most recent backup copy is kept in the safe** = nous mettons toujours la plus récente sauvegarde dans le coffre fort; *(alternative path for a signal around a network)* **backup path** = chemin *m* de sauvegarde; *(rules that take effect when normal operation has gone wrong)* **backup plan** = plan *m* de sauvegarde; **the normal UPS has gone wrong, so we will have to use our backup plan to try and restore power** = l'onduleur en service est tombé en panne, il faut donc mettre en oeuvre notre plan de sauvegarde; **backup procedure** = procédure *f* de sauvegarde; *(second computer that contains duplicate files)* **backup server** = serveur *m* de secours *or* de sauvegarde; *(software that simplifies backing up data)* **backup utility** = utilitaire *m* de sauvegarde; *(copy of a file made during a backup)* **backup version** = version *f or* copie *f* de sauvegarde; *(for volatile RAM chips)* **memory backup capacitor** = alimentation *f* de secours de la mémoire

BACKUP *noun (MS-DOS command)* (commande MS-DOS) BACKUP

Backus-Naur-Form (BNF) convention *f* BNF *or* métalangage *m* BNF

backward *or* **backwards** *adjective & adverb* à rebours *or* de retour *or* en arrière; **backward channel** = voie *f or* canal *m* de retour; *(used in artificial intelligence systems to calculate a goal)* **backward chaining** = chaînage *m* arrière *or* en amont; **backward error correction** = correction *f* d'erreurs par retransmission; *(in a broadband network)* **backward LAN channel** = voie *f* de retour du réseau local; **backward mode** = mode *m* à rebours *or* marche *f* arrière; **backward recovery** = reconstitution *f* de procédure *or* récupération *f* de fichier à rebours; *(search for data back to the beginning of the file)* **backwards search** = recherche arrière *or* en amont; **backwards supervision** = contrôle *m* par le récepteur

BACS = BANKERS AUTOMATED CLEARANCE SYSTEM

bacterium microbe *m or* virus *m see* VIRUS

bad break *noun (wrong way of splitting a word)* coupure *f* déplacée *or* impropre

◊ **bad copy** *noun* texte *m or* manuscrit *m* inacceptable *or* illisible

◊ **bad sector** *noun* secteur *m* défectueux *or* mauvais secteur; **you will receive error messages when you copy files that are stored on bad sectors on a disk** = vous obtiendrez des messages d'erreur si vous essayez de copier des fichiers implantés sur des secteurs défectueux d'une disquette

badge reader *noun* lecteur *m* de badges; **a badge reader makes sure that only authorized personnel can gain access to a computer room** = le lecteur de badges garantit que seules les personnes autorisées ont accès à la salle des ordinateurs

baffle *noun* (i) enceinte *f* acoustique; (ii) écran *m or* déflecteur *m* (de résonances parasites)

bag *noun (of elements)* éléments *mpl* en vrac

BAK file extension *noun (standard extension used in MS-DOS systems to signify a backup)* extension *f* BAK

balance 1 *noun* (a) *(of text and graphics)* équilibre *m* ; symétrie *f*; **the DTP package allows the user to see if the overall page balance is correct** = le logiciel de PAO permet à l'utilisateur de juger du bon équilibre *or* de la bonne disposition d'une page; *(making sure that the ends of two columns of text are level)* **column balance** = équilibrage *m* des colonnes (b) *(stereophonic)* balance *f* (c) *(amplitude control in a stereo system)* balance; *(on cine film)* **balance stripe** = bande *f* d'équilibrage **2** *verb* équilibrer *or* égaliser; **balanced circuit** = circuit équilibré; **you must use a balanced circuit at the end of the line to prevent signal reflections** = il faut utiliser un circuit équilibré en fin de ligne pour éviter la réflexion des signaux; **balanced error** = erreur équilibrée *or* à valeur moyenne nulle; **balanced line** = ligne équilibrée; *(using all possible routes)* **balanced routing** = équilibrage *m* des lignes de transmission

ball printer *noun (impact printer using a small metal ball)* imprimante *f* à boule; *see also* GOLF-BALL PRINTER

balun *noun (transformer)* équilibreur *m* d'impédance *or* balun *m*; **we have used a balun to connect the coaxial cable to the twisted-pair circuit** = nous avons utilisé un équilibreur d'impédance pour connecter le câble coaxial au circuit à paire torsadée

band *noun* (a) *(of frequencies)* bande *f* (de fréquences); **base band** = bande de base; **voice base band ranges from 20Hz to 15KHz** = la bande de base des fréquences vocales varie de 20Hz à 15KHz; **base band modem** = modem en bande de base; **do not use a base band modem with a normal phone line** = n'utilisez jamais un modem en bande de base sur une ligne téléphonique normale; **base band local area network** = réseau local en bande de base (b) *(on magnetic disk)* bande multipiste

◊ **banding** *noun (of an image)* **elastic banding** = recadrage *m* (d'une image sur l'écran); **elastic banding is much easier to control with a mouse** = le recadrage d'une image est plus facile à réaliser avec la souris

◊ **bandlimited** *adjective* (signal) filtré

◊ **bandpass filter** *noun* filtre *m* passe-bande

◊ **band printer** *noun* imprimante à bande

◊ **bandwidth** *noun* (a) *(range of frequencies)* bande *f* passante (b) *(amount of data that can be transmitted)* largeur *f* de bande (de fréquence) *or* bande *f* passante *or* capacité *f* de transfert (d'un câble); **telephone bandwidth is 3100Hz** = la largeur de bande d'un téléphone est de 3100Hz; **this fibre-optic cable has a greater bandwidth than the old copper cable and so it can carry data at higher speeds** = le câble en fibre optique a une bande passante plus étendue que les anciens câbles de cuivre et peut transporter les données à des vitesses plus grandes (c) *(measure of range of frequencies that a monitor or CRT will accept and display)* bande passante

bank *noun (collection of similar devices)* banque *f or* groupe *m or* bloc *m*; **a bank of minicomputers process all the raw data** = un groupe de mini-ordinateurs traite toutes les données brutes; **bank switching** = changement *m* de banque de mémoire *or* de bloc de mémoire; **memory bank** = banque de mémoire; **an add-on card has a 128KB memory bank made up of 16 chips** = la carte d'extension possède une banque de mémoire de 128Ko constituée de 16 puces

bankers automated clearance system (BACS) *noun (system to transfer money between banks)* système *m* interbancaire de télécompensation *or* SIT

banner *noun (newspapers)* **banner headlines** = gros titres *mpl* à la une *or* manchettes *fpl*

bar 1 *noun (thick line)* barre *f or* ligne *f or* trait *m*; *(printing rule)* filet *m* **2** *verb (to stop someone from doing something)* défendre *or* interdire; **to bar entry to a file** = interdire l'accès à un fichier

◊ **bar chart** *or* **bar graph** *noun* histogramme *m*

◊ **bar code** *US* **bar graph** *noun* code *m* (à) barres; **bar-code reader** = lecteur *m* (optique) de codes barres *or* stylo *m* optique; douchette *f*

◊ **bar printer** *noun* imprimante *f* à barres

bare board *noun* *(circuit board with no components)* carte *f* nue *or* carte d'extension sans mémoires *or* carte mémoire sans composants

barrel *noun* **(a)** tonneau *m or* baril *m* **(b)** borne *f* (de raccordement)

◊ **barrel distortion** *noun* *(of lens)* distorsion *f* en barillet *or* en oreiller *or* médiane (des bordures)

◊ **barrel printer** *noun* imprimante *f* à cylindre *or* à tambour

barrier box *noun* boîtier *m* d'arrêt *or* d'isolation

baryta paper *noun* papier *m* baryté

base 1 *noun* **(a)** *(lowest or first position)* base *f* **(b)** *(collection of files)* base *f* **(c)** *(initial or original position)* **base address** = adresse *f* de base; *(register used to store the base address)* **base address register** = registre *m* d'adresse de base; **base addressing** = adressage *m* de base *or* adressage relatif; *(frequency range)* **base band** = bande *f* de base; **base band modem** = modem *m* en bande de base; **base band local area network** = réseau *m* local en bande de base; *(default font)* **base font** = police *f* de caractères de base *or* par défaut; *(assembly language)* **base language** = langage *m* d'assemblage; *(printing)* **base line** = ligne *f* de base; *(in a PC, first 640Kb of RAM)* **base memory** *or* **conventional memory** *or* **base RAM** = mémoire *f* de base *or* mémoire conventionnelle; *compare* HIGH MEMORY *or* EXPANDED MEMORY; *(in a CPU)* **base register** = registre *m* d'adresse *or* registre de base; *(fixed radio transmitter/receiver)* **base station** = centrale *or* base de transmission **(d)** *(number system)* **base 2** = base binaire *or* base 2; **base 8** = base octale *or* base 8; **base 10** = base décimale *or* base 10; **base 16** = base hexadécimale *or* base 16 **2** *verb* *(to calculate from)* (se) baser (sur); **we based our calculations on the basic keyboarding rate** = nous avons basé nos calculs *or* nos calculs sont basés sur la vitesse standard de la saisie de texte (au clavier); **based on** = basé, -ée sur; **based on last year's figures** = d'après les résultats de l'an dernier; **the price is based on estimates of keyboarding costs** = ce prix est basé sur diverses estimations des coûts de saisie (au clavier); **disk-based system** = système utilisant un disque *or* des disquettes

◊ **baseband** *or* **base band** *noun* *(frequency range of a signal; digital signals without modulation; information modulated with a single carrier frequency)* bande *f* de base; *(transmission method)* **baseband local area network** = réseau *m* local en bande de base; **base band local area networks can support a maximum cable length of around 300m** = les réseaux locaux en bande de base peuvent avoir des longueurs de câbles d'environ 300m au maximum; *(transmitting data as varying voltage levels)* **baseband signalling** = transmission *f* en bande de base *or* en modulation de tension

BASIC = BEGINNER'S ALL-PURPOSE SYMBOLIC INSTRUCTION CODE langage *m* (de haut niveau) BASIC

basic *adjective* de base *or* fondamental, -e; standard; **the basic architecture is the same for all models in this range** = l'architecture de base est la même pour tous les modèles de la gamme; **basic code** = code *m* élémentaire *or* de base; **basic control system (satellite) (BCS)** = système *m* satellite de base; *(part of a communications controller)* **basic controller** = contrôleur *m* de base; *(method of directly updating or retrieving)* **basic direct access method (BDAM)** = méthode *f* d'accès direct de base; *(method of storing data on a disk)* **basic exchange format** = format *m* d'échange standard; **basic input/output operating system (BIOS)** = système *m* d'exploitation des entrées/sorties (adapté à chaque ordinateur) *or* système BIOS; **basic instruction** = instruction *f* de base *or* primitive; **basic mode link control** = protocole *m* standard de contrôle de liaisons; **basic operating system (BOS)** = système *m* d'exploitation de base; *(basic ISDN service that provides two data channels)* **basic rate access (BRA)** = débit de base (d'un RNIS); *(method of storing or retrieving blocks of data in a continuous sequence)* **basic sequential access method (BSAM)** = méthode d'accès séquentiel de base; **basic telecommunications access method (BTAM)** = protocole *m* d'accès de télécommunications (britannique) *or* méthode BTAM; *(for paper)* **basic weight** = poids *m* unitaire (d'une rame de papier)

◊ **basically** *adverb* en principe *or* fondamentalement; **the acoustic coupler is basically the same as a modem** = en principe, un coupleur acoustique est la même chose qu'un modem

◊ **basis** *noun* base *f*; **we calculated keyboarding costs on the basis of 5,500 keystrokes per hour** = le coût de la saisie du texte sur clavier a été établi sur une base de 5,500 frappes/heure

bass *noun* & *adjective* *(low sound)* (son) grave; **bass signal** = signal *m* de basse fréquence; *(knob)* **bass control** = contrôle *m* des (sons) graves; **bass driver** *or* **speaker** = haut-parleur *m* de basses fréquences *or* de graves; **bass response** = réponse *f* aux basses fréquences

BAT file extension *noun* *(file extension used in MS-DOS systems to signify a batch file)* extension *f* BAT

batch 1 *noun* **(a)** *(group of items)* lot *m*; **the last batch of disk drives are faulty** = les lecteurs de disquettes du dernier lot sont défectueux **(b)** *(documents or tasks or data processed as a single unit)* paquet *m or* lot; **batch file** = fichier *m* de commandes; **this batch file is used to save time and effort when carrying out a routine task** = ce fichier de commandes est utilisé pour économiser du temps et des efforts lorsqu'on traite une routine; **(processing data in) batch mode** = mode de traitement par lots *or* par paquets; **batch region** = partition *f or* zone *f* de traitement par lots; **batch system** = système de traitement par lots *or* par paquets; **batch total** = total *m* par groupe *or* par lot **2** *verb* **(a)** *(to group data or tasks)* grouper; **batched communication** = communications *fpl* groupées **(b)** *(to put items together)* (re)grouper

◊ **batch number** *noun* numéro *m* de lot

◊ **batch processing** *noun* traitement *m* par lots *or* par paquets

◊ **batch processor** *noun* processeur *m* de traitement par lots *or* par paquets

battery *noun* pile *f or* batterie *f or* accu *m*; **battery backup** = pile *or* alimentation *f* auxiliaire *or* de secours; **battery-backed** = équipé, -ée d'une pile auxiliaire *or* de secours; **battery voltage level** = niveau *m* de tension *or* différence *f* de potentiel d'une pile

baud *noun* baud *m*; **baud rate** = débit *m or* vitesse *f* de transmission; **the baud rate of the binary signal was 300 bits per second** = la vitesse de transmission du signal binaire était de 300 bits par seconde; **a modem with auto-baud scanner can automatically sense at which baud rate it should operate** = un modem équipé d'une reconnaissance de débit s'ajuste automatiquement à la vitesse à laquelle il doit fonctionner; **baud rate generator** = adaptateur *m* de vitesse de transmission; **split baud rate modem** = modem *m* à deux vitesses (réception et émission); **the viewdata modem uses a 1200/75 split baud rate** = le modem viewdata reçoit à 1200 bauds et transmet à 75

Baudot code *noun* *(five-bit character transmission code)* code *m* (télégraphique) Baudot

bay *or* **drive bay** *noun* *(space where a disk drive is fitted)* baie *f or* emplacement *m* (de lecteur de disque)

B box *noun* registre *m* secondaire

BBS = BULLETIN BOARD SYSTEM

BCC = BLOCK CHARACTER CHECK

BCD = BINARY CODED DECIMAL décimal codé binaire (DCB); **the BCD representation of decimal 8 is 1000** = le code binaire du nombre décimal 8 est 1000; **BCD adder** = additionneur *m* binaire *or* additionneur DCB

BCH code = BOSE-CHANDHURI-HOCQUENGHEM CODE

BCNF = BOYCE-CODD NORMAL FORM

BCPL *noun* langage *m* (de haut niveau) BCPL

BCS (a) = BRITISH COMPUTER SOCIETY **(b)** = BASIC CONTROL SYSTEM (SATELLITE)

BDAM = BASIC DIRECT ACCESS METHOD

beacon *noun* *(signal transmitted by a device that is malfunctioning)* alerteur *m* d'évènement *or* d'incident (sur un réseau)

◊ **beacon frame** *noun* *(frame that is sent after a network break has occurred)* trame *f* d'alerte; *see also* FDDI

bead *noun* *(small section of a program)* module

m or sous-ensemble *m or* sous-programme *m or* fonction *f*

beam *noun* rayon *m or* rayonnement *m*; faisceau *m*; **the laser produces a thin beam of light** = le laser émet un mince rayon lumineux; **a beam of laser light is used in this printer to produce high-resolution graphics** = l'imprimante utilise un rayon laser pour obtenir une haute résolution graphique; *(moving the electron beam across the screen)* **beam deflection** = déflexion *f or* déviation *f* de rayon; **a magnetic field is used for beam deflection in a CRT** = dans un tube à rayons cathodiques, la déflexion du faisceau est effectuée par un champ magnétique; **beam diversity** = dédoublement *m* du faisceau; **beam splitter** = diviseur *m* optique; **beam width** = largeur *f* d'un faisceau *or* d'un lobe

beard *noun* talon *m* de caractère

BEC = BUS EXTENSION CARD

beep 1 *noun* *(audible warning noise)* (tonalité) bip *m*; **the printer will make a beep when it runs out of paper** = l'imprimante émet un bip pour avertir qu'il ne reste plus de papier **2** *verb* émettre *or* faire un bip; **the computer beeped when the wrong key was hit** = chaque fois qu'on appuyait sur la mauvaise touche, l'ordinateur émettait un bip

beginning *noun* commencement *m or* début *m*; **beginning of file (bof** *or* **BOF)** = (caractère de) début de fichier; **beginning of information mark (bim)** = marque *f* de début d'enregistrement; **beginning of tape (bot) marker** = marque de début de bande

Beginner's All-Purpose Symbolic Instruction Code (BASIC) *noun* langage *m* (de haut niveau) BASIC

bel *noun* bel *m*

BEL *noun* *(bell character, equivalent to ASCII code 7)* caractère *m* BEL

bell character *noun* caractère *m* (d') alarme

◊ **Bell-compatible modem** *noun* *(modem that operates according to standards set by AT&T)* modem *m* compatible Bell

bells and whistles *plural noun* *(advanced features)* toute la panoplie; **this word-processor has all the bells and whistles you would expect - including page preview** = ce traitement de texte est doté de toute la panoplie y compris l'aperçu avant impression

below-the-line costs *noun* *(of TV crew & technicians)* frais *mpl* salariaux du personnel technique

benchmark *noun* **(a)** référence *f* **(b)** *(to test performance)* test *m* d'évaluation des performances *or* banc *m* d'essai *or* essai *m* comparatif; **the magazine gave the new program's benchmark test results** = la revue a publié les résultats du banc d'essai *or* du test d'évaluation des performances du nouveau programme

◊ **benchmark problem** *noun* problème *m* d'évaluation *or* d'étalonnage

◊ **benchmarking** *noun* étalonnage *m* des performances *or* évaluation *f* comparative des performances

BER = BIT ERROR RATE

Berkeley UNIX (BSD) *noun (version of UNIX developed by the University of California, Berkeley)* UNIX BSD

Bernoulli box *noun* boîte *f* de Bernoulli

> QUOTE I use a pair of Bernoulli boxes for back up and simply do a disk-to-disk copy
> *PC Business World*

best fit *noun* meilleur choix *m*

beta site *noun (company that tests new software before it is released)* site *m* de bêta test; site témoin

◊ **beta software** *noun (software that has not finished all its testing)* logiciel *m* (en version) bêta

◊ **beta test** *noun (second stage of tests performed on new software)* bêta test *m*; **the application has passed the alpha tests and is just entering the beta test phase** = cette application a passé le stade des tests alpha et entre juste en phase de bêta test.

◊ **beta version** *noun (version of software that is almost ready to be released)* version *f* bêta; **we'll try out the beta version on as many different PCs as possible to try and find all the bugs** = nous allons essayer la version bêta sur autant de PC différents que nous pourrons pour tenter de trouver toutes les bogues

> QUOTE The client was so eager to get his hands on the product that the managing director bypassed internal testing and decided to let it go straight out to beta test.
> *Computing*

bezel *noun (front cover of a computer's casing)* (panneau de) façade *f*

Bézier curve *noun (geometric curve)* courbe *f* de Bézier

> COMMENT: the overall shape is defined by two midpoints, called control handles. Bézier curves are a feature of many high-end design software packages; they allow a designer to create smooth curves by defining a number of points. The PostScript page description language uses Bézier curves to define the shapes of characters during printing.

bias *noun* **(a)** *(electrical reference level)* polarisation *f* **(b)** *(to minimize noise)* réducteur *m* de bruit *or* Dolby *m* **(c)** *(statistics)* écart *m*

◊ **biased** *adjective (electrical)* polarisé, -ée; *(orientated)* biaisé, -ée *or* partial, -e; **biased data** = données biaisées *or* orientées; *(in a floating point number)* **biased exponent** = exposant *m*

bibliographic *or* **bibliographical** *adjective*

bibliographique; **bibliographical information** = notice *f* bibliographique

◊ **bibliography** *noun* **(a)** *(list of references)* bibliographie *f*; **he printed a bibliography at the end of each chapter** = il a fait suivre chaque chapitre d'une bibliographie **(b)** *(catalogue of books)* bibliographie *or* liste *f* bibliographique

bid *verb (of a computer)* demander (la ligne); **the terminal had to bid three times before there was a gap in transmissions on the network** = le terminal a dû demander trois fois la ligne avant d'obtenir un créneau sur le réseau

bi-directional *adjective* bidirectionnel, -elle; **bi-directional file transfer** = transfert de fichier bidirectionnel; **bi-directional bus** = bus bidirectionnel; **bi-directional printer** = imprimante bidirectionnelle

bifurcation *noun* bifurcation *f*

Big Blue *(informal)* la société IBM

billion *(one thousand million or one million million)* million *m* de millions; *US* milliard *m*

BIM = BEGINNING OF INFORMATION MARK

bin *noun (for paper)* bac *m* à feuilles *or* à papier; **lower bin** = bac inférieur; **upper bin** = bac supérieur; *(icon in Windows)* **recycle bin** = corbeille *f*

binary *adjective & noun* binaire; **binary adder** = additionneur *m* binaire; **binary arithmetic** = calcul *m* binaire; **binary bit** = bit *m*; **binary cell** = cellule *f* binaire; **binary chop** = *see* BINARY SEARCH **binary code** = code *m* binaire; **binary coded characters** = caractères *mpl* codés binaires; **binary coded decimal (BCD)** = décimal codé binaire (DCB); **binary counter** = compteur *m* binaire; **binary digit** *or* **bit** = bit *m* *or* chiffre *m* binaire *or* élément *m* binaire; **binary dump** = vidage *m* binaire; **binary encoding** = codage *m* binaire; **binary exponent** = exposant *m* binaire; **binary file** = fichier *m* binaire; **the program instructions are stored in the binary file** = les instructions du programme sont stockées dans un fichier binaire; **your letter is a text file, not a binary file** = votre lettre est un fichier texte et non un fichier binaire; **binary fraction** = fraction *f* binaire; **the binary fraction 0.011 is equal to one quarter plus one eighth (i.e. three eighths)** = la fraction binaire 0,011 est égale à un quart plus un huitième (ou trois huitièmes); **binary half adder** = demi-additionneur *m* binaire; **binary loader** = chargeur *m* binaire; **binary mantissa** = mantisse *f* binaire; **binary notation** = numération *f* binaire; **binary number** = nombre *m* binaire; *(operation on two operands or on an operand in binary form)* **binary operation** = opération *f* binaire; **binary point** = virgule *f* binaire; **binary scale** = échelle *f* binaire; **in a four bit word, the binary scale is 1,2,4,8** = dans un mot à quatre bits, l'échelle binaire est 1,2,4,8; **binary search** *or* **chop** = recherche *f* (par coupe) binaire *or* recherche dichotomique *or* par dichotomie; **binary sequence** = séquence *f* binaire; **binary signalling** = transmission *f* de signaux en binaire; *(method of iteration)* **binary split** = séparation *f* binaire; **binary synchronous communications (BSC)** = communication *f* synchrone binaire; **binary system** = système *m* binaire; **binary-to-decimal conversion** = conversion *f* binaire-décimale; **binary tree (btree)** = arbre *m* binaire; **binary variable** = variable *f* binaire

> QUOTE with this type of compression you can only retrieve words by scanning the list sequentially, rather than by faster means such as a binary search
> *Practical Computing*

binaural *adjective* biaural, -e *or* binaural, -e

bind *verb* **(a)** *(to link)* établir des liens; *(address)* associer; **binding time** = temps *m* d'association (d'une adresse) **(b)** *(book)* relier; **the book is bound in laminated paper** = c'est un livre avec couverture pelliculée; **a paperbound book** = un livre broché; **the sheets have been sent to the bindery for binding** = les feuilles ont été envoyées à la reliure; *(extra wide margin on the inside of printed page)* **binding offset** = marge de reliure *or* d'agrafage (NOTE: **binding - bound**)

◊ **binder** *noun* **(a)** *(of books)* relieur, -euse **(b)** *(program that converts object code into a form that can be executed)* éditeur *m* de liens

◊ **bindery** *noun* atelier *m* de reliure

Bindery *noun* *(database used in a Novell NetWare network operating system)* fichier *m* *or* bibliothèque *f* de liens (Netware)

binding *noun* **(a)** (l'art de) la reliure **(b)** *(cover of a book)* reliure *or* couverture *f*; **the book has a soft plastic binding** = c'est un livre avec couverture plastique souple

BIOS = BASIC INPUT/OUTPUT SYSTEM

biosensor *noun* capteur *m* *or* électrode *f* *or* sonde *f*; **the nerve activity can be measured by attaching a biosensor to your arm** = l'activité nerveuse peut se mesurer en plaçant une électrode sur le bras

bipolar *adjective* bipolaire; **bipolar coding** = codage *m* bipolaire; **bipolar junction transistor (BJT)** = transistor *m* à jonction bipolaire; **bipolar signal** = signal *m* bipolaire; **bipolar transistor** = transistor bipolaire

biquinary code *noun* code *m* biquinaire

B-ISDN = BROADBAND ISDN RNIS bande étendue

bistable *adjective* bistable; **bistable circuit** *or* **multivibrator** = circuit *m* *or* multivibrateur *m* bistable *or* bascule *f*

bit *noun* **(a)** = BINARY DIGIT bit *m* *or* élément *m* *or* nombre *m* binaire **(b)** *(smallest unit of data)* bit; **bit addressing** = adressage *m* binaire; *(in computer graphics, to move a block of bits)* **bit blit** *or* **bitblt** = déplacement *m* de bit (en mémoire); *(in computer*

graphics, group of bits treated as one unit)* **bit block** = bloc *m* de bits; *(to move a block of bits from one memory location to another)* **bit block transfer** = transfert *m* de bits par blocs; *(memory into which data can be discarded)* **bit bucket** = panier *m* *or* poubelle *f* (à bit); **bit density** = densité *f* binaire; *(fibre optics: ratio of the number of bits received to the number of errors in a transmission)* **bit error rate (BER)** = taux *m* d'erreur de transmission (sur fibre optique); *(inverting the state of bits from 0 to 1 and 1 to 0)* **bit flipping** = inversion *f* binaire; **bit handling** = traitement *m* du bit; *(collection of bits that represent the pixels)* **bit image** = image *f* binaire; *(time domain multiplexing)* **bit interleaving** = entrelaçage *m* binaire; **bit manipulation** = manipulation *f* binaire; *(transmission of a collection of bits over a number of lines)* **bit parallel** = transmission *f* parallèle (bit par bit); **bit pattern** = arrangement *f* binaire; *(one layer of a multiple-layer image)* **bit plane** = plan *m* *or* couche *f* binaire (dans une image graphique); **bit position** = position *f* binaire; **bit rate** = débit *m* binaire; **bit significant** = qui détermine la valeur du bit significatif; **testing bit six of a byte containing an ASCII character is bit significant and determines if the ASCII character is upper or lower case** = la recherche du sixième bit d'un octet contenant un caractère ASCII détermine si le bit significatif indique un caractère en majuscule ou en minuscule; **bit slice design** = architecture (de processeur) en tranches; **the bit slice design uses four 4-bit word processors to construct a 16-bit processor** = le processeur en tranches utilise quatre processeurs à 4 bits pour réaliser un processeur à 16 bits; **bit stream** = flot *m* *or* train *m* de bits; **bit stuffing** = remplissage *m* *or* garnissage *m* de bits; *(on a magnetic disk)* **bit track** = piste *f* (de données binaires); *(carried out on each bit in a byte, one bit at a time)* **bit wise** = (opération effectuée) au niveau binaire; **bits per inch (bpi)** = (nombre de) bits par pouce; *(number of bits assigned to store the colour of each pixel)* **bits per pixel (BPP)** = bits par pixel; **bits per second (bps)** = (nombre de) bits par seconde (bps); **their transmission rate is 60,000 bits per second (bps) through a parallel connection** = leur débit est de 60 000 bits par seconde sur une liaison parallèle; **check bit** = bit de contrôle *or* clé *f* de contrôle; **mask bit** = masque *m* binaire; **sign bit** = bit de signe; **significant bit** = bit significatif; **least significant bit (LSB)** = bit de poids (le plus) faible; **most significant bit (MSB)** = bit de poids (le plus) fort *or* bit significatif

bitblt *see* BIT, BLIT

bit-map *verb* définir une table d'adressage binaire; **bit-mapped graphics** = infographie *f* par points *or* à adressage binaire

◊ **bit-map mode** *noun* mode *m* point

> QUOTE it became possible to store more than one bit per pixel
> *Practical Computing*

> QUOTE the expansion cards fit into the PC's expansion slot and convert bit-mapped screen images to video signals
> *Publish*

QUOTE it is easy to turn any page into a bit-mapped graphic

PC Business World

QUOTE microcomputers invariably use raster-scan cathode ray tube displays, and frequently use a bit-map to store graphic images

Soft

BJT = BIPOLAR JUNCTION TRANSISTOR

black *adjective* noir, -e; *(image in which each pixel is either black or white)* **black and white** = noir et blanc; *(screen)* monochrome; **black box** = boîte *f* noire; **black crush** = conversion *f* monochrome (d'une image couleur); **black level** = niveau *m* de noir

◊ **blackboard** *noun* tableau *m* noir; **electronic blackboard** = tableau noir électronique

◊ **blackout** *or* **black out** *noun (complete loss of electrical power)* coupure *f* (de courant) *or* panne *f* d'électricité *or* panne de secteur; *compare* BROWNOUT, BROWN-OUT

◊ **black writer** *noun* imprimante *f* à définition des noirs; *compare* WHITE WRITER

blank 1 *adjective* blanc, blanche; *(empty cell in a spreadsheet)* **blank cell** = cellule *f* vide; **blank character** = caractère (d')espace; **blank instruction** = instruction *f* de remplissage; **blank string** = (i) chaîne vide; (ii) chaîne contenant des caractères d'espace; **blank tape** *or* **blank disk** = bande *f* vierge *or* disque *m* vierge **2** *noun* blanc *m or* case *f* vide; **fill in the blanks and insert the form into the OCR** = complétez le formulaire et introduisez-le dans le lecteur optique

◊ **blanking** *noun* suppression *f or* inhibition *f* du signal; **blanking interval** = délai *m* de retour du signal en fin d'écran; **blanking pulse** = impulsion *f* d'inhibition du signal; **line blanking interval** = délai *m* de retour de ligne

blanket cylinder *noun* cylindre *m* porte-blanchet

◊ **blanketing** *noun* couverture *f* (d'une émission) *or* brouillage *m* (de la réception)

blast *verb* (a) brûler (une PROM) *or* programmer (une PROM) (b) libérer une partie de la mémoire *or* désallouer (une ressource)

◊ **blast-through alphanumerics** *noun* caractères *mpl* éclatés (sur un écran vidéotex)

bleed *noun (line that runs off the edge of the paper)* bavure *f (badly adjusted colour monitor)* écran *m* brouillé

◊ **bled off** *adjective* à fond(s) perdu(s); **the photo is bled off** = la photo est à fond perdu

bleep 1 *noun* bip *m or* signal *m* sonore; **the printer will make a bleep when it runs out of paper** = lorsqu'il n'y a plus de papier, l'imprimante émet un bip *or* un signal sonore **2** *verb* émettre *or* faire un bip; émettre un signal sonore; *see also* BEEP

◊ **bleeper** *noun* bip *m or* avertisseur *m* (pour

recherche de personne); **he is in the factory somewhere - we'll try to find him on his bleeper** = il doit être quelque part dans l'usine, nous essaierons de le joindre par son avertisseur

blessed folder *noun (the System Folder that contains files loaded when the Macintosh is switched on)* dossier *m* préférentiel (Macintosh)

blind *adjective* aveugle; **blind dialling** = transmission *f* en aveugle *or* sans décrochage; **blind keyboard** = clavier *m* aveugle

◊ **blind copy receipt** *noun (in electronic mail, method of sending a message to several users whose identities are not known)* avis *m* de réception de copie discrète; *compare* CARBON COPY

B-line counter *noun* registre *m* auxiliaire de routage d'adresse

blinking *noun* clignotement *m or* papillotement *m*

blip *noun (mark on a tape or film)* repère *m*

blister pack *noun* blister *m or* emballage *m* bulle

blit *or* **bitblt** *verb (in computer graphics, to move a block of bits from one memory location to another)* effectuer un déplacement de bit (en mémoire)

◊ **blitter** *noun (component designed to process or move a bit-mapped image)* accélérateur *m* binaire; **the new blitter chip speeds up the graphics display** = le nouvel accélérateur binaire accélère l'affichage des images graphiques

block 1 *noun* (a) bloc *m*; **block character check (BCC)** = contrôle *m* de bloc de caractères; **block code** = code *m* de contrôle de bloc; **block compaction** = compactage *m or* compression *f* de bloc; **block copy** = copie de bloc; **block delete** = suppression *f* de bloc; *(device that manipulates many bytes of data at once)* **block device** = manipulateur *m* de bloc; **the disk drive is a block device that can transfer 256 bytes of data at a time** = l'unité de disque est un manipulateur de blocs qui peut transférer 256 octets de données à la fois; *(illustration of how the main components in a system are connected)* **block diagram** = schéma *m* synoptique *or* fonctionnel; **the first step to designing a new computer is to draw out a block diagram of its main components** = la première étape de la conception d'un ordinateur consiste à établir le schéma synoptique de ses principaux composants; **block error rate** = taux *m* d'erreur par bloc; **block header** = en-tête *m* de bloc; *(when corrupt data are present)* **block ignore character** = caractère *m* de rejet de bloc (dont les données sont mauvaises); **block input processing** = traitement *m* de contrôle de bloc à l'entrée; **block length** = longueur *f or* taille *f* d'un bloc; **block list** = fichier *m* d'enregistrement des blocs; *(used to mark text to be moved)* **block mark** = marque *f* de sélection d'un bloc (de texte); *(move of the contents of an area of memory to another area of memory)* **block move** = déplacement *m* de bloc (en mémoire); **block operation** = manipulation *f* de blocs; **block**

parity = (contrôle de) parité *f* d'un bloc; *(prevent a block of text being split by an automatic page break)* **block protection** = protection *f* de bloc; **block retrieval** = recherche *f* or extraction *f* de bloc; **block synchronization** = synchronisation *f* de blocs; **block transfer** = transfert *m* or insertion *f* d'un bloc or d'un paragraphe; **building block** = élément *m* or module *m*; **data block** = bloc de données; **end of block (EOB)** = (marque de) fin *f* de bloc; **interblock gap (IBG)** = espace *m* interbloc **(b)** *(wide printed bar)* bloc; *(cursor like a solid rectangle that fills a character position)* **block cursor** = curseur *m* pavé; **block diagram** = graphe *m* or ordinogramme *m* à pavés **(c) block capitals** or **block letters** = (lettres) majuscules *fpl* or (lettres) capitales *fpl*; **write your name and address in block letters** = écrivez votre nom et votre adresse en capitales or en majuscules **2** *verb* **(a)** *(to stop)* empêcher or bloquer or faire opposition (à); **the system manager blocked his request for more CPU time** = le directeur du système a fait opposition à sa demande de temps supplémentaire sur l'unité centrale **(b) to block in** = esquisser (un design)

◊ **blocking factor** *noun (records in a block)* facteur *m* (de) bloc

bloom *noun* tache *f* lumineuse sur l'écran

bloop *verb* démagnétiser

blow *verb* **(a)** *(fuse)* faire sauter (les plombs) **(b)** *(burn)* brûler or programmer une PROM

blueprint *noun* (i) spécifications *fpl*; (ii) plan *m* or épure *f*

◊ **blue-ribbon program** *noun (informal)* programme *m* canon (qui tourne sans erreur du premier coup)

blur 1 *noun* flou *m* **2** *verb* rendre flou; **the image becomes blurred when you turn the focus knob** = en tournant le bouton de mise au point l'image devient floue or perd de sa netteté

BMP *noun (extension to a filename that indicates that the file contains a bit-mapped image)* extension *f* BMP (d'un fichier graphique); **this paint package lets you import BMP files** = ce logiciel de peinture permet l'importation de fichiers BMP

bn = BILLION

BNC connector *noun (cylindrical metal connector with a copper core)* adaptateur *m* BNC (coaxial)

◊ **BNC T-piece connector** *noun (T-shaped metal connector)* adaptateur *m* en T BNC

BNF = BACKUS-NAUR-FORM

board *noun* **(a)** *(for printed circuit)* carte *f* or plaque *f* (présensibilisée) pour circuit imprimé; **bulletin board system (BBS)** = messagerie *f* or BBS; tableau *m* or zone *f* d'affichage électronique; babillard *m*; **bus board** = carte bus or carte connecteur; **daughter board** = carte fille; **expansion board** or **add-on board** = carte

d'extension; **motherboard** = carte mère; **printed circuit board (PCB)** = (carte de) circuit *m* imprimé **(b)** *(people who run company, etc.)* conseil *m* d'administration or directoire *m*; **editorial board** = la rédaction

> QUOTE both models can be expanded to the current maximum of the terminals by adding further serial interface boards
> *Micro Decision*

body *noun (main section of text or program)* corps *m* (d'un texte or d'un programme); **body size** = *(of text)* dimension *f* (en points) du corps d'un texte; *(of character)* corps *m* (d'un caractère); **body type** = police de caractères (par défaut) utilisée pour le corps d'un texte

BOF or **bof** = BEGINNING OF FILE BOF or Bof or début *m* de fichier

boilerplate *noun* document *m* monté or créé (à partir de paragraphes standard)

◊ **boilerplating** *noun* montage *m* d'un document (à partir de paragraphes standard)

bold face *adjective & noun* (en) caractère(s) gras

bomb 1 *verb (informal - of software)* (faire) sauter or (se) planter; **the program bombed, and we lost all the data** = le programme s'est planté et nous avons perdu toutes les données; **the system can bomb if you set up several desk accessories or memory-resident programs at the same time** = le système peut se planter si vous installez en même temps plusieurs accessoires de bureau ou programmes résidents **2** *noun (routine designed to crash the system)* bombe *f*; **logic bomb** = bombe logique; **the system programmer installed a logic bomb when they made him redundant** = le programmeur système a installé une bombe logique lorsqu'il a été licencié

bond paper *noun* papier *m* à lettre commercial

book *noun* livre *m*; **they can print books of up to 96 pages** = ils peuvent imprimer des livres qui ont jusqu'à 96 pages; **the book is available in paperback and hard cover** = ce livre existe en édition brochée et en édition cartonnée

◊ **booklet** *noun* livret *m* or prospectus *m* or brochure *f*

◊ **bookmark** *noun (code inserted in a document that allows the user to move straight to that point)* signet *m* or marque *f* (qui permet de retrouver facilement une partie de programme)

◊ **bookseller** *noun* libraire *m&f*

◊ **bookshop** *noun* librairie *f*

◊ **bookstall** *noun* kiosque *m* (à livres)

◊ **bookstore** *noun US* librairie *f*

◊ **bookwork** *noun* **(a)** *(keeping of financial records)* comptabilité *f* or tenue *f* de livres **(b)** *(printing and binding of books)* imprimerie *f* et reliure

Boolean algebra or **Boolean logic** *noun* algèbre *f* de Boole or algèbre booléenne

◊ **Boolean connective** *noun* relation *f* booléenne

◊ **Boolean operation** *noun* opération booléenne; **Boolean operation table** = table *f* de Boole *or* table *f* de vérité; *(logical operation on only one word, such as NOT)* **monadic Boolean operation** = opération (booléenne) monadique *or* à un opérande; **dyadic Boolean operation** = opération (booléenne) dyadique *or* à deux opérandes; **Boolean operator** = opérateur *m* booléen; **Boolean value** = valeur *f* booléenne; **Boolean variable** = variable *f* booléenne

boom *noun (of microphone)* perche *f*

boost 1 *noun* encouragement *m or* augmentation *f*; **the prize was a real boost** = le prix a été un réel encouragement; **the new model gave a boost to the sales figures** = le nouveau modèle a fait monter les chiffres de vente **2** *verb* augmenter *or* gonfler; **the extra hard disk will boost our storage capacity by 25Mb** = le disque dur supplémentaire va augmenter *or* gonfler la capacité de mémoire de 25Mo

boot *verb* lancer un système *or* amorcer un système; *(first track - track 0 - on a boot disk)* **boot block** *or* **record** = bloc *m or* enregistrement *m* de lancement *or* d'amorçage; *(disk which contains a bootstrap program)* **boot disk** = disque *m or* disquette *f* de lancement *or* d'amorçage; **after you switch on the computer, insert the boot disk** = après avoir mis l'ordinateur en route, insérez la disquette de lancement *or* d'amorçage; *(on a hard disk the partition that contains the bootstrap)* **boot partition** = partition *f* de lancement *or* d'amorçage

◊ **bootup** *or* **booting** *noun (of system)* lancement *m or* amorçage *m*

bootleg *noun* copie *f* illégale *or* piratée

bootstrap (loader) *noun* amorce *f or* programme *m* d'amorçage *or* de lancement (d'un système)

QUOTE the digital signal processor includes special on-chip bootstrap hardware to allow easy loading of user programs into the program RAM

Electronics & Wireless World

---

booth *noun* cabine *f*; **telephone booth** = cabine téléphonique

border *noun* bordure *f or* cadre *m or* encadrement *m*

Borland *(software company)* Borland (éditeur de logiciels spécialisés dans les langages et les bases de données)

borrow *verb* **(a)** emprunter (de l'argent *or* un livre); **she borrowed a book on computer construction** = elle a emprunté un livre sur la fabrication des ordinateurs **(b)** *(in subtraction)* emprunter

BOS = BASIC OPERATING SYSTEM

Bose-Chandhuri-Hocquenghem code (BCH) *noun* code *m* BCH

bot *or* **BOT** = BEGINNING OF TAPE **BOT marker** = marque *f* de début de bande

bottom *noun* bas *m*; *(of page)* **bottom space** = bas de page *or* blanc *m* de pied

◊ **bottom up method** *noun* conception *f* ascendante (d'un programme)

bounce *noun (of key)* rebond *m* (d'une touche de clavier); **de-bounce** = *(on keyboard)* (dispositif) antirebond *m*

boundary *noun* limite *f*; **boundary protection** = protection *f* des limites (de mémoire); **boundary punctuation** = marquage *m* de limites (d'un fichier); **boundary register** = registre *m* (d'adresses) de limites

bounds *noun* bornes *fpl or* limites *fpl*; **array bounds** = limites *fpl* de tableau

box *noun* **(a)** *(container)* boîte *f*; **the keyboard is packed in expanded polystyrene before being put into the box** = le clavier est emballé dans du polystyrène expansé avant d'être mis dans son carton; *(d'un avion, etc.)* **black box** = boîte noire **(b)** **letter box** = boîte à *or* aux lettres **(c)** *(around text or illustration)* cadre *m*; **the comments and quotations are printed in boxes** = les commentaires et les citations sont dans des cadres *or* sont encadrés

◊ **box in** *verb* encadrer

Boyce-Codd normal form (BCNF) format *m* normal Boyce-Codd *or* format BCNF

bozo bit *noun (in an Apple Macintosh system: attribute bit that prevents a file being copied)* bit *m* de protection *or* bozo *m* (Apple Macintosh)

BPI *or* **bpi** = BITS PER INCH

BPP *or* **bpp** = BITS PER PIXEL

bps = BITS PER SECOND; *(rate at which information is sent)* **bps rate** = bps *or* bits *mpl* par seconde; *(ability of a modem to adjust the speed of its serial port to match the communications speed)* **bps rate adjust** = débit *m* corrigé en bps

Bps = BYTES PER SECOND

BRA = BASIC RATE ACCESS

braces *noun (curly bracket characters {})* accolades *fpl*

bracket 1 *noun (bracket characters {} used in some programming languages)* **curly bracket(s)** *or* **brace(s)** = accolade(s) *f(pl)*; *(bracket characters ())* **round bracket(s)** = parenthèse(s) *f(pl)*; *(bracket characters [])* **square bracket(s)** = crochet(s) *m(pl)* **2** *verb* **to bracket together** = (i) (re)grouper; (ii) mettre entre parenthèses *or* entre crochets

◊ **bracketed** *adjective* (caractère) avec empattements elzéviriens

◊ **bracketing** *noun* *(photography)* photographie *f* de la même scène avec plusieurs ouvertures

Braille *noun* (écriture) Braille; **she was reading a Braille book** = elle lisait un livre en (caractères) Braille; **the book has been published in Braille** = il existe une édition en Braille de ce livre; **Braille marks** = caractères *mpl* Braille

branch 1 *noun* **(a)** branche *f*; **branch instruction** = instruction *f* de branchement *or* de saut; *(table that defines where to jump to in a program)* **branch table** = table *f* de branchements; **program branch** = branche *f* d'un programme **(b)** *(of network)* branchement *m*; **the faulty station is on this branch** = le poste défectueux est connecté sur ce branchement **2** *verb* brancher

◊ **branchpoint** *noun* point *m* de branchement

breadboard *noun* *(device that allows prototype electronic circuits to be constructed easily)* carte *f* de montage (de circuits) sans soudure

break 1 *noun* **(a)** *(of program execution)* interruption *f* *(key on an IBM-compatible keyboard that halts execution of a program)* **Break key** = touche *f* d'interruption; **I stopped the problem by pressing Ctrl-Break** = j'ai résolu le problème en appuyant sur les touches CTRL et Interruption **(b)** *(hyphen)* coupure *f* (de mot) *or* césure *f*; **bad break** = coupure déplacée *or* impropre **2** *verb* **(a)** *(to decipher)* déchiffrer; **he finally broke the cipher system** = il a finalement réussi à déchiffrer le code *or* il a finalement trouvé la clé du code **(b) to break into a database** = piller une base de données (NOTE: **breaking - broke - has broken**)

◊ **break down** *verb* *(to stop working)* tomber en panne; **the modem has broken down** = ce modem ne fonctionne pas *or* est en dérangement *or* en panne; **what do you do when your line printer breaks down?** = que faut-il faire quand l'imprimante ligne tombe en panne?

◊ **breakdown** *noun* panne *f* *or* défaillance *f*; **we cannot communicate with our New York office because of the breakdown of the telex** = nous ne pouvons pas joindre notre bureau à New York à cause d'une panne de télex

◊ **breaker** *noun* **circuit breaker** = coupe-circuit *m or* interrupteur *m or* disjoncteur *m*

◊ **breakout box** *noun* *(device that displays the status of lines within an interface)* fenêtre *f* de contrôle d'interface; **the serial interface doesn't seem to be working - use the breakout box to see which signals are present** = l'interface série ne semble pas fonctionner - ouvrez la fenêtre de contrôle pour voir quels signaux fonctionnent

◊ **breakpoint** *noun* *(control point)* point *m* d'arrêt *or* d'interruption; **breakpoint instruction** = **halt** = instruction *f* d'arrêt (dans un programme); **breakpoint symbol** = symbole *m* d'arrêt (dynamique)

◊ **breakup** *noun* *(usually in video)* coupure *f*; perte *f or* distorsion *f* d'un signal

breezeway *noun* intervalle *m* de garde

B register *noun* registre *m* (d'adresse) indexé

bridge *or* **bridging product 1** *noun* **(a)** *(communications equipment between two networks)* pont *m or* gestionnaire *m* de transition; *see also* ROUTER, BROUTER **(b)** *(matching communications equipment)* pont *or* interface *f* de transition **(c)** *(hardware or software that allows part of an old system to be used with a new system)* interface *f or* logiciel *m* de transition; pont *m*; **a bridging product is available for companies with both generations of machines** = une interface de transition est fournie *or* un pont est fourni aux entreprises qui disposent des deux générations d'équipement **2** *verb* *(use bridgeware to help transfer programs, data files, etc.)* établir un pont *or* une transition

◊ **bridgeware** *noun* équipement *m or* logiciel *m* de transition *or* pont *m*

◊ **bridging** *noun* (i) mise en place d'une dérivation; (ii) transfert de programme avec l'aide d'un pont

QUOTE Lotus Development and IMRS are jointly developing a bridge linking their respective spreadsheet and client server reporting tools. It will allow users of IMRS' Hyperion reporting tool to manipulate live data from Lotus Improv.
Computing

COMMENT: A bridge connects two similar networks, a gateway connects two different networks. To connect two Ethernet networks, use a bridge.

brightness *noun* luminosité *f or* brillance *f*; **a control knob allows you to adjust brightness and contrast** = un bouton vous permet de régler la luminosité et les contrastes; **the brightness of the monitor can hurt the eyes** = une trop forte brillance peut causer une fatigue oculaire; **brightness range** = niveaux *mpl* de luminosité

QUOTE there is a brightness control on the front panel
Micro Decision

brilliant *adjective* brillant, -e; **the background colour is a brilliant red** = le fond est d'un rouge brillant; **he used brilliant white for the highlights** = il utilise un blanc brillant pour les mises en valeur

◊ **brilliance** *noun* brillance *f*

bring-up *verb* *(start a computer system)* mettre en marche *or* faire monter (un système)

British Standards Institute (BSI) *(British equivalent of)* Association française de normalisation (AFNOR)

broadband *or* **wideband** *noun* *(transmission method that combines several channels of data onto a carrier signal)* (transmission en) large bande *f*; **broadband radio** = radio à large bande

broadcast 1 *noun (message sent to a group of users)* diffusion *f (data transmission to many receivers)* émission *f or* diffusion *f* ; radiocommunication *f* (radiophonique); **broadcast homes** = foyers qui possèdent au moins un poste de télévision ou de radio; *(message sent to everyone on a network)* **broadcast message** = message *m* diffusé; **five minutes before we shut down the LAN, we send a broadcast message to all users** = cinq minutes avant de fermer le réseau local, nous diffusons un message à tous les utilisateurs; **broadcast network** = réseau *m* de diffusion; *(video image or signal that is the same as that used by professional television stations)* **broadcast quality** = qualité *f* de transmission *or* qualité broadcast; **we can use your multimedia presentation as the advert on TV if it's of broadcast quality** = nous pouvons utiliser votre présentation multimédia pour la publicité à condition qu'elle soit conforme aux normes télévision; **broadcast satellite technique** = technique *f* de diffusion par satellite **2** *verb* (radio)diffuser; **he broadcast the latest news over the radio** *or* **over the WAN** = il a diffusé les dernières informations à la radio *or* via le réseau étendu; **broadcasting station** = station *f* de radio

broadsheet *noun (printing)* placard *m*

broadside *noun US* prospectus *m* publicitaire

brochure *noun* brochure *f or* prospectus *m* (publicitaire); **we sent off for a brochure about maintenance services** = nous avons demandé une brochure sur les services de maintenance

bromide *or* **bromide print** *noun* **(a)** bromure *m*; **in 24 hours we had bromides ready to film** = 24 heures plus tard nous avions reçu les bromures et pouvions faire les films **(b)** *(photo sensitive paper)* bromure

brouter *noun (device that combines the functions of a router and bridge)* pont *m* de routage; **the brouter provides dynamic routing and can bridge two local area networks** = le pont de routage permet un routage dynamique entre deux réseaux locaux; *see also* BRIDGE; ROUTER

brown-out *noun* baisse *f or* chute *f* de courant

browse *verb* **(a)** *(to view data on online system)* visionner **(b)** *(to search database material without permission)* consulter une base de données sans autorisation *or* piller une base de données

brush *noun (tool in paint package software that draws pixels on screen)* pinceau *m or* brosse *f*; **the paint package lets you vary the width of the brush (in pixels) and the colour it produces** = le logiciel de dessin vous permet de changer la largeur du pinceau (en pixels) et la couleur qu'il étale; *(width and shape of the brush tool in a paint package)* **brush style** = type *m* de pinceau; **to fill in a big area, I select a wide, square brush style** = pour couvrir une grande surface, j'utilise un pinceau large et à bout carré

brute force method *noun* méthode *f* brutale

BS = BACKSPACE caractère *m* retour arrière *or* caractère BS

BSAM = BASIC SEQUENTIAL ACCESS METHOD

BSC = BINARY SYNCHRONOUS COMMUNICATIONS

BSI = BRITISH STANDARDS INSTITUTE

BTAM = BASIC TELECOMMUNICATIONS ACCESS METHOD

btree = BINARY TREE

bubble jet printer™ imprimante *f* à bulle d'encre; *see also* INK-JET PRINTER

bubble memory *noun* mémoire *f* à bulles (magnétiques); **bubble memory cassette** = cassette *f* mémoire à bulles (magnétiques)

◊ **bubble sort** *noun* tri *m* par permutation (de paires *or* de bulles)

bucket *noun* emplacement *m* de rangement (en mémoire)

buckling *noun (of film)* gondolage *m*

buffer 1 *noun* **(a)** *(circuit)* (circuit) tampon *m* **(b)** *(temporary storage area for data)* (mémoire) tampon *m*; **buffer register** = registre *m* tampon; **buffer size** = taille *f* de mémoire tampon; **data buffer** = (mémoire) tampon de données; **dynamic** *or* **elastic buffer** = tampon dynamique *or* variable; **I/O buffer** = mémoire tampon d'entrée/sortie; **printer buffer** = tampon d'imprimante **2** *verb* utiliser une mémoire tampon; **buffered input/output** = entrée/sortie utilisant une mémoire tampon; **buffered memory** = mémoire avec tampon; **buffering** = utilisation de mémoire tampon; **double buffering** = utilisation de double mémoire tampon

QUOTE the speed is enhanced by the 8K RAM printer buffer included

QUOTE the software allocates a portion of cache as a print buffer to restore program control faster after sending data to the printer
Which PC?

bug 1 *noun* **(a)** *(in software)* erreur *f or* bogue *f or* bug *m*; *(temporary correction made to a program)* **bug patches** = rustine *f or* replâtrage *m* **(b)** *(hidden microphone)* micro *m* espion *or* micro-espion *m or* dispositif *m* de surveillance **2** *verb* placer un micro espion *or* surveiller par micro espion; **the conference room was bugged** = il y avait des micros-espions dans la salle de conférence

buggy *noun (small computer-controlled vehicle)* chariot *m* piloté par ordinateur

build *noun (particular version of a program)* mouture *f or* version *f*; **this is the latest build of the new software** = c'est la dernière mouture du nouveau logiciel

building block *noun (self-contained unit to form a system)* élément *m or* module *m*

built-in *adjective* intégré, -ée *or* incorporé, -ée; **the built-in adapter card makes it fully IBM compatible** = la carte adaptateur intégrée rend l'appareil compatible IBM; **the computer has a built-in hard disk** = l'ordinateur est équipé d'un disque dur intégré; **built-in check** = système de contrôle intégré; **built-in function** = fonction incorporée

◊ **built into** *adjective* incorporé, -ée *or* intégré, -ée; **there are communications ports built into all modems** = tous les modems possèdent des ports de communication intégrés (NOTE: opposite is **add-on**)

bulk *noun* grande quantité *or* masse *f*; **in bulk** = en vrac *or* en grande quantité *or* en masse; **bulk erase** = effacement *m* en masse; **bulk storage medium** = support *m* de stockage de grande capacité *or* mémoire de masse; **magnetic tape is a reliable bulk storage medium** = la bande magnétique constitue un support de stockage de grande capacité très sûr; *(for videotex)* **bulk update terminal** = terminal *m* de mise à jour rapide

bullet *noun* **(a)** vignette *f or* point *m* indicateur de couleur *(filled circle or square in front of a line of text)* puce *f or* marqueur *m* d'énumération

bulletin board system (BBS) *noun* messagerie *f or* BBS; tableau *m or* zone *f* d'affichage; babillard *m*

bundle *noun* **(a)** *(of optic fibres)* faisceau *m* de fibres optiques **(b)** *(package containing a computer with software or accessories)* offre *f* groupée *or* offre *f* promotionnelle; **the bundle now includes a PC with spreadsheet and database applications for just £999** = l'offre comporte un PC avec un tableur et une base de données pour seulement 999£ **2** *verb (market a computer together with a range of software at a special price)* faire une offre groupée *or* promotionnelle; inclure un logiciel *or* des logiciels dans le prix d'achat d'un ordinateur

◊ **bundled software** *noun* logiciel *m* inclus à l'achat d'un ordinateur

bureau *noun* bureau *m or* société *f* de services; **the company offers a number of bureau services, such as printing and data collection** = la société offre, entre autres, des services d'imprimerie et de saisie de données; **our data manipulation is handled by a bureau** = nous faisons faire la manipulation de données par une société de services informatiques; **computer bureau** = société de services et d'ingénierie informatique (SSII); *(office that converts data from a DTP program into artwork)* **output bureau** = flasheur *m or* imprimeur *m*; **word-processing bureau** = société *or* bureau de traitement de texte; **we farm out the office typing to a local bureau** = nous confions notre correspondance à un bureau de secrétariat local (NOTE: the plural is **bureaux**)

burner *noun* programmeur *m* de ROM *or* de mémoire morte

◊ **burn-in** *noun (for electronic components)* test *m* à chaud

◊ **burn in** *verb* **(a)** *(television or monitor screen)* faire un brûlage *m* d'écran **(b)** *(PROM chip)* graver *or* programmer *or* brûler

◊ **burn out** *noun (electronic circuit or device)* panne *f* par échauffement

burst *noun (signals)* rafale *f or* paquet *m or* burst *m*; **burst mode** = mode *m* de transmission de données par paquets *or* par rafales; *(TV)* **colour burst** = rafale de signaux couleur; *(consecutive errors in a transmission)* **error burst** = rafale *f* d'erreurs *or* série *f* d'erreurs consécutives

burster *noun (for paper)* rupteur *m or* séparateur *m or* éclateur *m* (de feuilles)

bus *noun* **(a)** bus *m*; **bus address lines** = voies de liaison d'un bus d'adresses; **bus arbitration** = arbitrage *m or* gestion *f* de (l'utilisation d'un) bus; **bus board** = carte *f* bus; **bus control lines** = lignes *fpl* de contrôle; **bus data lines** = lignes de transmission de données; **bus driver** = bus driver; amplificateur *m* de courant du bus; **bus extender** *or* **bus extension card (BEC)** = carte *f* d'extension de bus; **bus master** = (émetteur de données) maître *m* d'un bus; *(adapter card that fits in a EISA or MCA expansion slot in a PC)* **bus master adapter** = adaptateur *m* maître; **the bus master network adapter provides much faster data throughput than the old adapter** = l'adaptateur maître du réseau a un débit de transfert beaucoup plus élevé que l'ancien; *(mouse that plugs into the main data bus of a computer)* **bus mouse** = souris (de) bus; **bus network** = réseau *m* de type bus; **bus slave** = (puits *or* collecteur de données) asservi à un bus *or* esclave *m* d'un bus; **bus structure** = structure *f* d'un bus; *(topology in which all devices are connected to a single cable)* **bus topology** = topologie en bus; **Ethernet is a network that uses the bus topology; token ring uses a ring topology** = Ethernet est un réseau qui utilise une topologie en bus; token ring utilise une topologie en anneau; *(bus carrying address data)* **address bus** = bus d'adresses; *(lines that can carry signals travelling in two directions)* **bi-directional bus** = bus bidirectionnel; **control bus** = bus de commande; **daisy chain bus** = bus série *or* bus de chaîne; **data bus** = bus de données; **dual bus system** = système *m* à bus double *or* à bus auxiliaire; **expansion bus** = bus d'expansion *or* d'extension; **input/output data bus (I/O bus)** = bus d'entrée/sortie; **memory bus** = bus de mémoire **(b)** carte connecteur *or* bus central

QUOTE both buses can be software controlled to operate as either a 16- or 32-bit interface

Electronics & Power

QUOTE The slot controller detects when a new board is inserted, it activates power up and assigns a bus arbitration and card slot ID to the board.

Computing

business *noun* **(a)** *(activity)* affaires *fpl*; **business computer** = ordinateur *m* de bureau; **business efficiency exhibition** = salon *m* de la bureautique; **business system** *or* **business package** = logiciel de comptabilité-gestion *or* logiciel de bureautique **(b)** *(company)* entreprise *f*; **he owns a small computer repair business** = il possède une petite entreprise de réparation d'ordinateurs; **he set up in business as an computer consultant** = il a ouvert son propre bureau d'ingénieur conseil en informatique

busy *adjective* **(a)** *(machine)* (appareil) en service; *(tone or signal)* (signal *or* tonalité) occupé, -ée; **when the busy line goes low, the printer will accept more data** = quand le signal 'occupé' s'éteint, l'imprimante peut de nouveau accepter des données; **the line is busy** = la ligne est occupée **(b)** *(background to a film shot)* fond *m* animé

button *noun* **(a)** *(switch that carries out an action)* bouton *m* (d'une souris ou d'une manette de jeu); **use the mouse to move the cursor to the icon and start the application by pressing the mouse button** = utilisez la souris pour placer le curseur sur l'icône et démarrez l'application en appuyant sur le bouton (de la souris) **(b)** *(square shape that*

can be selected by a pointer) bouton *m*; **there are two buttons at the bottom of the status line, select the left button to cancel the operation or the right to continue** = il y a deux boutons au bas de la ligne d'état, sélectionnez le bouton de gauche pour annuler l'opération et le bouton de droite pour continuer

buzz 1 *noun* vibration *f* sonore **2** *verb* émettre une vibration sonore *or* sonner

◊ **buzzer** *noun* buzzer *m or* sonnerie *f* d'avertissement *or* vibreur *m* sonore

◊ **buzzword** *noun* *(informal)* mot *m* à la mode *or* mot du jour

bypass *noun* dérivation *f*; **there is an automatic bypass around any faulty equipment** = il y a dérivation automatique lorsqu'une des machines tombe en panne

byte *noun* octet *m*; **byte addresses** = adresses *fpl* d'octets; *(variable word length computer)* **byte machine** = processeur *m* à mots variables; **byte manipulation** = manipulation *f* d'octets; *(familiar)* bidouillage *m* du bit; *(protocol which transmits data as characters)* **byte-orientated protocol** = protocole (de communication) caractère par caractère *or* à niveau octet; **byte serial transmission** *or* **mode** = transmission d'octets en série; *(measure of data storage capacity)* **bytes per inch** = octets par pouce; **bytes per second (Bps)** = octets *mpl* par seconde *or* Bps

QUOTE if you can find a way of packing two eight-bit values into a single byte, you save substantial amounts of RAM or disk space

Practical Computing

Cc

C *(hexadecimal number equivalent to decimal 12)* nombre hexadécimal équivalent du 12 décimal *or* C

C *(high level programming language)* langage *m* C

C++ *(high level programming language providing object oriented programming functions)* (langage de programmation orienté objets) C++

cable 1 *noun* **(a)** câble *m (connector at either end of a cable)* **cable connector** = connecteur *m* (de câble); *(impedance matching device)* **cable matcher** = accordeur *m* d'impédance; *(all the cables, etc. inside a building)* **cable plant** = câblage *m (equipment used to find faults in cabling)* **cable tester** = testeur *m* de câble **(b)** *(television)* **cable TV** = télévision câblée *or* le câble; **cable TV relay station** = relais *m* de télévision câblée **(c)** *(telegram)* câble *m or* câblogramme *m* ; télégramme *m*; **he sent a cable to his office asking for more money** = il a envoyé un câble au bureau pour redemander de l'argent; **cable address** = adresse *f* télégraphique **2** *verb* télégraphier *or* câbler *or* envoyer un câble *or* un télégramme; **he cabled his office to ask them to send more money** = il a envoyé un câble au bureau pour redemander de l'argent; **the office cabled him £1,000 to cover his expenses** = le bureau lui a envoyé un mandat télégraphique de 1000 livres sterling pour couvrir ses frais

◊ **cablegram** *noun* câblogramme *m*

◊ **cabling** *noun (cable as a material)* câblage *m or* câbles *mpl or* réseau *m* câblé; **using high-quality cabling will allow the user to achieve very high data transfer rates** = les câbles de haute qualité vont permettre à l'utilisateur d'obtenir un taux de transfert de données très élevé; **cabling costs up to £2 a foot** = le câble peut coûter jusqu'à 2 livres sterling les 30cm; *(drawing showing where a cable runs)* **cabling diagram** = schéma *m* de câblage *or* de circuit câblé

cache *or* **cache memory 1** *noun* cache *m or* mémoire *f* cache *or* antémémoire *f*; **file access time is much quicker if the most frequently used data is stored in cache memory** = le temps d'accès est réduit lorsque les données les plus fréquemment utilisées sont placées dans la mémoire cache;

(logic circuits that determine when to store data in cache memory) **cache controller** = contrôleur *m* de cache; **instruction cache** = cache *or* antémémoire d'instruction **2** *verb* stocker en mémoire cache; utiliser un cache; **this CPU caches instructions so improves performance by 15 percent** = ce processeur utilise un cache d'instructions et améliore ainsi les performances de 15 pour cent; **this program can cache any size font** = ce programme peut stocker une police de caractères, quelle qu'en soit la taille, dans la mémoire cache

CAD = COMPUTER AIDED DESIGN *or* COMPUTER ASSISTED DESIGN conception assistée par ordinateur *or* CAO; **all our engineers design on CAD workstations** = tous nos ingénieurs travaillent sur des stations de CAO

◊ **CAD/CAM** = COMPUTER AIDED DESIGN/COMPUTER AIDED MANUFACTURE; *see also* COMPUTER AIDED

CAI = COMPUTER AIDED INSTRUCTION *or* COMPUTER ASSISTED INSTRUCTION

CAL = COMPUTER AIDED LEARNING *or* COMPUTER ASSISTED LEARNING

calculate *verb* **(a)** calculer; **the DP manager calculated the rate for keyboarding** = le directeur du centre de traitement a calculé le coût de saisie de texte sur clavier; **you need to calculate the remaining disk space** = vous devez calculer l'espace libre sur la disquette **(b)** *(to estimate)* calculer *or* juger *or* estimer; **I calculate that we have six months' stock left** = j'estime que nous avons du stock pour six mois encore

◊ **calculated field** *noun (field that contains the results of calculations)* champ *m* calculé

◊ **calculation** *noun* calcul *m*; **rough calculation** = approximation *f or* calcul approximatif; **I made some rough calculations on the back of an envelope** = j'ai fait un calcul approximatif au dos d'une enveloppe; **according to my calculations, we have six months' stock left** = d'après mes calculs, il nous reste du stock pour six mois

◊ **calculator** *noun* calculatrice *f or* calculette *f*; **my pocket calculator needs a new battery** = j'ai besoin d'une pile pour ma calculatrice de poche; **he worked out the discount on his calculator** = il a calculé la remise sur sa calculatrice

calendar program *noun* (*software diary utility*) programme *m or* logiciel *m* de calendrier; **multi-user *or* network calendar program** = logiciel *m* de calendrier de groupe

calibration *noun* calibrage *m or* étalonnage *m*

call 1 *noun* **(a)** (*telephone*) appel *m or* communication *f*; **call diverter** = dispositif de réacheminement *or* de déroutage d'appel; **call forwarding** = transfert *m* d'appel (automatique); **we are having all calls forwarded from the office to home** = nous avons demandé le transfert à la maison des appels que nous recevons au bureau; (*for long-distance*) **call scheduling** = programmation *f* d'appels; **local call** = communication urbaine; **long-distance call *or* trunk call** = communication interurbaine; **person-to-person call** = communication avec préavis; **reverse charge call**, *US* **collect call** = appel en PCV; **to log calls** = enregistrer le nombre et la durée des appels; **to make a call** = appeler quelqu'un (au téléphone) *or* téléphoner (à quelqu'un); **to take a call** = répondre au téléphone **(b)** **call accepted signal** = signal *m* d'appel accepté *or* signal d'acceptation d'appel; **call control signal** = signal *m* de contrôle d'appel; **call duration** = durée *f* d'un appel; **call duration depends on the complexity of the transaction** = la durée de l'appel varie suivant la complexité de la transaction; **charges are related to call duration** = le prix est fonction de la durée de l'appel **(c)** (*computer*) appel (d'un programme); (*programming instruction that directs control to a routine*) **call instruction** = instruction *f* d'appel; **the subroutine call instruction should be at this point** = c'est ici qu'il faudrait introduire l'instruction d'appel **2** *verb* **(a)** téléphoner à quelqu'un *or* appeler quelqu'un; **I'll call you at your office tomorrow** = je vous appellerai au bureau demain; **called party** = correspondant, -e **(b)** (*modem that, on answering a call, immediately hangs up and calls the user back*) **call back modem** = modem *m* de rappel **(c)** (*to transfer control to a separate program or routine from a main program*) appeler un programme *or* un sous-programme *or* une routine

◊ **call box** *noun* cabine *f* téléphonique

◊ **caller** *noun* personne qui fait un appel téléphonique *or* demandeur *m*

◊ **call in** *verb* contacter (son bureau) par téléphone; **we ask the representatives to call in every Friday** = nous demandons aux représentants de communiquer par téléphone, chaque vendredi

◊ **calling** *noun* **(a)** (*signal to request attention, sent from a terminal or device to the main computer*) signal *m* d'appel; (*series of program commands*) **calling sequence** = séquence *f* d'appel **(b)** **calling unit** = unité *f or* système *m* d'appel

◊ **call up** *verb* appeler *or* rappeler *or* afficher à l'écran; **all the customers addresses were called up** = on a affiché à l'écran les adresses de tous les clients; **call up the previous file** = rappelez le fichier précédent à l'écran; **after an input is received, the first function is called up** = dès réception d'une entrée, on appelle la première fonction

callier effect *noun* effet *m* Callier *or* le flare

calligraphy *noun* calligraphie *f*

calloc (*in C programming: instruction to allocate memory to a program*) (instruction en langage C) calloc

CAM (a) = COMPUTER AIDED MANUFACTURE *or* COMPUTER ASSISTED MANUFACTURING **(b)** = CONTENT ADDRESSABLE MEMORY

Cambridge ring *noun* (réseau en) anneau *m* de Cambridge

camcorder *noun* Caméscope ™ *m*

cameo *noun* **(a)** impression inversée *or* blanc sur noir **(b)** (*on film*) contre-jour *m*

camera *noun* (*still photos*) appareil *m* photographique *or* appareil photo; (*film*) caméra *f*; (*TV*) caméra de télévision; **camera chain** = ensemble *m* caméra

campus environment *noun* (*large area that has lots of users connected by several networks*) environnement *m* universitaire

CAN = CANCEL CHARACTER

cancel *verb* annuler; **cancel character (CAN)** = caractère *m* d'annulation; **the software automatically sends a cancel character after any error** = le logiciel envoie automatiquement un caractère d'annulation après une erreur; (*in book*) **cancel page** = page *m* corrigée qui en remplace une autre

◊ **cancellation** *noun* annulation *f*

candela *noun* (*light intensity*) candela *f*

canned *adjective* **(a)** (*computer*) **canned program** = programme *m* portable *or* transportable (d'une machine à l'autre) *or* programme d'une grande portabilité; **canned software** = logiciel *m* de série *or* progiciel *m* **(b)** (*TV*) **canned programme** = programme filmé *or* en différé

canonical schema *noun* schéma *m* (de base de données) standard *or* canonique

capability *noun* capacité *f or* facilité *f* ; fonction *f* ; **resolution capabilities** = capacité de définition; **electronic mail capabilities** = (avec) fonction courrier électronique; **capability list** = liste *f* des fonctions *or* des possibilités

◊ **capable** *adjective* capable; **that is the highest speed that this printer is capable of** = c'est la vitesse maximum que peut atteindre cette imprimante; **the software is capable of far more complex functions** = ce logiciel permet d'exécuter des fonctions beaucoup plus complexes

capacitance *noun* capacitance *f*

◊ **capacitative** *or* **capacitive** *adjective* capacitif, -ive

◊ **capacitor** *noun* condensateur *m or* capacité *f* ; **capacitor microphone** = microphone *m* à condensateur; **ceramic capacitor** = condensateur céramique; **electrolytic capacitor** = condensateur électrolytique; **non-electrolytic capacitor** = condensateur non électrolytique; **variable capacitor** = condensateur variable *or* capacité variable; **capacitor storage** = mémoire capacitive *or* à condensateur; **memory backup capacitor** = condensateur pour mémoire RAM

capacity *noun* **(a)** *(production)* capacité *f* ; *(amount produced)* **industrial** *or* **manufacturing** *or* **production capacity** = rendement *m* ; **channel capacity** = capacité *f or* débit *m* d'une voie de transmission; **to work at full capacity** = travailler à plein régime *or* à plein rendement; **to use up spare** *or* **excess capacity** = utiliser la capacité en excédent **(b)** *(space)* capacité; **storage capacity** = capacité *f* de mémoire *or* taille *f* (de la) mémoire; **total storage capacity is now 3MB** = la capacité de mémoire est maintenant de 3Mo

capital *(informal)* **cap** *noun* (lettre) majuscule *f or* capitale *f* ; **the word BASIC is always written in caps** = BASIC s'écrit toujours avec des majuscules; **caps lock** = touche *f* de verrouillage des majuscules; **the LED lights up when caps lock is pressed** = le témoin s'allume quand la touche (des) majuscules est verrouillée

◊ **capitalization** *noun* *(converts text into capitals)* mise *f* en majuscule

capstan *noun* *(of tape player)* cabestan *m* (d'entraînement) *or* presseur *m* de bande

caption légende *f* ; **the captions are printed in italics** = les légendes sont (imprimées) en italique

capture 1 *noun* **data capture** = saisie *f* de données; **data capture starts when an interrupt is received** = la saisie commence dès réception du signal d'interruption **2** *verb* **(a)** saisir *or* capturer (des données); **the software allows captured images to be edited** = le logiciel permet d'éditer les images saisies *or* capturées; **this scanner captures images at a resolution of 300 dots per inch (dpi)** = ce scanner peut capturer des images avec définition *or*

résolution de 300 points par pouce (ppp) **(b)** *(remove a token from the network)* prélever un jeton (dans un réseau Token-Ring); *see also* TOKEN-RING

QUOTE images can then be captured, stored, manipulated and displayed
Electronics & Wireless World

QUOTE In July this year it signed a two-year outsourcing and disaster-recovery deal with Unisys for the operation and management of its Birmingham-based data-capture facility.
Computing

CAR = CURRENT ADDRESS REGISTER

carbon *noun* **(a)** (papier) carbone *m* ; **you forgot to put a carbon in the typewriter** = vous avez oublié de mettre un carbone dans votre machine à écrire **(b)** double *m or* copie *f* carbone; **make a top copy and two carbons** = faites un original et deux doubles

◊ **carbon copy** *noun* copie *f* carbone *or* double *m* ; **give me the original, and file the carbon copy** = passez-moi l'original et classez la copie dans le dossier

◊ **carbonless** *adjective* autocopiant, -e; **we use carbonless order pads** = nous utilisons des carnets de commandes autocopiants; **carbonless paper** = papier *m* autocopiant

◊ **carbon microphone** *noun* microphone *m* à charbon

◊ **carbon paper** *noun* (papier) carbone *m*

◊ **carbon ribbon** *noun* ruban *m* carbone

◊ **carbon set** *noun* formulaire *m* avec double carboné

◊ **carbon tissue** *noun* film *m* de transfert

card *noun* **(a)** *(material)* carton *m* ; **we have printed the instructions on thick white card** = nous avons fait imprimer les instructions sur carton blanc épais **(b)** *(plastic card)* carte *f* ; *(device which reads data from the magnetic strip on the back of a credit card)* **card reader** = lecteur *m* de carte(s); **cash card** = carte de retrait (bancaire); **charge card** = carte accréditive; **credit card** = carte de crédit; **smart card** = carte à puce *or* carte à mémoire *or* carte magnétique; **smart cards reduce fraud** = les cartes à puce aident à réduire le nombre de fraudes; **future smart cards could contain an image of the user's fingerprint for identification** = à l'avenir, on pourrait inclure les empreintes digitales de l'utilisateur sur ses cartes à mémoire à fin d'identification **(c)** **filing card** = fiche *f* ; **index card** = fiche *or* carte de fichier; *see also* CARD INDEX **(d)** *(punched card)* carte perforée; **card code** = code *m* de perforation de cartes; **card column** = colonne *f* de perforations (d'une carte perforée); **card feed** = (système d') alimentation *f or* entraînement *m* de cartes perforées; **card field** = champ *m* de carte (perforée); **card format** = format *m* de carte (perforée); **card frame** *or* **card chassis** = support *m* de cartes (de circuits imprimés) *or* chassis *m* avec guide-cartes *or* baie *f* ; **card image** = image *f* (mémoire) de carte; *(program that transfers data from a punched card into main memory)* **card loader** = chargeur *m* de cartes; **card punch (CP)** = poinçon *m* de perforation *or* perforateur *m* (pour cartes); **card reader** *or* **punched card reader** = lecteur *m* de cartes perforées; **card row** = colonne de perforations d'une carte **(e)** *(circuit card)* carte de circuit imprimé *or* plaque *f* (présensibilisée) pour circuit imprimé; **card cage** = support *f* de cartes *or* châssis *m* avec guide-cartes *or* baie *f*; **card edge connector** = connecteur *m* de carte; **card extender** = support *m* de carte d'extension; **expansion card** *or* **expansion board** = carte d'extension; **hard card** = carte de disque dur

◊ **cardboard** *noun (material)* carton *m*; **cardboard box** = carton *or* boîte *f* en carton

◊ **card index** *noun* fichier *m*

◊ **card-index** *verb* mettre sur fiches

◊ **card-indexing** *noun* mise *f* sur fiches; **no one can understand her card-indexing system** = personne ne comprend sa méthode de classement du fichier

```
QUOTE this card does not occupy system
memory space and provides fifty functions
including programmable character sets
                           Computing Today
```

```
QUOTE A smart card carries an encryption
chip, which codifies your ID and password prior
to their being transmitted across a network.
                                    Computing
```

cardinal *noun & adjective (positive integer)* cardinal, -e; **13, 19 and 27 are cardinal numbers, −2.3 and 7.45 are not** = 13, 19 et 27 sont des nombres cardinaux, −2,3 et 7,45 n'en sont pas

cardioid response *noun* (réponse) cardioïde *f*

caret mark *or* **sign** *noun* **(a)** *(used in proofreading)* signe *m* d'omission **(b)** *(symbol ^ used to mean the Control key)* caret *m* *or* symbole ^ (de la touche Ctrl)

carriage *noun (of typewriter or printer)* chariot *m*; **carriage control** = commande *f* de chariot; **carriage control codes can be used to move the paper forward two lines between each line of text** = les codes de commande de chariot peuvent être utilisés pour faire avancer le papier de deux interlignes; **carriage return (CR)** = touche *f* *or* signal *m* de retour du chariot; **the carriage return key is badly placed for touch-typists** = les clavistes trouvent que la touche de retour est mal placée; **carriage return/line feed (CR/LF)** = retour *m* (de) chariot/retour à la ligne

carrier *noun* **(a)** *(photocopying or printing processes)* support *m* (d'encrage) **(b)** *(microfilm)* support **(c)** *(high frequency waveform)* (onde) porteuse *f*; *(signal from a modem)* **carrier detect (CD)** = signal CD *or* signal de détection de porteuse; *(frequency of the carrier signal)* **carrier frequency** = fréquence de porteuse; *(method of controlling access to a network)* **carrier sense multiple access-collision detection (CSMA-CD)** =

méthode d'accès à test de porteuse et détection de collision *or* protocole de transmission CSMA-CD; *(waveform that can be modulated by a signal)* **carrier signal** = signal de porteuse; **carrier signalling** = transmission *f* par onde porteuse; **he's not using a modem - there's no carrier signal on the line** = il n'utilise pas de modem: il n'existe aucun signal de porteuse sur la ligne; **carrier system** = *(analog)* système *m* à courants porteurs; *(analog or digital)* système multiplex; **carrier telegraphy** = télégraphie *f* par onde porteuse; **carrier wave** = onde porteuse; **data carrier** = (i) support de données; (ii) onde porteuse de données; **data carrier detect (DCD)** = (signal) détecteur *m* d'onde porteuse *or* signal *m* de détection de porteuse; **the call is stopped if the software does not receive a DCD signal from the modem** = l'appel est bloqué si le logiciel ne reçoit pas de signal de détection de porteuse

carry 1 *noun (maths)* retenue *f* *or* report *m*; **when 5 and 7 are added, there is an answer of 2 and a carry which is put in the next column, giving 12** = lorsqu'on additionne 5 et 7, on pose 2 et on retient 1 sur la colonne des dizaines, ce qui fait 12; **carry bit** *or* **flag** = balise de *or* bit de report; **carry complete signal** = signal *m* de fin de report; **carry look ahead** = additionneur *m* à retenue automatique (très rapide); **carry time** = temps *m* de report; **cascade carry** = report en cascade; **end-around carry** = report circulaire *or* en boucle; **high speed carry** = report rapide; **partial carry** = report partiel; **ripple-through carry** = report rapide *or* simultané **2** *verb* transporter *or* transmettre *or* véhiculer; **the fibre optic link carried all the data** = toutes les données ont été transmises par fibres optiques; **the information-carrying abilities of this link are very good** = la capacité de transmission *or* de portage de cette liaison est excellente

cartesian coordinates *noun* coordonnées *fpl* cartésiennes

◊ **cartesian structure** *noun* structure cartésienne *f*

cartridge *noun* cartouche *f*; **data cartridge** = cartouche de données; **disk cartridge** = cartouche (de) disque dur *or* disque dur amovible; *(for use in printers)* **ink cartridge** = cartouche *f* d'encre; **ROM cartridge** = cartouche ROM *or* ROM amovible; **the portable computer has no disk drives, but has a slot for ROM cartridges** = cet ordinateur portatif n'est pas équipé de lecteur de disquettes mais possède un connecteur pour cartouches ROM; **tape cartridge** = cartouche (de) bande; **cartridge drive** = lecteur de cartouches; **cartridge fonts** = cartouche de police de caractères; *(for printers)* **cartridge ribbon** = ruban en cartouche

◊ **cartridge paper** *noun* papier *m* à dessin (de type 'cartridge')

cascade carry *noun* report *m* en cascade

◊ **cascade connection** *noun* connexion *f* (montée) en cascade

◊ **cascade control** *noun* contrôle *m* en cascade

◊ **cascading windows** *plural noun (windows that are displayed overlapping)* (disposition de fenêtres en) cascade *f*

case 1 *noun* **(a)** *(container)* boîtier *m* **(b)** *(typography)* casse *f*; **lower case** = minuscule *f or* bas *m* de casse; **upper case** = majuscule *f or* haut *m* de casse; **he corrected the word 'coMputer', replacing the upper case M with a lower case letter** = il a remplacé le M majuscule de 'coMputer' par une minuscule; **case change** = touche *f* des majuscules; *(command that will only work when the characters are entered in a particular case)* **case sensitive** = qui distingue les majuscules des minuscules; **the password is case sensitive** = le mot de passe tient compte des majuscules; *(search function)* **case sensitive search** = recherche *f* qui distingue les majuscules des minuscules *or* qui tient compte des majuscules **(c)** *(programming command)* (commande) CASE *or* commande de branchement conditionnel; *(branch to a part of a program)* **case branch** = branchement *m* conditionnel **(d)** *(cardboard cover for a book)* cartonnage *m*; **the library edition has a case and jacket** = l'édition pour bibliothèques est cartonnée avec jaquette; **case binding** = couverture *f* cartonnée **(e)** *(box)* carton *m or* boîte *f* en carton; **packing case** = caisse *f* **2** *verb* **(a)** *(to bind)* cartonner *or* relier avec couverture cartonnée; **cased book** = livre cartonné **(b)** *(to pack)* emballer *or* mettre dans une caisse

◊ **case-making machine** *noun (for books)* machine *f* à cartonner

casing *noun* boîtier *m or* coffret *m*

cassette *noun* cassette *f*; **you must back up the information from the computer onto a cassette** = il faut faire une cassette de sauvegarde pour vos données; **audio cassette** = audiocassette *f or* cassette audio; **data cassette** = cassette informatique; **video cassette** = vidéocassette *f*; **cassette recorder** = magnétophone à cassette; **cassette tape** = bande *f* magnétique *or* cassette

cast *noun (in a programming language, instruction that converts data)* (commande) CAST (de conversion); **to convert the variable from an integer to a character type, use the cast command** = pour convertir une variable de type nombre entier en une variable de type caractère, utilisez la commande CAST

caster machine *noun* fondeuse *f*

◊ **cast off 1** *noun* calibrage *m* d'un texte **2** *verb* calibrer un texte

◊ **casting off** *noun* calibrage d'un texte

CAT (a) = COMPUTER-AIDED *or* ASSISTED TRAINING **(b)** = COMPUTER-AIDED *or* ASSISTED TESTING

catalogue 1 *noun* catalogue *m*; *(directory)* **disk catalogue** = répertoire *m* des fichiers d'un disque *or* d'une disquette; **the entry in the disk catalogue is removed when the file is deleted** = le nom d'un fichier qui est effacé disparaît aussi du répertoire du disque **2** *verb* cataloguer *or* répertorier; **all the terminals are catalogued, with their location, call sign and attribute table** = tous les terminaux sont répertoriés avec (indication de) leur emplacement, leur code *or* signe d'appel et leur table d'attributs

◊ **cataloguer** *noun* archiviste *m&f*

catastrophe *noun* catastrophe *f*

◊ **catastrophic error** *noun* erreur *f* qui cause une catastrophe *or* erreur fatale; **catastrophic failure** = panne *f* fatale

catena *noun* (i) (nombre de) caractères *mpl* dans une chaîne; (ii) chaîne *f* de caractères

◊ **catenate** *verb* (en)chaîner *or* lier; concaténer *or* faire une concaténation

◊ **catenation** *noun (chain)* chaîne *f or* concaténation *f (chaining)* enchaînement *m or* concaténation

cathode *noun* cathode *f* (NOTE: opposite is **anode**)

◊ **cathode ray tube (CRT)** *noun* (i) tube *m* à rayons cathodiques *or* tube cathodique; (ii) écran (à tube cathodique); **cathode ray tube (storage)** = moniteur *m or* écran *m* (d'ordinateur)

CATV = COMMUNITY ANTENNA TELEVISION antenne *f* collective de télévision câblée *or* système de télévision (câblée) CATV; **CATV cable** = câble *m* de télévision (câblée) *or* câble CATV

C band *noun* (fréquence de) bande *f* C

CB = CITIZENS BAND (RADIO)

CBL = COMPUTER-BASED LEARNING

CBMS = COMPUTER-BASED MESSAGE SYSTEM

CBT = COMPUTER-BASED TRAINING

CBX = COMPUTERIZED BRANCH EXCHANGE

CCD = CHARGE COUPLED DEVICE dispositif *m* à couplage de charge; **CCD memory** = mémoire CCD *or* à couplage de charge

CCITT = COMITE CONSULTATIF INTERNATIONAL TELEGRAPHIQUE ET TELEPHONIQUE

CCP = COMMAND CONSOLE PROCESSOR

CCTV = CLOSED CIRCUIT TELEVISION

CCU = COMMUNICATIONS CONTROL UNIT

CD = CHANGE DIRECTORY; *(instruction in MS-DOS and UNIX)* (commande) CD (de changement de répertoire); **type in CD DOCS to move into the DOCS subdirectory** = entrez CD DOCS au clavier pour aller dans le sous-répertoire DOCS

CD = COMPACT DISC disque *m* compact *or* disque CD; **CD player** = platine *f* laser *or* platine (de) disques compacts; lecteur *m* de disques CD

◊ **CD-I** = COMPACT DISC-INTERACTIVE; *(standards that combine sound, data, video and text onto a CD)* disque compact interactif *or* (disque) CD interactif

◊ **CD-ROM** = COMPACT DISK-READ ONLY MEMORY; *(disc drive)* **CD-ROM player** = platine *f or* lecteur *m* de CD-ROM; *(extended CD-ROM format)* **CD-ROM Extended Architecture** *or* **CD-ROM/XA** = architecture *f* étendue multimédia *or* CD-ROM/XA

QUOTE Customers' images will be captured, digitised, and stored on optical disk or CD-ROM, and produced if queries arise about responsibility for ATM transactions.
Computing

cedilla *noun (typography)* cédille *f*

cell *noun* **(a)** *(single function in a spreadsheet)* cellule *f*; *(code that identifies the position of a cell by row and column)* **cell address** = adresse *f* de cellule; *(in a spreadsheet: formula contained in a cell)* **cell definition** = définition *f* de cellule; *(in a spreadsheet: way a cell is displayed)* **cell format** = format *m* de cellule; **the cell format is right-aligned and emboldened** = le format de cette cellule est justification à droite et caractères gras; *(prevent the contents of a cell from being changed)* **cell protection** = protection *f* de cellule; **cell reference variable** = variable *f* de référence d'une cellule; *(thicker line surrounding the cell being edited)* **current** *or* **active cell** = cellule courante *or* active **(b)** *(single memory location)* cellule

cellar *noun* pile *f* (de données en mémoire)

cell phone *noun* téléphone *m* cellulaire

cellular *adjective* cellulaire; **cellular phone** = téléphone cellulaire; **cellular radio** = radiotéléphone (de type) cellulaire; **cellular service** = réseau *m* radiotéléphonique

centi- *prefix* centi-; **centimetre** = centimètre *m*

central *adjective* central, -e *or* principal, -e; *(host computer)* **central computer** = ordinateur central *or* ordinateur hôte; **central memory (CM)** = mémoire centrale *or* principale; **central processing element (CPE)** = unité centrale de calcul (d'un processeur en tranches); **central processing unit (CPU)** *or* **central processor** = unité centrale (de traitement) *or* processeur central; **central terminal** = terminal principal *or* central

◊ **centralized** *adjective* centralisé, -ée; **centralized data processing** = traitement centralisé de l'information; **centralized computer network** = réseau informatique centralisé

centre, US center 1 *noun* centre *m*; *(of punched tape)* **centre holes** = perforations *fpl* centrales; **centre operator** = opérateur *m* central; *(on punched tape)* **centre sprocket feed** = canal *m* d'entraînement (avec perforations centrales) **2**

verb **(a)** *(to align read/write head)* centrer *or* aligner *or* ajuster (les têtes) **(b)** *(in text or on screen)* centrer; **which key do you press to centre the heading?** = sur quelle touche faut-il appuyer pour centrer l'en-tête?

◊ **centering** *noun (text)* centrage *m* (d'un texte); **centering of headings is easily done, using this function key** = il est plutôt facile de centrer les en-têtes avec cette touche (de fonction)

Centronics ™ interface *noun* interface parallèle (de type) Centronics

CEPT standard *noun (character standard defined by the Conference of European Post Telephone and Telegraph)* norme *f* CEPT

ceramic *noun & adjective* céramique *(f)*

CGA = COLOUR GRAPHICS ADAPTER

CGM = COMPUTER GRAPHICS METAFILE

chad *noun* confetti *m*; **chadded** *or* **chadless tape** = bande semi-perforée *or* à confettis non détachés

chain 1 *noun* chaîne *f*; **chain code** = code *m* en chaîne *or* code chaîné; *(for paper)* **chain delivery mechanism** = convoyeur *m* (d'alimentation du papier); **chain list** = liste *f* en chaîne *or* liste chaînée; **chain printer** = imprimante à chaîne; **command chain** = chaîne de commandes; **daisy chain** = chaîne *f*; **daisy chain bus** = bus *m* de chaîne **2** *verb (files or data items)* (s')enchaîner; **more than 1,000 articles or chapters can be chained together when printing** = plus de 1000 articles ou chapitres peuvent être enchaînés à l'impression; **chained** *or* **threaded file** = fichier *m* chaîné; **chained list** = liste *f* chaînée *or* concaténée; **chained record** = enregistrement *m or* article *m* chaîné; *(hardware)* **to daisy-chain** = relier en série *or* en chaîne *or* en cascade

◊ **chaining** *noun* (i) enchaînement *m* ; (ii) chaînage *m*; **chaining search** = recherche en chaîne; *(of hardware)* **daisy-chaining** = connexion *f* en chaîne *or* en cascade; **daisy-chaining saves a lot of cable** = la connexion en chaîne réduit le câblage; **data chaining** = liaison *f* de données en chaîne *or* chaînage de données

change 1 *verb (to modify)* changer *or* modifier; *(to transfer)* changer (de place *or* d'appareil) *or* transférer **2** *noun* changement *m or* modification *f*; **change dump** = vidage *m* de mouvements (sur imprimante); **change file** = fichier *m* (de) mouvements *or* de mise à jour; **change record** = enregistrement *m* de mouvements *or* de modifications; **change tape** = bande *f* (de) mouvements

◊ **change over** *verb* passer d'un système à un autre

◊ **change-over** *noun* transfert *m or* permutation *f*; **direct change-over** = transfert direct

◊ **changer** *noun* changeur *m*; *(of connectors)* **gender changer** = changeur de genre; **you can interconnect all these peripherals with just two** cables and a gender changer = il est possible de relier tous ces périphériques en utilisant seulement deux câbles et un changeur de genre; record changer = changeur (de disques) automatique

channel 1 *noun* (a) canal *m or* voie *f*; channel adapter = interface *f or* adaptateur *m* de canal de transmission; channel bank = banque *f* de canaux; channel capacity = débit *m* d'un canal *or* d'une voie; channel command = commande *f* de canal; channel group = groupement *m* de voies; channel isolation = isolation *f* de canaux; channel overload = surcharge *f or* saturation *f* d'un canal *or* d'une voie; channel queue = file *f* d'attente (de demandes de service *or* de données à transmettre); channel synchronizer = synchroniseur *m* de canaux *or* de voies; channel-to-channel connection = liaison directe entre canaux; data channel = canal de transmission de données; dedicated channel = voie spécialisée *or* canal dédié; I/O channel = canal *or* voie d'entrée/sortie (b) voie (de communication); to open up new channels of communication = créer de nouveaux circuits de communication 2 *verb* (*signals or data*) acheminer *or* transmettre *or* véhiculer

◊ **channelling** *noun* (*protective pipes*) conduite *f or* canalisation *f*

chapter *noun* (a) (*of program*) module *m* (b) (*on a video disk*) module; chapter stop = (code) fin *f* de module (c) (*of book, etc.*) chapitre *m*; chapter heading = tête *f* de chapitre; chapter headings are in 12 point bold = les têtes de chapitre sont en caractères gras de 12 points

char *noun* (*in programming*) (variable de type caractère) char

character *noun* caractère *m*; character assembly = assemblage *m or* groupage *m* de caractères; (*screen design using ASCII characters*) character-based = (écran) à base de caractères; character blink = caractère clignotant; character block = bloc *m* (de) caractères; character byte = octet *m* (de caractères); character check = contrôle *m* de caractère; character code = code *m* de caractères; the ASCII code is the most frequently used character coding system = le code ASCII est le code de caractères le plus fréquemment utilisé; character density = densité *f* de caractère; character display = affichage *m* de caractères *or* de texte; character fill = (i) remplissage *m* (avec caractères blancs); (ii) insertion *f* de caractères de remplissage (en mémoire); character generator = générateur *m* de caractères; the ROM used as a character generator can be changed to provide different fonts = on peut utiliser une ROM comme générateur de caractères pour obtenir les différentes polices; (*time division multiplexing*) character interleaving = entrelaçage *m* de caractères; (*word processor control*) character key = touche *f* caractère; character machine = processeur *m* en mode caractère *or* à mots variables; (*display adapter mode*) character mode = mode *m* caractère; character orientated (computer) = (ordinateur) à mode caractère; character printer = imprimante *f* caractère (par caractère); a daisy-wheel printer is a character

printer = l'imprimante à marguerite imprime un caractère à la fois; character recognition = reconnaissance *f* optique de caractères; character repertoire = répertoire *m* de caractères *or* répertoire typographique; character representation = expression *f* binaire d'un caractère; character set = (*codes*) jeu *m* de caractères; (*printing*) police *f* de caractères; character skew = angle *m or* oblique *f* (d'un caractère); character string = chaîne *f* de caractères; characters per inch (cpi) = (nombre de) caractères par pouce; you can select 10 or 12 cpi with the green button = le bouton vert vous permet de sélectionner 10 ou 12 caractères par pouce; characters per second (cps) = (nombre de) caractères par seconde (cps); character stuffing = (i) remplissage *m* (avec caractères blancs); (ii) insertion *f* de caractères blancs *or* de caractères de remplissage; alphanumeric characters = caractères alphanumériques; cancel character = caractère d'annulation; check character = caractère de contrôle; device control character = caractère de contrôle de périphérique

◊ **characteristic** 1 *noun* (a) (*maths*) exposant *m or* caractéristique *f*; the floating point number 1.345 x 10³, has a characteristic of 3 = la valeur de l'exposant du nombre à virgule flottante 1,345 x 10³ est 3; characteristic overflow = dépassement *m* de capacité de la caractéristique (b) (*properties of component*) caractéristique 2 *adjective* (*typical or special*) caractéristique; this fault is characteristic of this make and model of personal computer = c'est un défaut caractéristique de cette marque et de ce modèle d'ordinateur individuel; characteristic curve = courbe *f* caractéristique

charge 1 *noun* (*of electricity or of electrons*) charge *f*; charge-coupled device (CCD) = dispositif *m* CCD *or* à couplage de charge; charge-coupled device memory = mémoire *f* CCD *or* à couplage de charge; electric charge = charge électrique 2 *verb* charger; battery charging = (temps de) charge d'une pile

◊ **chargeable** *adjective* chargeable; re-chargeable battery = pile *f or* batterie *f* rechargeable; a re-chargeable battery is used for RAM back-up when the system is switched off = on utilise une pile rechargeable comme alimentation auxiliaire pour la mémoire RAM quand le système est éteint

chart *noun* diagramme *m or* graphique *m*; **bar chart** = graphique à barres *or* en tuyaux d'orgue; histogramme *m*; **logical chart** = diagramme logique; **pie chart** = diagramme à secteurs *or* (diagramme en) camembert *m*; **the memory allocation is shown on this pie chart** = l'attribution de mémoire est indiquée sur ce camembert; **chart recorder** = enregistreur *m* graphique; *see also* FLOWCHART

chassis *noun* châssis *m*

CHCP *(in MS-DOS OS/2: system command that selects which code page to use)* (commande) CHCP (de changement de page de code)

CHDIR = CHANGE DIRECTORY (commande) CHDIR (de changement de répertoire); *see also* CD

cheapernet *noun* *(informal: thin-Ethernet)* Ethernet câble fin; **cheapernet cable** = câblage *m* léger (et bon marché) Ethernet

check 1 *noun* **(a)** vérification *f or* test *m or* contrôle *m*; **character check** = contrôle de caractère; **check bit** = bit *m* de contrôle; *(in a GUI or front-end)* **check box** = case *f* à cocher *or* case de sélection *or* case de pointage; **select the option by moving the cursor to the check box and pressing the mouse button** = pour faire un choix, déplaçez le curseur sur une case de sélection et appuyez sur le bouton de la souris; **check character** = caractère *m* de contrôle; **check digit** *or* **number** = chiffre *m or* clé *f* (numérique) de contrôle; **check indicator** = indicateur *m* de contrôle; **check key** = clé de contrôle; **check point** = point *m* de contrôle *or* de reprise; **check point dump** = vidage *m* de contrôle (sur imprimante); **check register** = registre *m* de contrôle; **check total** = CHECKSUM; *(dry run of a program)* **desk check** = essai *m* à blanc *or* contrôle sur papier *m* (d'un programme) **(b)** arrêt *m* de courte durée (causé par un défaut du support magnétique); **data check** = brève interruption *f* de transmission de données (due à un défaut du support magnétique) **2** *verb* vérifier *or* tester *or* contrôler; **the separate parts of the system were all checked for faults before being packaged** = les différentes parties du système ont été contrôlées avant l'emballage; **he checked the computer printout against the invoices** = il a comparé la sortie d'imprimante avec les factures

QUOTE Four bits control three multiplexers within the function unit. The last bit is a check bit to read the block's output.
Computing

checker *see* SPELL

◊ **checkerboarding** *noun* caviardage *m* (de la mémoire)

◊ **checking** *noun* examen *m or* vérification *f or* contrôle *m*; **the maintenance engineer found some defects whilst checking the equipment** = l'ingénieur de maintenance a découvert des défauts en contrôlant le matériel; **checking program** = programme *m* de contrôle; **self-checking code** = code détecteur d'erreur

◊ **checksum** *or* **check total** *noun* total *m* de vérification *or* de contrôle; **the data must be corrupted if the checksum is different** = les données sont sûrement erronées si le total de contrôle est faux

chemical 1 *adjective* chimique; **chemical reaction** = réaction *f* chimique **2** *noun* produit *m* chimique

child process *or* **program** *noun* *(program called by another program)* procédure *f* fille *or* de deuxième génération

chip *noun* puce *f or* composant *m* ; circuit *m* intégré; **chip architecture** = architecture *f* d'un circuit intégré; **chip card** = carte *f* à puce *or* carte à mémoire; **chip count** = nombre de puces (sur une carte, etc.); **it's no good, the chip count is still too high** = le nombre de puces est malheureusement encore trop élevé; **chip select line** = ligne *f* de sélection *or* de validation d'un circuit intégré; **the data strobe line is connected to the latch chip select line** = la ligne de validation de données est reliée à la ligne de sélection de la bascule; **chip set** = ensemble *m* de circuits intégrés; **diagnostic chip** = puce de diagnostic; **they are carrying out research on diagnostic chips to test computers that contain processors** = ils font des recherches sur les puces de diagnostic destinées au contrôle des ordinateurs équipés de processeurs; **single chip computer** = ordinateur *m* monopuce *or* à puce unique; **sound chip** = (circuit intégré) générateur *m* de son

QUOTE Where the display is provided by an LCD system, high levels of performance must be achieved with the lowest cost, smallest chip count and lowest power consumption.
Computing

CHKDSK *(in MS-DOS: system command that checks the status of a disk drive)* (commande) CHKDSK (de contrôle de lecteur de disque)

choke *see* INDUCTOR

Chooser ™ *(Apple Macintosh operating system)* utilitaire *m* Chooser ™

chop *see* BINARY

chord keying *noun* action *f* d'appuyer sur deux touches en même temps

COMMENT: as an example, to access a second window, you may need to press control and F2; pressing shift and character delete keys at the same time will delete a line of text

chroma *noun* chrominance *f or* chroma *f*; *(TV)* **chroma control** = contrôle *m* chromatique; **chroma detector** = détecteur *m* chromatique

◊ **chromatic** *adjective* chromatique; **chromatic aberration** = aberration *f* chromatique; **chromatic dispersion** = dispersion *f* chromatique

◊ **chromaticity** *noun* chromaticité *f*

◊ **chrominance signal** *noun* signal *m* de chrominance

chronological order *noun* ordre *m* chronologique

CIM (a) = COMPUTER INPUT FROM MICROFILM **(b)** = COMPUTER-INTEGRATED MANUFACTURE

cine- *prefix* ciné-; **cine-camera** = caméra *f or* appareil *m* cinématographique; **cine-orientated image** = image orientée en film

◊ **cinema** *noun* **(a)** *(as an art)* **the cinema** = le cinéma *m or* l'art *m* cinématographique **(b)** *(building)* cinéma

◊ **cinematography** *noun* cinématographie *f*

cipher *noun* code *m* (chiffré) *or* écriture *f* chiffrée; **always use a secure cipher when sending data over a telephone line** = il faut toujours utiliser un code (chiffré) sûr quand vous transmettez des données par téléphone; **cipher key** = clé *f* de chiffrage *or* de cryptage; **cipher system** = code chiffré; **public key cipher** = code chiffré *m* à clé publique; **ciphertext** = message *m* chiffré *or* crypté (NOTE: opposite is **plaintext**)

CIR = CURRENT INSTRUCTION REGISTER

circuit *noun* circuit *m*; *(measures voltage in a circuit)* **circuit analyzer** = analyseur *m* de circuit; **circuit board** *or* **card** = carte *f* de circuit imprimé *or* plaque *f* (présensibilisée) pour circuit imprimé; *(with circuit printed)* **printed circuit board (PCB)** = (carte de) circuit imprimé (CI); **circuit breaker** = disjoncteur *m or* interrupteur *m* (de courant); **circuit capacity** = capacité *f* d'un circuit; **circuit diagram** = diagramme *m* d'un circuit; **the CAD program will plot the circuit diagram rapidly** = le programme de CAO peut tracer le circuit très rapidement; **circuit grade** = qualité *f or* caractéristique *f* d'un circuit; **circuit noise level** = niveau *m* de bruit d'un circuit; **circuit switched digital circuitry** = circuiterie numérique commutée; **circuit switched network** = réseau *m* commuté; *(link between two nodes established at the time of calling)* **circuit switching** = commutation *f* de circuit; **data circuit** = circuit (de transmission *or* d'échange) de données; **decision circuit** = circuit de décision; **digital circuit** = circuit numérique; **logic circuit** = circuit logique

◊ **circuitry** *noun* (ensemble de) circuits *mpl or* circuiterie *f*; **the circuitry is still too complex** = la circuiterie demeure trop complexe

> QUOTE The biggest shock was to open up the PC and find the motherboard smothered in patch wires (usually a sign that a design fault in the printed circuit board was rectified at the last minute).
> *Computing*

circular *adjective* circulaire *or* en boucle; **circular buffer** = tampon *m* circulaire; **circular file** = fichier *m* en boucle; **circular list** = liste *f* en boucle; **circular orbit** = orbite *f* circulaire; *(spreadsheet error condition)* **circular reference** = référence *f* circulaire; **circular shift** = décalage *m* circulaire; **circular waveguide** = guide *m* d'ondes circulaire

◊ **circulate** *verb* **(a)** *(to go in circle)* décrire un cercle **(b)** *(to send information to)* (faire) circuler *or* distribuer

◊ **circulating** *adjective* circulant, -e; **circulating register** = registre *m* à décalage circulaire *or* à bits circulants; **circulating storage** = mémoire circulante *or* mémoire dynamique

circulation *noun* **(a)** *(of information)* circulation *f*; **the company is trying to improve the circulation of information between departments** = la société essaie d'améliorer la circulation de l'information dans les services **(b)** *(of a newspaper)* tirage *m*; **what is the circulation of this computer magazine?** = quel est le tirage de cette revue d'informatique? *or* à combien d'exemplaires tire cette revue d'informatique?; **a specialized paper with a circulation of over 10,000** = un journal spécialisé qui tire à plus de 10 000 exemplaires

circumflex *noun* accent *m* circonflexe

CISC = COMPLEX INSTRUCTION SET COMPUTER

citizens band radio (CB) *noun* radio *f* CB *or* radio à bande CB

cladding *noun* *(surrounding a conducting core)* gaine *f*; **if the cladding is chipped, the fibre-optic cable will not function well** = la fibre optique sera moins performante si sa gaine est endommagée

claim frame *noun* *(FDDI protocol network: frame used to determine which station will initialise the network)* trame *f* d'initialisation (de réseau sous protocole FDDI)

clamp *verb* verrouiller le voltage (d'un signal)

clapper *noun* *(on printer)* presseur *m*

clarity *noun* clarté *f*; **the atmospheric conditions affect the clarity of the signal** = les conditions atmosphériques influencent la clarté du signal *or* le signal est plus ou moins clair suivant les conditions atmosphériques

class *noun* *(definition of what a software routine will do)* classe *f*; *(range of values that can be contained in a class)* **class interval** = intervalle *m* de classe

classify *verb* classer; **the diagnostic printouts have been classified under T for test results** = les sorties d'imprimante qui contiennent les diagnostics sont classées sous la rubrique 'Test', sous la lettre 'T'; **classified directory** = annuaire *m* téléphonique par professions

◊ **classification** *noun* classification *f*

clean 1 *adjective* *(not dirty)* propre; *(text)* (texte) sans erreur *or* sans correction; *(disk)* (disquette) vierge; **I'll have to start again - I just erased the only clean file** = il me faut tout recommencer; je viens d'effacer le seul fichier qui ne contenait aucune erreur; **clean copy** = copie *f* finale; **clean machine** = machine *f* nue; *(of* *memory*) **clean page** = page mémoire sans modification; **clean proof** = épreuve *f* sans correction; *(area where hard disks, wafers and chips are manufactured)* **clean room** = chambre *f* stérile **2** *verb (to make clean)* nettoyer; **data cleaning** = nettoyage *m* de données *or* correction *f* d'erreurs; **head cleaning disk** = disquette *f* de nettoyage (des têtes); **use a head cleaning disk every week** = il faut utiliser la disquette de nettoyage une fois par semaine; **write errors occur if you do not use a head cleaning kit regularly** = vous aurez des erreurs d'écriture si vous ne vous servez pas régulièrement de votre disquette de nettoyage; **screen cleaning kit** = kit *m* de nettoyage pour écran

clear 1 *adjective* **(a)** *(easily understood)* clair, -e; **the program manual is not clear on copying files** = le manuel d'utilisation n'explique pas clairement la marche à suivre pour copier un fichier; **the booklet gives clear instructions how to connect the different parts of the system** = la notice indique clairement comment relier les différents modules du système; **he made it clear that the system will only work on IBM-compatible hardware** = il a bien expliqué que le système ne fonctionne qu'avec les appareils IBM et les compatibles **(b)** *(free)* libre; **clear to send (CTS)** = (signal) CTS *or* (signal de) prêt à transmettre **2** *verb* **(a)** *(to wipe out)* effacer *or* vider; **type CLS to clear the screen** = tapez CLS pour effacer *or* faire disparaître ce qu'il y a sur l'écran; **all arrays are cleared each time the program is run** = tous les tableaux sont vidés chaque fois que le programme est lancé; **to clear an area of memory** = vider une zone de mémoire; **to clear the data register** = vider le registre de données **(b)** libérer la ligne (lorsque la transmission est terminée)

◊ **clearance** *noun* autorisation *f* (d'accès à un fichier); **you do not have the required clearance for this processor** = vous n'avez pas l'autorisation d'accéder à ce processeur

click 1 *noun* **(a)** *(short sound)* clic *m* **(b)** *(pressing a key or button especially of a mouse)* clic *m*; **you move through text and graphics with a click of the button** = un clic (sur la souris) vous permet de vous déplacer dans les textes et graphiques; **double-click** = double-clic *m* **2** *verb (to press a key or button or mouse)* cliquer; **use the mouse to enlarge a frame by clicking inside its border and dragging to the position wanted** = utilisez la souris pour agrandir le cadre: cliquez à l'intérieur des limites du cadre et glissez jusqu'à la position voulue; *(two press-release actions on a mouse button)* **double-click** = double-cliquer

client *noun (in a network, a workstation connected to a network)* client *m*

◊ **client-server architecture** *noun (in a network)* architecture *f* client-serveur

| COMMENT: a central server computer carries out the main tasks in response to instructions from terminals or workstations; the results are sent back across the network to be displayed on the terminal, the client (the terminal or workstation) does not need to be able to directly access the data stored on the server nor does it need to carry out a lot of processing

◊ **client-server network** *noun* réseau *m* client-serveur; *compare* PEER-TO-PEER NETWORK

| COMMENT: method of organising a network in which one central dedicated computer, the server, looks after tasks such as security, user accounts, printing and file sharing, while clients (the terminals or workstations connected to the server) run standard applications

clip 1 *noun (short piece of live film)* extrait *m* de film *or* clip *m*; **there was a clip of the disaster on the news** = un clip de l'accident a été passé aux informations **2** *verb* **(a)** attacher (avec un trombone, etc.); **the corrections are clipped to the computer printout** = les corrections sont attachées à la sortie d'imprimante **(b)** *(cut out)* couper *or* découper; **clipping service** = service *m* de coupures de presse **(c)** *(waveform)* écrêter; **the voltage signal was clipped to prevent excess signal level** = le signal a été écrêté pour éviter une amplitude excessive

◊ **clip-art** *or* **clipart** *noun* image *f* de bibliothèque *or* clipart *or* clip art *m*; **we have used some clip-art to enhance our presentation** = nous avons utilisé des images de bibliothèque pour améliorer la présentation

◊ **clipboard** *noun (temporary storage area for data)* stockage *m* temporaire (de données) *or* presse-papiers *m (utility that temporarily stores any type of data)* Presse-papiers ™ *m*; **copy the text to the clipboard, then paste it back into a new document** = copiez le texte dans le presse-papiers, puis collez-le dans le nouveau document

clock *noun* **(a)** horloge *f*; **the micro has a built-in clock** = le micro possède une horloge intégrée *or* incorporée; **the time is shown by the clock in the corner of the screen** = l'heure est affichée à l'horloge placée dans un coin de l'écran; **digital clock** = horloge numérique **(b)** *(used to synchronize equipment)* horloge; **clock cycle** = cycle *m* d'horloge; *(doubles the speed of the system clock)* **clock doubler** = doubleur *m* d'horloge; **the new CPU from Intel has an optional clock doubler that will double performance** = le nouveau processeur d'Intel a un doubleur d'horloge en option qui permet de doubler ses performances; **clock pulse** = impulsion *f* d'horloge *or* rythme *m*; **clock rate** = vitesse *f* d'horloge; **clock track** = piste *f* d'horloge; **main clock** = horloge centrale; **programmable clock** = horloge programmable **2** *verb* synchroniser; **clocked signals** = signaux synchrones aux impulsions d'horloge

clone *noun* clone *m*; **they have copied our new personal computer and brought out a cheaper clone** = ils ont copié notre nouveau modèle d'ordinateur pour commercialiser un clone qui se vend beaucoup moins cher; **higher performance clones are available for all the models in our range** = il existe des clones de tous nos modèles et tous sont plus performants

CLOSE *(in a programming language)* (commande) CLOSE (de fin d'accès à un équipement ou à un fichier)

close *verb* arrêter *or* fermer *or* terminer; **close file** = fermer un fichier *or* (opération de) fermeture *f* de fichier; *(computer with no expansion bus)* **closed bus system** = système *m* à bus fermé; **closed circuit television (CCTV)** = télévision *f* en circuit fermé; **closed loop** = boucle fermée; **closed subroutine** = sous-programme fermé; **closed user group (CUG)** = groupe *m* fermé d'utilisateurs

◊ **close-down** *noun* (a) *(end of braodcasting for the day)* fin *f* des émissions (b) *(stoppage)* **disorderly close-down** = panne *f* désordonnée

◊ **close up** *verb* *(typesetting)* refermer *or* rapprocher *or* resserrer; **if we close up the lines, we should save a page** = en resserrant les lignes, nous gagnerons une page

◊ **close-up** *noun* *(photography)* gros plan *m*

CLS *(in MS-DOS)* (commande MS-DOS) CLS (de vidage d'écran)

cluster *noun* (a) *(sectors on a hard disk)* secteurs *mpl* contigus *or* cluster *m* (b) *(of terminals)* grappe *f* (de périphériques, etc.); **cluster controller** = unité de contrôle de périphériques disposés en grappe

◊ **clustering** *noun* liaison *f* en grappe de plusieurs périphériques

CM = CENTRAL MEMORY

C-MAC multiplexeur *m* C-MAC

CMI = COMPUTER-MANAGED INSTRUCTION

CMIP = COMMON MANAGEMENT INFORMATION PROTOCOL

CMIS = COMMON MANAGEMENT INFORMATION SPECIFICATION

CML = COMPUTER-MANAGED LEARNING

CMOS = COMPLEMENTARY METAL OXIDE SEMICONDUCTOR

CMOT = CMIP/CMIS OVER TCP; *(using of CMIP and CMIS network management protocols to manage gateways)* gestionnaire de passerelle CMOT (à base de CMIS et de CMIP)

CMYK = CYAN-MAGENTA-YELLOW-BLACK; *(method of describing a colour)* CMYK (système de définition de couleurs: cyan, magenta, jaune, noir)

CNC = COMPUTER NUMERIC CONTROL

coalesce *verb* *(to merge files)* combiner *or* fusionner *or* fondre

coat *verb* recouvrir (de) *or* revêtir (de) *or* enduire (de); **coated paper** = papier *m* couché

◊ **coating** *noun* couche *f*; **paper which has a coating of clay** = papier enduit d'une fine couche de kaolin

co-axial cable *noun* câble *m* coaxial

COBOL = COMMON ORDINARY BUSINESS ORIENTED LANGUAGE langage *m* COBOL

code 1 *noun* (a) code *m*; **code conversion** = conversion *f* de code; *(in MS-DOS: table that defines characters produced from each key)* **code page** = page *f* de codes; **in order to enter Swedish characters from an English keyboard, you have to change the system code page** = pour entrer des caractères suédois avec un clavier britannique, il faut changer la page de codes du système (b) *(sequence of computer instructions)* code; **chain code** = code en chaîne *or* code chaîné; *(of main memory)* **code area** = zone *f* de code; *(of program)* **code line** = ligne *f* de code (d'un programme); *(area of memory)* **code segment** = segment *m* (mémoire) de code; **computer** *or* **machine code** = code d'instruction *or* code (en langage) machine; **direct** *or* **one-level** *or* **specific code** = code direct *or* à un niveau *or* code spécifique; **macro code** = macrocode *m*; **object code** = code objet; **optimum code** = code optimum *or* amélioré *or* accéléré; **source code** = code source; **symbolic code** = code symbolique (c) *(telephone)* **(dialling) code** = indicatif *m* (téléphonique); **area code** = indicatif de zone *(Quebec)* indicatif régional; **what is the code for Edinburgh?** = quel est l'indicatif d'Edimbourg?; **country code followed by area code followed by customer's number** = indicatif du pays suivi de l'indicatif de zone suivi du numéro de votre correspondant; **international dialling code** = indicatif (téléphonique) international (d) **bar code** = code (à) barres; **bar-code reader** = lecteur *m* de codes (à) barres; douchette *f*; *(smallest signalling element)* **code bit** = bit *m* de code; *(voltage or signal to represent binary digits)* **code element** = élément *m* d'un code; *(sequence of five code bits that represent an FDDI symbol)* **code group** = groupe *m* code (de distribution par fibre optique); **cyclic code** = code binaire réfléchi *or* code de Gray; *(for a peripheral)* **device code** = code d'identification (de périphérique); **error code** = code (indicateur) d'erreur; **error correcting code** = code correcteur (d'erreur); **error detecting code** = code détecteur d'erreur; **escape code** = code échappement *or* code 'escape'; **machine-readable**

codes = codes en langage machine; **post code** *US* **zip code** = code postal; **punched code** = code de perforation; **self-checking code** = code détecteur d'erreur; **stock code** = numéro *m* de stock **2** *verb* **(a)** *(cryptography)* coder *or* chiffrer *or* crypter **(b)** *(write in a programming language)* programmer *or* coder

◊ **coder** *noun* codeur *m*

◊ **coder/decoder** **(CODEC)** *noun* codeur/décodeur *m*

◊ **coding** *noun* codage *m* *or* programmation *f*; **coding sheet** *or* **coding form** = feuille *f or* formulaire *m* de programmation

CODEC = CODER/DECODER

coercivity *noun* coercibilité *f*

coherent *adjective* *(of waveforms)* cohérent, -e; **a laser produces coherent light** = le laser produit une lumière cohérente; *(of optical fibres)* **coherent bundle** = faisceau *m* cohérent

coil *noun* bobine *f*; **an inductor is made from a coil of (copper) wire** = un inducteur consiste en une bobine de fil (de cuivre)

coincidence circuit *or* **element** *noun* circuit *m* à coïncidence

cold *adjective* **(a)** froid, -e; **the machines work badly in cold weather** = les appareils fonctionnent mal par temps froid **(b)** *(without being prepared)* à froid *or* au démarrage; *(switching on a computer)* **cold boot** = démarrage *m* *or* mise *f* en route; **cold fault** = erreur au démarrage; *(backup system that will allow the equipment to continue running but with the loss of any volatile data)* **cold standby** = système de secours lancé manuellement; arrêt d'urgence manuel (avec perte du contenu des mémoires volatiles); **cold start** = *(switching on a computer)* démarrage *m* à froid *or* mise *f* en route; *(running a program from its original start point)* reprise *f* (après interruption de l'alimentation) *or* retour *m* à l'application quittée (après extinction); *compare* WARM START; WARM BOOT

collate *verb* *(documents)* (r)assembler *or* fusionner; interclasser; *(book signatures)* collationner

◊ **collating** *noun* *(documents)* fusionnement *m* *or* interclassement *m*; *(books)* collationnement *m*; **collating marks** = indices *mpl* de collationnement; **collating sequence** = séquence *f* de fusionnement *or* de classement; *(books)* ordre *m* des cahiers

◊ **collator** *noun* programme de fusionnement de données; *(machine for punched cards)* interclasseuse *f*; *(for signatures of books)* assembleuse *f*

collect *verb* *(data)* rassembler; **data collection** = collecte *f* de données; **data collection platform** = plate-forme *f* de collecte de données

◊ **collect transfer** *verb* récupérer les données et les transférer dans un registre

◊ **collection** *noun* *(gathering together)* collecte *f* *or* rassemblement *m*; *(series of items put together)* collection *f*

collision detection *noun* détection *f* de collision

colon (:) *noun* *(typography)* deux points; **semi-colon (;)** = point-virgule *m*

colophon *noun* colophon *m* ; marque *f* de l'éditeur *or* de l'imprimeur

colour *noun* couleur *f*; **colour balance** = équilibre *m* des couleurs; *(data bits assigned to a pixel)* **colour bits** = bits *mpl* (de description) de couleur; *(TV)* **colour burst** = rafale *f* de signaux couleur; **colour cell** = cellule *f* de contrôle des couleurs; **colour decoder** = décodeur *m* de couleurs; **colour display** = affichage *m* couleur; **colour encoder** = encodeur *m* de couleurs; **colour graphics adapter (CGA)** = adaptateur *m* graphique couleur CGA *or* carte *f* CGA; **colour monitor** = moniteur *m* couleur *or* écran *m* couleur; **the colour monitor is great for games** = le moniteur couleur est excellent pour les jeux électroniques; **colour printer** = imprimante *f* couleur; **colour saturation** = saturation *f* de couleur; **colour separation** = séparation *f or* sélection *f* des couleurs; *(unwanted change in colour)* **colour shift** = variation *m* chromatique; **colour temperature** = température *f* chromatique; **colour transparency** = diapositive *f* couleur

QUOTE as a minimum, a colour graphics adapter (CGA) is necessary, but for best quality of graphic presentation an enhanced graphics adapter (EGA) should be considered

Micro Decision

column *noun* **(a)** colonne *f*; **to add up a column of figures** = additionner une colonne de chiffres; **put the total at the bottom of the column** = écrivez le total au bas de la colonne; **card column** = colonne de perforations (de carte perforée); *(in a DTP application)* **column guide** = guide *m* *or* séparateur *m* de colonnes (dans une application de PAO); *(in word-processing software)* **column indicator** = indicateur *m* de colonne (dans un traitement de texte); **column parity** = parité *f* de colonnes; **80-column printer** = imprimante *f* (de) 80 colonnes; **an 80-column printer is included in the price** = le prix comprend une imprimante 80 colonnes **(b)** *(in newspaper or magazine)* colonne

◊ **columnar** *adjective* en colonne(s); **columnar graph** = diagramme *m* *or* graphique *m* en colonnes *or* en tuyaux d'orgue *or* histogramme *m*; **columnar working** = présentation *f* (graphique) sous forme de colonne(s) *or* sous forme d'histogramme(s)

COM = COMPUTER OUTPUT ON MICROFILM

COM file *noun* *(three-letter extension to a file name)* fichier COM *or* fichier binaire exécutable; **to start the program, type the name of the COM file at the MS-DOS prompt** = pour démarrer le programme, entrez au clavier le nom du fichier COM à l'invite MS-DOS

COM1 *(first serial port in a PC)* (port) COM1; *see also* AUX

coma *noun (lens aberration)* coma *f*

COMAL = COMMON ALGORITHMIC LANGUAGE langage (de programmation structurée) COMAL

combine *verb* combiner *or* joindre *or* fusionner; **combined head** = tête *f* de lecture/écriture; **combined station** = poste de contrôle mixte; **combined symbol matching (CSM)** = système de reconnaissance de caractères CSM (par identification des caractéristiques combinées)

◊ **combination** *noun* combinaison *f*

◊ **combinational** *adjective* combinatoire; **combinational circuit** = circuit *m* combinatoire; **combinational logic** = logique *f* combinatoire

comma (**,**) *noun (typography)* virgule *f*; **inverted commas** ('' *or* " ") = guillemets *mpl*

◊ **comma-delimited file** *noun* fichier délimité par virgule; **all databases can import and export to a comma-delimited file format** = à partir de toutes bases de données on peut soit importer des données d'un fichier délimité par virgule, soit en exporter

command *noun* **(a)** *(electrical pulse or signal)* commande *f or* instruction *f or* signal *m* **(b)** *(word recognized by a computer)* commande *or* instruction; **the command to execute the program is RUN** = RUN est la commande d'exécution du programme; **type the command 'DIR' to get the list of files** = tapez la commande DIR pour obtenir la liste des fichiers; **channel command** = commande de canal; **command code** = code *m* d'opération; **command console processor (CCP)** = processeur *m* de console; **command control language** = langage *m* de contrôle *or* de pilotage (de périphériques); **command-driven program** = programme *m* activé par commande; **command file** = fichier *m* de commandes; **command file processor** = processeur *m* de fichier de commandes; **command interface** = interface *f* de commande *or* de contrôle; *(program within an operating system that recognises a set of system commands)* **command interpreter** = interpréteur *m* de commandes; *(key on an Apple Macintosh that gives access to various special functions)* **command key** = touche *f* de commande; **command language** = langage *m* de commande; **command line** = ligne *f* de commande (d'un programme); *(items entered following a command)* **command line argument** = argument *m* de ligne de commande; **use the command 'DIR' to view the files on disk, add the command line argument 'A:' to view the files on drive A:** = utilisez la commande DIR pour afficher la liste des fichiers du disque et ajoutez l'argument de ligne A: pour voir les fichiers du disque A:; *(computer system software)* **command line operating system** = système de ligne de commande; **command prompt** = (message d') invite *f* (de commande); **command register** = registre *m* de commande *or* d'instruction; *(modem ready to accept commands)* **command state** = état *m* commande (d'un modem prêt à recevoir des commandes); **command window** = fenêtre *f* de commande; **the user can define the size of the command window** = l'utilisateur peut définir la taille de la fenêtre de

commande; **dot command** = commande (précédée d'un) point; *(printer control command inserted into test)* **embedded command** = commande imbriquée; **interrupt command** = commande d'interruption (de programme)

> QUOTE This gives Unix a friendly face instead of the terrifyingly complex command-line prompts that make most users reach for their manuals.
> *Computing*

COMMAND.COM *(program file that contains the command interpreter)* fichier *m* COMMAND.COM; **MS-DOS will not work because you deleted the COMMAND.COM file by mistake** = MS-DOS ne marche pas parce que vous avez effacé le fichier COMMAND.COM par erreur

comment *noun* note *f or* explication *f or* commentaire *m*; **BASIC allows comments to be written after a REM instruction** = en BASIC il est possible d'inclure des commentaires à la suite de l'instruction REM; **comment field** = champ *m* bloc-notes; *(temporarily disabling a command)* **comment out** = mise *f* en commentaire (d'une commande)

◊ **commentary** *noun* commentaire *m*

commercial *noun (TV)* pub *f or* message *m* publicitaire; **commercials** = la publicité

common *adjective* **(a)** *(which happens very often)* commun, -e *or* habituel, -elle *or* courant, -e; **this is a common fault with this printer model** = c'est un défaut courant de ce modèle d'imprimante **(b)** *(belonging to several people or programs)* commun; **common carrier** = *(information)* entreprise de diffusion d'informations grand public; *(network)* ligne banalisée *or* canal banal; **common channel signalling** = signalisation *f* par canal banal *or* par voie commune; **common business orientated language (COBOL)** = langage (de programmation) COBOL; **common hardware** = matériel *m* courant *or* banal *or* partagé; **common language** = langage commun *or* banal *or* partagé; **common mode noise** = (bruit) parasite courant; **common software** = logiciel commun *or* de réseau *or* partagé; **common storage area** = zone *f* commune de la mémoire; **the file server memory is mainly common storage area, with a section reserved for the operating system** = la mémoire centrale du serveur est en général banalisée en dehors de la partie réservée au système d'exploitation

◊ **common management information protocol (CMIP)** *noun (protocol adopted by the ISO used to carry network management information)* protocole *m* CMIP; *(powerful network management system)* **common management information specification (CMIS)** = (système de gestion de réseau) CMIS

comms = COMMUNICATIONS

communicate *verb* **(a)** communiquer; **he finds it impossible to communicate with his staff** = il n'arrive pas à communiquer avec son personnel; **communicating with head office has been quicker since we installed the fax machine** = communiquer avec le siège social est plus rapide depuis que nous avons installé un fax **(b)** *(computers)* communiquer *or* dialoguer; **communicating word processor (CWP)** = système de traitement de texte doté d'une interface de communication

communication *noun* **(a)** communication *f*; **communication with the head office has been made easier by the fax** = les communications avec le siège social ont été facilitées par le télécopieur **(b)** **communications** = transmission *f or* (télé)communication(s) *f(pl)*; **communications buffer** = (mémoire) tampon de transmission de données; **communications channel** = canal *f* de transmission; **communications computer** = ordinateur *f* de contrôle des transmissions; **communications control unit (CCU)** = contrôleur *m* de transmission *or* de communication; **communications executive** = gestionnaire *m* de télécommunication; **communications interface adapter** = adaptateur *m* d'interface de communication; **communications link** = ligne *f* de communication *or* de transmission; **communications link control** = contrôle *m* de ligne de communication *or* de transmission; **communications network** = réseau *m* de communication; **communications network processor** = processeur *m* de réseau (de communication); *(software to control a modem)* **communications package** = logiciel *m or* progiciel *m* de communication; **communications port** = port *m* de communication; **communications protocol** = protocole *m* de communication; **communications protocol for most dial-up online services is eight-bit words, no stop bit and even parity** = pour la plupart des services en lignes, le protocole de communication est un mot de huit bits, sans bit d'arrêt et bit de parité pair; **communications satellite** = satellite *m* de télécommunication; **communications scanner** = scanner *m* de contrôle d'appel *or* de demande de communication; *(computer with a modem or fax card attached)* **communications server** = serveur *m* de communication; **communications software** = logiciel de communication; **data communications** = téléinformatique *f or* transmission *f* de données; *(buffer on a receiver)* **data communications buffer** = mémoire tampon de transmission de données; **data communications equipment (DCE)** = appareils *mpl or* matériel *m* téléinformatique

QUOTE it requires no additional hardware, other than a communications board in the PC
Electronics & Power

community *noun* groupe *m or* communauté *f or* milieu *m*; **the local business community** = le milieu d'affaires local

◊ **community antenna television (CATV)** *noun* antenne *f* collective de télévision (câblée) *or* système de télévision câblée CATV

compact 1 *adjective* compact, -e *or* dense *or* serré, -e; **compact cassette** = cassette compacte;

compact code = code compacté; **compact disc (CD)** = disque *m* compact *or* disque CD; **compact disc player** = platine *f* laser *or* platine (de) disques compacts; lecteur *m* de disques CD; **compact disc ROM** *or* **compact disc-read only memory (CD-ROM)** = disque compact lecture seule *or* (disque) CD-ROM; **the compact disc ROM can store as much data as a dozen hard disks** = on peut stocker autant de données sur un (disque) CD-ROM que sur une douzaine de disques durs; *(memory model in the Intel 80x86 family of CPUs)* **compact model** = modèle *m* compact **2** *verb* compacter; *see also* CD-ROM

◊ **compacting** *noun* compactage *m*; **compacting algorithm** = algorithme *m* de compactage; **data compacting** = compactage de données

companding = COMPRESSING AND EXPANDING

◊ **compandor** = COMPRESSOR/EXPANDER

COMPAQ ™ *(US personal computer company)* (la société) Compaq ™

compare *verb* comparer

◊ **compare with** *verb* comparer à *or* avec

◊ **comparable** *adjective* comparable; **the two sets of figures are not comparable** = les deux séries de chiffres ne sont pas comparables

◊ **comparator** *noun* comparateur *m*

◊ **comparison** *noun* comparaison *f*; **there is no comparison between the speeds of the two word processors** = les vitesses de traitement de texte de ces deux logiciels ne sont pas comparables

compatible 1 *adjective* compatible; **is the hardware IBM-compatible?** = est-ce que le matériel est compatible IBM? **2** *noun* un compatible (IBM); **buy an IBM PC or a compatible** = achetez un IBM PC ou un compatible; **this computer is much cheaper than the other compatibles** = cet ordinateur et beaucoup moins cher que les autres compatibles

QUOTE the compatibles bring computing to the masses
PC Business World

QUOTE low-cost compatibles have begun to find homes as terminals on LANS
Minicomputer News

QUOTE it is a fairly standard feature on most low-cost PC compatibles
Which PC?

QUOTE this was the only piece of software I found that wouldn't work, but it does show that there is no such thing as a totally compatible PC clone
Personal Computer World

compatibility *noun* *(ability of two devices to function together)* **compatibility box** = fenêtre *f* de compatibilité; **OS/2 has a compatibility box to**

allow it to run DOS applications = OS/2 a une fenêtre de compatibilité qui permet de faire tourner les applications sous DOS

COMMENT: by conforming to the standards of another manufacturer or organization, compatibility of hardware and software allows programs and hardware to be interchanged without modification

QUOTE check for software compatibility before choosing a display or graphics adapter
PC Business World

QUOTE The manufacturer claims that this card does not require special drivers on the host machine, as a flash-memory card does, and therefore has fewer compatibility problems.
Computing

compile *verb* compiler; **compiling takes a long time with this old version** = il faut beaucoup de temps pour faire la compilation avec cette ancienne version du programme; **debug your program, then compile it** = déboguez votre programme avant de le compiler; **compiled BASIC programs run much faster than the interpreter version** = les programmes en BASIC qui sont compilés sont plus rapides que les versions interprétées; *(program)* **compile and go** = (instruction de) compilation et exécution; **compile phase** = phase *f* de compilation

◊ **compilation** *noun* compilation *f*; **compilation error** = erreur *f* de compilation; **compilation errors result in the job being aborted** = les erreurs de compilation provoquent l'interruption inopinée de la tâche; **compilation time** = temps *m* de compilation *or* durée *f* de compilation

QUOTE This utility divides the compilation of software into pieces and performs the compile in parallel across available machines on the network.
Computergram

◊ **compiler (program)** *noun* compilateur *m*; **the new compiler has an in-built editor** = le nouveau compilateur possède un éditeur intégré; **this compiler produces a more efficient program** = ce compilateur génère un programme plus performant; **compiler diagnostics** = outils de diagnostic du compilateur; **compiler language** = langage *m* de compilation; **cross-compiler** = compilateur croisé; **we can use the cross-compiler to develop the software before the new system arrives** = nous pouvons utiliser un compilateur croisé pour développer le logiciel avant l'arrivée du nouveau système; **language compiler** = compilateur (d'un langage évolué)

complement 1 *noun* complément *m*; **the complement is found by changing the 1s to 0s and 0s to 1s** = on trouve les compléments en remplaçant les 1 par des 0 et les 0 par des 1; **one's complement** = complément à 1; **two's complement** = complément à 2; **nine's complement** = complément à 9; **ten's complement** = complément à 10 2 *verb (to invert a binary digit)* calculer un complément; **complemented** = (nombre binaire, etc.) complémenté, -ée

◊ **complementary** *adjective* complémentaire; **complementary colours** = couleurs *fpl* complémentaires; **complementary operation** = opération *f* complémentaire

◊ **complementary metal oxide semiconductor (CMOS)** *noun* semi-conducteur *m* CMOS

complementation *noun* (ensemble des) nombres *mpl* complets

complete 1 *adjective* **(a)** *(finished)* complet, -ète *or* terminé, -ée; **the spelling check is complete** = la vérification orthographique est terminée; **when this job is complete, the next in the queue is processed** = une fois cette tâche exécutée, ce sera le tour de la suivante dans la file d'attente **(b)** *(total)* complet, -ète; au complet; **complete operation** = l'opération au complet 2 *verb* terminer *or* achever; **when you have completed the keyboarding, pass the text through the spelling checker** = une fois la saisie du texte terminée, servez-vous du correcteur orthographique pour corriger les fautes

◊ **completion** *noun* fin *f or* achèvement *m*; **completion date for the new software package is November 15th** = le nouveau progiciel sera achevé le 15 novembre

complex *adjective* complexe; **the complex mathematical formula was difficult to solve** = cette formule mathématique complexe était difficile à résoudre; **complex instruction set computer (CISC)** = ordinateur *m* à jeu d'instructions complexe (CISC)

◊ **complexity** *noun* complexité *f*; **complexity measure** = niveau *m* de complexité

complicated *adjective* compliqué, -ée; **this program is very complicated** = il s'agit d'un programme très compliqué; **the computer design is more complicated than necessary** = cet ordinateur est d'une conception plus compliquée que nécessaire

component *noun (piece of machinery)* pièce *f* (mécanique); *(electronic device)* composant *m*; *(of an array or of a matrix)* composant (d'un tableau *or* d'une matrice); **component density** = densité *f* des composants; **component density is so high on this motherboard** = il y a une telle densité de composants sur la carte-mère; **component density increases with production expertise** = la densité des composants augmente avec l'expertise du fabricant; **component error** = erreur *f* imputable à un composant défectueux; **component list** = nomenclature *f* des composants

compose *verb (typesetting)* composer; **composing room** = atelier *m* de composition *or* la composition

composite *adjective (electronic circuit made up of several circuits and components)* **composite circuit** = circuit *m* composite; *(video display unit)* **composite display** = écran *m* composite; affichage *m* composite; *(video signal which combines the colour signals and the monochrome signal into one)* composite video = (signal) vidéo composite; **most TV set and video players expect a composite video feed** = la plupart des postes de télévision et des lecteurs vidéo sont construits pour recevoir des signaux composites

composition *noun* composition *f*; *(printing)* **composition size** = taille *f* des caractères utilisés lors de la composition

◊ **compositor** *noun (person)* compositeur *m or* typo(graphe) *m*; *(machine)* **electronic compositor** = compositeur électronique

compound *adjective* composé, -ée; **compound logical element** = élément *m* logique composé *or* élément logique multiple; **compound statement** = instruction composée; **the debugger cannot handle compound statements** = le débogueur ne peut agir sur les instructions composées

compress *verb* comprimer; **use the archiving program to compress the file** = utilisez un programme d'archivage pour comprimer le fichier

◊ **compressing and expanding (companding)** *noun* compression et expansion (de données)

◊ **compression** *noun* compression *f*; **data compression** = compression de données; *(resident software that compresses data)* **disk compression software** = logiciel *m* de compression de disque

◊ **compressor** *noun (circuit or program)* compresseur *m*; **audio compressor** = limiteur *m or* réducteur *m* de signal audio; **compressor/expander (compandor)** = dispositif *m* de compression/expansion *or* concentrateur/déconcentrateur *m* (de données vidéo)

comptometer *noun* compteur *m*

CompuServe ™ *(one of the largest US-based online information services)* (service en ligne) CompuServe ™

compute *verb* calculer; **connect charges were computed on an hourly rate** = les frais de connection ont été calculés sur une base horaire

◊ **computable** *adjective* calculable

◊ **computation** *noun* calcul *m*

◊ **computational** *adjective* (de) calcul; **computational error** = erreur *f* de calcul

computer *noun* **(a)** ordinateur *m*; *(calculating machine)* calculateur *m*; **analog computer** = ordinateur analogique; **business computer** = ordinateur de gestion *or* de bureau *or* (pour usage) professionnel; **digital computer** = ordinateur numérique; **home computer** = ordinateur familial *or* pour la maison; **mainframe computer** = gros ordinateur *or* ordinateur central *or* mainframe *m*; **microcomputer** *or* **micro** = micro-ordinateur *or* micro *m*; **minicomputer** *or* **mini** = mini-ordinateur *or* mini *m*; **personal computer (PC)** = ordinateur individuel *or* personnel *or* PC; **single board computer (sbc)** = ordinateur monocarte *or* à carte

unique; **single chip computer** = calculateur *or* ordinateur monopuce *or* à puce unique; **supercomputer** = ordinateur géant *or* de grande puissance **(b) computer animation** = animation *f* (d'images) sur ordinateur; **computer applications** = applications *fpl* informatiques; **computer architecture** = architecture *f* d'un système; **computer bureau** = société de services et d'ingénierie informatique (SSII); **computer centre** = centre *m* de calcul; **computer code** = code *m* d'instruction *or* code (en langage) machine; **computer conferencing** = téléconférence *f* (sur réseau informatique); connexion *f* (d'ordinateurs) en mode conversationnel; communication *f or* dialogue *m* entre ordinateurs; **computer crime** *or* **computer fraud** = fraude *f* informatique (passible du tribunal correctionnel); **computer dating** = rencontre *f* matrimoniale assistée par ordinateur; **computer department** = service *m* informatique; **computer engineer** = ingénieur *m* informaticien; **computer error** = erreur *f* due à l'ordinateur; **computer file** = fichier *m* informatique *or* d'ordinateur; **computer graphics** = infographie *f*; *(device-independent file format)* **computer graphics metafile (CGM)** = métafichier *m or* fichier *m* graphique CGM; **computer image processing** = traitement *m* informatique de l'image; **computer independent language** = langage *m* standard *or* universel; langage informatique indépendant; **computer input from microfilm (CIM)** = entrée *f* à partir de *or* par lecture de microfilm; **computer language** = langage *m* informatique; **computer listing** = sortie *f* d'imprimante *or* listing *m*; **computer literacy** = (niveau de) connaissances *fpl* en informatique; **computer-literate** = (personne) qui a des connaissances en informatique; **the managing director is simply not computer-literate** = le directeur général n'a aucune notion d'informatique; **computer logic** = logique *f* des ordinateurs *or* logique informatique; **computer mail** *or* **electronic mail** = messagerie *f* électronique; courrier *m* électronique; **computer manager** = directeur, -trice (du service) informatique; **computer network** = réseau *m* informatique *or* réseau d'ordinateurs; **computer numeric control (CNC)** = (programme de) commandes *fpl* numériques de machines-outils; **computer office system** = système bureautique *or* système informatique pour bureau; **computer operator** = opérateur, -trice d'ordinateur; *(computer architecture)* **computer organization** = architecture *f* d'un système; **computer output** = données *fpl* de sortie; **computer output on microfilm (COM)** = stockage *m* sur microfilm *or* micromation *f*; **computer power** = puissance *f* d'un ordinateur; **computer program** = programme *m* (informatique); **the user cannot write a computer program with this system** = l'utilisateur ne peut pas écrire de programme avec ce système; **computer programmer** = programmeur, -euse; **computer run** = exécution *f* d'un programme; **computer science** = l'informatique *f*; **computer services** = services *mpl* informatiques; **computer stationery** = papier *m* listing; **computer system** = système informatique *or* système *m* temps *m* d'ordinateur; **running all those sales reports costs a lot in computer time** = tous ces rapports de vente coûtent cher en temps d'ordinateur; **computer** virus = virus *m* informatique; **computer word** = mot *m or* unité *f* d'information

COMMENT: a program which adds itself to an executable file and copies (or spreads) itself to other executable files each time an infected file is run; a virus can corrupt data, display a message or do nothing

◊ **computer generation** *noun* génération *f* d'ordinateurs

computer- *prefix*

◊ **computer-aided** *or* **computer-assisted** *adjective* assisté, -ée par ordinateur; **computer-aided** *or* **assisted design (CAD)** = conception *f or* création assistée par ordinateur (CAO); **computer-aided** *or* **assisted design/computer-aided** *or* **assisted manufacture (CAD/CAM)** = conception et fabrication assistées par ordinateur (CFAO); **computer-aided drafting** = dessin *m* assisté par ordinateur (DAO); **computer-aided** *or* **assisted engineering (CAE)** = ingénierie *f* assistée par ordinateur (IAO); **computer-aided** *or* **assisted instruction (CAI)** = enseignement *m* assisté par ordinateur (EAO); **computer-aided** *or* **assisted learning (CAL)** = formation *f* assistée par ordinateur (FAO); **computer-aided** *or* **assisted manufacture (CAM)** = fabrication *f* assistée par ordinateur (FAO); **computer-aided** *or* **assisted testing (CAT)** = test *m* assisté par ordinateur (TAO); **computer-aided** *or* **assisted training (CAT)** = apprentissage *m* assisté par ordinateur

◊ **computer-based** *adjective* = COMPUTER-AIDED **computer-based learning (CBL)** = formation assistée par ordinateur; **computer-based message system (CBMS)** = (système de) messagerie *f* électronique; **computer-based training (CBT)** = apprentissage *m* assisté par ordinateur

◊ **computer-generated** *adjective* conçu, -e *or* généré, -ée par ordinateur; **computer-generated graphics** = images *fpl* de synthèses (sur ordinateur) *or* infographie *f*

◊ **computer-integrated** *adjective* **computer-integrated manufacturing (CIM)** = productique intégrée; **computer-integrated systems** = systèmes (d'exploitation) intégrés; **this firm is a very well-known supplier of computer-integrated systems which allow both batch pagination of very long documents with alteration of individual pages** = cette entreprise est un fournisseur réputé de systèmes informatiques intégrés qui permettent à la fois la pagination de très longs documents et le traitement personnalisé de chaque page

◊ **computer-managed** *adjective* informatisé, -ée *or* géré, -ée par ordinateur; **computer-managed instruction (CMI)** = enseignement interactif assisté par ordinateur; **computer-managed learning (CML)** = formation *m* informatisée

◊ **computer-readable** *adjective* **computer-readable codes** = codes *mpl* (en langage) machine

computerize *verb* informatiser; **our stock control has been completely computerized** = notre gestion des stocks est totalement informatisée; **they operate a computerized invoicing system** =

leur facturation est informatisée; **computerized branch exchange (CBX)** = autocommutateur *m* électronique (privé) *or* PBX électronique

◊ **computerization** *noun* informatisation *f*; **computerization of the financial sector is proceeding very fast** = l'informatisation du secteur financier progresse très rapidement

computing *adjective & noun (science)* informatique *f (calculation)* calcul *m* (fait par un ordinateur); **computing power** = puissance *f* de calcul; **computing speed** = vitesse *f* de calcul (par ordinateur)

CON *(in IBM-PC compatible systems: name used to identify the console)* CON *or* console *f* (avec écran et clavier, des compatibles IBM PC)

concatenate *verb* enchaîner *or* concaténer; **concatenated data set** = concaténation *f* (de données) *or* données reliés en chaîne *or* données chaînées

◊ **concatenation** *noun* concaténation *f*

conceal *verb* cacher *or* dissimuler *or* masquer; **the hidden lines are concealed from view with this algorithm** = les lignes qu'on ne veut pas montrer sont masquées par cet algorithme

concentrate *verb (light ray)* concentrer; *(line or circuit or data)* condenser *or* compresser *or* compacter; **to concentrate a beam of light on a lens** = concentrer un rayon lumineux sur une lentille; **the concentrated data was transmitted cheaply** = les données compressées ont pu être transmises à peu de frais

◊ **concentrator** *noun* **(a)** *(in a Token-Ring network)* concentrateur *m* **(b)** *(in an FDDI network)* noeud *m* d'accès au réseau **(c)** *(in an 10Base-T Ethernet network)* concentrateur 10base-T **(d)** *(in general networking)* concentrateur de réseau

conceptual model *noun (description of a database)* modèle *m* conceptuel

concertina fold *noun* (papier) plié en paravent *or* en accordéon *or* en éventail; papier en continu

concurrent *adjective* simultané, -ée; **each concurrent process has its own window** = chacune des applications exécutées simultanément possède sa propre fenêtre; **concurrent processing** = multitraitement *m*; **three transputers provide concurrent processing capabilities for the entire department** = trois transordinateurs procurent une capacité de multitraitement suffisante pour tout le département; **concurrent operating system** = système d'exploitation multiprogramme; **concurrent programming** = multiprogrammation *f*

QUOTE The system uses parallel-processing technology to allow support for large numbers of concurrent users.

Computing

◊ **concurrently** *adverb* simultanément

condenser lens *noun* condensateur *m* optique

condition 1 *noun* condition *f*; **condition code register** = registre *m* des codes condition; **error condition** = condition *f* d'erreur **2** *verb* adapter *or* conditionner; **condition the raw data to a standard format** = adaptez les données brutes à un format standard

◊ **conditional** *adjective* conditionnel, -elle; **conditional breakpoint** = arrêt conditionnel; **conditional jump** *or* **branch** *or* **transfer** = branchement *or* saut conditionnel; **the conditional branch will select routine one if the response is yes and routine two if no** = le branchement conditionnel choisira le programme n° 1 ou 2 suivant que la réponse est oui ou non; **conditional statement** = commande *or* instruction conditionnelle

conduct *verb* conduire *or* transmettre; **to conduct electricity** = conduire l'électricité; **copper conducts well** = le cuivre est bon conducteur (d'électricité)

◊ **conduction** *noun* conductibilité *f or* conduction *f*; **the conduction of electricity by gold contacts** = conduction (d'électricité) par broches de contact (en) or

◊ **conductive** *adjective* conductible

◊ **conductor** *noun* conducteur *m*; **copper is a good conductor of electricity** = le cuivre est un bon conducteur

conduit *noun* conduite *f or* tube *m or* tuyau *m or* canalisation *f*; **the cables from each terminal are channelled to the computer centre by metal conduit** = les câbles de liaison de tous les terminaux sont acheminés par conduite métallique *or* par canalisation métallique *or* sous gaine métallique jusqu'au centre informatique

cone *noun* (*of loudspeaker*) cône *m or* membrane *f* conique

conference *noun* (*meeting*) réunion *f or* conférence *f*; (*large*) congrès *m*; **to be in conference** = être en conférence; **conference phone** = téléphone *m* de conférence; **conference room** = salle *f* de conférence(s); **conference call** = téléconférence; **press conference** = conférence de presse

◊ **conferencing** *or* **teleconferencing** *noun* (*discussion between remote users using computers linked by modem*) téléconférence *f*; **computer conferencing** = téléconférence (sur réseau informatique); communication *f or* dialogue *m* entre ordinateurs; connexion *f* (d'ordinateurs) en mode conversationnel; **the multi-user BBS has a computer conferencing facility** = l'affichage électronique du réseau permet aux systèmes reliés de communiquer entre eux

> QUOTE Small organisations and individuals find it convenient to use online services, offering email, conferencing and information services.
> *Computing*

confidence level *noun* (*statistics*) niveau *m* de confiance

CONFIG.SYS (*configuration text file*) (fichier de configuration MS-DOS) CONFIG.SYS; **if you add a new adapter card to your PC you will have to add a new command to the CONFIG.SYS file** = si vous installez une nouvelle carte adaptateur sur votre PC, il faudra ajouter une nouvelle commande dans le fichier CONFIG.SYS

configure *verb* configurer; **this terminal has been configured to display graphics** = ce terminal est configuré pour l'affichage de graphiques; **you only have to configure the PC once - when you first buy it** = il suffit de configurer l'ordinateur individuel une seule fois, à l'achat

◊ **configuration** *noun* configuration *f*; **configuration state** = (état de) configuration (d'un système)

◊ **configured-in** *adjective* (*device: ready*) (état) configuré; (avec) configuration validée; prêt à fonctionner *or* disponible

◊ **configured-off** *or* **configured out** *adjective* (avec) configuration invalidée; indisponible

> QUOTE He said only Banyan Vines had the network configuration and administration capabilities required for implementing an international business plan based on client-server computing.
> *Computing*

> QUOTE the machine uses RAM to store system configuration information
> *PC Business World*

> QUOTE several configuration files are provided to assign memory to the program, depending on the available RAM on your system
> *PC Business World*

> QUOTE users can configure four of the eight ports to handle links at speeds of 64K bit/sec
> *Computer News*

> QUOTE if you modify a program with the editor, or with a wordprocessor specified in the configuration file, it will know that the program has changed and will execute the new one accordingly
> *PC Business World*

confirm *verb* (*agree with a particular action*) confirmer; **click on the OK button to confirm that you want to delete all your files** = cliquez sur le bouton OK pour confirmer que vous voulez effacer tous les fichiers

conform *verb* obéir à *or* se conformer à; être conforme à; **the software will not run if it does not conform to the operating system standards** = le logiciel ne fonctionnera pas s'il ne répond pas aux normes du système d'exploitation

congestion *noun* (*of system*) encombrement *m*

conjunct *noun* (*in an logical function*) opérande *m* d'une opération ET *or* d'une conjonction

◊ **conjunction** *noun* (*logical function*) conjonction *f or* opération *f* ET *or* intersection *f*

connect *verb* connecter (à) *or* relier (à) *or* brancher (sur); *(cost per minute of time connected)* **connect charge** = coût *m* de connexion; *(state of a modem)* **connect state** = état *m* connecté (d'un modem); **connect time** = temps *m* de connexion

◊ **connection** *noun* connexion *f*; **parallel connection** = connexion parallèle; **their transmission rate is 60,000 bps through parallel connection** = leur débit est de 60 000 bps sur connexion parallèle

connective *noun* *(symbol between two operands)* connectif *m*

◊ **connectivity** *noun* *(ability of a device to connect with other devices)* connectivité *f*

connector *noun* connecteur *m*; **the connector at the end of the cable will fit any standard serial port** = le connecteur relié au câble s'adapte sur tout port série standard; **card edge connector** = connecteur de carte; **connector engineering** *or* **connector technology** = connectique *f (in an FDDI network)* **connector plug** = prise *f* mâle de connecteur; *(in an FDDI network)* **connector receptacle** = prise femelle de connecteur

conscious error *noun* erreur *f* consciente

consecutive *adjective* consécutif, -ive; **the computer ran three consecutive files** = l'ordinateur a exploité trois fichiers consécutifs

◊ **consecutively** *adverb* de façon consécutive *or* consécutivement *or* l'un(e) à la suite de l'autre; **the sections of the program run consecutively** = les différentes sections du programme s'exécutent l'une à la suite de l'autre

consistency check *noun* *(to make sure that data or items conform)* contrôle *m* de cohérence

console *noun* console *f or* poste *m* de travail; *(mainframe)* pupitre *m or* console (de commande); **the console consists of input device such as a keyboard, and an output device such as a printer or CRT** = la console comporte un périphérique d'entrée tel qu'un clavier, et un périphérique de sortie, soit une imprimante ou un écran

constant 1 *noun* *(as opposed to a variable)* constante *f* **2** *adjective* *(which does not change)* constant, -e *or* fixe; **the disk drive motor spins at a constant velocity** = le moteur du lecteur de disque tourne à une vitesse constante; **constant length field** = champ de taille fixe; **constant ratio code** = code *m* à rapport (de bits) constant *or* fixe

construct *verb* construire *or* fabriquer

◊ **construction** *noun* construction *f or* fabrication *f*; **construction of the prototype is advancing rapidly** = la construction du prototype progresse rapidement; **construction techniques have changed over the past few years** = les techniques de fabrication ont évolué au cours des dernières années

consult *verb* consulter *or* demander l'avis de quelqu'un; **he consulted the maintenance manager about the disk fault** = il a demandé l'avis du responsable de (la) maintenance sur le mauvais fonctionnement du disque

◊ **consultancy** *noun* assistance *f or* conseil *f*; **a consultancy firm** = cabinet-conseil *m or* société d'assistance technique *m*; **he offers a consultancy service** = il offre une assistance technique

◊ **consultant** *noun* expert *m or* spécialiste *m&f or* ingénieur-conseil *m*; **they called in a computer consultant to advise them on the system design** = ils ont fait venir un expert en informatique pour les conseiller sur la conception du système

◊ **consulting** *adjective* **a consulting engineer** = ingénieur-conseil *m*

consumables *plural noun* consommables *mpl*; **put all the printer leads and paper under the heading 'consumables'** = il faut inclure les câbles pour imprimantes et le papier sous la rubrique 'consommables'

contact 1 *noun* **(a)** *(section of a switch or connector)* contact *m or* connexion *f*; **gold contacts** = contacts (en) or; **the circuit is not working because the contact is dirty** = le circuit ne fonctionne pas parce que la connexion est encrassée; *(keyboard)* **contact bounce** = rebond *m* (de contact *or* de touche) **(b)** *(photography)* **contact negative** = (film) négatif *m* contact; **contact print** = épreuve *f* de contact **2** *verb* contacter *or* joindre

contain *verb* contenir; **each carton contains two computers and their peripherals** = chaque caisse contient deux ordinateurs et leurs périphériques; **we have lost a file containing important documents** = nous avons égaré un dossier contenant des documents importants

content *noun* *(ideas)* contenu *m* (d'une lettre)

◊ **contents** *plural noun* **(a)** *(things contained)* contenu (d'une boîte, etc.); **the contents of the bottle poured out onto the computer keyboard** = le contenu de la bouteille s'est répandu sur le clavier de l'ordinateur; **the customs officials inspected the contents of the box** = les douaniers ont examiné le contenu de la caisse; *(the words written in the letter)* **the contents of the letter** = le contenu *or* le texte de la lettre **(b)** *(list of items in a file)* répertoire *m or* liste *f*

◊ **content-addressable** *adjective* adressable par le contenu; **content-addressable file** *or* **location** = fichier *m or* location *f* adressable par le contenu; **content-addressable memory (CAM)** = mémoire *f* adressable par le contenu *or* mémoire associative

contention *noun* contention *f*; **contention bus** = bus *m* d'arbitrage *or* de régulation; **contention delay** = délai *m or* retard *m* de contention

context *noun* contexte *m*; **the example shows how the word is used in context** = l'exemple démontre l'emploi du mot dans son contexte

◊ **context-sensitive** *adjective (relating to the particular context)* en fonction du contexte; *(help message that gives useful information about a particular function)* **context-sensitive help** = aide (en ligne) liée au contexte

◊ **context-switching** *noun* basculement *m or* changement *m* d'application

COMMENT: unlike a true multitasking system which can load several programs into memory and run several programs at once, context-switching only allows one program to be run at a time

contiguous *adjective* contigu, -ë; **contiguous file** = fichier contigu; **contiguous graphics** = graphiques contigus; **most display units do not provide contiguous graphics: their characters have a small space on each side to improve legibility** = la plupart des écrans ne permettent pas l'affichage de graphiques contigus; chaque caractère (graphique) est bordé de chaque côté par un espace qui améliore sa lisibilité

QUOTE If you later edit the file again, some of the new data clusters will not be contiguous with the original clusters but spread around the disk.

Computing

contingency plan *noun* plan *m* d'urgence

continue *verb* continuer

◊ **continual** *adjective* continuel, -elle; **the continual system breakdowns have slowed down the processing** = les pannes continuelles du système ont ralenti le traitement

◊ **continually** *adverb* continuellement *or* sans cesse

◊ **continuation** *noun* continuation *f*; *(page or screen of text that follows)* **continuation page** = suite *f*

◊ **continuity** *noun* **(a)** *(conduction path)* continuité *f* **(b)** *(of scenes in film)* continuité

◊ **continuous** *adjective* continu, -e *or* en continu; **continuous data stream** = flux *m* continu *or* ininterrompu de données; **continuous feed** = alimentation (du papier) en continu; **continuous loop** = boucle *f* sans fin; **continuous signal** = signal *m* continu; **continuous stationery** = papier *m* en continu; **continuous wave** = onde *f* continue *or* entretenue

◊ **continuously** *adverb* continuellement *or* sans interruption; **the printer overheated after working continuously for five hours** = l'imprimante s'est mise à chauffer après cinq heures de marche sans interruption

contrast 1 *noun* **(a)** contraste *m*; **the control allows you to adjust brightness and contrast** = ce bouton vous permet de régler la luminosité et le contraste; **contrast enhancement filter** = filtre *m* d'amélioration du contraste **(b)** *(knob or key)* bouton *m or* touche *f* (de) contraste **2** *verb* comparer (à *or* avec); **the old data was contrasted with the latest information** = on a comparé les anciennes données aux informations les plus récentes

◊ **contrasting** *adjective* contrastant, -e *or* contrasté, -ée; **a cover design in contrasting colours** = un dessin de couverture aux couleurs contrastées

control 1 *verb (to manage)* contrôler *or* piloter; *(to monitor)* contrôler *or* surveiller *or* vérifier; **controlled vocabulary** = vocabulaire contrôlé (NOTE: **controlling - controlled**) **2** *noun* **(a)** contrôle *m or* surveillance *f or* vérification *f*; **control computer** = ordinateur dédié *or* de contrôle; **control total** = total *m* de vérification *or* de contrôle; **out of control** = hors de contrôle **(b)** *((i) section of computer or device that carries instructions; (ii) conditional program statements)* contrôle *or* pilote *m*; **control unit (CU)** = unité de contrôle (de processus); *(defines the actions in a process)* **control word** = mot *m* de contrôle *or* de commande; **device control character** = caractère *m* de contrôle *or* de commande de périphérique; **line control** = commandes *fpl or* protocole *m* de transmission **(c)** *(key or data)* (i) touche *f* de commande; (ii) données *fpl or* touche de contrôle; **control block** = bloc *m* (de données) de contrôle; **control bus** = bus *m* de commande; **control card** = carte *f* de contrôle; **control character** = caractère *m* de contrôle; **control cycle** = cycle *m* de contrôle; **control data** = données *fpl* de commande *or* de contrôle; **control driven** = commandé par les codes CTRL *or* asservi aux codes CTRL (générés par la touche contrôle); **control field** = champ *m* de contrôle; **control instruction** = instruction *f* de contrôle; **the next control instruction will switch to italics** = la prochaine instruction de contrôle vous donnera les italiques; *(special key on IBM-PC compatible systems)* **control key or Ctrl** = touche *f* de contrôle *or* Ctrl; **to halt a program, press Ctrl-C - the control key and letter C - at the same time** = pour arrêter un programme, appuyez sur Ctrl-C, c'est-à-dire appuyez sur la touche de contrôle et la touche C en même temps; **to reset your PC, press Ctrl-Alt-Del** = pour relancer votre PC, appuyez sur Ctrl-Alt-Del; **control language** = langage *m* de commande; **control memory or ROM** = mémoire fixe *or* ROM; *(in Microsoft Windows: menu that allows you to move)* **control menu** = menu *m* de contrôle (MS-Windows); **control mode** = mode *m* (de) contrôle *or* mode CTRL; *(in Windows, Macintosh and OS/2)* **control panel** = panneau *m* de contrôle *or* de commandes; **control program/ monitor or control program for microcomputers (CP/M)** = système *m* d'exploitation CP/M; **control register** = registre *m* de commande de contrôle; **control sequence** = séquence *f* de commande (d'exécution); **control signal** = signal *m* de contrôle *or* de commande; *(to the CPU)* **control statement** = instruction *f or* commande *f* de contrôle; **control token** = jeton *m* de contrôle (de réseau); *(to the CPU)* **control transfer** = transfert *m* de contrôle **(d)** **control group** = groupe *m* témoin *or* de contrôle; *(for benchmark)* **control systems** = systèmes de contrôle

◊ **controllable** *adjective* contrôlable *or* qui peut être contrôlé, -ée

◊ **controller** *noun* contrôleur *m or* pilote *m* de périphérique(s); **display controller** = contrôleur *or* pilote d'écran *or* d'affichage; **printer's controller** = contrôleur *or* pilote d'imprimante

convention *noun* convention *f*

◊ **conventional memory** *or* **RAM** *noun* (*in an IBM-PC compatible system: random access memory region*) mémoire conventionnelle *or* RAM; *compare* HIGH MEMORY, EXPANDED MEMORY

conversational *adjective* conversationnel, -elle *or* interactif, -ive; **conversational mode** mode *m* conversationnel *or* mode dialogué *or* mode interactif; **conversational terminal** = terminal conversationnel *or* interactif

conversion *noun* conversion *f*; **conversion equipment** = convertisseur *m*; **conversion tables** *or* **translation tables** = tables *fpl* d'équivalence *or* de conversion; **conversion tables may be created and used in conjunction with the customer's data to convert it to our systems codes** = on peut établir des tables d'équivalence qui serviront à convertir les données clients aux codes utilisés par notre système; **conversion program** = (programme) convertisseur *m or* programme *m* de conversion

◊ **convert** *verb* convertir *or* adapter

◊ **convertibility** *noun* convertibilité *f*

◊ **convertible** *adjective* convertible

◊ **converter** *or* **convertor** *noun* convertisseur *m*; **the convertor allowed the old data to be used on the new system** = grâce au convertisseur les anciennes données sont acceptées par le nouveau système; **analog to digital converter (ADC)** = convertisseur analogique-numérique; **digital to analog converter (DAC)** = convertisseur numérique-analogique

convey *verb* transmettre *or* transporter

◊ **conveyor** *noun* convoyeur *m or* bande *f* transporteuse

cooperative processing *noun* (*system in which computers in a distributed network can execute a part of a program*) processus *m* coopératif

coordinate 1 *noun* (*on a graph*) **coordinates** = coordonnées *fpl*; **coordinate graph** = graphe *m* (exprimé en coordonnées); **polar coordinates** = coordonnées polaires; **rectangular coordinates** = coordonnées rectangulaires **2** *verb* coordonner; **she has to coordinate the keyboarding of several parts of a file in six different locations** = elle doit coordonner la saisie des diverses parties d'un fichier qui se fait dans six centres différents

◊ **coordination** *noun* coordination *f*

copier = COPYING MACHINE, PHOTOCOPIER **copier paper** = papier *m* pour photocopieur

copper *noun* cuivre *m*

◊ **copperplate printing** *noun* impression *f* en taille douce

coprocessor *noun* co-processeur *m or* processeur *m* auxiliaire; **graphics coprocessor** = coprocesseur graphique; **maths coprocessor** = coprocesseur mathématique

copy 1 *noun* (**a**) copie *f or* double *m*; **file copy** = copie pour archivage (**b**) document *m*; **clean copy** = texte *m* sans erreur *or* sans modification; **fair copy** *or* **final copy** = texte *m* définitif; **hard copy** = sortie *f* d'imprimante; impression *f* d'écran; imprimé *m*; **rough copy** = brouillon *m or* ébauche *f*; **top copy** = original *m* (**c**) texte *m*; **Tuesday is the last date for copy for the advertisement** = le texte publicitaire doit nous arriver mardi, dernier délai; **copy reader** = lecteur, -trice (**d**) (*book or magazine or newspaper*) exemplaire *m*; (*issue of magazine or newspaper*) numéro *m*; **I kept yesterday's copy of 'The Times'** = j'ai toujours le 'Times' d'hier; **I read it in the office copy of 'Fortune'** = je l'ai lu dans l'exemplaire de 'Fortune' que nous avons au bureau **2** *verb* copier *or* faire une copie *or* reproduire (un document); **there is a memory resident utility which copies the latest files onto backing store every 40 minutes** = il existe un utilitaire résident qui copie les fichiers les plus récents sur un support de sauvegarde toutes les 40 minutes

◊ **copying machine** *or* **copier** *noun* photocopieur *m or* copieur *m*

◊ **copy protect 1** *noun* protection *f* (contre la copie) **2** *verb* protéger (contre la copie); **the program is not copy protected** = le programme n'est pas protégé (contre la copie); **all disks are copy protected** = toutes les disquettes sont munies d'un système de protection *or* tous les disques sont protégés contre la copie

◊ **copy protection** *noun* (système *or* dispositif *or* codage) anticopie *or* de protection contre la copie; **a hard disk may crash because of faulty copy protection** = il arrive qu'une protection anticopie défectueuse entraîne la détérioration du disque dur; **the new program will come without copy protection** = le nouveau programme ne sera pas protégé contre la copie

◊ **COPY** *noun* (*operating system command that copies*) (commande) COPY; **make a copy of your data using the COPY command before you edit it** = faites une copie de vos données avant de les modifier en utilisant la commande COPY

copyright 1 *noun* droit *m* d'auteur *or* copyright *m or* propriété *f* littéraire; **Copyright Act** = Convention *f* sur le droit d'auteur; **work which is**

out of copyright = oeuvre qui est dans le domaine public; **work still in copyright** = oeuvre protégée par un copyright *or* dont les droits de reproduction sont réservés; **infringement of copyright** *or* **copyright infringement** = contrefaçon *f or* reproduction *f* illégale *or* violation *f* du droit d'auteur; **copyright notice** = mention *f* de copyright (dans un livre); **copyright owner** = titulaire *m&f* d'un droit d'auteur *or* d'un copyright **2** *verb* déposer un copyright **3** *adjective* protégé, -ée (par un copyright); **it is illegal to take copies of a copyright work** = photocopier une oeuvre protégée par un copyright est illégal

◊ **copyrighted** *adjective* (oeuvre) sous copyright *or* protégé -ée par un copyright

CORAL = COMMON REAL-TIME APPLICATIONS LANGUAGE langage *m* (d'application temps réel) CORAL

cord *noun* fil *m* (de liaison) *or* cordon *m or* câble *m*

◊ **cordless telephone** *noun* téléphone *m or* poste *m* téléphonique sans cordon

core *noun* (a) *(of cable)* âme *f or* coeur *m* (b) **core memory** *or* **store** = mémoire *f* centrale; **core program** = programme en mémoire centrale

coresident *adjective (program)* co-résident, -e

corona *noun (electric discharge that charges toner)* charge *f* statique; *(thin wire that charges the toner particles)* **corona wire** = fil *m* de charge statique; **if your printouts are smudged, you may have to clean the corona wire** = si vos sorties d'imprimante sont sales, il faut nettoyer le fil de charge statique

coroutine *noun* module *m* d'accompagnement *or* coroutine *f*

correct 1 *adjective* correct, -e *or* exact, -e **2** *verb* corriger; **error correcting code** = code *m* correcteur d'erreur

◊ **correction** *noun* correction *f*

◊ **corrective maintenance** *noun* maintenance *f* corrective *or* dépannage *m or* réparation *f*

correspond *verb* (a) *(to write letters)* correspondre *or* écrire; **to correspond with someone** = correspondre avec quelqu'un (b) *(to fit or agree)* **to correspond with something** = correspondre à quelque chose

◊ **correspondence** *noun* (a) *(letter-writing)* correspondance *f*; **business correspondence** = correspondance commerciale *or* d'affaires; **to be in correspondence with someone** = être en correspondance avec quelqu'un (b) *(fitting or agreeing)* correspondance

◊ **correspondent** *noun* (a) *(person who writes letters)* correspondant, -e (b) *(journalist)* correspondant, -e *or* journaliste *m&f*; **the computer correspondent** = le correspondant (de la section) informatique; **the 'Times' business correspondent** = le correspondant économique du 'Times'

corrupt 1 *adjective* corrompu, -e *or* erroné, -ée **2** *verb* corrompre *or* détériorer *or* faire perdre l'intégrité; *(informal)* véroler; **power loss during disk access can corrupt the data** = un problème de tension pendant l'accès au disque peut détériorer *or* véroler les données *or* faire perdre l'intégrité des données

◊ **corruption** *noun* corruption *f or* détérioration *f*; **data corruption** = corruption *or* détérioration de données; **acoustic couplers suffer from data corruption more than the direct connect form of modem** = les coupleurs acoustiques sont plus susceptibles aux détériorations de données que les modems branchés directement sur la ligne; **data corruption on the disk has made one file unreadable** = la corruption de données sur la disquette a rendu le fichier impossible à lire

coulomb *noun* coulomb *m*

count *verb* compter

◊ **counter** *noun* compteur *m*; **the loop will repeat itself until the counter reaches 100** = la boucle se répétera jusqu'à ce que le compteur atteigne 100; **the number of items changed are recorded by the counter** = le nombre de changements est enregistré sur le compteur; **instruction** *or* **program counter** = compteur d'instruction *or* registre *m* compteur

counter- *prefix (opposite way to normal)* contre-; *(paths transmitted in opposite directions)* **counter-rotating ring** = anneau *m* de contre-rotation

counting perforator *noun* perforateur-compteur *m* (de composition)

country file *noun (file in an operating system that defines parameters)* fichier *m* localisation *or* pays

couple *verb* joindre *or* coupler; **the two systems are coupled together** = les deux systèmes sont couplés *or* connectés l'un à l'autre

◊ **coupler** *noun* coupleur *m*; **acoustic coupler** = coupleur acoustique

Courier *noun (typeface)* (police de caractères) Courier

courseware *noun* didacticiel *m*

coverage *noun (of newspaper)* couverture *f*; *(of broadcast)* potentiel *m* d'écoute; **press coverage** *or* **media coverage** = couverture médiatique; reportage *m*; **the company had good media coverage for the launch of its new model** = la société a eu une excellente couverture médiatique pour le lancement de son nouveau modèle

CP = CARD PUNCH

◊ **cp** *(UNIX command to copy a file)* (commande) cp (de copie de fichier UNIX)

CPE = CENTRAL PROCESSING ELEMENT

cpi = CHARACTERS PER INCH

CP/M = CONTROL PROGRAM/MONITOR

cps = CHARACTERS PER SECOND

CPU = CENTRAL PROCESSING UNIT unité *f* centrale (de traitement) *or* processeur *m* central; *(performance of a computer)* **CPU bound** = limité *or* bridé par l'unité centrale; **CPU cycle** = (temps de) cycle *m* de l'unité centrale *or* cycle d'horloge *or* cycle CPU; **CPU elements** = éléments de l'unité centrale *or* éléments CPU; **CPU handshaking** = protocole *m* de communication *or* d'échange d'informations (entre CPU et périphérique); handshaking *m*; **CPU time** = temps d'utilisation de l'unité centrale *or* du processeur *or* temps CPU

CR (a) = CARRIAGE RETURN **(b)** = CARD READER

crash 1 *noun* défaillance *f or* panne *f* ; crash *m or* plantage *m*; **disk crash** = détérioration *f or* destruction *f* (accidentelle) *or* crash du disque (dur) **2** *verb (of a computer)* tomber en panne (nécessitant une réparation); *(totale)* se planter; *(of disk)* détruire; (se) détériorer; **the disk head has crashed and the data may have been lost** = la tête de lecture du disque est tombée en panne et il se peut que les données aient été perdues

◊ **crash-protected** *adjective* protégé contre toute détérioration *or* destruction (accidentelle); **if the disk is crash-protected, you will never lose your data** = si vous vous servez d'un disque protégé contre la destruction accidentelle, vous ne perdrez jamais vos données

crawl *noun (of film)* dispositif *m* de défilement du générique *or* crawl *m*

CRC = CYCLIC REDUNDANCY CHECK

create *verb* créer *or* produire; **a new file was created on disk to store the document** = on a créé un nouveau fichier sur la disquette pour archiver le document; **move to the CREATE NEW FILE instruction on the menu** = allez à CREATION D'UN DOSSIER sur le menu

credit *noun* **(a)** *(finance)* crédit *m*; **credit card** = carte *f* de crédit **(b)** *(of films)* **credits** = générique *m*; *(magazine, etc.)* crédits *mpl*

crew *noun* équipe *f*; **camera crew** = équipe cinématographique *or* de cinéastes; **the camera crew had to film all day in the snow** = l'équipe de cinéastes a dû tourner toute la journée dans la neige

crippled leapfrog test *noun* test *m* sélectif limité *or* restreint; test saut de puce limité à un seul emplacement

criterion *noun* critère *m* (NOTE: plural is **criteria**)

critical *adjective* critique; *(error that crashes the computer)* **critical error** = erreur *f* critique; **critical fusion frequency** = fréquence *f* critique de fusion; **critical resource** = ressource *f* critique

◊ **critical path analysis** *noun* analyse *f* du chemin critique

QUOTE Surprisingly, critical path analysis and project management, frequently the next career step for engineers, did not seem to warrant a mention.

Computing

CR/LF = CARRIAGE RETURN/LINE FEED

crop *verb (reduce the size of an image)* découper (la bordure d'une image) *or* cadrer (une image)

◊ **crop mark** *noun (printed marks that show the edge of a page)* marque *f* de cadrage

◊ **cropping** *noun* cropping *m or* découpage *m*; **the photographs can be edited by cropping, sizing, touching up, etc.** = les photos peuvent être éditées par découpage, dimensionnement, retouche etc.

cross- *prefix* contre- *or* croisé, -ée; **cross fade** = fondu *m* enchaîné; **cross modulation** = intermodulation *f*

◊ **cross-assembler** *noun* assembleur *m* croisé *or* cross-assembleur *m*

◊ **cross-check** *noun* contrôle *m* croisé *or* double contrôle *or* contre-épreuve *f*

◊ **cross-compiler** *noun* compilateur *m* croisé

◊ **cross-linked files** *plural noun (error in which two files claim to be using the same cluster on disk)* fichiers mélangés *or* interférence *f* de fichiers

crossfire *noun* diaphonie *f or* interférence *f* induite

◊ **crossover** *noun* changement *m or* passage *m*; **the crossover to computerized file indexing was difficult** = il a été difficile de passer à un système d'index informatisé

◊ **cross-reference 1** *noun (in book)* renvoi *m or* référence *f*; *(to find a file)* référence croisée **2** *verb* faire un renvoi *or* référer (à une autre section d'un document); **the SI units are cross-referenced to the appendix** = les unités SI font l'objet d'un renvoi à l'appendice

◊ **cross-reference generator** *noun* générateur *m* de renvois

◊ **cross-section** *noun* coupe *f*; **the cross-section of the optical fibre showed the problem** = une coupe de la fibre optique a révélé la source du problème

◊ **crosstalk** *noun* diaphonie *f or* interférence *f* (entre deux canaux de communication); **the crosstalk was so bad, the signal was unreadable** = il y avait une telle diaphonie que le signal était illisible *or* l'interférence rendait le signal illisible

CRT = CATHODE RAY TUBE

cruncher, crunching *see* NUMBER

crushing *noun (TV)* écrasement *m* (de l'image)

cryogenic memory *noun* mémoire *f* cryogénique

cryptanalysis *noun* analyse *f* cryptographique

cryptography *noun* cryptographie *f*

◊ **cryptographic** *adjective* cryptographique; **cryptographic algorithm** = algorithme *m* cryptographique *or* de cryptage; **cryptographic key** = clé *f* de cryptage *or* de chiffrage

crystal *noun* cristal *m*; **liquid crystal display (LCD)** = affichage *m* à cristaux liquides; **crystal microphone** = microphone *m* à quartz; **crystal oscillator** = oscillateur *m* à quartz; *(page printer)* **crystal shutter printer** = imprimante *f* à transfert LCD; *see also* LASER PRINTER

CSDC = CIRCUIT SWITCHED DIGITAL CIRCUITRY

CSM = COMBINED SYMBOL MATCHING

CSMA-CD = CARRIER SENSE MULTIPLE ACCESS-COLLISION DETECTION

CTR *or* **CTRL** *or* **Ctrl** = CONTROL (touche) CTR *or* CTRL *or* Ctrl; touche *f* de contrôle

CTS = CLEAR TO SEND

CU = CONTROL UNIT

cue *noun* (message d') invitation *f* à taper une instruction

CUG = CLOSED USER GROUP

cumulative index *noun* index *m* cumulatif

cumulative trauma disorder *see* RSI

current 1 *adjective* courant, -e; **current address** = adresse *f* courante; **current address register (CAR)** = registre *m* d'adresse courante; *(directory which is currently being used)* **current directory** = répertoire *m* courant; *(disk drive that is currently being used)* **current drive** = lecteur de disque courant; **current instruction register (CIR)** = registre d'instruction courante **2** *noun (electric)* courant *m*; **direct current (DC)** = courant continu; **alternating current (AC)** = courant alternatif (CA)

cursor *noun* curseur *m*; **cursor control keys** = touches *fpl* de contrôle du curseur *or* touches fléchées; **cursor home** = coin *m* gauche supérieur (de l'écran) *or* début *m* de l'écran; **cursor pad** = touches de contrôle du curseur; **addressable cursor** = curseur adressable; **destructive cursor** = curseur effaceur

QUOTE above the cursor pad are the insert and delete keys, which when shifted produce clear and home respectively
Computing Today

QUOTE further quick cursor movements are available for editing by combining one of the arrow keys with the control function
Personal Computer World

QUOTE Probably the most exciting technology demonstrated was ScreenCam, which allows users to combine voice, cursor movement and on-screen activities into a movie which can be replayed.
Computing

curve *noun* courbe *f*; **to plot a curve** = tracer une courbe; **characteristic curve** = courbe caractéristique

customer *noun* client, -e; **customer engineering** = maintenance *f* du parc clients; **customer service department** = service *m* après-vente *or* service clients

◊ **custom-built** *adjective* personnalisé, -ée *or* (fait) sur mesure *or* sur commande

◊ **custom ROM (PROM)** *noun* ROM personnalisée

◊ **customize** *verb* fabriquer sur commande *or* personnaliser; **we use customized software** = nous utilisons des logiciels personnalisés *or* écrits sur commande

cut 1 *noun* coupure *f*; **the editors have asked for cuts in the first chapter** = les éditeurs ont demandé de faire des coupures au premier chapitre *or* de réduire le premier chapitre **2** *verb* **(a)** couper; **cut-in notes** = notes *fpl* marginales; *(for paper)* **cut sheet feeder** = (système d') alimentation *f* feuille à feuille **(b)** couper *or* réduire (un texte); **the author was asked to cut his manuscript to 250 pages** = on a demandé à l'auteur de réduire son manuscrit à 250 pages (NOTE: **cuts - cutting - has cut**)

◊ **cut and paste** *verb* (procédure) couper-coller *m*

◊ **cut off** *verb* **(a)** couper; **six metres of paper were cut off the reel** = on a coupé six mètres du rouleau de papier **(b)** couper *or* arrêter; **the electricity supply was cut off** = il y a eu une coupure de courant *or* une panne de secteur

◊ **cutoff** *noun & adjective* point *m* d'arrêt *or* coupure *f*; **cutoff frequency** = fréquence *f* de coupure

◊ **cutting** *noun* coupure *f*; *(in film studio)* **cutting room** = salle *f* de montage; **press cuttings** = coupures de journal

CWP = COMMUNICATING WORD PROCESSOR

cyan-magenta-yellow-black (CMYK) *(method of describing a colour)* (système soustractif de couleurs) CMYK *or* cyan-magenta-jaune-noir

cybernetics *noun* la cybernétique

cyberspace *noun* cyberspace *m*

cycle *noun* cycle *m*; **action cycle** = cycle fonctionnel; **clock cycle** = cycle d'horloge; **cycle availability** = (période de) disponibilité *f* dans le cycle; **cycle count** = nombre *m* de cycles; **cycle index** = index *m* de cycle; **cycle shift** = permutation *f* circulaire; **cycle stealing** = (exploitation par) vol *m* de cycle; *see also* DMA **cycle time** = temps *m* de cycle

◊ **cyclic** *adjective* cyclique *or* circulaire; **cyclic access** = accès *m* cyclique; **cyclic check** = contrôle *m* cyclique; **cyclic code** = code *m* binaire réfléchi *or* code de Gray; **cyclic decimal code** = code décimal réfléchi; **cyclic redundancy check (CRC)** = contrôle de redondance cyclique; **cyclic shift** = permutation *f or* décalage *m* circulaire

cylinder *noun (group of tracks on a disk; the tracks on a multidisk device)* cylindre *m*

cypher = CIPHER

Dd

D *(hexadecimal number equivalent to decimal 13)* nombre hexadécimal équivalent du 13 décimal *or* D

3D = THREE-DIMENSIONAL à trois dimensions *or* tridimensionnel, -elle

> QUOTE the software can create 3D images using data from a scanner or photographs from an electronic microscope
>
> *PC Business World*

DA = DESK ACCESSORY

DAC *or* **d/a converter** = DIGITAL TO ANALOG CONVERTER convertisseur *m* numérique-analogique; **speech is output from the computer via a D/A converter** = l'ordinateur émet un signal vocal via un convertisseur numérique-analogique; **the D/A converter on the output port controls the analog machine** = le convertisseur numérique-analogique du port de sortie contrôle la machine analogique

daemon *noun (utility program in a UNIX system)* (utilitaire UNIX) démon *m or* daemon *m*

dagger *noun (printing sign)* croix *f* (†); **double dagger** = croix double (‡)

daisy chain *noun* chaîne *f*; **daisy chain bus** = bus *m* de chaîne *or* bus série; **daisy chain interrupt** = interruption en série *or* en chaîne; **daisy chain recursion** = boucle *f* de récurrence

◊ **daisy-chain** *verb* relier en chaîne *or* en série *or* en cascade

> QUOTE you can often daisy-chain cards or plug them into expansion boxes
>
> *Byte*

daisy-wheel *noun* marguerite *f* (d'imprimante); **daisy-wheel printer** *or* **daisy-wheel typewriter** = imprimante *f* à marguerite; **a daisy-wheel printer produces much better quality text than a dot-matrix, but is slower** = l'imprimante à marguerite donne un bien meilleur résultat que l'imprimante matricielle mais elle est plus lente

DAMA = DEMAND ASSIGNED MULTIPLE ACCESS

damage 1 *noun* dommage *m or* avarie *f*; **to suffer damage** = subir des dommages; **to cause damage** = endommager; **the breakdown of the electricity supply caused damage estimated at £100,000** = les dommages causés par la panne d'électricité s'élèvent à environ 100 000 livres sterling **2** *verb* endommager *or* abîmer; *(file or data)* détériorer *or* corrompre; **the faulty read/write head appears to**

have **damaged the disks** = il semble que la tête de lecture défectueuse ait endommagé les disques; **the hard disk was damaged when it was dropped** = le disque dur a été endommagé quand on l'a laissé tomber

◊ **damaged** *adjective* endommagé, -ée *or* abîmé, -ée; *(file or data)* détérioré, -ée *or* corrompu,-e; **is it possible to repair the damaged files?** = est-il possible de récupérer les fichiers détériorés?

D to A converter = DIGITAL TO ANALOG CONVERTER

dark current *noun* courant *m* noir

◊ **dark trace tube** *noun* tube *m* ombré

darkroom *noun (photography)* chambre *f* noire

DAS = DUAL ATTACHMENT STATION

DASD = DIRECT ACCESS STORAGE DEVICE

dash *noun (short line in printing)* tiret *m*; *(typography)* **em dash** *or* **em rule** = tiret (dont la longueur équivaut à un 'm'); **en dash** *or* **en rule** = tiret de césure *or* tiret court

DAT = DIGITAL AUDIO TAPE; *(system of recording sound as digital information on DAT tape)* (système d') enregistrement *m* sur bande audionumérique; **DAT produces a very high quality sound** = l'enregistrement sur bande audionumérique produit un son de très haute qualité; *(drive that records data onto a DAT tape)* **DAT drive** = lecteur *m* de bande audionumérique; **we use a DAT drive as the backup device for our network** = la sauvegarde du réseau est assurée par un lecteur de bandes (audionumériques); **DAT tape** = bande *f* audionumérique *or* bande audio

data *noun* donnée(s) *f(pl)*; **data is input at one of several workstations** = les données sont saisies sur l'un des nombreux postes de travail; **the company stores data on customers in its main computer file** = les coordonnées des clients de la société sont entrées sur l'ordinateur principal; **a user needs a password to access data** = l'utilisateur doit utiliser un mot de passe pour accéder aux données; **raw data** = données brutes; **data above voice (DAV)** = (transmission de) données supravocales; **data access management** = gestion *f* d'accès aux données; **data acquisition** = acquisition *f* de données; **data adapter unit** = adaptateur *m* de canal de transmission de données; **data administrator** = gestionnaire *m* de données; **data aggregate** = agrégat *m* de données *or* données structurées *or* données agrégées; **data analysis** = analyse *f* de données; **data area** = zone *f* de données; **data below voice (DBV)** = (transmission de) données infravocales; **data block** = bloc *m* de données; **data break** = arrêt *m* de transmission de données; **data buffer** = (mémoire) tampon *m* de données; **data bus** = bus *m* de données; *see also* DB CONNECTOR; **data capture** = saisie *f or* capture *f* de données; **data carrier** = *(medium)* support *m* de données *or* d'information; *(waveform)* (onde) porteuse *f* de données; *(RS232C signal)* **data carrier detect (DCD)** = détecteur *m* d'onde porteuse *or* signal *m* de détection de porteuse; **the call is stopped if the software does not receive a DCD signal from the modem** = l'appel est bloqué si le logiciel ne reçoit pas de signal de détection de porteuse du modem; **data cartridge** = cartouche *f* de données; **data chaining** = liaison *f* (de données) en chaîne *or* chaînage de données; **data channel** = canal *m* de transmission de données; *(error in reading data)* **data check** = brève interruption de transmission de données (causée par un défaut du support magnétique); **data circuit** = circuit *m* d'échange (bi-directionnel) de données; **data cleaning** = nettoyage *m* des données *or* correction *f* d'erreurs; **data collection** = collecte *f* de données; **data collection platform** = plate-forme *f* de collecte de données; **data communications** = télématique *f or* téléinformatique *f or* transmission *f* de données; **data communications buffer** = (mémoire) tampon *m* de transmission de données; **data communications equipment (DCE)** = appareils *mpl or* matériel *m* (de) téléinformatique; **data communications network** = réseau *m* téléinformatique *or* de transmission de données; **data compacting** = compactage *m* de données; **all the files were stored on one disk with this new data compacting routine** = tous les fichiers ont pu être stockés sur une seule disquette grâce au nouveau programme de compactage; **data compression** = compression *f* de données; **scanners use a technique called data compression which manages to reduce, even by a third, the storage required** = les scanners utilisent la technique dite de compression de données qui peut réduire du tiers la mémoire nécessaire; **data concentrator** = concentrateur *m* de données; **data connection** = connexion *f* (pour transmission de données); **data control** = contrôle *m* de données; **data corruption** = corruption *f or* détérioration *f* de données; **data corruption occurs each time the motor is switched on** = chaque fois qu'on met le système sous tension, il y a corruption de données; **data delimiter** = (symbole) délimiteur *m* de données; **data description language (DDL)** = langage *m* de description de données; **data dictionary/directory (DD/D)** = dictionnaire/répertoire *m* de données; *(part of a COBOL progam)* **data division** = rubrique *f* de déclaration des données; **data-driven** = activé, -ée par reconnaissance des données; **data element** = élément *m* de données; **data element chain** = chaîne *f* d'éléments de données; **data encryption** = chiffrage *m or* chiffrement *m or* cryptage *m* de données; **data encryption standard (DES)** = norme *f or* standard *m* de cryptage de données; **data entry** = (mode d') entrée *f or* introduction *f or* (méthode de) saisie *f* de données; **data error** = erreur *f* de données; **data field** = champ *m* de données; **data file** = fichier *m* de données; **the data file has to be analysed** = il faut analyser le fichier de données; **data flow** = flux *m* de données; **data flowchart** = ordinogramme *m* de

données; **the data flowchart allowed us to improve throughput, by using a better structure** = l'ordinogramme des données nous a permis d'améliorer nos résultats à l'aide d'une meilleure structure; **data flow diagram (DFD)** = diagramme *m* de flux de données; **data format** = format *m* de données; **data hierarchy** = hiérarchie *f* des données; *(between a CPU and peripherals)* **data highway** = bus *m* de transfert de données; **data independence** = autonomie *f* des données; **data input** = saisie *f or* entrée *f* de données; **data input bus (DIB)** = bus *m* d'entrée; **data integrity** = intégrité *f* des données; *(standard method of storing spreadsheet data)* **data interchange format (DIF)** = format DIF; **data in voice (DIV)** = transmission *f* de données vocales; **data item** = élément *m* de données; **data level** = niveau *m* de données; **data link** = liaison *f* de données; **data link control** = contrôle *m* de liaison de données; **data link layer** = couche *f* (de) liaison de données; **data logging** = enregistrement *f* (automatique et chronologique) de données; **data management** = gestion *f* de données; **data manipulation language (DML)** = langage *m* de manipulation de données; **data medium** = support *m* de données; **data migration** = migration *f* de données *or* transfert *m* de données (sur dispositif hors ligne); **data network** = réseau *m* téléinformatique *or* de transmission de données; **data origination** = génération *f or* création *f* de données; **data path** = chemin *m or* trajet *m* (des données) *or* voie de transmission de données; **data pointer** = pointeur *m* (de position) de données; **data preparation** = préparation *f* de données; **data processing (DP or dp)** = traitement *m* de données *or* traitement de l'information; *(person)* **data processing manager (DPM)** = responsable *m&f* du service informatique; **data protection** = protection *f* des données; **Data Protection Act** = loi Informatique et Libertés; **data rate** = vitesse *f* de traitement *or* de transmission de données; **data record** = enregistrement *m* de données; **data reduction** = réduction *m* de données; **data register** = registre *m* de données; **data reliability** = qualité *f or* fiabilité *f* des données; **data retrieval** = (i) recherche *f* documentaire; (ii) extraction *f* de données; **data routing** = acheminement *m or* routage *m* des données; **data security** = sécurité *f* des données *or* de l'information; **data services** = service *m* de téléinformatique *or* de transmission de données; **data set ready (DSR)** = (signal de) prêt à recevoir; *(data that can be accessed by several users)* **data sharing** = partage *m* de données; données *fpl* partagées; **data signals** = signaux *mpl* (de transmission) de données; **data signalling rate** = débit *m or* vitesse *f* de transmission de données; **data sink** = collecteur *m* de données; puits *m or* terminal *m* récepteur (de données); **data source** = source *f or* émetteur *m* de données; **data station** = poste *m* informatique de télétransmission; **data storage** = *(medium)* mémoire *f* de données; *(storing)* stockage *m or* mise *f* en mémoire (de données); **data stream** = flot *m* de données; **data strobe** = (signal de) validation *f* de données transmises; **data structure** = structure *f* des données; **data switching exchange (DSE)** = centre *m* de commutation des données; **data tablet** = tablette *f* à numériser *or* tablette graphique; **data terminal** = terminal *m or* poste *m* informatique; **a** printer is a data terminal for computer output = l'imprimante est un terminal de sortie d'ordinateur; **data terminal equipment (DTE)** = (i) terminal *m* de traitement de données; (ii) terminal de transmission de données; **data terminal ready (DTR)** = (signal de) prêt à transmettre; **data transaction** = transaction *f* de données; **data transfer rate** = débit *m or* vitesse *f* de transfert de données; **data translation** = conversion *f* de données; **data transmission** = transmission *f* de données; **data type** = type *m* de données; **data under voice (DUV)** = transmission de données subvocales; **data validation** = validation *f* de données; **data vetting** = validation *or* vérification *f* de données; **data word** = mot *m* (de donnée); **data word length** = longueur *f* d'un mot

> QUOTE Zenith's new notebook models use the power-saving Intel 486 SL microprocessor which offers 32-bit internal and data bus operation.
> *Computing*

> QUOTE data compression is the art of squeezing more and more information into fewer and fewer bytes
> *Practical Computing*

◊ **databank** *noun* banque *f* de données

database *noun* base *f* de données; *(person)* **database administrator (DBA)** = responsable *m&f* de base de données; *(program that acts as interface)* **database engine** = moteur *m* de base de données; **database language** = langage *m* de base de données; **database machine** = machine *f* dédiée au traitement de bases de données; **database management system (DBMS)** *or* **database manager** = système *m* de gestion de base de données; gestionnaire *m* de base de données; **database mapping** = implantation *f or* configuration *f or* topologie *f* d'une base de données; **database schema** = schéma *m* de base de données; **database system** = système *m* de base de données; **on-line database** = base de données en ligne

> QUOTE This information could include hypertext references to information held within a computer database, or spreadsheet formulae.
> *Computing*

> QUOTE a database is a file of individual records of information which are stored in some kind of sequential order
> *Which PC?*

◊ **datagram** *noun* datagramme *m*

◊ **dataline** *noun* ligne *f* de communication de données

◊ **dataplex** *noun* multiplexage *m*

◊ **dataset** *noun* US modem *m*; *(RS232C signal)* **dataset ready (DSR)** = (signal de modem) prêt à transmettre/recevoir

date 1 *noun* date *f*; **I have received your message of yesterday's date** = j'ai bien reçu votre message en date d'hier; **the date of creation for the file was the 10th of June** = la date de création de ce fichier est le 10 juin **2** *verb* dater (un document)

◊ **out of date** *adjective & adverb* démodé, -ée *or* dépassé, -ée; **their computer system is years out of date** = leur système informatique est totalement dépassé; **they are still using out-of-date equipment** = ils utilisent toujours du matériel dépassé

◊ **up to date** *adjective & adverb* récent, -e *or* à jour *or* moderne *or* à la page; **an up-to-date computer system** = un système informatique de modèle récent; **to bring something up to date** = mettre à jour (un fichier, etc.); **to keep something up to date** = garder *or* maintenir (un fichier) à jour; **we spend a lot of time keeping our files up to date** = nous passons beaucoup de temps à maintenir nos fichiers à jour (NOTE: when used as adjective before a noun, **out-of-date** and **up-to-date** are hyphenated)

daughter board *noun* carte fille *f*

DAV = DATA ABOVE VOICE

dB *see* DECIBEL

DBA = DATABASE ADMINISTRATOR

dBASE ™ *(popular database software)* dBase ™

> COMMENT: dBASE has several versions, II, III and IV; the software development is currently carried out by Borland International. There have been several versions of dBASE, and files created in dBASE can normally be imported into other database programs

DB connector = DATA BUS CONNECTOR; *(D-shape connector)* connecteur *m* DB *or* connecteur en D; **the most common DB connectors are DB-9, DB-25 and DB-50 with 9, 25 and 50 connections respectively** = les connecteurs DB les plus répandus sont DB9, DB25 et DB50 qui portent respectivement 9, 25, 50 broches

DBMS = DATABASE MANAGEMENT SYSTEM

DBS = DIRECT BROADCAST SATELLITE

DBV = DATA BELOW VOICE

DC = DIRECT CURRENT courant *m* continu; **DC signalling** = transmission *f* directe de signaux

DCA = DOCUMENT CONTENT ARCHITECTURE

DCD = DATA CARRIER DETECT

DCE = DATA COMMUNICATIONS EQUIPMENT

DD = DOUBLE DENSITY

DDC = DIRECT DIGITAL CONTROL

DD/D = DATA DICTIONARY /DIRECTORY

DDE = DIRECT DATA ENTRY

DDE = DYNAMIC DATA EXCHANGE

DDL = DATA DESCRIPTION LANGUAGE langage *m* de description de données; **many of DDL's advantages come from the fact that it is a second generation language** = plusieurs des avantages d'un langage de description de données vient du fait qu'il s'agit d'un langage de deuxième génération

DDP = DISTRIBUTED DATA PROCESSING

dead *adjective* **(a)** *(not working)* hors service *or* inutilisable *or* mort, -e; **dead halt** *or* **drop dead halt** = arrêt *m* total; **the manual does not say what to do if a dead halt occurs** = le manuel n'explique pas la marche à suivre en cas d'arrêt total de la machine; **dead keys** = *(on computer)* touches *fpl* de fonction *or* d'intervention (qui ne produisent pas de caractères); *(on typewriter)* touches d'accents, etc. (qui ne font pas avancer le chariot); **dead matter** = sujet abandonné *or* affaire enterrée; **dead time** = temps *m* mort **(b)** *(room or space that has no acoustical reverberation)* (chambre, etc.) sourd, -e

◊ **deaden** *verb (sound)* assourdir *or* étouffer *or* amortir *or* atténuer (un son *or* bruit); *(colour)* adoucir *or* atténuer (une couleur); **acoustic hoods are used to deaden the noise of printers** = les capots *or* les hottes d'insonorisation servent à amortir *or* atténuer le bruit des imprimantes

deadline *noun* date *f* limite *or* délai *m* (impératif); **to meet a deadline** = respecter un délai; **we've missed our October 15th deadline** = nous avons dépassé notre date limite du 15 octobre

◊ **deadlock** *noun* impasse *f*

◊ **deadly embrace** *noun* = DEADLOCK

deal 1 *noun* accord *m* *or* marché *m* *or* contrat *m*; **package deal** = contrat global *or* forfait *m*; **they agreed a package deal, which involves the development of software, customizing hardware and training of staff** = il se sont mis d'accord sur un contrat global comprenant le développement d'un logiciel, la personnalisation du matériel et la formation du personnel **2** *verb* **to deal with** = prendre quelque chose en main(s) *or* s'occuper de quelque chose; **leave it to the DTP manager - he'll deal with it** = le responsable de la PAO s'en occupera!

◊ **dealer** *noun* marchand, -e *or* revendeur, -euse; **always buy hardware from a recognized dealer** = n'achetez votre matériel informatique que chez un revendeur agréé

deallocate *verb* libérer *or* désaffecter *or* désallouer; **when a reset button is pressed all resources are deallocated** = lorsque vous appuyez sur la touche *or* le bouton de ré-initialisation, toutes les ressources sont désallouées

debit *noun* débit *m* binaire

deblock *verb* éclater *or* dégrouper (les éléments d') un bloc

de-bounce *noun* (dispositif) antirebond *m*; **de-bounce circuit** = circuit antirebond

debug *verb* déboguer *or* déverminer *or* mettre au point; **they spent weeks debugging the system** = ils ont mis des semaines à déboguer le système; **debugging takes up more time than construction** = il faut plus de temps pour déboguer un programme que pour en créer un; **debugged program** = programme débogué *or* déverminé

◊ **debugger** *noun* logiciel *m* de débogage *or* de mise au point; débogueur *m*

> QUOTE the debug monitor makes development and testing very easy
> *Electronics & Wireless World*

> QUOTE Further questions, such as how you debug an application built from multisourced software to be run on multisourced hardware, must be resolved at this stage.
> *Computing*

DEBUG *noun* *(software utility in MS-DOS)* (utilitaire MS-DOS) DEBUG

decade *noun* dizaine *f* *or* décade *f*; **decade counter** = compteur *m* décadaire

decay 1 *noun* *(signal fading away)* extinction *f* *or* amortissement *m* (d'un son); **with a short decay, it sounds very sharp** = avec un amortissement court, le son est très aigu; *(of signal)* **decay time** = délai *m* d'amortissement d'un signal **2** *verb* s'amortir *or* s'affaiblir *or* s'atténuer; **the signal decayed rapidly** = le signal s'est amorti rapidement

deceleration time *noun* *(time taken for an access arm to come to a stop)* temps *m* de décélération

decentralized computer network *noun* réseau *m* décentralisé

◊ **decentralized data processing** *noun* traitement *m* décentralisé des données

deci- *prefix* déci-

decibel (dB) *noun* décibel (dB) *m*; **decibel meter** = décibelmètre *m* *or* analyseur *m* de bruit

decile *noun* décile *m*

decimal *adjective and noun* **decimal notation** = numération décimale; **correct to three places of decimals** = correct à la troisième décimale; **decimal point** = virgule *f* (décimale); **decimal system** = système *m* décimal *or* à base dix; **decimal tabbing** = tabulation *f* décimale *or* sur la virgule; **decimal tab key** = touche *f* de tabulation décimale; **decimal-to-binary conversion** = conversion *f* décimale-binaire

◊ **decimalization** *noun* décimalisation *f*

◊ **decimalize** *verb* décimaliser

decimonic ringing *noun* sonnerie *f* décimonique *or* sonnerie à résonance de fréquence *or* bip *m* d'appel

decipher *verb* déchiffrer

decision *noun* décision *f*; **to come to a decision** *or* **to reach a decision** = prendre une décision *or* se décider (à); **decision box** = symbole *m* de décision *or* de branchement *or* de condition; **decision circuit** *or* **element** = circuit *m* *or* élément *m* de décision; **decision** *or* **discrimination instruction** = décision *f* *or* instruction *f* conditionnelle; **decision support system (DSS)** = système *m* d'aide à la décision (SAID); **decision table** = table *f* de décision; **decision tree** = arbre *m* de décision

deck *noun* **(a)** **tape deck** = (i) platine *f* magnétophone; (ii) platine magnétocassette **(b)** jeu *m* *or* paquet *m* de cartes perforées

deckle edge *noun* (*rough edge of paper*) bord *m* déchiqueté *or* non rogné

declare *verb* déclarer *or* faire une déclaration; **he declared at the start of the program that X was equal to nine** = au début du programme X a été déclaré égal à 9

◊ **declaration** *or* **declarative statement** *noun* déclaration *f*; **procedure declaration** = déclaration de procédure

◊ **declarative language** *noun* langage *m* déclaratif

decode *verb* décoder *or* désembrouiller

◊ **decoder** *noun* décodeur *m*; **instruction decoder** = décodeur *m* d'instruction

◊ **decoding** *noun* décodage *m*

decollate *verb* (*continuous stationery*) déliasser

◊ **decollator** *noun* déliasseuse *f*

decompilation *noun* décompilation *f*; **incremental compilation and decompilation** = compilation et décompilation incrémentielles

decrement *verb* décrémenter; **the register contents were decremented until they reached zero** = le contenu du registre a été décrémenté à zéro

decrypt *verb* déchiffrer *or* décrypter

◊ **decryption** *noun* déchiffrage *m* *or* décryptage *m*; **decryption is done using hardware to increase speed** = le déchiffrage se fait avec l'ordinateur pour aller plus vite

QUOTE typically a file is encrypted using a password key and decrypted using the same key. A design fault of many systems means the use of the wrong password for decryption results in double and often irretrievable encryption
PC Business World

dedicated *adjective* (*reserved for a particular use*) dédié, -ée *or* spécialisé, -ée; **there's only one dedicated graphics workstation in this network** = il n'y a qu'un seul poste réservé aux graphiques sur ce réseau; **dedicated channel** = canal dédié *or* spécialisé *or* voie spécialisée; **dedicated computer** = ordinateur dédié; **dedicated line** = ligne téléphonique spécialisée *or* dédiée; **dedicated logic**

= fonction logique dédiée *or* spécialisée; **the person appointed should have a knowledge of micro-based hardware and dedicated logic** = la personne nommée devra connaître le matériel micro-informatique et la logique qui s'y rapporte; **dedicated logic cuts down the chip count** = la logique dédiée réduit le nombre de puces; **dedicated word processor** = appareil de traitement de texte dédié *or* spécialisé

QUOTE the server should reduce networking costs by using standard networking cable instead of dedicated links
PC Business World

QUOTE The PBX is changing from a dedicated proprietary hardware product into an open application software development platform.
Computing

deduct *verb* déduire *or* soustraire

de facto standard *noun* (*system which has become a standard*) norme *f* de fait *or* norme de facto

default *noun* défaut *m*; **by default** = par défaut *or* implicite; **default drive** = lecteur *m* par défaut; **the operating system allows the user to select the default drive** = ce système d'exploitation permet à l'utilisateur de choisir le lecteur par défaut; **default option** = option *f* implicite *or* par défaut *or* intrinsèque; **default rate** = débit *m* par défaut *or* prédéterminé d'un modem; **default response** = réponse *f* intrinsèque *or* par défaut; **default value** = valeur *f* par défaut *or* intrinsèque *or* prédéterminée; **screen width has a default value of 80** = la largeur par défaut de cet écran est de 80

QUOTE The default values of columns cannot be set in the database schema, so different applications can trash the database.
Computing

defect *noun* faute *f* *or* défaut *m*; **a computer defect** *or* **a defect in the computer** = un défaut de l'ordinateur

◊ **defective** *adjective* défectueux, -euse; **the machine broke down because of a defective cooling system** = l'appareil est tombé en panne parce que le système de refroidissement était défectueux; (*fault with a hard disk*) **defective sector** = secteur défectueux

defensive computing *noun* informatique *f* *or* programmation *f* défensive

deferred addressing *noun* adressage *m* indirect

define *verb* définir; **all the variables were defined at initialization** = toutes les variables ont été définies lors de l'initialisation

◊ **definition** *noun* (*of screen, value*) définition *f*; **macro definition** = macrodéfinition *f*

deflect *verb* (*object or beam*) (faire) dévier

◊ **deflection** *noun* déviation *f or* déflexion *f*; **deflection yokes** = déflecteurs *mpl or* armature *f* de déflexion

defocus *verb* dérégler la mise au point

DEFRAG *(defragmentation utility in MS-DOS)* (utilitaire de défragmentation) DEFRAG

defragmentation *noun (reorganisation of files)* défragmentation *f*; *(software utility that carries out defragmentation)* **defragmentation utility** = utilitaire *m* de défragmentation

> COMMENT: when a file is saved to disk, it is not always saved in adjacent sectors; this will increase the retrieval time. Defragmentation moves files back into adjacent sectors so that the read head does not have to move far across the disk, and it increases performance

degauss *verb* démagnétiser; **the R/W heads have to be degaussed each week to ensure optimum performance** = il faut démagnétiser les têtes de lecture/écriture une fois par semaine pour obtenir une performance optimale

◊ **degausser** *noun* effaceur *m* magnétique

degradation *noun* **(a)** *(loss of picture quality)* dégradation *f*; **image degradation** = dégradation de l'image **(b)** *(of computers)* dégradation *or* réduction *f* des performances; **graceful degradation** = dégradation limitée *or* douce *or* progressive

DEL = DELETE; *(MS-DOS command)* (commande) DEL (effacer); **to delete all files with the extension BAK, use the command DEL** *or* **.BAK** = pour effacer tous les fichiers avec l'extension BAK, entrez la commande DEL *or* .BAK; *(key on a keyboard)* **DEL key** = touche *f* d'effacement DEL; touche Suppr (sur claviers français); **to remove a word from the screen, press the DEL key repeatedly** = pour effacer un mot à l'écran, appuyez plusieurs fois de suite sur la touche DEL *or* sur la touche Suppr

◊ **deletion** *(allowing deleted files to be undeleted)* **deletion tracking** = suivi *m or* traçage *m* des suppressions

delay 1 *noun* délai *m or* retard *m*; **there was a delay of thirty seconds before the printer started printing** = l'imprimante a commencé à imprimer après un délai de trente secondes; **delay distortion** = distorsion due au retard du signal; **delay equalizer** = égaliseur *m or* compensateur *m* de phase; **delay line** = ligne *f* à *or* de retard; **delay line store** = mémoire *m* à ligne de retard; **delay vector** = vecteur *m* de retard **2** *verb* retarder

delete *verb* **(a)** *(word in text)* rayer *or* effacer *or* supprimer **(b)** *(text or data from a storage device)* effacer *or* détruire *or* supprimer; **the word-processor allows us to delete the whole file by pressing this key** = le traitement de texte permet de supprimer un fichier complet en appuyant sur cette touche; **delete character** = caractère *m* de suppression *or* d'effacement; *see also* UNDELETE

◊ **deletion** *noun (cutting)* suppression *f or*

coupure *f*; *(erasing)* effacement *m or* suppression *f*; **the editors asked the author to make several deletions in the last chapter** = les éditeurs ont demandé à l'auteur de faire plusieurs coupures dans le dernier chapitre; **deletion record** = fichier *m* de coupures *or* de corrections; *(allowing deleted files to be undeleted)* **deletion tracking** = suivi *m or* traçage *m* des suppressions

delimit *verb* délimiter; *(where each item is separated by a comma)* **comma delimited** = délimité par virgule

◊ **delimiter** *noun (symbol or code)* délimiteur *m or* séparateur *m* (d'information)

delta *noun* connexion *f* (en) triangle *or* (en) delta; **delta clock** = horloge *f* delta *or* à relance automatique; **delta-delta** = (connexion) delta-delta; **delta modulation** = modulation *f* (en) delta; **delta routing** = acheminement *m* (en) delta

demagnetize *verb* démagnétiser

◊ **demagnetizer** *noun* effaceur *m* magnétique; **he used the demagnetizer to degauss the tape heads** = il s'est servi d'un effaceur magnétique pour démagnétiser les têtes de lecture

demand 1 *noun* **(a)** demande *f* (impérative) *or* réclamation *f*; **demand assigned multiple access (DAMA)** = accès multiple asservi à la demande; **demand multiplexing** = multiplexage asservi à la demande; **demand paging** = appel *f* de page sur demande; **demand processing** = traitement *m* (de données) sur demande *or* immédiat; *(loading protocol stacks in memory)* **demand protocol architecture (DPA)** = architecture *f* DPA; *see also* PROTOCOL STACK; **demand reading/writing** = lecture-écriture sur demande *or* directe; *(moving data from a secondary storage)* **demand staging** = transfert *m* sur demande (d'une mémoire à une autre) **2** *verb* demander *or* réclamer *or* exiger; **she demanded her money back** = elle a exigé *or* réclamé un remboursement

demarcation *noun* (ligne de) démarcation *f*; **demarcation strip** = (mise à nu de) protection *f*

demo = DEMONSTRATION démo *f*

◊ **demo disk** *noun* version *f* de démonstration *or* démo *f*

democratic network *noun* réseau *m* démocratique

demodulation *noun* démodulation *f*

◊ **demodulator** *noun* démodulateur *m*; *see also* MODEM

demonstrate *verb* expliquer (le fonctionnement de quelque chose) *or* faire une démonstration *or* démontrer; **he demonstrated the file management program** = il a fait une démonstration du programme de gestion de fichiers

◊ **demonstration** *or* **demo** *noun* **(a)** démonstration *f*; **demonstration model** = modèle *m* de démonstration **(b)** *(software that shows what* *an application is like)* **demonstration software** = logiciel *m* de démonstration *or* version *f* de démonstration (d'un logiciel) *or* démo *f;* **the company gave away demonstration software that lets you do everything except save your data** = l'entreprise a distribué gratuitement des versions de démonstration *or* des démos qui permettent de tout faire sauf de sauvegarder les données

demultiplex *verb* démultiplexer

◊ **demultiplexor** *noun* démultiplexeur *m*

denary notation *noun* numérotation *f* décimale *or* dénaire

denial *noun* déni *m or* négation *f;* **alternative denial** = opération *f* NON-ET; **joint denial** = négation *f* connexe *or* opération NON-OU *or* NI

dense index *noun* index *m* complet; **dense list** = liste *f* complète

◊ **densitometer** *noun* densitomètre *m*

◊ **density** *noun* **(a)** *(amount of light that a negative blocks)* densité *f* **(b)** *(of printed image or text)* densité; **density dial** = (bouton de) réglage *m* de densité d'impression; **when fading occurs, turn the density dial on the printer to full black** = si l'impression est trop pâle, réglez le bouton de densité (d'impression) sur le noir **(c)** *(amount of data that can be packed into a space)* densité; **double density disk (DD)** = disquette *f* double densité (DD); **high density disk (HD)** = disquette haute densité (HD); **quad density disk (QD)** = disquette quadruple densité (QD); **single density disk (SD)** = disquette simple densité (SD); **packing** *or* **recording density** = densité d'enregistrement

---
QUOTE diode lasers with shorter wavelengths will make doubling of the bit and track densities possible

Byte
---

deny access (to) *verb* interdire l'accès (à un circuit *or* à un système)

dependent *adjective* dépendant, -e; **a process which is dependent on the result of another process** = procédé dépendant des résultats *or* relié aux résultats d'un autre procédé; **the output is dependent on the physical state of the link** = le résultat de sortie est fonction de l'état (physique) des liaisons; **machine dependent** = (logiciel) non standard *or* qui ne fonctionne que sur un type d'appareil

deposit 1 *noun (thin layer)* dépôt *m* **2** *verb* **(a)** *(to print out the content of memory)* vider (le contenu d'une mémoire) **(b)** *(to coat a surface)* enduire *or* recouvrir d'une couche **(c)** *(to write data)* enregistrer *or* mettre en registre *or* en mémoire auxilliaire

◊ **deposition** *noun (on semiconductor)* enduction *f or* dépôt *m or* pose *f* d'un enduit

depth of field *noun* profondeur *f* de champ; **depth of focus** = profondeur *f* de foyer

deque *noun* = DOUBLE-ENDED QUEUE

derive *verb* provenir (de) *or* dériver (de); **derived indexing** = indexage dérivé; **derived sound** = son dérivé

◊ **derivation graph** *noun* graphe *m* de relation

DES = DATA ENCRYPTION STANDARD

descender *noun (of 'q' or 'p')* jambage *m* (descendant)

de-scramble *verb (coded message)* déchiffrer *or* désembrouiller

◊ **de-scrambler** *noun* désembrouilleur *m or* décodeur *m*

describe *verb* décrire; **the leaflet describes the services the company can offer** = le prospectus contient une description des services offerts par la société; **the specifications are described in greater detail at the back of the manual** = on trouve une description plus détaillée des spécifications à la fin du manuel

◊ **description** *noun* description *f;* **description list** = liste *f* descriptive; **data description language (DDL)** = langage *m* de description de données; **page description language (PDL)** = langage de description de pages

◊ **descriptor** *noun* descripteur *m or* mot-clé *m*

design 1 *noun (planning)* conception *f or* design *m;* *(drawing)* esquisse *f;* **circuit design** = tracé *m* d'un circuit; **industrial design** = esthétique *f* industrielle; **product design** = conception *f* de produits; **design department** = bureau *m* d'études; **design parameters** = spécifications *fpl or* contraintes *fpl or* paramètres *mpl* de conception *or* de création; **design studio** = studio *m* de création *or* de design **2** *verb* dessiner *or* concevoir; **he designed a new chip factory** = il a fait les plans *or* l'étude de la nouvelle usine de composants

◊ **designer** *noun* dessinateur, -trice *or* concepteur, -trice *or* designer *m&f;* **she is the designer of the new computer** = c'est elle qui a conçu *or* réalisé le nouvel ordinateur

desk *noun* bureau *m;* **desk diary** = agenda *m* de bureau; **desk light** = lampe *f* de bureau; **desk check** = contrôle *m* (d'un programme) sur papier

◊ **desk accessory (DA)** *noun (Apple Macintosh utility that enhances the system)* accessoire *m* de bureau; **we have installed several DAs that help us manage our fonts** = nous avons installé plusieurs accessoires de bureau qui nous aident à gérer les polices de caractères

desktop *adjective* **(a) desktop computer (system)** = ordinateur *m* de bureau; *(Apple Macintosh system file)* **Desktop file** = fichier *m* bureau (Apple Macintosh); **desktop presentation** = présentation *f* de page assistée par ordinateur (PRéAO); **desktop publishing (DTP)** = publication *f* assistée par ordinateur (PAO) *or* édition *f* électronique **(b)** *(workspace that is a graphical representation of a real-life desktop)* bureau

COMMENT: a desktop makes it easier for a new user to operate a computer, they do not have to type in commands, instead they can point at icons on the desktop using a mouse

QUOTE desktop publishing or the ability to produce high-quality publications using a minicomputer, essentially boils down to combining words and images on pages

Byte

desolder *verb* dessouder

◊ **desoldering tool** *noun* dessoudeur *m*

despool *verb* imprimer la file d'attente

despotic network *noun* réseau *m* (avec synchronisation) despotique

de-spun antenna *noun* antenne *f* contrarotative

DESQview ™ *noun (multitasking function for MS-DOS)* (logiciel multitâche) DESQview ™

destination *noun* destination *f*

destructive addition *noun* addition *f* destructive

◊ **destructive cursor** *noun* curseur *m* destructif; **reading the screen becomes difficult without a destructive cursor** = l'écran devient presqu'illisible sans le curseur destructif; **destructive read** = lecture *f* destructive; **destructive readout (DRO)** = lecture destructive

detail 1 *noun* détail *m*; **detail file** = fichier *m* (de) mouvements; **in detail** = en détail; **the catalogue lists all the products in detail** = le catalogue présente une liste détaillée de tous les produits; **detail paper** = papier-calque *m* **2** *verb* énumérer *or* détailler *or* expliquer en détail

detect *verb* détecter *or* trouver; **the equipment can detect faint signals from the transducer** = l'appareil peut détecter les signaux faibles émis par le transducteur; **detected error** = erreur notifiée *or* détectée; **error detecting codes** = codes *mpl* de détection d'erreurs

◊ **detection** *noun* détection *f*; **the detection of the cause of the fault is proving difficult** = il est difficile de trouver la source du problème

◊ **detector** *noun* détecteur *m*; **metal detector** = détecteur de métal

deterministic *adjective* déterministe

develop *verb* **(a)** développer *or* mettre au point; **to develop a new product** = développer un nouveau produit **(b)** *(film)* développer

◊ **developer** *noun* **(a)** *(person)* **software developer** = créateur, -trice *or* concepteur, -trice *or* développeur *m* de logiciel *or* expert en création de logiciel **(b)** *(photography)* révélateur *m*

◊ **development** *noun* développement *m or* mise *f* au point; **research and development (R&D)** =

recherche *f* et développement (R et D); **development software** = logiciel *m* de développement; **development time** = temps de développement *or* de mise au point d'un nouveau produit

device *noun* dispositif *m or* (petit) appareil *m* *(linked to a computer)* périphérique *m*; *(location within memory used by a particular device)* **device address** = adresse *f* de contrôleur de périphérique; **device character control** = (système de) contrôle *m* de périphérique par caractère; **device code** = code *m* d'identification de périphérique; **device control character** = caractère de contrôle *or* de commande de périphérique; **device driver** = routine *f* de gestion de périphérique; **device flag** = marqueur *m or* témoin *m or* (bit) indicateur *m* d'utilisation *or* d'état; *(program)* **device independent** = (programme) indépendant *or* non tributaire *or* non spécialisé; *(abbreviation that denotes a device)* **device name** = nom *m* de périphérique (sous forme d'abréviation); **device priority** = priorité *f* d'un périphérique *or* d'un appareil; **the master console has a higher device priority than the printers and other terminals** = la console de commande a priorité sur l'imprimante et les autres terminaux; **device queue** = file *f* d'attente (de périphériques); **device status word (DSW)** = mot indicateur d'état; **this routine checks the device status word and will not transmit data if the busy bit is set** = cette routine vérifie l'indicateur d'état et ne transmet pas le signal si le bit occupé est présent; **I/O device** = appareil *or* périphérique *or* dispositif d'entrée/sortie; **output device** = appareil *or* périphérique *or* dispositif de sortie

QUOTE Users in remote locations can share ideas on the Liveboard through the use of a wireless pen-input device and network connections.

Computing

Dewey decimal classification *noun* *(library)* classification *f* (suivant la méthode de) Dewey

DFD = DATA FLOW DIAGRAM

Dhrystone benchmark *noun (benchmarking system)* test *m* comparatif de performance Dhrystone *or* benchmark *m* Dhrystone; *see also* BENCHMARK

diacritic *noun* signe *m* diacritique

diagnose *verb* diagnostiquer *or* trouver

◊ **diagnosis** *noun* diagnostic *m*

diagnostic *noun* diagnostic *m*; **diagnostic aid** = aide *f* au diagnostic; **diagnostic chip** = circuit *m* intégré *or* puce *f* de diagnostic; **diagnostic message** = message *m* de diagnostic; **diagnostic program** = logiciel *m* de diagnostic; **diagnostic routine** = routine *f* de diagnostic; **diagnostic test** = test *m* de diagnostic; **self-diagnostic** = auto-diagnostic *m*

◊ **diagnostics** *noun* outils *mpl* de diagnostic; **compiler diagnostics** = outils de diagnostic du compilateur; **thorough compiler diagnostics make**

debugging easy = les outils de diagnostic de compilation bien conçus facilitent le débogage; **error diagnostics** = outils de diagnostic d'erreurs

QUOTE the implementation of on-line diagnostic devices that measure key observable parameters

Byte

QUOTE to check for any hardware problems, a diagnostic disk is provided

Personal Computer World

diagonal cut *noun* coupe *f* (en) diagonale *or* en biseau

diagram *noun* diagramme *m or* graphique *m*; *(of data)* **flow diagram** = ordinogramme *m*

◊ **diagrammatic** *adjective* in diagrammatic **form** = sous forme de schéma; **the chart showed the sales pattern in diagrammatic form** = le tableau présentait la courbe des ventes sous forme de diagramme *or* de façon schématique

◊ **diagramatically** *adverb* sous forme de diagramme *or* de schéma; **the chart shows the sales pattern diagramatically** = le tableau présente la courbe des ventes sous forme de diagramme

dial 1 *verb (telephone)* **to dial a number** = composer *or* faire un numéro (de téléphone); **to dial the operator** = appeler la standardiste; **he dialled the code for the USA** = il a composé l'indicatif des Etats-Unis; **to dial direct** = appeler en direct; **you can dial New York direct from London** = vous pouvez appeler New York en direct depuis Londres; *(modem or telephone)* **auto-dial** = système d'appel *m* automatique (d'un correspondant) *or* système de numérotation automatique; **to dial into** = se connecter *or* entrer dans; **with the right access code it is possible to dial into a customer's computer to extract the files needed for the report** = avec un code d'accès valide, il est possible d'entrer dans le système du client et d'extraire les fichiers utiles pour établir le rapport (NOTE: GB English is **dialling - dialled**, but US spelling is **dialing - dialed**) **2** *noun (used to select or validate)* bouton *m or* réglage *m*; *(on telephone or clock)* cadran *m*; **to tune into the radio station, turn the dial** = pour obtenir la station de radio, tournez ce bouton; **dial conference** = (facilité de) téléconférence *f* par sélection *or* par composition; **dial pulse** = impulsion *f* de cadran; **dial tone** = tonalité *f* (d'appel); **dial-in modem** = modem *m* à appel automatique; **density dial** = bouton de densité; **if the text fades, turn the density dial on the printer to full black** = si l'impression est trop pâle, réglez le bouton de densité (d'impression) sur le noir

◊ **dialling** *noun* composition *f or* appel *f* (d'un numéro de téléphone) *or* numérotation *f*; **dialling code** = indicatif *m* téléphonique; **dialling tone** = tonalité *f* (d'appel); **direct dialling** = système d'acheminement direct des appels *or* l'automatique *m*; **international direct dialling (IDD)** = système *m* téléphonique automatique international

◊ **dialup** *or* **dial-up service** *noun (online information service)* service *m* d'appels

dialect *noun* dialecte *m*; **this manufacturer's dialect of BASIC is a little different to the one I'm used to** = cette version du BASIC offerte par le fabricant est légèrement différente de celle que j'utilise

dialogue *or* **dialog** *noun* dialogue *m*; *(on-screen message)* **dialogue box** = boîte *f or* fenêtre *f* de dialogue

diameter *noun* diamètre *m*

DIANE = DIRECT INFORMATION ACCESS NETWORK FOR EUROPE

diaphragm *noun* **(a)** *(photography)* diaphragme *m* **(b)** *(loudspeaker or microphone)* diaphragme; **the diaphragm in the microphone picks up sound waves** = le diaphragme d'un microphone capte les ondes sonores

diapositive *noun* diapositive *f or* diapo *f*

diary *noun* agenda *m or* journal *m*; **diary management** = (programme) agenda

diascope *noun* projecteur *m* de diapositives

diazo (process) *noun* diazocopie *f*

DIB = DATA INPUT BUS

dibit *noun* dibit *m or* groupe de 2 chiffres binaires

dichotomizing search *noun* (méthode de) recherche *f* dichotomique *or* par dichotomie

dichroic *adjective* dichroïque

dictate *verb* dicter; **to dictate a letter to a secretary** = dicter une lettre à une secrétaire; **he was dictating orders into his pocket dictating machine** = il enregistrait ses instructions sur son Dictaphone de poche; **dictating machine** = machine *f* à dicter *or* Dictaphone ™ *m*

◊ **dictation** *noun* dictée *f*; **to take dictation** = prendre en dictée; **dictation speed** = vitesse *f* de sténographie

dictionary *noun (reference book or spelling checker or data)* dictionnaire *m*; **exception dictionary** = liste *f or* répertoire *m* d'exceptions; *see also* SPELL-CHECKER

dielectric *noun* diélectrique *m*

DIF file = DATA INTERCHANGE FORMAT

differ *verb* différer *or* être différent (de); **the two products differ considerably - one has an external hard disk, the other has internal hard disk and external magnetic tape drive** = il existe une grande différence entre les deux produits: l'un d'eux possède un disque dur externe, tandis que l'autre est équipé d'un disque dur interne et d'un dérouleur de bande (magnétique) externe

◊ **difference** *noun* différence *f*; **symmetric difference** = exclusion réciproque *or* OU exclusif *or* non-équivalence

◊ **different** *adjective* différent, -e; **our product range is quite different in design from the Japanese models** = notre gamme de produits est d'une conception entièrement différente de celle des modèles japonais

◊ **differential** *adjective* différentiel, -elle; **differential pulse code modulation** *or* **differential PCM** = modulation *f* par impulsions et codage (MIC)

diffuse *verb* (se) diffuser *or* (se) répandre; **the smoke from the faulty machine rapidly diffused through the building** = la fumée produite par la machine défectueuse s'est répandue rapidement dans tout l'immeuble; **the chemical was diffused into the substrate** = il y a eu diffusion du produit chimique dans le substrat

◊ **diffusion** *noun* diffusion *f or* dopage *m* par diffusion

Digipulse ™ **telephone** *noun* téléphone *m* (à impulsion numérique) Digipulse

digit *noun* chiffre *m*; **a phone number with eight digits** *or* **an eight-digit phone number** = un numéro de téléphone de huit chiffres; **the decimal digit 8** = le chiffre décimal 8 *or* la décimale 8; **the decimal number system uses the digits 0123456789** = la base de numération décimale utilise les chiffres 0123456789; **check digit** = chiffre *or* clé *f* (numérique) de contrôle; **digit place** *or* **position** = place *f* d'un chiffre

◊ **digital** *adjective* numérique *or* digital, -e; **digital to analog converter** *or* **D to A converter (DAC)** = convertisseur *m* numérique-analogique; *(system of recording sound as digital information)* **digital audio tape (DAT)** = (système d') enregistrement *m* sur bande audionumérique; *see also* DAT TAPE; *(camera that uses a bank of CCD units to capture an image)* **digital camera** = caméra *f* numérique; **digital cassette** = cassette *f* audionumérique; **digital circuit** = circuit *m* numérique; **digital clock** = horloge *f* numérique; **digital computer** = ordinateur *m* numérique; **digital data** = données *fpl* numériques *or* numérisées; *(video display)* **digital display** = écran *m* numérique *or* digital; affichage *m* numérique; **digital logic** = logique *f* numérique; **digital multimeter (DMM)** = multimètre *m* numérique; **digital optical reading (DOR)** = lecture *f* optique de données numériques; **digital output** = sortie *f* numérique; **digital plotter** = traceur *m* numérique; **digital readout** = affichage *m* numérique; **digital recording** = enregistrement *m* numérique; **digital representation** = représentation *f* numérique; **digital resolution** = résolution *f* d'un nombre; **digital signal** = signal *m* numérique; *(IC used to manipulate digital signals)* **digital signal processing (DSP)** = circuit *m* DSP *or* de numérisation *f* des signaux; **digital signalling** = transmission *f* de signaux numériques; **digital signature** = signature numérique; **digital speech** = voix numérisée *or* de synthèse; **digital system** = système *m* numérique; **digital switching** = (système de) commutation *f* numérique; **digital transmission system** = système de transmission numérique; *(defines how video and audio signals should be compressed)* **digital video interactive**

(DV-I) = système *m* DV-I *or* vidéo numérisée interactive

> QUOTE Xerox Parc's LCD breakthrough promises the digital equivalent of paper, by producing thin, low-cost flat displays with a 600dpi resolution.
> *Computing*

◊ **digitally** *adverb* numériquement *or* sous forme numérique; **the machine takes digitally recorded data and generates an image** = l'appareil produit une image à partir de données enregistrées sous forme numérique

digitize *verb* numériser; **we can digitize your signature to allow it to be printed with any laser printer** = il nous est possible de numériser votre signature pour qu'elle puisse être imprimée par n'importe quelle imprimante (à) laser; **digitized photograph** = photographie *f* numérisée; **digitizing pad** = tablette *f* graphique *or* tablette à numériser

◊ **digitizer** *noun* convertisseur *m* analogique-numérique *or* numériseur *m*

> QUOTE The contract covers fibre optic cable and Synchronous Digital Hierarchy transmission equipment to be used to digitize the telecommunications network.
> *Computergram*

DIL = DUAL-IN-LINE PACKAGE

dimension *noun* dimension *f*; **the dimensions of the computer are small enough for it to fit into a case** = l'ordinateur est assez petit pour tenir dans un porte-documents

◊ **dimensioning** *noun* calcul *m* des dimensions; **array dimensioning occurs at this line** = le calcul des dimensions du tableau se fait à ce niveau-ci

diminished radix complement *noun* complément *m* restreint

DIN = DEUTSCHE INDUSTRIE NORM; *(German industry standards organisation)* DIN

Dingbat ™ *noun (font)* Dingbat ™ *or* police *f* de caractères spéciaux; **to insert a copyright symbol, use the Dingbat font** = pour insérer une marque de copyright, utilisez les caractères spéciaux

diode *noun* diode *f*; **light-emitting diode (LED)** = diode électroluminescente; *(indicator light)* lampe *f* témoin *or* voyant *m* (lumineux)

> QUOTE Sullivan would not reveal the launch power of the diode, except that it was twice that of existing LEDs because of the higher efficiency of electron injection in the part.
> *Electronic Times*

dioptre, *US* **diopter** *noun* dioptrie *f*; **diopter lens** = lentille *f* dioptrique

DIP = DOCUMENT IMAGE PROCESSING

DIP = DUAL-IN-LINE PACKAGE

diplex *noun* duplex *m*

dipole *noun* (i) dipôle *m* ; (ii) doublet *m*

DIP switch *noun* commutateur *m* DIP *or* à bascule

DIR = DIRECTORY; *(MS-DOS system command)* (commande) DIR (de recherche de fichier)

direct 1 *verb* diriger; **directed scan** = balayage *m* dirigé **2** *adjective* direct, -e; **direct access** = accès direct; **direct (access) address** = adresse absolue *or* directe; **direct access storage device (DASD)** = mémoire *f or* support *m* à accès direct; **direct addressing** = adressage direct; *(TV or radio)* **direct broadcast satellite (DBS)** = satellite *m* de diffusion directe; **direct change-over** = transfert direct; **direct code** = code direct *or* à un niveau; **direct coding** = codage direct; **direct connect** = connexion directe; **direct current (DC)** = courant *m* continu; **direct data entry (DDE)** = saisie *f* directe de données (au clavier) *or* entrée directe de données; *(telephone)* **direct dialling** = système d'acheminement direct des appels *or* l'automatique *m*; **direct digital control (DDC)** = commande numérique directe; **direct image film** = film *m* positif; **direct impression** = impression directe; **direct information access network for Europe (DIANE)** = DIANE; **direct-insert routine** *or* **subroutine** = programme *or* sous-programme d'insertion directe; **direct instruction** = instruction directe; *(automatic routing of phone calls in a private exchange)* **direct inward dialling** = accès direct à un poste; **direct memory access (DMA)** = accès direct à la mémoire (DMA); **direct memory access transfer between the main memory and the second processor** = transfert des données par accès direct (à la mémoire) entre la mémoire principale et le second processeur; **direct memory access channel** = voie d'accès direct à la mémoire; **direct mode** = mode direct; *(automatic access to a telephone network from a private exchange)* **direct outward dialling** = accès direct au réseau; *(of memory page)* **direct page register** = registre *m* de pagination à accès direct; **direct reference address** = adresse de référence directe; **direct transfer** = transfert direct **3** *adverb* directement *or* en direct; **to dial direct** = appeler *or* téléphoner en direct; **you can dial New York direct from London if you want** = vous pouvez appeler New York en direct depuis Londres

◊ **direction** *noun* **(a)** direction *f or* gestion *f*; **he took over the direction of a software distribution group** = c'est lui qui est maintenant à la tête du groupe de diffusion de logiciels **(b)** **directions for use** = mode *m* d'emploi

◊ **directional** *adjective* directionnel, -elle; **directional antenna** = antenne (uni)directionnelle; **directional pattern** = empreinte directionnelle

◊ **directive** **1** *noun* directive *f* **2** *adjective* **directive statement** = instruction directive

◊ **directly** *adverb* **(a)** *(immediately)* immédiatement **(b)** *(straight)* directement

◊ **director** *noun* **(a)** *(of company)* directeur, -trice; **managing director** = directeur général;

board of directors = conseil *m* d'administration **(b)** *(of project)* directeur, -trice *or* responsable *m&f*; **the director of the government computer research institute** = le directeur de l'institut de recherche informatique gouvernemental; **she was appointed director of the organization** = elle a été nommée directrice de l'organisation **(c)** *(of film or TV program)* réalisateur, -trice; **casting director** = responsable *m* de la distribution; **lighting director** = chef *m* éclairagiste; **technical director** = directeur technique

> QUOTE directives are very useful for selecting parts of the code for particular purposes
> *Personal Computer World*

directory *noun* **(a)** annuaire *m or* répertoire *m* d'adresses; **classified directory** = annuaire par professions; **commercial directory** *or* **trade directory** = répertoire d'entreprises; **street directory** = annuaire par rues *or* répertoire d'adresses par rues; **telephone directory** = annuaire téléphonique *or* des téléphones; le Bottin **(b)** *(method of organizing the files stored on a disk)* **disk directory** = répertoire (des fichiers); **the disk directory shows file name, date and time of creation** = on trouve les noms des fichiers, la date et l'heure de leur création dans le répertoire; **directory routing** = routage *m* par répertoire; *(MS-DOS, OS/2 and UNIX system command)* **change directory (CD or CHDR)** = (commande) CD (de changement de répertoire); *(MS-DOS and OS/2 system command)* **make directory (MD)** = (commande) MD (de création de répertoire); *(MS-DOS and OS/2 system command)* **remove directory (RD)** = (commande) RD (d'effacement de répertoire); *(directory from which all other directories branch)* **root directory** = répertoire racine *or* de départ; *(directory within a directory)* **sub-directory** = sous-répertoire *m*; *see also* TREE STRUCTURE

> COMMENT: a directory is best imagined as a folder within a drawer of a filing cabinet; the folder can contain files or other folders

dirty bit *noun* bit *m* marqué

disable *verb* invalider *or* mettre hors service; **he disabled the keyboard to prevent anyone changing the data** = il a mis le clavier hors service pour éviter qu'on change les données; **disable interrupt** = commande *f* d'invalidation d'interruption

disarm *verb* invalider *or* désactiver; **disarmed state** = état désactivé

disassemble *verb* désassembler

◊ **disassembler** *noun* désassembleur *m*

disaster dump *noun* vidage *m* irréversible

disc *noun* disque *m* compact; *see* COMPACT DISC (NOTE: the spelling 'disc' refers to compact discs, optical discs, etc.; magnetic media uses the spelling 'disk')

discard *verb* jeter *or* se défaire de (quelque chose) *or* mettre au rebut

disclose *verb* révéler

◊ **disclosure** *noun* révélation *f*

disconnect *verb* débrancher *or* déconnecter; **do not forget to disconnect the cable before moving the printer** = n'oubliez pas de débrancher (le câble de) l'imprimante avant de la changer de place

discrete *adjective* *(in small individual units)* discret, -ète; **a data word is made up of discrete bits** = le mot de données est formé de bits discrets

discretionary *adjective* discrétionnaire *or* au choix; **discretionary hyphen** *or* **soft hyphen** = trait d'union qui ne s'imprime pas *or* qui n'apparaît que sur l'écran

discrimination instruction *noun* instruction *f* (d'opération) conditionnelle

dish aerial *noun* antenne *f* parabolique; **we use a dish aerial to receive signals from the satellite** = nous utilisons une antenne parabolique pour capter les signaux transmis par satellite

disjointed *adjective* disjoint, -e *or* (données) qui n'ont aucune relation *or* aucun rapport (entre elles)

disjunction *noun* *(logical function)* disjonction *f or* opération *f* OU *or* opération de réunion *or* d'union

◊ **disjunctive search** *noun* recherche *f* par mots-clés

disk *noun* *(record or computer hard disk)* disque *m*; *(floppy)* disquette *f*; **backup disk** = disque *or* disquette de sauvegarde; **disk access** = accès *m* au disque; **disk-based (operating system)** = système d'exploitation utilisant un disque dur *or* des disquettes; **disk cartridge** = cartouche *f* disque *or* disque dur amovible *or* chargeur *m*; **disk controller** = contrôleur *m* de disque *or* de disquette; **disk-controller card** = carte *f* contrôleur de disque(tte); **disk crash** = crash *m or* panne *f* totale d'un disque *or* d'une disquette; **(hard) disk drive** = (unité de) disque dur; **(floppy) disk drive** = lecteur de disquette(s); unité *f* de disque *or* de disquette; **disk file** = fichier sur disque *or* sur disquette; **disk formatting** = formatage de disque *or* de disquette; **disk index holes** = perforations *fpl* de marquage (du bord) d'un disque; **disk map** = table *f* (de classement des fichiers) du disque; *(data protection system)* **disk mirroring** *or* **duplexing** = copie *f* miroir *or* duplication *f* de données sur un disque miroir *or* mirroring *m*; **disk operating system (DOS)** = système *m* d'exploitation de disque *or* (système) DOS; **MS disk operating system** *or* **Microsoft DOS (MS-DOS)** ™ = (système d'exploitation) MS-DOS™; **disk pack** = (pile de) plateaux *mpl* de disque dur; **disk sector** = secteur *m* de disque; **disk storage** = mémoire *f* sur disque; sauvegarde sur disque; *(capacity)* capacité *f* de mémoire (de disque *or* disquette); **disk track** = piste *f* d'un disque; **disk unit** = unité *f* de disque(s) *or* lecteur *m* de disque(s); **fixed disk** = disque (dur) fixe *or* non amovible; **floppy disk** = disquette *f*; **hard disk** = disque dur; **Winchester**

disk = disque (dur de type) Winchester; *see also* CD, COMPACT

◊ **diskette** *noun* disquette *f*

◊ **diskless** *adjective* sans disque; **diskless system** = système qui n'utilise pas de disque *or* de disquette; **they want to create a diskless workstation** = ils veulent créer un poste de travail qui n'utilise pas de disque

disorderly close-down *noun* panne désordonnée *or* arrêt désordonné

dispatch *or* **despatch** *noun* envoi *m*

dispenser *noun* distributeur *m*; **cash dispenser** = distributeur automatique de billets (de banque) (DAB) *or* billetterie *f*

dispersion *noun* **(a)** *(of beam)* dispersion *f* **(b)** *(logical function)* fonction *f* NON-ET

displacement *noun* déplacement *m*

display 1 *noun* affichage *m or* visualisation *f*; **character display** = affichage de caractères *or* de texte; **display adapter** = adaptateur *m* d'écran; **display attribute** = attribut *m* d'écran; **display character** = caractère *m* d'écran; **display character generator** = générateur *m* de caractères d'écran; **display colour** = couleur *f* d'affichage; **display controller** = contrôleur *m* d'écran; **display format** = format *m* d'affichage *or* format d'écran; **display highlights** = mots *mpl or* caractères *mpl* mis en évidence par affichage plus lumineux ou couleur contrastée; *(on screen)* mot *or* caractères en surbrillance; **display line** = ligne *f* d'écran; **display mode** = mode *m* affichage *or* visualisation; **display processor** = processeur *m* d'écran; **display register** = registre *m* d'affichage; **display resolution** = définition *f* de l'écran; **display screen** = écran *m* de visualisation; **display scrolling** = défilement *m* (du texte sur l'écran); **display size** = dimension *f* d'affichage; **display space** = espace *m* d'affichage; **display unit** = unité *f* de visualisation *or* de visu *or* écran (de visualisation); **backlit display** = écran *m* rétroéclairé; *(video display unit that can display any colours)* **composite display** = écran *m* composite; affichage *m* composite; *(video display unit that can display some colours)* **digital display** = écran numérique; **liquid crystal display (LCD)** = affichage à cristaux liquides **2** *verb* afficher; **the customer's details were displayed on the screen** = les coordonnées du client étaient affichées sur l'écran; **by keying HELP, the screen will display the options available to the user** = la touche HELP fera apparaître sur l'écran une description des différentes options; *see also* GAS

QUOTE the review machine also came with a monochrome display card plugged into one of the expansion slots
Personal Computer World

QUOTE Barco Chromatics is to supply colour display monitors to the IBM/Siemens Plessey consortium, which is installing the New En Route Centre for air-traffic control.
Computing

distance *noun* distance *f*; **signal distance** *or* **Hamming distance** = distance entre signaux *or* distance de Hamming

◊ **distant** *adjective* éloigné, -ée *or* distant, -e *or* à distance; **the distant printers are connected with cables** = les imprimantes à distance sont reliées par câbles

distinguish *verb* faire la distinction (entre une chose et une autre) *or* reconnaître (une chose); **an OCR has difficulty in distinguishing certain characters** = le lecteur optique reconnaît mal certains caractères

distort *verb* déformer

◊ **distortion** *noun* distorsion *f or* aberration *f or* altération *f*; **distortion optics** = lentille *f* déformante; **image distortion** = déformation *or* distorsion *or* aberration de l'image

distribute *verb* **(a)** distribuer; faire circuler; **distributed adaptive routing** = routage *m* adaptatif *or* flexible; **distributed database system** = système de base de données réparti *or* en réseau; **distributed data processing (DDP)** = informatique répartie; **distributed file system** = système de fichiers partagés *or* répartis; **distributed intelligence** = intelligence répartie; **distributed processing** = DISTRIBUTED DATA PROCESSING **distributed system** = système *m* décentralisé *or* réparti

QUOTE CORBA sets out a standard for how objects in applications, repositories or class libraries should make requests and receive responses across a distributed computing network.
Computing

◊ **distribution** *noun* distribution *f*; **distribution network** = réseau *m* de distribution; **distribution point** = point *m or* centre *m* de distribution

disturbance *noun* *(of the signal)* perturbation *f*

dither *verb* *(make a line smoother)* adoucir (une ligne)

dittogram *noun* *(printing error)* doublet *m*

DIV = DATA IN VOICE

divergence *noun* *(of beam)* divergence *f*

diversity *noun* diversité *f*; **beam diversity** = dédoublement *m* de faisceau

diverter *noun* dispositif *m* de transfert *or* de déroutage; **call diverter** = dispositif de transfert d'appel

divide *verb* **(a)** diviser; **to divide a number by four** = diviser un nombre par quatre; **twenty-one divided by three gives seven** = vingt-et-un divisé par trois égale sept **(b)** diviser *or* partager *or* couper (un mot); **in the hyphenation program, long words are automatically divided at the end of lines** = la coupure des mots trop longs se fait automatiquement en fin de ligne grâce au programme de césure

◊ **dividend** *noun* dividende *m*

◊ **divider** *noun* diviseur *m*; **frequency divider** = diviseur de fréquence

◊ **division** *noun* division *f or* partage *m*; *(of word)* coupure *f or* césure *f*

◊ **divisor** *noun* diviseur *m*

DLL = DYNAMIC LINK LIBRARY **DLL file** = fichier *m* DLL

DMA = DIRECT MEMORY ACCESS; *(interface IC that controls high-speed data transfer)* accès *m* direct à la mémoire *or* DMA; **DMA controller** = contrôleur *m* DMA *or* d'accès direct à la mémoire; **DMA cycle stealing** = accès direct à la mémoire par vol de cycle

QUOTE A 32-bit DMA controller, 16-bit video I/O ports and I/O filters complete the chip.
Computing

DML = DATA MANIPULATION LANGUAGE

DMM = DIGITAL MULTIMETER

DNS = DOMAIN NAME SYSTEM

document 1 *noun* document *m*; **document assembly** *or* **document merge** = fusion *f or* assemblage *m* de documents; *(IBM document format)* **document content architecture (DCA)** = architecture *f* de description de document *or* DCA; *(process of scanning paper documents)* **document image processing (DIP)** = procédé *m* de traitement d'image DIP; **document processing** = traitement *m* de texte *or* de document; **document reader** = lecteur *m* de documents; **document recovery** = récupération *f or* régénération *f* de document; **document retrieval system** = système de recherche documentaire *or* de documents 2 *verb* documenter *or* donner les renseignements appropriés *or* renseigner

◊ **documentation** *noun* **(a)** *(all documents)* documentation *f or* dossier *m* **(b)** *(information, notes, etc.)* documentation *or* renseignements *mpl*

dollar sign ($) *noun* signe *m* du dollar

domain *noun* **(a)** domaine *m*; **public domain** = domaine public; **program which is in the public domain** = programme du domaine public *or* qui n'est plus protégé par un copyright **(b)** *(area in a network)* domaine *m*; *(distributed database)* **domain name system (DNS)** = base *f* de données des adresses et des domaines (dans Internet) *or* DNS

domestic *adjective* domestique *or* national; **domestic satellite** = satellite *m* domestique

dongle *noun* circuit *m* crypté (de protection de logiciel) *or* clé *f* électronique

do-nothing (instruction) *noun* instruction *f* sans effet *or* ineffective

dope *verb* doper

◊ **dopant** *noun* dopant *m*

◊ **doped** *adjective* dopé, -ée *or* enduit, -e d'un dopant

◊ **doping** *noun* dopage *m*

DOR = DIGITAL OPTICAL READING

DOS = DISK OPERATING SYSTEM système d'exploitation de disque *or* (système) DOS; **boot up the DOS after you switch on the PC** = lancez le (système) DOS après la mise en route de l'ordinateur; *(operating system developed by Microsoft)* **MS-DOS** ™ = (système d'exploitation) MS-DOS ™; *(operating system developed by Digital Research)* **DR-DOS** ™ = (système d'exploitation) DR-DOS ™

dot *noun* point *m*; **dot command** = commande (précédée d'un) point; **dot matrix** = matrice *f* de points; **dots per inch** *or* **d.p.i.** *or* **dpi** = (nombre de) points par pouce *or* ppp; **some laser printers offer high resolution printing: 400 dpi** = certaines imprimantes (à) laser sont dotées d'une haute définition de 400 ppp *or* 400 points par pouce

◊ **dotted** *adjective* pointillé, -ée; **dotted line** = ligne pointillée *or* pointillé *m*

◊ **dot-matrix printer** *noun* imprimante *f* matricielle

QUOTE Star predicts that 500,000 customers will buy a dot matrix printer in the UK in the next 12 months.
Computing

QUOTE the characters are formed from an array of dots like in a dot-matrix printer, except that much higher resolution is used
Practical Computing

double *adjective* double; **double buffering** = utilisation *f* de double mémoire tampon; **double-click** = *(to click twice on the mouse)* double-cliquer; *(two clicks on the mouse)* double-clic *m*; **move the pointer to the icon then start the program with a double-click** = déplacer le pointeur sur l'icône puis démarrez le programme avec un double-clic; *(typography)* **double dagger** = croix *f* double (‡); **double density** = double densité; **double-density disk** = disquette *f* double densité; **double document** = doublon *m*; **double-ended queue (deque)** = file *f* d'attente à deux entrées *or* à deux extrémités; **double exposure** = double exposition; **double-length precision** *or* **double precision** = double précision; **double precision arithmetic** = calcul *m* en double précision; **double sideband** = double bande latérale; **double sideband suppressed carrier (DSBSC)** = (modulation d'amplitude à) double bande latérale sans porteuse *or* à porteuse inhibée; **double-sided disk** = disquette (à) double face; **double-sided disk drive** = lecteur *m* de disquettes (à) double face; **double-sided printed circuit board** = plaque (présensibilisée) double face pour circuit imprimé; **double word** = mot *m* double *or* long

doublet *or* **diad** *noun* doublet *m* *or* dyade *f*

down *adverb* **(a)** *(not working)* en panne; **the computer system went down twice during the afternoon** = l'ordinateur est tombé en panne deux fois cet après-midi; **down time** = temps *m* mort **(b)** *(of character)* **down stroke** = jambage *m* (descendant) (NOTE: opposite is **up**)

download *verb* *(to load a program or data from a remote computer via a telephone line; to load data from a CPU to a small computer; to send print font data stored on disk to a printer)* télécharger (des données, des polices de caractères, etc.); **there is no charge for downloading public domain software from the BBS** = il n'en coûte rien de télécharger, depuis le tableau d'affichage, un logiciel qui n'est pas protégé par un copyright

◊ **downloadable** *adjective* téléchargeable; **downloadable font** = police *f* de caractères téléchargeable

◊ **downloading** *noun* téléchargement *m*

QUOTE The cards will also download the latest version of the network drivers from the server.
Computing

downsize *verb* *(change from a central mainframe to a network)* réduire l'échelle (d'une configuration informatique); **downsizing is more cost effective and gives more processing power to the end-user** = la réduction d'échelle est très efficace sur le plan des coûts et donne plus de puissance de traitement à l'utilisateur

downward *adjective* vers le bas; **downward compatibility** = compatibilité *f* avec un système de niveau inférieur; **the mainframe is downward compatible with the micro** = le gros ordinateur est compatible avec le micro

dp *or* **DP** = DATA PROCESSING traitement *f* de l'information *or* traitement de données

DPA = DEMAND PROTOCOL ARCHITECTURE

d.p.i. *or* **dpi** = DOTS PER INCH (nombre de) points *mpl* par pouce *or* ppp; **a 300 d.p.i. black and white A4 monitor** = un moniteur monochrome format A4 avec une définition de 300 points par pouce; **a 300 dpi image scanner** = un scanner d'image avec définition de 300 ppp

DPM = DATA PROCESSING MANAGER

draft 1 *noun* brouillon *m* ; première mouture *f*; **draft printing** = (sortie d'imprimante) qualité *f* brouillon *or* qualité listing **2** *verb* faire un brouillon *or* ébaucher *or* esquisser; **he drafted out the details of the program on a piece of paper** = il a esquissé un projet de programme sur une feuille de papier

drag *verb* *(a mouse)* déplacer *or* glisser *or* traîner; *(a handle)* tirer; **you can enlarge a frame by clicking inside its border and dragging to the position wanted** = pour agrandir un cadre, vous cliquez à l'intérieur de ses limites et vous glissez jusqu'à la position voulue; *(to drag a section of text or icon or object onto another program icon)*

drag and drop = traîner/lâcher *or* glisser/lâcher; **drag and drop the document icon onto the word-processor icon and the system will start the program and load the document** = traînez l'icône document sur l'icône traitement de texte, puis lâchez la touche, le système démarrera le programme et chargera le document

QUOTE press the mouse button and drag the mouse: this produces a dotted rectangle on the screen

QUOTE you can easily enlarge the frame by dragging from any of the eight black rectangles round the border, showing that it is selected
Desktop Publishing

drain 1 *noun* courant *m* de décharge **2** *verb* épuiser *or* affaiblir *or* décharger

DRAM = DYNAMIC RANDOM ACCESS MEMORY

QUOTE cheap bulk memory systems are always built from DRAMs
Electronics & Power

DR-DOS™ *(operating system developed by Digital Research)* (système d'exploitation) DR-DOS ™

D-region *noun (ionosphere)* région *f* D; **the D-region is the main cause of attenuation in transmitted radio signals** = la région D est la principale cause d'affaiblissement des ondes radioélectriques

drift *noun (zone or resistance)* dérive *f*

drive 1 *noun (letter denoting the disk drive being used)* **drive letter** *or* **designator** = lettre *f* d'identification du lecteur *or* de l'unité de disque; **(hard) disk drive** = (unité de) disque dur; **(floppy) disk drive** = lecteur *m* de disquette(s); unité *f* de disque *or* de disquette; **tape drive** = lecteur *m or* dérouleur *m* de bande(s) magnétique(s) **2** *verb* faire marcher *or* faire fonctionner *or* entraîner; **the disk is driven by a motor** = un moteur entraîne le disque; *see also* NETWORK

◊ **driven** *adjective* (appareil) qui fonctionne (à l'électricité, etc.); **control driven** = commandé par les codes CTRL (générés par la touche contrôle) *or* asservi aux codes contrôle

◊ **driver** *or* **device driver** *or* **device handler** *noun* **(a)** logiciel *m* de commande de périphérique *or* gestionnaire *m* de périphérique; **printer driver** = gestionnaire *or* pilote *m* d'imprimante **(b) line driver** = amplificateur *m* de signal

DRO = DESTRUCTIVE READOUT

drop cable *noun (cable that links an adapter to the main network cable)* câble *m* de dérivation *or* de branchement

◊ **drop cap** *noun* lettrine *f*

◊ **drop dead halt** *or* **dead halt** *noun* arrêt *m* total

◊ **drop-down list box** *noun (list of options for an entry)* liste *f* déroulante *or* boîte *f* de liste

◊ **drop-down menu** *noun (menu that appears below a menu title)* menu *m* déroulant

◊ **drop in** *noun (on disk or tape)* parasite *m or* crasse *f*

◊ **drop line** *noun (cable television line running from a feeder cable to a user's home)* dérivation *f or* raccordement *m or* branchement *m*

◊ **drop out** *noun* **(a)** perte *f or* défaut *m* (de magnétisation) **(b)** *(of signal)* perte *f* de niveau

drum *noun* cylindre *m or* tambour *m*; **magnetic drum** = tambour magnétique; **drum plotter** = traceur *m or* enregistreur *m* à tambour

dry *adjective* sec, sèche; **dry cell** = pile *f* sèche *or* alcaline; **dry circuit** = circuit *m* vocal; **dry contact** = contact *m* sec *or* intermittent; **dry joint** = connexion *f* bricolée; **dry run** = essai *m* à blanc

DSBSC = DOUBLE SIDEBAND SUPPRESSED CARRIER

DSE = DATA SWITCHING EXCHANGE

DSP = DIGITAL SIGNAL PROCESSING

DSR = DATA SET READY

DSS = DECISION SUPPORT SYSTEM

DSW = DEVICE STATUS WORD

DTE = DATA TERMINAL EQUIPMENT

DTMF = DUAL TONE MULTI-FREQUENCY

DTP *or* **dtp** = DESKTOP PUBLISHING publication *f* assistée par ordinateur (PAO)

DTR = DATA TERMINAL READY

D-type connector *noun (connector shaped like the letter D)* connecteur *m* en D *or* de type D; **the serial port on a PC uses a 9-pin D-type connector** = le port série du PC utilise un connecteur à neuf broches de type D

dual *adjective* double; *(FDDI system station)* **dual attachment station (DAS)** = station *f* à double connexion (sur réseau FDDI); **dual channel** = voie *f* double; **dual clocking** = (à) double chronométrie *or* (à) décalage de fréquence; **dual column** = colonne *f* double; **dual-in-line package (DIL** *or* **DIP)** = système *m* à double rang de broches (parallèles); **dual port memory** = mémoire *f* à double accès; **dual processor** = processeur *m* double; **dual system** = système *m* double; **dual tone multi-frequency (DTMF)** = appel *m* à tonalité multifréquence; *compare with* PULSE DIALLING

dub *verb* doubler (un film); **dubbed sound** = effets *mpl* sonores postsynchronisés

◊ **dubbing** *noun* postsynchronisation *f or* doublage *m*

duct *noun* conduit *m*

dumb terminal *noun* terminal *m* non intelligent

dummy *noun* maquette *f*; **dummy instruction** = instruction *f* de remplissage; **dummy variable** = variable *f* factice

dump 1 *noun (data)* analyse *f* (de) mémoire; *(transferring of data)* vidage *m* or transfert *m* sur disque or sur support magnétique; *(copy)* vidage sur imprimante; **binary dump** = vidage binaire; **change dump** = vidage de mouvements (sur imprimante); **dump and restart** = (instruction de) vidage et reprise; **dump point** = point *m* de vidage; **memory dump** = listage *m* de mémoire or vidage de mémoire sur imprimante; **screen dump** = vidage d'écran sur imprimante **2** *verb* copier or transférer or vider; **the account results were dumped to the backup disk** = les résultats comptables ont été transférés sur le disque de sauvegarde

duodecimal number system *noun* système *m* duodécimal

duplex *noun* **(a)** *(photographic paper)* papier *m* photosensible double face **(b)** *(transmission of two signals)* (transmission) duplex *m*; **duplex circuit** = circuit *m* duplex; **duplex computer** = système duplex or ordinateurs jumelés; **duplex operation** = opération *f* or transmission *f* en duplex; **duplex printer** = imprimante *f* recto/verso

duplicate 1 *noun (copy)* copie *f* or double *m*; **in duplicate** = en double exemplaire or en deux exemplaires; **receipt in duplicate** = reçu *m* en double exemplaire; **to print an invoice in duplicate** = établir une facture en deux exemplaires **2** *verb* copier or dupliquer; **to duplicate a letter** = faire une copie d'une lettre

◊ **duplicating** *noun* duplication *f*; **duplicating machine** = duplicateur *m*; **duplicating paper** = papier *m* pour duplicateur

◊ **duplication** *noun* reproduction *f* or duplication *f* or copie *f*; **duplication of work** = travail qui fait double emploi

◊ **duplicator** *noun* duplicateur *m*; **duplicator paper** = papier pour duplicateur

durable *adjective* durable; **durable cartridge** = cartouche *f* longue durée

duration *noun* durée *f*; **pulse duration modulation (PDM)** = modulation *f* d'impulsions en durée

dustcover *noun (for a machine)* housse *f*

duty-rated *adjective* (système) évalué en cycles possibles par unité de temps or capacité de travail (d'un système)

DUV = DATA UNDER VOICE

DV-I = DIGITAL VIDEO INTERACTIVE

DVORAK keyboard *noun (special keyboard layout)* clavier *m* DVORAK

dyad *noun* dyade *f*

◊ **dyadic operation** *noun* opération *f* dyadique or à deux opérandes

dye-polymer recording *noun (optical disk recording method)* enregistrement *m* sur couche polymérisée

◊ **dye-sublimation printer** *noun (high-quality colour printer)* imprimante *f* à sublimation thermique; **the new dye-sublimation printer can produce colour images at a resolution of 300dpi** = la nouvelle imprimante à sublimation thermique peut fournir une image couleur avec une définition de 300 ppp

dynamic *adjective* dynamique; **dynamic allocation** = allocation *f* dynamique; **dynamic buffer** = mémoire *f* tampon dynamique; **dynamic data structure** = structure *f* de données dynamique; **dynamic dump** = vidage *m* dynamique; **dynamic memory** = mémoire dynamique; **dynamic RAM** or **dynamic random access memory (DRAM)** = RAM dynamique or mémoire vive dynamique; **dynamic microphone** = micro *m* à impulsion; **dynamic multiplexing** = multiplexage *m* dynamique; **dynamic range** = gamme *f* or amplitude *f* dynamique; **dynamic relocation (program)** = déplacement *m* dynamique; *(selecting a path for data)* **dynamic routing** = routage *m* dynamique or adaptatif

◊ **dynamic data exchange (DDE)** *noun (Microsoft Windows and OS/2 method of exchanging data)* échange *m* dynamique des données or DDE; **dynamic stop** = arrêt *m* dynamique; **dynamic storage allocation** = allocation *f* dynamique de la mémoire; **dynamic subroutine** = sous-programme *m* paramétrable; *compare* STATIC

◊ **dynamic link library (DLL)** *(Microsoft Windows and OS/2 library of utility programs)* bibliothèque *f* dynamique des liens or DLL; **the word-processor calls a spell-check program that is stored as a DLL** = le traitement de texte appelle le vérificateur d'orthographe stocké dans la (bibliothèque) DLL; *(file containing a library or routine)* **DLL file** = fichier DLL

◊ **dynamically** *adverb* dynamiquement or de façon dynamique; **dynamically redefinable character set** = police *f* de caractères vectorielle

Ee

E *(hexadecimal number equivalent to decimal 14)* nombre hexadécimal équivalent du 14 décimal *or* E

EAN = EUROPEAN ARTICLE NUMBER

EAPROM = ELECTRICALLY ALTERABLE PROGRAMMABLE READ-ONLY MEMORY

early token release *noun (Token-Ring or FDDI network system)* libération *f* anticipée du jeton

EAROM = ELECTRICALLY ALTERABLE READ-ONLY MEMORY

earth 1 *noun* **(a)** terre *f*; *(for satellite transmissions)* **earth coverage** = zone *f* terrestre de couverture *or* couverture *f* terrestre; **earth station** = station *f* terrestre **(b)** *(connection representing zero potential)* prise *f* de terre; **all loose wires should be tied to earth** = tous les fils non rattachés doivent être mis à la terre *or* à la masse; **earth wire** = fil *m* de terre *or* de mise à la masse **2** *verb (to connect an electrical device to earth)* mettre à la terre *or* à la masse; **all appliances must be earthed** = tous les appareils doivent être mis à la terre (NOTE: US English is **ground**)

easy-to-use *adjective* facile à utiliser *or* d'utilisation facile

> QUOTE it is a really easy-to-use, menu-driven program that allows you to produce presentation quality graphics with little or no training
>
> ***Soft***

EAX = ELECTRONIC AUTOMATIC EXCHANGE

EBCDIC = EXTENDED BINARY CODED DECIMAL INTERCHANGE CODE

EBNF = EXTENDED BACKUS-NAUR FORM

EBR = ELECTRON BEAM RECORDING

echo 1 *noun* écho *m*; **echo chamber** = chambre *f* à écho; **echo check** = contrôle *m* par écho; **echo suppressor** = éliminateur *m* d'écho *or* dispositif *m* anti-écho **2** *verb* faire écho

ECL = EMITTER COUPLED LOGIC

ECMA = EUROPEAN COMPUTER MANUFACTURERS ASSOCIATION syndicat *m* européen des constructeurs d'ordinateurs; *(used to draw flowcharts)* **ECMA symbols** = symboles *mpl* ECMA

EDAC = ERROR DETECTION AND CORRECTION

edge *noun* **(a)** *(of flat object or signal or clock pulse)* bordure *f* or bord *m* ; limite *f*; **edge board** *or* **card** = carte *f* à connecteur; **edge connector** = connecteur *m* de carte; **edge detection** = détection *f* de limites *or* de bordures; *(paper card)* **edge notched card** = carte *f* à encoches marginales **(b)** *(of process or circuit)* **edge-triggered** = déclenché par bascule de front d'impulsion

> QUOTE Connections to the target board are made via IC test clips or the edge connector.
>
> ***Electronics Today***

EDI = ELECTRONIC DATA INTERCHANGE

edit *verb (to format)* éditer; *(to correct text)* corriger *or* réviser (un texte avant l'impression); **edit commands** = commandes *f* d'édition; **edit key** = touche *f* (de fonction) d'édition; **there are several special edit keys - this one will re-format the text** = il y a plusieurs touches d'édition - celle-ci permet de reformater le texte; **edit window** = fenêtre *f* d'édition; *(film or TV program)* **editing plan** = maquette *f* d'édition; **editing run** = exécution *f* d'un programme d'édition (pour contrôle); *(on microfilm)* **editing symbol** = marque *f* *or* symbole *m* *or* repère *m* de positionnement (sur microfilm); **editing terms** = commandes et instructions d'édition; **linkage editing** = mise *f* en place de liens (à l'aide d'un éditeur de liens)

◊ **edition** *noun (books or newspapers printed at one time)* édition *f*; **the second edition has had some changes to the text** = le texte de la seconde édition a été modifié; **did you see the last edition of the evening paper?** = avez-vous lu la dernière édition du journal du soir?

◊ **editor** *noun* **(a)** *(person who edits films or books)* éditeur, -trice **(b)** **editor program** = (programme) éditeur; **line editor** = éditeur ligne à ligne; **linkage editor** = éditeur de liens; **text editor** = éditeur de texte *or* programme d'édition de texte **(c)** *(of a newspaper or magazine)* rédacteur, -trice; **the editor of 'The Times'** = le rédacteur en chef du 'Times'; **the paper's computer editor** = le rédacteur en chef de la rubrique informatique du journal

◊ **editorial 1** *adjective* éditorial, -e; **editorial processing centre** = centre *m* de traitement de texte **2** *noun (article written by the editor)* éditorial *m*

> QUOTE an object orientated graphics editor enables you to add text to graphics
>
> ***Byte***

> QUOTE while it has many formatting facilities, it does not include an editor with which to create the template for the report
> **Personal Computer World**

> QUOTE The Smartbook authoring system is a software product that integrates text and fractally compressed images, using any word-processor line editor.
> **Computing**

EDLIN *(MS-DOS system utility)* utilitaire *m* or éditeur *m* EDLIN *or* edlin

EDP = ELECTRONIC DATA PROCESSING traitement *m* électronique de données *or* de l'information; **EDP capability** = capacité *f* de traitement (électronique) de données (NOTE: **EDP** is more common in US English)

EDS = EXCHANGEABLE DISK STORAGE

educational *adjective* éducatif, -ive; **educational TV** *or* **ETV programme** = programme *m* de télévision (à caractère) éducatif

◊ **edutainment** *noun* le ludo-éducatif

EEMS = ENHANCED EXPANDED MEMORY SYSTEM

EEPROM = ELECTRICALLY ERASABLE PROGRAMMABLE READ-ONLY MEMORY

EEROM = ELECTRICALLY ERASABLE READ-ONLY MEMORY

effective *adjective* effectif, -ive; **effective address** = adresse effective; **effective bandwidth** = largeur de bande effective; **effective instruction** = instruction effective; **effective search speed** = vitesse de recherche effective; **effective throughput** = rendement effectif

◊ **effective aperture** *noun* **(a)** *(of aerial)* puissance *f* d'ouverture effective **(b)** *(of camera)* ouverture *f* utile

efficiency *noun* efficacité *f* or bonne performance *or* efficience *f*; **he is doubtful about the efficiency of the new networking system** = il n'est pas vraiment sûr que le nouveau système multiposte fonctionne bien *or* soit très performant

◊ **efficient** *adjective* efficace *or* performant, -e *or* efficient, -e; **the program is highly efficient at sorting files** = ce programme est excellent pour le tri des fichiers

◊ **efficiently** *adverb* efficacement; **the word-processing package has produced a series of addressed letters very efficiently** = ce progiciel de traitement de texte a produit, de façon très performante, une série de lettres personnalisées

EFT = ELECTRONIC FUNDS TRANSFER

◊ **EFTPOS** = ELECTRONIC FUNDS TRANSFER POINT-OF-SALE

> QUOTE Alphameric has extended its range specifically for the hospitality market and has developed an eftpos package which allows most credit and debit cards to be processed.
> **Computing**

EGA = ENHANCED GRAPHICS ADAPTER (carte) adaptateur *m* graphique couleur *or* carte EGA; **EGA screen** = écran EGA

> QUOTE although the video BIOS services are enhanced by adding an EGA card, the DOS functions are not
> **.EXE**

EHF = EXTREMELY HIGH FREQUENCY

EIA = ELECTRONICS INDUSTRY ASSOCIATION **EIA interface** = interface *f* aux normes EIA

eight-bit (system) *noun* (système) huit bits; **eight-bit byte** *or* **octet** = octet *m*

◊ **eight-inch disk** *noun* disquette *f* de huit pouces; **eight-inch drive** = lecteur *m* de disquettes de huit pouces

◊ **eighty-column screen** *noun* *(screen that displays 80 characters horizontally)* écran *m* de quatre-vingts colonnes

◊ **eighty-track disk** *noun* disque *m* de quatre-vingts pistes

EIS = EXECUTIVE INFORMATION SYSTEM

EISA = ELECTRONICS INDUSTRY STANDARDS ASSOCIATION (standard de bus) EISA

> COMMENT: the EISA expansion bus standard is backwards compatible with the older ISA standard of expansion cards, but also features 32-bit data path and allows bus mastering.

either-or operation *noun* *(logical function)* opération *f* OU inclusif *or* opération d'union *or* de réunion

◊ **either-way operation** *noun* mode de transmission bidirectionnelle à l'alternat

elapsed time *noun* temps *m* passé à une tâche *or* temps d'exécution d'une tâche

elastic banding *noun* *(defining the limits of an image on a screen)* recadrage *m* (d'une image sur l'écran)

◊ **elastic buffer** *noun* (mémoire) tampon *m* de capacité *or* de taille variable

electret *noun* électret *m*; **electret microphone** = microphone *m* à électret

electric *adjective* électrique; **electric current** = courant *m* électrique; **electric charge** = charge *f* électrique; **electric typewriter** = machine *f* à écrire électrique

◊ **electrical** *adjective* électrique; **the engineers are trying to repair an electrical fault** = les ingénieurs essaient de réparer une panne du système électrique

◊ **electrically** *adverb* à l'électricité *or* électriquement; **an electrically-powered motor** = un moteur électrique *or* un moteur qui marche *or* qui fonctionne à l'électricité; **electrically alterable, programmable read-only memory (EAPROM)** = mémoire *f* EAPROM *or* mémoire ROM programmable, modifiable électriquement; **electrically alterable read-only memory (EAROM)** = mémoire EAROM *or* mémoire ROM modifiable électriquement; **electrically erasable programmable read-only memory (EEPROM)** = mémoire EEPROM *or* mémoire ROM programmable et effaçable électriquement; **electrically erasable read-only memory (EEROM)** = mémoire EEROM *or* mémoire ROM effaçable électriquement

QUOTE conventional EEPROM requires two transistors to store each bit of data
Electronics & Power

electricity *noun* électricité *f*; **the electricity was cut off, and the computer crashed** = il y a eu une coupure de courant qui a été fatale à l'ordinateur; **electricity prices are an important factor in the production costs** = les frais d'électricité constituent un élément important des coûts de production

electrode *noun* électrode *f*

electrographic printer *noun* *see* ELECTROSTATIC PRINTER

electroluminescence *noun* électroluminescence *f*

◊ **electroluminescing** *adjective* électroluminescent, -e

◊ **electroluminescent** *adjective* électroluminescent, -e; **the screen coating is electroluminescent** = l'écran est recouvert d'une couche électroluminescente; **electroluminescent display** = affichage *or* écran électroluminescent

electrolytic capacitor *noun* condensateur *m* électrolytique; **non-electrolytic capacitor** = condensateur non électrolytique

electromagnet *noun* électro-aimant *m*

◊ **electromagnetic** *adjective* électromagnétique; **electromagnetic interference (EMI)** = interférence *f* électromagnétique; **electromagnetic radiation** = rayonnement *m* électromagnétique; **electromagnetic spectrum** = spectre *m* électromagnétique

◊ **electromagnetically** *adverb* (qui fonctionne) grâce à un électro-aimant

electromechanical switching *noun* commutation *f* électromécanique

electromotive force (EMF) *noun* force *f* électromotrice

electron *noun* électron *m*; **electron beam** = faisceau *m* électronique *or* d'électrons; **the electron beam draws the image on the inside of a CRT screen** = le faisceau électronique dessine l'image à l'intérieur de l'écran cathodique; *(onto microfilm)* **electron beam recording (EBR)** = enregistrement *m* par faisceau électronique (sur microfilm); **electron gun** = canon *m* à électrons

electronic *adjective* électronique; **electronic automatic exchange (EAX)** = central *m* automatique électronique *or* autocommutateur *m* électronique; **electronic banking** = la bancatique; **electronic blackboard** = tableau *m* noir électronique; **electronic composition** = composition *f* électronique; *(system of sending orders, paying invoices, etc. using electronic mail)* **electronic data interchange (EDI)** = système *m* électronique d'échange de données *or* système EDI; **electronic data processing (EDP)** = traitement *m* électronique de l'information *or* de données; **electronic data processing capability** = facilité *f* de traitement électronique de données; **electronic digital computer** = calculateur *m* *or* ordinateur *m* numérique; *(of video film)* **electronic editing** = montage *m* électronique; **electronic engineer** = ingénieur *m* électronicien; **electronic filing** = archivage *m* sur ordinateur; **electronic funds transfer (system) (EFT)** = transfert *m* *or* virement *m* électronique de fonds; **electronic funds transfer point of sale (EFTPOS)** = terminal *m* de transfert électronique de fonds; **electronic keyboard** = clavier *m* électronique; **electronic lock** = verrou *m* (de sécurité) électronique; **electronic mail** *or* **email** *or* **e-mail** = messagerie *f* *or* courrier *m* *or* poste *f* électronique; **electronic mailbox** = boîte *f* aux lettres électronique; **when I log onto the network, I always check my electronic mailbox for new messages** = lorsque je me connecte au réseau, je vérifie toujours s'il y a de nouveaux messages dans ma boîte aux lettres; **electronic money** = monnaie *f* électronique; **electronic news gathering (ENG)** = journalisme *m* *or* reportage *m* électronique; **electronic office** = bureau *m* informatisé; **electronic office system** = (système) bureautique *f*; **electronic pen** *or* **stylus** *or* **wand** = stylo *m* optique; **electronic point-of-sale (EPOS)** = point *m* de vente électronique; **electronic publishing** = édition *f* électronique *or* publication *f* assistée par ordinateur (PAO); **electronic pulse** = impulsion *f* électronique; **electronic shopping** = achats *mpl* sur *or* par ordinateur; **electronic signature** = signature *f* électronique; **electronic smog** = pollution *f* électronique; **electronic stylus** *or* **wand** = stylo *m* électronique; **electronic switching system (ESS)** = système *m* de commutation électronique *or* commutateur *m* électronique; **electronic traffic** = transmission électronique; **electronic typewriter** = machine *f* à écrire électronique; *(in TV or video camera)* **electronic viewfinder** = viseur *m* électronique; **electronic wand** = stylo *m* électronique

◊ **electronically** *adverb* électroniquement *or* par système électronique; **the text is electronically transmitted to an outside typesetter** = le texte est transmis au compositeur externe par système électronique

◊ **electronics** noun (science) l'électronique f; the electronics industry = l'industrie f électronique; **Electronics Industry Association interface (EIA)** = interface f aux normes EIA; **Electronics Industry Standards Association (EISA)** = (standard de bus) EISA; **electronics specialist** = expert m en électronique; (technician) électronicien, -ienne

QUOTE electronic mail is a system which allows computer users to send information to each other via a central computer
Which PC?

QUOTE electronic publishing will be used for printing on paper, but it can be applied equally to data storage on a database, transmission via telecommunications or for use with visual presentation media such as AV slides or television
Electronic Publishing & Print Show

electro-optic effect noun effet m optronique

◊ **electrophotography** noun électro-photographie f

◊ **electrosensitive** adjective **electrosensitive paper** = papier m électrosensible or à transfert thermique; **electrosensitive printing** = impression f thermique

◊ **electrostatic** adjective électrostatique; **electrostatic printer** = imprimante f électrostatique; **electrostatic screen** = écran m électrostatique; **electrostatic speaker** = haut-parleur m électrostatique; **electrostatic storage** = mémoire f électrostatique

◊ **electrostatically** adverb par charge électrostatique

◊ **electrothermal printer** noun imprimante f thermique

elegant adjective **elegant programming** = programmation élégante or bien conçue

element noun **(a)** élément m or composant m; **logic element** = élément logique; **picture element** or **pixel** = pixel m; **signal element** = élément d'un signal **(b)** (cell) élément or cellule f; **array element** = élément d'un tableau **(c)** (coil of resistive wire) élément **(d)** (substance) élément

◊ **elementary** adjective (made of many similar small sections or objects) élémentaire; **elementary cable section** = section f élémentaire de câble

ELF = EXTREMELY LOW FREQUENCY

eliminate verb (to remove) éliminer; **using a computer should eliminate all possibility of error in the address system** = l'ordinateur devrait servir à éliminer toute possibilité d'erreur dans le système d'adresses; **a spelling checker does not eliminate all spelling mistakes** = un correcteur orthographique n'élimine pas toutes les fautes d'orthographe

◊ **elimination** noun élimination f; **elimination factor** = facteur m d'élimination

QUOTE pointing with the cursor and pressing the joystick button eliminates use of the keyboard almost entirely
Soft

elite noun (typeface) caractères mpl Elite

ellipse noun ellipse f

◊ **elliptical orbit** noun orbite f or trajectoire f elliptique

else rule noun instruction ELSE (sinon); **IF X=20 THEN PRINT 'X is 20' ELSE PRINT 'X not 20'** = si X=20 imprimer 'X égale 20' sinon imprimer 'X différent de 20'

ELT = ELECTRONIC TYPEWRITER

em noun (measure equal to the width of the letter 'm') **em dash** or **em rule** = tiret m (dont la longueur équivaut à un 'm'); (space) **em quad** or **em space** = cadratin m; **ems per hour** = débit m d'une imprimante (mesuré en 'ems')

EM = END OF MEDIUM

email or **e-mail** = ELECTRONIC MAIL messagerie f or courrier m or poste f électronique

QUOTE to collect telex messages from an e-mail system, you have to remember to dial the system and check whether there are any telex messages in your mailbox
Which PC?

embedded code noun code m (d'instruction) imbriqué (dans un programme); **embedded command** = commande imbriquée (dans le texte); **embedded computer** or **system** = ordinateur or système imbriqué (dans un autre)

embolden verb (to make a word print in bold type) (donner une instruction d') imprimer en caractères gras

embrace see DEADLY

emf = ELECTROMOTIVE FORCE

EMI = ELECTROMAGNETIC INTERFERENCE

emission noun (of a signal or radiation, etc.) émission f; **the emission of the electron beam** = l'émission du faisceau électronique; **the receiver picked up the radio emission** = le récepteur a capté l'émission radiophonique

◊ **emit** verb émettre

◊ **emitter** noun émetteur m; **emitter-coupled logic (ECL)** = logique f ECL

EMM = EXPANDED MEMORY MANAGER

empty adjective vide; **empty** or **null list** = liste f vide; **empty medium** = support m magnétique vierge; **empty** or **null set** = jeu m or ensemble m de caractères nuls; **empty slot** = (i) case f vide; (ii) connecteur m or créneau m (pour carte additionnelle) inutilisé; **empty** or **null string** = chaîne f vide

EMS = EXPANDED MEMORY SYSTEM; *see also* LIM EMS

emulate *verb* émuler; **laser printer which emulates a wide range of office printers** = une imprimante laser qui peut émuler une série d'autres imprimantes de bureau

◊ **emulation** *noun* émulation f; **emulation facility** = capacité f d'émulation

◊ **emulator** *noun* émulateur m

QUOTE some application programs do not have the right drivers for a laser printer, so look out for laser printers which are able to emulate the more popular office printers

Publish

QUOTE full communications error checking built into the software ensures reliable file transfers and a terminal emulation facility enables a user's terminal to be used as if it were a terminal to the remote computer

Byte

QUOTE The London Borough of Hackney has standardised on terminal emulator software from Omniplex to allow its networked desktop users to select Unix or DOS applications from a single menu.

Computing

emulsion *noun* (*on photographic film or paper*) émulsion f; **emulsion laser storage** = mémoire f laser sur couche haute définition

en *noun* (*half the width of an em*) **en dash** or **en rule** = tiret m court; tiret de césure (dont la longueur équivaut à un 'n'); (*space*) **en quad** = demi-cadratin m

enable *verb* (a) (*to allow to happen*) permettre or rendre possible; **a spooling program enables editing work to be carried out while printing is going on** = un programme de 'spooling' permet d'éditer un texte tout en imprimant (b) (*to use an electronic signal to start a process*) sélectionner or activer or valider; **enabling signal** = signal m de sélection or de validation or d'activation

encapsulated *adjective* (*contained in something else*) encapsulé, -ée; (*PostScript commands*) **encapsulated PostScript (EPS)** = PostScript encapsulé or EPS; (*file containing encapsulated PostScript instructions*) **encapsulated PostScript file (EPSF)** = fichier PostScript encapsulé or EPSF

◊ **encapsulation** *noun* (*system of sending a frame of data in another frame*) encapsulation f

encipher *verb* chiffrer or crypter; **our competitors cannot understand our files - they have all been enciphered** = nos concurrents ne peuvent lire nos fichiers qui sont en langage chiffré

enclose *verb* (*to surround*) enfermer; (*to contain*) inclure or contenir

◊ **enclosure** *noun* (*protective casing for equipment*) boîtier m (protecteur)

encode *verb* encoder or coder

◊ **encoder** *noun* encodeur m; **colour encoder** = encodeur de couleurs; **magnetic tape encoder** = encodeur pour bandes magnétiques

◊ **encoding** *noun* encodage m or codage m; **binary encoding** = encodage binaire; **encoding format** = format m d'encodage; **magnetic encoding** = encodage magnétique

encrypt *verb* chiffrer or crypter; **the encrypted text can be sent along ordinary telephone lines, and no one will be able to understand it** = le message chiffré or crypté peut être transmis par téléphone sans que personne ne puisse le lire

◊ **encryption** *noun* chiffrage m or chiffrement m or cryptage m; **data encryption standard (DES)** = norme f or standard m de cryptage de données

end 1 *noun* (a) (*final point or last part*) fin f; **at the end of the data transmission** = à la fin de la transmission des données; **end product** = produit m fini; **far end** or **receiving end** = (point d') arrivée f or (point de) réception f; **in the end** = finalement or à la fin (b) (*character*) fin (de fichier); **end-around carry** = report m circulaire or en boucle; **end about shift** = décalage m circulaire; (*IBM PC keyboard key*) **end key** = touche f End; touche Fin (sur un clavier français); **end of address (EOA)** = (code de) fin d'adresse; **end of block (EOB)** = (code de) fin de bloc; **end of data (EOD)** = (code de) fin de données; **end of document** or **end of file (EOF)** = (code de) fin de document; **end of job (EOJ)** = (code de) fin de tâche; **end of line (EOL)** = fin f de ligne; **end of medium (EM)** = (code de) fin de support (de données); **end of message (EOM)** = (code de) fin de message; (*on typewriter*) **end of page indicator** = signal m de fin de page; **end of record (EOR)** = (code de) fin d'enregistrement; **end of run routines** = routines fpl de clôture (d'exécution); **end of tape (EOT)** = (code de) fin de la bande (magnétique); **end of text (EOT** or **ETX)** = (code de) fin de texte; **end of transmission (EOT)** = (code or signal de) fin de la transmission **2** *verb* finir or arrêter

◊ **ending** *noun* (a) (*action*) fin f or arrêt m (b) (*end part*) fin or bout m; **line endings** = bouts or fins de lignes

◊ **endless** *adjective* sans fin or continu, -e; **endless loop** = boucle sans fin or continue or infinie

◊ **end user** *noun* utilisateur, -trice (final); **the company is creating a computer with a specific end user in mind** = la société cherche à créer un ordinateur adapté aux besoins de l'utilisateur

energy *noun* (a) (*force*) énergie f (b) (*power from electricity, etc.*) énergie; **we try to save energy by switching off the lights when the rooms are empty** = nous essayons d'économiser de l'énergie or du courant en éteignant les lumières lorsque les pièces sont vides; **if you reduce the room temperature to eighteen degrees, you will save energy** = vous économiserez de l'énergie en limitant la température de la pièce à 18 degrés

◊ **energy-saving** *adjective* qui économise l'énergie; **our company is introducing energy-saving measures** = notre société met en place des mesures d'économie d'énergie

ENG = ELECTRONIC NEWS GATHERING

enhance *verb* optimiser *or* améliorer *or* relever; **enhanced dot matrix** = matrice *f* d'impression à haute définition; *(IBM PC development of EMS)* **enhanced expanded memory specification (EEMS)** = gestion *f* avancée de la mémoire étendue *or* paginée; mémoire EEMS; **enhanced graphics adapter (EGA)** = (carte) adaptateur *m* graphique couleur *or* carte EGA; **enhanced graphics adapter screen** *or* **EGA screen** = écran *m* EGA; *(IBM PC keyboard)* **enhanced keyboard** = clavier *m* étendu; *(IBM PC operation)* **enhanced mode** = mode *m* étendu; **enhanced small device interface (ESDI)** = interface *f* ESDI

◊ **enhancement** *noun* optimisation *f* or amélioration *f*

◊ **enhancer** *noun* optimiseur *m*

> QUOTE the typefaces are fairly rudimentary, especially if you are not using an enhanced graphics adapter screen
> **Desktop Publishing**

enlarge *verb* agrandir *or* grossir

◊ **enlargement** *noun* agrandissement *m* or grossissement *m*; **an enlargement of the photograph was used to provide better detail** = on a utilisé un agrandissement de la photo pour voir les détails plus clairement

ENQ = ENQUIRY

enquiry (ENQ) *noun* (i) demande *f* ; (ii) interrogation *f* or requête *f*; **enquiry character** = caractère *m* de requête

ensure *verb* assurer; **pushing the write-protect tab will ensure that the data on the disk cannot be erased** = en mettant en place le dispositif de protection d'écriture vous vous assurez de ne pas perdre vos données

enter *verb* *(data or code)* entrer *or* saisir *or* introduire (des données) *or* taper (un code); **to enter a name on a list** = entrer *or* inscrire un nom sur une liste; **the data has been entered** = les données ont été saisies; **enter key** = touche *f* Enter; touche Entrée (sur clavier français)

◊ **entering** *noun* *(action)* entrée *f* or saisie *f* or introduction *f* (de données)

enterprise network *noun* *(network connecting all the workstations in a company)* réseau *m* d'entreprise

entity *noun* entité *f*

entry *noun* **(a)** *(single record)* entrée *f* **(b)** *(place where you can enter)* entrée; *(before a routine can be entered)* **entry condition** = condition *f* d'entrée; *(in a called subroutine)* **entry instruction** =

instruction *f* d'entrée; **entry point** = point *m* or adresse d'entrée; **entry time** = heure *f* d'entrée

enumerated type *noun* classement *m* énumératif

envelope *noun* **(a)** *(for sending letters)* enveloppe *f*; **air mail envelope** = enveloppe avion; **window envelope** = enveloppe à fenêtre; **sealed envelope** = enveloppe fermée *or* cachetée; **unsealed envelope** = enveloppe ouverte *or* non cachetée; *(add-on to a printer)* **envelope feeder** = bac *m* d'alimentation pour enveloppes; *(printer used to print addresses)* **envelope printer** = imprimante *f* d'enveloppes **(b)** *(variation of amplitude of signal or sound)* enveloppe; **attack envelope** = enveloppe d'attaque (d'un signal); **envelope delay** = (temps de) propagation *f* d'une enveloppe; **envelope detection** = détection *f* d'enveloppe **(c)** *(transmitted packet of data containing error-detection and control information)* enveloppe **(d)** *(in electronic mail)* enveloppe (de message)

environment *noun* **(a)** *(condition in a computer system of all registers and memory locations)* environnement *m* *(amount of memory free)* **environment space** = taille *f* de l'environnement; *(variable set by the system)* **environment variable** = variable *f* d'environnement **(b)** *(surroundings)* environnement

> QUOTE one of the advantages of working in a PC-based environment is the enormous range of software which can run on the same computer
> **ESL Newsletter**

EOA = END OF ADDRESS

EOB = END OF BLOCK

EOD = END OF DATA

EOF = END OF FILE

EOJ = END OF JOB

EOL = END OF LINE

EOM = END OF MESSAGE

EOR = END OF RECORD

EOT = END OF TEXT *or* END OF TRANSMISSION

episcope *or* **epidiascope** *noun* épidiascope *m* or projecteur *m* de documents opaques

epitaxy *noun* épitaxie *f*

◊ **epitaxial layer** *noun* couche *f* épitaxiale

EPOS = ELECTRONIC POINT-OF-SALE

EPROM *noun* **(a)** = ELECTRICALLY PROGRAMMABLE READ-ONLY MEMORY mémoire *f* EPROM *or* mémoire ROM programmable électriquement **(b)** = ERASABLE PROGRAMMABLE READ-ONLY MEMORY mémoire EPROM *or* mémoire ROM programmable et effaçable

> QUOTE the densest EPROMs commercially available today are at the 1 Mbit level
>
> *Electronics & Power*

EPS = ENCAPSULATED POSTSCRIPT

◊ **EPSF** = ENCAPSULATED POSTSCRIPT FILE

equal 1 *adjective* égal, -e **2** *verb* être égal à (NOTE: **equalling - equalled** but US: **equaling - equaled**)

◊ **equality** *noun* égalité *f*

◊ **equalize** *verb* égaliser *or* corriger (à l'aide d'un filtre); **the received signal was equalized to an optimum shape** = le signal d'entrée a été filtré pour obtenir une forme optimale

◊ **equalization** *noun* égalisation *f*

◊ **equalizer** *noun* égaliseur *m*; **frequency equalizer** = égaliseur de fréquence *or* filtre *m* de bande de fréquence

◊ **equally** *adverb* également

equate *verb* égaler; **the variable was equated to the input data** = la variable a pris la valeur de la donnée saisie

◊ **equation** *noun* équation *f*; **machine equation** = équation machine

equator *noun* équateur *m*

◊ **equatorial orbit** *noun* orbite *f* équatoriale

equip *verb* (s') équiper

◊ **equipment** *noun* équipement *m* *or* matériel *m*; **computer equipment supplier** = fournisseur *m* *or* revendeur *m* d'équipements informatiques; **equipment failure** = défaillance *f* du matériel *or* de l'ordinateur

equivalence *noun* **(a)** *(being equivalent)* équivalence *f* **(b)** *(logical operation)* equivalence; **equivalence function** *or* **operation** = (i) fonction *f* *or* opération *f* d'équivalence ; (ii) équivalence logique; **equivalence gate** = porte *f* *or* circuit *m* d'équivalence; **non-equivalence function (NEQ)** = fonction de disjonction *or* OU exclusif; **non-equivalence gate** = porte *f* *or* circuit OU exclusif

◊ **equivalent** *adjective* équivalent, -e; **to be equivalent to** = être équivalent (à) *or* équivaloir (à); **the total number of characters keyboarded so far is equivalent to one day's printing time** = le nombre de caractères saisis jusqu'ici équivaut à une journée d'impression

erase *verb* **(a)** effacer; *(of memory)* effacer; remettre à zéro **(b)** *(data)* effacer *or* détruire; **erase character** = caractère *m* d'effacement; **erase head** = tête *f* d'effacement

◊ **erasable** *adjective* effaçable *or* qui peut être effacé, -ée; **erasable storage** *or* **erasable memory** = (i) support (magnétique) effaçable *or* réutilisable ; (ii) mémoire temporaire; **erasable programmable read-only memory (EPROM)** = mémoire EPROM *or* mémoire ROM programmable et effaçable

◊ **eraser** *noun* dispositif *m* *or* méthode *f* d'effacement; *(graphics program function)* **eraser tool** = outil *m* d'effacement *or* gomme *f*

ERCC = ERROR CHECKING AND CORRECTING

E-region *or* **Heaviside-Kennelly layer** *noun (section of the ionosphere)* couche *f* E

ergonomics *noun* ergonomie *f*

◊ **ergonomist** *noun* ergonome *m&f* *or* ergonomiste *m&f*

EROM = ERASABLE READ-ONLY MEMORY

erratum *noun* erratum *m* (NOTE: plural is **errata)**

error *noun* erreur *f* *or* faute *f* *or* anomalie *f*; **he made an error in calculating the total** = il a fait une erreur de total; **the secretary must have made a typing error** = la secrétaire doit avoir fait une faute de frappe; **in error** *or* **by error** = par erreur; **margin of error** = marge *f* d'erreur; **error ambiguity** = erreur d'ambiguïté; **error burst** = rafale *f* d'erreurs *or* série *f* d'erreurs consécutives; **error checking and correcting code (ECCC)** = code *m* de vérification et correction d'erreurs; **error code** = code d'erreur; **error condition** = condition *f* d'erreur; **error control** = contrôle *m* d'erreurs; **error correcting codes** = codes de correction d'erreurs; *see also* GRAY CODE; **error correction** = correction *f* d'erreurs; **error detecting codes** = codes *mpl* de détection d'erreurs; **error detection** = détection d'erreurs; **error detection and correction (EDAC)** = détection et correction d'erreurs; **error diagnosis** = diagnostic *m* d'erreurs; **error diagnostics** = outils *m* de diagnostic d'erreurs; **error handling** *or* **management** = procédure *f* de traitement des erreurs *or* gestion *f* des erreurs; **error interrupt** = (signal d') interruption *f* sur (une) erreur *or* sur (un) incident; **error logging** = enregistrement *m* automatique des erreurs; **features of the program include error logging** = ce programme permet l'enregistrement (automatique) des erreurs; **error message** = message *m* d'erreur; **error propagation** = propagation *f* d'erreur; **error rate** = taux *m* d'erreur; **the error rate is less than 1%** = le taux d'erreur est inférieur à 1%; **error recovery** = reprise *f* après erreur *or* après incident (sans repartir à zéro); **error routine** = routine *f* (de traitement) d'erreur; **error trapping** = détection *or* recherche *or* prévention *f* d'erreurs; **compilation error** = erreur de compilation; **diagnostic (error) message** = message *m* de diagnostic d'erreur; **execution error** = erreur d'exécution; **logical error** = erreur logique; *(number of mistakes which are acceptable)* **margin of error** = marge *f* d'erreur; **permanent error** = erreur permanente; **quantization error** = erreur de quantification; **recoverable error** = erreur qui peut être corrigée *or* redressée; **rejection error** = erreur de rejet *or* de refus; **scanning error** = erreur de balayage; **a wrinkled or torn page may be the cause of scanning errors** = un pli ou une déchirure dans une page peut être la cause d'une erreur de balayage *or* d'un balayage incorrect; **substitution error** = erreur de substitution; **syntax error** = faute de syntaxe; **transient error** = erreur passagère *or* momentanée; **undetected error** = erreur non détectée

---

QUOTE syntax errors, like omitting a bracket, will produce an error message from the compiler

Personal Computer World

QUOTE Microcom has launched a new version of its MNP proprietary error correction protocol, MNP10, which automatically slows down the transmission rate when it detects line interference and speeds up again when conditions improve.

Computing

ESC échappement *m or* code *m* ESC

escape character *noun* caractère *m* d'échappement; **escape codes** = codes *mpl* d'échappement; **escape key** = touche *f* ESC *or* touche d'échappement *or* touche ECHAPPEMENT

◊ **escapement** *noun* (*of paper in a printer*) échappement *m*

ESDI = ENHANCED SMALL DEVICE INTERFACE

ESS = ELECTRONIC SWITCHING SYSTEM

establish *verb* établir; **they established which component was faulty** = ils ont repéré le composant défectueux

etch *verb* graver; **etched type** = caractère gravé (gravure ionique *or* chimique)

Ethernet (réseau) Ethernet; (*network using thick cable*) **thick-Ethernet** = Ethernet câble lourd; (*network using thin cable*) **thin-Ethernet** = Ethernet câble fin; *compare* ARCNET, TOKEN-RING

COMMENT: Ethernet has several implementations: 10Base5 (the most common) is a bus-based topology running over coaxial cable; 10BaseT uses unshielded-twisted-pair cable in a ring-based topology; Ethernet normally has a data transmission rate of 10Mbps

◊ **EtherTalk** (*Apple Macintosh variation of Ethernet*) (version Apple) EtherTalk

ETV = EDUCATIONAL TELEVISION

ETX = END OF TEXT

Euronet *noun* (*telephone connected network*) Euronet *m*

European Article Number (EAN) *noun* numérotation *f* européenne des articles (NEA)

European Computer Manufacturers Association (ECMA) syndicat *m* européen des constructeurs d'ordinateurs; (*used to draw flowcharts*) **ECMA symbols** = symboles *mpl* ECMA

evaluate *verb* évaluer

◊ **evaluation** *noun* évaluation *f*

◊ **evaluative abstract** *noun* extrait *m or* résumé *m* critique

even *adjective* (*number*) pair, -e; **the first three even numbers are 2, 4, 6** = les trois premiers nombres pairs: 2,4 et 6; **even parity (check)** = contrôle *m* de parité paire; **even working** = pliage *m* en cahiers de 16, 32 ou 64 pages

event *noun* évènement *m*

◊ **event-driven** *adjective* activé, -ée *or* actionné, -ée par évènement

---

QUOTE Forthcoming language extensions will include object-oriented features, including classes with full inheritance, as well as event-driven programming.

Computing

---

except *preposition & conjunction* sauf *or* excepté; **all the text has been keyboarded, except the last ten pages** = le texte a été saisi, sauf les dix dernières pages; (*logical function*) **except gate** = porte *f or* circuit *m* OU exclusif

◊ **exception** *noun* exception *f*; **exception dictionary** = liste *f or* répertoire *m* d'exceptions; (*routines that diagnose and correct errors*) **exception handling** *or* **error handling** = traitement *m* des exceptions *or* des erreurs; **exception report** = rapport *m* d'exceptions *or* d'anomalies

excess *noun* excès *m*; **excess-3 code** = code *m* (binaire) plus 3; **the excess-3 code representation of 6 is 1001** = pour 6, le code (binaire) plus 3 est 1001

◊ **excessive** *adjective* excessif, -ive; **the program used an excessive amount of memory to accomplish the job** = ce programme a utilisé une quantité excessive de mémoire pour exécuter la tâche en question

exchange 1 *noun* (a) (*giving of one thing for another*) échange *m*; **part exchange** = reprise *f* (b) (*telephone equipment*) central *m* téléphonique; (*local loop*) **electronic automatic exchange** = central automatique *or* autocommutateur *m* electronique; **exchange line** = ligne *f* de jonction d'abonné (au centre téléphonique); *see also* PABX 2 *verb* (a) faire un échange *or* échanger (une chose contre une autre); **exchange selection** = tri *m* par échange (b) (*to swap data between two locations*) échanger *or* permuter *or* basculer (des données)

◊ **exchangeable** *adjective* (*returnable*) échangeable; (*moveable*) amovible; **exchangeable disk storage (EDS)** = disque *m* dur amovible

exclamation mark (!) *noun* point *m* d'exclamation

exclude *verb* exclure; **the interest charges have been excluded from the document** = les frais financiers n'ont pas été inclus dans le document; **the password is supposed to exclude hackers from the database** = le mot de passe est censé protéger la base de données contre le piratage

◊ **excluding** *preposition* à l'exception de

◊ **exclusion** *noun* **(a)** *(action)* exclusion *f* **(b)** *(restriction of access to a telephone line)* exclusion

◊ **exclusive** *adjective* exclusif, -ive; *(logical function)* **exclusive NOR (EXNOR)** = NI exclusif; **exclusive NOR gate** = porte *f* *or* circuit *m* NI exclusif; **exclusive OR (EXOR)** = OU exclusif; **exclusive OR gate** = porte *f* *or* circuit *m* OU exclusif

EXE file *noun* *(three-letter extension to a filename)* fichier *m* (à extension) EXE; **in DOS, to start a program type in its EXE file name** = pour démarrer un programme sous DOS, tapez le nom de son fichier EXE

executable file *noun* *(file containing a program)* fichier *m* exécutable

◊ **executable form** *noun* programme *m* prêt à être exécuté

execute *verb* *(computer program)* exécuter; **execute cycle** = cycle *m* d'exécution; **execute mode** = mode *m* d'exécution; **execute phase** = phase *f* d'exécution; **execute signal** = signal *m* d'exécution; **execute statement** = déclaration *f or* message *m* d'exécution; **execute time** durée *f or* temps *m* d'exécution; **fetch-execute cycle** = EXECUTE CYCLE

◊ **execution** *noun* *(carrying out of a computer program)* exécution *f*; **execution address** = adresse *f* d'exécution; **execution cycle** = cycle *m* d'exécution; **execution error** = erreur *f* d'exécution; **execution phase** = phase *f* d'exécution; **execution time** = temps *f* d'exécution

> QUOTE fast execution speed is the single most important feature of a C compiler
> **.EXE**

executive *adjective* *(refers to the operating system of a computer)* superviseur; **executive program** *or* **supervisor program** = programme *m* superviseur; **executive control program** = OPERATING SYSTEM **executive instruction** = instruction *f* de superviseur

◊ **executive information system (EIS)** *noun* *(software providing information to a manager)* système *m* d'information pour la direction *or* SID; **the EIS software is very easy to use** = le logiciel de SID est très facile à utiliser; **with this EIS software, we can see how every part of the company performs** = avec ce logiciel de SID on peut connaître l'efficacité de chaque section de l'entreprise

exerciser *noun* testeur *m or* programme *m* de test

exhaustive search *noun* recherche *f* exhaustive *or* très poussée

exit *verb* *(to stop program execution)* abandonner; *(to leave a program or a loop)* quitter *or* sortir (de); **exit point** = point *m* de sortie; **you have to exit to another editing system to add headlines** = pour mettre des en-têtes, il faut quitter ce programme et entrer dans un autre

◊ **EXIT** *(MS-DOS system command)* (commande MS-DOS) EXIT

exjunction *noun* *(logical function)* disjonction *f*

EXNOR = EXCLUSIVE NOR; *(logical function)* NI exclusif; **EXNOR gate** = porte *f or* circuit *m* NI exclusif

EXOR = EXCLUSIVE OR; *(logical function)* OU exclusif; **EXOR gate** = porte *f or* circuit *m* OU exclusif

expand *verb* augmenter *or* élargir *or* agrandir; **if you want to hold so much data, you will have to expand the disk capacity** = pour conserver une telle quantité de données, il vous faudra une extension de votre disque

◊ **expandable** *adjective* extensible *or* qui peut être augmenté, -ée; **expandable system** = système *m* extensible

◊ **expanded memory** *noun* *(IBM PC standard)* mémoire *f* étendue; *(expansion card)* **expanded memory board** = carte *f* d'extension de mémoire; *(utility which manages extra expanded memory)* **expanded memory manager (EMM)** = gestionnaire *m* de mémoire étendue *or* paginée; **expanded memory specification (EMS)** = mémoire EMS *or* standard *m* d'extension de la mémoire (RAM)

◊ **expander** *noun* **video expander** = déconcentrateur *m* pour transmission vidéo

◊ **expansion** *noun* expansion *f or* extension *f*; *(device that provides more free expansion slots)* **expansion box** = boîtier *m* d'expansion; *(lines allowing expansion cards to control data)* **expansion bus** = bus *m* d'extension; **expansion card** *or* **expansion board** = carte *f* d'extension; **expansion slot** = créneau *m or* connecteur *m or* emplacement *m* pour carte d'extension; **insert the board in the free expansion slot** = enfichez la carte d'extension dans l'emplacement libre; **macro expansion** = macro-expansion *f*

> QUOTE it can be attached to most kinds of printer, and, if that is not enough, an expansion box can be fitted to the bus connector
> ***Personal Computer World***

expert *noun* expert *m or* spécialiste *m&f*; **he is a computer expert** = c'est un spécialiste en informatique; **she is an expert in programming languages** = c'est une spécialiste des langages de programmation; **expert system** = système expert

expire *verb* expirer

◊ **expiration** *noun* expiration *f*; **expiration date** = *(sell-by date)* date *f* de péremption; *(time limit)* date limite *or* date d'expiration d'un délai

explicit address *noun* adresse *f* explicite

exponent *noun* *(maths)* exposant *m*; **binary exponent** = exposant binaire

◊ **exponential** *adjective* exponentiel, -elle

◊ **exponentiate** *verb* élever (un nombre) à la puissance x

◊ **exponentiation** *noun* élévation *f* (d'un nombre) à la puissance x

export *verb* (*save data*) exporter; **to use this data with dBASE, you will have to export it as a DBF file** = pour utiliser ces données avec dBase, il faut les exporter sous la forme d'un fichier de format dBase

express *verb* exprimer *or* formuler; **express the formula in its simplest form** = réduire la formule à sa plus simple expression; **the computer structure was expressed graphically** = l'architecture *or* la structure de l'ordinateur était représentée graphiquement

◊ **expression** *noun* **(a)** (*mathematical formula*) expression *f or* formule *f* **(b)** (*definition of a variable in a program*) expression

extend *verb* (*to make longer*) étendre *or* allonger; **extended arithmetic element** = élément arithmétique étendu; **extended binary coded decimal interchange code (EBCDIC)** = code EBCDIC *or* code binaire à 8 bits; **extended BNF (EBNF)** = métalangage BNF étendu *or* BNF étendu; (*high resolution graphics standard*) **extended graphics array (XGA)** = standard *m* XGA; (*standard method of adding extra memory*) **extended memory** = mémoire *f* étendue; (*software utility that configures extra memory*) **extended memory manager** = gestionnaire *m* de mémoire étendue; (*defining how a program should access extended memory*) **extended memory specification (XMS)** = standard *m* XMS (de mémoire étendue); **extending serial file** = fichier *m* série extensible

◊ **extender** *noun* **card extender** = support *m* de carte d'extension; **line extender** = unité *f* d'extension d'une ligne

◊ **extensible** *adjective* extensible; **extensible language** = langage *m* extensible *or* adaptable

◊ **extension** *noun* extension *f or* expansion *f*; **extension cable** = câble *m* d'extension; **extension memory** = mémoire d'extension; (*of photographic lens*) **extension tube** = bague *m* d'extension; **filename extension** = extension *or* spécification *f* du nom du fichier

◊ **extent** *noun* longueur *f* (d'un document) *or* nombre *m* total de pages (d'un document); **by adding the appendix, we will increase the page**

extent to 256 = en comptant l'appendice, nous ferons 256 pages au total

external *adjective* externe *or* extérieur, -e; **external clock** = horloge *f* externe *or* extérieure; **external data file** = fichier *m* de données externe; **external device** = dispositif *m* externe; (*peripheral*) périphérique *m*; **external disk drive** = lecteur *m* externe; **external interrupt** = signal *m* d'interrution externe *or* émis par un périphérique; **external label** = étiquette *f* extérieure *or* apposée à l'extérieur; **external memory** = mémoire *f* externe; (*self-contained modem*) **external modem** = modem *m* externe; **external register** = registre *m* externe; (*of system*) **external schema** = schéma *m* (du point de vue) de l'utilisateur *or* vision *f* d'utilisateur; **external sort** = tri *m* sur disque *or* sur support externe; **external storage** *or* **external store** = mémoire externe

extra 1 *adjective* supplémentaire **2** *noun* **(a)** (*additionnal item*) article *m* en sus *or* en option; **the mouse and cabling are sold as extras** = la souris et le câble sont en option **(b)** (*mark at the end of a telegraphic transmission*) traînée *f* de transmission **(c) extra-terrestrial noise** = bruit *m* extra-terrestre

◊ **extracode** *noun* extracode *m*

extract *verb* extraire; **we can extract the files required for typesetting** = nous pouvons extraire les dossiers qui doivent aller à la composition; **extract instruction** = instruction d'extraction

◊ **extractor** *noun* extracteur *m*

extrapolation *noun* extrapolation *f*

extremely *adverb* extrêmement; (*from 30-300GHz*) **extremely high frequency (EHF)** = onde(s) *f(pl)* millimétrique(s); (*of less than 100Hz*) **extremely low frequency (ELF)** = onde(s) myriamétrique(s)

eyepiece *noun* (*camera viewfinder*) viseur *m or* oculaire *m*

◊ **eye-strain** *noun* fatigue *f* oculaire

> QUOTE to minimize eye-strain, it is vital to have good lighting conditions with this LCD system
> *Personal Computer World*

Ff

F = FARAD

F *(hexadecimal number equivalent to decimal 15)* nombre hexadécimal équivalent du 15 décimal *or* F

f = FEMTO- *prefix (equal to one thousandth of a million millionth or 10^{15})* f *or* femto-

face *see* TYPEFACE

facet *noun* facette *f*

◊ **faceted code** *noun* code *m* à facettes

facility *noun* **(a)** *(being able to do something easily)* facilité *f*; *(service)* service *m*; **we offer facilities for processing a customer's own disks** = nous offrons à nos clients un service de traitement de leurs propres disquettes **(b)** *(communications path)* chemin *m or* voie *f or* dispositif *m* d'accès **(c)** *US* centre *m or* bureau *m*; **we have opened our new data processing facility** = nous avons ouvert un nouveau centre *or* bureau de traitement de l'information **(d)** **facilities** = *(equipment)* équipement *m*; *(buildings)* locaux *mpl*; **storage facilities** = entrepôt *m*

facsimile *noun* fac-similé *m*; **facsimile character generator** = générateur *m* de caractères fac-similés; **facsimile copy** = fac-similé; *(fax)* télécopie *f or* fax *m*; **facsimile transmission (fax or FAX)** = (système de) télécopie *or* fax *m*; *see also* FAX

factor *noun* **(a)** facteur *m*; **deciding factor** = facteur *or* argument *m* décisif; **the deciding factor was the superb graphics** = l'excellence des graphiques a constitué l'argument décisif; **elimination factor** = facteur *m* d'élimination **(b)** *(number)* facteur; **by a factor of ten** = dix fois *or* multiplié par dix

◊ **factorial** *noun* factorielle *f*; **4 factorial (written 4!) or 1x2x3x4 equals 24** = la factorielle de 4 (qui s'écrit 4!) ou 1x2x3x4 est 24

◊ **factorize** *verb* factoriser *or* mettre en facteur; **when factorized, 15 gives the factors 1, 15 or 3, 5** = la mise en facteur de 15 nous donne les facteurs suivants: 1, 15 ou 3, 5

factory *noun* usine *f*; **computer factory** = usine de construction d'ordinateurs; **they have opened a new components factory** = ils ont ouvert une nouvelle usine de composants électroniques; **factory price** *or* **price ex factory** = prix *m* départ usine

fade *verb* **(a)** *(radio or electrical signal)* faiblir *or* baisser *or* perdre de l'intensité *or* s'atténuer **(b)** *(colour or photograph)* (se) faner *or* pâlir *or*

s'atténuer; **to fade out** = faire disparaître progressivement; faire un fondu

◊ **fading** *noun* **(a)** *(of radio or TV signal)* affaiblissement *m or* baisse *f or* perte *f* d'intensité (du signal) **(b)** *(of photograph or colour)* atténuation *f*; **when fading occurs turn the density dial on the printer to full black** = si l'impression est trop pâle, réglez le bouton de densité (d'impression) sur le noir

fail *verb* **(a)** (i) ne pas faire quelque chose; (ii) rater *or* échouer *or* ne pas réussir quelque chose; **the company failed to carry out routine maintenance of its equipment** = la société ne s'est pas souciée d'effectuer la maintenance de routine de son matériel; **the prototype disk drive failed its first test** = le premier essai du prototype de lecteur de disquettes a été un échec **(b)** *(of machine)* tomber en panne; **a computer has failed if you turn on the power supply and nothing happens** = on peut dire que l'ordinateur est en panne si rien ne se produit à la mise sous tension; **fail-safe system** = système *m* de sécurité (en cas de défaillance *or* de coupure de courant); **fail soft system** = système *m* disjoncteur progressif

◊ **failure** *noun* **(a)** *(not doing something)* manquement *m*; *(lack of success)* insuccès *m or* échec *m* **(b)** *(of equipment)* défaillance *f or* panne *f or* arrêt *m or* incident *m or* dérangement *m*; **failure logging** = enregistrement *m* (automatique) des états d'incidents; **failure rate** = taux *m* de défaillance; **failure recovery** = reprise *f* sur incident; **induced failure** = défaillance provoquée par une cause externe *or* défaillance induite; **mean time between failures (MTBF)** = moyenne de temps de bon fonctionnement (entre les défaillances) (MTBF) *or* durée moyenne de bon fonctionnement; **power failure** = coupure *f* (de courant) *or* panne *f* d'électricité *or* de courant *or* de secteur

QUOTE if one processor system fails, the other takes recovery action on the database, before taking on the workload of the failed system
Computer News

QUOTE The DTI is publishing a new code of best practice which covers hardware reliability and fail-safe software systems.
Computing

fall back *noun* (procédure, etc. de) secours *m*; *(resuming a program after a fault has been fixed)* **fall back recovery** = reprise *f* au point d'appel *or* remise *f* en marche au point de reprise *or* au point d'arrêt; **fall back routines** = routines *fpl or* procédures *fpl* de secours (à utiliser en cas de panne)

false *adjective* *(not true or wrong)* faux, fausse *or* incorrect, -e *or* erroné, -ée; *(logic)* faux, fausse; **false code** = code erroné *or* erreur de code; **false drop** *or* **retrieval** = résultat *m* erroné (d'une recherche); *(error warning when no error has occurred)* **false error** = fausse erreur

FAM = FAST ACCESS MEMORY

family *noun* **(a)** *(range of typefaces)* famille *f* **(b)** *(range of machines)* famille *or* gamme *f or* série *f* (de produits)

fan 1 *noun* *(machine)* ventilateur *m*; *(spread)* éventail *m*; **if the fan fails, the system will rapidly overheat** = si le ventilateur tombe en panne, le système va bientôt (sur)chauffer; **fan antenna** = antenne *f* (en) éventail *or* semi-circulaire; **2** *verb* *(to cool or to spread)* ventiler; **fan-in** = entrance *f or* facteur *m* pyramidal d'entrée; **fan-out** = sortance *f or* facteur *m* pyramidal de sortie; **fanning strip** = tresse *f* de mise à la masse

◊ **fanfold** *or* **accordion paper** *noun* papier (plié) en paravent *or* en accordéon *or* en éventail; papier en continu

QUOTE a filtered fan maintains positive air pressure within the cabinet, to keep dust and dirt from entering
Personal Computer World

QUOTE Intel is investigating other options to solve the Pentium system overheating problems, including selling the chip with its own miniature fan.
Computing

farad (F) *noun* farad *m*

Faraday cage *noun* cage *f* de Faraday

far *adjective* lointain, -e *or* distant, -e; *(receiving end)* **far end** = (point d') arrivée *f or* (point de) réception *f*

fascia plate *noun* panneau *m* avant *or* antérieur; **the fascia plate on the disk drive of this model is smaller than those on other models** = le panneau avant du lecteur de disquettes de ce modèle est plus petit que celui des autres modèles

fast *adjective* **(a)** rapide; **fast program execution** = exécution *f* rapide d'un programme; **this hard disk is fast, it has an access time of 28ms** = c'est un disque dur très rapide avec un temps d'accès de 28ms; **fast access memory (FAM)** = mémoire *f* à accès rapide; **fast core** = mémoire centrale rapide; **the fast core is used as a scratchpad for all calculations in this system** = dans ce système, la mémoire centrale rapide sert de bloc- notes pour tous les calculs; *(for 48 or 96 baud rates)* **fast line** = ligne *f* de transmission rapide; **fast peripheral** = périphérique *m* rapide; **fast time-scale** = base *f* de temps réduite **(b)** *(lens or film)* rapide *or* sensible

FAT = FILE ALLOCATION TABLE

fatal error *noun* erreur *f* fatale

father file *noun* fichier *m* père

fault *noun* *(defect)* défaut *m*; *(mistake)* faute *f or* erreur *f*; *(stoppage)* panne *f or* incident *m*; **the technical staff are trying to correct a programming fault** = les techniciens essayent de corriger une erreur de programmation; **we think there is a basic fault in the product design** = nous estimons qu'il y a une erreur fondamentale dans la conception du produit; *(in a circuit)* **fault detection** = localisation *f* (automatique) de panne; **fault diagnosis** = diagnostic *m* de localisation de panne *or* de défaillance; **fault location program** = programme *m* de localisation de panne; **fault time** = durée *f* d'une panne; **fault trace** = enregistrement *m or* traçage *m* de panne

◊ **fault tolerance** *noun* (marge de) tolérance *f* de panne

◊ **fault-tolerant** *adjective* (système) à tolérance de panne; **they market a highly successful range of fault-tolerant minis** = ils ont commercialisé, avec beaucoup de succès, une gamme de minis à tolérance de panne

◊ **faulty** *adjective* défectueux, -euse; **there must be a faulty piece of equipment in the system** = il doit sûrement y avoir un composant défectueux dans le système; **they traced the fault to a faulty cable** = ils ont découvert que la défaillance était due à un câble défectueux; **faulty sector** = secteur *m* défectueux

QUOTE before fault-tolerant systems, users had to rely on cold standby

QUOTE fault tolerance is usually associated with a system's reliability
Computer News

QUOTE Hampshire fire brigade is investing £2 million in a command and control system based on the new SeriesFT fault-tolerant Unix machine from Motorola.
Computing

fax *or* **FAX 1** *noun* télécopie *f or* fax *m*; **we will send a fax of the design plan** = nous enverrons les plans par télécopie *or* par fax; *(card which allows a computer to send or receive faxes)* **fax card** *or* **board** *or* **adapter** = carte *f* fax; **fax machine** = télécopieur *m or* fax *m*; **the fax machine is next to the telephone switchboard** = notre fax est tout à côté du standard téléphonique; **fax paper** = papier pour télécopieur; *(computer fitted with a fax card)* **fax server** = serveur *m* de télécopie *or* de fax **2** *verb* envoyer par télécopie *or* envoyer par fax *or* faxer; **I've faxed the documents to our New York office** = j'ai faxé les documents *or* j'ai envoyé les documents par télécopie à notre bureau de New York

QUOTE investment in a good modem and communications system could reduce your costs considerably on both courier and fax services
Which PC?

FCB = FILE CONTROL BLOCK

fd *or* **FD** **(a)** = FULL DUPLEX **(b)** = FLOPPY DISK

fdc = FLOPPY DISK CONTROLLER

FDDI = FIBRE DISTRIBUTED DATA INTERFACE; *(extension to FDDI standard)* **FDDI II** = standard FDDI II

FDISK *(MS-DOS system utility)* (utilitaire) FDISK (de formatage de disque)

FDM = FREQUENCY DIVISION MULTIPLEXING

fdx *or* **FDX** = FULL DUPLEX

feature *noun* caractéristique *f*; **key feature** = caractéristique principale *or* la plus importante; **the key features of this system are: 20Mb of formatted storage with an access time of 60ms** = les principales caractéristiques de ce système sont les suivantes: 20Mo de mémoire formatée avec temps d'accès de 60ms

FEDS = FIXED AND EXCHANGEABLE DISK STORAGE

feed 1 *noun (printer or photocopier)* (dispositif d') entraînement *m or* alimentation *f*; **continuous feed** = (système d') alimentation en continu; *(command)* **feed form** = (instruction de) saut *m* de page; **feed holes** = perforations *fpl* d'entraînement *or* perforations marginales; **feed horn** = (dispositif de) guidage *m* directionnel; **feed reel** = bobine *f* d'alimentation; **friction feed** = entraînement par friction *or* par rouleaux; **front feed** = alimentation par l'avant; **paper feed** = (dispositif d') alimentation *or* entraînement du papier; **sheet feed** = alimentation feuille à feuille; **sheet feed attachment** = bac d'alimentation feuille à feuille; **tractor feed** = entraînement par picots **2** *verb* alimenter *or* introduire; **the paper should be manually fed into the printer** = le papier doit être chargé manuellement dans l'imprimante; **data is fed into the computer** = les données sont introduites dans l'ordinateur (NOTE: **feeding - fed**)

◊ **feedback** *noun* **(a)** feedback *m or* rétroaction *f or* (action en) retour *m or* réaction *f*; **feedback control** = contrôle *m* par retour; **feedback loop** = boucle *f* de feedback *or* de réaction *or* de rétroaction; **negative feedback** = rétroaction négative; **positive feedback** = rétroaction positive *or* feedback positif *or* boucle d'amplification **(b)** réaction; **we are getting customer feedback on the new system** = nous commençons à connaître les réactions des clients face au nouveau système

feeder *noun* **(a)** *(channel)* voie *f* d'acheminement *or* de transmission de signaux; **feeder cable** = câble *m* d'acheminement des signaux *or* câble antenne-circuit **(b)** *(for paper)* système d'alimentation *or* d'entraînement (du papier); *see also* ENVELOPE

feevee *noun* US *(informal)* télévision *f* câblée (payante)

feint *noun* (papier à) lignes *fpl* très pâles

female *adjective* femelle; **female connector** = connecteur *m* femelle; **female socket** = prise *f* femelle

femto- **(f)** *prefix* femto-; **femtosecond** = femtoseconde *f*

FEP = FRONT-END PROCESSOR

ferric oxide *noun* oxyde *m* de fer

ferrite *noun* ferrite *f*; **ferrite core** = noyau *m* de ferrite

ferromagnetic material *noun* matériau *m* ferromagnétique

FET = FIELD EFFECT TRANSISTOR

fetch *verb (command)* aller chercher et lire (une instruction); **demand fetching** = accès *m* sur demande à la mémoire paginée; **fetch cycle** = cycle *m* de lecture d'une instruction; **fetch-execute cycle** *or* **execute cycle** = cycle de lecture/exécution *or* cycle d'exécution (d'une instruction); **fetch instruction** = instruction de lecture d'une instruction; **fetch phase** = phase *f* de lecture d'une instruction; **fetch protect** = protection *f* des accès mémoire; **fetch signal** = signal *m* de lecture d'instruction

FF (a) = FORM FEED **(b)** = FLIP-FLOP

fibre *noun* fibre *f*; **fibre ribbon** = ruban *m* (en) tissu (pour machine à écrire)

◊ **fibre distributed data interface (FDDI)** *noun (ANSI standard for high-speed networks)* norme FDDI (pour réseau à fibre optique); *see also* FDDI

> QUOTE Honeywell has won a contract worth £380,000 to cable Abbey National's Milton Keynes-based administration offices. The installation will be based on copper wire and fibre optics and will be carried out by Honeywell's PDS Group.
>
> *Computing*

◊ **fibre optic cable** *or* **connection** *noun* câble *m or* liaison *f* à fibres optiques *or* câble optique; **fibre optic connections enabling nodes up to one kilometre apart to be used** = les câbles à fibres optiques permettent de placer les noeuds jusqu'à un kilomètre l'un de l'autre

◊ **fibre optics** *noun* technologie *f* de la fibre optique *or* de la transmission par fibre optique

fiche *see* MICROFICHE

fidelity *noun* fidélité *f*; **high fidelity system (hi-fi)** = système haute-fidélité *or* chaîne *f* hi-fi

field *noun* **(a)** *(area of force)* champ *m*; **field effect transistor (FET)** = transistor *m* à effet de champ (TEC); **field programmable device** = dispositif à champ programmable; **field programming** = programmation *f* de champ; **field strength** = intensité *f* de champ **(b)** *(in a record)* champ; **the employee record has a field for age** = le dossier 'employés' possède un champ 'âge';

address field = champ (d') adresse; **card field** = champ d'une carte magnétique; **data field** = zone *f* de données; **operand field** = champ (d') opérande; **field label** = label *m or* étiquette *f* d'un champ; **field length** = taille *f* d'un champ; **field marker** *or* **separator** = séparateur *m* de champs; **protected field** = champ protégé **(c)** *(of picture on a television screen)* trame *f* d'image; **field blanking (interval)** = intervalle *m* de trame *or* suppression *f* verticale de la trame; **field frequency** = fréquence *f* de trame; **field flyback** = retour *m* de trame; **field sweep** = balayage *m* vertical; **field sync pulse** = impulsion *f* de contrôle *or* de synchronisation du balayage **(d)** *(photography)* champ (d'image) **(e)** **field engineer** = ingénieur *m* d'entretien *or* d'après-vente *or* de maintenance (sur le site)

◊ **fielding** *noun* zonage *m*

FIFO = FIRST IN FIRST OUT (méthode du) premier entré premier sorti (FIFO); **FIFO memory** = mémoire *f* FIFO *or* mémoire qui fonctionne sur le principe du premier entré premier sorti; **the two computers operate at different rates, but can transmit data using a FIFO memory** = les deux ordinateurs fonctionnent à des vitesses différentes mais peuvent transmettre des données en utilisant une mémoire tampon fonctionnant sur le système 'premier entré premier sorti'; **FIFO queue** = file *f* d'attente qui fonctionne sur le principe 'premier entré premier sorti'

fifth generation computer *noun* ordinateur *m* de cinquième génération

figure *noun* **(a)** *(line illustration)* figure *f*; **see figure 10 for a chart of ASCII codes** = voir figure 10: tableau des codes ASCII **(b)** *(number)* chiffre *m*; **figures case** = chiffres et signes en code télégraphique; **in round figures** = en chiffres ronds; **they have a workforce of 2,500 in round figures** = leur personnel tourne autour de 2500 employés

file 1 *noun* **(a)** *(cardboard holder)* chemise *f or* classeur *m or* dossier *m*; **put these letters in the customer file** = classez ces lettres dans le dossier 'clients' **(b)** *(documents)* dossier; **to place (something) on file** = insérer (un document) au dossier; mettre (une information) sur fiche **(c)** *(section of data on a computer)* fichier *m*; **data file** = fichier de données; **disk file** = fichier *m* sur disque(tte); **distributed file system** = système à fichiers répartis *or* partagés; **file activity ratio** = ratio *m or* taux *m* d'activité d'un fichier; *(file containing the names of each file)* **file allocation table (FAT)** = table *f* d'allocation des fichiers *or* table FAT; *(control bits of data stored with each file)* **file attributes** = attributs *mpl* de fichiers; **file cleanup** = nettoyage *m or* vidage *m* de fichier; **file collating** = fusion *f or* interclassement *m* de fichier(s); **file control block (FCB)** = bloc *m* de contrôle de fichier; **file conversion** = conversion *f* de fichier; **file creation** = création *f* de fichier; **file defragmentation** = défragmentation *f* de fichier; *see* DEFRAGMENTATION **file deletion** = annulation *f or* destruction *f* de fichier; **file descriptor** = descripteur *m* de fichier; **file directory** = répertoire *m* de fichiers; **file extent** = taille *f* d'un fichier; *(file stored in non-contiguous sectors)* **file**

fragmentation = fragmentation *f* de fichier; **file gap** = espace *m* neutre (séparant deux fichiers); *(number by which a file is identified)* **file handle** = numéro *m* de fichier; **the new data is written to the file identified by file handle 1** = les nouvelles données sont écrites dans un fichier identifié par le numéro 1; **file handling routine** = routine *f* de manipulation de fichier; *(information about the file stored at the beginning of the file)* **file header** = en-tête *m* de fichier; **the file header in the database file shows the total number of records and lists the index fields** = l'en-tête du fichier indique le nombre total d'enregistrements et la liste des champs indexés; **file identification** = identification *f* de fichier; **file index** = index *m* des fichiers; **file label** = label *m or* étiquette *f or* descripteur *m* de fichier; **file layout** = structure *f* d'un fichier; *(software that prevents data in a file being updated by two different users)* **file locking** = protection *f or* verrouillage *m* de fichier; **file maintenance** = mise *f* à jour *or* maintenance *f* de fichier; **file management** = gestion *f* de fichier; **file manager** = gestionnaire *m* de fichier; **file merger** = fusion *f* de fichiers; **file name** = nom *m* d'un fichier; **file organization** = FILE LAYOUT **file processing** = traitement *m* de fichier; **file protection** = (logiciel *or* dispositif de) protection *f or* sécurisation *f* de fichiers; **file protect tab** = dispositif *m* de protection d'écriture (de fichier); **file purge** = vidage *m* de fichier; **file-recovery utility** = logiciel *m* de récupération de fichiers (après incident); **a lost file cannot be found without a file-recovery utility** = il est impossible de retrouver un fichier perdu sans l'aide d'un logiciel de récupération de fichiers; **file security** = protection *f or* sécurisation *f* de fichiers; **file server** = serveur *m*; **file set** = groupe *m* de fichiers (connexes); *(file that can be used by two users)* **file sharing** = partage *m* de fichier; *(number of bytes occupied by a file)* **file size** = taille *f* de fichier; **file sort** = tri *m* de fichiers; **file storage** = *(action)* mise *f* en mémoire *or* stockage *m* de fichier; *(storage medium)* support *m* de données (d'un fichier); *(memory)* mémoire *f* (contenant des fichiers); **file store** = (ensemble des) fichiers en mémoire; **file structure** = structure *f* d'un fichier; **file transfer** = transfert *m* de fichier; *(method of transferring files)* **file transfer access and management (FTAM)** = (méthode de) gestion, accès et transfert de fichiers *or* méthode FTAM; *(TCP/IP standard for transferring files)* **file transfer protocol (FTP)** = protocole *m* de transfert de fichiers *or* protocole FTP; *(utility that links two computers together)* **file transfer utility** = utilitaire *m* de transfert de fichiers; *(method of classifying what a file contains)* **file type** = type *m* de fichier; **files with the extension EXE are file types that contain program code** = les fichiers avec une extension EXE contiennent un code exécutable; **file update** = *(action)* mise à jour d'un fichier; *(corrected version)* nouvelle version d'un fichier; **file validation** = validation *f* de fichier; **change** *or* **movement file** = fichier de mouvements *or* de modifications *or* de mise à jour; **indexed file** = fichier indexé; **inverted file** = fichier inversé; **output file** = fichier de sortie; **program file** = fichier programme; **text file** = fichier texte; **threaded file** = fichier avec articles chaînés; **transaction file** = fichier de transactions **2** *verb* **to file documents** =

classer des documents *see also* BATCH, COMMAND

◊ **filename** *noun* nom *m* d'un fichier; *(MS-DOS: three-character name used together with a filename)* **filename extension** = extension *f* du nom d'un fichier *or* suffixe *m* d'un fichier; **the filename extension SYS indicates that this is a system file** = l'extension SYS ajoutée au nom du fichier indique qu'il s'agit d'un fichier système; **in MS-DOS, a filename can be up to eight characters long together with a three character filename extension** = sous MS-DOS, le nom de fichier peut comporter jusqu'à huit caractères et une extension (de nom) de trois caractères

> QUOTE it allows users to back up or restore read-only security files and hidden system files independently
> *Minicomputer News*

> QUOTE the lost file, while inaccessible without a file-recovery utility, remains on disk until new information writes over it
> *Publish*

> QUOTE when the filename is entered at the prompt, the operating system looks in the file and executes any instructions stored there
> *PC User*

filing *noun (putting documents in order)* classement *m* ; rangement *m*; *(documents to be put in order)* le classement *or* documents *mpl* à classer; **filing cabinet** = classeur *m*; **filing card** = fiche *f*

◊ **filing system** *noun* **(a)** *(way of putting documents in order)* méthode *f* de classement *or* d'archivage **(b)** *(software)* logiciel *m* d'archivage

fill *verb* **(a)** *(to make something full)* remplir **(b)** *(to put characters into gaps)* remplir; **fill character** = caractère *m* de remplissage; **filled cable** = câble *m* étanche **(c)** *(to draw)* combler

◊ **fill up** *verb* remplir; **the disk was quickly filled up** = la disquette a été très vite pleine

film 1 *noun* **(a)** *(for photographs)* pellicule *f* photographique *or* film *m*; **film advance** = *(of film roll)* entraînement *m* d'un film; *(of phototypesetting machine)* avance *f* *or* pas *m* *or* espacement *m*; **film assembly** = montage *m* d'un film; **film base** = pellicule *f*; **film chain** = l'équipement de prise de vue et de projection de films; **film optical scanning device for input into computers (FOSDIC)** = lecteur optique de microfilms pour entrée de données sur ordinateur; **film pickup** = repiquage *m* vidéo d'un film; *(teaching device)* **film strip** = film fixe; **photographic film** = pellicule photographique **(b)** *(cinema)* film; **film caméra** = camera *f* **2** *verb* **(a)** *(cinema)* filmer *or* tourner un film **(b)** *(printing)* filmer (un texte)

◊ **filming** *noun* **(a)** *(cinema)* tournage *m*; **filming will start next week if the weather is fine** = le tournage commencera la semaine prochaine s'il fait beau **(b)** *(printing)* flashage *m* (d'un texte)

◊ **filmsetting** *noun* photocomposition *f*

filter 1 *noun* **(a)** *(electronic circuit)* filtre *m*;

bandpass filter = filtre passe-bande; **high pass filter** = filtre passe-haut; **low pass filter** = filtre passe-bas **(b)** *(coloured glass)* filtre chromatique; **absorption filter** = filtre d'absorption; *(placed over a monitor)* **character enhancement filter** = filtre d'optimisation de caractères et de protection de la vue; **filter factor** = facteur *m* de filtre **(c)** *(pattern of binary digits)* masque *m* **2** *verb* **(a)** *(to remove unwanted elements)* filtrer **(b)** *(to select various bits)* séparer *or* éliminer par filtrage *or* sélectionner

final *adjective* dernier, -ière *or* final, -e; **to keyboard the final data files** = saisir (au clavier) les derniers fichiers de données; **to make the final changes to a document** = apporter les dernières corrections à un document

find 1 *verb* trouver *or* retrouver *or* repérer; **it took a lot of time to find the faulty chip** = il a fallu beaucoup de temps pour trouver la puce défectueuse; **the debugger found the error very quickly** = le débogueur a repéré la faute très rapidement (NOTE: **finding - found**) **2** *noun* **find and replace** = (procédure) chercher et remplacer

◊ **Finder** ™ *noun (Apple Macintosh graphical user interface)* Finder ™

fine *adjective* **(a)** *(very thin)* fin, fine *or* mince; **the engraving has some very fine lines** = on trouve quelques lignes très fines dans cette gravure **(b)** *(excellent)* très bon, bonne *or* excellent, -e

◊ **fine tune** *verb* mettre au point *or* régler (avec grande précision); **fine-tuning improved the speed by ten per cent** = une mise au point très précise améliore la vitesse de dix pour cent

finish 1 *noun* **(a)** *(final appearance)* fini *m* *or* finition *f*; **the product has an attractive finish** = ce produit a un très beau fini *or* présente une belle finition **(b)** *(end)* fin *f* **2** *verb* **(a)** terminer *or* finir; **she finished all the keyboarding before lunch** = elle a terminé la saisie (sur clavier) avant le déjeuner **(b)** se terminer *or* prendre fin

◊ **finished** *adjective* fini, -e *or* final, -e *or* définitif, -ive; **finished document** = document définitif

finite-precision numbers *noun* nombres *mpl* à précision finie

firmware *noun (stored in a hardware memory chip)* logiciel *m* de système sur puce *or* logiciel microprogrammé; firmware *m*

first *adjective* premier, -ière; **first fit** = (algorithme du) premier emplacement capable; *(original computer made with valve-based electronic technology)* **first generation computer** = ordinateur *m* de première génération; *(master copy)* **first generation image** = image *f* originale *or* de première génération; **first in first out (FIFO)** = (méthode du) premier entré premier sorti *or* (stockage) FIFO; **first-level address** = adresse *f* de premier niveau *or* adresse réelle; *(communications)* **first party release** = coupure *f* au premier raccroché

fisheye lens *noun* fisheye *m*

fit *verb (calculate a curve)* ajuster

fix *verb* **(a)** *(to attach something permanently)* fixer *or* attacher; **the computer is fixed to the workstation** = l'ordinateur est fixé au poste de travail; **fixed and exchangeable disk storage (FEDS)** = unité comprenant des disques fixes et des disques amovibles; **fixed cycle operation** = opération *f* en cycle fixe *or* opération synchronisée; **fixed data** = données constantes *or* permanentes; **fixed disk** = disque dur fixe *or* non amovible; **fixed field** = champ de taille constante *or* fixe; **fixed head (disk) drive** = lecteur (de disque) à tête de lecture fixe; **fixed-length record** = enregistrement *m* de longueur fixe *or* déterminée; **fixed-length word** = mot de longueur fixe *or* déterminée; **fixed program computer** = ordinateur à logique câblée; **fixed routing** = acheminement *m* pré-sélectionné; **fixed word length** = (ordinateur) à longueur de mots fixe **(b)** *(to mend)* réparer; **the technicians are trying to fix the switchboard** = les techniciens essayent de réparer le standard téléphonique; **can you fix the photocopier?** = pouvez-vous réparer le photocopieur?

◊ **fixed-point notation** *noun* notation à virgule fixe; **storage of fixed point numbers has two bytes allocated for the whole number and one byte for the fraction part** = la mise en mémoire de nombres à virgule fixe utilise deux octets pour le nombre entier et un octet pour la partie décimale; **fixed-point arithmetic** = arithmétique *f* à virgule fixe

◊ **fixing** *noun (photography)* fixage *m or* fixation *f*

flag 1 *noun (for block or field)* marqueur *m or* drapeau *m or* balise *f*; *(for status)* indicateur *m or* témoin *m or* drapeau *m*; **if the result is zero, the zero flag is set** = si le résultat est zéro, l'indicateur zéro est activé; **carry flag** = témoin *or* indicateur de retenue; **device flag** = (bit) indicateur *or* témoin (d'utilisation); **overflow bit** *or* **flag** = bit *m or* indicateur binaire de dépassement de capacité; **zero flag** = indicateur (binaire) zéro; **flag bit** = bit indicateur *or* indicateur binaire; **flag code** = code *m* drapeau; **flag event** = fonction *f or* condition *f* de balisage *or* de mise en place d'un drapeau; **flag register** = registre *m* des témoins *or* des drapeaux; **flag sequence** = séquence *f* de marqueurs *or* d'indicateurs *or* de drapeaux 2 *verb* marquer *or* baliser

◊ **flagging** *noun* **(a)** *(putting an indicator)* balisage *m or* marquage *m or* mise *f* en place d'un drapeau **(b)** *(picture distortion)* battement *m*

flare *noun* reflet *m or* tache *f* lumineuse *or* interférence *f* (lumineuse)

◊ **flared** *adjective* marqué, -e d'un reflet *or* taché, -e

flash *verb* (faire) clignoter; **flash A/D** = convertisseur analogique-numérique parallèle; *(nonvolatile memory)* **flash memory** = mémoire *f* flash; **flashing character** = caractère *m* clignotant

flat *adjective* **(a)** *(in an image or photograph)* sans contraste *or* plat, -e **(b)** *(area of memory)* **flat address space** = espace *m* d'adressage simple; *compare* SEGMENTED ADDRESS SPACE **flat**

file = fichier plat *or* bidimensionnel; *(database program)* **flat file database** = base *f* de données linéaire (non relationnelle); **flat pack** = boîtier *m* plat

◊ **flatbed** *noun (printer or scanner)* à plat *or* de type 'flatbed'; **scanners are either flatbed models or platen type, paper-fed models** = les scanners sont de type 'flatbed', ou possèdent un système d'entraînement du papier par rouleau(x); **paper cannot be rolled through flatbed scanners** = le papier n'est pas entraîné par rouleau(x) dans les scanners à plat; **flatbed plotter** = traceur *m* à plat; **flatbed press** = presse *f* à platine (horizontale); **flatbed transmitter** = lecteur *m* de transmission à plat *or* de type 'flatbed'

◊ **flatplan** *noun* maquette *f* d'édition *or* chemin de fer

flex *noun* câble *m or* fil *m* (de liaison) *or* cordon *m* (souple) (NOTE: no plural; say **pieces of flex**)

flexible *adjective* flexible *or* souple; **flexible array** = tableau *m* à dimensions variables; **flexible disk** = disque *m* souple *or* disquette *f*; **flexible disk cartridge** = cartouche *f* de disquette; **flexible machining system (FMS)** = système de machines-outils à commandes numériques; *(use of automated devices in manufacturing)* **flexible manufacturing system (FMS)** = atelier *m* flexible

◊ **flexibility** *noun* flexibilité *f or* souplesse *f*

flicker 1 *noun* **(a)** *(variation of brightness)* scintillement *m or* vacillement *m or* papillotement *m* **(b)** *(video disk)* scintillement **(c)** *(computer graphic image)* vacillement *or* tremblement *m* 2 *verb* clignoter *or* vaciller *or* papilloter; **the image flickers when the printer is switched on** = l'image sur l'écran vacille à la mise sous tension de l'imprimante

◊ **flicker-free** *adjective* (image *or* affichage) sans vacillement *or* sans clignotement *or* sans papillotement *or* sans reflet

QUOTE the new 640 by 480 pixel standard, coupled with the flicker- free displays on the four new monitors and a maximum of 256 colours from a palette of more than quarter of a million

PC User

flip-flop (FF) *noun* commutateur *m* à bascule; **JK-flip-flop** = commutateur à bascule de type JK; **D-flip-flop** = commutateur à bascule de type D

flippy *noun* disquette *f* réversible

float *noun* décalage *m or* déplacement *m*; **float factor** = facteur *m* de déplacement (d'une adresse relative); **float relocate** = ré-adressage *m* par déplacement (en ajoutant une adresse origine à une adresse relative)

◊ **floating** *adjective* flottant, -e; **floating accent** = accent flottant; **floating address** = adresse relative; **floating head** = FLYING HEAD **floating point** = virgule flottante; **floating point arithmetic** = calcul *m* en virgule flottante; **the fixed number 56.47 in floating-point arithmetic would be 0.5647 and a** power of 2 = dans un calcul en virgule flottante, le nombre 56,47 serait écrit 0,5647 puissance 2; **floating point notation** = notation à virgule flottante; **floating point number** = nombre à virgule flottante; **floating point operation (FLOP)** = opération en virgule flottante; *(CPU that can process floating point numbers)* **floating point unit** *or* **processor (FPU)** = processeur *m* à virgule flottante; **the floating point processor speeds up the processing of the graphics software** = le processeur à virgule flottante accélère la vitesse de traitement des logiciels graphiques; **this model includes a built-in floating point processor** = ce modèle est livré avec un processeur à virgule flottante installé; **floating symbolic address** = adresse symbolique *or* relative; **floating voltage** = courant *m* flottant

flooding *noun* routage *m* par dispersion *or* par redistribution

FLOP = FLOATING POINT OPERATION opération *f* en virgule flottante; **FLOPs per second** = (nombre d') opérations en virgule flottante par seconde

floppy disk *or* **floppy** *or* **FD** *or* **fd** *noun* disquette *f* *or* disque *m* souple; **floppy disk controller (FDC)** = contrôleur *m* de disquettes; **floppy disk sector** = secteur *m* de disquette; **floppy disk drive** *or* **unit** = lecteur *m* de disquette(s) *or* unité *f* de disquette(s); **floppy tape** *or* **tape streamer** = streamer *m*

flow 1 *noun* flux *m* *or* flot *m*; **automatic text flow across pages** = texte au kilomètre avec changement de page automatique; **the device controls the copy flow** = ce dispositif contrôle le mouvement des feuilles *or* l'alimentation du papier (en) feuille à feuille; **current flow is regulated by a resistor** = le débit d'électricité est régularisé par une résistance; **data flow** = flux des données; **flow control** = contrôle *m* du flux (de données); **flow direction** = direction *f* du flux **2** *verb* couler *or* circuler; **work is flowing normally again after the breakdown of the printer** = le travail reprend normalement après la panne de l'imprimante; *(insert text into page format)* **flow text** = verser *or* injecter du texte (dans un cadre PAO)

◊ **flowchart** *or* **flow diagram** *noun* ordinogramme *m* ; diagramme *m* d'opérations; **a flowchart is the first step to a well designed program** = l'ordinogramme est à la base d'un programme bien conçu; **data flowchart** = ordinogramme de données; **flowchart symbols** = symboles d'un ordinogramme; **flowchart template** = grille *f* *or* modèle *m* pour ordinogramme; **logical flowchart** = ordinogramme logique

◊ **flowline** *noun* ligne *f* de jonction des symboles d'un ordinogramme

fluctuate *verb* fluctuer *or* varier; **the electric current fluctuates between 1Amp and 1.3Amp** = le courant fluctue entre 1Amp et 1,3Amp

◊ **fluctuating** *adjective* variable *or* qui fluctue *or* qui varie; **fluctuating signal strength** = intensité *f* variable du signal

◊ **fluctuation** *noun* fluctuation *f* *or* variation *f* *or* saute *f* (de courant); **voltage fluctuations can affect the functioning of the computer system** = les sautes *or* les fluctuations de courant peuvent nuire au bon fonctionnement de l'ordinateur

flush 1 *verb* vider; **flush buffers** = vider la mémoire tampon **2** *adjective* **(a)** au même niveau *or* de niveau; **the cover is trimmed flush with the pages** = la couverture est rognée de niveau avec les pages **(b)** *(of text)* **flush left** = justifier à gauche *or* (au) fer à gauche; **flush right** = justifier à droite *or* (au) fer à droite

flutter *noun* variation *f* de vitesse *or* scintillement *m*; **wow and flutter are common faults on cheap tape recorders** = le pleurage et les variations de vitesse *or* le scintillement sont des défauts courants des magnétophones bon marché

flux *noun* **magnetic flux** = flux *m* magnétique

fly *verb* voler; **flying spot scan** = balayage *m* par faisceau mobile

◊ **flyback** *noun* retour *m* (d'un balayage); **field flyback** = retour de trame; **line flyback** = retour de ligne

flying head *noun* *(floating head)* tête *f* flottante

FM = FREQUENCY MODULATION

FMS (a) = FLEXIBLE MACHINING SYSTEM **(b)** = FLEXIBLE MANUFACTURING SYSTEM

FNP = FRONT END NETWORK PROCESSOR

f-number *noun* ouverture *f* de diaphragme *or* diaph *m*

focal length *noun* distance *f* focale

focus 1 *noun* foyer *m*; **the picture is out of focus** *or* **is not in focus** = l'image est floue *or* n'est pas au point **2** *verb* mettre au point; **the camera is focused on the foreground** = la camera est réglée pour le premier plan *or* est dirigée sur le premier plan; **they adjusted the lens position so that the beam focused correctly** = la position de la lentille a été ajustée de façon à bien mettre au point le rayon lumineux

◊ **focusing** *noun* **magnetic focusing** = concentration *f* *or* mise *f* au point magnétique

fog *noun* *(photography)* voile *m*

fold 1 *verb* plier *or* replier **2** *noun* pli *m* *or* pliage *m*; *(listing paper)* **accordion fold** *or* **fanfold** = papier (plié) en paravent *or* en éventail *or* en accordéon *or* en continu

◊ **-fold** *suffix* *(times)* **four-fold** = quatre fois

◊ **folder** *noun* chemise *f* *or* classeur *m* *(Apple Macintosh group of files)* dossier *m* (Macintosh, eMAIL); *see also* DIRECTORY

◊ **folding (a)** *noun* *(hashing method)* folding *m* *or* réassemblage *m* **(b)** pliage *m* *or* pliure *f*

◊ **folding machine** *noun* plieuse *f*

folio 1 *noun* **(a)** feuillet *m* or folio *m*; *(book)* in-folio *m* **(b)** numéro *m* de page 2 *verb* folioter or paginer

font or **fount** *noun* police *f* de caractères or fonte *f*; *(device that adds another resident font)* **font card** = carte *f* de police de caractères; **font change** = changement de police de caractères; *(Apple Macintosh system utility)* **Font/DA Mover** = gestionnaire *m* de polices et d'accessoires de bureau or Mover (Apple Macintosh); **font disk** = disquette de fontes or de polices de caractères; **downloadable fonts** = polices (de caractères) téléchargeables; **resident font** = police résidente

QUOTE laser printers store fonts in several ways: as resident, cartridge and downloadable fonts

Desktop Publishing Today

QUOTE Word Assistant is designed to help word-processing users produce better-looking documents. It has style templates and forms providing 25 TrueType fonts, 100 clip-art images and two font utility programs.

Computing

foolscap *noun* *(paper)* (papier) format *m* ministre; **the letter was on six sheets of foolscap** = la lettre était écrite sur six feuilles format ministre; **a foolscap envelope** = enveloppe longue (pour papier ministre)

foot *noun* **(a)** *(bottom part)* pied *m* or base *f*; bas *m*; **he signed his name at the foot of the letter** = il a signé au bas de la lettre **(b)** *(measurement = 0.3048m)* pied *m*

◊ **foot candle** *noun* *(amount of light)* candela *f* par pied carré

◊ **footer** or **footing** *noun* *(message at the bottom of pages)* pied *m* de page

◊ **footnote** *noun* note *f* or renvoi *m* en bas de page

◊ **footprint** *noun* **(a)** empreinte *f* (d'un faisceau, etc.) **(b)** encombrement *m* (d'un ordinateur)

QUOTE Acer has overhauled its desktop PC range with the launch of 16 new models ranging from small-footprint, single-processing systems to large multiprocessing boxes.

Computing

forbid *verb* interdire (quelque chose or de faire quelque chose); **forbidden character** or **combination** = caractère interdit or chaîne (de caractères) interdite (NOTE: **forbidding - forbade - forbidden**)

force 1 *noun* force *f*; **to come into force** = entrer en vigueur; **the new regulations will come into force on January 1st** = les nouveaux règlements entreront en vigueur le 1er janvier 2 *verb* forcer (quelqu'un à faire quelque chose); **forced page break** = saut *f* de page obligatoire or programmé

foreground *noun* **(a)** *(front part)* premier plan; **foreground colour** = couleur *f* de premier plan **(b)** *(high priority task)* (tâche) de premier plan or prioritaire; **foreground/background modes** = mode d'exécution frontal/masqué; **foreground processing** or **foregrounding** = traitement *m* frontal; *(region of a system in which high priority jobs are executed)* **foreground processing memory** = mémoire *f* de traitement frontal; **foreground program** = programme prioritaire

◊ **foregrounding** *noun* traitement frontal

QUOTE This brighter - but still anti-glare - type of screen is especially useful for people using colourful graphic applications, where both the background and foreground are visually important.

Computing

forest *noun* arborescence *f*

form 1 *noun* **(a)** *(preprinted document)* formulaire *m* ; bordereau *m*; *(preset computer layout for addresses, etc.)* masque *m* de saisie or format *m* d'écran de saisie; **it's been easy to train the operators to use the new software since its display looks like the existing printed forms** = il a été facile de former les opérateurs à l'utilisation de ce nouveau logiciel, parce que les formats d'écran ressemblent aux rapports d'impression existants **(b)** *(plate or block of type)* forme *f* d'impression **(c)** *(page of computer stationery)* feuillet *m* or page *f*; **form feed (FF)** = (instruction de) changement *m* de page; **form flash** = en-tête *m* préétabli (gardé en mémoire); **form handling equipment** = équipement de traitement de formulaires or de papier listing (en sortie d'imprimante); **form letter** = lettre *f* type or lettre standard; **form mode** = mode *m* masque (de saisie); **form overlay** = texte *m* or graphique *m* préétabli (gardé en mémoire); **form stop** = (i) arrêt *m* pour manque de papier; (ii) indicateur *m* de fin de papier 2 *verb* constituer or former or construire; **the system is formed of five separate modules** = le système est constitué de cinq modules indépendants

format 1 *noun* **(a)** *(of book)* format *m*; **the printer can deal with all formats up to quarto** = l'imprimante peut accommoder tous les formats jusqu'au quarto **(b)** *(of text)* format; *(in memory)* **address format** = format d'adresse; *(rows and columns of punched card)* **card format** = format de carte perforée; **data format** = format de données; **display format** = format d'affichage or format d'écran; **instruction format** = format d'instruction; **local format storage** = (mise en) mémoire *f* du format courant; **variable format** = format variable **(c)** *(syntax of instructions)* format; **symbolic-coding format** = format de langage symbolique **(d)** *(TV programme)* grille *f* d'émission; **magazine format** = format magazine 2 *verb* **(a)** *(to arrange text)* formater or mettre en forme; **style sheets are used to format documents** = on utilise des feuilles de style pour formater les documents or mettre les documents en forme; **formatted dump** = vidage *m* au format **(b)** **to format a disk** = formater un disque or une disquette; **disk formatting** = formatage *m* de disque or de disquette; **disk formatting has to be done before you can use a new floppy disk** = il faut formater toutes les nouvelles disquettes avant de les utiliser; *(defines the physical pattern of tracks)* **low-level formatting** = formatage *m* de bas niveau

> QUOTE As an increasing amount of information within businesses is generated in word-processed format, text retrieval tools are becoming a highly attractive pragmatic solution.

◊ **formatter** *noun* matériel *m or* logiciel *m* de formatage; **print formatter** = logiciel *m* de formatage d'impression; **text formatter** = logiciel de formatage de texte

> QUOTE there are three models, offering 53, 80 and 160 Mb of formatted capacity
> *Minicomputer News*

formula *noun* formule *f*; **formula portability** = portabilité *f* d'une formule; **formula translator (FORTRAN)** = traducteur *m* de formule *or* langage *m* FORTRAN (NOTE: plural is **formulae**)

for-next loop *noun* boucle *f* conditionnelle FOR...NEXT; **for X=1 to 5: print X: next X - this will print out 1 2 3 4 5** = pour X=1 à 5: imprimer X: calculer la valeur suivante de X - le résultat imprimé sera 1 2 3 4 5

FORTH langage *m* FORTH

> QUOTE the main attraction of FORTH over other computer languages is that it is not simply a language, rather it is a programming tool in which it is possible to write other application specific languages
> *Electronics & Power*

FORTRAN = FORMULA TRANSLATOR langage *m* FORTRAN

forty-track disk *noun* disquette *f* (de) quarante pistes

forward 1 *adjective* avant *or* en avant; en avance *or* d'avance; **forward channel** = canal (de transmission) aller; **forward clearing** = remise à l'état initial commandée par l'émetteur; **forward error correction** = correction d'erreur en cours de transmission; *(pointer that contains the address of the next item in the list)* **forward pointer** = pointeur *m* avant; **forward reference** = référence par anticipation; **forward scatter** = onde éclatée progressante **2** *verb* transmettre; *(a letter or a call)* faire suivre *or* réacheminer

◊ **forward mode** *noun* (tri, etc.) en ordre croissant

◊ **forwarding** *noun see* REDIRECTION

FOSDIC = FILM OPTICAL SCANNING DEVICE FOR INPUT INTO COMPUTERS

fount = FONT

four-address instruction *noun* instruction *f* à quatre adresses; **four-plus-one address** = quatre adresses plus une

◊ **four-part** *adjective* **four-part invoices** = factures *fpl* en quatre exemplaires *or* en quatre épaisseurs

Fourier series *noun* série *f* de Fourier

fourth generation computers *noun* ordinateurs de quatrième génération; **fourth generation languages** = langages de quatrième génération

four-track recorder *noun* magnétophone *m* à quatre pistes

fps = FRAMES PER SECOND

FPU = FLOATING POINT UNIT

fractal *noun (shape that repeats itself)* fractal *m*

fraction *noun* fraction *f*

◊ **fractional** *adjective* fractionnaire; **the root is the fractional power of a number** = la racine est la puissance fractionnaire d'un nombre; **fractional part** = partie *f* fractionnaire *or* mantisse *f* *(allocation of parts of a bandwidth)* **fractional services** = services *mpl* partagés; **the commercial carrier will sell you fractional services that provide 64Kbps data transmission** = l'opérateur (commercial) vous vendra des services partagés qui permettent de transmettre des données à 64K bps

fragmentation *noun (memory allocation to a number of files)* fragmentation *f or* segmentation *f or* fractionnement *m* *(files stored across non-contiguous sectors)* fragmentation; *see also* DEFRAGMENTATION

> COMMENT: when a file is saved to disk, it is not always saved in adjacent sectors; this will increase the retrieval time. Defragmentation moves files back into adjacent sectors so that the read head does not have to move far across the disk, so it increases performance.

frame *noun* **(a)** *(on magnetic tape)* trame *f*; *(of transmitted data)* bloc *m*; *(on magnetic tape)* **frame error** = erreur *f* de trame; *(communications protocol)* **frame relay** = échange *m* de trames **(b)** *(for printed circuit boards)* support *m* de cartes (de circuits imprimés) *m* avec guide-cartes *or* baie *f* (pour cartes) **(c)** *(one image)* image *f* complète; **video frame** = image vidéo; **with the image processor you can freeze a video frame** = le processeur d'images permet de figer une image *or* de faire un arrêt sur image; **frame flyback** = saut *m* d'image; **frame frequency** = fréquence *f* de l'image; **in the UK the frame frequency is 25 fps** = la télévision britannique utilise une fréquence de 25 images par seconde *or* 25 images/seconde; **frame grabber** = capteur *m* d'image vidéo; **frame store** = mémoire *f* image; **the image processor allows you to store a video frame in a built-in 8-bit frame store** = le processeur d'images permet le stockage d'une image vidéo dans une mémoire intégrée de 8 bits; **the frame store can be used to display weather satellite pictures** = la mémoire image peut servir à l'affichage des images météorologiques transmises par satellite

◊ **frames per second (fps)** noun (motion or TV picture) (nombre d') images f par seconde or images/seconde

◊ **framework** noun cadre m or structure f; **the program framework was designed first** = on a d'abord établi le cadre or la structure du programme

◊ **framing** noun (a) cadrage m (b) (of data on tape) synchronisation f de trames; **framing bit** = bit m de synchronisation; **framing code** = code m de synchronisation

fraud noun fraude f; **computer fraud** = fraude f informatique

QUOTE the offences led to the arrest of nine teenagers who were all charged with computer fraud

Computer News

free 1 adjective libre; (database that can store any type of data) **free form database** = base f de données à structure (de champs) libre; **free indexing** = indexage m libre; **free line** = ligne f libre; **free running mode** = mode m multi-utilisateur; **free space loss** = perte f dans l'espace; **free space media** = l'espace f, **free wheeling** = transmission f sans contrôle de retour **2** verb libérer (de l'espace dans la mémoire)

◊ **freedom** noun liberté f; **freedom of information** = liberté d'accès à l'information; **freedom of the press** = liberté de la presse; **freedom of speech** = liberté d'expression

◊ **freely** adverb librement

◊ **freeware** noun (software in the public domain) logiciel m gratuit or en libre service

freeze verb figer; **to freeze (frame)** = figer une image or faire un arrêt sur image; **the image processor will freeze a single TV frame** = le processeur d'image peut figer une image de télévision isolée; see also CRASH, HANG

F-region (astronomy) région f F

frequency noun fréquence f; **frequency changer** = convertisseur m de fréquence; **frequency divider** = réducteur m de fréquence; **frequency division multiplexing (FDM)** = multiplexage m (par répartition) en fréquence or FDM; **using FDM we can transmit 100 telephone calls along one main cable** = le multiplexage en fréquence permet de transférer 100 appels téléphoniques sur un seul câble; **frequency domain** = domaine m de fréquence; **frequency modulation (FM)** = modulation f de fréquence; **frequency range** = gamme f de fréquences; **frequency response** = réponse f en fréquence; **frequency shift keying (FSK)** = (système) de modulation f par déplacement or décalage de fréquence; **frequency variation** = variation f de fréquence; **clock frequency** = fréquence d'horloge; **the main clock frequency is 10MHz** = la principale fréquence d'horloge est de 10MHz; (number of times the picture beam scans) **line frequency** = fréquence (de balayage) de lignes; (from 30 - 300 GHz) **extremely high frequency (EHF)** = ondes fpl

millimétriques; (of less than 100 Hz) **extremely low frequency (ELF)** = ondes myriamétriques; see also LOW, HIGH, VERY, INFRA, MEDIUM, ULTRA

◊ **frequent** adjective fréquent, -e; **we send frequent telexes to New York** = nous envoyons fréquemment des télex à New York

◊ **frequently** adverb souvent or fréquemment; **the photocopier is frequently out of use** = il n'est pas rare de voir le photocopieur en dérangement

friction feed noun entraînement m par friction or par rouleaux

friendly front-end noun (display that is easy to use and understand) interface f utilisateur conviviale

FROM = FUSIBLE READ ONLY MEMORY

front 1 noun avant m or face f or panneau m avant; **the disks are inserted in slots in the front of the terminal** = on insère les disquettes dans les fentes du panneau avant du terminal **2** adjective avant; **front panel** = panneau avant or antérieur or de commande; **front porch** = palier m avant; **front projection** = rétroprojection f

◊ **front-end 1** adjective frontal, -e; **front-end computer** = ordinateur frontal or frontal m; **front-end processor (FEP)** = processeur frontal; **front-end network processor (FNP)** = processeur frontal de réseau; **front-end system** = système frontal **2** noun (program that is seen by an end user) interface f utilisateur; **the program is very easy to use thanks to the uncomplicated front-end** = ce programme est très facile à utiliser du fait de la simplicité de son interface utilisateur; (display that is easy to use and understand) **friendly front-end** = interface f utilisateur conviviale

FSK = FREQUENCY SHIFT KEYING

FTAM = FILE TRANSFER ACCESS AND MANAGEMENT

FTP = FILE TRANSFER PROTOCOL

full adjective (a) plein, -e or complet, -ète; **the disk is full, so the material will have to be stored on another disk** = cette disquette est pleine, il faudra donc saisir les données sur une autre disquette (b) (complete) exhaustif, -ive; **full adder** = additionneur complet or à trois entrées; **full duplex (FDX or fdx)** = full duplex; **full-frame time code** = comptage m d'images (complètes); (computer with a digitising card) **full motion video adapter** = carte f vidéo pleine animation or à grand débit; (position of a directory) **full path** = chemin m complet; (display that uses all the screen) **full-screen** = plein écran; **full-size display** = écran m pleine page; **full subtractor** = soustracteur complet or à trois entrées; (search for something through all the text) **full-text search** = recherche f globale or dans tout le texte

QUOTE transmitter and receiver can be operated independently, making full duplex communication possible

Electronics & Power

◊ **fully** *adverb* complètement; **fully connected network** = réseau totalement maillé; **fully formed character** = caractère complet; **a daisy wheel printer produces fully formed characters** = la marguerite imprime des caractères complets; *(circuit board which has all components)* **fully populated board** = carte *f* équipée *or* avec (tous ses) composants

QUOTE transmitter and receiver can be operated independently, making full duplex communication possible
Electronics & Power

function 1 *noun* **(a)** *(mathematical formula)* fonction *f* **(b)** *(computer program instructions)* fonction; **function call** = appel *m* de fonction; **function digit** = code *m* *or* caractère *m* de fonction; *(collection of functions)* **function library** = bibliothèque *f* de fonctions; *(programming system)* **function overloading** = système *m* de programmation à surcharge de fonctions; **function table** = table *f* de fonctions **(c)** *(special feature on a computer)* fonction; **the word-processor had a spelling-checker function but no built-in text-editing function** = cette machine de traitement de texte possédait une fonction correction orthographique *or* possédait un correcteur orthographique mais n'était pas équipée d'éditeur intégré; **function code** = code *m* de fonction **2** *verb* fonctionner *or* marcher; **the new system has not functioned properly since it was installed** = le nouvel ordinateur n'a jamais bien fonctionné depuis qu'on l'a installé

◊ **functional** *adjective* fonctionnel, -elle; **functional diagram** = schéma *or* diagramme fonctionnel; **functional specification** = spécification *f* *or* analyse *f* fonctionnelle; **functional unit** = appareil *m* en bon état de marche

◊ **function key** *or* **programmable function key** *noun* touche *f* de fonction; **tags can be allocated to function keys** = on peut allouer des étiquettes aux touches de fonction; **hitting F5 will put you into insert mode** = en appuyant sur la touche de fonction F5 on se met en mode entrée

QUOTE they made it clear that the PC was to take its place as part of a much larger computing function that comprised of local area networks, wide area networks, small systems, distributed systems and mainframes
Minicomputer News

QUOTE if your computer has a MOD function, you will not need the function defined in line 3010
Computing Today

QUOTE the final set of keys are to be found above the main keyboard and comprise 5 function keys, which together with shift, give 10 user-defined keys
Computing Today

fundamental frequency *noun* fréquence *f* fondamentale

fuse 1 *noun* fusible *m*; **to blow a fuse** = faire sauter un plomb **2** *verb* faire sauter un fusible *or* un plomb; **when the air-conditioning was switched on, it fused the whole system** = on a fait sauter les plombs en branchant le climatiseur

◊ **fusible link** *noun* élément *m* fusible

◊ **fusible read only memory (FROM)** *noun* ROM *or* mémoire *f* morte à fusibles

◊ **fusion** *noun* *(combining programs, etc.)* fusion *f*

fuzzy *noun* flou, -e; **top quality paper will eliminate fuzzy characters** = un papier de qualité supérieure donnera des caractères plus nets; **fuzzy logic** *or* **fuzzy theory** = logique floue

Gg

G = GIGA *prefix* giga; **GHz** = gigahertz *m or* GHz

GaAs = GALLIUM ARSENIDE

gaffer *noun (in a studio or office)* homme à tout faire *or* gaffeur *m;* US chef-électricien *m; (US - black adhesive tape)* **gaffer tape** = bande *f* adhésive noire (qui sert à tout dans un studio) *or* outil favori du gaffeur

gain 1 *noun* gain *m;* **gain control** = contrôle *m* de gain; **automatic gain control** = contrôle de gain automatique **2** *verb* **to gain access to a file** = avoir accès à *or* accéder à un fichier; **the user cannot gain access to the confidential information in the file without a password** = il est impossible d'accéder aux renseignements confidentiels du fichier sans utiliser le mot de passe

galactic noise *noun* bruits *mpl* cosmiques

galley proof *noun* épreuve *f* en placard *or* en première

gallium arsenide (GaAs) *noun* arséniure *m* de gallium

game *noun* jeu *m;* **computer game** = jeu électronique; **game paddle** = manette *f* (de jeu); *(ROM device that contains the program for a computer game)* **game cartridge** = cartouche *f* de jeu; *(dedicated computer designed to be only used to play games)* **game console** = console *f* de jeu; *(connection for a joystick)* **game port** = port *m* (de) jeu; **games software** = ludiciel *m*

gamma *noun (measure of light on photographic or TV image)* gamma *m*

ganged *adjective (mechanically linked)* (re)groupé, -ée *or* monté, -ée en série; **ganged switch** = (re)groupement *m* de commutateurs *or* commutateurs montés en série; **a ganged switch is used to select which data bus a printer will respond to** = avec des commutateurs montés en série, il est possible de choisir le bus de données qui va activer l'imprimante

gap *noun* **(a)** *(between recorded data)* espace *m or* intervalle *m;* **block gap** *or* **interblock gap (IBG)** = espace interbloc *or* entre blocs; **gap character** = caractère *m* de remplissage; **gap digit** = chiffre *m* de remplissage; **record gap** = intervalle blanc entre deux enregistrements **(b)** *(between read head and medium)* **air gap** *or* **head gap** = entrefer *m;* **gap loss** = perte *f* d'alignement **(c)** *(radio communications)* créneau *m or* intervalle *m*

garbage *noun* **(a)** *(radio interference)* signaux *mpl* parasites; brouillage *m or* interférences *fpl*

radio **(b)** *(information no longer required)* informations *fpl* sans intérêt *or* de rebut; *(from memory)* **garbage collection** = nettoyage *m* de mémoire; **garbage in garbage out (GIGO)** = à données erronées, résultats erronés *or* des données douteuses produisent des résultats douteux

gas discharge display *or* **gas plasma display** *noun* affichage *m or* écran *m* à plasma

gate *noun* **(a)** *(logical electronic switch)* porte *f;* **AND gate** = porte *or* circuit *m* ET; **coincidence gate** = porte *or* circuit ET; **EXNOR gate** = porte *or* circuit NI exclusif; **EXOR gate** = porte *or* circuit OU exclusif; **NAND gate** = porte *or* circuit NON-ET; **negation** *or* **NOT gate** = porte *or* circuit NON; **NOR gate** = porte *or* circuit NON-OU *or* NI; **OR gate** = porte *or* circuit OU; **gate array** = circuit *m* logique complexe *or* en réseau; **gate circuit** = circuit *m* logique; **gate delay** = délai *m or* temps *m* de réponse *or* de propagation **(b)** *(connection pin of a FET device)* connecteur *m* (d'un transistor à effet de champ) **(c)** *(for film or slide)* couloir *m*

◊ **gateway** *noun* **(a)** *(device or software that links two dissimilar networks)* passerelle *f* (de communication); **we use a gateway to link the LAN to WAN** = nous avons utilisé une passerelle pour relier le réseau local au réseau étendu **(b)** *(electronic mail software)* passerelle; *(allows users to send messages as a fax)* **fax gateway** = passerelle fax *or* de télécopie; **to send messages by fax instead of across the network, you'll need to install a fax gateway** = pour envoyer des messages par fax au lieu de les envoyer par le réseau, vous devez installer une passerelle fax; *compare* BRIDGE

gather *verb* regrouper *or* rassembler; *(data)* **gather write** = grouper *or* agglomérer (des données)

gauge 1 *noun (for measuring thickness)* calibre *m; (for petrol)* jauge *f; (for air pressure)* manomètre *m* **2** *verb (thickness)* calibrer; *(petrol)* jauger *or* vérifier le niveau; *(air)* mesurer *or* vérifier la pression

gender changer *noun (for connectors)* changeur *m* de genre

general *adjective* **(a)** *(not special)* ordinaire *or* commun, -e **(b)** *(dealing with everything)* général, -e; **general purpose computer** = ordinateur *m* non dédié *or* non spécialisé; ordinateur polyvalent; **general purpose interface bus (GPIB)** = bus *m* d'interface universel *or* banalisé; **general purpose program** = programme *m* à usage multiple *or* multifonction; **general register** *or* **general purpose register (gpr)** = registre banalisé *or* général *or* polyvalent

generate *verb* produire *or* générer *or* créer; **to generate an image from digitally recorded data** = créer une image à partir de données numériques; **the graphics tablet generates a pair of co-ordinates each time the pen is moved** = une tablette graphique permet de générer deux coordonnées à chaque position du stylo; **computer-generated** = créé, -ée *or* produit, -e à l'aide d'un ordinateur; **computer-generated graphics** = représentations *fpl* graphiques sur ordinateur *or* infographie *f*; **they analyzed the computer-generated image** = ils ont fait l'analyse de l'image créée par l'ordinateur; **generated address** = adresse générée *or* calculée; **generated error** = erreur générée (par des arrondis)

◊ **generation** *noun* **(a)** *(producing data)* production *f or* création *f*; **the computer is used in the generation of graphic images** = on utilise l'ordinateur pour produire des images graphiques; **code generation is automatic** = le code est produit *or* généré automatiquement; **program generation** = création d'un programme **(b)** *(age of the technology)* génération *f*; *(earliest type of technology)* **first generation** = première génération; **first generation computers** = ordinateurs de première génération; *(master copy)* **first generation image** = image originale; *(computers with transistors)* **second generation computers** = ordinateurs de deuxième génération; *(computers with integrated circuits)* **third generation computers** = ordinateurs de troisième génération; *(computers using LSI circuits from around 1970)* **fourth generation computers** = ordinateurs de quatrième génération; **fourth generation languages** = langages de quatrième génération; *(computers using fast VLSI circuits)* **fifth generation computers** = ordinateurs de cinquième génération **(c)** *(of file)* génération; **the father file is a first generation backup** = le fichier père est un fichier de sauvegarde de première génération

◊ **generator** *noun* **(a)** *(program)* générateur *m* de programmes; **character generator** = générateur de caractères **(b)** *(device generating electricity)* (appareil) générateur *m or* génératrice *f* (d'électricité); **the computer centre has its own independent generator, in case of mains power failure** = le centre informatique possède sa propre génératrice (d'électricité), en cas de panne de courant

QUOTE vector and character generation are executed in hardware by a graphics display processor
Computing Today

generic *adjective* générique

genuine *adjective* vrai, -e *or* véritable; **authentication allows the system to recognize that a sender's message is genuine** = la procédure d'authentification permet au système de reconnaître si un message est émis par un utilisateur autorisé

geometric distortion *noun* *(of television picture)* distorsion *f* géométrique

geostationary satellite *noun* satellite *m* géostationnaire

germanium (Ge) *noun* *(material for semiconductors)* germanium *m*

get *noun* instruction *f* 'GET' *or* instruction 'chercher'

GHz = GIGAHERTZ

GFLOPS = GIGAFLOPS

ghost *noun* image *f* fantôme; *(second cursor)* **ghost cursor** = curseur *m* secondaire

GHz = GIGAHERTZ

gibberish *noun* caractères *mpl* parasites

GIF file *noun* *(graphics file format)* fichier *m* (graphique) GIF

giga- *or* **G** *prefix (meaning one thousand million)* giga- *or* G; *(10⁹ bytes)* **gigabyte** = giga-octet (Go) *m*

◊ **gigaflop** *noun* *(one thousand million floating-point operations per second)* gigaflop *m or* GFLOPS

◊ **gigahertz (GHz)** *(frequency of one thousand million cycles per second)* gigahertz (GHz) *m*

GIGO = GARBAGE IN GARBAGE OUT

GINO = GRAPHICAL INPUT OUTPUT

gizmo *noun* truc *m*

QUOTE During 1996 we will see changes that will turn the net from an elitist gizmo into the business tool no company can afford to ignore
The Times

GKS = GRAPHICS KERNEL SYSTEM

glare *noun* reflets *mpl* ; réflexion *f*; **the glare from the screen makes my eyes hurt** = la réflexion sur l'écran me fatigue la vue; *(sheet placed in front of a screen)* **glare filter** = filtre *m* décran *or* filtre antireflets

glitch *noun* *(informal)* problème *m or* défaillance *f or* pépin *m*

QUOTE The programmer was upgrading a verification system at Visa's UK data centre when his work triggered a software glitch causing hundreds of valid cards to be rejected for several hours.
Computing

global *adjective* global, -e *or* total, -e; *(backup of all data; backup of all files)* **global backup** = sauvegarde *f* globale du réseau; sauvegarde globale d'un disque dur *or* d'un serveur; **global knowledge** = connaissance *f* globale *or* exhaustive; **global replace** = remplacer globalement *or* dans tout le texte; **global search and replace** =

(procédure) chercher et remplacer globalement *or* dans tout le texte; **global variable** = variable *f* globale *or* commune *or* générale

QUOTE In an attempt to bring order to an electronic Tower of Babel, pharmaceutical giant Rhone-Poulenc has assembled an X.400-based global messaging network and a patchwork directory system that will be used until a single email system is deployed worldwide.

Computing

glossy 1 *adjective* (papier couché) satiné *or* brillant; **the illustrations are printed on glossy art paper** = les illustrations sont imprimées sur papier brillant **2** *noun (informal - expensive magazines)* **the glossies** = les revues de luxe

GND = GROUND

go ahead *noun* (signal d') invitation *f* à transmettre

goal *noun* but *m* (visé *or* atteint)

gofer *noun US (informal)* homme à tout faire *or* gaffeur *m*

gold contacts *noun* contacts *mpl* (en) or

golf-ball *noun (which produces printed characters)* boule *f* d'impression; **golf-ball printer** = imprimante *f* à boule

GOSIP = GOVERNMENT OPEN SYSTEMS INTERCONNECT PROFILE

GOSUB *(programming command to execute a routine)* commande *f* GOSUB

GOTO *(command which instructs a jump)* instruction *f* GOTO *or* instruction de saut; **GOTO 105 instructs a jump to line 105** = GOTO 105 indique un saut à la ligne 105

GPIB = GENERAL PURPOSE INTERFACE BUS

gpr = GENERAL PURPOSE REGISTER

government *noun* gouvernement *m (standards defined by the government of a country)* **government open systems interconnect profile** = standard *m* GOSIP (de compatibilité)

grab *verb* capturer *or* saisir

◊ **grabber** *noun (of video images)* **frame grabber** = capteur *m* d'images *or* dispositif d'enregistrement d'images

QUOTE sometimes a program can grab all the available memory, even if it is not going to use it

Byte

QUOTE the frame grabber is distinguished by its ability to acquire a TV image in a single frame interval

Electronics & Wireless World

graceful degradation *noun* dégradation *f* limitée *or* douce *or* progressive

grade *noun* classe *f or* qualité *f*; **a top-grade computer expert** = un expert informaticien de première classe; *(quality of telephone service)* **grade of service** = niveau *m* (de qualité) d'un service téléphonique

◊ **graduated** *adjective* gradué, -ée

grain *noun (on fast photographic films)* grain *m*

gram *or* **gramme** *noun* gramme *m*; **the book is printed on 70 gram paper** = le livre est imprimé sur du papier de 70g; *see also* GSM

◊ **grammage** *noun (weight of paper)* grammage *m* (NOTE: often written as **gsm : 80 gsm paper**)

grammar *noun (rules for language use)* syntaxe *f or* grammaire *f*; *(software used to check a document)* **grammar checker** = vérificateur *m* grammatical *or* utilitaire *m* de vérification de grammaire

◊ **grammatical error** *noun* faute *f* de syntaxe

◊ **grammar** *noun* grammaire *f*

grandfather file *noun (when followed by two other files: father and son)* fichier *m* grand-père; fichier de première génération; **grandfather cycle** = cycle *m* de rotation des fichiers de sauvegarde

granularity *noun (size of memory segments)* granularité *f or* modularité *f* de la mémoire; degré *m* de segmentation de la mémoire

graph *noun* graphique *m or* graphe *m or* courbe *f*; **graph paper** = papier *m* quadrillé; papier millimétré; **graph plotter** = traceur *m or* grapheur *m*

◊ **graphic** *adjective* graphique; **graphic data** = données *fpl* graphiques; **graphic display** = représentation *f or* affichage *m* graphique; **graphic display resolution** = définition *f* de l'affichage graphique; **graphic language** = langage *m* graphique; **this graphic language can plot lines, circles and graphs with a single command** = avec ce langage graphique, on peut tracer des lignes, cercles et graphes avec une seule commande

◊ **graphical** *adjective* graphique; **graphical input/output (GINO)** = entrée/sortie *f* graphique

◊ **graphical user interface (GUI)** *noun (interface between an operating system and the user)* interface *f* graphique (d'utilisateur) *or* GUI; *compare* COMMAND LINE INTERFACE

COMMENT: GUIs normally use a combination of windows, icons and a mouse to control the operating system. In many GUIs, such as Microsoft Windows, Apple Macintosh System 7 and DR-GEM, you can control all the functions of the operating system just using the mouse. Icons represent programs and files; instead of entering the file name, you select it by moving a pointer with a mouse

◊ **graphically** *adverb* graphiquement *or* à l'aide d'un graphique; **the sales figures are graphically represented as a pie chart** = les chiffres de vente sont reproduits graphiquement sous forme de camembert

◊ **graphics** *noun* représentations *f* graphiques; **graphics output such as bar charts, pie charts, etc.** = les représentations graphiques telles que histogrammes, camemberts, etc; *(electronic device)* **graphics adapter** = adaptateur *m or* carte *f* graphique; **the new graphics adapter is capable of displaying higher resolution graphics** = cette nouvelle carte graphique permet un affichage de haute résolution; **graphics art terminal** = terminal *m* graphique *or* avec écran (à affichage) graphique; **graphics character** = caractère *m* graphique; *(graphics processor)* **graphics coprocessor** = coprocesseur *m* graphique; *(file containing data describing an image)* **graphics file** = fichier *m* graphique; **there are many standards for graphics files including TIFF, IMG and EPS** = il existe de nombreux formats de fichiers graphiques comme TIFF, IMG et EPS; *(way in which data describing an image is stored)* **graphics file format** = format *m* de fichier graphique; **graphics interface** = interface *f* graphique; **graphics kernel system (GKS)** = fonctions *fpl* graphiques GKS; **graphics library** = bibliothèque *f* graphique; **graphics light pen** = stylo *m* optique graphique; **graphics mode** = mode *m* graphique; **graphics pad** *or* **tablet** = tablette *f* graphique *or* à numériser; *(basic shape)* **graphics primitive** = forme *f* primitive *or* de base (dans un programme de graphisme); *(printer capable of printing bit-mapped images)* **graphics printer** = imprimante *f* graphique; *(secondary processor)* **graphics processor** *or* **graphics coprocessor** = processeur *m or* coprocesseur *m* graphique; **this graphics adapter has a graphics coprocessor fitted and is much faster** = cette carte graphique, équipée d'un coprocesseur graphique, est beaucoup plus rapide; **graphics software** = logiciel *m* graphique; logiciel de dessin; **graphics terminal** = terminal graphique *or* terminal de CAO; **graphics VDU** = écran (à affichage) graphique; **computer graphics** = représentations *fpl* graphiques sur ordinateur *or* infographie *f*; **high resolution graphics** = graphiques haute définition; **interactive graphics** = graphiques interactifs *or* infographie interactive

QUOTE one interesting feature of this model is graphics amplification, which permits graphic or text enlargement of up to 800 per cent

QUOTE the custom graphics chips can display an image that has 640 columns by 400 rows of 4-bit pixel

QUOTE several tools exist for manipulating image and graphical data: some were designed for graphics manipulation

Byte

gravure *see* PHOTOGRAVURE

Gray code *noun* code *m* (de) Gray

◊ **gray scale** = GREY SCALE

greeked *adjective* *(font with a point size too small to display)* en faux texte *or* en texte muet *or* en bolo-bolo

green phosphor *noun* phosphore *m* vert

gremlin *noun* *(unexplained fault in a system)* schmilblic *m or* erreur *f* inexplicable; **line gremlin** = schmilblic sur la ligne *or* perte de transmission inexplicable

grey scale *noun* **(a)** *(used to measure the correct exposure when filming)* échelle *f* de gris **(b)** *(shades of grey on a monochrome monitor)* niveaux *mpl* de gris (NOTE: US spelling is usually **gray scale**)

grid *noun* grille *f* *(patterns on screen limited to the points of a grid)* **grid snap** = ancrage *m* (du pointage); **if you want to draw accurate lines, you'll find it easier with grid snap turned on** = le plus simple pour tracer des lignes de manière précise est d'utiliser le dispositif d'ancrage du pointage

grip 1 *noun* *(person)* machiniste *m* **2** *verb* saisir *or* retenir; **in friction feed, the paper is gripped by the rollers** = dans l'entraînement par friction le papier est saisi par les rouleaux

ground 1 *noun* **(a)** *(electrical connection to earth or GND)* prise *f* de terre **(b)** *(earth)* sol *m*; **ground absorption** = perte *f* de terre; **ground station** = station *f* au sol **2** *verb* US *(to connect electrical device to ground)* mettre à la terre *or* à la masse (NOTE: **ground** is more common in US English; the UK English is **earth**)

group 1 *noun* **(a)** *(set of computer records)* groupe *m*; **group mark** *or* **marker** = marqueur *m* (de début *or* de fin) de groupe; *(of devices)* **group poll** = appel *m* sélectif de groupe **(b)** *(in telegraphic communications)* groupe (de caractères *or* de mots) **(c)** *(collection of icons in a GUI)* groupe *m* de programmes; groupe d'icônes; **all the icons in this group are to do with painting** = toutes les icônes de ce groupe concernent la peinture; *(icon that represents a window containing a collection of icons)* **group icon** = icône de groupe **(d)** *(collection of users)* groupe (d'utilisateurs); **the group ACCOUNTS contains all the users who work in the accounts department** = le groupe ACCOUNTS contient tous les utilisateurs des services comptables **2** *verb* *(bring together)* grouper

◊ **groupware** *noun* *(software written to be used by a group)* logiciel *m* de groupe (de travail)

gsm *or* **g/m²** = GRAMS PER SQUARE METRE (PER SHEET); *(weight of paper used in printing)* gramme *m* au mètre carré; **the book is printed on 70 gsm coated paper** = ce livre est imprimé sur papier couché de 70g

guarantee *noun* garantie *f*; **the system is still under guarantee and will be repaired free of charge** = le système est toujours sous garantie et la réparation sera faite gratuitement

guard band *noun* **(a)** bande *f* de fréquence intercalaire *or* bande de protection **(b)** *(on a tape)* bande intermédiaire

◊ **guard bit** *noun* bit *m* de protection

◊ **guarding** *noun* *(joining a single sheet to a book or magazine)* montage *m* (d'une feuille isolée *or* d'une illustration) sur onglet

GUI *(pronounced 'gooey')* = GRAPHICAL USER INTERFACE

COMMENT: GUIs normally use a combination of windows, icons and a mouse to control the operating system. In many GUIs, such as Microsoft Windows, Apple Macintosh System 7 and DR-GEM, you can control all the functions of the operating system just using the mouse. Icons represent programs and files; instead of entering the file name, you select it by moving a pointer with a mouse

guide bars *noun (in a bar code)* lignes *fpl* guides *or* lignes de référence; **the standard guide bars are** two thin lines that are a little longer than the coding lines = les lignes guides standard se présentent sous la forme de deux lignes fines un peu plus longues que les lignes codes

guillotine *noun* massicot *m*

gulp *noun* multiplet *m or* groupe *m* d'octets

gun *or* **electron gun** *noun* canon *m* à électrons

gutter *noun (inner margin between two facing pages of a book)* marge *f* intérieure

Hh

hack *verb (for criminal purposes)* s'introduire sans autorisation dans un système *or* faire du piratage informatique *or* pirater un système

◊ **hacker** **(a)** *(person who explores computer software and hardware)* passionné, -ée d'informatique **(b)** *(person who breaks into a computer system for criminal purposes)* pirate *m* informatique

QUOTE The two were also charged with offences under the Computer Misuse Act and found guilty of the very actions upon which every hacker is intent.
Computing

QUOTE software manufacturers try more and more sophisticated methods to protect their programs and the hackers use equally clever methods to break into them
Electronics & Wireless World

QUOTE the hackers used their own software to break into the credit card centre
Computer News

QUOTE any computer linked to the system will be alerted if a hacker uses its code number
Practical Computing

hairline rule *noun (in DTP system: very thin line)* filet *m* ultra-fin

halation *noun (photography)* (effet de) halo *m*

half *noun* moitié *f or* demie *f or* demi *m*; **half the data was lost in transmission** = la moitié des données a été perdue *or* ont été perdues au cours de la transmission; **the second half of the program contains some errors** = la seconde partie du programme contient des erreurs; **half adder** = additionneur *m* à deux entrées *or* demi-additionneur *m*; *(half length expansion card)* **half card** = carte *f* demi-longueur *or* demi-carte *f or* carte courte; **half duplex (HD** *or* **HDX)** = half duplex *(m) or* bidirectionnel, -elle à l'alternat; **half-duplex modem** = modem *m* half duplex; **some modems can operate in half-duplex mode if required** = certains modems peuvent fonctionner en mode half duplex si nécessaire; **half-height drive** = lecteur *m* de disquette(s) (de) demi-hauteur; **half-intensity** = demi-intensité *f*; *(printing)* **half space** = demi-espace *m*; *(first page of book)* **half title** = faux-titre *m*; **half wave rectifier** = redresseur *m* (de) simple alternance; **half word** = demi-mot *m*

◊ **halftone** *or* **half-tone** *noun* **(a)** demi-teinte *f*; *(printing method)* **halftone process** *or* **half-toning** = (procédé de) similigravure *f or* simili *f* **(b)** *(illustration)* similigravure *or* simili *or* gravure *f* en demi-teinte; **the book is illustrated with twenty halftones** = ce livre est contient vingt planches en demi-teinte *or* vingt similigravures

halide *noun* halogénure *m* (d'argent)

Hall effect *noun* effet *m* (de champ) Hall; **Hall effect switch** = commutateur *m* à effet (de champ) Hall

halo *noun (photography)* halo *m*

halt **1** *noun* arrêt *m*; **dead halt** *or* **drop-dead halt** = arrêt total; **halt instruction** = instruction *f* d'arrêt; **programmed halt** = arrêt programmé; **halt condition** = condition *f* d'arrêt **2** *verb* arrêter *or* interrompre; **hitting CTRL S will halt the program** = taper CTRL S pour interrompre le programme

ham *noun* **radio ham** = radio-amateur *m*

Hamming code *noun* code *m or* codage *m* de Hamming; **Hamming distance** = distance *f* de Hamming

hand *noun* main *f*; **hands off** = *(automatic)* (système) automatique *or* sans intervention manuelle; *(training)* (formation) théorique *or* sans accès à l'ordinateur; **hands on** = *(manual)* (système) manuel; *(training)* (formation) pratique *or* mise *f* en main; **the sales representatives have received hands-on experience of the new computer** = une mise en main du nouvel ordinateur a été organisée pour les délégués commerciaux; **the computer firm gives a two day hands-on training course** = la société informatique offre une formation pratique de deux jours; **hand portable set** = radiotéléphone *m* portatif; **hand receiver** = récepteur *m* portatif; **hand viewer** = petite visionneuse *f* (qu'on tient à la main)

◊ **hand-held** *adj* (petit appareil) qu'on tient à la main *or* (appareil) de poche; **hand-held computer** = petit ordinateur qu'on tient à la main *or* ordinateur de poche; ultraportatif *m*

QUOTE A year ago the hand-held computer business resembled that of PCs a decade ago, with a large number of incompatible models, often software incompatible and using proprietary displays, operating systems and storage media.
Computing

handle *noun* **(a)** *(number to identify an active file)* numéro *m* d'identification de fichier **(b)** *(small square to change a shape)* poignée *f* (de manipulation); **to stretch the box in the DTP program, select it once to display the handles then**

drag one handle to change its shape = dans ce programme de PAO, on sélectionne d'abord la boîte qu'on veut agrandir pour faire apparaître les poignées, puis on tire une des poignées pour modifier la taille de la boîte

◊ **handler** *noun (driver)* logiciel *m* de commande *or* gestionnaire *m* de périphérique; **the disk drive handler code is supplied in the library** = le code du gestionnaire de lecteur de disque se trouve dans la bibliothèque; *see also* DEVICE DRIVER; *(software routine)* **error handler** = gestionnaire *m* d'erreurs

◊ **hand off** *verb* basculer *or* transférer la communication d'un émetteur à l'autre

◊ **handset** *noun* combiné *m*

◊ **handy talkies** *or* **HTs** *noun* radiotéléphones *mpl* portatifs

handshake *or* **handshaking** *noun (between transmitter and receptor)* protocole *m* de validation de transfert de données *or* d'échange d'informations; **full handshaking** = protocole de communication (entre deux postes); *(between computer and slower peripheral)* **handshake I/O control** = contrôle *m* de mise en communication

handwriting *noun* écriture *f*; **the keyboarders are having difficulty in reading the author's handwriting** = les clavistes trouvent que l'écriture de l'auteur est difficile à lire

◊ **handwriting recognition** *noun (software that recognises handwritten text)* reconnaissance *f* d'écriture (à la main); **the new PDA has excellent handwriting recognition** = ce nouvel APC (assistant personnel de communication) est doté d'un excellent système de reconnaissance de l'écriture

◊ **handwritten** *adjective* écrit, -e à la main *or* manuscrit, -e; **the author sent in two hundred pages of handwritten manuscript** = l'auteur a envoyé un manuscrit de deux cents pages entièrement écrit à la main

QUOTE all acquisition, data reduction, processing, and memory circuitry is contained in the single hand-held unit
Byte

QUOTE if a line is free, the device waits another 400ms before reserving the line with a quick handshake process
Practical Computing

hang *verb* se perdre *or* être accroché dans une boucle

◊ **hangover** *noun* **(a)** *(on a TV screen)* traînée *f* *or* rémanence *f* d'image **(b)** *(of fax machine)* déréglage *m* de la qualité d'impression

◊ **hang up** *verb (communications line)* raccrocher; **after she had finished talking on the telephone, she hung up** = à la fin de la conversation téléphonique, elle a raccroché

◊ **hangup** *noun* arrêt *m* inattendu

hard *adjective* **(a)** *(solid)* dur, -e; *(not programmable)* fermé, -e; **hard card** = carte *f* de disque dur; **hard copy** = sortie *f* d'imprimante; imprimé *m* *or* texte *m* imprimé; **hard copy interface** = interface *f* d'imprimante; **hard disk** = disque dur; **hard disk drive** = contrôleur *m* de disque dur; (unité de) disque dur; **hard disk model** = modèle d'ordinateur avec disque dur; **hard error** = erreur *f* *or* anomalie *f* persistante; **hard failure** = panne sérieuse (d'équipement); **the hard failure was due to a burnt-out chip** = la panne était due à la défaillance d'un composant; **hard hyphen** = trait *m* d'union obligatoire; *(code that indicates the end of a paragraph)* **hard return** = (code de) fin de paragraphe **(b)** *(contrast)* fort, -e

◊ **hardback** *noun & adjective* édition *f* cartonnée *or* reliée

◊ **hardbound** *adjective (book)* (livre) avec couverture cartonnée

◊ **hardcover** *noun & adjective* édition *f* cartonnée *or* reliée; **we printed 4,000 copies of the hardcover edition, and 10,000 of the paperback** = nous avons imprimé 4000 exemplaires cartonnés et 10 000 brochés

◊ **hard-sectored** *adjective* (disque) avec formatage physique; **hard-sectoring** formatage *m* physique de secteurs *or* formatage par perforations

hardware *noun* matériel *m* informatique; **hardware compatibility** = compatibilité *f* du matériel; **hardware configuration** = configuration *f* du matériel; *(something which will only work with a particular model)* **hardware dependent** = dépendant, -e du matériel; **the communications software is hardware dependent and will only work with Hayes-compatible modems** = le logiciel de communication est dépendant du matériel et ne fonctionne qu'avec un modem compatible Hayes; *(fault with hardware)* **hardware failure** = défaillance *f* du matériel *or* panne *f* provoquée par le matériel; **hardware interrupt** = (signal d') interruption *f* provenant d'une machine; *(standard of a particular computer)* **hardware platform** = plate-forme *f* de matériel; **hardware reliability** = fiabilité *f* *or* bonne qualité du matériel; *(switch to reset the CPU)* **hardware reset** = interrupteur *m* de reprise; **hardware security** = sécurité *f* du matériel; *compare* SOFTWARE

QUOTE Sequent's Platform division will focus on hardware and software manufacture, procurement and marketing, with the Enterprise division concentrating on services and client-server implementation.
Computing

hardwired connection *noun* câblage *m* permanent *or* connexion *f* fixe

◊ **hardwired logic** *noun* logique *f* câblée

◊ **hardwired program** *noun* programme en logique câblée

harmonic *noun* harmonique *f*; **harmonic distortion** = distorsion *f* d'harmoniques; **harmonic telephone ringer** = sonnerie *f* d'appel à harmoniques

hartley *noun (unit of information equal to 3.32 bits)* hartley *m*

hash 1 *verb* générer un hash code; **hashing function** = algorithme *m or* fonction *f* hash **2** *noun* **(a)** *see* HASHMARK **(b) hash code** = hash code *m*; **hash-code system** = système de hash code; **hash index** = index hash code; **hash table** = table *f* des adresses hash codées; **hash total** = total *m* de vérification (pour hash code); **hash value** = valeur *f* d'un hash code

◊ **hashmark** *or* **hash mark** *noun (printed sign #)* signe typographique #

> COMMENT: in US usage # means number: #32 = number 32 (apartment number in an address, paragraph number in a text, etc.). In computer usage, the pound sign (£) is often used in the US instead of the hash to avoid confusion

Hayes Corporation™ *(modem manufacturer)* Hayes Corporation™; *(commands to control a modem)* **Hayes AT command set** = jeu *m* de commandes Hayes AT; **to dial the number 1234, use the Hayes AT command ATD1234** = pour appeler le numéro 1234, utilisez la commande Hayes ATD1234; *(modem compatible with the Hayes AT command set)* **Hayes compatible** = compatible Hayes

hazard *noun* erreur *f or* défaut *m* d'horloge; **hazard-free implementation** = application *f* qui tolère toutes les erreurs possibles

HD = HALF DUPLEX

HDLC = HIGH LEVEL DATA LINK CONTROL

HDVS = HIGH DEFINITION VIDEO SYSTEM

HDX = HALF DUPLEX

head 1 *noun* **(a) combined head** *or* **read/write head** = tête *f* de lecture/écriture *or* tête de lecture; **head alignment** = alignement *m* de la tête de lecture; **head cleaning disk** = disquette *f* de nettoyage; **head crash** = crash *m* (du disque dur) causé par la tête de lecture *or* atterrissage *m* de la tête de lecture; **head demagnetizer** = démagnétiseur *m* de tête; **head park** = mise en position de transport de la tête *or* parcage *m* de la tête; *(moving the read/write head)* **head positioning** = positionnement *m* de la tête; **head wheel** = molette *f* de pressage *or* galet *m* presseur; **disk head** = tête de lecture *or* de lecture/écriture de disquettes; **fixed head** = tête fixe; **floating head** *or* **flying head** = tête flottante; **playback head** = tête de lecture; **read head** = tête de lecture; **tape head** = tête de lecture *or* d'écriture de bande magnétique; **write head** = tête d'écriture **(b)** (données de) début *m* de fichier **(c)** *(of book or page)* **head of form (HOF)** = tête *or* début *m* d'une page (de papier listing) **(d)** tête de bobine *or* amorce *f* **(e)** *(of film or tape)* tête; **head end** = tête de réseau **2** *verb* être en tête de liste; **the queue was headed by my file** = mon fichier était en tête de la file d'attente

◊ **header** *noun* **(a)** *(in a local area network)* bloc *m* d'identification **(b)** *(at top of a list of data)* en-tête *m* de fichier; metadata *f(pl)*; **header block**

= bloc *m* d'identification; **header card** = carte *f* en-tête; *(on tape)* **header label** = label *m* d'identification *or* de reconnaisance de bande; **tape header** = en-tête *m or* début *m* de bande **(c)** *(at top of page)* en-tête *or* titre courant

◊ **heading** *noun* **(a)** en-tête *m or* titre *m* ; rubrique *f* *(title of document or file)* nom *m* **(b)** *(at the top of each page)* titre courant

◊ **headlife** *noun* durée *f* de vie de la tête

◊ **headline** *noun* = HEADING

◊ **headset** *or* **headphones** *noun* casque *m* (d'écoute)

◊ **headword** *noun* *(in a printed dictionary)* entrée *f*

heap *noun* **(a)** *(temporary storage area)* pile *f* **(b)** *(binary tree)* pile binaire

heat sensitive paper *noun* papier *m* thermique

heat sink *noun* dissipateur *m* thermique; radiateur *m* à ailette(s)

Heaviside-Kennelly layer *see* E-REGION

helical scan *noun* lecture *f* hélicoïdale

helios noise *noun* bruit *m* atmosphérique causé par le soleil

help *noun* **(a)** *(which makes things easy)* aide *f*; **he finds his word-processor a great help in the office** = il trouve la machine de traitement de texte très utile pour le travail de bureau; **they need some help with their programming** = ils ont besoin d'aide pour la programmation **(b)** *(function)* aide; *(help message)* **context sensitive help** = aide *f* en ligne *or* aide contextuelle; *(key that displays help information)* **help key** = touche *f* d'aide; touche AIDE; **hit the HELP key if you want information about what to do next** = appuyez sur la touche AIDE *or* sur la touche d'aide pour connaître la marche à suivre; *(display of help information)* **help screen** = écran *m* d'aide

> COMMENT: most software applications for IBM PCs have standardized the use of the F1 function key to display help text explaining how something can be done

Hercules graphics adapter (HGA)™ *noun* *(standard for high-resolution mono graphics adapter)* carte *f* graphique Hercules™

Hertz *noun* hertz *m*

heterodyne *noun* hétérodyne *f*

heterogeneous network *noun* réseau *m* informatique hétérogène; **heterogeneous multiplexing** = multiplexage *m* hétérogène

heuristic *adjective* heuristique; **a heuristic program learns from its previous actions and decisions** = un programme heuristique exploite ses actions et décisions antérieures

Hewlett Packard™ *(manufacturer of computers, etc.)* (la société) Hewlett Packard™; *(standard set of commands to describe graphics)* **Hewlett Packard Graphics Language (HPGL)** = langage *m* graphique HP *or* langage HPGL; *(standard method of interfacing peripheral devices)* **Hewlett Packard Interface Bus (HPIB)** = bus *m* d'interface HP; *(laser printer)* **Hewlett Packard LaserJet** *or* **HP LaserJet** = imprimante *f* graphique HP Laserjet; *(standard set of commands)* **Hewlett Packard Printer Control Language (HP-PCL)** = langage *m* de contrôle d'imprimante HP *or* langage HP-PCL

hex *or* **hexadecimal notation** *noun* notation *f* hexadécimale; **hex dump** = vidage hexadécimal; **hex pad** = clavier hexadécimal

HF = HIGH FREQUENCY

HFS = HIERARCHICAL FILE SYSTEM

HGA = HERCULES GRAPHICS ADAPTER

hidden *adjective* caché, -ée; **hidden defect in a program** = vice *or* défaut caché; **hidden files** = fichiers cachés; **it allows users to backup or restore hidden system files independently** = cela permet aux utilisateurs de sauvegarder ou de restaurer un par un les fichiers cachés; *(on 2-D images)* **hidden lines** = lignes cachées; **hidden line algorithm** = algorithme *m* d'effacement de lignes cachées; **hidden line removal** = effacement *m* des lignes cachées

hierarchical *adjective* hiérarchique *or* hiérarchisé, -ée; **hierarchical classification** = classification *f* hiérarchique; **hierarchical communications system** = système de communication hiérarchisé; **hierarchical computer network** = réseau (d'ordinateurs) hiérarchisé; **hierarchical database** = base de données hiérarchisées; **hierarchical directory** = répertoire *m* hiérarchique; *(method used to store and organise files)* **hierarchical file system (HFS)** = système *m* de fichiers hiérarchisés

hierarchy *noun* hiérarchie *f*; **data hierarchy** = structure *f* hiérarchique de données

hi fi *or* **hi-fi** *or* **hifi** = HIGH FIDELITY haute fidélité *or* hi-fi; **a hi fi system** *or* **a hi fi** = une chaîne haute fidélité *or* une chaîne hi-fi

high 1 *adjective* haut, -e; **high definition** = haute définition; **high definition video system (HDVS)** = système vidéo haute définition; **high density storage** = mémoire *f* *or* support *m* magnétique haute densité; **a hard disk is a high density storage medium compared to paper tape** = un disque dur est un support de haute densité par rapport à une bande perforée; *(device)* **high-end** = haut de gamme; **high fidelity** *or* **hifi** *or* **hi fi** = haute fidélité *or* hi-fi; **high frequency (HF)** = haute fréquence *f*; *(allows several computers to be linked)* **high-level data link control (HDLC)** = contrôle de liaison de données de haut niveau *or* protocole d'interfaçage HDLC; **high-level data link control station** = équipement interfacé HDLC; **high-level (programming) language (HLL)** = langage *m* de

programmation évolué *or* de haut niveau; **programmers should have a knowledge of high-level languages, particularly PASCAL** = on demande aux programmeurs une connaissance des langages de haut niveau, dont PASCAL; *(between 640KB and 1MB)* **high memory** = mémoire haute; **high memory area (HMA)** = zone de mémoire supérieure; **high order** = (chiffre) de poids fort; **high-order language** = HIGH-LEVEL LANGUAGE **high pass filter** = filtre *m* passe-haut; **high performance equipment** = matériel *m* (de) haute performance; *(method of storing file information)* **high performance filing system (HPFS)** = gestionnaire *m* de fichiers HPFS; **high priority program** = programme *m* prioritaire; **high reduction** = forte réduction; **high specification** *or* **high spec** = (de) haute précision *or* (de) haute technologie; **high spec cabling needs to be very carefully handled** = les câbles (de) haute technologie doivent être manipulés avec soin; **high speed carry** = report *m* en cascade; **high usage trunk** = ligne *f* de grand débit **2** *noun* **active high** = signal *m* haut actif; **logical high** = état *m* logique haut *or* vrai *or* 1

> QUOTE they have proposed a standardized high-level language for importing image data into desktop publishing and other applications programs
>
> *Byte*

◊ **highlight 1** *noun* **highlights** = mots *mpl or* caractères *mpl* (mis) en évidence; *(on screen)* mots *or* caractères en surbrillance; *(main characteristics)* caractéristiques *fpl* principales **2** *verb* mettre en évidence *or* faire ressortir; *(on screen)* mettre en surbrillance; **the headings are highlighted in bold** = les titres sont en caractères gras pour les faire ressortir

◊ **high-resolution** *or* **hi-res** *noun* haute définition *or* haute résolution; **high-resolution graphics** = graphiques *mpl* haute définition; **this high-resolution monitor can display 640 x 320 pixels** = ce moniteur haute définition permet un affichage de 640 x 320 pixels

> QUOTE the computer is uniquely suited to image processing because of its high-resolution graphics
>
> *Byte*

◊ **high Sierra specification** *noun* *(standard method of storing data)* norme *f* de stockage High Sierra

◊ **high-speed** *adjective* ultra-rapide *or* grande vitesse; *(film)* ultrasensible; **high-speed duplicator** = duplicateur *m* grande vitesse; *(of printer)* **high-speed skip** = saut *m* rapide

◊ **high-tech** *or* **high technology** *adjective* *(advanced)* technologie *f* avancée *or* high tech

highway *noun* *(bus)* bus *m*; **address highway** = bus d'adresses; **data highway** = bus de transfert de données

hill climbing *noun* *(in an expert system)* escalade *f or* méthode *f* ascendante

hi-res = HIGH RESOLUTION haute définition *f* *or* haute résolution; **hi-res graphics** = graphiques *mpl* haute définition; **this hi-res monitor can display 640 x 320 pixels** = ce moniteur haute définition permet un affichage de 640 x 320 pixels; **the new hi-res optical scanner can detect 300 dots per inch** = le nouveau scanner optique haute définition peut lire 300 points par pouce

hiss *noun* sifflement *f*

histogram *noun* histogramme *m*

hit 1 *noun* (a) *(successful search)* réussite *f or* trouvaille *f* ; (bonne) réponse *f*; **there was a hit after just a few seconds** = il n'a fallu que quelques secondes pour trouver la réponse *or* pour obtenir la donnée; **there are three hits for this search key** = cette clé produit trois réponses; *(data retrieved from cache memory)* **cache hit** = donnée *f* extraite (directement) du cache (b) *(noise)* **hit on the line** = courte perturbation sur la ligne **2** *verb* *(to press a key)* appuyer (sur une touche) *or* taper; **to save the text, hit ESCAPE S** = pour effectuer la sauvegarde, tapez ESCAPE S

> QUOTE the cause of the data disaster is usually due to your finger hitting the wrong key
> **PC Business World**

HLL = HIGH-LEVEL LANGUAGE

HMA = HIGH MEMORY AREA

HMI = HUMAN-MACHINE INTERFACE

HOF = HEAD OF FORM

hold 1 *noun* *(TV)* signal *m* de synchronisation; *(oscilloscope)* commande *f* de stabilisation du signal (après échantillonnage) **2** *verb* *(in memory)* garder; *(value)* garder; *(telephone)* mettre en attente; **hold current** = courant *m* de maintien *or* de veille; *(artwork)* **holding line** = ligne *f* de délimitation *or* d'arrêt; **holding loop** = boucle *f* de maintien; *(of communications circuit)* **holding time** = temps *m* d'occupation de la ligne

◊ **holdup** *noun* *(period over which power will be supplied by a UPS)* temps *m* de débit d'un onduleur *or* d'un dispositif de secours; *(pause in a program)* pause *f* accidentelle *or* décrochage *m*

hole *noun* (a) *(in punched tape or card)* perforation *f or* trou *m*; *(of hard-sectored disk)* **index hole** = perforation de marquage (du bord d'un disque) (b) *(absence of an electron)* trou

Hollerith code *noun* code *m* (de) Hollerith

hologram *noun* hologramme *m*

◊ **holographic image** *noun* hologramme; **holographic storage** = stockage *m or* mémoire *f* holographique *or* d'hologramme

◊ **holography** *noun* holographie *f*

home *noun* (a) *(of person)* domicile *m*; **home banking** = télébanque *f or* consultation *f* des comptes à domicile; **home computer** = ordinateur *m* familial *or* pour la maison (b) *(starting point for*

printing on a screen) position *f* initiale *or* de départ; *(key that moves the cursor to the beginning)* **home key** = touche *f* Home; touche Début (sur un clavier français); **home record** = début *m* d'enregistrement

◊ **homing** *noun* retour *m* à la source *or* à l'origine

homogeneous computer network *noun* réseau *m* informatique homogène; **homogeneous multiplexing** = multiplexage *m* homogène

hood *noun* capot *m*; **acoustic hood** = capot *m or* hotte *f* d'insonorisation

hook *noun* *(point where a programmer can insert test code or debugging code)* point *m* d'accrochage *or* d'insertion (de code)

hooking *noun* *(distortion of video image)* décrochage *m*

hop *noun* *(transmission)* bond *m*

hopper *noun* chargeur *m* de cartes perforées

horizontal *adjective* horizontal, -e; **horizontal blanking** = inhibition *or* suppression horizontale (du signal); **horizontal check** = contrôle horizontal; *(bar along the bottom of a window)* **horizontal scrollbar** = barre *f* de défilement horizontal; *(across a page)* **horizontal scrolling** = défilement *m* horizontal; **horizontal synchronization pulse** = impulsion *f* de synchronisation horizontale; *(movement of the cursor)* **horizontal wraparound** = enroulement *m or* retour *m* à la ligne (automatique)

horn *noun* *(radio device)* capteur *m* directionnel; *(for microwaves)* **feed horn** = dispositif *m* de guidage directionnel

host *noun* & *adjective* hôte *m*; **host adapter** = adaptateur *m* de l'ordinateur hôte; **the cable to connect the scanner to the host adapter is included** = le cordon qui relie le scanner et l'adaptateur de l'ordinateur hôte est fourni

◊ **host computer** *noun* (a) *(main controlling computer)* ordinateur *m* principal *or* ordinateur hôte (b) *(used to write and debug software)* ordinateur hôte *or* serveur *m* (c) *(in a network)* serveur

> QUOTE you select fonts manually or through commands sent from the host computer along with the text
> **Byte**

hot *adjective* chaud, -e; *(detects and prevents the use of a faulty sector)* **hot fix** = correction *f or* action *f* immédiate (en cas de secteur défectueux); réparation *f* à chaud; *(key which starts a process)* **hot key** = touche *f* d'activation

◊ **hot chassis** *noun* châssis *m* sous tension

◊ **hot frame** *noun* image *f* surexposée

◊ **hotline** *noun* service *m* d'assistance (par téléphone)

◊ **hot metal composition** *noun* composition *f* au plomb *or* composition chaude

◊ **hot spot** *noun* point chaud; *(area on an image)* zone *f* active *or* point *m* chaud; **the image of the trumpet is a hotspot and will play a sound when you move the pointer over it** = l'image de la trompette est une zone active qui produira un son lorsqu'on la sélectionne avec le pointeur

◊ **hot standby** *noun* système *m* de secours prêt à fonctionner

◊ **hot type** *noun* caractère *m or* ligne-bloc *f* fondu(e) au moment de la composition; composition *f* chaude *or* au plomb

◊ **hot zone** *noun* zone *f* de texte

house 1 *noun* *(especially a printing or publishing company)* société *f or* maison *f* (d'édition, etc.); **one of the biggest software houses in the US** = une des plus grandes maisons de logiciel aux Etats-Unis; **house corrections** = corrections *fpl* de l'imprimeur; **house style** = style *m* (de la) maison **2** *verb* loger *or* placer *or* insérer *or* ranger; **the magnetic tape is housed in a solid plastic case** = la bande magnétique est (contenue) dans un boîtier en plastique solide

◊ **housekeeping** *noun* maintenance *f* courante; **housekeeping routine** = programme *m* de maintenance *or* (programme) utilitaire *m*

◊ **housing** *noun* boîtier *m*; **the computer housing was damaged when it fell on the floor** = quand on a laissé tomber l'ordinateur, son boîtier s'est abîmé

howler *noun* **(a)** avertisseur *m* (sonore) **(b)** *(mistake)* erreur *f* monstre

HPFS = HIGH PERFORMANCE FILING SYSTEM

HPGL = HEWLETT PACKARD GRAPHICS LANGUAGE

◊ **HPIB** = HEWLETT PACKARD INTERFACE BUS

◊ **HP-PCL** = HEWLETT PACKARD PRINTER CONTROL LANGUAGE

HRG = HIGH RESOLUTION GRAPHICS graphiques *mpl* haute définition; **the HRG board can control up to 300 pixels per inch** = la carte graphique haute définition contrôle jusqu'à 300 pixels par pouce

HT = HANDY TALKIES

hub *noun* **(a)** *(of disk)* moyeu *m* **(b)** *(central ring in a star-topology network)* concentrateur *m or* hub *m*

Huffman code *noun* *(data compression code)* code *m* de Huffman

huge model *noun* *(memory model)* modèle *m* géant

hum *noun* bourdonnement *m or* ronflement *m*

human-computer *or* **human-machine interface (HMI)** *noun* interface *f* utilisateur/machine *or* interface homme/machine

hung *adjective* *(crash)* plantage *m*

hunting *noun* recherche *f*

hybrid circuit *noun* circuit *m* hybride *or* mixte *or* composite; **hybrid computer** = ordinateur *m* hybride; **hybrid interface** = interface *f* hybride; **hybrid system** = système *m* hybride

HyperCard™ *noun* *(database system)* HyperCard™

◊ **hypermedia** *noun* *(hypertext document)* hypermédia *m*

◊ **HyperTalk™** *noun* *(programming language)* HyperTalk™

◊ **hypertext** *adjective* *(system of organising information)* hypertext(e) *m*; **in this hypertext page, click once on the word 'computer' and it will tell you what a computer is** = dans cette page hypertext(e), cliquez sur le mot 'ordinateur' et on vous expliquera ce qu'est un ordinateur

hyphen *noun* trait *m* d'union; **hard hyphen** = trait d'union obligatoire; **soft** *or* **discretionary hyphen** = césure *f* d'écran

◊ **hyphenated** *adjective* (mot) qui s'écrit avec un trait d'union; **the word 'high-level' is usually hyphenated** = le mot 'high-level' s'écrit habituellement avec un trait d'union

◊ **hyphenation** *noun* césure *f or* coupure *f*; **hyphenation and justification** *or* **H & J** = césure et justification; **an American hyphenation and justification program will not work with British English spellings** = un programme de césure et justification établi aux Etats-Unis ne peut être utilisé pour un texte en anglais britannique

QUOTE the hyphenation program is useful for giving a professional appearance to documents and for getting as many words onto the page as possible

Micro Decision

hypo *abbreviation* *(photographic fixing solution)* hyposulfite *m or* thiosulfate *m* de sodium

Hz = HERTZ

Ii

IAM = INTERMEDIATE ACCESS MEMORY

IAR = INSTRUCTION ADDRESS REGISTER

IAS = IMMEDIATE ACCESS STORE

I-beam *noun (cursor shaped like 'I')* curseur *m* (en) bâton *or* en I

IBG = INTERBLOCK GAP

IBM *(the largest computer company in the world)* = INTERNATIONAL BUSINESS MACHINE; *(personal computer based on the Intel 80286)* **IBM AT** = ordinateur IBM AT; *(keyboard layout)* **IBM AT keyboard** = clavier (IBM) AT; *(personal computer that is compatible with the IBM PC)* **IBM compatible** = compatible IBM; *(personal computer)* **IBM PC** = (ordinateur) IBM PC; *(keyboard layout)* **IBM PC keyboard** = clavier IBM PC; *(range of personal computers)* **IBM PS/2** *or* **IBM Personal System/2** = (ordinateur) IBM PS/2; *(personal computer based on the IBM PC)* **IBM XT** = (ordinateur) IBM-XT

IC = INTEGRATED CIRCUIT (NOTE: plural is **ICs)**

icand = MULTIPLICAND

icon *or* **ikon** *noun* icône *f*; **the icon for the graphics program is a small picture of a palette** = l'icône du programme graphique à la forme d'une petite palette; **click twice over the wordprocessor icon - the picture of the typewriter** = cliquez deux fois sur l'icône Machine à écrire pour accéder au traitement de texte

QUOTE the system has on-screen icons and pop-up menus and is easy to control using the mouse

Electronics & Power =

QUOTE an icon-based system allows easy use of a computer without the need to memorize the complicated command structure of the native operating system

Micro Decision

QUOTE Despite (or because of?) the swap file, loading was slow and the hourglass icon of the mouse pointer frequently returned to the arrow symbol well before loading was complete.

Computing

ID = IDENTIFICATION **ID card** = carte *f* d'identité; **ID code** = code *m* personnel *or* code d'identification; **after you wake up the system, you have to input your ID code then your password** = après la mise en route du système, il faut tapez votre code personnel et votre mot de passe

IDA = INTEGRATED DIGITAL ACCESS

IDD = INTERNATIONAL DIRECT DIALLING

IDE = INTEGRATED DRIVE ELECTRONICS *or* INTELLIGENT DEVICE ELECTRONICS **IDE drives are the standard fitted to most PCs** = le disque IDE est devenu l'équipement standard de la plupart des PC

ideal *adjective* idéal, -e; *(for negatives)* **ideal format** = format professionnel

identical *adjective* identique *or* semblable; **the two systems use identical software** = les deux systèmes utilisent des logiciels identiques; **the performance of the two clones is identical** = du point de vue performance, les deux clones se valent

identify *verb* identifier; **the user has to identify himself to the system by using a password before access is allowed** = l'utilisateur doit s'identifier par un mot de passe qui lui permet d'avoir accès au système; **the maintenance engineers have identified the cause of the system failure** = les ingénieurs de maintenance ont repéré la source de la panne du système

◊ **identification** *noun* identification *f*; **identification character** = caractère *m* d'identification; *(in COBOL)* **identification division** = division *f* avec paramètres d'identification (d'un programme en COBOL)

◊ **identifier** *noun* identificateur *m or* caractère *m* d'identification; **identifier word** = identificateur *or* mot *m* d'identification

◊ **identity** *noun* identité *f*; **identity burst** = séquence *f* d'identification; **identity card** = carte *f* d'identité; **identity gate** *or* **element** = porte *f* d'identité; **identity number** = numéro *m* de code personnel; **don't forget to log in your identity number** = n'oublie pas d'entrer ton numéro de code personnel; **identity operation** = opération *f* d'identité

idiot tape *noun (tape containing unformatted text)* bande *f* idiote *or* bande de texte non formaté *or* sans paramètres d'impression

idle *adjective (machine)* au repos; *(code that means 'do nothing')* **idle character** = caractère nul; **idle time** = temps *m* mort *or* temps d'attente (entre deux opérations)

IDP = INTEGRATED DATA PROCESSING

IEC connector *noun (standard for a three-pin connector)* connecteur *m* IEC; **all PCs use a male IEC connector and a mains lead with a female IEC**

connector = tous les PC utilisent un connecteur mâle IEC et un câble d'alimentation avec un connecteur femelle IEC

IEE *UK* = INSTITUTION OF ELECTRICAL ENGINEERS

IEEE *USA* = INSTITUTE OF ELECTRICAL AND ELECTRONIC ENGINEERS **IEEE bus** = bus *m* (conforme aux normes du) IEEE; *(interfacing standard)* **IEEE-488** = (norme d'interface parallèle standard) IEEE-488; *(standard defining data links)* **IEEE-802.2** = standard IEEE 802.2 (définissant les liens entre données); *(standard defining Ethernet network)* **IEEE-802.3** = standard IEEE 802.3 (définissant le système de réseau Ethernet); *(standard defining Token Bus)* **IEEE-802.4** = standard IEEE 802.4 (définissant le bus Token-Ring); *(standard defining IBM Token-Ring network)* **IEEE-802.5** = standard IEEE-802.5 (définissant le réseau Token-Ring IBM)

ier *noun* = MULTIPLIER

if *or* **IF** = INTERMEDIATE FREQUENCY

IF statement *noun* instruction *f* IF (si); **IF-THEN-ELSE** = instructions IF-THEN-ELSE (branchement conditionnel)

ignore *verb* ne pas reconnaître *or* ne pas tenir compte de *or* ignorer *or* rejeter; **this command instructs the computer to ignore all punctuation** = cette commande donne ordre à l'ordinateur de ne pas tenir compte de la ponctuation; **ignore character** = caractère *m* de remplissage

IH = INTERRUPT HANDLER

IIL = INTEGRATED INJECTION LOGIC

IKBS = INTELLIGENT KNOWLEDGE-BASED SYSTEM

ikon *or* **icon** *noun* icône *m see also* ICON

ILF = INFRA LOW FREQUENCY

ILL = INTER-LIBRARY LOAN

illegal *adjective (against the law)* illégal, -e; *(against the rules)* invalide *or* qui va contre les règles de la syntaxe; **illegal character** = caractère *m* invalide; **illegal instruction** = instruction *f* invalide; **illegal operation** = opération *f* invalide

◊ **illegally** *adverb (against the law)* illégalement; *(against the rules)* de façon invalide *or* contre les règles de la syntaxe; **the company has been illegally copying copyright software** = depuis quelque temps déjà, la société fait des copies frauduleuses de logiciels protégés par copyright

illegible *adjective* illisible; **if the manuscript is illegible, send it back to the author to have it typed** = si le manuscrit est illisible, il faut le renvoyer à l'auteur et lui demander de le faire taper à la machine

illiterate *adjective* analphabète *or* illéttré, -ée; **computer illiterate** = (personne) qui ne possède aucune connaissance informatique *or* qui ne comprend pas le jargon informatique

QUOTE three years ago the number of people who were computer illiterate was much higher than today

Minicomputer News

illuminate *verb* éclairer *or* illuminer; **the screen is illuminated by a low-power light** = l'écran est éclairé par une lampe de très faible puissance

◊ **illumination** *noun* illumination *f* ; éclairage *m*; *(of antenna)* **aperture illumination** = illumination *f* de l'ouverture

◊ **illuminance** *noun (amount of light)* éclairement *m*

illustrate *verb* illustrer; **the book is illustrated in colour** = ce livre comporte des illustrations en couleur; **the manual is illustrated with charts and pictures of the networking connections** = le manuel contient des graphiques et des illustrations de configurations de réseaux

◊ **illustration** *noun (in a book)* illustration *f*; **the book has twenty-five pages of full-colour illustrations** = on trouve dans le livre 25 pages d'illustrations en couleur

image *noun* (a) *(of an area of memory)* image *f* (b) *(picture)* image; **image area** = zone *f* d'image; **image carrier** = *(in phototypesetting)* support *m* de polices de caractères; *(video)* porteuse *f* d'image *or* de signal vidéo; *(compressing the data forming an image)* **image compression** = compression *f* d'image; **image degradation** = dégradation *f* de l'image; **image distortion** = distorsion *f* de l'image; **image enhancer** = amplificateur *m or* intensificateur *m* d'image; *(describing character shapes)* **image master** = feuille *f* de style; *(in a camera)* **image plane** = plan *m* focal; **image processing** = traitement *m* de l'image; **image processor** = (i) système *m* de traitement de l'image *or* analyseur *m* d'image; (ii) processeur *m* d'image; **image retention** = rémanence *f* de l'image; **image scanner** = scanner *m* d'image; **image sensor** = capteur *m* d'image; **image stability** = stabilité *f* de l'image; **image storage space** = espace *m* mémoire de l'image *or* zone de stockage de l'image; **image table** = table *f* d'attributs

◊ **imaging** *noun* imagerie *f* médicale *or* de synthèse; **magnetic resonance imaging (MRI)** = imagerie *f* par résonance magnétique (IRM); **X-ray imaging** = radioscopie *f*

immediate *adjective* immédiat, -e; **immediate access store (IAS)** = mémoire *f* interne à accès immédiat; **immediate addressing** = adressage immédiat; **immediate instruction** = instruction immédiate; **immediate mode** = mode immédiat; **immediate operand** = opérande immédiat; **immediate processing** = traitement *m* immédiat

immunity *see* INTERFERENCE

impact *noun (striking)* impact *m*; **impact printer** = imprimante *f* à impact

QUOTE Lexmark is shipping the Wheelwriter family of typewriters that can be connected to a PC using the parallel printer port, making it act like a PC impact printer.

Computing

impedance *noun* impédance *f*; **impedance matching** = accord *m* d'impédance; **impedance matching between a transmitter and a receiver minimizes power losses to transmitted signals** = l'accord d'impédance entre un émetteur et un récepteur réduit la perte de puissance des signaux transmis; **impedance mismatch** = désaccord *m* d'impédance

implant *verb* implanter; **the dopant is implanted into the substrate** = le dopant est implanté dans le substrat

implement *verb* réaliser *or* implémenter *or* exécuter

◊ **implementation** *noun* réalisation *f or* implémentation *f* ; version *f*; **the latest implementation of the software runs much faster** = la dernière version du logiciel est beaucoup plus rapide

implication *noun* (*logical operation*) implication *f*

implied addressing *noun* adressage *m* implicite; **implied addressing for the accumulator is used in the instruction LDA,16** = l'adressage implicite pour l'accumulateur est inclus dans l'instruction LDA,16

import *verb* (**a**) (*goods*) importer (**b**) (*bring something in from outside a system*) importer; **you can import images from the CAD package into the DTP program** = il est possible d'importer des images d'un logiciel CAO dans un programme de PAO; **imported signal** = signal *m* importé

◊ **importation** *noun* (*into a system*) importation *f*

QUOTE text and graphics importation from other systems is possible

Publish

QUOTE At the moment, Acrobat supports only the sending and viewing of documents. There are legal implications associated with allowing users to edit documents in the style of the original application, without having the tool itself on their desks, and there is no import facility back into applications.

Computing

impression *noun* (*printrun*) tirage *m*; (*printing*) impression *f*; **impression cylinder** = cylindre *m or* tambour *m* d'impression

imprint *noun* (*publisher's or printer's name*) nom *f* de l'éditeur *or* de l'imprimeur

impulse *noun* impulsion *f or* excitation *f*

◊ **impulsive** *adjective* de courte durée; **impulsive noise** = bruit *m or* interférence *f* de courte durée

inaccurate *adjective* incorrect, -e *or* inexact, -e; **he entered an inaccurate password** = il a tapé le mauvais mot de passe *or* il y avait une erreur dans le mot de passe qu'il a tapé

◊ **inaccuracy** *noun* erreur *f or* inexactitude *f*; **the bibliography is full of inaccuracies** = on trouve des tas d'erreurs dans la bibliographie

inactive *adjective* inactif, -ive *or* au repos *or* à l'arrêt; (*window displayed, but not being used*) **inactive window** = fenêtre *f* inactive

in-band signalling *noun* transmission *f* de signaux sur bande passante

inbuilt *adjective* intégré, -ée; **this software has inbuilt error correction** = ce logiciel possède un système de correction d'erreurs intégré

in camera process *noun* traitement *m* instantané d'un film

incandescence *noun* incandescence *f*

◊ **incandescent** *adjective* incandescent, -e; **current passing through gas and heating a filament in a light bulb causes it to produce incandescent light** = le passage du courant qui chauffe le filament dans une ampoule contenant un gaz, produit une lumière incandescente

inches-per-second (ips) (nombre de) pouces *mpl* par seconde *or* pouce(s)/seconde

in-circuit emulator *noun* émulateur *m* intégré au circuit; **this in-circuit emulator is used to test the floppy disk controller by emulating a disk drive** = cet émulateur intégré au circuit sert à tester le contrôleur de la disquette, en simulant le fonctionnement d'un lecteur de disquette(s)

inclined orbit *noun* orbite *f* inclinée

inclusion *noun* inclusion *f*

◊ **inclusive** *adjective* inclusif, -ive; (*logical function*) **inclusive OR** = OU inclusif

incoming *adjective* qui vient de l'extérieur; **incoming message** = message *m* reçu; **incoming traffic** = (nombre de) messages reçus *or* données reçues

incompatible *adjective* incompatible *or* non compatible; **they tried to link the two systems, but found they were incompatible** = en essayant de relier les deux systèmes, ils ont trouvé qu'ils étaient incompatibles

incorrect *adjective* incorrect, -e *or* inexact, -e *or* erroné, -ée; **the input data was incorrect, so the output was also incorrect** = les données saisies étant incorrectes, les résultats à la sortie étaient par le fait même erronés

◊ **incorrectly** *adverb* incorrectement *or* mal; **the data was incorrectly keyboarded** = les données ont été incorrectement saisies *or* les données saisies contenaient des erreurs

increment 1 *noun* **(a)** *(addition of a number)* incrémentation *f or* augmentation *f*; **an increment is added to the counter each time a pulse is detected** = le compteur est incrémenté à chaque impulsion **(b)** *(number added)* incrément *m*; **increase the increment to three** = augmentez l'incrément à trois **2** *verb* **(a)** *(to increase a number)* augmenter *or* incrémenter; **the counter is incremented each time an instruction is executed** = le compteur est incrémenté à chaque instruction exécutée **(b)** *(to move forward)* avancer d'un pas *or* d'une instruction **(c)** *(to move a document forward)* faire avancer d'un pas

◊ **incremental computer** *noun* ordinateur incrémentiel *or* à valeurs variables; **incremental backup** = sauvegarde *f* incrémentielle; **incremental data** = donnée(s) incrémentielle(s); **incremental plotter** = traceur incrémentiel

indent 1 *noun* alinéa *m* **2** *verb* faire un alinéa; **the first line of the paragraph is indented two spaces** = comptez deux espaces pour l'alinéa du premier paragraphe

◊ **indentation** *noun* alinéa *m*

independent *adjective* indépendant, -e; **machine-independent language** = langage *m* standard *or* universel

◊ **independently** *adverb* indépendamment *or* séparément; **in spooling, the printer is acting independently of the keyboard** = lors d'un spooling, l'imprimante fonctionne indépendamment du clavier; **each item is indexed independently** = ces articles sont indexés séparément

indeterminate system *noun* système *m* indéterminé

index 1 *noun* **(a)** *(in a computer memory)* index *m*; **index build** = indexation *m*; *(of videotext)* **index page** = page *f* index **(b)** *(of book)* index **(c)** *(list)* index *or* répertoire *m*; **index card** = fiche *f*; **(d) index letter** = indicatif *m* littéral; **index number** = indicatif numérique **(e)** *(computer address)* adresse indexée; **index register (IR)** = registre *m* d'index; **index value word** = mot *m* d'index **(f)** *(guide mark on film or microfilm)* index *m* de position; *(in the edge of a disk)* **index hole** = perforation *f* de marquage (du bord d'un disque) **2** *verb* **(a)** *(a book)* préparer un index *or* indexer; **the book was sent out for indexing** = le livre a été envoyé à l'extérieur pour la préparation de l'index; **the book has been badly indexed** = l'index de ce livre est très mal fait **(b)** *(to mark with an index)* indexer; **indexed address** = adresse *f* indexée; **indexed addressing** = adressage indexé; **indexed file** = fichier *m* indexé; **indexed instruction** = instruction *f* indexée; **indexed sequential access method (ISAM)** = méthode *f* d'accès séquentiel indexé (ISAM); **indexed sequential storage** = mémoire *f* séquentielle indexée

◊ **indexer** *noun* *(of a book)* personne qui prépare un index *or* auteur *m* d'un index

◊ **indexing** *noun* **(a)** *(in a computer)* indexation *f* **(b)** *(list of records)* classement *m or* indexation *f*; **indexing language** = langage *m* d'indexation **(c)** *(book)* préparation de l'index d'un livre; **computer indexing** = indexation sur ordinateur *or* préparation d'un index à l'aide d'un ordinateur

indicate *verb* indiquer *or* montrer

◊ **indication** *noun* indication *f*

◊ **indicator** *noun* indicateur *m*; **indicator chart** = tableau *m* des indicateurs; **indicator flag** = indicateur *or* balise *f or* témoin *m or* marqueur *m or* drapeau *m*; **indicator light** = voyant *m* (lumineux)

indirect *adjective* indirect, -e; **indirect addressing** = adressage *m* indirect; **indirect ray** = rayonnement *m* indirect

individual 1 *noun* individu *m or* personne *f*; **each individual has his own password to access the system** = chaque personne possède son propre mot de passe pour accéder au système **2** *adjective* individuel, -elle *or* personnel, -elle; **the individual workstations are all linked to the mainframe** = les divers postes de travail individuels sont tous reliés à l'ordinateur principal

induce *verb* *(electricity)* induire *or* produire un courant induit *or* produire une induction; *(mathematics)* induire; **induced failure** = défaillance *f* induite *or* ayant une cause externe; **induced interference** = interférence *f* induite *or* causée par une autre machine

◊ **inductance** *noun* inductance *f*

◊ **induction** *noun* *(electricity or mathematics)* induction *f*; **induction coil** = bobine *f* d'induction

◊ **inductive coordination** *noun* coordination *f* inductive

◊ **inductor** *noun* inducteur *m or* bobine d'induction

Industry Standard Architecture (ISA) *noun* *(standard for 16-bit expansion bus)* architecture *f* (de bus) ISA; *compare* EISA, MCA

inequality operator *noun* *(symbol indicating that two variables are not equal)* opérateur *m* d'inégalité; **the C programming language uses the symbol '!=' as its inequality operator** = le langage C utilise le symbole '!=' comme opérateur d'inégalité

inequivalence *noun* *(logical function)* exclusion *f* réciproque

inert gas *adjective* gaz *m* inerte

infected computer *noun* *(computer with a virus program)* ordinateur *m* infecté

inference *noun* **(a)** *(operation)* inférence *f or* déduction *f*; **inference engine** *or* **machine** = moteur *m* d'inférence **(b)** *(result)* déduction *f or* inférence; **inference control** = contrôle *m* d'inférence

inferior figures *noun* *(smaller numbers printed slightly below normal characters)* indices *mpl*

infinite *adjective* infini, -e; **infinite loop** = boucle *f* sans fin *or* infinie

◊ **infinity** *noun* *(quantity or distance)* infini *m*

infix notation *noun* notation *f* infixée

informatics *noun* (science de) l'informatique *f*

information *noun* **(a)** *(knowledge)* information *f* **(b)** *(data)* information *or* données *fpl*; **information bearer channel** = voie *f* de transmission d'informations; **information content** = quantité *f* d'information; **information flow control** = contrôle *m* de flux d'informations; **information input** = saisie *f* de données; *(on screen)* **information line** = ligne *f* d'état *or* d'information; **information management system** = système *m* de gestion de l'information; **information networks** = réseaux *mpl* d'information *or* réseaux informatiques; **information output** = *(on screen)* affichage *m* de données; *(on printer)* sortie *f* d'imprimante; **information processing** = traitement *m* de données *or* de l'information; **information processor** = ordinateur *m* (utilisé pour le traitement de l'information); **information provider (IP)** = source *f* d'information; service *m* (fournisseur) d'information *or* agence d'information; **information rate** = vitesse *f* de sortie de l'information; **information retrieval (IR)** = (i) recherche *f* documentaire; (ii) extraction *f or* restitution *f* de données; **information retrieval centre** = centre de recherche documentaire *or* centre serveur *or* banque de données; **information storage** = stockage *m* de données *or* de l'information; **information storage and retrieval (ISR)** = stockage et restitution de données; **information structure** = structure *f* de données; **information system** = système *m* informatique; **information technology (IT)** = informatique *f or* techniques *f* de l'information; **information theory** = théorie *f* de l'information; **information transfer channel** = canal *m or* voie de transmission de l'information

QUOTE Racal-Datacom has picked up a £1.5 million order for its ISDN digital access multiplexers from financial information provider Telerate, its second from the company this year.

Computing

infra- *prefix* infra-

infrared *adjective* infrarouge; **infrared camera** = caméra *f* de vision nocturne; **infrared communications** = communication *f* par infrarouge; **infrared detector** = détecteur *m* d'infrarouge; *(process)* **infrared photography** = photo *f* avec film sensible aux infrarouges; **infrared sights** = instruments *mpl* de vision aux infrarouges

◊ **infrasonic frequency** *noun* fréquence *f* infrasonique

◊ **infrastructure** *noun* infrastructure *f*

infringement *noun* *(breaking the law)* violation *f or* transgression *f or* délit *m*; **copyright infringement** = contrefaçon *f* (d'une oeuvre protégée par un copyright) *or* violation *f* du droit d'auteur; délit de contrefaçon

inherent addressing *noun* adressage *m* inhérent *or* particulier

inherit *verb* *(acquire the characteristics of another data type)* hériter (des caractéristiques d'un autre objet)

◊ **inheritance** *noun* *(passing the characteristics of one data type to another)* héritage *m* ; transmission *f* (des caractéristiques d'un objet ou d'une classe)

◊ **inherited error** *noun* erreur *f* transmise *or* héritée

inhibit *verb* inhiber *or* arrêter *or* stopper; **inhibiting input** = signal *m* d'invalidation *or* d'interdiction de transmission

in-house *adverb & adjective* sur place *or* dans l'entreprise; interne *or* de la maison; **all the data processing is done in-house** = tout le travail informatique se fait dans l'entreprise; **the in-house maintenance staff deal with all our equipment** = tous nos équipements sont suivis par l'équipe de maintenance de la maison

initial 1 *adjective* *(at the beginning)* initial, -e *or* au départ; **initial address** = adresse initiale *or* de lancement; **initial condition** = condition initiale; **initial error** = erreur *f* au départ; **initial instructions** = instructions *f* de lancement *or* instructions initiales; **initial program header** = lanceur *m* de programme de chargement; **initial program loader (IPL)** = chargeur *m* de programme de lancement; **initial value** = valeur initiale **2** *noun* *(first letter)* initiale *f*; **(set of) initials** = sigle *m*; **what do the initials IBM stand for?** = que signifie le sigle IBM?

◊ **initialization** *noun* *(process)* initialisation *f*; **initialization is often carried out without the user knowing** = l'initialisation peut souvent s'effectuer à l'insu de l'utilisateur

◊ **initialize** *verb* *(a system)* initialiser

injection laser *noun* laser *m* de portance

◊ **injection logic** *see* INTEGRATED

ink 1 *noun* encre *f*; **ink-jet printer** = imprimante *f* à jet d'encre; **colour ink-jet technology and thermal transfer technology compete with each other** = les techniques du jet d'encre couleur et du transfert thermique sont non concurrentielles; **magnetic ink** = encre magnétique; **magnetic ink character recognition (MICR)** = reconnaissance *f* de caractères magnétiques **2** *verb* imprégner *or* couvrir d'encre

QUOTE ink-jet printers work by squirting a fine stream of ink onto the paper

Personal Computer World

inlay card *noun* (*inside tape or disk box*) étiquette *f* interne

in-line 1 *noun* (*connection pins arranged in one or two rows*) (connecteur avec broches disposées) en ligne **2** *adverb* (*that contains no loops*) **in-line program** = programme *m* linéaire; **in-line processing** = traitement *m* linéaire

inner loop *noun* boucle *f* intérieure

in phase *adverb* **(a)** (*signal*) en phase *or* synchronisé, -ée **(b)** (*film*) synchronisé, -ée

input (i/p *or* **I/P) 1** *verb* entrer *or* saisir *or* introduire (des données); **the data is input via a modem** = les données sont chargées à l'aide d'un modem **2** *noun* **(a)** (*action*) entrée *f or* saisie *f or* introduction *f* (de données); (*data*) données *fpl* d'entrée *or* données saisies; **input area** = zone *f* d'entrée; **input block** = bloc *m* d'entrée; (*computer or device in which the slowest part is data transfer*) **input bound** = (ordinateur) limité par les entrées *or* par le débit d'entrée des données; **input buffer register** = registre *m* tampon des entrées; **input device** = périphérique *m* d'entrée; **input lead** = câble *m* d'entrée *or* (câble de) liaison *f* d'un périphérique d'entrée; (*not running fast*) **input limited (program)** = (programme) limité par l'entrée des données; (*program*) **input mode** = mode *m* (d') entrée; **input port** = port *m* (d') entrée; **input register** = registre *m* d'entrée; **input routine** = routine *f* d'entrée *or* d'introduction de données; (*routine or area*) **input section** = section *f* d'entrée; **input speed** = débit *m* des entrées; **input statement** = déclaration *f or* message *m* d'entrée; **input storage** = mémoire *f* d'entrée; **input unit** = périphérique *m* d'entrée; **input work queue** = file *f* d'attente des données d'entrée **(b)** (*electrical signal*) signal *m* d'entrée

> QUOTE In fact, the non-Qwerty format of the Maltron keyboard did cause a few gasps when it was first shown to the staff, but within a month all the Maltron users had regained normal input speeds.
> *Computing*

◊ **input/output (I/O)** *noun* entrée/sortie *f*; **input/output buffer** = tampon *m* (d') entrée/sortie; **input/output bus** = bus *m* (d') entrée/sortie; **input/output channel** = canal *m or* voie *f* d'entrée/sortie; **input/output control program** = programme de contrôle d'entrée/sortie; **input/output controller** = contrôleur *m* d'entrée/sortie; **input/output device** *or* **unit** = périphérique *m* d'entrée/sortie; **input/output executive** = superviseur *m* d'entrée/sortie; **input/output instruction** = instruction *f* d'entrée/sortie; **input/output interface** = interface *f* d'entrée/sortie; (*signal*) **input/output interrupt** = (signal d') interruption *f* d'entrée/sortie; **input/output library** = bibliothèque *f* de programmes d'entrée/sortie; **input/output mapping** = configuration *f* d'entrée/sortie; **input/output port** = port *m* (d') entrée/sortie; **the joystick can be connected to the input/output port** = le manche à balai peut être connecté sur le port entrée/sortie; **input/output processor (IOP)** = processeur *m* d'entrée/sortie; **input/output**

referencing = référençage *m* d'entrée/sortie; **input/output register** = registre *m* d'entrée/sortie; **input/output request (IORQ)** = requête *f* d'entrée/sortie; **input/output status word** = mot *m* d'état d'entrée/sortie; **parallel input/output (PIO)** = entrée/sortie *f* parallèle

inquiry *noun* demande *f or* requête *f or* interrogation *f*; **inquiry character (ENQ)** = caractère *m* de requête *or* d'interrogation; **inquiry station** = poste *m* d'interrogation; **inquiry/response (function)** = (fonction) demande/réponse *or* interrogation/réponse

Ins *or* **insert key** *noun* (*key that switches into insert mode*) touche *f* Ins; touche Inser *or* insertion (sur un clavier français)

insert *verb* **(a)** introduire; **first insert the system disk in the left slot** = introduire d'abord la disquette système dans le lecteur de gauche **(b)** (*to add new text*) ajouter; (*key that switches into insert mode*) **insert key** *or* **Ins key** = touche *f* Ins; touche Inser *or* insertion (sur un clavier français); **inserted subroutine** = sous-programme *m* additionnel

◊ **insert mode** *noun* mode *m* insertion

insertion loss *noun* (*attenuation to a signal*) perte *f or* affaiblissement *m* d'insertion

install *verb* mettre en place *or* installer; **the system is easy to install and simple to use** = ce système est facile à mettre en place et à utiliser; (*software utility*) **install program** = programme *m* d'installation

◊ **installable device driver** *noun* (*device driver loaded into memory*) gestionnaire *m* de périphérique installable

◊ **installation** *noun* **(a)** (*equipment*) matériel *m or* équipement *m* informatique; **the engineers are still testing the new installation** = les ingénieurs n'ont pas terminé l'essai du nouveau système **(b)** (*setting up*) mise *f* en place *or* installation *f*; **the installation of the equipment took only a few hours** = il n'a fallu que quelques heures pour mettre l'équipement en place

instance *noun* (*duplicate object that has been created*) objet *m* disponible *or* instance *f* (en programmation orientée objet)

instantaneous access *noun* accès *m* instantané

instant replay *noun* (*of video film*) visionnage *m* immédiat

instruct *verb* donner des instructions à quelqu'un *or* à un ordinateur

◊ **instruction** *noun* instruction *f*; **the instruction PRINT is used in this BASIC dialect as an operand to display the following data** = l'instruction PRINT est un opérande employé en langage BASIC pour l'affichage des données suivantes; **instruction address** = adresse *f* d'instruction; **instruction address register (IAR)** = registre *m* d'adresse d'instruction; **instruction area** = zone *f* d'instruction (dans une mémoire); **instruction cache** = antémémoire *f* d'instruction; **instruction character** = caractère *m* d'instruction; **instruction codes** = codes d'instruction; *(IAR or program counter)* **instruction counter** = compteur *m* d'instruction *or* registre d'adresse d'instruction; **instruction cycle** = cycle *m* d'instruction; **instruction cycle time** = temps *m* de cycle d'instruction; **instruction decoder** = décodeur *m* d'instructions; **instruction execution time** = temps *m* d'exécution d'une instruction; **instruction format** = format *m* d'instruction; **instruction modification** = modification *f* d'une instruction; **instruction pipelining** = mode d'exécution d'instructions en pipeline *or* enchaînement d'instructions avec recouvrement; *(register in a CPU)* **instruction pointer** = pointeur *m* d'instruction; **instruction processor** = processeur *m* d'instruction; **instruction register (IR)** = registre d'instruction; **instruction repertoire** *or* **set** = jeu *m* d'instructions; **instruction storage** = *(area)* mémoire *f* d'instruction; *(storing)* mise *f* en mémoire *or* stockage *m* d'instruction; **instruction time** = temps *m* d'exécution d'une instruction *or* temps d'instruction; **instruction word** = (mot) instruction; **the manufacturers of this CPU have decided that JMP will be the instruction word to call the jump function** = les constructeurs du CPU ont décidé que l'instruction JMP servirait à indiquer un branchement *or* un saut; **absolute instruction** = instruction *f* absolue; **arithmetic instruction** = instruction arithmétique; **blank** *or* **dummy** *or* **null instruction** = instruction nulle *or* de remplissage; **breakpoint instruction** = instruction d'arrêt; **decision** *or* **discrimination instruction** = instruction (d'opération) conditionnelle; **dummy instruction** = *see* BLANK INSTRUCTION **executive instruction** = instruction de superviseur; **four-address instruction** = instruction à quatre adresses; **indexed instruction** = instruction indexée; **input/output instruction** = instruction d'entrée/sortie; **jump instruction** = instruction de branchement *or* de saut; **macro instruction** = macro-instruction *f*; **no-op instruction** = instruction vide *or* factice *or* de remplissage; **n-plus-one instruction** = instruction à n adresse(s) plus une; **supervisory instruction** = instruction de contrôle *or* de surveillance; **three-address-instruction** = instruction à trois adresses; **two-address-instruction** = instruction à deux adresses; **two-plus-one-address instruction** = instruction à deux adresses plus une

instrumentation *noun (set of tools)* instruments *mpl*; *(electronic devices)* instrumentation *f*; **we've improved the instrumentation on this model to keep you better informed of the machine's position** = nous avons amélioré l'instrumentation se rapportant à ce modèle pour que vous puissiez mieux suivre l'état de la machine

insufficient *adjective* insuffisant, -e; **there is insufficient time to train the keyboarders properly** = il est impossible de former convenablement un opérateur dans un délai aussi court

insulate *verb* isoler

◊ **insulation material** *noun* isolant *m or* matériau *m* isolant

◊ **insulator** *noun* isolant *m or* matériau *m* isolant; **plastic is a good insulator** = le plastique est un bon isolant

integer *noun* (nombre) entier *m*; **double-precision integer** = nombre entier en double précision; *(faster version of BASIC)* **integer BASIC** = integer BASIC

◊ **integral** *noun (device)* intégré, -ée; **the integral disk drives and modem reduce desk space** = puisque les lecteurs de disquettes et le modem sont intégrés, l'encombrement est réduit

QUOTE an integral 7 inch amber display screen, two half-height disk drives and modem emulation for easy interfacing with mainframes
Computing Today

integrated *adjective* intégré -ée; **integrated database** = base *f* de données intégrée; **integrated data processing (IDP)** = (système de) traitement de données intégré; **integrated device** = dispositif intégré; **our competitor's computer doesn't have an integrated disk drive like this model** = l'ordinateur concurrent ne possède pas de lecteur de disquettes intégré comme ce modèle-ci; *(standard for hard disk drive unit)* **integrated device electronics (IDE)** = contrôleur *m* de disque IDE; **IDE drives are the standard fitted to most PCs** = le disque IDE est devenu l'équipement standard de la plupart des PC; **integrated digital access (IDA)** = accès au réseau numérique intégré; **integrated digital network** = réseau numérique intégré (RNI); **integrated emulator** = émulateur intégré; **integrated injection logic (IIL)** = logique *f* intégrée à injection *or* logique IIL *or* logique I2L; **integrated modem** = modem intégré; **integrated office** = (système de) bureautique intégrée; **integrated optical circuit** = circuit optique intégré; **integrated program** = programme *m* intégré; **integrated services digital network (ISDN)** = réseau *m* numérique à intégration de services (RNIS); **integrated software** = logiciel intégré

◊ **integrated circuit (IC)** *noun* circuit intégré

◊ **integration** *noun* intégration *f*; **small scale integration (SSI)** = intégration à petite échelle; **medium scale integration (MSI)** = intégration à moyenne échelle; **large scale integration (LSI)** = intégration à grande échelle; **super large scale integration (SLSI)** = intégration à super grande échelle; **very large scale integration (VLSI)** = intégration à très grande échelle; **wafer scale integration** = intégration sur tranche de silicium

integrity *noun* intégrité *f*; **integrity of a file** = intégrité d'un fichier; **the data in this file has integrity** = les données de ce fichier n'ont pas été corrompues

QUOTE it is intended for use in applications demanding high data integrity, such as archival storage or permanent databases
Minicomputer News

Intel ™ *(company which developed the first microprocessor)* (la société) Intel ™; *(Intel microprocessors)* **Intel 8086, 8088, 80286, 80386, 80486** = (microprocesseurs) Intel 8086, 8088, 80286, 80386, 80486; **Intel Pentium** ™ = Intel Pentium ™

intelligence *noun (of person or machine)* intelligence *f*; **artificial intelligence (AI)** = intelligence artificielle (IA)

◊ **intelligent** *noun (person or program or machine)* intelligent, -e; **intelligent device** = machine intelligente; **intelligent knowledge-based system (IKBS)** *or* **expert system** = système intelligent à base de connaissances *or* système expert; **intelligent spacer** = fonction césure intelligente; **intelligent tutoring system** = formation assistée par système expert; *(terminal which contains a CPU and memory)* **intelligent terminal** = terminal intelligent (NOTE: the opposite is **dumb terminal**) *(wiring hub that can be controlled from a workstation)* **intelligent wiring hub** = boîtier *m* de câblage intelligent

INTELSAT = INTERNATIONAL TELECOMMUNICATIONS SATELLITE ORGANIZATION INTELSAT

intensity *noun (of signal or light or sound)* intensité *f*

inter- *prefix (between)* inter-; **interblock** = entre blocs *or* interbloc

interact *verb (of two things)* interagir

◊ **interaction** *noun* interaction *f*

◊ **interactive** *adjective (system or software)* interactif, -ive; *(mode)* dialogué, -ée *or* conversationnel, -elle; **interactive cable television** = télévision câblée interactive; **interactive debugging system** = système de déverminage *or* de débogage interactif; **interactive graphics** = représentations graphiques interactives *or* infographie interactive; **the space invaders machine has great interactive graphics, the player controls the position of his spaceship with the joystick** = le jeu (électronique) 'les envahisseurs de l'espace' présente d'excellents graphiques interactifs; le joueur contrôle la position de son vaisseau spatial avec la manette (de jeu); **interactive media** = média interactif; **interactive mode** *or* **processing** = mode interactif *or* mode dialogué *or* mode conversationnel; *(multimedia system)* **interactive multimedia** = (système) multimédia interactif; **this interactive multimedia title allows a user to make music with a synthesizer program** = ce logiciel multimédia interactif permet à l'utilisateur de faire de la musique avec un programme de synthétiseur; **interactive routine** = routine interactive; **interactive system** = système interactif; **interactive terminal** = terminal interactif *or* conversationnel; **interactive video** = vidéo *or* vidéographie interactive; **interactive videotext** = dialogue *m* vidéotex *or* vidéographie interactive

◊ **interactivity** *noun* interactivité *f*

> QUOTE soon pupils will be able to go shopping in a French town from the comfort of their classroom - carried to their destination by interactive video, a medium which combines the power of the computer with the audiovisual impact of video
> *Electronics & Power*

> QUOTE interactivity is a buzzword you've been hearing a lot lately. Resign yourself to it because you're going to be hearing a lot more of it
> *Music Technology*

> QUOTE Oracle today details its interactive information superhighway aims, endorsed by 17 industry partners. The lynchpin to the announcement will be software based on the Oracle Media Server, a multimedia database designed to run on massively parallel computers.
> *Computing*

interblock gap (IBG) *noun* espace *m* interbloc

intercarrier noise *noun* interférence *f* entre porteuses; **television intercarrier noise is noticed when the picture and the sound signal carriers clash** = on note des interférences de porteuses sur une télévision lorsque la porteuse son et la porteuse image se rencontrent

interchange 1 *noun* échange *m or* transfert *m or* permutation *f*; **the machine allows document interchange between it and other machines without reformatting** = avec cette machine, on peut transférer des documents d'une machine à l'autre sans qu'il soit nécessaire de reformater **2** *verb* permuter; mettre une chose à la place d'une autre

◊ **interchangeable** *adjective* interchangeable

intercharacter spacing *noun (wordprocessing)* espacement *m* (proportionnel) de caractères

intercom *noun* Interphone ™ *m*

interconnect *verb (of several things)* interconnecter *or* relier les un(e)s aux autres; **a series of interconnected terminals** = une série de postes reliés les uns aux autres

◊ **interconnection** *noun* **(a)** *(connecting material)* interconnexion *f or* liaison *f* (entre plusieurs machines *or* dispositifs) **(b)** *(connection)* raccordement *m* (au réseau téléphonique)

interface 1 *noun* interface *f*; **EIA interface** = interface EIA; **general purpose interface adapter (GPIA)** = interface universelle GPIA; **general purpose interface bus (GPIB)** = bus universel GPIB; **input/output interface** = interface d'entrée/sortie; **interface card** = carte *f* (d') interface; **interface message processor** = serveur *m* de message; **interface processor** = processeur *m* d'interface; **interface routines** = routines *fpl* d'interface; **parallel interface** = interface parallèle (NOTE: parallel interfaces are usually used to drive printers) **serial interface** = interface série (NOTE: the most common serial interface is RS232C) **2** *verb* **to interface with** = relier à (utilisant une interface) *or* interfacer avec

◊ **interfacing** *noun (hardware or software)* (d') interface *f*

interfere *verb* **to interfere with something** = interférer *or* nuire (à)

◊ **interference** *noun* **(a)** *(unwanted addition of signal)* brouillage *m*; **electromagnetic interference (EMI)** = perturbation *f* électromagnétique; **induced interference** = brouillage induit *or* causé par des machines **(b)** *(effect seen when two signals are added)* interférence *f*; **interference fading** = affaiblissement *m* (du signal) dû à l'interférence; **interference immunity** = tolérance *f* à l'interférence; **interference pattern** = empreinte *f* d'interférence; **constructive interference** = interférence constructive; **destructive interference** = interférence destructive

interior label *noun* label *m* d'identification (sur le support magnétique)

interlace *verb* entrelacer

interleave factor *noun (ratio of sectors skipped between access operations)* facteur *m* d'entrelacement

> COMMENT: in a hard disk with an interleave of 3, the first sector is read, then three sectors are skipped and the next sector is read. This is used to allow hard disks with slow access time to store more data on the disk.

interleaved *adjective* **(a)** *(sheets of paper)* interfolié -ée *or* placé, -ée entre deux feuilles; **blank paper was interleaved with the newly printed text to prevent the ink running** = on avait placé des feuilles blanches entre les pages nouvellement imprimées pour éviter les coulures d'encre **(b)** *(sections of programs)* imbriqué,-ée *or* entrelacé, -ée; *(two banks of memory used in sequence)* **interleaved memory** = mémoire imbriquée *or* entrelacée

◊ **interleaving** *noun* **(a)** *(putting blank paper between printed sheets)* interfoliage *m* **(b)** *(dealing with processes alternately)* entrelacement *m or* emboîtement *m*; **multiprocessor interleaving** = multiprogrammation *f* **(c)** *(dividing data into sections)* entrelacement

> QUOTE there are two separate 40-bit arrays on each card to allow interleaved operation, achieving data access every 170ns machine cycle
> *Minicomputer News*

inter-library loan (ILL) *noun* prêt *m* interbibliothèque

interlinear spacing *noun (on a phototypesetter)* interligne *m*

interlock 1 *noun* **(a)** *(security device)* verrouillage *m or* protection *f* (par mot de passe)

(b) *(synchronizing)* synchronisation *f*; **interlock projector** = projecteur *m* synchronisé **2** *verb* verrouiller

interlude *noun (routine)* interlude *m*

intermediate *adjective* intermédiaire; **intermediate access memory (IAM)** = mémoire *f* à accès intermédiaire; **intermediate code** = code *m* intermédiaire; **intermediate file** = fichier *m* intermédiaire; **intermediate material** = support *m* intermédiaire; **those slides and photographs are the intermediate materials to be mastered onto the video disk** = ces diapositives et ces photos sont les supports intermédiaires qui doivent être recopiés sur le vidéodisque; **intermediate storage** = mémoire intermédiaire; **intermediate user** = utilisateur *m* intermédiaire

◊ **intermediate frequency (if** *or* **IF)** *noun* moyenne fréquence *or* fréquence intermédiaire

intermittent error *noun* erreur *f* intermittente

internal *adjective* interne *or* intérieur, -e; **internal arithmetic** = arithmétique *f* interne; **internal character code** = code *m* de caractères interne; *(part of the operating system)* **internal command** = commande *f* interne; **in MS-DOS, the internal command DIR is used frequently** = la commande interne DIR est fréquemment employée lorsqu'on travaille sous MS-DOS; *(font stored on a ROM in a printer)* **internal** *or* **resident font** = police *f* (de caractères) résidente; **internal format** = format *m* interne; *(hard disk inside the main case of a computer)* **internal hard disk** = disque *m* dur interne; **internal language** = langage *m* interne *or* langage machine

◊ **internal memory** *or* **store** *noun* mémoire *f* interne

◊ **internal modem** *noun (modem that transfers information to the processor through the bus)* carte *f* modem

◊ **internal sort** *noun* tri *m* en mémoire interne

◊ **internally stored program** *noun* programme *m* résident

international *adjective* international, -e; **international direct dialling (IDD)** = système téléphonique automatique international; **international (dialling) code** = indicatif *m* (téléphonique) international; *(ten-digit identifying number allocated to every new book published)* **international standard book number (ISBN)** = ISBN *m*; *(identifying number for journals or magazines)* **international standard serial number (ISSN)** = ISSN *m*

◊ **International Standards Organization (ISO)** *noun* organisme international de normalisation ISO; **International Standards Organization/Open System Interconnection (ISO/OSI)** = architecture *f* ISO/OSI

internet *noun (wide area network formed of many local area networks)* internet *m*; *(TCP/IP standard)* **internet protocol (IP)** = protocole *m* internet *or* protocole TCP/IP (assurant l'interconnexion de réseaux); *(unique number)* **internet protocol address (IP Address)** = adresse *f* internet; *(packet of data)* **internet protocol datagram (IP Datagram)** = paquet *m* IP

◊ **Internet** *noun (international wide area network)* (réseau public étendu) Internet

interpolation *noun* interpolation *f*

interpret *verb* interpréter *or* traduire; *(programming language)* **interpreted language** = langage interprété

◊ **interpretative** *adjective* interprétatif, -ive; **interpretative code** = code interprétatif; **interpretative program** = programme interprétatif

◊ **interpreter** *noun (software)* (programme) interpréteur *m*

interrecord gap = INTERBLOCK GAP

interrogation *noun* interrogation *f*; **file interrogation** = interrogation de fichier

interrupt 1 *verb* interrompre *or* arrêter *or* stopper **2** *noun* **(a)** *(stopping of a transmission)* interruption *f* **(b)** *(signal)* interruption; **this printer port design uses an interrupt line to let the CPU know it is ready to receive data** = ce modèle de connecteur d'imprimante utilise une ligne d'interruption pour avertir l'unité centrale qu'il est prêt à recevoir des données; **armed interrupt** = interruption validée *or* activée; **interrupt disable** = invalider *or* interdire une interruption; **interrupt enable** = valider une interruption; **interrupt handler (IH)** = gestionnaire *m* d'interruption; **interrupt level** = niveau *m* d'interruption; **interrupt line** = ligne *f* d'interruption; **interrupt mask** = masque *m* d'interruption; **interrupt priorities** = priorités *fpl* d'interruption; *see also* NON-MASKABLE INTERRUPT **interrupt request** = demande *f* d'interruption; **interrupt servicing** = (opérations de) contrôle et exécution d'interruption; **interrupt signal** = signal *m* d'interruption; **interrupt stacking** = constitution de pile d'interruptions; **maskable interrupt** = interruption qui peut être invalidée *or* masquée; **non-maskable interrupt (NMI)** = interruption obligatoire *or* qui ne peut être invalidée *or* qui ne peut être masquée; **polled interrupt** = interruption d'appel; *(list of peripherals and their priorities)* **priority interrupt table** = table *f* de priorité des interruptions; **transparent interrupt** = interruption transparente *or* contrôlée; **vectored interrupt** = interruption vectorisée

intersection *noun* intersection *f*

interstation muting *noun* réduction *f* du bruit d'interférence interstation

interval *noun* intervalle *m* ; délai *m*; **there was an interval between pressing the key and the starting of the printout** = il y a eu un intervalle entre le moment où on a appuyé sur la touche et la mise en marche de l'imprimante

intervention *noun* intervention *f*

interword spacing *noun* espacement *m* entre les mots

intimate *adjective (software)* (logiciel) sur mesure *or* de constructeur *or* adapté à un ordinateur

intrinsic *adjective* intrinsèque; **the base material for ICs is an intrinsic semiconductor which is then doped** = le matériau de base utilisé dans la fabrication des circuits intégrés est un semi-conducteur intrinsèque auquel on ajoute un dopant

introduce *verb* introduire *or* insérer *or* glisser; **errors were introduced into the text at keyboarding** = il s'est glissé des erreurs au cours de la saisie du texte (au clavier)

intruder *noun (person who is not authorized to use a computer)* intrus *m or* resquilleur *m*

intrusion *noun* intrusion *f*

invalid *adjective* invalide; **he tried to use an invalid password** = il a tenté d'utiliser un mot de passe qui n'était pas valide; **the message was that the instruction was invalid** = d'après le message, l'instruction était invalide

inverse *noun* contraire *m or* inverse *m or* opposé *m*; **the inverse of true is false** = le contraire de vrai est faux; **the inverse of 1 is 0** = l'opposé de 1 est 0; **inverse video** = vidéo inverse *or* inversion vidéo

◊ **inversion** *noun* inversion *f*; **the inversion of a binary digit takes place in one's complement** = il y a inversion du chiffre binaire dans le complément à un

◊ **invert** *verb* inverser; **inverted commas (" ")** = guillemets *mpl*; **inverted file** = fichier inversé

◊ **inverter** *noun* **(a)** *(logical gate)* inverseur *m* **(b)** *(circuit)* **inverter (AC/DC)** = inverseur *m* de courant

invitation *noun* invitation *f*; **invitation to send (ITS)** = (signal d') invitation à transmettre

◊ **invite** *verb* inviter (quelqu'un à faire quelque chose)

invoke *verb (a program)* appeler

QUOTE when an error is detected, the editor may be invoked and positioned at the statement in error

Personal Computer World

involve *verb* comprendre *or* inclure; **backing up involves copying current working files onto a separate storage disk** = sauvegarder signifie faire la copie du fichier de travail actuel sur une deuxième disquette

I/O = INPUT/OUTPUT entrée/sortie *f*; *(memory location used by an I/O port)* **I/O address** = adresse *f* des ports d'entrée/sortie; **I/O bound** = (programme) limité par le débit d'entrée/sortie *or* avec contrainte de vitesse d'entrée/sortie; **I/O buffer** = tampon *m* (d') entrée/sortie; **I/O bus** = bus *m* (d') entrée/sortie; **I/O channel** = voie *f* *or* canal *m* (d') entrée/sortie; **I/O device** =

périphérique *m* (d') entrée/sortie; **I/O file** = fichier (d') entrée/sortie; **I/O instruction** = instruction *f* (d') entrée/sortie; **I/O mapping** = configuration *m* d'entrées/sorties; *compare with* MEMORY MAPPING; **I/O port** = port *m* (d') entrée/sortie; **I/O request** = requête *f* d'entrée/sortie; **I/O processor** = processeur *m* (d') entrée/sortie

ion *noun* ion *m*

◊ **ionosphere** *noun* ionosphère *f*

IOP = INPUT/OUTPUT PROCESSOR

IORQ = INPUT/OUTPUT REQUEST

i/p *or* **I/P** = INPUT

ip = INFORMATION PROVIDER; *(company or user providing information for use in videotext system)* source *f* d'information *or* service (fournisseur) d'information *or* service de base de données spécialisée (pour vidéotex); **ip terminal** = terminal *m* d'entrée (de données) vidéotex

◊ **IP** = INTERNET PROTOCOL **IP Address** = adresse *f* internet; *(packet of data)* **IP Datagram** = paquet *m* IP

IPL = INITIAL PROGRAM LOADER

ips = INCHES PER SECOND

IR (a) = INFORMATION RETRIEVAL **(b)** = INDEX REGISTER **(c)** = INSTRUCTION REGISTER

IRC = INFORMATION RETRIEVAL CENTRE

irretrievable *adjective* qui ne peut être restitué, -ée *or* extrait, -e; **the files are irretrievable since the computer crashed** = il est impossible de restituer *or* d'extraire les fichiers depuis la panne

irreversible process *noun* processus *m* irréversible

ISA = INDUSTRY STANDARD ARCHITECTURE

ISAM = INDEXED SEQUENTIAL ACCESS METHOD

ISBN = INTERNATIONAL STANDARD BOOK NUMBER

ISDN = INTEGRATED SERVICES DIGITAL NETWORK

ISO = INTERNATIONAL STANDARDS ORGANIZATION

◊ **ISO/OSI** = INTERNATIONAL STANDARDS ORGANIZATION/OPEN SYSTEMS INTERCONNECTION

isolate *verb (to separate or to insulate)* isoler; **isolated adaptive routing** = routage *m* adaptatif protégé; **isolated location** = zone *f* protégée

◊ **isolation** *noun* isolation *f*; **isolation transformer** = transformateur *m* d'isolement *or* de protection

◊ **isolator** *noun (device or material which isolates)* isolateur *m*

isotropic *adjective* isotrope; **isotropic radiator** = émetteur *m* *or* antenne *f* isotrope

ISR = INFORMATION STORAGE AND RETRIEVAL

ISSN = INTERNATIONAL STANDARD SERIAL NUMBER

IT = INFORMATION TECHNOLOGY

italic *adjective & noun* italique *(m)*; **the headline is printed in italic and underlined** = le titre est en italique souligné; **all the footnotes are printed in italics** = les notes de bas de page sont toutes en italique; **hit CTRL I to print the text in italics** = tapez CTRL I pour imprimer les italiques; **italics** = lettres italiques *or* italiques

item *noun* item *m* *or* unité *f*; **a data item can be a word or a series of figures or a record in a file** = une unité d'information peut être soit un mot, une série de chiffres ou une entrée dans un fichier; **item size** = dimension *f* d'une unité d'information *or* d'un item

iterate *or* **iterative routine** *noun* routine *f* itérative

◊ **iteration** *noun* itération *f*

◊ **iterative process** *noun* processus *m* itératif

ITS = INVITATION TO SEND

Jj

jabber *noun (continuous random signal)* bruit *m* parasite

jack *noun* fiche *f or* jack *m*; *(for modem)* **data jack** = fiche *f* TELECOM (pour modem)

jacket *noun (of book)* jaquette *f*; *(of record)* pochette *f*; **the book jacket has the author's name on it** = on trouve le nom de l'auteur sur la jaquette du livre

jaggies *plural noun (jagged edges)* crénelage *m or* effet *m* d'escalier; *see also* ALIASING, ANTI-ALIASING

jam 1 *noun (of mechanism)* coincement *m*; **jam in the paper feed** = bourrage *m* (de l'entraînement de l'imprimante) **2** *verb* **(a)** *(to block)* (se) coincer *or* bloquer; **the recorder's not working because the tape is jammed in the motor** = le magnétophone ne fonctionne pas parce que la bande est coincée dans le moteur; **lightweight copier paper will feed without jamming** = l'emploi de papier plus mince évite le bourrage **(b)** *(to prevent transmission)* brouiller; **the TV signals are being jammed from that tower** = cette tour brouille la transmission des émissions de télévision

jar *verb* déplacer brusquement *or* secouer; **you can cause trouble by turning off or jarring the PC while the disk read head is moving** = éteindre l'ordinateur ou lui donner un coup quand la tête de lecture est en marche peut causer des ennuis; **hard disks are very sensitive to jarring** = les disques durs sont très sensibles aux secousses *or* aux chocs

JCL = JOB CONTROL LANGUAGE

jet *see* INK-JET

jitter 1 *noun* tremblotement *m or* sautillement *m or* papillotement *m* (de l'image); **looking at this screen jitter is giving me a headache** = j'ai mal à la tête à force de regarder cet écran qui tremblote **2** *verb (image or screen)* trembloter

JK-flip-flop *noun* (commutateur à) bascule *f* de type JK

job *noun* tâche *f or* travail *m*; **the next job to be processed is to sort all the records** = la tâche suivante consistera à trier tous les enregistrements; **job control file** = fichier *m* de contrôle de tâche; **job control language (JCL)** = langage *m* de commande de tâche; **job control program** = programme *m* de contrôle de tâche; **job file** = fichier de travaux *or* de tâches (à exécuter); **job mix** = ensemble des travaux *or* des tâches en cours d'exécution; **job number** = numéro *m* (de suite) d'une tâche dans la file d'attente; **job-orientated language** = langage d'application; **job-orientated terminal** = terminal d'application *or* terminal spécialisé; **job priority** = priorité *f* d'une tâche; **job processing** = traitement *m* de tâche; **job queue** *or* **job stream** = file *f* d'attente (des tâches *or* des travaux à exécuter); **job scheduling** = planification *f* de la séquence d'exécution des tâches *or* répartition *f* des tâches; **job statement control** = contrôle *m* d'exécution des tâches; **job step** = étape *f* d'un travail; **job stream** = suite *f* de tâches; **remote job entry (RJE)** = lancement *m or* commande *f* de tâches à distance; **stacked job control** = contrôle de travaux (groupés) en pile

◊ **jobbing printer** *noun* imprimeur *m* à façon

jog *verb* (faire) avancer image par image *or* pas à pas

joggle *verb (punched cards)* taquer

join 1 *verb* **(a)** *(to put together)* joindre *or* relier **(b)** *(to combine pieces of information)* assembler *or* fusionner; **join files** = (instruction de) fusion *f* de fichiers **2** *noun (logical function)* fonction *f* d'union *or* opération *f* OU

joint denial *noun (logical function)* négation *f* connexe *or* opération *f* NON-OU *or* NI

journal *noun* **(a)** *(record of communications)* journal *m*; **journal file** = fichier *m* chronologique *or* fichier-journal **(b)** *(list of changes to a file)* journal *m or* liste *f* des modifications; **the modified records were added to the master file and noted in the journal** = les enregistrements modifiés ont été ajoutés au fichier maître et inscrits au journal des modifications **(c)** **learned journal** = revue *f* spécialisée *or* revue savante

◊ **journalist** *noun* journaliste *m&f*

joystick *noun* manette *f* de jeu *or* manche *m* à balai *or* joystick *m*; **joystick port** = connecteur *m or* port *m* pour manette de jeu *or* pour joystick; port jeu; **a joystick port is provided with the home computer** = l'ordinateur pour la maison possède un port (pour manette de) jeu

judder *noun* vibration *f*

jumbo chip *noun* puce *f* géante *or* circuit *m* à très haut niveau d'intégration

jump (instruction) 1 *noun* (instruction de) branchement *m or* saut *m*; **conditional jump** = branchement *m* conditionnel; **jump operation** = opération *f* de branchement; **unconditional jump** = branchement inconditionnel **2** *verb* **(a)** effectuer un branchement *or* sauter; **jump on zero** = effectuer un branchement (conditionnel) à zéro **(b)**

(to miss) sauter; **the typewriter jumped two lines** = la machine à écrire a sauté deux lignes; **the paging system has jumped two folio numbers** = le système de pagination a sauté deux numéros de pages

◊ **jumper** *noun (on circuit board)* cavalier *m or* connecteur *m* mâle à deux broches; **jumper-selectable** = (circuit *or* dispositif) qui peut être sélectionné *or* validé par cavalier; **the printer's typeface is jumper-selectable** = sur cette imprimante, la police de caractères peut être sélectionnée par cavalier

junction *noun* **(a)** *(connection)* jonction *f*; **junction box** = boîte *f* de jonction *or* de raccordement **(b)** *(on semiconductor)* jonction; **bipolar junction transistor (BJT)** = transistor à jonction bipolaire

junk 1 *noun* camelote *f or* rebut *m*; **junk mail** = prospectus *mpl* publicitaires sans intérêt; **space junk** = satellites *mpl* hors d'usage *or* de rebut (qui tournent dans l'espace) **2** *verb* virer *or* éjecter *or*

mettre à la poubelle; **to junk a file** = virer *or* effacer un fichier

◊ **junky** *see* TERMINAL JUNKY

justification *noun* justification *f*; **hyphenation and justification** *or* **H & J** = césure *f* et justification; **an American hyphenation and justification program will not work with British English spellings** = un programme de césure et justification établi aux Etats-Unis ne peut être utilisé pour un texte en anglais britannique; *see also* LEFT JUSTIFICATION, RIGHT JUSTIFICATION

◊ **justify** *verb* **(a)** justifier; **justify inhibit** = (instruction d') invalider la justification; **justify margin** = *see* LEFT JUSTIFY, RIGHT JUSTIFY **hyphenate and justify** = (fonction de) césure et justification; **left justify** = (instruction de) justifier à gauche; **right justify** = (instruction de) justifier à droite **(b)** *(computer register)* justifier (la pile)

juxtaposition *noun* juxtaposition *f*

Kk

K *prefix* **(a)** = KILO; *(thousand)* k *or* kilo *m* **(b)** *(represents 1,024 or 2^{10})* K *or* kilo

◊ **KB** *or* **Kb** *or* **Kbyte** = KILOBYTE; *(1,024 bytes)* ko *or* Ko *or* Koctet *or* kilo-octet *m*; **the new disk drive has a 100Kb capacity** = le nouveau lecteur de disquettes a une capacité de 100Ko; **the original PC cannot access more than 640Kbytes of RAM** = le premier ordinateur individuel de la série ne peut accéder à plus de 640Ko de RAM

◊ **Kb** *or* **Kbit** = KILOBIT

Karnaugh map *noun* table *f* de Karnaugh; **the prototype was checked for hazards with a Karnaugh map** = le prototype a fait l'objet d'un contrôle de fiabilité statistique sur la base des tables de Karnaugh

Kermit *noun (file transfer protocol)* (protocole de communication) Kermit

kern *verb (adjust space between letters)* serrer *or* réduire l'espace entre deux caractères; **we have kerned 'T' and 'o' so they are closer together** = nous avons réduit l'espace entre le T et le o pour les rapprocher

kernel *noun* noyau *m* (du système d'exploitation); **graphics kernel system (GKS)** = fonctions *fpl* graphiques GKS

kerning *noun (printing)* crénage *m or* kerning *m*

key 1 *noun* **(a)** *(on a keyboard)* touche *f*; **there are 84 keys on the keyboard** = le clavier comporte 84 touches; **key click** = clic *m* témoin (de fonctionnement) de touche; **key force** = pression *f* nécessaire pour actionner une touche; **key matrix** = implantation *f* des touches sur un clavier; **key number** = code *m* numérique d'une touche; **key overlay** = grille *f* d'aide *or* mémento *m* de fonction des touches (de clavier); **without the key overlay, I would never remember which function key does what** = sans la grille d'aide, je ne saurais jamais quelle touche de fonction je dois utiliser; **key punch** = perforatrice (à clavier) *f*; **key rollover** = clavier à mémoire tampon *or* clavier rapide; **key strip** = marquage *m* (mnémotechnique) *or* pense-bête *m* (indiquant la fonction d'une touche); **key travel** = jeu vertical *or* course *f* d'une touche **(b)** **alphanumeric key** = touche alphanumérique; **character key** = touche de caractère; **carriage return key** = touche de retour du chariot; **function key** = touche de fonction; **tags can be allocated to function keys** = on peut allouer une étiquette aux touches de fonction; **shift key** = touche des majuscules **(c)** *(important)* clé *or* clef *f*; *(printing)* **key plate** = cliché *f* de base; **key terminal** = terminal *m* principal **(d)** *(numbers to encrypt or decrypt a message)* clé (de cryptage et décryptage)

d'un code; **type this key into the machine, that will decode the last message** = tapez la clé et vous pourrez décoder le dernier message; **key management** = gestion *f* de clé **(e)** *(identification code)* clé d'identification *or* clé de recherche *or* mot-clé *m*; **we selected all the records with the word DISK in their keys** = nous avons sélectionné les enregistrements en utilisant le mot DISK comme clé de recherche; **index key** = clé d'index; **key field** = champ *m* clé; **keyed sequential access method (KSAM)** = méthode d'accès séquentiel indexé multiclé(s) **2** *verb* actionner une touche; **to key in** = saisir (un texte *or* des données) au *or* sur *or* par clavier; taper (une commande, un texte); **they keyed in the latest data** = ils ont saisi les toutes dernières données (sur clavier)

◊ **keyboard 1** *noun* clavier *m*; **keyboard to disk entry** = saisie *f* directe sur disque(tte), par clavier; **ANSI keyboard** = clavier ANSI; **ASCII keyboard** = clavier ASCII; **ASR keyboard** = clavier émetteur/récepteur *or* de téléscripteur; **AZERTY keyboard** = clavier AZERTY (utilisé surtout dans les pays francophones) *or* clavier français accentué; **interactive keyboard** = clavier interactif; **keyboard contact bounce** = rebond *m* d'une touche de clavier; **keyboard encoder** = encodeur *m* des touches; **keyboard layout** = disposition *f or* implantation *f* des touches d'un clavier; **keyboard overlay** = grille *f* d'aide *or* mémento *m* (de fonction des touches) de clavier; *(method of control)* **keyboard scan** = contrôle *m* de clavier *or* d'utilisation de touches; **keyboard send/receive (KSR)** = terminal *m* entrée/sortie *or* émetteur/récepteur à clavier; **QWERTY keyboard** = clavier QWERTY *or* clavier international (utilisé surtout dans les pays anglo-saxons); **touch sensitive keyboard** = clavier sensitif *or* tactile *or* à effleurement **2** *verb* saisir (des données) au *or* sur *or* par clavier; taper; **it was cheaper to have the manuscript keyboarded by another company** = il était plus économique de faire saisir *or* de faire taper le manuscrit par une société de service informatique

◊ **keyboarder** *noun* claviste *m&f or* opérateur, -trice de saisie

◊ **keyboarding** *noun* saisie *f* (au *or* sur *or* par clavier); **the cost of keyboarding is calculated in keystrokes per hour** = le coût de saisie (au clavier) est calculé sur une base de frappes/heure

◊ **keypad** *noun* clavier auxiliaire *or* pavé *m*; **hex keypad** = clavier hexadécimal; **numeric keypad** = pavé numérique; **you can use the numeric keypad to enter the figures** = utilisez le pavé numérique pour saisir les chiffres

◊ **keystroke** *noun* frappe *f*; **he keyboards at a rate of 3500 keystrokes per hour** = il peut saisir un texte au rythme de 3500 frappes/heure; **keystroke count** = nombre *m* de frappes; **keystrokes per hour**

= (nombre de) frappes par heure *or* frappes/heure; **keystroke rate** = vitesse *f* de frappe; **keystroke verification** = contrôle *m* des touches

◊ **key-to-disk** *noun* saisie *f* directe sur disque(tte) (par clavier)

◊ **keyword** *noun* **(a)** *(command word)* (mot de) commande *f*; *(important word in a title or text or subject)* mot-clé *m or* mot principal; **the BASIC keyword PRINT will display text on the screen** = en langage BASIC, la commande PRINT fera apparaître le texte sur l'écran; **computer is a keyword in IT** = le mot computer est un mot-clé en informatique **(b)** *(library system)* **keyword and context (KWAC)** = (système de) thésaurus *m or* mot-clé et contexte; **keyword in context (KWIC)** = mot-clé en contexte; **keyword out of context (KWOC)** = mot-clé hors contexte

QUOTE where large orders are being placed over the telephone it is easy to key them into the micro
Micro Decision

QUOTE the new keyboard is almost unchanged, and features sixteen programmable function keys
Micro Decision

QUOTE it uses a six button keypad to select the devices and functions
Byte

QUOTE the main QWERTY typing area is in the centre of the keyboard with the 10 function keys on the left
Personal Computer World

kHz = KILOHERTZ

kill *verb* détruire *or* effacer; **kill file** = (instruction de) détruire un fichier; **kill job** = (instruction d') arrêter *or* (de) virer une tâche

kilo *prefix* **(a)** *(one thousand)* kilo *m*; **kilobaud** = kilobaud *m*; **kilohertz (kHz)** = kilohertz *m* (kHz); **kilo instructions per second (KIPS)** = millier d'instructions par seconde (KIPS); **kilo-ohm** = kilo-ohm *m*; **kiloVolt-Ampere output rating (KVA)** = mesure *f* du travail en kva; **kilowatt (kW)** = kilowatt *m* (kW) **(b)** *(1,024 units, equal to 2^{10})*

kilo *m*; *(1,024 bits of data)* **kilobit** *or* **Kbit** *or* **Kb** = kilobit *m*; *(1,024 bytes of data)* **kilobyte** *or* **Kbyte (KB** *or* **Kb)** = kilo-octet *m* (Ko); **kiloword (KW)** = kilo-mot *m*

kilogram *or* **kilogramme (kg)** *noun* kilogramme (kg) *m*

kimball tag *noun* étiquette *f* Kimball

KIPS = KILO INSTRUCTIONS PER SECOND

kit *noun* trousse *f or* kit *m*; **screen cleaning kit** = kit de nettoyage d'écran

kludge *noun* *(software or hardware)* programme *or* système retapé *or* hâtivement bricolé

◊ **kludged** *adjective* retapé, -ée *or* bricolé, -ée

knob *noun* bouton *m* (de réglage, etc.); **turn the on/off knob** = tourner le bouton marche/arrêt; **the brightness can be regulated by turning a knob at the back of the monitor** = pour ajuster la luminosité de l'écran, tourner le bouton placé à l'arrière du moniteur

knowledge *noun* connaissance *f*; **intelligent knowledge-based system (IKBS)** = système intelligent à base de connaissances *or* intelligence *f* artificielle; **knowledge-based system** = système à base de connaissances *or* système expert; **knowledge engineer** = cogniticien, -ienne; **knowledge engineering** = ingénierie *f* de la connaissance

KSAM = KEYED SEQUENTIAL ACCESS METHOD

KSR = KEYBOARD SEND/RECEIVE

KVA = KILOVOLT-AMPERE OUTPUT RATING

kW = KILOWATT

KW = KILOWORD

KWAC = KEYWORD AND CONTEXT

◊ **KWIC** = KEYWORD IN CONTEXT

◊ **KWOC** = KEYWORD OUT OF CONTEXT

LI

label 1 (a) *noun (in a computer program)* étiquette *f or* label *m or* identificateur *m*; **BASIC uses many program labels such as line numbers** = les programmes en langage BASIC contiennent plusieurs labels dont la numérotation des lignes; **label field** = champ label *or* champ d'identification; **label record** = enregistrement de labels *or* d'étiquettes *or* d'identificateurs; **internal label** = label d'identification (sur le support magnétique) **(b)** *(piece of paper)* étiquette *f or* label; *(for quality)* label de qualité; *(adhesive labels on a backing sheet)* **continuous labels** = étiquettes *fpl* en continu; **external label** = étiquette externe *or* étiquette extérieure *or* apposée à l'extérieur (d'une bande, etc.); *(printer used to print onto labels)* **label printer** = imprimante d'étiquettes **2** *verb (to put a label on a product)* étiqueter; *(to put a label on a program)* produire un label *or* une étiquette (pour un programme) (NOTE: **labelling - labelled** but US **labeling - labeled**)

◊ **labelling** *noun (putting a label on a product)* étiquetage *m*; *(printing labels)* impression *f* d'étiquettes; **the word-processor has a special utility allowing simple and rapid labelling** = le traitement de texte possède un utilitaire qui permet d'imprimer des étiquettes facilement et rapidement

laboratory *noun* laboratoire *m*; **the new chip is being developed in the university laboratories** = le travail de recherche et développement sur la nouvelle puce se fait dans les laboratoires de l'université

lag *noun* **(a)** *(of signal)* retard *m or* décalage *m*; **time lag is noticeable on international phone calls** = le décalage est perceptible sur les lignes téléphoniques internationales **(b)** *(of image on a CRT screen)* rémanence *f or* persistance *f*; retard d'effacement *m*

laminate *verb* pelliculer; **the book has a laminated cover** = c'est un livre avec couverture pelliculée

LAN *or* **lan** = LOCAL AREA NETWORK réseau *m* local (d'entreprise); *(part of a network)* **LAN segment** = segment *m* de réseau local; *(computer which runs a network operating system)* **LAN server** = serveur *m* de réseau local; *see also* PEER-TO-PEER; *compare* WAN

◊ **LAN Manager** ™ *noun (MicroSoft network operating system)* LAN Manager ™

◊ **LAN Server** ™ *noun (IBM network operating system)* LAN Server ™

landing zone *noun (area of a hard disk which does not carry data)* zone *f* de parcage (de la tête de lecture); *see also* PARKING

landline *noun (cable)* câble *m or* liaison *f or* ligne *f* terrestre

landscape *noun (page where the longest edge is horizontal)* paysage *m; compare* PORTRAIT

language *noun* **(a)** *(spoken or written)* langue *f*; **he speaks several European languages** = il parle plusieurs langues européennes; **foreign language** = langue étrangère **(b)** *(for computers)* langage *m*; **language assembler** = (programme) assembleur *m*; **language compiler** = (programme) compilateur *m*; **language interpreter** = (programme) interpréteur *m*; **language processor** = processeur *m* de langage; **language rules** = syntaxe *f or* règles *fpl* propres à un langage; **language support environment** = aides *mpl* à la programmation (dans un langage déterminé); *(of programming language)* **language translation** = traduction *f* d'un langage (en un autre langage); **language translator** = (programme) traducteur *m* (de langage); **assembly language** *or* **assembler language** = langage d'assemblage; **command language** = langage de commande *or* d'instruction; **compiler language** = langage de compilation; **control language** = langage de commande *or* de contrôle; **graphic language** = langage graphique; **high-level language (HLL)** = langage de haut niveau *or* langage évolué; **low-level language (LLL)** = langage de bas niveau *or* langage peu évolué; **machine language** = langage machine; **programming language** = langage de programmation; **query language (QL)** = langage de requête *or* d'interrogation; **source language** = langage source

LAP = LINK ACCESS PROTOCOL; *(CCITT standard protocol)* standard LAP; *(CCITT standard setup routine)* **LAP-B** = routine d'installation LAP-B; *(variation of LAP-B protocol)* **LAP-M** = LINK ACCESS PROTOCOL FOR MODEMS protocole LAP-M

lap *noun* **(a)** *(of person)* genoux *mpl*; **he placed the computer on his lap and keyboarded some orders while sitting in his car** = il a posé l'ordinateur sur ses genoux et saisi quelques commandes alors qu'il était assis dans sa voiture **(b)** *(overlap)* chevauchement *m*

◊ **lapheld** *or* **laptop (computer)** *noun (light computer)* (petit ordinateur) portable *m or* laptop *m*

QUOTE Michael Business Systems has provided research company BMRB with 240 Toshiba laptop computers in a deal valued at {300,000. The deal includes a three-year maintenance contract.

Computing

QUOTE in our summary of seven laphelds we found features to admire in every machine

QUOTE the idea of a hard disk in a lapheld machine which runs on batteries is not brand new

PC Business World

lapel microphone *noun* micro-cravate *m*

large model *noun (memory model in an Intel processor)* grand modèle (de mémoire des processeurs INTEL)

large-scale computer *noun* gros ordinateur *m*

◊ **large-scale integration (LSI)** *noun* intégration *f* à grande échelle

laser *noun* = LIGHT AMPLIFICATION BY STIMULATED EMISSION OF RADIATION laser *m*; **laser beam recording (LBR)** = enregistrement *m* par rayon laser; **laser beam communications** = communication *f* par rayon laser; *(compact disc)* **laser disc** = disque *m* laser; **emulsion laser storage** = mémoire (à) laser sur couche haute définition; **laser printer** = imprimante *f* (à) laser; *(in optical fibre)* **injection laser** = laser d'injection (dans une fibre optique)

LaserJet ™ *or* **Hewlett Packard LaserJet** *or* **HP LaserJet** *noun (Hewlett Packard laser printer)* imprimante *f* Hewlett Packard LaserJet

LaserWriter ™ *noun (Apple laser printer)* imprimante *f* Apple LaserWriter ™

last in first out (LIFO) *noun* (méthode du) dernier entré premier sorti *or* méthode LIFO; **this computer stack uses a last in first out data retrieval method** = cet ordinateur gère la pile suivant la méthode du dernier entré premier sorti *or* suivant la méthode LIFO

latch 1 *noun (electronic component that*

maintains an output value) bascule *f or* dispositif *m* de verrouillage **2** *verb* verrouiller; **the output latched high until we reset the computer** = la sortie est restée verrouillée *or* bloquée au plus haut niveau jusqu'à la ré-initialisation du système

QUOTE other features of the device include a programmable latch bypass which allows any number of latches from 0 to 8 so that this device may be used as latched or combinatorial

Electronics & Power

latency *noun* période *f or* temps *m* de latence

◊ **latent image** *noun (on light-sensitive films)* image *f* latente

lateral reversal *noun* inversion *f* latérale *or* effet *m* (de) miroir

launch 1 *noun (of new product)* lancement *m*; *(satellite)* mise *f* en orbite; **the launch of the new PC has been put back six months** = le lancement du nouvel ordinateur individuel se fera avec six mois de retard; **the launch date for the network will be September** = le lancement du réseau aura lieu en septembre **2** *verb* **(a)** *(new product)* lancer; *(satellite)* mettre en orbite; **the new PC was launched at the Personal Computer Show** = on a lancé le nouvel ordinateur personnel au Salon de l'Informatique **(b)** *(start a program)* lancer; **you launch the word-processor by double-clicking on this icon** = on lance le traitement de texte avec un double clic sur cette icône

◊ **launch amplifier** *noun* amplificateur *m* de signal

◊ **launch vehicle** *noun (for satellite)* fusée *f* porteuse *or* de lancement

layer *noun* **(a)** *(division of space)* couche *f* **(b)** *(ISO/OSI standards)* couche (de protocole); **application layer** = couche application; **data link layer** = couche liaison de données; **network layer** = couche réseau; **physical layer** = couche physique; **presentation layer** = couche présentation; **session layer** = couche session; **transport layer** = couche transport

◊ **layered** *adjective* disposé, -ée en couches; **the kernel has a layered structure according to user priority** = le noyau possède une structure en couches adaptée aux besoins de l'utilisateur

lay in *verb (to synchronize film and sound tracks)* synchroniser

◊ **layout** *noun* **(a)** mise *f* en page; **the design team is working on the layouts for the new magazine** = les designers travaillent à la mise en page de la nouvelle revue **(b)** spécifications *fpl* de présentation des données **(c) keyboard layout** = disposition *f or* implantation *f* des touches d'un clavier

◊ **lay out** *verb* mettre en page; **the designers have laid out the pages in A4 format** = les designers ont décidé de mettre en page sur format A4

LBR = LASER BEAM RECORDING

LC circuit *noun* circuit *m* LC

LCD = LIQUID CRYSTAL DISPLAY

> QUOTE LCD screens can run for long periods on ordinary or rechargeable batteries
> ***Micro Decision***

LCP = LINK CONTROL PROCEDURE

LDS = LOCAL DISTRIBUTION SERVICE

lead[1] *noun (wire)* conducteur *m or* câble *m or* fil *m* (conducteur)

◊ **lead-in page** *noun (videotext page)* sommaire *m or* page *f* guide

◊ **leader** *noun* **(a)** *(beginning of the reel)* amorce *f*; **leader record** = enregistrement *m* de tête **(b)** *(row of dots)* pointillé *m*

◊ **leading edge** *noun (of punched card)* bord *m* d'introduction *or* bord avant

◊ **leading zero** *noun* zéro *m* de tête

lead[2] *noun (metal rod)* interligne *f*

◊ **leading** *noun (space in printing)* interligne *m*; *(action)* interlignage *m*

leaf *noun* **(a)** feuille *f* (de papier); *(of book)* page *f* **(b)** *(in a data tree)* élément *m* final d'une arborescence

◊ **leaflet** *noun* feuillet *m* (publicitaire)

leak 1 *noun* **(a)** *(of secret)* fuite *f*; **a leak informed the press of our new designs** = c'est grâce à une fuite que la presse a eu vent de notre nouveau modèle **(b)** *(of charge, etc.)* fuite *or* perte *f* 2 *verb* **(a)** *(information)* dévoiler *or* divulguer **(b)** *(charge, etc.)* fuir *or* perdre (sa charge); **in this circuit, the capacitor charge leaks out at 10% per second** = dans ce circuit, le condensateur perd 10% de sa charge par seconde

◊ **leakage** *noun (of signal)* fuite *f or* perte *f or* affaiblissement *m* (de signal)

> QUOTE signal leakages in both directions can be a major problem in co-axial cable systems
> ***Electronics & Wireless World***

leapfrog test *noun* test *m* sélectif; test de lecture/écriture aléatoire des mémoires *or* test saut de puce; **crippled leapfrog test** = test sélectif limité *or* restreint; test saut de puce limité à un seul emplacement

learning curve *noun (graph of how someone can acquire knowledge)* courbe *f* d'apprentissage; *(difficult to use)* **steep learning curve** = (produit d') apprentissage *m* difficile

lease 1 *noun* bail *m* (de location) 2 *verb* louer; **the company leases all its computers** = la société loue tous ses ordinateurs; **the company has a policy of only using leased equipment** = la société a pour politique de louer son matériel; **leased circuit** = circuit loué *or* de location; **leased line** = ligne louée *or* de location

least cost design *noun* conception *f or* design

m économique; **the budget is only £1,000, we need the least cost design for the new circuit** = le budget n'étant que de 1000 livres, il nous faut une conception économique pour ce nouveau circuit

◊ **least recently used algorithm** *noun* algorithme *m* d'ancienneté (des pages de mémoire paginée) *or* algorithme de la page la moins récemment utilisée

◊ **least significant digit (LSD)** *noun* chiffre *m* le moins significatif *or* de poids faible; **least significant bit (LSB)** = bit *m* le moins significatif *or* de poids faible

leaving files open *phrase* laisse le fichier ouvert

LED = LIGHT-EMITTING DIODE diode *f* électroluminescente; *(page printer)* **LED printer** = imprimante *f* à diodes *or* imprimante LED

left justification *noun (printing)* justification *f* à gauche

◊ **left justify** *verb (printing or binary number)* justifier à gauche

◊ **left shift** 1 *noun (of bits)* décalage *m or* glissement *m* à gauche 2 *verb* effectuer un décalage à gauche

leg *noun* branchement *m*

legal *adjective* légal, -e *or* valide *or* permis, -e *or* autorisé, -ée

legible *adjective* lisible; **the manuscript is written in pencil and is hardly legible** = le manuscrit est écrit au crayon et est à peine lisible

◊ **legibility** *noun* lisibilité *f*; **the keyboarders find the manuscript lacks legibility** = les opérateurs de saisie trouvent ce manuscrit difficile à lire *or* trouvent que la lisibilité du manuscrit laisse à désirer

length *noun* longueur *f*; **block length** = longueur d'un bloc; **buffer length** = taille *f* de la mémoire tampon; **field length** = dimension *f or* taille d'un champ; **file length** = longueur *or* dimension d'un fichier; **length of filename** = longueur du nom d'un fichier; **line length** = longueur d'une ligne; **record length** = longueur *or* taille d'un enregistrement; **register length** = dimension d'un registre

lens *noun* lentille *f*; **concave lens** = lentille concave; **convex lens** = lentille convexe; **lens speed** = vitesse *f* d'ouverture d'un objectif; **lens stop** = ouverture *f* d'objectif

letter *noun* **(a)** *(piece of writing)* lettre *f*; **form letter** *or* **standard letter** = lettre type *or* lettre standard **(b)** *(A, B, C, etc.)* lettre; **capital letter** = (lettre) majuscule *f*; **his name was written in capital letters** = son nom était écrit en majuscules

◊ **letterhead** *noun* en-tête *m* de lettre; **business forms and letterheads can now be designed on a PC** = formulaires et en-têtes peuvent être conçus sur ordinateur

◊ **near-letter-quality (NLQ) printing** *noun (of dot-matrix printer)* qualité *f* courrier

level *noun* **(a)** *(of electrical signal)* niveau *m*; *(of sound)* volume *m*; **turn the sound level down, it's far too loud** = baissez le volume (du son) qui est vraiment trop fort; **sound pressure level (SPL)** = niveau de pression acoustique **(b)** *(quantity of bits)* niveau d'un signal

lexical analysis *noun* analyse *f* lexicale

lexicographical order *noun* ordre *m* lexicographique

LF (a) = LOW FREQUENCY **(b)** = LINE FEED

library *noun* **(a)** bibliothèque *f*; **the editors have checked all the references in the local library** = les éditeurs ont vérifié toutes les références à la bibliothèque locale; **a copy of each new book has to be deposited in the British Library** = il faut déposer un exemplaire de toute nouvelle publication à la British Library; **look up the bibliographical details in the library catalogue** = consultez le catalogue de la bibliothèque pour obtenir les renseignements bibliographiques **(b)** *(of programs)* bibliothèque; *(collection of programs)* **program library** *or* **software library** = bibliothèque de programmes *or* de logiciels; **he has a large library of computer games** = il possède une importante bibliothèque de jeux informatiques **(c)** *(software routine)* **library function** = fonction *f* bibliothèque; **library program** = programme *m* de bibliothèque; **the square root function is already in the library program** = la fonction racine carrée se trouve déjà dans le programme de bibliothèque; **library routine** = routine de bibliothèque; **library subroutine** = sous-programme *m* de bibliothèque; *(on disk)* **library track** = piste *f* de référence; **graphics library** = bibliothèque graphique; **macro library** = bibliothèque de macros

◊ **librarian** *noun* bibliothécaire *m&f*

licence *noun* permis *m* *or* licence *f*; **this software is manufactured under licence** = ce logiciel est fabriqué sous licence

lifetime *noun* *(time during which a device is useful)* durée *f* de vie; **this new computer has a four-year lifetime** = ce nouvel ordinateur a une durée de vie de quatre ans

LIFO = LAST IN FIRST OUT

lifter *noun* écarteur *m* de bande

ligature *noun* ligature *f*

light 1 *noun* lumière *f*; **the VDU should not be placed under a bright light** = il faut éviter de placer l'écran sous une lumière trop forte; **light conduit** = conducteur *m* de lumière; **light-emitting diode (LED)** = diode *f* électroluminescente; **light guide** = guide *m* optique; **light pen** = stylo *m* optique; **light pipe** = LIGHT GUIDE **coherent light** = lumière cohérente *or* monochrome; **visible light** = lumière visible; **ultra-violet light (UV light)** = lumière ultra-violette *or* rayonnement ultra-violet; **infrared light (IR light)** = rayons *mpl* infrarouges **2** *adjective (not dark)* clair, -e; *(typeface)* **light face** = caractères *mpl* maigres

◊ **light-sensitive** *adjective* photosensible *or* sensible à la lumière; **the photograph is printed on light-sensitive paper** = la photo est imprimée sur papier photosensible; **light-sensitive device** = dispositif *m* photosensible

lightweight *adjective* léger, -ère; **a lightweight computer which can easily fit into a suitcase** = un ordinateur léger qui tient facilement dans une valise

LIM EMS = LOTUS, INTEL, MICROSOFT EXPANDED MEMORY SYSTEM; *(standard in an IBM PC)* mémoire *f* étendue LIM EMS

limited distance modem *noun* modem *m* pour réseau local *or* à distance de transmission limitée

◊ **limiter** *noun* limitateur *m*

◊ **limiting resolution** *noun* définition *f* maximum

◊ **limits** *noun (for numbers in a computer)* limites *fpl*

line *noun* **(a)** *(cable)* ligne *f* *or* liaison *f*; **access line** = ligne d'accès; **fast line** = ligne rapide; **telephone line** = ligne *f* téléphonique; *(electronic circuit)* **line adapter** = équilibreur *m* de ligne *or* d'impédance; *(test equipment)* **line analyzer** = analyseur *m* de ligne; *(signal to indicate that a line is in use)* **line busy tone** = signal *m* ligne occupée *or* tonalité *f* 'occupé'; **line communications** = communication *f* par câble; *(techniques used to maintain the quality on a line)* **line conditioning** = maintenance *f* de ligne; **line control** = commandes *fpl* *or* protocole *m* de communication; **line driver** = amplificateur *m* de signal; *(in cable TV)* **line extender** = unité *f* d'extension d'une ligne; **line impedance** = impédance *f* de ligne; **line level** = niveau *m* de transmission (d'une ligne); **line load** = trafic *m* *or* charge *f* d'une ligne; **line speed** = débit *m* d'une ligne; **line switching** = commutation *f* de ligne; **line terminator** = dispositif *m* de fin de ligne; **line transient** = courant *m* transitoire d'une ligne **(b)** *(thin mark)* ligne *or* trait *m*; *(printing)* filet *m*; **the printer has difficulty in reproducing very fine lines** = l'imprimante ne réussit pas très bien à imprimer les lignes trop fines; **line art** = graphisme *m*; **line drawing** = dessin *m* au trait; **the book is illustrated with line drawings and halftones** = on trouve dans ce livre des dessins (au trait) et des illustrations en demi-teinte **(c)** *(on screen)* ligne *f*; **line blanking interval** = délai *m* de retour de ligne; **line drive signal** = signal (de début) de balayage; **line flyback** = retour de ligne; **line frequency** = fréquence *f* (de balayage) de ligne **(d)** *(of text)* ligne (de texte); **each page has 52 lines of text** = on compte 52 lignes de texte par page; **several lines of the**

manuscript have been missed by the keyboarder = le claviste a sauté plusieurs lignes du manuscrit; **can we insert an extra line of spacing between the paragraphs?** = est-il possible d'ajouter un interligne supplémentaire entre les paragraphes?; *(of program)* **command line** = ligne de commande; *(of program)* **information line** *or* **status line** = ligne d'état; **line editor** = éditeur *m* de ligne; **line ending** = caractère *m or* symbole *m* de fin de ligne; **line feed (LF)** = saut *m* de ligne *or* interlignage *m*; **line folding** = enroulement *m* d'une ligne; *(between two lines of type)* **line increment** = incrément *m* de ligne; **line length** = longueur *f* d'une ligne *or* nombre de caractères par ligne; *(space between lines)* **line spacing** = interligne *m*; *(printing)* **lines per minute (LPM)** = (nombre de) lignes par minute *or* débit *m* **(e)** *(characters received as a single input)* ligne; **line input** = (commande de) validation *f* de ligne **(f)** *(row of commands)* ligne de programme; **line number** = numéro *f* d'une ligne (de programme)

> QUOTE straight lines are drawn by clicking the points on the screen where you would like the line to start and finish
> *Personal Computer World*

> QUOTE while pixel editing is handy for line art, most desktop scanners have trouble producing the shades of grey or half-tones found in black and white photography
> *Publish*

line of sight *noun* ligne *f* optique *or* directe

line printer *noun* imprimante *f* ligne à ligne

linear *adjective* linéaire *or* séquentiel, -elle; *(antenna)* **linear array** = antenne *f* linéaire; **linear function** = fonction *f* linéaire; **the expression Y = 10 + 5X - 3W is a linear function** = l'expression Y = 10 + 5X - 3W est une fonction linéaire; **the expression Y = (10 + 5X²) is not a linear function** = l'expression Y = (10 + 5X²) n'est pas une fonction linéaire; **linear integrated circuit** = circuit *m* intégré linéaire; **linear list** = liste séquentielle; **linear program** = programme *m* linéaire; **linear programming** = programmation *f* linéaire; **linear search** = recherche séquentielle

link 1 *noun* **(a)** *(communication path)* liaison *f*; **to transmit faster, you can use the direct link with the mainframe** = pour une transmission plus rapide, vous pouvez utiliser la liaison directe avec le gros ordinateur; *(ISO/OSI layer)* **data link layer** = couche *f* liaison de données; **link access protocol** = *see* LAP **link control procedure (LCP)** = protocole *m* de communication; **link loss** = perte *f* de transmission; **satellite link** = liaison *or* transmission *f* par satellite **(b)** *(software routine)* lien *m*; **link trials** = tests *mpl* de contrôle de liens **2** *verb* relier *or* connecter; *(with interface)* interfacer; **the two computers are linked** = les deux ordinateurs sont reliés; **link files** = (instruction d') assemblage *m or* (instruction de) concaténation *f* de fichiers; **linked list** = liste chaînée *or* concaténée; **linked subroutine** = sous-programme chaîné

◊ **linkage** *noun (of devices)* couplage *m*; *(for program)* création *f* de liens; **linkage editing** =

mise *f* en place de liens (à l'aide d'un éditeur de liens); **linkage software** = (programme) générateur *m* de liens; **graphics and text are joined without linkage software** = les graphiques et le texte sont assemblés sans l'aide d'un générateur de liens

◊ **linking** *noun* liaison *f or* enchaînement *m or* assemblage *m*; **linking loader** = chargeur/éditeur *m* de liens

LIPS = LOGICAL INFERENCES PER SECOND

liquid crystal display (LCD) *noun* écran *m* à cristaux liquides; affichage *m* à cristaux liquides; *(page printer)* **liquid crystal display shutter printer** *or* **LCD shutter printer** = imprimante *f* à transfert LCD

LISP = LIST PROCESSING langage *m* LISP

list 1 *noun* liste *f*; **chained list** = liste chaînée *or* concaténée; **linear list** = liste séquentielle; **linked list** = liste chaînée *or* concaténée; **pushdown list** = liste inversée *or* en mode LIFO; **reference list** = liste de référence; **stop list** = liste d'interdictions; **list processing** = (i) traitement *m* de liste; (ii) langage *m* LISP **2** *verb* lister *or* éditer sous forme de liste; **to list a program** = lister (les lignes d'instruction d') un programme

◊ **listing** *noun* **(a)** listage *m or* listing *m*; **computer listing** = listing *or* sortie *f* d'imprimante; **a program listing** = listage *or* listing d'un programme; **listing paper** = papier *m* listing *or* papier en continu **(b)** *(of cinema times, etc.)* **listings** = liste *f or* répertoire *m* (des films *or* pièces à l'affiche)

literacy *noun* (le fait de) savoir lire; **computer literacy** = (niveau de) connaissances *fpl* en informatique

literal *noun* **(a)** *(operand)* (symbole) littéral *m* **(b)** *(printing error)* coquille *f*

literate *adjective (person who can read)* (personne) qui sait lire *or* lettré, -ée; **computer-literate** = (personne) qui a des connaissances en informatique

lith film *noun* film *m* lith

◊ **lithography** *or* **litho** *noun* lithographie *f or* litho *f*; **offset lithography** = (lithographie) offset *m*

◊ **lithographic** *adjective* lithographique; **lithographic film** = LITH FILM

liveware *noun* personnel *m* informatique

LLC = LOGICAL LINK CONTROL

LLL = LOW-LEVEL LANGUAGE

load 1 *noun* **(a)** *(job)* tâche *f*; charge *f*; **load sharing** = partage *m* des tâches; **line load** = trafic *m or* charge d'une ligne; **work load** = charge de travail *or* (nombre de) tâches *fpl* **(b)** *(impedance)* charge *or* facteur *m* de charge; **load impedance** = impédance *f* de charge; **load life** = temps *m* de décharge; **matched load** = charge équilibrée **2** *verb*

(a) *(file or program)* charger; **scatter load** = faire un chargement dispersé des données; **load and run** *or* **load and go** = (programme de) chargement *m* et exécution; *(MS-DOS command: transfers a program into high memory)* **load high** = commande LOAD HIGH *or* LH (sous MS-DOS) **(b)** *(disk or cartridge, etc.)* mettre en place *or* insérer *or* introduire *or* charger; **load lower bin** = introduire le bac inférieur **(c)** *(to place an impedance)* charger une ligne

◊ **loading** *noun (of file)* chargement *m*; **loading can be a long process** = le chargement (d'un programme) peut être assez long à effectuer

◊ **loader** *noun (program)* chargeur *m*; **absolute loader** = chargeur absolu; **binary loader** = chargeur binaire; *(program)* **card loader** = chargeur de cartes; **initial program loader (IPL)** = chargeur de programme de lancement

◊ **loadpoint** *noun (start of a recording section)* point *m* de début d'enregistrement

QUOTE this windowing system is particularly handy when you want to load or save a file or change directories
Byte

lobe *noun (of response curve)* lobe *m*

local *adjective* **(a)** *(used in a certain section of a computer program)* local, -e; **local declaration** = déclaration *f* d'une variable locale; **local variable** = variable *f* locale **(b)** *(system with limited access)* local, -e *or* localisé, -ée; **local mode** = mode *m* local; *(of terminal)* **on local** = (terminal *or* unité) autonome **(c)** *(device that is physically attached and close to the controlling computer)* local, -e; *(bridge linking two local networks)* **local bridge** = pont *m* local; **we use a local bridge to link the two LANs in the office** = nous utilisons un pont local pour connecter les deux réseaux (locaux) du bureau; *(direct link between a device and the processor)* **local bus** = bus local *or* local bus (LB); **the fastest expansion cards fit into this local bus connector** = les cartes d'extension les plus rapides se placent dans ce connecteur local bus; *(disk drive attached to a computer)* **local drive** = lecteur (de disquette) local *or* non partagé; **local memory** = mémoire locale; *(printer attached to a computer)* **local printer** = imprimante locale *or* non partagée

◊ **local area network (LAN** *or* **lan)** *noun* réseau *m* local d'entreprise; **local area network server** = serveur *m* de réseau local (d'entreprise)

local distribution service (LDS) = *noun* station *f* relais

LocalTalk ™ *noun (cabling system in AppleTalk network)* réseau LocalTalk ™

locate *verb* (i) se trouver; (ii) trouver *or* repérer *or* localiser *or* situer; **the computer is located in the main office building** = l'ordinateur se trouve dans l'édifice principal; **have you managed to locate the programming fault?** = avez-vous réussi à localiser l'erreur de programmation?

◊ **location** *noun* **(a)** *(absolute address)* emplacement *m* (de mémoire) **(b)** *(filming)* **on location** = (prise de vue) en extérieur; **location shots** = les extérieurs *mpl* (d'un film); **the programme was shot on location in Spain** = les extérieurs pour ce programme ont été tournés en Espagne

lock *verb* verrouiller; **locking a file** = verrouiller (l'accès à) un fichier

◊ **lock onto** *verb* coupler *or* synchroniser

◊ **lockout** *noun (over a network)* lockout *m*

◊ **lock up** *noun (of computer)* blocage *m or* accrochage *m or* plantage *m*

log 1 *noun* **(a)** enregistrement *m or* entrée *f* (dans un journal *or* livre de bord) **(b)** journal *m* de bord; **system log** = journal de bord d'un système **2** *verb* **(a)** enregistrer; tenir un journal **(b)** *(telephone)* **to log calls** = enregistrer les appels **(c)** *(computer)* **to log in** *or* **log on** = ouvrir *or* débuter une session; *(make a connection)* se connecter; *(series of batch instructions)* **log on script** = instructions *fpl or* séquence *f* d'initialisation; *(computer that checks user identification)* **log on server** = serveur *m* de contrôle des accès; **automatic log on** = ouverture *f* automatique d'une session; **to log off** *or* **log out** = clore *or* fermer *or* terminer une session (NOTE: the verbs can be spelled **log on, log-on,** or **logon; log off, log-off** or **logoff)**

◊ **logger** *noun* enregistreur *m* (chronologique); **call logger** = enregistreur d'appels

◊ **logging** *noun (input of data)* acquisition *f or* saisie *f* de données; *(recording)* enregistrement *m*; **logging in** *or* **logging on** = ouverture *f* de session; **logging off** *or* **logging out** = clôture *f* de session; **call logging** = enregistrement d'appels; **error logging** = enregistrement automatique des erreurs; **features of the program include error logging** = ce programme permet l'enregistrement (automatique) des erreurs

QUOTE logging on and off from terminals is simple, requiring only a user name and password

QUOTE once the server is up and running it is possible for users to log-on
Micro Decision

QUOTE facilities for protection against hardware failure and software malfunction include log files
Computer News

logarithm *noun* logarithme *m*; **decimal logarithm of 1,000 is 3 (= 10 x 10 x 10)** = le logarithme décimal de 1000 est 3 (= 10 x 10 x 10)

◊ **logarithmic** *adjective* logarithmique; **bel is a unit in the logarithmic scale** = le 'bel' est mesuré sur une échelle logarithmique; **logarithmic graph** = graphe *m* logarithmique

logic *noun* **(a)** *(thought and reasoning)* logique *f*; **formal logic** = logique formelle **(b)** *(mathematical treatment)* logique; **logic map** = configuration *f* logique; **logic state** = état *m* logique; **logic state**

analyzer = analyseur *m* d'état logique; **logic symbol** = symbole *m* logique **(c)** *(for deducing results from binary data)* logique binaire; **logic bomb** = bombe *f* logique; **logic level** = niveau *m* logique; **logic operation** = opération *f* logique **(d)** *(components of a computer system)* la logique (d'un système); **sequential logic** = logique séquentielle; **logic array** = réseau *m* *or* circuit *m* logique; **programmable logic array (PLA)** = circuit logique programmable *or* logique câblée programmable; **uncommitted logic array (ULA)** = circuit logique non connecté; **logic card** *or* **logic board** = carte *f* logique; **logic circuit** = circuit *m* logique; **logic element** = élément *m* logique; **logic flowchart** = diagramme *m* logique; **logic gate** = porte *f* *or* circuit *m* logique

◊ **logical** *adjective* logique; **logical reasoning can be simulated by an artificial intelligence machine** = le raisonnement logique peut être simulé par une machine intelligente *or* un système expert; **logical channel** = voie *f* logique; **logical chart** = diagramme logique; **logical comparison** = comparaison *f* logique; **logical decision** = décision *f* logique; *(letter assigned to a disk drive)* **logical drive** = unité *f* logique; lettre *f* désignant une unité de disque; **the logical drive F: actually stores data on part of the server's disk drive** = l'unité logique F: est, en fait, une partie du disque du serveur utilisée pour stocker les données; **logical error** = erreur *f* logique; **logical expression** = expression *f* logique; **logical high** = état logique haut *or* binon 1 *or* tension haute; *(standard for the measurement of processing power of an inference engine)* **logical inferences per second (LIPS)** = (nombre d') inférences logiques par seconde *or* LIPS; *(IEEE 802.2 standard)* **logical link control (LLC)** = standard *m* LLC; **logical low** = état logique bas *or* binon 0 *or* tension faible; **logical operator** = opérateur *m* logique; **logical record** = enregistrement *m* *or* article *m* logique; *(the path a token follows)* **logical ring** = anneau *m* *or* chemin *m* logique; **logical shift** = décalage *m* logique

◊ **logic-seeking** *adjective* (imprimante à) recherche *f* logique

login = LOGGING IN

LOGO *noun (high level programming language)* langage *m* LOGO

logo *noun* logotype *m* *or* logo *m*

logoff = LOG OFF, LOGGING OFF

◊ **logon** = LOG ON, LOGGING ON

◊ **logout** = LOG OUT, LOGGING OUT

long haul network *noun* réseau *m* très étendu

long integer *noun* *(integer represented by several bytes of data)* nombre *m* entier long (représenté par plusieurs octets de données)

longitudinal *adjective* **longitudinal redundancy check** = contrôle *m* par redondance longitudinale

long persistence phosphor *noun* phosphore *m* *or* couche *f* phosphorée à grande persistance

look ahead *noun* lecture *f* anticipée; **carry look ahead** = retenue *f* anticipée

◊ **binary look-up** *noun* recherche *f* binaire

◊ **look-up table (LUT)** *noun* table d'équivalence *or* de référence; **look-up tables are preprogrammed then used in processing so saving calculations for each result required** = les tables d'équivalence sont préprogrammées et permettent de gagner du temps de traitement en évitant de recalculer les mêmes valeurs

loop 1 *noun* **(a)** *(instruction in a computer program)* boucle *f*; **closed loop** = boucle fermée; **endless loop** *or* **infinite loop** = boucle sans fin; **holding loop** = boucle de maintien; **modification loop** = boucle de modification; **nested loop** = boucle imbriquée *or* emboîtée; **loop body** = corps *m* de la boucle; **loop check** = vérification *f* *or* contrôle *m* de boucle; **loop counter** = compteur *m* de boucles; **loop program** = boucle d'itération *or* boucle de programme *or* boucle de fond *or* programme *m* itératif **(b) loop film** = film *m* en boucle; **loop network** = réseau en anneau *or* en boucle **(c)** *(coiled in circle)* boucle *or* tour *m*; **loop antenna** = antenne en boucle **2** *verb* créer une boucle *or* boucler; **looping program** = boucle d'itération *or* boucle de programme *or* boucle de fond *or* programme itératif

◊ **loopback** *noun (diagnostic test)* boucle *f* de rétroaction *or* de correction

lose *verb* perdre; **we have lost the signal in the noise** = le signal a été masqué par le bruit; **all the current files were lost when the system crashed and we had no backup copies** = tous les fichiers courants ont été perdus lors de la panne d'ordinateur parce que nous n'avions pas de copie de sauvegarde; **lost call** = demande *f* de communication qui ne peut être établie *or* qui ne passe pas; **lost time** = temps *m* mort

lost cluster *noun (sectors on a disk whose identification bits have been corrupted)* grappe *f* de données perdue *or* cluster *m* perdu

loss *noun (of signal)* perte *f* *or* atténuation *f* *or* affaiblissement *m* (d'un signal)

Lotus ™ *(software company)* (la société) Lotus ™; *see also* LIM EMS

loudness *noun* volume *m*

◊ **loudspeaker** *noun* haut-parleur *m*; *(system)* enceinte *f* acoustique

low 1 *noun* **active low** = signal *m* bas actif **2** *adjective* bas, basse

◊ **low end** *noun (hardware that is not very powerful or sophisticated)* bas *m* de gamme

◊ **low frequency (LF)** *noun (radio: 30 - 300kHz)* basse fréquence *f or* onde *f* kilométrique; *(audio: 5 - 300 Hz)* basse fréquence *or* audiofréquence *f see also* VERY

◊ **low-level format** *noun (defines the pattern of tracks on a disk)* formatage *m* de bas niveau

◊ **low-level language (LLL)** *noun (programming language similar to assembler)* langage *m* de bas niveau *or* LLL; *compare* HIGH-LEVEL LANGUAGE

◊ **low-memory** *noun (memory locations in a PC)* mémoire *f* basse; *compare* HIGH MEMORY

◊ **low-order digit** *noun* chiffre *m* de poids faible *or* chiffre le moins significatif; **the number 234156 has a low-order digit of 6** = 6 est le chiffre le moins significatif du nombre 234156

◊ **low pass filter** *noun* filtre *m* passe-bas

◊ **low-priority work** *noun* tâche *f* non prioritaire *or* d'arrière-plan

◊ **low-res** *see* LOW-RESOLUTION

◊ **low-resolution graphics** *or* **low-res graphics** *noun* graphiques *mpl* de basse définition *or* de basse résolution

◊ **low speed communications** *noun* communication *f* à faible débit

◊ **lower case** *noun* (lettre) minuscule *f or* bas *m* de casse

LPM = LINES PER MINUTE

LPT1 *(first parallel printer port)* (sur un PC) port *m* parallèle LPT1

LQ = LETTER QUALITY

LRU = LEAST RECENTLY USED ALGORITHM

LSB = LEAST SIGNIFICANT BIT

LSD = LEAST SIGNIFICANT DIGIT

LSI = LARGE SCALE INTEGRATION

luggable *noun & adjective* ordinateur *m* déplaçable *or* à peu près portable

lumen *noun (SI unit of illumination)* lumen *m*

luminance *noun* luminance *f*; **luminance signal** = signal *m* de luminance

LUT = LOOK-UP TABLE

QUOTE an image processing system can have three LUTs that map the image memory to the display device
Byte

lux *noun (SI unit of measurement of one lumen per square metre)* lux *m*

Mm

m *prefix* = MILLI; *(one thousandth)* m *or* milli-

M *prefix* = MEGA **(a)** *(one million)* M *or* méga-; **Mbps** = MEGA BITS PER SECOND; *(number of million bits transmitted every second)* Mbps *or* (nombre de) mégabits *mpl* par seconde; **MFLOPS** = MEGA FLOATING POINT OPERATIONS PER SECOND; *(one million floating point operations per second)* mégaflops *mpl or* (nombre de) millions d'opérations en virgule flottante par seconde **(b)** *(equal to 1,048,576 or 2^{20})* M; **Mbyte (MB)** = Moctet *or* Mo; **the latest model has a 30Mbyte hard disk** = le modèle le plus récent possède un disque dur d'une capacité de 30Mo

mA = MILLIAMPERE

◊ **Mac** *see* Macintosh

◊ **MacBinary** ™ *noun (file storage and transfer system)* MacBinary ™

MAC **(a)** = MULTIPLEXED ANALOG COMPONENTS **(b)** = MESSAGE AUTHENTICATION CODE

machine *noun* **(a)** machine *f*; **copying machine** *or* **duplicating machine** = photocopieur *m or* copieur *m*; **dictating machine** = Dictaphone ™ *m*; *(proof sheets of a book)* **machine proof** = épreuve *f* de machine **(b)** ordinateur *m or* processeur *m or* machine; *(contains only the minimum of ROM based code to boot its system from disk)* **clean machine** = processeur *m* nu; *(computer which can compile source code)* **source machine** = machine source *or* processeur *m* de programme source; **virtual machine** = machine virtuelle; **machine address** = adresse *f* absolue; *(fault)* **machine check** = arrêt *m* dû à une défaillance de l'appareil; **machine code** = code *m* machine; **machine code format** = format de code machine; **machine code instruction** = instruction *f* en code *or* en langage machine; **machine cycle** = cycle *m* de machine; *(software)* **machine-dependent** = (logiciel) non standard *or* qui ne fonctionne que sur un type d'ordinateur; (logiciel) de constructeur *or* de propriétaire; **machine equation** = équation *f or* logique *f* machine; *(caused by a hardware malfunction)* **machine error** = erreur *f* (causée par la) machine; *(software)* **machine-independent** = standard *or* universel, -elle *or* qui fonctionne sur la plupart des ordinateurs; **machine-independent language** = langage *m* standard *or* universel; **machine instruction** = instruction en langage machine; **machine intelligence** = intelligence artificielle; **machine-intimate** = (logiciel) propre à la machine *or* sur mesure *or* de constructeur *or* adapté à l'ordinateur; **machine language** = langage *m* machine; **machine language compile** = compiler en langage machine; **machine language**

programming = programmation *f* en langage machine; *(command or data)* **machine-readable** = (instruction *or* donnée) en langage machine *or* exploitable par l'ordinateur; **the disk stores data in machine-readable form** = le disque garde en mémoire des données sous une forme exploitable par l'ordinateur; **machine run** = exécution *f* d'un programme; *(of foreign language)* **machine translation** = traduction *f* assistée par ordinateur; **machine word** = mot *m* machine

◊ **machinery** *noun* (l'ensemble des) machines *fpl*

◊ **machining** *noun* **(a)** *(making a product)* usinage *m* **(b)** *(books)* impression *f*

◊ **machinist** *noun* machiniste *m&f*

Macintosh ™ *noun (range of computers designed by Apple Corporation)* (ordinateurs) Macintosh ™; **Macintosh computers are not compatible with an IBM PC unless you use special emulation software** = les ordinateurs Macintosh ne sont pas compatibles IBM PC à moins d'utiliser un logiciel d'émulation spécialement conçu à cet effet; **Macintosh filing system (MFS)** = logiciel d'archivage MFS

macro- *prefix* macro(-)

◊ **macro** *noun* macro-instruction *f or* macro *f*; **macro assembler** *or* **assembly program** = macro-assembleur *m or* programme *m* assembleur pour macrolangage; **macro call** = macro-instruction *f*; **macro code** = macrocode *m*; **macro command** = macrocommande *f*; **macro definition** = macrodéfinition *f*; **macroelement** = macro-élément *m*; **macro expansion** = macro-expansion *f or* désassemblage *m* de macro; **macro flowchart** = macro-ordinogramme *m*; **macro instruction** = macro-instruction *f or* macro *f*; **macro language** = macrolangage *m*; **macro library** = bibliothèque *f* de macros; **macro programming** = macroprogrammation *f*

> QUOTE Microsoft has released a developer's kit for its Word 6.0 for Windows word-processing package. The 900-page kit explains how to use the WordBasic macro language supplied with the software.
> *Computing*

magazine *noun* **(a)** *(review)* revue *f or* magazine *m or* périodique *m*; **a weekly magazine** = une revue hebdomadaire; **he edits a computer magazine** = il travaille à la rédaction d'une revue de micro-informatique **(b)** *(pages of videotext system)* (nombre de) pages d'un système vidéotex **(c)** *(containing photographic film)* magasin *m*

magnet *noun* aimant *m*

◊ **magnetic** *adjective* magnétique *or* aimanté, -ée; **magnetic bubble memory** = mémoire *f* à bulles magnétiques; **magnetic card** = carte *f* magnétique; **magnetic card reader** = lecteur *m* de cartes (magnétiques); **magnetic cartridge** = cartouche *f* (de bande magnétique); **magnetic cassette** = cassette *f* (de bande magnétique); **magnetic cell** = cellule *f* magnétique; **magnetic core** = tore *m* magnétique; **magnetic disk** = disque *m* magnétique; **magnetic disk unit** = unité *f* de disque *or* de disquette; **magnetic drum** = tambour *m* magnétique; **magnetic encoding** = encodage *m* magnétique *or* sur support magnétique; **magnetic field** = champ *m* magnétique; **magnetic flux** = flux *m* magnétique; *(of beam of electrons)* **magnetic focusing** = concentration *f* *or* mise *f* au point magnétique; **magnetic head** = tête *f* magnétique; **magnetic ink** = encre *f* magnétique; **magnetic ink character recognition (MICR)** = reconnaissance *f* de caractères magnétiques; **magnetic master** = support *m* magnétique original *or* bande originale *or* disque original; **magnetic material** *or* **medium** = support *m* magnétique; **magnetic media** = les supports magnétiques; **magnetic memory** *or* **store** = mémoire *m* magnétique; **magnetic recording** = enregistrement *m* sur support magnétique; **magnetic screen** = écran *m* magnétique; **magnetic storm** = orage *m* magnétique; **magnetic strip** = piste *f* magnétique; **magnetic thin film storage** = mémoire à couches minces (magnétiques); **magnetic transfer** = transfert *m* d'un support magnétique à un autre *or* transfert magnétique

◊ **magnetic tape** *or* **mag tape** *noun* bande *f* magnétique; **magnetic tape cartridge** *or* **cassette** = cartouche *f* *or* cassette *f* de bande magnétique; **magnetic tape encoder** = encodeur *m* pour bandes magnétiques; **magnetic tape reader** = lecteur *m* de bandes magnétiques; **magnetic tape recorder** = enregistreur *m* de bandes; magnétophone *m*; **magnetic tape transport** = dérouleur *m* *or* dispositif d'entraînement de bandes magnétiques

◊ **magnetize** *verb* magnétiser

◊ **magneto-optical disc** *noun* *(optical disc)* disque *m* (magnéto)optique numérique (DON) (réinscriptible)

◊ **magneto-optical recording** *noun* *(storage using an optical disc)* enregistrement *m* sur disque (magnéto)optique numérique

COMMENT: the optical disk has a thin layer of magnetic film which is heated by a laser, the particles are then polarised by a weak magnetic field. Magneto-optical media has very high capacity (over 600Mb) and is re-writable

magnify *verb* *(image)* agrandir *or* grossir *or* amplifier; **the photograph has been magnified 200 times** = cette photo a été agrandie 200 fois

◊ **magnification** *noun* agrandissement *m* *or* grossissement *m* *or* amplification *f*; **the lens gives a magnification of 10 times** = cette lentille grossit 10 fois

magnitude *noun* *(of a signal)* amplitude *f* *or* grandeur *f*; **signal magnitude** = amplitude d'un signal

mag tape *noun* *(informal)* = MAGNETIC TAPE

mail 1 *noun* **(a)** *(postal system)* poste *f* **(b)** *(letters sent or received)* courrier *m* **(c)** *(electronic messages)* **electronic mail** *or* **email** *or* **e-mail** = messagerie *f* *or* poste *f* *or* courrier *m* électronique **2** *verb* mettre à la poste; **to mail a letter** = poster une lettre

◊ **mailbox** *or* **mail box** *noun* *(electronic)* boîte *f* aux lettres (électronique)

◊ **mail-enabled** *adjective* *(application that has access to an electronic mail system)* utilisable avec une messagerie électronique; **this word-processor is mail-enabled - you can send messages to other users from within it** = ce traitement de texte peut être utlisé avec la messagerie électronique: vous pouvez envoyer des messages aux autres utilisateurs sans sortir du programme

◊ **mailing** *noun* envoi *m* par la poste *or* mailing *m*; **the mailing of publicity material** = l'envoi (par la poste) de prospectus publicitaires; **direct mailing** = publipostage *m* *or* publicité *f* directe *or* mailing *m*; **mailing list** = fichier *m* d'adresses (destiné aux mailings); **his name is on our mailing list** = son nom figure sur notre fichier d'adresses; **to build up a mailing list** = établir un fichier d'adresses; **to buy a mailing list** = acheter un fichier d'adresses; **mailing piece** = prospectus *m* envoyé par la poste; **mailing shot** = envoi *m* de prospectus publicitaires

◊ **mail-merge** *or* **mailmerge** *noun* (programme d') édition *f* de lettres types; (fonction) publipostage *m*

QUOTE Spreadsheet views for data and graphical forms for data entry have been added to the Q&A database, with the traditional reporting, mailmerge, and labels improved through Windows facilities.
Computing

main *adjective* principal, -e; *(of antenna transmission)* **main beam** = porteuse principale; *(main part of a program)* **main body (of a program)** = corps principal (d'un programme); **main clock** = horloge *f* maîtresse; **main distributing frame** = tableau de distribution principal; *(in a catalogue)* **main entry** = entrée principale; **main index** = index général *or* principal; *(instructions performed repeatedly)* **main loop (of a program)** = boucle principale (d'un programme; **main memory** *or* **main storage** = mémoire principale *or* centrale; **the 16-bit system includes up to 3Mb of main memory** = le système de 16 bits contient une mémoire principale d'une capacité allant jusqu'à 3Mo; **main routine** = routine principale

◊ **mainframe (computer)** *noun* gros ordinateur *or* ordinateur central *or* ordinateur principal; **mainframe access** = accès à l'ordinateur principal (par l'intermédiaire d'un micro)

mains electricity *noun* le secteur

maintain *verb* entretenir; **well maintained** = bien entretenu, -e

◊ **maintainability** *noun* maintenabilité *f*

◊ **maintenance** *noun* maintenance *f* *or*

entretien *m (service)* service *m* de maintenance *or* service après-vente; **file maintenance** = mise *f* à jour de fichier *or* maintenance de fichier; **on-site maintenance** = service *m* d'assistance technique sur le lieu de travail *or* sur site; *(service)* **preventive maintenance** = maintenance préventive; vérification *f or* entretien régulier; *(repair)* **remedial maintenance** = maintenance curative *or* corrective; réparation *f*; **maintenance contract** = contrat *m* de maintenance; *(revision that corrects a minor problem)* **maintenance release** = mise *f* à jour corrective; **the maintenance release of the database program, version 2.01, corrects the problem with the margins** = la mise à jour corrective de ce programme de base de données, version 2.01, corrige le problème des marges; **maintenance routine** = programme de diagnostic *or* de maintenance; **remote maintenance** = télémaintenance *f*

major cycle *noun* cycle *m* principal

majuscule *noun* (lettre) majuscule *f or* capitale *f* (d'imprimerie)

make-ready time *noun* temps *m* de préparation

◊ **make up** *verb (book)* mettre en page; *(text on computer)* formater *or* mettre en forme

◊ **make up** *or* **makeup** *noun (of book)* mise *f* en page; *(of text, on computer)* formatage *m*; **corrections after the page makeup are very expensive** = les corrections faites après la mise en page coûtent très cher

male connector *noun* connecteur *m* mâle

malfunction **1** *noun (of hardware or software)* défaillance *f or* dysfonctionnement *m*; **the data was lost due to a software malfunction** = les données ont été perdues par suite d'une défaillance du logiciel; **malfunction routine** = (programme) diagnostic *m* de dysfonctionnement **2** *verb* mal fonctionner *or* être en dérangement; **some of the keys on the keyboard have started to malfunction** = quelques-unes des touches du clavier ne fonctionnent déjà plus très bien

◊ **malfunctioning** *noun* mauvais fonctionnement *or* dysfonctionnement *m*

MAN = METROPOLITAN AREA NETWORK

man/machine interface (MMI) *noun* interface *f* homme/machine *or* interface utilisateur/machine

◊ **man-made** *adjective* artificiel, -elle; **man-made noise** = bruit parasite causé par une machine

manage *verb* gérer *or* diriger

◊ **manageable** *adjective* qui peut être maîtrisé, -ée *or* résolu, -e; **processing problems which are still manageable** = problèmes de traitement qui peuvent être résolus; **data should be split into manageable files** = les données devraient être réparties en fichiers plus courts et plus faciles à utiliser

◊ **management** *noun* gestion *f*; **management**

programme = gestionnaire *m*; **network management** = gestion de réseau

◊ **management information service (MIS)** *noun (department within a company)* service *m* informatique

◊ **management information system (MIS)** *noun (software for managers)* logiciel *m* de gestion

◊ **manager** *noun* **(a)** *(software)* gestionnaire *m*; **file manager** = gestionnaire de fichiers; **queue manager** = gestionnaire de file d'attente; **records manager** = gestionnaire d'enregistrements; **text manager** = gestionnaire de texte **(b)** *(person)* manager *m or* chef *m or* responsable *m* (de service); **data processing manager** = responsable *or* chef du service informatique

Manchester coding *noun (method of encoding data)* encodage *m* Manchester

Mandlebrot set *noun (mathematical equation)* équation *f* de Mandlebrot; *see also* FRACTAL

manipulate *verb* manipuler; **an image processor that captures, displays and manipulates video images** = un processeur d'images qui peut lire, afficher et manipuler les images vidéo

◊ **manipulation** *noun* manipulation *f* (de données *or* d'images); **a high-speed database management program allows the manipulation of very large amounts of data** = un gestionnaire de base de données ultra-rapide permet la manipulation d'une très grande quantité de données

mantissa *noun* mantisse *f*; **the mantissa of the number 45.897 is 0.897** = la mantisse du nombre 45,897 est 0,897

manual **1** *noun (book or booklet)* manuel *m* (d'utilisation); **the manual is included with the system** = un manuel d'utilisation est fourni avec le système; **installation manual** = manuel d'installation *or* manuel technique; **instruction manual** = manuel d'utilisation; **technical manual** = manuel technique *or* manuel d'installation; **user manual** = manuel d'utilisation **2** *adjective* manuel, -elle; **manual data processing** = traitement de l'information sans l'aide d'un ordinateur; **manual entry** *or* **manual input** = saisie *f* de données par *or* au *or* sur clavier

◊ **manually** *adverb* manuellement *or* à la main; **the paper has to be fed into the printer manually** = l'alimentation en papier de l'imprimante se fait manuellement

manufacture *verb* fabriquer *or* manufacturer; **the company manufactures diskettes and magnetic tape** = cette société fabrique des disquettes et des bandes magnétiques

◊ **manufacturer** *noun* fabricant *m*; **if the system develops a fault it should be returned to the manufacturer for checking** = en cas de mauvais fonctionnement, renvoyer le système au fabricant; **the manufacturer guarantees the system for 12 months** = le fabricant garantit le système 12 mois

manuscript *or* **MS** *noun* manuscrit *m*; **this manuscript was all written on computer** = ce manuscrit a été écrit directement sur ordinateur

map 1 *noun (internal layout of computer's memory or communication regions)* configuration *f*; **logic map** = configuration logique; **memory map** = configuration de la mémoire **2** *verb* **to map out** = configurer; organiser *or* planifier; **database mapping** = configuration de base de données; **I/O mapping** = configuration d'entrée/sortie; *(with addresses allocated to input or output devices)* **memory-mapped** = configuré en mémoire; **a memory-mapped screen has an address allocated to each pixel, allowing direct access to the screen by the CPU** = chaque pixel de cet écran configuré en mémoire a une adresse allouée en mémoire, ce qui permet au processeur d'y accéder directement; *(I/O port which can be accessed as if it were a memory location)* **memory-mapped input/output** *or* **memory-mapped I/O** = entrée/sortie configurée en mémoire; *see also* BIT-MAP, BIT-MAPPED

MAR = MEMORY ADDRESS REGISTER

marching display *noun* visualisation *f* de contrôle d'entrée

margin *noun* **(a)** *(blank space)* marge *f*; **the left margin and right margin are the two sections of blank paper on either side of the page** = les marges de droite et de gauche sont les blancs de chaque côté d'une page; **when typing the contract leave wide margins** = en tapant le contrat à la machine, n'oubliez pas de laisser des marges très larges; **foot margin** = blanc *m* de pied; **top margin** = blanc de tête; **to set a margin** = fixer *or* paramétrer une marge **(b)** *(extra time or space)* marge; **safety margin** = marge de sécurité; **margin of error** = marge d'erreur

◊ **margination** *noun* paramétrage *m* de marges

mark 1 *noun* **(a)** *(sign)* marque *f or* signe *m*; **proof correction marks** = signes *mpl* de correction (d'épreuves d'imprimerie) **(b)** *(signal)* marque logique; **mark hold** = marque attente; **mark space** = marque espace **2** *verb* marquer *or* indiquer; **mark block** = (instruction de) marquer un bloc; **marking interval** = intervalle de marquage; **mark sense** = graphiter (une marque); **mark sense device** *or* **reader** = lecteur de marques magnétiques; **mark sensing card** = carte graphitée

◊ **marker** *noun* **(a)** **marker pen** = marqueur *m or* surligneur *m* **(b)** *(code)* marqueur *m or* indicateur *m or* marque; **block markers** = délimiteurs *mpl or* marques *fpl* de bloc; **field marker** = marqueur *m* de champ; **word marker** = marque *f* de début de mot

◊ **mark up** *verb* annoter une copie (en spécifiant la typographie)

◊ **marking up** *noun* annotation *f* typographique

MASER = MICROWAVE AMPLIFICATION BY STIMULATED EMISSION OF RADIATION

mask 1 *noun* **(a)** *(circuit layout stencil)* masque *m*; **a mask or stencil is used to transfer the transistor design onto silicon** = on se sert d'un masque ou d'un stencil pour reproduire le tracé du circuit du transistor sur le silicium **(b)** *(photographic)* masque **(c)** *(pattern of binary digits)* masque; **mask bit** = bit masque; **mask register** = registre de masque; **interrupt mask** = masque d'interruption **2** *verb* masquer; **masked ROM** = mémoire morte masquée

◊ **maskable** *adjective* qui peut être masqué, -ée; **maskable interrupt** = interruption *f* qui peut être masquée *or* invalidée; **non-maskable interrupt (NMI)** = interruption obligatoire *or* qui ne peut être invalidée *or* qui ne peut être masquée

◊ **masking** *noun* masquage *m*

QUOTE the device features a maskable interrupt feature which reduces CPU overheads
Electronics & Power

mass media *noun* les mass-medias *mpl or* les médias *mpl*

◊ **mass storage** *noun* mémoire *f* de masse; **mass storage device** = support *m* de stockage de grande capacité *or* de mémoire de masse; **a hard disk is definitely a mass storage device** = un disque dur constitue un véritable support de stockage de grande capacité; **mass storage system** = mémoire de masse

mast *noun* **radio mast** *or* **TV mast** = pylône *m* de radio *or* de télévision

master 1 *noun* maître *m*; **master antenna television system (MATV)** = antenne *f* de relais régional; **master card** = carte *f* maîtresse; **master clock** *or* **timing master** = horloge *f* maîtresse *or* horloge principale; **master computer** = ordinateur *m* maître *or* principal; **the master computer controls everything else** = l'ordinateur maître contrôle tout; **master control program (MCP)** = programme *m* de commande; **master data** = données permanentes *or* de base; **master disk** = disque *m* original; **master file** = fichier *m* principal *or* fichier maître *or* fichier permanent; **master/master computer system** = système *m* maître/maître; **master program file** = fichier de programme maître; **master proof** = épreuve *f* finale; **master/slave computer system** = système *m* maître/esclave; **master tape** = bande *f* originale; **master terminal** = terminal *m* principal *or* maître; **image master** = feuille *f* de style **2** *verb* **(a)** réussir (à faire quelque chose) *or* apprendre (quelque chose); **we mastered the new word-processor quite quickly** = nous avons appris à utiliser le nouveau système de traitement de texte assez rapidement **(b)** reporter *or* copier *or* recopier; **those slides and photographs are the intermediate materials to be mastered onto the video disk** = ces diapos et photos sont les supports intermédiaires qui doivent être recopiés sur le vidéodisque

◊ **mastergroup** *noun* *(600 voice channels)* groupe *m* tertiaire

match *verb* **(a)** assortir **(b)** *(to set a register)* accorder *or* équilibrer; **matched load** = charge accordée *or* équilibrée; **matching transformer** =

transformateur *m* de couplage; **impedance matching** = accord *m* d'impédance

material *noun* **(a)** *(substance to make a finished product)* matériau *m*; **gold is the ideal material for electrical connections** = l'or est le matériau idéal pour la fabrication des connecteurs électriques; **synthetic materials** = matériaux synthétiques; **materials control** = contrôle d'approvisionnement en matériaux; **materials handling** = manutention *f* **(b)** matériel *m*; **display material** = matériel publicitaire

mathematics *noun* mathématiques *fpl*

◊ **mathematical** *adjective* mathématique; **mathematical model** = modèle mathématique; **mathematical subroutine** = sous-programme mathématique

◊ **maths** *or* US **math** *(informal)* = MATHEMATICS math *or* maths; **maths chip** *or* **coprocessor** = coprocesseur *m* mathématique

matrix *noun* **(a)** *(array of numbers)* matrice *f*; **matrix rotation** = rotation *f* de matrice **(b)** *(array of connections)* matrice de relation; **key matrix** = implantation *f* *or* matrice des touches sur un clavier **(c)** *(printing)* matrice graphique; **matrix printer** *or* **dot-matrix printer** = imprimante matricielle; **character matrix** = matrice de caractères; *see also* ACTIVE

matt *or* **matte** 1 *noun* *(mask for film)* cache *m* *or* gobo *m* 2 *adjective* *(which is not shiny)* mat, matte

matter *noun* **(a)** question *f* *or* point *m* **(b)** *(main section of text)* corps *m* du texte; **printed matter** = imprimé *m*; **publicity matter** = imprimé *or* matériel *m* publicitaire

MATV = MASTER ANTENNA TELEVISION SYSTEM

maximise *verb* maximiser *or* maximaliser; porter à son maximum; *(expand an application icon)* agrandir au plein écran (une fenêtre MS-Windows); *compare* MINIMISE

| COMMENT: you maximise a window by clicking once on the up arrow in the top right hand corner

maximum 1 *noun* maximum *m* 2 *adjective* maximum *or* maximal, -e; **maximum capacity** = capacité *f* maximale; *(of signal)* **maximum reading** = amplitude maximum enregistrée; **maximum transmission rate** = vitesse *f* maximale *or* débit *m* maximal de transmission; **maximum usable frequency** = fréquence *f* maximum *or* maximale utilisable; **maximum users** = nombre *m* maximum d'utilisateurs

Mb *or* **Mbit** = MEGABIT Mb *or* mégabit *m*

MB *or* **Mb** *or* **Mbyte** = MEGABYTE Mo *or* méga-octet *m*

QUOTE the maximum storage capacity is restricted to 8 Mbytes
Micro Decision

Mbps = MEGABITS PER SECOND (nombre de) mégabits par seconde

MBR = MEMORY BUFFER REGISTER

mC = MILLICOULOMB

MCA = MICROCHANNEL ARCHITECTURE; *(components)* **MCA chipset** = jeu *m* de composants MCA

MCGA = MULTICOLOR GRAPHICS ADAPTER

MCP = MASTER CONTROL PROGRAM

MD *or* **MKDIR** = MAKE DIRECTORY; *(DOS command to create a new directory)* commande MD *or* MKDIR (de création de répertoire)

MDA = MONOCHROME DISPLAY ADAPTER

MDR = MEMORY DATA REGISTER

mean 1 *noun* moyenne *f* 2 *adjective* moyen, -enne; **mean time between failures (MTBF)** = durée *f* moyenne de bon fonctionnement *or* moyenne de temps de bon fonctionnement entre les défaillances (MTBF); **mean time to failure (MTF)** = durée moyenne de bon fonctionnement; **mean time to repair** = moyenne de temps requis pour réparation 2 *verb* signifier *or* vouloir dire; **the message DISK FULL means that there is no more room on the disk for further data** = le message DISK FULL signifie que le disque n'a plus l'espace voulu pour enregistrer de nouvelles données

measure 1 *noun* **(a)** *(way of calculating size)* mesure *f*; **square measure** = mesure de surface **(b)** **tape measure** = mètre *m* (à ruban) **(c)** *(width of a printed line)* largeur *f* d'une ligne **(d)** *(action)* mesure; **to take measures to prevent something happening** = prendre des mesures pour éviter quelque chose; **safety measures** = mesures de sécurité 2 *verb* mesurer

◊ **measurement** *noun* **(a)** **measurements** = dimensions *fpl* *or* encombrement *m*; **to write down the measurements of a package** = noter les dimensions d'un paquet **(b)** évaluation *f*; **performance measurement** *or* **measurement of performance is carried out by running a benchmark program** = la performance est mesurée à l'aide d'un programme test

mechanical *adjective* mécanique; *(device that is operated by moving it across a flat surface)* **mechanical mouse** = souris *f* mécanique; *compare* OPTICAL MOUSE; **mechanical paper** = papier *m* journal

◊ **mechanism** *noun* mécanisme *m*; **the printer mechanism is very simple** = l'imprimante possède un mécanisme très simple; **the drive mechanism appears to be faulty** = il semble que le mécanisme du lecteur ne fonctionne pas très bien

media **(a)** *(means of communicating information to the public)* media *or* média *m*; **the media** = les médias; **the product attracted a lot of interest in the media** *or* **a lot of media interest** = le produit a beaucoup fait parler de lui dans les medias *or* a suscité un grand intérêt médiatique; **media analysis** *or* **media research** = analyse *f* des médias; **media coverage** = couverture *f* médiatique; **we got good media coverage for the launch of the new model** = nous avons eu une bonne couverture médiatique pour le lancement du nouveau modèle (NOTE: **media** is followed by a singular or plural verb) **(b)** *(physical material that can be used to store data)* média *m or* support *m*; **computers can store data on a variety of media, such as disk, punched card or CD-ROM** = les ordinateurs peuvent stocker des données sur différents types de supports: disques, cartes perforées ou CD-ROM; *(copying data)* **media conversion** = conversion *f* de support; **to transfer from magnetic tape to floppy disk, you need a media conversion device** = pour transférer le contenu d'une bande magnétique sur disquette, vous avez besoin d'un équipement de conversion de support.; *(fault in storage media)* **media error** = erreur causée par le support; **magnetic media** = supports *mpl* magnétiques; *see also* MEDIUM

QUOTE The Kontron IN Lite notebook, said to continue working even when fully immersed in a metre of liquid, includes an Intel i386 25MHz processor, between 4MB and 20MB of RAM, a 80MB or 200MB hard disk and a 40Mb removable media option.
Computing

medium 1 *adjective (middle or average)* moyen, -enne; **a medium-sized computer system** = un système informatique de taille moyenne; *(memory model)* **medium model** = modèle *m* moyen (de gestion de mémoire, pour processeurs Intel 8086) **2** *noun* **(a)** moyen *m or* support *m*; **advertising medium** = support *m* publicitaire; **the product was advertised through the medium of the trade press** = la publicité pour le produit s'est faite par voie de presse spécialisée **(b)** **storage medium** = support *m* de stockage; **data storage mediums such as paper tape, magnetic disk, magnetic tape, card and microfiche are available** = il existe différents types de supports de stockage dont les bandes papier, les disques et bandes magnétiques, les cartes et microfiches; **data medium** = support de données *or* d'information; **empty medium** = support vierge; **magnetic medium** *or* **material** = support magnétique (NOTE: plural is **mediums** or **media)**

◊ **medium frequency** *noun (300-3000kHz)* moyenne fréquence; onde *f* hectométrique

◊ **medium lens** *noun* objectif *m* standard *or* de focale moyenne

◊ **medium scale integration (MSI)** *noun* intégration *f* à moyenne échelle

◊ **medium speed** *noun* vitesse moyenne *or* débit moyen (de transmission)

◊ **medium wave (MW)** = MEDIUM FREQUENCY

meet *noun (logical function)* conjonction *f*

meg = MEGABYTE méga (= Méga-octet); **this computer has a ninety-meg hard disk** = l'ordinateur a un disque de quatre-vingt-dix mégas

mega- *prefix* **(a)** *(one million)* méga-; **megabits per second (Mbps)** = (nombre de) mégabits *mpl* par seconde; **megaflops (MFLOPS)** = million d'opérations en virgule flottante par seconde *or* mégaflops *mpl* (Mflops); *(one million cycles per second)* **megahertz (MHz)** = mégahertz *m* MHz; *(data link provided by British Telecom)* **Megastream** ™ = connexion *f* Megastream ™ **(b)** *(meaning 1,048,576 (2^{20}) and used only in computing and electronic related applications)* méga-; **megabit (Mb)** = mégabit *m* (Mb); **megabyte (MB** *or* **Mb)** = méga-octet *m* (Mo); *(display adapter and monitor)* **megapixel display** = adaptateur d'écran de résolution supérieure à 1024x1024 pixels

QUOTE adding multiple megabytes of memory is a simple matter of plugging memory cards into the internal bus
Byte

QUOTE The component manufacturers sell flash memory at an average price of $30 a megabyte. By comparison, the hard-disk components sell at $3 a megabyte.
Computing

member *noun* élément *m* (d'un champ)

membrane keyboard *noun (keyboard using a thin plastic sheet)* clavier *m* à membrane

COMMENT: the keys in a membrane keyboard have less travel than normal mechanical keys, but since they have no moving parts, they are more robust and reliable

memo field *noun (field in a database)* champ *m* mémo

memomotion *noun* prise *f* de vue à cadence lente *or* décomposition *f* de mouvements

memorize *verb* mémoriser; mettre en mémoire

memory *noun* mémoire *f*; **associative memory** = mémoire associative; **backing memory** = mémoire auxiliaire; **bootstrap memory** = mémoire de lancement; **bubble memory** = mémoire à bulles; **cache memory** = mémoire cache *or or* cache *m or* antémémoire *f*; **charge coupled device (CCD) memory** = (dispositif) mémoire à couplage de charge; **content-addressable memory** = mémoire adressable par son contenu; **control memory** = mémoire fixe; **core memory** *or* **primary memory** = mémoire centrale *or* à accès direct; **disk memory** = mémoire sur disque(tte); **dynamic memory** = mémoire dynamique; **external memory** = mémoire externe *or* auxiliaire; **fast access memory (FAM)** = mémoire à accès rapide; **FIFO memory** *or* **first in first out memory** = mémoire basée sur le principe 'premier entré premier sorti' *or* mémoire FIFO; **internal memory** = mémoire interne; **magnetic memory** = mémoire magnétique; **main memory** = mémoire principale *or* centrale; **non-volatile memory** = mémoire non-volatile; **paged memory** = mémoire paginée; **random access memory (RAM)** = mémoire vive *or* mémoire RAM; **read only memory (ROM)** = mémoire morte *or* mémoire ROM; **scratchpad memory** =

mémoire 'bloc-notes' *or* mémoire banale; **serial memory** = mémoire séquentielle; **magnetic tape is a high capacity serial memory** = la bande magnétique constitue une mémoire séquentielle d'une grande capacité; **static memory** = mémoire statique; **virtual memory** = mémoire virtuelle; **volatile memory** = mémoire volatile; **memory access time** = temps d'accès à la mémoire; **memory address register (MAR)** = registre *m* d'adresse en mémoire; **memory bank** = bloc *m or* banque *f* de mémoire; **memory board** = carte *f* mémoire; **memory buffer register (MBR)** = registre de mémoire tampon; **memory capacity** = capacité *f* de mémoire; **memory cell** = cellule *f* de mémoire; **memory chip** = puce *f* mémoire; **memory cycle** = cycle *m* de mémoire; **memory data register (MDR)** = registre des données en mémoire; **memory diagnostic** = diagnostic *m* de la mémoire; **memory dump** = listage *m* de mémoire *or* vidage *m* de mémoire (sur imprimante); **memory edit** = changement *m* d'adresse en mémoire; **memory hierarchy** = hiérarchie *f* des mémoires; **memory-intensive software** = logiciel qui requiert beaucoup de mémoire *or* grand consommateur de mémoire *or* gourmand en mémoire; **memory location** = emplacement *m* de mémoire; **memory management** = gestion *f* de mémoire; *(electronic logic circuits)* **memory management unit (MMU)** = unité *f* de gestion de la mémoire; **memory map** = configuration *f or* topographie *f* de la mémoire; image mémoire; **memory-mapped** = configuré, -ée en mémoire; **a memory-mapped screen has an address allocated to each pixel, allowing direct access to the screen by the CPU** = chaque pixel de cet écran configuré en mémoire a une adresse allouée en mémoire, ce qui permet au processeur d'y accéder directement; **memory-mapped input/output** *or* **memory-mapped I/O** = entrée/sortie configurée en mémoire; **memory page** = page *f* mémoire; *(method of addressing the code and data used in a program)* **memory model** = modèle de (gestion des accès à la) mémoire; **memory protect** = (dispositif de) protection *f* de la mémoire; **memory-resident** = résident, -e; **the system can bomb if you set up too many memory-resident programs at the same time** = le système peut planter si vous introduisez un trop grand nombre de programmes résidents; **memory switching system** = système à transfert de mémoire; **memory workspace** = zone *f* de travail (en mémoire); *see also* HIGH, UPPER

QUOTE when a program is loaded into memory, some is used for the code, some for the permanent data, and some is reserved for the stack which grows and shrinks for function calls and local data
Personal Computer World

QUOTE The lower-power design, together with an additional 8Kb of on-board cache memory, will increase the chip's performance to 75 million instructions per second.
Computing

menu *noun* menu *m*; *(list of options available in a GUI)* **menu-bar** = barre *f* de menu; **menu-driven software** = logiciel *m* avec menu *or* à base de menu; *(one of the choices in a menu)* **menu item** = élément

m de menu; **menu selection** = sélection *f* par menu; **main menu** = menu principal; *(set of options displayed in the centre of the screen)* **pop-up menu** *or* **pop-down menu** = fenêtre *f* de menu; *(set of options displayed below an entry on a menu-bar)* **pull-down menu** = menu déroulant; **the pull-down menu is viewed by clicking on the menu bar at the top of the screen** = le menu déroulant est affiché en cliquant sur la barre de menu au sommet de l'écran

QUOTE when the operator is required to make a choice a menu is displayed
Micro Decision

QUOTE The London Borough of Hackney has standardised on terminal emulator software from Omniplex to allow its networked desktop users to select Unix or DOS applications from a single menu.
Computing

mercury delay line *noun (old method of storing data)* ligne *f* à *or* de retard au mercure

merge *verb* fusionner *or* intégrer *or* combiner; **the system automatically merges text and illustrations into the document** = ce système assure l'intégration automatique du texte et des illustrations dans le document; **merge sort** = (fonction de) tri *m* et fusion; *see also* MAIL-MERGE

mesh *noun* maille *f*; **mesh network** = réseau maillé *m*

message *noun* message *m*; **error message** = message d'erreur; **message authentication code (MAC)** = code d'identification de message; **message format** = format *m* de message; *(sequence of data at the beginning of a message)* **message header** = en-tête *m* de message; **message numbering** = numérotation *f* des messages; **message routing** = acheminement *m* des messages; *(number of bits)* **message slot** = créneau *m* pour message; **message switching** = commutation *f* de message; **message text** = texte *m* d'un message

metabit *noun* métabit *m*

◊ **metacompilation** *noun* métacompilation *f*

◊ **metafile** *noun (file that contains other files or that defines data about other files)* métafichier *m*; **the operating system uses a metafile to hold data that defines where each file is stored on disk** = le système d'exploitation utilise un métafichier qui contient les données qui définissent l'emplacement de chaque fichier sur le disque

◊ **metalanguage** *noun* métalangage *m*

metal oxide semiconductor (MOS) *noun* semi-conducteur *m* MOS; **metal oxide semiconductor field effect transistor (MOSFET)** = semi-conducteur à effet de champ MOSFET; **complementary metal oxide semiconductor (CMOS)** = semi-conducteur CMOS; **p-channel metal oxide semiconductor (PMOS)** = semi-conducteur PMOS

meter 1 *noun* compteur *m*; **electricity meter** =

compteur d'électricité; **a meter attached to the photocopier records the number of copies made** = un compteur relié au photocopieur enregistre le nombre de photocopies **2** *verb* enregistrer (le nombre et la durée); **the calls from each office are metered by the call logger** = le nombre et la durée des appels effectués dans chacun des bureaux sont enregistrés sur l'enregistreur d'appels

metre, *US* **meter** *noun (measure)* mètre *m*; **metre kilogram second (Ampere) (MKS(A)** = mètre kilogramme seconde (ampère) *or* mks(A)

metropolitan area network (MAN) *noun (network extending over a limited area)* réseau *m* urbain; *compare* LAN, WAN

MF = MEDIUM FREQUENCY

MFLOPS = MEGA FLOATING POINT OPERATIONS PER SECOND

MFM = MODIFIED FREQUENCY MODULATION

MFS = MACINTOSH FILING SYSTEM

MHz = MEGAHERTZ

MICR = MAGNETIC INK CHARACTER RECOGNITION

micro *noun* = MICROCOMPUTER

micro- *prefix* **(a)** *(one millionth)* micro-; **micrometre** = micromètre *m or* micron *m* **(b)** *(very small)* **microcassette** = microcassette *f*; **microchip** = puce *f*; **microcircuit** = microcircuit *m*; **microcode** = microcode *m or* micro-instruction *f*

Micro Channel Architecture (MCA) *(design of expansion bus in the PS/2 range of PCs)* architecture *f* MCA; *(number of electronic components)* **Micro Channel Architecture chipset** *or* **MCA chipset** = jeu *m* de composants MCA ◊ **Micro Channel Bus** *noun (32-bit expansion bus defined by IBM)* bus *m* Micro-Channel *or* bus MCA

Microcom Networking Protocol ™ **(MNP)** *(error detection and correction system developed by Microcom)* protocole *m* de communication de réseau Microcom (MNP)

microcomputer *or* **micro** *noun* micro-ordinateur *m or* micro *m*; **microcomputer architecture** = architecture *f* de micro-ordinateur; **microcomputer backplane** = fond *m* de panier *or* carte *f* mère d'un micro-ordinateur; **microcomputer bus** = bus *m* d'un micro-ordinateur; **microcomputer development kit** = kit *m* d'extension de micro-ordinateur; **single board microcomputer** = micro-ordinateur monocarte *or* à carte unique

◊ **microcomputing** *noun* micro-informatique *f*; **the microcomputing industry** = l'industrie *f* des micro-ordinateurs

microcontroller *noun* micro-ordinateur *m* de contrôle *or* de commande; **single-chip microcontroller** = micro-ordinateur de contrôle à puce unique

◊ **microcycle** *noun* microcycle *m*

◊ **microdevice** *noun* dispositif *m or* composant *m* de très petite dimension; *(microprocessor)* microprocesseur *m*

◊ **microelectronics** *noun* la micro-électronique

◊ **microfiche** *noun* microfiche *f*

◊ **microfilm 1** *noun* microfilm *m*; **we hold all our records on microfilm** = toutes nos archives sont sur microfilms **2** *verb* microfilmer; **the 1989 records have been sent away for microfilming** = nous avons envoyé les archives de 1989 pour les faire microfilmer *or* pour les faire mettre sur microfilm(s); *see also* CIM, COM

◊ **microfloppy** *noun (usually refers to 3.5 inch disks)* microdisquette *f or* disquette 3,5″

◊ **microform** *noun* microfiche *f*

micrographics *noun* micrographie *f*

◊ **microimage** *noun* micro-image *f*

microinstruction *noun* micro-instruction *f*

microphone *noun* microphone *m or* micro *m*; **dynamic microphone** = micro(phone) dynamique; **lapel microphone** = micro-cravate *m*; **moving coil microphone** = micro(phone) à aimant mobile

microphotography *noun* microphotographie *f*

microprocessor *noun* microprocesseur *m*; **bit-slice microprocessor** = microprocesseur en tranches; **the bit-slice microprocessor uses four 4-bit processors to make a 16-bit word processor** = le microprocesseur en tranches utilise quatre processeurs à 4 bits pour réaliser un microprocesseur à 16 bits; **microprocessor addressing capabilities** = capacité *or* facilité *f* d'adressage mémoire d'un microprocesseur; **microprocessor architecture** = architecture *f* d'un microprocesseur; **microprocessor chip** = puce *f or* microprocesseur; **microprocessor unit (MPU)** = microprocesseur

microprogram *noun* microprogramme *m*; **microprogram assembly language** = langage *m* d'assemblage pour microprogramme; **microprogram counter** = registre *m or* compteur *m* de microprogramme; **microprogram instruction set** = ensemble des instructions *or* jeu *m* d'instructions d'un microprogramme; **microprogram store** = mémoire *f* qui contient un microprogramme

◊ **microprogramming** *noun* micro-programmation *f*

microsecond (ms) *noun* microseconde *f*

microsequence *noun* séquence *f* de micro-instructions *or* d'instructions d'un microprogramme

Microsoft ™ *(developer and publisher of software)* (la société) Microsoft ™; *(operating system for IBM PC range)* **Microsoft DOS (MS-DOS)** = (système d'exploitation) MS-DOS; *(multi-tasking graphical operating system software)* **Microsoft Windows** = Microsoft Windows

microwave *noun* micro-onde *f*; *(frequency)* hyperfréquence *f*; **microwave amplification by stimulated emission of radiation (MASER)** = (amplificateur) MASER; **microwave communications link** = liaison *f* hertzienne *or* liaison de transmission par hyperfréquence; **microwave relay** = relais *m* hertzien; **microwave transmission** = transmission *f* hertzienne *or* par hyperfréquence

middleware *noun* progiciel *m* adapté aux besoins de l'utilisateur *or* progiciel personnalisé *or* sur mesure

MIDI = MUSICAL INSTRUMENT DIGITAL INTERFACE

mid-user *noun* utilisateur *m* intermédiaire

migration *noun* *(moving users from one hardware platform to another)* migration *f*; **data migration** = transfert *m* *or* migration de données

mike *noun* *(familiar)* microphone *m* *or* micro *m*

milk disk *noun* disque *m* à traiter *or* disque relais

◊ **milking machine** *noun* concentrateur *m* de données *or* capteur *m* de données (à traiter)

milli- *prefix* *(one thousandth)* milli-; **milliampere (mA)** = milliampère (mA) *m*; **millicoulomb (mC)** = millicoulomb (mC) *m*; **millisecond (ms)** = milliseconde (ms) *f*

million *number (1,000,000)* million *m* *(measure of processor speed)* **million instructions per second (MIPS)** = million d'instructions par seconde *or* MIPS

MIMD = MULTIPLE INSTRUCTION STREAM - MULTIPLE DATA STREAM

mini- *prefix* *(small)* mini; *(usually 3.5 inch)* **minidisk** = (mini)disquette *f*; *(slang)* **miniwinny** = minidisque dur (de type Winchester)

◊ **miniaturization** *noun* miniaturisation *f*

minicomputer *or* **mini** *noun* mini-ordinateur *m* *or* mini *m*

minimal *adjective* minimal, -e *or* minimum

◊ **minimal latency coding** *see* MINIMUM ACCESS CODE

◊ **minimal tree** *noun* arborescence *f* optimale

minmax *noun* méthode *f* mini/maxi

minimise *verb* **(a)** minimiser *or* réduire; **we minimized costs by cutting down the number of**

components = nous avons réduit les frais en diminuant le nombre des composants **(b)** *(shrink an application window to an icon)* réduire une fenêtre en icône; *compare* MAXIMISE

COMMENT: the application can continue to run in the background; you minimise a window by clicking once on the down arrow in the top right hand corner

◊ **minimize** = MINIMISE

minimum *noun* minimum *m*; **minimum access code** *or* **minimum delay code** *or* **minimum latency coding** = code *m* à temps d'accès optimisé; **minimum weight routing** = routage *m* optimisé

minuend *noun* nombre *m* duquel on soustrait

minus *or* **minus sign (-)** *noun* signe de la soustraction *or* (le signe) moins *m*

minuscule *noun* (lettre) minuscule *f*

MIPS = MILLION INSTRUCTIONS PER SECOND

QUOTE ICL has staked its claim to the massively parallel market with the launch of the Goldrush MegaServer, providing up to 16,000 Unix MIPS of processing power.
Computing

mirror 1 *noun* miroir *m* *or* glace *f*; **mirror disk** = disque *m* miroir; **mirror image** = image *f* inversée **2** *verb* **(a)** *(make an identical copy)* copier à l'identique **(b)** *(duplicate all disk operations onto a second disk)* faire une copie-miroir; **there's less chance of losing your data now that you have mirrored the server's disk drive** = vous avez moins de chance de perdre vos données, maintenant que vous avez fait une copie-miroir du disque du serveur

QUOTE disks are also mirrored so that the system can continue to run in the event of a disk crash

QUOTE mirroring of the database is handled automatically by systems software
Computer News

MIS **(a)** = MANAGEMENT INFORMATION SERVICE **(b)** = MANAGEMENT INFORMATION SYSTEM

MISD = MULTIPLE INSTRUCTION STREAM - SINGLE DATA STREAM

mismatch *noun* non accord *m* *or* désaccord *m* *or* discordance *f*; **impedance mismatch** = désaccord d'impédance

mission-critical *adjective* *(on which a company depends)* critique *or* vital, -e (pour l'entreprise); *(program on which a company depends)* **mission-critical application** = application *f* vitale *or* critique pour l'entreprise

mix 1 *noun* mélange *m* (sonore) *or* mixage *m* **2**

verb (signals) mélanger *or* faire un mixage; **to mix down** = mélanger *or* mixer

◊ **mixer** *noun* mélangeur *m or* mixeur *m*

◊ **mixing** *noun* **(a)** *(signals)* mixage *m*; **mixing studio** = studio de mixage **(b)** *(different typefaces)* (composition d'une ligne avec) mixage de polices de caractères *or* utilisant plusieurs polices de caractères

MKS(A) = METRE KILOGRAM SECOND (AMPERE)

MMI = MAN MACHINE INTERFACE

MMU = MEMORY MANAGEMENT UNIT

MNP ™ = MICROCOM NETWORKING PROTOCOL

mnemonic *noun* (procédé) mnémonique *m*; **assembler mnemonics** *or* **mnemonic operation codes** = codes *mpl* mnémoniques d'assemblage

mobile *adjective* mobile; **mobile earth terminal** = station *f* terrestre mobile; **mobile phone** = téléphone *m* mobile; **mobile unit** = unité *f* mobile

mock-up *noun* maquette *f*

modal *adjective* modal, -e

mode *noun* **(a)** *(way of doing something)* mode *m*; **when you want to type in text, press this function key which will put the terminal in its alphanumeric mode** = pour saisir un texte, appuyer d'abord sur cette touche de fonction qui met le terminal en mode alphanumérique; **bit-map mode** = mode point; **burst mode** = mode (de transfert par) paquets; **byte mode** = mode octet; **control mode** = mode de contrôle; **deferred mode** = mode différé *or* en (mode) différé; **direct mode** = mode direct *or* en (mode) direct; **execute mode** = mode (d') exécution; **form mode** = mode masque; **input mode** = mode (d') entrée; **insert mode** = mode insertion; **interactive mode** = mode interactif; **noisy mode** = mode bruyant; **replace mode** = mode remplacement; **sequential mode** = mode séquentiel **(b)** *(number of paths taken by light)* mode; **mode dispersion** = dispersion *f* modale **(c)** *(number that occurs most frequently)* mode (de la distribution)

model 1 *noun* **(a)** *(small-size copy)* maquette *f or* modèle *m* réduit; **he showed us a model of the new computer centre building** = il nous a fait voir la maquette du nouveau centre informatique **(b)** *(version)* modèle; **the new model B has taken the place of model A** = le nouveau modèle B remplace

le modèle A; **this is the latest model** = voici notre dernier modèle; **demonstration model** = modèle de démonstration **2** *verb* modéliser (NOTE: **modelling - modelled** but US **modeling - modeled**)

◊ **modelling** *noun* création *f* de modèles de programmes

modem = MODULATOR/DEMODULATOR modem *m*; *(cable that allows two computers to communicate via their serial ports)* **modem eliminator** = câble de liaison directe *or* de connexion série (sans modem); **dial-in modem** = modem à appel automatique; *(circuit that allows two computers to communicate via their serial ports)* **null modem** = (circuit *or* câble) de liaison directe *or* null modem; **this cable is configured as a null modem, which will allow me to connect these 2 computers together easily** = ce câble est configuré pour fonctionner sans modem et me permet de connecter ces deux ordinateurs facilement; *see also* STANDARD; *compare* ACOUSTIC COUPLER

modify *verb* modifier *or* adapter; **the keyboard was modified for European users** = le clavier a été adapté pour la vente en Europe; **we are running a modified version of the mail-merge system** = nous utilisons une version modifiée du programme d'édition de lettres types *or* de publipostage; **the software will have to be modified to run on a small PC** = il faudra modifier le logiciel pour pouvoir l'utiliser sur un PC

◊ **modification** *noun* modification *f or* changement *m*; **the modifications to the system allow it to be run as part of a LAN** = les modifications apportées au système permettent de l'utiliser sur un réseau local d'entreprise; **modification loop** = boucle *f* de modification

◊ **modified frequency modulation (MFM)** *noun* *(method of storing data on magnetic media)* norme *f* de codage MFM

◊ **modifier** *noun* modificateur *m*

Modula-2 *noun* *(high-level programming language derived from Pascal)* langage *m* Modula-2

modular *adjective* modulaire; **modular programming** = programmation *f* modulaire

◊ **modularity** *noun* modularité *f*; **the modularity of the software or hardware allows the system to be changed** = la modularité du logiciel ou du matériel permet de modifier le système

◊ **modularization** *noun* programmation *f* modulaire

modulate *verb* moduler; **modulated signal** = signal *m* modulé; **modulating signal** = signal *m* de modulation

◊ **modulation** *noun* modulation *f*; **amplitude**

modulation (AM) = modulation d'amplitude (MA); **frequency modulation (FM)** = modulation de fréquence (MF); **pulse modulation** = modulation d'impulsion

◊ **modulator** *noun* modulateur *m*; **modulator/demodulator (modem)** = modulateur-démodulateur *or* modem *m*

module *noun* **(a)** *(section of program)* module *m* **(b)** *(piece of hardware)* module; **a multifunction analog interface module includes analog to digital and digital to analog converters** = un module d'interface analogique multifonction comprend un convertisseur analogique-numérique et un convertisseur numérique-analogique

modulo arithmetic *noun* arithmétique à modulo; **modulo-N** = modulo-n; **modulo-N check** = contrôle *m* par modulo-n

modulus *or* **MOD** *or* **mod** *noun* modulo; **7 mod 3 = 1** = 7 modulo-3 = 1

momentary switch *noun* interrupteur *m* temporaire

monadic (Boolean) operator *noun* opérateur *m* monadique *or* à un opérande; **the monadic operator NOT can be used here** = l'opérateur monadique NOT peut être utilisé ici; **monadic operation** = opération *f* monadique

monitor 1 *noun* **(a)** moniteur *m* *or* écran *m* (de visualisation); **multi-scan** *or* **multi-sync monitor** = écran multistandard; **monitor unit** = moniteur **(b)** *(loudspeaker)* moniteur (retour de son); *(TV control screen)* moniteur (de contrôle d'image) **(c)** *(software)* **monitor program** = programme *m* de contrôle *or* programme moniteur; **firmware monitor** = moniteur intégré **(d)** *(system that watches for faults)* (dispositif de) contrôle *m*; **power monitor** = (dispositif de) contrôle de l'alimentation **2** *verb* vérifier; contrôler *or* surveiller *or* suivre; **he is monitoring the progress of the trainee programmers** = il contrôle *or* suit le progrès des programmeurs débutants; **the machine monitors each signal as it is sent out** = l'appareil contrôle chaque signal de sortie

mono- *prefix* mono

◊ **monoaural** *adjective* monaural, -e

◊ **monochrome** *adjective* & *noun* monochrome *or* noir et blanc; **monochrome monitor** = écran *m* monochrome *or* écran noir et blanc; *(video adapter standard)* **monochrome display adapter (MDA)** = standard d'affichage MDA; adaptateur (monochrome) MDA *or* carte MDA

◊ **monolithic** *adjective* (circuit intégré) monolithique

◊ **monomode fibre** *noun* fibre *f* optique monomode

◊ **monophonic** *adjective* monophonique

◊ **monoprogramming system** *noun* système *m* de monoprogrammation

◊ **monospacing** *noun* espacement *m* uniforme

◊ **monostable** *noun* (circuit) monostable *m*

Monte Carlo method *noun* méthode *f* de Monte Carlo

Morse code *noun* morse *m* *or* alphabet *m* morse; **morse key** = télégraphe *m* *or* manipulateur *m* morse

MOS = METAL OXIDE SEMICONDUCTOR semi-conducteur *m* MOS; *see also* MOSFET **MOS memory** = mémoire *f* MOS; **CMOS** = COMPLEMENTARY METAL OXIDE SEMICONDUCTOR semi-conducteur CMOS

QUOTE integrated circuits fall into one of two distinct classes, based either on bipolar or metal oxide semiconductor (MOS) transistors
Electronics & Power

mosaic *noun* mosaïque *f*

MOSFET = METAL OXIDE SEMICONDUCTOR FIELD EFFECT TRANSISTOR

most significant bit *or* **msb** *or* **MSB** *noun* bit de poids fort *or* le bit le plus significatif; **the most significant bit in an eight bit binary word represents 128 in decimal notation** = le bit le plus significatif dans un mot de huit bits représente 128 en numération décimale

◊ **most significant character** *or* **most significant digit (MSD)** *noun* chiffre de poids fort *or* le chiffre le plus significatif (NOTE: the opposite is **LSB, LSD**)

motherboard *noun* carte *f* mère

motion picture *noun* film *m* (cinématographique)

motor *noun* moteur *m*

Motorola ™ *(manufacturer of electronic components)* (la société) Motorola ™; *(processor used in the Macintosh)* **Motorola 68000, 68020, 68030** = (puces) Motorola 68000, 68020, 68030

mount *verb* **(a)** monter *or* fixer; **the chips are mounted in sockets on the PCB** = les puces sont montées dans des prises de la carte de circuit imprimé **(b)** *(insert a disk in a disk drive)* monter un disque

mouse *noun* souris *f*; *(mouse that connects to a special expansion card)* **bus mouse** = souris (de) bus; *(pointing device operated by moving it across a flat surface)* **mechanical mouse** = souris mécanique; *(pointing device operated by moving it across a special flat mat)* **optical mouse** = souris optique; *(mouse that connects to the serial port of a PC)* **serial mouse** = souris série; **mouse-driven (software)** = (logiciel) contrôlé *or* piloté par une souris; *(program)* **mouse driver** = (programme) pilote *m* de souris; *(small arrow on screen)* **mouse pointer** = pointeur *m* de souris *or* contrôlé par la souris (NOTE: the plural is **mice**)

QUOTE a powerful new mouse-based editor:- you can cut, paste and copy with the mouse
Personal Computer World

> QUOTE you can use a mouse to access pop-up menus and a keyboard for a word-processor
> *Byte*

> QUOTE This project has now borne fruit, with the announcement last week of Windots, a project which allows users to 'see' Windows screens in a Braille form of Ascii. Other areas of research include a sound system which allows a sound to 'move', mirroring the movement of a mouse.
> *Computing*

mouth *noun* ouverture *f or* bouche *f*

M out of N code *noun* code *m* N dont M

move *verb* déplacer *or* changer de place; **move block** = (instruction de) déplacer un bloc; **moving coil microphone** = microphone *m* à bobine *or* à aimant mobile

◊ **movable** *adjective (which can be moved)* mobile; *(which can be removed)* amovible

◊ **movement** *noun* mouvement *m*; **movement file** = fichier *m* (de) mouvements

MPU = MICROPROCESSOR UNIT

ms = MILLISECOND

MS = MANUSCRIPT (NOTE: plural is **MSS**)

msb *or* **MSB** = MOST SIGNIFICANT BIT

MSD = MOST SIGNIFICANT DIGIT

MS-DOS ™ = MICROSOFT DOS MS-DOS

MSI = MEDIUM SCALE INTEGRATION

M signal *noun* signal *m* groupé

MS-Windows = MICROSOFT WINDOWS

MSX *noun* norme *f or* standard *m* MSX

MTBF = MEAN TIME BETWEEN FAILURES

MTF = MEAN TIME TO FAILURE

multi- *prefix (many or more than one)* multi-; **multimegabyte memory card** = carte mémoire de plusieurs méga-octets; **a multistandard unit** = unité *f* multinorme *or* unité multistandard; **multi-access system** = système *m* à accès multiple *or* système multi-accès; **multi-address** *or* **multi-address instruction** = instruction *f* multi-adresse

◊ **multi-board computer** *noun* ordinateur *m* multicarte

◊ **multiburst signal** *noun* signal *m* multipaquet

◊ **multi-bus system** *noun* système *m* multibus *or* à bus multiples

◊ **multicasting** *noun* transmission *f* multicible

◊ **multichannel** *adjective* (système) multivoie

◊ **multicolour** *adjective* multicolore; *(colour graphics adapter standard)* **multicolor graphics adapter (MCGA)** = carte MCGA; standard MCGA (d'adaptateur graphique couleur)

◊ **multidimensional** *adjective* multidimensionnel, -elle; **multidimensional array** = tableau multidimensionnel; **multidimensional language** = langage multidimensionnel *or* multiniveau

◊ **multi-disk** *adjective* multidisque; **multi-disk option** = option *f* multidisque; **multi-disk reader** = lecteur *m* multidisque

◊ **multidrop circuit** *noun* circuit multipoint

MultiFinder ™ *(Apple Macintosh Finder that supports multitasking)* MultiFinder ™

multifrequency *noun* multifréquence *f*; **dual tone, multifrequency (DTMF)** = signalisation *f* multifréquence DTMF

◊ **multifunction** *adjective* multifonction *f*; **a multifunction analog interface module includes analog to digital and digital to analog converters** = un module d'interface analogique multifonction comprend un convertisseur analogique-numérique et un convertisseur numérique-analogique; **multifunction card** = carte *f* d'extension multifonction; **multifunction workstation** = poste *m* de travail multifonction

◊ **multifunctional** *adjective* multifonction; **a multifunctional scanner** = scanner *m* multifonction

◊ **multilayer** *noun* multicouche *or* à couches multiples

◊ **multilevel** *noun* multiniveau *or* à plusieurs niveaux

◊ **multilink system** *noun* système multiligne *or* à multiples connexions *or* système maillé

multimedia *adjective (combination of sound, graphics, etc.)* multimédia; **multimedia mail** = message multimédia; *(computer that can run multimedia applications)* **multimedia PC** = PC multimédia

> QUOTE The Oracle Media Server is a multimedia database designed to run on massively parallel computers, running hundreds of transactions per second and managing multiple data types, such as video, audio and text.
> *Computing*

multimeter *noun* multimètre *m*; **analog multimeter (AMM)** = multimètre analogique; **digital multimeter (DMM)** = multimètre numérique

◊ **multimode fibre** *noun* fibre *f* optique multimode

◊ **multi-part stationery** *noun* papier *m* (listing) en plusieurs épaisseurs

◊ **multipass overlap** *noun* impression *f* à passages multiples

◊ **multiphase program** *noun* programme *m* multiphase

multiple *adjective* multiple; **multiple access** = (à) accès *m* multiple; *see* MULTI-ACCESS **multiple address code** = code *m* multi-adresse; **multiple bus architecture** = architecture *f* à bus multiples; **multiple instruction stream - multiple data stream (MIMD)** = architecture *f* MIMD *or* architecture multiflux d'instruction - multiflux de données; **multiple instruction stream - single data stream (MISD)** = architecture *f* MISD *or* architecture multiflux d'instruction - monoflux de données; **multiple precision** = (en) multiple précision

multiplex *verb* multiplexer; **multiplexed analog components (MAC)** = format *m* MAC; **multiplexed bus** = bus *m* multiplexé

◊ **multiplexing** *noun* multiplexage *m*; **dynamic multiplexing** = multiplexage dynamique; **homogeneous multiplexing** = multiplexage homogène; **optical multiplexing** = multiplexage optique; *see also* TIME, FREQUENCY

◊ **multiplexor (MUX)** *noun* multiplexeur *m*; **a 4 to 1 multiplexor combines four inputs into a single output** = un multiplexeur 4/1 reçoit sur 4 canaux et émet sur un seul

> QUOTE the displays use BCD input signals and can be multiplexed to provide up to six digits
> *Electronics & Power*

multiplicand *noun* multiplicande *m*

◊ **multiplication** *noun* multiplication *f*; **the multiplication of 5 and 3 equals 15** = la multiplication de 5 par 3 donne 15 comme résultat; **multiplication sign (x)** = signe *m* de la multiplication

◊ **multiplier** *noun* multiplicateur *m*

◊ **multiply** *verb* (*perform the multiplication of a number by another number*) multiplier

multipoint *adjective* multipoint

◊ **multiprecision** *noun* (en) multiple précision

◊ **multiprocessing** *noun* multitraitement *m*

◊ **multiprocessing system** *noun* système *m* multiprocesseur *m*

◊ **multiprocessor** *noun* multiprocesseur *m*; **multiprocessor interleaving** = multitraitement *m*

◊ **multi-programming** *noun* multi-programmation *f*

multi-scan monitor *noun* (*can lock onto the scanning frequency of any type of graphics card*) moniteur *m* multistandard

multi-statement line *noun* ligne *f* multi-instruction

◊ **multi-strike printer ribbon** *noun* ruban *m* multifrappe

multitasking *or* **multi-tasking** *noun* multitâche *f*; **the system is multi-user and multi-tasking** = c'est un système multi-utilisateur et multitâche; **real-time multitasking** = multitâche en temps réel

> QUOTE this is a true multi-tasking system, meaning that several computer applications can be running at the same time
> *Which PC?*

> QUOTE page management programs are so greedy for memory that it is not a good idea to ask them to share RAM space with anything else, so the question of multi-tasking does not arise here
> *Desktop Publishing*

> QUOTE X is the underlying technology which allows Unix applications to run under a multiuser, multitasking GUI. It has been adopted as the standard for the Common Open Software Environment, proposed recently by top Unix vendors including Digital, IBM and Sun.
> *Computing*

multi-terminal system *noun* système *m* à plusieurs terminaux *or* système multiposte

◊ **multithread** *noun* programme *m* à plusieurs branches

◊ **multi-user system** *noun* système multi-utilisateur *or* système multiposte; **the program runs on a standalone machine or a multi-user system** = on peut exécuter le programme sur un ordinateur indépendant ou sur un système multiposte

◊ **multivibrator** *noun* multivibrateur *m*; **astable multivibrator** = multivibrateur astable

◊ **multi-window editor** *noun* logiciel *m* (de traitement de texte) multifenêtre

◊ **multi-windowing** *noun* multifenêtrage *m*

mung up *verb* (*informal*) bouffer *or* altérer *or* ruiner (des données *or* un fichier)

mush *noun* (*informal*) purée *f or* brouillard *m*; **mush area** = zone *f* de brouillage *or* de purée

music chip *noun* circuit *m* intégré générateur de son; **music synthesizer** = synthétiseur *m* de son

◊ **musical instrument digital interface (MIDI)** *noun* (*interface that connects electronic instruments*) interface *f* numérisée pour instruments de musique *or* interface *f* MIDI

> COMMENT: the MIDI interface carries signals from a controller or computer that instructs the different instruments to play notes

muting *noun* assourdissement *m or* réduction *f* de bruit; **interstation muting** = réduction du bruit d'interférence interstation

MUX = MULTIPLEXOR multiplexeur *m*

MW = MEDIUM WAVE

Nn

n *prefix (nano-)* n *or* nano-

NAK *or* **NACK** = NEGATIVE ACKNOWLEDGEMENT

name *noun* **(a)** nom *m*; **brand name** = (nom de) marque *f* **(b)** *(to identify an address)* nom; **file name** = nom de fichier; **program name** = nom de programme; *(symbol table)* **name table** = table de noms *or* de symboles; **variable name** = nom de variable

NAND function *noun* fonction *f* NON-ET *or* NAND; **NAND gate** = porte *f or* circuit *m* NON-ET *or* NAND

nano- *or* **n** *prefix (one thousand millionth or one billionth)* nano- (n); **nanocircuit** *or* **nanosecond circuit** = circuit *m* (électronique *or* logique) à délai de réponse de l'ordre de la nanoseconde; **nanometre (nm)** = nanomètre *m*; **nanosecond** *or* **ns** = nanoseconde (ns) *f* (NOTE: US billion is the same as UK one thousand million (10 to the power of nine); UK billion is one million million (10 to the power of 10)

narrative *noun (explanatory notes)* commentaire *m*

◊ **narrative statement** *noun* déclaration *f* (de procédure)

narrow band *noun* bande *f* étroite; **narrow band FM (NBFM)** = (système de) modulation *f* de fréquence à bande étroite

National Television System Committee (NTSC) *noun (used mainly in the USA and in Japan)* Comité National de Normalisation de la Télévision; **NTSC standards** = normes *fpl* NTSC; *see also* VIDEO STANDARDS

native *adjective* natif, -ive; *(compiler that produces code that will run on the same system)* **native compiler** = compilateur natif *or* originel; *(default file format)* **native file format** = format de fichier natif; *(first format)* **native format** = format natif; *(language that can be executed without any special software)* **native language** = langage natif *or* de constructeur

natural *adjective* naturel, -elle; **natural binary coded decimal (NBCD)** = (codage) décimal codé binaire naturel; **natural language** = langage *m* naturel; **the expert system can be programmed in a natural language** = le système expert peut être programmé en langage naturel

NBCD = NATURAL BINARY CODED DECIMAL

NBFM = NARROW BAND FREQUENCY MODULATION

NC = NUMERICAL CONTROL

n-channel metal oxide semiconductor *noun* semi-conducteur *m* MOS à canal (de type) N

NCR paper = NO CARBON REQUIRED paper; *(special type of carbonless paper)* papier NCR *or* autocopiant

NDIS = NETWORK DRIVER INTERFACE SPECIFICATION

NDR = NON DESTRUCTIVE READOUT

near-letter-quality (NLQ) *noun (of dot-matrix printer)* qualité *f* courrier; **switch the printer to NLQ for these form letters** = mettez l'imprimante en mode courrier pour imprimer ces lettres types

needle *noun (on dot matrix printer)* aiguille *f*

negate *verb (to reverse the sign of a number)* inverser *or* affecter d'un signe négatif *or* qualifier négativement; **if you negate 23.4 the result is −23.4** = la valeur négative *or* l'opposé de 23,4 est −23,4

◊ **negation** *noun (reversing the sign of a number)* négation *f or* inversion *f*

◊ **negative 1** *adjective (meaning 'no')* négatif, -ive; *(indicates signal incorrectly or incompletely received)* **negative acknowledgement (NAK *or* NACK)** = accusé *m* de réception négatif (NACK); **negative feedback** = rétroaction négative; **negative number** = nombre négatif; **negative-true logic** = logique *f* négative **2** *noun (film)* négatif *m or* épreuve *f* négative; **contact negative** = (film) négatif contact

neither-nor function *noun (logical function)* fonction *f* NON-OU *or* NI

NEQ = NON-EQUIVALENCE **NEQ function** = *(logical function)* fonction *f* de disjonction *or* OU exclusif; **NEQ gate** = porte *f or* circuit *m* OU-exclusif

nest *verb (loop or subroutine)* imbriquer *or*

emboîter; **nested loop** = boucle *f* imbriquée *or* emboîtée; *(macro called from within another macro)* **nested macro call** = appel *m* de macro imbriqué; *(section of a program)* **nested structure** = structure imbriquée; *(of loops)* **nesting level** = niveau *m* d'imbrication (de boucles); **nesting store** = mémoire *f* à liste permutée

net *noun* = INTERNET

> QUOTE During 1996 we will see changes that will turn the net from an elitist gizmo into the business tool no company can afford to ignore
> *The Times*

NetBIOS = NETWORK BASIC INPUT OUTPUT SYSTEM

netsurfer *noun see* SURFER

◊ **netsurfing** *noun see* SURFING

network 1 *noun* réseau *m*; **communications network** = réseau de communication *or* de télécommunications; **computer network** = réseau d'ordinateurs *or* réseau informatique; **information network** = réseau informatique; **local area network (LAN)** = réseau local (d'entreprise); **long haul network** = réseau à (grande) distance; *(system running an artificial intelligence program)* **neural network** = réseau neural *or* neuro-réseau *m*; **radio network** = réseau radiophonique; **television network** = réseau de télévision; **wide area network (WAN)** = réseau étendu *or* à distance; *(board that connects a computer to a network)* **network adapter** = carte *f* réseau; *(person responsible for looking after a network)* **network administrator** = administrateur *m* de réseau; **network analysis** = analyse *f* de réseaux; **network architecture** = architecture *f* de réseau; *(standard set of commands)* **Network Basic Input Output System (NetBIOS)** = NetBIOS (système *or* noyau de base pour gérer les entrées et sorties de réseau); **this software uses NetBIOS calls to manage file sharing** = ce logiciel utilise les appels NetBIOS pour gérer le partage des fichiers; **network control program** = programme *m* de contrôle de réseau; **network controller** = contrôleur *m* de réseau; **network database** = base *f* de données en réseau; *(software which controls a network adapter card)* **network device driver** = gestionnaire *m* de périphérique de réseau; **network diagram** = diagramme *m* (de configuration *or* de topologie) de réseau; *(directory stored on a disk drive on another computer in the network)* **network directory** = répertoire *m* de réseau; *(disk drive that is part of another computer on a network)* **network drive** = disque *m* serveur *or* unité *f* de disque (dur) d'un réseau; *(standard command interface between network driver software and network adapter card - defined by Microsoft)* **network driver interface specification (NDIS)** = norme *f* NDIS *or* norme d'interface gestionnaire de réseaux; **network hardware** = matériel *m* *or* équipements *mpl* de réseau (informatique); *(board that connects a computer to a network)* **network interface card (NIC)** = carte *f* (interface de) réseau; *(ISO/OSI standard layer)* **network layer** = couche *f* réseau; *see also* LAYER **network management** = gestion *f* de réseau; **network manager** = gestionnaire *m* de

réseau; *(operating system running on a server computer)* **network operating system (NOS)** = système d'exploitation de réseau *or* NOS; *(printer attached to a server)* **network printer** = imprimante *f* de réseau *or* imprimante partagée; **network processor** = processeur *m* de réseau; *(handshaking signals)* **network protocol** = protocole *m* (de communication) de réseau; *(extra links)* **network redundancy** = liaisons *fpl* redondantes *or* auxiliaires d'un réseau; *(computer which runs a network operating system)* **network server** = serveur *m* de réseau; **network software** = logiciel *m* de réseau; **network structure** = structure *f* en réseau; **network timing** = synchronisation *f* de réseau; *(arrangement of links within a network)* **network topology** = configuration *f* *or* topologie *f* de réseau **2** *verb* disposer *or* configurer en réseau; **they run a system of networked micros** = ils exploitent un réseau de micros; **the workstations have been networked together rather than used as standalone systems** = les postes de travail ont été reliés en réseau plutôt que d'être utilisés indépendamment; **networked TV programme** = programme *m* transmis sur (tout) un réseau de télévision

◊ **networking** *noun* **(a)** *(TV or radio)* transmission *f* *or* diffusion *f* sur (tout) un réseau **(b)** *(organization of a computer network)* configuration *f* de réseau; *(interconnecting computers)* mise *f* en réseau (d'ordinateurs); **networking hardware** *or* **network hardware** = matériel *m* *or* équipements *mpl* de réseau *or* en réseau; **networking software** *or* **network software** = logiciel *m* de *or* pour réseau; **networking specialist** = expert *m* *or* spécialiste *m&f* en réseaux informatiques; **this computer firm is a UK networking specialist** = cette société informatique est une société britannique spécialisée en réseaux

> QUOTE the traditional way of operating networks involves having a network manager and training network users to familiarize themselves with a special set of new commands
> *Which PC?*

> QUOTE workstations are cheaper the more you buy, because they are usually networked and share resources
> *PC Business World*

> QUOTE Asante Technologies has expanded its range of Ethernet-to-LocalTalk converters with the release of AsantePrint 8, which connects up to eight LocalTalk printers, or other LocalTalk devices, to a high-speed Ethernet network.
> *Computing*

neutral *adjective* neutre; **neutral transmission** = transmission *f* neutre

new *adjective (recent)* nouveau, nouvelle *or* récent, -e; **they have installed a new computer system** = ils ont installé un nouveau système informatique *or* un nouvel ordinateur; *(command)* **new (command)** = (commande de lancement d'une) nouvelle tâche; **new line character** = caractère *m* indiquant d'aller à la ligne *or* de retour à la ligne; *see also* CARRIAGE RETURN (CR); LINEFEED (LF); **new technology** = nouvelle technologie *or* techniques nouvelles

◊ **news** *noun (radio or TV)* informations *fpl or* nouvelles *fpl; (in newpapers)* **business news** = chronique *f* économique; **financial news** = chronique financière; **news agency** = agence *f* de presse; **news release** = communiqué *m* de presse; **the company sent out a news release about the new laser printer** = la société a diffusé un communiqué au sujet de la nouvelle imprimante laser

◊ **newsletter** *noun* **company newsletter** = bulletin *m* (d'informations) de la société

◊ **newsprint** *noun* papier *m* journal

next instruction register *noun* registre *m* d'instruction à exécuter *or* de la prochaine instruction

nexus *noun* connexion *f*

nibble *or* **nybble** *noun (half the length of a standard byte)* demi-octet *m* (NOTE: a nibble is normally 4 bits, but can vary according to different micros or people)

NIC = NETWORK INTERFACE CARD

nil pointer *noun* marqueur *m* de fin de liste

nine's complement *noun* complément *m* à neuf

n-key rollover *noun (using a buffer to provide key stroke storage)* mémoire *f* tampon (de clavier) chronologique à n positions

n-level logic *noun* logique *f* à n niveau(x)

NLQ = NEAR-LETTER-QUALITY

nm = NANOMETRE

NMI = NON-MASKABLE INTERRUPT

NMOS = N-CHANNEL METAL OXIDE SEMICONDUCTOR

no-address operation *noun* opération *f* sans adresse *or* non adressable

no-op = NO-OPERATION

◊ **no-operation** *or* **no-op instruction** *noun* instruction *f* vide *or* factice *or* de remplissage

◊ **no parity** *noun (data transmission which does not use a parity bit)* sans (bit de) parité

node *noun* noeud *m*; **a tree is made of branches that connect together at nodes** = une arborescence est formée de branches reliées les unes aux autres par des points de liaison ou noeuds; **this network has fibre optic connection with nodes up to one kilometre apart** = ce réseau est relié par fibres optiques avec des noeuds pouvant être positionnés jusqu'à un kilomètre les uns des autres

noise *noun* bruit *m or* (bruits) parasites *(mpl) or* brouillage *m*; **noise immunity** = insensibilité *f or* tolérance *f* au bruit; **noise margin** = marge *f* de bruit *or* limite *f* de tolérance au bruit; **noise temperature** = température *f* de bruit; **galactic noise** = bruits cosmiques; **impulsive noise** = bruit intermittent; **thermal noise** = bruit thermique

QUOTE the photographs were grainy, out of focus, and distorted by signal noise

Byte

nomenclature *noun* nomenclature *f*

nomogram *or* **nomograph** *noun* nomographe *m or* abaque *m*

non- *prefix* non-

◊ **nonaligned** *adjective* désaligné, -ée *or* non-aligné, -ée; **nonaligned read head** = tête de lecture désalignée

◊ **non-arithmetic shift** *noun* décalage *m* logique; *also* LOGICAL SHIFT

◊ **non-breaking space** *noun (space character that prevents two words being separated)* espace *m* sans rupture

◊ **noncompatibility** *noun* incompatibilité *f or* non compatibilité

◊ **non-dedicated server** *noun (computer that runs a network operating system in the background)* serveur *m* non-dédié

◊ **non-destructive cursor** *noun* curseur *m* non destructif; **the screen quickly becomes unreadable when using a non-destructive cursor** = l'écran devient rapidement illisible lorsqu'on utilise le curseur non destructif; **non-destructive readout (NDR)** = lecture *f* non destructive; **non-destructive test** = essai *m* non destructif; **I will carry out a number of non-destructive tests on your computer: if it passes, you can start using it again** = je vais effectuer une série de tests non destructifs sur votre machine; si tout se passe bien, vous pourrez vous en servir de nouveau

◊ **non-equivalence function (NEQ)** *noun* fonction *f* de disjonction *or* OU exclusif; **non-equivalence gate** = porte *f or* circuit *m* OU exclusif

◊ **nonerasable storage** *noun* mémoire *f* permanente *or* qui ne peut être effacée *or* ineffaçable; **paper tape is a nonerasable storage** = une bande papier perforée est une mémoire qui ne peut être effacée

◊ **non-impact printer** *noun* imprimante *f* sans impact

◊ **non-interlaced** *adjective (system in which the picture electron beam scans each line of the display once)* non entrelacé, -ée

◊ **nonlinear** *adjective* non-linéaire

◊ **non-maskable interrupt (NMI)** *noun* interruption *f* obligatoire *or* qui ne peut être invalidée *or* qui ne peut être masquée

◊ **non-operable instruction** *noun* instruction *f* factice *or* nulle *or* de remplissage

◊ **non-printing codes** *noun* code *m*

paramétrique *or* de paramétrage de l'imprimante; **the line width can be set using one of the non-printing codes, .LW, then a number** = la largeur des lignes peut être définie par le code paramétrique .LW suivi d'un chiffre

◊ **non return to zero (NRZ)** *noun* non-retour *m or* non-remise *f* à zéro

◊ **non-scrollable** *adjective* qu'on ne peut pas faire défiler (sur l'écran)

◊ **non-volatile** *adjective (retains data even when the power has been switched off)* non-volatile; **non-volatile memory** *or* **non-volatile store** *or* **storage** = mémoire *f* non-volatile; **bubble memory is a non-volatile storage** = la mémoire à bulles est une mémoire non-volatile; **using magnetic tape provides non-volatile memory** = une bande magnétique constitue une mémoire non-volatile (NOTE: opposite is **volatile)**

> QUOTE 100 sets of test results can be stored in non-volatile memory for later hard-copy printout.
>
> *Computing*

NOR function *noun (logical function)* fonction *f* NON-OU *or* NI; **NOR gate** = porte *f or* circuit *m* NON-OU *or* NI

normal *adjective* normal, -e; **the normal procedure is for backup copies to be made at the end of each day's work** = la procédure normale préconise une sauvegarde de tout le travail en fin de journée; *(structuring information in a database)* **normal form** = forme normale; **normal format** = format normal *or* standard; **normal range** = gamme *or* fourchette *or* plage normale

◊ **normalize** *verb* **(a)** *(to convert data)* normaliser **(b)** *(to convert characters)* uniformiser (en majuscule *or* en minuscules); mettre en mode majuscule *or* minuscule **(c)** *(to store and represent numbers)* normaliser *or* formater (un nombre, une donnée); **all the new data has been normalized to 10 decimal places** = toutes les nouvelles données sont normalisées à dix positions décimales; *(floating point number)* **normalized form** = forme normalisée

◊ **normalization** *noun* normalisation *f or* formatage *m*; *(normalizes a floating point number)* **normalization routine** = routine *f* de normalisation

NOS = NETWORK OPERATING SYSTEM

NOT function *noun (logical inverse function)* fonction *f* NON *or* fonction complément; **NOT gate** = porte *f or* circuit *m* NON *or* circuit inverseur; **NOT-AND (NAND)** = fonction NON-ET *or* NAND

notation *noun* **(a)** numération *f*; **binary notation** = numération binaire; **decimal notation** = numération décimale; **hexadecimal notation** = numération hexadécimale **(b)** notation *f*; **infix notation** = notation infixée; **octal notation** = notation octale; **postfix notation** = notation suffixée *or* notation polonaise inversée; **normal notation: (x-y) + z, but using postfix notation: xy - z**

+ = alors que la notation conventionnelle s'écrit: (x-y) + z, la notation polonaise inversée s'écrit: xy- z+; **prefix notation** = notation préfixée *or* notation polonaise (préfixée); **normal notation: (x-y) + z, but using prefix notation: - xy + z** = notation normale: (x-y) + z, notation polonaise (préfixée): - xy + z

notched *see* EDGE NOTCHED CARD

notepad *noun* bloc-notes *m*; **screen notepad** = bloc-notes d'écran *or* fenêtre *f* bloc-notes

notice board *noun* tableau *m* d'affichage

Novell ™ *(company that produces network software)* (la société) Novell ™

n-plus-one address instruction *noun* instruction à n adresse(s) plus une

npn transistor *noun* transistor *m* (de type) npn

NRZ = NON RETURN TO ZERO

ns = NANOSECOND

NTSC = NATIONAL TELEVISION SYSTEM COMMITTEE

> QUOTE the system has a composite video output port that conforms to the NTSC video specification
>
> *Byte*

n-type material *or* **N-type material** *or* **n-type semiconductor** *noun* matériau *m* semi-conducteur de type N; *see also* NPN TRANSISTOR

NuBus ™ *noun (high-speed expansion bus)* NuBus ™ (extension de bus à 96 connecteurs utilisé par les Macintosh de Apple)

null *noun (nothing)* nul, nulle; **null character** = caractère nul *or* de remplissage; **null instruction** = instruction nulle *or* factice *or* de remplissage; **null list** = liste vide; **null modem** = sans modem *or* null modem; **this cable is configured as a null modem, which will allow me to connect these two computers together easily** = ce câble est configuré sans modem ce qui permet de connecter les deux ordinateurs sans difficulté; *(that only contains zeros)* **null set** = jeu *m* de caractères nuls; *(that contains no characters)* **null string** = chaîne *f* vide; *(has a null character to indicate the end)* **null terminated string** = chaîne *f* de caractères terminée par le caractère nul

> QUOTE you have to connect the two RS232 ports together using a crossed cable, or null modem
>
> *PC Business World*

Num Lock key *noun (key on a keyboard)* touche *f* de blocage du pavé numérique

number 1 *noun* **(a)** nombre *m*; **number cruncher** = processeur *m* mathématique pour calcul ultra-rapide; **number crunching** = calcul ultra-rapide *or* opérations numériques ultra-rapides; **a very powerful processor is needed for graphics applications which require extensive number crunching capabilities** = il faut un processeur très puissant pour les applications graphiques qui exigent une capabilité de calcul ultra-rapide; **number range** = gamme *f* de valeurs **(b)** *(written figure)* chiffre *m or* numéro *m*; **each piece of hardware has a production number** = chacune des pièces de l'ordinateur possède un numéro de fabrication; *(for parity or error detection)* **check number** = chiffre *m or* clé *f* (numérique) de contrôle **2** *verb* **(a)** *(a document)* numéroter; **the pages of the manual are numbered 1 to 395** = les pages de ce manuel sont numérotées de 1 à 395 **(b)** *(items on a list)* numéroter

◊ **numeral** *noun* chiffre *m*; *(written 1, 2, 3, 4, etc.)* **Arabic numerals** = chiffres arabes; *(written I, II, III, IV, etc.)* **Roman numerals** = chiffres romains

◊ **numeric** *adjective* numérique *or* numéral, -e;

numeric array = tableau *m* numérique *or* de chiffres; **numeric character** = lettre *f* numérale *or* caractère *m* (à valeur) numérique; **numeric keypad** = pavé *m or* clavier *m* numérique; **numeric operand** = opérande *m* numérique; **numeric pad** = pavé *or* clavier numérique; **numeric punch** = perforation *f* numérique

QUOTE Hewlett-Packard's 100LX Palmtop PC weighs 11oz and has a separate numeric keypad.

Computing

◊ **numerical** *adjective (referring to numbers)* numérique; **numerical analysis** = analyse *f* numérique; **numerical control (NC)** *or* **computer numerical control (CNC)** = commande *f or* contrôle *m* numérique

nybble *or* **nibble** *noun (informal) (half the length of a standard byte)* demi-octet *m* (NOTE: a nybble is normally 4 bits, but can vary according to different micros)

Oo

OA = OFFICE AUTOMATION

object *noun* **(a)** *(data that makes a particular image)* objet *m* **(b)** *(variable in expert system)* objet *m* **(c)** *(data in a statement)* objet; **object architecture** *or* **object-orientated architecture** = architecture orientée vers l'objet *or* adaptée à l'ojet; **object code** = code *m* objet; **object computer** = ordinateur *m* d'exécution de programme objet; *(punched cards that contain a program)* **object deck** = jeu *m* (de cartes) objet; *(file containing object code)* **object file** = fichier *m* objet; **object language** = langage *m* objet; *compare with* SOURCE LANGUAGE; **object program** = programme *m* objet

◊ **object linking and embedding (OLE)** *noun (in Microsoft Windows: method of sharing data)* procédé *m* de liaison et incorporation d'objets *or* (procédé) OLE

◊ **object-oriented** *adjective (that uses objects)* orienté objet; *(image which uses vector definitions)* **object-oriented graphics** = graphique *m* orienté objet; **this object-oriented graphics program lets you move shapes around very easily** = ce programme graphique orienté objet vous permet de déplacer les formes très facilement; *(programming language used for object-oriented programming)* **object-oriented language** = langage orienté objet; *(method of programming, in which each element of the program is treated as an object)* **object-oriented programming (OOP)** = programmation orientée objet *or* POO

◊ **objective** *noun* **(a)** *(aim)* but *m or* objectif *m* **(b)** *(lens)* objectif

obtain *verb* obtenir *or* recevoir; **to obtain data from a storage device** = extraire des données rangées en mémoire; **a clear signal is obtained after filtering** = le filtrage permet d'obtenir un signal très clair

OCCAM langage *m* (de programmation) OCCAM

occur *verb* se produire *or* avoir lieu *or* survenir; **data loss can occur because of power supply variations** = les fluctuations de courant peuvent entraîner la perte de données

OCP = ORDER CODE PROCESSOR

OCR **(a)** = OPTICAL CHARACTER READER **(b)** = OPTICAL CHARACTER RECOGNITION **OCR font** = police *f* de caractères reconnaissable par lecteur optique

octal *adjective* octal, -e; *(digit 0 to 7 in the octal system)* **octal digit** = nombre *m* en base octale; **octal notation** = numération octale *or* en base 8; **octal scale** = base 8

octave *noun (series of eight musical notes)* octave *f*

octet *noun (group of eight bits)* octet *m*

odd *adjective (number)* impair, -e; **odd-even check** = contrôle *m* de parité paire-impaire; **odd parity (check)** = (contrôle de) parité *f* impaire

ODI = OPEN DATALINK INTERFACE

OEM = ORIGINAL EQUIPMENT MANUFACTURER

off-cut *noun (paper)* tombée *f*

off-hook *adverb (condition in a modem)* (mode) décroché

office *noun (room or building)* bureau *m*; **office automation (OA)** = bureautique *f*; **office computer** = ordinateur *m* de bureau *or* à usage professionnel; **office equipment** = équipement(s) *m(pl)* de bureau; **office of the future** = le bureau du futur; *see also* PAPERLESS OFFICE

off-line *adverb & adjective (peripheral or processing, etc.)* hors ligne *or* off-line; *(peripheral)* non-connecté, -ée *or* autonome; *(processing, etc.)* hors ligne *or* en différé; **before changing the paper in the printer, switch it off-line** = avant de remplacer le papier de l'imprimante, assurez-vous que l'imprimante est hors ligne *or* off-line; **off-line printing** = impression *f* hors ligne *or* en différé *or* par imprimante autonome; **off-line processing** = traitement *m* hors ligne *or* off-line *or* en différé; *(storage not currently available for access)* **off-line**

storage = stockage *m* hors ligne (NOTE: opposite is **on-line**)

offprint *noun* tiré *m* à part *or* copie *f*

off screen *adverb (TV action)* (action) hors champ

offset 1 *noun* **(a)** *(printing)* offset *m*; **offset lithography** = lithographie *f* offset; **offset printing** = impression *f* (en) offset **(b)** *(quantity added to a number)* valeur *f* complémentaire; *(value to be added to a base address)* **offset value** *or* **offset word** = valeur *or* adresse *f* relative

ohm *noun* ohm *m*; **this resistance has a value of 100 ohms** = la valeur de cette résistance est de 100 ohms; *(one thousand ohms)* **kilo-ohm** = kilo-ohm

◊ **Ohm's Law** *noun* loi *f* d'Ohm

OK *(prompt meaning 'ready')* OK; *(in a GUI: button used to start an action)* **OK button** = bouton OK

OLE = OBJECT LINKING AND EMBEDDING

omega wrap *noun (for threading video tape)* enrouleur-presseur *m* (de bande)

omission factor *noun* facteur *m* d'omission *or* de silence

omnidirectional *adjective* omnidirectionnel, -elle; **omnidirectional aerial** = antenne omnidirectionnelle; **omnidirectional microphone** = microphone omnidirectionnel

OMR (a) = OPTICAL MARK READER **(b)** = OPTICAL MARK RECOGNITION

on-board *adjective (on main PCB)* intégré, -ée au circuit

QUOTE the electronic page is converted to a printer-readable video image by the on-board raster image processor

QUOTE the key intelligence features of these laser printers are emulation modes and on-board memory

Byte

on chip *noun (circuit)* circuit *m* intégré à une puce

◊ **on-chip** *adjective* intégré, -ée à une puce; **the processor uses on-chip bootstrap software to allow programs to be loaded rapidly** = le processeur utilise un logiciel de lancement intégré à la puce, pour permettre le chargement rapide des programmes

one address computer *noun* ordinateur *m* à adresse unique; **one address instruction** = instruction *f* à adresse unique *or* à adresse directe

◊ **one element** *noun (logical function)* (opération) constante *f*

◊ **one for one** *noun (programming language)* (langage de programmation) un pour un

◊ **one-level address** *noun* adresse *f* directe *or* à un niveau; **one-level code** = code direct *or* à un niveau; **one-level store** = mémoire *f* à un niveau; **one-level subroutine** = sous-programme direct

one's complement *noun* complément *m* à 1; **the one's complement of 10011 is 01100** = le complément à 1 de 10011 est 01100

one-pass assembler *noun* assembleur *m* une passe; **this new one-pass assembler is very quick in operation** = ce nouvel assembleur une passe travaille très vite

◊ **one-plus-one address** *noun* une adresse plus une

one-time pad *noun (for coding system)* clé *f* (à usage) unique

one to zero ratio *noun* rapport *m* de discrimination *or* rapport un à zéro

on hook *adverb (modem)* (mode) (r)accroché

onion skin architecture *noun (computer design)* architecture *f* en pelure d'oignon; **the onion skin architecture of this computer is made up of a kernel at the centre, an operating system, a low-level language and then the user's program** = cet ordinateur possède une architecture en pelure d'oignon comprenant un noyau central, un système d'exploitation, un langage de bas niveau et le programme utilisateur

◊ **onion skin language** *noun* langage *m* en pelure d'oignon

on-line *adverb & adjective (processing or peripheral, etc.)* en ligne *or* on-line; *(peripheral)* relié, -ée *or* connecté, -ée; **the terminal is on-line to the mainframe** = le terminal est en ligne *or* relié à l'ordinateur principal *or* connecté à l'ordinateur principal; **on-line database** = base *f* de données en ligne; *(screen text that explains how to use the application)* **on-line help** = aide *f* en ligne; **on-line information retrieval** = recherche *f* documentaire en ligne; **on-line processing** = traitement *m* en ligne; **on-line storage** = stockage *m* de données en ligne; **on-line system** = système *m* en ligne *or* relié à l'ordinateur principal; **on-line transaction processing** = traitement transactionnel en ligne

on-screen *adjective (displayed on a screen)* (affiché, -ée) à l'écran *or* visualisé, -ée

on-site *adjective* sur place; **on-site maintainance** = service *m* d'assistance technique sur le lieu de travail; maintenance *f* sur site; **the new model has an on-site upgrade facility** = le nouveau modèle peut être optimisé sans renvoi chez le fournisseur

on the fly *adverb (without stopping the run)* à la volée

OOP = OBJECT ORIENTED PROGRAMMING

O/P *or* **o/p** = OUTPUT

opacity *noun (of optical lens)* opacité *f* (NOTE: opposite is **transmittance**)

op amp = OPERATIONAL AMPLIFIER

op code = OPERATION CODE

> QUOTE the subroutine at 3300 is used to find the op code corresponding to the byte whose hex value is in B
>
> *Computing Today*

opaque *adjective* opaque; **the screen is opaque - you cannot see through it** = l'écran étant opaque, il est impossible de voir au travers; **opaque projector** = épidiascope *m or* projecteur *m* de documents opaques

open 1 *adjective* **(a)** *(file)* ouvert, -e; **you cannot access the data unless the file is open** = vous ne pouvez accéder aux données que si le fichier est ouvert; *(file that can be read from or written to)* **open file** = fichier ouvert **(b)** *(not closed)* ouvert, -e; **open access** = (poste de travail) ouvert *or* à accès illimité *or* banalisé; *(computer designed to allow add-on hardware to be plugged in)* **open architecture** = architecture ouverte; **open code** = code ouvert; *(standard interface)* **open datalink interface (ODI)** = interface *f* ODI; *compare* NDIS **open-ended program** = programme extensible *or* ouvert; **open loop** = boucle ouverte; **open reel tape** = bande *f* sur bobine ouverte; **open routine** = routine ouverte; **open subroutine** = sous-programme ouvert; *(which can work with other systems)* **open system** = système ouvert; **Open Systems Interconnection (OSI)** = interconnexion *f* de systèmes ouverts (aux normes ISO); *see also* ISO/OSI LAYERS, INTERNATIONAL **2** *verb* **(a)** *(door or cover)* ouvrir; **first, open the disk drive door** = ouvrez d'abord la porte du lecteur de disquettes; **open the top of the computer by lifting** = soulevez le couvercle de l'ordinateur pour l'ouvrir **(b)** *(file)* ouvrir (un fichier); **you cannot access the data unless the file has been opened** = vous ne pouvez pas accéder aux données avant d'avoir ouvert le fichier

operand *noun* opérande *m*; **in the instruction ADD 74, the operator ADD will add the operand 74 to the accumulator** = par effet de l'instruction ADD 74, l'opérateur ADD va ajouter l'opérande 74 à l'accumulateur; **immediate operand** = opérande immédiat; **literal operand** = opérande littéral; **numeric operand** = opérande numérique; **operand field** = champ *m* d'opérande

operate *verb* faire marcher *or* faire fonctionner *or* mettre en marche; **do you know how to operate the telephone switchboard?** = savez-vous comment fonctionne le standard téléphonique?

◊ **operating** *noun* **operating code (op code)** = code *m* d'opération *or* de commande; **operating console** = poste *m or* station *f* de travail; **operating instructions** = commandes *fpl*; **operating system (OS)** = système *m* d'exploitation; **disk operating system (DOS)** = système *m* d'exploitation DOS; **operating time** = temps *m* d'exécution (d'une tâche)

◊ **operation** *noun* opération *f*; **arithmetic operation** = opération arithmétique; **binary operation** = opération binaire; **block operation** = manipulation *f* de bloc; **Boolean operation** = opération booléenne; **complete operation** = cycle *m* complet d'exécution d'une opération; **dyadic Boolean operation** = opération booléenne dyadique *or* à deux opérandes; **no-address operation** = opération non adressable; **no-operation instruction (no-op)** = instruction *f* vide *or* factice *or* de remplissage; **operation code (op code)** = code *m* d'opération; **operation cycle** = cycle d'opération; *see also* FETCH-EXECUTE CYCLE, MACHINE CYCLE **operation decoder** = décodeur *m* d'instruction; **operation field** = champ *m* d'opération; **operation priority** = ordre *m* de priorité des opérations; **operation register** = registre *m* d'opération; **operation time** = temps *m* d'exécution d'une opération; **operation trial** = essai *m or* test *m* opérationnel; **operations manual** = manuel *m* d'utilisation

◊ **operational** *adjective* opérationnel, -elle; **operational information** = notice *f* d'utilisation

◊ **operational amplifier (op amp)** *noun* amplificateur *m* operationnel

operator *noun* **(a)** *(person)* opérateur, -trice; **the operator was sitting at his console** = l'opérateur était assis devant l'écran de son ordinateur *or* à son pupitre; **computer operator** = opérateur *m*; **operator's console** = console *f or* pupitre *m* de commande *or* poste *m* de travail d'un opérateur; *(to work a machine)* **operator procedure (b)** *(character or symbol or word that defines a function or operation)* opérateur *m*; **x is the multiplication operator** = x est l'opérateur de la multiplication; **arithmetic operator** = opérateur *or* symbole *m* (d'une opération) arithmétique; *(assigning more than one function to an operator)* **operator overloading** = surcharge *f* d'un opérateur; *(order in which operations will be carried out)* **operator precedence** = ordre *m* de priorité des opérateurs; ordre d'enchaînement des opérations

op register *noun* registre *m* de code d'opération

optic fibres = OPTICAL FIBRES

optical *adjective* *(referring to or making use of light)* optique; **an optical reader uses a light beam to scan characters, patterns or lines** = un lecteur optique utilise un rayon lumineux qui balaye les caractères, les symboles ou les lignes; **optical bar reader** *or* **bar code reader** *or* **optical wand** = lecteur (optique) de codes barres *or* stylo *m* optique; **optical character reader (OCR)** = lecteur optique de caractères; **optical character recognition (OCR)** = reconnaissance *f* optique de caractères; **optical communications system** = système de communication optoélectronique; **optical data link** = liaison *f* optique pour transmission de données; **optical disc** = disque *m* optique; **optical fibre** = fibre *f* optique; **optical font** *or* **OCR font** = police *f* de caractères reconnaissable par lecture optique; **optical mark reader (OMR)** = lecteur optique de marques; **optical mark recognition (OMR)** = reconnaissance *f* optique de marques *or* de signes *or* de symboles; **optical memory** = mémoire *f* optique; *(pointing device operated by moving it across a special flat mat)* **optical mouse** =

souris *f* optique; **optical scanner** = scanner *m* (à reconnaissance optique); **optical storage** = *(action)* stockage *m* de données sur support optique; *(place)* mémoire *f* optique; **optical transmission** = transmission *f* par système optoélectronique; **optical wand** *or* **optical bar reader** = stylo *m* optique

optimization *noun* optimisation *f*

◊ **optimize** *verb* optimiser; **optimized code** = code accéléré *or* amélioré *or* optimisé

◊ **optimizer** *noun (program)* optimiseur *m*

◊ **optimizing compiler** *noun (compiler that analyses the machine code it produces to improve efficiency)* compilateur *m* d'optimisation

optimum *noun & adjective (best possible)* optimum *(m) or* optimal, -e; **optimum code** = code *m* optimal *or* code à temps d'accès minimum

option *noun* option *f*; **there are usually four options along the top of the screen** = on trouve habituellement quatre options affichées en haut de l'écran; **the options available are described in the main menu** = les options disponibles sont décrites dans le menu principal

◊ **optional** *adjective* optionnel, -elle; **the system comes with optional 3.5 or 5.25 disk drives** = le système est équipé d'un lecteur de disquettes 3,5 ou 5,25 pouces au choix

QUOTE with the colour palette option, remarkable colour effects can be achieved on an RGB colour monitor
Electronics & Wireless World

optoelectrical *adjective (which converts light to electrical signals or electrical signals into light)* optoélectrique

◊ **optoelectronic** *adjective* optoélectronique *or* optronique

◊ **optoelectronics** *noun* l'optoélectronique *f or* l'optronique *f*

optomechanical mouse *noun* souris *f* optomécanique; *see also* MOUSE

OR function *noun (logical function)* fonction *f* OU *or* OR; **OR gate** = porte *f or* circuit *m* OU *or* OR

orbit 1 *noun* orbite *f*; **the satellite's orbit is 100km from the earth's surface** = le satellite se déplace sur une orbite à 100km de la terre; **elliptical orbit** = orbite elliptique; **geostationary orbit** = orbite géostationnaire; **polar orbit** = orbite polaire 2 *verb* orbiter *or* parcourir une orbite *or* décrire une orbite; **this weather satellite orbits the earth every four hours** = ce satellite météorologique décrit une orbite autour de la terre toutes les quatre heures

order *noun* **(a)** *(instruction)* commande *f or* instruction *f*; **order code** = code *m* de commande *or* d'opération; *(in a multiprocessor system)* **order code processor (OCP)** = processeur *m* de codes de commande **(b)** *(disposition)* ordre *m*; **in**

alphabetical order = en *or* par ordre alphabétique 2 *verb* **(a)** *(to instruct)* donner une instruction **(b)** *(to put in order)* ordonner *or* classer; trier par clé(s); **ordered list** = liste dont les éléments sont classés (suivant un ordre déterminé)

organize *verb* organiser

◊ **organization** *noun* **(a)** *(way of arranging)* organisation *f*; **organization chart** = organigramme *m* **(b)** *(group of people)* organisation

◊ **organizational** *adjective* organisationnel, -elle

orientated *adjective* orienté, -ée; **problem-orientated language (POL)** = langage *m* de résolution de problèmes *or* langage adapté aux problèmes *or* langage d'application

◊ **orientation** *noun (direction of a page)* orientation *f* (paysage ou portrait)

origin *noun* **(a)** *(position on a screen)* origine *f* **(b)** *(location in memory)* adresse *f* origine

original 1 *adjective* original, -e 2 *noun* **(a)** *(document)* original *m*; **the original is too faint to photocopy well** = l'original n'est pas assez contrasté pour être photocopié **(b)** *(first disk or film or recording)* disque *or* film original *or* bande originale

◊ **original equipment manufacturer (OEM)** *noun (manufacturer of basic parts)* constructeur *m* de matériel informatique *or* OEM; *(company which produces equipment using basic parts made by other manufacturers)* assembleur *m or* OEM; **he started in business as a manufacturer of PCs for the OEM market** = il a commencé sa carrière comme assembleur de PC pour le marché OEM

originate *verb (to start)* produire *or* créer; *(to come from)* venir de *or* sortir de; **the data originated from the new computer** = les données viennent *or* sortent du nouvel ordinateur; *(modem that makes a call to another modem)* **originate modem** = modem d'appel *or* modem demandeur

◊ **origination** *noun* création *f or* production *f*; **the origination of the artwork will take several weeks** = la création de la maquette demandera plusieurs semaines; **data origination** = création de données

ortho film *or* **orthochromatic film** *noun* film *m* orthochromatique

orthogonal *adjective* orthogonal, -e

OS = OPERATING SYSTEM système *m* d'exploitation

◊ **OS/2** ™ *(multitasking operating system for PCs)* (système d'exploitation) OS/2 ™

oscillator *noun* oscillateur *m*

oscilloscope *noun* oscilloscope *m*

OSI = OPEN SYSTEMS INTERCONNECTION; *see also* ISO/OSI

out of band signalling *noun* signalisation *f* hors bande (vocale)

◊ **out of phase** *adverb* déphasé, -ée

◊ **out of range** *adjective* hors de portée *or* inaccessible *or* qui dépasse la capacité (d'un ordinateur, etc.)

outage *noun (of machine)* (temps de) non disponibilité *or* interruption *f* de service (d'un appareil)

outdent *verb* faire ressortir *or* faire déborder une ligne (dans la marge de gauche) (NOTE: opposite is **indent**)

outlet *noun* (point de) sortie *f*; *(electrical)* prise *f* de courant

outline *noun* profil *m* *or* esquisse *f*; **outline flowchart** = schéma *m* directeur; *(font stored as a set of outlines)* **outline font** = modèle de fonte *or* de police de caractères; *see also* BIT-MAP FONTS

◊ **outliner** *noun (program used to help a user order sections of a list)* utilitaire *m* de plan *or* description *f* de projet

output (o/p *or* **O/P) 1** *noun* **(a)** *(data)* sortie *f*; **computer output** = données *fpl* de sortie *or* sortie d'ordinateur (NOTE opposite is **input**) **(b)** *(action)* sortie; **output area** *or* **block** = zone *f* sortie (de la mémoire); *(processor)* **output bound** *or* **limited** = (processeur) limité *or* contraint par la vitesse de sortie des données *or* par le débit des données; **output buffer register** = registre *m* tampon de sortie; **output device** = périphérique *m* de sortie; **output file** = fichier de sortie; **output formatter** = formateur *m* de données de sortie; **output mode** = mode *m* sortie; *(allow a computer to output data)* **output port** = port *m* (de) sortie; **connect the printer to the printer output port** = connectez l'imprimante au port de sortie (d') imprimante; **output register** = registre *m* (de) sortie; **output stream** = flux *m* (de données) de sortie; **input/output (I/O)** = entrée/sortie *f*; *see also* INPUT **2** *verb* **(a)** *(data)* produire *or* sortir (des données) **(b)** transmettre *or* transférer; **finished documents can be output to the laser printer** = les documents qui sont prêts peuvent être transmis à l'imprimante laser (NOTE: **outputting - output**)

QUOTE most CAD users output to a colour plotter
PC Business World

OV = OVERFLOW

overflow (OV) *noun* **(a)** *(of storage system)* dépassement *m* de capacité; **overflow bit** *or* **flag** *or* **indicator** = bit *m* *or* drapeau *m* *or* indicateur *m* *or* balise *f* de dépassement de capacité; **overflow check** = contrôle *m* de dépassement de capacité **(b)** *(of line capacity)* débordement *m* de capacité (d'une ligne)

overhead *noun* **(a)** *(extra code)* code *m* *or* élément *m* de structure; **the line numbers in a BASIC program are an overhead** = les numéros de lignes sont des éléments de structure en BASIC;

overhead bit = bit *m* supplémentaire; **polling overhead** = temps *m* d'appels sélectifs **(b) overhead projector** = rétroprojecteur *m* **(c) routing overheads** = procédure *f* de contrôle d'acheminement *or* protocole *m* de routage (d'un message)

overheat *verb* chauffer *or* surchauffer; **the system may overheat if the room is not air-conditioned** = il se peut que le système chauffe si la pièce n'est pas climatisée

overink *verb* mettre trop d'encre *or* encrer de façon excessive

◊ **overinking** *noun* excès *m* d'encre; **two signatures were spoilt by overinking** = deux cahiers ont été gâchés par un excès d'encre

overlap 1 *noun* chevauchement *m* *or* recouvrement *m* *or* superposition *f*; *(printing)* **multipass overlap** = impression *f* à plusieurs passages légèrement décalés *or* surimpression *f* **2** *verb* (se) chevaucher *or* (se) recouvrir *or* (se) superposer

overlay *noun* **(a)** *(strip of paper placed over keys)* **keyboard overlay** = grille *f* d'aide *or* mémento *m* de fonction des touches de clavier **(b)** *(small section of a program)* section *f* de programme superposable *or* overlay *m* *or* fichier OVL; **form overlay** = texte *m* *or* graphique *m* préétabli (gardé en mémoire); *(software)* **overlay manager** = gestionnaire *m* de segment de recouvrement *or* d'overlay; *(area of main memory)* **overlay region** = zone *f* de segment de recouvrement *or* d'overlay; *(short sections of a long program)* **overlay segment** = segment *m* superposable *or* segment d'overlay

◊ **overlay network** *noun* réseau *m* à zone de recouvrement

◊ **overlaying** *noun* utilisation *f* d'une technique de recouvrement

QUOTE Many packages also boast useful drawing and overlay facilities which enable the user to annotate specific maps.
Computing

overload 1 *verb* surcharger; **the computer is overloaded with that amount of processing** = l'ordinateur est vraiment surchargé par tout ce travail **2** *noun* surcharge *f*; **channel overload** = surcharge de la voie

overmodulation *noun* surmodulation *f*

overpunching *noun* surperforation *f*

overrun 1 *noun* engorgement *m* **2** *verb* faire une erreur de synchronisation (en transmettant trop vite)

overscan *noun* balayage *m* hors champ *or* en dehors des limites

overstrike *verb (to print on top of an existing character)* faire une surcharge *or* faire une surimpression *or* superposer des caractères (pour créer un nouveau caractère)

overtones *noun see* HARMONICS

over-voltage protection *noun* (dispositif de) protection *f* contre le survoltage *or* la surtension

overwrite *verb (data)* (i) superposer des données *or* faire une superposition d'écriture (et détruire les données en mémoire); (ii) remplacer *or* effacer *or* détruire des données par superposition d'écriture; **the latest data input has overwritten the old information** = les nouvelles données ont remplacé les anciennes (par superposition d'écriture)

oxide *noun* oxyde *m*; **ferric oxide** = oxyde ferrique; **metal oxide semiconductors (MOS)** = semi-conducteurs *m* MOS; *see also* MOSFET, CMOS, NMOS

Pp

P = PETA

p = PICO-

PA = PUBLIC ADDRESS

PB = PETABYTE

p-channel *noun* canal (de type) P; **p-channel MOS** = semi-conducteur *m* MOS à canal de type P; *see also* P-TYPE SEMICONDUCTOR

P-code *noun* pseudocode *m or* pseudo-instruction *f*

PABX = PRIVATE AUTOMATIC BRANCH EXCHANGE

pack 1 *noun* **(a)** *(punched cards)* paquet *m*; **disk pack** = (pile de) plateaux *mpl* du disque dur **(b)** kit *m or* trousse *f* (d'outils *or* de nettoyage, etc.); **power pack** = bloc *m* d'alimentation **2** *verb* **(a)** *(goods)* emballer *or* conditionner; **the diskettes are packed in plastic wrappers** = les disquettes sont présentées sous emballage plastique **(b)** *(to store data in a reduced form)* condenser *or* comprimer *or* compacter; **packed decimal** = décimale condensée; **packed format** = format *m* condensé

package *noun* **(a) package deal** = contrat *m* global; forfait *m*; **we are offering a package deal which includes the whole office computer system, staff training and hardware maintenance** = nous offrons un contrat global comprenant un système informatique complet pour le bureau, la formation du personnel et l'entretien du matériel **(b) applications package** = programme *m* d'application *or* progiciel *m*; **software package** = progiciel *m or* package *m* (logiciel); **the computer is sold with accounting and word-processing packages** = l'ordinateur est vendu avec un progiciel de comptabilité et un progiciel de traitement de texte

◊ **packaged software** *noun* = SOFTWARE PACKAGE

◊ **packaging** *noun* **(a)** *(material)* emballage *m or* conditionnement *m*; **airtight packaging** = emballage hermétique **(b)** *(creating books for publishers)* création *f* de livres (par des maisons spécialisées) *or* packaging *m*

◊ **packager** *noun* *(of books)* packager *m or* packageur *m*

packet *noun* *(group of bits)* paquet *m*; **packet assembler/disassembler (PAD)** = assembleur/désassembleur *m* (de paquets); **the remote terminal is connected to a PAD device through which it accesses the host computer** = le terminal à distance est relié à un assembleur/désassembleur de paquets qui lui permet d'accéder à l'ordinateur hôte; **packet switched data service** *or* **packet switched network (PSN)** = réseau *m* de commutation de données par paquets; **packet switching** = commutation *f* (de messages) par paquets; **packet switching system (PSS)** = système *m* de transmission par paquets *or* PSS; *compare* STORE-AND-FORWARD

packing *noun* **(a)** *(of goods)* emballage *m or* conditionnement *m* **(b)** *(data)* compression *f or* condensation *m or* compactage *m*; **packing density** = densité *f* d'enregistrement; **packing routine** = routine *f* de compression *or* routine de compactage (NOTE: opposite is **padding**)

PAD = PACKET ASSEMBLER/DISASSEMBLER

pad 1 *noun* **(a)** *(of keys)* clavier *m or* pavé *m*; **cursor pad** = touches *fpl* fléchées *or* touches de contrôle (du curseur) *or* pavé *m* de commandes du curseur; **keypad** = pavé *or* clavier (numérique, etc.); **hex keypad** = clavier hexadécimal; **numerical keypad** = pavé *or* clavier numérique **(b) digitizing pad** = tablette *f* à numériser *or* tablette graphique; **graphics pad** = tablette graphique **2** *verb* remplir *or* rembourrer; **pad character** = caractère *m* de remplissage

◊ **padding** *noun* remplissage *m* *(characters added to fill out)* (caractères de) remplissage *m* (d'une chaîne de caractères) (NOTE: opposite is **packing**)

paddle *noun* manette *f*; **games paddle** = manette de jeu

page *noun* **(a)** *(sheet of paper)* page *f* **(b)** *(side of a printed sheet or text held on a computer screen)* page; **page break** = *(point at which a page ends)* fin *f* de page; *(marker)* caractère *m* de fin de page; **page description language (PDL)** = langage *m* de description de page; **page display** = affichage *m* d'une page; *(key that moves the cursor down)* **page down key** = touche *f* PgDn; touche page suivante; *(memory that holds the image)* **page image buffer** = mémoire *f* image de page; *(arrangement of a page)* **page layout** = mise *f* en page *or* présentation *f* de page; **we do all our page layouts using desktop publishing software** = nous faisons toute notre présentation *or* toute notre mise en page avec un logiciel de PAO; *(in wordprocessing)* **page length** = longueur *f* de page *or* nombre de lignes par page;

(pasting images and text into a page) **page makeup** = mise *f* en page(s); *(direction of the long edge of a page)* **page orientation** = orientation *f* de la page; *see* PORTRAIT, LANDSCAPE; *(speed of printer)* **pages per minute (ppm)** = (nombre de) pages par minute (ppm); **this laser printer can output eight pages per minute** = cette imprimante laser peut imprimer huit pages par minute; *(representation of how a page will look when printed)* **page preview** = aperçu *m* avant impression *or* prévisualisation *f*; **page printer** = imprimante *f* (par) page; **this dot-matrix printer is not a page printer, it only prints one line at a time** = cette imprimante matricielle n'est pas une imprimante page, elle n'imprime qu'une ligne à la fois; *(device which converts written information to a form that a computer can read)* **page reader** = lecteur *m* de page *or* scanner *m* page (avec reconnaissance de caractères); *(allowing a user to set up the margins, size of paper, etc.)* **page setup** = mise en page *or* définition *f* de page *or* édition *f* de page; *(key that moves the cursor up)* **page up key** = touche PgUp; touche page précédente **(c)** *(section of main store)* page (de mémoire); **multiple base page** = système *m* multipage; **page addressing** = adressage *m* de page; **page boundary** = limite *f* de page; *(address to which a page of memory can be mapped)* **page frame** = trame *f* de page; *(RAM designed to access sequential memory locations)* **page-mode RAM** = mémoire *f* RAM en mode page; **the video adapter uses page-mode RAM to speed up the display** = l'adaptateur vidéo utilise la mémoire vive en mode page pour accélérer l'affichage; **page protection** = protection *f* de page; **page table** = table *f* page *or* table de pages (de la mémoire paginée) **(d)** *(section of a main program)* page **2** *verb* **(a)** *(to use a radio-pager)* **to page someone** = appeler *or* chercher à joindre quelqu'un par système d'appel (de personne) *or* par signaleur d'appel *or* par bip **(b)** *(to make a text into page)* mettre en page; *(to put numbers onto pages)* paginer **(c)** *(to divide computer store into sections)* paginer

> QUOTE Mannesmann Tally has launched the T9005, a five-page-a-minute page printer designed to handle over 3,000 pages a month.
> *Computing*

◊ **paged address** *noun* *(physical memory address)* adresse *f* paginée; **paged memory** = mémoire *f* paginée; *(divides memory into pages)* **paged-memory scheme** = méthode de pagination (de la mémoire); *(electronic logic circuit)* **paged-memory management unit** = unité *f* de gestion de la mémoire paginée

◊ **pager** *noun* récepteur *m* de poche *or* signaleur *m* d'appel (pour système d'appel de personne) *or* bip *m*

◊ **pagination** *noun* *(dividing text into pages)* pagination *f*

◊ **paging** *noun* **(a)** *(technique that splits main memory)* pagination *f*; **paging algorithm** = algorithme *m* de pagination **(b)** *(calling someone on his pager)* appel *m* de personne *or* recherche *f* de

personne (par système d'appel); *see also* RADIO PAGING

paint 1 *noun* *(in a graphics program)* peinture *f* **2** *verb* *(in a graphics program)* peindre *or* colorier

◊ **paint program** *noun* *(allows a user to draw on screen in different colours)* logiciel *m* de dessin *or* de peinture; **I drew a rough of our new logo with this paint program** = j'ai fait une esquisse de notre nouveau logo en utilisant ce logiciel de dessin

> COMMENT: paint programs normally operate on bitmap images; drafting or design software normally works with vector-based images

paired registers *noun* registres *mpl* appariés *or* associés; **the 8-bit CPU uses a paired register to provide a 16-bit address register** = pour obtenir un registre d'adresse de 16 bits avec un processeur de 8 bits, on lui associe un deuxième registre (de 8 bits)

PAL = PHASE ALTERNATING LINE

palette *noun* palette *f* de couleurs

> QUOTE the colour palette option offers sixteen colours from a range of over four thousand
> *Electronics & Wireless World*

palmtop *noun* *(very small PC)* ordinateur *m* qu'on tient à la main; ordinateur de poche; **this palmtop has a tiny keyboard and twenty-line LCD screen** = cet ordinateur de poche a un clavier minuscule et un écran à cristaux liquides de 20 lignes

PAM = PULSE AMPLITUDE MODULATION

pan *verb* *(move a viewing window horizontally)* afficher (une image) par déplacement horizontal

panel *noun* *(flat section of a casing)* panneau *m*; **the socket is on the back panel** = la prise est située sur le panneau arrière; *(panel at the rear of a computer)* **back panel** = panneau *m* arrière; **control panel** = panneau de contrôle; **front panel** = panneau avant

Pantone Matching System ™ (PMS) *(method of matching colours)* système *m* (de référence de couleurs) Pantone ™; nuancier *m* Pantone

paper *noun* papier *m*; **the book is printed on 80gsm paper** = le livre est imprimé sur du papier 80 grammes; **glossy paper is used for printing half-tones** = on utilise du papier glacé pour l'impression de similigravures; **bad quality paper gives too much show-through** = un papier de mauvaise qualité est beaucoup trop transparent; **paper feed** = (dispositif d') entraînement *m* *or* alimentation *f* du papier; *US* **paper slew** = PAPER THROW **paper tape** = bande *f* papier; **paper tape punch** = poinçon *m* de perforation (pour bandes papier); **paper tape reader** = lecteur *m* de bandes perforées; **paper tape feed** = (dispositif d') entraînement de la bande papier; **paper throw** = saut *m* du papier; *(of printer)* **paper tray** *or* **paper**

bin = bac *m* à papier (pour l'alimentation en feuille à feuille) *or* bac à feuilles; *(used in printing)* **paper weight** = grammage *m*

◊ **paperback** *noun* livre *m* broché; livre de poche; **we are publishing the book as a hardback and as a paperback** = ce livre paraîtra en édition cartonnée et en livre de poche

◊ **paperbound** *adjective* (livre) broché *or* (édition) brochée

◊ **paper-fed** *adjective* **paper-fed scanner** = scanner *m* avec alimentation automatique du papier

◊ **paperless** *adjective* **paperless office** = bureau *m* sans papier *or* le bureau électronique

◊ **paper-white monitor** *noun (displays black text on a white background)* écran *m* à fond blanc avec texte en noir

QUOTE Indeed, the concept of the paperless office may have been a direct attack on Xerox and its close ties to the paper document. Yet, as we all know, the paperless office has so far been an empty promise.

Computing

paragraph *noun* **(a)** *(in a document)* paragraphe *m*; *(character that shows where a carriage return is)* **paragraph marker** = marqueur *m* de paragraphe **(b)** *(in a memory map)* bloc *m* paragraphe (de mémoire)

parallel *adjective* parallèle; **parallel access** = accès *m* parallèle; **parallel adder** = additionneur *m* parallèle; **parallel computer** = ordinateur *m* parallèle; **parallel connection** = connexion *f* (en) parallèle; **their average transmission rate is 60,000 bps through parallel connection** = leur débit de transmission est de 60 000 bits par seconde en connexion parallèle; **parallel data transmission** = transmission *f* de données en parallèle; **parallel input/output (PIO)** = entrée/sortie *f* (en) parallèle; **parallel input/output chip** = circuit intégré d'entrée/sortie en parallèle; **parallel input/parallel output (PIPO)** = entrée parallèle/sortie parallèle; **parallel input/serial output (PISO)** = entrée parallèle/sortie série; **parallel interface** = interface *f* parallèle; **parallel operation** = opération *f* (en) parallèle; **parallel port** = port *m* parallèle; **parallel priority system** = système de gestion des priorités en (fonctionnement) parallèle; **parallel printer** = imprimante *f* (qui fonctionne) sur port parallèle; **parallel processing** = traitement *m* (en) parallèle; *(running an old and a new computer together)* **parallel running** = exploitation *f* en parallèle *or* en double; **parallel search storage** = mémoire *f* associative; **parallel transfer** = transfert *m* (en) parallèle; *(data transmitted over a number of data lines)* **parallel transmission** = transmission *f* (en) parallèle

parameter *noun* paramètre *m*; **the X parameter defines the number of characters displayed across a screen** = le paramètre X définit le nombre de caractères contenus dans une ligne d'écran; **the size of the array is set with this parameter** = la taille du tableau est fixée par ce paramètre; **parameter-driven software** = *(with values not yet fixed)*

logiciel *m* paramétrable; *(with values fixed)* logiciel paramétré *or* paramétrique; *(value passed to a routine)* **parameter passing** = passage *m* de paramètre; *(using a program to examine parameters)* **parameter testing** = test *m* des paramètres; **parameter word** = mot-paramètre *m*; **physical parameter** = paramètre physique *or* donnée descriptive

◊ **parametric (subroutine)** *noun* sous-programme *m* paramétré *or* paramétrique

◊ **parameterization** *noun* paramétrage *m*

parent directory *noun (directory above a sub-directory)* répertoire *m* parent

◊ **parent folder** *noun (Macintosh system: folder that contains other folders)* fichier *m* parent

◊ **parent program** *noun (program that starts another program)* programme *m* parent

parity *noun* parité *f*; **parity bit** = bit *m* de parité; **parity check** = contrôle *m* de parité; **parity flag** = indicateur *m* de contrôle de parité; **parity interrupt** = interruption *f* (de contrôle) de parité; **parity track** = piste *f* de parité; **block parity** = parité de bloc; **column parity** = parité de colonne; **even parity (check)** = (contrôle de) parité paire; *(data transmission which does not use a parity bit)* **no parity** = sans (bit de) parité; **odd parity (check)** = (contrôle de) parité impaire

QUOTE The difference between them is that RAID level one offers mirroring, whereas level five stripes records in parity across the disks in the system.

Computing

park *verb (move the read/write head over a point on the disk where no data is stored)* parquer (la tête de lecture du disque); **when parked, the disk head will not damage any data if it touches the disk surface** = en position parquée, la tête du disque ne peut plus endommager les données en touchant la surface du disque; *see also* HEAD

parse *verb (break down high-level language code into its parts)* faire l'analyse grammaticale *or* syntaxique

◊ **parsing** *noun (of high-level language)* analyse *f* grammaticale *or* syntaxique

part *noun* **(a)** section *f or* partie *f*; **part page display** = affichage *m* réduit *or* d'une partie de page **(b)** **spare part** = pièce *f* détachée; **the printer won't work - we need to get a spare part** = l'imprimante est en panne, il faut remplacer une pièce **(c)** *(listing paper)* **two part stationery** = (papier listing) en double épaisseur; *see also* MULTIPART

partial carry *noun* report *m* partiel

◊ **partial RAM** *noun* (mémoire) RAM partielle *or* incomplète

particle *noun* particule *f*

partition 1 *noun* division *f (area of hard disk treated as a logical drive)* partition *f*; **I defined two**

partitions on this hard disk - called drive C: and D:
= j'ai défini deux partitions sur ce disque dur
désignées par C: et D: **2** *verb* subdiviser *or* diviser *or*
découper; *(divide a hard disk into logical drives)*
effectuer une partition; **partitioned file** = fichier *m*
subdivisé *or* fichier divisé en plusieurs parties

party line *or* **shared line** *noun (telephone line)*
ligne *f* partagée

PASCAL *(programming language)* langage *m*
PASCAL

pass 1 *noun* passe *f or* passage *m*; **single-pass
assembler** = assembleur *m* une passe; **sorting pass**
= passage de tri **2** *verb (magnétic tape)* (faire)
défiler

password *noun* mot *m* de passe; **the user has to
key in the password before he can access the
database** = l'utilisateur doit d'abord taper le mot
de passe pour avoir accès à la base de données;
password-protected = protégé, -ée par mot de
passe; **password protection** = protection *f* par mot
de passe

QUOTE the system's security features let you
divide the disk into up to 256 password-
protected sections
Byte

paste *verb (insert text that has been cut)* coller;
**now that I have cut this paragraph from the end of
the document, I can paste it in here** = après avoir
coupé ce paragraphe à la fin du document, je peux
le coller ici; *(taking text from one point and
inserting it at another)* **cut-and-paste** =
couper/coller

patch *noun (temporary correction made to a
program; small correction made to software by the
user on the instruction of the publisher)*
modification *f or* correction *f* provisoire; patch *m*
(short cable with a connector at each end) **patch
cord** = câble *m* de raccordement; *(allows quick
and simple reconfiguration of a network using
patch cords)* **patch panel** = panneau *m* de
raccordement

path *noun* **(a)** *(possible route or sequence of
events or instructions)* chemin *m or* filière *f* **(b)**
(route from one point in a network to another)
chemin *m* **(c)** *(in the DOS system: list of
subdirectories)* chemin d'accès (DOS); **you cannot
run the program from the root directory until its
directory is added to the path** = vous ne pouvez pas
lancer le programme à partir du répertoire racine
si vous n'avez pas ajouté le nom de son répertoire
dans la commande de chemins d'accès

◊ **pathname** *noun (location of a file with a
listing of the subdirectories)* nom *m* du chemin; **the
pathname for the letter file is
\FILES\SIMON\DOCS\LETTER.DOC** = le
nom du chemin du fichier lettre est:
\FILES\SIMON\DOCS\LETTER.DOC

pattern *noun (shapes or lines)* motif *m or* forme *f*
or dessin *f*; **pattern recognition** = reconnaissance *f*
de formes; *(TV)* **test pattern** = mire *f* de contrôle

◊ **patterned** *adjective* avec motifs *or* avec
dessins

pause key *noun (key that stops a process)*
touche *f* Pause

pay TV *noun* télévision *f* câblée (payante)

◊ **paycable** *noun US* télévision câblée (payante)

PAX = PRIVATE AUTOMATIC EXCHANGE

PBX = PRIVATE BRANCH EXCHANGE

PC (a) = PERSONAL COMPUTER ordinateur *m*
personnel *or* ordinateur individuel *or* PC;
(computer compatible with the IBM PC) **PC
compatible** = compatible PC; *(IBM PC
compatible computer)* **PC/AT** = PC/AT;
(keyboard with twelve function keys) **PC/AT
keyboard** = clavier PC/AT; *(IBM PC compatible)*
PC/XT = PC/XT; *(keyboard with ten function
keys)* **PC/XT keyboard** = clavier PC/XT **(b)** =
PRINTED CIRCUIT (BOARD) **(c)** = PROGRAM
COUNTER

QUOTE in the UK, the company is known not for
PCs but for PC printers
Which PC?

PCB = PRINTED CIRCUIT BOARD

PC-DOS ™ *(version of MS-DOS sold by IBM)*
PC-DOS (version IBM de MS-DOS)

PCI = PERIPHERAL COMPONENT
INTERCONNECT

PCL ™ = PRINTER CONTROL LANGUAGE

PCM (a) = PULSE CODE MODULATION **(b)** =
PLUG-COMPATIBLE MANUFACTURER

PCMCIA = PERSONAL COMPUTER
MEMORY CARD INTERNATIONAL
ASSOCIATION; *(specification for add-in
expansion cards)* (norme de carte d'extension)
PCMCIA; *(complies with the PCMCIA
standard)* **PCMCIA card** = carte *f* PCMCIA; **the
extra memory is stored on this PCMCIA card and I
use it on my laptop** = la mémoire additionnelle est
stockée sur une carte PCMCIA et je l'utilise sur
mon (ordinateur) portable; *(connector inside a
PCMCIA slot)* **PCMCIA connector** = connecteur
m PCMCIA; *(expansion slot that can accept a
PCMCIA card)* **PCMCIA slot** = emplacement *m*
pour carte PCMCIA

PCU = PERIPHERAL CONTROL UNIT

PDA = PERSONAL DIGITAL ASSISTANT

PDL (a) = PAGE DESCRIPTION LANGUAGE
(b) = PROGRAM DESIGN LANGUAGE

PDM = PULSE DURATION MODULATION

PDN = PUBLIC DATA NETWORK

peak 1 *noun* pic *m or* crête *f or* pointe *f*; **keep the**

peak power below 60 watts or the amplifier will overheat = veillez à ce que la tension de crête ne dépasse pas 60 watts sinon l'amplificateur surchauffera; **the marker on the thermometer shows the peak temperature for today** = le marqueur du thermomètre indique la température maximum d'aujourd'hui; *(of waveform)* **peaks and troughs** = les pointes et les creux; **peak period** = heure(s) *f(pl)* de pointe; **time of peak demand** = période *f* de demande maximum; **peak output** = niveau *m* maximum de production *or* production *f* record **2** *verb* atteindre un niveau maximum; **the power peaked at 1,200 volts** = la tension a atteint le niveau maximum de 1200 volts

peek *noun* instruction *f* PEEK (de lecture directe de la mémoire); **you need the instruction PEEK 1452 here to examine the contents of memory location 1452** = vous devez utliser l'instruction PEEK 1452 pour regarder le contenu de la mémoire à l'emplacement 1452; *compare* POKE

peer *noun (any two similar devices)* égal *m or* pair *m*

◊ **peer-to-peer network** *noun (local area network)* réseau *m* égal à égal *or* sans serveur dédié; **we have linked the four PCs in our small office using a peer-to-peer network** = nous avons connecté les quatre PCs de notre petit bureau avec un réseau sans serveur

peg *verb* **(a)** bloquer *or* verrouiller **(b)** marquer *or* atteindre (un niveau); **after he turned up the input level, the signal level meter was pegging on its maximum stop** = lorsqu'il a augmenté le niveau d'entrée, l'aiguille du mesureur de niveau a bondi en butée *or* a atteint son maximum

pel *see* PIXEL

pen *noun* **(a)** stylo *m* **(b)** *(computer that uses a pen instead of a keyboard)* **pen computer** = ordinateur à crayon optique *or* sans clavier **(c)** *(used with plotters)* plume *f (plotter that uses pens to draw on paper)* **pen plotter** = traceur *m* à plumes; **pen recorder** = traceur *m or* enregistreur *m* graphique; **plotter pen** = plume pour traceur; *see also* ELECTRONIC PEN, LIGHT PEN

Pentium ™ *noun (processor developed by Intel)* (processeur 32 bits développé par Intel) Pentium

per *preposition* **(a)** **as per** = suivant *or* selon; **as per sample** = selon échantillon; **as per specification** = selon les spécifications **(b)** *(at a rate of)* par; **per day** = par jour; **per hour** = (à *or* de) l'heure; **per week** = par semaine; **per year** = par année **(c)** *(out of)* pour; **the rate is twenty-five per thousand** = le taux s'élève à vingt-cinq pour mille; **the error rate has fallen to twelve per hundred** = le taux d'erreur est tombé à douze pour cent

◊ **per cent** *adjective & adverb* pour cent; **10 per cent** = dix pour cent; **what is the increase per cent?** = quel est le pourcentage d'augmentation?; **fifty per cent of nothing is still nothing** = cinquante pour cent de rien est toujours rien

◊ **percentage** *noun* pourcentage *m*; **percentage**

increase = pourcentage d'augmentation; **percentage point** = un pour cent

◊ **percentile** *noun* centile *m*

perfect 1 *adjective* parfait, -e *or* impeccable; **we check each batch to make sure it is perfect** = nous vérifions chaque lot pour nous assurer de la qualité **2** *verb* mettre au point; **he perfected the process for making high grade steel** = il a mis au point le procédé de fabrication d'un acier de haute qualité

◊ **perfect binding** *noun (of books which are trimmed and glued to the cover)* reliure *f* sans couture *or* perfect binding

◊ **perfect bound** *adjective* (livre) relié sans couture *or* (livre) avec perfect binding

◊ **perfectly** *adverb* parfaitement *or* impeccablement

perforations *noun* ligne *f or* colonne *f* de perforations *or* ligne perforée

◊ **perforated tape** *noun* bande perforée *or* ruban perforé

◊ **perforator** *noun* poinçon *m* de perforation; *(machine)* perforatrice *f*

perform *verb (machine)* marcher *or* fonctionner (bien *or* mal)

◊ **performance** *noun* performance *f*; **as a measure of the system's performance** = pour juger de la performance du système; **in benchmarking, the performances of several systems or devices are tested against a standard benchmark** = les bancs d'essais consistent à évaluer la performance de plusieurs systèmes ou périphériques en utilisant le même test standard; **high performance** = (de) haute performance

perigee *noun* périgée *m*

period *noun* **(a)** période *f*; **for a period of time** = pendant quelque temps *or* pendant un certain temps; **for a period of months** = pendant quelques mois; **for a six-year period** = pendant six ans *or* sur une période de six ans **(b)** *US (typography)* point *m* (NOTE: GB English is **full stop**)

◊ **periodic** *or* **periodical 1** *adjective* **(a)** *(from time to time)* périodique *or* de temps en temps **(b)** *(that occurs regularly)* **periodic** = périodique *or* à intervalles réguliers; **the clock signal is periodic** = l'horloge émet un signal à intervalles réguliers **2** *noun (magazine)* **periodical** = périodique *m*

◊ **periodically** *adverb* périodiquement *or* de temps en temps

peripheral 1 *adjective* périphérique **2** *noun* périphérique *m*; **peripherals such as disk drives or printers allow data transfer and are controlled by a system, but contain independent circuits for their operation** = les périphériques, tels que les lecteurs de disquettes et imprimantes, qui permettent le transfert de données sont asservis à un système (central) mais fonctionnent grâce à des circuits indépendants; **fast peripheral** = périphérique rapide; **slow peripheral** = périphérique lent;

(specification defining a type of fast local bus) **peripheral component interconnect (PCI)** = (modèle de) bus local PCI; **peripheral control unit (PCU)** = unité *f* de commande *or* unité de contrôle de périphérique *or* contrôleur *m* de périphérique; *(program or routine)* **peripheral driver** = gestionnaire *m or* pilote *m* de périphérique; **peripheral equipment** = *(piece of equipment)* un périphérique; *(all equipment)* les périphériques; **peripheral interface adapter (PIA)** = contrôleur *m* d'interface de périphérique; **peripheral limited** = limité par (la vitesse d') un périphérique *or* avec contrainte de vitesse de périphérique; **peripheral memory** = mémoire *f* (de) périphérique; **peripheral processing unit (PPU)** = processeur *m* périphérique; *(device driver)* **peripheral software driver** = routine *f* de gestion de périphérique; **peripheral transfer** = échange *m* d'informations *or* de données entre unité centrale et périphérique; **peripheral unit** = périphérique

permanent *adjective* permanent, -e; **permanent dynamic memory** = mémoire *f* dynamique permanente; **permanent error** = erreur *f* permanente; **permanent file** = fichier *m* permanent; **permanent memory** = mémoire *f* permanente; *(file which stores a swap file)* **permanent swap file** = fichier *m* d'échange permanent

◊ **permanently** *adverb* en permanence *or* de façon permanente *or* définitivement; **the production number is permanently engraved on the back of the computer casing** = le numéro de fabrication est gravé de façon permanente sur le panneau arrière du boîtier de l'ordinateur

permeability *noun* perméabilité *f*

permission *noun (authorization to access)* autorisation *f* d'accès; **this user cannot access the file on the server because he does not have permission** = cet utilisateur ne peut pas accéder au fichier du serveur parce qu'il n'a pas d'autorisation d'accès; *see also* RIGHTS

permutation *noun* permutation *f*; **this cipher system is very secure since there are so many possible permutations for the key** = ce code chiffré est très sûr puisqu'il comporte une clé avec un très grand nombre de permutations possibles

persistence *noun* persistance *f*; **slow scan rate monitors need long persistence phosphor to prevent the image flickering** = les écrans à faible fréquence de balayage ont besoin de phosphore à longue persistance pour éviter l'instabilité de l'image

person *noun* personne *f*; *(telephone)* **person-to-person call** = appel *m* avec préavis

◊ **personal** *adjective* personnel, -elle; **personal computer (PC)** = ordinateur *m* individuel *or* ordinateur personnel *or* PC *m*; *(lightweight palmtop computer)* **personal digital assistant (PDA)** = assistant personnel de communication (APC); **personal identification device (PID)** = dispositif *m* électronique d'identification; carte *f* magnétique; **personal identification number (PIN)** = numéro *m* de code confidentiel *or* personnel;

(utility that stores and manages everyday data) **personal information manager (PIM)** = gestionnaire personnel d'information (GPI) *or* PIM

◊ **personalize** *verb* personnaliser

PERT = PROGRAM EVALUATION AND REVIEW TECHNIQUE

peta (P) *(one quadrillion (2^{50}))* péta *m*

◊ **petabyte (PB)** *noun (one quadrillion bytes)* péta-octet *m*

petal printer = DAISY WHEEL PRINTER

pF = PICOFARAD picofarad (pF) *m*

phantom ROM *noun (duplicate area of read-only memory)* (mémoire) ROM fantôme

phase 1 *noun* **(a)** *(part of a larger process)* phase *f*; **compile phase** = phase de compilation; **run phase** *or* **target phase** = phase d'exécution *or* (en) code objet **(b)** *(delay)* phase; **in phase** = en phase; **out of phase** = déphasé, -ée; **phase alternating line (PAL)** = norme *f* de télévision couleur PAL; **phase angle** = angle *m* de phase *or* déphasage *m*; **phase clipping** = écrêtage *m* de phase; **phase equalizer** = égaliseur *m or* compensateur *m* de phase; **phase modulation** = modulation *f* de phase **2** *verb* **to phase in** = commencer *or* démarrer *or* introduire quelque chose graduellement; **to phase out** = arrêter *or* mettre fin à quelque chose graduellement; **phased change-over** = changement *m* graduel *or* progressif

phon *noun (measure of sound)* phone *m*

phone 1 *noun* téléphone *m*; **we had a new phone system installed last week** = nous avons une nouvelle installation téléphonique depuis la semaine dernière; **house phone** *or* **internal phone** = téléphone interne; **by phone** = par téléphone *or* téléphonique; **to be on the phone** = parler au téléphone; être en ligne (avec quelqu'un); **she has been on the phone all morning** = elle a passé la matinée (à parler) au téléphone; **he spoke to the manager on the phone** = il a eu le directeur au téléphone; **card phone** = téléphone à carte; **phone book** = annuaire *m* téléphonique *or* des téléphones; **look up his address in the phone book** = cherche son adresse dans l'annuaire; **phone call** = appel *m* (téléphonique); **to make a phone call** = téléphoner *or* appeler *or* faire un appel *or* passer un coup de fil; **to answer the phone** *or* **to take a phone call** = répondre au téléphone; **phonecard** = Télécarte ™ *f*; **phone number** = numéro *m* de téléphone; **he keeps a list of phone numbers in a little black book** = il a une liste de numéros de téléphone dans un petit carnet noir; **the phone number is on the company notepaper** = le numéro de téléphone figure sur le papier à en-tête de la société; **can you give me your phone number?** = pouvez-vous me donner votre numéro de téléphone? **2** *verb* **to phone someone** = appeler quelqu'un *or* téléphoner à quelqu'un; **don't phone me, I'll phone you** = ne me téléphonez pas, c'est moi qui vous appellerai; **his secretary phoned to say he would be late** = sa secrétaire a téléphoné pour prévenir de son retard; **he phoned the order through to the warehouse** = il a téléphoné directement à l'entrepôt pour passer la commande; **to phone for something** = demander quelque chose par téléphone *or* appeler pour faire venir quelque chose; **he phoned for a taxi** = il a appelé un taxi; **to phone about something** = téléphoner au sujet de quelque chose; **he phoned about the order for computer stationery** = il a appelé à propos de la commande de papier listing

◊ **phone back** *verb* rappeler; **the chairman is in a meeting, can you phone back in about half an hour?** = le président est en conférence, pourriez-vous rappeler dans une demi-heure environ?; **Mr Smith called while you were out and asked if you would phone him back** = M. Smith a téléphoné en votre absence et a demandé que vous le rappeliez

phoneme *noun* phonème *m*; **the phoneme 'oo' is present in the words too and zoo** = les mots 'too' et 'zoo' contiennent le phonème 'oo'

◊ **phonetic** *adjective* phonétique; **the pronunciation is indicated in phonetic script** = il y a une transcription phonétique de la prononciation

◊ **phonetics** *noun* la phonétique

phosphor *noun* phosphore *m*; **phosphor coating** = couche *f* de phosphore *or* couche phosphorescente; **phosphor dots** = points *mpl* de phosphore *or* de phosphorescence; **phosphor efficiency** = rendement *m* de phosphorescence; **long persistence phosphor** = phosphore à longue persistance

phosphorescence *noun* phosphorescence *f*

photo 1 = PHOTOGRAPH **2** *prefix (referring to light)* photo-

◊ **photocell** *noun* cellule *f* photoélectrique *or* photocellule *f*

◊ **photocomposition** *noun* photo-composition *f*

◊ **photoconductivity** *noun* photo-conductivité *f*

◊ **photoconductor** *noun* cellule *f* photo-conductrice

◊ **photocopier** *noun* photocopieur *m or* copieur *m*

◊ **photocopy 1** *noun* photocopie *f*; **make six photocopies of the contract** = faites six photocopies du contrat **2** *verb* photocopier; **she photocopied the contract** = elle a photocopié le contrat

◊ **photocopying** *noun (making photocopies)* photocopie *f*; **photocopying costs are rising each year** = les frais de photocopie augmentent d'année en année; **photocopying bureau** = bureau *m* de photocopie; **there is a mass of photocopying to be done** = il y a une grande quantité de photocopies à faire

◊ **photodigital memory** *noun* mémoire *f* optonumérique

◊ **photodiode** *noun* photodiode *f*

◊ **photoelectric** *adjective* photoélectrique; **photoelectric cell** = cellule *f* photoélectrique *or* photocellule *f*; **the photoelectric cell detects the amount of light passing through the liquid** = la cellule photoélectrique décèle la quantité de lumière qui traverse le liquide

◊ **photoelectricity** *noun* photoélectricité *f*

◊ **photoemission** *noun* photoémission *f*

photograph *noun* photographie *f or* photo *f*; **colour photograph** = photographie en couleur *or* photo couleur; **black and white photograph** = photo en noir et blanc; **it's a photograph of the author** = c'est une photo de l'auteur; **he took six photographs of the new machine** = il a fait six photos du nouvel appareil; **we will be using a colour photograph of the author on the back of the jacket** = il y aura une photographie en couleur de l'auteur au dos de la jaquette

◊ **photographic** *adjective* photographique; **the copier makes a photographic reproduction of the printed page** = le copieur photographie le texte imprimé pour le reproduire

◊ **photographically** *adverb* photographiquement; **the text film can be reproduced photographically** = le film du texte peut être reproduit par photographie

◊ **photography** *noun* la photographie

photogravure *noun* photogravure *f*

◊ **photolithography** *noun* photolithographie *f or* photo-litho *f*

◊ **photomechanical transfer (PMT)** *noun* transfert *m* photomécanique

◊ **photometry** *noun* photométrie *f*

◊ **photon** *noun* photon *m*

◊ **photoprint** *noun (in typesetting)* épreuve *f* positive

◊ **photoresist** *noun* résine *f* photosensible; **to make the PCB, coat the board with photoresist, place the opaque pattern above, expose, then develop and etch, leaving the conducting tracks** = pour faire un circuit imprimé il faut d'abord recouvrir la carte d'une résine photosensible puis appliquer le masque du circuit, exposer, développer et graver pour finalement obtenir le tracé; **positive photoresist** = (méthode de la) résine photosensible en positif

◊ **photosensor** *noun* détecteur *m* photoélectrique *or* photosensible

◊ **photostat 1** *noun* photostat *m or* photocopie *f* **2** *verb* faire un photostat (d'un document) *or* photocopier

◊ **phototelegraphy** *noun* transmission *f* de fac-similé

◊ **phototext** *noun* texte *m* photocomposé

◊ **phototransistor** *noun* phototransistor *m*

phototypesetter *noun* photocomposeuse *f*

◊ **phototypesetting** *noun* photocomposition *f*

photovoltaic *adjective* photovoltaïque

physical *adjective* physique; *(memory address)* **physical address** = adresse *f* physique; **physical database** = base de données physique; **physical layer** = couche *f* physique; *(memory fitted in a computer)* **physical memory** = mémoire *f* physique; *compare* VIRTUAL MEMORY; *(arrangement of cables in a network)* **physical topology** = topologie *f* physique

◊ **physical record** *noun* **(a)** *(unit of data that can be transmitted)* unité *f* physique **(b)** *(all the information for one record)* enregistrement *m* physique

PIA = PERIPHERAL INTERFACE ADAPTER

pica *noun* **(a)** *(printing measurement)* pica *or* 12 points anglais (= environ 11 points Didot) **(b)** *(on a printer - ten characters to the inch)* caractère *m* pica (de 12 points anglais, environ 11 points Didot)

PICK ™ *noun* *(operating system)* système *m* d'exploitation PICK ™

pickup *noun* *(arm and cartridge to playback music)* pick-up *m*

◊ **pickup reel** *noun* bobine *f* réceptrice *or* d'enroulement

pico- **(p)** *prefix* *(one million millionth)* pico-; **picofarad (pF)** = picofarad (pF) *m*; **picosecond (ps)** = picoseconde (ps) *f*

picture **1** *noun* *(drawing)* dessin *m*; *(book)* illustration *f*; *(TV or book)* image *f*; *(photograph)* photo *f*; **this picture shows the new design** = vous pouvez voir le nouveau modèle sur cette représentation *or* cette photo *or* ce dessin; **picture beam** = faisceau *m* d'image; **picture element** *or* **pixel** = élément *m*; d'image *or* pixel *m*; *see also* PIXEL; **picture phone** = visiophone *m*; **picture processing** = traitement *m* de l'image; **picture transmission** = transmission *f* d'image **2** *verb* imaginer *or* visualiser; **try to picture the layout before starting to draw it in** = essayer de visualiser l'implantation avant de commencer à dessiner

PID = PERSONAL IDENTIFICATION DEVICE

piece accent *noun* accent *m* mobile *or* caractère *m* accent

◊ **piece fraction** *noun* caractère *m* de fraction

pie chart *noun* diagramme *m* en secteurs *or* en camembert

piezoelectric *adjective* piézoélectrique

PIF = PROGRAM INFORMATION FILE

piggyback *verb* superposer; monter *or* mettre en piggyback; **piggyback those two memory chips to boost the memory capacity** = superposez ces deux puces pour augmenter la capacité de la mémoire; **piggyback entry** = entrée *f* sur un système avec un mot de passe piraté *or* sur un terminal mal verrouillé

◊ **piggybacking** *noun* *(messages)* mise *f* en

piggyback *or* superposition *f* d'un accusé de réception au message suivant

PILOT *(programming language)* langage *m* PILOT

pilot **1** *noun* *(used as a test)* pilote *m or* test *m*; **the company set up a pilot project to see if the proposed manufacturing system was efficient** = la société a mis sur pied un projet-pilote pour évaluer le procédé de fabrication proposé; **the pilot factory has been built to test the new production process** = l'usine-pilote a été construite pour tester le nouveau procédé de fabrication; **pilot system** = système-pilote *m* **2** *verb* faire l'essai (d'un système); **they are piloting the new system** = ils font l'essai du nouveau système

PIM = PERSONAL INFORMATION MANAGER

PIN = PERSONAL IDENTIFICATION NUMBER numéro *m* de code confidentiel *or* personnel

pin *noun* **(a)** *(short piece of wire attached to an IC)* broche *f or* contact *m*; *(chip that can directly replace another)* **pin compatible** = compatible à l'enfichage; **it's easy to upgrade the processor because the new one is pin-compatible** = il est facile d'augmenter la puissance de ce processeur, la nouvelle puce est compatible à l'enfichage avec l'ancienne **(b)** *(part of a plug)* broche; **use a three-pin plug to connect the printer to the mains** = il faut une fiche à trois broches pour connecter *or* brancher le système sur le secteur; **three-pin mains plug** = fiche secteur à trois broches; **two-pin mains plug** = fiche secteur à deux broches

◊ **pin cushion distortion** *noun* distorsion *f* en oreiller *or* en coussinet *or* en barillet

◊ **pinfeed** *noun* entraînement *m* (du papier) par picots; *see* TRACTOR FEED

◊ **pinout** *noun* *(position of pins on an IC)* disposition *f* des broches; configuration *f* d'un connecteur

◊ **pin photodiode** *noun* photodiode *f* (de type) PIN

pinchwheel *noun* molette *f* de serrage

PIO = PARALLEL INPUT/OUTPUT; *see also* PIPO, PISO

pipe *noun* *(symbol, normally (¦), that tells the operating system to send output)* opérateur *m* de dérivation *or* de transfert (de données)

pipeline (computer) **1** *noun* (architecture) en pipeline *or* en pipe-line **2** *verb* **(a)** *(to schedule inputs)* organiser en pipeline; faire du pipeline **(b)** *(to begin processing of a second instruction while still processing the first)* traiter *or* exécuter (des instructions) en pipeline

◊ **pipelining** *noun* **(a)** *(scheduling inputs)* organisation *f* en pipeline **(b)** *(processing a third instruction while still processing the second)* mode *m* de traitement *or* d'exécution en pipeline

PIPO = PARALLEL INPUT/PARALLEL OUTPUT

pirate 1 *noun* pirate *m*; **the company is trying to take the software pirates to court** = la société tente d'amener les pirates de logiciel devant les tribunaux; **pirate copy of a computer program** = exemplaire *m* d'un logiciel piraté **2** *adjective (illegal copy)* **pirate copy** = copie pirate *or* piratée *or* illégale; **a pirate copy of a computer program** = exemplaire piraté d'un programme d'ordinateur **3** *verb* pirater; **a pirated tape** = une bande piratée; **the designs for the new system were pirated in the Far East** = les schémas du nouveau système ont été piratés en Extrême-Orient; **he used a cheap pirated disk and found the program had bugs in it** = il a utilisé une disquette piratée bon marché et a découvert que le programme contenait des bogues

◊ **piracy** *noun* piratage *m*

PISO = PARALLEL INPUT/SERIAL OUTPUT

pitch *noun* **(a)** *(horizontal spacing)* espacement *m or* pas *m or* pitch *m*; *(of characters)* densité *f* de caractères *or* nombre *m* de caractères par pouce **(b)** *(of sound)* hauteur *f* d'un son; **pitch envelope** = enveloppe *f* tonale **(c)** *(movement about an axis)* tangage *m*

pix *noun* images *fpl or* illustrations *fpl or* photos *fpl*

◊ **pix lock** *noun* *(in video recording)* synchronisation *f or* topage *m*

◊ **pixel** *or* **picture element** *noun* pixel *m or* élément *m* d'image

> QUOTE an EGA display and driver give a resolution of 640 x 350 pixels and support sixteen colours
>
> *PC Business World*

> QUOTE adding 40 to each pixel brightens the image and can improve the display's appearance
>
> *Byte*

PL/1 = PROGRAMMING LANGUAGE/1 langage *m* de programmation PL/1

PLA = PROGRAMMABLE LOGIC ARRAY

place *noun* place *f or* position *f*

plaintext *noun* texte *m* en clair *or* non chiffré; **the messages were sent as plaintext by telephone** = le texte du message a été transmis en clair par téléphone; **enter the plaintext message into the cipher machine** = introduire le texte non chiffré dans la machine à chiffrer (NOTE: opposite is **ciphertext**)

PLAN *(low-level programming language)* langage *m* PLAN

plan 1 *noun* **(a)** plan *m or* projet *m* **(b)** *(drawing)* plan; **plans** = jeu *m* de plans *or* les plans; **floor plan** = plan d'ensemble (d'un étage); **street plan** *or* **town plan** = plan des rues *or* plan de la ville **2** *verb* planifier *or* projeter (NOTE: **planning - planned**)

◊ **planar** *noun* **(a)** *(method of producing ICs)* procédé *m* planar (de production de circuits intégrés) **(b)** *(graphical images arranged on the same plane)* graphe *m* planar

◊ **planchest** *noun* armoire *f or* meuble *m* à plans (d'architecte)

◊ **planner** *noun* **(a)** *(software)* agenda *m* **(b)** **wall planner** = agenda *m* mural

◊ **planning** *noun* planification *f or* planning *m*; **long-term planning** = planification à longue échéance; **short-term planning** = planification à courte échéance

planet *noun* planète *f*

◊ **planetary camera** *noun* caméra *f* de poursuite

plant *verb* *(in memory)* ranger *or* implanter *or* stocker (dans la *or* en mémoire)

plasma display *or* **gas plasma display** *noun* affichage *m* (au) plasma

> QUOTE the disadvantage of using plasma technology is that it really needs mains power to work for any length of time

> QUOTE the plasma panel came out of the extended use test well
>
> *Micro Decision*

plate *noun* **(a)** *(in book)* planche *f* **(b)** *(printing)* cliché *m* **(c)** *(photograph)* plaque *f* photographique *or* plaque photosensible; **plate camera** = appareil (photo) *m* à plaques

platen *noun* **(a)** *(roller for paper)* rouleau *m or* cylindre *m* **(b)** *(for film in camera)* presseur *m*

platform *noun* *(standard type of hardware)* plate-forme *f or* environnement *m*; **this software will only work on the IBM PC platform** = ce logiciel ne fonctionne que dans un environnement IBM; **data collection platform** = plate-forme de collecte de données; *(can work with different types of hardware)* **platform independence** = indépendance *f* de la plate-forme *or* de l'environnement (de travail)

platter *noun* *(one disk in a hard disk drive)* plateau *m* (d'un disque dur) *or* disque *m* simple

> COMMENT: the disks are made of metal or glass and coated with a magnetic compound; each platter has a read/write head that moves across its surface to access stored data

play back *verb* *(music)* (re)jouer; *(film, etc.)* passer *or* visionner; **after you have recorded the music, press this button to play back the tape and hear what it sounds like** = après avoir enregistré la musique, appuyez sur ce bouton-ci pour faire jouer la bande et vous assurer de la bonne qualité du son enregistré

◊ **playback head** *noun* tête *f* de lecture; **disk playback head** = tête de lecture de disques; **tape playback head** = tête de lecture de bandes

player *noun* **CD player** = platine *f* laser *or* platine disques compacts *or* lecteur *m* de disques CD

◊ **player missile graphics** *see* SPRITES

PLD = PROGRAMMABLE LOGIC DEVICE

plex database *noun* base *f* de données relationnelle

◊ **plex structure** *noun* structure *f* à maillage intégral *or* réseau *m* intégralement interconnecté

PL/M = PROGRAMMING LANGUAGE FOR MICROPROCESSORS

plot 1 *noun (graph or map)* graphe *m or* courbe *f or* tracé *m* **2** *verb* tracer une courbe *or* un graphe (par points numérisés); **plotting mode** = mode *m* graphe

◊ **plotter** *noun* traceur *m*; **plotter driver** = pilote *m* de traceur; **plotter pen** = plume *f* de traceur; **digital plotter** = traceur numérique; **drum plotter** = traceur à tambour; **flatbed plotter** = traceur à plat; **incremental plotter** = traceur à incrémentation; *(uses pens to draw an image on paper)* **pen plotter** = traceur *m* à plumes; **printer-plotter** = imprimante *f* graphique; **X-Y plotter** *or* **graph plotter** = traceur de courbes *or* de graphiques

plug 1 *noun* fiche *f*; **the printer is supplied with a plug** = la fiche est fournie avec l'imprimante; **adapter plug** = adaptateur *m*; **plug-compatible** = à connecteur compatible *or* directement enfichable; **this new plug-compatible board works much faster than any of its rivals, we can install it by simply plugging it into the expansion port** = cette nouvelle carte directement enfichable travaille beaucoup plus vite que ses concurrentes, vous l'installez en l'enfichant simplement dans le connecteur d'extension; **plug-compatible manufacturer (PCM)** = fabricant *m* de produits (à connecteurs) compatibles **2** *verb* brancher; **to plug in** = *(a machine)* brancher *or* connecter; *(a board)* enficher; **no wonder the computer does nothing, you haven't plugged it in at the mains** = ne soyez pas surpris si l'ordinateur ne fonctionne pas, vous ne l'avez pas branché sur le secteur; **plug-in unit** = extension *f* enfichable **(b)** *(to publicize)* promouvoir *or* vanter; **they ran six commercials plugging holidays in Spain** = ils ont fait un véritable matraquage publicitaire avec leurs six pubs sur les séjours en Espagne

◊ **plugboard** *or* **patchboard** *noun* panneau *m* de raccordement

QUOTE it allows room for up to 40K of RAM via plug-in memory cartridges
Which PC?

QUOTE adding memory is simply a matter of plugging a card into an expansion bus connector
Byte

plus *or* **plus sign (+)** *noun* le signe plus *or* le signe de l'addition

PMBX = PRIVATE MANUAL BRANCH EXCHANGE

PMOS = P-channel METAL OXIDE SEMICONDUCTOR

PMS = PANTONE MATCHING SYSTEM

PMT = PHOTOMECHANICAL TRANSFER

pn-junction *noun* zone *f* interface pn *or* jonction *f* pn; **diffused pn-junction** = zone interface *or* jonction pn à diffusion; **step pn-junction** = zone interface pn *or* jonction pn à seuil

◊ **pnp** *or* **p-n-p transistor** *noun* transistor (de type) pnp

pocket *noun* poche *f* ; de poche; **pocket calculator** = calculatrice *f* de poche

point 1 *noun* **(a)** endroit *m or* point *m*; **access point** = point d'accès *or* d'entrée; **re-entry point** = point de ré-entrée *or* de rentrée; **starting point** = point de départ; *see also* BREAKPOINT **(b) binary point** = virgule *f* binaire; **decimal point** = virgule *f* (décimale); **percentage point** = un pour cent **(c)** *(British measurement in typesetting)* point (anglais) *or* un douzième de pica *or* 0,351 mm; *(French measurement)* point Didot *or* point typographique *or* 0,324 mm; **the text of the book is set in 9 point Times** = le texte du livre est (composé) en Times 9 points; **if we increase the point size to 10, will the page extent increase?** = est-ce qu'en augmentant la taille des caractères à 10 points on augmente ainsi le nombre de pages? (NOTE: usually written **pt** after figures: **10pt Times Bold**) **2** *verb* **to point out** = indiquer *or* montrer; faire remarquer

◊ **point-of-sale (POS)** *noun* point *m* de vente; **electronic point-of-sale (EPOS)** = point de vente électronique; **point-of-sale material** = publicité *f* lieu de vente (PLV); **point-of-sale terminal** *or* **POS terminal** = terminal *m* de point de vente

◊ **pointer** *noun* **(a)** *(in a computer program)* pointeur *m*; **increment the contents of the pointer to the address of the next instruction** = incrémenter le pointeur jusqu'à l'adresse (d'instruction) suivante; **data pointer** = pointeur de position de données; **pointer file** = fichier de pointeurs **(b)** *(graphical symbol)* pointeur; **desktop publishing on a PC is greatly helped by the use of a pointer and mouse** = il est beaucoup plus facile de faire de la PAO sur un ordinateur personnel si on utilise un pointeur et une souris

◊ **pointing device** *noun* *(device that controls the position of a cursor)* dispositif *m* de pointage; *see also* MOUSE

QUOTE the arrow keys, the spacebar or the mouse are used for pointing, and the enter key or the left mouse button are to pick
PC User

QUOTE pointing with the cursor and pressing the joystick button eliminates use of the keyboard entirely
Soft

point to point *noun* (liaison) point à point; **point to point protocol (PPP)** = protocole *m* point à point

poke *noun* instruction POKE (d'insertion); **poke**

1423,74 will write the data 74 into location 1423 = l'instruction POKE 1423,74 écrira 74 à l'emplacement 1423; *compare* PEEK

POL = PROBLEM-ORIENTATED LANGUAGE

polar *adjective* polaire; **polar coordinates** = coordonnées *fpl* polaires; **polar diagram** = diagramme *m* en coordonnées polaires; **polar orbit** = orbite *f* polaire

◊ **polarity** *noun* polarité *f*; **electrical polarity** = polarité électrique; **magnetic polarity** = polarité magnétique; **polarity test** = test *m* de polarité; **reverse polarity** = polarité inversée

◊ **polarization** *noun* polarisation *f*

◊ **polarized** *adjective* **(a)** polarisé, -ée; **vertically polarized** = (antenne, etc.) à polarisation verticale **(b) polarized plug** = connecteur *m* à une seule position d'enfichage; **polarized edge connector** = connecteur à enfichage dirigé *or* à un seul bord d'enfichage

polaroid filter *noun* filtre *m* polaroïde

Polish notation *see* REVERSE

poll *verb (of computer)* appeler *or* interroger *or* inviter à émettre; **polled interrupt** = interruption *f* d'appel

◊ **polling** *noun (from controlling computer to terminal)* interrogation *f or* appel *m* sélectif *or* invitation *f* à émettre; **polling characters** = caractères *mpl* d'appel sélectif; **polling interval** = intervalle *m* d'appels; **polling list** = ordre *m* d'interrogation *or* d'appel (des terminaux); **polling overhead** = temps *m* d'appels sélectifs

polynomial code *noun* code *m* polynomial (de détection d'erreur par algorithme de calcul)

POP 2 langage *m* (de traitement de listes) POP 2

pop *verb* pop-down menu *or* pop-up menu = fenêtre *f* de menu; **to pop off** *or* **pop on** = effacer *or* afficher (une image) à un moment déterminé; **this is the last frame of the film so pop on the titles** = c'est la dernière image du film, faites apparaître les titres

◊ **pop filter** *noun* filtre *m* de micro; **every time you say a 'p' you overload the tape recorder, so put this pop filter in to stop it** = chaque fois que vous prononcez un 'p' vous saturez l'enregistrement, placez donc ce filtre pour que cela cesse

QUOTE you can use a mouse to access pop-up menus and a keyboard for word processing
Byte

populate *verb (fill the sockets on a printed circuit board with components)* habiller *or* garnir une carte; **fully-populated** = *(all the options fitted into a computer)* avec toutes les options; *(PCB with components in all free sockets)* carte complètement garnie (de composants)

porch *see* FRONT PORCH

port *noun* port *m or* point *m* d'accès *or*

d'entrée/sortie; **asynchronous port** = port asynchrone; **input port** = port (d') entrée; **joystick port** = port (de) manche à balai *or* port (de manette de) jeu; **output port** = port (de) sortie; **parallel port** = port parallèle; **printer port** = port (d')imprimante; **serial port** = port série; **port selector** = sélecteur *m* de port; **port sharing** = (en) port partagé *or* partage *m* de port

QUOTE the 40 Mbyte hard disk model is provided with eight terminal ports
Micro Decision

portable **1** *noun (computer)* portable *m*; *(typewriter)* (machine à écrire) portative *f* **2** *adjective (machine)* portable; portatif, -ive; *(program)* **portable software** *or* **portable programs** = programme *m* portable

◊ **portable operating system interface (POSIX)** *noun (IEEE standard)* standard IEEE POSIX (de portabilité des services d'un système d'exploitation)

◊ **portability** *noun (of program)* portabilité *f*

QUOTE although portability between machines is there in theory, in practice it just isn't that simple
Personal Computer World

POS = POINT-OF-SALE

position 1 *noun* endroit *m or* position *f*; **this is the position of that chip on the PCB** = voici le point de connexion de cette puce sur la carte **2** *verb* positionner *or* placer *or* mettre (en place); **the VDU should not be positioned in front of a window** = il faut éviter de placer l'écran devant une fenêtre; **position this photograph at the top right-hand corner of the page** = positionnez la photo dans le coin droit du haut de la page; *(accessing data)* **positioning time** = temps *m* de mise en place *or* temps d'accès

◊ **positional** *adjective* positionnel, -elle

positive *adjective* **(a)** *(meaning 'yes')* affirmatif, -ive; **positive response** = réponse *f* affirmative *or* positive **(b)** *(photographie)* épreuve *f* positive; **positive display** = affichage *m* noir sur fond blanc; **positive presentation** = affichage en positif **(c)** *(electrical)* positif; **positive logic** = logique *f* positive; **positive terminal** = borne *f* positive

◊ **positive feedback** *noun* rétroaction positive *or* feedback positif *or* boucle *f* d'amplification; **make sure the microphone is not too close to the loudspeaker or positive feedback will occur and you will overload the amplifier** = ne placez pas le micro trop près du haut-parleur sinon le retour va saturer l'ampli

POSIX = PORTABLE OPERATING SYSTEM INTERFACE

post 1 *verb (to enter data)* enregistrer **2** *prefix* post-; **post-editing** = édition *f* après compilation *or* après calculs; *(text)* **post-formatted** = (texte) mis en forme à l'impression; **post mortem (dump)** = (vidage par) autopsie *f*

◊ **postbyte** *noun* octet *m* de placement

◊ **postfix** *noun* suffixe *m*; **postfix notation** = notation suffixée *or* notation polonaise inversée; **normal notation: (x-y) + z, but using postfix notation: xy - z +** = en notation normale on écrit: (x-y) + z, en notation inversée on écrira: xy - z + (NOTE: often referred to as **reverse Polish notation**)

◊ **postprocessor** *noun* **(a)** *(microporcessor)* post-processeur *m* **(b)** *(program)* programme *m* de retraitement

poster *noun* poster *m or* affiche *f*

PostScript ™ *(standard page description language developed by Adobe Systems)* (langage de description de page) PostScript ™; **if you do a lot of DTP work, you will benefit from a PostScript printer** = si vous utilisez beaucoup la PAO, vous tirerez profit d'une imprimante PostScript; *(graphics language system)* **Display PostScript** = affichage PostScript

pot = POTENTIOMETER

potential *noun* potentiel *m*; **potential difference** = différence *f* de potentiel

◊ **potentiometer** *noun* potentiomètre *m*

power 1 *noun* **(a)** *(measured in Watts)* puissance *f*; **automatic power off** = (dispositif d') arrêt *m or* de mise hors tension automatique; **power dump** = coupure *m* de courant; **power failure** = panne *f* de courant *or* de secteur; **power loss** = chute *f* de tension; **'power off'** = 'arrêt' *or* 'hors tension'; **'power on'** = 'marche' *or* 'sous tension'; **power-on reset** = réinitialisation *f* automatique à la mise sous tension; *(hardware tests carried out when a computer is switched on)* **power-on self test (POST)** = autotest *m* à la mise sous tension; **power pack** = bloc *m* d'alimentation; **power supply** alimentation *f*; **power supply unit (PSU)** = bloc d'alimentation; **uninterruptable power supply (UPS)** = onduleur *m* **(b)** *(user who needs the latest model of computer)* **power user** = utilisateur avancé *or* ayant besoin d'une configuration puissante **(c)** *(mathematical term)* puissance *f*; **5 to the power 2 is equal to 25** = 5 à la puissance deux *or* 5 au carré égale 25 (NOTE: written as small figures in superscript: 10^5: say: 'ten to the power five') **2** *verb (provide electrical energy to a device)* alimenter (en courant électrique); **the monitor is powered from a supply in the main PC** = l'écran est alimenté par le transformateur du PC principal; *(turn off the power)* **power down** *or* **power off** = éteindre *or* mettre hors tension; **once you have shut down the software, you can power off the server** = lorsque vous avez quitté le programme, vous pouvez mettre le serveur hors tension; **to power up** = mettre sous tension *or* mettre en marche; **powered (by)** (appareil) qui marche *or* qui fonctionne (à l'électricité, etc.)

PowerBook ™ *noun (laptop version of a Macintosh)* PowerBook ™

PPM = PULSE POSITION MODULATION

ppm = PAGES PER MINUTE

pre- *prefix (before)* pré- *or* d'avance; **pre-agreed** = accepté, -ée d'avance *or* suivant accord préalable; **pre-allocation** = préallocation *f*; **pre-fetch** = appel *m* d'instruction anticipé

◊ **pre-amplifier** *noun* préamplificateur *m or* préampli *m*

precede *verb* précéder; **instruction which cancels the instruction which precedes it** = instruction qui annule l'instruction antérieure

◊ **precedence** *noun* priorité *f*; *(mathematical)* **operator precedence** = ordre *m* d'enchaînement des opérations *or* ordre de priorité

precise *adjective* précis, -e *or* exact, -e; **the atomic clock will give the precise time of starting the process** = l'horloge atomique indiquera l'heure précise du début du processus

◊ **precision** *noun* précision *f or* exactitude *f*; **double precision** = double précision; **multiple precision** = multiple précision; *(number of digits in a number)* **precision of a number** = précision d'un nombre; **single precision** = simple précision

precompiled code *noun* code *m* précompilé

precondition *verb* préconditionner

predefined *adjective* défini, -e d'avance *or* prédéfini, -e

◊ **predesigned** *adjective* établi, -e d'avance *or* préétabli, -e; **a wide selection of predesigned layouts help you automatically format typical business and technical documents** = un grand choix de modèles de mise en page préétablis vous permet de formater automatiquement vos documents d'affaires ou vos documents techniques

◊ **predetermined** *adjective* déterminé, -ée *or* établi, -e d'avance; prédéterminé, -ée *or* préétabli, -e

predicate *noun* prédicat *m*

QUOTE we should stick to systems which we know are formally sound, such as predicate logic

Personal Computer World

pre-edit *verb* prééditer

pre-emphasise *verb (to boost signal)* préamplifier

preemptive multitasking *noun* (système) multitâche préemptif *or* multitâche en temps partagé

prefix *noun* **(a)** *(code)* préfixe *m* **(b)** *(word)* préfixe

◊ **prefix notation** *noun* notation *f* préfixée *or* notation polonaise (préfixée); **normal notation: (x-y) + z, but using prefix notation: - xy + z** = la notation normale: (x-y) + z, la notation polonaise: - xy + z =

preformatted *adjective* formaté, -ée d'avance

or préformaté, -ée; **a preformatted disk** = disquette *f* préformatée

premix *noun (of signals)* prémixage *m*

preparation *noun* préparation *f*; *(conversion into machine-readable form)* **data preparation** = préparation *f* de données

preprinted *adjective* imprimé, -ée d'avance *or* préimprimé, -ée; **preprinted form** = formulaire *m* préimprimé; **preprinted stationery** = papier *m* à en-tête; papier préimprimé; papier personnalisé

preprocessor *noun* **(a)** *(software)* programme *m* de prétraitement **(b)** *(small computer)* préprocesseur *m*

◊ **preprocess** *verb* prétraiter des données

QUOTE the C preprocessor is in the first stage of converting a written program into machine instructions

QUOTE the preprocessor can be directed to read in another file before completion, perhaps because the same information is needed in each module of the program
Personal Computer World

preproduction *noun* avant-production *f or* préproduction *f*

preprogrammed *adjective* programmé, -ée d'avance *or* préprogrammé, -ée

prerecord **1** *verb* enregistrer (d'avance) *or* préenregistrer; **the answerphone plays a prerecorded message** = le répondeur téléphonique fait entendre un message enregistré **2** *noun* (module de) texte *m* préenregistré

presentation graphics *noun (used to represent business information)* graphique(s) *m(pl) or* diagramme(s) *m(pl)* ; présentation *f* graphique; **the sales for last month looked even better thanks to the use of presentation graphics** = les ventes du mois dernier avaient meilleure mine grâce à une présentation graphique *or* grâce à l'utilisation de diagrammes

◊ **presentation layer** *noun (network layer)* couche *f* présentation

◊ **Presentation Manager** ™ *noun (graphical user interface)* (interface graphique OS/2) Presentation Manager ™

preset *verb* établir *or* fixer *or* programmer d'avance; **the printer was preset with new page parameters** = on avait programmé d'avance les nouveaux paramètres de page de l'imprimante (NOTE: **presetting - preset**)

press 1 *noun* **(a)** *(newspapers and magazines)* la presse *or* les journaux; **the local press** = les journaux régionaux; **the national press** = les grands journaux *or* les grands quotidiens *or* les journaux à gros tirage *or* la presse nationale; **the new car has been advertised in the national press** = la publicité pour la nouvelle voiture a été faite

dans la presse nationale; **we plan to give the product a lot of press publicity** = nous avons l'intention de faire beaucoup de publicité dans la presse pour le produit; **there was no mention of the new product in the press** = aucun journal n'a mentionné le nouveau produit; **press conference** = conférence *f* de presse; **press coverage** = couverture *f* médiatique; **we were very disappointed by the press coverage of the new PC** = nous avons été très déçus par ce que la presse a écrit sur le nouveau PC; **press cutting** = coupure *f* de journal *or* de presse; **we have kept a file of press cuttings about the new software package** = nous avons constitué un dossier de coupures de presse sur le nouveau progiciel; **press release** = communiqué *m* de presse; **the company sent out a press release about the launch of the new scanner** = la société a publié un communiqué de presse au sujet du lancement du nouveau scanner **(b)** **printing press** = presse *f* **2** *verb (to push)* appuyer; **to end the program, press ESCAPE** = appuyez sur la touche ECHAPPEMENT pour arrêter le programme

pressure pad *noun* capteur *m* de pression; **the pressure pad under the carpet will set off the burglar alarm if anyone steps on it** = le détecteur de pression caché sous le tapis déclenche une alarme si quelqu'un marche dessus

prestore *verb* stocker (des données) avant traitement

presumptive address *noun* adresse *f* de base *or* adresse origine *or* adresse primitive

◊ **presumptive instruction** *noun* instruction *f* de base *or* primitive *or* d'origine

prevent *verb* empêcher; **we have changed the passwords to prevent hackers getting into the database** = nous avons changé les mots de passe pour empêcher le piratage de la base de données

◊ **preventive** *or* **preventative** *adjective* préventif, -ive; *(service)* **preventive maintenance** = maintenance *f* préventive; vérification *f or* entretien *m* régulier; **we offer a preventive maintenance contract for the system** = nous offrons un contrat de maintenance préventive qui s'applique à ce système

◊ **prevention** *noun* prévention *f*

preview 1 *verb* prévisualiser **2** *noun* prévisualisation *f*; présentation-aperçu *f*; aperçu *m* avant impression; **page preview** = (fonction de) prévisualisation de page (avant impression)

◊ **previewer** *noun (procedure)* prévisualisation *f* ; présentation-aperçu *f* ; aperçu *m* avant impression

previous *adjective* antérieur, -e *or* précédent, -e; **copy data into the present workspace from the previous file** = copiez les données du fichier précédent dans le fichier actuel

◊ **previously** *adverb* antérieurement *or* précédemment; **the data is copied onto previously formatted disks** = ces données ont été copiées sur des disquettes préformatées

primary *adjective* primaire *or* élémentaire *or* fondamental, -e; *(channel that carries data transmission between two devices)* **primary channel** = canal principal; *compare* SECONDARY CHANNEL; *((i) red, green, blue; (ii) magenta, cyan, yellow)* **primary colours** = couleurs *fpl* fondamentales *or* primaires; *(12 voice channels)* **primary group** = groupe *m* primaire; **primary key** = clé *f* primaire *or* principale; *(main memory)* **primary memory** *or* **storage** *or* **main memory** = mémoire *f* principale; **primary station** = station *f* primaire

◊ **primarily** *adverb* principalement *or* surtout

prime 1 *adjective (very important)* très important, -e *or* essentiel, -elle; **prime attribute** = caractéristique essentielle; *(TV)* **prime time** = heures *fpl* de grande écoute *or* d'écoute maximale; **we are putting out a series of prime-time commercials** = nous commençons à diffuser des spots publicitaires aux heures de grande écoute **2** *noun (number)* nombre *m* premier; **the number seven is a prime** = sept est un nombre premier

primer *noun* guide *m* élémentaire *or* manuel *m* d'utilisation élémentaire

primitive *noun (in programming)* primitive *f or* routine *f* primitive *or* instructions *f* de base; *(in graphics)* forme *f* primitive *or* de base *or* de bibliothèque (dans un programme de graphisme)

print 1 *noun* **(a)** *(etched)* gravure *f*; **he collects 18th century prints** = il fait collection de gravures du 18e siècle **(b)** *(photograph)* épreuve *f or* tirage *m*; **print contrast ratio** = rapport *m* de contraste d'un imprimé **(c)** *(characters on paper)* impression *f*; **he was very pleased to see his book in print** = il était ravi de voir son livre imprimé; **the print from the daisy-wheel printer is clearer than that from the line printer** = l'imprimante à marguerite donne un meilleur résultat que l'imprimante ligne à ligne; **print control character** = caractère de contrôle d'impression; **print format** = format *m* d'impression; **print hammer** = marteau *m* d'impression; *(file that contains all the characters and printer control codes)* **print job** = tâche *f* d'impression; **print life** = durée *f* de vie d'une imprimante; **the printhead has a print life of over 400 million characters** = la tête d'impression peut imprimer plus de 400 millions de caractères; **print modifiers** = modificateurs *mpl or* paramètres *mpl* d'impression; **print pause** = arrêt *m* de l'impression; *(quality of the text or graphics printed)* **print quality** = qualité *f* d'impression; **a desktop printer with a resolution of 600dpi provides good print quality** = une imprimante graphique avec une résolution de 600 dpi fournit une bonne qualité d'impression; *(memory that stores print jobs)* **print queue** = file *f* d'attente à l'impression; *(computer dedicated to managing print queues)* **print server** = serveur *m* d'impression; **print spooling** = impression en différé *or* en arrière-plan *or* par spooling; **print style** = style *m* d'impression **2** *verb* **(a)** imprimer; **the printer prints at 60 characters per second** = cette imprimante a un débit de 60 caractères/seconde; **printed document** = document *m* imprimé; écrit *m*; **printed regulations** = règlements *m* écrits **(b)** *(book)* imprimer; **the book was printed in Hong Kong** = ce livre a été imprimé à Hong Kong; **the book is printing at the moment, so we will have bound copies at the end of the month** = le livre est sous presse, nous recevrons donc les exemplaires reliés vers la fin du mois **(c)** *(to write in capital letters)* écrire en majuscules *or* en capitales *or* en caractères d'imprimerie; **please print your name and address at the top of the form** = écrivez votre nom et votre adresse en majuscules en haut du formulaire

◊ **printed circuit** *or* **printed circuit board (PCB)** *noun* (carte de) circuit *m* imprimé

◊ **printer** *noun* **(a)** computer printer = imprimante *f* (pour ordinateur); **barrel printer** = imprimante à tambour; **bi-directional printer** = imprimante bidirectionnelle; *(produces characters by sending a stream of tiny drops of ink)* **bubble-jet printer** = imprimante à bulle d'encre; **chain printer** = imprimante à chaîne; *(prints information from a computer)* **computer printer** = imprimante d'ordinateur; **daisy-wheel printer** = imprimante à marguerite; **dot-matrix printer** = imprimante matricielle; **duplex printer** = imprimante recto/verso; **graphics printer** = imprimante graphique; **impact printer** = imprimante à impact; **ink-jet printer** = imprimante à jet d'encre; **laser printer** = imprimante laser; **line printer** = imprimante ligne (à ligne); **page printer** = imprimante (en mode) page; **thermal printer** = imprimante thermique; **printer buffer** = tampon *m* d'imprimante; **printer control characters** = caractères *mpl* de contrôle d'impression; *(standard set of commands)* **printer control language (PCL)** = langage PCL *or* jeu de commandes de contrôle d'imprimante PCL; *(software)* **printer driver** = gestionnaire *m or* pilote *m* d'imprimante; *(can interpret the set of commands used to control another brand of printer)* **printer emulation** = émulation *f* d'imprimante; **this printer emulation allows my NEC printer to emulate an Epsom** = cette émulation permet à mon imprimante NEC d'émuler une Epsom; **printer-plotter** = traceur *m*; **printer port** = port *m* (d')imprimante; **printer quality** = qualité *f* d'impression (d'une imprimante); **printer-readable** = imprimable *or* qui peut être lu, -e *or* accepté, -ée par l'imprimante; **printer ribbon** = ruban *m* d'imprimante **(b)** *(company)* imprimeur *m or* imprimerie *f*; **the book will be sent to the printer next week** = on doit envoyer le livre chez l'imprimeur la semaine prochaine; **we are using Japanese printers for some of our magazines** = nous faisons imprimer quelques-unes de nos revues au Japon

◊ **printhead** *noun* tête *f* d'impression

◊ **printing** *noun (action)* impression *f*

◊ **print out** *verb* imprimer (des données)

◊ **printout** *noun* sortie *f* d'imprimante *or* listing *m*; **computer printout** = sortie *f* d'imprimante; **the sales director asked for a printout of the agents' commissions** = le directeur des ventes a demandé un listing des commissions d'agents

◊ **printrun** *noun* tirage *m*

◊ **print shop** *noun* imprimerie *f* à façon

◊ **printwheel** *noun* marguerite *f*

prior 1 *adjective* antérieur, -e *or* précédent, -e **2** *adverb* **prior to** = avant *or* antérieurement à; **the password has to be keyed in prior to accessing the system** = il faut taper le mot de passe avant d'accéder au système

◊ **priority** *noun* (ordre de) priorité *f*; **the operating system has priority over the application when disk space is allocated** = le système d'exploitation a priorité sur les applications en ce qui concerne l'espace alloué sur la disquette; **the disk drive is more important than the printer, so it has a higher priority** = le lecteur de disquettes est plus important que l'imprimante, il a donc la priorité sur cette dernière; **interrupt priority** = priorité d'interruption; **job priority** = priorité d'une tâche; **priority interrupt** = interruption *f* prioritaire; **priority interrupt table** = table *f* des priorités d'interruption; **priority sequence** = ordre *m* de priorité; **priority scheduler** = gestionnaire *m* de priorités

privacy *noun* confidentialité *f*; **privacy of data** = confidentialité *f* des données; **privacy of information** = confidentialité de l'information; **privacy transformation** = cryptage *m* de l'information pour en assurer la confidentialité

private *adjective* privé, -e *or* privatif, -ive; **private address space** = partition *f* privée *or* espace *m* mémoire réservé (à l'usage d'un utilisateur); **private automatic branch exchange (PABX)** = autocommutateur privatif (raccordé au réseau public) (PABX); **private automatic exchange (PAX)** = central téléphonique privatif (non raccordé au réseau public); **private branch exchange (PBX)** = autocommutateur privatif (raccordé au réseau public); **private dial port** = port privatif *or* réservé; **private line** = ligne *f* privée *or* réservée *or* privative; **private manual branch exchange (PMBX)** = central téléphonique manuel privatif (raccordé au secteur public); **private telephone system** = système *m* téléphonique privatif

privilege *noun* privilège *m*

◊ **privileged** *adjective* privilégié, -ée; **privileged account** = partition privilégiée (avec niveau d'accès prioritaire); **the system manager can access anyone else's account from his privileged account** = le gestionnaire du système peut accéder à toutes les partitions à partir de sa partition privilégiée; **privileged instructions** = instructions privilégiées; **the systems manager has a privileged status so he can access any file on the system** = le gestionnaire d'un système jouit d'une partition privilégiée qui lui permet d'accéder à tous les fichiers de ce système; *(mode of an Intel 80286 processor)* **privileged mode** = mode *m* protégé

PRN = PRINTER; *(represents the standard printer port in MS-DOS)* PRN (abréviation pour désigner l'imprimante sous MS-DOS)

problem *noun* **(a)** *(question)* problème *m*; **to solve a problem** = résoudre un problème; **problem definition** = exposé *m* d'un problème; **problem-orientated language (POL)** = langage *m* de résolution de problème *or* langage adapté au problème *or* langage d'application **(b)** *(fault)* mauvais fonctionnement *m or* dysfonctionnement *m or* défaillance *f*; **problem diagnosis** = diagnostic *m* (de cause) de défaillance

procedure *noun* **(a)** *(instruction code)* procédure *f*; **this procedure sorts all the files into alphabetic order, you can call it from the main program by the instruction SORT** = cette procédure qui sert à classer les fichiers par ordre alphabétique peut être sélectionnée depuis le programme principal par la commande SORT **(b)** *(route used)* procédure *or* méthode *f or* marche *f* à suivre; **you should use this procedure to retrieve lost files** = voici la marche à suivre pour retrouver des fichiers perdus; **the procedure is given in the manual** = la procédure est expliquée dans le manuel d'utilisation; **procedure-orientated language** = langage *m* de procédure *or* langage adapté à la procédure

◊ **procedural** *adjective* à base de procédure; **procedural language** = langage de procédure

proceed *verb* continuer *or* passer à; **after spellchecking the text, you can proceed to the printing stage** = vérifiez d'abord l'orthographe, vous pourrez ensuite imprimer votre texte

process 1 *noun* (i) procédé *m or* processus *m* ; (ii) traitement *m*; **the process of setting up the computer takes a long time** = il faut quand même un certain temps pour mettre en route l'ordinateur; **there are five stages in the process** = le processus compte cinq étapes; **process bound** = (programme) limité par le traitement *or* avec contrainte de traitement; **process camera** = caméra *f* de traitement de l'image couleur; **process chart** = schéma *m or* diagramme *m* de procédure; **process control** = commande *f or* contrôle *m* de processus; **process control computer** = ordinateur *m* de contrôle de processus *or* ordinateur industriel; **process control system** = système *m* de contrôle ou de conduite de processus **2** *verb* traiter (des données, etc.) *or* effectuer un traitement; **we processed the new data** = nous avons traité les données; **processing all the information will take a long time** = le traitement des données sera assez long

◊ **processing** *noun* traitement *m*; **page processing time depends on the complexity of a given page** = le temps d'ordinateur requis pour le traitement d'une page de texte varie en fonction de la complexité du document; **batch processing** = traitement par lots *or* par paquets; **data processing** *or* **information processing** = traitement (automatique) de données *or* de l'information; **distributed (data) processing (DDP)** = informatique *f* répartie; **image processing** = traitement de l'image; **immediate processing** = traitement immédiat *or* sur demande; **off-line processing** = traitement (en) différé *or* hors ligne *or* off-line; **on-line processing** = traitement en ligne *or* on-line; **query processing** = traitement de requête; **real-time processing** = traitement en temps réel; **serial processing** = traitement en série; *see also* PARALLEL PROCESSING; **word-processing** *or* **text processing** = traitement de texte; *see also* INFORMATION

processor *noun* processeur *m*; **array processor** = processeur vectoriel; **associative processor** = processeur à mémoire associative; **attached processor** = processeur auxiliaire relié au processeur central; **auxiliary processor** = processeur auxiliaire; **back-end processor** = processeur de fond *or* principal; **bit-slice processor** = processeur en tranches; **central processor** = processeur central; **front-end processor (FEP)** = processeur frontal; **input/output processor** = processeur d'entrée/sortie; **language processor** = processeur de langage; **network processor** = processeur de réseau; *(in a multiprocessor system)* **order code processor** = processeur de code commande; **processor-controlled keying** = saisie *f* au clavier contrôlée par ordinateur; **processor interrupt** = (instruction d') interruption *f* du processeur *or* du traitement; **processor status word (PSW)** = mot *m* d'état d'un processeur; *(operation)* **processor-limited** = dépendant, -e du processeur *or* limité, -ée par le processeur; **dual processor** = double processeur; **image processor** = machine *f* de traitement d'image *or* processeur d'image; **word-processor** *or* **text processor** = *(hardware)* machine *f* de traitement de texte; *(software)* programme *m* *or* logiciel *m* de traitement de texte

---

QUOTE each chip will contain 128 processors
and one million transistors

Computer News

---

producer *noun* *(TV or film)* réalisateur, -trice; **executive producer** = directeur *m* de production

product *noun* **(a** *(item)* produit *m* **(b)** *(result of multiplication)* produit

◊ **production** *noun* *(making or manufacturing)* production *f or* fabrication *f*; **production run** = *(of product)* cycle *m* de production; *(of program)* exécution *f* d'un programme

◊ **productive** *adjective* productif, -ive; *(error-free time)* **productive time** = temps productif

PROFS ™ *(electronic mail system)* (messagerie électronique) PROFS ™

program 1 *noun* *(software)* programme *m*; **assembly program** = assembleur *m or* programme d'assemblage; **background program** = programme non prioritaire; **blue-ribbon program** = programme canon (qui tourne sans erreur du premier coup); **control program/monitor** *or* **control program for microcomputers (CP/M)** = système *m* d'exploitation CP/M; **diagnostic program** = logiciel *m* de diagnostic; **executive program** = programme superviseur; **foreground program** = programme prioritaire; **hardwired program** = programme en logique câblée; **job control program** = programme de contrôle de tâche; **library program** = programme de bibliothèque; **linear program** = programme linéaire; **user program** = programme (d') utilisateur; **program address counter** = PROGRAM COUNTER; **program branch** = branche *f* d'un programme; **program cards** = cartes *fpl* programme; programme sur cartes perforées; **program coding sheet** = formulaire *m* de programmation; **program**

compatibility = compatibilité *f* de logiciel; **program compilation** = compilation *f* de programme; **program counter (PC)** *or* **instruction address register (IAR)** = compteur *m* d'instruction *or* registre *m* compteur; **program crash** = défaillance *f or* crash *m* d'un programme; **I forgot to insert an important instruction which caused a program to crash, erasing all the files on the disk!** = j'ai omis une instruction importante dans le programme ce qui a produit le crash du programme et détruit tous les fichiers contenus sur le disque; **program design language (PDL)** = langage *m* de conception de programme; **program development** = développement *m* d'un programme; **program development system** = environnement *m* de développement de programme; **program documentation** = documentation *f* relative à l'utilisation d'un programme; **program editor** = éditeur *m* de programme; **program evaluation and review technique (PERT)** = technique *f* d'évaluation et de révision de programme; **program execution** = exécution *f* d'un programme; **program file** = fichier *m* programme; **program flowchart** = organigramme *m* de programmation; **program generator** = générateur *m* de programme; *(icon that represents an executable program file)* **program icon** = icône de programme; **to run the program, double-click on the program icon** = pour lancer le programme, faites un double clic sur l'icône du programme; *(Microsoft Windows: file that contains environment settings)* **program information file (PIF)** = fichier PIF (fichier d'information d'un programme, sous MS-Windows); *(single word that represents one operation)* **program instruction** = instruction *f* (dans un programme); *(icon that represents a program)* **program item** = élément *m* de programme; **program library** = bibliothèque *f* de programmes; **program line** = ligne *f* (d'instruction) d'un programme; **program line number** = numéro *m* de référence d'une ligne d'un programme; **program listing** = édition listée d'un programme sur imprimante *or* listing *m or* listage *m* d'un programme; **program maintenance** = maintenance *f* d'un programme; **program name** = nom *m* d'un programme; **program origin** = adresse origine (de la première instruction d'un programme); **program register** = registre *m* d'instruction; *(moving a stored program)* **program relocation** = translation *f or* déplacement (en mémoire) *m or* transfert *m* d'un programme (relogeable); *(software)* **program report generator** = (programme) générateur *m* d'application; **program run** = exécution *f* d'un programme; **program segment** = segment *m* de programme; **program specifications** = spécifications *fpl* d'un programme; **program stack** = pile *f* d'instructions d'un programme; **program statement** = instruction *f or* déclaration *f*; **program step** = pas *m or* étape *f* de programmation; **program storage** = mémoire *f* (de) programme; **program structure** = structure *f* d'un programme; **program testing** = essai *m or* test *m* d'un programme; **program verification** = vérification *f* (du bon fonctionnement) d'un programme **2** *verb* écrire un programme *or* programmer; **programmed halt** = arrêt *m* programmé; **programmed learning** =

formation *f* à l'aide de didacticiel (NOTE: **programs - programming - programmed**)

◊ **programmable** **1** *adjective* *(device)* programmable; **programmable calculator** = calculatrice *f* programmable; **programmable logic array (PLA)** *or* **programmable logic device (PLD)** = circuit *m* logique programmable *or* logique câblée programmable; **programmable interrupt controller** = contrôleur *m* d'interruption programmable; **programmable key** = touche *f* (de fonction) programmable; **programmable memory (PROM)** = mémoire *f* programmable *or* (mémoire) PROM; **programmable read only memory (PROM)** = mémoire morte programmable *or* (mémoire) PROM; *see also* EAROM, EEPROM, EPROM, ROM **2** *noun* ordinateur *m*; **hand-held programmable** = ordinateur de poche

◊ **programmer** *noun* **(a)** *(person)* programmeur, -euse; **the programmer is still working on the new software** = le programmeur n'a pas encore terminé le nouveau logiciel; **analyst/programmer** *or* **programmer/analyst** = analyste-programmeur, -euse; **applications programmer** = programmeur d'application; **systems programmer** = programmeur (de) systèmes **(b)** *(device)* programmateur *m* (d'EPROM)

◊ **programming** *noun* **(a)** programmation *f*; **programming in logic** *or* **PROLOG** = langage *m* PROLOG; **programming language** = langage *m* de programmation; **programming language for microprocessor (PL/M)** = langage *m* PL/M (pour microprocesseurs); **programming standards** = normes *fpl* *or* standards *mpl* de programmation **(b)** programmation d'une PROM

QUOTE we've included some useful program tools to make your job easier. Like the symbolic debugger

Personal Computer World

QUOTE the other use for the socket is to program 2, 4, 8 or 16Kbyte EPROMS

Electronics & Wireless World

QUOTE each of the 16 programmable function keys has two modes - normal and shift - giving 32 possible functions

Micro Decision

---

programme *or US* **program** *noun* *(TV or radio)* programme *m* de radio *or* de télévision; **they were filming a wild life programme** = ils tournaient un programme sur les animaux sauvages; **children's programmes are scheduled for early evening viewing** = les programmes destinés aux enfants sont présentés tôt dans la soirée

project 1 *noun* projet *m*; **his latest project is computerizing the sales team** = il projette maintenant d'informatiser le service des ventes; **the design project was entirely worked out on computer** = le design a été complètement exécuté sur ordinateur *or* la conception a été entièrement assistée par ordinateur; **CAD is essential for accurate project design** = un logiciel de CAO est indispensable à la réalisation d'une conception

très précise **2** *verb* *(to forecast)* prévoir; **the projected sales of the new PC** = les prévisions de vente du nouvel ordinateur individuel *or* du nouveau PC

◊ **projection** *noun* **(a)** *(of sales, etc.)* prévision *f* *or* projection *f* **(b)** *(of film, etc.)* projection *f*; **projection room** = salle *f* de projection

◊ **projector** *noun* **film projector** = projecteur *m* de cinéma *or* de films; **slide projector** = projecteur de diapositives *or* de diapos; *see also* OVERHEAD

PROLOG = PROGRAMMING IN LOGIC

PROM **(a)** = PROGRAMMABLE READ-ONLY MEMORY mémoire *f* morte programmable *or* PROM; **PROM burner** *or* **programmer** = programmeur *m* de PROM; *see also* EPROM **(b)** = PROGRAMMABLE MEMORY mémoire *f* programmable

prompt *noun* message *m* d'invitation à taper une instruction, etc.; invite *f*; **the prompt READY indicates that the system is available to receive instructions** = le message READY signifie que le système est prêt à recevoir des instructions; **command prompt** = invite *f* de commande; **MS-DOS normally displays the command prompt C:\> to indicate that it is ready to process instructions typed in by a user** = MS-DOS affiche normalement l'invite (de commande) C:\> pour indiquer qu'il est prêt à traiter les commandes entrées par l'utilisateur; **system prompt** = invite du système

proof 1 *noun* *(from a printer)* épreuve *f*; **galley proofs** = épreuves en placards *or* en seconde; **page proof** = dernière épreuve *or* épreuve de mise en page *or* tierce *f* **2** *verb* tirer les épreuves (d'un texte)

◊ **proofer** *noun* imprimante *f* (destinée au tirage) d'épreuves; **output devices such as laser proofers and typesetters** = des périphériques tels que les imprimantes laser destinées au tirage d'épreuves et les photocomposeuses

◊ **proofing** *noun* *(producing proofs)* tirage *m* d'épreuves

◊ **proofread** *verb* corriger des épreuves; **has all the text been proofread yet?** = la relecture des épreuves est-elle terminée?

◊ **proofreader** *noun* lecteur, -trice *or* correcteur, -trice d'épreuves

◊ **proofreading** *noun* relecture *f* d'épreuves; correction *f* d'épreuves

propagate *verb* (se) propager *or* (s') étendre; **propagated error** = erreur propagée; **propagating error** = erreur qui se propage

◊ **propagation delay** *noun* délai *m* de propagation; **propagation delay in the transmission path causes signal distortion** = le délai de propagation dans une voie de communication crée une distorsion du signal

proportion *noun* proportion *f*

◊ **proportional spacing** *noun* espacement *m* proportionnel

proprietary file format *noun (data storing method devised by a company)* format *m* de fichier (de) propriétaire *or* (de) constructeur; **you cannot read this spreadsheet file because my software saves it in a proprietary file format** = vous ne pouvez pas lire ce fichier de tableur parce que mon logiciel le sauvegarde en format (de) constructeur

protect *verb* protéger; *(memory location)* **protected location** = emplacement *m* protégé; **protected storage** = mémoire *f* protégée; *(switch or device)* **copy protect** = dispositif *m* anticopie *or* dispositif de protection contre la copie; **all the disks are copy protected** = toutes les disquettes sont munies d'un dispositif anticopie *or* tous les disques sont protégés contre la copie; **crash protected** = protégé contre la détérioration *or* contre la destruction (accidentelle); **if the disk is crash protected, you will never lose your work** = si vous vous servez d'un disque protégé contre la détérioration, vous ne perdrez jamais vos fichiers

◊ **write protect** *verb* protéger (une disquette) contre l'écriture indésirée

◊ **protection** *noun* protection *f or* sécurité *f*; **protection key** = clé *f* de protection; **protection master** = original *m* sauvegardé *or* copie *f* d'original; **copy protection** = (système *or* dispositif *or* codage) anticopie *or* (de) protection contre la copie; **a hard disk may crash because of faulty copy protection** = il arrive qu'une protection anticopie défectueuse entraîne la détérioration du disque dur; **the new program will come without copy protection** = la nouvelle version du logiciel ne sera pas protégée contre la copie; **data protection** = protection *or* sécurité des données; **Data Protection Act** = loi *f* Informatique et Libertés

◊ **protective** *adjective* protecteur, -trice *or* de protection; **the disks are housed in hard protective cases** = les disques sont dans des boîtes de rangement rigides par mesure de protection

protocol *noun* protocole *m*; **protocol standards** = normes *fpl* de protocoles (de transmission)

QUOTE there is a very simple protocol that would exclude hackers from computer networks using the telephone system
Practical Computing

prototype *noun* prototype *m*

◊ **prototyping** *noun* fabrication *f* de prototype *or* prototypage *m*

provider *noun* **information provider (IP)** = source *f* d'information *or* service *m* (fournisseur) d'information *or* service de base de données spécialisées (pour vidéotex)

PrtSc = PRINT SCREEN; *(key that sends the contents of the screen to the printer)* touche PrtSc *or* touche Print Screen; touche Imp Ecran (impression d'écran) (sur un clavier français)

ps = PICOSECOND

PS/2 ™ *(IBM PC computers)* PS/2 ™ (modèle de PC IBM avec bus d'extension MCA); *see also* MCA

PSA *US* = PUBLIC SERVICE ANNOUNCEMENT

pseudo- *prefix* pseudo-

◊ **pseudo-code** *noun* pseudocode *m*

◊ **pseudo-digital** *adjective* (signal) analogique modulé

◊ **pseudo-instruction** *noun* instruction *f* de remplissage *or* pseudo-instruction *f*

◊ **pseudo-operation** *noun* instruction d'assemblage

◊ **pseudo-random** *adjective* pseudo-aléatoire; **pseudo-random number generator** = générateur *m* de nombres pseudo-aléatoires

PSN = PACKET SWITCHED NETWORK

PSS = PACKET SWITCHING SYSTEM

PSTN = PUBLIC SWITCHED TELEPHONE NETWORK

PSU = POWER SUPPLY UNIT

PSW = PROCESSOR STATUS WORD

PTR = PAPER TAPE READER

p-type semiconductor *noun* semi-conducteur *m* de type P

public *adjective* public, publique; **public address system (PA)** = système de sonorisation *f*; **public data network** = réseau *m* public (de transmission de données); **public dial port** = point *m* d'accès au réseau public commuté; *(refers to a document which is not protected by a copyright)* **public domain (PD)** = domaine *m* public; **public key cipher system** = cryptage *m* à clé publique; **public service announcement (PSA)** = *US* publicité *f* de services publics; **public switched telephone network (PSTN)** = réseau *m* téléphonique (public) commuté

publication *noun* **(a)** publication *f or* parution *f*; **the publication of the report on data protection** = la publication du rapport sur la confidentialité de l'information; **the publication date of the book is November 15th** = la date de parution du livre est fixée au 15 novembre **(b)** *(book or leaflet, etc.)* publication; **government publications can be bought at special shops** = les textes ministériels sont en vente dans des librairies spécialisées; **the company specializes in publications for the business reader** = la maison publie des revues destinées aux hommes/femmes d'affaires

publicity *noun* publicité *f or* réclame *f*; **publicity matter** = matériel *mpl* publicitaire

publish *verb* publier; **the institute has published a list of sales figures for different home computers** = l'institut a publié une liste des statistiques de vente d'une série d'ordinateurs personnels; **the company specializes in publishing reference books** = cette maison d'édition publie principalement des livres de référence

◇ **publisher** *noun* (i) éditeur *m* ; (ii) maison *f* d'édition

◇ **publishing** *noun* édition *f or* publication *f*; **desktop publishing (DTP)** = publication *f* assistée par ordinateur (PAO); **electronic publishing** = édition électronique *or* publication assistée par ordinateur (PAO); **professional publishing** = l'édition spécialisée *or* professionnelle

---

QUOTE desktop publishing or the ability to produce high-quality publications using a minicomputer, essentially boils down to combining words and images on pages

Byte

---

pull *verb (to remove data from a stack)* extraire *or* retirer

pull-down *or* **pull-up menu** *noun (options displayed below the entry on a menu-bar)* menu *m* déroulant; **the pull-down menu is viewed by clicking on the menu bar at the top of the screen** = on affiche le menu déroulant en cliquant sur la barre de menu au sommet de l'écran; *compare* POP-UP MENU

◇ **pull up** *verb* **to pull up a line** = élever le potentiel d'une ligne *or* brancher une ligne sur une source d'alimentation; **pull up the input line to a logic one by connecting it to 5 volts** = élever le potentiel de la ligne de réception au niveau logique un, en la connectant sur une source de courant de 5 volts

---

QUOTE the gated inputs lower the standby current and also eliminate the need for input pull-up or pull-down resistors

Electronics & Power

---

pulse 1 *noun* impulsion *f*; **pulse amplitude modulation (PAM)** = modulation *f* d'impulsions en amplitude (MIA); **pulse code modulation (PCM)** = modulation par impulsions et codage (MIC); **pulse duration modulation (PDM)** = modulation d'impulsions en durée (MID); **pulse generator** = générateur *m* d'impulsions; **pulse modulation** = modulation d'impulsion; **pulse position modulation (PPM)** = modulation d'impulsions en position (MIP); **pulse stream** *or* **train** = train *m* d'impulsions; **pulse width modulation (PWM)** = modulation d'impulsions en largeur *or* en durée (MIL *or* MID) **2** *verb* émettre des impulsions; **we pulsed the input but it**

still **would not work** = nous avons émis le signal d'entrée mais toujours sans succès

---

COMMENT: electric pulse can be used to transmit information, as the binary digits 0 and 1 correspond to 'no pulse' and 'pulse' (the voltage level used to distinguish the binary digits 0 and 1, is often zero and 5 or 12 volts, with the pulse width depending on transmission rate)

◇ **pulse-dialling** *noun (telephone dialling that sends a series of pulses)* (composition de numéro d') appel par impulsion *or* au cadran (rotatif); **pulse-dialling takes longer to dial than the newer tone-dialling system** = composer un numéro au cadran prend plus de temps qu'en utilisant le nouveau système à touches

punch 1 *noun* poinçon *m* (de perforation) **2** *verb* perforer; **punch card** *or* **punched card** = carte *f* perforée; **punched card reader** = lecteur *m* de cartes perforées; **punched tag** = étiquette *f* perforée; **punched (paper) tape** = bande (papier) perforée

◇ **punch-down block** *noun (device used to connect UTP cable)* bloc *m* d'enfichage (de câble de réseau local)

punctuation mark *noun* signe *m* de ponctuation

pure *adjective* pur, -e; **pure code** = code pur *or* code binaire; **pure semiconductor** = semi-conducteur simple; **pure tone** = son pur

purge *verb (remove unnecessary data from a file)* vider *or* purger (la mémoire); **each month, I purge the disk of all the old email messages** = chaque mois, je purge le disque de tous les messages périmés

push *verb (to press)* appuyer (sur quelque chose) *or* enfoncer (une touche); *(to move)* (re)pousser (quelque chose); **push-down list** *or* **stack** = pile inversée *or* en mode LIFO; *see also* LIFO; **push instruction** *or* **operation** = instruction *f* d'entrée dans la pile; **push-up list** *or* **stack** = pile en file d'attente *or* en mode FIFO; *see also* FIFO

◇ **pushbutton** *noun* bouton-poussoir *m* *(on telephone)* touche *f*; **pushbutton dialling** = numérotation *f* sur clavier; **pushbutton telephone** = téléphone *m* à clavier

put *verb (to place data onto a stack)* introduire *or* mettre (des données) dans la pile

PWM = PULSE WIDTH MODULATION

Qq

QAM = QUADRATURE AMPLITUDE MODULATION

QBE = QUERY BY EXAMPLE

QISAM = QUEUED INDEXED SEQUENTIAL ACCESS METHOD

QSAM = QUEUED SEQUENTIAL ACCESS METHOD

QL = QUERY LANGUAGE

quad 1 *noun* **(a)** *(sheet of paper)* quadrat *m* **(b)** *(space in printing)* **em quad** = cadratin *m*; **en quad** = demi-cadratin *m* **2** *adjective (four times)* quadruple; *(four bits of data)* **quad density** = quadruple densité

◊ **quadbit** *noun (four bits used by modems to increase transmission rates)* mot *m* de quatre bits

◊ **quadding** *noun (insertion of spaces)* insertion d'espaces

QUOTE in this case, interfacing is done by a single quad-wide adapter
Minicomputer News

quadr- *prefix (meaning four)* quadr- *or* tétra-

quadrature *noun (video playback error)* (erreur de) quadrature *f*

◊ **quadrature amplitude modulation (QAM)** *noun (data encoding method)* modulation d'amplitude en quadrature (MAQ)

◊ **quadrature encoding** *noun (determines the direction of a mouse)* encodage *m* en quadrature

quadrophonic *adjective (using four speakers)* tétraphonique *or* quadriphonique

◊ **quadruple** *adjective* quadruple

◊ **quadruplex** *noun (four signals)* quadruplex *m*

◊ **quadruplicate** *noun* in **quadruplicate** = en quatre exemplaires; **the statements are printed in quadruplicate** = les relevés sont imprimés en quatre exemplaires

quality *noun* qualité *f*; **there is a market for good quality secondhand computers** = il existe un marché pour les ordinateurs d'occasion de bonne qualité; **high quality** *or* **top quality** = de qualité supérieure *or* de choix *or* de luxe; haut de gamme; **printer quality** = qualité *f* d'impression d'une imprimante; *see also* NEAR-LETTER, DRAFT **quality control** = contrôle *m* de (la) qualité; **quality**

controller = responsable *m&f* du contrôle de (la) qualité

QUOTE the computer operates at 120cps in draft quality mode and 30cps in near letter-quality mode
Minicomputer News

quantify *verb* to quantify the effect of something = quantifier; **it is impossible to quantify the effect of the new computer system on our production** = il est impossible de quantifier l'effet du nouveau système informatique sur notre production

◊ **quantifiable** *adjective* quantifiable

◊ **quantifier** *noun* quantificateur *m*

quantity *noun* **(a)** *(amount)* quantité *f*; **a small quantity of illegal copies of the program have been imported** = un petit nombre de disquettes piratées de ce programme se sont infiltrées à l'importation; **he bought a large quantity of spare parts** = il a acheté une grande quantité de pièces détachées **(b)** *(large amount)* grande quantité; **the company offers a discount for quantity purchases** = la société fait une remise sur les achats en nombre

quantization *noun* quantification *f*; **quantization error** = erreur *f* de quantification

◊ **quantize** *verb* quantifier; **quantizing noise** = bruit(s) *m(pl)* de quantification

◊ **quantizer** *noun* quantificateur *m*

quantum *noun (in communications: packet of data)* quantum *m*

quartile *noun* quartile *m*

quarto *noun (paper size)* (format) in-quarto

quartz (crystal) clock *noun* horloge *f* à quartz

quasi- *prefix* quasi-; *(in an assembly program)* **quasi-instruction** = label *m* *or* étiquette *f* *or* pseudo-instruction *f*

quaternary *adjective* quaternaire; **quaternary level quantization** = quantification *f* de niveau quatre

query 1 *noun (question)* question *f* *or* interrogation *f* *or* demande *f*; *(for data retrieval)* requête *f*; *(simple language used to retrieve information from a database management system)* **query by example (QBE)** = langage *m* QBE *or* langage de requête; **in most QBE databases, the query form looks like the record format in the**

database - retrieving data is as easy as filling in a form = dans la plupart des base de données QBE, les requêtes ont sensiblement la même forme que les enregistrements dans la base de données; faire une requête est aussi facile que remplir un formulaire; **query facility** = utilitaire *m* de requête *or* d'interrogation; **query language (QL)** = langage *m* de requête; **query processing** = traitement *m* de requête **2** *verb* interroger *or* poser une question *or* se renseigner (sur)

> QUOTE The Query By Example features now found on some database packages, Foxpro in particular, are easy to use and very powerful.
>
> *Computing*

question 1 *noun* **(a)** *(query)* question *f*; **she refused to answer questions about faulty keyboards** = elle a refusé de répondre aux questions concernant les claviers défectueux **(b)** *(problem)* problème *m or* sujet *m*; **the main question is that of cost** = le problème essentiel est celui du coût; **the board discussed the question of launching a new business computer** = la direction a discuté du lancement d'un nouvel ordinateur de bureau **2** *verb* **(a)** *(to ask questions)* interroger (quelqu'un) *or* poser une question (à quelqu'un) **(b)** *(to query)* mettre en doute *or* se demander; **we all question how accurate the computer printout is** = nous nous demandons tous jusqu'à quel point la sortie d'imprimante est correcte *or* juste

◊ **question mark** *noun* *(the character?)* point *m* d'interrogation; *(often used as a wildcard)* caractère *m* joker; **to find all the letters, use the command DIR LETTER?.DOC which will list LETTER1.DOC, LETTER2.DOC and LETTER3.DOC** = pour trouver toutes les lettres, utilisez la commande DIR LETTER?.DOC qui produira la liste LETTER1.DOC, LETTER2.DOC, LETTER3.DOC; *see also* ASTERISK

◊ **questionnaire** *noun* questionnaire *m*; **to send out a questionnaire to test the opinions of users of the system** = envoyer un questionnaire concernant le système pour faire un sondage d'opinion auprès des utilisateurs; **to answer** *or* **to fill in a questionnaire** = remplir *or* compléter un questionnaire

queue 1 *noun* **(a)** *(of people)* file *f* d'attente; **to form a queue** *or* **to join a queue** = se joindre à la file d'attente **(b)** *(of data)* file *f* d'attente; **channel queue** = file d'attente (du service de transmission *or* de données à transmettre); **file queue** = fichiers *mpl* dans une file d'attente; file d'attente de fichiers; **output devices such as laser printers are connected on-line with an automatic file queue** = les périphériques tels que les imprimantes laser sont reliés en ligne et les fichiers sont gérés par un système de file d'attente automatique; **job queue** = file d'attente de tâches *or* de travaux; **queue discipline** = procédure *f* de file d'attente; **queue management** = gestion *f* de file d'attente; **queue manager** = gestionnaire *m* de file d'attente; **this is a new software spooler with built-in queue management** = il s'agit d'un nouveau logiciel de

spouling avec gestionnaire de file d'attente intégré **2** *verb* prendre la file *or* placer (des données *or* des tâches) dans la file d'attente; *(programming method)* **queued access method** = méthode *f* de gestion de la file d'attente; **queued indexed sequential access method (QISAM)** = méthode *f* d'accès séquentiel indexé en file; **queued sequential access method (QSAM)** = méthode d'accès séquentiel en file; **queuing time** = temps *m* d'attente dans la file

> QUOTE Citibank Global Asset Management had two weeks of parallel running, which threw out some problems. For example, you can have 120 elements in a System/36 job queue, but you can only have 30 elements in a Baby/36 environment.
>
> *Computing*

quick *adjective* rapide

◊ **quickly** *adverb* rapidement

◊ **QuickDraw** ™ *(Apple Macintosh graphics routines)* QuickDraw ™

◊ **quicksort** *noun* tri *m* rapide

◊ **QuickTime** ™ *(Apple Macintosh graphics routines)* QuickTime ™

quiescent *adjective* à l'état de repos *or* au repos

quiet *adjective* silencieux, -ieuse; **laser printers are much quieter than dot-matrix** = les imprimantes laser sont beaucoup plus silencieuses *or* moins bruyantes que les imprimantes matricielles

quintet *noun* *(five bits)* quintet *m*

quit *verb* *(system or program)* quitter *or* abandonner; **do not forget to save your text before you quit the system** = n'oubliez pas de sauvegarder votre texte avant de quitter le système (NOTE: **quitting - quit**)

quotation *noun* *(text borrowed from another text)* citation *f*

◊ **quotation marks** *noun* *(inverted commas)* guillemets *mpl*

quote 1 *verb* **(a)** *(to repeat)* citer *or* mentionner *or* rappeler; **he quoted figures from the newspaper report** = il a cité des chiffres mentionnés dans le journal; **in reply please quote this number** = veuillez rappeler ce numéro de référence dans votre réponse; **when making a complaint please quote the batch number printed on the computer case** = en cas de réclamation, mentionnez toujours le numéro de lot qui apparaît sur le boîtier de l'ordinateur **(b)** *(to estimate)* faire un devis *or* donner des prix; **to quote a price for supplying stationery** = faire un devis *or* donner un prix pour les fournitures de bureau **2** *noun* **(a)** *(quotation)* citation *f or* extrait *m* (référencé) **(b)** *(inverted commas)* **quotes** = guillemets *mpl*; **single quotes** = guillemets simples; **double quotes** = guillemets doubles; **the name of the company should be put in double quotes** = il faut mettre le nom de la société entre guillemets doubles

quotient *noun* quotient *m*

QWERTY *noun* **QWERTY keyboard** = clavier *m* QWERTY; **the computer has a normal QWERTY keyboard** = l'ordinateur possède un clavier QWERTY ordinaire; *see also* AZERTY

QUOTE the keyboard does not have a QWERTY layout but is easy to use

Micro Decision

Rr

R & D = RESEARCH AND DEVELOPMENT **R & D department** = service *m* R et D *or* service de recherche et développement

race *noun (error condition in digital circuit)* pompage *m*

rack *noun* **(a)** *(in shop)* présentoir *m or* étagère *f*; **a rack for holding mag tapes** = un ratelier à *or* pour bandes magnétiques **(b)** *(for electronic circuit boards and peripheral devices)* baie *f or* châssis *m or* coffret *m* avec guide-cartes; **rack mounted** = monté, -ée sur supports

radar *noun* radar *m*

radial transfer *noun* transfert *m* radial (de données *or* programmes)

radiant *adjective* rayonnant, -e *or* de rayonnement; **radiant energy** = énergie rayonnante *or* de rayonnement

◊ **radiate** *verb* **(a)** *(to go in all directions from a central point)* rayonner **(b)** *(to send out rays)* irradier *or* rayonner; *(of antenna)* rayonner; *(of antenna)* **radiating element** = élément *m* rayonnant

◊ **radiator** *noun* radiateur *m*; *(of antenna)* élément rayonnant (d'une antenne)

◊ **radiation** *noun (waves of energy)* radiation *f or* rayonnement *m*; *(from antenna)* rayonnement

radio *noun* radio *f*; *(electromagnetic spectrum)* **radio frequency (RF)** = fréquence *f* radio *or* radiofréquence *f*; **the radio frequency range extends from a few hertz to hundreds of gigahertz** = la gamme des radiofréquences s'étend de quelques hertz seulement à des centaines de gigahertz; **radio microphone** = micro *m* sans fil *or* micro radio; **radio pager** *or* **radio paging device** = récepteur *m* de poche *or* signaleur *m* d'appel (pour système d'appel de personne); **you could contact your salesman if he had a radio pager** = vous pourriez contacter votre vendeur s'il était équipé d'un récepteur de poche; **radio paging** = appel *m* de personne *or* recherche *f* de personne (par système d'appel); **radio phone** *or* **radio telephone** = radiotéléphone *m*; **radio receiver** = récepteur *m* radio; **radio spectrum** = spectre *m* de fréquences radio; **radio telegraphy** = radiotélégraphie *f*; **radio transmission of data** = transmission *f* de données par radio *or* radiotransmission *f*; **radio waves** = ondes *f* radioélectriques

◊ **radio button** *noun (in a GUI: circle displayed beside an option)* bouton *m* radio

◊ **radiocommunications** *noun* radiocommunication *f*

radix *noun (of a number system)* base *f*; **the hexadecimal number has a radix of 16** = le nombre hexadécimal est à base 16; **radix complement** = complément à la base; *see* TEN'S, TWO'S COMPLEMENT; **radix notation** = numération *f* à base

ragged *adjective* en dents de scie *or* déchiqueté, -ée; *(book)* non rogné; *(text)* **ragged left** = (texte) non justifié à gauche; **ragged right** = (texte) non justifié à droite; **ragged text** = texte non justifié

RAID = REDUNDANT ARRAY of INEXPENSIVE DISKS

RAM = RANDOM ACCESS MEMORY mémoire *f* vive *or* (mémoire) RAM *or* mémoire à accès aléatoire; *(RAM used to buffer data transfers)* **RAM cache** = mémoire cache *or* antémémoire *f*; *(memory expansion card which contains RAM chips)* **RAM card** = carte RAM; *(device that contains RAM chips)* **RAM cartridge** = cartouche RAM; **you can increase the printer's memory by plugging in another RAM cartridge** = vous pouvez augmenter la mémoire de l'imprimante en enfichant une cartouche RAM supplémentaire; **RAM chip** = puce *f* RAM; **RAM disk** = disque *m* RAM *or* disque mémoire; **RAM loader** = (programme) chargeur *m or* programme de chargement de la mémoire vive; **RAM refresh** = (signal de) rafraîchissement *m* de la mémoire RAM; **RAM refresh rate** = fréquence *f* de rafraîchissement de la mémoire RAM; *(program that loads itself into main memory)* **RAM resident program** *or* **TSR** = programme résident *or* TSR; **when you hit Ctrl-F5, you will activate the RAM resident program and it will display your day's diary** = en appuyant sur les touches Ctrl-F5, vous activez le programme résident et ouvrez l'agenda de la journée; **dynamic RAM** = (mémoire) RAM dynamique; **partial RAM** = RAM partielle; **self-refreshing RAM** = RAM auto-rafraîchie *or* auto-entretenue; **static RAM** = (mémoire) RAM statique (NOTE: there is no plural for RAM, and it often has no article: **512K of RAM; the file is stored in RAM**)

QUOTE in addition the board features 512K of video RAM, expandable up to a massive 1MB
PC Business World

QUOTE fast memory is RAM that does not have to share bus access with the chip that manages the video display
Byte

QUOTE The HP Enterprise Desktops have hard-disk capacities of between 260Mb and 1Gb, with RAM ranging from 16Mb up to 128Mb.
Computing

random *adjective* aléatoire; **random process** = processus *m* *or* procédé *m* aléatoire

◊ **random access** *noun* accès *m* aléatoire *or* sélectif *or* direct; **disk drives are random access, magnetic tape is sequential access memory** = les lecteurs de disquettes permettent l'accès aléatoire *or* direct des données alors qu'une bande magnétique en permet l'accès séquentiel; **random access device** = dispositif *m* mémoire à accès aléatoire; **random access files** = fichiers *mpl* à accès direct *or* sélectif; **random access storage** = mémoire à accès aléatoire *or* sélectif *or* direct; **random access memory (RAM)** = mémoire *f* vive *or* mémoire à accès aléatoire *or* (mémoire) RAM; *see* RAM

◊ **random number** *noun* nombre aléatoire *or* choisi au hasard; *(creating a sequence of numbers which appears to be random)* **random number generation** = génération *f* de nombres aléatoires; **random number generator** = générateur *m* de nombres aléatoires

◊ **random processing** *noun* traitement *m* aléatoire *or* direct (des données)

range 1 *noun* **(a)** *(series of items)* gamme *f*; **a wide range of products** = toute une gamme de produits; **the catalogue lists a wide range of computer stationery** = on trouve dans le catalogue toute une gamme de papiers listing **(b)** *(reach)* portée *f* *or* étendue *f* **(c)** *(set of values)* gamme *or* fourchette *f*; **number range** = gamme de valeurs; **frequency range** = gamme de fréquences; **the telephone channel can accept signals in the frequency range 300 - 3400Hz** la transmission par téléphone accepte des signaux dans la gamme de fréquences 300 à 3400 Hz; **magnetic tape is stable within a temperature range of 0° to 40°C** = la bande magnétique est stable entre 0° et 40°C **2** *verb* **(a)** *(to vary)* varier *or* s'étendre *or* aller (de ... à); **the company's products range from a cheap lapheld micro to a multistation mainframe** = la gamme des produits de la société va du micro portatif au gros ordinateur multiposte **(b)** *(to put text in order)* aligner *or* justifier; **range left** = aligner à gauche

rank *verb* classer par rang *or* par ordre d'importance

rapid *adjective* rapide; **rapid access** = accès *m* rapide; **rapid access memory** *or* **fast access memory (FAM)** = mémoire *f* à accès rapide

raster *noun* raster *m*; **raster graphics** = infographie *f* *or* graphisme *m* par balayage de trame; **raster image processor (RIP)** = raster (RIP) *or* processeur *m* graphique à balayage de trame *or* processeur d'image matricielle; **an electronic page can be converted to a printer-readable video image by an on-board raster image processor** = une page électronique peut être convertie en image vidéo imprimable à l'aide d'un raster *or* d'un processeur d'image matricielle; *(one sweep)* **raster scan** = passe *f* de balayage; *(action)* **raster scanning** = balayage *m* récurrent *or* balayage (vertical) de trame

rate 1 *noun* *(ratio)* taux *m*; *(speed)* vitesse *f*; **the processor's instruction execution rate is better than the older version** = la vitesse d'exécution des commandes de ce processeur est plus grande qu'avec l'ancienne version; **error rate** = taux d'erreur; *(transmitted per second)* **information rate** = débit *m* de transmission d'informations **2** *verb* *(to evaluate)* évaluer; **rated throughput** = rendement *m* estimé

◊ **ratings** *noun* *(of TV programmes)* taux *m* d'écoute; **ratings battle** *or* **war** = guerre *f* de taux d'écoute *or* bataille *f* d'audimat

ratio *noun* ratio *m* *or* rapport *m* *or* taux *m*; **the ratio of 10 to 5 is 2:1** = le rapport 10 sur 5 est (égal à) 2:1; **the ratio of corrupt bits per transmitted message is falling with new technology** = le taux des bits corrompus par message transmis est moins élevé grâce aux nouvelles techniques

◊ **rational number** *noun* nombre *m* rationnel; **24 over 7 is a rational number** = 24/7 est un nombre rationnel; **0.333 can be written as the rational number 1/3** = on peut écrire 0,333 sous la forme du nombre rationnel 1/3

raw *adjective* *(not processed)* brut, -e; **raw data** = données *fpl* brutes *or* non traitées; **this small computer collects raw data from the sensors, converts it and transmits it to the mainframe** = ce petit ordinateur recueille les données brutes venant des capteurs, les convertit et les transmet au gros ordinateur; *(method of accessing a file)* **raw mode** = mode brut *or* direct

ray *noun* rayon *m* *or* rayonnement *m*; **the rays of light pass down the optical fibre** = les rayons lumineux se propagent dans la fibre optique

◊ **ray tracing** *noun* *(method of creating computer-generated graphics)* tracé *m* filaire; **to generate this picture with ray tracing will take several hours on this powerful PC** = générer cette image en mode filaire va prendre plusieurs heures sur ce PC puissant

react *verb* réagir; **to react to something** = réagir à quelque chose; *(of substance)* **to react with something** = entrer en réaction avec une autre substance

◊ **reactance** *noun* réactance *f*

◊ **reaction** *noun* réaction *f*

◊ **reactive mode** *noun* mode *m* réactif

RD = REMOVE DIRECTORY; *(DOS command to remove an empty subdirectory)* (commande) RD *or* Remove Directory (pour supprimer un répertoire DOS)

RDBMS = RELATIONAL DATABASE MANAGEMENT SYSTEM

read *verb* **(a)** lire; **conditions of sale are printed in such small characters that they are difficult to read** = les conditions de vente sont imprimées en caractères si petits qu'il est très difficile de les lire; **can the OCR read typeset characters?** = est-ce qu'un lecteur optique peut lire les caractères d'imprimerie? **(b)** *(to retrieve data)* lire *or* extraire; **this instruction reads the first record of a file** = cette instruction va lire le premier enregistrement du fichier; **access time can be the time taken to read from a record** = le temps d'accès peut être le temps requis pour la lecture de données (rangées) en mémoire; **destructive read** = lecture *f* destructive; **read back check** = contrôle *m* par relecture; **read cycle** = cycle *m* de lecture; *(error during a read operation)* **read error** = erreur *f* de lecture; **read head** = tête *f* de lecture; *(device)* **read only** = (mémoire) à lecture seule; *(attribute bit of a file)* **read only attribute** = attribut *m* lecture seule; **read only memory (ROM)** = mémoire *f* morte *or* (mémoire) ROM; **read rate** = vitesse *f* de lecture; **read/write channel** = voie *f* de lecture/écriture; **read/write cycle** = cycle *m* de lecture/écriture; **read/write head** = tête *f* de lecture/écriture; **read/write memory** = mémoire *f* lecture/écriture

◊ **readable** *adjective* qui peut être lu, -e; **the electronic page is converted to a printer-readable video image** = le texte électronique est converti en image vidéo qui peut être lue par l'imprimante; *(command or data)* **machine-readable** = (commande *or* donnée) en langage machine *or* directement exploitable

◊ **reader** *noun (device)* lecteur *m*; **card reader** = lecteur de cartes (magnétiques); **tape reader** = lecteur de bandes magnétiques; *see also* BAR CODE READER, OPTICAL CHARACTER READER

◊ **read-in** *or* **read in** *verb (to transfer data from an external source to main memory)* introduire *or* entrer *or* enregistrer; **the computer automatically read-in thirty values from the A/D converter** = l'ordinateur a lu *or* enregistré automatiquement trente valeurs données par le convertisseur analogique-numérique

◊ **reading** *noun* lecture *f*; **optical reading** = lecture optique

◊ **readout** *noun* affichage *m* *or* lecture *f*; **the readout displayed the time** = l'heure était affichée; **the clock had a digital readout** = cette horloge avait un affichage numérique; **destructive readout** = lecture *f* destructive; **readout device** = dispositif *m* *or* écran *m* d'affichage

QUOTE some OCR programs can be taught to read typefaces that are not in their library
Publish

QUOTE the machine easily reads in text from typewriters and daisy- wheel printers
PC Business World

ready *adjective* prêt, -e; **the green light indicates the system is ready for another program** = le voyant vert allumé signifie que le système est prêt à accepter le programme suivant; **the programming will not be ready until next week** = la programmation ne sera pas terminée avant la semaine prochaine; **the maintenance people hope that the system will be ready for use in 24 hours** = le service de maintenance espère que le système sera de nouveau en état de fonctionner dans les 24 heures; *(of line or device)* **ready state** = état prêt

real *adjective* réel, réelle

◊ **real address** *noun (directly accesses a memory location)* adresse *f* absolue; *compare* PAGED ADDRESS

◊ **real memory** *noun* mémoire *f* réelle; *compare with* VIRTUAL MEMORY

◊ **real mode** *noun (default operating mode for an IBM PC)* mode *m* réel *or* non protégé

◊ **real number** *noun* nombre *m* réel

◊ **real time** *noun* temps *m* réel; **a navigation system needs to be able to process the position of a ship in real time and take suitable action before she hits a rock** = un système de navigation doit pouvoir faire le point en temps réel et prendre les mesures nécessaires pour éviter de heurter un écueil; **program shown in real time** = émission *f* en direct; *(objects appear to move at the same speed as they would in real life)* **real-time animation** = animation en temps réel; **US real-time clock** = horloge *f* en temps réel; **real time execution (RTE)** = exécution *f* (d'un programme) en temps réel; **real-time input** = entrée *f* en temps réel; **real-time multi-tasking** = traitement *m* multitâche en temps réel; *(control a real-time system)* **real-time operating system** = système d'exploitation en temps réel; **real-time processing** = traitement en temps réel; **real-time simulation** = simulation *f* en temps réel

◊ **real-time system** *noun* système *m* en temps réel; **in a real-time system, as you move the joystick left, the image on the screen moves left. If there is a pause for processing it is not a true real-time system** = dans un système en temps réel, le déplacement de l'image vers la gauche est parfaitement synchronisé au mouvement du manche à balai vers la gauche; s'il se produit un délai entre l'action et le résultat, il ne s'agit pas d'un véritable système en temps réel

QUOTE a real-time process is one which interacts with a real external activity and respects deadlines imposed by that activity
.EXE

QUOTE define a real-time system as any system which is expected to interact with its environment within certain timing constraints
British Telecom Technology Journal

QUOTE Quotron provides real-time quotes, news and analysis on equity securities through a network of 40,000 terminals to US brokers and investors.
Computing

reboot *verb* relancer; **we rebooted and the files reappeared** = nous avons relancé le système et les fichiers ont réapparu sur l'écran

recall 1 *noun* rappel *m* **2** *verb* rappeler

QUOTE automatic recall provides the facility to recall the last twenty commands and to edit and re-use them
Practical Computing

receive *verb* recevoir; **the computer received data via the telephone line** = les données ont été transmises à l'ordinateur par l'intermédiaire de la ligne téléphonique; **receive only terminal** = terminal d'arrivée

◊ **receiver** *noun* récepteur *m*; **radio receiver** = récepteur radio; **the radio receiver picked up your signal very strongly** = votre signal a été capté très clairement par le récepteur radio; **receiver register** = registre *m* des entrées

reception *noun (of radio or TV signal)* réception *f*; **signal reception is bad with that aerial** = cette antenne ne donne pas un bonne réception

rechargeable *adjective (battery)* rechargeable

recode *verb* modifier les codes d'un programme

recognition *noun* reconnaissance *f*; **recognition logic** = logique *f* de reconnaissance; **optical character recognition** = reconnaissance optique de caractères; **optical mark recognition** = reconnaissance optique de marques *or* de signes *or* de symboles; **voice recognition** = reconnaissance de la parole *or* reconnaissance vocale

◊ **recognizable** *adjective* reconnaissable

◊ **recognize** *verb* reconnaître; **the scanner will recognize most character fonts** = le scanner reconnaît la plupart des polices de caractères

recompile *verb* effectuer une nouvelle compilation

reconfiguration *noun* reconfiguration *f*

◊ **reconfigure** *verb* reconfigurer; **I reconfigured the field structure in the file** = j'ai reconfiguré la structure des champs du fichier; **this program allows us to reconfigure the system to our own requirements** = avec ce programme, il est possible de reconfigurer le système selon nos besoins

reconnect *verb* reconnecter *or* rétablir une liaison; **the telephone engineers are trying to reconnect the telephone** = les techniciens (du téléphone) essayent de rétablir la liaison téléphonique

reconstitute *verb (after crash or corruption)* reconstituer *or* restaurer (des données)

record 1 *noun* **(a)** *(items of data)* article *m or* enregistrement *m*; **your record contains several fields that have been grouped together under the one heading** = votre article *or* enregistrement contient divers champs regroupés sous une même rubrique; **this record contains all their personal details** = cet enregistrement contient toutes leurs coordonnées; **chained record** = article *or* enregistrement chaîné; **change** *or* **transaction record** = enregistrement d'une modification *or* d'une transaction; **logical record** = enregistrement logique; **physical record** = enregistrement physique; **record count** = (nombre d') enregistrements dans un fichier; **record format** *or* **layout** = format *m or* présentation *f* d'un enregistrement; **record length** = longueur *f or* dimension *f* d'un enregistrement; *(method of preventing more than one user writing data)* **record locking** = verrouillage *m* des enregistrements;

(fields which make up a record) **record structure** = structure *f* d'un enregistrement; **records manager** = gestionnaire *m* d'enregistrements; **records management** = programme de gestion d'enregistrements *or* de fichiers **(b)** *(disk)* disque *m*; **record changer** = changeur *m* de disques automatique **2** *verb* inscrire; *(data)* enregistrer; **record the results in this column** = inscrivez les résultats dans cette colonne; **this device records signals onto magnetic tape** = ce dispositif enregistre les signaux sur bande magnétique; **digitally recorded data are used to generate images** = des données enregistrées numériquement servent à générer des images; **record button** = touche *f or* bouton *m* d'enregistrement; **record gap** = espace *m* entre deux enregistrements; **record head** *or* **write head** = tête *f* d'écriture *or* d'enregistrement

QUOTE you can echo the previous record if a lot of replication is involved

QUOTE records may be sorted before the report is created, using up to nine sort fields
Byte

QUOTE file and record-locking procedures have to be implemented to make sure that files cannot be corrupted when two users try to read or write to the same record simultaneously
Micro Decision

QUOTE Micro Focus provides Fileshare 2, which it claims substantially reduces network traffic, and provides features such as full record locking, update logging and roll-forward recovery.
Computing

recorder *noun (equipment)* enregistreur *m*; **magnetic tape recorder** = enregistreur de bandes magnétiques; magnétophone *m*

recording *noun* **(a)** *(process of storing signals, etc.)* enregistrement *m*; **recording density** = densité *f* d'enregistrement; *(telephone line)* **recording trunk** = ligne *f* de jonction **(b)** *(on record or tape)* enregistrement; **a new recording of Beethoven's quartets** = un nouvel enregistrement des quatuors de Beethoven

QUOTE file and record-locking procedures have to be implemented to make sure that files cannot be corrupted when two users try to read or write to the same record simultaneously
Micro Decision

recover *verb* retrouver *or* récupérer; **it is possible to recover the data but it can take a long time** = les données sont récupérables mais il faudra beaucoup de temps pour y arriver

◊ **recoverable error** *noun* erreur récupérable *or* réparable

◊ **recovery** *noun* **(a)** *(return to normal)* restauration *f or* remise *f* en état; **automatic recovery program** = programme de restauration *or* de remise en état automatique; **failure recovery** = remise en marche *or* remise en route *or* reprise sur

incident; **fall back recovery** = reprise *f* au point
d'appel *or* remise *f* en marche au point de reprise *or*
au point d'arrêt; *(from read to write)* **sense
recovery time** = délai *m* de conversion; *(processes
to return a system to normal)* **recovery procedure** =
procédure *f* de restauration **(b)** *(getting back
something)* récupération *f*; **the recovery of lost files
can be carried out using a recovery procedure** = les
fichiers perdus peuvent être récupérés en suivant
une procédure de récupération de données

rectangular waveguide *noun* guide *m*
d'ondes rectangulaire

rectify *verb* **(a)** *(to correct)* corriger; **they had to
rectify the error at the printout stage** = ils ont dû
corriger l'erreur à l'impression **(b)** *(to remove the
positive or negative sections of a signal)* redresser

◊ **rectifier** *noun* *(electronic circuit)* circuit *m*
redresseur

recto *noun* *(of page)* endroit *m or* recto *m*; *(page
of book)* page *f* de droite *or* belle page

recursion *or* **recursive routine** *noun* routine
f récursive; **daisy-chain recursion** = boucle *f* de
récurrence; **recursive call** = appel récursif *or*
procédure récursive

redefine *verb* redéfinir *or* définir de nouveau;
reprogrammer; établir de nouveaux paramètres;
we redefined the initial parameters = nous avons
redéfini les premiers paramètres; **to redefine a key**
= redéfinir la fonction d'une touche *or*
reprogrammer une touche; **I have redefined this
key to display the figure five when pressed** = j'ai
reprogrammé cette touche pour obtenir un 5

◊ **redefinable** *adjective* qui peut être redéfini, -e
or reprogrammé, -ée; reprogrammable

red, green, blue (RGB) *noun* *(the three
colour picture beams used in a colour TV)* rouge,
vert, bleu *or* RVB; *see also* RGB

redial *verb* *(telephone)* composer (le numéro) de
nouveau; **auto-redial** = (modem *or* téléphone avec)
système *m* de rappel automatique

redirect *verb* réacheminer

◊ **redirection** *noun* **(a)** réacheminement *m*; **call
forwarding is automatic redirection of calls** = faire
suivre des appels veut dire les réacheminer
automatiquement **(b)** *(treating the output of one
program as input for another)* acheminer *or*
rediriger; ré-injecter; **you can sort the results from
a DIR command by redirecting to the SORT
command** = vous pouvez trier les résultats d'une
commande DIR en les ré-injectant dans la
commande SORT; *(character > used to show that*

*the output of one program is to be sent as input to
another)* **redirect** *or* **redirection operator** =
opérateur *m or* caractère *m* de redirection (sous
DOS)

redliner *noun* *(highlights text in a different
colour)* surligné *m* rouge

redo *verb* refaire; **redo from start** = (à) refaire à
partir du début

redraw *verb* redessiner *or* dessiner de nouveau;
**can the computer redraw the graphics showing the
product from the top view?** = est-ce que
l'ordinateur peut refaire le graphique du produit
de façon à en présenter une vue plongeante?

reduce *verb* **(a)** *(to make smaller)* réduire **(b)**
(to convert data into a more compact form)
comprimer

◊ **reduced instruction set computer
(RISC)** *noun* processeur à jeu d'instructions
réduit *or* à architecture RISC; *compare with* WISC

◊ **reduction** *noun* réduction *f*; **we need a 25%
reduction to fit the halftone in the space** = il nous
faut réduire la reproduction en simili de 25% pour
pouvoir l'insérer dans l'espace fixé

redundancy *noun* redondance *f*; **redundancy
checking** = contrôle par redondance; **longitudinal
redundancy check** = contrôle *m* par redondance
longitudinale; **network redundancy** = liaisons
redondantes *or* auxiliaires d'un réseau; **vertical
redundancy check** = contrôle par redondance
verticale

◊ **redundant** *adjective* **(a)** *(data that can be
removed without losing any information)* en trop *or*
superflu, -e; redondant, -e *or* de redondance; **the
parity bits on the received data are redundant and
can be removed** = les bits de parité des données
reçues sont redondants et peuvent être supprimés;
(disk drive system) **redundant array of inexpensive
disks (RAID)** = système de stockage rapide sur
disques multiples (RAID); **redundant character** =
caractère de redondance; **redundant code** = code
de redondance **(b)** *(equipment kept ready)*
suréquipement *m* de sécurité *or* équipement
redondant

reel *noun* bobine *f*; **he dropped the reel on the floor
and the tape unwound itself** = il a laissé tomber la
bobine et le ruban s'est déroulé; **pick-up reel** =
bobine réceptrice *or* d'enroulement; **open reel tape**
= bande *f* sur bobine ouverte

◊ **reel to reel** *adjective* (copie) de bobine à
bobine; **reel to reel recorder** = enregistreur *m*
bobine à bobine

re-entrant program *or* **code** *or* **routine** *noun*
programme *m* ré-entrant

◊ **re-entry** *noun* rentrée *f or* ré-entrée *f*; **re-entry point** = point *m* de rentrée *or* de reprise

refer *verb* *(mentionner)* mentionner *or* faire référence (à) *or* se référer (à); **the manual refers to the serial port, but I cannot find it** = le manuel mentionne un port série, mais je n'en vois aucun

◊ **reference 1** *noun* **(a)** *(value used as a starting point)* référence *f*; **reference address** = adresse *f* de référence; *(of signal)* **reference level** = niveau *m* de référence; **reference time** = période *f* de référence **(b)** *(file of data)* **reference file** = fichier *m* de référence; **reference instruction** = instruction *f* de base; *(of stored data)* **reference list** = liste *f* de références; **reference mark** = renvoi *m*; **reference retrieval system** = système *m* de référence *or* (système d') index *m*; **reference table** = table *f or* tableau *m* de référence **2** *verb* référencer; **the access time taken to reference an item in memory is short** = le temps d'accès à une donnée (en mémoire) est très court

◊ **referencing** *noun* référençage *m*

> QUOTE a referencing function dynamically links all references throughout a document
> *Byte*

reflect *verb* *(light or image)* réfléchir; **in a reflex camera, the image is reflected by an inbuilt mirror** = dans un appareil reflex, l'image est refléchie par un miroir interne

◊ **reflectance** *noun* réflectance *f* (NOTE: the opposite is **absorptance)**

◊ **reflected code** *noun* code *m* réfléchi

◊ **reflection** *noun* réflexion *f*; **signal reflection** = coefficient *m* de réflexion d'un signal

◊ **reflective disc** *noun* disque *m* laser à réflexion *or* disque à surface réfléchissante

reflex (camera) *noun* appareil *m* (photo) reflex

reformat *verb* reformater; **do not reformat your hard disk unless you can't do anything else** = évitez de reformater votre disque dur à moins qu'il n'y ait aucune autre solution

◊ **reformatting** *noun* reformatage *m*; **reformatting destroys all the data on a disk** = toutes les données contenues sur un disque sont détruites par le reformatage

refract *verb* (se) réfracter

◊ **refraction** *noun* réfraction *f*

◊ **refractive index** *noun* indice *m* de réfraction

refresh *verb* **(a)** *(to update a memory)* rafraîchir *or* entretenir; *(time during which a controller updates the contents of dynamic RAM chips)* **refresh cycle** = cycle *m or* temps *m* de rafraîchissement; **memory refresh signal** = signal *m* de rafraîchissement de la mémoire; **RAM refresh rate** = fréquence *f* de rafraîchissement de la mémoire vive; **self-refreshing RAM** = RAM auto-entretenue *or* autorafraîchie **(b)** *(image)* **screen refresh** = (i) rafraîchir l'écran; (ii) rafraîchissement d'écran; **refresh rate** = fréquence de rafraîchissement (de l'écran)

> QUOTE Philips autoscan colour monitor, the 4CM6099, has SVGA refresh rates of 72Hz (800 x 600) and EVGA refresh rates of 70Hz (1,024 x 768).
> *Computing*

regenerate *verb* recréer *or* régénérer

◊ **regeneration** *noun* *(of signal)* régénération *f* (du signal)

◊ **regenerative memory** *noun* mémoire *f* qui demande à être rafraîchie; **dynamic RAM is regenerative memory - it needs to be refreshed every 250ns** = une RAM dynamique demande à être rafraîchie toutes les 250ns; **the CRT display can be thought of as regenerative memory, it requires regular refresh picture scans to prevent flicker** = l'écran peut être comparé à une mémoire qui demande à être rafraîchie, il doit être balayé régulièrement pour éviter de présenter des images instables; *(reading that regenerates data)* **regenerative reading** = lecture *f* régénératrice (de données)

◊ **regenerator** *noun* *(device that regenerates a received signal)* régénérateur *m or* amplificateur *m* de signal

region *noun* *(area of memory or program)* zone *f or* région *f* *(fill an area with a particular colour)* **region fill** = remplissage *m* de zone

◊ **regional breakpoint** *noun* point *m* d'arrêt variable (de déroulement d'un programme)

register 1 *noun* **(a)** *(for data)* registre *m*; **accumulator register** = accumulateur *m*; **address register** = registre d'adresse; **base register** = registre de base; **buffer register** = registre tampon; **circulating register** = registre à *or* de décalage *or* registre permutable *or* à bits circulants; **control register** = registre de contrôle *or* de commande; **data register** = registre de données; **external register** = accumulateur *or* registre externe; **index register** = registre d'index; **input/output register** = registre d'entrée/sortie; **instruction register** = registre d'instruction; **instruction address register (IAR)** = registre d'adresse d'instruction; **memory address register (MAR)** = registre des adresses (en mémoire); **next instruction register** = registre d'instruction à exécuter *or* de la prochaine instruction; **program status word register (PSW register)** = registre des mots d'état; **sequence control register (SCR)** = registre d'instruction à suivre *or* à exécuter; **shift register** = registre à *or* de décalage; **register addressing** = adressage *m* de registre; **register file** = fichier *m* des registres; *(size in bits)* **register length** = taille *f* d'un registre; **register map** = (affichage du) contenu des registres *or* (affichage de la) configuration des registres **(b)** *(printing)* **register marks** = repères *mpl*; **in register** = en repérage; **the two colours are out of register** = les deux couleurs ne sont pas superposées **2** *verb* **(a)** *(to react)* réagir; **light-sensitive films register light intensity** = la réaction des films photosensibles varie suivant l'intensité de la lumière **(b)** *(to superimpose two images)* faire coïncider *or* positionner sur repères

regulate *verb* contrôler *or* ajuster *or* régler *or*

réguler; **regulated power supply** = courant *m* régulé *or* contrôlé

rehyphenation *noun* remplacement *m* de césures *or* des traits d'union

reject *verb* rejeter; **the computer rejects all incoming data from incompatible sources** = l'ordinateur rejette toute donnée venant de sources non compatibles

◊ **rejection** *noun* rejet *m*; **rejection error** = erreur *f* de rejet

relational database *noun (database in which all the items of data can be interconnected)* base *f* de données relationnelle; **if you search the relational database for the surname, you can pull out his salary from the related accounts database** = lorsque vous cherchez un patronyme dans une base de données relationnelle, il est aussi possible d'extraire le salaire (de la personne) du Livre de comptes qui lui est relié; **relational database management system (RDBMS)** = système de gestion de base de données relationnelle (SGBDR); **relational operator** *or* **logical operator** = opérateur *m* relationnel *or* logique; **relational query** = requête *f* relationnelle; **the relational query 'find all men under 35 years old' will not work on this system** = la requête relationnelle: 'trouver tous les individus mâles de moins de 35 ans' ne peut pas être traitée par ce système

> QUOTE Data replication is the process of duplicating data on, or distributing it between, databases, usually on different servers. It is not new, having been around for many years: nor is it confined to relational databases.
> *Computing*

◊ **relationship** *noun* rapport *m* *or* relation *f*

relative *adjective* relatif, -ive; *(location in relation to a reference address)* **relative address** *or* **indirect address** = adresse relative *or* indirecte *or* calculée; **relative coding** = codage relatif; **relative coordinates** = coordonnées relatives; **relative data** = données relatives; **relative error** = erreur relative; *(input device such as a mouse)* **relative pointing device** = dispositif de pointage relatif *or* pointeur relatif; **relative-time clock** = horloge relative

relay 1 *noun (switch)* relais *m*; **there is a relay in the circuit** = ce circuit comporte un relais; **it is relay-rated at 5 Amps** = il est protégé par un relais de 5A; **microwave relay** = relais hertzien **2** *verb* retransmettre; **all messages are relayed through this small micro** = tous les messages sont retransmis par l'intermédiaire de ce petit micro

release 1 *noun* **(a)** *(version of a product)* version *f*; **the latest software is release 5** = la dernière version du logiciel porte le numéro 5; *(number of the version of a product)* **release number** = numéro *m* de version; *see also* VERSION **(b)** *(putting a new product on the market)* mise *f* sur le marché *or* commercialisation *f*; *(records)* **new releases** = nouveaux enregistrements *or* nouveaux disques; nouveautés *fpl*; **on general release** = *(available)*

(produit) sur le marché; *(shown)* (film) à l'écran **(c)** **press release** = communiqué *m* de presse **2** *verb* **(a)** *(new product)* mettre (un nouveau produit) sur le marché; lancer *or* commercialiser (un nouveau produit); *(a new software version)* publier une nouvelle version *or* une mise à jour **(b)** *(of software: relinquish control)* relâcher *or* libérer (un bloc de mémoire ou un fichier)

relevance *noun* relation pertinente *f* ; pertinence *f*

◊ **relevant** *adjective* pertinent, -e

reliability *noun* fiabilité *f*; **it has an excellent reliability record** = il est reconnu pour sa fiabilité; **the product has passed its reliability tests** = ce produit a réussi tous les tests de fiabilité

◊ **reliable** *adjective* fiable *or* sur lequel on peut compter *or* auquel on peut se fier *or* qui donne satisfaction; **the early versions of the software were not completely reliable** = les premières versions du logiciel ne donnaient pas complète satisfaction

relief printing *noun* impression *f* en relief

reload *verb* recharger *or* relancer; **we reloaded the program after the crash** = nous avons rechargé le programme après la panne

relocatable *adjective (to another area of memory)* réadressable; relogeable; **relocatable program** = programme relogeable; **the operating system can load and run a relocatable program from any area of memory** = ce système d'exploitation peut charger et exécuter un programme relogeable sans distinction de la zone d'origine

◊ **relocate** *verb (to move data)* déplacer *or* reloger; changer d'adresse; **the data is relocated during execution** = l'adresse de cette donnée est changée au cours de l'éxécution; **self-relocating program** = programme auto-relogeable

◊ **relocation** *noun* réadressage *m* ; déplacement *m* *or* translation *f* *or* relogement *m* (en mémoire); **dynamic relocation** = relogement *or* translation dynamique; **relocation constant** = constante *f* de translation *or* de réadressage; **static relocation** = relogement *or* translation statique

REM = REMARK

remainder 1 *noun (in division)* reste *m*; **7 divided by 3 is equal to 2 remainder 1** = 7 divisé par 3 égale 2 reste 1 **2** *verb (to sell - mainly books - below cost price)* vendre à bas prix *or* solder; **this computer model is out of date so we have to remainder the rest of the stock** = ce modèle d'ordinateur est dépassé, il faut donc solder le stock qui nous reste

remark (REM) *(statement ignored by the interpreter)* REM *or* déclaration *f* de remarque (dans un programme en BASIC)

remedial maintenance *noun (repair)* maintenance *f* curative *or* corrective; réparation *f*

remote *adjective* éloigné, -ée *or* à distance; **users**

can print reports on remote printers = les utilisateurs peuvent imprimer leurs rapports sur des imprimantes à distance; *(allows access to a computer from a distance)* **remote access** = accès à distance; **remote console** *or* **device** = console *f or* poste *m* de commande *or* périphérique éloigné *or* à distance; **remote control** = *(of TV set)* télécommande *f*; *(allows a user to control a computer from a distance)* contrôle *m* à distance *or* pilotage *m* à distance; **the video recorder has a remote control facility** = ce magnétoscope est équipé d'une télécommande; *(allows a user to control the remote computer)* **remote control software** = logiciel de prise de contrôle à distance *or* de pilotage à distance; **this remote control software will work with Windows and lets me operate my office PC from home over a modem link** = ce logiciel de prise de contrôle à distance travaille sous Windows et me permet d'utiliser de chez moi le PC de mon bureau relié par un modem; **remote job entry (RJE)** = (système de) lancement *m* de tâches à distance; *(communication between two programs running on two connected computers)* **remote procedure call (RPC)** = appel *m* de procédure à distance *or* appel RPC; **remote station** = poste à distance *or* éloigné; **remote terminal** = terminal à distance *or* éloigné

removable *adjective* amovible; **a removable hard disk** = un disque dur amovible

◊ **removal** *noun* annulation *f or* suppression *f*; **the removal of this instruction could solve the problem** = l'annulation de cette instruction résoudrait le problème

◊ **remove** *verb* annuler *or* enlever *or* faire disparaître *or* supprimer; **the file entry was removed from the floppy disk directory** = le fichier a été effacé *or* supprimé du répertoire de la disquette; *see also* RD

rename *verb* changer le nom (d'un fichier); **save the file and rename it CLIENT** = sauvegarder le fichier mais changez-en le nom et appelez-le CLIENT

renumber *noun* *(line, etc.)* refaire la numérotation; *(page)* repaginer

reorganize *verb* réorganiser; **wait while the spelling checker database is being reorganized** = il faut attendre que la base de données du correcteur orthographique soit réorganisée

repaginate *verb* *(to change the lengths of pages)* repaginer *or* paginer de nouveau *or* refaire la pagination; **the dtp package allows simple repagination** = le système de PAO permet de repaginer; **the text was repaginated with a new line width** = la pagination a été refaite avec une nouvelle largeur de ligne

◊ **repagination** *noun* *(changing pages lengths)* repagination *f*; **the dtp package allows simple repagination** = le logiciel de PAO permet de faire une simple repagination

repair 1 *verb* réparer **2** *noun* réparation *f*

repeat *verb* répéter *or* reprendre; **repeat counter**

= compteur *m* de répétitions; **repeat key** = touche *f* répétition

◊ **repeater** *noun* *(device that repeats a signal)* répétiteur *m* *(device that amplifies or regenerates a received signal)* répéteur *m or* amplificateur *m* intermédiaire; **this cheap repeater does not regenerate the signals** = ce répéteur bon marché ne régénère pas les signaux

◊ **repeating group** *noun* groupe *m* (de données) à répétition *or* qui se répètent de façon périodique

reperforator *noun* (re)perforatrice *f*

repertoire *noun* répertoire *m*; **the manual describes the full repertoire** = le répertoire entier est inclus dans le manuel; **character repertoire** = police *f* de caractères; **instruction repertoire** = répertoire d'instructions

QUOTE the only omissions in the editing repertoire are dump, to list variables currently in use, and find

Computing Today

repetitive letter *noun* lettre *f* standard *or* lettre type

replace *verb* **(a)** remplacer; **a printer ribbon needs replacing after several thousand characters** = un ruban qui a imprimé plusieurs milliers de caractères a besoin d'être changé **(b)** *(instruction)* (instruction) remplacer *m*; *see also* SEARCH AND REPLACE, GLOBAL

replay 1 *noun* **(a)** *(data or music)* relecture *f* **(b)** *(film or video)* visionnage *m* (d'une séquence de film, au ralenti); **the replay clearly showed the winner** = le visionnage du ralenti ne laisse aucun doute sur le vainqueur; **this video recorder has a replay feature** = ce magnétoscope possède une fonction 'visionnage'; **instant replay** = visionnage *m* immédiat *or* instantané **2** *verb* *(something which has been recorded)* (i) faire jouer (une bande nouvellement enregistrée); (ii) rejouer une bande; (iii) faire passer *or* projeter (un film); visionner; **he replayed the tape** = il a repassé la bande *or* il a remis la bande; **she recorded the TV programme on video tape and replayed it the next evening** = elle a enregistré le programme de télévision sur une bande vidéo et l'a visionné le lendemain soir

replenish *verb* *(a battery)* recharger (une batterie d'accumulateurs)

replicate *verb* copier *or* dupliquer; **the routine will replicate your results with very little effort** = cette routine va dupliquer *or* copier vos résulats sans aucun problème

◊ **replication** *noun* *(copying a record)* duplication *f*; *(copy)* double *m*

report generator *noun* *(software)* générateur *m* de rapport *or* d'état

◊ **report program generator (RPG)** *noun* générateur *m* d'application

represent *verb* représenter *or* signifier; **the hash**

sign is used to represent a number in a series = le symbole # s'utilise devant un numéro de série

◊ **representation** *noun* représentation *f*; **character representation** = expression *f* binaire d'un caractère

◊ **representative** *adjective* représentatif, -ive

reprint 1 *verb* réimprimer *or* faire une réimpression 2 *noun* réimpression *f*; **we have ordered a 10,000 copy reprint** = nous réimprimons 10 000 exemplaires

repro *noun* (*informal*) repro(graphie) *f*; **repro proof** = épreuve *f* de reproduction

reproduce *verb* reproduire

◊ **reproduction** *noun* reproduction *f*

reprogram *verb* reprogrammer *or* programmer de nouveau

request 1 *noun* demande *f or* requête *f*; **request to send signal (RTS)** = (signal de) demande *f* de transmission 2 *verb* demander (quelque chose)

require *verb* (*to need something*) avoir besoin de (quelque chose); (*to demand something*) demander *or* exiger (quelque chose); **delicate computer systems require careful handling** = les systèmes informatiques sont très fragiles et demandent à être manipulés avec soin

◊ **required hyphen** *or* **hard hyphen** *noun* trait *m* d'union obligatoire; *see also* SOFT

◊ **requirements** *noun* (i) besoins *mpl* ; (ii) exigences *fpl*; **memory requirements depend on the application software in use** = la quantité de mémoire nécessaire varie suivant le logiciel utilisé

re-route *verb* réacheminer; **the call diverter re-routes a call** = le dispositif de transfert d'appel sert à réacheminer les appels

rerun *verb* recommencer *or* reprendre l'exécution; **rerun point** = point *m* de reprise

res *see* RESOLUTION; **hi-res** = HIGH RESOLUTION; **low-res** = LOW RESOLUTION

resave *verb* sauvegarder de nouveau; **it automatically resaves the text** = cela permet de sauvegarder le texte de nouveau automatiquement

rescue dump *noun* vidage *m* de sauvegarde

research *noun* recherche *f*; **research and development (R & D)** = recherche et développement; **the company has spent millions of dollars on R & D** = la société a dépensé des millions de dollars pour la recherche et le développement

reserved character *noun* (*special character used by the operating system*) caractère réservé; **in DOS, the reserved character \ is used to represent a directory path** = sous DOS, le caractère \ est réservé pour représenter un chemin du répertoire

◊ **reserved sector** *noun* (*area of disk*) secteur *m* réservé; (*word or phrase used as an identifier*) **reserved word** = mot *m* réservé

reset *verb* (**a**) ré-initialiser; **reset button** *or* **key** = bouton *m* de ré-initialisation; **hard reset** = ré-initialisation (du système en) utilisant le contacteur; **soft reset** = ré-initialisation (du système) par commande (**b**) (*register or counter*) remettre à zéro; **when it reaches 999 this counter resets to zero** = le compteur revient automatiquement à zéro dès qu'il atteint 999 (**c**) (*to set data to zero*) remettre à zéro

resident *adjective* (*data or program*) résident, -e; **resident engineer** = ingénieur *m* de l'entreprise; (*font data always present in a printer*) **resident font** = police (de caractères) *or* fonte résidente; **resident software** *or* **memory-resident software** = logiciel *m* résident; (*program started from the command line*) **terminate and stay resident software (TSR)** = programme résident *or* TSR

residual *adjective* résiduel, -elle; **residual error rate** = taux d'erreur résiduel

◊ **residue check** *noun* contrôle *m* sur reste

resist 1 *verb* résister (à) 2 *noun* (*substance not affected by etching chemicals*) substance *f* résistante (à un produit chimique); *see also* PHOTORESIST

◊ **resistance** *noun* (*measure of the voltage*) résistance *f*

◊ **resistor** *noun* (*electronic component*) résistance *f*; **resistor transistor logic (RTL)** = logique *f* (à) transistors (et) résistances *or* logique RTL; **variable resistor** = résistance variable

resolution *noun* (*number of pixels*) résolution *f* *or* définition *f*; **the resolution of most personal computer screens is not much more than 70 dpi (dots per inch)** = la plupart des écrans d'ordinateurs individuels ont une définition qui est à peine supérieure à 70 ppp (points par pouce); **graphic display resolution** = définition d'affichage graphique; **high resolution (hi-res)** = haute définition; **the high resolution screen can display 640 by 450 pixels** = avec un écran haute définition on obtient un affichage de 640 par 450 pixels; **limiting resolution** = définition maximum; **low resolution** *or* **low-res** = basse définition

resolving power *noun* (*of an optical system*) pouvoir *m* de résolution

resonance *noun* résonance *f or* résonnance *f*

resource *noun* ressource *f*; **resource allocation** = allocation *f* de ressources; *(Apple Macintosh: one of two forks of a file)* **resource fork** = fourche *f* de ressources; **resource sharing** = partage *m* de ressources

respond *verb* répondre (à)

◊ **response** *noun* réponse *f or* réaction *f*; *(page in a videotext)* **response frame** = cadre-réponse *m*; **response position** = emplacement *m or* case *f* réservé(e) à la réponse; **response time** = (i) temps *m* d'accès; (ii) temps de réponse; **the response time of this flight simulator is very good** = le temps de réponse de ce simulateur de vol est excellent

restart 1 *noun* remise *f* en marche *or* redémarrage *m or* relance *f* **2** *verb* redémarrer *or* remettre en marche *or* relancer; **first try to restart your system** = essayez d'abord de relancer (votre système) *or* de remettre votre système en marche

restore *verb* restaurer *or* remettre en bon état; récupérer

QUOTE first you have to restore the directory that contains the list of deleted files
Personal Computer World

restrict *verb* limiter l'accès *or* l'utilisation (de quelque chose) *or* imposer une contrainte (à quelque chose); **the document is restricted, and cannot be placed on open access** = ce document de diffusion restreinte ne doit pas être rendu public

◊ **restriction** *noun* restriction *f or* limite *f or* contrainte *f*

result *noun* résultat *m*

◊ **result code** *noun* *(indicates the state of a modem)* code *m* résultat

resume *verb* *(to restart)* continuer *or* repartir *or* reprendre

retain *verb* conserver *or* maintenir

◊ **retention** *noun* rétention *f*; **image retention** = rémanence *f or* persistance *f* de l'image

retouch *verb* *(image, photo, etc.)* retoucher; **the artwork for the line drawings needs retouching in places** = il y a quelques retouches à faire au dessin

retrain *verb* *(re-establish a better quality connection)* recycler *or* rafraîchir une connexion

retransmit *verb* transmettre de nouveau *or* retransmettre

◊ **retransmission** *noun* retransmission *f*

retrieval *noun* (i) recherche *f* (documentaire); (ii) extraction *f* (de données); **information retrieval** = recherche *f* documentaire; **information retrieval centre** = centre *m* de recherche documentaire *or* centrale *f* d'information; **text retrieval** = recherche (et extraction) de texte

◊ **retrieve** *verb* extraire *or* récupérer; **these are the records retrieved in that search** = voici les informations extraites au cours de cette recherche; **this command will retrieve all names beginning with S** = on utilise cette commande pour extraire la liste de tous les noms qui commencent par S

retro- *prefix* rétro-; *(device or accessory)* **retrofit** = dispositif *m* d'actualisation (d'un système)

retrospective parallel running *noun* test rétrospectif en parallèle

◊ **retrospective search** *noun* recherche *f* rétrospective

return *noun* **(a)** (instruction de) retour *m*; **the program is not working because you missed out the return instruction at the end of the subroutine** = ce programme ne marche pas parce que vous avez oublié de placer un retour à la fin de cette routine; *(after a called routine finishes)* **return address** = adresse *f* de retour **(b)** *(key on a keyboard)* (touche) entrée; **you type in your name and code number then press return** = tapez votre nom et numéro de code, puis appuyez sur la touche 'entrée' **(c)** *(at end of line)* (symbole de) fin *f* de ligne; *(code or key)* **carriage return (CR)** = (code *or* touche de) retour (du) chariot *or* retour à la ligne

◊ **return to zero signal** *noun* signal *m* de remise à zéro *or* de ré-initialisation (NOTE: opposite is **non return to zero**)

reveal *verb* révéler *or* mettre à jour *or* faire apparaître

reverse 1 *adjective* inversé, -ée *or* inverse; **reverse channel** = canal *m* de retour; **reverse index** = index *m* inversé; **reverse interrupt** = interruption *f* d'inversion; *(product design in which the finished item is analysed to determine how it should be constructed)* **reverse engineering** = rétro-ingénierie *f*; **reverse polarity** = polarité inversée; **reverse Polish notation (RPN)** = notation *f* polonaise inversée; **three plus four, minus two is written in RPN as 3 4 + 2 - = 5** = suivant la notation polonaise inversée, trois plus quatre moins deux s'écrit 3 4 + 2 - = 5; **normal notation: (x-y) + z, but using RPN: xy - z+** = alors que la notation conventionnelle s'écrit: (x-y) + z, la notation polonaise inversée s'écrit: xy - z+; **reverse video** = vidéo *f* inversée **2** *verb* inverser; *(with movement)* faire marche arrière

QUOTE the options are listed on the left side of the screen, with active options shown at the top left in reverse video
PC User

revert *verb* revenir (à) *or* reprendre; **after the rush order, we reverted back to our normal speed** = une fois le travail urgent terminé, nous avons repris notre rythme normal; *(returns a formatted page to its original form)* **revert command** = commande *f* de retour à la situation de départ

review *verb* réviser *or* vérifier; **the program allows the user to review all wrongly spelled words** = le programme permet de vérifier l'orthographe

revise *verb* revoir *or* réviser; **the revised version has no mistakes** = la version revue et corrigée ne contient aucune erreur

rewind *verb* rembobiner; **the tape rewinds onto the spool automatically** = le film s'enroule automatiquement sur la bobine

rewrite 1 *verb* réécrire *or* écrire de nouveau **2** *noun* nouvelle version *f*; **the program is in its second rewrite** = le programme en est à sa troisième version *or* à sa troisième mouture

RF = RADIO FREQUENCY; *(electromagnetic spectrum)* radiofréquence *f or* fréquence radio; **RF modulator** *or* **radio frequency modulator** = modulateur *m* de fréquence radio; *(metal foil wrapped around a cable)* **RF shielding** = blindage *m* (d'un câble); déparasitage *m*; **without RF shielding, the transmitted signal would be distorted by the interference** = sans blindage, le signal transmis serait perturbé par les interférences

RGB = RED, GREEN, BLUE; *(producing colours by mixing three primary colours red, green and blue)* RVB (rouge, vert, bleu)

◊ **RGB display** *or* **monitor** *noun (system using three input signals controlling red, green and blue)* moniteur *m* couleur RVB

rheostat *noun* rhéostat *m* (NOTE: also called **variable potential divider)**

RI = RING INDICATOR

ribbon *noun* ruban *m*; **printer ribbon** = ruban d'imprimante; **ribbon cable** = câble *m* ruban *or* câble plat

right 1 *adjective* droit, -e; **right justification** = justification *f* à droite; **right shift** = décalage *m or* glissement *m* à droite **2** *noun* droite *f*

◊ **right justify** *verb (printing)* justifier *f* à droite

◊ **right shift** *verb (maths)* effectuer un décalage à droite; *see also* LOGICAL SHIFT, ARITHMETIC SHIFT

rightsizing *noun (changing a company's IT structure to a new hardware platform)* mise *f* à la bonne échelle d'un système informatique

rigid *adjective* rigide *or* dur, -e; *(disk that is able to store many times more data than a floppy disk)* **rigid disk** = disque *m* dur

ring 1 *noun* **(a)** *(data list whose last entry points back to the first entry)* liste *f* circulaire; *see also* CHAINED LIST **(b)** anneau *m*; *(network topology)* en anneau; **ring (data) network** = réseau *m* en anneau; *(IEEE 802.5 standard)* **Token Ring network** = réseau *m* Token Ring; **Token Ring networks are very democratic and retain performance against increasing load** = les réseaux Token Ring sont très démocratiques et conservent leurs performances en cas d'augmentation de la charge (de travail); *compare* BUS NETWORK, ETHERNET **2** *verb* téléphoner; **ring back system** = système de rappel

automatique; **ring down** = faire un appel groupé; **ring indicator (RI)** = indicateur *m* d'appel

◊ **ring counter** *noun* compteur *m* (à décalage) circulaire *or* compteur annulaire

◊ **ring shift** *noun* permutation *f or* décalage *m* circulaire

RIP = RASTER IMAGE PROCESSOR

RIP = REST IN PROPORTION; *(typography)* augmenter *or* réduire l'échelle; augmenter *or* réduire proportionnellement

ripple *noun* frisure *f or* oscillations *fpl* résiduelles (sur un courant)

◊ **ripple-through carry** *noun* report *m* simultané *or* rapide

◊ **ripple-through effect** *noun (changes in a spreadsheet when the value in one cell is changed)* effet *m* de cascade *or* mise *f* à jour en cascade (dans un tableur à la suite d'un changement de valeur dans une cellule)

RISC = REDUCED INSTRUCTION SET COMPUTER

rise time *noun* temps *m* de montée; **the circuit has a fast rise time** = le temps de montée du circuit est très rapide

RJE = REMOTE JOB ENTRY

RJ11 connector *noun (standard four-wire modular connector)* connecteur *m* RJ11

◊ **RJ45 connector** *noun (modular connector)* connecteur *m* de réseau RJ45

RLL encoding = RUN-LENGTH LIMITED ENCODING

rm *(UNIX command to remove an empty subdirectory)* (commande) rm (de suppression d'un sous-répertoire UNIX)

◊ **RMDIR** *or* **RD** = REMOVE DIRECTORY; *(DOS command to remove an empty subdirectory)* (commande) RD *or* Remove Directory (pour supprimer un répertoire sous DOS)

RMS = ROOT MEAN SQUARE; valeur *f* efficace (d'amplitude *or* d'intensité, etc.); **RMS line current** = intensité *f* efficace d'une ligne

RO = RECEIVE ONLY terminal *m* d'arrivée

roam *verb (in wireless communications)* bouger *or* se déplacer (avec un téléphone sans cordon)

robot *noun* robot *m*

◊ **robotics** *noun* la robotique

QUOTE so far no robot sensor has been devised which can operate quickly enough to halt the robot if a human being is in its path of work
IEE News

robust *adjective* robuste; **this hard disk is not very robust** = ce disque dur n'est pas très robuste

◊ **robustness** *noun* **(a)** *(strength of a casing)* robustesse *f or* solidité *f* **(b)** *(ability to continue functioning even with faults)* (à) tolérance de pannes

rogue indicator *noun* indicateur *m* de contrôle

◊ **rogue value** *noun* *(terminator)* marque *f or* marqueur *m* de fin de fichier

role indicator *noun* indicateur *m* de fonction

roll 1 *noun (film or tape)* rouleau *m*; **he put a new roll of film into the camera** = il a mis une nouvelle pellicule dans son appareil photo **2** *verb* **(a)** *(to rotate)* faire tourner *or* basculer; **roll in** = déplacer de mémoire auxiliaire en mémoire centrale; **roll out** = rappeler de mémoire centrale en mémoire auxiliaire **(b)** tourner

◊ **rollback** *noun* rechargement *m* d'un programme (après incident)

◊ **rolling headers** *noun* titres *mpl* et en-têtes courants

◊ **rollover** *noun* mémoire *f* tampon de clavier; **key rollover** = clavier *m* rapide *or* à mémoire

◊ **roll scroll** *verb* faire défiler ligne à ligne sur l'écran

ROM = READ ONLY MEMORY; *(small disk used as a high capacity ROM device)* **CD-ROM** *or* **compact disc-ROM** = (disque) CD-ROM *m (code which makes up the BIOS routines stored in a ROM chip)* **ROM BIOS** = BIOS sur ROM *or* ROM BIOS; **ROM cartridge** = cartouche *f* ROM *or* ROM *f* enfichable; **the manufacturer provided the monitor program in two ROM chips** = le constructeur a fourni le programme de commande sur deux circuits ROM (NOTE: there is no plural for ROM, and it is often used without the article: **the file is stored in ROM**)

◊ **romware** *noun* programmes *mpl* sur ROM

roman *noun (typeface)* romain *m*; **the text is set in Times Roman** = le texte est imprimé en Times Romain

◊ **Roman numerals** *noun (figures written I, II, III, IV, etc.)* chiffres *m* romains

root *noun* **(a)** *(in a data tree structure)* racine *f*; *(topmost directory)* **root directory** = répertoire *m* racine; **in DOS, the root directory on drive C: is called C:** = sous DOS, le répertoire racine du disque C: est désigné par C:\ **(b)** *(fractional power of a number)* puissance *f* fractionnaire *or* racine *f*; **square root** = racine carrée; **the square root of 25 is 5** = la racine carrée de 25 est 5; **root mean square (RMS)** = valeur *f* efficace (d'amplitude *or* d'intensité, etc.); **the root mean square of the pure sinusoidal signal is 0.7071 of its amplitude** = la valeur efficace d'une sinusoïde parfaite équivaut à 0,7071 de son amplitude

rotary *adjective* rotatif, -ive; **rotary camera** = caméra rotative; **rotary press** = (presse) rotative *f*

◊ **rotate** *verb* tourner (autour d'un axe)

◊ **rotation** *noun* rotation *f*; **bit rotation** *or* **rotate**

operation = permutation *f* de bits; **matrix rotation** = rotation de matrice

round 1 *adjective* rond, -e *or* qui tourne en rond; **round robin** = (utilisation d'un appareil) à tour de rôle **2** *verb* **to round down** = arrondir un nombre par défaut; **we can round down 2.651 to 2.65** = on peut arrondir 2,651 à 2,65 par défaut; **to round off** = arrondir (au plus près); **round off 23.456 to 23.46** = arrondir 23,456 à 23,46; **round off error** = erreur *f* d'arrondi; **to round up** = arrondir par excès; **we can round up 2.647 to 2.65** = on peut arrondir 2,647 à 2,65 par excès

◊ **rounding** *noun* **(a)** *(of a number)* arrondi *m* (au plus près) *or* troncature *f*; **rounding error** = erreur d'arrondi *or* de troncature **(b)** *(giving a smoother look)* arrondissement *m* (d'angles); **character rounding** = arrondissement de caractère

route *noun* *(of message)* chemin *m or* cheminement *m or* itinéraire *m*; **the route taken was not the most direct since a lot of nodes were busy** = le chemin choisi ne s'est pas révélé le plus direct puisque de nombreux noeuds étaient occupés; **alternate route** = voie *f* de déroutement *or* déviation *f*

◊ **router** *noun* *(communications device that receives data packets)* gestionnaire *m* de routage; *(LAN: device that connects two or more LANs)* routeur *m or* dispositif *m* de routage

◊ **routing** *noun* acheminement *m or* routage *m*; **there is a new way of routing data to the central computer** = il existe une nouvelle façon d'acheminer les données vers l'ordinateur central; **routing overheads** = procédure *f* de contrôle d'acheminement *or* protocole *m* de routage (d'un message); **the information transfer rate is very much less once all routing overheads have been accommodated** = la vitesse de transmission d'informations est beaucoup moins grande une fois qu'on tient compte du protocole de routage; **routing page** = page *f* de routage; **routing table** = table *f* de routage

routine *noun* routine *f*; **the routine copies the screen display onto a printer** = la routine permet d'imprimer le contenu de l'écran; **the RETURN instruction at the end of the routine sends control back to the main program** = l'instruction RETOUR à la fin de la routine permet de redonner la main au programme principal; **fall back routines** = routines de secours; **floating-point routines** = routines de traitement de la virgule flottante; **input routine** = routine d'entrée; **open routine** = routine ouverte *or* auxiliaire; **packing routine** = routine de compactage de données

row *noun* **(a)** *(of characters)* ligne *f*; *(of perforations)* rang *m*; **the figures are presented in rows, not in columns** = les chiffres sont alignés l'un à la suite de l'autre plutôt que d'être présentés en colonnes; **each entry is separated by a row of dots** = une ligne pointillée sépare les entrées les unes des autres **(b)** *(in an array or matrix)* ligne d'un tableau *or* d'une matrice

RPC = REMOTE PROCEDURE CALL

RPG = REPORT PROGRAM GENERATOR

RPN = REVERSE POLISH NOTATION

RS-232C *(EIA approved standard used in serial data transmission, covering voltage and control signals)* norme RS-232C (pour interface série) *or* (interface série normalisée) RS-232C

◊ **RS-422** *(EIA approved standards)* norme RS-422; **RS-423** = norme RS-423

RS-flip-flop = RESET-SET FLIP-FLOP commutateur *m* à bascule à deux états

RSA cipher system *(the Rivest, Shamir and Adleman public key cipher system)* code *m* de cryptage RSA

RTE = REAL TIME EXECUTION

RTL = RESISTOR-TRANSISTOR LOGIC

RTS = REQUEST TO SEND SIGNAL

rubber banding *see* ELASTIC BANDING

rub out *see* ERASE

rubric *noun* rubrique *f*

rule *noun* **(a)** règle *f*; **the rule states that you wait for the clear signal before transmitting** = il est de règle d'attendre le signal CTS avant de commencer à transmettre, c'est la règle; **rule-based system** = système *m* à base de règles **(b)** *(thin line)* réglure *f*; **em rule** = tiret *m* long (dont la longueur équivaut à un 'm'); **en rule** = tiret court (dont la longueur équivaut à un 'n')

◊ **ruler** *noun* règle *f* graduée; *(bar on screen that is a unit of measurement)* règle *f*; **ruler line** = règle de tabulation

run 1 *noun* exécution *f*; **the next invoice run will be on Friday** = nous n'imprimons pas les prochaines factures avant vendredi; **program run** = exécution d'un programme; **run indicator** = indicateur *m* (lumineux) de marche **2** *verb* fonctionner *or* être en marche; *(a program)* exécuter (un programme); **the computer has been running ten hours a day** = l'ordinateur fonctionne jusqu'à dix heures par jour; **do not interrupt the spelling checker while it is running** = n'arrêtez pas la vérification de l'orthographe en cours de route; **the new package runs on our PC** = le nouveau progiciel peut être utilisé sur notre PC; **parallel running** = exploitation *f* en parallèle *or* en double; *(to fit text around an image)* **run around** = faire l'habillage *m* d'une illustration *or* d'une gravure; **run in** = roder

◊ **runaway** *noun* opération *f* incontrôlable

◊ **run-length limited encoding (RLL)** *(method of storing data onto a disk)* encodage *m* RLL

◊ **running head** *noun* titre *m* courant

◊ **run on** *verb* **(a)** *(text)* composer à la suite *or* laisser courir le texte (sans interruption *or* sans alinéa); **the line can run on to the next without any space** = le texte peut courir sans alinéa **(b)** *(to print more copies)* tirer à la suite; **we decided to run on 3,000 copies to the first printing** = nous avons décidé de faire un tirage à la suite de 3000 exemplaires; **run-on price** = prix *m* d'un tirage à la suite

◊ **run-time** *or* **run-duration 1** *noun* **(a)** *(length of time a program takes to run)* durée *f* d'exécution (d'un programme) **(b)** *(time when a computer is executing a program)* temps *m* d'exécution (d'un programme) *or* temps de traitement **2** *adjective* **run-time error** = erreur *f* à l'exécution; *(library of routines)* **run-time library** = bibliothèque *f* des routines d'applications; **the software is designed with all the graphics routines in this run-time library file** = ce logiciel a été conçu avec toutes les routines graphiques accessibles dans la bibliothèque des routines d'applications; *(licence granted to run an application)* **run-time licence** = licence *f* d'utilisation; *(software)* **run-time system** = (programme) superviseur *m*; **run-time version** = *(program code that can be directly executed by the computer)* version *f* exécutable; *(program that is sold with an application developed in a high-level language)* version run-time (utilisable seulement avec l'interpréteur d'une application maître)

R/W = READ/WRITE

◊ **R/W cycle** = READ/WRITE CYCLE

◊ **R/W head** = READ/WRITE HEAD

RX = RECEIVE, RECEIVER; **the RXed signal needs to be amplified** = le signal reçu devrait être amplifié

Ss

S100 bus *or* **S-100 bus** *noun (IEEE-696 standard bus)* bus *m* (de type) S-100 (NOTE: say: 'S one hundred bus')

SAA = SYSTEMS APPLICATION ARCHITECTURE

SAFE = SIGNATURE ANALYSIS USING FUNCTIONAL ANALYSIS

safe area *noun* zone *f* d'image reçue

◊ **safety net** *noun* (i) mesure *f* de précaution; (ii) dispositif *m* de sécurité *or* auxiliaire *or* de secours; **if there is a power failure, we have a safety net in the form of a UPS** = en cas de panne d'électricité, nous avons un onduleur qui peut prendre la relève

◊ **safe format** *noun (format operation that does not destroy the existing data)* formatage *m* de sécurité

SAM = SERIAL ACCESS MEMORY

sample 1 *noun* échantillon *m*; **the sample at three seconds showed an increase** = la prise d'échantillon toutes les trois secondes a révélé une augmentation; **sample and hold circuit** = (circuit) échantillonneur-bloqueur *m* **2** *verb* échantillonner

◊ **sampler** *noun (electronic circuit)* échantillonneur *m*

◊ **sampling** *noun* échantillonnage *m*; **sampling interval** = pas *m* d'échantillonnage; **sampling rate** = fréquence *f* d'échantillonnage

sans serif *noun (typography)* (caractère) sans empattement *m*

sapphire *noun (precious stone)* saphir *m*

SAR = STORE ADDRESS REGISTER

SAS = SINGLE ATTACHMENT STATION

satellite *noun* **(a)** *(device)* satellite *m*; **communications satellite** = satellite de télécommunication; **direct broadcast satellite (DBS)** = satellite de diffusion directe; **weather satellite** = satellite météorologique; **satellite broadcasting** = radiodiffusion *f* par satellite; **satellite link** = liaison *f* (par) satellite **(b)** *(small system)* système satellite *or* système auxiliaire; **satellite computer** = ordinateur *m* satellite; **satellite terminal** = terminal *m* satellite

saturation *noun (magnetic)* saturation *f* (magnétique); **saturation noise** = bruit *m* de saturation (magnétique); *(of data and messages)* **saturation testing** = tests *mpl* de saturation

save *verb (to store data)* sauvegarder; **this WP saves the text every 15 minutes in case of a fault** = ce système de traitement de texte fait une sauvegarde toutes les 15 minutes pour prévenir une défaillance; **don't forget to save the file before switching off** = n'oubliez pas de sauvegarder le fichier avant d'éteindre votre appareil; **save area** = zone *f* de sauvegarde; *(save the current work in a file with a different name)* **save as** = enregistrer sous

sawtooth waveform *noun* onde *f* en dents de scie

SBC = SINGLE BOARD COMPUTER

S-box *noun* schéma *m* itératif de cryptage DES

scalable font *noun (produces characters of different sizes)* fonte *f* vectorielle *or* police *f* de caractères à échelle variable; *see also* OUTLINE FONT

◊ **scalable software** *noun (groupware application)* logiciel *m* à échelle variable (adaptable au nombre d'utilisateurs)

scalar *noun* grandeur *f* scalaire; **a scalar has a single magnitude value, a vector has two or more positional values** = une grandeur scalaire n'a qu'une dimension, un vecteur en possède au moins deux; *(containing single values which are predictable)* **scalar data** = données *fpl* scalaires; *(processor designed to operate on scalar values)* **scalar processor** = processeur *m* scalaire; *(RISC processor)* **Scalar Processor Architecture (SPARC)** ™ = architecture *f* de processeur scalaire *or* architecture SPARC ™; *(variable which can contain a single value)* **scalar variable** = variable *f* scalaire; *(single value)* **scalar value** = valeur *f* scalaire

◊ **scale 1** *noun* échelle *f*; **large scale** = grande échelle; **small scale** = petite échelle; *(of circuit with 500 - 10,000 components)* **large scale integration (LSI)** = intégration *f* à grande échelle; *(10 - 500 components)* **medium scale integration (MSI)** = intégration à moyenne échelle; *(1 - 10 components)* **small scale integration (SSI)** = intégration à petite échelle; *(with several microprocessors)* **super large scale integration (SLSI)** = intégration à super grande échelle; *(10,000 - 100,000 components)* **very large scale integration (VLSI)** = intégration à très grande échelle; **wafer scale integration** = intégration sur tranche de silicium **2** *verb* **to scale down** = réduire l'échelle; **to scale up** = augmenter l'échelle

scan 1 *noun* balayage *m* *or* scan *m*; **the heat scan of the computer quickly showed which component was overheating** = le scanner a très vite repéré le composant qui surchauffait; **the scan revealed which records were now out of date** = un balayage a fait apparaître les données périmées; **scan area** = zone *f* de balayage; *(number to identify a key)* **scan code** = code *m* d'identification de touche; *(device used to turn an image into a pattern of pixels)* **scan head** = tête *f* de scanner; **this model uses a scan head that can distinguish 256 different colours** = ce modèle utilise une tête de scanner qui reconnaît 256 couleurs; **scan length** = étendue *f* de la zone de balayage; *(horizontal line of phosphor)* **scan line** = ligne *f* de balayage; *(one sweep of the picture beam horizontally across the front of the CRT screen)* **raster scan** = (passe de) balayage *m* **2** *verb (electronic)* scanner *or* faire un balayage *or* un scanning *or* un scannage; *(to look closely at something)* lire *or* examiner (quelque chose) attentivement; **he scanned the map for Teddington** = il a cherché Teddington sur la carte; **a facsimile machine scans the picture and converts this to digital form before transmission** = le fax balaye l'image et la convertit en format numérique *or* la numérise avant transmission; **the machine scans at up to 300 dpi resolution** = la lecture par scanner se fait avec une définition allant jusqu'à 300 points par pouce

◊ **scanner** *noun (device which converts an image into graphical data)* scanner *m or* scanneur *m*; **a scanner reads the bar-code on the product label using a laser beam and photodiode** = le scanneur peut lire les codes barres sur les étiquettes des produits grâce à un rayon laser et une photodiode; **scanner memory** = mémoire d'images optiques; *(with flat sheet of glass)* **flat-bed scanner** = scanner à plat; *(scanner held in the hand)* **hand-held scanner** = scanner à main; **image scanner** = scanner d'images; **optical scanner** = lecteur *m* optique *or* scanner (à reconnaissance optique)

scanning *noun* scanning *m or* scannage *m or* balayage *m or* lecture *f* (par scanner); **scanning device** = scanner *m or* scanneur *m or* dispositif *m* de lecture par balayage; **scanning error** = erreur de balayage; **scanning line** = ligne *f* de balayage; **scanning radio receiver** = récepteur *m* à recherche de signal; **scanning rate** = fréquence *f* de balayage; **scanning resolution** = définition *f* de lecture *or* de balayage; **scanning software** = logiciel *m* de saisie (par balayage); **scanning speed** = vitesse *f* de balayage; **throughput is 1.3 inches per second scanning speed** = la vitesse de lecture par balayage est de 1,3 pouces par seconde; **its scanning speed is 9.9 seconds for an 8.5 inch by 11 inch document** = il lui faut 9,9 secondes pour lire un document de 8,5 x 11 pouces; **auto-baud scanning** *or* **auto-baud sensing** = sélection *f* automatique de vitesse de transmission *or* reconnaissance *f* automatique de débit d'une ligne; **raster scanning** = balayage de trame

◊ **scanning spot** *noun* **(a)** *(small area of an*

image) spot *m* de balayage *or* point *m* d'image **(b)** *(on a TV screen)* spot *m* de balayage; *(of satellite)* **scanning spot beam** = faisceau *m* de balayage *or* d'exploration

scatter *noun* onde *f* diffusée; **scatter graph** = graphique de points; **scatter proofs** = épreuves *fpl* en vrac; *see also* BACKSCATTER

◊ **scatter load** *verb* faire un chargement éclaté; **scatter read** = faire une lecture sélective

scavenge *verb* piller (une base de données)

schedule *noun* **1** *noun* programme *m or* horaire *m or* plan *m* **2** *verb (TV or radio programmes)* établir un horaire (de programme de télévision *or* radio)

◊ **scheduled circuits** *noun* lignes *fpl* spécialisées

◊ **scheduler** *noun* **(a)** *(computer program which organizes the use of a CPU)* (programme) superviseur *m* (de multiprogrammation) *or* gestionnaire *m* de tâches **(b)** *(person)* personne *f* qui établit l'horaire (de programme de télévision *or* radio); *(utility software used to help organise meetings, etc.)* logiciel *m* d'agenda *or* logiciel de plan de travail; ordonnanceur *m*

◊ **scheduling** *noun* **(a)** *(share of CPU)* détermination *f* de l'ordre de priorité *or* constitution *f* de file d'attente; *(of production)* ordonnancement *m*; *(production)* **job scheduling** = détermination de priorité des tâches *or* gestion *f* de tâches; *(production)* ordonnancement des travaux **(b)** **programme scheduling** = établissement *m* d'un horaire de programme de télévision *or* radio

schema *noun* graphique *m or* schéma *m or* diagramme *m*

◊ **schematic** **1** *adjective* schématique *or* sous forme de schéma *or* de diagramme **2** *noun* plan *m* schématique *or* diagramme *m or* schéma *m*

scientific *adjective* scientifique; **scientific calculator** = calculatrice *f* avec fonctions scientifiques

scissor *verb (text or graphics)* couper

SCR = SEQUENCE CONTROL REGISTER

scramble *verb (message)* embrouiller

◊ **scrambler** *noun (device that codes a data stream in pseudorandom form)* embrouilleur *m*

scrapbook *noun (Apple Macintosh utility)* utilitaire *m* de stockage de dessin *or* album *m* de croquis; **we store our logo in the scrapbook** = nous conservons le logo dans l'album (de croquis)

scratch **1** *noun (mark on disk or film)* rayure *f or* éraflure *f or* égratignure *f or* défaut *m* de surface;

this scratch makes the disk unreadable = cette rayure rend la lecture du disque impossible **2** *verb* *(file or data)* supprimer *or* détruire

◊ **scratch file** *or* **work file** *noun (work area)* fichier *m* de travail *or* de manoeuvre; **scratch tape** = bande *f* de travail

◊ **scratchpad** *noun* (mémoire) bloc-notes *m (used to buffer data between a fast processor and a slow I/O device)* **scratchpad memory** = mémoire *f* cache

> QUOTE Mathcad is described as an easy-to-use 'handy scratch pad for quick number crunching', which is positioned as an alternative to popular spreadsheets.
>
> *Computing*

screen 1 *noun* **(a)** *(display device)* écran *m*; *(defines how each character will be displayed on screen)* **screen attribute** = attribut *m* d'écran; **screen border** = bordure *f* d'écran; **screen buffer** = mémoire *f* tampon d'écran; **screen dump** = vidage *m* d'écran (sur imprimante); **screen editor** = éditeur *m* d'écran; *(image that moves slightly)* **screen flicker** = scintillement *m* *or* papillotement *m*; *(typeface used to display text on screen)* **screen font** = police *f* d'écran; **the screen font is displayed at 72dpi on a monitor, rather than printed at 300dpi on this laser printer** = la police d'écran est affichée à 72 ppp sur le moniteur plutôt qu'à 300 ppp pour l'imprimante laser; **screen format** = format *m* d'écran; *(capturing what is displayed and storing it)* **screen grab** = capture *f* d'écran; **screen memory** = mémoire *f* écran; *(replaces the image on screen with moving image)* **screen saver** = économiseur *m* d'écran; **screen shot** = capture *f* d'écran; *(displayed on a screen)* **on-screen** = à l'écran; **on-screen display** = affichage *m*; **the dtp package offers on-screen font display** = le logiciel PAO permet l'affichage des polices de caractères; **text screen** = écran de texte; **touch screen** = écran tactile **(b)** *(which protects)* écran de protection; **magnetic screen** = blindage *m* *or* écran magnétique; **without the metal screen over the power supply unit, the computer just produced garbage** = lorsqu'on enlevait le blindage métallique du bloc d'alimentation, l'ordinateur ne donnait plus rien de bon **2** *verb* **(a)** *(to protect)* protéger à l'aide d'un écran; **the PSU is screened against interference** = un blindage du bloc d'alimentation réduit les perturbations **(b)** *(to display) (data)* afficher; *(film)* projeter; **the film is now being screened** = la projection du film est commencée **(c)** *(to select)* sélectionner *or* trier

◊ **screenful** *noun* plein écran

> QUOTE the screen memory is, in fact a total of 4K in size, the first 2K hold the character codes, of which 1K is displayed. Scrolling brings the remaining area into view
>
> *Computing Today*

script *noun (instructions which carry out a function)* script *m*; **I log in automatically using this script with my communications software** = je débute automatiquement la session en utilisant ce script avec mon logiciel de communication; *(simple programming language)* **scripting**

language = langage *m* de script; **this communications software has a scripting language that lets me dial and log in automatically** = ce logiciel de communication possède un langage de script qui me permet de composer les numéros d'appels et de débuter la session automatiquement

◊ **scriptwriter** *noun* scénariste *m&f*

scroll *verb* faire défiler (un texte); *(arrows that move the contents of the window)* **scroll arrows** = flèches *fpl* de défilement; *(bar along the side of a window)* **scroll bar** = barre *f* de défilement *or* ascenseur *m*; **the marker is in the middle of the scroll bar so I know I am in the middle of the document** = le marqueur est situé au milieu de la barre de défilement; je sais ainsi que je suis au milieu du document; *(key that changes how the cursor control keys operate)* **Scroll Lock key** = touche *f* Scroll lock; touche Arrêt Défilement (sur un clavier français); **roll scroll** = faire défiler (un texte) ligne à ligne sur l'écran; **scroll mode** = mode défilement; **smooth scroll** = faire défiler (un texte) point par point

◊ **scrolling down** *noun* défilement *m* descendant *or* vers le bas; **scrolling up** = défilement ascendant *or* vers le haut

scrub *verb* effacer *or* supprimer *or* détruire; **scrub all files with the .BAK extension** = détruisez tous les fichiers avec l'extension .BAK

SCSI = SMALL COMPUTER SYSTEMS INTERFACE interface SCSI; *(standard that provides a wider data bus)* **SCSI-2** = interface SCSI-2; *(allows data to be transferred at a higher rate)* **Fast-SCSI** = interface Fast-SCSI; *(provides a wider data bus)* **Wide-SCSI** = interface Wide-SCSI (SCSI large)

> COMMENT: SCSI is the current standard used to interface high-capacity, high-performance disk drives to computers, smaller disk drives are connected with an IDE interface, which is slower, but cheaper. SCSI replaced the older ESDI interface and allows several (normally eight) peripherals to be connected, in a daisy-chain, to one controller

> QUOTE The Tricord ES4000 is an entry-level superserver machine, with 525Mb of SCSI-2 fixed disk, 64Mb of ECC memory, and support for Raid levels 0, 1 and 10.
>
> *Computing*

> QUOTE the system uses SCSI for connecting to the host and ESDI for interconnecting among drives within a multidrive system
>
> *Byte*

SD = SINGLE DENSITY (DISK)

SDLC = SYNCHRONOUS DATA LINK CONTROL

SDR = STORE DATA REGISTER

seal *verb* fermer hermétiquement *or* sceller; **the hard disk is in a sealed case** = le disque dur est contenu dans un boîtier scellé

seamless integration *noun (including a new device or software without any problems)* intégration *f* parfaite *or* sans couture *or* sans hiatus; **it took a lot of careful planning, but we succeeded in a seamless integration of the new application** = après beaucoup de travail, nous avons finalement réussi une intégration sans couture de la nouvelle application

search 1 *noun* recherche *f*; **chaining search** = recherche associative *or* en chaîne; **linear search** *or* **sequential search** = recherche séquentielle; **retrospective search** = recherche rétrospective; **sequential search** = recherche séquentielle; **search key** = clé *f* de recherche; **search memory** = mémoire associative *or* adressable par le contenu; *(on word processors)* **search and replace** = (fonction *or* procédure) chercher et remplacer; *(search and replace function covering a complete file)* **global search and replace** = chercher et remplacer globalement *or* dans tout le texte **2** *verb (look for an item of data)* (re)chercher (une donnée) *or* faire une recherche

◊ **searching storage** *noun* mémoire associative *or* adressable par le contenu

> QUOTE a linear search of 1,000 items takes 500 comparisons to find the target, and 1,000 to report that it isn't present. A binary search of the same set of items takes roughly ten divisions either to find or not to find the target
> *Personal Computer World*

SECAM = SEQUENTIEL COULEUR A MEMOIRE

second *adjective* deuxième *or* second, -e; **we have two computers, the second one being used if the first is being repaired** = nous possédons un second ordinateur pour assurer la relève si le premier tombe en panne; **second generation computers** = ordinateurs de deuxième génération; **second-level addressing** = adressage *m* indirect; **second-sourcing** = utilisation *f* d'une seconde source de composants; **second-user** *or* **second-hand** = (équipement) d'occasion

◊ **secondary** *adjective* secondaire; **secondary channel** = canal *m* *or* voie *f* secondaire; *(from two primary colours)* **secondary colour** = couleur *f* secondaire; **secondary station** = station *f* secondaire; **secondary storage** = mémoire *f* auxiliaire

section *noun (of main program)* segment *m* (exécutable)

sector 1 *noun (on magnetic disk)* secteur *m* (de disque); *(faulty sector)* **bad sector** = mauvais secteur *or* secteur inutilisable; *(ratio of sectors skipped between access operations on a hard disk)* **sector interleave** = entrelacement *m* de secteurs; *(contains the addresses of unusable sectors on a hard disk)* **sector map** = table d'adresse des secteurs marqués inutilisables **2** *verb (disk)* diviser en secteur *or* sectoriser; **(disk) sector formatting** = formatage *m* de secteurs (d'un disque); **sectoring hole** = perforation *f* de positionnement; **hard-sectored** = (disque) avec

formatage physique; **soft-sectored** = (disque) formaté *or* sectorisé par logiciel; *see also* FORMAT

secure system *noun* système *m* sécurisé *or* verrouillé

◊ **secured** *adjective (file)* sécurisé, -ée

◊ **security** *noun* sécurité *f*; **the system has been designed to assure the security of the stored data** = la conception du système assure la sécurité des données en mémoire; **security backup** = copie *f* de sauvegarde; *(of users)* **security check** = contrôle *m* de sécurité

seed *noun (starting value when generating random numbers)* valeur *f* de départ *or* amorce *f* théorique

seek *verb* chercher; *(section of memory to be searched)* **seek area** = zone *f* de recherche; **seek time** = temps *m* d'accès; **the new hard disk drive has a seek time of 35ms** = le nouveau disque a un temps d'accès de 35 ms

segment 1 *noun (section of a main program)* segment *m*; **LAN segment** = *(continuous piece of cable)* segment *m* de câble; *(part of a network)* segment (isolable) de réseau local **2** *verb (a long program)* segmenter *or* diviser; *(memory address space divided into segments)* **segmented address space** = espace *m* d'adresse segmenté; *see also* OVERLAY

> QUOTE you can also write in smaller program segments. This simplifies debugging and testing
> *Personal Computer World*

select *verb* sélectionner; valider *or* activer; *(line or signal)* **chip select (CS)** = valider *or* activer un circuit intégré

◊ **selectable** *adjective* qui peut être sélectionné *or* validé; qui peut être programmé; **jumper-selectable** = (circuit *or* dispositif) qui peut être sélectionné *or* validé par cavalier; **selectable attributes** = attributs programmables (par l'utilisateur); **user-selectable** = programmable *or* définissable *or* réglable (par l'utilisateur); qui peut être modifié *or* programmé *or* sélectionné *or* validé *or* réglé suivant les besoins de l'utilisateur; **this modem has user-selectable baud rates** = les vitesses (de réception et de transmission) de ce modem sont réglables

◊ **selection** *noun* choix *m* *or* sélection *f*; **selection of information from a large database may take some time** = la sélection d'informations contenues dans une très grande base de données peut prendre un certain temps

◊ **selective** *adjective* sélectif, -ive; **selective calling** = appel sélectif; **selective dump** = vidage sélectif; **selective sort** = tri sélectif

◊ **selectivity** *noun* sélectivité *f*

◊ **selector** *noun* sélecteur *m*; **the selector knob for the amplification is located there** = c'est là que se trouve le sélecteur d'amplitude; **turn the selector control** = tournez le sélecteur; **selector channel** = canal *m* sélecteur *or* de sélection

self- *prefix (referring to oneself)* auto-; **self-**

adapting system = système *m* auto-adaptatif; **self-checking system** = système avec contrôle automatique *or* avec autocontrôle; **self-checking code** = code *m* (auto)détecteur (d'erreurs); **self-correcting codes** = codes (auto)correcteurs; **self-diagnostic** = autodiagnostic *m*; **self-documenting program** = programme *m* avec documentation en ligne; *(expert system)* **self-learning** = système auto-enrichissant *or* à acquisition de connaissances et de régles *or* autodidacte; **self-refreshing RAM** = (mémoire) RAM auto-rafraîchie *or* auto-entretenue; **self-relocating program** = programme relogeable automatiquement; **self-resetting** *or* **self-restoring loop** = boucle *f* avec retour automatique à zéro *or* avec retour automatique aux paramètres de départ

semantics *noun* sémantique *f*; *(use of incorrect symbol)* **semantic error** = erreur *f* (de) sémantique

semaphore *noun* **(a)** *(flags)* (fonction) sémaphore *m* **(b)** *(signalling system)* (technique) sémaphore

semi- *prefix* semi- *or* demi-; **semi-processed data** = données partiellement (pré)traitées

semicolon (;) *noun* point-virgule *m*

semicompiled *adjective* (programme) semi-compilé

semiconductor *noun* semi-conducteur *m*; **semiconductor device** = (composant) semi-conducteur; **semiconductor memory** = mémoire à semi-conducteur; *(solid-state laser)* **semiconductor laser** = laser *m* transistorisé

sender *noun (person)* émetteur, -euse

◊ **send-only device** *noun* émetteur *m*

sense 1 *verb* détecter *or* lire; **the condition of the switch was sensed by the program** = le programme a pu détecter l'état du connecteur; **this device senses the holes punched in a paper tape** = ce dispositif lit les perforations de la bande papier; **mark sense** = graphiter **2** *noun* détection *f or* lecture *f or* reconnaissance *f*; **sense recovery time** = délai *m* de retournement *or* de conversion; **sense switch** = (commutateur) détecteur *m or* indicateur *m* d'état

◊ **sensing** *noun* détection *f* ; reconnaissance *f*; **auto-baud sensing** = reconnaissance *f* automatique du débit d'une ligne

◊ **sensitive** *adjective* sensible; **the computer is sensitive even to very slight changes in current** = cet ordinateur est sensible aux moindres variations du courant; **light-sensitive films change when exposed to light** = les films photosensibles réagissent à la lumière; **touch-sensitive keyboard** = clavier *m* tactile *or* à effleurement

◊ **sensitivity** *noun* **(a)** sensibilité *f*; **the scanner's sensitivity to small objects** = la sensibilité du scanner aux petits objets **(b)** *(minimum power necessary for a receiver to distinguish a signal)* sensibilité *f*

sensor *noun* capteur *m*; **the sensor's output varies with temperature** = le signal de sortie du capteur varie suivant la température; **the process is monitored by a bank of sensors** = le processus est contrôlé par une batterie de capteurs; **image sensor** = capteur d'images

sentinel *noun (marker or pointer)* drapeau *m or* marqueur *m*

separate 1 *adjective* indépendant, -e *or* différent, -e; **separate channel signalling** = émission de signaux par canaux indépendants **2** *verb* séparer; *(display option)* **separated graphics** = caractères graphiques espacés *or* séparés

◊ **separation** *noun* séparation *f*; **colour separation** = séparation *f or* sélection *f* des couleurs; **colour separations** = négatifs *mpl* de séparation des couleurs

◊ **separator** *noun (symbol or code in a program)* (symbole *or* code) séparateur *m* (d'information) *or* symbole *m* intercalaire

septet *noun (word made up of seven bits)* septet *m*

sequence *noun* séquence *f or* ordre *m*; **the sequence of names is arranged alphabetically** = les noms sont classés par ordre alphabétique; **the program instructions are arranged in sequence according to line numbers** = les instructions sont ordonnées suivant le numéro de ligne; **binary sequence** = séquence binaire; **control sequence** = séquence de commande (d'exécution); **sequence check** = contrôle *m* de séquence; **sequence control register (SCR)** *or* **sequence counter** *or* **sequence register** = registre *m* de contrôle de séquence; **the logon sequence** = séquence d'ouverture de session *or* d'identification

◊ **sequencer** *noun* séquenceur *m*

◊ **sequential** *adjective* séquentiel, -elle; **sequential batch processing** = traitement *m* par lots en mode séquentiel; **sequential computer** = ordinateur *m* série; **sequential file** *or* **serial file** = fichier *m* à accès séquentiel; **sequential logic** = logique séquentielle; **if the input sequence to the sequential logic circuit is 1101 the output will always be zero (0)** = si l'entrée dans le circuit séquentiel logique est 1101, la sortie sera toujours zéro (0); **sequential mode** = mode séquentiel; **sequential operation** = opération séquentielle; **sequential processing** = traitement séquentiel (de données); **sequential search** = recherche séquentielle

◊ **sequential access** *noun* accès séquentiel; **sequential access storage** = mémoire *f* à accès séquentiel; **queued indexed sequential access method (QISAM)** = méthode d'accès séquentiel indexé en file; **queued sequential access method (QSAM)** = méthode d'accès séquentiel en file

◊ **sequentially** *adverb* (exécuté) en série *or* suivant un ordre séquentiel

Séquentiel Couleur à Mémoire (SECAM) standard de télévision SECAM

serial *adjective* (en) série *or* séquentiel, -elle;

serial access = accès *m* séquentiel *or* accès série; **serial-access memory (SAM)** = mémoire *f* à accès séquentiel; **serial adder** = additionneur *m* (en) série; **serial computer** = ordinateur *m* série; **serial data transmission** *or* **communication** = communication *f* *or* transmission *f* (en mode) série; **serial file** = fichier *m* à accès séquentiel; **serial input/output (SIO)** = entrée/sortie *f* (en) série; *see* SERIAL TRANSMISSION **serial input/parallel output (SIPO)** = entrée série/sortie parallèle; **serial input/serial output (SISO)** = entrée série/sortie série; **serial interface** = interface *f* série; **parallel connections are usually less trouble to set up and use than serial interfaces, but are usually limited to 20 feet in length** = de façon générale, les connexions parallèles sont moins difficiles à mettre en place et à utiliser que les interfaces série, mais leur longueur est limitée à environ 6 mètres; **serial memory** = mémoire *f* séquentielle; *(mouse which connects to the serial port of a PC)* **serial mouse** = souris *f* série; *(working on data in a sequential manner)* **serial operation** = opération séquentielle; **serial port** = port *m* série; **serial printer** = imprimante *f* série; **serial processing** = traitement séquentiel; **serial storage** = *(action)* stockage *m* séquentiel; *(place)* mémoire *f* à accès séquentiel; **serial to parallel converter** = convertisseur *m* série/parallèle; **serial transmission** *or* **serial input/output** = transmission (en) série *or* entrée/sortie (en) série; **word serial** = transfert *m* en série (de mots binaires)

◊ **serially** *adverb* (disposé *or* monté) en série; **their transmission rate is 64,000 bits per second through a parallel connection or 19,200 serially** = leur vitesse de transmission est de 64 000 bits par seconde en connexion parallèle ou 19 200 en connexion série

◊ **series** *noun* série *f*; **series circuit** = circuit *m* (disposé en) série *or* montage *m* en série

serif *noun* *(typography)* empattement *m* (d'un caractère); **sans serif** = (caractère) sans empattement

server *noun* *(dedicated computer or peripheral)* serveur *m*; *(computer which runs a network operating system software)* **file server** = serveur de fichiers; *(facility used by terminals and operators of a LAN)* **LAN server** = serveur de réseau local; *(IBM network operating system)* **LAN Server** ™ = Lan Server ™; *(computer dedicated to managing print queues and printers)* **print server** = serveur d'impression; *(application program which can be accessed by several users)* **server-based application** = application sur serveur *or* partagée; *(allows a user to access another computer's files over a network)* **server message block (SMB)** = système SMB (de partage de fichiers)

QUOTE Sequent Computer Systems' Platform division will focus on hardware and software manufacture, procurement and marketing, with the Enterprise division concentrating on services and server implementation.
Computing

service 1 *verb* *(system)* réviser *or* réparer; **the disk drives were serviced yesterday and are working well** = nous avons fait réviser *or* réparer les lecteurs de disquettes hier et tout fonctionne très bien **2** *noun* **(a)** contrôle *m*; **service bit** = bit *m* de contrôle **(b)** (opération de) maintenance *f* *or* (d') entretien *m*; **service contract** = contrat *m* de maintenance; **service program** = programme *m* de maintenance *or* utilitaire *m* de maintenance

◊ **services** *noun* *(functions provided by a device)* services *m* *or* fonctions *fpl* de service

servo *or* **servomechanism** *noun* servomécanisme *m*

session *noun* *(time when a program is running)* session *f* *or* période *f* de travail; **session key** = clé d'ouverture d'une session; **session layer** = couche *f* session

set 1 *noun* **(a)** ensemble *m* *or* jeu *m* *or* série *f*; **character set** = *(code)* jeu *or* ensemble de caractères; *(typeface)* fonte *f* *or* police *f* de caractères; *(maths)* **set theory** = théorie *f* des ensembles **(b)** *(typeface)* corps *m* d'un caractère; **set size** = taille *f* d'un caractère (mesuré en points); **set width** = chasse *f* **(c)** *(radio or TV receiver)* poste *m* (de télévision *or* radio); **set-top converter** = convertisseur *m* de signal *or* de fréquence **(d)** *(of play or film or TV)* décors *mpl* **2** *verb* **(a)** *(to define a value)* fixer *or* programmer *or* paramétrer *or* régler; **we set the right-hand margin at 80 characters** = nous avons programmé *or* fixé la marge de droite à 80 caractères; **to set breakpoints** = programmer les points d'arrêt **(b)** *(to give a bit the value of 1)* charger *or* affecter (la valeur 1 à un bit) **(c)** *(to compose a text into typeset characters)* composer; **the text is set in 12 point Times Roman** = le texte est (composé) en Times romain corps 12

◊ **setting** *noun* **(a)** réglage *m*; *(adjusting)* **brightness setting** = réglage de la luminosité; **contrast setting** = réglage des contrastes; **tab settings** = tabulation *f* **(b)** *(typesetting of text)* composition *f*; **the MS has been sent to the typesetter for setting** = le manuscrit a été envoyé à l'atelier de composition; **setting charges have increased since last year** = les frais de composition ont augmenté depuis l'an dernier; **computer setting** = composition informatisée *or* assistée par ordinateur

◊ **set up** *verb* *(to install or configure)* installer *or* configurer *or* définir; *(to initialize or start)* initialiser *or* mettre en route; **the new computer worked well as soon as the engineer had set it up** = dès qu'il a été configuré par l'ingénieur, le nouvel ordinateur a bien fonctionné; *(choices)* **set-up option** = option *f* de configuration; *(between signal and start)* **set-up time** = délai *m* de configuration *or* d'installation

sex changer *noun* *(device for changing a connection)* changeur *m* de genre; adaptateur *m* mâle/femelle *or* adaptateur femelle/mâle

sextet *noun* *(byte made up of six bits)* sextet *m*

sf signalling = SINGLE FREQUENCY SIGNALLING

SGML = STANDARD GENERALIZED MARKUP LANGUAGE

shade *noun (of colour)* ton *m or* nuance *f*; **shades of grey** = niveaux *mpl* de gris

◊ **shading** *noun (of drawing)* ombre *f or* ombrage *m*; *(lines)* hachures *fpl*; *(of colour)* dégradé *m*

shadow *noun (area where signals cannot be received)* ombre *f*; **the mountain casts a shadow over those houses, so they cannot receive any radio broadcasts** = la montagne fait écran à ces habitations qui ne reçoivent aucune émission radio

◊ **shadowmask** *noun (to separate three-colour picture beams)* masque *m* filtre

◊ **shadow memory** *or* **shadow page** *noun* shadow RAM; **shadow page table** = table *f* pages de shadow RAM

◊ **shadow RAM** *noun (UMB)* shadow RAM

shannon *noun* shannon *m*

◊ **Shannon's Law** *noun* loi *f* de Shannon

share *verb* partager; **the system is shared by several independent companies** = plusieurs sociétés indépendantes se partagent le système; *(network operating system)* **share level security** = sécurité *f* par niveau d'opération; **shared access** = accès *m* partagé; *see also* TIME-SHARING SYSTEM, MULTI-USER; **shared bus** = bus *m* partagé; *(directory which can be accessed by several users)* **shared directory** = répertoire *m* partagé; **shared file** = fichier *m* commun *or* partagé; **shared line** *or* **party line** = ligne *f* partagée; **shared logic system** = système logique partagé; **shared logic text processor** = processeur *m* de traitement de texte à logique partagée; **shared memory** = mémoire partagée; **shared network directory** = répertoire de réseau partagé; **shared resources system** = système à ressources partagées *or* système multi-utilisateur; **resource sharing** = partage *m* de ressources; **time-sharing** = partage de temps *or* (système) en temps partagé

◊ **shareware** *noun* logiciel *m* pour lequel une contribution volontaire est demandée *or* shareware *m*

> QUOTE Bulletin board users know the dangers of 'flaming' (receiving hostile comments following a naïve or ridiculous assertion) and of being seen 'troughing' (grabbing every bit of shareware on the network).
>
> *Computing*

sheet *noun* feuille *f* (de papier); *(paper feed system)* **(single) sheet feed** = alimentation *f* feuille à feuille; **sheet feed attachment** = bac *m* d'alimentation feuille à feuille (automatique)

shelf life *noun* durée *f* de vie (à l'étalage) *or* date *f* de péremption (d'un produit en magasin); **the developer has a shelf life of one year** = le révélateur doit être utilisé dans un délai d'un an

shell *noun (software operating between the user and the system)* (programme) shell *or* de définition de l'environnement; **MS-DOS's**

COMMAND.COM **is a basic shell that interprets commands typed in at the prompt** = COMMAND.COM de MS.DOS est un programme shell indispensable qui interprète les commandes entrées au clavier en réponse à l'invite de DOS; **the Macintosh Finder is a sophisticated shell with a GUI front-end** = Finder de Macintosh est un programme shell intelligent qui utilise une interface (graphique) GUI

◊ **shell out** *verb (to exit to the operating system)* sortir du program (en cours) et revenir au DOS; **I shelled out from the word-processor to check which files were on the floppy, then went back to the program** = je suis sorti du traitement de texte pour vérifier quels étaient les fichiers disponibles sur la disquette, puis je suis retourné dans le programme

◊ **shell sort** *noun* (algorithme de) tri *m* enveloppe

SHF = SUPER HIGH FREQUENCY

shield 1 *noun* écran *m* ; blindage *m* (de protection) **2** *verb* protéger; blinder; **shielded cable** = câble *m* blindé; *(two insulated copper wires twisted around each other, wrapped in an insulating layer)* **shielded twisted pair (STP) cable** = câble *m* en paires torsadées blindé; *(two insulated copper wires twisted around each other)* **unshielded twisted pair (UTP) cable** = câble en paires torsadées non blindé *or* sans blindage

shift 1 *verb* **(a)** *(to move)* déplacer *or* décaler *or* permuter; **shift instruction** = instruction *f* de décalage; **shift left** = faire un décalage à gauche; **0110 left shifted once is 1100** = 0110 décalé à gauche d'un pas, devient 1100; **shift right** = faire un décalage à droite **(b)** *(typewriter, etc.)* passer en majuscule **2** *noun* **(a)** décalage *m or* permutation *f*; **arithmetic shift** = décalage arithmétique; **cyclic shift** = permutation *or* décalage circulaire; **logical shift** = décalage logique *or* non arithmétique; **shift character** = caractère *m* de déplacement; **shift code** = code *m* de déplacement; **shift register** = registre *m* à *or* de décalage **(b)** *(on typewriter, etc.)* **shift key** = touche *f* majuscule

shoot *verb (to film)* tourner (un film) *or* filmer; **they shot hundreds of feet of film, but none of it was any good** = ils ont pris des centaines de mètres de pellicule sans rien obtenir d'intéressant; **the programme was shot on location in Spain** = les extérieurs pour ce programme ont été tournés en Espagne (NOTE: **shooting - shot**)

short *adjective* court, -e; *(expansion board)* **short card** = carte *f* de taille réduite *or* carte courte; *(half card)* carte demi-longueur; **short haul modem** = modem *m* de courte portée

short circuit 1 *noun* court-circuit *m* **2** *verb* créer un court-circuit *or* court-circuiter; **short-circuited** = (qui a été) mis en court-circuit *or* court-circuité, -ée

shorten *verb* raccourcir *or* couper *or* réduire; **we had to shorten the file to be able to save it on one floppy** = nous avons dû raccourcir *or* couper le fichier pour réussir à le sauvegarder sur une seule disquette

short-run *adjective* tirage *m* réduit *or* limité; **a printer specializing in short-run printing** = un imprimeur qui se spécialise dans les petits tirages; **the laser printer is good for short-run leaflets** = l'imprimante laser est très utile pour les feuillets à tirage limité

short wave (SW) *noun (frequency below 60 metres)* ondes *fpl* courtes; **short-wave receiver** = récepteur *m or* radio à ondes courtes

shotgun microphone *noun* microphone *m* 'canon'

show-through *noun* transparence *f*; **bad quality paper gives too much show-through** = un papier de mauvaise qualité est beaucoup trop transparent

shrink *verb* réduire *or* condenser *or* comprimer; **the drawing was shrunk to fit the space** = on a réduit le dessin pour le faire entrer dans l'emplacement prévu (NOTE: **shrinks - shrank - has shrunk)**

shut down *verb* arrêter *or* fermer *or* éteindre

◊ **shut-off mechanism** *noun* mécanisme *m* d'arrêt

shutter *noun (of camera)* obturateur *m*

SI units = SYSTEME INTERNATIONAL d'unités

sibilance *noun* sibilance *f or* sifflement *m*

sideband *noun* bande *f* latérale; **upper sideband** = bande latérale supérieure; **lower sideband** = bande latérale inférieure; **double sideband** = double bande latérale; **double sideband suppressed carrier (DSBSC)** = (modulation d'amplitude à) double bande latérale sans porteuse *or* à porteuse inhibée; **single sideband** = bande latérale unique

side lobe *noun (of aerial's response pattern)* lobe *m* latéral

sideways ROM *noun* ROM auxiliaire *or* mémoire *f* morte auxiliaire

SIG = SPECIAL INTEREST GROUP

sign 1 *noun* signe *m* (de polarité); **sign and modulus** = signe et modulo; **sign bit** *or* **sign indicator** = bit *m* de signe *or* indicateur *m* de signe; **sign digit** = binaire *m* de signe *or* chiffre (indicateur) de signe; **sign and magnitude** *or* **signed magnitude** = chiffre (de) signe; **sign position** = position *f* du signe **2** *verb* **(a)** signer; *(to logoff)* **to sign off** = terminer une session; *(to logon)* **to sign on** = débuter *or* ouvrir une session (en s'identifiant) **(b) signed field** = champ (de) signe

signal 1 *noun* signal *m*; **the signal received from the computer contained the answer** = le signal émis par l'ordinateur contenait la réponse; **interrupt**

signal = signal (d') interruption; **signal conditioning** = mise *f* en forme *or* conversion *f* de signaux; **signal conversion** = conversion de signaux; **signal converter** = convertisseur *m* de signaux; **signal distance** = distance de Hamming; **signal element** = élément (d'un) signal; **the signal element in this system is a short voltage pulse, indicating a binary one** = l'élément signal de ce système est une courte impulsion de tension qui représente un 1 binaire; **the signal elements for the radio transmission system are 10ms of 40KHz and 10ms of 60KHz for binary 0 and 1 respectively** = les signaux élémentaires de ce système de radiotransmission sont 10 ms à 40 kHz, pour le bit zéro (0) et 10 ms à 60 kHz, pour le bit chargé (1); **signal generator** = générateur *m* de signaux; **signal processing** = traitement *m* du signal; **the system is used by students doing research on signal processing techniques** = ce système est à la disposition des étudiants qui se spécialisent dans la recherche sur les techniques de traitement du signal; *(difference between the power of the signal and the noise on the line)* **signal to noise ratio (S/N)** = rapport signal/bruit **2** *verb* émettre *or* transmettre un signal; **signal to the network that we are busy** = signale au réseau que nous sommes occupés *or* envoie un signal au réseau pour prévenir que nous sommes occupés

◊ **signalling** *noun* signalisation *f*; **in band signalling** = transmission *f* de signaux sur bande vocale

signature *noun* **(a)** *(name)* signature *f*; **do you recognize the signature on the cheque?** = reconnaissez-vous la signature sur le chèque? **(b)** *(of book)* cahier *m*; **signature (mark)** = signature **(c)** *(authentication code)* identification *f or* signature *or* code *m* personnel *or* code confidentiel; **safe signature analysis using functional analysis (SAFE)** = technique *f* d'identification SAFE

signify *verb (to mean)* signifier *or* vouloir dire; **a carriage return code signifies the end of an input line** = l'envoi du code CR signifie que la ligne saisie est terminée

◊ **significance** *noun* signification *f*

◊ **significant** *adjective* significatif, -ive *or* important, -e; **significant digit codes** *or* **faceted codes** = codes *mpl* significatifs; *see also* BIT

silicon *noun* silicium *m*; **silicon chip** = puce *f or* pastille *f* de silicium; **silicon disk** *or* **RAM disk** = disque *m* RAM *or* virtuel; **silicon foundry** = fonderie *f* de silicium; **silicon gate** = semi-conducteur *m* au silicium; **silicon on sapphire (SOS)** = silicium sur saphir; **silicon transistor** = transistor *m* silicium; *(area of California)* **Silicon Valley** = Silicon Valley (région de la Californie où l'on trouve une forte concentration de sociétés productrices de semi-conducteurs); **silicon wafer** = tranche *f* de silicium

SIMD = SINGLE INSTRUCTION STREAM MULTIPLE DATA STREAM

SIMM = SINGLE IN-LINE MEMORY MODULE

simple *adjective (not complicated)* simple;

(hardware or software) **simple to use** = (machine or logiciel) d'utilisation facile

◊ **simple mail transfer protocol (SMTP)** *(protocol for electronic mail messages)* protocole *m* SMTP (de messagerie électronique)

◊ **simple network management protocol (SNMP)** *(network management system)* protocole SNMP (de gestion de réseau)

simplex *noun (transmission in one direction)* simplex *m or* transmission *f* unidirectionnelle

simplify *verb* simplifier *or* rendre plus facile; **function keys simplify program operation** = les touches de fonction simplifient l'exploitation d'un programme

simulate *verb* simuler; **this software simulates the action of an aeroplane** = ce logiciel simule les manoeuvres aériennes *or* est un simulateur de vol

◊ **simulator** *noun* simulateur *m*; **flight simulator** = simulateur de vol

◊ **simulation** *noun* simulation *f*; **simulation software** = logiciel *m* de simulation; **simulation techniques have reached a high degree of sophistication** = les techniques de simulation sont devenues très sophistiquées

simultaneity *adjective* simultanéité *f*

simultaneous *adjective* simultané, -ée; **simultaneous processing** = traitement *m* simultané; **simultaneous transmission** = transmission *f* simultanée (NOTE: same as **duplex)**

◊ **simultaneously** *adverb* de façon simultanée *or* simultanément

sin *or* **sine** *noun (geometry)* sinus *m*

◊ **sine wave** *noun* sinusoïde *f or* onde *f* sinusoïdale

single *adjective (only one)* unique *or* simple *or* seul, -e; **single address code** = code *m* d'instruction à adresse unique *or* directe; **single address instruction** = instruction *f* à adresse unique *or* directe; **single address message** = message *m* à une seule adresse; *(station with only one port)* **single attachment station (SAS)** = station *f* à connexion unique *or* à liaison unique; **single board computer (SBC)** = ordinateur *m* à carte unique *or* ordinateur monocarte; **single chip computer** = ordinateur *m* à puce unique *or* ordinateur monopuce; **single density disk (SD)** = disquette *f* à simple densité; **single frequency signalling** *or* **SF signalling** = signalisation *f* monofréquence; **single function software** = logiciel *m* d'application spécialisée; *(circuit board with an edge connector along one edge)* **single in-line memory module (SIMM)** = barrette *f* de mémoire (de type) SIMM; **you can expand the main memory of your PC by plugging in two more SIMMs** = pour augmenter la mémoire de votre ordinateur, installez deux barrettes SIMM supplémentaires; *(component which has all its leads on one side)* **single in-line package (SIP)** = composant *m or* barrette (de type) SIP;

(architecture of a parallel computer) **single instruction stream multiple data stream (SIMD)** = architecture *f* SIMD *or* flux simple d'instructions, flux multiple de données; **single instruction stream single data stream (SISD)** = architecture SISD *or* flux simple d'instructions, flux simple de données; **single key response** = (logiciel) activé par une seule touche; *(by one computer word)* **single length precision** = (en) simple précision; **single length working** = opération *f* en simple mot; **single line display** = écran *m* d'une ligne *or* (écran avec) affichage d'une ligne (à la fois); *(optic fibre)* **single mode** *or* **monomode** = monomode; **single operand instruction** = instruction à un opérande; *(transmission in one direction)* **single operation** = transmission *f* unidirectionnelle *or* simplex *m*; **single pass operation** = opération (en) une passe *or* opération monopasse; **single pole (switch)** = (commutateur) unipolaire; **single precision** = (en) simple précision; **single scan non segmented** = balayage *m* une passe sans segmentation d'image *or* balayage d'image complète en une passe; **single sheet feed** = alimentation *f or* entraînement *m* feuille à feuille; **single sideband** = bande *f* latérale unique; **single-sided disk (SSD)** = disquette *f* simple face; *(one instruction at a time)* **single step** = (exécution) pas à pas; **single strike ribbon** = ruban *m* à un seul passage *or* non réutilisable; **single tasking** = monotâche *f*; **single user system** = système *m* mono-utilisateur *or* ordinateur *m* individuel

sink *noun (end of line)* puits *m or* collecteur *m* de données; *(conducts heat away from component)* **heat sink** = dissipateur *m* thermique *or* radiateur *m* à ailette(s); *(paths in a network)* **sink tree** = arborescence *f* en puits

sinusoidal *adjective* sinusoïdal, -e; **the carrier has a sinusoidal waveform** = la porteuse est une onde sinusoïde

SIO = SERIAL INPUT/OUTPUT

SIP = SINGLE IN-LINE PACKAGE

siphoning *noun* siphonage *m*

SIPO = SERIAL INPUT/PARALLEL OUTPUT

SISD = SINGLE INSTRUCTION STREAM SINGLE DATA STREAM

SISO = SERIAL INPUT/SERIAL OUTPUT

site *noun* emplacement *m or* site *m*; *(licence which allows any number of users in one site)* **site licence** = licence *f* de site; **we have negotiated a good deal for the site licence for our 1200 employees in our HQ** = nous avons négocié longtemps pour obtenir une licence de site pour les 1200 employés du siège; *see also* ON-SITE

◊ **site poll** *verb* appel *m* (à émettre) à tous les terminaux d'un site; *see also* POLLING

sixteen-bit *or* **16-bit** *adjective* (système à) seize bits

sixteenmo *or* **16mo** *noun* in-16 *or* in seize *or* (à) quatre plis

size 1 *noun* dimension *f or* taille *f or* grandeur *f*; **the size of the print has been increased to make it easier to read** = la taille des caractères a été augmentée pour rendre la lecture plus facile; **page size** = taille *or* grandeur *or* format *m* de la page; **our page sizes vary from 220 x 110 to 360 x 220** = nos formats de pages varient de 220 x 110mm à 360 x 220mm; **screen size** = dimension de l'écran **2** *verb* dimensionner

◊ **sizing** *noun* modification *f* des dimensions *or* mise *f* à la taille; **photographs can be edited by cropping, sizing, touching up, etc.** = les photos peuvent être éditées par découpage, dimensionnement, retouche, etc.

skeletal code *noun* code *m* incomplet *or* code de base *or* code support *or* code paramétrable

sketch 1 *noun* esquisse *f* **2** *verb* esquisser *or* faire une esquisse

skew *noun* *(amount by which something which is not correctly aligned)* inclinaison *f or* biais *m* ; défaut *m* d'alignement **2** *verb* *(align incorrectly)* réaliser un mauvais alignement; **this page is badly skewed** = cette page est mal alignée

skip *verb* **(a)** *(to transmit over an abnormally long distance)* réfléchir **(b)** sauter *or* passer *or* omettre; **the printer skipped the next three lines of text** = l'imprimante a sauté les trois lignes suivantes; **skip capability** = capacité *f* de saut; **skip instruction** = instruction *f* de saut; *(of paper in a printer)* **high-speed skip** = avance *f* rapide du papier

slash *or* **oblique stroke (/)** *noun* trait *m* oblique

◊ **slashed zero** *noun* *(sign θ used to distinguish a zero from the letter O)* zéro *m* barré d'un trait oblique

slave *noun* esclave *m*; **bus slave** = (puits de données) asservi à un bus *or* esclave d'un bus; **slave cache** *or* **store** = mémoire *f* auxiliaire; **slave processor** = processeur *m* asservi; **slave terminal** = terminal *m* asservi; *(second CRT showing the same image)* **slave tube** = écran *m* asservi *or* second écran

sleep *noun* (système) en attente; *see also* WAKE-UP

sleeve *noun* pochette *f*

slew *noun* *(of paper in a printer)* avance *f* rapide de papier

slice *noun* tranche *f*; **bit-slice architecture** = architecture *f* en tranches; **the bit-slice design uses four four-bit word processors to make a sixteen-bit processor** = le principe du processeur en tranches est de prendre quatre processeurs quatre bits pour en faire un processeur seize bits; **time slice** = tranche de temps

◊ **slicing** *noun* *(from a bar of silicon crystal)* découpe *f* en pastille

slide 1 *noun* diapositive *f*; **slide projector** =

projecteur *m* de diapositives; **slide/sync recorder** = magnétophone *m* avec interface synchro pour projecteur de diapos **2** *verb* glisser; **the disk cover slides on and off easily** = la disquette se glisse dans sa pochette et s'en retire tout aussi facilement

slip pages *or* **slip proofs** *noun* épreuves *fpl* en placard

slot 1 *noun* **(a)** *(long thin hole)* ouverture *f or* fente *f*; **the system disk should be inserted into the left-hand slot on the front of the computer** = la disquette système s'insère dans la fente gauche du panneau avant de l'ordinateur; *(connector into which an expansion card can be plugged)* **expansion slot** = connecteur *m* d'extension *or* emplacement *m* (avec connecteur) pour carte d'extension *or* slot *m*; **there are two free slots in the micro, you only need one for the add-on board** = il y a deux connecteurs *or* deux emplacements libres sur ce micro, un seul suffit pour ajouter la carte d'extension **(b)** *(in a ring network)* **message slot** = trame *f*; **time slot** = créneau (de temps) **2** *verb* insérer dans une fente *or* une ouverture; **the disk slots into one of the floppy drive apertures** = la disquette s'insère dans l'une des deux fentes du lecteur de disquettes

slow motion *noun* ralenti *m*; **the film switches to slow motion** = le film enchaîne sur un ralenti; **play the film again in slow motion** = repassez ce film au ralenti

◊ **slow scan television** *noun* télévision *f* à balayage lent

SLSI = SUPER LARGE SCALE INTEGRATION

slug *noun* *(printing)* ligne-bloc *f*

slur *noun* *(blur of image)* bavure *f or* macule *f*; *(distortion of voice)* bredouillage *m*

small *adjective* petit, -e; **small caps** = petites capitales

◊ **small computer systems interface (SCSI)** *noun* *(interface used to connect computers to peripherals)* interface *f* SCSI (se prononce 'scousi'); *see also* SCSI

◊ **small scale integration (SSI)** *noun* intégration *f* à petite échelle

Smalltalk ™ *(programming language developed by Xerox)* (langage) Smalltalk ™

smart *adjective* *(intelligent)* intelligent, -e; **smart card** = carte *f* magnétique *or* à mémoire; *(intelligent terminal)* **smart terminal** = terminal intelligent; *(network hub which can transmit status information back to a managing station)* **smart wiring hub** = concentrateur *m or* hub *m* intelligent; **using this management software, I can shut down Tom's port on the remote smart wiring hub** = avec ce logiciel de gestion, je peux fermer à distance le port de Tom sur le concentrateur intelligent

SMB = SERVER MESSAGE BLOCK

smog *noun* **electronic smog** = pollution *f* électronique (par rayonnement)

smoke test *noun (informal)* test *m* de la fumée

smooth *verb (signal)* lisser

SMT = SURFACE-MOUNT TECHNOLOGY

SMTP = SIMPLE MAIL TRANSFER PROTOCOL

SNA = SYSTEMS NETWORK ARCHITECTURE

snapshot *noun* instantané *m*; **snapshot dump** = vidage *m* instantané sur imprimante

SNMP = SIMPLE NETWORK MANAGEMENT PROTOCOL

SNOBOL = STRING ORIENTATED SYMBOLIC LANGUAGE

snow *noun (TV image distortion)* (effet de) neige *f* sur l'écran

s/n ratio = SIGNAL TO NOISE RATIO rapport *m* signal/bruit

soak *verb* tester en continu sur une longue période *or* torturer; **the device was soak-tested prior to delivery** = l'appareil a été testé sous tous les angles avant la livraison

socket *noun* prise *f or* douille *f*; **female socket** = prise femelle

QUOTE the mouse and keyboard sockets are the same, and could lead to the kind of confusion that arose with the early PCs when the keyboard could be connected to the tape socket
PC User

soft *adjective* **(a)** *(material that loses magnetic effects)* doux, douce **(b)** *(data not permanently stored)* (données) sur support magnétique *or* effaçables; **soft copy** = texte *m* (d') écran; **soft error** = erreur *f* de logiciel; *(font stored on a disk)* **soft font** = fonte *f* logicielle *or* téléchargeable; *compare with* HARD ERROR; **soft-fail** = panne douce; **soft hyphen** = césure *f* d'écran; **soft keys** = touches *fpl* programmables; **soft keyboard** = clavier *m* à touches programmables; *(instruction)* **soft-reset** = ré-initialisation *f* par logiciel; *compare with* HARD RESET; **soft-sectored disk** = disque formaté *or* sectorisé par logiciel; *(wordprocessing)* **soft zone** = zone *f* de texte

software *noun* logiciel *m*; **applications software** = logiciel d'application *or* progiciel *m*; **bundled software** = logiciel inclus *or* fourni à l'achat d'un ordinateur; **common software** = logiciel commun; **graphics software** = logiciel graphique; **network software** = logiciel de réseau; **pirate software** = logiciel (qui a été) piraté; **system software** = logiciel système; **unbundled software** = logiciel non inclus *or* non fourni à l'achat d'un ordinateur; **user-friendly software** = logiciel convivial; **software compatible** = (système) compatible avec des logiciels écrits pour d'autres systèmes *or* compatible logiciels; **software developer** = développeur *m* de logiciel(s); **software**

development = développement *m* d'un logiciel; **software documentation** = notice *f* d'utilisation d'un logiciel; **software engineer** = ingénieur *m* logiciel *or* ingénieur programmeur; **software engineering** = génie *m* logiciel; **software house** = société *f* spécialisée en logiciels; **software interrupt** = interruption *f* programmée *or* générée par logiciel; **software library** = bibliothèque *f* de logiciels *or* logithèque *f*; **software licence** = autorisation *f* de copie (d'un logiciel); **software life cycle** = cycle *m* de vie d'un logiciel; **software maintenance** = maintenance *f* de logiciel; **software package** = progiciel *m*; **software piracy** = piratage *m* de logiciel; **software quality assurance (SQA)** = assurance *f* qualité dans le domaine du génie logiciel; **software reliability** = fiabilité *f* d'un logiciel; **software specification** = spécifications *fpl* d'un logiciel *or* définition *f* et standards de qualité d'un logiciel; **software system** = progiciel; **software tool** = outil *m* de programmation (NOTE: no plural for **software;** for the plural say **pieces of software)**

solar *adjective* solaire; **solar cell** = pile *f* solaire; **solar power** = énergie *f* solaire; **solar-powered calculator** = calculatrice *f* à batteries photovoltaïques *or* à pile(s) solaire(s)

solder 1 *noun (soft lead used to join wires)* soudure *f* **2** *verb* souder

◊ **solderless** *adjective (board)* sans soudure; *(component, etc.)* enfichable

solenoid *noun* solénoïde *m*

solid *adjective (printed text)* (texte) sans interligne; **solid error** = erreur *f* certaine; **solid font printer** = imprimante *f* à caractères pleins

◊ **solid-state** *adjective* transistorisé, ée *or* à base de semi-conducteurs; **solid-state device** = dispositif transistorisé *or* à semi-conducteurs; **solid-state laser** = laser *m* à composant solide; **solid-state memory device** = mémoire transistorisée

solve *verb* résoudre (un problème)

solution *noun* **(a)** *(answer)* solution *f* (à un problème) **(b)** *(liquid)* solution

son file *noun* fichier *m* fils *or* fichier de troisième génération; *compare with* FATHER FILE, GRANDFATHER FILE

sonar *noun* sonar *m*

◊ **sonic** *adjective (within the human hearing range or 20 - 20,000Hz)* sonique; *(above 20kHz)* **ultrasonic** = ultrasonique

sophisticated *adjective* sophistiqué, -ée *or* évolué, -ée *or* recherché, -ée *or* avancé, -ée; **a sophisticated desktop publishing program** = un programme de PAO évolué *or* avancé

◊ **sophistication** *noun* sophistication *f or* avance *f* technologique; **the sophistication of the new package is remarkable** = le nouveau progiciel est tout à fait sophistiqué

sort 1 *noun* tri *m* **2** *verb* classer *or* trier; **to sort addresses into alphabetical order** = classer les adresses en *or* par ordre alphabétique; **bubble sort** = effectuer un tri bulle *or* un tri par permutation de paires *or* de bulles; **shell sort** = effectuer un tri 'enveloppe' *or* un tri 'bloc par bloc'; **sort/merge** = (fonction de) trier/fusionner; **tree selection sort** = tri en arborescence

◊ **sortkey** *or* **sort field** *noun* clé *f* de tri; champ *m* de tri; **the orders were sorted according to dates by assigning the date field as the sortkey** = les commandes ont été triées par dates en designant le champ date comme clé de tri

SOS = SILICON ON SAPPHIRE

sound *noun* son *m* *or* bruit *m*; **sound advance** = décalage *m* en avance de la bande son; *(expansion card which produces analog sound)* **sound card** = carte *f* audio *or* carte son; **this software lets you create almost any sound - but you can only hear them if you have a sound card fitted** = ce logiciel vous permet de créer presque tous les sons, mais il vous faut une carte audio *or* une carte son pour pouvoir les écouter; *(conversion of an analog sound into digital)* **sound capture** = capture *f* *or* prise *f* de son *or* enregistrement *m* digital; **sound chip** = circuit *m* intégré générateur de son; **sound effects** = effets *m* sonores; **all the sound effects for the film are produced electronically** = tous les effets sonores du film sont produits électroniquement; **sound head** = tête *f* de lecture; *(cover which cuts down noise from a printer)* **sound hood** = capot *m* *or* hotte *f* d'insonorisation; **sound pressure level (SPL)** = niveau *m* de pression acoustique; **sound synthesizer** = synthétiseur *m* de son; **sound track** = piste *f* sonore

◊ **soundproof** *adjective* insonorisé, -ée; **the telephone is installed in a soundproof booth** = le téléphone est dans une cabine insonorisée

source *noun* **(a)** *(point where a signal enters a network)* source *f* (NOTE: opposite is **sink**) **(b)** *(terminal on an FET device)* borne *f* d'entrée **(c)** *(initial point)* source *or* origine *f*; *(detects a particular address)* **source address filtering** = filtrage *m* des adresses sources; **source code** = code *m* source; *(set of punched cards)* **source deck** *or* **pack** = jeu *m* original; **source document** = document original *or* d'origine; *(software)* **source editor** = éditeur *m* de programme source; **source file** = fichier *m* source; **source language** = *(computer)* langage *m* source *or* d'origine; *(translation)* langue *f* de départ; **source listing** = *(text in its original form)* listage *m* *or* liste *f* du texte source; *(of source program)* listage d'un programme source; **source machine** = compilateur *m* de programme source; **source program** = programme *m* source *or* d'origine; *(moving data between two networks)* **source routing** = routage *m* source

SP = STACK POINTER

space 1 *noun* **(a)** *(gap between characters or lines)* espace *m* *or* espacement *m* (entre caractères *or* lignes); **space character** = caractère *m* d'espacement *or* caractère espace *or* caractère

blanc; **space bar** = barre *f* d'espacement **(b)** *(in communications)* (signal d') espace (NOTE: opposite is **mark**) **(c)** *(atmosphere)* espace; **space craft** = véhicule *m* *or* engin *m* spatial; **space station** = station *f* spatiale **2** *verb* espacer; **the line of characters was evenly spaced out across the page** = les caractères régulièrement espacés s'alignaient sur la page

◊ **spacer** *noun* gestionnaire *m* d'espaces; **intelligent spacer** = gestionnaire d'espaces intelligent

◊ **spacing** *noun* espaces *mpl*; **the spacing on some lines is very uneven** = il y a quelques lignes où les espaces sont très inégaux

span *noun* fourchette *f*

◊ **spanning tree** *noun* *(creating a logical topology)* arborescence *f*

SPARC ™ = SCALAR PROCESSOR ARCHITECTURE

spark printer *noun* imprimante *f* thermique à étincelle

sparse array *noun* tableau réduit *or* matrice réduite

speaker *see* LOUDSPEAKER

spec *(informal)* = SPECIFICATION **high-spec** = de haute précision *or* de haute technologie

special *adjective* spécial, -e; **special character** = caractère spécial; **special effects** = effets spéciaux; *(system)* **special purpose** = spécial *or* dédié, -ée; **special sort** = fonte spéciale

◊ **special interest group (SIG)** *noun* *(group of people)* groupe *m* d'intérêt particulier; **our local computer club has a SIG for comms and networking** = notre club informatique local a constitué un groupe de travail qui s'intéresse aux communications et aux réseaux

◊ **specialist** *noun* expert *m* *or* spécialiste *m&f*; **you need a specialist programmer to help devise a new word-processing program** = demandez l'aide d'un bon programmeur qui vous aidera à créer un nouveau (programme de) traitement de texte

◊ **specialize** *verb* se spécialiser *or* être spécialiste *or* être expert; **he specializes in the design of CAD systems** = c'est un spécialiste *or* un expert en CAO

specify *verb* spécifier *or* indiquer *or* préciser *or* préconiser

◊ **specification** *noun* spécification *f*; **to work to standard specifications** = travailler suivant des normes établies; **the work is not up to specification** *or* **does not meet the customer's specifications** = le travail ne répond pas au cahier des charges *or* aux spécifications du client; **high specification** *or* **high spec** = (de) haute technologie *or* (de) haute précision *or* (de) technologie avancée; **high spec cabling needs to be very carefully handled** = les câbles de haute technologie doivent être manipulés avec grand soin; **program specification** = spécifications relatives à un programme

specific address *noun* adresse *f* spécifique

◊ **specific code** *noun* code (binaire) absolu *or* code spécifique; **specific coding** = codage (binaire) à adresse absolue *or* codage spécifique

◊ **specificity** *noun* spécificité *f*

spectrum *noun* spectre *m*; **electromagnetic spectrum** = spectre électromagnétique; **spectrum analyzer** = analyseur *m* de spectre

speech *noun* parole *f or* voix *f*; **speech chip** = puce *f* de synthèse vocale; **speech plus** = transmission *f* vocale étendue; **speech processor** = processeur *m* de la parole *or* du signal vocal; **speech recognition** = reconnaissance *f* vocale *or* de la parole; **speech signal** = signal *m* vocal; **speech synthesis** = synthèse *f* vocale *or* de la parole; **speech synthesizer** = synthétiseur *m* vocal *or* de la parole

QUOTE speech conveys information, and the primary task of computer speech processing is the transmission and reception of that information
Personal Computer World

speed *noun* **(a)** *(of film)* rapidité *f or* sensibilité *f*; **high speed film is very sensitive to light** = un film ultra-rapide est extrêmement sensible à la lumière **(b)** *(time taken for a movement)* vitesse *or* rapidité *f*; **speed of loop** = fréquence *f* de boucle *or* de bouclage; **playback speed** = vitesse de défilement (d'une bande magnétique)

spellcheck *verb* vérifier l'orthographe *or* faire une vérification orthographique

◊ **spellchecker** *or* **spelling checker** *noun* vérificateur *m* d'orthographe *or* programme de vérification orthographique; **the program will be upgraded with a word-processor and a spelling checker** = on va optimiser le programme en ajoutant un traitement de texte et un vérificateur d'orthographe

spherical aberration *noun* aberration *f* sphérique

spike *noun* *(of voltage pulse)* pointe *f* de tension

spillage *noun* débordement *m or* excès *m*

spin *verb* (faire) tourner; **the disk was spun by the drive** = le lecteur faisait tourner la disquette; **the disk drive motor spins at a constant velocity** = le moteur du lecteur de disquettes tourne à vitesse constante (NOTE: **spinning - span - spun**)

spindle *noun* *(for disk)* axe *m*

◊ **spindling** *noun* *(turning a disk by hand)* mouvement *m* de rotation (transmis manuellement)

spine *noun* *(of book)* dos *m*; **the author's name and the title usually are shown on the spine as well as on the title page** = de façon générale, le nom de l'auteur et le titre apparaissent au dos du livre et sur la page de titre

spirit duplicator *noun* *(short-run printing machine)* duplicateur *m* à alcool

SPL = SOUND PRESSURE LEVEL

splice *verb* *(to join ends of tape or film)* coller *or* faire un raccord; **you can use glue or splicing tape to splice the ends** = utilisez de la colle ou du ruban gommé pour raccorder les extrémités (du film); **splicing block** = colleuse *f* de film *or* de bande; **splicing tape** = ruban *m* de raccord

split screen *noun* écran *m* divisé *or* partagé; **we use split screen mode to show the text being worked on and another text from memory for comparison** = nous utilisons le mode d'écran partagé pour comparer le texte en cours de travail à un texte de référence conservé en mémoire

◊ **splitter** *noun* répartiteur *m*; **beam splitter** = diviseur *m* optique

spool 1 *noun* *(for tape or ribbon)* bobine *f* **2** *verb* faire un spooling *or* faire un spouling *or* transférer des données en mémoire tampon auxiliaire (entre périphérique lent et processeur rapide)

◊ **spooler** *or* **spooling device** *noun* spoule *m or* dispositif *m* de stockage temporaire

◊ **spooling** *noun* spouling *m or* spooling *m or* utilisation de mémoire tampon auxiliaire (entre périphérique lent et processeur rapide)

sporadic fault *noun* erreur *f* sporadique

spot *noun* point *m*

◊ **spot beam** *noun* *(of satellite antenna)* (antenne à) faisceau *m* étroit

spreadsheet *noun* *(program)* tableur *m*; *(printout)* tableau *m*

sprite *noun* *(in computer graphics)* esprit *m or* sprite *m*

sprocket *or* **sprocket wheel** *noun* roue *f* à picots

◊ **sprocket feed** *noun* entraînement *m* par picots; *see also* TRACTOR FEED

◊ **sprocket holes** *noun* perforations *fpl* d'entraînement *or* perforations marginales

spur *noun* jonction *f or* noeud *m*

SPX = SIMPLEX

SQA = SOFTWARE QUALITY ASSURANCE

SQL = STRUCTURED QUERY LANGUAGE

square wave *noun* onde *f* carrée

SS = SINGLE-SIDED

SSBSC = SINGLE SIDEBAND SUPPRESSED CARRIER

SSD = SINGLE-SIDED DISK

SSI = SMALL SCALE INTEGRATION

ST connector *noun* *(connector used to terminate optical fibres)* connecteur *m* ST

ST506 standard *noun (old disk interface standard)* standard *m* ST506 (d'interface de disques durs); **the ST506 standard has now been replaced by IDE and SCSI** = le standard ST506 a été remplacé par les normes IDE et SCSI

stable *adjective* stable; **stable state** = état *m* stable

◊ **stability** *noun* stabilité *f*; **image stability** = stabilité de l'image

stack *noun* pile *f* (de données en mémoire); **push-down stack** = pile inversée (utilisée suivant la méthode LIFO); **virtual memory stack** = pile de mémoire virtuelle; **stack address** = adresse *f* de pile; **stack base** = (adresse de) base *f* de la pile; **stack job processor** = processeur *m* de pile de tâches; **stack pointer (SP)** = pointeur *m* de pile

stage *noun* étape *f* or phase *f* or stade *m*; **the text is ready for the printing stage** = le texte est prêt pour l'impression; **we are in the first stage of running in the new computer system** = nous n'en sommes qu'à la phase de rodage du système d'exploitation

◊ **staged** *adjective* graduel, -elle *or* effectué, -ée par étapes *or* par paliers; **staged change-over** = passage *m* graduel (à un nouveau système)

stand-alone *or* **standalone** *noun & adjective* poste *m* autonome *or* individuel; **stand-alone system** = système *m* autonome; **stand-alone terminal** = terminal *m* autonome; **the workstations have been networked together rather than used as stand-alone systems** = les postes ont été reliés en réseau plutôt que d'être utilisés comme postes autonomes *or* comme postes individuels

standard *adjective (normal or usual)* standard *or* courant, -e *or* normal, -e; **standard document** *or* **standard form** *or* **standard paragraph** *or* **standard text** = document *m* *or* formulaire *m* *or* paragraphe *m* *or* texte *m* standard; **standard function** = fonction *f* standard; **Standard Generalized Markup Language** = langage *m* de balisage SGML; **standard interface** = interface *f* standard *or* universelle; **standard letter** = lettre *f* type *or* lettre standard; *(mode of operation of Microsoft Windows)* **standard mode** = mode non protégé *or* mode standard; **standard subroutine** = sous-programme *m* standard

◊ **standardize** *verb* standardiser *or* normaliser; **the standardized control of transmission links** = le contrôle standardisé *or* normalisé des voies de transmission

◊ **standards** *noun* normes *fpl* *or* standards *mpl*; **production standards** = normes *or* standards de production; **up to standard** = (qui est) conforme aux normes; **this batch of disks is not up to standard** = ce lot de disquettes ne répond pas aux normes; **standards converter** = convertisseur *m* de normes; **the standards converter allows us to watch US television** = c'est grâce à un convertisseur (de normes) que nous pouvons regarder la télévision américaine; **video standards** = normes vidéo; *see* VIDEO; **modem standards** = normes pour modems

standby *noun* (appareil *or* dispositif) de secours *or* de réserve *or* auxiliaire; **standby equipment** = équipement *m* *or* système *m* auxiliaire *or* de secours; **cold standby** = système de secours lancé manuellement; **hot standby** = système de secours prêt à fonctionner; **warm standby** = équipement de secours à démarrage semi-automatique

QUOTE before fault-tolerant systems, users had to rely on the cold standby, that is switching on a second machine when the first developed a fault; the alternative was the hot standby, where a second computer was kept running continuously

Computer News

star network *noun* réseau *m* en étoile

◊ **star program** *noun* programme *m* vedette

start *noun (of file)* début *m*; *(of machine)* démarrage *m* *or* mise *f* en route; **cold start** = démarrage à froid *or* reprise *f* totale; **start bit** *or* **start element** = bit *m* *or* élément *m* de début; **start of header** = (code de) début d'en-tête; **start of text (SOT** *or* **STX)** = (code de) début de texte; *(of program)* **warm start** = reprise *f* au point d'arrêt

◊ **startup disk** *noun (disk which holds the operating system and system configuration files)* disquette *f* d'amorçage *or* de lancement

stat *(informal)* = PHOTOSTAT

state *noun* état *m*; **active state** = mode *m* actif; **steady state** = état stationnaire

statement *noun* déclaration *f* *or* instruction *f*; **conditional statement** = instruction conditionnelle; **control statement** = *(to another branch)* instruction de branchement; *(for the CPU)* (instruction de) commande *f*; **directive statement** = directive *f*; **input statement** = instruction *or* déclaration d'entrée; **multi-statement line** = ligne multi-instruction; **narrative statement** = instruction déclarative; **statement number** = numéro *m* d'instruction

state-of-the-art *adjective (technology, etc.)* de pointe *or* avancé, -ée

QUOTE the main PCB is decidedly non-state-of-the-art

Personal Computer World

static 1 *noun* **(a)** *(TV or radio)* (bruits) parasites *mpl*; *(in recorded signal)* interférence *f* *or* bruit(s) *m(pl)* **(b)** *(charge)* électricité *f* statique **2** *adjective (not dynamic)* statique *or* qui n'évolue pas; **static dump** = vidage *m* statique; **static memory** = mémoire *f* statique; **static RAM** = mémoire *f* vive statique *or* RAM *f* statique; **static subroutine** = sous-programme statique

station *noun* **(a)** station *f* *or* poste *m* *or* terminal *m*; **secondary station** = station auxiliaire; *(software and hardware within the FDDI specification)* **station management (SMT)** = gestion *f* de station SMT; **workstation** = poste de travail **(b)** **earth station** = station *f* terrestre; **radio station** = station radio; **the signal from this radio**

station is very weak = le signal de cette station émettrice *or* de cet émetteur radio est très faible; **we are trying to jam the signals from that station** = nous essayons de brouiller les signaux émis par cette station

stationary *adjective* stationnaire; **geostationary orbit** = orbite *f* (de satellite) géostationnaire

stationery *noun* papeterie *f*; **computer stationery** = papier *m* listing (pour imprimante); **continuous stationery** = papier listing *or* papier en continu; **preprinted stationery** = formulaires *mpl* préimprimés; papier à en-tête

statistics *noun (science)* statistique *f*

◊ **statistical** *adjective* statistique; **statistical time division multiplexing (STDM)** = multiplexage temporel statistique *or* en fonction des appels

◊ **statistician** *noun* statisticien, -ienne

status *noun* statut *m or* état *m*; **status bit** = bit *m* d'état; **status line** = ligne *f* d'état; **status poll** = (appel de) contrôle *m* d'état; **status register** = registre *m* d'état; **status window** = fenêtre *f* d'état; **processor status word (PSW)** = mot *m* d'état (d'un processeur)

STD = SUBSCRIBER TRUNK DIALLING

STDM = STATISTICAL TIME DIVISION MULTIPLEXING

steady state *noun* état *m* stationnaire

stencil *noun (pre-shaped pattern)* pochoir *m* de traçage; *(for duplicating)* stencil *m*; **the stencil has all the electronic components on it** = ce pochoir contient toutes les formes pour composants électroniques; **flowchart stencil** = grille *f or* modèle *m* pour ordinogramme

step 1 *noun* étape *f or* pas *m*; **single step** = (opération) pas à pas **2** *verb (to move forwards)* faire un pas *or* avancer d'un pas; *(to move backwards)* reculer d'un pas; **we stepped forward through the file one record at a time** = nous avons repris le fichier, entrée par entrée; **we stepped forward the film one frame at a time** = nous avons projeté le film image par image

◊ **stepper motor** *or* **stepping motor** *noun* moteur *m* à pas

steradian *noun* stéradian *m*

stereo *informal* = STEREOPHONIC

stereophonic *adjective* stéréophonique *or* stéréo; **stereophonic microphone** = microphone *m* stéréophonique; **stereophonic recorder** = magnétophone *m* stéréophonique

still frame *noun* image *f* fixe

stochastic model *noun* modèle *m* stochastique

stop 1 *verb* (s') arrêter *or* (s') immobiliser;

stopper; *(in communications)* **stop and wait protocol** = protocole *m* de contrôle par signal d'arrêt **2** *noun (not doing any action)* arrêt *m*; **tab stop** = arrêt de tabulation

◊ **stop bit** *or* **stop element** *noun* bit *m or* élément *m* d'arrêt; **stop code** = code *m* d'arrêt; **stop instruction** = instruction *f* d'arrêt; **stop list** = liste *f* des mots interdits (dans une indexation); **stop time** = temps *m* d'arrêt *or* de décélération

storage *noun (place)* mémoire *f*; *(action)* stockage; **archive storage** = mémoire d'archivage; **auxiliary storage** = mémoire auxiliaire; **dynamic storage** *or* **memory** = mémoire dynamique; **external storage** = mémoire externe; **information storage** = mise *f* en mémoire *or* stockage de données; **instruction storage** = mémoire d'instruction; **intermediate storage** = mémoire intermédiaire; **mass storage system** = mémoire de masse; **nonerasable storage** = mémoire ineffaçable *or* permanente; **primary storage** = mémoire principale; **secondary storage** = mémoire secondaire *or* intermédiaire; **static storage** = mémoire statique; **temporary storage** = mémoire temporaire; **volatile storage** = mémoire volatile; **storage allocation** = allocation *f* de mémoire; **storage capacity** = capacité *f* de la mémoire *or* taille *f* de la mémoire; **storage density** = densité *f* de mémoire; **storage device** = dispositif de stockage; **storage disk** = disquette *f or* disque *m* (de) mémoire; **storage dump** = vidage *m or* listage *m* de mémoire (sur imprimante); **storage media** = supports *mpl* de mémoire *or* de stockage; **storage size** = taille *f* de la mémoire; **storage tube** = écran *m or* tube *m* à mémoire

store 1 *noun* mémoire *f*; **store address register (SAR)** = registre *m* d'adresse en mémoire; **store data register (SDR)** = registre des données en mémoire; **store cell** = cellule *f* de mémoire; **store location** = emplacement *m* de mémoire **2** *verb (to save data)* mettre en mémoire *or* ranger en mémoire *or* mémoriser; **storing a page of high resolution graphics can require 3Mb** = il faudra jusqu'à 3Mo pour mémoriser une page de données graphiques haute-définition; *(communications)* **store and forward (system)** = (système d') envoi *m* différé; **stored program** = programme *m* mis en mémoire *or* mémorisé *or* enregistré; **stored program signalling** = signalisation *f* à contrôle programmé en mémoire

STP cable = SHIELDED TWISTED PAIR CABLE

straight-line coding *noun* codage *m* en ligne directe

stray *adjective* égaré, -ée *or* perdu, -e; **the metal screen protects the CPU against stray electromagnetic effects from the PSU** = le blindage protège l'unité centrale des pertes *or* fuites electromagnétiques du bloc d'alimentation

streaking *noun* rayures *fpl or* zébrures *fpl or* traînage *m*

stream *noun* flux *m* (continu) *or* flot *m*; **job stream** = flux des tâches

◊ **streamer** *noun* tape streamer *or* **streaming tape drive** = unité *f* de sauvegarde rapide (sur bande magnétique) *or* dévideur *m or* streamer *m*

> QUOTE the product has 16Mb of memory, 45Mb of Winchester disk storage and 95Mb streaming tape storage
>
> *Minicomputer News*

string *noun* chaîne *f or* séquence *f*; **alphanumeric string** = chaîne de caractères alphanumériques; **character string** = chaîne de caractères; **numeric string** = chaîne de caractères numériques; **null** *or* **blank string** = chaîne vide; **string area** = zone *f* mémoire *or* zone de stockage des variables; **string concatenation** = concaténation *f* de (plusieurs) chaînes; **string function** = fonction *f* (de) chaîne; **string length** = taille *f* d'une chaîne; **string matching** = comparaison *f* de chaînes; **string name** = nom *m* de chaîne; **string orientated symbolic language (SNOBOL)** = langage *m* SNOBOL (de traitement et de manipulation de chaîne); **string scanning** = balayage *m* de chaînes; **string variable** = variable *f* de chaîne

◊ **stringy floppy** *or* **tape streamer** *noun* unité *f* de sauvegarde rapide sur bande magnétique *or* streamer *m*

strip 1 *noun* bande *f or* ruban *m*; **strip window** = fenêtre *f* d'une ligne; *(on plastic cards)* **magnetic strip** = piste *f* magnétique **2** *verb* dépouiller (un message)

stripe *noun* bande *f or* raie *f* (de couleur); **balance stripe** = bande d'équilibrage (de tension)

strobe 1 *verb* émettre une impulsion *or* un signal (d'échantillonnage *or* de validation); échantillonner *or* valider **2** *noun (pulse of an electric circuit)* impulsion *f* électrique; **address strobe** = signal de validation d'adresse; **data strobe** = signal de validation de données (transmises)

◊ **stroboscope** *or* **strobe** *noun* stroboscope *m*

stroke *noun* frappe *f*

strowger exchange *noun* central *m* téléphonique électromécanique *or* central Strowger

structure 1 *noun* structure *f*; **network structure** = structure en réseau **2** *verb* structurer *or* organiser; **you first structure a document to meet your requirements and then fill in the blanks** = vous organisez d'abord le document pour répondre à vos besoins, puis vous remplissez les blancs; *(using UTP cable feeding into hubs)* **structured cabling** = câblage *m* structuré; **structured design** = modèle *m* structuré; *(standard database programming language)* **structured query language (SQL)** = langage *m* SQL *or* langage de requête; **structured programming** = programmation *f* structurée

stub *noun (short program routine)* (programme) souche *f*

stuck beacon *noun (error where a station*

continuously transmits beacon frames) alerteur *f* bloqué

studio *noun* studio *m* (de création, d'enregistrement, de prise de vues)

STX = START OF TEXT

style sheet *noun* feuille *f* de style

stylus *noun* **(a)** *(for audio record)* aiguille *f or* pointe *f or* diamant *m* de lecture; *(for video disk)* lecteur *m* **(b)** *(pen-like device)* stylet *m*; **use the stylus on the graphics tablet to draw** = pour dessiner, utilisez un stylet et une tablette graphique **(c)** **stylus printer** = imprimante *f* matricielle *or* à aiguilles

sub- *prefix* sous- *or* secondaire; **subaddress** = adresse *f* secondaire; **subaudio frequencies** = fréquences *fpl* inaudibles *or* infrasonores; **subclass** = sous-classe *f*

◊ **sub-edit** *or* **sub** *verb (text)* réviser; **subbing** *or* **sub-editing** = vérification *f or* révision *f*

subdirectory *noun* sous-répertoire *m*

> QUOTE if you delete a file and then delete the subdirectory where it was located, you cannot restore the file because the directory does not exist
>
> *Personal Computer World*

subprogram *noun* sous-programme *m*

subroutine *noun* sous-programme *m*; **closed subroutine** *or* **linked subroutine** = sous-programme fermé *or* ré-entrant; **open subroutine** = sous-programme ouvert; **static subroutine** = sous-programme statique; **two-level subroutine** = sous-programme à deux niveaux; **subroutine call** = appel *m* d'un sous-programme

subscriber *noun (telephone or service)* abonné, -ée; **subscriber trunk dialling (STD)** = l'automatique *m*

subscript *noun* indice *m*; *see also* SUPERSCRIPT (NOTE: used in chemical formulae: CO_2) **subscripted variable** = variable indicée *or* caractérisée par un indice

◊ **subset** *noun* sous-ensemble *m*

◊ **subsegment** *noun* sous-segment *m*

substance *noun* substance *f*

substitute *verb* substituer

◊ **substitute character** *noun (character displayed if a received character is not recognized)* caractère *m* de substitution (NOTE: you substitute one thing **for** another)

◊ **substitution** *noun* substitution *f*; **substitution error** = erreur *f* de substitution; **substitution table** = table *f* de substitution *or* d'équivalence

substrate *noun (base material)* substrat *m*

subsystem *noun (smaller part of a large system)* sous-système *m*

subtotal *noun* sous-total *m*

subtract *verb* soustraire

◊ **subtraction** *noun* soustraction *f*

◊ **subtrahend** *noun* nombre *m* à soustraire d'un autre *or* diminuteur *m*

subvoice grade channel *noun* canal *m* de fréquences subvocales

successive *adjective* successif, -ive *or* qui suit; **each successive operation adds further characters to the string** = chacune des opérations successives ajoute de nouveaux caractères à la chaîne

suffix notation *noun* *(postfix notation)* notation *f* suffixée *or* notation polonaise inversée

suitcase *noun* *(Apple Macintosh icon which contains a screen font)* valise *f or* icône *f* de police de caractères

suite of programs *noun* suite *f* de programmes *or* série *f* de programmes l'un à la suite de l'autre; **the word-processing system uses a suite of three programs, editor, spelling checker and printing controller** = le système de traitement de texte utilise une série de trois programmes reliés: un éditeur de texte, un correcteur d'orthographe et un contrôleur d'impression

sum *noun* somme *f or* addition *f*

◊ **summation check** *noun* contrôle *m* par totalisation

sun outage *noun* durée *f* de non ensoleillement *or* d'ombre

super- *prefix* super- *or* sur-; **supercomputer** = ordinateur *m* géant; *(60 voice channels)* **supergroup** = groupe *m* secondaire; *(900 voice channels)* **super mastergroup** = groupe quaternaire; *(enhancement to the standard VGA graphics system)* **super VGA (SVGA)** = (standard d'écran) super VGA *or* SVGA

◊ **super high frequency (SHF)** *noun* ultra-haute fréquence

◊ **super large scale integration (SLSI)** *noun* intégration *f* à super grande échelle

superheterodyne radio *noun* radio *f* superhétérodyne

superhighway *noun* **information superhighway** = autoroute *f* de l'information

superimpose *verb* surimposer

superior number *noun* chiffre *m* en exposant *or* exposant *m*

superscript *noun* exposant *m* (NOTE: used often in mathematics: 10^5 (say: ten to the power five)

supersede *verb* remplacer; **the new program supersedes the earlier one, and is much faster** = le

nouveau programme, qui remplace le précédent, est beaucoup plus rapide

superstation *noun* *US* superstation *f*

supervise *verb* superviser *or* surveiller *or* contrôler; **the manufacture of circuit boards is very carefully supervised** = la confection des cartes de circuits imprimés est étroitement surveillée

◊ **supervision** *noun* supervision *f or* surveillance *f or* contrôle *m*

◊ **supervisor** *noun* *(person)* surveillant, -e *or* contrôleur, -euse *or* superviseur *m*; *(program)* programme *m* superviseur

◊ **supervisory** *adjective* de supervision *or* de surveillance *or* de contrôle; **supervisory program** *or* **executive program** = programme *m* superviseur; **supervisory sequence** = séquence *f* de contrôle; **supervisory signal** = signal *m* de contrôle *or* de supervision

supply 1 *noun* fourniture *f or* approvisionnement *m*; **the electricity supply has failed** = il y a une panne de courant; **they signed a contract for the supply of computer stationery** = ils ont signé un contrat pour la fourniture de papier listing **2** *verb* fournir *or* approvisionner; **the computer was supplied by a recognized dealer** = l'ordinateur vient de chez un fournisseur connu; **they have signed a contract to supply on-line information** = ils ont signé un contrat pour fournir des informations en ligne

◊ **supplier** *noun* fournisseur *m*; **a supplier of computer parts** = un fournisseur de composants pour ordinateurs; **a supplier of disk drives** *or* **a disk drive supplier** = un fournisseur de lecteurs de disquettes; **our Japanese suppliers have set up a warehouse in England** = nos fournisseurs japonais ont ouvert un entrepôt en Angleterre

support 1 *verb* supporter; **the main computer supports six workstations** = l'ordinateur principal accepte jusqu'à six postes de travail *or* contrôle six postes de travail **2** *noun* **(a)** support *m*; **support chip** = processeur *m* auxiliaire; **the maths support chip can be plugged in here** = le processeur arithmétique auxiliaire peut être enfiché à cet endroit **(b)** assistance *f*; **support hotline** = service *m* d'assistance technique par téléphone; **support service** = service d'assistance technique; **system support** = assistance *f* technique destinée à un système

suppress *verb* *(to remove)* supprimer; **the filter is used to suppress the noise due to static interference** = ce filtre sert à supprimer les bruits parasites; **suppressed carrier modulation** = modulation d'amplitude sans porteuse *or* à porteuse inhibée; **double sideband suppressed carrier (DSBSC)** = double bande latérale sans porteuse *or* à porteuse inhibée; **single sideband suppressed carrier (SSBSC)** = bande latérale unique sans porteuse *or* à porteuse inhibée

◊ **suppression** *noun* suppression *f*

◊ **suppressor** *noun* dispositif *m* antiparasite; **echo suppressor** = dispositif *m* anti-écho *or* éliminateur *m* d'écho

surf *verb* to surf the Internet *or* to surf the net = naviguer sur Internet *or* se balader sur Internet

◊ **surfer** *noun (netsurfer)* utilisateur *m* qui se balade *or* qui navigue sur Internet

◊ **surfing** *noun (netsurfing)* navigation *f* sur Internet *or* balade *f* sur Internet

> QUOTE surfing the net on the software of today is rather like driving a Ferrari across a ploughed field
>
> *The Times*

surface-mount technology (SMT) *noun (manufacturing circuit boards)* procédé *m* d'assemblage SMT; **surface-mount technology is faster and more space-efficient than soldering** = la technologie d'assemblage SMT est plus rapide et utilise mieux l'espace que la soudure

surge *noun (electrical)* surtension *f or* pointe *f* de tension; **surge protector** = limiteur *m* de tension

sustain *verb* maintenir

SVGA = SUPER VGA

SW = SHORT WAVE

swap 1 *noun* = SWAPPING **2** *verb* permuter *or* basculer

◊ **swapping** *or* **swap** *noun* permutation *f or* basculement *m* (de programme)

sweep *noun* balayage *m*

swim *noun* flottement *m*

switch 1 *noun* **(a)** *(additional character)* commutateur *m* (de commande); **add the switch '/W' to the DOS command DIR and the directory listing will be displayed across the screen** = ajoutez le commutateur '/W' à la commande DIR (sous DOS) pour afficher le répertoire sur toute la largeur de l'écran **(b)** *(point in a computer program)* aiguillage *m or* bifurcation *f* **(c)** *(device)* commutateur *m*; **switch train** = série *f* de commutateurs *or* commutateurs en série **(d)** aiguillage *m* **2** *verb (connect two lines)* connecter (à l'aide d'un commutateur); *(system, etc.)* **to switch on** = mettre en marche *or* mettre sous tension; **to switch off** = éteindre *or* mettre hors tension; *(to use something else)* **to switch over to** = changer (de); **switched network backup** = commutation *f* de secours; **switched star** = réseau *m* commuté en étoile; **switched virtual call** = communication *f* virtuelle commutée

◊ **switchboard** *noun* standard *m* téléphonique; **switchboard operator** = standardiste *m&f*

◊ **switching** *noun* commutation *f or* connexion *f*; **switching centre** = centre *m* de commutation; **switching circuit** = circuit *m* de commutation; **line switching** = commutation de ligne *or* de circuit

symbol *noun* symbole *m*; **this language uses the symbol ? to represent the print command** = ce langage utilise le symbole ? pour la commande d'impression; **graphic symbol** = symbole graphique; **logic symbol** = symbole logique; **symbol table** *or* **library** = table *f or* bibliothèque *f* de symboles

◊ **symbolic** *adjective* symbolique; **symbolic address** = adresse *f* symbolique; **symbolic code** *or* **instruction** = code *m or* instruction *f* symbolique; **symbolic debugging** = (programme de) débogage *m* symbolique; **symbolic language** = langage *m* symbolique; **symbolic logic** = logique *f* symbolique; **symbolic name** = nom *m* symbolique; **symbolic programming** = programmation *f* symbolique

symmetric difference *noun (logical function)* exclusion *f* réciproque

sync *noun (informal)* = SYNCHRONIZATION synchro *or* synchronisation *f*; **sync bit** = bit *m* de synchro; **sync character** = caractère *m* de synchro; **sync pulses** = impulsions *fpl* de synchro; *(synchronized)* **in sync** = synchronisé, -ée *or* synchrone *or* en synchronisme; **the two devices are out of sync** = ces deux dispositifs ne sont pas parfaitement synchronisés

◊ **synchronization** *noun* synchronisation *f*; **synchronization pulses** = impulsions *fpl* de synchronisation

◊ **synchronize** *verb* synchroniser

◊ **synchronizer** *noun* synchroniseur *m or* unité *f* de synchronisation

◊ **synchronous** *adjective* synchrone; **synchronous computer** = ordinateur *m* synchrone; *(data transmission protocol)* **synchronous data link control (SDLC)** = protocole *m* SDLC (de transmission de données en mode synchrone); **synchronous data network** = réseau *m* de données synchrone; **synchronous detection** = repérage *m* synchrone; **synchronous idle character** = caractère *m* de synchronisation; **synchronous mode** = mode *m* synchrone; **synchronous network** = réseau *m* synchrone; **synchronous system** = système *m* synchrone; **synchronous transmission** = transmission *f* synchrone

synonym *noun* synonyme *m*

◊ **synonymous** *adjective* synonyme; **the words 'error' and 'mistake' are synonymous** = 'erreur' et 'faute' sont des synonymes

syntactic error *noun* faute *f* de syntaxe

◊ **syntactical** *adjective* syntaxique *or* de syntaxe

syntax *noun* syntaxe *f*; **syntax analysis** = analyse *f* syntaxique; **syntax error** = faute *f* de syntaxe

synthesis *noun* synthèse *f*

◊ **synthesize** *verb* synthétiser

◊ **synthesizer** *noun* synthétiseur *m*; **music synthesizer** = synthétiseur de son; **speech synthesizer** = synthétiseur vocal *or* de la parole

◊ **synthetic address** *noun* adresse calculée; **synthetic language** = langage de synthèse

> QUOTE despite the fact that speech can now be synthesized with very acceptable quality, all it conveys is linguistic information
>
> *Personal Computer World*

sysgen = SYSTEM GENERATION

system *noun* système *m*; **adaptive system** = système auto-adaptable *or* dynamique; **computer system** = système informatique *or* ordinateur *m*; *(software to help solve a problem)* **expert system** = système expert; **information system** = système informatique; **interactive system** = système interactif; **operating system (op sys)** = système d'exploitation; **secure system** = système sécurisé; **system check** = diagnostic *m* de système; *(terminal or control centre)* **system console** = console *f* système; **system control panel** = panneau *m* de commandes d'un système; **system crash** = panne *f* de système *or* crash *m*; **system design** = conception *f or* modèle *m or* design *m* d'un système; **system diagnostics** = outils *mpl* de diagnostic d'un système; **system disk** = disquette *f* (de programme) système; **system firmware** = logiciel *m* (de) système *or* microprogrammé; **system flowchart** = ordinogramme *m* d'un système; *(Apple Macintosh folder)* **system folder** = dossier *m* système; **system generation** *or* **sysgen** = génération *f* d'un système *or* à laquelle appartient un système; **system library** = bibliothèque *f* d'un système; **system life cycle** = durée *f* de vie d'un système; **system log** = journal *m* d'un système; *(which indicates the operating system is ready)* **system prompt** = invite *f* du système *or* prompt *m*; **system security** = sécurisation *f* d'un système;

system software = logiciel *m* d'exploitation; **system specifications** = spécifications *fpl* d'un système; **system support** = assistance *f* technique pour un système; *(terminal or control centre for a computer)* **system unit** = unité *f* système *or* poste *m*

◊ **System 7** ™ *(operating system for the Apple Macintosh)* System 7 ™ *or* Système 7

◊ **Système international** *see* SI

◊ **systems analysis** *noun* analyse *f* de systèmes; **systems analyst** = informaticien, -ienne analyste; **systems engineer** = ingénieur *m* système; *(combining different products to create a system)* **systems integration** = intégration *f* de systèmes; **systems network architecture (SNA)** = architecture *f* de réseau; **systems program** = programme *m* système; **systems programmer** = programmeur *m* système

QUOTE the core of an expert system is its database of rules
Personal Computer World

◊ **Systems Application Architecture (SAA)** *noun* *(standard which defines the look and feel of an application)* norme *m* SAA *or* architecture *f* de système d'application

◊ **Systems Network Architecture (SNA)** *noun* *(design methods developed by IBM)* architecture *f* de réseau *or* architecture SNA

Tt

T = TERA-

T carrier *noun* (*US standard for digital data transmission lines*) porteuse *f* T

T connector *noun* (*coaxial connector shaped like a 'T'*) connecteur *m* en T

T junction *noun* jonction *f* en T

◊ **T network** *noun* réseau *m* en T

T1 committee *noun* (*ANSI committee which sets digital communications standards*) commission *f* (ANSI) T1

T1 link *noun* (*long distance data transmission link*) liaison *f* T1

TAB = TABULATE

tab 1 *verb* tabuler (des données) *or* disposer (des données) en tableau *or* en table *or* en colonne(s); **the list was neatly lined up by tabbing to column 10 at the start of each new line** = en appuyant sur la touche de tabulation en début de ligne, pour se placer à la colonne 10, la liste avait été parfaitement alignée; (*ASCII character used to align text at a tab stop*) **tab character** = caractère tab; (*key used to insert a tab character*) **tab key** = touche *f* de tabulation *or* touche Tab; **tab memory** = mémoire *f* de tabulation; **tab rack** *or* **ruler line** = règle *f* de tabulation; **a tab rack shows you the left and right margins** = la règle de tabulation indique les marges de gauche et de droite; **tab stops** = arrêts *mpl* de tabulation **2** *noun* (**a**) (*on disks*) **write-protect tab** = volet *m* de protection d'écriture (**b**) (*of windows in Windows 95*) onglet *m*

◊ **tabbing** *noun* tabulation *f*; **tabbing can be done from inside the program** = la tabulation peut être incorporée au programme; **decimal tabbing** = tabulation décimale

table *noun* table *f or* tableau *m*; **decision table** = table de décision; **lookup table (LUT)** = table de référence *or* d'équivalence; **this is the value of the key pressed, use a lookup table to find its ASCII value** = voici la fonction de cette touche, pour la traduire en ASCII consultez la table d'équivalence; **table lookup** = consultation *f* d'une table de référence; (*of books*) **table of contents** = table *f* des matières; (*list of variables, routines and macros*) **reference program table** = table de référence de programme; **symbol table** = table des symboles; (*in DOS*) **system file table** = table des fichiers système

tablet *noun* **graphics tablet** = tablette *f* graphique *or* à numériser; **it is much easier to draw accurately with a tablet than with a mouse** = un dessin précis s'obtient beaucoup plus facilement avec une tablette graphique qu'avec une souris

tabular *adjective* **in tabular form** = tabulaire *or* disposé, -ée en tableau *or* en table *or* en colonne(s)

◊ **tabulate** *verb* tabuler (des données) *or* disposer (des données) en tableau *or* en table *or* en colonne(s)

◊ **tabulating** *noun* (*punched cards*) traitement *m* de données (sur cartes perforées) par tabulatrice

◊ **tabulation** *noun* tabulation *f*; **tabulation markers** = repères *mpl* de tabulation; **tabulation stops** = arrêts *mpl* de tabulation

◊ **tabulator** *noun* (*on typewriters, etc.*) tabulateur *m*

TACS = TOTAL ACCESS COMMUNICATION SYSTEM

tactile *adjective* tactile; **tactile feedback** = information *f* tactile; **tactile keyboard** = clavier *m* tactile *or* sensitif *or* à effleurement

tag *noun* (**a**) (*section of computer instruction*) étiquette *f*; (*in machine language*) adresse *f* symbolique (**b**) (*of file or item of data*) étiquette *f*; **each file has a three letter tag for rapid identification** = chaque fichier est identifié rapidement par son étiquette de trois lettres (**c**) (*of windows in Windows 95*) onglet *m*

◊ **tag image file format (TIFF)** *noun* (*file format used to store graphic images*) format *m* de fichier image *or* format TIFF

tail *noun* (**a**) (*data which is the end of a list*) fin *f* de liste (**b**) (*code which signals the end of a message*) (code de) fin de message

takedown *verb* désinstaller *or* démonter *m* (entre deux tâches); **takedown time** = temps *m* de préparation entre deux tâches

take-up reel *noun* bobine *f* réceptrice *or* de réception *or* d'enroulement; **put the full reel on this spindle, and feed the tape into the take-up reel on the other spindle** = placez la bobine pleine sur cet axe-ci et la bobine de réception sur celui-là

talk *verb* (*computers*) dialoguer

◊ **talkback** *noun* conversation *f or* dialogue *m*

tandem *noun* **working in tandem** =

fonctionnement *m* en tandem; *(two processors connected)* **tandem processors** = processeurs *mpl* en tandem; **tandem switching** = commutation *f* (en) tandem

tap 1 *verb* brancher une ligne sur une table d'écoute **2** *noun* **wiretap** = table *f* d'écoute

tape *noun* bande *f*; **cassette tape** = cassette *f*; **cassette tape is mainly used with home computers** = c'est en général avec les ordinateurs utilisés à la maison qu'on se sert de cassettes; **(magnetic) tape** = bande magnétique; **master tape** = bande originale; **paper tape** *or* **punched tape** = bande perforée *or* bande papier; **open reel tape** = bande sur bobine ouverte; **streaming tape drive** = unité *f* de sauvegarde (rapide) sur bande *or* streamer *m*; **tape backup** = sauvegarde *f* sur bande; **tape cable** *or* **ribbon cable** = câble *m* plat *or* ruban *m*; **tape cartridge** = cartouche *f*; **tape cassette** = cassette *f*; **tape code** = code *m* de perforation *or* de marquage (de bande papier); **tape counter** = compteur *m* de déroulement; **tape deck** = platine *f* magnétophone; platine magnétocassette *m*; **tape drive** = lecteur *m* de bandes (magnétiques) *or* dérouleur *m* de bandes; **our new product has a 96Mb streaming tape drive** = notre nouveau modèle est équipé d'un streamer de 96 Mo; **tape format** = format *m* de bande; **tape guide** = guide-bande *m*; **the tape is out of alignment because one of the tape guides has broken** = la bande est désalignée parce qu'un guide-bande est cassé; **tape head** = tête *f* de lecture (pour bandes magnétiques); **tape header** = en-tête *m* de bande; **tape label** = label *m* *or* étiquette *f* en-tête de bande; **tape library** = bibliothèque *f* de bandes *or* bandothèque *f*; **tape loadpoint** = point *m* de début d'enregistrement (d'une bande magnétique); **tape punch** = poinçon *m* (de perforation) pour bandes papier; **tape reader** = lecteur *m* de bandes perforées; **tape recorder** = enregistreur *m* de bandes; magnétophone *m*; **tape streamer** = streamer *m*; **tape timer** = compteur *m* de défilement; **tape to card converter** = convertisseur *m* bande magnétique/carte perforée; **tape transmitter** = émetteur *m* à bande; **tape trailer** = label *m* de fin de bande; **tape transport** = dérouleur *m* *or* dispositif *m* d'entraînement de bande; **tape unit** = magnétophone *m* *or* magnétocassette *m*; **video cassette tape** = bande vidéo

target *noun* cible *f* *or* objectif *m* *or* but *m*; **target computer** = ordinateur *m* cible *or* ordinateur d'exécution; *(disk onto which a file is to be copied)* **target disk** = disque *m* cible; **target language** = *(translation)* langue *f* d'arrivée; *(computing)* langage *m* objet; **the target language for this PASCAL program is machine code** = pour ce qui est de ce programme en PASCAL, le langage machine constitue le langage objet; **target level** = niveau *m* cible; **target phase** *or* **run phase** = phase *f* exécution *or* (en) code objet; **target program** = programme *m* objet

> QUOTE the target board is connected to the machine through the incircuit emulator cable
> *Electronics & Wireless World*

tariff *noun (charge)* tarif *m*; **there is a set tariff for**

logging on, then a rate for every minute of computer time used = il existe un tarif forfaitaire d'utilisation plus un taux/minute de temps d'ordinateur

TASI = TIME ASSIGNED SPEECH INTERPOLATION

task *noun* tâche *f*; **task management** = gestion *f* de tâches; **task queue** = file *f* d'attente des tâches à exécuter; *(exchanging one program for another)* **task swapping** *or* **switching** = permutation *f* *or* basculement *m* de tâches; passage *m* d'une tâche à une autre; *see also* MULTITASKING

TAT = TURNAROUND TIME

TCP = TRANSMISSION CONTROL PROTOCOL

TCP/IP = TRANSMISSION CONTROL PROTOCOL/INTERFACE PROGRAM

TDM = TIME DIVISION MULTIPLEXING

TDR = TIME DOMAIN REFLECTOMETRY

TDS = TRANSACTION-DRIVEN SYSTEM

tearing *noun (distortion of image)* déchirure *f*

technical *adjective* technique; **the document gives all the technical details on the new computer** = ce document contient tous les renseignements d'ordre technique concernant le nouvel ordinateur; *(advice to a user)* **technical support** = assistance *f* technique

◊ **technician** *noun* technicien, -ienne; **the computer technicians installed the new system** = le nouveau système a été mis en place par les techniciens *or* ce sont les techniciens qui ont installé le nouveau système; **laboratory technician** = technicien, -ienne de laboratoire

◊ **technique** *noun* technique *f* *or* méthode *f*; **the company has developed a new technique for processing customers' disks** = la société a mis au point une nouvelle technique de traitement des disquettes clients

technology *noun* technologie *f* *or* techniques *fpl*; **information technology (IT)** = informatique *f* *or* techniques *fpl* de l'information; **new technology** = techniques nouvelles *or* techniques de pointe *or* nouvelle technologie; **the introduction of new technology** = l'introduction *f* de techniques nouvelles

◊ **technological** *adjective* technologique *or* technique; **the technological revolution** = la révolution technologique

tel = TELEPHONE

tele- *prefix (referring to TV or long distance)* télé-; **telebanking** = bancatique *f*; **telecine** = télécinéma *m*

◊ **telecommunications** *noun (passing and receiving messages over a distance)* télécommunications *fpl*

◊ **telecommuting** *noun* *(working on a computer from home)* télétravail *m*

◊ **teleconferencing** *noun* *(linking video, audio and computer signals as if in a conference room)* téléconférence *f*

◊ **telecontrol** *noun* télécommande *f*

◊ **telegram** *noun* télégramme *m*; **to send a telegram** = envoyer un télégramme

◊ **telegraph** 1 *noun* télégraphe *m*; **telegraph office** = bureau *m* de poste (d'où on envoie un télégramme) 2 *verb* télégraphier *or* envoyer un télégramme; **they telegraphed their agreement** = ils ont envoyé un télégramme confirmant leur accord; **the photographs were telegraphed to New York** = on a télégraphié les photos à New York

◊ **telegraphic** *adjective* télégraphique; **telegraphic address** = adresse *f* télégraphique

◊ **telegraphy** *noun* télégraphie *f*; **carrier telegraphy** = radiotélégraphie *f*

teleinformatic services *noun* services *mpl* de téléinformatique

telematics *noun* télématique *f*

telemessage *noun* GB télégramme *m or* message *m* télégraphié

telemetry *noun* télémétrie *f*

teleordering *noun* *(book ordering system)* système de réapprovisionnement informatisé *or* géré par ordinateur

telephone 1 *noun* téléphone *m*; **we had a new telephone system installed last week** = nous avons une nouvelle installation téléphonique depuis la semaine dernière; **to be on the telephone** = parler au téléphone *or* être en ligne; **she is on the telephone to Hong Kong** = elle est en ligne avec Hong Kong; **by telephone** = par téléphone; **to place an order by telephone** = faire une commmande par téléphone; **cellular telephone** = téléphone cellulaire; **conference telephone** = téléphone de *or* pour conférence; **house telephone** *or* **internal telephone** = téléphone interne; **telephone answering machine** = répondeur *m* téléphonique; **telephone book** *or* **telephone directory** = annuaire *m* des téléphones *or* annuaire téléphonique; **telephone call** = appel *m* (téléphonique); **to make a telephone call** = faire un appel *or* téléphoner *or* appeler; **to answer the telephone** *or* **to take a telephone call** = répondre au téléphone *or* prendre un appel; **telephone (data carrier)** = transmission de données par téléphone *or* sur le réseau commuté; **telephone exchange** = central *m* téléphonique; **telephone number** = numéro *m* de téléphone; **can you give me your telephone number?** = pouvez-vous me donner votre numéro de téléphone?; **telephone operator** = standardiste *m&f*; **telephone repeater** = amplificateur *m or* répéteur *m* de téléphone; **telephone subscriber** = abonné, -ée du téléphone; **telephone switchboard** = standard *m* téléphonique 2 *verb* appeler (quelqu'un) *or* téléphoner (à quelqu'un); **he telephoned about the order for computer stationery** = il a téléphoné au sujet de la commande de papier listing

◊ **telephonist** *noun* téléphoniste *m&f or* standardiste *m&f*

◊ **telephony** *noun* téléphonie *f*

teleprinter *noun* téléimprimeur *m or* téléscripteur *m or* télétype *m*; **you can drive a teleprinter from this modified serial port** = vous pouvez connecter un téléimprimeur sur ce port série modifié; **teleprinter interface** = interface *f* (pour) téléimprimeur; **teleprinter operator** = opérateur, -trice de téléimprimeur *or* télétypiste *m&f*; **teleprinter roll** = rouleau *m* de papier de *or* pour téléimprimeur

teleprocessing (TP) *noun* télétraitement *m*

telesales *noun* *(sales made by telephone)* ventes *fpl* par téléphone

◊ **teleshopping** *noun* achats *mpl* par téléphone

telesoftware (TSW) *noun* logiciel *m* téléchargé; **the telesoftware was downloaded yesterday** = on a téléchargé le logiciel hier

Teletext ™ *noun* *(over television)* Télétexte ™ *m*

teletype (TTY) *noun* téléscripteur *m*

◊ **teletypewriter** *noun* téléimprimeur *m*

◊ **teletypsetting** *noun* télécomposition *f*

television (TV) *noun* *(system)* la télévision; *(device or set)* téléviseur *m or* poste *m* (de) télévision; **television camera** = caméra *f* de télévision; **television monitor** = moniteur *m* (de) télévision; **television projector** = projecteur *m* (de) télévision; **television receiver** = téléviseur *m or* poste *m* (de) télévision; **television receiver/monitor** = moniteur/téléviseur *m*; **television scan** = balayage *m* d'écran; **television tube** = tube *m* cathodique (pour téléviseur)

telex 1 *noun* **(a)** *(system)* télex *m*; **to send information by telex** = envoyer des renseignements par télex *or* télexer des renseignements; **the order came by telex** = la commande nous a été télexée; **telex line** = ligne *f* (de) télex; **we cannot communicate with our Nigerian office because of the breakdown of the telex lines** = il nous est impossible de joindre nos bureaux au Nigéria parce que le télex est en panne; **telex operator** = opérateur, -trice de télex *or* télexiste *m&f*; **telex subscriber** = abonné, -ée du télex **(b)** *(machine or message)* **a telex** = télex *m*; **we don't have a telex** = nous n'avons pas le télex; **he sent a telex to his office** = il a envoyé un télex à son bureau; **we received his telex this morning** = nous avons reçu son télex ce matin 2 *verb* télexer *or* envoyer un télex; **can you telex the Canadian office before they open?** = pouvez-vous envoyer un télex au bureau canadien avant son ouverture?

template *noun* **(a)** *(cut-out shape)* gabarit *m* (de traçage) **(b)** *(standard letter)* lettre *f* type; *(standard paragraph)* paragraphe *m* standard; **template command** = commande *f* de formatage (de paragraphe, etc.); **a template paragraph command enables the user to specify the number of**

spaces each paragraph should be indented = une commande de formatage permet à l'utilisateur de préciser l'alinéa de chaque paragraphe **(c)** *(blank form for addresses, etc.)* masque *m* (de saisie)

temporary *adjective* temporaire; **temporary register** = registre *m* temporaire; **temporary storage** = *(place)* mémoire *f* temporaire; *(action)* stockage *m* temporaire; *(file used to store data temporarily)* **temporary swap file** = fichier *m* d'échange temporaire

◊ **temporarily** *adverb* temporairement

ten's complement *noun* complément *m* à dix

10Base2 *(IEEE standard specifications)* standard 10Base2; *see also* ETHERNET

◊ **10Base5** standard 10Base5

◊ **10BaseT** standard 10BaseT

tera- *prefix (10^{12}; one million million)* téra-

◊ **terabyte** *noun (one thousand gigabytes or one million megabytes)* téraoctet *m*

◊ **terahertz** *noun* térahertz *m*

terminal 1 *noun* **(a)** *(display unit and keyboard)* terminal *m or* poste *m* de travail; **addressable terminal** = terminal à adressage protégé; **all the messages go to all the terminals since none are addressable terminals** = tous les messages sont transmis à tous les terminaux puisqu'aucun d'eux ne possède un adressage protégé; **applications terminal** = terminal dédié *or* spécialisé; **central terminal** = terminal principal *or* central; **dumb terminal** = terminal non intelligent; **intelligent terminal** = terminal intelligent; **the new intelligent terminal has a built-in text editor** = le nouveau terminal intelligent comporte un éditeur de texte; **master terminal** = terminal maître *or* terminal principal; **the system manager uses the master terminal to restart the system** = le gestionnaire de système utilise le terminal principal pour relancer le système; **remote terminal** = terminal à distance; **slave terminal** = terminal asservi *or* esclave; **terminal character set** = police *f* de caractères utilisable par un terminal; *(hardware device or IC)* **terminal controller** = contrôleur *m* de terminal; *(emulate the functions of another type of terminal)* **terminal emulation** = émulation *f* de terminal; **terminal identity** = (code d') identification *f* d'un terminal; **terminal interface** = interface *f* de *or* pour terminal; **the network controller has 16 terminal interfaces** = le contrôleur de réseau possède 16 interfaces pour terminaux; **terminal junky (TJ)** = fou *m or* fana *m&f* d'informatique *or* infomaniaque *m&f*; **my son has turned into a real terminal junky** = mon fils est devenu un véritable infomaniaque; *(time when a terminal is in use)* **terminal keyboard** = clavier *m* relié à un terminal; **terminal session** = session *f or* temps *m* de connexion d'un terminal **(b)** *(electrical connection point)* borne *f or* point *m* de connexion *or* de raccordement; **terminal area** = zone *f* de connexions; **terminal block** = bloc *m* de raccordement; *(electrical connectors)* **terminal strip** = barrette *f* de connexion du terminal **(c)** *(point in a network where a message can be*

transmitted and received) terminal (de réseau) **2** *adjective* fatal, -e; **the computer has a terminal fault** = l'ordinateur ne peut être réparé *or* souffre d'une panne irréparable

> QUOTE The London Borough of Hackney has standardised on terminal emulator software from Omniplex to allow its networked desktop users to select Unix or DOS applications from a single menu.
> *Computing*

terminate *verb* terminer

◊ **terminate and stay resident (TSR) program** *noun (program which loads itself into main memory and carries out a function)* programme résident *or* programme TSR; **when you hit Ctrl-F5, you will activate the TSR program and it will display your day's diary** = lorsque vous tapez Ctrl-F5 vous activez le module résident et il affiche l'agenda du jour

◊ **termination** *noun (stopping)* arrêt *m*; *(ending)* terminaison *f*; *(caused by a fault or power failure)* **abnormal termination** = arrêt *m* anormal

◊ **terminator** *noun* **(a)** *(LAN resistor)* terminateur *m* de réseau; *(SCSI resistor)* terminateur SCSI **(b)** *(indicates the end of a list)* marqueur *m* de fin de liste **(c)** *(connection)* **line terminator** = dispositif *m* de fin de ligne

ternary *adjective* ternaire

test 1 *noun* test *m or* essai *m*; *(for software)* **test bed** = banc *m* d'essai; **test data** = données *f* de contrôle; **test equipment** = testeur *m or* équipement *m* pour tests; **the engineer has special test equipment for this model** = l'ingénieur possède un équipement spécialisé pour effectuer les tests sur ce modèle; *see also* BENCHMARK; *(of software)* **test run** = essai (de programme) *or* test d'évaluation des performances; **a test run will soon show up any errors** = un essai fera tout de suite apparaître les erreurs **2** *verb* tester *or* contrôler *or* faire un test *or* faire un essai; **saturation testing** = tests de saturation

text *noun* texte *m*; **ragged text** = texte non justifié (à droite); **start-of-text (SOT *or* STX)** = (code de) début *m* de texte; **text compression** = compression *f* de texte; **text-editing facilities** = (système de) traitement de texte; **text-editing function** = fonction *f* (de) traitement de texte; **the program includes a built-in text-editing function** = une fonction traitement de texte est intégrée au programme; *(software)* **text editor** = éditeur *m* de texte; **the text editor will only read files smaller than 64Kbytes long** = cet éditeur de texte ne peut lire que les fichiers de moins de 64Ko; **text file** = fichier *m* texte; **text formatter** = programme *m* de formatage de texte; **people use the text formatter as a basic desk-top publishing program** = on utilise le formatage de texte comme programme de base de PAO; **text management** = gestion *f* de texte; **text manipulation** = manipulation *f* de texte; **text processing** = traitement *m* de texte; **text processor** = *(hardware)* machine *f* de traitement de texte; *(software)* logiciel *m* de traitement de texte; **text register** = registre *m* de texte; **text retrieval** =

recherche *f* (et extraction) de texte; **text screen** = zone *f* d'affichage de texte *or* écran *m* texte; **text-to-speech converter** = convertisseur *m* texte/signal vocal

◊ **textual** *adjective* textuel, -elle; **the editors made several textual changes before the proofs were sent back for correction** = les éditeurs ont généreusement annoté le texte avant le renvoi des épreuves pour correction

TFT screen = THIN FILM TRANSISTOR SCREEN

thermal *adjective* thermique; *(sends stream of drops of electrically charged ink)* **thermal inkjet printer** = imprimante *f* à jet d'encre thermique; *(paper with a special coating which turns black when heated)* **thermal paper** = papier *m* thermique; **thermal printer** = imprimante *f* thermique

| COMMENT: this type of printer is very quiet in operation since the printing head does not strike the paper

◊ **thermal transfer** *or* **thermal wax** *or* **thermal wax transfer printer** *noun (where the colours are produced by melting couloured wax onto the paper)* imprimante à transfert thermique *or* à sublimation thermique; **thermal wax transfer technology still provides the best colour representation on paper for PC output** = la technologie du transfert thermique produit encore les meilleures représentations de couleurs sur papier pour les sorties sur PC

thermistor *noun* thermistor *m*

thermo-sensitive *adjective* thermosensible

thesaurus *noun (file containing synonyms)* thésaurus *m* *or* dictionnaire *m* de synonymes; dictionnaire par thèmes

thick *adjective* épais, épaisse; *(for circuit design)* **thick film** = couche *f* épaisse

◊ **thick-Ethernet** *noun (network using thick coaxial cable)* Ethernet câble lourd; *see also* ETHERNET, THIN-ETHERNET

thimble printer *noun* imprimante *f* à tulipe

thin *adjective* mince; *(for ICs)* **thin film** = couche *f* mince; **thin film memory** = mémoire *f* à couches minces; **thin film transistor (TFT) screen** = écran *m* plat à matrice active; **thin window** = fenêtre *f* étroite *or* fenêtre d'une ligne

◊ **thin-Ethernet** *noun (network using thin coaxial cable)* Ethernet câble fin

third 1 *noun* tiers *m*; **one third** = un tiers **2** *adjective* **(a)** troisième; **third generation computer** = ordinateur *m* de troisième génération **(b) third party** = tiers *m*·

| QUOTE they expect third party developers to enhance the operating systems by adding their own libraries
| *PC Business World*

thirty-two bit system *noun* système *m* (informatique) de 32 bits

thousand *noun* mille *m* *or* millier *m*

thrashing *noun (excessive disk activity)* emballement *m* *(fault in virtual memory system)* pompage *m* *or* transferts *mpl* de page incontrôlés (entre la mémoire et le disque)

thread *noun* programme *m* en chapelet

◊ **threaded** *adjective* **threaded file** = fichier *m* chaîné; **threaded language** = langage chaîné; **threaded tree** = arborescence chaînée

| QUOTE WigWam makes it easier for a user to follow a thread in a bulletin-board conference topic by ordering responses using a hierarchical indent similar to that found in outline processor.
| *Computing*

three-address instruction *noun* instruction *f* à trois adresses

◊ **three-dimensional** *or* **3D** *adjective* tridimensionnel, -elle *or* à trois dimensions *or* 3D

◊ **three input adder** *see* FULL ADDER

three-pin plug *noun* fiche *f* *or* connecteur *m* à trois broches

three state logic *noun* circuit *m* logique à trois états

threshold *noun* seuil *m*; **threshold gate** = circuit *m* à seuil; **threshold value** = valeur *f* de seuil

throughput *noun* rendement *m* *or* débit *m*; **for this machine throughput is 1.3 inches per second (ips) scanning speed** = la vitesse de balayage de cette machine est de 1,3 pouce par seconde; **rated throughput** = débit *m* théorique *or* nominal

thyristor *noun* thyristor *m*

tie line *or* **tie trunk** *noun* ligne *f* de jonction privée

TIFF = TAG IMAGE FILE FORMAT

tilde *noun (sign over a letter ñ)* tilde *m*

tile 1 *verb (in a GUI: to arrange windows side by side)* disposer en mosaïque **2** *noun* (disposition en) mosaïque *f*

tilt and swivel *adjective* (écran) orientable

time 1 *noun* temps *m*; **addition time** = temps *m* d'addition; **cycle time** = temps de cycle; **queuing time** = temps d'attente (dans une file d'attente); **real time** = temps réel; **response time** = temps de réponse; **stop time** = temps d'arrêt *or* d'immobilisation; **time address code** = signal de contrôle du temps écoulé; **time assigned speech interpolation (TASI)** = interpolation *f* de signaux sur bande vocale; **time base** = base *f* de temps; **time coded page** = page *f* (vidéotex) à enchaînement programmé; **time derived channel** = voie *f* dérivée en temps; **time display** = horloge *f* numérique (qui affiche l'heure sur l'écran); **time division multiple access** = accès temporel multiplexé *or* accès multiple par division dans le temps; *(combining several signals into one carrier)* **time division multiplexing (TDM)** = multiplexage *m* temporel *or* multiplexage par répartition dans le temps (MRT); **time division switching** = commutation *f* temporelle; **time domain analysis** = analyse *f* du signal dans le temps; *(test for cable faults)* **time domain reflectometry (TDR)** = test *m* de câble par réflectométrie; **time shift viewing** = visionnage *m* en temps différé; **time slice** = tranche *f* de temps *or* tranche horaire; **time slot** = créneau *m* (de temps) **2** *verb* minuter; **microprocessor timing** = fréquence *f* d'horloge du processeur; **network timing** = synchronisation *f* de réseau; *(automatic backup)* **timed backup** = sauvegarde *f* programmée; **timing loop** = boucle *f* de temporisation *or* de synchronisation; **timing master** = horloge *f* maîtresse

◊ **time out** *verb (to become no longer valid)* invalider (une option ou un évènement) lorsque le temps imparti est écoulé; **if you do not answer this question within one minute, the program times out and moves onto the next question** = si vous ne répondez pas à la question dans la minute qui suit, le programme déclenche la question suivante parce que vous avez dépassé les délais

◊ **timeout** *noun* sortie *f* de session

◊ **timer** *noun* chronomètre *m*

◊ **time-sharing** *noun (system)* partage *m* de temps *or* (système en) temps partagé

tiny model *noun (memory model)* petit modèle (de mémoire Intel de 64Ko)

title *noun* titre *m or* nom *m*; **title of disk** = nom d'une disquette; *(first main page)* **title page** = page *f* de titre

TJ = TERMINAL JUNKY

toggle *verb (to switch)* basculer *or* valider (à l'aide d'un commutateur à bascule); **toggle switch** = commutateur *m* à bascule

> QUOTE the symbols can be toggled on or off the display
> *Micro Decision*

token *noun* **(a)** *(internal code)* jeton *m* **(b)** *(control packet)* jeton *m*

◊ **token bus network** *noun (IEEE 802.4 standard for a LAN)* réseau *m* en bus à jeton

◊ **token passing** *noun (controlling access to a LAN)* passage *m* du jeton

◊ **token ring network** *noun (IEEE 802.5 standard)* réseau *m* Token Ring *or* réseau à jeton; **control token** = jeton de contrôle; **Token Ring networks are very democratic and retain performance against increasing load** = les réseaux Token Ring sont très démocratiques et conservent leurs performances en cas d'accroissement de la charge

tomo- *prefix* tomo-

◊ **tomogram** *noun* image *f* tomographique

◊ **tomography** *noun* tomographie *f*; **computerized axial tomography (CAT)** = tomodensitométrie *f*

tone *noun* **(a)** *(sound)* tonalité *f*; **dialling tone** = tonalité d'appel; **engaged tone** = tonalité 'occupé'; **tone dialling** = numérotation *f* sur clavier tonal; **tone signalling** = signalisation tonale **(b)** *(shade)* ton *m or* nuance *f*; **the graphics package can give several tones of blue** = le progiciel graphique offre plusieurs nuances de bleu

◊ **toner** *noun (powdered ink for photocopier or printer)* (poudre d') encre *f or* toner *m*; **if you get toner on your hands, you can only wash it off with cold water** = si vous vous êtes mis du toner sur les mains, il faut les laver à l'eau froide; **toner cartridge** = cartouche *f* de toner; **change toner and toner cartridge according to the manual** = pour remettre du toner ou changer la cartouche, voir la marche à suivre dans le manuel d'utilisation; **the toner cartridge and the imaging drum can be replaced as one unit when the toner runs out** = lorsque l'encre est épuisée, on remplace la cartouche et le tambour en une seule opération

toolbox *noun (set of predefined routines)* boîte *f* à outils

◊ **Toolbox** ™ *noun (Apple Macintosh: set of utility programs)* Toolbox *or* boîte *f* à outils Macintosh

◊ **toolkit** *noun (for programs)* (boîte à) outils *or* (programmes) utilitaires *mpl*

◊ **tools** *noun (for programs)* outils *mpl* (de programmation)

top *noun* haut *m or* partie *f* supérieure; *(structured programming)* **top-down programming** = programmation *f* structurée suivant un ordre décroissant; **top of stack** = dessus *m* de la pile; *(of page)* **top space** = blanc *m* de tête *or* marge *f* supérieure

topology *noun* topologie *f*; *(topology in which all devices are connected to a single cable)* **bus topology** = topologie en bus; **Ethernet is a network that uses the bus topology** = Ethernet est un réseau qui utilise une topologie en bus; **token ring uses a ring topology** = token ring utilise une topologie en anneau; **network topology** = topologie de réseau; *(topology in which all devices are connected by individual cables)* **star topology** = topologie en étoile; **if one workstation cable snaps in a star topology, the rest continue, unlike a bus topology** = dans un réseau en étoile, si le câble d'une station est défaillant, les autres stations continuent à travailler, ce qui n'est pas le cas dans une topologie en bus

TOPS ™ *(software that allows IBM PCs and Apple Macintoshes to share files)* logiciel *m* de communication TOPS

torn tape *noun (communication switching method)* bande *f* perforée (pour télex hors ligne)

total *noun* total *m*; **hash total** = total de vérification (pour hash codes); **total access communication system (TACS)** = norme TACS (pour système de radio-téléphone cellulaire)

touch *verb* toucher *or* appuyer (sur); **touch pad** = pavé *m* tactile *or* à effleurement; **touch screen** = écran *m* tactile; **touch-sensitive keyboard** = clavier *m* tactile *or* à effleurement

◊ **touch up** *verb* retoucher

TP = TELEPROCESSING, TRANSACTION PROCESSING

TPI = TRACKS PER INCH

trace *noun* traçage *m* d'un programme *or* d'un procédé; **trace program** = programme de traçage; **trace trap** = point *m* de contrôle (du registre) dans un programme de traçage

track 1 *noun* piste *f*; **address track** = piste adresse; **track address** = adresse de piste; **tracks per inch (TPI)** = (nombre de) pistes par pouce **2** *verb* localiser; **the read head is not tracking the recorded track correctly** = la tête de lecture fait une erreur de piste

trackball *noun* boule *f* (de pointeur)

tractor feed *noun* entraînement *m* (du papier) par picots

QUOTE the printer is fairly standard with both tractor and cut sheet feed system
Which PC?

traffic *noun* (*messages and signals*) trafic *m* *or* mouvements *mpl*; **our Ethernet network begins to slow down if the traffic reaches 60 per cent of the bandwidth** = notre réseau Ethernet commence à ralentir lorsque le trafic atteint 60 pour cent de la bande passante; **traffic analysis** = analyse *f* du trafic (sur une ligne); **traffic density** = densité *f* du trafic; **traffic intensity** = intensité *f* de trafic; **incoming traffic** = trafic *m* d'entrée *or* d'arrivée

trail *noun* trace *f*; **audit trail** = protocole *m* de traçage *or* de contrôle *or* de vérification

◊ **trailer** *noun* (*final byte of file*) label *m* de fin de fichier; **trailer record** = dernier enregistrement *or* enregistrement *m* de fin de fichier; **tape trailer** = label de fin de bande

transaction *noun* transaction *f* *or* mouvement *m*; **transaction-driven system (TDS)** = système *m* transactionnel; (*movement file*) **transaction file** = fichier *m* de transactions *or* fichier mouvements *or* fichier de mise à jour; **transaction processing (TP)** = traitement de mouvements; (*change record*) **transaction record** = enregistrement de mouvements *or* de transactions

QUOTE At present, users implementing client-server strategies are focusing on decision support systems before implementing online transaction processing and other mission-critical applications.
Computing

transborder data flow *noun* flux *m* de données passant les frontières *or* flux transfrontière

transceiver *noun* émetteur/récepteur *m*; **radio transceiver** = émetteur/récepteur radio

transcoder *noun* transcodeur *m*; **use the transcoder to convert PAL to SECAM** = utilisez le transcodeur pour la conversion de PAL en SECAM

transcribe *verb* transcrire

◊ **transcription** *noun* transcription *f*

transducer *noun* transducteur *m*; **a pressure transducer converts physical pressure signals into electrical signals** = un transducteur de pression transforme un signal physique de pression en signal électrique

transfer 1 *verb* (a) (*to change command*) transférer; **all processing activities have been transferred to the mainframe** = toutes les opérations de traitement ont été transférées sur l'ordinateur principal (b) (*to copy a section of memory*) transférer **2** *noun* (a) (*between devices or memory*) transfert *m*; **radial transfer** = (*between peripherals*) transfert radial; (*between layers*) transfert intercouche *or* radial; **transfer check** = contrôle *m* de transfert; (*between devices and locations*) **transfer rate** = taux *m* *or* vitesse *f* de transfert; **with a good telephone line, this pair of modems can achieve a transfer rate of 14.4Kbps** = avec une bonne ligne téléphonique, cette paire de modems peut atteindre un taux de transfert de 14,4 Kops; **transfer time** = temps *m* de transfert (b) (*within program*) **conditional transfer** = transfert *or* branchement *m* conditionnel; **transfer command** = instruction *f* de transfert *or* de branchement; **transfer control** = contrôle *m* de transfert *or* de branchement; *see also* THERMAL

transform *verb* transformer

◊ **transformation** *noun* transformation *f*

◊ **transformational rules** *noun* régles *fpl* de transformation

◊ **transformer** *noun* transformateur *m*

transient 1 *adjective* passager, -ère *or* de courte durée *or* éphémère; **transient area** = zone *f* (de mémoire) des programmes non résidents; **transient error** = erreur *f* passagère *or* momentanée **2** *noun* (*something which is present for a short time only*) effet *m* transitoire; **voltage transient** = pointe *f* de tension; **power transient** = courant *m* transitoire; **transient suppressor** = limiteur *m* *or* éliminateur *m* de courant transitoire

transistor *noun* transistor *m*; **bipolar (junction) transistor (BJT)** = transistor bipolaire *or* à jonction pnp *or* à jonction npn; **field effect transistor (FET)** = transistor à effet de champ (TEC); **transistor-resistor logic (TRL)** = logique *f* transistor résistance (LTR); **transistor-transistor logic (TTL)** = logique transistor transistor (LTT); **unipolar transistor** = transistor unipolaire

transition *noun* transition *f*; **transition point** = point *m* de transition

translate *verb* *(to convert data)* traduire *or* convertir

◊ **translation tables** *or* **conversion tables** *noun* tables *f* de conversion *or* d'équivalence *or* de référence

◊ **translator (program)** *noun* traducteur *m or* programme *m* de traduction

transmission *noun* transmission *f*; **neutral transmission** = transmission neutre; **parallel transmission** = transmission (en) parallèle; **serial transmission** = transmission (en) série; **synchronous transmission** = transmission synchrone; **transmission channel** = voie *f or* canal *m* de transmission; *(data transmission protocol)* **transmission control protocol (TCP)** = protocole *m* de contrôle de transmission *or* protocole TCP (de transmission); *(data transfer protocol)* **transmission control protocol/interface program (TCP/IP)** = protocole *m* TCP/IP (de communication de réseau); **transmission error** = erreur *f* de transmission; **transmission media** = moyens *mpl or* supports *mpl* de transmission; **transmission rate** = vitesse *f* de transmission *or* débit *m*; **their average transmission is 64,000 bits per second (bps) through a parallel connection or 19,200 bps through a serial connection** = la vitesse moyenne de transmission est de 64 000 bits par seconde en connexion parallèle et 19 200 bits par seconde en connexion série; **transmission window** = fenêtre *f* de transmission

◊ **transmissive disc** *noun* disque *m* optique transitif

◊ **transmit** *verb* transmettre

◊ **transmittance** *noun* transmittance *f*

◊ **transmitter (TX)** *noun* transmetteur *m*

QUOTE an X-ray picture can be digitized and transmitted from one hospital to a specialist at another for diagnosis
Electronics & Business World

QUOTE modern high-power transmitters are much reduced in size and a simple and uncluttered appearance
Electronics & Power

transparent *adjective* **(a)** transparent, -e; **transparent interrupts** = interruptions transparentes; **transparent paging** = pagination *f* tranparente **(b)** *(device or network)* transparent,-e

◊ **transparency** *noun* *(for overhead projector)* transparent *m*; *(positive film)* diapositive *f*

transphasor *noun* transphaseur *m*

transponder *noun* transpondeur *m or* transmetteur/répondeur *m*

transport 1 *verb* transporter 2 *noun* **(a)** *(device)* **(magnetic) tape transport** = dérouleur *m or* dispositif *m* d'entraînement de bandes (magnétiques) **(b)** *(ISO/OSI standard)* **transport layer** = couche *f* transport

◊ **transportable** *adjective* transportable; **a transportable computer is not as small as a portable** = un ordinateur transportable n'est pas aussi petit *or* aussi léger qu'un portable

transposition *noun* transposition *f or* inversion *f or* interversion *f*; **a series of transposition errors caused faulty results** = une série d'interversions a donné de faux résultats

transputer *noun* *(single large very powerful chip)* transordinateur *m*

QUOTE TAOS kernels are now available from TKS for the Intel 486 and Pentium, the Apple/Olivetti ARM, the Inmos T800/T9000 transputer and the Mips R3000 series.
Computing

transverse mode noise *noun* interférence *f* interligne

◊ **transverse scan** *noun* balayage transversal *or* lecture transversale

trap *noun* piège *m or* trappe *f*; **trace trap** = point *m* de contrôle (du registre) dans un programme de traçage; *(accepts interrupt signals and acts on them)* **trap handler** = manipulateur *m* d'interruption

◊ **trapdoor** *noun* point d'entrée dans un système

trashcan *noun* *(icon which looks like a dustbin)* corbeille *f*; *see also* WASTEPAPER BASKET, BIN

tray *noun* bac *m* (à papier *or* à feuilles)

tree *noun* **tree (structure)** = (structure en) arbre *m or* arborescence *f*; **tree and branch network system** = système *m* arborescent; **tree selection sort** = tri *m* en arborescence; **binary tree** = arbre binaire

trellis coding *noun* *(modulating a signal)* codage *m* treillis

triad *noun* triade *f*

trial *noun* essai *m or* test *m*; **trials engineer** = ingénieur *m* d'essai

tributary station *noun* station *f* secondaire

trim *verb* couper (très peu) *or* régulariser la coupe; *(pages of a book)* rogner; **the printed pages are trimmed to 198 x 129mm** = après l'impression, on rogne pour obtenir des pages de 198 x 129mm; **you will need to trim the top part of the photograph to make it fit** = il vous faudra couper légèrement le bord supérieur de la photo pour qu'elle ait les dimensions désirées

TRL = TRANSISTOR-RESISTOR LOGIC

Trojan Horse *noun* *(program)* cheval *m* de Troie

troposphere *noun* troposphère *f*; *see also* IONOSPHERE

troubleshoot *verb* *(to debug)* déboguer (un

logiciel); *(to locate and repair faults)* localiser (et réparer) une panne

◊ **troubleshooter** *noun (for debugging)* spécialiste *m&f* en débogage; *(technician)* technicien/réparateur *m*

trough *noun (in a waveform)* creux *m*

TRUE *noun (logical condition)* VRAI

TrueType ™ *(outline font technology)* caractères TrueType ™

truncate *verb* (a) *(to cut short)* tronquer (b) *(to give an approximate value)* arrondir par défaut *or* tronquer; **3.5678 truncated to 3.56** = 3,5678 tronqué *or* arrondi par défaut à 3,56

◊ **truncation** *noun (of value)* troncature *f*; **truncation error** = erreur *f* de troncature *or* d'arrondi

trunk *noun* circuit *m or* faisceau *m* de jonction

◊ **trunk call** *noun GB (long-distance call)* appel *m* interurbain *or* communication interurbaine

◊ **trunk exchange** *noun GB (telephone exchange)* central *m* téléphonique pour réseau interurbain

truth table *noun* table *f* de vérité; **truth value** = valeur *f* binaire *or* booléenne

TSR = TERMINATE AND STAY RESIDENT (PROGRAM)

TSW = TELESOFTWARE

TTL = TRANSISTOR-TRANSISTOR LOGIC logique *f* transistor-transistor (LTT); **TTL compatible** = compatible (avec) LTT; **TTL logic** = logique transistor-transistor *or* logique LTT; *(monitor which can only accept digital signals)* **TTL monitor** = moniteur *m* TTL

TTY = TELETYPE

tube *noun (TV)* tube *m*

tune *verb* (a) *(a system)* ajuster *or* régler *or* mettre au point; **to fine tune** = régler avec grande précision (b) *(radio frequency)* régler

Turing machine *noun* machine *f* de Turing *or* simulateur *m* (de) Turing

◊ **Turing test** *noun* test *m* de Turing

turn off *verb (to switch off)* éteindre *or* mettre hors tension; **turn off the power before unplugging the monitor** = il faut éteindre l'appareil avant de déconnecter le moniteur

◊ **turn on** *verb (to switch on)* allumer *or* mettre en marche *or* mettre sous tension

turnaround document *noun* document *m* circulant

◊ **turnaround time (TAT)** *noun* (a) *(time to switch data flow direction)* délai *m* d'inversion *or*

de retournement (b) *US (time to activate a program and get results)* temps *m* d'exécution

◊ **turnkey system** *noun* système *m* clé en main

turtle *noun* tortue *f*; **turtle graphics** = graphisme généré à l'aide d'une tortue; **the charts were prepared using turtle graphics** = la présentation graphique a été préparée avec une tortue

tutorial *noun* tutoriel *m*

TV = TELEVISION **TV camera** = caméra *f* de télévision

tweak *verb (make small adjustments)* mettre au point *or* fignoler un programme *or* un détail d'installation

tweening *noun (calculating intermediate images in computer graphics)* transformation *f* sérielle *or* calcul *m* des déformées intermédiaires; **using tweening, we can show how a frog turns into a princess in five steps** = en utilisant le procédé de transformation sérielle nous pouvons montrer une grenouille qui se transforme en princesse en cinq étapes

tweeter *noun (informal)* haut-parleur *m* d'aigus *or* de hautes fréquences

twisted pair cable *noun (two insulated copper wires twisted around each other)* câble *m* en paire(s) torsadée(s); *(two insulated copper wires twisted around each other, then wrapped in a shielding layer)* **shielded twisted pair (STP) cable** = câble en paires torsadées blindé; *(two insulated copper wires twisted around each other)* **unshielded twisted pair (UTP) cable** = câble en paires torsadées sans blindage

two-address instruction *noun* instruction *f* à deux adresses; **two-plus-one instruction** = instruction à deux adresses plus une

◊ **two-dimensional** *adjective* à deux dimensions *or* bidimensionnel, -elle; **two-dimensional array** = tableau *m* à deux dimensions *or* bidimensionnel

◊ **two input adder** *noun* additionneur *m* à deux entrées

◊ **two-level subroutine** *noun* sous-programme à deux niveaux

◊ **two-part** *noun (paper)* (papier) double *or* en double épaisseur; **two-part stationery** = papier commercial, factures, etc. en double épaisseur

◊ **two-pass assembler** *noun* assembleur *m* deux passes

two's complement *noun* complément *m* à deux

two way cable *noun US* câble *m* bidirectionnel

two way radio *noun* poste *m* émetteur-récepteur

two wire circuit *noun* circuit *m* à deux fils *or* bidirectionnel *or* bifilaire

TX = TRANSMITTER

type 1 *noun* **(a)** *(metal)* caractères *mpl* **(b)** *(shape)* (police de) caractères (d'imprimerie); **they switched to italic type for the heading** = ils ont changé de police de caractères et composé l'entête en italique; *(size of a font)* **type size** = taille *f* de caractères (mesurée en points); *(weight and angle of a font)* **type style** = style *m* de caractère **(c)** *(variety)* type *m*; **variable data type** = variable *f* (de type non précisé); **string type** = variable chaînée *or* de type chaîne de caractères **2** *verb* **(a)** taper *or* écrire à la machine; **he can type quite fast** = il a une vitesse de frappe assez rapide; **all his reports are typed on his portable typewriter** = il tape tous ses rapports sur sa machine à écrire portative **(b)** *(enter data via a keyboard)* entrer *or* taper (au clavier); **I typed in the command again, but it still didn't work** = j'ai retapé cette commande, mais ça ne marche pas

◊ **typeface** *or* **typestyle** *noun* *(font or characters in a particular design)* modèle *m or* type *m* de caractères; fonte *f or* police *f* de caractères; **most of this book is set in the Times typeface** = ce livre a été imprimé presque entièrement en (caractères) Times

typescript *noun* texte *m or* manuscrit *m* dactylographié

typeset *verb* composer *or* faire la composition (d'un texte); **in desktop publishing, the finished work should look almost as if it had been typeset** = la PAO devrait produire un texte dont la qualité est à peu près égale à celle de la photocomposition

◊ **typesetter** *noun* compositeur *m or* typographe *m*; **the text is ready to be sent to the typesetter** = le texte est prêt à être envoyé au compositeur

◊ **typesetting** *noun* composition *f*; **typesetting costs can be reduced by supplying the typesetter with prekeyed disks** = les frais de composition sont moins élevés si le texte est saisi sur disquette avant d'être envoyé au compositeur

typesize *noun* corps *m or* taille *f* de caractères (en points)

typewriter *noun* machine *f* à écrire; **she wrote the letter on her portable typewriter** = elle a écrit la lettre sur sa petite portative; **he makes fewer mistakes now he is using an electronic typewriter** = il fait moins d'erreurs depuis qu'il utilise une machine à écrire électronique; **typewriter faces** = caractères *mpl* de machine à écrire

◊ **typewritten** *adjective* dactylographié, -ée *or* écrit, -e à la machine

◊ **typing** *noun* dactylographie *f*; **typing error** = faute *f* de frappe; **she must have made a typing error** = elle doit avoir fait une faute de frappe; **typing pool** = pool *m* de dactylos; **copy typing** = dactylographie *f*

◊ **typist** *noun* **copy typist** = dactylo *f*; **shorthand typist** = sténo-dactylo *f*

typo *noun* *(typographical error)* coquille *f*

◊ **typographer** *noun* typographe *m&f*

◊ **typographic** *or* **typographical** *adjective* typographique; **no typographical skills are required for this job** = ce travail ne demande aucune expérience en typographie; **a typographical error made while typesetting is called a 'typo'** = une erreur typographique à la composition donne ce qu'on appelle une 'coquille'; **typographical error** = coquille *f*

◊ **typography** *noun* typographie *f*

Uu

UART = UNIVERSAL ASYNCHRONOUS RECEIVER/TRANSMITTER émetteur/récepteur *m* asynchrone universel; **UART controller** = contrôleur *m* d'émetteur/récepteur asynchrone universel

UBC = UNIVERSAL BLOCK CHANNEL

UHF = ULTRA HIGH FREQUENCY

ULA = UNCOMMITTED LOGIC ARRAY

ultra- *prefix* ultra *or* hyper *or* très; **ultra high frequency (UHF)** = ultra-haute fréquence (UHF) *or* onde *f* décimétrique; *(reduced by more than 90X)* **ultrafiche** = microfiche *f* (avec réduction de plus de 90X); *(above 20KHz)* **ultrasonic** = ultrasonore *or* ultrasonique; **ultrasound** = ultrason *m or* ultra-son *m*; **ultraviolet (UV) light** *or* **radiation** = rayonnement *m* ultraviolet; (l') ultraviolet; rayons *mpl* ultraviolets *or* les ultraviolets *mpl*; **ultraviolet erasable PROM** = mémoire morte programmable (PROM) effaçable par ultraviolet

UMB = UPPER MEMORY BLOCKS

umlaut *noun (typography)* tréma *m*

un- *prefix (meaning not)* non *or* in-; *(illegal combination of bits)* **unallowable digit** = chiffre *m* non affectable; **unauthorized** = *(person)* non autorisé, -ée; *(access)* interdit, -e; **the use of a password is to prevent unauthorized access to the data** = le mot de passe interdit aux personnes non autorisées d'avoir accès aux données; *(pages of book)* **uncut** = (livre) dont les pages ne sont pas rognées

unary operation *noun* opération *f* monadique *or* à un opérande

unattended operation *noun* tâche qui peut être exécutée automatiquement; fonctionnement automatique (d'un système)

◊ **unbundled software** *noun* logiciel *m* non compris *or* non inclus à l'achat d'un ordinateur

◊ **unclocked** *adjective (circuit)* asynchrone *or* non asservi,-e à l'horloge

◊ **uncommitted logic array (ULA)** *noun* circuit *m* logique non connecté; **uncommitted storage list** = liste *f* des emplacements disponibles *or* non alloués

◊ **unconditional** *adjective* sans réserve *or* systématique *or* inconditionnel, -elle; **unconditional branch** *or* **jump** = branchement *m or* saut *m* inconditionnel; **unconditional transfer** = transfert *m* systématique *or* automatique (NOTE: opposite is **conditional)**

undelete *verb (restore deleted information)* récupérer (un fichier *or* un texte supprimé); **don't worry, this function will undelete your cuts to the letter** = ne vous faites pas de soucis, cette fonction vous permet de récupérer les parties coupées de votre lettre; **thankfully we could undelete the files** = par bonheur, nous avons pu récupérer ce fichier

underexposed *adjective (photograph)* sous-exposé, -ée

underflow *noun* dépassement *m or* débordement *m* négatif

underline *or* **underscore** **1** *noun* soulignement *m or* soulignage *m or* trait *m* (sous un mot ou une ligne de texte); **the chapter headings are given a double underline and the paragraphs a single underline** = on souligne deux fois l'en-tête d'un chapitre et une seule fois celui d'un paragraphe **2** *verb* souligner

◊ **underlining** *noun* soulignement *m or* soulignage *m*

undertake *verb* entreprendre; **he has undertaken to reprogram the whole system** = il a entrepris de refaire la totalité des programmes du système (NOTE: **undertaking - undertaken - undertook)**

undetected *adjective* non décelé, -ée *or* non détecté, -ée; **the programming error was undetected for some time** = l'erreur de programmation n'a été détectée qu'après un certain temps

undo *verb (reverse the previous action)* annuler (une action) *or* undo; **you've just deleted the paragraph, but you can undo it from the option in the Edit menu** = vous venez de supprimer un paragraphe, vous pouvez annuler cette action avec l'option 'annuler frappe' du menu Edition

unedited *adjective (text)* non édité, -ée *or* non corrigé, -ée

unformatted *adjective (contains no formatting commands)* non formaté, -ée; *(capacity of a disk before it has been formatted)* **unformatted capacity** = capacité non formatée; *(which has not been formatted)* **unformatted disk** = disque non formaté; **it is impossible to copy to an unformatted disk** = il est impossible de copier quoi que ce soit sur une disquette non formatée; **the cartridge drive provides 12.7Mbyte of unformatted storage** = le lecteur de cartouche donne une capacité de mémoire non formatée de 12.7Mo

uni- *prefix (meaning one)* uni-

◊ **unidirectional microphone** *noun*

microphone *m* unidirectionnel; *compare with* OMNIDIRECTIONAL

union *noun (logical function)* union *f or* opération *f* OU

uninterruptable power supply (UPS) *noun* onduleur *m*

unipolar *adjective* **(a)** *(transistor)* unipolaire **(b)** *(transmission system)* unipolaire; **unipolar signal** = signal unipolaire; *compare* POLAR

unique *adjective* unique; **each separate memory byte has its own unique address** = chaque octet de mémoire a une adresse unique

unit *noun* **(a)** *(smallest element)* unité *f or* élément *m*; **unit buffer** = tampon *m* élémentaire; **unit record** = enregistrement *m* unique **(b)** *(single machine)* unité *or* organe *m*; **arithmetic and logic unit (ALU)** = unité arithmétique et logique; **central processing unit (CPU)** = unité centrale (de traitement) *or* processeur central; **control unit** = unité de contrôle; **desk top unit** = ordinateur *m* de bureau; **input/output unit** *or* **device** = périphérique *m or* organe d'entrée/sortie

universal *adjective* universel, -elle; standard; **universal asynchronous receiver/transmitter (UART)** = émetteur/récepteur *m* asynchrone universel; **universal block channel (UBC)** = canal universel de transmission par blocs; **universal device (UART, USRT, USART)** = dispositif universel; **universal product code (UPC)** = code *m* barres; **universal programming** = programmation *f* en langage universel; **universal set** = ensemble *m* référentiel; **the universal set of prime numbers less than ten and greater than two is 3,5,7** = l'ensemble référentiel des nombres premiers inférieurs à dix et plus grands que deux est 3,5,7; **universal synchronous asynchronous receiver-transmitter (USART)** = émetteur/récepteur *m* synchrone asynchrone universel; **universal synchronous receiver/transmitter (USRT)** = émetteur/récepteur synchrone universel

Unix ™ *noun (operating system developed by AT&T Bell)* (système d'exploitation) UNIX; *(utilities that help a user to copy data)* **UNIX-to-UNIX copy (UUCP)** = utilitaire *m* UUCP

unlock *verb (allow other users to write to a file or access a system)* déverrouiller

unmodified instruction *noun* instruction *f* dans sa forme initiale

unmodulated *adjective (signal)* non modulé, -ée; *see also* BASE BAND

unmount *verb* **(a)** *(remove a disk from a disk drive)* enlever un disque dur **(b)** *(inform the operating system that a disk drive is no longer in use)* (instruction) 'unmount' (qui indique que le disque n'est pas utilisable)

unpack *verb* dégrouper *or* décondenser *or* décomprimer; **this routine unpacks the archived file** = cette routine permet de décomprimer les fichiers archivés

unplug *verb* débrancher *or* déconnecter; **do not move the system without unplugging it** = ne déplacez pas le système sans l'avoir d'abord débranché; **simply unplug the old drive and plug-in a new one** = vous n'avez qu'à déconnecter le lecteur et en connecter un nouveau à sa place

unpopulated *adjective (PCB which does not contain any components)* (carte) nue *or* non équipée *or* sans composant; **you can buy an unpopulated RAM card and fit your own RAM chips** = vous pouvez acheter une carte d'extension RAM nue et installer vos propres plaquettes

unprotected *adjective (data that can be modified)* non protégé, -ée; **unprotected field** = champ non protégé

unrecoverable error *noun* erreur *f* irrécupérable *or* impossible à corriger

unshielded twisted-pair (UTP) cable *noun (two insulated copper wires twisted around each other)* câble *m* en paire(s) torsadée(s) sans blindage *or* câble UTP

COMMENT: UTP is normally used for telephone cabling, but is also the cabling used in the IEEE 802.3 (10BaseT) standard that defines Ethernet running over UTP at rates of up to 10Mbits per second

unsigned *adjective (number system)* sans signe *or* en valeur absolue

unsorted *adjective (data)* non classé, -ée *or* non trié, -ée; **it took four times as long to search the unsorted file** = il a fallu quatre fois plus de temps pour chercher dans les fichiers non classés

unwanted *adjective* non requis, -e; **use the global delete command to remove large areas of unwanted text** = lorsqu'il s'agit de supprimer un texte assez long, servez-vous de la commande qui permet d'effacer en bloc

up *adverb (working or running)* en (bon) état de marche; **they must have found the fault - the computer is finally up and running** = ils ont sûrement trouvé la source du problème puisque l'ordinateur fonctionne à merveille; **up time** *or* **uptime** = temps *m* productif *or* de bon fonctionnement (NOTE: opposite is **down**)

◊ **up and down propagation time** *noun* temps *m* de propagation aller (et) retour

UPC = UNIVERSAL PRODUCT CODE

update 1 *noun (file)* fichier *m* mis à jour *or* corrigé; *(action)* mise *f* à jour *or* correction (d'un fichier, etc.); *(system)* nouvelle version (d'un progiciel); **update file** *or* **transaction file** = fichier *m* (de) mouvements **2** *verb* mettre à jour *or* corriger; **we have the original and updated documents on disks** = le document original et le document corrigé se trouvent tous les deux sur disquettes

QUOTE it means that any item of data stored in the system need be updated only once

Which PC?

up/down counter *noun* compteur *m* incrémenteur/décrémenteur

upgrade *verb* optimiser *or* rendre plus efficace; améliorer; **they can upgrade the printer** = ils peuvent optimiser l'imprimante; **the single processor with 2Mbytes of memory can be upgraded to 4Mbytes** = il est possible d'augmenter la mémoire du processeur unique de 2Mo jusqu'à 4Mo *or* le processeur unique possède une mémoire de 2Mo extensible jusqu'à 4Mo; **all three models have an on-site upgrade facility** = les trois modèles offrent des possibilités d'extension sur site

QUOTE the cost of upgrading a PC to support CAD clearly depends on the peripheral devices added

PC Business World

upkeep *noun (software)* mise *f* à jour; *(hardware)* entretien *m* *or* maintenance *f*; **the upkeep of the files means reviewing them every six months** = la mise à jour des fichiers doit se faire tous les six mois

uplink *noun (link from an earth station to a satellite)* liaison *f* terre/satellite

upload *verb* télécharger *or* transférer des données (d'un petit ordinateur à un plus gros); **the user can upload PC data to update mainframe applications** = l'utilisateur peut transférer les données d'un micro sur un gros ordinateur, pour mettre les applications à jour (NOTE: the opposite is **download**)

◊ **uploading** *noun* téléchargement *m*; **the image can be manipulated before uploading to the host computer** = on peut manipuler l'image avant son téléchargement sur l'ordinateur hôte

upper case *noun* (lettre) majuscule *f or* haut *m* de casse; **upper case M** = M majuscule

upper memory *noun (IBM PC: memory located between the 640Kb and 1 Mb limits)* bloc *m* de mémoire haute

UPS = UNINTERRUPTABLE POWER SUPPLY onduleur *m*

QUOTE Magnum Power Systems has launched a new UPS for PCs. The BI-UPS prevents loss of data due to power dips or 'brown-outs' - voltage drops because of circuit overload.

Computing

uptime *noun (time when a computer is functioning correctly)* temps *m* productif *or* de bon fonctionnement (NOTE: opposite is **downtime**)

upwards compatible *or US* **upward compatible** *adjective (hardware or software)* compatible avec système de niveau supérieur

usability *noun (ease of use)* facilité *f* d'utilisation; convivialité *f*; **we have studied usability tests and found that a GUI is easier for new users than a command line** = nous avons étudié les tests de convivialité et trouvé que l'interface graphique (GUI) est plus facile à maîtriser pour les nouveaux utilisateurs que les lignes de commandes

◊ **usable** *adjective* utilisable; **the PC has 512K of usable memory** = cet ordinateur individuel possède 512K de mémoire utilisable; **maximum usable frequency** = maximum *m* de fréquence utilisable

USART = UNIVERSAL SYNCHRONOUS ASYNCHRONOUS RECEIVER-TRANSMITTER

USASCII *US* = USA STANDARD CODE FOR INFORMATION INTERCHANGE; *see* ASCII

use 1 *noun* **(a)** *(way in which something can be used)* usage *m*; **the use of that file is restricted** = l'accès à ce fichier est limité; **to make use of something** = faire usage de *or* utiliser *or* employer quelque chose; **in use** = en service *or* utilisé, -ée; **sorry, the printer is already in use** = je regrette, mais il y a déjà quelqu'un qui se sert de l'imprimante; **the printer has been in use for the last two hours** = l'imprimante fonctionne depuis deux heures **(b)** *(being useful)* utilité *f*; **what use is an extra disk drive?** je ne vois pas l'utilité d'un deuxième lecteur; **it's no use, I cannot find the error** = à quoi bon, je ne réussis pas à trouver l'erreur **2** *verb* **(a)** *(to operate something)* utiliser *or* employer *or* se servir de (quelque chose); **if you use the computer for processing the labels, it will be much quicker** = la préparation de ces étiquettes se fera beaucoup plus rapidement avec l'ordinateur; **the computer is used too often by the sales staff** = les commerciaux utilisent l'ordinateur trop souvent **(b)** *(to consume power)* consommer; **it's using too much electricity** = la consommation d'électricité de cette machine est beaucoup trop forte

◊ **used** *adjective (not new)* d'occasion; **special offer on used terminals** = prix spécial pour terminaux d'occasion *or* de seconde main

user *noun* utilisateur, -trice; **user area** = zone *f* utilisateur *or* pour programme utilisateur; *(record which identifies a user)* **user account** = compte *m* (d') utilisateur; **I have a new user account on this LAN but I cannot remember my password** = j'ai un nouveau compte d'utilisateur sur ce réseau, mais j'ai oublié mon mot de passe; **user-definable** = programmable par l'utilisateur *or* selon les besoins de l'utilisateur; **the style sheet contains 125 user-definable symbols** = la feuille de style comporte 125 symboles programmables (selon les besoins de l'utilisateur); **user-defined characters** = caractères programmés par l'utilisateur; **user documentation** = notice *f* d'utilisation destinée à l'utilisateur; **using the package was easy with the excellent user documentation** = l'excellente notice facilitait l'utilisation du progiciel; **user group** = groupe *m* d'utilisateurs; **I found how to solve the problem by asking people at the user group meeting** = j'ai trouvé la solution au problème en me renseignant auprès des autres utilisateurs rencontrés à la réunion des membres du groupe; **user guide** = manuel *m* d'utilisation; **user ID** = mot *m* de passe; code *m* personnel *or* d'identification d'un utilisateur; **if you forget your user ID, you will not be able to logon** = il faut vous rappeler votre mot de passe sinon vous ne pourrez pas avoir accès au système; **user interface** = interface *m* système/utilisateur; *(name by which a user is known)* **user name** = nom d'utilisateur; **user-operated language** = langage *m* (d')utilisateur; **user port** = port *m* pour périphérique(s); **user's program** = programme *m* écrit par l'utilisateur *or* programme (d') utilisateur; **user-selectable** = programmable *or* définissable *or* réglable par l'utilisateur; qui peut être modifié *or* programmé *or* sélectionné *or* validé *or* réglé suivant les besoins de l'utilisateur; **the video resolution of 640 by 300, 240 or 200 pixels is user-selectable** = l'utilisateur peut sélectionner une résolution d'écran de 640 x 300, 240 ou 200 pixels

◊ **user-friendly** *adjective (language or system or program)* convivial, -e *or* d'utilisation facile *or* facile à utiliser; **it's such a user-friendly machine** = c'est un appareil vraiment convivial *or* extrêmement facile à utiliser; **compared with the previous version this one is very user- friendly** = comparée à la version précédente, celle-ci est très facile à utiliser *or* très conviviale

---

QUOTE the user's guides are designed for people who have never seen a computer, but some sections have been spoiled by careless checking

PC User

QUOTE the first popular microcomputer to have a user-friendly interface built into its operating system

Micro Decision

QUOTE ModelMaker saves researchers a great deal of time and effort, and provides a highly user-friendly environment using menus and 'buttons', instant output, and instant access to a wide variety of mathematical techniques built into the system.

Computing

USRT = UNIVERSAL SYNCHRONOUS RECEIVER/TRANSMITTER

utility (program) *noun* (programme) utilitaire *m*; **a lost file cannot be found without a file-recovery utility** = il est impossible de récupérer un fichier perdu sans l'aide d'un utilitaire de récupération de fichier; **there is a utility for backing up a hard disk** = il y a un utilitaire qui permet de copier tous les fichiers du disque dur

UTP cable = UNSHIELDED TWISTED-PAIR CABLE

UUCP = UNIX-TO-UNIX COPY

UV light = ULTRAVIOLET LIGHT

Vv

V = VOLTAGE

V & V = VERIFICATION AND VALIDATION

V20, V30 *(processor chips made by NEC, which are compatible with the Intel 8088 and 8086)* processeurs V20, V30

V format *noun* format *m* variable

V series avis *mpl* de série V; *(300 bits/second transmit and receive, full duplex)* **V.21** = norme V21 (transmission en duplex à 300 bits par seconde en émission et réception); *(1200 bits/second transmit and receive, half duplex)* **V.22** = norme V22 (transmission en semi-duplex à 1200 bits par seconde en émission et réception); *(1200 bits/second transmit and receive, full duplex)* **V.22 BIS** = norme V22 bis (transmission en duplex à 1200 bits par seconde en émission et réception); *(75 bits/second transmit, 1200 bits/second receive, half duplex)* **V.23** = norme V23 (transmission en semi-duplex à 75 bits par seconde en émission et 1200 bits par seconde en réception); *(interchange circuits between a DTE and a DCE)* **V.24** = norme V24 (circuits d'échange entre système central et terminal); *(automatic calling and answering equipment on a PSTN)* **V.25 BIS** = norme V25 bis (équipement d'appel et de réponse automatique sur le réseau public commuté); *(2400 bits/second transmission over leased lines)* **V.26** = norme V26 (transmission à 2400 bits par seconde sur des lignes louées); *(2400 bits/second transmit, 1200 bits/second receive, half duplex for use on a PSTN)* **V.26 BIS** = norme V26 bis (transmission en semi-duplex à 2400 bits par seconde en émission et 1200 bits par seconde en réception sur le réseau public commuté); *(2400 bits/second transmit, 1200 bits/second receive, full duplex for use on a PSTN)* **V.26 TER** = norme V26 ter (transmission en duplex à 2400 bits par seconde en émission et 1200 bits par seconde en réception sur le réseau public commuté); *(4800 bits/second modem for use on a leased line)* **V.27** = norme V27 (modem à 4800 bits par seconde sur lignes louées); *(4800 bits/second transmit, 2400 bits/second receive for use on a leased line)* **V.27 BIS** = norme V27 bis (transmission à 4800 bits par seconde en émission et 2400 bits par seconde en réception sur lignes louées); *(4800 bits/second transmit, 2400 bits/second receive for use on a PSTN)* **V.27 TER** = norme V27 ter (transmission à 4800 bits par seconde en émission et 2400 bits par seconde en réception sur le réseau public commuté); *(9600 bits/second modem for use on a PSTN or leased line)* **V.29** = norme V29 (modem à 9600 bits par seconde sur le réseau public commuté ou sur lignes louées); *(error control and correction protocol)* **V.42** = norme V42 (protocole de contrôle et de correction d'erreurs); *(data compression used with V.42 error control)* **V.42 BIS** = norme V42 bis (compression de données avec contrôle d'erreurs V42)

vaccine *noun (utility to check a system to see if viruses are present)* logiciel *m or* utilitaire *m* antivirus

vacuum *noun* vide *m or* vacuum *m*; **there is a vacuum in the sealed CRT** = on a fait le vide dans le tube cathodique scellé; **vacuum tube** = tube *m* à vide

valid *adjective* valide; **valid memory address** = adresse *f* valide

◊ **validate** *verb* valider

◊ **validation** *noun* validation *f*

◊ **validity** *noun* validité *f*; **validity check** = (test de) vérification *f* de validité des données

value *noun* valeur *f*; **absolute value** = valeur absolue; **the absolute value of −62.34 is 62.34** = la valeur absolue de −62,34 est 62,34; **initial value** = valeur initiale

◊ **value-added** *adjective (with extra benefit for a user)* valeur ajoutée; *(network which offers information services)* **value-added network (VAN)** = réseau *m* à valeur ajoutée *or* réseau à intégration de service (RIS); *(buys material and adds other features)* **value-added reseller (VAR)** = revendeur *m* à valeur ajoutée *or* revendeur à intégration de service

valve *noun (vacuum tube)* tube *m* (à vide) *or* valve *f or* lampe *f*

VAN = VALUE ADDED NETWORK

vapourware *noun (informal) (products which exist in name only)* rideau *m* de fumée; produits *mpl* fictifs

> QUOTE Rivals dismissed the initiative as IBM vapourware, designed to protect its installed base of machines running under widely differing operating systems.
> *Computing*

VAR = VALUE ADDED RESELLER

variable 1 *adjective* variable; **variable data** = donnée(s) *f(pl)* variable(s); **variable length record** = enregistrement *m* à longueur variable; **variable word length computer** = ordinateur *m* à mots de longueur variable **2** *noun* variable *f*; **global variable** = variable globale; **local variable** = variable locale

◊ **vary** *verb* varier *or* modifier *or* changer; **the** clarity of the signal can vary with the power supply = la clarté du signal peut varier avec la tension du courant d'alimentation

VCR = VIDEO CASSETTE RECORDER

VDT *or* **VDU** = VISUAL DISPLAY TERMINAL, VISUAL DISPLAY UNIT écran *m* de visualisation *or* visuel *m*

> QUOTE it normally consists of a keyboard to input information and either a printing terminal or a VDU screen to display messages and results
> **Practical Computing**

> QUOTE a VDU is a device used with a computer that displays information in the form of characters and drawings on a screen
> **Electronics & Power**

vector *noun* **(a)** *(address to a new memory location)* vecteur *m* **(b)** *(coordinate)* vecteur; **vector graphics** *or* **vector image** *or* **vector scan** = infographie *f or* image *f* vectorisée; **vector processor** = processeur *m* vectoriel

◊ **vectored interrupt** *noun* interruption *f* vectorielle

> QUOTE the great advantage of the vector-scan display is that it requires little memory to store a picture
> **Electronics & Power**

Veitch diagram *noun* diagramme *m* de Veitch

velocity *noun* vitesse *f*; **the disk drive motor spins at a constant velocity** = le moteur du lecteur de disquettes tourne à vitesse constante

vendor *noun* *(seller)* vendeur *m*; *(works with hardware and software manufactured by someone else)* **vendor independent** = indépendant, -e du constructeur; *opposite is* PROPRIETARY

Venn diagram *noun* diagramme *m* de Venn

verify *verb* vérifier *or* contrôler

◊ **verification** *noun* vérification *f or* contrôle *m*; **keystroke verification** = contrôle *m* de la frappe; **verification and validation (V & V)** = vérification et validation *or* contrôle et validation

◊ **verifier** *noun* *(device)* vérificatrice *f*

version *noun* version *f*; **the latest version of the software includes an improved graphics routine** = la dernière version du logiciel comprend une routine graphique améliorée; *(allows several programmers to work on a source file)* **version control** = utilitaire de suivi de version *or* de modifications; *(number of the version of a product)* **version number** = numéro *m* de version

verso *noun* *(of page)* verso *m*

vertical *adjective* vertical, -e; *(software designed for a specific use)* **vertical application** = application verticale; **your new software to** manage a florist's is a good vertical application = votre nouveau progiciel pour gérer une boutique de fleuriste est une bonne application verticale; **vertical blanking interval** = délai *m* de retour vertical; **vertical format unit (VFU)** = unité *f* de formatage vertical; **vertical justification** = justification *f* verticale; **vertical parity check** = contrôle *m* de parité verticale; **vertical redundancy check (VRC)** = contrôle *m* par redondance verticale; **vertical scrolling** = défilement *m* vertical; *(indicates the end of the display)* **vertical sync signal** = signal vidéo vertical; **vertical tab** = tabulation *f* verticale

◊ **vertically** *adverb* verticalement; **vertically polarized signal** = signal *m* avec polarisation verticale *or* signal polarisé verticalement

very high frequency (VHF) *noun* *(between 30 - 300MHz)* très haute fréquence (THF); onde *f* métrique

very large scale integration (VLSI) *noun* intégration *f* à très grande échelle

very low frequency (VLF) *noun* *(between 3 - 30KHz)* très basse fréquence (TBF); onde *f* myriamétrique

VESA = VIDEO ELECTRONICS STANDARDS ASSOCIATION; *(allows three special expansion slots)* **VESA local bus** *or* **VL-bus** = bus local VESA *or* bus VLB; **for a high-performance PC, choose one with a VESA bus** = pour avoir un PC de hautes performances, choisissez un modèle avec bus local VESA

vestigial sideband *noun* bande *f* latérale résiduelle

vf band = VOICE FREQUENCY BAND; *see* BAND

VFU = VERTICAL FORMAT UNIT

VGA = VIDEO GRAPHICS ARRAY; *(standard of video adapter developed by IBM)* (adaptateur) VGA; *(enhancement to the standard VGA graphics display)* **super VGA (SVGA)** = (adaptateur *or* carte) Super VGA *or* SVGA

VHD = VERY HIGH DENSITY; *(of disk)* très haute densité

VHF = VERY HIGH FREQUENCY

via *preposition* via *or* par *or* par l'intermédiaire de *or* en passant par; **the signals have reached us via satellite** = les signaux nous ont été transmis par satellite; **you can download the data to the CPU via a modem** = le téléchargement des données dans l'unité centrale peut se faire par l'intermédiaire d'un modem

video *noun* vidéo *f*; *(add-in board)* **video adapter** *or* **board** *or* **controller** = carte vidéo; **video bandwidth** = largeur *f* de bande vidéo; *(memory used to store the bit-map of the image)* **video buffer** = mémoire *f* (tampon) vidéo; **video camera** = vidéocaméra *f*; **infrared video camera** =

vidéocamera à infrarouge; **some instructors monitor their trainees with infrared video cameras** = certains instructeurs utilisent une vidéocaméra à infrarouge pour suivre leurs élèves; **video card** = carte *f* vidéo; **video cassette** = vidéocassette *f*; **video cassette recorder (VCR)** = magnétoscope *m*; **video compressor** = concentrateur *m or* réducteur *m* (de largeur de bande) vidéo; **video conferencing** = vidéoconférence *f*; *(digital sampling circuit)* **video digitiser** = numériseur *m* vidéo; **videodisk** = disque *m* vidéo *or* vidéodisque *m*; **video display** = écran *m or* moniteur *m* vidéo; **video expander** = déconcentrateur *m* pour transmission vidéo; **video frame** = image *f* vidéo; **with an image processor you can freeze a video frame** = le processeur d'images permet de figer une image *or* de faire un arrêt sur image; **video game** = jeu *m* vidéo; *(IBM PC standard of video adapter)* **video graphics array (VGA)** = (norme d'écran) VGA; **video image** = image *f* vidéo; **a printer-readable video image can be sent to a basic laser printer through a video port** = une image vidéo imprimable peut être envoyée sur une imprimante laser classique par le port vidéo; **video interface chip** = circuit intégré de carte vidéo; **video library** = vidéothèque *f*; *(pre-calculated values of different colours)* **video lookup table** = table *f* de contrôle des paramètres d'écran couleur; **video memory** *or* **video RAM (VRAM)** = RAM *f* vidéo *or* mémoire *f* vidéo *or* mémoire image; **video monitor** = moniteur *m or* écran *m* vidéo; *(informal)* **video nasties** = films *mpl* d'épouvante *or* d'horreur sur vidéocassettes *or* sur bandes vidéo; **video phone** = vidéophone *m or* visiophone *m*; **video player** = lecteur *m* vidéo; **video port** = port *m* vidéo; **video random access memory (VRAM)** = mémoire vidéo à accès aléatoire (VRAM); **video recorder** = magnétoscope *m*; *(allows images to be entered into a computer)* **video scanner** = scanner vidéo *m or* scanner d'images; **new video scanners are designed to scan three-dimensional objects** = les nouveaux scanners d'images sont construits pour saisir des objets en trois dimensions; **video signal** = signal *m* vidéo; **video standards** = standards *mpl or* normes *fpl* vidéo; **videotape** = bande *f* vidéo; **videotape recorder** = magnétoscope *m*; **video terminal** = terminal *m* vidéo *or* écran vidéo avec clavier

QUOTE Vision Dynamics has upgraded its video capture and display boards for PCs. Elvis II will now display TV pictures on a VGA screen at a resolution of 1,024 x 768 square pixels and 2 million colours to provide enhanced picture quality from PAL, NTSC and S-VHS sources.

Computing

◊ **videotext** *or* **videotex** *noun* vidéotex *m or* vidéographie *f* interactive

view *verb (film, etc.)* visionner; *(display)* visualiser; **the user has to pay a charge for viewing pages on a bulletin board** = l'utilisateur paie un droit pour visualiser le tableau d'affichage

◊ **Viewdata** ™ *noun* système britannique équivalent au Minitel ™

◊ **viewer** *noun* **(a)** *(person)* téléspectateur, -trice **(b)** *(device)* visionneuse *f*

◊ **viewfinder** *noun (eyepiece)* viseur *m*; **electronic viewfinder** = viseur électronique

◊ **viewing** *noun (film)* visionnage *m*; *(display)* visualisation *f*

virgin *adjective (tape or disk)* (disquette *or* bande) vierge

virtual *adjective* virtuel, -elle; **virtual address** = adresse virtuelle; **virtual circuit** = circuit virtuel; **virtual disk** = disque virtuel; **virtual machine** = machine virtuelle; **virtual memory** *or* **virtual storage (VS)** = mémoire virtuelle; *(simulation of a real-life scene)* **virtual reality** = réalité virtuelle; **this new virtual reality software can create a three-dimensional room that you can navigate around** = ce nouveau logiciel de réalité virtuelle peut créer une pièce en trois dimensions dans laquelle vous pouvez vous déplacer; **virtual terminal** = terminal virtuel

QUOTE Autodesk suggests that anyone wishing to build Virtual Reality applications with the Cyberspace Developer's Kit should have solid knowledge of programming in C++ along with general knowledge of computer graphics.

Computing

virus *noun (program which can corrupt data)* virus *m*; **if your PC is infected with a virus, your data is at risk** = si vous avez un virus dans votre PC, vos données sont en danger; *(removes a virus from a file)* **anti-virus software** = logiciel *m or* utilitaire *m* antivirus; *(checks files to see if they contain a virus)* **virus detector** = détecteur *m* de virus

COMMENT: viruses are spread by downloading unchecked files from a bulletin board system or via unregulated networks or by inserting an unchecked floppy disk into your PC - always use virus detector.

visible *adjective* visible; **visible light** = lumière *f* visible

visual **1** *adjective* visuel, -elle; **visual programming** = programmation *f* visuelle **2** *noun* visuel *m*; *(illustratiions)* **visuals** = illustrations *fpl or* iconographie *f*

◊ **visual display terminal (VDT)** *or* **visual display unit (VDU)** *noun* écran *m* (de visualisation) *or* visuel *m*

◊ **visualize** *verb* visualiser

VL-bus *or* **VL local bus** *noun (allows three special expansion slots)* bus VLB *or* bus local VESA; **for a high-performance PC, choose one with a VL-bus** = pour avoir un PC de hautes performances, choisissez un modèle avec bus VLB

VLF = VERY LOW FREQUENCY

VLSI = VERY LARGE SCALE INTEGRATION

voice *noun* voix *f*; **voice answer back** = répondeur *m* avec message vocal de synthèse; *(usually 300 - 3400 Hz)* **voice band** = bande *f* (de fréquences) vocale *or* bande de basses fréquences *or* bande téléphonique; **voice data entry** *or* **input** = saisie *f* vocale; **voice grade channel** = canal de basses fréquences; *(computer linked to a telephone exchange that answers a person's telephone when no one is there)* **voice mail** = messagerie *f* vocale; **I checked my voice mail to see if anyone had left me a message** = j'ai vérifié ma boîte à lettre vocale pour voir si quelqu'un m'avait laissé un message; **voice output** = sortie *f* vocale; synthèse vocale; **voice print** = empreinte *f* vocale; **voice recognition** = reconnaissance *f* vocale *or* de la parole; **voice response** = VOICE OUTPUT; **voice synthesis** = synthèse *f* vocale; **voice synthesizer** = synthétiseur *m* vocal

---

QUOTE the technology of voice output is reasonably difficult, but the technology of voice recognition is much more complex
Personal Computer World

◊ **voice-over** *noun* voix *f* hors champ *or* voix off

◊ **voice unit** *noun* unité *f* de puissance vocale

volatile memory *or* **volatile store** *or* **volatile dynamic storage** *noun* mémoire *f* volatile (NOTE: opposite is **non-volatile memory**)

◊ **volatility** *noun* volatilité *f*

volt *noun* volt *m*

◊ **voltage** *noun* voltage *m or* tension *f*; **voltage dip** *or* **dip in voltage** = chute *f or* baisse *f* de tension; **voltage regulator** = régulateur *m* de tension; **voltage transient** = pointe *f* de tension

volume *noun* **(a)** *(total space)* volume *m* *(space occupied by data)* volume (occupé par les données sur un dispositif de stockage) **(b)** *(identifies a disk or tape)* **volume label** *or* **name** = nom *or* étiquette *or* label de volume **(c)** *(sound)* volume; **volume control** = réglage *m or* contrôle *m or* bouton *m* du volume

VRAM = VIDEO RANDOM ACCESS MEMORY

VRC = VERTICAL REDUNDANCY CHECK

VS = VIRTUAL STORAGE

VT-terminal emulation *noun* *(set of codes developed by Digital Equipment Corporation)* émulation *f* de terminal VT (de DEC); *(standard of a terminal)* **VT-52** = standard VT-52

VTR = VIDEO TAPE RECORDER

VU = VOICE UNIT

Ww

wafer *noun (slice of silicon)* tranche *f* (de silicium)

◊ **wafer scale integration** *noun* intégration *f* sur tranche de silicium

wait condition *or* **state** *noun (processor not active)* état *m* d'attente *or* de latence

◊ **wait loop** *noun* boucle *f* d'attente

◊ **wait time** *noun* délai *m* d'attente *or* latence *f*

◊ **waiting list** *noun* file *f* d'attente

◊ **waiting state** *noun (computer state)* attente *f*

wake up *verb (to start or initiate)* activer *or* alerter; *(from a remote terminal)* **wake up a system** = alerter un système

walk through *verb (to examine each step of a piece of software)* réviser

wallpaper *noun (background in a window)* papier *m* peint (fond d'écran du bureau Windows)

WAN = WIDE AREA NETWORK

wand *noun (bar code reader or optical device)* stylo *m* optique

warm boot *noun (reloads operating system)* amorçage *m* à chaud; *compare* HARD RESET

◊ **warm standby** *noun (secondary backup device)* équipement *m* de secours à démarrage semi-automatique

◊ **warm start** *noun (of programme)* reprise *f* sur l'instruction d'arrêt *or* reprise au point d'arrêt

◊ **warm up** *verb (machine)* amorcer

warn *verb* avertir; **he warned the keyboarders that the system might become overloaded** = il a averti les opérateurs de saisie d'une surcharge possible du système (NOTE: you warn someone **of** something, or **that** something may happen)

◊ **warning** *noun* avertissement *m*; **to issue a warning** = donner un avertissement; **warning light** = voyant *m* d'alarme; **when the warning light on** the front panel comes on, switch off the system = lorsque le voyant placé sur le panneau avant s'allume, il faut éteindre le système

wash PROM *verb* effacer une PROM

waste instruction *noun* instruction *f* de remplissage

◊ **wastepaper basket** *noun (icon)* corbeille *f*

Watt (W) *noun (measurement of electrical power)* watt *m*

wave *noun* onde *f*; **microwave** = micro-onde *f*; **sound wave** = onde sonore

◊ **waveform** *noun* (forme d') onde; **waveform digitization** = conversion *f* d'une onde en numérique *or* numérisation *f* d'une onde

◊ **waveguide** *noun* guide *m* d'onde

◊ **wavelength** *noun* longueur *f* d'onde

WBFM = WIDEBAND FREQUENCY MODULATION

weigh *verb* peser *or* pondérer

◊ **weight** *noun* poids *m*; **gross weight** = poids brut; **net weight** = poids net; **paper weight** = grammage *m*; **our paper weight is 70 - 90 gsm** = nous avons du papier de 70 - 90 grammes

◊ **weighted** *adjective* pondéré, -ée; **weighted average** = moyenne *f* pondérée; **weighted bit** = bit *m* de poids fort *or* bit lourd

◊ **weighting** *noun* pondération *f*

well-behaved *adjective (program)* (programme) policé; *(informal)* non bidouillé

wetware *noun US (informal)* le cerveau humain *or* la matière grise

What-You-See-Is-All-You-Get (WYSIAYG) *noun* ce que vous voyez est tout ce que vous obtenez

What-You-See-Is-What-You-Get (WYSIWYG) *noun* ce que vous voyez est ce que vous obtenez

while-loop *noun* boucle *f* conditionnelle 'WHILE'

white *adjective & noun* blanc, blanche; *(on video disk)* **white flag** = signal *m* blanc; *(on monitor)* **white level** = niveau *m* de blanc; **white noise** = bruit *m* blanc; **white writer** = imprimante *f* à définition des blancs (NOTE: the opposite is **black writer)**

wide angle lens *noun* grand-angle *m or* objectif *m* grand-angle *or* grand-angulaire

◊ **wide area network (WAN)** *noun* réseau *m* étendu; *compare with* LAN

wideband *noun (transmission method that combines several channels)* (communication) en bande large; **wideband frequency modulation (WBFM)** = modulation *f* de fréquence à large bande; *compare* BASEBAND

widow *noun (single line)* (dernière) ligne *f* (d'un paragraphe) isolée en tête de page; *compare* ORPHAN

width *noun* largeur *f*; **line width** = longueur *f* de ligne (en caractères); **page width** = largeur de page (en caractères)

wild card character *noun (symbol used when searching)* caractère *m* joker; **a wild card can be used to find all file names beginning with DIC** = on peut utiliser un caractère joker pour trouver tous les noms de fichiers commençant par DIC

> COMMENT: in DOS, UNIX and PC operating systems, the wild card character '?' will match any single character in this position; the wild card character '*' means: match any number of characters

WIMP = WINDOW, ICON, MOUSE, POINTERS

> COMMENT: WIMPs normally use a combination of windows, icons and a mouse to control the operating system. In many GUIs, such as Microsoft Windows, Apple Macintosh System 7 and DR-GEM, you can control all the functions of the operating system just using the mouse. Icons represent programs and files; instead of entering the file name, you select it by moving a pointer with a mouse

Winchester™ disk *noun* disque *m* (dur) Winchester; **Winchester drive** = lecteur *m* de disque Winchester; **removable Winchester** = disque Winchester amovible

window 1 *noun* fenêtre *f*; **several remote stations are connected to the network and each has its own window onto the hard disk** = plusieurs postes de travail à distance sont connectés au réseau, chacun disposant d'une fenêtre sur le disque dur; **the operating system will allow other programs to be displayed on-screen at the same time in different windows** = le système d'exploitation permet d'afficher d'autres programmes simultanément, chacun dans une fenêtre différente; **active window** = fenêtre active; **command window** = fenêtre de commande; **the command window is a single line at the bottom of the screen** = la fenêtre de commande est une seule ligne au bas de l'écran; **edit window** = fenêtre d'édition; **text window** = fenêtre de texte; **window, icon, mouse, pointer (WIMP)** = environnement *m* graphique WIMP (avec fenêtre, icône, souris, pointeur) 2 *verb* fenêtrer

◊ **windowing** *noun* fenêtrage *m*

> QUOTE when an output window overlaps another, the interpreter does not save the contents of the obscured window
> *Personal Computer World*

> QUOTE windowing facilities make use of virtual screens as well as physical screens
> *Byte*

> QUOTE you can connect more satellites to the network, each having its own window onto the hard disk
> *PC Plus*

> QUOTE the network system uses the latest windowing techniques
> *Desktop Publishing*

> QUOTE the functions are integrated via a windowing system with pull-down menus used to select different operations
> *Byte*

> QUOTE For instance, if you define a screen window using PowerBuilder, you can build a whole family of windows, which automatically inherit the characteristics of the first.
> *Computing*

Windows ™ *(graphical user interface developed by Microsoft)* (interface graphique) Windows ™ (de Microsoft); *(Windows that includes peer-to-peer file-sharing functions)* **Windows for Workgroups** ™ = Windows for Workgroups ™; *(GUI derived from Windows)* **Windows NT** ™ = (système d'exploitation) Windows NT ™

◊ **Windows 95** *(operating system software)* (programme système) Windows 95; **new software for Windows 95** = nouveaux logiciels pour Windows 95

wipe *verb (to clean data from a disk)* effacer *or* détruire (des données); blanchir (un disque); **by reformatting you will wipe the disk clean** = si vous reformatez, vous détruirez toutes les données du disque *or* vous blanchirez le disque

◊ **wiper** *noun (of potentiometer, etc.)* curseur *m or* variateur *m*

wire 1 *noun* fil *m* (métallique *or* électrique *or* de liaison); **telephone wires** = fils téléphoniques; *(dot-matrix printer)* **wire printer** = imprimante *f* matricielle; **wire wrap** = connexion *f* enroulée 2 *verb (to install wiring)* câbler; **the studio is wired for sound** = le studio est câblé pour la sonorisation; **wired** *or* **hardwired program computer** = ordinateur à logique câblée

◊ **wireless** 1 *noun (old use)* poste *m* (de) radio *or* (de) T.S.F. 2 *adjective* sans fil; **wireless microphone** = microphone *m* sans fil (pour transmission) *or* micro-cravate *m*

◊ **wiretap** *noun* table *f* d'écoute

◊ **wiring** *noun* câblage *m*; **the wiring in the system had to be replaced** = il a fallu refaire le câblage du système; *(box for cabling)* **wiring closet** = boîte *f or* armoire *f* de câblage; *(structure used to support cables)* **wiring frame** = châssis *m or* cadre *m* de câblage

WISC = WRITABLE INSTRUCTION SET COMPUTER

woofer *noun* *(informal)* haut-parleur *m* de graves *or* de basses fréquences

word *noun* **(a)** mot *m*; **words per minute (wpm** *or* **WPM)** = (nombre de) mots par minute; **word break** = coupure *f* *or* césure *f*; **word count** = nombre de mots contenus dans un fichier *or* un texte; *(wordprocessing)* **word wrap** *or* **wraparound** = retour *m* à la ligne automatique **(b)** *(separate item of data)* mot; **word length** = longueur *f* d'un mot; **word marker** = marque *f* de début de mot; **word serial** = série *f* de mots (l'un à la suite de l'autre); **word time** = temps *m* de transfert d'un mot

◊ **Word** ™ *(word-processing application)* (progiciel de traitement de texte) Word ™

◊ **WordPerfect** ™ *(word-processing application)* (progiciel de traitement de texte) WordPerfect ™

◊ **word-process** *verb* éditer *or* traiter *or* composer un texte sur ordinateur; **it is quite easy to read word-processed files** = on lit facilement les fichiers de texte composés sur ordinateur

◊ **wordprocessing** *or* **word-processing(WP)** *noun* *(using a computer to keyboard, edit, and output text)* traitement *m* de texte; **load the word-processing program before you start keyboarding** = chargez le programme de traitement de texte avant de commencer à taper au clavier; *(office which specializes in word-processing)* **wordprocessing bureau** = société *f* de services en PAO

◊ **word-processor** *noun* **(a)** *(machine)* machine *f* de traitement de texte **(b)** *(software)* logiciel *m* de traitement de texte

◊ **WordStar** ™ *(word-processing application developed by MicroPro International)* (logiciel de traitement de texte) WordStar ™

work 1 *noun* travail *m*; **work area** = espace *m* de travail *or* zone *f* de travail; **work disk** = disque *m* de travail *or* de manoeuvre *or* d'enregistrement; *(scratch file)* **work file** = fichier *m* de travail *or* de manoeuvre **2** *verb* travailler; fonctionner *or* marcher; **the computer system has never worked properly since it was installed** = ce système informatique n'a jamais bien marché depuis son installation

◊ **workflow** *noun* *(software designed to improve the flow of electronic documents)* (logiciel de gestion de) flux *m* de travaux

◊ **workgroup** *noun* *(group of users)* groupe *m* de travail *or* de projet (relié par réseau ou messagerie); *(added to standard software to appeal to a group of users)* **workgroup enabled** = qui permet *or* qui facilite le travail de groupe; **this word-processor is workgroup enabled which adds an email gateway from the standard menus** = ce traitement de texte est orienté sur les groupes de travail et comporte un passerelle de messagerie électronique dans le menu courant; *(designed to be used by many users)* **workgroup software** = logiciel de groupe (de travail)

◊ **working** *adjective* **(a)** (appareil) en état de marche **(b)** **working store** *or* **scratchpad** = mémoire temporaire *or* mémoire banale *or* (mémoire) bloc-notes *m*

◊ **workload** *noun* charge *f* de travail

◊ **worksheet** *noun* *(two-dimensional matrix of rows and columns)* feuille *f* de travail

◊ **workspace** *noun* *(space in memory)* espace *m* de manoeuvre *or* de travail

◊ **workstation** *noun* *(PC)* poste *m* de travail *or* station *f* de travail; **the system includes five workstations linked together in a ring network** = le système comprend cinq postes de travail reliés en anneau; **the archive storage has a total capacity of 1200 Mb between seven workstations** = la mémoire d'archivage a une capacité de 1200 Mo pour sept stations de travail

> QUOTE an image processing workstation must provide three basic facilities: the means to digitize, display and manipulate the image data
> *Byte*

WORM = WRITE ONCE READ MANY times memory

wow *noun* pleurage *m*

WP = WORD-PROCESSING

WPM *or* **wpm** = WORDS PER MINUTE

wrap *noun* *(system of threading video tape)* **omega wrap** = enrouleur-presseur *m* de bande magnétique

◊ **wraparound** *or* **word wrap** *noun* *(word-processing)* retour *m* à la ligne automatique; *(of cursor)* **horizontal wraparound** = retour à la ligne *or* saut *m* de ligne automatique (en limite d'écran)

writable instruction set computer (WISC) *noun* *(CPU design)* ordinateur *m* à jeu d'instructions modifiable

write *verb* **(a)** écrire **(b)** *(data onto a disk or tape)* enregistrer *or* ranger une donnée en mémoire; **access time is the time taken to read from or write to a location in memory** = le temps d'accès est le temps requis pour consulter une donnée en mémoire ou pour ranger une donnée en mémoire; *(temporary storage used to hold data)* **write** *or* **write-back** *or* **write-behind cache** = mémoire cache à écriture différée; **write-back cacheing improves performance, but can be dangerous** = le cache à écriture différée améliore les performances mais ne doit être utilisé que par les experts; *see also* CACHE, READ CACHE; *(error when trying to save data)* **write error** = erreur d'écriture; **write head** = tête *f* d'enregistrement *or* d'écriture; **write once, read many times memory (WORM)** = disque *m* optique WORM (permettant une seule écriture et des lectures multiples); **write time** = temps d'écriture *or* d'enregistrement (NOTE: you write data **to** a file. Note also: **writing - wrote - has written**)

◊ **write black printer** *noun (printer where toner sticks to points hit by a laser beam)* imprimante *f* à transfert d'encre; *compare* WHITE WRITER

COMMENT: a write black printer produces sharp edges and graphics, but large areas of black are muddy

◊ **write-permit ring** *noun* anneau *m or* bague *f* de protection d'écriture

◊ **write protect** *verb* protéger (une disquette contre l'écriture indésirée); **write-protect tab** = volet *m* de protection d'écriture

◊ **writer** *noun see* BLACK, WHITE

◊ **writing** *noun (handwriting)* écriture *f*; *(text)* écrit *m*; **in writing** = par écrit; **to put the agreement in writing** = rédiger un accord; **he has difficulty in reading my writing** = il trouve mon écriture difficile à lire; *(special device that allows computers to read in handwritten characters which have been written onto a special pad)* **writing pad** = tablette *f* à numériser (pour saisie de texte écrit à la main)

WWW = WORLD WIDE WEB

WYSIAYG = WHAT YOU SEE IS ALL YOU GET

WYSIWYG = WHAT YOU SEE IS WHAT YOU GET (NOTE: say 'wiziwig')

Xx

X = EXTENSION

X.25 *(defines the connection between a terminal and a packet-switching network)* standard CCITT X 25 (connexion entre un terminal et un réseau de transfert par paquets)

◊ **X.400** *(defines an electronic mail transfer method)* standard CCITT X 400 (transfert de messages électroniques)

◊ **X.500** *(defines a method of global naming)* standard CCITT X 500 (gestion des noms et des transferts de messages)

X-axis *noun* axe *m* d'abscisse *or* axe des X

◊ **X-coordinate** *noun* abscisse *f or* coordonnée *f* horizontale

◊ **X direction** *noun* horizontale *f*

◊ **X distance** *noun* distance *f* sur l'axe des X

xerographic printer *noun* imprimante *f* xérographique

◊ **xerography** *noun* xérographie *f*

Xerox ™ 1 *noun* (a) *(photocopier)* photocopieur de marque Xerox; **to make a xerox copy of a letter** = photocopier une lettre (avec une machine Xerox); **we must order some more Xerox paper for the copier** = il faut commander de nouveau du papier Xerox pour le photocopieur; **we are having a new Xerox machine installed tomorrow** = on nous installera une nouvelle machine *or* un nouveau photocopieur Xerox demain **(b)** *(photocopy made with a xerox machine)* photocopie *f* (faite avec une machine Xerox); **to send the other party a xerox of the contract** = envoyer une photocopie du contrat à l'autre partie; **we have sent xeroxes to each of the agents** = nous avons envoyé des photocopies à chacun des agents 2 *verb (to make a photocopy with a xerox machine)* photocopier; **to xerox a document** = photocopier un document; **she xeroxed all the file** = elle a photocopié tout le dossier

XMODEM *(file transfer and error-detecting protocol)* protocole *m* de transmission de fichiers XMODEM; *(transfers 1024-byte blocks of data)* **XMODEM 1K** = protocole XMODEM 1K; *(enhanced version of XMODEM)* **XMODEM**

CRC = protocole XMODEM CRC (comprend un dispositif de contrôle d'erreurs)

XMS = EXTENDED MEMORY SPECIFICATION; *(define how a program should access extended memory)* spécifications de mémoire étendue *or* XMS

XNS = XEROX NETWORKING SYSTEM; *(protocol developed by Xerox)* protocole XNS

XON/XOFF *(asynchronous transmission protocol)* (protocole de transmission asynchrone) XON/XOFF

X/OPEN *(group promoting open systems)* groupe X/OPEN

x punch *noun* perforation *f* (de la ligne) 11 *or* perforation X

X-ray 1 *noun* **(a)** *(ray)* rayon *m* X; **X-ray imaging** = radioscopie *f* **(b)** *(photograph)* radiographie *f or* radio *f* **2** *verb* radiographier

X-series *noun* protocoles *mpl* de télétransmission de la série X

XT *(version of the original IBM PC)* version XT (basée sur le processeur Inter 8088); *(keyboard used with the IBM PC)* **XT keyboard** = clavier XT

X-Window System *or* **X-Windows** *(set of API commands and display handling routines)* (système d'API) X-Window

> QUOTE X is the underlying technology which allows Unix applications to run under a multi-user, multitasking GUI. It has been adopted as the standard for the Common Open Software Environment, proposed recently by top Unix vendors including Digital, IBM and Sun.
> *Computing*

X-Y *noun* coordonnées *fpl*; **X-Y plotter** = traceur *m* de courbes *or* de graphiques

Yy

yaw *noun (of a satellite)* (mouvement de) lacet *m*

Y-axis *noun* axe *m* de l'ordonnée *or* axe des Y

◊ **Y-coordinate** *noun* ordonnée *f* *or* coordonnée *f* verticale

◊ **Y-direction** *noun* verticale *f*

◊ **Y-distance** *noun* distance *f* sur l'axe des Y

Yellow, magenta, cyan, black (YMCK) *(colour definition based on four colours)* YMCK

(définition de couleurs basée sur: jaune, magenta, cyan, noir)

YMCK = YELLOW, MAGENTA, CYAN, BLACK

YMODEM *(variation of the XMODEM file transfer protocol)* (protocole) YMODEM

yoke *noun (coils around a TV tube)* **deflection yoke** = déflecteur *m* à enroulement

y punch *noun* perforation *f* (de ligne) 12 *or* perforation Y

Zz

Z = IMPEDANCE

Z80 *(processor developed by Zilog)* processeur *m* Z80

zap *verb* faire disparaître de l'écran *or* nettoyer *or* vider l'écran; **he pressed CONTROL Z and zapped all the text** = il a tapé CONTROL Z pour vider l'écran

Z-axis *noun* axe *m* des Z

zero 1 *noun* zéro *m*; **in Britain, the code for international calls is zero zero (00)** = en Grande-Bretagne, l'indicatif des appels internationaux est zéro zéro (00); **jump on zero** = effectuer un branchement (conditionnel) à zéro; **zero compression** *or* **zero suppression** = élimination *f* des zéros (non significatifs); **zero flag** = indicateur *m* zéro; **the jump on zero instruction tests the zero flag** = l'instruction de branchement conditionnel à zéro teste l'indicateur zéro; **zero-level address** *or* **immediate address** = adresse *f* immédiate *or* directe **2** *verb* remettre à zéro *or* effacer un fichier; **to zero a device** = remettre à zéro *or* nettoyer un dispositif programmable; **to zero fill** = garnir de zéros

◊ **zero insertion force (ZIF)** *noun (of connector)* insertion *f* sans friction *or* force *f* d'insertion zéro

◊ **zero slot LAN** *noun (LAN that does not use internal expansion adapters)* réseau *m* local utilisant les ports séries ou un adaptateur externe

◊ **zero wait state** *noun (fast enough to run at the same speed as other components)* sans état d'attente

ZIF = ZERO INSERTION FORCE

ZIP code *noun US (US postal delivery areas)* code *m* postal (aux E.-U.) (NOTE: the GB equivalent for this is **post code)**

ZMODEM *(enhanced version of the XMODEM file transfer protocol)* (protocole) ZMODEM

zone *noun (part of a screen)* zone *f*; *(in wordprocessing)* **hot zone** = zone de texte

zoom *verb* faire un zoom

◊ **zooming** *noun* zoom *m*

◊ **zoom lens** *noun* zoom *m or* objectif *m* à focale variable

QUOTE there are many options to allow you to zoom into an area for precision work
Electronics & Wireless World

QUOTE any window can be zoomed to full-screen size by pressing the F-5 function key
Byte

SPECIALIST FRENCH DICTIONARIES

COMPUTING & IT
FRENCH DICTIONARY
FRENCH-ENGLISH/ENGLISH-FRENCH

An up-to-date bilingual dictionary that provides accurate translations and comprehensive coverage of over 35,000 terms from computing and information technology. Each entry includes part of speech and example sentences (that are also translated) to show how words are used in context.
The terms cover all aspects of computing, programming, electronics, hardware, software, networking and multimedia.

ISBN 0-948549-65-3   hardback   608pages

BUSINESS FRENCH
DICTIONARY
FRENCH-ENGLISH/ENGLISH-FRENCH

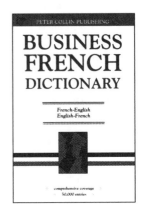

The second edition of this respected dictionary. The dictionary is a fully bilingual edition that has been revised and updated to provide one of the most comprehensive and up-to-date dictionaries available. The dictionary includes accurate translation for over 50,000 terms that cover all aspects of business usage. Each entry includes example sentences, part of speech, grammar notes and comments.

ISBN 0-948549-64-5   hardback   600pages
ISBN 0-948549-77-7   CD-ROM   demo on our website

DICTIONARY OF
ECOLOGY & ENVIRONMENT

A full, bilingual English-French/French-English dictionary providing comprehensive coverage of the areas of ecology and the environment. Includes terms that cover pollution, waste disposal, natural and man-made disasters and conservation.

ISBN 0-948549-29-7   hardback   608pages

BUSINESS GLOSSARY SERIES

A range of bilingual business glossaries that provide accurate translations for over 5,000 business terms. Each glossary is in a convenient paperback format with 196 pages.

French-English/English-French   ISBN 0-948549-52-1

For full details of all our English and bilingual titles, please request a catalogue or visit our website.
tel: +44 020 8943 3386 fax: +44 020 8943 1673   email: info@petercollin.com
www.petercollin.com